The New York Paralegal

Essential Rules, Documents, and Resources

The New York Paralegal

Essential Rules, Documents, and Resources

INCLUDES

- A Comprehensive Legal Dictionary
- New York Code of Professional Responsibility
- Paralegal Ethics
- Paralegal Registration
- Paralegal Certification
- Employment Resources
- Court Opinions on Paralegals
- CLE for Paralegals
- Employment Law Governing Paralegals
- Litigation Timelines
- Sample Documents
- State Research and Citation

William P. Statsky

Robert A. Sarachan

DELMAR
CENGAGE Learning

Australia • Brazil • Japan • Korea • Mexico • Singapore • Spain • United Kingdom • United States

The New York Paralegal: Essential Rules, Documents, and Resources
William P. Statsky and Robert A. Sarachan

Vice President, Career and Professional Editorial: Dave Garza

Director of Learning Solutions: Sandy Clark

Senior Acquisitions Editor: Shelley Esposito

Managing Editor: Larry Main

Senior Product Manager: Melissa Riveglia

Editorial Assistant: Danielle Klahr

Vice President, Career and Professional Marketing: Jennifer Baker

Marketing Director: Deborah Yarnell

Marketing Manager: Erin Brennan

Marketing Coordinator: Jonathan Sheehan

Production Director: Wendy Troeger

Production Manager: Mark Bernard

Senior Content Project Manager: Betty Dickson

Senior Art Director: Joy Kocsis

Senior Technology Product Manager: Joe Pliss

Content Project Management: Pre-Press PMG

Production Service/Compositor: Pre-Press PMG

Library of Congress Control Number: 2010925096

ISBN-13: 978-1-4180-1302-8

ISBN-10: 1-4180-1302-1

Delmar
5 Maxwell Drive
Clifton Park, NY 12065-2919
USA

Cengage Learning is a leading provider of customized learning solutions with office locations around the globe, including Singapore, the United Kingdom, Australia, Mexico, Brazil, and Japan. Locate your local office at **www.cengage.com/global**

Cengage Learning products are represented in Canada by Nelson Education, Ltd.

To learn more about Delmar, visit **www.cengage.com/delmar**

Purchase any of our products at your local college store or at our preferred online store **www.cengagebrain.com**

Notice to the Reader

Publisher does not warrant or guarantee any of the products described herein or perform any independent analysis in connection with any of the product information contained herein. Publisher does not assume, and expressly disclaims, any obligation to obtain and include information other than that provided to it by the manufacturer. The reader is expressly warned to consider and adopt all safety precautions that might be indicated by the activities described herein and to avoid all potential hazards. By following the instructions contained herein, the reader willingly assumes all risks in connection with such instructions. The publisher makes no representations or warranties of any kind, including but not limited to, the warranties of fitness for particular purpose or merchantability, nor are any such representations implied with respect to the material set forth herein, and the publisher takes no responsibility with respect to such material. The publisher shall not be liable for any special, consequential, or exemplary damages resulting, in whole or part, from the readers' use of, or reliance upon, this material.

Printed in the United States of America
2 3 4 5 6   24 23 22 21 20

Dedication

For Ava, Hailey, Myles, and Kaia.
WPS

For Ella, Ezra, Michelle, and in memory of Sonya.
RAS

Contents

Preface

What does it take to be an outstanding paralegal in New York? Three key ingredients in your success are your paralegal education, native intelligence, and determination. This book seeks to complement all three by bringing together in one volume a vast amount of material that is either essential for all paralegals or useful for many.

Our focus is on the state of New York—state resources, state laws, and state associations. Some federal laws and institutions will also be included when they are directly relevant to the state, e.g., federal government jobs for paralegals in federal agencies located in New York.

The book has eight parts:

Part 1. Paralegal Profession
Part 2. Paralegal Employment
Part 3. Ethics, Paralegals, and Attorneys
Part 4. Legal System
Part 5. Legal Research and Records Research
Part 6. Procedure: Some Basics
Part 7. Sample Documents
Part 8. Comprehensive Legal Dictionary

The last part contains a comprehensive legal dictionary with selected definitions specifically keyed to New York law. Within each of the first seven parts of the book, the sections will often include the following features:

Introduction: An overview of what is in the section and why it was included in the book

Table of Contents: A list of the main topics or areas covered in the section

Abbreviations Used in the Section

Materials and Resources: The heart of the section

More Information: Leads to further materials, usually on the Internet

Something to Check: Questions that will help you expand and build on the material in the section

For updates and related material, go to *www.paralegal.delmar.cengage.com*.

The New York Paralegal Reviewers

Janet Holmgren
NALA

Steven Kempisty
Bryant and Stratton College
Liverpool, NY

Roger Stone
Hilbert College
Hamburg, NY

Marcelle Veater
Paralegal Association of Rochester

Paralegal Profession

A. Introduction

In the United States, a paralegal (also called a legal assistant) is a person with substantive legal skills whose authority to use those skills is based on attorney supervision or special authorization from the government. By substantive skills, we mean skills that (a) are obtained through sophisticated training and (b) are significantly more advanced than those possessed by clerical personnel in most law offices.

According to the paralegal guidelines of the New York State Bar Association, the legal profession recognizes paralegals "as dedicated professionals with skills and abilities" that "contribute to the delivery of cost-effective, high quality legal services." The Bar uses the following definition for this field:

> A legal assistant/paralegal is a person who is qualified through education, training or work experience to be employed or retained by a lawyer, law office, governmental agency, or other entity in a capacity or function that involves the performance, under the ultimate direction and supervision of, and/or accountability to, an attorney, of substantive legal work, that requires a sufficient knowledge of legal concepts such that, absent such legal assistant/paralegal, the attorney would perform the task. The terms "legal assistant" and "paralegal" are synonymous and are not to be confused with numerous other legal titles which have proliferated with the public and within the legal community. *Guidelines for Utilization by Lawyers of the Services of Legal Assistants* approved by the New York State Bar Association House of Delegates on June 28, 1997.
> (*www.cdpa.info/files/NY_Paralegal_guidelines.pdf*)

Also adopting this definition is the Empire State Alliance of Paralegal Associations, an organization we will examine in section 1.2. The Alliance is a major promoter of professionalism among paralegals, as evidenced by its recommendations for minimum educational requirements for paralegals in the state. *Position Statement on Paralegal Education Standards in New York State* (2006). (*www.empirestateparalegals.org/position_papers*)

The New York State Department of Civil Service also has a definition of a paralegal that it uses for the examinations for the Legal Assistant 1 and 2 positions that we will discuss later in section 2.2:

> A paralegal is someone who applies knowledge of the law and legal procedures in rendering direct assistance to lawyers, clients, and courts; prepares and interprets legal documents; researches, compiles, and uses information from legal materials; and analyzes and handles procedural problems that involve independent decisions. NY State Department of Civil Service (S5/TC2 BXO-dmb). (*www.cs.state.ny.us/announarchive/announcements/24-830.cfm*)

This is a fascinating time to be a paralegal in New York. Paralegals, working in a wide variety of settings, have made major contributions in the delivery of legal services. The state has a rich paralegal history. Our objective in this book is to give you the perspective of this history and to provide resources that will help you:

- Find paralegal employment
- Understand many of the unique features of our state government
- Find laws that are the foundation of paralegal work
- Examine some of the major documents that paralegals prepare or help prepare on behalf of clients
- Abide by the ethics rules
- Participate in organized efforts to continue the growth of the paralegal profession
- Provide a comprehensive legal dictionary that defines the legal terms that give the legal system its distinctive character

In recognition of the value of the paralegal profession, the governor has issued a proclamation that declares July 20th to be Paralegal Day in the state. See Exhibit 1.1A.

B. Paralegals in the Twenty-First Century

Highlights

- About 7 out of 10 paralegals in the country work for law firms; others work for corporate legal departments, government agencies, legal aid/legal service offices, and special interest organizations.
- Employment is projected to grow much faster than average, as employers try to reduce costs by hiring paralegals to perform tasks that attorneys would otherwise have to perform.
- Formally trained paralegals have the best employment opportunities as competition for jobs increases. (*www.bls.gov/oco/ocos114.htm*)

EXHIBIT 1.1A Paralegal Day: Governor's Proclamation

State of New York
Executive Chamber

Proclamation

Whereas, the Empire State recognizes members of the legal community who share a common professional affiliation and high degree of dedication to their work through which they contribute to the integrity of our judicial system, and we join to acknowledge the significant role that paralegals, also called legal assistants, serve within this state; and

Whereas, of vital importance to the attorneys they assist and under whose supervision they work, paralegals are generally responsible for researching, analyzing, and managing the daily tasks for legal cases; and

Whereas, paralegals perform nearly all the functions of lawyers, except for those strictly constituting the practice of law, and they assist lawyers with virtually all aspects of legal work – including specialized areas of law, such as family law, corporate law, real estate, government, estate planning, litigation and criminal trials; and

Whereas, the duties of paralegals primarily involve researching and writing reports about pertinent sections of statutes or cases to help lawyers prepare for legal proceedings, as well as drafting documents for litigation; and

Whereas, paralegals also help lawyers speak with clients to uncover all the facts of a case by obtaining affidavits and assisting with depositions and other materials relevant to cases; and

Whereas, many paralegals work in government maintaining reference files, analyzing material for internal use and preparing informational guides on the law, and other paralegals work in community legal services helping disadvantaged people obtain legal advice and aid, while yet others work for corporations where they help draw up employee benefit plans, shareholder agreements and stock options; and

Whereas, in whatever capacity they work, paralegals are an important component of any legal team, and, not only is their work invaluable to lawyers, but also to the public which benefits from their efforts that promote the efficiency and effectiveness of the judicial process, and it is fitting that New Yorkers join to recognize this hardworking and dedicated community of professionals;

Now, Therefore, I, David A. Paterson, Governor of the State of New York, do hereby proclaim July 20, 2008 as

PARALEGAL DAY

in the Empire State.

Given under my hand and the Privy Seal of the State at the Capitol in the City of Albany this twenty-sixth day of June in the year two thousand eight.

David A. Paterson
Governor

Secretary to the Governor

Source: *www.state.ny.us/governor/keydocs/proclamations/proc_paralegal.html*

Work Settings

Most paralegals are employed by law firms, corporate legal departments, and government offices. In these organizations, they can work in many different areas of the law, including:

- Litigation
- Personal injury
- Corporate law
- Criminal law
- Intellectual property
- Labor and employment law

- Bankruptcy
- Immigration
- Family law
- Real estate
- Probate (wills, trusts, estates)

As the law has become more complex, paralegals have responded by becoming more specialized. Within specialties, functions often are broken down further so that paralegals may deal with a specific area. For example, paralegals specializing in labor law may concentrate exclusively on employee benefits. The U.S. Department of Labor has estimated that there are just over 263,000 paralegal jobs in the country. Bureau of Labor Statistics, U.S. Department of Labor, *Occupational Outlook Handbook*, 2008–09 Edition (*www.bls.gov/oco/ocos114.htm*).

A small number of paralegals own their own businesses and work as independent or freelance paralegals, contracting their services to attorneys or corporate legal departments. At some administrative agencies (e.g., Social Security Administration) paralegals are authorized to provide client representation at agency hearings without attorney supervision. Finally, some independent paralegals offer limited law-related services directly to the public without attorney supervision. (Substantial restrictions exist on what these individuals are able to do, as we will see later in sections 3.1 and 3.3.)

Paralegal Work

While attorneys assume ultimate responsibility for legal work, they often delegate tasks to paralegals. In fact, paralegals are continuing to assume a growing range of tasks in the nation's legal offices and perform some of the same tasks as attorneys. Nevertheless, paralegals cannot give legal advice, set fees, represent clients in court, or engage in other categories of activities that constitute the unauthorized practice of law.

The variety and complexity of paralegal tasks depend on the kind of law practiced in the office, the competence and initiative of the paralegal, and the willingness of the attorney to delegate. Here are some examples of tasks and skills that demonstrate this variety and complexity:

- Provide litigation assistance by helping attorneys prepare for hearings and trials
- Investigate the facts of cases and help ensure that all relevant information is considered

- Perform cite checks, help determine the current validity of laws (through a process called shepardizing and keyciting), and perform other research tasks
- Prepare pleadings and motions, summarize pretrial testimony, perform further factual research, and assist attorneys during the trial itself
- Help with file organization and tracking so that the numerous documents involved in client representation can be easily accessible to attorneys
- Help draft contracts, mortgages, separation agreements, trust instruments, tax returns, and estate plans
- Coordinate and supervise the activities of other paralegals and support staff (paralegal supervisors have formed their own association, the International Paralegal Management Association; *www.paralegalmanagement.org*)

Transactional paralegals provide paralegal services for attorneys who represent clients in transactions such as entering contracts, incorporating a business, closing a real estate sale, or planning an estate. Paralegals who work for corporations often assist attorneys with employee contracts, shareholder agreements, stock-option plans, employee benefit plans, and other transactional documents. They may help prepare and file annual financial reports, corporate minutes, and corporate resolutions. They perform compliance work by monitoring and reviewing government regulations to ensure that the corporation is aware of new requirements and is operating within the law. Increasingly, experienced paralegals are assuming additional supervisory responsibilities such as overseeing team projects and serving as a communications link between the legal team and the business staff of the corporation. When the corporation retains outside counsel, the corporate paralegal has additional liaison responsibilities.

Paralegals who work in government agencies analyze legal material for internal use, maintain office files, conduct factual and legal research for attorneys, and collect evidence for agency hearings. They may help prepare informative or explanatory material on laws, agency regulations, and agency policy for general use by the agency and the public. Paralegals employed in legal aid or legal service offices in the community help disadvantaged individuals who cannot afford private law firms. They file forms, conduct research, prepare documents, and, when authorized by law, represent clients at administrative hearings.

Paralegals in small and medium-size law firms often perform a variety of duties that require a general knowledge of several areas of law. Those employed by large law firms, government agencies, and corporations, however, are more likely to specialize in one area of law.

Familiarity with the use of computers has become essential to paralegal work. Software is used to search documents and data stored in computer databases and CD-ROM. The Internet is also a valuable research tool. In litigation involving many supporting documents, paralegals often use computer databases to retrieve, organize, and index various materials. Imaging software allows paralegals to scan documents directly into a database, while billing programs help them track hours that will be billed to clients. Computer software packages are also used to prepare tax returns, assemble legal documents, create trial exhibits, maintain calendars and dockets, etc.

Certification

Although few employers require certification, earning a voluntary certificate from a professional association may offer advantages in the labor market. Some paralegals feel that certification is important because it indicates professionalism, demonstrates a level of proficiency, and enhances the profession as a whole. Here is an overview of the major certification programs that are available:

- CLA/CP certification of the National Association of Legal Assistants (NALA). Passing an exam and fulfilling the other requirements of NALA entitle you to be called a Certified Legal Assistant (CLA) or a Certified Paralegal (CP) (*www.nala.org*). NALA also has an advanced certification credential, Advanced Certified Paralegal (ACP) (*www.nala.org/apc.aspx*).
- PACE certification of the National Federation of Paralegal Associations (NFPA). Passing an exam and fulfilling the other requirements of NFPA entitle you to be called a Registered Paralegal (RP) or a PACE Registered Paralegal (*www.paralegals.org*).
- PP certification of NALS, the Association for Legal Professionals. Passing an exam and fulfilling the other requirements of NALS entitle you to be called a Professional Paralegal (PP) (*www.nals.org*).
- AACP certification of the American Alliance of Paralegals Inc. (AAPI). Fulfilling the requirements of AAPI (which does not include an examination) entitles you to be called an American Alliance Certified Paralegal (AACP) (*www.aapipara.org*).

National Job Outlook According to the U.S. Department of Labor

Employment for paralegals and legal assistants is projected to grow much faster than the average for all occupations through 2018. Employers are trying to reduce costs and increase the availability and efficiency of legal services by hiring paralegals to perform tasks formerly carried out by attorneys. Besides new jobs created by employment growth, additional job openings will arise as people retire and leave the field. Despite projections of rapid employment growth, competition for jobs should continue as many people seek to go into this profession. Experienced, formally trained paralegals often have the best employment opportunities.

Private law firms will continue to be the largest employers of paralegals, but a growing array of other organizations, such as corporate legal departments, insurance companies, real estate and title insurance firms, and banks hire paralegals. Corporations in particular are boosting their in-house legal departments to cut costs. Demand for paralegals is expected to grow as an expanding population increasingly requires legal services, especially in areas such as intellectual property, health care, elder law issues, criminal law, environmental law, and the global economy. Paralegals who specialize in areas such as real estate, bankruptcy, medical malpractice, and product liability are often in demand. The growth of prepaid legal plans should also contribute to the demand for legal services. (A prepaid plan is like health insurance in which a person pays an ongoing fee or premium for legal service needs that might arise in the future.) A growing number of experienced paralegals are expected to establish their own businesses as independent paralegals, mainly as contract paralegals who sell their services to attorneys.

Job opportunities for paralegals will expand in the public sector as well. Community legal aid or legal service programs (which provide assistance to the poor, elderly, minorities, and middle-income families), will employ additional paralegals to minimize expenses and serve the most people. Federal, state, and local government agencies, consumer organizations, and the courts also should continue to hire paralegals in increasing numbers.

To a limited extent, paralegal jobs are affected by the business cycle. During recessions, demand declines for some discretionary legal services, such as estate planning, drafting wills, and handling real estate transactions. Corporations may be less inclined to initiate certain types of litigation when falling sales and profits lead to fiscal belt tightening. As a result, full-time paralegals employed in offices adversely affected by a recession may be laid off or have their work hours reduced. However, during recessions, corporations and individuals are more likely to face other problems that require legal assistance, such as bankruptcies, foreclosures, and divorces. Bureau of Labor Statistics, U.S. Department of Labor, *Occupational Outlook Handbook*, 2008–09 Edition (*www.bls.gov/oco/ocos114.htm*).

Career Video on Paralegals

To watch a video on the paralegal career:

- Go to *www.acinet.org/acinet*.
- Click "Videos" then "Cluster and Career Videos" then "Law and Public Safety" then "Paralegals and Legal Assistants."
- Also type "career videos" in the search box; click "Cluster and Career Videos" and scroll down to "Paralegals and Legal Assistants."

C. Statistics on Paralegal Employment in New York

Exhibit 1.1B presents an overview of paralegal employment in New York in comparison with related occupations.

Earnings of paralegals vary greatly. Salaries depend on education, training, experience, the type and size of employer, and the geographic location of the job. In general, paralegals who work for large law firms or in large metropolitan areas earn more than those who work for smaller firms or in less populated regions. In addition to earning a salary, many paralegals receive bonuses.

Average New York Wages
Average wage for entry-level paralegal: $39,810
Average wage for experienced paralegal: $66,010
Source: Career Zone
(*www.nycareerzone.org/graphic/profile.jsp?onetsoc=23-2011.00*)

Exhibit 1.1C provides a more detailed overview of national and New York data on compensation.

D. More Information

Paralegal Associations in New York
See section 1.2 for information on every paralegal and related legal association in New York.

Career Zone: Paralegals and Legal Assistants in New York
www.nycareerzone.org
(Click "Career Information"; sign up for a free job assistance account)
www.nycareerzone.org/graphic/profile.jsp?onetsoc=23-2011.00

U.S. Department of Labor, Paralegals and Legal Assistants
www.bls.gov/oco/ocos114.htm

American Bar Association Standing Committee on Paralegals (SCOP)
www.abanet.org/legalservices/paralegals

American Bar Association
Associate Membership for Paralegals
www.abanet.org/join

National Federation of Paralegal Associations (NFPA)
www.paralegals.org

National Association of Legal Assistants (NALA)
www.nala.org

NALS, the Association for Legal Professionals
www.nals.org

International Paralegal Management Association
www.paralegalmanagement.org

American Association for Paralegal Education
www.aafpe.org

EXHIBIT 1.1B	Employment Growth of Paralegals Compared with Other Legal Occupations in the Nation and in New York			
United States	**Employment**		**Percentage Change**	**Job Openings***
	2008	**2018**		
Paralegals and legal assistants	263,800	337,900	+ 28 %	10,400
Lawyers	759,200	857,700	+ 13 %	24,040
Legal support workers, all other	48,100	53,400	+ 11 %	1,240
Court reporters	21,500	25,400	+ 28 %	710
New York	**Employment**		**Percentage Change**	**Job Openings***
	2006	**2016**		
Paralegals and legal assistants	25,580	29,760	+ 16 %	760
Lawyers	85,610	90,960	+ 6 %	2,160
Legal support workers, all other	2,670	2,620	− 2 %	40
Court reporters	1,970	2,060	+ 4 %	40

* Job openings refers to the average annual job openings due to growth and net replacement.

Source: Bureau of Labor Statistics, Office of Occupational Statistics and Employment Projections; New York State Department of Labor, Labor Market Information. Career InfoNet; Bureau of Labor Statistics, Office of Occupational Statistics and Employment Projections; New York Labor Market Information (*www.acinet.org/acinet*) (click "Occupation Information" then "Compare Employment Trends" then "New York" then "Legal" then "Paralegals and Legal Assistants" plus other legal occupations).

EXHIBIT 1.1C Paralegal Wages Nationally and in New York State						
Location	**Pay Period**	**2008**				
		10%	**25%**	**Median**	**75%**	**90%**
United States	Hourly	$14.07	$17.34	$22.18	$28.51	$35.31
	Yearly	$29,300	$36,100	$46,100	$59,300	$73,400
Albany-Schenectady-Troy	Hourly	$15.30	$17.90	$21.33	$24.74	$29.32
	Yearly	$31,800	$37,200	$44,400	$51,500	$61,000
Binghamton	Hourly	$13.37	$16.01	$18.21	$22.73	$37.63
	Yearly	$27,800	$33,300	$37,900	$47,300	$78,300
Buffalo-Niagara Falls	Hourly	$14.23	$17.17	$21.27	$26.77	$31.52
	Yearly	$29,600	$35,700	$44,200	$55,700	$65,600
Glens Falls	Hourly	$13.52	$15.14	$17.67	$27.10	$34.33
	Yearly	$28,100	$31,500	$36,800	$56,400	$71,400
Nassau-Suffolk	Hourly	$18.28	$21.59	$25.73	$30.06	$34.79
	Yearly	$38,000	$44,900	$53,500	$62,500	$72,400
New York-White Plains-Wayne, NY-NJ	Hourly	$18.75	$22.48	$28.98	$35.71	$40.14
	Yearly	$39,000	$46,800	$60,300	$74,300	$83,500
Poughkeepsie-Newburgh-Middletown	Hourly	$16.46	$20.72	$25.36	$31.79	$37.53
	Yearly	$34,200	$43,100	$52,700	$66,100	$78,100
Rochester	Hourly	$15.95	$17.48	$20.19	$24.21	$28.71
	Yearly	$33,200	$36,400	$42,000	$50,400	$59,700
Syracuse	Hourly	$15.91	$18.17	$22.61	$28.34	$31.78
	Yearly	$33,100	$37,800	$47,000	$58,900	$66,100
Utica-Rome	Hourly	$15.39	$17.13	$19.46	$25.92	$31.04
	Yearly	$32,000	$35,600	$40,500	$53,900	$64,600

Source: Career InfoNet; Bureau of Labor Statistics, Occupational Employment Statistics Survey; the Labor Market Information Office within the State Employment Security Agency (*www.acinet.org*) (click "Occupation Information" then "Compare Metro Wages" then "Legal" then "Paralegals and Legal Assistants" then the cities desired)

American Association for Justice
Paralegal Affiliates
www.justice.org/cps/rde/xchg/justice/hs.xsl/1090.htm

Law Firms in New York
www.hg.org/northam-firms.html
lawyers.findlaw.com
www.findlaw.com/11stategov/ny/index.html

America's Largest Law Firms
www.ilrg.com/nlj250

National Association of Legal Employers (NALP)
www.nalpdirectory.com

Law Firm Salaries
www.infirmation.com/shared/insider/payscale.tcl
swz.salary.com

(type "paralegal" in the "Search by" box and your zip code in "Location")

Wikipedia on Paralegals
en.wikipedia.org/wiki/Paralegal

E. Something to Check

1. Watch the video mentioned in this section (just before Exhibit 1.1B). What is your evaluation of the video?

2. The New York State Bar Association's definition of a paralegal is presented at the beginning of section A. Compare this definition to the definitions of a paralegal found on the Web sites of NFPA, NALA, and SCOP. (See their Internet addresses

above.) List the similarities and differences among the definitions.

3. Pick an area of practice that interests you. Find and compare three law firm descriptions of that area online. In what ways are the descriptions similar and different? To find law firms online, go to Google (*www.google.com*) or any general search engine. Type "New York law firm" and the area of law you are checking. For example:

"New York law firm" "criminal law"
"New York law firm" "adoption law"
"New York law firm" "estate planning"

1.2 Paralegal Associations and Related Groups in New York

A. Introduction

B. Paralegal Associations and Bar Associations That Allow Paralegal Affiliate Membership

C. National Paralegal Associations

D. Other Law-Related Groups

E. Something to Check

A. Introduction

There are many vibrant paralegal associations in New York that have had a major impact on the development of the field. We will be examining paralegal associations as well as bar associations that have various categories of paralegal membership. All of these organizations can be helpful in finding employment and in continuing your legal education while employed. For example, one of the best networking opportunities available to you will be the various meetings regularly held by paralegal associations. The essence of networking is locating other paralegals and exchanging ideas, resources, leads, and business cards with them. Such exchanges can be important even if the subject matter of a particular meeting does not interest you. Furthermore, your involvement in a paralegal association will help strengthen the association and the profession itself.

Here is a list of the paralegal associations and bar associations with paralegal membership categories that we will be covering:

Paralegal and Related Associations

- Associations affiliated with the Empire State Alliance of Paralegal Associations (*www.empirestateparalegals.org*):

Adirondack Paralegal Association (APA)
Capital District Paralegal Association (CDPA)
Long Island Paralegal Association (LIPA)
New York City Paralegal Association (NYCPA)
Paralegal Association of Rochester (PAR)
Western New York Paralegal Association (WNYPA)

- Also affiliated with the Alliance:
Onondaga County Bar Association Paralegals Committee
Oswego County Bar Association

- Associations affiliated with NALS, the Association for Legal Professionals (*www.nals.org*):
Central NY Chapter of NALS
NALS of New York
NALS of New York City
NALS of Nassau County

Not all associations in New York are alike. Some are large and highly structured, while others may be small, more informal, and not as easy to reach. When an organization has a Web site, visit it often to explore its mission and services. You'll want to find out, for example, if the organization offers a job bank that lists current paralegal openings in the area. Note the date and location of the next meeting of the group nearest you. For many paralegals, as indicated, regular participation in organization activities is richly rewarding.

Bar Associations That Have Paralegal Membership Categories

Albany County Bar Association
Asian American Bar Association of New York
Bar Association of Erie County
Capital District Women's Bar Association
Greater Rochester Association for Women Attorneys
Lesbian, Gay, Bisexual and Transgender Law Association of Greater New York
Metropolitan Black Lawyers Association
Monroe County Bar Association
Nassau Lawyers' Association of Long Island
New York Association of Collaborative Professionals
New York City Chapter, National Lawyers Guild
New York State Academy of Trial Lawyers
New York State Association of Criminal Defense Lawyers
New York State Defenders Association
New York State Trial Lawyers Association
Onondaga County Bar Association
Oswego County Bar Association
Saratoga County Bar Association
Westchester County Bar Association

B. Paralegal Associations and Bar Associations That Allow Paralegal Affiliate Membership

ADIRONDACK PARALEGAL ASSOCIATION (APA)

www.empirestateparalegals.org/member_associations
bushmanmlds@gmail.com

Background: APA was founded in 1989 for paralegals who work in the "North Country."

Number of Members: 60+

Publications: *President's Message*

Services Offered: In addition to providing a support network, APA offers a job bank, makes speakers available on the paralegal career to high school and college students, provides updates of legal issues in its newsletter, provides scholarships to high school students, and holds monthly meetings from September through May.

ALBANY COUNTY BAR ASSOCIATION (ACBA)

www.albanycountybar.com/membership/
Affiliate membership dues for paralegals: $25
("Any legal secretary or paralegal employed by or working under the direction of any member of the Association who is a member of the Bar of the State of New York in good standing is entitled to all privileges of the Association except for voting or holding office.")

ASIAN AMERICAN BAR ASSOCIATION OF NEW YORK

www.aabany.org
Paralegal membership dues: $30
www.aabany.org/registernewmembers.cfm
(A "Paralegal Member shall be entitled to all privileges and rights of Active Members, excluding the right to vote at any/all meetings and/or hold office.")

BAR ASSOCIATION OF ERIE COUNTY (BAEC)

Affiliate membership for paralegals
www.eriebar.org/displaycommon.cfm?an=9
www.eriebar.org/displaycommon.cfm?an=1&subarticlenbr=79
(BAEC "is a professional organization with more than 3,800 member lawyers, judges, law students, legal administrators and paralegals.")

CAPITAL DISTRICT PARALEGAL ASSOCIATION (CDPA)

P.O. Box 12562
Albany, NY 12212-2562
info@cdpa.info; president@cdpa.info
www.cdpa.info

Background: CDPA was founded in 1993. (It was formerly known as the Albany Legal Assistants Association.) The goal of CDPA is to "promote and improve the image of paralegals as professionals" in the Albany/Capital District area.

Membership: CDPA offers four classes of membership: Voting ($55), Student ($35), Affiliate ($40), and Sustaining ($150).

National Affiliation: CDPA is affiliated with the National Federation of Paralegal Associations (*www.paralegals.org*).

Number of Members: 100+

Publications: *Para-News*
(*www.cdpa.info/NewsletterCommittee.html*)

Services Offered: Salary and benefits surveys, continuing legal education dinner/seminars, roundtable discussions on the paralegal career for area paralegal students, participation in pro bono activities (e.g., assisting in divorce in domestic violence cases) through the Albany County Bar Association.

CAPITAL DISTRICT WOMEN'S BAR ASSOCIATION

Non-attorney membership dues: $50
cdwba.org
www.wbasny.bluestep.net
(click "Chapters")

CENTRAL NY CHAPTER OF NALS

www.nalsofnewyorkinc.org/onondaga.html

National Affiliation: Central NY Chapter **of** NALS is affiliated with the NALS, the Association for Legal Professionals (*www.nals.org*).

Publications: *Monthly Bulletin*

Services Offered: Networking, job bank, continuing legal education.

GREATER ROCHESTER ASSOCIATION FOR WOMEN ATTORNEYS

Non-attorney affiliate membership dues: $60
grawa.org
grawa.org/grawa_join.htm

LESBIAN, GAY, BISEXUAL AND TRANSGENDER LAW ASSOCIATION OF GREATER NEW YORK

Legal assistant membership dues: $75
www.le-gal.org/site/form.pdf
www.le-gal.org/join/legalform.html

LONG ISLAND PARALEGAL ASSOCIATION (LIPA)

1877 Bly Road
East Meadow, NY 11554
516-357-9820
www.liparalegals.org

Background: LIPA was established as an independent association in 1983 after it ceased being a chapter of the Greater New York Paralegal Association (the latter no longer being in existence).

Membership: LIPA offers four classes of membership: Voting ($70), Associate ($70), Student ($55), and Contributing ($85).

National Affiliation: LIPA is affiliated with the National Federation of Paralegal Associations (*www.paralegals.org*).

Publications: Newsletter (*www.liparalegals.org/main_web/newsletter_main.htm*)

Services Offered: Job bank, continuing legal education programs, e-mail alerts on developments in the field.

METROPOLITAN BLACK LAWYERS ASSOCIATION
Non-lawyer membership dues: $25
www.mbbanyc.org
www.facebook.com/group.php?gid=53833336360

MONROE COUNTY BAR ASSOCIATION
Paralegal affiliate membership dues: $90
www.mcba.org
www.mcba.org/Members/Memberservices

NALS OF THE LOWER HUDSON VALLEY
www.nalsofnewyorkinc.org/lowerhudsonvalley.html

National Affiliation: NALS of the Lower Hudson Valley is affiliated with NALS, the Association for Legal Professionals (*www.nals.org*)

Publications: *Monthly Bulletin*

Services Offered: Networking, job bank, continuing legal education.

NALS OF NASSAU COUNTY
www.nalsofnewyorkinc.org/nassau.html

National Affiliation: NALS of Nassau County is affiliated with NALS, the Association for Legal Professionals (*www.nals.org*).

Publications: *Monthly Bulletin*

Services Offered: Networking, job bank, continuing legal education.

NALS OF NEW YORK
www.nalsofnewyorkinc.org

Chapters: *www.nalsofnewyorkinc.org/chapters.html*

National Affiliation: NALS of New York is affiliated with NALS, the Association for Legal Professionals (*www.nals.org*).

Publications: *Monthly Bulletin*

Services Offered: Networking, job bank, continuing legal education.

NALS OF NEW YORK CITY
www.nalsofnewyorkinc.org/newyorkcity.html

National Affiliation: NALS of New York City is affiliated with NALS, the Association for Legal Professionals (*www.nals.org*).

Publications: *Monthly Bulletin*

Services Offered: Networking, job bank, continuing legal education.

NALS OF SUFFOLK COUNTY
www.nalsofnewyorkinc.org/suffolk.html

National Affiliation: NALS of Suffolk County is affiliated with NALS, the Association for Legal Professionals (*www.nals.org*).

Publications: *Monthly Bulletin*

Services Offered: Networking, job bank, continuing legal education.

NASSAU LAWYERS ASSOCIATION OF LONG ISLAND
Non-lawyer associate membership dues: $50
www.nassaulawyersassociation.com

NEW YORK CITY CHAPTER, NATIONAL LAWYERS GUILD
Non-lawyer/legal worker membership dues: $45+
www.nlgnyc.org

NEW YORK ASSOCIATION OF COLLABORATIVE PROFESSIONALS
Non-lawyer membership dues: $1,000
www.collaborativelawny.com
www.collaborativelawny.com/join.php

NEW YORK CITY PARALEGAL ASSOCIATION (NYCPA)
P.O. Box 4484
Grand Central Station
New York, NY 10163-4484
www.nyc-pa.org
www.linkedin.com (after signing in, type "New York City Paralegal Association" in the search box)

Background: NYCPA was formed in 2007 to be "a viable medium for the progress and professional advancement of all paralegals working within the five Boroughs, Westchester and Rockland." NYCPA is an expansion of the Manhattan Paralegal Association (the latter no longer being in existence).

Membership: NYCPA offers three classes of membership: Voting ($100), Associate ($75), and Student ($50).

National Affiliation: NYCPA is affiliated with the National Federation of Paralegal Associations (*www.paralegals.org*).

Publications: *The New York City Paralegal Times* (*www.nyc-pa.org/new-york-paralegal-times*).

Services Offered: Job bank, networking events, study groups, online forum (listserv), partnering with legal employment agencies.

NEW YORK STATE ACADEMY OF TRIAL LAWYERS
Paralegal membership dues: $75
www.trialacademy.org
www.trialacademy.org/NYSA/index.cfm?event=showPage&
pg=MemberApp

NEW YORK STATE ASSOCIATION OF CRIMINAL DEFENSE LAWYERS
Non-lawyer associate membership dues: $175
www.nysacdl.org
www.nysacdl.org/index.php?doc_id=6

NEW YORK STATE DEFENDERS ASSOCIATION
Non-lawyer associate membership dues: $40
www.nysda.org
www.nysda.org/html/about_nysda.html#Membership

NEW YORK STATE TRIAL LAWYERS ASSOCIATION (NYSTLA)
132 Nassau Street
New York, NY 10038
212-349-5890
info@nystla.org
www.nystla.org

Paralegal membership: $75

Paralegal discussion forum: 68.166.193.91/jive4/index.
jspa (*paralegalforum@nystla.org*)

Paralegal articles: type "paralegal" in search box (*www.nystla.org*)

ONONDAGA COUNTY BAR ASSOCIATION (OCBA)
Paralegal Committee
109 South Warren Street
Syracuse, NY 13202
315-471-2667
www.onbar.org
(click "About the OCBA" then "Sections" and then "Paralegals")
(also click "About the OCBA" "Renew OCBA Membership")

Paralegals Committee membership dues: $65
www.onbar.org/about/joininstructions.htm

Attorney attestation: To become a member, there must be a certification from a sponsoring attorney stating: "I certify that I am an attorney who is a member of the Onondaga County Bar Association, and that this applicant is employed by me and that a majority of his/her work is in the capacity of a legal assistant or paralegal."

Committees: Affiliate members then become members of committees, including the paralegal committee.

Services offered: Monthly mini-seminars, listserv for paralegal members, job bank, networking, and participation in events offered by other sections and committees of OCBA. The bar's publication (the OCBA Bar Reporter) has a column devoted to the Paralegals Committee.

OSWEGO COUNTY BAR ASSOCIATION (OSCBA)
(Oswego County Paralegal Association)
P.O. Box 5453
Oswego, NY 13126
315-343-4016
www.oswego-bar.org

Affiliate membership dues: $25
www.empirestateparalegals.org/member_associations

PARALEGAL ASSOCIATION OF ROCHESTER (PAR)
P.O. Box 40567
Rochester, NY 14604
www.rochesterparalegal.org
www.par.itgo.com

Background: PAR was established in 1975 to be an organized voice of paralegals in the Rochester area and to promote the profession.

Membership: PAR offers three classes of membership: Voting ($60), Student ($30), and Affiliate ($50).

National Affiliation: PAR is affiliated with the National Federation of Paralegal Associations (*www.paralegals.org*).

Publications: Monthly Calendar of Events. In addition, PAR writes a monthly article on the paralegal profession in the *Daily Record* (click "Press Releases" under "What's New" on PAR's home page).

Services offered: Monthly luncheon meetings with guest speakers, workshops, continuing legal education, pro bono opportunities, networking.

SARATOGA COUNTY BAR ASSOCIATION
Paralegal associate membership dues: $25
www.saratogacountybar.org
www.saratogacountybar.org/membership.html

WESTCHESTER COUNTY BAR ASSOCIATION
Non-lawyer affiliate membership dues: $80
www.wcbany.org
www.wcbany.org/displaycommon.cfm?an=4

WESTERN NEW YORK PARALEGAL ASSOCIATION (WNYPA)
P.O. Box 207
Buffalo, NY 14201
contact@wnyparalegals.org
www.wnyparalegals.org

Background: WNYPA was formed in 1976 "to promote the professional development and continuing legal education of paralegals in the Western New York area."

History of WNYPA:
www.wnyparalegals.org/docs/WNYPA_Footprints.pdf#
search=%22%22ADIRONDACK%20PARALEGAL%20
ASSOCIATION%22%22

Membership: WNYPA offers four classes of membership: Active ($60), Associate ($50), Student ($40), and Sustaining ($100).

National Affiliation: WNYPA is affiliated with the National Federation of Paralegal Associations (*www.paralegals.org*).

Number of Members: 200+

Publications: *Paramount*

Services offered: Annual Paralegal/Attorney Dinner, salary survey, scholarship assistance, job bank, bulletin board discussion forums, continuing legal education.

C. National Paralegal Associations

There are a number of national paralegal associations that New York paralegals have joined either directly or through one of their affiliates:

National Association of Legal Assistants (NALA)
National Federation of Paralegal Associations (NFPA)
NALS, the Association of Legal Professionals (NALS)
American Alliance of Paralegals (AAPI)

National Association of Legal Assistants (NALA)

www.nala.org
Certification Awarded: Certified Legal Assistant (CLA); Certified Paralegal (CP); Advanced Certified Paralegal (ACP)
Certification Requirements: *www.nala.org/Certification.aspx* (*www.nala.org/apcweb/index.html*)
Ethics Code: *www.nala.org/code.aspx*
Newsletter: *Facts and Findings*
Continuing Legal Education: *www.nalacampus.com*
Affiliated Associations: *www.nala.org/factsandfindings.aspx*

National Federation of Paralegal Associations (NFPA)

www.paralegals.org
Certification Awarded: PACE Registered Paralegal (RP)
Certification Requirements: *www.paralegals.org* (click "PACE/RP")
Ethics Code: *www.paralegals.org* (click "Positions & Issues")
Newsletter: *National Paralegal Reporter* (*www.paralegals.org*)
Continuing Legal Education: *www.paralegals.org* (click "CLE")
Career Center: *www.paralegals.org*

Affiliated Associations: *www.paralegals.org* (click "About NFPA" then "Local Member Associations")

NALS, the Association of Legal Professionals (Nals)

www.nals.org
Certification Awarded: Professional Paralegal (PP)
Certification Requirements: *www.nals.org/certification*
Ethics Code: *www.nals.org/aboutnals/Code*
Newsletter: *@Law* (*www.nals.org/newsletters/index.html*)
Continuing Legal Education: *www.nals.org/education/index.html*
Career Center: *www.nals.org/careercenter/index.html*
Affiliated Associations: *www.nals.org/membership/states/index.html*

American Alliance of Paralegals (Aapi)

www.aapipara.org
Certification Awarded: American Alliance Certified Paralegal (AACP)
Certification Requirements: *www.aapipara.org/Certification.htm*
Ethics Code: *www.aapipara.org/Ethicalstandards.htm*
Newsletter: *Alliance Echo* (*www.aapipara.org/Newsletter.htm*)
Job Bank: *www.aapipara.org/Jobbank.htm*
Continuing Legal Education: *www.aapipara.org*

D. Other Law-Related Groups

New York State Bar Association
www.nysba.org

Other Bar Associations in New York
See section 3.4

American Bar Association
Associate Membership for Paralegals ($175)
www.abanet.org/join

American Association for Justice
Paralegal Affiliates ($50)
www.justice.org/cps/rde/xchg/justice/hs.xsl/2636.htm

American Association of Legal Nurse Consultants, New York
www.nyccaalnc.org

American Association of Legal Nurse Consultants, Rochester
www.rochesterlnn.com

Association of Legal Administrators—Buffalo
www.alabuffalo.org

Association of Legal Administrators—Hudson Valley
www.hudsonvalleyala.org

Association of Legal Administrators—New York City
www.alanyc.org

East Coast Association of Litigation Support Managers
www.ecalsm.com

Legal Marketing Association, Metropolitan New York
www.nylma.org
www.legalmarketing.org/nylma

New York State Dispute Resolution Association
www.nysdra.org

Association of Law Libraries of Upstate New York
www.aallnet.org/chapter/alluny

Law Library Association of Greater New York
www.aallnet.org/chapter/llagny

New York State Society of Enrolled Agents
www.nyssea.org

New York State Court Reporters Association
www.nyscra.org

Self-Advocacy Association of New York State
(persons with disabilities)
www.sanys.org/advocacy.htm

E. Something to Check

1. Examine any two online paralegal newsletters. Find an article or position statement in each that covers the same ethical issue. Compare what each says about the issue.
2. For each of the following three topics, which paralegal association has the most comprehensive links: (a) New York law, (b) paralegal employment, and (c) litigation services?

1.3 Sources of CLE for Paralegals

   A. Introduction

   B. CLE Options

   C. Something to Check

A. Introduction

CLE (continuing legal education) is training in the law (often short term) that one receives after completing formal legal training. The training usually takes place at a rented hotel facility or other accessible location, often in a larger city. Increasingly, more flexible alternatives have become available through audio tapes, video tapes, and online offerings.

There are several reasons CLE is important for New York paralegals:

- First, CLE allows paralegals to keep current on changing laws, new developments in law office management, and the dynamics of the practice of law.

- Second, CLE programs can be an excellent way to network with paralegals and other professionals in the field of law.
- Third, if you have received voluntary paralegal certification from a national organization, you must submit proof of compliance with the CLE requirements for maintaining your certification. For an explanation of these requirements, see:

  - National Association of Legal Assistants (*www.nala.org*) for being a Certified Legal Assistant/Certified Paralegal
  - National Federation of Paralegal Associations (*www.paralegals.org*) for being a PACE Registered Paralegal
  - American Alliance of Paralegals (*www.aapipara.org*) for being an American Alliance Certified Paralegal
  - NALS, the Association for Legal Professionals (*www.nals.org*) for being a Professional Paralegal

- Fourth, if you move to a state such as California that has mandatory/minimum continuing legal education (MCLE) requirements, you may be able to argue that the CLE you took in New York will satisfy some of the CLE requirements of that state (on California's requirements, see *www.caparalegal.org*).

Keep careful records of your attendance at CLE courses and events even if you do not need to do so for certification. CLE helps demonstrate your expertise and can be a marketing tool when seeking a raise or other employment.

On the tax deductibility of CLE, see Appendix A of Part 2.

B. CLE Options

Your Paralegal School

Many paralegal schools offer excellent CLE opportunities for their own graduates as well as for paralegals educated at other schools. Check the Web sites of schools in your area as well as elsewhere in the state. Some of the CLE programs are offered online so that they can be taken anywhere.

Your Local Paralegal Association

Go to the Web site of your paralegal association (see section 1.2). On the site, look for links that might be labeled "education," "continuing legal education," "CLE," "professional development," "career center," "events," etc. Click these links to find out if the association sponsors or links to CLE programs. If there is a search box on the site, type in these terms. If there is an e-mail link to the association, send a message inquiring about CLE opportunities.

Also check the Web sites of related associations in New York such as chapters of the Association of Legal Administrators (see the links at the end of section 1.2). They may lead you to additional CLE options you should consider.

National Paralegal Associations

National Federation of Paralegal Associations
www.paralegals.org
(click "CLE")

National Association of Legal Assistants
www.nala.org
(click "Continuing Education for Paralegals")

NALS, the Association for Legal Professionals
www.nals.org
(click "Online Learning Center")

New York State Bar Association Attorney CLE
www.nysba.org
(click "CLE")

Many paralegals take some of the same CLE programs offered to attorneys. Most New York attorneys are required to attend 24 hours of CLE every two years, including four hours of ethics and professionalism (32 hours total for newly admitted attorneys). There is a wide variety of CLE programs and CLE providers, but the New York State Bar Association is considered by many lawyers to be one of the best, with a wide range of subjects and formats available. Paralegal employers are often willing to pay for a paralegal's participation in CLE programs offered by quality providers such as the state bar.

New York State's Continuing Legal Education Board
www.courts.state.ny.us/attorneys/cle/index.shtml

See the links to the list of accredited providers of CLE in New York.

Your Local Bar Association

Local bar associations are active in CLE. Bigger cities and counties typically have many offerings, but even smaller areas usually have choices worth considering. Go to the Web site of your local bar association (see section 3.4). If you live in a rural area, try the Web sites of nearby larger cities. Click "education," "CLE," "continuing legal education," or "professional development" to find out what is offered by the local bar.

Specialty Bar Associations

Also check what is available from the specialty bar associations (see section 3.4 for their Web addresses).

New York State Trial Lawyers Association
www.nystla.org
(click "CLE")

Women's Bar Association of the State of New York
www.wbasny.bluestep.net
(click "CLE")

West Legal Education Center
westlegaledcenter.com

- In the CLE pull-down menus, find New York programs. Type "New York" as a keyword in the search box.
- Under "Browse Programs" click "Paralegal Studies."

Findlaw CLE
www.findlaw.com/07cle/list.html

Paralegal Gateway CLE
www.legalspan.com/plg/catalog.asp

Law.Com CLE Center, New York
clecenter.com/programs/bundles.aspx?stateCode=NY

Institute for Paralegal Education
www.nbi-sems.com/instituteforparalegaleducation.aspx
(type in your zip code)

National Business Institute
www.nbi-sems.com
(under "Paralegal Knowledge" type your zip code)

International Paralegal Management Association
paralegalmanagement.org
(click "Events" then "Webinar")

American Bar Association CLE
www.abanet.org/cle/clenow
www.abanet.org/cle/ecle/home.html

Taecan
www.taecan.com
(click "NY" in the pull-down menu)

Practicing Law Institute
www.pli.edu

General Search Engines
Type "ny cle" or "nys cle" in
www.google.com
www.yahoo.com
www.bing.com

C. Something to Check

Pick an area of New York law and practice. For that area, find five different CLE courses or offerings from different CLE providers. Describe and compare the five.

Paralegals in Court Opinions
A. Introduction
B. Abbreviations
C. Case Summaries and Excerpts
D. Something to Check

A. Introduction

One sign of the prominence of paralegals is the extent to which paralegal issues have been discussed in court opinions. This section demonstrates this prominence by presenting excerpts from a wide range of these opinions. Some of the opinions raise ethical issues, although most of the opinions cover broader themes such as the award of paralegal fees, the consequences of paralegal mistakes, the attorney-client privilege, and the division of a paralegal degree in a divorce action. Of course, even these themes can have ethical implications, but a more comprehensive treatment of ethics will come later in sections 3.2 and 3.3. Most of the cases involving the unauthorized practice of law (and defining the practice of law) are covered in section 3.1.

To compile the material for this section, we did a search on Westlaw (WL) that asked for every case that mentions paralegal, legal assistant, lay assistant, or bankruptcy petition preparer.

Westlaw Query:

paralegal "legal assistant" "lay assistant" "bankruptcy petition preparer"

The database in Westlaw selected to run this query was NY-CS-ALL. It contains all published and unpublished cases from the following courts:

New York state courts
United States Court of Appeals for the 2d Circuit
United States District Courts in New York
United States Bankruptcy Courts in New York

The query produced over 2,250 "hits" from which excerpts have been selected for this section. We have included summaries of opinions that will be (or have been) published in traditional reporters such as *New York Supplement*, *Federal Supplement*, and the *Bankruptcy Reporter*. We have also included excerpts from those unpublished opinions (i.e., opinions that have not been certified for publication) whenever they say something of interest to the paralegal community. If you wish further information about any of the cases,

e.g., whether any of the cases have been reversed or otherwise modified on appeal, check the citations in citators such as WestCite and Shepard's. (For information on citators on New York law, see the chart in section 5.1.)

A similar query could have been run on Lexis-Nexis, yielding a comparable response.

B. Abbreviations

- **A.D.2d, A.D.3d** *Appellate Division Reports* 2d and 3d Series
- **Bkrtcy.** United States Bankruptcy Court
- **B.R.** *Bankruptcy Reporter*
- **C.A.N.Y.** (also **C.A.2**) United States Court of Appeals for the 2d Circuit (case arising out of New York)
- **E.D.N.Y.** United States District Court for the Eastern District
- **F.2d; F.3d** *Federal Reporter* 2d and 3d Series
- **Fed. Appx.** *Federal Appendix Reporter*
- **F.R.D.** Federal Rules Decisions
- **F. Supp.; F. Supp. 2d** *Federal Supplement Reporter* 1st and 2d Series
- **Misc. 2d, Misc. 3d** *Miscellaneous Reports* 2d and 3d Series
- **N.D.N.Y.** United States District Court for the Northern District
- **N.Y. City Civ. Ct.** New York City Civil Court
- **N.Y.2d** *New York Reports* 2d Series
- **N.Y.S.2d** *New York Supplement* 2d Series
- **N.Y. Sup.** New York Supreme Court
- **N.Y. Sur.** Surrogate's Court
- **S.D.N.Y.** United States District Court for the Southern District
- **W.D.N.Y.** United States District Court for the Western District
- **WL** Westlaw

Westlaw citations are provided by year and document number. For example, 2003 WL 365353 refers to document number 365353 for the year 2003 in the Westlaw system.

C. Case Summaries and Excerpts

Here are the major categories of issues covered by these courts when they mentioned paralegals, legal assistants, or other nonattorneys involved in the delivery of legal services:

- The Value of Paralegals
- Paralegal Fees: Introduction
- Paralegal Fees: Documentation Required
- Paralegal Fees: Clerical vs. Paralegal Tasks
- Paralegal Fees: Failure to Delegate
- Paralegal Fees: Excessive, Duplicative, Overstaffing
- Conflict of Interest: Switching Sides
- Conflict of Interest: Witness Involvement
- Supervision
- Blaming a Paralegal
- Paralegal Mistakes
- Paralegal Misconduct
- Attorney-Client Privilege and Paralegals
- Work Product Rule and Paralegals
- Paralegals and Unemployment Compensation
- Miscellaneous Cases Involving Paralegals

The Value of Paralegals

- The employment of educated and trained legal assistants presents an opportunity to expand the public's accessibility to legal services at a reduced cost while preserving attorneys' time for attention to legal services which require the independent exercise of an attorney's judgment. *Guidelines for the Utilization by Lawyers of the Service of Legal Assistants*, NYSBA Subcommittee on Legal Assistants, 1997 (p. 1). Quoted in *Sussman v. Grado*, 192 Misc. 2d 628, 629, 746 N.Y.S.2d 548, 550 (Dist. Ct., Nas. Co., 2002)
- The Court is keenly aware of the necessity for paralegals with specialized skills in today's legal arena. *In re Bennett Funding Group, Inc.*, 213 B.R. 234 (Bkrtcy. N.D.N.Y., 1997)
- The appropriate use of legal assistants facilitates the delivery of legal services at reasonable cost in fulfillment of the obligation of lawyers to make legal counsel available to the public. *Matter of Parker*, 241 A.D.2d 208, 670 N.Y.S.2d 414 (1st Dept., 1998)
- Paralegals often competently perform certain services equivalent to those done by attorneys, while generally charging their time at a lesser rate than attorneys, thus benefitting those who pay the fees. *First Deposit Nat. Bank v. Moreno*, 159 Misc. 2d 920, 606 N.Y.S.2d 938 (N.Y. City Civ. Ct., N.Y. Co., 1993)
- There is credible testimony that attorneys would be able to operate more efficiently by utilizing the services of paralegals to perform the work that the attorneys are now performing. *New York County Lawyers' Ass'n v. State*, 196 Misc. 2d 761, 763 N.Y.S.2d 397 (Sup. Ct., N.Y. Co., 2003)

- The handling of cases by more than one lawyer and the use of paralegals is commonplace today. Frequently the complexity of matters requires it. The economic interests of clients usually is served by it because the more routine tasks can be done at lower cost by personnel with less training and experience who consequently are paid less and billed at lower rates. Thus, the conduct of litigation frequently is a joint endeavor involving the efforts of a number of individuals. *Etna Products Co., Inc. v. Q Marketing Group, Ltd.*, 2005 WL 2254465 (S.D.N.Y., 2005)
- Non-inclusion of paralegal fees in an award of attorney fees is counterproductive, since this penalized attorneys who saved costs by assigning work to paralegal assistants. *Blue Cross and Blue Shield of New Jersey, Inc. v. Philip Morris, Inc.*, 190 F. Supp. 2d 407 (E.D.N.Y., 2002)

Paralegal Fees: Introduction

Market rates for paralegal fees

- Paralegal time, like attorney time, is measured by the prevailing market rate. *DaimlerChrysler Corp. v. Karman*, 5 Misc 3d 567, 782 N.Y.S.2d 343 (Sup. Ct., Albany Co., 2004)
- New York and federal courts routinely include fees for paralegal services billed at market rates in an award of attorney's fees. *Soberman v. Groff Studios Corp.*, 2000 WL 1010288 (S.D.N.Y., 2000)
- We reject the argument that compensation for paralegals at rates above "cost" would yield a "windfall" for the prevailing attorney. Neither petitioners nor anyone else, to our knowledge, has ever suggested that the hourly rate applied to the work of an associate attorney in a law firm creates a windfall for the firm's partners or is otherwise improper under § 1988, merely because it exceeds the cost of the attorney's services. If the fees are consistent with market rates and practices, the "windfall" argument has no more force with regard to paralegals than it does for associates. And it would hardly accord with Congress's intent to provide a "fully compensatory fee" if the prevailing plaintiff's attorney in a civil rights lawsuit were not permitted to bill separately for paralegals, while the defense attorney in the same litigation was able to take advantage of the prevailing practice and obtain market rates for such work. *Irish v. City of New York*, 2004 WL 444544 (S.D.N.Y., 2004)

Lodestar calculation

- In civil rights cases, including cases brought pursuant to Title VII, determination of a reasonable attorneys' fee has traditionally begun with a calculation of the "lodestar": the number of hours reasonably expended multiplied by the appropriate hourly rate for each attorney or paralegal. Paralegals engaged in compensable activities, including collating and labeling trial exhibits and preparing witness binders. *Rozell v. Ross-Holst*, 2008 WL 229842 (S.D.N.Y., 2008)

Paralegal fees are not determined by playing "beat the clock"

- There is no reason to doubt that counsel, in fact, worked all hours claimed and that all hours claimed were actually and necessarily incurred for the advancement of the class action suit. However, much of the work could have been done by lawyers, paralegals, technology experts, or secretaries billing at much lower rates with a net efficiency. It may well be that if "beat the clock" were played between a paralegal undertaking a task (subject to the senior lawyer's supervision and review) and the senior lawyer performing the same task alone, the senior lawyer could complete the task in less time. That, of course, is not the measure of efficiency because the amount billed to the client may still be lower if a combination of paralegal and senior lawyer time is used. Counsel is free to have his preferences. He may do all work by himself (or with minimal assistance) and a private client is free to pay for such work at the lawyer's usual billing rate. My responsibility is to ensure that a fee award is reasonable. *Sines v. Service Corp. Intern.*, 2006 WL 1148725 (S.D.N.Y., 2006)

NFPA data used to calculate paralegal fees

- Yurman has calculated its hourly rate for paralegals in New York City to be $162.35. The 1999 Compensation and Benefits Survey of the National Federation of Paralegal Associations (NFPA) contains a listed billing rate range of $90.00 which, when multiplied by the ratio of the average New York base salary ($48,277) to the average base salary nationally ($38,085) (1.2676), produces an average hourly billing rate for paralegals in New York of $114.08. *Yurman Designs, Inc. v. PAJ, Inc.*, 125 F. Supp. 2d 54 (S.D.N.Y., 2000)

Paralegal fees in capital cases

- Judiciary Law § 35-b, which permits attorney compensation for capital murder cases, also applies to paralegal compensation. *Mahoney v. Pataki*, 98 N.Y.2d 45, 772 N.E.2d 1118, 745 N.Y.S.2d 760 (2002)

Paralegal fees in consumer protection cases

- Paralegal fees are includable in attorney fee award under New York consumer protection statute. N.Y. General Business Law § 349(h) (McKinney, 2008). *Blue Cross and Blue Shield of New Jersey, Inc. v. Philip Morris, Inc.*, 190 F. Supp. 2d 407 (E.D.N.Y., 2002)

Paralegal fees under the Surrogate's Court Procedure Act

- Section 2110 of the Surrogate's Court Procedure Act (SCPA) provides that "the court shall consider the time and value of services performed by a person who is not an attorney, provided such services are performed under the supervision of an attorney and would, if performed by an attorney, be considered by the court in determining the attorney's compensation." McKinney's SCPA § 2110(4). Paralegal fees, however, cannot be awarded for secretarial tasks performed by paralegals. *In re Brannen*, 14 Misc. 3d 1222(A), 836 N.Y.S.2d 483 (Sur. Ct., Dutchess Co., 2007)

Paralegal experience justifies a higher fee

- As for the two paralegals on the case, we find that Reigel's services are compensable at the standard hourly rate of $100 but that Ajashvilli's substantial experience as a paralegal commands a higher rate of $140. *Simmonds v. New York City Dept. of Corrections*, 2008 WL 4303474 (S.D.N.Y., 2008)

- Counsel offers no evidence regarding the experience or training of its paralegal who billed 256 hours at an hourly rate of $150. Paralegal rates vary based on experience. *Comm'n Express Nat'l, Inc. v. Rikhy*, 2006 WL 385323 (E.D.N.Y., 2006) (reciting paralegals' professional biographies before determining that the rates being sought should be reduced to $75 per hour). Because counsel failed in its burden, the Court will award an hourly rate near the lower end of the paralegal market, or $75 an hour. *In re Zyprexa Products Liability Litigation*, 2008 WL 1844000 (E.D.N.Y., 2008)

Pro se litigants are not entitled to paralegal fees

- Where attorney's fees are provided by statute, a pro se litigant who is not an attorney is not entitled to an award of such fees. *Mayerson ex rel. M.M. v. DeBuono*, 181 Misc. 2d 55, 694 N.Y.S.2d 269. (Sup.Ct., Westchester Co., 1999)

- While it is undisputed that paralegal work may qualify for fee-shifting awards, no such payment can be awarded to plaintiff for his own work as a paralegal in his own case. Otherwise time spent by clients in support of their own litigation would become a major additional cost to be imposed on their adversaries, thereby adding a currently absent additional encouragement to litigation generally— something there is no suggestion that Congress intended in enacting fee-shifting legislation. *Heldman on Behalf of T.H. v. Sobol*, 846 F. Supp. 285 (S.D.N.Y., 1994)

- Title VII plaintiff's use of a paralegal during parts of the trial was reasonable for purposes of an attorney fee award; according to an affidavit of the plaintiff's attorney, the paralegal not only brought research and other needed material to court, but also took notes during important parts of the trial so that attorneys would have an accurate record on which to base questions at trial and closing arguments. *Dailey v. Societe Generale*, 915 F. Supp. 1315 (S.D.N.Y., 1996)

- Plaintiffs' request for paralegal fees of $125 per hour does not appear to be reasonable. Generally, courts in this district and within the Second Circuit have awarded paralegal fees ranging from $50 per hour to $80 per hour in ERISA cases. *Trustees of Local 531 Pension Plan v. Corner Distributors, Inc.*, 2008 WL 2687085 (E.D.N.Y., 2008)

- Although scanning letters and forwarding documents on their own could be categorized as typical secretarial duties, the Court finds that the enormity of the undertaking renders the work more akin to paralegal tasks. *In re Zyprexa Products Liability Litigation*, 2008 WL 1844000 (E.D.N.Y., 2008)

Paralegal Fees: Documentation Required

Who are these nonlegal personnel?

- An application for attorney fees stating that legal and nonlegal personnel under lawyer's supervision performed various services is insufficient; the application did not designate how much work was performed by attorneys, how much by nonlegal personnel, and their status. Who are these nonlegal personnel? Are they paralegals? Are they secretaries or clerks? *First Deposit Nat. Bank v. Moreno*, 159 Misc. 2d 920, 606 N.Y.S.2d 938 (N.Y. City Civ. Ct., N.Y. Co., 1993)

- In a request for paralegal billing at $230, counsel has failed to present an affirmation with any itemized detail of the actual legal services performed and an explanation of the billing rates. *Transamerica Financial Life Ins. Co. v. Simmonds*, 2008 WL 4302491 (N.Y. Sup. Ct., Kings Co., 2008)

- Many of the paralegal time entries are too imprecise and vague for meaningful review, including, among other things, billings for "legal research," "file review," and "document inspection and review." *Ayers v. SGS Control Services, Inc.*, 2008 WL 4185813 (S.D.N.Y., 2008)

Improper block billing for paralegal fees

- Counsel submitted contemporaneous time records showing that paralegals spent 2.0 hours on this case. Although the time records contain separate daily entries for the work completed, the attorneys utilized "block billing" for their daily entries. As such, many of the entries are not sufficiently detailed to enable an adequate determination of the reasonableness of the hours claimed for any given task. Because "block billing" prevents the court from identifying hours billed for specific activities, a percentage reduction or other reduction of the requested hours is warranted. *Trustees of Local 531 Pension Plan v. Corner Distributors, Inc.*, 2008 WL 2687085 (E.D.N.Y., 2008)

Contemporaneous time records required

- The party seeking an award of attorney's fees must support its application by providing contemporaneous time records that detail for each attorney and legal assistant, the date, the hours expended, and the nature of the work done. *Bobrow Palumbo Sales, Inc. v. Broan-Nutone, LLC*, 549 F. Supp. 2d 274 (E.D.N.Y., 2008). See also: *Pugach v. M & T Mortg. Corp.*, 564 F. Supp. 2d 153 (E.D.N.Y., 2008)

- The application for attorney fees in this case does not include any contemporaneous time records. Instead, it lists the attorney and paralegal along with a date, number of hours, and description of the work. A party seeking an award of attorneys' fees must support the request with contemporaneous time records that show the date, the hours expended, and the nature of the work done. *Kingvision Pay-Per-View Ltd. v. Espinosa*, 2007 WL 625362 (S.D.N.Y., 2007)

- Defendants also seek payment for paralegal services at the rate of $200 per hour but fail to include an affidavit from any paralegal attesting to the accuracy, validity, and reasonableness of these charges. *Morgenthau v. Figliolia*, 2004 WL 2113355 (Sup. Ct., N.Y. Co., 2004)

- The relevant entry in the case of one paralegal states that nine hours were spent on "deposition prep, including reviewing and retrieving files and documents for use in preparation and as possible exhibits." No breakdown of the time spent on each item is provided. Consequently, since the paralegals' time entries are too vague to allow the Court to evaluate the reasonableness of the time spent, the total number of hours claimed in this category should be reduced by fifty percent (50%). *Marathon Ashland Petroleum LLC v. Equili Co., L.P.*, 2003 WL 21355216 (S.D.N.Y., 2003)

- Plaintiffs note that their paralegals performed numerous tasks, including organizing the case file, preparing materials for attorneys, and keeping track of discovery documents. Since plaintiffs' time records list the attorney or paralegal by their initials, not their full name, it is not reasonable for this court to look through the submissions to find what tasks each paralegal was performing. While perhaps there may have been some billing for clerical tasks such as "putting documents into boxes," that should have been billed at lower rate, I do not see any specific evidence that the use of paralegals by Yamanouchi and Merck was essentially unreasonable in other ways. *Yamanouchi Pharmaceutical Co., Ltd. v. Danbury Pharmacal, Inc.*, 51 F. Supp. 2d 302 (S.D.N.Y., 1999)

Paralegal Fees: Clerical vs. Paralegal Tasks

No paralegal fees for administrative tasks

- Fifteen hours of paralegal time were expended upon matters that were administrative or executorial in nature and did not require legal expertise. *In re Estate of Smith*, 15 Misc. 3d 1117(A) (2007)

- Some of the services billed appear to be secretarial in nature and should not be billed separately as paralegal services. Secretarial services are part of an attorney's office overhead factored into the hourly rate charged by counsel. The court does not disparage the efforts of the paralegals or question that actual paralegal services may be billed when legal work is performed by a nonattorney in lieu of an attorney's efforts. *In re Brannen*, 14 Misc. 3d 1222(A), 839 N.Y.S.2d 437 (Sur. Ct., Dutchess Co., 2007)

- Pegus-Neptune is a paralegal at Wotorson's law office. Wotorson submits that $75 per hour is a reasonable rate for Pegus-Neptune's services. City Defendants do not directly assert that $75 per hour is unreasonable, but instead, they claim that many of the tasks listed in her work log were those of a secretary, whose work would more properly be considered overhead at the firm and not billed to clients at an hourly rate. After reviewing Pegus-Neptune's work log, the Court concludes that she was in fact performing paralegal, not secretarial, duties, including: document reviewing, organizing trial documents, and preparing trial subpoenas. Accordingly, the reasonable paralegal fees attributable to Pegus-Neptune's services amount to $4,492. *Kinneary v. City of New York*, 536 F. Supp. 2d 326 (S.D.N.Y., 2008)

- Plaintiff's counsel have deleted from their final fee application 33.5 hours of paralegal time devoted to clerical tasks, such as velobinding, organizing case files, and preparing documents for mailing. *Rozell v. Ross-Holst*, 2008 WL 229842 (S.D.N.Y., 2008)

- Certain activities identified were by their nature more appropriately categorized as clerical or administrative, for which professional or paraprofessional billing rates were inappropriate. Thus, the court would disallow fees requested for entries such as "prepared papers for filing," "copying documents for distribution," "file same with court," and "checked faxes and delivered them to appropriate persons." *In re Bennett Funding Group, Inc.*, 213 B.R. 234 (Bkrtcy. N.D.N.Y., 1997)

- The bankruptcy court should review fee applications not for whether each particular service undertaken by a paralegal is clerical or paraprofessional by nature, but for whether non-bankruptcy attorneys typically charge and collect from their clients fees for that particular service when performed by a member of that profession, and the rates charged and collected therefor. *In re Poseidon Pools of America, Inc.*, 180 B.R. 718 (Bkrtcy. E.D.N.Y., 1995)

- In determining the number of hours reasonably expended on litigation, legal work should be differentiated from nonlegal work such as investigation, clerical work, the compilation of facts and other types of work, which can be accomplished by nonlawyers who command lesser rates. *Goldberg v. Blue Ridge Farms, Inc.*, 2005 WL 1796116 (E.D.N.Y., 2005)

Paralegal Fees: Failure to Delegate

Court criticizes firm for parsimonious use of paralegals; firm promises to reform

- The Court heard argument on the motion for attorneys' fees. At that time, the Court voiced certain concerns with regard to the number of attorney hours. The number of hours was especially remarkable when juxtaposed with the parsimonious use of paralegals. Counsel explained that it had made extensive use of contract attorneys in lieu of paralegals and advised the Court that it would give "great consideration" to modifying this practice in the future. *In re Polaroid*, 2007 WL 2116398 (S.D.N.Y., 2007)

- Class Counsel have also inflated the lodestar by inappropriately staffing persons billing at higher rates for tasks that could have been performed by paralegals. The time records of Weiss and Cauley are striking for the relatively small percentage of hours for work performed by paralegals even though extensive document review was required. Out of the 2,985 hours billed by Weiss & Lurie, approximately 88 hours, or three percent, was for work by paralegals. Similarly, Cauley Bowman's paralegals accounted for 53 hours, or two percent of total time billed by that firm. Notwithstanding Mr. Weiss's general claim that the document review in this case needed to be performed by persons with a legal background, there is nothing about the claims raised nor any discussion in the submissions in this case that suggest that there were particularly difficult or complex issues that required a person with formal legal training, as opposed to a trained paralegal, to perform much of the work. *In re KeySpan Corp. Securities Litigation*, 2005 WL 3093399 (E.D.N.Y., 2005)

Attorney comfort level in delegating tasks to paralegals

- Whether a task is appropriate for assignment to a paralegal is a matter of professional judgment. In exercising this judgment, attorneys must consider the assignment's complexity, the skill and experience of the available staff, and the attorneys' own level of comfort regarding their ability to exercise supervision. This Court will not substitute its own judgment for that of the attorneys who are charged with responsibility for a client's representation. When attorneys believe that their existing paralegal staff lacks sufficient skill to complete a particular task, that judgment is to be respected, and is not to become the basis for challenge of the attorney's fee application. *In re St. Rita's Associates Private Placement, L.P.*, 216 B.R. 490 (Bkrtcy. W.D.N.Y., 1998)

Appellate brief written by a paralegal

- The court rejected an argument by a criminal defendant that his assigned counsel used (but failed to supervise) a paralegal to research and write the appellate brief on his case. The constitution "does not place limits on the ability of a retained attorney to delegate work to others." *Munoz v. U.S.*, 2008 WL 4104462 (E.D.N.Y., 2008)

Cite-checking is not necessarily a paralegal task

- We disagree with the plaintiff's criticism of the billing that cite-checking by a junior associate should not be charged at her rate because a paralegal could do the same job for less. With due respect for the marvels of computerized research and cite-checking, in determining whether a case stands for the proposition for which it is cited (one essential element of cite-checking), an attorney's role is essential and certainly not an unreasonable allocation of responsibility. *Malletier v. Dooney & Bourke, Inc.*, 2007 WL 1284013 (S.D.N.Y., 2007)

Overdelegation to paralegals is not required

- Many of the tasks identified by defendants involve substantive legal work such as "Research re: substitution of next friend," and "find case and Shepardize case for CL." While a paralegal may have been able to perform these tasks, the tasks constitute work that attorneys typically engage in and there is no reason why the attorneys here should not be compensated at their hourly rate for choosing to do the work themselves. Although some of the entries identified by defendants describe insignificant tasks such as "Retrieve documents that came up in conversation with Linda Stanch that I said I would fax," each of these tasks did not take up much of the attorneys' time. It would be unreasonable to expect attorneys to delegate every ministerial duty they perform because the time spent delegating the task could well exceed the time spent by the attorney performing the task herself. Therefore, the Court will not eliminate these hours from plaintiffs' fee application. *Marisol A. ex rel. Forbes v. Giuliani*, 111 F. Supp. 2d 381 (S.D.N.Y., 2000)

Delegation to a paralegal by a sole practitioner is sometimes inefficient

- The court dismisses defendant's remaining objections that plaintiff's attorney claimed an attorney

rate for purely ministerial tasks and an inordinate amount of time for telephone conferences. The court finds that Mr. Price used a reasonable amount of time to complete the necessary work of this case. As to the objection to ministerial tasks, the court finds that as a sole practitioner, it would have been inefficient for Mr. Price to train a paralegal to complete the tasks which defendant characterizes as ministerial. *Jackson v. Cassellas*, 959 F. Supp. 164 (W.D.N.Y., 1997)

Electronic filing should have been performed by a paralegal

- Some of the work performed by an associate attorney, specifically, 0.42 hours to file the complaint (presumably via Electronic Case Filing) involves a task that could have been performed by a legal assistant. Clerical tasks such as faxing, filing, photocopying, delivery, drafting affidavits of service, and service of papers should be billed at clerical rates. This time spent on filing papers should not have been billed at the higher hourly rate for associate attorneys. Therefore, the time charge involving clerical work should be recoverable at an hourly rate of $70, rather than $200, reducing that time charge from $83.33 to $29.40. *King v. Northern Bay Contractors, Inc.*, 2006 WL 3335118 (E.D.N.Y., 2006)

Bates and deposition indexing should have been delegated to a paralegal

- The defendants further object to the fee application insofar as it is based on time spent by an attorney preparing and indexing a Bates folder. I assume that this 27.5 hours of work ($9,625) involved some degree of legal expertise, rather than mere mechanical sorting, but it obviously is a task that largely could have been performed by a skilled paralegal. Accordingly, I will reduce the billings for this work to $2,750 based on a billing rate of $100 per hour, which I find to be reasonable for a paralegal at a small firm in Manhattan. The defendants similarly object to 163.8 hours of time ($57,330) spent on the review and indexing of deposition transcripts. This work involved reviewing the particular transcript in preparation for trial, but also evaluating and cross-referencing all of the facts and contentions recorded in that transcript with other related evidence adduced during the course of the litigation. While I sympathize with trial counsel's desire to be fully conversant with all of the facts and to have them be readily accessible for trial, some of this work clearly could have been performed by a paralegal. Accordingly, I will reduce these time charges by one-third, allowing $38,000 to be recovered. *Sylvester v. City of New York*, 2006 WL 3230152 (S.D.N.Y., 2006)

No attorney fees for filing

- Further examination of the time sheets reveals that some of the attorney's time was spent performing the tasks of a legal assistant. For example, he expended 0.10 hours personally filing the complaint, 0.30 hours personally filing the civil cover sheet, and 0.10 hours personally filing the proof of service. These are unnecessary expenses insofar as they are billed at an attorney's hourly rate and I reduce this time accordingly. *Entertainment By J&J, Inc. v. Ramsarran*, 2002 WL 720480 (E.D.N.Y., 2002)

- The attorney's affidavit describes her contributions as "coordinating the reproduction of trial exhibits and cross referencing same with witnesses and issues to be tried." These tasks are more akin to paralegal duties. *Cruz v. Henry Modell & Co., Inc.*, 2008 WL 905351 (E.D.N.Y., 2008)

- Fees at an attorney's rate should not be paid for tasks more appropriately handled by paralegal, such as traveling to court to file papers, ensuring that service was effected, and forwarding copies of documents. *Whitten v. Cross Garage Corp.*, 2003 WL 21744088 (S.D.N.Y., 2003)

- In calculation of attorney fee award in a civil rights case under § 1988, time spent by attorneys completing tasks that could have been completed by experienced paralegal would be compensated at hourly rate of $75, rather than at the hourly rate for attorney time. Tasks such as checking tenant statistics by race, checking reports for completeness, and discussing preparation of declarations and proofreading of brief constituted attorney time. *Davis v. New York City Housing Authority*, 2002 WL 31748586 (S.D.N.Y., 2002)

- A partner charging $500 an hour billed for certain tasks that could have been performed by a more junior attorney, paralegal, or secretary including, among other things, legal research on retaliation standards; review all files to determine defendant's outstanding obligations; get train schedule; found round trip travel to deposition; review and print deposition notices; help get out mailing of class notice; and apply stamps to envelopes. *Ayers v. SGS Control Services, Inc.*, 2008 WL 4185813 (S.D.N.Y., 2008)

- This Court also found instances where plaintiff's firm inefficiently allocated work among attorneys, paralegals, and other law firm employees. One associate who bills at a rate of $305–$355 per hour billed approximately 10.5 hours for filing papers with the court and coordinating the service of papers with other attorneys. Another associate, whose rate is $265–310 per hour, billed approximately 115 hours to such paralegal and clerical tasks as proofreading, Bates labeling, and assembling documents and exhibits for use at depositions. Such

fees are not recoverable. The court also found that paralegals sometimes billed the client (at rates of $120 per hour) for totally nonlegal tasks that involved purely physical skills (e.g., moving boxes) and that required a minimum of sentience. Such services are part of overhead. *Daiwa Special Asset Corp. v. Desnick*, 2002 WL 31767817 (S.D.N.Y., 2002)

- Some of the billing entries for attorney time reflect purely ministerial work that should have been performed by a paralegal or even a secretary (for example, over six hours for "mailing" and "transmission" of letters and motions). *Latimore v. Schilling*, 2008 WL 2421628 (S.D.N.Y., 2008)

- Counsel spent part of 2.75 hours assembling courtesy copies of documents for the court. He billed at an hourly rate of $205 for time he spent performing these clerical tasks, all of which could have been done by a paralegal at a substantially lower hourly rate. *DCH Auto Group (USA) Inc. v. Fit You Best Auto., Inc.*, 2006 WL 279055 (E.D.N.Y., 2006)

- The court reduced the charges for factotum duties such as faxing papers that could have been more economically performed by a nonattorney and that inflate the costs when performed by an attorney. *315 Berry Street Corp. v. Huang*, 2003 WL 22901027 (N.Y. City Civ. Ct., 2003)

- Counsel performed administrative work that a paralegal could have performed at a significant savings, such as obtaining a transcript and reviewing the file for a particular document. *Agamede Ltd. v. Life Energy & Technology Holdings, Inc.*, 2007 WL 1074599 (E.D.N.Y., 2007)

- Counsel argues that this Court should reduce the total hours claimed by opposing counsel because of his failure to delegate proper work to associates and paralegals. I agree that counsel did not delegate their work appropriately by utilizing associates and paralegals when necessary. The tasks performed by a partner that should have been performed by either an associate or paralegal will be charged at the proper associate ($180) and/or paralegal ($95) rate. In addition, any tasks performed by an associate that could have been performed by a paralegal will be charged at the hourly rate of $95. Moreover, any time spent for clerical activity will be billed at the clerical rate of $50 per hour. *Klimbach v. Spherion Corp.*, 467 F. Supp. 2d 323 (W.D.N.Y., 2006)

- An attorney should not be compensated $200 per hour for any work performed which would typically be performed by an administrative assistant or paralegal. For example, an attorney spent 1.25 hours personally filing the complaint and forwarding the papers to the process server, the client, and the judge; 0.50 hours personally filing the dismissal papers; 0.50 hours personally speaking to the process server; and 1.0 hours preparing and filing the "Notation of Default." These expenses represent services that may not be billed at an attorney's hourly rate. *Entertainment by J&J, Inc. v. Friends II, Inc.*, 2003 WL 1990414 (S.D.N.Y., 2003)

- In addition to the excessive, redundant, and at times vague billing, the attorney billed at associate rates for work that appears to be administrative paralegal tasks. Accordingly, tasks described as "open and categorize new file," "prepare civil cover sheet and summons," "prepare new captions for all pleadings," and "prepare all pleadings for filing with court," which total 3.5 hours, shall be compensated at a paralegal rate. *Rotella v. Board of Educ. of City of New York*, 2002 WL 59106 (E.D.N.Y., 2002)

Paralegal Fees: Excessive, Duplicative, Overstaffing

602 paralegal hours at $166 per hour is excessive

- There were sixteen members of the law firm's support staff, presumably paralegals, who posted 602 hours at an average hourly rate of $166 for a total of $100,566. The paralegal rate is reduced to $75 per hour based on prevailing attorney fee awards in employment discrimination suits. *Bell v. Helmsley*, 2003 WL 21057630 (Sup. Ct., N.Y. Co., 2003)

Paralegal fee approved, but not for sitting and waiting

- The reasonable value of attorney's professional services included $100 per hour in paralegal time. However, there is no justification for charging for both the attorney and the paralegal to sit and wait for a trial assignment. *Koeth v. Koeth*, 2002 WL 523109 (Sup. Ct., Nassau Co., 2002)

Seven paralegals for one motion is too much

- With respect to the legal assistants, seven is an extremely large number of staff to have involved in this case, which produced only one motion. The total amount of those fees should be reduced by 10% to account for the excess staffing. *BNP-Dresdner Bank ZAO v. Haque*, 1998 WL 831353 (S.D.N.Y., 1998)

One hour to update a case binder is excessive

- As to paralegal Sarah Thomas's hours, I reduce by half the one hour charged for updating case binders with new court papers as excessive. *Entral Group Intern., LLC v. Honey Cafe on 5th, Inc.*, 2006 WL 3694584 (E.D.N.Y., 2006)

It should not take 1.3 hours to instruct a paralegal on filing procedures

- The court shall reduce counsel's claim of a total of 1.3 hours for instructing his paralegal on filing procedures and other administrative tasks to a more reasonable 0.5 hours. *Cornett v. Capital Management Services, Inc.*, 2006 WL 2270346 (W.D.N.Y., 2006)

Twenty-one hours to determine the relationship between two parties is excessive

- A paralegal expended some 21 hours in an apparent attempt to discern the relationship between Schenectady County and EMSA. Having reviewed the complaint, and based upon my familiarity with the case and others of this nature, I find these amounts to be excessive. *Lake v. Schoharie County Com'r of Social Services*, 2006 WL 1891141 (N.D.N.Y., 2006)

- Counsel have not provided justification for billing paralegal services at the rate charged. Many of the services rendered by counsel for the firm were unnecessarily duplicative. In most circumstances where an attorney or paralegal discussed any aspect of this matter with a colleague, both individuals billed for the full amount of time spent in the discussion. Additionally, counsel billed for the same legal services that were also being performed and billed by a paralegal. *In re Brannen*, 14 Misc. 3d 1222(A), 836 N.Y.S.2d 483 (Sur. Ct., Dutchess Co., 2007)

- Billings by two of a cable television provider's paralegals were excessive and duplicative, or, in any event, so ministerial as not properly chargeable to the client, thus warranting reduction of requested fees for the paralegals in an action brought under the Federal Communications Act; one paralegal twice billed simultaneous calendar entries as three distinct billing events and once billed two simultaneous calendar entries as two billing events. *Cablevision Systems New York City Corp. v. Torres*, 2003 WL 22078938 (S.D.N.Y., 2003)

- The court finds that 30.7 hours of legal assistant time were expended upon matters that were executorial in nature, duplicated services provided by other counsel, were expended upon assets that were of no value to the estate, or duplicated services provided by other staff in the office. *In re Estate of Hopkins*, 17 Misc. 3d 1129, 851 N.Y.S.2d 69 (Sur. Ct., Wym. Co., 2007)

- I have carefully reviewed each of the time entries. In the category of "Employment and Fee Applications," a paralegal recorded 57.3 hours of service. This time included at least 25.8 hours spent on the application to employ Hodgson Russ LLP, and 15.5 hours spent on the application to appoint an accountant for the Official Committee of Unsecured Creditors. Moreover, this work was only preliminary, as it was then reviewed by counsel. Although the paralegal did perform some work on the resolution of conflicts, the employment applications were generally routine. Particularly with respect to the accountant, the paralegal appears to have spent an excessive amount of time in preparing what was essentially a preliminary draft of the application for appointment. For any particular provider of services, billing rates should appropriately reflect several factors, including education, competence, experience, accountability, and risk. Most paralegals lack the training derived from the rigors of law school. Without a license to practice law, they have no duty to account professionally as an officer of the court. Nor do they share the same risks of liability for malpractice. For these reasons, the court will carefully review any proposal to compensate a firm for paralegal services at rates that approach those allowed for attorneys. *In re The Colad Group, Inc.,* 336 B.R. 36 (Bkrtcy. W.D.N.Y., 2005)

Paralegal tasks billed at attorney rates

- Attorney disciplined for billing clients for work performed by paralegals at the higher attorney rate. *In re Lowell,* 14 A.D.3d 41, 784 N.Y.S.2d 69 (1st Dept., 2004)

Conflict of Interest: Switching Sides

Screening of paralegal prevents disqualification

- The fact that the law firm of a plaintiff employs a secretary/paralegal who was previously employed by defense counsel and assisted an attorney on this case does not require disqualification of the plaintiff's counsel even though the secretary/paralegal was in a position to acquire confidential information. Existing ethical rules do not require automatic disqualification of law firms merely because they hire nonlawyers who have had access to confidences of their opponents. The hiring firm can avoid disqualification by taking steps to ensure that nonlawyer employees with confidential information are kept from divulging or using confidences obtained at the prior firm. Here, plaintiff's counsel demonstrated that it did a satisfactory job of ensuring that its employee was and continues to be effectively isolated from defendant's case. Before hiring the secretary/paralegal, the firm determined which cases she had worked on in the prior job, established that she was to have no contact with those working on the cases at the current firm, and obtained her agreement to follow those procedures. *Mulhern v. Calder,* 196 Misc. 2d 818, 763 N.Y.S.2d 741 (Sup. Ct., Albany Co., 2003)

Disqualification motion granted

- Disqualification of defendant's firm is ordered. The defendants' attorneys hired a paralegal who had previously been employed by the plaintiff's counsel and had worked on the litigation pending between the parties and had interviewed the plaintiff's manager concerning the facts of this case. *Glover Bottled Gas Corp. v. Circle M. Beverage Barn, Inc.,* 129 A.D.2d 678 (2d Dept., 1987). Note: this case has been criticized for failing to indicate precisely what conduct of the paralegal justified the disqualification. See *Mulhern v. Calder,* 196 Misc. 2d 818, 763 N.Y.S.2d 741 (Sup. Ct., Albany Co., 2003)

Paralegal says he cannot remember the names of any clients while working at other firms

- In a prior employment, a paralegal worked on cases that were adverse to clients of his current employer. This was not disclosed because the paralegal told his current employer that he could not recall the names of clients at his prior employment. When the current firm found out about the conflict, it fired the paralegal. The court denied the disqualification motion, being satisfied that confidences had not been revealed. The paralegal did not work on the same case at the opposing firms even though the two firms had clients with adverse interests. *Riddell Sports, Inc. v. Brooks,* 1994 WL 67836 (S.D.N.Y., 1994)

- Attorney disciplined for directing a paralegal in her employ, who formerly worked for the adversary in a pending case, to work on that case, and for questioning the paralegal about her adversary's litigation strategy. *In re Lowell,* 14 A.D.3d 41, 784 N.Y.S.2d 69 (1st Dept., 2004)

Conflict of Interest: Witness Involvement

Deposition of a paralegal leads to disqualification

- Disqualification of the law firm representing the purchaser was warranted in the purchaser's legal malpractice action against the attorney who represented her in connection with the underlying real estate transaction, where one of firm's attorneys and a paralegal then employed by the firm were deposed as fact witnesses in connection with the transaction. *Fernandes v. Jamron,* 9 A.D.3d 379, 780 N.Y.S.2d 164 (2d Dept., 2004)

- A nonlawyer clerk employed by the law firm in its mailroom, in charge of the mailing of plaintiff's bills and proof of claim, will not cause the law firm to be disqualified from representing the plaintiff, simply because the clerk's testimony is necessary in establishing the elements of plaintiff's prima facie case. The disqualification rules governing lawyers do not apply to nonlawyer employees of a law firm. *NYC Medical & Neurodiagnostic, P.C. v. Republic Western Ins. Co.,* 6 Misc. 3d 275, 784 N.Y.S.2d 840 (N.Y. City Civ. Ct., Kings Co., 2004)

- Paralegals and interns of law firm that currently represented plaintiffs were not barred by advocate-witness rule from testifying on behalf of plaintiffs in civil rights action. *M.K.B. v. Eggleston*, 414 F. Supp. 2d 469 (S.D.N.Y., 2006)

Conflict caused by paralegal exposure to discovery materials

- The trial court could disqualify an attorney from Office of Federal Public Defender from representing a defendant charged with racketeering offenses upon disclosure that another Federal Defender attorney had been briefly assigned to a potential government witness and Federal Defender paralegals had been exposed to that witness and to relevant discovery files. *U.S. v. Pappa*, 37 Fed. Appx. 551 (2d Cir., 2002)

Supervision

- An attorney was suspended from practice, in part, for failing to properly supervise his staff. Problems included having his paralegal meeting with a client at a medical clinic but failing to properly prepare the papers, having a paralegal prepare a document with false statements that was submitted to the Office of Court Administration, and having a law clerk negotiate directly with an insurance company, with his permission, when the law clerk made false statements. *In re Wiss*, 3 A.D.3d 182, 772 N.Y.S.2d 9 (1st Dept., 2004)
- An attorney was suspended for three years for misconduct, which included the failure to supervise his paralegal and continuing to employ the paralegal after discovering misconduct by the paralegal. *In re Gaesser*, 290 A.D.2d 58, 737 N.Y.S.2d 719 (4th Dept., 2001)
- Attorney abdicated "his responsibility to manage his law practice" by allowing a paralegal to finalize an estate without attorney supervision. *In re Carrigan*, 283 A.D.2d 63, 726 N.Y.S.2d 538 (4th Dept., 2001)
- "A lawyer may ethically outsource legal support services overseas to a non-lawyer if the lawyer (a) rigorously supervises the non-lawyer, so as to avoid aiding the non-lawyer in the unauthorized practice of law and to ensure that the non-lawyer's work contributes to the lawyer's competent representation of the client." *Opinion 2006-3* (8/06) Association of the Bar of the City of New York Committee on Professional and Judicial Ethics (*www.nycbar. org/Ethics/eth2006.htm*) (2006 WL 2389364). For more on this opinion, see section 3.3.

Blaming a Paralegal

- Attorney is disciplined for lying when he claimed that his paralegal "doctored" divorce papers. *In the*

Matter of Saltz, 142 A.D.2d 272, 536 N.Y.S.2d 126 (2d Dept., 1988)
- DR 1-104(D)(2) prevents a lawyer from attempting to lay blame upon a partner, associate, or non-lawyer employee for misconduct that occurs in the lawyer's office. This provision recognizes that a lawyer is under a duty to know how a client's file is being handled and cannot simply claim ignorance of another's misconduct. *Heritage East-West v. Chung & Choi*, 6 Misc. 3d 523, 785 N.Y.S.2d 317 (N.Y. City Civ. Ct., Queens Co., 2004)
- The attorney attempts to place the blame on his staff, claiming that one of his staff members (a paralegal) did not timely notice the filing of the motion. Regardless of whether the paralegal was responsible within the attorney's office for being aware of filings in this case, the attorney retains full responsibility. Paralegals work under the supervision of attorneys, who are fully responsible for such representation. *Friedman v. State University of New York at Binghamton*, 2006 WL 2882980 (N.D.N.Y., 2006)

Paralegal Mistakes

Paralegal mistakenly files a satisfaction of judgment

- Counsel asserted that "a paralegal in my office mistakenly filed a satisfaction of judgment entered in this court. The court denied the request to vacate the satisfaction of judgment. The remedy the plaintiff seeks, vacating the satisfaction, would wreak havoc on a system that third parties rely on when extending credit and therefore public policy requires the court to uphold the integrity and reliability of public records. *DaimlerChrysler Services North America v. Granger*, 5 Misc. 3d 865, 784 N.Y.S.2d 357 (Watertown City Ct. Jeff. Co., 2004)

Paralegal misplaces pleadings

- Not only did respondent's paralegal "misplace" both the Article 78 pleadings and the subsequent default judgment with notice of entry, but he twice provided false information as to the status of the case. Motion to vacate default judgment denied. *Rownd v. Teachers Retirement System of City of New York*, 52 A.D.3d 321, 859 N.Y.S.2d 190 (1st Dept., 2008)

Paralegal #2 fails to catch paralegal #1's venue error

- Counsel maintains that, at all times, it intended to file collection suits, such as the underlying suit, in the county in which the debtor resides. First, Suzanne Jones, the paralegal responsible for entering Katz's data into the firm's electronic filing system, asserts that she mistakenly entered the incorrect venue code in the file as the result of an "unintentional clerical error." Second, Anne Marie

Kielty, a paralegal in the firm's litigation department, attests that she did not catch the mistake in venue when preparing the draft complaint for the underlying suit and, thus, unintentionally designated New York County as the venue. *Katz v. Asset Acceptance, LLC,* 2006 WL 3483921 (E.D.N.Y., 2006)

Errors attributed to a paralegal deemed judicial admissions

- Petitioners argued that since references in their predicate notices to attorney fee provisions in a lease were due to their paralegal's errors, they should not constitute judicial admissions, but the court rejected this argument based on the doctrine of judicial estoppel (not related to the paralegal's conduct). *Marbru Associates and the Berkeley Associates, L.P. v. White,* 24 Misc. 3d 1219(A), 2009 WL 2049982 (N.Y.C. Civ. Ct., N.Y. Co., 2009)

Paralegal errs in thinking the client had 30 days to file

- A paralegal's ignorance of the rule establishing a ten-day deadline for filing criminal appeals did not constitute "excusable neglect" justifying late filing of defendant's appeal from his conviction of cocaine and firearm offenses. On the day of sentencing, defendant's attorney instructed his paralegal to prepare a notice of appeal for defendant and file it immediately, but the paralegal did not do so because of her mistaken belief that she had 30 days to file, rather than ten. *U.S. v. Hooper,* 43 F.3d 26 (2d Cir., 1994)

(Mis)advice by paralegal on what was on the calendar

- With respect to plaintiff's excuse for the delay, counsel avers that he had been (mis)advised by a paralegal assistant that the matter had already been placed back on the trial calendar and was simply awaiting a trial date. "While counsel might be faulted for failing to keep track of the status of the case, such an oversight amounts to law office failure, which may be accepted as an excuse for delay." *Negron v. New York City Housing Authority,* 2 Misc. 2d 138(A), 784 N.Y.S.2d 922 (1st Dept., 2004)
- A paralegal's failure to restore an action to the calendar when told to do so was not deemed to be an acceptable excuse when the total delay in moving to restore the action to the calendar was one year and eight months. *Collins v. New York City Health and Hosp. Corp.,* 266 A.D.2d 178, 697 N.Y.S.2d 341 (2d Dept., 1999)
- The affidavit and other opposition papers, although timely prepared, were not served or filed due to the failure of a law office paralegal to properly diary the date for the opposition to be served. The court found reasonable excuse. *De Bartolo v. De Bartolo,* 46 A.D.3d 739, 849 N.Y.S.2d 282 (2d Dept., 2007)

Due to defendant's counsel's trial commitments at that time, his firm's paralegal requested, and was granted, an adjournment of the motion return date to February 12. However, no opposition papers were filed or served on behalf of defendant and, thus, on March 28, plaintiff's motion for leave to enter a default judgment was granted. The failure of the attorney to answer a default judgment motion was allegedly based on his paralegal's failure to dairy the return date. The court held that this was excusable law office failure. *Mothon v. ITT Hartford Group, Inc.,* 301 A.D.2d 999, 755 N.Y.S.2d 468 (3d Dept., 2003)

- Counsel asserted that his paralegal, who was unfamiliar with the procedure to be followed when an action has been commenced by summons with notice, had improperly commenced the action. *Splinters, Inc. v. Greenfield,* 880 N.Y.S.2d 328 (2d Dept., 2009)

Paralegal ships privileged material to opponent!

- Paralegals numbered approximately 16,000 documents retrieved from Prescient Partners' storage facility, and made three copies: the "pristine set," the "attorney set," and the "paralegal set." Ms. Diaz personally reviewed the "attorney set" and marked the privileged documents with a yellow sticker. She then gave the color-coded "attorney set" to paralegal Joseph Ramirez, who was to remove the specified documents from his "paralegal set" before shipping them to the defendants. Mr. Ramirez delegated this task to another paralegal, who shipped the documents without removing all the privileged material. *Prescient Partners, L.P. v. Fieldcrest Cannon, Inc.,* 1997 WL 736726 (S.D.N.Y., 1997)

Inadvertent disclosure of privileged documents by paralegal

- Inadvertent disclosure during discovery of documents as to which attorney-client privilege was asserted did not waive the privilege, as counsel took reasonable steps to prevent disclosure and disclosure occurred in the course of large-scale litigation; before discovery documents were presented to opposing party, they had been reviewed and those considered nonresponsive or privileged had been removed, parties had produced more than 70,000 pages of documents, paralegals apparently neglected to remove some documents before production, and counsel asserted the privilege as soon as they were alerted to the production. *Bank Brussels Lambert v. Credit Lyonnais (Suisse) S.A.,* 160 F.R.D. 437 (S.D.N.Y., 1995)

Paralegal relies on wrong account statement

- The paralegal, assigned to review the stipulation for factual error, relied on the wrong account statement in coming up with the number of shares of corporation secured margin account. Relief granted to avoid unjust enrichment. *Cox v. Lehman Bros., Inc.,* 15 A.D.3d 239, 790 N.Y.S.2d 16 (1st Dept., 2005)

Counsel fails to explain his paralegal's confusion

- One of the reasons given by plaintiffs' attorney for the failure to respond was a paralegal's mistaken belief that the response to Defendant's Local Rule 56.1 Statement was the response to the Request to Admit. Plaintiffs' counsel does not explain how a paralegal could have confused the Request to Admit with the Local Rule 56.1 Statement, given that the answer to the Request to Admit was due October 13, but defendant's initial Local Rule 56.1 Statement was not filed until November 15. *Sook Kim v. Goldstein,* 2007 WL 1649902 (S.D.N.Y., 2007)

Paralegal neglects to file papers with federal agency on time, and files others incorrectly

- Important papers were not timely filed by the paralegal with the Immigration and Naturalization Service, as clients had been promised, or such papers were filed without required supporting information. *In re Meltzer,* 293 A.D.2d 202, 741 N.Y.S.2d 240 (1st Dept., 2002)

Failure to serve due to paralegal neglect

- Due to this paralegal's misconduct and failure to fulfill his professional duties, the opposition papers were never filed or served on defendants. This court, under similar circumstances, has previously held that the defalcations of a law firm employee that result in a default may constitute excusable law office failure. *Goldman v. Cotter,* 10 A.D.3d 289, 781 N.Y.S.2d 28 (1st Dept., 2004)

Nonlawyer representative error on adjournment

- In turnover proceeding where nonlawyer representative of respondent inadvertently thought that his request for four-week adjournment from Clerk of Court to obtain counsel had been granted and where respondent's defense had merit, default judgment against respondent should have been vacated. *Theatre Row Phase II Associates v. H & I, Inc.,* 27 A.D.3d 216, 810 N.Y.S.2d 461 (1st Dept., 2006)

Paralegal Misconduct

Paralegal continues to improperly engage in a document preparation business

- The respondent operated a paralegal and document preparation business and was accused of repeated deceptive and fraudulent practices. He was permanently enjoined by court order to refrain from providing paralegal and document preparation and filing services, later modified to prohibit him from engaging in a similar business in any capacity whatsoever. Although denying charges that he had again engaged in paralegal and document preparation work as alleged, he admitted working as an "informational receptionist," notary, and process server for a similar business operated by his daughter, and was held in both civil and criminal contempt by the court. *People, ex rel. Spitzer v. Hooks,* 64 A.D.3d 1075, 883 N.Y.S.2d 378 (3rd Dept., 2009)

Paralegal inappropriately interferes with psychiatric examination

- Plaintiff was accompanied to the psychiatric examination by a paralegal from the plaintiff's law firm. The paralegal was also present during another evaluation of the plaintiff. During the evaluation, the paralegal instructed plaintiff to not respond to certain questions. Under these circumstances, the paralegal's interference was not appropriate. Assuming her objections were proper, the paralegal is not a physician, and, as such, did not have the ability to make determinations on the appropriateness of the doctor's questions. *Ardolic v. New Water Street Corp.,* 6 Misc. 3d 1036(A), 800 NYS2d 342 (NY Civ. Ct., NY Co., 2005)

Improper signature by paralegal

- A paralegal improperly signed the client's name and the attorney's name as the notary—at the direction of the attorney. *In re Raskind,* 46 A.D.3d 129 843 N.Y.S.2d 841 (2d Dept., 2007)
- An attorney is disciplined for allowing submissions to civil court of documents requiring his attestation to be signed by a nonattorney in his office. *In re Moroff,* 55 A.D.3d 200, 863 N.Y.S.2d 800 (2d Dept., 2008)
- An attorney is disciplined for improperly permitting a nonattorney (his secretary) to be an authorized signatory on his escrow account. *In re Gebo,* 19 A.D.3d 932, 798 N.Y.S.2d 162 (3d Dept., 2005)

Paralegal letter challenged as improper

- The letter by the paralegal is, conservatively construed, a blatant attempt to coach a witness, and may reasonably be understood as an attempt to persuade a witness to change his testimony. As such, the letter could subject counsel, at a minimum, to sanctions. While the letter was written by a paralegal and not an attorney, Cobb and Cobb is a small firm comprised of two attorneys who are husband and wife, and a paralegal, who is their son. Under these circumstances, the inference that the letter was written under the close supervision of counsel is a strong one. *Hogan v. Higgins*, 2008 WL 3200252 (E.D.N.Y., 2008)

A nonlawyer should not be making decisions on withdrawal from representation

- A withdrawal can never be justified when the decision to withdraw is made by a nonlawyer, even if, or particularly if, the nonlawyer is acting pursuant to an "office policy" that requires withdrawal for the sole reason that the client is not current on billed fees or will not pay an additional advance. *Dar v. Nadel & Associates, P.C.*, 5 Misc. 3d 1016(A), 798 N.Y.S.2d 708 (N.Y. City Civ. Ct., Kings Co., 2004)

Paralegal fraud in asbestos cases

- Allegations that paralegals for law firm "fixed" affidavits of clients, who were plaintiffs in asbestos litigation, by adding omitted product identification information and false signatures to affidavits, and that such affidavits were then filed in asbestos litigation against manufacturer and others, were adequately specific for manufacturer to plead mail and wire fraud claims against the law firm under the Racketeer Influenced and Corrupt Organizations Act (RICO). *G-I Holdings, Inc. v. Baron & Budd*, 238 F. Supp. 2d 521 (S.D.N.Y., 2002)

Insider trading information from a paralegal

- An attorney is disciplined for professional misconduct. He became privy to material, nonpublic inside information concerning the proposed acquisition of a corporation known as Parisian. His brother and his cousin obtained this information from a paralegal employed by the firm of Skadden, Arps. The respondent knew that the subject information had been illegally misappropriated from this law firm and its client. To conceal the illegal trading, the attorney advised his cousin not to purchase Parisian securities in his own name or in the name of the paralegal. *Matter of Laboz*, 200 A.D.2d 239, 614 N.Y.S.2d 444 (2d Dept., 1994)

Paralegal steals Kennedy memorabilia

- A paralegal was prosecuted for mail and wire fraud in selling forged documents falsely attributed to President John F. Kennedy. There was a theft of authentic Kennedy deeds from the client's vault to which defendant had unsupervised access as a paralegal in the law firm. *U.S. v. Cusack*, 229 F.3d 344 (2d Cir., 2000)

Attorney-Client Privilege and Paralegals

- The attorney-client privilege is not limited to communications directly between the client and counsel.

It also encompasses communications between attorney and a client's agent or representative provided the communications are intended to facilitate the provision of legal services by the attorney to the client. It does not, however, cover communications between a nonlawyer and a client that involve the conveyance of legal advice offered by the nonattorney, except perhaps when the nonlawyer is acting under the supervision or the direction of an attorney. *Delta Financial Corp. v. Morrison*, 15 Misc. 3d 308, 829 N.Y.S.2d 877 (Sup. Ct., Nassau Co., 2007)

- Although the Code of Professional Responsibility does not apply to nonlawyers, it places a burden on attorneys to insure that their nonlawyer employees, including paralegals, comply with all provisions of the Code applicable to attorneys. Thus, pursuant to the Code's Canons, Ethical Considerations, and mandatory Disciplinary Rules, nonlawyer employees of an attorney, including agents, law clerks, paralegals, and legal secretaries, are charged, *inter alia*, with the preservation of matters within the attorney-client privilege that are revealed to them through such employment. *People v. Seal*, 9 Misc. 3d 239, 800 N.Y.S.2d 825 (Sup. Ct., Kings Co., 2005)

- A letter from a nonattorney, registered patent agent, describing results of prior art search to a patent prosecution attorney, who retained the patent agent while providing legal representation to a client, was entitled to attorney-client protection. *Cargill, Inc. v. Sears Petroleum & Transport Corp.*, 2003 WL 22225580 (N.D.N.Y., 2003)

- Witness's documents were not shielded from production by the attorney-client privilege based on the witness's asserted status as a "paralegal" for the defense team during related criminal prosecution, where witness was not acting as the agent of the attorney when she gathered information contained in documents. *Von Bulow by Auersperg v. von Bulow*, 811 F.2d 136 (2d Cir., 1987)

- An individual representing himself as a paralegal assisting his attorney-employer regarding a matter within the attorney-client privilege, telephoned the police, allegedly pursuant to the attorney-employer's direction, to advise of the attorney's representation of defendant. Thus, the issue presented herein is whether a paralegal who makes such a telephone call at the direction of his attorney-employer similarly serves to invoke the right to counsel, thereby requiring that custodial questioning cease. For the following reasons, this court holds in the affirmative. *People v. Seal*, 9 Misc. 3d 239, 800 N.Y.S.2d 825 (Sup. Ct., Kings Co., 2005)

Work-Product Rule and Paralegals

- A lawyer can perform work of a legal or nonlegal nature. The legal work performed by the lawyer need not be done directly by the lawyer himself or herself, but can qualify for the attorney work-product exclusion even if done by a nonlawyer, acting under the direction of a lawyer. *Delta Financial Corp. v. Morrison*, 15 Misc. 3d 308, 829 N.Y.S.2d 877 (Sup. Ct., Nassau Co., 2007)

- Under the work-product doctrine, handwritten notes on an aircraft manufacturer's document, made by paralegal in course of discovery in another case, were protected from disclosure in a products liability action. *Fine v. Facet Aerospace Products Co.*, 133 F.R.D. 439 (S.D.N.Y., 1990)

- Like the federal work-product rule, under New York law, material prepared by nonattorneys in anticipation of litigation, such as accident reports, is immune from discovery only where the material is prepared exclusively and in specific response to imminent litigation. *Calabro v. Stone*, 225 F.R.D. 96 (E.D.N.Y., 2004)

- Government took sufficient steps to ensure confidentiality of an agency paralegal's work product, for purposes of determining whether inadvertent disclosure of such material to criminal defendants waived the work-product privilege. The paralegal's files were maintained on agency's secure computer network, which could be accessed only by authorized individuals with security clearance; the paralegal's work was stored within private, password-protected account on that network; the vendor hired by defendants to copy hard drives of business at agency's main office, for discovery purposes, was prohibited from accessing the agency's network and was supervised by an agency employee throughout duration of visit; and government took reasonable precautions to protect the integrity of business's hard drives themselves. *U.S. v. Rigas*, 281 F. Supp. 2d 733 (S.D.N.Y., 2003)

Paralegals and Unemployment Compensation

Former paralegal is not required to take a legal secretary position

- A former paralegal should not be denied unemployment compensation benefits for refusing to take a position as a legal secretary. While both the paralegal position and the legal secretary position were characterized as legal support staff, the paralegal duties are more extensive and required different skills than that of a legal secretary. The legal secretary position did not "bear a reasonable relationship to claimant's skills" as a paralegal. *In re Feldman*, 13 A.D.3d 713, 785 N.Y.S.2d 600 (3d Dept., 2004)

- A paralegal who was hired as a full-time employee asked to become part time. The request was denied. Her application for unemployment compensation

was denied because she voluntarily left her employment without good cause. Continuing work was available and her dissatisfaction with her work schedule did not constitute good cause for resigning. *In re Anthony*, 257 A.D.2d 876 (3d Dept., 1999)

- A paralegal aide was disqualified from receiving unemployment insurance benefits because he voluntarily left his employment without good cause. He resigned after a coworker made anti-Semitic remarks without giving the employer a reasonable opportunity to investigate and address the matter. *In re Schwartz*, 62 A.D.3d 1231, 881 N.Y.S.2d 515 (3d Dept., 2009)

Paralegal was an employee, not an independent contractor

- An attorney fails to make unemployment insurance contributions for paralegals and other workers in the office, claiming that they were independent contractors rather than employees. The court disagreed. The attorney exercised sufficient overall control of their work to establish employer status by assigning the specific work, giving directions how the work was to be completed, paying them hourly, reimbursing their expenses, and having the work performed at his office using his office equipment and supplies. *In re Spinnell*, 300 A.D.2d 770, 751 N.Y.S.2d 643 (3d Dept., 2002)

Paralegal leaves without just cause

- Claimant worked as a paralegal for a law firm for just under one year. One morning, she returned from an errand much later than the employer expected and, as a result, she and the employer became involved in an argument during which the employer told her to get out of his office but did not fire her. Nevertheless, claimant left the employer's premises and did not go back to work. She was subsequently disqualified from receiving unemployment insurance benefits on the basis that she voluntarily left her employment without good cause. Criticism from a supervisor, even where it is perceived as unjust or unduly critical, does not necessarily constitute good cause for leaving employment. *In re Orrijola*, 55 A.D.3d 1201, 867 N.Y.S.2d 228 (3d Dept., 2008)

Paralegal misconduct as to smoking

- A paralegal at a law firm was ineligible to receive unemployment insurance benefits because her employment was terminated due to misconduct, where, after the firm adopted a policy prohibiting hourly employees from taking breaks during the workday, except for a midday lunch break, claimant was fired after she violated the policy by taking breaks to smoke cigarettes, as she had done before the policy was adopted. *In re Kridel*, 54 A.D.3d 465, 863 N.Y.S.2d 287 (3d Dept., 2008)

- A terminated senior paralegal is denied unemployment insurance because of misconduct. She received both written and verbal warnings regarding her tardiness and had been warned that further incidents could result in her termination. *In re Shorte*, 270 A.D.2d 554, 703 N.Y.S.2d 587 (3d Dept., 2000)

Miscellaneous Cases Involving Paralegals

Corrective step taken by a lawyer in ethical trouble: Hire a paralegal

- The attorney has undertaken corrective measures to avoid a repetition of bookkeeping irregularities. These include modernizing his bookkeeping system, utilizing QuickBooks software, and hiring a paralegal who is thoroughly familiar with the system. *In re Martin*, 62 A.D.3d (2d Dept., 2009)

Paralegal's husband seeks 50 percent of the value of her paralegal degree in a divorce action

- The court refused to distribute the marital portion of the wife's paralegal degree. All of paralegal education took place after her husband vacated the marital premises, and approximately one half of that education took place prior to the commencement of the action for divorce, which represents the cutoff date for acquisition of marital property. Although the husband appears not to have provided the wife with any particular encouragement or assistance during her one-year course of paralegal study, he was providing her with maintenance, child support, and other financial assistance at the time. We conclude that 50% of the value of defendant's paralegal degree constitutes marital property but that, under all the circumstances, it would be inequitable to distribute any part of that marital property to the husband. *Gandhi v. Gandhi*, 283 A.D.2d 782, 724 N.Y.S.2d 541 (3d Dept., 2001)

Paralegal designated as executor of a will

- Decedent's will designated petitioner, a paralegal for the attorney who drafted the will, as executor of his estate. As such the paralegal was entitled to the full statutory executor's commission. A reduction in the commission due to a failure to file a disclosure statement applied to attorney executors, not to paralegal executors. *In re Estate of Wagoner*, 30 A.D.3d 805, 816 N.Y.S.2d 599 (3d Dept., 2006)

Nonattorney excused from written disclosure to testator

- Good cause existed for excusing an attorney's legal secretary, who prepared a will, from making written disclosure to the testator where she was the executor. The court found her actions reasonable because

she was a non lawyer who had retired nine years before the disclosure requirement was adopted and because the will was drafted 13 years before the disclosure requirement was extended to law office employees. *In re Will of Winters*, 25 Misc. 3d 631, 883 N.Y.S.2d 703 (Sur. Ct., Broome Co., 2009)

Sexual harassment of a paralegal

- On one occasion, plaintiff invited a paralegal intern to lunch under the guise of helping her study for the "Law School Aptitude Test" but later propositioned her for a date. When the paralegal declined, plaintiff repeatedly harassed her for a date, putting pressure on her to accept. Eventually, plaintiff represented to co-workers that he was "seeing her." As a result, the paralegal confronted plaintiff and asked him to stop misrepresenting the nature of their relationship. *LaBella v. New York City Admin. for Children's Services*, 2005 WL 2077192 (E.D.N.Y., 2005)

Paralegal as an at-will employee

- A paralegal was hired as a consultant (independent contractor). When terminated without notice, she sued for breach of contract, asserting a contractual right to a ten-day termination notice. It is well established that if a definite term is not set for employment, then it is at-will, irrespective of the fact that a salary is determined on a weekly, monthly, or yearly basis. The failure to give the ten-day notice was a breach of contract. *Latimi v. Metropolitan Transp. Authority*, 17 Misc. 3d 1115, 851 N.Y.S.2d 64 (N.Y. City Civ. Ct., Kings Co., 2007)

Paralegal statement does not overcome presumption

- Under CPLR 2103(b)(2), service is complete upon mailing. The appellant failed to raise any issue regarding the validity of the affidavit of service. The statement by appellant's paralegal that appellant did not receive the order with notice of entry is insufficient to defeat the presumption that a proper mailing occurred. *Goldman v. Akl*, 3 Misc. 3d 131, 787 N.Y.S.2d 677 (Sup. Ct., App. Term, 2004)

Paralegal affidavit in a summary judgment motion

- Plaintiffs cite no cases allowing unsubstantiated assertions in affidavits by paralegals or legal assistants to be submitted in support of a summary judgment motion. Indeed, such evidence is clearly insufficient, in view of the principle that the conclusory assertions in the affirmation of an attorney, who fails to demonstrate personal knowledge of the facts, does not constitute "evidentiary proof in admissible form" which can be submitted in support of or in opposition to a summary judgment motion. *Tower Mineola Ltd. Partnership v. Potomac Ins.*

Co. of Illinois, 14 Misc. 3d 1288(A), 836 N.Y.S.2d 504 (Sup. Ct., New York Co., 2007)

Paralegal school brings antitrust suit against the ABA

- The court dismissed the paralegal school's antitrust suit against the American Bar Association. The guidelines and program of accreditation developed by ABA were reasonable insofar as they affected paralegal field and, hence, were not violative of antitrust law. *Paralegal Institute, Inc. v. American Bar Ass'n*, 475 F. Supp. 1123 (S.D.N.Y., 1979)

Paralegal allowed same access to inmates as other legal personnel

- Petitioner, in his capacity as a paralegal for an attorney, is allowed unmonitored contact visitation with inmates at the Erie County Holding Center, such as accorded other legal personnel. *Hicks v. Schoetz*, 261 A.D.2d 944, 691 N.Y.S.2d 219 (4th Dept., 1999)
- The county's unwritten policy of prohibiting paralegals with felony convictions from obtaining privileged access to a prison did not violate paralegals' due process rights. *Hicks v. Erie County, New York*, 65 Fed. Appx. 746, 2003 WL 21105337 (2d Cir., 2003)

The right to counsel and the right to speak to a paralegal

- The right of an accused to counsel did not attach when he requested permission to speak to his girlfriend, a paralegal who was being interviewed by police at the time of defendant's request. "Counsel"

as the word is used in the Sixth Amendment can mean nothing less than a licensed attorney at law. *People v. Starks*, 46 A.D.3d 1426, 848 N.Y.S.2d 467 (4th Dept., 2007)

Disbarred attorney as paralegal

- In a disbarment proceeding, the court noted that the respondent afforded so little regard to his law license as to allow a disbarred felon to use his name freely on court papers and to advertise himself as his paralegal. *In re Hancock*, 55 A.D.3d 216, 863 N.Y.S.2d 804 (2d Dept., 2008)

The court will not be the party's paralegal

- It is not the role of this court to operate as the paralegal for movants and ferret out legal authority to justify their requests for relief. The litigants, through their counsel, are obligated to present for acceptance by the court the precise legal theories upon which their arguments are based and the legal authority supporting these contentions. *Manessis v. Chang-Nam Song*, 8 Misc. 3d 1018(A), 803 N.Y.S.2d 19 (Sup. Ct., Queens Co., 2005)

D. Something to Check

Go to the online sources that provide free access to state court opinions in New York. (See chart in section 5.1.) Do a search for the terms "paralegal" or "legal assistant." Summarize (brief) one of the cases you find.

Becoming an Attorney in New York

A. Introduction

A question that arises in the minds of some paralegals during their career is: "Should I become an attorney?" The answer of most paralegals is *no*, particularly in light of the stress that they see in the lives of many practicing attorneys and the massive law school debt that they carry well into the early years of their career. In addition, the competition for jobs is keen (particularly in large cities), as over 9,200 new attorneys are licensed in New York each year. Yet some paralegals wish to pursue the law school option. If you look at the résumé of New York attorneys posted on their law firm web sites, you will occasionally see references to prior employment as paralegals before going to law school. Some attorneys worked part-time as paralegals while going to law school. In this section we explore what is involved in becoming an attorney in this state.

For a statistical overview of attorneys in New York (including salaries and bar passage rates), see section 3.4. For a timeline of the disciplinary process in New York, see Part 3, Appendix A.

B. Requirements to Become a New York Attorney

The rules for admission to practice law in New York were promulgated by the New York Court of Appeals and are found at 22 NYCRR 520.1 et. seq.

To be admitted to practice law, an applicant needs an order from the Appellate Division of the Supreme Court. Generally, to obtain an order, an applicant shall:

(A) Be at least 21 years of age

(B) Have earned a degree from a law school that was approved by the American Bar Association at the time the degree was earned

(C) Have passed both the New York bar examination and the Multistate Professional Responsibility Examination (MPRE)

(D) Have demonstrated that the applicant possesses the requisite character, fitness, and moral qualifications for admission to the practice of law

(E) Have taken the oath of office

Bar Exam Handbook and Rules
www.nybarexam.org (click "Bar Exam Handbook")
www.nybarexam.org/Rules/Rules.htm

Attorneys are admitted to the practice of law in New York State through one of the four Appellate Divisions of the Supreme Court. After passing the bar exam, the next step is an inquiry by the Committee on Character and Fitness of the Appellate Division. The process includes filing a completed application and appearing for a personal interview conducted by a member of the Committee on Character and Fitness.

C. Law Office Study: Taking the Bar Exam without Three Years of Law School

It is possible to take the bar exam without attending three years of law school. This option, sometimes called reading for the law or law office study, is relatively narrow. Here are the requirements:

- You have completed one year of an approved law school curriculum after your eighteenth birthday
- You are eligible to continue onto your second and third year, but decide not to do so
- You study law in a New York law office under the supervision of one or more New York lawyers for a minimum of three years 22 NYCRR 520.4 (*www.nybarexam.org/Rules/Rules.htm#520.4*)

Filing Requirements for the Law Office Study Option

(a) An Applicant's Affidavit of Law Office Study

(b) A certified copy of the Certificate of Commencement of Clerkship that was filed with the Office of the Clerk of the Court of Appeals

(c) An official law school transcript

(d) A completed handwriting sample certified by the attorney for whom you clerked

(e) An affidavit from the attorney(s) for whom you clerked

www.nybarexam.org/forms/forms.htm (click "Download" at "Law Office Study")

D. The Bar Exam

The New York State Bar Exam is administered by the New York State Board of Law Examiners:

New York State Board of Law Examiners
Corporate Plaza, Building 3
254 Washington Avenue Extension
Albany, NY 12203-5195
800-342-3335; 518-452-8700
www.nybarexam.org

The exam is challenging. Most applicants enroll in an intensive (and expensive) bar preparation course from a commercial company prior to taking the exam. (See Part F for examples of bar preparation courses.) For information about the bar pass rate, see section 3.4 and click "Past Exam Results" at the Board's site (*www.nybarexam.org*).

Bar Exam Structure

The bar examination (administered over two days) contains two sections: the New York section and the Multistate Bar Examination (MBE). The New York section consists of five essay questions and 50 multiple choice questions prepared by the New York Board, and one Multistate Performance Test (MPT) question, developed by the National Conference of Bar Examiners. The second day of the exam is the MBE section, which consists of 200 multiple choice questions. Applicants must also pass a separate exam, the Multistate Professional Responsibility Exam (MPRE), given at a different time.

- **Essay Questions:** The essay portion of the exam tests on 13 subject areas.

  (1) Business relationships (e.g., corporations)
  (2) Conflict of laws
  (3) New York and federal constitutional law
  (4) Contracts and contract remedies
  (5) Criminal law and procedure
  (6) Evidence
  (7) Matrimonial and family law
  (8) New York and federal civil jurisdiction and procedure
  (9) Professional responsibility
  (10) Real property
  (11) Torts and tort remedies
  (12) Trusts, wills, and estates
  (13) Uniform Commercial Code (UCC) articles 2, 3, and 9
  www.nybarexam.org/ExamQuestions/ExamQuestions.htm

- **Multistate Bar Exam (MBE):** The MBE is a six-hour, 200-question, multiple choice examination covering contracts, torts, constitutional law, criminal law, evidence, and real property.
  www.ncbex.org
  www.ncbex.org/multistate-tests/mbe

- **Multistate Performance Test (MPT):** The MPT is a practice-oriented test. The applicant is given a set of facts along with documents (e.g., a police report, a contract, a letter, a statute). A task must then be performed such as drafting of a legal memo or preparing a discovery strategy. The practice skills being tested can include legal analysis, fact analysis, problem solving, resolution of ethical dilemmas, organization and management of a lawyering task, and communication.
  www.ncbex.org/multistate-tests/mpt

- **Multistate Professional Responsibility Examination (MPRE):** The MPRE is a 60-question, two-hour, multiple choice legal ethics examination administered three times a year, on dates that are not used for the two-day exam described above. Applicants often take this exam before graduating from law school.
  www.ncbex.org/multistate-tests/mpre

Fees

Bar exam: $250 (NY Judiciary Law § 465)
Multistate Professional Responsibility Examination (MPRE): $55

E. Law Schools in New York

To practice law in New York, one does not need to attend a law school in New York. Most New York attorneys, however, do attend one of the following schools in the state:

Albany Law School
www.albanylaw.edu

Cardozo Law School
www.cardozo.yu.edu

Brooklyn Law School
www.brooklaw.edu

CUNY School of Law
www.law.cuny.edu

Columbia Law School
www.law.columbia.edu

Cornell University Law School
www.lawschool.cornell.edu

Fordham University School of Law
law.fordham.edu

Hofstra University School of Law
www.hofstra.edu/Academics/Law

New York Law School
www.nyls.edu

New York University School of Law
www.law.nyu.edu

Pace University School of Law
www.law.pace.edu

St. John's University School of Law
www.stjohns.edu/academics/graduate/law

SUNY Buffalo School of Law
www.law.buffalo.edu

Syracuse University College of Law
www.law.syr.edu

Touro Law Center
www.tourolaw.edu

F. More Information

New York State Board of Bar Examiners
www.nybarexam.org

Authority to Regulate Admission of Attorneys
6A New York Jurisprudence 2d, *Attorneys at Law* § 9

New York State Bar Association
www.nysba.org

National Conference of Bar Examiners
www.ncbex.org

Multistate Bar Exam Study Aids
www.ncbex.org (click "NCBE Online Store")

Bar Review Courses
www.thebarexam.com (click "New York")
www.supremebarreview.com (click "NY")
www.barbri.com (click "New York")
www.micromashbar.com (click "State Bar Reviews" "NY")
stu.findlaw.com/thebar/barreview.html

Bar Exam Resources
www.nyls.edu/library/for_students/bar_exam_resources
www.megalaw.com/lawstudent/studentcenter.php

The Cost of Law School: Some Examples
www.albanylaw.edu/sub.php?navigation_id=120
www.lawschool.cornell.edu/admissions/tuition/index.cfm
*law.hofstra.edu/CurrentStudents/FinancialAid/finaid_
    tuition.html*

Financial Aid For Law School
www.lsac.org/Financing/financial-aid-introduction.asp
studentaid.ed.gov
www.fafsa.ed.gov
www.fedmoney.org
www.megalaw.com/lawstudent/studentcenter.php

College Scholarship Search
www.fastweb.com

Law School Admission Council
www.lsac.org

Bar Admission and Law Schools in All States
www.abanet.org (click "Legal Education")

New York Lawyer's Guide to Passing the Bar Exam
www.nylawyer.com/display.php/file=/exam/index

Top Ten Mistakes to Avoid in Applying to Law School
www.chss.montclair.edu/leclair/LS/lsprep.html
www.accepted.com/Law/vault_article.aspx

Why Law School Is So Stressful
*www.law.fsu.edu/academic_programs/humanizing_lawschool/
    images/EP.pdf*

Bar Admission in All States
www.abanet.org/legaled/baradmissions/basicoverview.html
www.abanet.org/legaled/baradmissions/barcont.html

G. Something to Check

1. Law school library web sites often have excellent legal research guides. Select any three law schools listed in section E above. At the web sites of these law schools, click their law library link. At these law library sites, compare the information provided (including further links) on New York legal research. Describe what you are led to. Which law library leads you to the most comprehensive collection of New York law?

2. Run the following search in Google or other search engine:

   "Should I go to law school?"
   What categories of results does this search yield?

PART
2
Paralegal Employment

A. Introduction

How do new paralegals find their first job? How do experienced paralegals interested in a job change find opportunities that build on their experience? In this section we present ideas and resources that can be helpful in answering these questions for full-time and part-time work. In addition to general strategies, you will find specific Internet sites that should be checked. Some of the sites cover the entire state, while others focus on specific areas of the state.

Most of the leads will be to traditional employment agencies that match employers with applicants. In addition, staffing agencies are included. A staffing agency is an employment agency that places temporary workers, often directly paying the workers and handling all of the financial aspects of the placement. A law office will pay the staffing agency, which in turn pays the paralegal's salary for work at the law office. Many employment and staffing agencies do not charge job applicants for their services. Of course, you should confirm that this is true before deciding to work with any agency.

B. General Strategies for Finding Employment

Here are strategies that can be helpful in finding leads to employment:

▶ *School Connections.* Start with your paralegal school. It often has employment resources that can be tapped into. If there is an alumni association, it can be a rich source of networking opportunities. Is there is a listserv of school graduates? Check lists of social networking sites (*en.wikipedia.org/wiki/List_of_social_networking_websites*) to find out if any graduates of your school have formed any groups. Sites such as Facebook (*www.facebook.com*) can be particularly fruitful.

▶ *Paralegal Associations.* Section 1.2 lists every paralegal association in the state. It also gives you related groups such as legal administrator associations. Go to the web site of every association near the cities or towns where you want to work. Find out if any job leads are available on these web sites. Some associations give current openings that nonmembers can access. If the newsletter of an association is online, look through recent issues. They may list job openings that are not found elsewhere on the association's web site. Send an e-mail to the association in which you ask for leads to employment and staffing agencies in the area. If there is a search box on the site, type in search words such as "employment," "job bank," "paralegal work," and "legal assistant employment."

▶ *National Paralegal Associations.* Check the career resources of the national paralegal associations:

National Federation of Paralegal Associations
www.paralegals.org
(click "NFPA Career Center")

NALS, the Association for Legal Professionals
www.nals.org
(click "Career Center")

▶ *Paralegal Positions Listed on the Career Center.* The New York State Bar Association has a Career Center that lists paralegal positions in the state:

- Go to the bar's main site (*www.nysba.org*).
- Under "For Attorneys," click "Jobs and Careers."
- Under "Job Type" select "Paralegal."
- Or type "paralegal" in the keyword box.

▶ *Attorney Job Search Resources.* There are many resources in the state that focus on the search for attorney employment. (Some are listed below.) Don't be reluctant to check out web sites for attorney employment, since many have pages or links on paralegal employment. If not, call them or send them an e-mail message, asking for leads on paralegal employment in the area. In the search box on the site, type in search words such as "paralegal" and "legal assistant."

▶ *Bar Associations.* Bar associations sometimes have employment services for their members. The Career Center mentioned above covers attorney and paralegal employment. Some of this information might be available to the general public. (The list of bar associations in the state is in section 3.4.) Go to the web sites of the associations to find out if any leads are available on paralegal employment. Consider sending the bar association an e-mail message asking about paralegal employment and staffing agencies in the area.

▶ *Paralegal Résumé Bank.* Some bar associations allow paralegals to post their résumés online. When you check a bar association web site, check whether this option is available.

Example:
wcba.legalstaff.com/Common/HomePage.aspx?abbr=
L.WCBA

► *CareerZone* (Workforce New York). In the online CareerZone, you can sign up for a free account, which will lead you to information about paralegal careers in New York and allow you to search for job openings within a designated number of miles from your zip code.
www.nycareerzone.org
(click "Find a Job" and then follow the instructions to set up an account)

Overview of Paralegals at CareerZone
www.nycareerzone.org/graphic/profile.jsp?onetsoc=
23-2011.00

NYSJE: New York State Job Exchange
www.americasjobexchange.com/ny
(under "Job Category," click "Legal" and a New York city or zip code)

► *General Circulation and Legal Newspapers.* General circulation newspapers often have want ads for paralegals. These newspapers are worth checking, particularly their online editions. Also find out what the legal newspaper is for your area—hard copy and online. It may have want ads for paralegals.

New York State Newspapers Online
newslink.org/nynews.html
www.usnpl.com/nynews.php
www.onlinenewspapers.com/usstate/usnewyor.htm

Examples of Online Newspapers
- Albany (*timesunion.com*) (*albany.bizjournals.com*)
- Buffalo (*buffalonews.com*) (*buffalo.bizjournals.com*)
- Long Island (*newsday.com*) (*longislandpress.com*)
- New York City (*www.law.com/jsp/nylj/index.jsp*)
(*nytimes.com*) (*nypost.com*) (*nydailynews.com*)
- Rochester (*democratandchronicle.com*)
- Schenectady (*dailygazette.com*)
- Syracuse (*www.syracuse.com/poststandard*)
- Utica (*uticaod.com*)

► *General Search Engines.* Go to general search engines (examples: *www.google.com, www.bing.com, www.yahoo.com, www.ask.com*). In these engines, try the following searches that include the name of the state or the city where you want to work:

paralegal job "New York"
paralegal job Albany
paralegal job Buffalo

► *Google Legal Employment Directory.*
directory.google.com/Top/Society/Law/Employment

► *Legal Search Engines.*

Findlaw
www.findlaw.com
(click "Jobs")
careers.findlaw.com

Catalaw
www.catalaw.com/catextra/Profession_Employment.shtml
(type "paralegal jobs New York" (without the quotation marks))

Hieros Gamos
www.hg.org
(see the entries under "Law Employment Center")
(Under "Job Listings" select "Paralegal")

LawGuru
www.lawguru.com/pro.php
(click "Legal Career Center")

► *Networking.* Many paralegals find employment through the networking contacts they make with attorneys, paralegals, legal secretaries, etc. whom they meet at school, at paralegal associations, at social clubs, at church, at synagogue, etc. At these settings, always be ready to ask, "Who do you know who might be looking for paralegals?" There is not a more powerful question that could be asked of anyone with any connection to the practice of law.

► *Legal Assistant Today Job Bank.*
www.legalassistanttoday.com/jobbank

► *Paralegal Jobs in the Public Sector.* If you are seeking employment in the public sector:

New York Legal Aid and Legal Services Offices
www.nlada.org/Jobs
(click "New York")

New York State Defenders Association
www.nysda.org
www.llrx.com/features/publicdefense.htm

- See section 2.2 for employment in state government
- See section 2.3 for employment in federal agencies located in New York
- See section 4.2 for links to employment in New York state courts and 4.3 for links to employment in federal courts in the state
- See section 2.4 for the links to legal aid/legal services offices and other public sector offices in New York

► *Paralegal Jobs in Corporations.*

Association of Corporate Counsel
www.acc.com

- Click "Careers" and "Find a Job"
- Click "New York"
- Look through the attorney jobs to see if any paralegal (or related) jobs are listed

- For attorney jobs, contact some of the offices or agencies listed to determine if they place paralegals in corporations or can direct you to agencies that do
- In the search box, type "paralegal" or "legal assistant"

Largest Employers in New York
www.careerinfonet.org
(in Google, type "largest employers in New York state" without the quotation marks)
Go to the web sites of large corporate employers in the state; find employment links on the site to inquire about paralegal openings.

▶ *Law Firm Web Sites.* Most law firms have a web site and the largest ones invariably have a job section, often under the caption "careers" or "employment." Look for links to "legal support," "staff & support," "careers," "professional legal staff," "legal assistants," "paralegals," and the like. These sections usually include a description of the firm, specific jobs available, and instructions on how to apply for a job. For lists of some New York law offices, check:

lawyers.findlaw.com/lawyer/state.jsp
www.lawresearchservices.com/firms/lawfirmUS.htm
washlaw.edu/lfirms/index.php?c=8
www.nalpdirectory.com
www.hg.org/northam-firms.html

▶ *Legal Management Links.* Paralegal positions are often posted on the web sites of legal management associations.

International Paralegal Management Association
www.paralegalmanagement.org
(click "Job Bank")

Association of Legal Administrators
www.alanet.org
(under "Career Center/Job Bank" select "Job Seekers"; type "paralegal" as a keyword and as a location, select "New York")

C. Additional Resources

AARDVARC
www.aardvarc.org/dv/states/nydv.shtml
(This site contains an extensive list of legal aid/legal services offices in the counties of the state. Although the focus of the site is domestic violence, the links to the offices can be used to inquire about job opportunities in general.)

Career Builder
www.careerbuilder.com
(type "paralegal" and a specific city in New York)

Craigslist
www.craigslist.org
(click "New York" and a city; under "Jobs," click "legal/paralegal")

Detod.com
detod.legalstaff.com

Indeed
www.indeed.com
(type "paralegal" and a zip code or city in New York)

IntJobs
intjobs.org/law/paralegal.html

Job Search
legal.jobsearch.com

JobsNet, New York
legal.jobs.net/newyork.htm

Law Crossing
www.lawcrossing.com/lclegalstaff.php

LawJobs
www.lawjobs.com
(select "Paralegal" job type and "New York" under region)

Lawyers Weekly Jobs
www.lawyersweeklyjobs.com
(select "paralegal" and "New York")

Legal Staff
www.legalstaff.com

Litigation Support Jobs
www.litigationsupportjobs.com

Monster, New York
legal.monster.com
www.monster.com
jobsearch.monster.com

Nation Job Network
www.nationjob.com/legal

Paralegal Gateway
paralegalgateway.com

Robert Half Legal
800-870-8367
www.roberthalflegal.com

SimplyHired
www.simplyhired.com
(type "paralegal" and "New York")

Smart Hunt
smarthunt.com
(type "paralegal" and a city in New York)

Vault
www.vault.com
(click "Jobs" then "New York" and type "paralegal" as a keyword)

Yahoo Hotjobs, Legaljobs, NY
hotjobs.yahoo.com/jobs/NY/legal-jobs

Selected Areas of the State

Albany
albany.craigslist.org/lgl
legal.jobs.net/NewYork-Albany.htm
legal.careers.com/NewYork-Albany.htm

Buffalo
buffalo.craigslist.org/lgl
legal.jobs.net/NewYork-Buffalo.htm

Long Island
newyork.craigslist.org/lgi/lgl
legal.jobs.net/NewYork-LongIsland.htm
legal.careers.com/NewYork-LongIsland.htm

New York City
newyork.craigslist.org/lgl
www.filcro.com
hotjobs.yahoo.com/jobs/NY/New-York/Legal-jobs
www.nbocellistaffing.com/aboutus.asp
abcny.legalstaff.com/Common/HomePage.aspx?abbr=ABCNY

Rochester
rochester.craigslist.org/lgl
legal.jobs.net/NewYork-Rochester.htm
legal.careers.com/NewYork-Rochester.htm

Schenectady
legal.jobs.net/NewYork-Schenectady.htm
legal.careers.com/NewYork-Schenectady.htm

Syracuse
syracuse.craigslist.org/lgl
lycos.syracuse.oodle.com/job/legal

Utica
utica.craigslist.org/lgl
legal.jobs.net/NewYork-Utica.htm
legal.careers.com/NewYork-Utica.htm

Yonkers
legal.jobs.net/NewYork-Melville.htm
hotjobs.yahoo.com/jobs/NY/Yonkers/Legal-jobs

D. More Information

U.S. Department of Labor
Paralegals and Legal Assistants
www.bls.gov/oco/ocos114.htm

Paralegal Salaries
See section 1.1.

Job Strategy Toolbox for Paralegals (Gailynne Ferguson)
www.law.com/jsp/law/careercenter/lawArticleCareerCenter.
  jsp?id=1176973460690&rss=careercenter

25 Things You Should Never Include on a Resume
www.hrworld.com/features/25-things-not-to-put-on-
  resume-121807

E. Something to Check

1. List and compare the services of two paralegal employment sites that allow you to submit your résumé online.
2. What direct or indirect paralegal employment services are available to you at two paralegal associations and two bar associations closest to your area?
3. What useful information can you obtain at any of the legal administrator or legal secretary association sites in the state?
   (See section 1.2 for a list of these sites.)

2.2 Sample Paralegal Job Descriptions in State Government

A. Introduction

B. Legal Assistant Series

C. Examinations

D. Related Civil Service Positions

E. Court Positions

F. More Information

G. Something to Check

A. Introduction

In this section we will explore paralegal positions that are part of the civil service system. Different rules and procedures apply when seeking comparable positions in the court system and in the state legislature.

Seeking a State or Local Government Position

Overview of the job application process
www.cs.state.ny.us/jobseeker

Searching for a position in state government
www.cs.state.ny.us/jobseeker/public/index.cfm
nyjobsource.com/gov.html

Searching for a position in local government
www.cs.state.ny.us/jobseeker/local/index.cfm
www.cs.state.ny.us/home/msd.cfm
www.cs.state.ny.us/employees/local/local.cfm
nyjobsource.com/gov.html

Searching for civil service positions
www.statejobsny.com/search.asp
(type the keywords "legal assistant paralegal")

Searching for court positions
www.nycourts.gov/careers/statewide

Searching for positions in the state legislature
(inquire through the office of your assemblymember or state senator)
assembly.state.ny.us
www.senate.state.ny.us

**Understanding the examination process
(where required)**
www.cs.state.ny.us/jobseeker/public/stateexam.cfm

New York State Department of Civil Service
Alfred E. Smith State Office Building
Albany, NY 12239
877-NYS-JOBS; 518-457-2487
www.cs.state.ny.us

B. Legal Assistant Series

Most state and local government paralegal jobs fall under the rules of the civil service. Civil service appointments and promotions are made by merit and fitness as mandated by the New York State Constitution. This can include taking a standardized test.

The major paralegal positions in state government are legal assistant 1 and legal assistant 2. Here are the specifications for these positions:

Positions

Legal Assistant 1, Grade 14
Legal Assistant 2, Grade 17
Occupational Code: 2522210
Salary Range:
Legal Assistant 1: (grade 14) $41,349 to $59,861
Legal Assistant 2: (grade 17) $48,504 to $69,510
(*www.cs.state.ny.us/tsplan/tsp_display2.cfm?specCode= 2522210F*)

Brief Description of Class Series

In close association with an attorney, legal assistants perform a variety of paralegal tasks that require formal education and certification as a paralegal. When classified in agencies other than the Office of the Attorney General, legal assistants are typically assigned to Counsel's Offices.

Distinguishing Characteristics

The preponderance of duties performed by legal assistants is legal work, rather than office management or secretarial keyboarding work.

Legal Assistant 1: performs less complex paralegal work, e.g., legal research in areas where precedent may be expected; may perform limited analysis of the research obtained; has limited program or case involvement.

Legal Assistant 2: functions at highest level in the series; independently performs more complex paralegal work, e.g., legal research in areas where clear precedent may not exist; provides an analysis of the information gathered with minimal direction from attorneys; reviews and analyzes complex materials; has varied assignments and requires extensive involvement in the program area or cases.

Illustrative Duties

Legal Assistant 1:

- Schedules witnesses, takes depositions, and determines and collects information relevant to the case.
- Reviews case-related materials for lines of questioning.
- Assembles exhibits and briefs.
- Assists at trials or hearings by managing the exhibits and suggesting relevant questions for the attorney to raise.
- Prepares and files with the courts associated court papers.
- Performs preliminary background work for administrative review processes.
- Calculates monies owed to the State, determines responsible parties, and locates and notifies them of the amount.
- Reviews administrative procedures and makes initial determinations on information releasable under the Freedom of Information Act.
- Negotiates and proposes preliminary settlements of fines.
- Completes routine investigative work for attorney review.
- Reviews draft legislative proposals for compliance with bill drafting requirements.
- Uses Shepard's Citations or other reference sources to check the cases cited to ensure that the case law is still relevant.
- Maintains or oversees tracking systems, calendars, and reporting systems.
- Opens and closes files or cases.
- Performs activities related to docketing, the placement of court-related activities on the court calendar and on the attorney's calendar.
- Prepares portions of briefs.
- Answers routine questions from the public.
- Prepares findings of decisions and findings of fact.
- Prepares opinions on routine matters.
- Prepares reports.

Legal Assistant 2:

- Prepares arguments in court for pro se and other similar cases or for materials related to administrative hearings. (Pro se refers to cases in which a litigant or claimant against the State represents him/herself before the courts or before a judge.)

- Develops assigned cases or files to the point where an attorney need only sign off on the related papers or present the case before the court.
- Prepares correspondence and all relevant case materials for the record.
- Drafts various legal documents and assists in the preparation for litigation.
- Drafts responsive motions or answers, affidavits, or discovery demands.
- Organizes exhibits for examination before trial (EBT).
- Organizes, drafts, and prepares motions for summary judgment.
- Works with the assigned attorney to restyle papers as needed.
- Serves subpoenas or arranges service.
- Arranges for filing pleadings and other legal papers with the court clerk of record.
- Analyzes adversaries' responses for their sufficiency and evaluates any objections received.
- Reviews discovery demands received.
- Drafts responses to interrogatories, notices to admit, and requests for documents.
- Digests transcripts from EBTs or excerpts from trial transcripts.
- Prepares final documents for file closing.
- Writes briefs.
- Drafts opinions for review by an attorney.
- Performs detailed, open-ended investigations.
- Reviews and proposes changes in legislation, including drafting language and making revisions, and manages related bill-tracking activities.
- Drafts contracts and participates in the negotiation of contracts.

Minimum Qualifications (may be modified in examination announcements)

Legal Assistant 1

An associate's degree or certificate in legal studies, paralegal studies, or legal assistant studies from an accredited institution or one approved by the American Bar Association.

Legal Assistant 2

Either I: A bachelor's degree in legal studies, paralegal studies, or legal assistant studies from an accredited institution or one approved by the American Bar Association;

OR II: An associate's degree or certificate in legal studies, paralegal studies, or legal assistant studies from an accredited institution or one approved by the American Bar Association AND one year of subsequent full-time experience as a paralegal.

For the purposes of this examination, a paralegal is someone who applies knowledge of the law and legal procedures in rendering direct assistance to lawyers, clients, and courts; prepares and interprets legal documents; researches, compiles, and uses information from legal materials; and analyzes and handles procedural problems that involve independent decisions.

For the purposes of the examination, experience limited solely to general clerical or secretarial duties performed in a law office is NOT considered to be qualifying experience.

C. Examinations

You need to check examination announcements for information on required examinations for legal assistant positions. Here is an example of such information from a recent announcement:

Subject of Examination

There will be a written test which you must pass in order to be considered for appointment. The written test is designed to test for knowledge, skills, and/or abilities in such areas as:

1. **Conducting research into legal matters**—These questions test for the ability to use various reference materials and legal research techniques. You will be required to know where to find a particular law, subject, or topic, and be familiar with various legal reference texts. Upon being provided with special commands and symbols for setting the parameters of a search, you will be expected to know how to perform legal research through the use of the computer. These questions also test for a knowledge of legal citations.

2. **Interviewing**—These questions test for knowledge of the principles and practices employed in obtaining information from individuals through structured conversations. These questions require you to apply the principles, practices, and techniques of effective interviewing to hypothetical interviewing situations. Included are questions that present a problem arising from an interviewing situation, and you must choose the most appropriate course of action to take.

3. **Office record keeping**—These questions test your ability to perform common office record keeping tasks. The test consists of two or more "sets" of questions, each set concerning a different problem. Typical record keeping problems might involve the organization or collation of data from several sources; scheduling; maintaining a record system using running balances; or completion of a table summarizing data using totals, subtotals, averages, and percents.

4. **Preparing written material**—These questions test for the ability to present information clearly and accurately, and to organize paragraphs logically

and comprehensibly. For some questions, you will be given information in two or three sentences followed by four restatements of the information. You must then choose the best version. For other questions, you will be given paragraphs with their sentences out of order. You must then choose, from four suggestions, the best order for the sentences.

5. **Legal terminology, documents and forms**—These questions test for the ability to recognize definitions of specific common legal terms or the term which fits a certain description. The questions are presented in various forms such as simple definitions, examples of terminology, and the use of this terminology within documents and forms related to the legal field.

6. **Understanding and interpreting legal material**—These questions test for the ability to read, interpret, and apply legal passages. You will be provided with brief reading selections based on or taken from legal text, each followed by one or more questions. All the information needed to answer the questions is contained in the reading selections. No prior knowledge of the subject is required. The subject matter of the selections may not be specific to the title(s) for which you are being tested. The purpose of these questions is only to test for the ability to read this type of material at this level of difficulty.

The final score must be 70 or higher in order to pass. Rank on the eligible list will be determined after adding any wartime veterans' and Civil Service Law Section 85-a credits to the final passing score.

D. Related Civil Service Positions

You may also want to explore the following state civil service positions:

Collection and Civil Prosecution Specialists

- *Duties:* In close association with Department of Law attorneys, Collection and Civil Prosecution Specialists trace, locate, and contact debtors referred for nonpayment of their State obligations, and upon making contact, either arrange voluntary compliance or extract it through income executions, fines, and court action. They also perform related paralegal work, such as monitoring files in which legal process has been served, drafting papers for review by attorneys, performing occasional legal research, monitoring enforcement of judgment, and closing files.
- *Qualifications:* Two years of full-range debt-collection work experience; or two years of work experience as a paralegal; or an associate's or higher degree

in paralegal studies; or a general practice legal specialty certificate (normally comprised of at least 150 classroom hours) from an accredited or ABA-cited institution.
(*www.cs.state.ny.us/tsplan/tsp_display2.cfm?specCode= 2592100F*)

Law Department Document Specialists

- *Duties:* Serve as legal document preparation assistant to litigation attorneys in the Department of Law. Specialists must possess knowledge of legal terminology and court formatting requirements; must be able to verify legal citations and perform other paralegal functions related to the production of legal papers for filing with courts and opposing counsel, e.g., assembly of documents and exhibits, and creation of a table of contents page. This work requires the skilled use of keyboarding and information processing equipment.
- *Qualifications:* Successful performance on a job-related examination.
(*www.cs.state.ny.us/tsplan/tsp_display2.cfm?specCode= 2602200F*)

E. Court Positions

Positions for all New York State courts are administered by the Office of Court Administration (OCA).

Current Openings:
www.nycourts.gov/careers/statewide/index.shtml

Although there are no titles in the court system for "paralegal" or "legal assistant," there are many similar positions for which a paralegal may be qualified, such as court office assistant. Here is an example of such a position:

Position Title: Supervisor of Records, Surrogate's Court
Grade: JG-16
Location: Surrogate's Court, New York County, New York City
Salary: $39,160 (plus $1,302 location pay)
Classification: Non-competitive
Duties: Supervise subordinate personnel engaged in (a) maintaining records of wills and other legal documents pertaining to the taxation and distribution of estates and (b) searching for and providing certified copies of such documents to the public.
Qualifications: Two years of work experience; or associate's degree (or completion of 60 college-level credits) from an accredited college or university; or an equivalent combination of education and experience. Thirty college-level credits may be substituted for one year of work experience.

Justice Courts (town and village courts) have a separate hiring system.

F. More Information

Careers in State Government
www.cs.state.ny.us/jobseeker/gettingajob/empnys.cfm

Example of Notification of Legal Assistant Examination
www.cs.state.ny.us/announarchive/announcements/24-830.cfm

Questions and Answers about NYS Civil Service Exams
www.cs.state.ny.us/jobseeker/local/qanda.cfm
www.niagaracounty.com/Dept_FAQs.asp

Sign up to Receive E-mail Notification of New Examination Announcements
www.cs.state.ny.us/announ/emaillist.cfm

Examination Announcements for Local Government Positions
www.cs.state.ny.us/jobseeker/local/map.cfm

New York State Department of Civil Service
www.cs.state.ny.us

Civil Service Positions in State Government
www.cs.state.ny.us/jobseeker/public

Civil Service Positions in Local Government
www.cs.state.ny.us/employees/local/local.cfm

State Jobs New York
www.statejobsny.com

New York Job Source
nyjobsource.com/gov.html

Local Government Civil Service Offices
www.cs.state.ny.us/jobseeker/local.cfm

New York State Department of Labor: Finding a Job
www.labor.state.ny.us/careerservices/CareerServicesIndex.shtm

Employment Guide
nysegov.com/citGuide.cfm?superCat=36&cat=75&content=main

New York City Public Employment
www.nyc.gov/html/dcas/html/employment/employ.shtml

Court Employment
Careers at the Unified Court System
www.nycourts.gov/careers/statewide/index.shtml

G. Something to Check

1. Use the links above to find an example of a current job opening for a legal assistant in state government.
2. Go to the web site of the state courts in your county (see above). Find a current job opening for a paralegal-related position. If nothing is open, try other counties.
3. Are there any current job openings for paralegals in any of the federal courts sitting in New York? See section 4.3 for sites to check.

2.3 Sample Paralegal Job Description in a Federal Agency Located in New York

A. Introduction
B. Sample Job Description
C. More Information
D. Something to Check

A. Introduction

The federal government is the largest employer of paralegals in the United States. Its paralegal position is the Paralegal Specialist. (There is also a Legal Assistant position that has substantial clerical responsibility.) The role of the Paralegal Specialist in the federal government can be somewhat different from what exists in the private sector. A Paralegal Specialist can be a document examiner, an investigator, or a law clerk, among other descriptions. He or she may work independently in the federal government and does not always work directly for or under the supervision of an attorney.

There is an official, centralized web site called USAJobs that posts federal job vacancies. It is managed by the Office of Personnel Management (OPM), the agency responsible for federal personnel matters. Vacancies from all federal agencies may be posted at USAJobs.

Using USAJobs
www.usajobs.opm.gov

- Type "paralegal" and click Search
- Also, click "Search Jobs" and select "Legal and Claims Examining"

In addition to the USAJobs web site, many agencies list vacancies on their individual web sites. Look for links to "Jobs" or "Employment" on their sites. The agencies might advertise their employment openings in local newspapers and other local employment agency publications. Calling local federal agencies directly can also lead to information about potential employment opportunities. Check standard telephone directories for a list of U.S. government offices in your area. For a list of federal agencies and additional leads to finding a federal job, see "More Information" at the end of this section.

The government identification code for the Paralegal Specialist is GS-950. For the Legal Assistant, it is GS-986. The Paralegal Specialist positions range from GS-5 to GS-11 on the federal General Schedule (GS) pay scale and from GS-5 to GS-7 for the Legal Assistant. See the salary link below. The pay levels include yearly cost-of-living increases passed by Congress, as well as locality pay.

Elsewhere in this book you will find additional information on employment:

- In state government agencies (section 2.2)
- In private law firms (section 2.1)
- In corporations (section 2.1)
- In legal aid/legal service offices (sections 2.1 and 2.4)

B. Sample Job Description

The following job description is for a paralegal position in a federal government agency located in New York. It is an example only. The position may no longer be open. We present it here solely to give you an idea of the kinds of positions available in the federal government for New York paralegals. Note that the listing also includes the equivalent of interview questions ("Sample Questions Used in Evaluating Applicants"). You should consider preparing answers to such questions when applying for *any* paralegal job.

Basics

Title: Paralegal Specialist
Series, Grade: GS-0950-07
Salary Range: $32,534 to $42,290
Promotion Potential: To GS-11
Vacancy Announcement Number: ATR-05-17
Duty Location: Department of Justice, Federal Bureau of Investigation, New York City
Number of Vacancies: 2
Level: This is an entry-level, trainee position.
Appointment: Two-year appointment, which may be renewable up to a total of four years, subject to a one-year trial period in accordance with 5 CFR § 316.304. Full-time, competitive position.
Who May Apply: This announcement is open to all qualified applicants within the New York City commuting area only.

This position is advertised concurrently under Merit Promotion procedures in Announcement Number NY-2006-0084. Candidates who wish to be considered under both External and Merit Promotion procedures must apply to both announcements. Applications will not be accepted from outside the area of consideration.

Duties of a Paralegal Specialist Functioning at a GS-7 Level

In a developmental capacity and under the direction of the Chief Division Counsel (CDC), performs a variety of analytical, research, and procedural duties to provide legal assistance to the CDC and to increase the effectiveness and efficiency of operations within the legal unit of the field office:

- oversees the administrative management of administrative claims arising from accidents involving Bureau vehicles;

- advises office personnel of the procedures and policy for reporting automobile accidents;
- assists in processing administrative claims;
- verifies citations and legal references;
- prepares summaries of testimony and depositions;
- provides paralegal instruction and guidance to Special Agents within field office;
- maintains the law library for the unit and ensures that reference materials and files are kept up-to-date;
- reviews court dockets and obtains copies of pertinent filings.

Duties of a Paralegal Specialist Functioning at a GS-9 Level

Under the direction of the Chief Division Counsel (CDC), performs a variety of complex analytical, research, and procedural duties to provide legal assistance to the CDC and to increase the effectiveness and efficiency of operations within the legal unit of the field office:

- analyzes information related to legal matters arising from automobile accidents, property damage, and casualty claims;
- reviews case information to become familiar with questions under consideration;
- recommends additional investigation where necessary;
- reviews and analyzes information on claims submitted under the Federal Tort Claims Act and Title 31;
- processes discovery requests for information maintained by the FBI;
- maintains liaison with counterparts in insurance companies, U.S. Attorney's Office, third parties, outside attorneys, and FBI headquarters.

Qualifications of GS-7 Candidates

Must have one year of specialized experience equivalent to the GS-5 level. Specialized experience is experience in conducting research for preparation of legal opinions on matters of interest to the agency and performing substantive legal analysis of requests for information under the provisions of various acts.

Qualifications of GS-9 Candidates

Must have one year of specialized experience equivalent to the GS-7 level. Specialized experience is experience in conducting research for the preparation of legal opinions on matters of interest to the agency and performing substantive legal analysis of requests for information under the provisions of various acts.

Education of a GS-7 Candidate That May Be Substituted for Specialized Experience

Superior Academic Achievement—a GPA of 3.0 or higher out of a 4.0, as recorded on an official transcript, or based on courses completed during final two years of curriculum; or a GPA of 3.5 or higher out of 4.0, based on the average of required courses completed in major or required courses in major completed during the final two years of curriculum or at least one year of graduate-level education.

Education of a GS-9 Candidate That May Be Substituted for Specialized Experience

Two full academic years of progressively higher-level graduate education OR master's degree OR equivalent graduate degree such as LL.B. or J.D.

The selectee may be required to serve a one-year probationary period.

How to Apply

Applications (résumé and application questions) for this vacancy must be submitted online via the FBI jobs Online Application system (*www.fbijobs.gov*) BEFORE midnight Eastern Time (Washington, DC time) on the closing date of this announcement. If you fail to submit a complete online résumé, you will not be considered for this position. Requests for an extension will not be granted.

Sample Questions Used in Evaluating Applicants

For some federal positions, the following kinds of questions are used to help the agency evaluate applicants. The questions are the equivalent of interview questions. You should consider preparing answers to such questions when applying for any paralegal job. (Note: Your responses are subject to verification through background checks, job interviews, or any other information obtained during the application process.)

- In the past three years how many different paying jobs have you held for more than two weeks?
- On your present or most recent job, how did your supervisor rate you: outstanding; above average; average; below average; not employed or received no rating?
- How many civic or social organizations (which have regular meetings and a defined membership) have you belonged to?
- Have you successfully done work where your primary responsibility was to help others work out their problems?
- Have you successfully done work that constantly required you to work under difficult time constraints?
- Have you successfully planned an event such as a conference, fund-raiser, etc.?
- Have you successfully learned a hobby or leisure activity requiring extensive study or use of complex directions?
- Have you effectively served on a problem-solving, planning, or goal-setting committee or team?

- Have you successfully completed a long-term project outside of work where you were solely responsible for doing the work?
- Have you successfully done work that required extensive on-the-job training?
- Have you worked on several major assignments or projects at the same time with minimal supervision and completed the work on time or ahead of schedule?
- Have you often been asked to proofread or edit the writing of others for content, punctuation, spelling, and grammar?
- Have you suggested or made changes to products or procedures that resulted in better meeting customer needs?
- Have you successfully done work that required you to interact with people at many levels in an organization?
- Have you successfully done work that regularly involved composing letters or writing reports containing several short paragraphs, such as investigation reports, accident reports, performance evaluations, etc.?
- Have you successfully done work that regularly involved answering questions, gathering nonsensitive information, or providing assistance to others, either in person or by telephone?
- Have you successfully done work where you had to coordinate vacation schedules, lunch breaks, etc., with other workers?
- Have you designed or developed something, on your own initiative, to help you or other employees better complete assignments?
- Have you successfully done work that regularly involved being on duty by yourself, or completing nonroutine assignments with minimal or no close supervision?
- Have you taught yourself skills that improved your performance in school or at work (e.g., taught yourself typing, computer skills, a foreign language, etc.)?
- Have you successfully completed a complex research project that included collecting and analyzing information, and reporting conclusions or recommendations?
- Have you successfully done work where your supervisor regularly relied on you to make decisions while he or she was in meetings or out of the office?
- Have you taken the initiative to learn new skills or acquire additional knowledge that improved your performance at work or school, or in leisure activities?
- Have you participated in training classes, workshops, or seminars outside of school that helped you improve your teamwork skills?
- Have you been given additional responsibilities because of your ability to organize and complete your regular work more quickly than expected?

C. More Information

General Search Engines

In a general search engine (e.g., *www.google.com*, *www.yahoo.com*, *www.bing.com*, *www.ask.com*), run the following search: federal government jobs "New York".

Finding a Federal Job
USA Jobs
www.usajobs.opm.gov
jobsearch.usajobs.opm.gov/a9opm.asp

Federal Job Search
www.federaljobsearch.com
(in Career Field, click "Legal, Law and Claims"; in Location, click "New York")

Applying for a Federal Job
www.gpo.gov/careers/pdfs/of0510.pdf

Official/Standard Forms Used in Federal Hiring
www.opm.gov/forms

FedWorld
www.fedworld.gov/jobs/jobsearch.html

Federal Jobs Digest
www.jobsfed.com
(click "New York" on the map)

Yahoo HotJobs/Government
hotjobs.yahoo.com/governmentjobs

Lists of U.S. Government Departments and Agencies
www.firstgov.gov
(click "A–Z Agency Index")
www.congress.org
(click "Federal Agencies")

Federal Salaries
www.opm.gov/oca/06tables/index.asp

Federal Job Benefits
www.usajobs.gov/jobextrainfo.asp

Qualification Standards for General Schedule (GS) Positions
www.opm.gov/qualifications/SEC-IV/A/gs-admin.asp

D. Something to Check

1. Use the links above to find three examples of federal job openings for paralegals in agencies located in New York.
2. Go to a list of the web sites of U.S. senators (*www.senate.gov*) and U.S. representatives (*www.house.gov*) in Congress for New York. Give examples of information on these sites that might be helpful for someone looking for work as a paralegal in the federal government.

2.4 Pro Bono Opportunities for Paralegals

A. Introduction
B. Finding Pro Bono Opportunities
C. More Information
D. Something to Check

A. Introduction

In this section you will learn a great deal about working in the public sector as we explore pro bono opportunities for paralegals. Pro bono (or pro bono publico) means *for the public good*. It refers to work performed without fee or compensation for the benefit of society. Certain kinds of law offices often welcome volunteer or pro bono help. Here are some examples:

- Legal aid societies that provide free legal services to the poor
- Public interest law offices (e.g., American Civil Liberties Union) that focus on test cases that raise broad issues of social justice
- Government offices (e.g., the domestic violence unit in the office of the local district attorney)

Paralegals with full-time jobs might devote an evening a month or every other Saturday to pro bono work. Some employers give their paralegals time off during the work week to do such work. Pro bono service by paralegals is strongly encouraged by paralegal associations (see, e.g., Guideline 4 of the Model Standards and Guidelines for Utilization of Legal Assistants/Paralegals ("public service activities") of the National Association of Legal Assistants).

There is a great range of pro bono tasks that paralegals perform. For example, they might:

- Interview prospective clients to help screen applicants for the services that the office provides
- Perform factual research
- Draft pleadings, particularly in high-volume categories of cases such as divorce or petitions for restraining orders

For example, in Onondaga County, paralegals have been an integral part of pro bono activities, such as projects in housing court, will clinics, social security disability, insurance claimant representation, and simple divorce proceedings. New York State Bar Association Ad Hoc Committee on Non-Lawyer Practice, *Final Report* (May 1995) (*www.cdpa.info/files/NY_Paralegal_guidelines.pdf*)

In addition to substantive tasks, pro bono paralegals might be asked to perform administrative and clerical tasks such as photocopying documents or entering data in a computer database.

Why Paralegals Engage in Pro Bono Work

Why do paralegals engage in pro bono work? Here are some of the major reasons:

- *Personal Satisfaction.* The primary reason is the personal satisfaction derived by working for organizations or agencies engaged in socially worthy ventures. Many paralegals feel a professional responsibility to help ensure that disadvantaged individuals have greater access to our justice system. (According to a major law department, "Participation in the pro bono program gives attorneys, paralegals and support staff the opportunity to serve the diverse people of the community as well as to increase his/her ability, understanding and compassion." Pro Bono Activity of the Sears Law Department (*www.cpbo.org/ resources/displayResource.cfm?resourceID=1239*)

- *Ethical Obligation.* Associations often say that pro bono work is an ethical obligation that is either required or strongly encouraged. See for example:

  - Guideline 4 of the model standards and guidelines of the National Association of Legal Assistants (Comment) (*www.nala.org/model.aspx#guide4*)
  - Guideline 10 of the model guidelines of the American Bar Association Standing Committee on Paralegals (*www.abanet.org/legalservices/paralegals/ downloads/modelguidelines.pdf*).
  - Guideline VII of *Guidelines for the Utilization by Lawyers of the Services of Legal Assistants* (see full text in section 3.3) states that "a lawyer should promote the professional development of the legal assistant." The commentary to this guideline states that legal assistants should be provided with the chance to participate in pro bono work.

- *New Experiences.* Through pro bono work, paralegals often gain practical experience in areas of the law outside their primary expertise.

- *Networking.* Even if pro bono work in some offices is more administrative or clerical than legal, paralegals can obtain valuable insights and networking contacts by interacting with the staff (including other volunteers) at these offices.

- *Résumé Building.* Unemployed paralegals, particularly those just out of school, have an added incentive to do pro bono work. Anything you can say on your résumé about real-world law office experience might help distinguish your résumé from that of someone without such experience.

- *Possible Job Leads.* All or most of the offices that accept volunteers have regular salaried employees. It is not uncommon for a paralegal to be hired by a law office where he or she once did work as a pro bono volunteer.

Ethical Concerns

Before outlining some of the major ways to explore pro bono opportunities, two ethical cautions should be covered: confidentiality and conflict of interest.

- *Confidentiality.* Everything you learn about a client when working pro bono should be kept confidential. The fact that some of these clients do not pay for their services is irrelevant. A poor person seeking a divorce in a legal aid office has the same right of confidentiality as a *Fortune* 500 company involved in complex litigation.

- *Conflict of Interest.* As you know from courses that cover ethics (and as will be examined later in sections 3.1, 3.2, and 3.3), you need to be aware of the danger that prior client work by an attorney or paralegal could create a conflict of interest for another client in another office. One of the ways this can occur is when the prior work was on behalf of a client who now has an *adverse interest* with a current client in a different office.

Example: Jim works on behalf of a client named Smith in the case of *Smith vs. Jones* while Jim is volunteering at the ABC law office. Later, Jim applies for work at the XYZ law office. One of the clients of this firm is Jones, who is now suing Smith in a case that is different from (yet related to) the case Smith had at the ABC office.

If XYZ hires Jim, there may be a conflict of interest because of Jim's prior work on behalf of Smith. Hiring Jim might eventually disqualify XYZ from continuing to represent Jones, particularly if Jim gives an XYZ attorney confidential information about Smith that Jim learned while at the ABC office. If this occurs, the prior work of the paralegal at the ABC office has "contaminated" the XYZ office.

It is unlikely that pro bono work will create such conflicts of interest, but the cautious paralegal needs to be alert to the possibility. Keep a *personal journal* in which you note the names of all the parties involved in cases on which you work in *any* law office. The journal should be private because it contains confidential information. (Client names, for example, are confidential.) Yet when applying for a job, one of the ways an office can determine whether you pose conflict-of-interest risks is to find out what cases you have worked on in the past. It is ethically permissible for you to reveal this information when you are in serious discussions about a new position.

B. Finding Pro Bono Opportunities

1. Your Office

Find out if the law office, corporation, or association where you work already has a pro bono program. Does it encourage its employees to perform pro bono work? Does it give time off for such work? Your supervisor (or someone else in the office) is probably already engaged in pro bono cases on which you might be allowed to contribute. Paralegals often do pro bono work in the same offices where attorneys do such work.

2. Networking

From your network of contacts in the area, find out from other paralegals if they have done any pro bono work, and, if not, whether they know of others who have. Make similar inquiries of attorneys you have met professionally and socially.

3. Pro Bono Opportunities Guide, Paralegals

Go to the Pro Bono Opportunities Guide of the New York State Bar Association (*www.probono.net/ny/ NYSBA_oppsguide.cfm*). In the "Projects For" box, click "Paralegals" to find offices in the state that welcome pro bono help by paralegals.

4. Paralegal Associations

Check with the local paralegal associations near you (see the addresses of all state associations in section 1.2). Follow these steps:

(a) Find out if the association's web site lists pro bono opportunities or a pro bono coordinator for the association.
(b) Check the titles of board members and officers of the association to see if anyone on the list covers pro bono matters.
(c) If the newsletter of the association is online, find out if there are any leads in it on offices that use pro bono help.
(d) E-mail the president of the association or the association's general-information e-mail address to inquire about leads to pro bono work.
(e) If there is a search box on the site, type in "pro bono."
(f) Click the e-mail address of any paralegal on the site, introduce yourself, state that you are trying to learn about pro bono opportunities in the area, and ask if this person has any leads. Often all you need to get started is the name of one paralegal doing pro bono work. Such a person will tell you where he or she does such work and who would know if additional volunteers are needed.

5. CASA: Court Appointed Special Advocate

Advocates for Children of New York State
877-80-VOICE
www.casanys.org
Find a Local Program
www.casanys.org/programs.php

CASA means Court Appointed Special Advocate. When a court must intervene to help a child in abuse

and neglect cases, CASA volunteers (who do not have to be attorneys) are there to tell the child's story and to help protect the child's future. "A volunteer's role in abuse and neglect proceedings is to present the court with a neutral perspective regarding what is in the best interests of the child." Volunteers do not work under attorney supervision but are given training to serve as an informed, independent, and objective voice in court for abused and neglected children. Volunteers work as fact finders, interviewers, and investigators. They gather pertinent information relative to the child's case and report on these findings to the court. Their goal is to gather as much information as possible to help the court make the best decision regarding the child's future. They also help monitor the case to ensure that the child's needs are being met.

6. Attorney Pro Bono as a Lead to Paralegal Pro Bono

Very often, a law office that accepts pro bono volunteer work by attorneys also accepts (or would be willing to consider) pro bono volunteer work by paralegals. (New York attorneys are urged to provide a designated number of hours of pro bono legal services annually.) Hence you need to know what offices in New York welcome pro bono work by attorneys. Here are steps to take to find out where attorneys do pro bono work:

(a) Go to the Pro Bono Opportunities Guide of the New York State Bar Association (*www.probono.net/ny/ NYSBA_oppsguide.cfm*). Enter the county and other relevant information. You will receive a list of local pro bono organizations with contact information.
(b) If you work for a corporation, find out if the corporation has adopted the attorney and paralegal pro bono policy recommended by the Corporate Counsel Section of the New York State Bar Association. The policy states:

"Each new attorney and paralegal will be given a copy of this Policy and will be asked to complete a survey to indicate areas of interest in pro bono work. The Chairman of the Pro Bono Committee and the Pro Bono Coordinator will meet with each new attorney and paralegal to emphasize the Department's commitment to pro bono work, to explain the process, to describe available opportunities and to determine a specific timetable for getting involved in a pro bono matter."
(*www.nysba.org/Content/NavigationMenu5/Corporate ProBonoModel/default.htm*)

(c) *Probono.net*
www.probono.net/ny
"This site contains helpful resources for pro bono and legal services attorneys, law professionals, and law students to assist in your representation of low income or disadvantaged clients."

(d) Go to the web site of the local bar associations in your area (see the addresses in section 3.4). Look for committees, sections, or special programs on pro bono. Type "pro bono" in the association's search box. Send an e-mail to the information office at the association in which you say, "I'm looking for leads to law offices that accept pro bono work by paralegals and would appreciate any help you can provide."

(e) *LawHelp*
www.lawhelp.org/ny
This comprehensive site lists numerous programs in the state that provide legal services to low income persons. Almost all of these programs accept pro bono assistance.

(f) *Consumer's Guide to Legal Help, Pro Bono*
www.abanet.org/legalservices/findlegalhelp/pb.cfm?id=NY

(g) *ABA Directory of Local Pro Bono Programs*
www.abanet.org/legalservices/probono
Click "Directory of Local Pro Bono Programs." Then click New York on the map. These steps lead you to a site that lists pro bono programs throughout the state (*www. abanet.org/legalservices/probono/ directory/newyork.html*)

(h) *ABA National Domestic Violence Pro Bono Directory*
www.probono.net/dv

(i) In Google, run a search that contains the name of your city or county, the phrase "pro bono," and the word ~attorney. The tilde (~) before the word *attorney* means you want to include synonyms of attorney such as lawyer and counsel. Here are examples of such queries:

"Albany" "pro bono" ~attorney
"Kings County" "pro bono" ~attorney

(j) Do the following search in Google or any search engine:

"volunteer lawyers" "New York"

(k) Go to the web sites of the specialty bar associations that interest you (see section 3.4 for web sites). Find out if the sites provide information or links to pro bono needs. If not, try to e-mail someone at the association to ask about leads.

(l) *Legal Services Corporation*
Check the links on the site for the Legal Services Corporation (LSC), the federal government agency that funds legal service programs.

Legal Services Corporation
www.lsc.gov
(Click New York on the map or type "New York" in the search box. You will be led to a list of all of the legal service programs in the state, many of which welcome pro bono assistance.)

(m) *Volunteer Match*
www.volunteermatch.org
(Type in your zip code and "law" as a keyword. You will be led to organizations seeking people who can provide direct or indirect legal help.)

(n) *Second Circuit*
www.ca2.uscourts.gov/ProBono.htm

7. Specific Categories of Law Offices That May Need Pro Bono Help

The steps listed above for paralegal and attorney pro bono work will lead you to most of the offices in the state that serve indigent (poor) clients as well as clients in specialty groups. Here are some additional routes to such offices. At the following sites, look for contact links and e-mail addresses where you can inquire about pro bono opportunities for paralegals in your area. If a site does not cover your area of the state, the site will probably be able to tell you (via e-mail) where you might find something closer to you.

American Civil Liberties Union
www.nyclu.org
www.aclu.org/affiliates/newyork.html

Empire Justice Center
www.empirejustice.org

Frank H. Hiscock Legal Aid Society (Syracuse)
www.hiscocklegalaid.org
www.hiscocklegalaid.org/membership.html

HIV/AIDS Information Outreach Project
Links to NYC Legal Services
www.aidsnyc.org/servicesnyc/legal.html

Lambda Legal Defense and Education Fund
www.lambdalegal.org

Legal Aid/Legal Services Offices
The Legal Aid Society of New York City
www.legal-aid.org
(click "NYC Pro Bono Center")

The Legal Aid Society of Mid-New York (Binghamton, Syracuse)
www.lasmny.org
(click "Pro Bono Opportunities")

Legal Aid Society of Northeastern New York (Albany)
www.lasnny.org
(click "Pro Bono Opportunities")

Legal Aid Society of Rochester
www.lasroc.org

Legal Assistance of Western New York
www.lawny.org

Legal Service for New York City
www.lsny.org
(click "Pro Bono")

Legal Services of the Hudson Valley
www.lshv.org

Nassau/Suffolk Law Services Committee Inc.
www.nslawservices.org

National Health Law Program
www.healthlaw.org

Northwestern Legal Services (Buffalo)
www.nls.org
www.eriebar.com/lpsa_legal_aid.htm

Other Legal Aid Locations
www.lawhelp.org/NY

C. More Information

NY Law Journal Pro Bono Information
www.law.com/jsp/nylj/probono.jsp

New York Lawyer Pro Bono Information
nylj.com/nylawyer/probono

ABA Pro Bono Sites by State
www.abanet.org/legalservices/probono/directory.html#

Miscellaneous Pro Bono Links
www.ptla.org/ptlasite/probono.htm

National Association of Pro Bono Professionals
www.abanet.org/legalservices/probono/napbpro/home.html

Pro Bono Institute
www.probonoinst.org

Lawyer Referral Services
www.abanet.org/legalservices/lris
www.legal-aid.com/lawyer_referral_services.html

D. Something to Check

1. Find any three offices in New York that accept pro bono help for adopted children seeking information and possible contact with birth parents.
2. Pick any other area of the law. Find three offices in New York that accept pro bono help for that area of the law.

2.5 Becoming a Notary Public
   A. Introduction
   B. Laws Governing Notaries
   C. More Information
   D. Something to Check

A. Introduction

Very often, law offices work with documents that must be notarized. This is particularly true in offices that do transactional work. (Transactional paralegals provide paralegal services for attorneys who represent clients in transactions such as entering contracts, incorporating a business, closing a real estate sale, or planning an estate.) A notary is a public officer commissioned or licensed by the New York State Secretary of State to witness the signing of important documents in order to render them admissible as evidence of the facts that are contained in those documents. (NY Executive Law § 135; see powers below in part B.)

Paralegals should consider becoming notaries whether or not specifically requested to do so by their employer. Being a notary can be valuable even if this credential is used only occasionally as a backup when others are not readily available inside or outside the office to notarize documents.

Caution, however, is needed when performing notary services. Attorney supervisors have been known to pressure their employees to notarize documents improperly, such as by asking them to notarize a signature that the employee did not personally observe being placed on the document involved. False notarization can result in the paralegal being joined as a defendant in a lawsuit.

Qualifications

The county clerk for each county administers the licensing of notaries for the New York State Secretary of State. Notaries are commissioned in their county of residence. For a nonattorney to receive a notary public commission, you must:

1. Complete a notary application (which includes the oath of office; see Exhibit 2.5A)
2. Be at least 18 years old
3. Be a U.S. citizen
4. Be a citizen of New York and have a place of business or an office in New York or be a former citizen and have a place of business or an office in New York
5. Submit a Certificate of Official Character, which includes a statement that the applicant has not been convicted in any place of a felony or of certain other offenses listed in NY Executive Law § 130
6. Take the notary examination (fee: $15) and provide a "pass slip" (proof of passing the examination)
7. Pay a $60 fee

A New York attorney can become a notary without taking the examination. When a notary license is issued, it is valid for four years.

EXHIBIT 2.5A Oath of Office of a Notary Public

"I do solemnly swear that I will support the Constitution of the United States and the Constitution of the State of New York, and that I will faithfully discharge the duties of the office of Notary Public to the best of my ability." N.Y. Const. Art. XIII, § 1

Steps

1. Obtain an application packet and information about test dates and locations from the County Clerk's Office or the Department of State office. Also ask for a study booklet.
2. Take the test. (It is a walk-in test; you can register for the exam at the test center on the day of the exam.)
3. Mail the application, $60, and the "pass slip" to the New York State Licensing Commission (see address below).
4. After receiving and approving an applicant for a notary public commission, the Secretary of State forwards the commission, the oath of office, and the signature of the notary public to the appropriate county clerk. The county clerk maintains a record of the commission and signature.

Study Booklet for the Notary Test
www.dos.state.ny.us/lcns/lawbooks/notary.html

Addresses

New York State Department of State
Division of Licensing Services
84 Holland Avenue, Basement
Albany, NY 12208
518-474-4429
www.dos.state.ny.us/lcns/licensing.html

Department of State Local Numbers
Albany: 518-474-4429
Binghamton: 607-721-8757
Buffalo: 716-847-7110
Hauppauge: 631-952-6579
New York City: 212-417-5747
Syracuse: 315-428-4258
Utica: 315-793-2533

New York State Licensing Commission
41 State Street
Albany, NY 12231
518-474-4429

New York State County Clerks
www.realmarketing.com/county_recorders/new_york_county_ recorders.htm

B. Laws Governing Notaries

Powers

A notary public is authorized and empowered within and throughout the state:

- To administer oaths and affirmations
- To take affidavits and depositions
- To receive and certify acknowledgments or proof of deeds, mortgages, and powers of attorney and other instruments in writing

- To demand acceptance or payment of foreign and inland bills of exchange, promissory notes, and obligations in writing, and to protest the same for non-acceptance or non-payment. (NY Executive Law § 135)

Prohibitions

1. Notaries may not give advice on the law. The notary may not draw any kind of legal papers, such as wills, deeds, bills of sale, mortgages, chattel mortgages, contracts, leases, offers, options, incorporation papers, releases, mechanics liens, power of attorney, complaints and all legal pleadings, papers in summary proceedings to evict a tenant, or in bankruptcy, affidavits, or any papers which our courts have said are legal documents or papers.
2. A notary public is cautioned not to execute an acknowledgment of the execution of a will. Such acknowledgment cannot be deemed equivalent to an attestation clause accompanying a will.
3. Notaries may not ask for and get legal business to send to a lawyer or lawyers with whom the notary has any business connection or from whom the notary receives any money or other consideration for sending the business.
4. Notaries may not divide or agree to divide notary fees with a lawyer, or accept any part of a lawyer's fee on any legal business.
5. Notaries may not advertise in, or circulate in any manner, any paper or advertisement, or say to anyone that he or she has any powers or rights not given to the notary by the laws under which the notary was appointed.

Fees

A notary public shall be entitled to the following fees:

- For administering an oath or affirmation, and certifying the same when required, except where another fee is specifically prescribed by statute, $2.
- For taking and certifying the acknowledgment or proof of execution of a written instrument, by one person, $2, and by each additional person, $2, for swearing such witness thereto, $2. (NY Executive Law § 136)

C. More Information

Important Information about Becoming a New York Notary
www.dos.state.ny.us/lcns/professions/notary/notary1.htm
www.notarytrainer.com/NotaryFAQNY.html

Notary Public License Law
www.dos.state.ny.us/lcns/lawbooks/notary.html

Search for New York Notaries Public
appsext8.dos.state.ny.us/lcns_public/chk_load

National Notary Organizations and Resources
www.americannotaryexchange.com
www.nationalnotary.org
www.nanotary.com
www.enotary.org

D. Something to Check

1. Go to the New York Executive Law § 135 (*www.dos. state.ny.us/lcns/lawbooks/notary.html*). What authorization is given to attorneys in this section?
2. On Google (*www.google.com*) or any other general search engine, run the following search: "New York notary public." Summarize the categories of information found with this search.

2.6 An Employee or an Independent Contractor?
A. Introduction
B. Standards under New York Law
C. Standards under Federal Law
D. More Information
E. Something to Check

A. Introduction

Most paralegals are employees of law firms, corporations, or other groups where they work in full-time or part-time positions. There are, however, a fair number of paralegals who have left the security of a regular paycheck in order to open their own business. They have become independent contractors (sometimes called freelance paralegals or independent paralegals) who offer services to more than one law office, usually charging the office an hourly rate or a per-project flat fee. We are not referring to individuals who offer their services directly to the public without attorney supervision. Our focus is the independent who works under the supervision of an attorney. Yet this person is not on the traditional payroll of a single law office.

Paralegals as independent contractors provide a variety of services to law firms. For example, they might:

- Digest the transcript of depositions or other litigation documents
- Encode or enter documents into a computer database
- Collect and help interpret medical records
- Prepare a 706 federal estate tax return
- Prepare all the documents needed to probate an estate
- Prepare trial exhibits
- Conduct an asset search
- Compile a chain-of-title report on real property

Such work is performed in the paralegal's office (often in his or her home) or at the law firms that have retained the paralegal.

The problem is that New York and the federal government (particularly the Internal Revenue Service) may conclude that these independent paralegals are not independent enough. They might be considered *employees* regardless of their title or where they do their work.

For its *employees*, a law office is required to withhold federal income taxes, withhold and pay Social Security and Medicare taxes, pay unemployment tax on wages, pay overtime compensation, provide workers' compensation coverage, etc. In general, however, none of this is required for *independent contractors* the office hires. In light of this disparity of treatment, offices are occasionally charged with improperly classifying workers as independent contractors in order to avoid their tax withholding and other employee-related obligations.

This raises the basic question: What is an employee? The answer to this question is not always clear.

- The sole test is *not* whether you are on the payroll.
- The sole test is *not* your title.
- The sole test is *not* whether you work full-time or part-time.
- The sole test is *not* whether the law office considers you an independent contractor nor whether you consider yourself to be one.
- The sole test is *not* whether you have signed an agreement with the law office specifying that you are an independent contractor rather than an employee.

It is quite possible for everyone to consider a worker to be an independent contractor—*except the government!* The New York state government and/or the federal government may take the position that the "independent contractor" is in fact an employee in disguise. When such a conclusion is reached, back employment taxes must be paid and penalties are possible. The law office may not be trying to avoid its tax and other responsibilities. It may simply have been mistaken in its definition of an employee. This is not uncommon. Many businesses have been told that workers being paid as independent contractors should have been classified as employees.

Sometimes the issue arises through tort law. For example:

> The ABC law firm hires Mary as an "independent contractor." One of Mary's tasks for the firm is to file pleadings in court. While driving to court one day in her own car, Mary has an accident. The other driver now wants to sue Mary *and* the ABC law firm as her employer.

Whether the driver can also recover against ABC depends, in part, on whether Mary is an employee of ABC.

The key to determining whether someone is an independent contractor is the amount of control that exists over what he or she does and how he or she does it.

EXHIBIT 2.6A	**Independent Contractor or Employee?**

General Guidelines for Determining Who Is an Independent Contractor and Who Is an Employee

- An individual is an independent contractor if the person for whom the services are performed:
  - Has the right to control or direct only the result of the work
  - Does not have the right to control or direct the means and methods of accomplishing the result
- Anyone who performs services for an office is an employee if the office can control what will be done *and* how it will be done through instructions, training, or other means. This is so even when the office gives the worker freedom of action. What matters is that the office has the *right* to control the details of how the services are performed.

Related factors are also considered, but control is key. Exhibit 2.6A summarizes the test.

No two independent paralegals operate exactly alike. Different paralegals have different relationships with their attorney clients. Some are given much more independence than others. Hence there is no one answer to the question of whether a particular independent paralegal is an employee or an independent contractor. Each case must be examined separately.

There is both New York and federal law on when a worker is an employee as opposed to an independent contractor. New York applies its own law on state issues such as whether a worker must be covered by unemployment insurance or workers' compensation and whether the boss is liable for a tort committed by someone the boss has hired. The federal government applies its law when the issue is whether federal income and Social Security taxes must be withheld. Yet there is substantial similarity between New York and federal law on the question. The right of control is central under both laws.

B. Standards under New York Law

According to the New York State Department of Labor (which administers the unemployment insurance program), the existence of an employer-employee relationship depends on the degree of supervision, direction, and control the office has over the services of the worker. In general, independent contractors are free from supervision, direction, and control in the performance of their duties. They are in business for themselves, offering their services to the general public.

No single factor or group of factors conclusively define an employer-employee relationship. Rather, all factors must be examined to determine the degree of supervision, direction, and control. An office is an employer if it controls what will be done and how it will be done, i.e., the manner, means, and results. See Exhibit 2.6B for the factors considered.

EXHIBIT 2.6B	**Factors That Indicate Control under New York Law**

Factors That May Be Indicators of Employee Status:

- Determining when, where, and how services will be performed
- Providing facilities, equipment, tools, and supplies
- Directly supervising the services
- Stipulating the hours of work
- Requiring exclusive services
- Setting the rate of pay
- Requiring attendance at meetings and/or training sessions
- Requiring oral or written reports
- Reserving the right to review and approve the work product
- Evaluating job performance
- Requiring prior permission for absences
- Reserving the right to terminate the services

Factors That May Be Indicators of Independent Contractor Status:

- Having an established business
- Advertising in the electronic and/or print media
- Maintaining a listing in the commercial pages of the telephone directory
- Using business cards, business stationery, and billheads
- Carrying insurance
- Maintaining a place of business and making a significant investment in facilities, equipment, and supplies
- Paying one's own expenses
- Assuming risk for profit or loss in providing services
- Determining one's own schedule
- Setting or negotiating own pay rate
- Providing services concurrently for other businesses, competitive or non-competitive
- Being free to refuse work offers
- Being free to hire help

Factors That Do Not Necessarily Prove a Worker Is an Independent Contractor:

- The office gives the worker a 1099 form rather than a W-2 form
- The office asks the worker to sign a statement claiming independent contractor status
- The office asks the worker to waive any rights as an employee
- The office requires the worker to obtain a DBA (doing business as) filing

Source: New York State Department of Labor, The Employer-Employee Relationship (*www.labor.state.ny.us/ui/dande/ic.shtm*).

How an individual is compensated is another indicator of status. Employees typically are paid a salary or an hourly rate of pay, or they draw against future commissions with no requirement for repayment of unearned commissions. Employees may also receive certain fringe benefits, including an allowance or reimbursement for business or travel expenses.

The nature of the services performed can be significant. Unskilled or casual labor is usually employment because such services are typically subject to supervision. However, even professionals such as doctors and lawyers who have considerable freedom in the performance of their duties can be determined to be employees if they are subject to significant control.

An employer-employee relationship may exist if the employer controls important aspects of the services performed other than results and means. For example, a referral agency usually does not directly supervise the individuals it refers for assignments but it could be their employer if it controls such important aspects of the services as client contact, the individual's wages and billing, and collection from clients. (*www.labor.state.ny. us/ui/dande/ic.shtm*) (2A NY Jur 2d, Agency and Independent Contractors § 379)

C. Standards under Federal Law

Federal law reaches substantially the same conclusion, but uses different terminology in describing the factors involved. Under federal law, three categories of evidence on control and independence are considered: (1) behavioral control, (2) financial control, and (3) type of relationship. Evidence in these categories present factors to be weighed; they are not absolute guidelines or definitions.

(1) Behavioral Control

Does the office have the right to direct and control *how* the worker does the task for which he or she is hired? Two behavioral facts that help answer this question are the type and degree of instructions received and the training provided.

- *Instructions the office gives the worker.* In general, employees are subject to instructions about when, where, and how to work. Here are examples of the kinds of instructions an office could give on how work should be done:

  - When and where to do the work
  - What tools or equipment to use
  - What other workers to use to assist with the work
  - Where to purchase supplies and services
  - What work must be performed by a specified individual
  - What order or sequence to follow

- *The amount of instruction needed varies among different jobs.* Even if no instructions are given, sufficient behavioral control may exist if the office has the right to control how the work results are achieved. An office may lack the knowledge to instruct some highly specialized professionals; in other cases, the task may require little or no instruction. The key consideration is whether the office has retained the right to control the details of a worker's performance or has given up this right.
- *Training the office gives the worker.* An employee may be given training on performing the services in a particular manner. Independent contractors, on the other hand, ordinarily use their own methods.

(2) Financial Control

Factors that show whether the office has a right to control the business aspects of the worker's job include:

- *The extent to which the worker has unreimbursed business expenses.* Independent contractors are more likely to have unreimbursed expenses than are employees. Fixed ongoing costs that are incurred regardless of whether work is currently being performed are especially important. Note, however, that it is possible for employees to incur unreimbursed expenses in connection with the services they perform for their office.
- *The extent of the worker's investment.* An independent contractor (unlike an employee) often has a significant investment in the facilities he or she uses in performing services for someone else. This is not to say, however, that a significant investment is required for independent contractor status.
- *The extent to which the worker makes services available to the relevant market.* An independent contractor is generally free to seek out business opportunities. Independent contractors often advertise, maintain a visible business location, and are available to work in the relevant market.
- *How the office pays the worker.* Assume that a worker is guaranteed a regular wage amount for an hourly, weekly, or other period of time. This usually indicates that he or she is an employee, even when the wage or salary is supplemented by a commission. An independent contractor is usually paid a flat fee for the job. In some professions, however, such as law, independent contractors are often paid hourly.
- *The extent to which the worker can realize a profit or loss.* An independent contractor can make a profit or suffer a loss.

(3) Type of Relationship

Facts that show the parties' type of relationship include:

- *Written contracts describing the relationship the parties intended to create.* Employees often do not have such contracts.

- *Whether the office provides the worker with employee-type benefits, such as insurance, a pension plan, vacation pay, or sick pay.* Independent contractors are seldom given such benefits.
- *The permanency of the relationship.* If the office engages a worker with the expectation that the relationship will continue indefinitely, rather than for a specific project or period, this is generally considered evidence that the intent of the office was to create an employer-employee relationship.
- *The extent to which services performed by the worker are a key aspect of the regular business of the office.* If a worker provides services that are a key aspect of the office's regular business activity, it is more likely that it will have the right to direct and control his or her activities and, therefore, this factor indicates an employer-employee relationship.

Conclusion

When the status of a paralegal is challenged, the various factors under New York or federal law will be weighed one by one. The evidence may conflict. Some aspects of what a paralegal does may clearly indicate an independent contractor status, while others may point to an employee-employer relationship. A court will examine the factors to determine where, on balance, a particular worker fits.

D. More Information

Independent Contractor vs. Employee: NY Unemployment Insurance
www.labor.state.ny.us/ui/PDFs/ia31814.pdf
www.labor.state.ny.us/ui/dande/ic.shtm

More New York Sites on the Distinction
www.osc.state.ny.us/agencies/gbull/g_233.htm
www.brockport.edu/hr/procedures/cntremp.html
www.ilr.cornell.edu/news/061807_misclassificationStudy.html

IRS Guidance
www.irs.gov/pub/irs-pdf/p15a.pdf
www.irs.gov/businesses/small/article/0,,id=115041,00.html
www.irs.gov/businesses/small/article/0,,id=115045,00.html
www.irs.gov/businesses/small/article/0,,id=99921,00.html

IRS Telephone Help for Employment Questions
800-829-4933

Other Useful Sites
www.alllaw.com/articles/employment/article5.asp
sbinformation.about.com/cs/laborlaws/a/contractor_2.htm
www.mbda.gov/?section_id=2&bucket_id=128&content_id =2325&well=well_2

E. Something to Check

1. Using any general search engine (e.g., *www.google. com*) or legal search engine (e.g., *www.findlaw.com*), find and summarize a court opinion from any court in which the issue was whether a worker was an employee or independent contractor.

2. Interview an independent or freelance paralegal who has his or her own office in New York. Find out how they typically provide their services to law firms. Then apply the state and federal factors to identify evidence of both independent contractor and employee status.

2.7 Overtime Pay under Federal and State Law

A. Introduction
B. The Three Exemptions
C. Filing a Complaint
D. More Information
E. Something to Check

A. Introduction

Overtime rules are contained in both state and federal law. NY Labor Law § 220 states that a workday is eight hours per day, that there are five days in a workweek, and that any work performed in excess of that is overtime. The federal Fair Labor Standards Act (FLSA) specifies categories of employees that are excluded (exempt) from overtime provisions. Generally state exemptions from the overtime pay requirement are the same as federal overtime exemptions outlined in the FLSA. If there is a conflict between federal and state overtime law, the law providing greater benefits to the employee applies.

Eligibility for overtime depends on job duties, not on job titles. Regardless of what an employee is called, his or her right to overtime compensation will depend on a close analysis of the nature of the actual work performed by individual employees. Furthermore, if an employee is eligible for overtime, he or she cannot be asked to waive this entitlement as a condition of obtaining or maintaining employment.

Some paralegals prefer *not* to receive overtime compensation even if they are entitled to it. They would rather have their extra work hours rewarded by bonuses and other perks, similar to the way attorneys are rewarded. Yet even these paralegals should know the law in the event that they may one day need to use it, particularly when leaving a position.

In general, as you will see in the following discussion, many paralegal *supervisors* are not eligible for overtime compensation; they are exempt. Most paralegals who do not have managerial or supervisory responsibility, however, are entitled to overtime compensation; they are not exempt. Our discussion assumes that a paralegal at a particular job site is *not* covered by a union contract, which can provide greater wage benefits than either federal or state law.

B. The Three Exemptions

Workers earning over $455 a week ($23,660 a year) on a salary basis are entitled to overtime compensation unless they are exempt. (No exemptions exist for workers earning less than this amount.) There are three main categories of exempt employees: executive, professional, or administrative. They are referred to as the *white collar exemptions.*

Do paralegals fit within any of the three exemptions? The answer depends on their primary duties, meaning the main or most important tasks they perform. It does not depend on their title, which can vary from employer to employer. Furthermore, because paralegals perform a wide variety of tasks in many different settings, the question of whether they are exempt must be determined on a person-by-person basis, one paralegal at a time. It is possible for a paralegal in an office to be exempt while another paralegal in the same office is nonexempt.

Here is an overview of the three exemptions and how they might apply to paralegals:

Executive Exemption. The employee (1) manages an enterprise such as a department or subdivision that has a permanent status or function in the office; (2) customarily and regularly directs the work of two or more employees; and (3) either has the authority to hire, promote, or fire other employees or can recommend such action and the recommendation is given particular weight.

Many paralegal supervisors meet all three tests of the executive exemption. They often manage the paralegal unit of the firm, supervise more than two employees, and have great influence on who is hired, promoted, or fired in their department. This is not so, however, for nonsupervisory paralegals. Hence the latter are not exempt under the executive exemption, but many paralegal supervisors are.

Professional Exemption. The employee performs work that requires advanced knowledge that is customarily acquired by a prolonged course of specialized intellectual instruction. (Advanced knowledge means work that is predominantly intellectual in character and includes work requiring the consistent exercise of discretion and judgment.) There are two categories of exempt professional employees: learned professionals (whose specialized academic training is a standard prerequisite for entrance into the profession) and creative professionals (who work mainly in the creative arts).

Paralegals do not fit within the professional exemption. They are not "creative professionals" because law is not in the same category as music, theater, or one of the other creative arts. Nor are they "learned professionals" because prolonged specialized instruction is not a standard prerequisite to entering the field. A bachelor's degree, for example, is not a prerequisite to becoming a paralegal.

According to the regulations of the U.S. Department of Labor in the Code of Federal Regulations, "Paralegals and legal assistants generally do not qualify as exempt learned professionals because an advanced specialized academic degree is not a standard prerequisite for entry into the field. Although many paralegals possess general four-year advanced degrees, most specialized paralegal programs are two-year associate's degree programs from a community college or equivalent institution. However, the learned professional exemption is available for paralegals who possess advanced specialized degrees in other professional fields and apply advanced knowledge in that field in the performance of their duties. For example, if a law firm hires an engineer as a paralegal to provide expert advice on product liability cases or to assist on patent matters, that engineer would qualify for exemption." 29 C.F.R. § 541.301(e)(7)

Administrative Exemption. The employee (1) performs office work that is directly related to the management or general business operations of the employer or of the employer's customers, and (2) exercises discretion and independent judgment with respect to matters of significance.

The question of whether the administrative exemption applies to paralegals is less clear. The first test under the administrative exemption is that the employees perform office work that is "directly related to the management or general business operations of the employer or of the employer's customers." This means "assisting with the running or servicing of the business" such as working on budgets, purchasing equipment, or administering the office's computer database. Such tasks, however, are not the primary duties of most paralegals, although they may help out in these areas. In the main, paralegals spend most of their time working on individual cases and hence do not meet the first test.

The second test (which also must be met for the administrative exemption to apply) is that the employees exercise "discretion and independent judgment with respect to matters of significance." The phrase "discretion and independent judgment" involves (a) comparing and evaluating possible courses of conduct and (b) acting or making a decision after the various possibilities have been considered. The phrase implies that the employee has authority to make an independent choice, "free from immediate direction or supervision." An employee does *not* exercise discretion and independent judgment if he or she merely uses skills in applying well-established techniques, procedures, or standards described in manuals or other sources.

Do paralegals meet the second test, of exercising "discretion and independent judgment with respect to matters of significance"? They certainly work on "matters of significance." Yet it is not clear whether they exercise "discretion and independent judgment." Paralegals are often given some leeway in the performance of their work. Yet if they operate "within closely prescribed limits," they are not exercising discretion and independent judgment. Federal officials argue that paralegals could not have the kind of independence this exemption requires in light of the ethical obligation of attorneys to supervise and approve the work of paralegals. If paralegals make independent choices on client matters, they run the risk of being charged with engaging in the unauthorized practice of law (UPL) and their attorneys could be charged with violating their ethical duty of supervision.

Summary of Overtime Law

- Most nonsupervisory paralegals are not exempt under the executive exemption (therefore, they are entitled to overtime pay).
- Many paralegal supervisors are exempt under the executive exemption.
- Most paralegals are not exempt under the professional exemption unless they have an advanced degree.
- Most paralegals are probably not exempt under the administrative exemption.

New York Law

As indicated, New York follows federal law (the FLSA) on eligibility for overtime compensation. According to the New York State Department of Labor: "Some categories of employees are excluded from New York State's overtime provisions. These state exemptions from the requirement for overtime pay are identical to the federal overtime exemptions outlined in the Fair Labor Standards Act (FLSA), listed by the U.S. Department of Labor, Wage and Hour Division." (*www.labor. state.ny.us/workerprotection/laborstandards/faq.shtm#4*)

C. Filing a Complaint

The federal and state agencies primarily responsible for enforcing wage laws are as follows:

U.S. Department of Labor
Employment Standards Administration
Wage and Hour Division
200 Constitution Avenue, NW
Washington, DC 20210
866-4-USWAGE
www.dol.gov/whd/index.htm

NYS Department of Labor
W. Averell Harriman State Office Campus
Building 12
Albany, NY 12240
518-457-9000; 800-HIRE-992
www.labor.state.ny.us/index.htm

For information about filing a complaint for the failure to receive overtime compensation, contact one of the following district offices of the Wage and Hour Division of the U.S. Department of Labor:

Albany District Office
U.S. Dept. of Labor
ESA Wage & Hour Division
O'Brien Federal Bldg.
Albany, NY 12207
518-431-4278; 866-4-USWAGE

Brooklyn Area Office
U.S. Dept. of Labor
ESA Wage & Hour Division
625 Fulton St., 7th Floor
Brooklyn, NY 11201
718-254-9410; 866-4-USWAGE

Buffalo Area Office
U.S. Dept. of Labor
ESA Wage & Hour Division
111 West Huron St.
Buffalo, NY 14202
716-842-2950; 866-4-USWAGE

Long Island District Office
U.S. Dept. of Labor
ESA Wage & Hour Division
1400 Old Country Rd.
Westbury, NY 11590-5119
516-338-1890; 866-4-USWAGE

New York City District Office
U.S. Dept. of Labor
ESA Wage & Hour Division
26 Federal Plaza, Room 3700
New York, NY 10278
212-264-8185; 866-4-USWAGE

Syracuse Area Office
U.S. Dept. of Labor
ESA Wage & Hour Division
100 South Clinton St.
Syracuse, NY 13260
315-448-0630; 866-4-USWAGE

Hudson Valley Area Office
U.S. Dept. of Labor
ESA Wage & Hour Division
140 Grand St., Suite 304
White Plains, NY 10601
914-682-6348; 866-4-USWAGE

For overtime claims, there is a two-year statute of limitations (three years for willful violations). Failure to file a federal claim within this period may mean that the claim is lost.

D. More Information

New York Paralegal Wins Overtime Claim
www.newyorkemploymentlawyerblog.com/2009/12/new_york_paralegal_wins_overti.html

Opinion of Wage and Hour Division of the U.S. Department of Labor on Paralegal Entitlement to Overtime Compensation
www.dol.gov/whd/opinion/FLSA/2005/2005_12_16_54_FLSA.htm

Federal Overtime Law: Fair Labor Standards Act (FLSA)
www.dol.gov
www.dol.gov/whd/flsa/index.htm

Fair Labor Standards Act
www.gpoaccess.gov/uscode
(type "Fair Labor Standards Act" in the search box)

NYS Department of Labor
www.labor.state.ny.us/index.htm

NYS Consolidated Laws: Labor Law (LAB)
public.leginfo.state.ny.us/menugetf.cgi?COMMONQUERY=LAWS

NYS Department of Labor FAQ
www.labor.state.ny.us/workerprotection/laborstandards/faq.shtm

E. Something to Check

1. Go to Labor Law in New York State Consolidated Laws (see site above under More Information). Quote any sentence that mentions overtime compensation.
2. Go to the FLSA in the United States Code (see site above under More Information). Quote any sentence that mentions any of the exemptions from overtime laws.

2.8 Laid-Off Paralegals and Unemployment Compensation

A. Introduction
B. Eligibility for UI Benefits
C. Applying for UI Benefits
D. Appeals
E. More Information
F. Something to Check

A. Introduction

It can happen. You're working as a paralegal and suddenly find yourself out of work with no immediate prospects for new employment. One resource to consider while continuing to look for work is unemployment insurance (UI), which provides weekly unemployment insurance payments ("partial wage replacement"). Even if you are still able to work part-time, you may be eligible for UI benefits.

UI is temporary income for eligible workers who become unemployed through no fault of their own; who are ready, willing, and able to work; and who meet the other requirements for benefits. The funding for UI payments comes from taxes paid by employers. The benefits are not funded by deductions from a worker's paycheck. (Note, however, that UI benefits are subject to federal, state, and local income taxes.)

There is another reason paralegals should know about UI in addition to the fact that they may someday need to check their own eligibility for UI benefits due to being laid off. Nonattorneys are permitted to represent claimants in most administrative hearings, including unemployment insurance hearings. In New York City, nonattorney representatives can charge their clients fees, as we will see here and in section 3.1.

B. Eligibility for UI Benefits

The Unemployment Insurance Division is part of the New York State Department of Labor:

New York State Department of Labor (NYSDOL)
Unemployment Insurance Division
W.A. Harriman Campus, Building 12
Albany, NY 12240
888-209-8124 (Claims Center)
www.labor.state.ny.us/ui/ui_index.shtm

Summary

You are eligible for UI if you:

(1) Have worked long enough and earned sufficient wages in "covered" employment during the "base period" of your claim
(2) Have lost your job through no fault of your own
(3) Are available for work
(4) Are actively seeking work

- *Covered Employment.* Unless specifically excluded by law, all employment performed by a liable employer is covered, whether part-time or full-time. Independent contractors cannot receive unemployment compensation. On the definition of an independent contractor, see section 2.6.
- *Base Period.* There are two base periods that can be used: basic and alternate. You may use the one that will provide the higher benefit rate. (a) The primary basic base period is the first four of the last five completed calendar quarters prior to the calendar quarter in which your claim is effective. (b) The alternate base period is the last four completed

calendar quarters prior to the calendar quarter in which your claim is effective.

- *Earnings Needed to Qualify.* In the basic base period or in the alternate base period:

    (a) You must have worked and been paid wages for employment in at least two calendar quarters in your base period, AND

    (b) You must have been paid at least $1,600 in wages in one of the calendar quarters in your base period, AND

    (c) The total wages paid to you in your base period must be one and one-half times your high quarter wages. The amount of high quarter earnings used to determine if you meet this requirement will not be greater than $8,910. Earnings in the other base period quarters must total at least $4,455 (one-half of $8,910)

Note, however, that wages paid to you for employment that you lost because of misconduct or a criminal act cannot be used to establish a claim or in the calculation of the benefit rate.

Weekly Benefit Rate; Maximum Amount of Benefits

The weekly benefit rate is one twenty-sixth (1/26) of the high quarter wages paid to you in your base period. (Exception: If your high quarter wages are $3,575 or less, your weekly benefit rate is one twenty-fifth (1/25) of your high quarter wages.) Wages are applied to the quarter in which they are paid.

The benefit year is the one-year period beginning with the Monday following the week you filed your claim. You may be paid up to 26 weeks during a benefit year.

Reason for Being Unemployed

You are not eligible for UI benefits if your departure from work was a "voluntary quit" or discharge for misconduct. No benefits are paid if:

- You quit a job without good cause; or
- You quit a job due to marriage; or
- You lost a job because of misconduct; and
- You have subsequently worked and earned five times your benefit rate.

Able to Work

You must be able to take a job immediately. If you are not physically or mentally capable of employment, you will not be paid benefits until you satisfy the Department of Labor that you are again available for employment, are capable of working, and are making diligent efforts to find a job.

Available for Work; Suitable Work

You must be ready and willing to take suitable work. Suitable work is work for which you are reasonably fitted by training and/or experience. This means that you have to look for work in all your recent occupations, especially if the prospect of obtaining work in your primary skill area is not good. After 13 full weeks of benefits are claimed, suitable work will also include *any* work that you are capable of performing whether or not you have any experience or training in such work, unless you obtain employment through a union hiring hall or have a definite date to return to work. You must also be willing to travel a reasonable distance to obtain employment. As a general rule, travel of one hour by private transportation or one and one half hours by public transportation is considered reasonable.

You may not be paid for weeks in which your own restrictions on hours, wages, or conditions of employment limit your chances of obtaining work. You must be available to demonstrate your availability by actively seeking employment while you are claiming benefits. You must keep a written record of all your efforts to find employment. (Looking for self-employment only does not satisfy the search-for-work requirement.)

C. Applying for UI Benefits

Ways to Apply

There are two ways to apply for benefits:

- Online. The online application is at: *ui.labor.state.ny.us/UBC/home.do?FF_LOCALE=1*
- Phone. To apply by phone, call: 888-209-8124

Information and Documents Needed When You Apply

- Your Social Security number
- Your New York State driver's license or Motor Vehicle ID card number if you have one
- Your mailing address and zip code
- A telephone number where you can be contacted for additional information
- Your alien registration card number, if you have one
- The names and addresses of all employers for whom you've worked within the last 18 months, including those in another state
- Copies of forms SF8 and SF50, if you had federal employment within the last 18 months
- Copy of separation form DD 214, if you are an exservice member claiming benefits based on your military service

D. Appeals

Requesting a Hearing

If you are denied benefits, a Notice of Determination will be mailed to you telling you why. This notice will also explain for what period of time benefits are being denied, how to requalify, and how to ask for a hearing. If you disagree with any determination of the amount of weekly benefits or with a determination denying you benefits, you have a right to a hearing before an administrative law judge (ALJ). (A hearing on your claim may also be requested by your last employer or any employer for whom you worked in your base period.) To request a hearing, notify the UI Telephone Claims Center in writing by mail within 30 days after the determination is mailed to you. When you request a hearing, send your hearing request to:

NYS Department of Labor
P.O. Box 15131
Albany, NY 12212-5131

Hearing before an Administrative Law Judge (ALJ)

The Administrative Law Judge Section will notify you of the time and place of the hearing on your claim. The ALJ makes a decision after reviewing the evidence introduced at the hearing.

You have the right to inspect the file on your case prior to the hearing at the hearing site. At the hearing, you may testify and present witnesses and documents. If you cannot obtain necessary witnesses or documents, you may ask the ALJ to have them brought in under subpoena. You may question opposing parties and witnesses, and you also may request an adjournment for a good reason.

Attorney and Nonattorney Representatives at the Hearing

New York City Residents
New York City residents have the right to be represented at a hearing by an attorney or other person. Some nonattorneys have been registered by the Unemployment Insurance Appeal Board (UIAB) as claimant representatives. Only an attorney or a registered representative may charge a fee for services. The fee must be approved by the Unemployment Insurance Appeal Board before the attorney or registered representative can be paid. A listing of attorneys and registered representatives who are available to represent claimants can be found by calling 212-352-6982 or may be obtained by writing to the Unemployment Insurance Appeal Board, P.O. Box 15126, Albany, NY 12212-5126, or the Administrative Law Judge Section at P.O. Box 697, New York, NY 10014-0697.

Persons Living outside New York City
New Yorkers living outside New York City have the right to be represented at a hearing by an attorney or other person. Only attorneys, however, may charge a fee for that service. The fee must be approved by the UIAB. *A nonattorney may not charge a fee for representing a UI claimant outside New York City.*

Unemployment Insurance Appeal Board (UIAB)

Twenty days after the ALJ's decision is mailed, there can be an appeal to the Unemployment Insurance Appeal Board (UIAB). A claimant, the employer, and the Commissioner of Labor have the right to appeal. If, however, you or the employer appeal, the party making the appeal must have been present or represented at the hearing. Only the Commissioner of Labor may appeal without being represented at the hearing. If you did not appear, you can apply to reopen the ALJ's decision, giving the reasons why you did not appear.

After your appeal has been filed, you will receive a notice of receipt of appeal. It will explain your rights and the time limits for you to inspect the file, to submit a written statement, and to reply to statements submitted by other parties.

Appellate Division of the State Supreme Court, Third Department

Within 30 days after the decision of the UIAB is mailed, if you are dissatisfied with the decision, you can appeal to the Appellate Division of the State Supreme Court, Third Department. To appeal, you must notify the UIAB in writing within this 30-day period. The decision of the Appellate Division may be appealed to the Court of Appeals.

E. More Information

UI Overview
www.labor.state.ny.us/ui/ui_index.shtm
www.labor.state.ny.us/ui/faq.shtm

Filing a UI Claim
ui.labor.state.ny.us/UBC/home.do

UI Hearings and Appeals
www.labor.state.ny.us/ui/aso/hearingsandappeals.shtm
www.labor.state.ny.us/ui/claimantinfo/HearingProcess.shtm

Statutes on UI
www.labor.state.ny.us/ui/dande/article18.shtm
public.leginfo.state.ny.us/menugetf.cgi?COMMONQUERY=
* LAWS*
(click "LAB" then "Article 18")

Regulations on UI
www.labor.state.ny.us/ui/dande/regintro.shtm

Agency Decisions and Court Opinions Interpreting UI Law
www.labor.state.ny.us/ui/aso/interpservice.shtm

Glossary of UI Terms
www.labor.state.ny.us/ui/bpta/Glossary.shtm

U.S Department of Labor: "About Unemployment Insurance"
workforcesecurity.doleta.gov/unemploy/aboutui.asp

Taxation of Unemployment Compensation Benefits
www.irs.gov/taxtopics/tc418.html

A. Introduction

There are two main reasons New York paralegals should know about workers' compensation law: (1) understanding your rights when injured on the job and (2) being aware of one of the major state agencies in which paralegals are allowed to represent clients at administrative hearings.

What happens if you are injured on your paralegal job? Although paralegal work certainly does not qualify as inherently dangerous work, accidents can occur.

Examples

- You have an accident while driving to a court clerk's office to file a pleading
- You slip in the hallway on the way back from your supervisor's office
- You develop carpel tunnel syndrome as a result of repetitive computer work

The primary system covering such mishaps is workers' compensation insurance. This mandatory program provides weekly cash payments and coverage for medical treatment, including rehabilitation, for employees who become disabled as a result of a disease or injury connected with their employment. It also provides payments for qualified dependents of a worker who dies from a compensable injury or illness. With few exceptions, all employers must provide workers' compensation coverage for their employees. Employers purchase workers' compensation insurance or are self-insured if they can demonstrate that they can pay benefits out of their own resources.

Workers' compensation is a no-fault system. In a workers' compensation case, no one party is determined to be at fault. The amount that a claimant receives is not decreased by his or her carelessness, nor increased by an employer's fault. However, a worker loses the right to workers' compensation if the injury results solely from his or her intoxication from drugs or alcohol, or from the intent to injure him or herself or someone else.

A claim is paid if the employer or insurance carrier agrees that the injury or illness is work-related. If the employer or insurance carrier disputes the claim, no cash benefits are paid until a Workers' Compensation Law Judge decides who is right. If a worker is not receiving benefits because the employer or insurance carrier is arguing that the injury is not job-related, the worker may be eligible for *disability benefits* in the meantime. Any payments made under the disability program, however, will be subtracted from future workers' compensation awards.

Workers' compensation is administered by the Workers' Compensation Board (WCB) (*www.wcb.state.ny.us*). The WCB:

- Processes over 150,000 benefit claims a year
- Conducts hearings to resolve disputes on eligibility

B. Paralegals as Licensed Representatives

Paralegals are allowed to represent claimants before the Workers' Compensation Board (WCB). When qualified, they are called one of the following:

- Licensed Representative
- Licensed Claimant Representative
- New York State Workers' Compensation Board Licensed Representative

To become licensed, a paralegal must pass an examination:

Licensed Representative Examination
www.wcb.state.ny.us
(click "Licensed Representatives")

For more on this license, see section 3.1.

C. Benefits

Medical Benefits

The injured or ill worker receives necessary medical care directly related to the original injury or illness and the recovery from his or her disability. The worker is free to choose any health care provider who is authorized by the Workers' Compensation Board (WCB), except in an emergency situation.

The cost of necessary medical services is paid by the employer or the employer's insurance carrier. The doctor may not collect a fee from the patient. If, however, the workers' compensation claim is disputed by the employer or insurance carrier, the doctor may require the worker to guarantee payment in the event that the WCB disallows the claim or the worker does not pursue the claim.

Cash Benefits

Cash benefits are not paid for the first 7 days of the disability, unless it extends beyond 14 days. In that case, the worker may receive cash benefits from the first work day off the job. Necessary medical care is provided no matter how short or how long the length of the disability.

Claimants who are totally or partially disabled and unable to work for more than seven days receive cash benefits. The amount that a worker receives is based on his/her average weekly wage for the previous year. Benefits are calculated by the formula presented in Exhibit 2.9A. For example, a claimant who was earning $400 per week and is totally (100%) disabled would receive $266.67 per week. A partially disabled claimant (50%) would receive $133.34 per week. Note, however, that the weekly benefit cannot exceed designated maximums based on the date of the accident. (*www.wcb.state.ny.us/content/main/onthejob/CashBenefits.jsp*)

EXHIBIT 2.9A	**Formula Used to Calculate Workers' Compensation Benefits**
2/3 x average weekly wage x % of disability = weekly benefit	

Death Benefits

If a worker dies from a compensable injury, the surviving spouse and/or minor children are entitled to weekly cash benefits. The amount is equal to two-thirds of the deceased worker's average weekly wage for the year before the accident. The weekly compensation may not exceed the weekly maximum, despite the number of dependents.

D. Resolving Disputes: Hearings and Appeals

The Board may hold a hearing or hearings before a Workers' Compensation Law Judge. The Judge may take testimony, review medical and other evidence, and decide whether the claimant is entitled to benefits. If the claim is determined to be compensable, the Judge determines the amount and duration of the compensation award.

Either side may appeal the decision within 30 days of the filing of the Judge's decision. This is done by applying in writing for Board review. If the application is granted, a panel of three Board Members will review the case. This panel may affirm, modify, or rescind the Judge's decision, or restore the case to the Law Judge for further development of the record. In the event the panel is not unanimous, any interested party may make application in writing for a full Board review. The full Board must review and either affirm, modify, or rescind such decision.

Appeals of Board Panel decisions may be taken to the Appellate Division, Third Department, Supreme Court of the State of New York, within 30 days. The decision of the Appellate Division may be appealed to the Court of Appeals.

E. Contacts

Workers' Compensation Board (WCB)
20 Park Street
Albany, NY 12207
877-632-4996; 518-474-6670
www.wcb.state.ny.us
www.wcb.state.ny.us/content/main/Contact.jsp

Locating your Local District Office and Service Center

The WCB has 11 district offices and 30 satellite service centers throughout the state:
www.wcb.state.ny.us/content/main/DistrictOffices/MainPage.jsp

Albany	866-750-5157
Binghamton	866-802-3604
Brooklyn	800-877-1373
Buffalo	866-211-0645
Hauppauge	866-681-5354
Hempstead	866-805-3630
Manhattan	800-877-1373
Peekskill	866-746-0552
Queens	800-877-1373
Rochester	866-211-0644
Syracuse	866-802-3730

Advocate for Injured Workers
800-580-6665

Questions about Workers' Compensation
866-298-7830

Questions about Disability Benefits
800-353-3092

Fraud Referral Hotline
888-363-6001

Office of Appeals
877-258-3441

Overview of New York State Workers' Compensation Law
www.wcb.state.ny.us/index.htm
www.albanylaw.edu/sub.php?navigation_id=846
www.nycosh.org/workers_comp/compensation.html

Filing a Claim
www.wcb.state.ny.us/content/main/onthejob/howto.jsp

Workers' Compensation Law and Regulations
www.wcb.state.ny.us/content/main/wclaws/newlaws.jsp

New York State Insurance Fund
(Workers' Compensation and Disability Benefits)
ww3.nysif.com

Glossary of Workers' Compensation Terms
www.wcb.state.ny.us/content/main/TheBoard/glossary.jsp

Advocate for Injured Workers
www.wcb.state.ny.us/content/main/Workers/WhatIsAdvocate InjuredWkrs.jsp

Injured Workers Bar Association
www.injuredworkersbar.org

New York Committee for Occupational Safety and Health
www.nycosh.org

Workers Injury Law & Advocacy Group
www.wilg.org

U.S. Occupational Safety & Health Administration (OSHA)
www.osha.gov

WorkersCompensation.com
www.workerscompensation.com
(click "New York")

Workers Comp Rx
www.workerscomprx.com

1. Read Workers' Compensation Law, § 24-a and § 50-3-b(b) (*public.leginfo.state.ny.us/menugetf.cgi? COMMONQUERY=LAWS*) (click "WKC"). What are the requirements for being an attorney or nonattorney representative of a workers' compensation claimant?

2. Go to the Constitution of the State of New York (*public.leginfo.state.ny.us/menugetf.cgi?COMMONQUERY =LAWS*) (click "CNS") (scroll down to Article I, section 18). Summarize what this section says about workers' compensation.

3. Find three New York law firms online that represent clients in workers' compensation cases. Compare their descriptions of the services they offer.

APPENDIX A

Deductibility of Paralegal Education or Training

A. **Introduction**
B. **Qualifying Work-Related Education (QWRE) That Is Deductible**
C. **More Information**
D. **Something to Check**

A. Introduction

Paralegals can incur education and training expenses (1) before they obtain their first job, (2) while employed, and (3) while looking for a new position after leaving an old one. In addition, the cost of obtaining a paralegal education by way of a bachelor's degree, associate's degree, or certificate can, of course, be significant.

Also, there are the costs of earning the credits required to maintain one's credentials in voluntary certification programs. For example, continuing legal education (CLE) obligations exist for certification by the National Association of Legal Assistants (as a Certified Legal Assistant, Certified Paralegal, or Advanced Certified Paralegal) and the National Federation of Paralegal Associations (as a PACE Registered Paralegal). Paralegals also participate in CLE to keep current in their field even if they have not sought voluntary certification.

A working paralegal's first choice should be to request reimbursement for CLE from an employer, but that is not always feasible. When paralegals spend their own money for any of these purposes, are the expenses deductible on their income tax returns as business expenses? In this section, we examine the tax law governing this question.

B. Qualifying Work-Related Education (QWRE) That Is Deductible

You can deduct education costs as a business expense if the education can be classified as *qualifying work-related education* (QWRE). What is QWRE? The following three principles apply:

1. The education must fit within *either* (a) or (b):
   (a) The education is required by your employer or by the law to keep your present salary, status, or job, and this required education serves a bona fide business purpose of the employer.
   (b) The education is used to maintain or improve skills that are needed in your present work.
2. Education that meets the minimum educational requirements of your present trade or business is *not* a QWRE.

3. Education that is part of a program of study to qualify you for a new trade or business is *not* a QWRE.

Exhibit A summarizes these principles.

CLE Expenses

New York paralegals often purchase continuing legal education (CLE) courses offered by associations, schools, or institutes. (See section 1.3 on CLE for paralegals.) Although CLE is not required to be a paralegal in New York, it helps paralegals maintain or improve their legal skills. Indeed, skill maintenance or skill improvement is a major purpose of CLE. Consequently, when you pay for such CLE yourself, the cost constitutes deductible QWRE.

Certification Expenses

The same is true of expenses to become certified and maintain that certification by associations such as NALA and NFPA. The application and testing fees, for example, would constitute deductible QWRE. Certification, although voluntary, is designed to enhance the status of the profession and of one's employability.

Initial Education Expenses

Of course, your largest education expense will probably be for your *initial* paralegal training. Can this be QWRE? For most students the answer is *no* because it is a program of study to qualify you for a "new trade or business."

Suppose, however, that you are a legal secretary paying your own way to go to paralegal school part-time or during an extended break from work. Can the cost of this education be QWRE? This is a more difficult question to answer. If as a secretary you were performing some paralegal tasks (even though you were not called a paralegal), an argument can be made that you are not trying to enter a "new trade or business." You are simply expanding (improving) what you already do. It's not clear whether the IRS would accept this argument. If it does, the cost of the paralegal education would be QWRE.

Suppose that you are an experienced paralegal who wants to become an attorney. Can your law school education be QWRE? Since the requirements for being

EXHIBIT A	When Does Your Education or Training Constitute Qualified Work-Related Education (QWRE)?

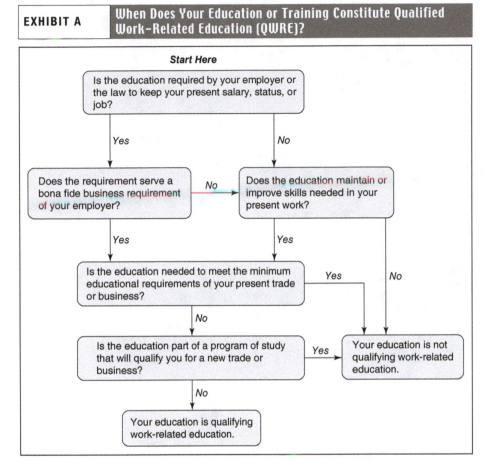

Source: Internal Revenue Service, *Tax Benefits for Education,* 65, Figure 12-1 (2008) (*www.irs.gov/pub/irs-pdf/ p970.pdf*)

an attorney are substantially different from what is required to be a paralegal, the IRS would probably take the position that going from paralegal to attorney is entering a "new trade or business." In an example provided by the IRS, if an accountant decides to become an attorney, his or her law school education would not be QWRE even if the employer requires the accountant to obtain a law degree. According to the IRS, going from accountant to attorney qualifies the accountant for a "new trade or business."

C.	More Information

Federal Tax Benefits for Education
www.irs.gov/pub/irs-pdf/p970.pdf
www.irs.gov/publications/p970/ch12.html
taxguide.completetax.com/text/Q04_5120.asp
www.jacksonhewitt.com/Resource-Center/Tax-Topics/ Education-Credits—Deductions
www.unclefed.com/TaxHelpArchives/2002/HTML/ p508toc.html

New York State College Tuition Credit and Itemized Deduction
www.tax.state.ny.us/pdf/publications/income/pub10w.pdf

New York Department of Taxation
800-225-5829
www.tax.state.ny.us

D.	Something to Check

Go to the Internal Revenue Service site (*www.irs.gov*). Use its search boxes to try to find material relevant to the following case. Mary is a legal investigator who works for a New York law firm. She wants to take an evidence course at a local paralegal school. If she pays for the course herself, under what circumstances, if any, can she deduct the cost as QWRE?

P A R T

3

Ethics, Paralegals, and Attorneys

A. Introduction

In this section we examine the practice of law in order to understand the unauthorized practice of law (UPL). See also the following related sections:

- Section 3.2 (the Rules of Professional Conduct, some of which cover UPL)
- Section 3.3 (ethical opinions, some of which cover UPL)
- Appendix A of Part 1 (paralegals in court opinions, some of which cover UPL)
- Appendix A of Part 3 (attorney discipline for offenses such as aiding nonattorneys in UPL)

B. Themes Covered

- Who can practice law (§ 478)
- Purpose of the prohibition of the UPL
- Deciding who can practice law
- Criminal penalties for UPL
- Defining the practice of law
- General information vs. legal advice
- Selling legal forms and kits
- Real estate transactions
- The absence of attorney supervision and UPL
- Outsourcing and UPL
- Summary of tasks that can and cannot be delegated to a supervised nonlawyer
- Improper delegation and UPL
- Answering calendar calls
- Paralegals representing workers' compensation claimants
- Paralegals representing unemployment insurance claimants

- Paralegals representing public assistance claimants
- Paralegals representing Social Security claimants
- Other agency authorizations of nonattorney representation
- Small claims court representation by nonattorneys
- Bankruptcy petition preparers
- Corporations represented by nonlawyers
- Accountants and tax law
- Attorney in fact cannot practice law
- Attorney disciplined in cases involving paralegal UPL
- Nonlawyer posing as a lawyer
- Action for the unauthorized practice of law
- Disbarred or suspended attorneys
- Miscellaneous

C. Applicable Laws

Who Can Practice Law (NY Judiciary Law § 478)

▶ It is unlawful for anyone to practice law without having first been duly licensed and admitted to practice law in the courts of record of New York. "It shall be unlawful for any natural person to practice or appear as an . . . attorney . . . for a person other than himself in a court of record in this state, or to furnish attorneys or counsel or an attorney and counsel to render legal services, or to hold himself out to the public as being entitled to practice law as aforesaid, or in any other manner, or to assume to be an attorney or counselor-at-law, or to assume, use, or advertise the title of lawyer, or attorney . . . or equivalent terms in any language, in such manner as to convey the impression that he is a legal practitioner of law or in any manner to advertise that he either alone or together with any other persons or person has, owns, conducts or maintains a law office or law and collection office, or office of any kind for the practice of law, without having first been duly and regularly licensed and admitted to practice law in the courts of record of this state, and without having taken the constitutional oath." (NY Judiciary § 478.)

Although § 478 Is Not a Model of Clarity . . .

▶ While Judiciary Law section 478 is not a model of clarity, it clearly prohibits a non-licensed individual from practicing law in this State as follows: to appear as an attorney in a court of record in this State, to render legal services, or to hold himself out as being entitled to practice law . . . in any other manner. Moreover, the prohibited practice of law includes the rendering of legal advice and preparation of legal papers in New York even if performed out of court and with respect to foreign law. *People v. Jakubowitz*, 184 Misc.2d 559, 710 N.Y.S.2d 844 (Sup. Ct., Bronx Co., 2000).

Purpose of the Prohibition of the UPL

▶ The purpose of the statute prohibiting the practice of law by non attorneys is to protect citizens against the dangers of legal representation and advice given by persons not trained, examined, and licensed for such work, whether they are laymen or lawyers from other jurisdictions. *Spivak v. Sachs*, 16 N.Y.2d 163, 211 N.E.2d 329, 263 N.Y.S.2d 953 (1965).

▶ The prohibition against the practice of law by a nonlawyer is grounded in the need of the public for integrity and competence of those who undertake to render legal services. Because of the fiduciary and personal character of the lawyer-client relationship and the inherently complex nature of our legal system, the public can better be assured of the requisite responsibility and competence if the practice of law is confined to those who are subject to the requirements and regulations imposed upon members of the legal profession. Lawyer's Code of Professional Responsibility, EC 3-1.

▶ The reason why preparatory study, educational qualifications, experience, examination, and license by the courts are required, is not to protect the bar, but to protect the public. Similar preparation and license are now demanded for the practice of medicine, surgery, dentistry, and other callings, and the list is constantly increasing as the danger to the citizen becomes manifest, and knowledge reveals how it may be avoided. *People v. Alfani*, 227 N.Y. 334, 125 N.E. 671 (1919).

Deciding Who Can Practice Law

▶ Admissions to and removal from the practice of law is controlled by the appellate divisions. NY Judiciary § 90, NY CPLR Art. 94.

▶ A person shall be admitted to practice law in the courts of the State of New York only by an order of the Appellate Division of the Supreme Court upon compliance with these rules. 22 NYCRR 520.1 et. seq.

Criminal Penalties for UPL

▶ Any person who violates the provisions of section 478, 479 (soliciting business on behalf of an attorney), 480 (entering a hospital to negotiate settlement or obtain release or statement), 481 (aiding, assisting, or abetting the solicitation of persons or the procurement of a retainer for an attorney), 482 (employment by attorney of person to aid, assist, or abet in the solicitation of business or the procurement through solicitation of a retainer to perform legal services), 483 (signs advertising services as attorney-at-law), or 484 of the Judiciary Law is guilty of a misdemeanor, with a maximum penalty of one year in jail, or three years' probation and a $1,000 fine. NY Judiciary Law § 485.

Defining the Practice of Law

▶ It is neither necessary nor desirable to attempt the formulation of a single, specific definition of what constitutes the practice of law. Functionally, the practice of law relates to the rendition of services for others that call for the professional judgment of a lawyer. The essence of the professional judgment of the lawyer is the educated ability to relate the general body and philosophy of law to a specific legal problem of a client; and thus, the public interest will be better served if only lawyers are permitted to act in matters involving professional judgment. Where this professional judgment is not involved, nonlawyers, such as court clerks, police officers, abstracters, and many governmental employees, may engage in occupations that require a special knowledge of law in certain areas. But the services of a lawyer are essential in the public interest whenever the exercise of professional legal judgment is required. Lawyer's Code of Professional Responsibility, EC 3-5.

▶ The practice of law is not limited to the conduct of cases in courts. According to the generally understood definition of the practice of law in this country, it embraces the preparation of pleadings and other papers incident to actions and special proceedings and the management of such actions and proceedings on behalf of clients before judges and courts, and in addition conveyancing, the preparation of legal instruments of all kinds, and in general all advice to clients and all action taken for them in matters connected with the law. *People v. Alfani*, 227 N.Y. 334, 125 N.E. 671 (1919).

▶ The practice of law includes legal advice and counsel as well as appearing in court on behalf of another and holding oneself out as a lawyer. *Spivak v. Sachs*, 16 N.Y.2d 163, 211 N.E.2d 329, 263 N.Y.S.2d 953 (1965).

▶ "No natural person shall ask or receive, directly or indirectly, compensation for appearing for a person other than himself as attorney in any court or before any magistrate, or for preparing deeds, mortgages, assignments, discharges, leases or any other instruments affecting real estate, wills, codicils, or any other instrument affecting the disposition of property after death, or decedents' estates, or pleadings of any kind in any action brought before any court of record in this state . . . unless he has been regularly admitted to practice, as an attorney or counselor, in the courts of record in the state." NY Judiciary § 484.

▶ "No voluntary association or corporation shall ask or receive directly or indirectly, compensation for preparing deeds, mortgages, assignments, discharges, leases, or any other instruments affecting real estate, wills, codicils, or any other instruments affecting disposition of property after death or decedents' estates, or pleadings of any kind in actions or proceedings of any nature." NY Judiciary § 495(3).

▶ "It shall be unlawful for any natural person to practice or appear as an . . . attorney . . . for a person other than himself in a court of record in this state, or to furnish attorneys or counsel or an attorney and counsel to render legal services, or to hold himself out to the public as being entitled to practice law as aforesaid, or in any other manner, or to assume to be an attorney or counselor-at-law, or to assume, use, or advertise the title of lawyer, or attorney . . . or equivalent terms in any language, in such manner as to convey the impression that he is a legal practitioner of law or in any manner to advertise that he either alone or together with any other persons or person has, owns, conducts or maintains a law office or law and collection office, or office of any kind for the practice of law, without having first been duly and regularly licensed and admitted to practice law in the courts of record of this state, and without having taken the constitutional oath." NY Judiciary § 478.

▶ For purposes of this section [on the attorney's obligation to file a registration statement], the "practice of law" shall mean the giving of legal advice or counsel to, or providing legal representation for, particular body or individual in a particular situation in either the public or private sector in the State of New York or elsewhere, it shall include the appearance as an attorney before any court or administrative agency. 22 NYCRR 118.1(g).

General Information vs. Legal Advice

▶ The practice of law (prohibited to nonattorneys) covers advice or services rendered to particular clients. Publishing of general legal information without personal contract or relationship to a specific individual is not unauthorized practice of law. *El Gemayel v. Seaman*, 72 N.Y.2d 701, 533 N.E.2d 245, 536 N.Y.S.2d 406 (1988).

▶ Providing "information" with respect to administrative proceedings in the school system will involve advising as to procedural as well as substantive rights. The giving of such advice is peculiarly within the province of the practice of law which is limited to duly-licensed lawyers. *In re Queens Lay Advocate Service, Inc.*, 71 Misc.2d 33, 335 N.Y.S.2d 583 (Sup. Ct. Queens Co., 1972).

Selling Legal Forms and Kits

▶ Dacey sold a self-help forms book to the general public called "How to Avoid Probate." The Court of Appeals rejected the position that Dacey was practicing law. He was not providing advice to particular persons. It could not be claimed that the publication of a legal text, which purported to say what the law is, amounts to legal practice. The mere fact that the principles or rules stated in the text may be accepted by a particular reader as a solution to his problem, does not affect the matter. The publication of a multitude of forms for all manner of legal situations is a commonplace activity and their use by the Bar and public is general. The conjoining of the text and the forms with advice as to how the forms should be filled out does not constitute the unlawful practice of law. *New York Lawyers' Assn. v. Dacey*, 21 N.Y.2d 694, 234 N.E.2d 694, 287 N.Y.S.2d 422 (1967).

▶ The publication and sale of divorce-yourself kits did not constitute the unlawful practice of law. There would be unauthorized practice, however, if the author of the kits gave legal advice to a buyer of a kit concerning that person's particular matrimonial problems or remedies and provided assistance in preparing the documents involved. *State v. Winder*, 42 A.D.2d 1039, 348 N.Y.S.2d 270 (4th Dept. 1973).

▶ In New York it is not a violation of the unauthorized practice of law to provide legal material, or even specific forms for legal use as long as there is no attorney-client relationship. See, e.g., *In re N.Y. County Lawyers' Ass'n*, 21 N.Y.2d 694, 234 N.E.2d 459, 287 N.Y.S.2d 422 (1967) (finding that "the publication of a legal text which purported to say what the law is . . . and that the conjoining of the text and the forms with advice as to how the forms should be filled out does not constitute the unauthorized practice of law."). *In re Tomlinson*, 343 B.R. 400 (E.D.N.Y. 2006).

Real Estate Transactions

▶ The line between such permitted acts by real estate brokers and the unauthorized practice of the law has been recognized as thin and difficult to define and, at times, to discern. *Duncan & Hill Realty, Inc. v. Department of State*, 62 A.D.2d 690, 405 N.Y.S.2d 339 (4th Dept., 1978).

▶ **Filling out real estate forms.** The courts have distinguished between the mere filling out and completion of forms by a nonlawyer, which is not a violation of the Judiciary Law, and acts which require independent judgment regarding whether documents have been prepared in accordance with New York law, which constitutes the unlawful practice of law. The line is crossed when the person who is not licensed to practice law provides professional advice to a specific client on a specific legal problem or issue. nonlawyers, such as paralegals, may assist attorneys in preparing documents such as mortgages and contracts and other documents related to real estate transactions, provided that the work is properly and adequately supervised by an attorney. See The Association of the Bar of the City of New York, Committee on Professional and Judicial Ethics, Formal Opinion 1995-11. *Fuchs v. Wachovia Mortg. Corp.*, 9 Misc.3d 1129(A), 862 N.Y.S.2d 808 (Sup. Ct., Nassau Co., 2005).

▶ It is not proper for a licensed real estate broker to undertake to devise the detailed terms of a purchase money mortgage or other legal terms beyond the general description of property, the price, and the mortgage to be assumed or given. *Duncan & Hill Realty, Inc. v. Department of State*, 62 A.D.2d 690, 405 N.Y.S.2d 339 (3rd Dept., 1978).

▶ Real estate brokers are not engaged in the unauthorized practice of law if they prepare purchase-and-sale contracts that expressly state the documents are subject to review by the parties' attorneys, or if they use forms approved by the appropriate organizations and do not insert any material requiring legal expertise. This limited privilege must be narrowly circumscribed. 1996 N.Y. Op. Atty. Gen. 46, 1996 WL 710801.

▶ A real estate broker engaged in the unlawful practice of law, by drafting a clause in the purchase offer that was of considerable legal significance in degree to which it permitted the buyer to be relieved of its obligations under contract, and advising the buyer of the legal effect of certain provisions of the second purchase offer, and receiving a $100 fee that was at least in part for the preparation of operative legal instruments. *Mulford v. Shaffer*, 124 A.D.2d 876, 508 N.Y.S.2d 302 (3rd Dept., 1986).

Affiliation with a Nonlawyer

▶ A lawyer may not affiliate with a nonlawyer to represent homeowners in small claims proceedings to reduce real estate taxes, even if the lawyer refrains from holding himself or herself out as an attorney. "We have no difficulty in concluding that the activity proposed here—a lawyer representing homeowners in judicial or administrative proceedings challenging real estate taxes—constitutes the practice of law. When a lawyer represents a client in a litigation or quasi-litigation proceeding, the lawyer is practicing law whether or not a nonlawyer is legally permitted to perform the same function. . . . It therefore follows that a lawyer may not affiliate with a nonlawyer real estate broker in prosecuting small claims petitions to reduce real property taxes if the lawyer holds himself or herself out as a lawyer in doing so. In addition, it is likely that such an arrangement would also violate DR 3-102(A), which prohibits sharing of legal fees with a nonlawyer. See N.Y. State 644 (1992)(lawyer may not form corporation with nonlawyers to assist homeowners in obtaining real

estate tax reductions because of violation of state judiciary law and violation of DR 3-102[A])." Opinion 662 (5/15/94) New York State Bar Association Committee on Professional Ethics. (*www.nysba.org/AM/ Template.cfm?Section=Ethics_Opinions&TEMPLATE=/ CM/ContentDisplay.cfm&CONTENTID=18750*) (1994 WL 120206)

The Absence of Attorney Supervision and UPL

▶ As we will see in section 3.2, the new Rules of Professional Conduct impose on attorneys the duty to supervise paralegals "adequately." The failure to provide this supervision can involve the paralegal in the unauthorized practice of law. "A law firm shall ensure that the work of nonlawyers who work for the firm is adequately supervised, as appropriate. A lawyer with direct supervisory authority over a nonlawyer shall adequately supervise the work of the nonlawyer, as appropriate. In either case, the degree of supervision required is that which is reasonable under the circumstances, taking into account factors such as the experience of the person whose work is being supervised, the amount of work involved in a particular matter and the likelihood that ethical problems might arise in the course of working on the matter." Rule 5.2(a), Rules of Professional Conduct. (*www.nycourts.gov/rules/jointappellate/ NY%20Rules%20of%20Prof%20Conduct.pdf*)

▶ An independent paralegal has, in this Court's opinion, crossed the line between filling out forms and engaging in the practice of law by rendering legal services in trying to help a particular debtor collect a debt. A paralegal cannot practice law—an "act requiring the exercise of 'independent professional legal judgment,'" NYSBA Committee on Professional Ethics Opinion 304 (1973). When a paralegal declines to work under the direct supervision of an attorney, problems may occur. In this case a debtor went to an independent paralegal who did not work under attorney supervision. Dissatisfied with the paralegal's work, the debtor sued the paralegal. The paralegal made serious errors in the case. "The defendant testified that she's a graduate from a paralegal certificate program and has been a paralegal for thirteen (13) years and she "help[s] a lot of people." The American Bar Association has defined an independent paralegal as "a person who is not supervised by a lawyer, provides services to clients with regard to a process in which the law is involved, is not functioning at the time as a paralegal or a document preparer, and for whose work no lawyer is accountable," Nonlawyer Practice in the United States: Summary of the Factual Record before the American Bar Association Commission on Nonlawyer Practice (1994). However, New York State bar associations have not recognized the "legal technician/independent paralegal" for reasons obvious from this case—the independent paralegal, working without the supervision of an attorney, may cross the line between assisting a person in need to hurting a person in need through lack of knowledge and supervision, see, e.g., N.Y. County Lawyers Association Ethics Committee opinion 641 (1975), Association of the Bar of the City of New York Ethics Committee opinion 1995-11 ["Supervision within the law firm thus is a key consideration."]. This Court finds that the defendant used independent judgment on a subject with which she had insufficient knowledge. Regardless of her intentions to help the plaintiff, this independent paralegal operated without the supervision of an attorney. She tried to create a legal document without the required knowledge, skill, or training. Just as a law school graduate, not admitted to practice law, cannot undertake to collect overdue accounts on behalf of prospective clients [see Nassau County Bar Association Ethics Committee opinion 3 (1980)], so is an independent paralegal barred from attempting to collect a judgment. The court awarded the debtor treble damages against the paralegal for engaging in deceptive "acts or practices in the conduct" of a business under NY General Business Law § 349. *Sussman v. Grado*, 192 Misc.2d 628, 746 N.Y.S.2d 548 (Dist. Ct., Nas. Co., 2002).

▶ The attorney aided a nonattorney in the unauthorized practice of law. He was associated with a collection agency where, among other things, he allowed the agency to use his name, letterhead, and signature without actually reviewing letters sent out under his name. *Matter of Scheck*, 171 A.D.2d 33, 574 N.Y.S.2d 372 (2nd Dept., 1991).

▶ A law firm may not enter into arrangement with a staff leasing company (SLC) to provide debt consolidation services to law firm's clients, where law firm does not supervise work or maintain direct relationship with clients. . . . There are circumstances under which a nonlawyer may provide services to a law firm's clients in conjunction with the lawyers of the firm. The lawyers, however, must supervise the work delegated to the nonlawyers and maintain a direct relationship with the clients. EC 3-6. Under the proposed arrangement, the lawyers of the firm would not supervise the SLC and the lawyers would have minimal contact with the clients. Instead, the SLC would perform most of the work on its own and refer only "difficult" legal questions to the law firm. Based on these facts, the proposed arrangement is prohibited by DR 3-101(A) of the Code. Opinion 633 (5/3/92) New York State Bar Association Committee on Professional Ethics. (*www .nysba.org/AM/Template.cfm?Section= Ethics_Opinions& TEMPLATE=/CM/ContentDisplay.cfm&CONTENTID= 18722*) (1992 WL 348745)

Outsourcing and UPL

▶ A New York lawyer may ethically outsource legal support services overseas to a nonlawyer, if the New York lawyer (a) rigorously supervises the nonlawyer, so as to avoid aiding the nonlawyer in the unauthorized practice of law and to ensure that the nonlawyer's work contributes to the lawyer's competent representation of the client; (b) preserves the client's confidences and secrets when outsourcing; (c) avoids conflicts of interest when outsourcing; (d) bills for outsourcing appropriately; and (e) when necessary, obtains advance client consent to outsourcing. Opinion 2006-3 (8/06) Association of the Bar of the City of New York Committee on Professional and Judicial Ethics. (*www.nycbar.org/ Ethics/eth2006.htm*) (2006 WL 2389364)

Summary of Tasks That Can and Cannot Be Delegated to a Supervised Nonlawyer

▶ Nonlawyers may engage in a variety of activities under the supervision and direction of a lawyer. See N.Y. County 641 (1975), quoting N.Y. County 420 (1953). Various ethics opinions have established guidelines consisting of permitted and non-permitted activities for legal assistants and unadmitted lawyers. For convenience, we summarize them here. A person not admitted to the bar:

- May not counsel clients about legal matters. See N.Y. City 884 (1974); N.Y. State 44 (1967); ABA 316 (1967); N.Y. City 78 (1927–28).
- May not appear in court. N.Y. City 884 (1974); N.Y. City 78 (1927–28); ABA 316 (1967).
- May not argue motions. N.Y. State 44 (1967).
- May not take depositions or EBTs, even if supervised throughout the deposition by a lawyer admitted to practice in New York. N.Y. State 304 (1973), N.Y. State 44 (1967).
- May not supervise the execution of a will. N.Y. State 343 (1974).
- May interview witnesses. N.Y. City 884 (1974).
- May draft documents of all kinds, including process, affidavits, deeds, contracts, pleadings, briefs, and other legal papers, under the supervision of an admitted lawyer. N.Y. City 884 (1974), N.Y. City 78 (1927–28).
- May research questions of law. Id.
- May answer calendar calls provided no argument is necessary, and role is confined to purely ministerial activity. N.Y. State 44 (1967).
- May attend title or mortgage closings if it merely involves formalities, such as receipt or delivery of a deed or payment or receipt of money. N.Y. City 884 (1974), N.Y. City 78 (1927–28).

Opinion 682 (11/11/90) New York County Lawyers' Association Committee on Professional Ethics. (*www.nycla.org/siteFiles/Publications/Publications455_0 .pdf*) (1990 WL 677024)

▶ To ensure that its objectives are nonetheless met, the Code requires lawyers to effectively supervise nonlawyers in their employ, to refrain from aiding or encouraging the unauthorized practice of law; to ascertain that client confidences are maintained and the public not misled as to the status of nonlawyers. In delegating tasks, the lawyer should provide instruction regarding the ethical constraints under which those in the law office must work. While the nonlawyer may receive some guidance in this regard elsewhere, as for instance through the Code of Ethics and Professional Responsibility and Model Standards and Guidelines adopted by the NALA and NFPA, the lawyer should not rely on others to perform this important task. Given that the Code holds the attorney accountable, the tasks a nonlawyer may undertake under the supervision of an attorney should be more expansive than those without either supervision or legislation. Supervision within the law firm thus is a key consideration. The standard of supervision is fairly strict. A lawyer should not permit a paralegal within his or her employ:

- to give advice regarding legal relationships, rights, or obligations which he or she has developed independent of or unbeknownst to a supervising attorney;

- to counsel on the legal consequences of actions or the application of legal precepts to facts.

Paralegals may:

- communicate with clients and witnesses to obtain facts for purposes of legal representation;

- complete legal forms for attorney review and signature;

- engage in such activity as the organizing, indexing, reviewing, summarizing and proofreading of documents;

- draft correspondence, briefs, and affidavits under the direction and supervision of an attorney. Formal Opinion 1995-11 (July 6, 1995) Association of the Bar of the City of New York Committee on Professional and Judicial Ethics. (*www.nycbar.org/Ethics/eth1995-11.htm*) (1995 WL 607778)

▶ In simplest terms, a legal assistant may not perform those functions which only lawyers may perform. Moreover, legal assistants "may never perform services which involve the exercise of the professional judgment of a lawyer [and may not advise clients with respect to their legal rights]" N.Y. County 641. As an employee of a lawyer, but not as an independent entrepreneur (Judiciary Law, §§ 478, 479, 484, and 486; cf. *Spivak v. Sacks*, 16 N.Y.2d 163, 263 N.E.2d 329, 263 N.Y.S.2d 953 (1965), he or she, may, however, perform virtually any other task of a ministerial or clerical nature. He or she may:

- conduct legal research

- prepare memoranda of law and briefs and may be credited in a footnote or other appropriate notation provided the fact that the assistant is a nonlawyer is made clear. N.Y. State 299 (1973)

- prepare all legal papers

- interview prospective witnesses

- deal directly with the public either by oral or written communication, provided that he or she properly identifies him or herself from the outset as a nonlawyer (N.Y. City 884; N.Y. State 500 [1978]) and, again, provided that such dealings do not call for the independent exercise of professional judgment

- deal directly with and appear before courts and other tribunals on routine matters, such as responding to calendar calls, provided no oral argument or exercise of judgment of any kind is required (N.Y. City 884; N.Y. State 44) and, of course, provided that such appearance would not contravene a standing rule of the court of tribunal. See DR7-106(A); see also Canons 1 and 9

- may attend closings of title, if it merely involves formalities such as receipt or delivery of a deed, or payment or receipt of money; if it involves argument or decision in behalf of a client, the nonlawyer would be acting as an attorney and consequently should not attend or close. N.Y. City 78; N.Y. City 884. (Patently, the supervising lawyer should know or determine in advance whether a particular closing involves formalities only and thus is merely ministerial or whether decisions of a substantive nature will be involved.)

▶ The essence of the legal assistant's role is that he or she may perform any delegated duty, under the supervision of a lawyer who is responsible to the client and any tribunal for the assistant's acts (ABA 316; N.Y. City 884; EC 3-6) and provided that the assistant may not counsel any client nor exercise independent professional judgment. The determination of what matters, moreover, require the exercise of professional judgment is not one which should be left to the legal assistant. Rather, before delegating any task, the lawyer should determine whether any such matters may arise. If it appears that any questions may arise calling for the exercise of such judgment during the performance of the task, the lawyer should not delegate it to the legal assistant or so circumscribe the assignment as to avoid the need for the legal assistant to exercise judgment. Should any questions calling for the exercise of professional judgment arise unexpectedly, it is the duty of the legal assistant to immediately refer such matters to the lawyer under whose supervision he or she is performing the work. Opinion 666 (October 29, 1985), New York County Lawyers' Association Committee on Professional Ethics. (*www.nycla.org/siteFiles/Publications/Publications440_0.pdf*) (1985 WL 287691)

▶ Nonlawyers may research questions of law and draft documents of all kinds, including process, affidavits, pleadings, briefs, and other legal papers as long as the work is performed under the supervision of an admitted lawyer. N.Y. County 682 (1990). See also N.Y. City 1995-11, N.Y. City 884 (1974). In N.Y. State 677, we determined that proper supervision involves considering in advance the work that will be done and reviewing after the fact what in fact occurred, assuring its soundness. Opinion 721 (9/27/99) New York State Bar Association Committee on Professional Ethics. (*www.nysba.org/AM/Template.cfm?Section=Ethics_Opinions& TEMPLATE=/CM/ContentDisplay.cfm&CONTENTID= 18918*) (1999 WL 1756189)

Pension Work

▶ A lawyer may hire nonlawyers to prepare and negotiate orders pertaining to the division of pension rights in matrimonial actions, provided that the lawyer assumes overall responsibility to the client and conducts all judicial proceedings. Moreover, an attorney-employee of a retirement system may deal with nonlawyers in passing upon the enforceability of such orders. Opinion 713 (5/28/96) New York County Lawyers' Association Committee on Professional Ethics. (*www.nycla.org/siteFiles/Publications/ Publications488_0.pdf*) (1996 WL 592655)

Improper Delegation and UPL

▶ "A lawyer shall not aid a nonlawyer in the unauthorized practice of law." Rule 5.5(b), Rules of Professional Conduct. (*www.nycourts.gov/rules/jointappellate/ NY%20Rules%20of%20Prof%20Conduct.pdf*)

▶ Attorney's actions in allowing a nonlawyer to prepare a contract of sale and appear on a client's behalf in order to postpone a foreclosure sale, which was conduct that aided nonlawyer in unauthorized practice of law and resulted in attorney's failure to adequately practice law under the circumstances, warranted three-month suspension from practice of law. *Matter of Parker*, 241 A.D.2d 208, 670 N.Y.S.2d 414 (1st Dept., 1998).

▶ Nonlawyer staff member was allowed to discuss substantive legal issues with a client and with opposing counsel. This was an improper delegation of professional responsibility to a nonlawyer who was engaged in the unauthorized practice of law. *Lester & Associates, P.C. v. Eneman*, 69 A.D.3d 906, 983 N.Y.S.2d 611 (2nd Dept., 2010).

Answering Calendar Calls

▶ In some courtrooms around the State, legal assistants are allowed to answer calendar calls and submit affidavits of engagement or unopposed motions; in others they are not. . . . If a court requires the presence of an individual in the trial assignment part pending assignment to a nonjury part or for

jury selection, the legal assistant can perform these responsibilities in lieu of a lawyer. The result would be cost savings to the client and better use of the attorney's time, which can be spent working on other legal matters. While this is permitted in some localities, elsewhere it is not. New York State Bar Association Ad Hoc Committee on NonLawyer Practice, *Final Report* (May 1995). (*www.cdpa.info/files/ NY_Paralegal_guidelines.pdf*)

▶ A legal assistant may deal directly with and appear before courts and other tribunals on routine matters, such as responding to calendar calls, provided no oral argument or exercise of judgment of any kind is required (N.Y. City 884; N.Y. State 44) and, of course, provided that such appearance would not contravene a standing rule of the court of tribunal. See DR7-106(A); see also Canons 1 and 9. Opinion 666 (October 29, 1985), New York County Lawyers' Association Committee on Professional Ethics. (*www.nycla.org/siteFiles/Publications/Publications440_0 .pdf*) (1985 WL 287691)

Paralegals Representing Workers' Compensation Claimants

▶ A paralegal can become a New York State Workers' Compensation Board Licensed Representative by applying for a license from the Workers' Compensation Board. The applicant must take an exam, given twice a year, and then appear before a board committee for an interview on the character and fitness. Licenses are valid for three years and may be renewed. Licensed representatives can not represent claimants on appeals taken to courts of law. NY Workers' Compensation Law § 24-a.

▶ To be licensed, an applicant must be over 18 years of age, be of good moral character, and show that he or she "has a competent knowledge of the law and regulations relating to workers' compensation matters and the necessary qualifications to render service to his or her client." 12 NYCRR 302-1.2(a). (*www.wcb.state.ny.us/content/main/wclaws/30213.jsp*)

▶ No representative licensed under section 24-a shall exact or accept any fee or other payment unless and until it shall have been authorized by order of the board or referee. Division of any fee with another licensed representative or a lawyer shall be based upon division of service or responsibility and shall be improper unless fully disclosed to the board and referee before the fee is authorized. 12 NYCRR 302-2.4(a)&(b). (*www.wcb.state.ny.us/ content/main/wclaws/30213.jsp*)

▶ A lawyer may employ a licensed representative (a layman) to appear on behalf of the lawyer's client to represent claimants or self-insurers in proceedings held before the Workers' Compensation Board if the lawyer discloses the nonlawyer status of the licensed representative, obtains the consent of the client, and assumes responsibility for the conduct of the representative. Opinion 446 (12/3/76) New York State Bar Association Committee on Professional Ethics. (*http://www.nysba.org/AM/Template .cfm?Section=Ethics_Opinions&CONTENTID=18203& TEMPLATE=/CM/ContentDisplay.cfm*)

▶ A lawyer may employ a law licensed representative on a salary basis to appear for him and try cases before the Workers' Compensation Board as long as the layman restricts his activities to those which may lawfully be undertaken by him. In fairness to the client the lawyer must disclose the fact that he is retaining a layman to try the client's case. Moreover, the lawyer must assume responsibility for the layman's conduct of the action. Joint opinion: Opinion 833 (1958) (Association of the Bar of the City of New York Committee on Professional and Judicial Ethics) and Opinion 463 (1958) (New York County Lawyers' Association Committee on Professional Ethics). (*www.nycla.org/siteFiles/Publications/ Publications534_0.PDF*)

Paralegals Representing Unemployment Insurance Claimants

▶ A paralegal can be a representative at unemployment insurance hearings. There are no special requirements to be an agent.

"Any party may appear in person or be represented by an attorney or agent. . . . All parties and their attorney or agent shall have the right to call, examine and cross-examine parties and witnesses, . . . offer relevant documents, records and other evidence, . . . [and] request that subpoenas be issued to compel the appearance of relevant witnesses or the production of relevant documents." 12 NYCRR 461.4(c).

▶ In New York City, some nonattorneys are registered by the Unemployment Insurance Appeal Board (UIAB) as claimant representatives. Only an attorney or a registered representative may charge a fee for their services. The fee must be approved by the UIAB. (*www.labor.state.ny.us/ui/claimantinfo/hearingfaq.shtm*)

▶ New Yorkers living *outside* New York City also have the right to be represented at a hearing by an attorney or other person. Only attorneys, however, may charge a fee for that service. "Only a lawyer or a registered agent can charge a fee to help you (and then only if you win). Anyone can help you who does not charge a fee." (*www.labor.state.ny.us/ui/ claimantinfo/hearingfaq.shtm*)

Paralegals Representing Public Assistance Claimants

▶ A paralegal can be a representative at public assistance hearings. When an applicant for designated public assistance (e.g., family assistance, food stamps) requests a fair hearing, he or she becomes the appellant and has a right to representation. "As an appellant you have the right . . . to be represented by an attorney or other representative at any conference and hearing." 18 NYCRR 358-3.4(e).

Paralegals Representing Social Security Claimants

▶ The administrative law judge (ALJ) must not only weigh the evidence but must assist the plaintiff affirmatively in developing the record. It may be true, as the Secretary contends, that plaintiff was represented by Harlem Legal Services, which has considerable expertise in litigating Social Security Claims. But plaintiff's actual representative before the ALJ was a paralegal. The proceedings in cases involving social security benefits are not designed to be adversarial. The ALJ's duty to develop the comprehensive record requisite for an equitable determination of disability is greatest when claimant is unrepresented; but the duty still exists when plaintiff is represented and even more, as here, where plaintiff is represented at hearing by a paralegal. *Smith v. Bowen*, 687 F. Supp. 902 (S.D.N.Y., 1988).

▶ It is true that the claimant herein was represented by a nonattorney at the administrative level. However, the regulations of the Social Security Administration permit a claimant to be represented by a nonattorney, including a parent, throughout the administrative process. See 20 C.F.R. § 416.1505(b). But as the Court of Appeals has pointed out, while representation by a nonattorney is authorized by the Social Security Act, that authorization extends only to proceedings before the Commissioner. *Iannaccone v. Law*, 142 F.3d 553 (2d Cir. 1998); see 42 U.S.C § 406(a)(1). There is no parallel provision in the Act authorizing the Commissioner to permit nonattorney representation of claimants in proceedings before the courts. *Rosario v. Apfel*, 1998 WL 685173 (S.D.N.Y., 1998).

▶ A nonattorney parent may bring an action relating to a claim for Supplemental Security Income (SSI) benefits on behalf of his or her child without representation by an attorney where a district court, after appropriate inquiry into the particular circumstances of the matter at hand, determines that the parent has a sufficient interest in the case and meets basic standards of competence. In the absence of this interest, attorney representation is required. *Machadio v. Apfel*, 276 F.3d 103 (2d Cir. 2002).

Other Agency Authorizations of Nonattorney Representation

▶ **Program for the Elderly Pharmaceutical Insurance Coverage.** "When an applicant or participant requests a fair hearing, he/she becomes the appellant and has the right to . . . be represented by an attorney or other representative." 9 NYCRR 9720.5(d).

▸ **Department of Health WIC program.** When an applicant is denied or disqualified from the WIC program, he or she may be represented by an attorney or other representative at the conference and, if necessary, the subsequent fair hearing. 10 NYCRR 60-1.3 and 60-1.5.

▸ **Public Employment Relations Board.** At the hearing before the Public Employment Relations Board, the union was represented by a nonlawyer, a labor relations specialist. Petitioner objected to this procedure, contending that such representation constituted the unauthorized practice of law in violation of Judiciary Law § 478. We cannot agree. Judiciary Law § 478 provides, in relevant part, that "[i]t shall be unlawful for any natural person to practice or appear as an attorney-at-law or as an attorney and counselor-at-law for a person other than himself *in a court of record in this state*" (emphasis supplied). An administrative hearing, however, is not a court of record (see, Judiciary Law § 2); it is an adjudicatory proceeding governed by the State Administrative Procedure Act (see, State Administrative Procedure Act § 102[3]; § 301 et seq.) and, as such, no violation of Judiciary Law § 478 occurred. *Board of Educ. of Union-Endicott Cent. School Dist. v. New York State Public Employment Relations Bd.*, 233 A.D.2d 602, 649 N.Y.S.2d 523 (3rd Dept., 1996).

▸ **Residential property tax assessment disputes.** Nonattorneys may act on behalf of petitioners in small claims assessment review procedures even though the procedure is designated a "judicial review" process. The informal nature of the hearing, the specialized nature of the expertise required, and the clear authorization in the statute for nonattorney preparation of the initiating petition, all support this conclusion. In addition, such representation furthers the intent of the legislature to establish a specialized and efficient forum for residential assessment disputes. *Cipollone v. City of White Plains*, 181 A.D.2d 887, 581 N.Y.S.2d 421 (2d Dept., 1992).

▸ Proceedings to review property assessments in New York may not be initiated by one not authorized to practice law. *Property Valuation Analysts, Inc. v. Williams*, 164 A.D.2d 131, 563 N.Y.S.2d 545 (3rd Dept. 1990).

▸ A contract employing plaintiff as the defendant's agent to appear before the tax commission of the city and before any other person or authority having jurisdiction over assessment of property, and authorizing the plaintiff to take necessary or proper steps, as defendant's agent, to obtain adjustment or reduction in assessment of certain properties for certain

tax year, did not necessarily involve unauthorized practice of law, and therefore such agreement was not unenforceable and void on its face. However, where the representation entails the performance of legal services, only a duly licensed lawyer should be permitted to act for the owner. The legality of the transaction, therefore, depends upon the nature of the services rendered, or contemplated to be performed, under the agreement of hire. *Realty Appraisals Co. v. Astor-Broadway Holding Corp.*, 5 A.D.2d 36, 169 N.Y.S.2d 121 (1st Dept., 1957).

▸ The Federal Administrative Procedure Act, Title 5, U.S.C. § 555(b), authorizes federal administrative agencies to permit representation by nonlawyers. *Sperry v. Florida ex rel. Florida Bar*, 373 U.S. 379 (1963). *Sperry* held that no state may prohibit, through its UPL provisions, a nonlawyer from practice before a federal administrative agency if the agency itself and federal statute authorizes such practice. Examples of Federal Agencies That Authorize Nonlawyer Practice:
- Bureau of Indian Affairs: 25 CFR § 20
- Consumer Product Safety Commission: 16 CFR § 1025.61
- Department of Agriculture (food stamps): 7 CFR § 273
- Department of Health and Human Services: 45 CFR § 205
- Department of Homeland Security (Immigration and Naturalization): 8 CFR §§ 292.1–3
- Department of Veterans Affairs: 38 CFR § 14
- Internal Revenue Service: 13 CFR Part 10; 31 U.S.C. § 330
- Patent & Trademark Office: 35 CFR §§ 31–33
- Social Security Administration: 42 U.S.C. § 406(a)

▸ Many New York State agencies permit nonlawyer advocacy pursuant to statute and regulation. According to a survey of the New York County Lawyers' Association, fourteen New York State agencies permit nonlawyer advocacy and twelve New York City agencies permit it. Examples of New York City Agencies That Authorize Nonlawyer Practice:
- Office of Administrative Trials and Hearings
- Department of Agriculture and Markets
- Department of Consumer Affairs
- Department of Transportation
- Housing Authority
- Tax Commission
- Taxi and Limousine Commission

New York State Bar Association, *Guidelines for Utilization by Lawyers of the Services of Legal Assistants* (1997). (*www.cdpa.info/files/NY_Paralegal_guidelines.pdf*)

Small Claims Court Representation by Nonattorneys

▸ The court may permit, upon the request of a party, that a nonattorney representative, who is related by consanguinity or affinity to such party, be allowed to appear on behalf of such party when the court finds that due to the age, mental or physical capacity, or other disability of such party that it is in the interests of justice to permit such representation. No person acting as a nonattorney representative shall be permitted to charge a fee or be allowed to accept any form of remuneration for such services. NY Uniform Dist. Ct. Act § 1815, NY Uniform City Ct. Act § 1815; NY Uniform Justice Ct. Act § 1815; NY City Civ. Ct. Act § 1815.

▶ Any plaintiff may appear in a small claims proceeding by a nonlawyer. A tenant was not entitled to recover a default judgment against a landlord on basis that the landlord's manager, a nonlawyer, appeared in a small claims proceeding to defend against the tenant's action to recover rent she paid the landlord for an apartment she never occupied, as the law permitted a nonlawyer to defend such a proceeding. The power of a small claims court to allow a nonlawyer to appear may be found in UCCA 1802. *Newsome v. Potter*, 128 Misc.2d 779, 491 N.Y.S.2d 257 (Albany City Ct., 1985).

▶ Representation by a nonattorney was not permissible in a small claims action before the effective date of statutes permitting representation by nonattorneys in some instances. NY Uniform City Ct. Act § 1815; NY Uniform Dist. Ct. Act § 1815;N.Y. City Civ. Ct. Act § 1815; NY Uniform Justice Court Act § 1815. *Urgo v. Jamaica Sav. Bank*, 150 Misc.2d 983, 578 N.Y.S.2d 805 (Sup. Ct. Appellate Term, 1991).

Bankruptcy Petition Preparers

▶ A bankruptcy petition preparer is "a person, other than an attorney for the debtor or an employee of such attorney under the direct supervision of such attorney, who prepares for compensation a document for filing." 11 U.S.C. § 110(a)(1). A document for filing is defined as a petition or any other document prepared for filing by a debtor in a United States bankruptcy court or a United States District Court in connection with a bankruptcy case. 11 U.S.C. § 110(a)(2). As a bankruptcy petition preparer only prepares a document for filing, the Bankruptcy Code prohibits a bankruptcy petition preparer from collecting or receiving any payment from the debtor or on behalf of the debtor for the court fees in connection with the filing the petition. 11 U.S.C. § 110(g). The role of a bankruptcy petition preparer is solely to type information on bankruptcy forms. He or she may not offer a potential bankruptcy debtor any legal advice. *In re Taub*, 2008 WL 728927 (Bkrtcy. E.D.N.Y. 2008).

▶ Congress enacted Section 110 of the Bankruptcy Code to provide a remedy against a growing number of nonattorneys who were rendering quasi-legal (and legal) services in bankruptcy cases to the detriment of both the bankruptcy system and the consuming public. Section 110(g) was enacted for three reasons: (1) to prevent the unauthorized filing of petitions; (2) to prevent or curtail the preparer's influence on a debtor's decision and timing on petition filing; and (3) to prevent a preparer's misrepresentation, or misquoting of the filing fee. *In re McDonald*, 318 B.R. 37, 43 (Bkrtcy. E.D.N.Y. 2004).

▶ A non attorney bankruptcy petition preparer violated the statute that regulated his conduct by failing to list his name, address, or social security number on any of the petitions which he either prepared or instructed the debtor on how to prepare, by failing to furnish the debtor with a copy of petitions, and by not filing a declaration disclosing all fees received. *In re France*, 271 B.R. 748 (Bkrtcy. E.D.N.Y., 2002).

▶ By telling a layman customer that she could not list her sister as a creditor on forms and by filling out her workbook, the nonattorney bankruptcy petition preparer violated New York state's rules against the unauthorized practice of law, and thus violated the Bankruptcy Code provision prohibiting fraudulent, unfair, or deceptive acts. *In re Tomlinson*, 343 B.R. 400 (E.D. N.Y. 2006).

Corporations Represented by Nonlawyers

▶ A corporation may appear as a party in any action brought pursuant to this act [Uniform Justice Court Act] except as otherwise provided in section eighteen hundred nine thereof by an attorney as well as by any authorized officer, director or employee of the corporation provided that the appearance by a nonlawyer on behalf of a corporation shall be deemed to constitute the requisite authority to bind the corporation in a settlement or trial. The court or arbitrator may make reasonable inquiry to determine the authority of any person who appears for the corporation in a case. Uniform Justice Court Act § 501.

▶ A corporation may appear in the defense of any small claim action brought pursuant to this article by an attorney as well as by any authorized officer, director, or employee of the corporation provided that the appearance by a nonlawyer on behalf of a corporation shall be deemed to constitute the requisite authority to bind the corporation in a settlement or trial. The court or arbitrator may make reasonable inquiry to determine the authority of any person who appears for the corporation in defense of a small claims court case. Uniform Justice Court Act § 1809(2). See also NY Uniform City Civ. Ct. Act § 1809(2); NY Uniform City Ct. Act § 1809(2); and NY Uniform Dist. Ct. Act § 1809(2).

Accountants and Tax Law

▶ In many fields of endeavor laymen acquire specialized knowledge which is relevant to the practice of law in that area. Thus accountants may know a great deal about tax law and labor relations consultants much about labor law. A specialized area of competence does not, however, entitle these laymen to engage in the business of giving legal advice based on their knowledge of the subjects. When legal documents are prepared for a layman by a person in the business of preparing such documents, that person is practicing law whether the documents be prepared in conformity with the law of New York or any other law. *In re Roel*, 3 N.Y.2d 224, 144 N.E.2d 24, 165 N.Y.S.2d 31 (1957).

▶ The accountant serves in setting up or auditing books, or advising with respect to the keeping of books and records, the making of entries therein and the handling of transactions for tax purposes and the preparation of tax returns. Naturally his work and advice must take cognizance of the law and conform with the law, particularly the tax law. The application of legal knowledge in such work, however, is only incidental to the accounting functions. It is not expected or permitted of the accountant, despite his knowledge or use of the law, to give legal advice which is unconnected with accounting work. *Application of New York County Lawyers' Ass'n*, 273 A.D. 524, 78 N.Y.S.2d 209 (1st Dept., 1948).

▶ A certified public accountant, who never stated or represented or conveyed the impression to any one that he was an attorney or entitled to practice law, was not engaged in unlawful "practice of law," though in expectation of compensation from taxpayer accountant submitted a memorandum giving his opinion that certain deductions could be legally made by taxpayer in its income tax return. *In re Bercu*, 188 Misc. 406, 69 N.Y.S.2d 730 (Sup. Ct., N.Y. Co., 1947).

▶ The ethics committee answered no to the following three questions: (1) May a lawyer form a "professional relationship" with an accountant, who is not a lawyer, for the purpose of providing clients with tax-related legal and accounting services? (2) May a lawyer share legal fees with an accountant? (3) May a lawyer state that he or she is a lawyer on stationery shared with an accountant who is not a lawyer? Opinion 557 (2/17/84) New York State Bar Association Committee on Professional Ethics. (*www.nysba.org/AM/Template.cfm?Section=Ethics_Opinions&TEMPLATE=/CM/ContentDisplay.cfm&CONTENTID=18446*) (1984 WL 50012)

Scope of a Power of Attorney

▶ May a nonattorney armed with a power of attorney appear in the place of a pro se party at trial in small claims court? New York law contains several provisions that permit a nonlawyer to appear in court in the place of a party, such as CPLR article 12 [pertaining to the appointment of a guardian ad litem, see *New York Life Insurance Co. v. V.K.*, 184 Misc. 2d 727, 711 N.Y.S.2d 90 (N.Y.C. Civ. Ct., N.Y. Co., 1999)]; NYCCA § 1809 [pertaining to the appearance on a small claim of a corporation by a nonlawyer, who is an officer, director, or employee with requisite authority]; and NYCCA § 1815 [pertaining to court permission in the interest of justice that a nonlawyer related by consanguinity or affinity represent a party due to that party's age, mental or physical capacity, or other disability]. Citing the "substantial justice" criterion in small claims actions under NYCCA § 1804, judges have also allowed a mother in her own name to prosecute her infant's personal injury action, *Buonomo v. Stalker*, 40 A.D.2d 733, 336 N.Y.S.2d 687 (3rd Dept., 1972), and a wife, where there was no personal representative appointed, to pursue property damages on behalf of her husband who died during the pendency of the claim, *Bogart v. Imports of Wantagh*, 142 Misc.2d 105, 536 N.Y.S.2d 391 (Long Beach City Ct., 1988). None of those provisions or exigent circumstances are present to justify a claimant presenting his attorney in fact in his own stead on the trial of the claim at bar. Judiciary Law §§ 478 and 484 prohibit persons from appearing as an attorney-at-law for a person other than himself in any court of record unless such person is licensed and admitted to the practice of law. *Gilman v. Kipp*, 136 Misc.2d 860, 519 N.Y.S.2d 314 (Syracuse City Court, 1987). While an individual has the right to appear pro se (that is, personally or for one's self), such individual may not be represented in court by another person who is not an attorney. By this holding, the court does not necessarily diverge from the holdings, of *Buonomo* and *Bogart*, which, based upon the substantial justice standard of the small claims part, permitted, respectively, a mother to appear for her child and a wife to appear for her deceased husband. Neither case is precedent for the right of a solo practitioner medical doctor to delegate to a paralegal his right to testify about medical necessity or other matters only within the doctor's knowledge. *Richstone v. Bell Atlantic*, 2001 WL 1537394 (N.Y. City Civ. Ct., N.Y. Co., 2001).

Attorney in Fact Cannot Practice Law

▶ An attorney in fact is one authorized to act in place of or for another. The statutory short form power of attorney, however, does not give a nonattorney authority to practice law in the court of record on behalf of his or her principal. *Stokes v. Village of Wurtsboro*, 123 Misc.2d 694, 474 N.Y.S.2d 660 (Sup. Ct., Sull. Co., 1984).

Attorney Disciplined in Cases Involving Paralegal UPL

▶ Attorneys have supervisory responsibility over non-lawyers in a law office. 22 NYCRR 1200.39.

▶ Attorney censured. The attorney's paralegal engaged in the unauthorized practice of immigration law. In addition, he became partners with a non-lawyer and shared fees with her, both violations of disciplinary rules. *In re Meltzer*, 293 A.D.2d 202, 741 N.Y.S.2d 240 (1st Dept., 2002).

▶ Attorney censured. The attorney's inadequate supervision of his paralegal led to the paralegal's engaging in the unauthorized practice of law. *Matter of Bonanno*, 208 A.D.2d 1117, 741 N.Y.S.2d 240 (3rd Dept., 1994).

Nonlawyer Posing as a Lawyer

▶ In a criminal prosecution, where a defendant had been at all times represented by an admitted attorney, the mere participation of a nonlawyer in the defense did not, without more, deprive defendant of his right to effective assistance of counsel or mandate reversal. Earlier this Court held that when a defendant in a criminal proceeding has unwittingly been represented by a layman masquerading as an attorney but in fact not licensed to practice law, his conviction must be set aside without regard to whether he was individually prejudiced by such representation. We decline to extend this rule of per se reversal to every situation, such as that before us, in which a nonlawyer participates in a trial as co-counsel with an admitted attorney. *People v. Jacobs*, 6 N.Y.3d 188, 844 N.E.2d 1126, 811 N.Y.S.2d 604 (2005).

▶ An attorney was censured for aiding someone in the unauthorized practice of law. The attorney sent his paralegal to a child support hearing with his client. The paralegal acknowledged that she did not correct the hearing officer's misunderstanding that she was an attorney. The paralegal entered an appearance on the record, allowed herself to be addressed as counselor, and acted as an advocate for the client. *In the Matter of Pomper*, 889 N.Y.S.2d 868 (2nd Dept., 2009).

Action for the Unauthorized Practice of Law

▶ The attorney-general may maintain an action upon his own information or upon the complaint of a private person or of a bar association organized and existing under the laws of this state against any person, partnership, corporation, or association, and any employee, agent, director, or officer thereof who commits any act or engages in any conduct prohibited by law as constituting the unlawful practice of the law. NY Judiciary Law § 476-a(1).

Disbarred or Suspended Attorneys

▶ Judiciary Law § 90 directs the Appellate Divisions to "command" every lawyer who is disbarred or suspended "to desist and refrain from the practice of law *in any form*, either as principal or *as agent, clerk or employee of another*" [emphasis supplied]. The danger that an unsuspecting member of the public or even other lawyers may be misled as to the status of a disbarred lawyer who is employed by a law firm is too grave to ignore. Moreover, such employment, especially for the purposes stated in the present inquiry, runs counter to the intent of the order imposing discipline. It is always the lawyer's duty to uphold the orders of a court and to avoid the appearance of impropriety. Consequently it is the opinion of this Committee that it is improper for a licensed lawyer to employ a disbarred lawyer for any purpose, or in any capacity, related to the practice of law. We express no opinion as to whether a disbarred lawyer may be employed in some other capacity such as a process server, messenger, secretary, investigator, etc. In Kentucky, a disbarred lawyer can prepare title abstracts and do legal research. Kentucky E-255 (1982): "We do not so approve as these activities are clearly related to the practice of law." Opinion 666 (October 29, 1985), New York County Lawyers' Association Committee on Professional Ethics. (*www.nycla.org/siteFiles/Publications/Publications440_0.pdf*) (1985 WL 287691)

▶ It is worth repeating that N.Y. County 666 declined to opine on whether a disbarred lawyer might properly be employed by a law firm as a process server, messenger, secretary, or investigator; and we concur that only the Appellate Division, on proper application, can decide such an issue or, for that matter, whether there are circumstances in which a disbarred attorney might be able to act as a paralegal while "desist[ing] and refrain[ing] from the practice of law in any form." Opinion 1998-1 (12/21/98) Association of the Bar of the City of New York Committee on Professional and judicial Ethics. (*www.nycbar.org/Ethics/eth1998.htm*) (1998 WL 1557150)

▶ An attorney may not aid a nonlawyer, including a disbarred or suspended attorney, in the unauthorized practice of law. It is improper for an attorney or law firm to employ a disbarred or suspended attorney in any capacity related to practice of law. Opinion 1998-1 (12/21/98) Association of the Bar of the City of New York Committee on Professional and Judicial Ethics. (*http://www.nycbar.org/Ethics/eth1998.htm*) (1998 WL 1557150)

▶ Whether an attorney may ethically employ a suspended attorney to draft pleadings, contracts, trust agreements and wills, and to perform legal research as a "litigation analyst," depends on the scope of the rules and statutes governing the unauthorized practice of law and the scope of the specific suspension order at issue. If the employing attorney knows that the suspended attorney would be violating the suspension order or engaging in the unauthorized practice of law, the employing attorney may not ethically employ the suspended attorney in the described capacity. Opinion 95-15 (8/30/95) Nassau County Bar Association Committee on Professional Ethics. (*www.nassaubar.org/Ethics%20Opinions/Archive/Opinion 95-15.aspx*)

Miscellaneous

▸ **A "pro se paralegal" cannot file a motion for another.** In this case the defendant is neither proceeding pro se nor is he represented by counsel. He has a self-styled "pro se paralegal" representing him. A layperson, regardless of his educational qualifications or experience, is not a substitute for a member of the Bar. The right to counsel means the right to an attorney. It does not mean that a criminal defendant has the right to choose to be represented by a layperson. Therefore, Woodrow Flemming, as "pro se paralegal," does not have the authority to file the instant motion on behalf of the defendant. *People v. Smith*, 12 Misc.3d 1190(A), 824 N.Y.S.2d 769 (Sup. Ct., Queens Co., 2006).

▸ **Solicitation.** An attorney may hire a nonlawyer to assist in administrative and non-professional tasks with regard to a direct mail solicitation and the interaction with clients acquired through this solicitation as long as the attorney retains his or her supervisory role. The attorney's nonlawyer consultant, however, should not contact by telephone those who do not respond to the direct mail solicitation. NYSBA Opinion 720 (5/5/97) (1997 WL 232467).

▸ **A nonattorney cannot be a district attorney.** A nonattorney was not eligible for election to the position as county district attorney, since the legal nature of important public responsibilities entrusted to state district attorneys require that such individuals be lawyers admitted to practice. *Curry v. Hosley*, 86 N.Y.2d 470, 657 N.E.2d 1311, 634 N.Y.S.2d 28 (1995).

▸ **Nonattorney can prosecute petty cases.** There is an exception to the prohibition against the unlicensed practice of law for petty prosecutions due to the historical high volume of such prosecutions, which district attorneys cannot handle. District attorneys, however, must prosecute all felonies. *People v. Jackson*, 145 Misc.2d 1020, 548 N.Y.S.2d 987 (Sup. Ct., Kings Co., 1989).

▸ **Paralegals staffing a help line at a corporation.** A paralegal can be part of a help line for a compliance program at a corporation, but must not be allowed to exercise professional judgment such as determining whether a conflict of interest ("adversity") exists between the caller and the corporation. While the Code of Professional Responsibility is addressed to lawyers, not paralegals, attorneys must be diligent in the supervision of nonlawyer employees in order that the obligations of the attorney be met. See EC 4-4, EC 4-5. Further, tasks assigned paralegals must not violate DR 3-101(A). A determination of "adversity," for example, might require professional judgment. If so, it cannot properly be delegated to a legal assistant. Opinion 650 (6/30/93) New York State Bar Association Committee on Professional Ethics. (*www.nysba.org/AM/ Template.cfm?Section=Home&TEMPLATE=/CM/Content Display.cfm&CONTENTID=18737*) (1993 WL 560291)

▸ A lawyer who continues to represent a client in a transaction in which the counter-party has chosen to be represented by a nonlawyer is not thereby aiding the unauthorized practice of law. Opinion 809 (2/12/07) New York State Bar Association Committee on Professional Ethics. (*www .nysba.org/AM/Template.cfm?Section=Ethics_Opinions& TEMPLATE=/CM/ContentDisplay.cfm&CONTENTID= 13670*) (2007 WL 833429)

▸ **Nonattorney judges.** Absent some showing that the interests of justice required removal, defendant was not entitled to have misdemeanor charges of operating a vehicle with a suspended license prosecuted by way of formal indictment rather than trial by town justice, especially as there were no complex legal issues and no mens rea to be determined, and due process did not mandate removal notwithstanding that the town justice was a nonlawyer. *People v. Mossow*, 118 Misc.2d 522, 461 N.Y.S.2d 191 (County Ct., Oswego Co., 1983).

D. Recommendations of State Bar Committee on Nonlawyer Practice

In the mid-1990s, the American Bar Association conducted a study of independents who provide services to the public without attorney supervision. The ABA referred to these individuals as legal technicians. It issued a report that outlined the steps that should be followed by the state when it is deciding whether to expand the scope of what legal technicians and other independents are allowed to do. American Bar Association, Commission on Nonlawyer Practice, *Nonlawyer Activity in Law-Related Situations* (1995).

The New York State Bar Association established an Ad Hoc Committee on Nonlawyer Practice to respond to the work of the ABA. This committee did not favor expanding the role of the legal technician. Although New York has not expanded the role of legal technicians or other independents (only a few states, e.g., Washington State, have done so), the arguments of the ad hoc committee are important in understanding the parameters of the practice of law in New York.

New York State Bar Association Ad Hoc Committee on NonLawyer Practice, *Final Report* (May 1995) (*www.cdpa.info/files/NY_Paralegal_guidelines.pdf*).

A. The Ad Hoc Committee on Nonlawyer Practice Supports the Expanded Use and Role of the Traditional Paralegal as an Approach Preferable to the Recognition of the Legal Technician.

---

1. The Committee believes that only an attorney should be responsible for analyzing legal problems and giving legal advice

A matter may come into an office sounding in "tort" but may require an attorney's knowledge of bankruptcy, labor law or some other area with which a legal technician may not be familiar. The attorney, through his or her training and education, and under the Code of Professional Responsibility which states that the lawyer shall not take on a matter which the lawyer is not competent to handle, is better able to "see the whole picture" that may develop in the course of representation.

For instance, if an Executrix under a will comes into the office to probate the will, she may have to be counseled, in addition to collecting and accounting for assets and payment of debts, in the following activities: selling real property (release of liens, transfer of property, possible partition action); bankruptcy of borrower to whom decedent lent money; after-born children contesting the will; etc.

While a traditional legal assistant should not independently advise a client concerning legal rights and duties (NYSBA Ethics Opinion 44 [1967]), the chances of such advice-offering increase dramatically with the legal technician.

So long as the attorney is present in the relationship, the client may be counseled by the attorney as to his or her rights and responsibilities.

2. The Committee recommends that court rules and ethical rules be developed to encourage the expanded use of the traditional paralegal

In some courtrooms around the State, legal assistants are allowed to answer calendar calls and submit affidavits of engagement or unopposed motions; in others they are not. The Uniform Court Rules should be expanded to permit the use of paralegals for calendar calls, motions, adjournments and submissions of consent orders for disclosure.

For example, if a court requires the presence of an individual in the trial assignment part pending assignment to a nonjury part or for jury selection, the legal assistant can perform these responsibilities in lieu of a lawyer. The result would be cost savings to the client and better use of the attorney's time, which can be spent working on other legal matters. While this is permitted in some localities, elsewhere it is not.

In some communities, legal assistants perform most, if not all, of the legal work at real estate closings, without the physical presence of an attorney. While the Committee has not attempted to assess the feasibility or desirability of any particular localized practices, we urge NYSBA, perhaps under the leadership of the [Law Practice Management] Committee and with the assistance of the Ethics Committee, to review existing ethical guidelines with a view towards expanding the use and role of legal assistants in a more uniform manner statewide.

3. The Committee believes that the expanded use of the professional traditional paralegal will benefit both client and bar

The traditional paralegal, through training, education and/or experience, has the capacity to make a greater contribution to the public. It goes without saying that some legal assistants know more about some technical aspects of practice areas than do some lawyers. While the lawyer must continue to maintain an involved relationship with clients, the paralegal can serve as a liaison and provide individual contact with the client. The client has a contact when the attorney is in court or otherwise unavailable and a relationship of trust may be developed, benefiting both public and bar.

Fiscally, the use of paralegals makes sense. In addition, the United States Supreme Court has stated that "reasonable attorney's fees" include compensation for a paralegal's time on work of a nonclerical nature. (*Missouri v. Jenkins*, 491 U.S. 274 (1989).)

The expanded use of traditional legal assistants also presents an opportunity to service poor and lower middle income persons. As explained by the Chief Judge's Committee to Improve the Availability of Legal Services (otherwise known as the "Marrero Committee"):

Certified paralegals, under the supervision of attorneys, are capable of performing many vital functions such as interviewing, screening, research and drafting. Many perform similar work in private law firms and could help relieve the workload of attorneys in legal services programs. Recruitment and training of paralegals can be achieved under the auspices of existing legal services organizations and bar associations. Further, the increased use of traditional paralegals may help reduce the cost of legal services, thereby helping to serve those people who cannot afford lawyers' fees. (*Report of the Chief Judge's Committee to Improve the Availability of Legal Services*, April 1990.)

Indeed, these expectations have been partially realized in New York. For example, in Onondaga County, legal assistants have been an integral part of pro bono projects in housing court, will clinics, and simple divorce proceedings. Similar service is being provided across the state in various pro bono programs. These are being provided by volunteer legal assistants with no formal "obligation" to do so.

4. The Committee recommends the increased use of bar publications and CLE programs to promote the use of paralegals, such as a series of articles informing the bar about the qualifications, ability and professionalism of legal assistants

Despite the considerable evidence built over many years supporting the premise that legal assistants are valuable members of the legal "team," the legal profession still fails to fully avail itself of the talent such individuals offer. Attorneys are still not aware of the capabilities of legal assistants.

The bar must be educated that the traditional legal assistant is a true professional. Articles should be written in NYSBA publications about the utilization and role of legal assistants. Economic benefits to the attorney without compromising quality should be stressed, as well as benefits to the client.

In addition, [Continuing Legal Education and Law Practice Management] programs on the state and local bar association level should be offered on a more frequent basis for legal assistants and for attorneys. The Nassau Academy of Law, for instance, has given programs in which the attorney and paralegal spoke as a team on various substantive topics, reinforcing the image of the paralegal as a professional.

> **B. The Committee Supports Continued Study of Regulation of NonLawyers and Recommends Against Imposition of a New System of Regulation at This Time.**

Although there has been considerable study of various forms of regulation in other jurisdictions, in the opinion of the Committee, there is no clearly superior form of proposed regulation. The following points highlight the major issues related to regulation.

1. Need to protect the public

Of those jurisdictions that have surveyed or studied the topic, there is uniform consensus that consumers are accessing the justice system without the aid of lawyers. Moreover, such activity is on the increase. Frequently, the consumer fares well. However, there are many instances when grave harm befalls the consumer and there is little or no recourse to be had. Such harm is most prevalent in the areas of family law (divorces), immigration law, bankruptcy, consumer law, and landlord/tenant practice.

It is possible that much of this harm can be eliminated by a regulatory system that makes affordable legal services available to those consumers who now seek services from nonlawyers. Usually, the reason for avoiding attorney representation is economic.

Even regulation, however, cannot cure the fundamental problem associated with the degree of knowledge and experience that is necessary to render competent legal advice. For any particular set of facts there may be other rights, more appropriate remedies, or opportunities involved than are presented by the initial inquiry. A lawyer is trained to recognize these. Therefore, it is extremely difficult to predict when a lawyer will never be needed, regardless of the regulatory system.

2. Mandatory versus voluntary regulation

Legal assistants will be the principal profession affected by regulation. In fact, depending upon the definitions and scope of any specific regulatory scheme, legal assistants may be the only profession affected. When one considers the current status of the legal assistant profession and the wide disparity of education, experience and function of legal assistants, it can be easily concluded that mandatory across-the-board regulation will be opposed by both lawyers and legal assistants. Legitimate concerns about the time and cost of training, refresher courses, examination fees and annual registration fees will be raised.

Moreover, across-the-board mandatory regulation is likely to increase the cost of legal services to some extent and possibly decrease the "supply" of nonlawyer practitioners. Many attorneys and legal assistants, for their own individual reasons, may prefer the status quo ante.

On the other hand, a regulatory scheme that enhances the role of nonlawyer practitioners will attract the interest of many legal assistants. If the costs of the regulatory scheme are properly controlled, such individuals will ultimately be in a position to reduce the cost of some legal services by allowing the supervisory lawyer to delegate less complex activities and concentrate on more complex issues.

3. Regulatory authority

Many administrative agencies already regulate nonlawyer representation. [In the Federal tax area, for example, there is extensive regulation of nonlawyer services. The Internal Revenue Code requires that tax return preparers sign returns, and provides civil and criminal penalties for improper conduct. Representation before the Internal Revenue Service by other than lawyers and accountants requires qualification as an enrolled agent, including an examination process. Also, the Internal Revenue Service has issued extensive regulations governing tax practice. The Director of Practice monitors reports of incompetence or misconduct, and has substantial disciplinary authority over tax practitioners. The bar has an important role in consulting with the Service concerning its standards of tax practice and in reporting any serious incompetence or misconduct, but in this area of practice there may be little need to replace or significantly supplement the existing regulatory structure.]

[I]f there is to be broader regulation [of legal assistants], consideration should be given to who would administer the regulatory scheme. Should it be the New York State Department of Education, which now administers most licenses, or should it be the courts? If the courts, should it be as comprehensive as lawyer regulation or something different? Should a private entity such as the bar association, NALA or NFPA be considered? This issue is sure to engender discussion and controversy. With ever increasing demands on the public fisc, it is unlikely that a state or court administered program would be funded with taxpayer dollars.

Some nonlawyers have expressed reservations about being regulated by lawyers rather than members of their own profession. Although in New York the integrity of the practice of law is entrusted to the courts and therein is the likely seat of regulation, the costs and other associated burdens may make some alternative more attractive, especially if a voluntary scheme is implemented.

4. Qualifications

The issue of who qualifies for the "title" ("Registrant," "Licensee," "Certified") will cause great study and debate. How much weight should be given to education? How much weight should be given to experience? Typically, lawyers have little or no experience when they are granted a license. Should different criteria apply to legal assistants? Many proposals have been made in various states and provinces. None are identical. All require a combination of education and experience. Formal education in legal assistant programs is typically given greater weight than a bachelor's degree in a social science. Sometimes ABA-approved legal assistant training programs are given greater weight than non-ABA-approved programs. The issue of what qualifications are appropriate in New York will require careful consideration.

5. *Scope of activity*

A critical issue that must be defined (and thereafter will require constant vigilance) is the nature and extent of services and activities that the regulated person will be authorized to perform. At the present time there are, apparently, differences among New York jurisdictions as to the latitude granted to nonlawyer practitioners. A formal definition of what is and what is not allowed will be required.

6. *Supervision*

[A proposal of a Minnesota Supreme Court Study Committee] would limit the registered lawyer to the supervision of two registered legal assistants. This is admittedly an arbitrary constraint and the Minnesota study committee considered it to be a "pilot project" until some practical experience was gained.

The issue of supervision is an important one. It is difficult not to acknowledge that some legal assistants know more about the nuts and bolts of some processes than their supervising attorneys. Real estate transactions may be a good example. The legal assistant is probably more familiar with the currently required affidavits and fees than the attorney. However, the attorney is better able to assess the essence of the transaction and the overall legal position of the client.

Although the NYSBA has promulgated Guidelines for the Utilization of Legal Assistants, a comprehensive review of these guidelines would be required as part of the imposition of a regulatory scheme.

7. *Cost/benefit analysis*

It is difficult to perform a cost/benefit analysis of a regulatory scheme in the abstract. However, some fundamental points may be recognized. The implementation of a regulatory scheme presumes that certain legal assistants will be allowed to perform legal services presently reserved only to attorneys. If it can also be assumed that these services will be performed at lower rates, then access to legal services will be opened to a larger segment of the public. That segment includes the lower to moderate income sector which frequently forgoes proper legal representation. Assuming further that attorney supervision is part of the scheme, proper legal representation may become available to more of the public, thereby greatly enhancing the goal of access to justice.

The cost of a regulatory scheme depends upon many factors. Private administration (such as the NALA-CLA Program) versus regulation by state agency must be considered. Expansion of the current OCA (Office of Court Administration) program must be considered (*www.courts.state.ny.us/admin/oca.shtml*). Clearly, fees will be required to offset the costs associated with administration. It must also be recognized that such fees will ultimately be borne by the client. Also, to the extent that fees do not adequately cover administrative expenses, the general public may be forced to fund some part of the regulatory scheme.

8. *Conclusion*

The Committee was impressed with the analytical framework utilized by the Minnesota Supreme Court Study Committee and believes it useful to reiterate several themes expressed by that committee. First, the

Minnesota committee attempted to identify certain categories of legal services that could be provided by a legal assistant without supervision by an attorney. They concluded, however, that

> the practice of law does not lend itself to the identification of discrete routine services. Few clients seek the services of an attorney to perform a clearly defined task . . . Although a legal assistant may be competent to prepare a simple deed after it is determined that the client needs a deed, preparing the deed is a small part of the legal services rendered. *Determining that the deed is what the client needs is the more significant service provided by an attorney.* (Emphasis supplied)

The Minnesota committee also expressed concern that granting licenses to legal assistants to practice in a specialty area will not guarantee proper representation in that such a person might not recognize aspects of a case that involve areas of the law outside that specialty. Thus, the committee determined that it was not "feasible to specify certain legal procedures that a legal assistant would be allowed to provide without attorney supervision."

Furthermore, the Minnesota committee expressed concern over the creation of another regulatory system similar to that for lawyers. In language which this Committee finds persuasive, they stated:

> Although there is no inherent bar to the creation of a regulatory system for legal assistants, an elaborate system is already in place for lawyers. Creating a second system would be justified if it would result in significantly cheaper costs to the consumers of legal services without unacceptable risk, but it was not apparent to the committee how independent licensure would achieve these goals.

With so many unresolved problematic issues, the Committee cannot conclude the public interest would be served by any system of regulation, licensing or mandated certification at this time.

C. The Committee Recommends Active Enforcement of U.P.L. Statutes.

Preventing the practice of law by those unqualified to provide legal services not only safeguards against harm to the public, but enhances the image of attorneys who are licensed to practice. Those who provide legal services under the guise of nonlawyers, such as disbarred lawyers, document preparers or unregulated legal technicians, are wholly unaccountable for their malfeasance.

The Committee feels that the NYSBA has a legitimate role to play in monitoring the unauthorized practice of law and assisting those charged by law with enforcing our unlawful practice statutes. However, this role must be viewed as only a part of a total effort and larger initiative to bring access to justice to the entire populace. We believe that implementation of alternative delivery systems (see D.) and enhanced utilization of traditional legal assistants should be significant aspects of such an initiative. We, therefore, recommend that the U.P.L. Committee be reconstituted to its former active role, including the issuance of advisory opinions. We understand there are certain safeguards, which have been recommended to our association, to ensure that the NYSBA does not encounter anti-trust objections to our activities. Those safeguards, such as appropriate disclaimers in written opinions, we find to be quite manageable.

The State Bar should encourage continued vigorous activity by the Attorney General and local District Attorneys in enjoining violations of the statutes prohibiting the practice of law without a license. Through the various outreach media available (e.g., the *State Bar Journal, State Bar News,* etc.), the NYSBA should educate its members as to the various Attorney General offices which handle unauthorized practice complaints. The Committee also recommends that the District Grievance Committees, which often receive complaints of unauthorized practice, sometimes by disbarred or suspended lawyers, be supplied with the same information and be encouraged to report instances of U.P.L. when detected.

D. The Committee Recommends Consideration and Implementation of Alternative Delivery Systems for Lawyers' Services.

The growing unmet legal needs of New Yorkers of modest and moderate means demand that legal services be provided effectively and be affordable. Sometimes this simply means making available attorneys accessible to clients. Other times this means that legal services must be provided in an affordable manner that is responsive to the needs of clients and attorneys. Viable alternatives to the traditional delivery system should be considered and implemented to protect New Yorkers from the unfortunate consequences which may arise if legal services are provided without attorney involvement. Among these alternatives are prepaid legal services programs, assisted pro se litigation programs, modest means fee panels, and programs to match under-utilized attorneys with clients with unmet legal needs.

The Committee understands that Association President Witmer has now appointed a Commission on Legal Services for the Middle Income, to be chaired by Robert L. Geltzer of New York City. The Committee applauds this step which is designed to identify the major problems confronting middle income consumers of legal services and to devise workable solutions. In hopes that our work can provide useful suggestions to Mr. Geltzer's Commission, we offer the following recommendations.

1. *Matching under-utilized attorneys and clients with unmet legal needs*

Although the Committee is unable to point to working models, the Committee is struck by the anomaly which exists in the marketplace for legal services. At the same time so many decry the unavailability of legal services at affordable rates, many of our members and many newly admitted lawyers are unable to find full-time employment or maintain economically viable practices. This suggests that experimentation is in order with programs which provide a matching mechanism for under-utilized attorneys and clients of modest means. Perhaps the organized bar can establish umbrella organizations, possibly modeled after the Legal Services Corporation, but privately funded and operating on a non-profit basis, which will actually employ attorneys, provide legal assistant and secretarial staffing, back office functions and equipment, eligibility screening and billing/collection services, all designed to provide legal representation at reduced rates; that is, non-profit legal clinics that provide employment to lawyers and legal services to those who otherwise cannot afford lawyers.

2. *Prepaid legal service plans present an effective vehicle for providing legal services from the perspective of both clients and attorneys*

The client is relieved of anxiety over the amount and method of payment for legal services, and the attorney is guaranteed that he or she will be paid an agreed-upon fee for the services provided. The ABA and NYSBA have encouraged the development of such panels. (See *Civil Justice: An Agenda for the 1990's*, Report of the American Bar Association National Conference on Access to Justice in the 1990s, 39 (1991).) The ABA has urged Congress to permanently enact revisions to the Internal Revenue Code encouraging employer-funded prepaid plans. Both the ABA and NYSBA encourage attorney participation in prepaid panels. While concerns persist about profitability and quality control, these programs nonetheless provide a vehicle for increased access to attorneys for affordable legal services.

Credit card payment for legal services, whether as an adjunct to prepaid plans or otherwise, should be considered as a means of providing legal services to persons who cannot afford to pay fees out of current income.

3. *Modest means panels*

While various programs exist designed to address the legal needs of the poor and near-poor (those with incomes no greater than 125% of the poverty level), there are few programs devoted to the great number of our citizens who fail to qualify for Legal Aid Society or Legal Services Corporation services, or are not eligible for pro bono services.

In response to this problem, many local bar associations have recently begun to implement and/or experiment with modest/moderate means panels. These panels consist of attorneys who are willing to provide legal services at reduced rates to screened clients who meet income qualifications for such services. The screening process is similar to that utilized by pro bono and legal services organizations.

These modest/moderate means panels are administered by local bar associations, usually in conjunction with the local lawyer referral service. That service matches clients of modest means with the empaneled attorneys.

4. *Pro se assistance programs and clinics*

Certain jurisdictions utilize pro bono/pro se assistance programs to assist unrepresented litigants. In some cases, a court-appointed attorney presents defenses which would probably not be raised in the absence of an attorney. In the event more extensive legal work is required, the case could be transferred to a local legal services corporation office, if the client meets financial eligibility guidelines.

Pro se clinics are also offered to pro se litigants by pro bono organizations in matters such as bankruptcy and divorce. Attorneys would meet the client outside of court. However, as with the in-court programs, persons of modest means usually do not qualify for the services of a pro se clinic.

A most innovative program is under way in Maricopa County, Arizona, where a kiosk is set up in the courthouse, using computer programming, to lead pro se litigants through the maze of forms and procedures involved in litigation matters. Although New York courts do not seem well disposed to the idea, in the view of the Committee, pro se clerks in various court settings can make a major contribution to improving the public's access to the legal system.

Unless the profession can find alternatives to traditionally delivered legal services to meet the challenges of the marketplace, we will be unable to effectively respond to calls for de-licensing of legal services or licensing of nonlawyer services. In our view, both the public and the bar will suffer as a result.

E. Recommendations of City Bar Committee on Nonlawyer Practice

The Committee on the Profession of the Association of the Bar of the City of New York in its 1992 report, *Is Professionalism Declining?*, and the ABA Commission on Professionalism in its 1986 report, advocated a greater role [for paralegals]. Recently, the City Bar's Committee on Professional Responsibility gave its "preliminary endorsement to a deregulated licensing approach that permits greater nonlawyer practice in specified areas but [which] establishes minimal requirements . . . ." *Prohibition on Nonlawyer Practice: An Overview and Preliminary Assessment*, 50 Record 190, 209 (1995). Formal Opinion 1995-11, Association of the Bar of the City of New York Committee on Professional and Judicial Ethics (1995).

F. Position on the Unauthorized Practice of Law by the Empire State Alliance of Paralegal Associations

Position Statement on the Unauthorized Practice Of Law In New York State (Adopted February 1, 2003), Empire State Alliance of Paralegal Associations (*www .empirestateparalegals.org/position_papers*). Reprinted with the permission of the Empire State Alliance of Paralegal Associations.

The Empire State Alliance of Paralegal Associations and its member associations ("ESAPA") are concerned with increased unauthorized practice of law activity in New York State. The unauthorized practice of law damages the legal profession and the public it serves.

Misuse of the title "paralegal" and "legal assistant" confuses the public and negatively impacts the paralegal profession. The ESAPA does not support paralegals or other nonlawyers who participate in the unauthorized practice of law.

In response to the need to effectively curb the unauthorized practice of law in New York State, the ESAPA has chosen to take a pro-active position on this issue by:

- Investigating and reporting UPL activity
- Participating in legislative activity involving UPL issues
- Developing and expanding working relationships with bar associations and other law-related entities against UPL
- Increasing efforts to educate the public on nonlawyer services, attorneys on paralegal utilization, paralegals and other nonlawyers on ethical boundaries of nonlawyers and the practice of law, and acting as an information resource on the paralegal profession

This Position Statement is respectfully submitted for your consideration in an effort to foster continuing dialogue on this issue with those who share the common goal of the delivery of quality legal services by legal professionals in accordance with the laws of the State of New York.

Unauthorized Practice of Law ("UPL") and The State of New York.

UPL Defined or Undefined

The "practice of law" has yet to be clearly defined. Ethics Opinion #304 issued in 1973 by the New York State Bar Association ("NYSBA") Committee on Professional Ethics states: "It would be violative of accepted professional standards to delegate to a law clerk studying in a law office under a certificate of clerkship, or to a law school graduate awaiting bar admission, or to a paralegal employee, or to any unlicensed individual any function which calls for the professional judgment of a lawyer."

The Opinion further states that the delegation of certain tasks to nonlawyer employees permitted by EC3-6 and Ethics Opinion #255 issued in 1972 "does not extend to any matter where the exercise of professional legal judgment is required."

Prohibition of the unauthorized practice of law has been addressed in the NYSBA Code of Professional Responsibility ("NYSBA Code"), court decisions and statues. New York Judiciary Laws 478 and 484 restrict the practice of law to those who are "regularly admitted to practice, as an attorney or counselor, in the courts of record in the state."

The *Guidelines for Utilization by Lawyers of the Services of Legal Assistants* approved by the NYSBA House of Delegates on June 28, 1997 ("Guidelines") include:

- **Guideline II. Unauthorized Practice of Law.** A lawyer shall not assist a legal assistant in the performance of an activity that constitutes the unauthorized practice of law.
- **Guideline III. Authorized Practice of Law.** A legal assistant may perform certain functions otherwise prohibited when and only to the extent authorized by statute, court rule or decision, or administrative rule or regulation.

Further, the Commentary for Guideline III states: "A legal assistant is not engaged in the unauthorized practice of law when acting in compliance with statutes, court rules or decisions, or administrative rules and regulations which establish authority in specific areas for a lay person to appear on behalf of parties to proceedings before administrative agencies."

Professional Ethics and UPL

The NYSBA Code states in Canon 3 that a "lawyer should assist in preventing the unauthorized practice of law." Paralegals are not directly bound by the NYSBA

Code; however, similar principles are recited in the codes of paralegal associations:

- **National Association of Legal Assistants.** Code of Ethics and Professional Responsibility:

  Canon 3—A legal assistant must not: a. engage in, encourage, or contribute to any act which would constitute the unauthorized practice of law. . . .

  Canon 4—A legal assistant must use discretion commensurate with knowledge and experience but must not render independent legal judgment in place of an attorney. The services of an attorney are essential in the public interest whenever such legal judgment is required.

- **National Federation of Paralegal Associations.** Model Code of Ethics and Professional Responsibility and Guidelines for Enforcement:

  1.8 A paralegal shall not engage in the unauthorized practice of law.

  EC-1.8(a) A paralegal shall comply with the applicable legal authority governing the unauthorized practice of law in the jurisdiction in which the paralegal practices.

In the *Final Report*, NYSBA Ad Hoc Committee on NonLawyer Practice, May 1995 ("Ad Hoc Committee Report"), the Committee recommended active enforcement of the unauthorized practice of law statute:

- The State Bar should encourage continued vigorous activity by the Attorney General and local District Attorneys in enjoining violations of the statutes prohibiting the practice of law without a license.
- Preventing the practice of law by those unqualified to provide legal services not only safeguards against harm to the public, but enhances the images of attorneys who are licensed to practice law. Those who provide legal services under the guise of nonlawyers, such as disbarred lawyers, document preparers or unregulated legal technicians, are wholly unaccountable for their malfeasance.

Actions to Be Taken against the Unauthorized Practice of Law in New York State

---

Investigate and Report UPL Activity

Each ESAPA member association shall investigate UPL activity within its geographic area. If such investigation affirms UPL activity, the ESAPA member association shall report its findings to the local bar association and/or Office of the Attorney General as is customary in the area.

In the event the offender is a member of an ESAPA member association, direct contact shall be made with the offender to provide education materials and work to halt those activities which constitute the unauthorized

practice of law. Inadequate response by the offender shall result in termination of the offender's membership.

Participate in Legislative Activity Involving UPL Issues

The ESAPA shall monitor legislative activity involving UPL issues. When warranted, it shall establish contact with legislators to state its position against UPL and offer its services as an information resource.

Develop and Expand Working Relationships with Bar Associations and Other Law-Related Entities Against UPL

Each ESAPA member association shall communicate its position against UPL to law-related entities within its local legal community and offer its services as a co-worker in efforts to curb UPL activity. This Position Statement may be distributed for this purpose.

Increase Efforts to Educate the Public, Attorneys, Paralegals and Other NonLawyers

Each ESAPA member association shall work to increase understanding of the role of paralegals in the practice of law. The Guidelines may be used as an information resource. Further, the ESAPA shall pursue education efforts through the NYSBA, local bar associations and other law-related entities within its local legal community, as recommended in the Ad Hoc Committee Report: "The Committee recommends the increased use of bar publications and CLE programs to promote the use of paralegals, such as series of articles informing the bar about qualifications, ability and professionalism of legal assistants."

These education efforts may include distributing education materials, organizing and speaking at seminars, and authoring articles for bar association and other legal publications, on topics such as:

- paralegal utilization (generally and by law practice area)
- paralegal ethics (professional codes and NYSBA Ethics Opinions)
- issues surrounding nonlawyer services
- paralegal education standards and programs
- the paralegal profession, past, present and future

Act as an Information Resource on the Paralegal Profession

The ESAPA shall be the state-wide information resource on the paralegal profession and shall respond to inquiries, distribute information and provide speakers on paralegal utilization. Member associations may be contacted individually or through the ESAPA. [For a list of ESAPA members, see section 1.2.]

G. More Information

New York Rules of Professional Conduct
www.nycourts.gov/rules/jointappellate/NY%20Rules%20of%20Prof%20Conduct_09.pdf

www.nysba.org
(click "For Attorneys" then "Professional Standards for Attorneys")

Lawyer's Code of Professional Responsibility
www.law.cornell.edu/ethics/ny/code

www.nysba.org
(click "For Attorneys" then "Professional Standards for Attorneys")

Ethical Complaints against Attorneys
www.nysba.org
(click "For the Community" then "Resolving Conflict with a New York Attorney?")

American Legal Ethics Library
www.law.cornell.edu/ethics
(click "Listing by Jurisdiction" then "New York")

Defender Ethics Resources
www.nysda.org/html/ethics_resources.html

New York State Research Resources (including ethics)
www.ll.georgetown.edu/states/newyork-in-depth.cfm

Legal Ethics Resources on the Web
ww3.lawschool.cornell.edu/faculty-pages/wendel/ethlinks.htm

H. Something to Check

1. Run the following search ("unauthorized practice of law New York") in any three general search engines (e.g., *www.google.com, www.yahoo.com, www.bing.com, www.ask.com*). Prepare a report on the categories of sites to which each search engine leads you. Cluster the same kinds of sites you find into categories, e.g., sites giving you cases on UPL in New York, sites giving you bar associations in New York that have UPL resources, sites that give you law firms that represent clients suing other attorneys for UPL, etc. Give a brief description of each category with examples of web sites under each category. After you finish the report for the three general search engines, comment on which engine was the most productive and why.

2. Pick any three legal search engines (e.g., *www.findlaw.com, scholar.google.com, www.washlaw.edu, www.lawguru.com, www.rominger legal.com*). How effective is each in leading you to material about the unauthorized practice of law in New York? Describe what you are able to find.

3.2 New York Rules of Professional Conduct (RPC) and Related Judiciary Law Statutes

A. Introduction

B. Rules of Particular Relevance to Paralegals and Other Nonlawyers

C. Table of Contents of RPC

D. Index to the RPC

E. Text of the RPC

F. Selected Statutes from Judiciary Law (Article 15, Attorneys and Counsellors)

G. More Information

H. Something to Check

A. Introduction

The authority to practice law in New York is regulated by the Appellate Division Departments and the disciplinary committees. The Departments oversee the licensure of attorneys and their continued eligibility to practice, including discipline of attorneys through the disciplinary committees, payment of the biennial registration fee, and monitoring completion of mandatory CLE requirements. In addition, each Department has some substantive practice rules:

- Appellate Division, First Department, Part 603
- Appellate Division, Second Department, Part 691
- Appellate Division, Third Department, Part 806
- Appellate Division, Fourth Department, Part 1022

In general, attorneys are governed by (and can be disciplined by) the Department that admitted them to practice or the Department within whose geographical boundaries they practice:

"The supreme court shall have power and control over attorneys and counsellors-at-law and all persons practicing or assuming to practice law, and the appellate division of the supreme court in each department is authorized to censure, suspend from practice or remove from office any attorney and counsellor-at-law admitted to practice who is guilty of professional misconduct, malpractice, fraud, deceit, crime or misdemeanor, or any conduct prejudicial to the administration of justice; and the appellate division of the supreme court is hereby authorized to revoke such admission for any misrepresentation or suppression of any information in connection with the application for admission to practice." Judiciary Law § 90(2)

Rules of Professional Conduct

www.nycourts.gov/rules/jointappellate/NY%20Rules%20of%20Prof%20Conduct_09.pdf
(22 NYCRR 1200.0 to 22 NYCRR 1200.59.)

Effective in 2009, a new ethics code was approved by the Appellate Divisions of the State Supreme Court. The Rules of Professional Conduct (RPC) replace the Code of Professional Responsibility (CPR). The RPC sets out the minimum standards of conduct below which no lawyer can fall without being subject to disciplinary action.

We present the text of the RPC in its entirety. The RPC is based on the American Bar Association's Model Rules of Professional Conduct, as modified by the Appellate Divisions. Rules of particular note to paralegals and other nonlawyers are highlighted.

Judiciary Law

public.leginfo.state.ny.us/menugetf.cgi?COMMONQUERY=LAWS
(click "JUD" then "Article 15")

The Judiciary Law in the state's statutory code, particularly article 15, also contains regulatory provisions governing attorneys. It does not contain a comprehensive set of rules. It is primarily concerned with administrative requirements relating to admissions and registration, and a few substance matters such as the unauthorized practice of law (UPL), retainer agreements, contingency fees, solicitation, and Interest on Lawyer Account Fund (IOLA).

In this section we have included selected statutes in the Judiciary Law that are relevant to some of the ethical rules in the RPC, particular fees, and solicitation.

For other material on or related to ethics, see also:

- Part 1, Appendix A. Paralegals in Court Opinions (some of the court opinions summarized in Appendix A of Part 1 cover ethical issues)
- Section 3.1. Defining the Practice of Law and the Unauthorized Practice of Law
- Section 3.3. Ethical Opinions and Guidelines on Paralegals and Other Employees
- Part 3, Appendix A. Disciplinary Proceedings against an Attorney

---

B. Rules of Particular Relevance to Paralegals and Other Nonlawyers

Although all of the rules and official comments in the RPC are important, some are of particular relevance to paralegals and other nonlawyers. The section numbers (§) refer to related statutory provisions in the Judiciary Law.

> **Rules of Particular Relevance to Paralegals and other Nonlawyers**

Rule 1.0(t) Definition of screening (paralegals are sometimes screened to prevent disqualification due to conflict of interest)

Rule 1.5(a) When a fee is excessive

Rule 1.6(b) A lawyer may reveal confidential information when reasonably necessary to defend a paralegal or other employee against an accusation of wrongful conduct

Rule 1.6(c) A lawyer shall exercise reasonable care to prevent paralegals and other employees from disclosing or using confidential information

Rule 1.10(e) Conflicts-checking systems to avoid disqualification due to conflict of interest

Rule 1.15(e) Paralegals and other nonlawyers cannot be authorized signatories of client accounts

Rule 1.18(d) Notice to paralegals and other nonlawyer personnel of screening steps

Rule 4.2(a) A lawyer shall not allow another (e.g., a nonlawyer employee) to communicate with a party represented by counsel without the permission of the latter

Rule 4.5(a) A lawyer's employee shall not contact potential personal injury/wrongful death clients within a designated number of days after the incident involved

Rule 5.3 Ethical responsibilities for supervising paralegals and other nonlawyers

Rule 5.4(a) A lawyer must not share fees with nonlawyers

Rule 5.4(a)(3) Lawyers can compensate nonlawyer employees based on a profit-sharing arrangement

Rule 5.4(b) Lawyers cannot form a partnership with nonlawyers involving the practice of law

Rule 5.4(d) Nonlawyers cannot own or control the law firm or other entity engaged in the practice of law

Rule 5.5(b) A lawyer cannot aid a nonlawyer in the unauthorized practice of law

Rule 5.7(b) A nonlawyer cannot direct or regulate the professional legal judgment of a lawyer when the lawyer is engaged in providing nonlegal services

Rule 5.8(a) A lawyer cannot form a multi-disciplinary practice with a nonlawyer but can enter contracts with nonlegal professionals

Rule 7.5(a)(1) The use of business cards and letterheads by a law firm ("a law firm may also give the names of members and associates")

Rule 7.5(b) Nonlawyer names may not be part of the law firm's name

§§ 479, 482 It is unlawful for a lawyer's employee to solicit legal business

C. Table of Contents of RPC

D. Index to the RPC

(Section numbers (§) refer to sections of the Judiciary Law. All other numbers refer to rule numbers of the Rules of Professional Conduct.)

E. Text of the RPC

Rule 1.0: Terminology

> Text of the Rules

(a) "Advertisement" means any public or private communication made by or on behalf of a lawyer or law firm about that lawyer or law firm's services, the primary purpose of which is for the retention of the lawyer or law firm. It does not include communications to existing clients or other lawyers.

(b) "Belief" or "believes" denotes that the person involved actually believes the fact in question to be true. A person's belief may be inferred from circumstances.

(c) "Computer-accessed communication" means any communication made by or on behalf of a lawyer or law firm that is disseminated through the use of a computer or related electronic device, including, but not limited to, web sites, weblogs, search engines, electronic mail, banner advertisements, pop-up and pop-under advertisements, chat rooms, list servers, instant messaging, or other internet presences, and any attachments or links related thereto.

(d) "Confidential information" is defined in Rule 1.6.

(e) "Confirmed in writing" denotes (i) a writing from the person to the lawyer confirming that the person has given consent, (ii) a writing that the lawyer promptly transmits to the person confirming the person's oral consent, or (iii) a statement by the person made on the record of any proceeding before a tribunal. If it is not feasible to obtain or transmit the writing at the time the person gives oral consent, then the lawyer must obtain or transmit it within a reasonable time thereafter.

(f) "Differing interests" include every interest that will adversely affect either the judgment or the loyalty of a lawyer to a client, whether it be a conflicting, inconsistent, diverse, or other interest.

(g) "Domestic relations matter" denotes representation of a client in a claim, action or proceeding, or preliminary to the filing of a claim, action or proceeding, in either Supreme Court or Family Court, or in any court of appellate jurisdiction, for divorce, separation, annulment, custody, visitation, maintenance, child support, alimony, or to enforce or modify a judgment or order in connection with any such claim, action or proceeding.

(h) "Firm" or "law firm" includes, but is not limited to, a lawyer or lawyers in a law partnership, professional corporation, sole proprietorship or other association authorized to practice law; or lawyers employed in a qualified legal assistance organization, a government law office, or the legal department of a corporation or other organization.

(i) "Fraud" or "fraudulent" denotes conduct that is fraudulent under the substantive or procedural law

> **Definition of Fraud**

of the applicable jurisdiction or has a purpose to deceive, provided that it does not include conduct that, although characterized as fraudulent by statute or administrative rule, lacks an element of scienter, deceit, intent to mislead, or knowing failure to correct misrepresentations that can be reasonably expected to induce detrimental reliance by another.

(j) "Informed consent" denotes the agreement by a person to a proposed course of conduct after the lawyer has communicated information adequate for the person to make an informed decision, and after the lawyer has adequately explained to the person the material risks of the proposed course of conduct and reasonably available alternatives.

(k) "Knowingly," "known," "know," or "knows" denotes actual knowledge of the fact in question. A person's knowledge may be inferred from circumstances.

(l) "Matter" includes any litigation, judicial or administrative proceeding, case, claim, application, request for a ruling or other determination, contract, controversy, investigation, charge, accusation, arrest, negotiation, arbitration, mediation or any other representation involving a specific party or parties.

(m) "Partner" denotes a member of a partnership, a shareholder in a law firm organized as a professional legal corporation or a member of an association authorized to practice law.

(n) "Person" includes an individual, a corporation, an association, a trust, a partnership, and any other organization or entity.

(o) "Professional legal corporation" means a corporation, or an association treated as a corporation, authorized by law to practice law for profit.

(p) "Qualified legal assistance organization" means an office or organization of one of the four types listed in Rule 7.2(b)(1)–(4) that meets all of the requirements thereof.

(q) "Reasonable" or "reasonably," when used in relation to conduct by a lawyer, denotes the conduct of a reasonably prudent and competent lawyer. When used in the context of conflict of interest determinations, "reasonable lawyer" denotes a lawyer acting from the perspective of a reasonably prudent and competent lawyer who is personally disinterested in commencing or continuing the representation.

(r) "Reasonable belief" or "reasonably believes," when used in reference to a lawyer, denotes that the lawyer believes the matter in question and that the circumstances are such that the belief is reasonable.

(s) "Reasonably should know," when used in reference to a lawyer, denotes that a lawyer of reasonable prudence and competence would ascertain the matter in question.

(t) "Screened" or "screening" denotes the isolation of a lawyer from any participation in a matter through

> **Definition of Screening**

the timely imposition of procedures within a firm that are reasonably adequate under the circumstances to protect information that the isolated lawyer or the firm is obligated to protect under these Rules or other law.

(u) "Sexual relations" denotes sexual intercourse or the touching of an intimate part of the lawyer or another person for the purpose of sexual arousal, sexual gratification or sexual abuse.

(v) "State" includes the District of Columbia, Puerto Rico, and other federal territories and possessions.

(w) "Tribunal" denotes a court, an arbitrator in an arbitration proceeding or a legislative body, administrative agency or other body acting in an adjudicative capacity. A legislative body, administrative agency or other body acts in an adjudicative capacity when a neutral official, after the presentation of evidence or legal argument by a party or parties, will render a legal judgment directly affecting a party's interests in a particular matter.

(x) "Writing" or "written" denotes a tangible or electronic record of a communication or representation, including handwriting, typewriting, printing, photocopying, photography, audio or video recording and email. A "signed" writing includes an electronic sound, symbol or process attached to or logically associated with a writing and executed or adopted by a person with the intent to sign the writing.

Rule 1.1 Competence

(a) A lawyer should provide competent representation to a client. Competent representation requires the legal knowledge, skill, thoroughness and preparation reasonably necessary for the representation.

> **Competent Representation: Knowledge, Skill, Thoroughness, and Preparation**

(b) A lawyer shall not handle a legal matter that the lawyer knows or should know that the lawyer is not competent to handle, without associating with a lawyer who is competent to handle it.

(c) A lawyer shall not intentionally:
   (1) fail to seek the objectives of the client through reasonably available means permitted by law and these Rules; or
   (2) prejudice or damage the client during the course of the representation except as permitted or required by these Rules.

Rule 1.2 Scope of Representation and Allocation of Authority Between Client and Lawyer

(a) Subject to the provisions herein, a lawyer shall abide by a client's decisions concerning the objectives of representation and, as required by Rule 1.4, shall consult with the client as to the means by which they are to be pursued. A lawyer shall abide by a client's decision whether to settle a matter. In a criminal case, the lawyer shall abide by the client's decision, after consultation with the lawyer, as to a plea to be entered, whether to waive jury trial and whether the client will testify.

> **Following Client Objectives**

(b) A lawyer's representation of a client, including representation by appointment, does not constitute an endorsement of the client's political, economic, social or moral views or activities.

(c) A lawyer may limit the scope of the representation if the limitation is reasonable under the circumstances, the client gives informed consent and where necessary notice is provided to the tribunal and/or opposing counsel.

> **Unbundled Legal Services**

(d) A lawyer shall not counsel a client to engage, or assist a client, in conduct that the lawyer knows is illegal or fraudulent, except that the lawyer may discuss the legal consequences of any proposed course of conduct with a client.

> **Counseling Illegal or Fraudulent Conduct**

(e) A lawyer may exercise professional judgment to waive or fail to assert a right or position of the client, or accede to reasonable requests of opposing

counsel, when doing so does not prejudice the rights of the client.

(f) A lawyer may refuse to aid or participate in conduct that the lawyer believes to be unlawful, even though there is some support for an argument that the conduct is legal.

(g) A lawyer does not violate this Rule by being punctual in fulfilling all professional commitments, by avoiding offensive tactics, and by treating with courtesy and consideration all persons involved in the legal process.

> **Refusing to Be Offensive Is Not Unethical**

Rule 1.3 Diligence

(a) A lawyer shall act with reasonable diligence and promptness in representing a client.

> **Diligence and Promptness**

(b) A lawyer shall not neglect a legal matter entrusted to the lawyer.

(c) A lawyer shall not intentionally fail to carry out a contract of employment entered into with a client for professional services, but the lawyer may withdraw as permitted under these Rules.

1.4 Communication

(a) A lawyer shall:

> **Client Communication**

   (1) promptly inform the client of:
       (i) any decision or circumstance with respect to which the client's informed consent, as defined in Rule 1.0(j), is required by these Rules;
       (ii) any information required by court rule or other law to be communicated to a client; and
       (iii) material developments in the matter including settlement or plea offers.
   (2) reasonably consult with the client about the means by which the client's objectives are to be accomplished;
   (3) keep the client reasonably informed about the status of the matter;
   (4) promptly comply with a client's reasonable requests for information; and
   (5) consult with the client about any relevant limitation on the lawyer's conduct when the lawyer knows that the client expects assistance not permitted by these Rules or other law.

(b) A lawyer shall explain a matter to the extent reasonably necessary to permit the client to make informed decisions regarding the representation.

1.5 Fees and Division of Fees

(a) A lawyer shall not make an agreement for, charge, or collect an excessive or illegal fee or expense.

> **When Is a Fee Excessive?**

A fee is excessive when, after a review of the facts, a reasonable lawyer would be left with a definite and firm conviction that the fee is excessive. The factors to be considered in determining whether a fee is excessive may include the following:

(1) the time and labor required, the novelty and difficulty of the questions involved, and the skill requisite to perform the legal service properly;

(2) the likelihood, if apparent or made known to the client, that the acceptance of the particular employment will preclude other employment by the lawyer;

(3) the fee customarily charged in the locality for similar legal services;

(4) the amount involved and the results obtained;

(5) the time limitations imposed by the client or by circumstances;

(6) the nature and length of the professional relationship with the client;

(7) the experience, reputation and ability of the lawyer or lawyers performing the services; and

(8) whether the fee is fixed or contingent. [See Exhibit 3.2A]

EXHIBIT 3.2A	Factors That Determine Whether a Fee Is Excessive
• the time and labor required	• amount involved
• novelty and difficulty of the questions	• results obtained
• skill needed for the service	• time limitations
• the known likelihood of other employment being precluded	• prior work with client
• customary fee in locality	• experience of lawyer
	• reputation of lawyer
	• ability of lawyer
	• whether the fee is fixed or contingent

Source: Rule 1.5(a)

(b) A lawyer shall communicate to a client the scope of the representation and the basis or rate of the fee and expenses for which the client will be responsi-

The Fee Agreement ble. This information shall be communicated to the client before or within a reasonable time after commencement of the representation and shall be in writing where required by statute or court rule. This provision shall not apply when the lawyer will charge a regularly represented client on the same basis or rate and perform services that are of the same general kind as previously rendered to and paid for by the client. Any changes in the scope of the representation or the basis or rate of the fee or expenses shall also be communicated to the client.

(c) A fee may be contingent on the outcome of the matter for which the service is rendered, except in a

matter in which a contingent fee is prohibited by paragraph (d) or other law. Promptly after a lawyer

Contingent Fee Requirements

has been employed in a contingent fee matter, the lawyer shall provide the client with a writing stating the method by which the fee is to be determined, including the percentage or percentages that shall accrue to the lawyer in the event of settlement, trial or appeal; litigation and other expenses to be deducted from the recovery; and whether such expenses are to be deducted before or, if not prohibited by statute or court rule, after the contingent fee is calculated. The writing must clearly notify the client of any expenses for which the client will be liable regardless of whether the client is the prevailing party. Upon conclusion of a contingent fee matter, the lawyer shall provide the client with a writing stating the outcome of the matter and, if there is a recovery, showing the remittance to the client and the method of its determination.

(d) A lawyer shall not enter into an arrangement for, charge or collect:

(1) a contingent fee for representing a defendant in a criminal matter;

(2) a fee prohibited by law or rule of court;

(3) a fee based on fraudulent billing;

(4) a nonrefundable retainer fee. A lawyer may enter into a retainer agreement with a client

Nonrefundable Retainer Fee

containing a reasonable minimum fee clause, if it defines in plain language and sets forth the circumstances under which such fee may be incurred and how it will be calculated; or

(5) any fee in a domestic relations matter if:

Contingent Fees in Domestic Relations Cases

(i) the payment or amount of the fee is contingent upon the securing of a divorce or of obtaining child custody or visitation or is in any way determined by reference to the amount of maintenance, support, equitable distribution, or property settlement;

(ii) a written retainer agreement has not been signed by the lawyer and client setting forth in plain language the nature of the relationship and the details of the fee arrangement; or

(iii) the written retainer agreement includes a security interest, confession of judgment or other lien without prior notice being provided to the client in a signed retainer agreement and approval from a tribunal after notice to the adversary. A lawyer shall not foreclose on a mortgage placed on the marital residence while the spouse who consents to the mortgage remains the titleholder and the residence remains the spouse's primary residence.

(e) In domestic relations matters, a lawyer shall provide a prospective client with a statement of client's rights and responsibilities at the initial conference and prior to the signing of a written retainer agreement.

| Statement of Client Rights and Responsibilities |

(f) Where applicable, a lawyer shall resolve fee disputes by arbitration at the election of the client pursuant to a fee arbitration program established by the Chief Administrator of the Courts and approved by the Administrative Board of the Courts.

| Fee Disputes |

(g) A lawyer shall not divide a fee for legal services with another lawyer who is not associated in the same law firm unless:

| Dividing Fees among Lawyers |

(1) the division is in proportion to the services performed by each lawyer or, by a writing given to the client, each lawyer assumes joint responsibility for the representation;

(2) the client agrees to employment of the other lawyer after a full disclosure that a division of fees will be made, including the share each lawyer will receive, and the client's agreement is confirmed in writing; and

(3) the total fee is not excessive.
   [See Exhibit 3.2B]

| EXHIBIT 3.2B | **Dividing Fees between Lawyers in Different Firms** |

A division of fees between lawyers in different firms is ethical if:
- the division is proportional to the professional services performed by each lawyer, *or*
- the lawyers assume joint responsibility for the representation, *and*
- prior consent is obtained from the client in writing
- the total fee is not excessive

Source: Rule 1.5(g)

(h) Rule 1.5(g) does not prohibit payment to a lawyer formerly associated in a law firm pursuant to a separation or retirement agreement.

1.6 Confidentiality of Information

(a) A lawyer shall not knowingly reveal confidential information, as defined in this Rule, or use such information to the disadvantage of a client or for the advantage of the lawyer or a third person, unless:

| When Confidential Information May Be Revealed |

(1) the client gives informed consent, as defined in Rule 1.0(j);

(2) the disclosure is impliedly authorized to advance the best interests of the client and is either reasonable under the circumstances or customary in the professional community; or

(3) the disclosure is permitted by paragraph (b).

"Confidential information" consists of information gained during or relating to the representation of a client, whatever its source, that is (a) protected by the attorney-client privilege, (b) likely to be embarrassing or detrimental to the client if disclosed, or (c) information that the client has requested be kept confidential. "Confidential information" does not ordinarily include (i) a lawyer's legal knowledge or legal research or (ii) information that is generally known in the local community or in the trade, field or profession to which the information relates.
[See Exhibit 3.2C]

| When Is Information Confidential? |

| EXHIBIT 3.2C | **Defining Confidential Information** |

What is confidential:
- information gained during or relating to the representation of a client, whatever its source
- information protected by the attorney-client privilege, or
- information likely to be embarrassing or detrimental to the client if disclosed, or
- information that the client has requested be kept confidential

What is not confidential:
- a lawyer's legal knowledge
- the results of a lawyer's legal research
- information that is generally known in the local community, or
- information generally known in the trade, field or profession to which the information relates

Source: Rule 1.6(a)

(b) A lawyer may reveal or use confidential information to the extent that the lawyer reasonably believes necessary:

| When Confidential Information May Be Revealed |

(1) to prevent reasonably certain death or substantial bodily harm;

(2) to prevent the client from committing a crime;

(3) to withdraw a written or oral opinion or representation previously given by the lawyer and reasonably believed by the lawyer still to be relied upon by a third person, where the lawyer has discovered that the opinion or representation was based on materially inaccurate information or is being used to further a crime or fraud;

(4) to secure legal advice about compliance with these Rules or other law by the lawyer, another lawyer associated with the lawyer's firm or the law firm;

(5) (i) to defend the lawyer or the lawyer's employees and associates against an accusation of wrongful conduct; or

    (ii) to establish or collect a fee; or

(6) when permitted or required under these Rules or to comply with other law or court order. [See Exhibit 3.2D]

EXHIBIT 3.2D	Disclosure of Confidential Information

WHEN CONFIDENTIAL INFORMATION MAY BE REVEALED

- To prevent reasonably certain death
- To prevent reasonably certain substantial bodily harm
- To prevent the client from committing a crime
- To withdraw advice that may still be relied upon by a third person if the advice is based on materially inaccurate information or is being used to further a crime or fraud
- To secure legal advice about compliance with ethical rules or other laws
- To defend the lawyer or the lawyer's employees and associates against an accusation of wrongful conduct
- To establish or collect a fee
- When otherwise permitted or required by law

Source: Rule 1.6(b)

(c) A lawyer shall exercise reasonable care to prevent the

Paralegals and Other Employees

lawyer's employees, associates, and others whose services are utilized by the lawyer from disclosing or using confidential information of a client, except that a lawyer may reveal the information permitted to be disclosed by paragraph (b) through an employee.

1.7 Conflict of Interest: Current Clients

(a) Except as provided in paragraph (b), a lawyer shall

Concurrent Conflicts of Interest

not represent a client if a reasonable lawyer would conclude that either:

(1) the representation will involve the lawyer in representing differing interests; or

(2) there is a significant risk that the lawyer's professional judgment on behalf of a client will be adversely affected by the lawyer's own financial, business, property or other personal interests.

(b) Notwithstanding the existence of a concurrent conflict of interest under paragraph (a), a lawyer may represent a client if:

(1) the lawyer reasonably believes that the lawyer will be able to provide competent and diligent representation to each affected client;

(2) the representation is not prohibited by law;

(3) the representation does not involve the assertion of a claim by one client against another client

represented by the lawyer in the same litigation or other proceeding before a tribunal; and

(4) each affected client gives informed consent, confirmed in writing.

1.8 Current Clients: Specific Conflict of Interest Rules

(a) A lawyer shall not enter into a

Entering a Business Transaction with a Client

business transaction with a client if they have differing interests therein and if the client expects the lawyer to exercise professional judgment therein for the protection of the client, unless:

(1) the transaction is fair and reasonable to the client and the terms of the transaction are fully disclosed and transmitted in writing in a manner that can be reasonably understood by the client;

(2) the client is advised in writing of the desirability of seeking, and is given a reasonable opportunity to seek, the advice of independent legal counsel on the transaction; and

(3) the client gives informed consent, in a writing signed by the client, to the essential terms of the transaction and the lawyer's role in the transaction, including whether the lawyer is representing the client in the transaction.

(b) A lawyer shall not use information relating to representation of a client to the disadvantage of the client unless the client gives informed consent, except as permitted or required by these Rules.

(c) A lawyer shall not:

Gifts from a Client

(1) solicit any gift from a client, including a testamentary gift, for the benefit of the lawyer or a person related to the lawyer; or

(2) prepare on behalf of a client an instrument giving the lawyer or a person related to the lawyer any gift, unless the lawyer or other recipient of the gift is related to the client and a reasonable lawyer would conclude that the transaction is fair and reasonable. For purposes of this paragraph, related persons include a spouse, child, grandchild, parent, grandparent or other relative or individual with whom the lawyer or the client maintains a close, familial relationship.

(d) Prior to conclusion of all

Literary or Media Rights

aspects of the matter giving rise to the representation or proposed representation of the client or prospective client, a lawyer shall not negotiate or enter into any arrangement or understanding with:

(1) a client or a prospective client by which the lawyer acquires an interest in literary or media rights with respect to the subject matter of the representation or proposed representation; or

(2) any person by which the lawyer transfers or assigns any interest in literary or media rights with respect to the subject matter of the representation of a client or prospective client.

(e) While representing a client in connection with contemplated or pending litigation, a lawyer shall not advance or guarantee financial assistance to the client, except that:

| Giving Financial Assistance to a Client |

(1) a lawyer may advance court costs and expenses of litigation, the repayment of which may be contingent on the outcome of the matter;

(2) a lawyer representing an indigent or pro bono client may pay court costs and expenses of litigation on behalf of the client; and

(3) a lawyer, in an action in which an attorney's fee is payable in whole or in part as a percentage of the recovery in the action, may pay on the lawyer's own account court costs and expenses of litigation. In such case, the fee paid to the lawyer from the proceeds of the action may include an amount equal to such costs and expenses incurred.

(f) A lawyer shall not accept compensation for representing a client, or anything of value related to the lawyer's representation of the client, from one other than the client unless:

| Payment for Services by Someone Other Than the Client |

(1) the client gives informed consent;

(2) there is no interference with the lawyer's independent professional judgment or with the client-lawyer relationship; and

(3) the client's confidential information is protected as required by Rule 1.6.

(g) A lawyer who represents two or more clients shall not participate in making an aggregate settlement of the claims of or against the clients, absent court approval, unless each client gives informed consent in a writing signed by the client. The lawyer's disclosure shall include the existence and nature of all the claims involved and of the participation of each person in the settlement.

(h) A lawyer shall not:

(1) make an agreement prospectively limiting the lawyer's liability to a client for malpractice; or

(2) settle a claim or potential claim for such liability with an unrepresented client or former client unless that person is advised in writing of the desirability of seeking, and is given a reasonable opportunity to seek, the advice of independent legal counsel in connection therewith.

| Agreements Limiting a Lawyer's Liability |

(i) A lawyer shall not acquire a proprietary interest in the cause of action or subject matter of litigation the lawyer is conducting for a client, except that the lawyer may:

(1) acquire a lien authorized by law to secure the lawyer's fee or expenses; and

(2) contract with a client for a reasonable contingent fee in a civil matter subject to Rule 1.5(d) or other law or court rule.

(j) (1) A lawyer shall not:

| Inappropriate Sexual Relations |

(i) as a condition of entering into or continuing any professional representation by the lawyer or the lawyer's firm, require or demand sexual relations with any person;

(ii) employ coercion, intimidation or undue influence in entering into sexual relations incident to any professional representation by the lawyer or the lawyer's firm; or

(iii) in domestic relations matters, enter into sexual relations with a client during the course of the lawyer's representation of the client.

(2) Rule 1.8(j)(1) shall not apply to sexual relations between lawyers and their spouses or to ongoing consensual sexual relationships that predate the initiation of the client-lawyer relationship.

(k) Where a lawyer in a firm has sexual relations with a client but does not participate in the representation of that client, the lawyers in the firm shall not be subject to discipline under this Rule solely because of the occurrence of such sexual relations.

1.9 Duties to Former Clients

(a) A lawyer who has formerly represented a client in a matter shall not thereafter represent another person in the same or a substantially related matter in which

| Adverse Interests in the Same or a Substantially Related Matter |

that person's interests are materially adverse to the interests of the former client unless the former client gives informed consent, confirmed in writing.

(b) Unless the former client gives informed consent, confirmed in writing, a lawyer shall not knowingly represent a person in the same or a substantially related matter in which a firm with which the lawyer formerly was associated had previously represented a client:

(1) whose interests are materially adverse to that person; and

(2) about whom the lawyer had acquired information protected by Rules 1.6 and paragraph (c) that is material to the matter.

(c) A lawyer who has formerly represented a client in a matter or whose present or former firm has formerly represented a client in a matter shall not thereafter:

(1) use confidential information of the former client protected by Rule 1.6 to the disadvantage of the former client, except as these Rules would permit or require with respect to a current client or when the information has become generally known; or

EXHIBIT 3.2E — Kinds of Conflicts of Interest Covered in the Rules	
SITUATIONS THAT MIGHT INVOLVE A CONFLICT OF INTEREST	**WHERE ETHICAL IMPLICATIONS ARE COVERED IN THE RULES**
Representing current clients with differing interests	Rule 1.7(a)(1)
Representing a current client who would be adversely affected by the lawyer's own financial, business, property, or other personal interests	Rule 1.6(b)
Representing a client when the lawyer's personal interest may adversely limit the representation of the client	Rule 1.6(b)(2)
Representing a client with whom the lawyer has entered a business transaction	Rule 1.8(a)
Soliciting a gift from a client to the lawyer or to someone related to the lawyer	Rule 1.8(c)(1)
Preparing a will or other instrument that will allow a client to give a gift to the lawyer or to someone related to the lawyer	Rule 1.8(c)(2)
Acquiring literary or media rights in the case of the client	Rule 1.8(d)
Advancing or guaranteeing the court costs or other litigation expenses of the client	Rule 1.8(e)
Receiving payment from a third party for legal services provided to a client	Rule 1.8(f)
Making a settlement that pertains to the cases of two or more clients	Rule 1.8(g)
Making an agreement with a client that limits liability for legal malpractice	Rule 1.8(h)
Acquiring a proprietary interest in the cause of action	Rule 1.8(i)
Engaging in sexual relations with a client	Rule 1.8(j)
Representing a client who has adverse interests with a former client in the same or a substantially related matter	Rule 1.9(a)
Lawyers related to other lawyers	Rule 1.10(h)
Former government lawyers now in private practice	Rule 1.11
Former judges now in private practice	Rule 1.12
Corporate lawyer responding to corporate issues that may conflict with issues involving directors and officers	Rule 1.13
Representing someone who has materially adverse interests with a prospective client	Rule 1.18(c)
Representing a client when the lawyer may have to act as a witness in the case	Rule 3.7
Communicating with represented and unrepresented opposing parties	Rules 4.2, 4.3
Acting as a director, officer, or member of a legal services or law reform group that serves clients with interests that differ from the lawyer's own clients	Rules 6.3, 6.4, 6.5

(2) reveal confidential information of the former client protected by Rule 1.6 except as these Rules would permit or require with respect to a current client.

[See Exhibit 3.2E for a summary of conflict issues.]

1.10 Imputation of Conflicts of Interest

(a) While lawyers are associated in a firm, none of them shall knowingly represent a client when any one of them practicing alone would be prohibited from doing so by Rule 1.7, 1.8 or 1.9, except as otherwise provided therein.

> **Vicarious Disqualification**

(b) When a lawyer has terminated an association with a firm, the firm is prohibited from thereafter representing a person with interests that the firm knows or reasonably should know are materially adverse to those of a client represented by the formerly associated lawyer and not currently represented by the firm if the firm or any lawyer remaining in the firm has information protected by Rule 1.6 or Rule 1.9(c) that is material to the matter.

(c) When a lawyer becomes associated with a firm, the firm may not knowingly represent a client in a matter that is the same as or substantially related to a matter in which the newly associated lawyer, or a firm with which that lawyer was associated, formerly represented a client whose interests are materially adverse to the prospective or current client unless the newly associated lawyer did not acquire any information protected by Rule 1.6 or Rule 1.9(c) that is material to the current matter.

(d) A disqualification prescribed by this Rule may be waived by the affected client or former client under the conditions stated in Rule 1.7.

(e) A law firm shall make a written record of its engagements, at or near the time of each new engagement, and shall implement and maintain a system by which proposed engagements are checked against current and previous engagements when:

> **Conflicts-Checking System**

(1) the firm agrees to represent a new client;
(2) the firm agrees to represent an existing client in a new matter;
(3) the firm hires or associates with another lawyer; or
(4) an additional party is named or appears in a pending matter.

(f) Substantial failure to keep records or to implement or maintain a conflict-checking system that complies with paragraph (e) shall be a violation thereof regardless of whether there is another violation of these Rules.

(g) Where a violation of paragraph (e) by a law firm is a substantial factor in causing a violation of paragraph (a) by a lawyer, the law firm, as well as the individual lawyer, shall be responsible for the violation of paragraph (a).

(h) A lawyer related to another lawyer as parent, child, sibling or spouse shall not represent in any matter a

| Lawyers Related to Other Lawyers |

client whose interests differ from those of another party to the matter who the lawyer knows is represented by the other lawyer unless the client consents to the representation after full disclosure and the lawyer concludes that the lawyer can adequately represent the interests of the client.

1.11 Special Conflicts of Interest for Former and Current Government Officers and Employees

(a) Except as law may otherwise expressly provide, a lawyer who has formerly served as a public officer or employee of the government:

(1) shall comply with Rule 1.9(c); and

(2) shall not represent a client in connection with a matter in which the lawyer participated per-

| Former Government Lawyers Now in Private Practice |

sonally and substantially as a public officer or employee, unless the appropriate government agency gives its informed consent, confirmed in writing, to the representation. This provision shall not apply to matters governed by Rule 1.12(a).

(b) When a lawyer is disqualified from representation

| Screening Procedures |

under paragraph (a), no lawyer in a firm with which that lawyer is associated may knowingly undertake or continue representation in such a matter unless the firm acts promptly and reasonably to:

(1) notify, as appropriate, lawyers and nonlawyer personnel within the firm that the personally disqualified lawyer is prohibited from participating in the representation of the current client;

(2) implement effective screening procedures to prevent the flow of information about the matter between the personally disqualified lawyer and the others in the firm;

(3) the disqualified lawyer is apportioned no part of the fee therefrom;

(4) written notice is promptly given to the appro-

| Appearance of Impropriety |

priate government agency to enable it to ascertain compliance with the provisions of this Rule; and

(5) there are no other circumstances in the particular representation that create an appearance of impropriety.

(c) Except as law may otherwise expressly provide, a lawyer having information that the lawyer knows is confidential government information about a person, acquired when the lawyer was a public officer or employee, may not represent a private client whose interests are adverse to that person in a matter in which the information could be used to the material disadvantage of that person. As used in this Rule, the term "confidential government information" means information that has been obtained under governmental authority and that, at the time this Rule is applied, the government is prohibited by law from disclosing to the public or has a legal privilege not to disclose, and that is not otherwise available to the public. A firm with which that lawyer is associated may undertake or continue representation in the matter only if the disqualified lawyer is timely and effectively screened from any participation in the matter in accordance with the provisions of paragraph (b).

(d) Except as law may otherwise expressly provide, a lawyer currently serving as a public officer or employee shall not:

(1) participate in a matter in which the lawyer participated personally and substantially while in private practice or nongovernmental employment, unless under applicable law no one is, or by lawful delegation may be, authorized to act in the lawyer's stead in the matter; or

(2) negotiate for private employment with any person who is involved as a party or as lawyer for a party in a matter in which the lawyer is participating personally and substantially.

(e) As used in this Rule, the term "matter" as defined in Rule 1.0(l) does not include or apply to agency rule making functions.

(f) A lawyer who holds public office shall not:

(1) use the public position to obtain, or attempt to obtain, a special advantage in legislative matters for the lawyer or for a client under circumstances where the lawyer knows or it is obvious that such action is not in the public interest;

(2) use the public position to influence, or attempt to influence, a tribunal to act in favor of the lawyer or of a client; or

(3) accept anything of value from any person when the lawyer knows or it is obvious that the offer is for the purpose of influencing the lawyer's action as a public official.

1.12 Specific Conflicts of Interest for Former Judges, Arbitrators, Mediators, and Other Third-Party Neutrals

(a) A lawyer shall not accept private employment in a matter upon the merits of which the lawyer has acted in a judicial capacity.

(b) Except as stated in paragraph (e), and unless all parties to the proceeding give informed consent, confirmed in writing, a lawyer shall not represent anyone in connection with a matter in which the lawyer participated personally and substantially as:

(1) an arbitrator, mediator or other third-party neutral; or

(2) a law clerk to a judge or other adjudicative officer or an arbitrator, mediator or other third-party neutral.

(c) A lawyer shall not negotiate for employment with any person who is involved as a party or as lawyer for a party in a matter in which the lawyer is participating personally and substantially as a judge or other adjudicative officer or as an arbitrator, mediator or other third-party neutral.

(d) When a lawyer is disqualified from representation under this Rule, no lawyer in a firm with which that lawyer is associated may knowingly undertake or continue representation in such a matter unless the firm acts promptly and reasonably to:

(1) notify, as appropriate, lawyers and nonlawyer personnel within the firm that the personally disqualified lawyer is prohibited from participating in the representation of the current client;

(2) implement effective screening procedures to prevent the flow of information about the matter between the personally disqualified lawyer and the others in the firm;

(3) the disqualified lawyer is apportioned no part of the fee therefrom;

(4) written notice is promptly given to the parties and any appropriate tribunal to enable it to ascertain compliance with the provisions of this Rule; and

(5) there are no other circumstances in the particular representation that create an appearance of impropriety.

(e) An arbitrator selected as a partisan of a party in a multimember arbitration panel is not prohibited from subsequently representing that party.

1.13 Organization as a Client

(a) When a lawyer employed or retained by an organization is dealing with the organization's directors,

| Lawyers for Corporations and Other Organizations |

officers, employees, members, shareholders or other constituents, and it appears that the organization's interests may differ from those of the constituents with whom the lawyer is dealing, the lawyer shall explain that the lawyer is the lawyer for the organization and not for any of the constituents.

(b) If a lawyer for an organization knows that an officer,

| Ethical Duty of Corporate Lawyers When They Become Aware of Corporate Wrongdoing |

employee or other person associated with the organization is engaged in action or intends to

act or refuses to act in a matter related to the representation that (i) is a violation of a legal obligation to the organization or a violation of law that reasonably might be imputed to the organization, and (ii) is likely to result in substantial injury to the organization, the lawyer shall proceed as is reasonably necessary in the best interest of the organization. In determining how to proceed, the lawyer shall give due consideration to the seriousness of the violation and its consequences, the scope and nature of the lawyer's representation, the responsibility in the organization and the apparent motivation of the person involved, the policies of the organization concerning such matters and any other relevant considerations. Any measures taken shall be designed to minimize disruption of the organization and the risk of revealing information relating to the representation to persons outside the organization. Such measures may include, among others:

(1) Asking reconsideration of the matter;

(2) Advising that a separate legal opinion on the matter be sought for presentation to an appropriate authority in the organization; and

(3) Referring the matter to higher authority in the organization, including, if warranted by the seriousness of the matter, referral to the highest authority that can act in behalf of the organization as determined by applicable law.

(c) If, despite the lawyer's efforts in accordance with paragraph (b), the highest authority that can act on behalf of the organization insists upon action, or a refusal to act, that is clearly in violation of law and is likely to result in a substantial injury to the organization, the lawyer may reveal confidential information only if permitted by Rule 1.6, and may resign in accordance with Rule 1.16.

(d) A lawyer representing an organization may also represent any of its directors, officers, employees, members, shareholders or other constituents, subject to the provisions of Rule 1.7. If the organization's consent to the concurrent representation is required by Rule 1.7, the consent shall be given by an appropriate official of the organization other than the individual who is to be represented, or by the shareholders.

1.14 Client with Diminished Capacity

(a) When a client's capacity to make adequately considered decisions in connection is di-

| Clients Who Are Minors or Are Mentally Impaired |

minished, whether because of minority, mental impairment or for some other reason, the lawyer shall, as far as reasonably possible, maintain a conventional relationship with the client.

(b) When the lawyer reasonably believes that the client has diminished capacity, is at risk of substantial physical, financial or other harm unless action is taken and cannot adequately act in the client's own interest, the lawyer may take reasonably necessary protective action, including consulting with individuals or entities that have the ability to take action to protect the client and, in appropriate cases, seeking the appointment of a guardian ad litem, conservator or guardian.

(c) Information relating to the representation of a client with diminished capacity is protected by Rule 1.6. When taking protective action pursuant to paragraph (b), the lawyer is impliedly authorized under Rule 1.6(a) to reveal information about the client, but only to the extent reasonably necessary to protect the client's interests.

1.15 Preserving Identity of Funds and Property of Others; Fiduciary Responsibility; Commingling and Misappropriation of Client Funds or Property; Maintenance of Bank Accounts; Record Keeping; Examination of Records

(a) Prohibition Against Commingling and Misappropriation of Client Funds or Property.

| Lawyer as Fiduciary |
A lawyer in possession of any funds or other property belonging to another person, where such possession is incident to his or her practice of law, is a fiduciary, and must not misappropriate such funds or property or commingle such funds or property with his or her own.

(b) Separate Accounts.

(1) A lawyer who is in possession of funds belonging to another person incident to the lawyer's practice of law shall maintain such funds in a banking institution within New York

| Prohibition of Commingling |
State that agrees to provide dishonored check reports in accordance with the provisions of 22 N.Y.C.R.R. Part 1300. "Banking institution" means a state or national bank, trust company, savings bank, savings and loan association or credit union. Such funds shall be maintained, in the lawyer's own name, or in the name of a firm of lawyers of which the lawyer is a member, or in the name of the lawyer or firm of lawyers by whom the lawyer is employed, in a special account or accounts, separate from any business or personal accounts of the lawyer or lawyer's firm, and separate from any accounts that the lawyer may maintain as executor, guardian, trustee or receiver, or in any other fiduciary capacity; into such special account or accounts all funds held in escrow or otherwise entrusted to the lawyer or firm shall be deposited; provided, however, that such funds may be maintained in

a banking institution located outside New York State if such banking institution complies with 22 N.Y.C.R.R. Part 1300 and the lawyer has obtained the prior written approval of the person to whom such funds belong specifying the name and address of the office or branch of the banking institution where such funds are to be maintained.

(2) A lawyer or the lawyer's firm shall identify the special bank account or accounts required by Rule 1.15(b)(1) as an "Attorney Special Account," or "Attorney Trust Account," or "Attorney Escrow Account," and shall obtain checks and deposit slips that bear such title. Such title may be accompanied by such other descriptive language as the lawyer may deem appropriate, provided that such additional language distinguishes such special account or accounts from other bank accounts that are maintained by the lawyer or the lawyer's firm.

(3) Funds reasonably sufficient to maintain the account or to pay account charges may be deposited therein.

(4) Funds belonging in part to a client or third person and in part currently or potentially to the lawyer or law firm shall be kept in such special account or accounts, but the portion belonging to the lawyer or law firm may be withdrawn when due unless the right of the lawyer or law firm to receive it is disputed by the client or third person, in which event the disputed portion shall not be withdrawn until the dispute is finally resolved.

(c) Notification of Receipt of Property; Safekeeping; Rendering Accounts; Payment or Delivery of Property.

A lawyer shall:

(1) promptly notify a client or third person of the receipt of funds, securities, or other properties in which the client or third person has an interest;

(2) identify and label securities and properties of a client or third person promptly upon receipt and place them in a safe deposit box or other place of safekeeping as soon as practicable;

(3) maintain complete records of all funds, securities, and other properties of a client | Required Record Keeping | or third person coming into the possession of the lawyer and render appropriate accounts to the client or third person regarding them; and

(4) promptly pay or deliver to the client or third person as requested by the client or third person the funds, securities, or other properties in the possession of the lawyer that the client or third person is entitled to receive.

(d) Required Bookkeeping Records.

    (1) A lawyer shall maintain for seven years after the events that they record:

        (i) the records of all deposits in and withdrawals from the accounts specified in Rule 1.15(b) and of any other bank account that concerns or affects the lawyer's practice of law; these records shall specifically identify the date, source and description of each item deposited, as well as the date, payee and purpose of each withdrawal or disbursement;

> **Seven-Year Rule on Client Financial Records**

        (ii) a record for special accounts, showing the source of all funds deposited in such accounts, the names of all persons for whom the funds are or were held, the amount of such funds, the description and amounts, and the names of all persons to whom such funds were disbursed;

        (iii) copies of all retainer and compensation agreements with clients;

        (iv) copies of all statements to clients or other persons showing the disbursement of funds to them or on their behalf;

        (v) copies of all bills rendered to clients;

        (vi) copies of all records showing payments to lawyers, investigators or other persons, not in the lawyer's regular employ, for services rendered or performed;

        (vii) copies of all retainer and closing statements filed with the Office of Court Administration; and

        (viii) all checkbooks and check stubs, bank statements, prenumbered canceled checks and duplicate deposit slips.

    (2) Lawyers shall make accurate entries of all financial transactions in their records of receipts and disbursements, in their special accounts, in their ledger books or similar records, and in any other books of account kept by them in the regular course of their practice, which entries shall be made at or near the time of the act, condition or event recorded.

    (3) For purposes of Rule 1.15(d), a lawyer may satisfy the requirements of maintaining "copies" by maintaining any of the following items: original records, photocopies, microfilm, optical imaging, and any other medium that preserves an image of the document that cannot be altered without detection.

(e) Authorized Signatories.

> **Prohibition on Withdrawals to Cash; A Nonlawyer Cannot Be an Authorized Signatory**

All special account withdrawals shall be made only to a named payee and not to cash. Such withdrawals shall be made by check or, with the prior written approval of the party entitled to the proceeds, by bank transfer. Only a lawyer admitted to practice law in New York State shall be an authorized signatory of a special account.

(f) Missing Clients.

Whenever any sum of money is payable to a client and the lawyer is unable to locate the client, the lawyer shall apply to the court in which the action was brought if in the unified court system, or, if no action was commenced in the unified court system, to the Supreme Court in the county in which the lawyer maintains an office for the practice of law, for an order directing payment to the lawyer of any fees and disbursements that are owed by the client and the balance, if any, to the Lawyers' Fund for Client Protection for safeguarding and disbursement to persons who are entitled thereto.

(g) Designation of Successor Signatories.

    (1) Upon the death of a lawyer who was the sole signatory on an attorney trust, escrow or special account, an application may be made to the Supreme Court for an order designating a successor signatory for such trust, escrow or special account, who shall be a member of the bar in good standing and admitted to the practice of law in New York State.

    (2) An application to designate a successor signatory shall be made to the Supreme Court in the judicial district in which the deceased lawyer maintained an office for the practice of law. The application may be made by the legal representative of the deceased lawyer's estate; a lawyer who was affiliated with the deceased lawyer in the practice of law; any person who has a beneficial interest in such trust, escrow or special account; an officer of a city or county bar association; or counsel for an attorney disciplinary committee. No lawyer may charge a legal fee for assisting with an application to designate a successor signatory pursuant to this Rule.

    (3) The Supreme Court may designate a successor signatory and may direct the safeguarding of funds from such trust, escrow or special account, and the disbursement of such funds to persons who are entitled thereto, and may order that funds in such account be deposited with the Lawyers' Fund for Client Protection for safeguarding and disbursement to persons who are entitled thereto.

(h) Dissolution of a Firm.

Upon the dissolution of any firm of lawyers, the former partners or members shall make appropriate arrangements for the maintenance, by one of them or by a successor firm, of the records specified in Rule 1.15(d).

> **Record Keeping upon Dissolution of a Law Firm**

(i) Availability of Bookkeeping Records: Records Subject to Production in Disciplinary Investigations and Proceedings.

The financial records required by this Rule shall be located, or made available, at the principal New York State office of the lawyers subject hereto, and any such records shall be produced in response to a notice or subpoena duces tecum issued in connection with a complaint before or any investigation by the appropriate grievance or departmental disciplinary committee, or shall be produced at the direction of the appropriate Appellate Division before any person designated by it. All books and records produced pursuant to this Rule shall be kept confidential, except for the purpose of the particular proceeding, and their contents shall not be disclosed by anyone in violation of the attorney-client privilege.

(j) Disciplinary Action.

A lawyer who does not maintain and keep the accounts and records as specified and required by this Rule, or who does not produce any such records pursuant to this Rule, shall be deemed in violation of these Rules and shall be subject to disciplinary proceedings.

1.16 Declining or Terminating Representation

(a) A lawyer shall not accept employment on behalf of

> **When a Lawyer Must Refuse Representation**

a person if the lawyer knows or reasonably should know that such person wishes to:

(1) bring a legal action, conduct a defense, or assert a position in a matter, or otherwise have steps taken for such person, merely for the purpose of harassing or maliciously injuring any person; or

(2) present a claim or defense in a matter that is not warranted under existing law, unless it can be supported by a good faith argument for an extension, modification, or reversal of existing law.

(b) Except as stated in paragraph (d), a lawyer shall withdraw from the representation of a client when:

(1) the lawyer knows or reasonably should know

> **Mandatory Withdrawal**

that the representation will result in a violation of these Rules or of law;

(2) the lawyer's physical or mental condition materially impairs the lawyer's ability to represent the client;

(3) the lawyer is discharged; or

(4) the lawyer knows or reasonably should know that the client is bringing the legal action, conducting the defense, or asserting a position in the matter, or is otherwise having steps taken, merely for the purpose of harassing or maliciously injuring any person.

(c) Except as stated in paragraph (d), a

> **Permissive Withdrawal**

lawyer may withdraw from representing a client when:

(1) withdrawal can be accomplished without material adverse effect on the interests of the client;

(2) the client persists in a course of action involving the lawyer's services that the lawyer reasonably believes is criminal or fraudulent;

(3) the client has used the lawyer's services to perpetrate a crime or fraud;

(4) the client insists upon taking action with which the lawyer has a fundamental disagreement;

(5) the client deliberately disregards an agreement or obligation to the lawyer as to expenses or fees;

(6) the client insists upon presenting a claim or defense that is not warranted under existing law and cannot be supported by good faith argument for an extension, modification, or reversal of existing law;

(7) the client fails to cooperate in the representation or otherwise renders the representation unreasonably difficult for the lawyer to carry out employment;

(8) the lawyer's inability to work with co-counsel indicates that the best interest of the client likely will be served by withdrawal;

(9) the lawyer's mental or physical condition renders it difficult for the lawyer to carry out the representation effectively;

(10) the client knowingly and freely assents to termination of the employment;

(11) withdrawal is permitted under Rule 1.13(c) or other law;

(12) the lawyer believes in good faith, in a matter pending before a tribunal, that the tribunal will find the existence of other good cause for withdrawal; or

(13) the client insists that the lawyer pursue a course of conduct which is illegal or prohibited under these Rules.

(d) If permission for withdrawal from employment is required by the rules of a tribunal, a lawyer shall not withdraw from employment in a matter before that tribunal without its permission. When ordered to do so by a tribunal, a lawyer shall continue representation notwithstanding good cause for terminating the representation.

(e) Even when withdrawal is otherwise permitted or required, upon termination of representation, a lawyer shall take steps, to the extent reasonably practicable, to avoid foreseeable prejudice to the rights of the client, including giving reasonable notice to the client, allowing time for employment of other counsel, delivering to the client all papers and property to which the client is entitled, promptly refunding any part of a fee paid in

EXHIBIT 3.2F	Mandatory and Permissive Withdrawal

MANDATORY WITHDRAWAL: WHEN LAWYERS MUST WITHDRAW

(1) the lawyer knows or reasonably should know that the representation will result in a violation of these Rules or of law;
(2) the lawyer's physical or mental condition materially impairs the lawyer's ability to represent the client;
(3) the lawyer is discharged; or
(4) the lawyer knows or reasonably should know that the client is bringing the legal action, conducting the defense, or asserting a position in the matter, or is otherwise having steps taken, merely for the purpose of harassing or maliciously injuring any person.

PERMISSIVE WITHDRAWAL: WHEN LAWYERS MAY WITHDRAW

(1) withdrawal can be accomplished without material adverse effect on the interests of the client;
(2) the client persists in a course of action involving the lawyer's services that the lawyer reasonably believes is criminal or fraudulent;
(3) the client has used the lawyer's services to perpetrate a crime or fraud;
(4) the client insists upon taking action with which the lawyer has a fundamental disagreement;
(5) the client deliberately disregards an agreement or obligation to the lawyer as to expenses or fees;
(6) the client insists upon presenting a claim or defense that is not warranted under existing law and cannot be supported by good faith argument for an extension, modification, or reversal of existing law;
(7) the client fails to cooperate in the representation or otherwise renders the representation unreasonably difficult for the lawyer to carry out employment;
(8) the lawyer's inability to work with co-counsel indicates that the best interest of the client likely will be served by withdrawal;
(9) the lawyer's mental or physical condition renders it difficult for the lawyer to carry out the representation effectively;
(10) the client knowingly and freely assents to termination of the employment;
(11) withdrawal is permitted under Rule 1.13(c) or other law;
(12) the lawyer believes in good faith, in a matter pending before a tribunal, that the tribunal will find the existence of other good cause for withdrawal; or
(13) the client insists that the lawyer pursue a course of conduct which is illegal or prohibited under these Rules.

Source: Rules 1.16(b), 1.16(c)

advance that has not been earned and complying with applicable laws and rules.
[See Exhibit 3.2F]

1.17 Sale of Law Practice

(a) A lawyer retiring from a private practice of law; a law firm, one or more members of which are retiring from the private practice of law with the firm; or the personal representative of a deceased, disabled or missing lawyer, may sell a law practice, including goodwill, to one or more lawyers or law firms, who may purchase the practice. The seller and the buyer may agree on reasonable restrictions on the seller's private practice of law, notwithstanding any other provision of these Rules. Retirement shall include the cessation of the private practice of law in the geographic area, that is, the county and city and any county or city contiguous thereto, in which the practice to be sold has been conducted.

> Confidentiality, Privilege, and Conflicts Rules When a Law Practice Is Sold

(b) Confidential information
(1) With respect to each matter subject to the contemplated sale, the seller may provide prospective buyers with any information not protected as confidential information under Rule 1.6.
(2) Notwithstanding Rule 1.6, the seller may provide the prospective buyer with information as to individual clients:
   (i) concerning the identity of the client, except as provided in paragraph (b)(6);
   (ii) concerning the status and general nature of the matter;
   (iii) available in public court files; and
   (iv) concerning the financial terms of the client-lawyer relationship and the payment status of the client's account.
(3) Prior to making any disclosure of confidential information that may be permitted under paragraph (b)(2), the seller shall provide the prospective buyer with information regarding the matters involved in the proposed sale sufficient to enable the prospective buyer to determine whether any conflicts of interest exist. Where sufficient information cannot be disclosed without revealing client confidential information, the seller may make the disclosures necessary for the prospective buyer to determine whether any conflict of interest

exists, subject to paragraph (b)(6). If the prospective buyer determines that conflicts of interest exist prior to reviewing the information, or determines during the course of review that a conflict of interest exists, the prospective buyer shall not review or continue to review the information unless the seller shall have obtained the consent of the client in accordance with Rule 1.6(a)(1).

(4) Prospective buyers shall maintain the confidentiality of and shall not use any client information received in connection with the proposed sale in the same manner and to the same extent as if the prospective buyers represented the client.

(5) Absent the consent of the client after full disclosure, a seller shall not provide a prospective buyer with information if doing so would cause a violation of the attorney-client privilege.

(6) If the seller has reason to believe that the identity of the client or the fact of the representation itself constitutes confidential information in the circumstances, the seller may not provide such information to a prospective buyer without first advising the client of the identity of the prospective buyer and obtaining the client's consent to the proposed disclosure.

(c) Written notice of the sale shall be given jointly by the seller and the buyer to each of the seller's clients and shall include information regarding:

(1) the client's right to retain other counsel or to take possession of the file;

(2) the fact that the client's consent to the transfer of the client's file or matter to the buyer will be presumed if the client does not take any action or otherwise object within 90 days of the sending of the notice, subject to any court rule or statute requiring express approval by the client or a court;

(3) the fact that agreements between the seller and the seller's clients as to fees will be honored by the buyer;

(4) proposed fee increases, if any, permitted under paragraph (e); and

(5) the identity and background of the buyer or buyers, including principal office address, bar admissions, number of years in practice in New York State, whether the buyer has ever been disciplined for professional misconduct or convicted of a crime, and whether the buyer currently intends to resell the practice.

(d) When the buyer's representation of a client of the seller would give rise to a waivable conflict of interest, the buyer shall not undertake such representation unless the necessary waiver or waivers have been obtained in writing.

(e) The fee charged a client by the buyer shall not be increased by reason of the sale, unless permitted by a retainer agreement with the client or otherwise specifically agreed to by the client.

1.18 Duties to Prospective Clients

(a) A person who discusses with a lawyer the possibility of forming a client-lawyer relationship with respect to a matter is a "prospective client."

(b) Even when no client-lawyer relationship ensues, a lawyer who has had discussions with a prospective client shall not use or reveal information learned in the consultation, except as Rule 1.9 would permit with respect to information of a former client.

(c) A lawyer subject to paragraph (b) shall not represent a client with interests materially adverse to those of a prospective client in the same or a substantially related matter if the lawyer received information from the prospective client that could be significantly harmful to that person in the matter, except as provided in paragraph (d). If a lawyer is disqualified from representation under this paragraph, no lawyer in a firm with which that lawyer is associated may knowingly undertake or continue representation in such a matter, except as provided in paragraph (d).

(d) When the lawyer has received disqualifying information as defined in paragraph (c), representation is permissible if:

(1) both the affected client and the prospective client have given informed consent, confirmed in writing; or

(2) the lawyer who received the information took reasonable measures to avoid exposure to more disqualifying information than was reasonably necessary to determine whether to represent the prospective client; and

> **Notice of Screening Given to Nonlawyer Personnel**

(i) the firm acts promptly and reasonably to notify, as appropriate, lawyers and nonlawyer personnel within the firm that the personally disqualified lawyer is prohibited from participating in the representation of the current client;

(ii) the firm implements effective screening procedures to prevent the flow of information about the matter between the disqualified lawyer and the others in the firm;

(iii) the disqualified lawyer is apportioned no part of the fee therefrom; and

(iv) written notice is promptly given to the prospective client; and

(3) a reasonable lawyer would conclude that the law firm will be able to provide competent and diligent representation in the matter.

(e) A person who: (1) communicates information unilaterally to a lawyer, without any reasonable expectation that the lawyer is willing to discuss the possibility of forming a client-lawyer relationship; or (2) communicates with a lawyer for the purpose of disqualifying the lawyer from handling a materially adverse representation on the same or a substantially related matter, is not a prospective client with the meaning of paragraph (a).

2.1 Advisor

In representing a client, a lawyer shall exercise independent professional judgment and render candid advice. In rendering advice, a lawyer may refer not only

| Independent Professional Judgment |

to law but to other considerations such as moral, economic, social, psychological, and political factors that may be relevant to the client's situation.

2.2 Reserved

2.3 Evaluation for Use by Third Persons

(a) A lawyer may provide an evaluation of a matter affecting a client for the use of someone other than

| Reliance on a Lawyer's Advice by Nonclients |

the client if the lawyer reasonably believes that making the evaluation is compatible with other aspects of the lawyer's relationship with the client.

(b) When the lawyer knows or reasonably should know that the evaluation is likely to affect the client's interests materially and adversely, the lawyer shall not provide the evaluation unless the client gives informed consent.

(c) Unless disclosure is authorized in connection with a report of an evaluation, information relating to the evaluation is protected by Rule 1.6.

2.4 Lawyer Serving as Third-Party Neutral

(a) A lawyer serves as a "third-party neutral" when the lawyer assists two or more persons who are not

| Lawyer as Arbitrator or Mediator |

clients of the lawyer to reach a resolution of a dispute or other matter that has arisen between them. Service as a third-party neutral may include service as an arbitrator, a mediator or in such other capacity as will enable the lawyer to assist the parties to resolve the matter.

(b) A lawyer serving as a third-party neutral shall inform unrepresented parties that the lawyer is not representing them. When the lawyer knows or reasonably should know that a party does not understand the lawyer's role in the matter, the lawyer shall explain the difference between the lawyer's role as a third-party neutral and a lawyer's role as one who represents a client.

3.1 Non-Meritorious Claims and Contentions

(a) A lawyer shall not bring or defend a proceeding, or assert or controvert an issue therein, unless there is a basis in law and fact for doing so that is not frivolous. A lawyer for the defendant

| Frivolous Claims or Defenses |

in a criminal proceeding or for the respondent in a proceeding that could result in incarceration may nevertheless so defend the proceeding as to require that every element of the case be established.

(b) A lawyer's conduct is "frivolous" for purposes of this Rule if:

(1) the lawyer knowingly advances a claim or defense that is unwarranted under existing law, except that the lawyer may advance such claim or defense if it can be supported by good faith argument for an extension, modification, or reversal of existing law;

(2) the conduct has no reasonable purpose other than to delay or prolong the resolution of litigation, in violation of Rule 3.2, or serves merely to harass or maliciously injure another; or

(3) the lawyer knowingly asserts material factual statements that are false.

3.2 Delay of Litigation

In representing a client, a lawyer shall not use means that have no substantial purpose other than to delay or prolong the proceeding or to cause needless expense.

| Dilatory Tactics |

3.3 Conduct Before a Tribunal

(a) A lawyer shall not knowingly:

(1) make a false statement of fact or law to a tribunal or fail to correct a false statement of material fact or law previously made to the tribunal by the lawyer;

| Making False Statements |

(2) fail to disclose to the tribunal controlling legal authority known to the lawyer to be directly adverse to the position of the client and not disclosed by opposing counsel; or

| Failure to Disclose Contrary Authority |

(3) offer or use evidence that the lawyer knows to be false. If a lawyer, the lawyer's client, or a witness called by the lawyer has offered material evidence and the lawyer comes to know of its falsity, the lawyer shall take reasonable remedial measures, including, if necessary, disclosure to the tribunal. A lawyer may refuse to offer evidence, other than the testimony of a defendant in a criminal matter, that the lawyer reasonably believes is false.

| Using False Evidence |

(b) A lawyer who represents a client before a tribunal and who knows that a person intends to engage, is engaging or has engaged in criminal or fraudulent conduct related to the proceeding shall take reasonable remedial measures, including, if necessary, disclosure to the tribunal.

(c) The duties stated in paragraphs (a) and (b) apply even if compliance requires disclosure of information otherwise protected by Rule 1.6.

(d) In an ex parte proceeding, a lawyer shall inform the tribunal of all material facts known to the lawyer that will enable the tribunal to make an informed decision, whether or not the facts are adverse.

(e) In presenting a matter to a tribunal, a lawyer shall disclose, unless privileged or irrelevant, the identities of the clients the lawyer represents and of the persons who employed the lawyer.

(f) In appearing as a lawyer before a tribunal, a lawyer shall not:

> | Unethical Discourtesy |

    (1) fail to comply with known local customs of courtesy or practice of the bar or a particular tribunal without giving to opposing counsel timely notice of the intent not to comply;

    (2) engage in undignified or discourteous conduct;

    (3) intentionally or habitually violate any established rule of procedure or of evidence; or

    (4) engage in conduct intended to disrupt the tribunal.

3.4 Fairness to Opposing Party and Counsel

A lawyer shall not:

(a) (1) suppress any evidence that the lawyer or the client has a legal obligation to reveal or produce;

> | Suppressing Evidence and Other Improper Tactics |

    (2) advise or cause a person to hide or leave the jurisdiction of a tribunal for the purpose of making the person unavailable as a witness therein;

    (3) conceal or knowingly fail to disclose that which the lawyer is required by law to reveal;

    (4) knowingly use perjured testimony or false evidence;

    (5) participate in the creation or preservation of evidence when the lawyer knows or it is obvious that the evidence is false; or

    (6) knowingly engage in other illegal conduct or conduct contrary to these Rules;

(b) offer an inducement to a witness that is prohibited by law or pay, offer to pay or acquiesce in the payment of compensation to a witness contingent upon the content of the witness's testimony or the outcome of

> | Prohibited Witness Fees |

the matter. A lawyer may advance, guarantee or acquiesce in the payment of:

    (1) reasonable compensation to a witness for the loss of time in attending, testifying, preparing to testify or otherwise assisting counsel, and reasonable related expenses; or

    (2) a reasonable fee for the professional services of an expert witness and reasonable related expenses;

(c) disregard or advise the client to disregard a standing rule of a tribunal or a ruling of a tribunal made in the course of a proceeding, but the lawyer may take appropriate steps in good faith to test the validity of such rule or ruling;

(d) in appearing before a tribunal on behalf of a client:

    (1) state or allude to any matter that the lawyer does not reasonably believe is relevant or that will not be supported by admissible evidence;

> | Asserting Personal Knowledge or Opinions |

    (2) assert personal knowledge of facts in issue except when testifying as a witness;

    (3) assert a personal opinion as to the justness of a cause, the credibility of a witness, the culpability of a civil litigant or the guilt or innocence of an accused but the lawyer may argue, upon analysis of the evidence, for any position or conclusion with respect to the matters stated herein;

    (4) ask any question that the lawyer has no reasonable basis to believe is relevant to the case and that is intended to degrade a witness or other person; or

(e) present, participate in presenting, or threaten to present criminal charges solely to obtain an advantage in a civil matter.

> | Improper Threats |

3.5 Maintaining and Preserving the Impartiality of Tribunals and Jurors

(a) A lawyer shall not:

> | Improper Influence |

    (1) seek to or cause another person to influence a judge, official or employee of a tribunal by means prohibited by law or give or lend anything of value to such judge, official, or employee of a tribunal when the recipient is prohibited from accepting the gift or loan but a lawyer may make a contribution to the campaign fund of a candidate for judicial office in conformity with Part 100 of the Rules of the Chief Administrator of the Courts;

    (2) in an adversary proceeding communicate or cause another person to do so on the lawyer's behalf, as to the merits of the matter with a judge or

> | Ex Parte Contacts |

official of a tribunal or an employee thereof before whom the matter is pending, except:

   (i) in the course of official proceedings in the matter;

   (ii) in writing, if the lawyer promptly delivers a copy of the writing to counsel for other parties and to a party who is not represented by a lawyer;

   (iii) orally, upon adequate notice to counsel for the other parties and to any party who is not represented by a lawyer; or

   (iv) as otherwise authorized by law, or by Part 100 of the Rules of the Chief Administrator of the Courts;

(3) seek to or cause another to influence a juror or prospective juror by means prohibited by law;

(4) communicate or cause another to communicate with a member of the jury venire from which the jury will be selected for the trial of a case or, during the trial of a case, with any member of the jury unless authorized to do so by law or court order;

(5) communicate with a juror or prospective juror after discharge of the jury if:

   (i) the communication is prohibited by law or court order;

   (ii) the juror has made known to the lawyer a desire not to communicate;

   (iii) the communication involves misrepresentation, coercion, duress or harassment; or

   (iv) the communication is an attempt to influence the juror's actions in future jury service; or

(6) conduct a vexatious or harassing investigation of either a member of the venire or a juror or, by financial support or otherwise, cause another to do so.

(b) During the trial of a case a lawyer who is not connected therewith shall not communicate with or cause another to communicate with a juror concerning the case.

(c) All restrictions imposed by this Rule also apply to communications with or investigations of members of a family of a member of the venire or a juror.

(d) A lawyer shall reveal promptly to the court improper conduct by a member of the venire or a juror, or by another toward a member of the venire or a juror or a member of his or her family of which the lawyer has knowledge.

3.6 Trial Publicity

(a) A lawyer who is participating in or has participated in a criminal or civil matter shall not make

> **Inappropriate Extrajudicial Statements**

an extrajudicial statement that the lawyer knows or reasonably should know will be disseminated by means of public communication and will have a substantial likelihood of materially prejudicing an adjudicative proceeding in the matter.

(b) A statement ordinarily is likely to prejudice materially an adjudicative proceeding when it refers to a civil matter triable to a jury, a criminal matter or any other proceeding that could result in incarceration, and the statement relates to:

(1) the character, credibility, reputation or criminal record of a party, suspect in a criminal investigation or witness, or the identity of a witness or the expected testimony of a party or witness;

(2) in a criminal matter that could result in incarceration, the possibility of a plea of guilty to the offense or the existence or contents of any confession, admission or statement given by a defendant or suspect, or that person's refusal or failure to make a statement;

(3) the performance or results of any examination or test, or the refusal or failure of a person to submit to an examination or test, or the identity or nature of physical evidence expected to be presented;

(4) any opinion as to the guilt or innocence of a defendant or suspect in a criminal matter that could result in incarceration;

(5) information the lawyer knows or reasonably should know is likely to be inadmissible as evidence in a trial and would, if disclosed, create a substantial risk of prejudicing an impartial trial; or

(6) the fact that a defendant has been charged with a crime, unless there is included therein a statement explaining that the charge is merely an accusation and that the defendant is presumed innocent until and unless proven guilty.

(c) Provided that the statement complies with paragraph (a), a lawyer may state the following without elaboration:

> **Appropriate Extrajudicial Statements**

(1) the claim, offense or defense and, except when prohibited by law, the identity of the persons involved;

(2) information contained in a public record;

(3) that an investigation of a matter is in progress;

(4) the scheduling or result of any step in litigation;

(5) a request for assistance in obtaining evidence and information necessary thereto;

(6) a warning of danger concerning the behavior of a person involved, when there is reason to believe that there exists the likelihood of substantial harm to an individual or to the public interest; and

(7) in a criminal matter:

   (i) the identity, age, residence, occupation and family status of the accused;

(ii) if the accused has not been apprehended, information necessary to aid in apprehension of that person;

(iii) the identity of investigating and arresting officers or agencies and the length of the investigation; and

(iv) the fact, time and place of arrest, resistance, pursuit and use of weapons, and a description of physical evidence seized, other than as contained only in a confession, admission or statement.

(d) Notwithstanding paragraph (a), a lawyer may make a statement that a reasonable lawyer would believe is required to protect a client from the substantial prejudicial effect of recent publicity not initiated by the lawyer or the lawyer's client. A statement made pursuant to this paragraph shall be limited to such information as is necessary to mitigate the recent adverse publicity.

(e) No lawyer associated in a firm or government agency with a lawyer subject to paragraph (a) shall make a statement prohibited by paragraph (a).

3.7 Lawyer as Witness

(a) A lawyer shall not act as advocate before a tribunal in a matter in which the lawyer is likely to be a witness on a significant issue of fact unless:

> Lawyer as Advocate vs. Lawyer as Witness

(1) the testimony relates solely to an uncontested issue;

(2) the testimony relates solely to the nature and value of legal services rendered in the matter;

(3) disqualification of the lawyer would work substantial hardship on the client;

(4) the testimony will relate solely to a matter of formality, and there is no reason to believe that substantial evidence will be offered in opposition to the testimony; or

(5) the testimony is authorized by the tribunal.

(b) A lawyer may not act as advocate before a tribunal in a matter if:

(1) another lawyer in the lawyer's firm is likely to be called as a witness on a significant issue other than on behalf of the client, and it is apparent that the testimony may be prejudicial to the client; or

(2) the lawyer is precluded from doing so by Rule 1.7 or Rule 1.9.

3.8 Special Responsibilities of Prosecutors and Other Government Lawyers

(a) A prosecutor or other government lawyer shall not institute, cause to be instituted or maintain a criminal charge when the prosecutor or other government lawyer knows

> Probable Cause; Disclosing Exculpatory Evidence

or it is obvious that the charge is not supported by probable cause.

(b) A prosecutor or other government lawyer in criminal litigation shall make timely disclosure to counsel for the defendant or to a defendant who has no counsel of the existence of evidence or information known to the prosecutor or other government lawyer that tends to negate the guilt of the accused, mitigate the degree of the offense, or reduce the sentence, except when relieved of this responsibility by a protective order of a tribunal.

3.9 Advocate in Non-Adjudicative Matters

A lawyer communicating in a representative capacity with a legislative body or administrative agency in connection with a pending non-adjudicative matter or proceeding shall disclose that the appearance is in a representative capacity, except when the lawyer seeks information from an agency that is available to the public.

4.1 Truthfulness in Statements to Others

In the course of representing a client, a lawyer shall not knowingly make a false statement of fact or law to a third person.

> Making False Statements

4.2 Communication with Person Represented by Counsel

(a) In representing a client, a lawyer shall not communicate or cause another to communicate about the subject of the representation with a party the lawyer knows to be represented by another lawyer in the matter, unless the lawyer has the prior consent of the other lawyer or is authorized to do so by law.

> No-Contact Rule: Opposing Party Represented by Counsel

(b) Notwithstanding the prohibitions of paragraph (a), and unless otherwise prohibited by law, a lawyer may cause a client to communicate with a represented person unless the represented person is not legally competent, and may counsel the client with respect to those communications, provided the lawyer gives reasonable advance notice to the represented person's counsel that such communications will be taking place.

4.3 Communicating with Unrepresented Persons

In communicating on behalf of a client with a person who is not represented by counsel, a lawyer shall not state or imply that the lawyer is disinterested. When the lawyer knows or reasonably should know that the unrepresented person

> No-Contact Rule: Opposing Party Who Is Unrepresented

misunderstands the lawyer's role in the matter, the lawyer shall make reasonable efforts to correct the misunderstanding. The lawyer shall not give legal advice to an unrepresented person other than the advice to secure counsel if the lawyer knows or reasonably should know that the interests of such person are or have a reasonable possibility of being in conflict with the interests of the client.

4.4 Respect for Rights of Third Persons

(a) In representing a client, a lawyer shall not use means that have no substantial purpose other than to embarrass or harm a third person or use methods of obtaining evidence that violate the legal rights of such a person.

(b) A lawyer who receives a document relating to the representation of the lawyer's client and knows or reasonably should know that the document was inadvertently sent shall promptly notify the sender.

> **Misdelivered Communications**

4.5 Communication after Incidents Involving Personal Injury or Wrongful Death

(a) In the event of a specific incident involving potential claims for personal injury or wrongful death, no unsolicited communication shall be made to an individual injured in the incident or to a family member or legal representative of such an individual, by a lawyer or law firm, or by any associate, agent, employee or other representative of a lawyer or law firm representing actual or potential defendants or entities that may defend and/or indemnify said defendants, before the 30th day after the date of the incident, unless a filing must be made within 30 days of the incident as a legal prerequisite to the particular claim, in which case no unsolicited communication shall be made before the 15th day after the date of the incident.

> **Solicitation: Thirty-Day Rule**

(b) An unsolicited communication by a lawyer or law firm, seeking to represent an injured individual or the legal representative thereof under the circumstance described in paragraph (a) shall comply with Rule 7.3(e).

5.1 Responsibilities of Law Firms, Partners, Managers, and Supervisory Lawyers

(a) A law firm shall make reasonable efforts to ensure that all lawyers in the firm conform to these Rules.

(b) (1) A lawyer with management responsibility in a law firm shall make reasonable efforts to ensure that other lawyers in the law firm conform to these Rules.

> **One Lawyer's Responsibility for the Ethical Conduct of Another Lawyer**

(2) A lawyer with direct supervisory authority over another lawyer shall make reasonable efforts to ensure that the supervised lawyer conforms to these Rules.

(c) A law firm shall ensure that the work of partners and associates is adequately supervised, as appropriate. A lawyer with direct supervisory authority over another lawyer shall adequately supervise the work of the other lawyer, as appropriate. In either case, the degree of supervision required is that which is reasonable under the circumstances, taking into account factors such as the experience of the person whose work is being supervised, the amount of work involved in a particular matter, and the likelihood that ethical problems might arise in the course of working on the matter.

> **Required Supervision of Other Lawyers**

(d) A lawyer shall be responsible for a violation of these Rules by another lawyer if:

(1) the lawyer orders or directs the specific conduct or, with knowledge of the specific conduct, ratifies it; or

(2) the lawyer is a partner in a law firm or is a lawyer who individually or together with other lawyers possesses comparable managerial responsibility in a law firm in which the other lawyer practices or is a lawyer who has supervisory authority over the other lawyer; and

  (i) knows of such conduct at a time when it could be prevented or its consequences avoided or mitigated but fails to take reasonable remedial action; or

  (ii) in the exercise of reasonable management or supervisory authority should have known of the conduct so that reasonable remedial action could have been taken at a time when the consequences of the conduct could have been avoided or mitigated.

5.2 Responsibilities of a Subordinate Lawyer

(a) A lawyer is bound by these Rules notwithstanding that the lawyer acted at the direction of another person.

(b) A subordinate lawyer does not violate these Rules if that lawyer acts in accordance with a supervisory lawyer's reasonable resolution of an arguable question of professional duty.

5.3 Lawyer's Responsibility for Conduct of Nonlawyers

(a) A law firm shall ensure that the work of nonlawyers who work for the firm is

> **Required Supervision of Paralegals and Other Nonlawyers**

adequately supervised, as appropriate. A lawyer with direct supervisory authority over a nonlawyer shall adequately supervise the work of the nonlawyer, as appropriate. In either case, the degree of supervision required is that which is reasonable under the circumstances, taking into account factors such as the experience of the person whose work is being supervised, the amount of work involved in a particular matter and the likelihood that ethical problems might arise in the course of working on the matter.

(b) A lawyer shall be responsible for conduct of a nonlawyer employed or retained by or associated with the lawyer that would be a violation of these Rules if engaged in by a lawyer, if:

(1) the lawyer orders or directs the specific conduct or, with knowledge of the specific conduct, ratifies it; or

(2) the lawyer is a partner in a law firm or is a lawyer who individually or together with other lawyers possesses comparable managerial responsibility in a law firm in which the nonlawyer is employed or is a lawyer who has supervisory authority over the nonlawyer; and

(i) knows of such conduct at a time when it could be prevented or its consequences avoided or mitigated but fails to take reasonable remedial action; or

(ii) in the exercise of reasonable management or supervisory authority should have known of the conduct so that reasonable remedial action could have been taken at a time when the consequences of the conduct could have been avoided or mitigated. [See Exhibits 3.2G and 3.2H]

5.4 Professional Independence of a Lawyer

(a) A lawyer or law firm shall not share legal fees with a nonlawyer, except that:

Sharing Fees with Nonlawyers

(1) an agreement by a lawyer with the lawyer's firm or another lawyer associated in the firm may provide for the payment of money, over a reasonable period of time after the lawyer's death, to the lawyer's estate or to one or more specified persons;

(2) a lawyer who undertakes to complete unfinished legal business of a deceased lawyer may

EXHIBIT 3.2G	Factors Determining the Adequacy of Paralegal Supervision under Rule 5.3
GENERAL RULE	Paralegals and other nonlawyers must be adequately supervised as appropriate; the degree of supervision required is that which is reasonable under the circumstances.
FACTORS THAT DETERMINE THE ADEQUACY/REASONABLENESS OF SUPERVISION	• the experience of the person whose work is being supervised • the amount of work involved in a particular matter • the likelihood that ethical problems might arise in the course of working on the matter

Source: Rule 5.3

EXHIBIT 3.2H	Ethical Duties and Consequences Concerning Paralegals and Other Nonlawyers under Rule 5.3
LAWYER IN THE OFFICE	**ETHICAL DUTY OR CONSEQUENCES**
A lawyer who has direct supervisory authority over a nonlawyer	This lawyer must provide adequate supervision; the degree of supervision required is that which is reasonable under the circumstances. (See Exhibit 3.2G.)
Any lawyer in the office who orders or directs the unethical conduct of the nonlawyer, or with knowledge of the conduct, ratifies it	This lawyer will be responsible for the conduct of the nonlawyer.
Any partner, attorney manager, or lawyer with supervisory authority over the nonlawyer who had *knowledge* of the nonlawyer's unethical conduct in time to take reasonable remedial action to avoid or mitigate the conduct	This lawyer will be responsible for the conduct of the nonlawyer.
Any partner, attorney manager, or lawyer with supervisory authority over the nonlawyer who *should have known* of the nonlawyer's conduct in time to take reasonable remedial action to avoid or mitigate the conduct	This lawyer will be responsible for the conduct of the nonlawyer.

Source: Rule 5.3

pay to the estate of the deceased lawyer that portion of the total compensation that fairly represents the services rendered by the deceased lawyer; and

(3) a lawyer or law firm may compensate a non-

| Nonlawyer Compensation Based on a Profit-sharing Arrangement |

lawyer employee or include a nonlawyer employee in a retirement plan based in whole or in part on a profit-sharing arrangement.

(b) A lawyer shall not form a partnership with a non-

| Forming a Partnership with a Nonlawyer |

lawyer if any of the activities of the partnership consist of the practice of law.

(c) Unless authorized by law, a lawyer shall not permit a person who recommends, employs or pays the lawyer to render legal service for another to direct or regulate the lawyer's professional judgment in rendering such legal services or to cause the lawyer to compromise the lawyer's duty to maintain the confidential information of the client under Rule 1.6.

(d) A lawyer shall not practice with or in the form of an entity authorized to practice law for profit, if:

(1) a nonlawyer owns any interest therein, except

| Prohibited Nonlawyer Ownership or Control |

that a fiduciary representative of the estate of a lawyer may hold the stock or interest of the lawyer for a reasonable time during administration;

(2) a nonlawyer is a member, corporate director or officer thereof or occupies a position of similar responsibility in any form of association other than a corporation; or

(3) a nonlawyer has the right to direct or control the professional judgment of a lawyer.

5.5 Unauthorized Practice of Law

(a) A lawyer shall not practice law in a jurisdiction in violation of the regulation of the legal profession in that jurisdiction.

| Aiding a Nonlawyer in the Unauthorized Practice of Law |

(b) A lawyer shall not aid a nonlawyer in the unauthorized practice of law.

5.6 Restrictions on Right to Practice

(a) A lawyer shall not participate in offering or making:

(1) a partnership, shareholder, operating, employment, or other similar type of agreement that restricts the right of a lawyer to practice after termination of the relationship, except an agreement concerning benefits upon retirement; or

(2) an agreement in which a restriction on a lawyer's right to practice is part of the settlement of a client controversy.

(b) This Rule does not prohibit restrictions that may be included in the terms of the sale of a law practice pursuant to Rule 1.17.

5.7 Responsibilities Regarding Nonlegal Services

(a) With respect to lawyers or law firms providing nonlegal services to clients or other persons:

(1) A lawyer or law firm that provides nonlegal services to a person that are not distinct from legal services being provided to that person by the lawyer or law firm is subject to these Rules with respect to the provision of both legal and nonlegal services.

(2) A lawyer or law firm that pro-

| Confusion on Whether a Client-Lawyer Relationship Exists |

vides nonlegal services to a person that are distinct from legal services being provided to that person by the lawyer or law firm is subject to these Rules with respect to the nonlegal services if the person receiving the services could reasonably believe that the nonlegal services are the subject of a client-lawyer relationship.

(3) A lawyer or law firm that is an owner, controlling party or agent of, or that is otherwise affiliated with, an entity that the lawyer or law firm knows to be providing nonlegal services to a person is subject to these Rules with respect to the nonlegal services if the person receiving the services could reasonably believe that the nonlegal services are the subject of a client-lawyer relationship.

(4) For purposes of paragraphs (a)(2) and (a)(3), it will be presumed that the person receiving nonlegal services believes the services to be the subject of a client-lawyer relationship unless the lawyer or law firm has advised the person receiving the services in writing that the services are not legal services and that the protection of a client-lawyer relationship does not exist with respect to the nonlegal services, or if the interest of the lawyer or law firm in the entity providing nonlegal services is de minimis.

(b) Notwithstanding the provisions of paragraph (a), a lawyer or law firm that is an owner, controlling party, agent, or is otherwise affiliated with an entity that the lawyer or law firm knows is

| Inappropriate Control by a Nonlawyer |

providing nonlegal services to a person shall not permit any nonlawyer providing such services or affiliated with that entity to direct or regulate the professional judgment of the lawyer or law firm in rendering legal services to any person, or to cause the lawyer or law firm to compromise its duty under Rule 1.6(a) and (c) with respect to the confidential information of a client receiving legal services.

(c) For purposes of this Rule, "nonlegal services" shall mean those services that lawyers may lawfully provide and that are not prohibited as an unauthorized practice of law when provided by a nonlawyer.

5.8 Contractual Relationship between Lawyers and Nonlegal Professionals

(a) The practice of law has an essential tradition of complete independence and uncompromised

Multi-disciplinary Practices; Special Contract Relationships with Designated Nonlawyers

loyalty to those it serves. Recognizing this tradition, clients of lawyers practicing in New York State are guaranteed "independent professional judgment and undivided loyalty uncompromised by conflicts of interest." Indeed, these guarantees represent the very foundation of the profession and allow and foster its continued role as a protector of the system of law. Therefore, a lawyer must remain completely responsible for his or her own independent professional judgment, maintain the confidences and secrets of clients, preserve funds of clients and third parties in his or her control, and otherwise comply with the legal and ethical principles governing lawyers in New York State. Multi-disciplinary practice between lawyers and nonlawyers is incompatible with the core values of the legal profession and therefore, a strict division between services provided by lawyers and those provided by nonlawyers is essential to protect those values. However, a lawyer or law firm may enter into and maintain a contractual relationship with a nonlegal professional or nonlegal professional service firm for the purpose of offering to the public, on a systematic and continuing basis, legal services performed by the lawyer or law firm as well as other nonlegal professional services, notwithstanding the provisions of Rule 1.7(a), provided that:

(1) the profession of the nonlegal professional or nonlegal professional service firm is included in a list jointly established and maintained by the Appellate Divisions pursuant to Section 1205.3 of the Joint Appellate Division Rules;

(2) the lawyer or law firm neither grants to the nonlegal professional or nonlegal professional service firm, nor permits such person or firm to obtain, hold or exercise, directly or indirectly, any ownership or investment interest in, or managerial or supervisory right, power or position in connection with the practice of law by the lawyer or law firm, nor, as provided in Rule 7.2(a)(1), shares legal fees with a nonlawyer or receives or gives any monetary or other tangible benefit for giving or receiving a referral; and

(3) the fact that the contractual relationship exists is disclosed by the lawyer or law firm to any

Statement of Client's Rights in Cooperative Business Arrangements

client of the lawyer or law firm before the client is referred to the nonlegal professional service firm, or to any client of the nonlegal professional service firm before that client receives legal services from the lawyer or law firm; and the client has given informed written consent and has been provided with a copy of the "Statement of Client's Rights in Cooperative Business Arrangements" pursuant to section 1205.4 of the Joint Appellate Divisions Rules.

(b) For purposes of paragraph (a):

(1) each profession on the list maintained pursuant to a joint rule of the Appellate Divisions shall have been designated sua sponte, or approved by the Appellate Divisions upon application of a member of a nonlegal profession or nonlegal professional service firm, upon a determination that the profession is composed of individuals who, with respect to their profession:

(a) have been awarded a Bachelor's Degree or its equivalent from an accredited college or university, or have attained an equivalent combination of educational credit from such a college or university and work experience;

(b) are licensed to practice the profession by an agency of the State of New York or the United States Government; and

(c) are required under penalty of suspension or revocation of license to adhere to a code of ethical conduct that is reasonably comparable to that of the legal profession;

(2) the term "ownership or investment interest" shall mean any such interest in any form of debt or equity, and shall include any interest commonly considered to be an interest accruing to or enjoyed by an owner or investor.

(c) This Rule shall not apply to relationships consisting solely of non-exclusive reciprocal referral agreements or understandings between a lawyer or law firm and a nonlegal professional or nonlegal professional service firm.

6.1 Voluntary Pro Bono Service

Lawyers are strongly encouraged to provide pro bono legal services to benefit poor persons.

Assisting Poor Persons— Nonbinding Pro Bono Goals

(a) Every lawyer should aspire:

(1) to provide at least 20 hours of pro bono legal services each year to poor persons; and

(2) to contribute financially to organizations that provide legal services to poor persons.

(b) Pro bono legal services that meet this goal are:

(1) professional services rendered in civil matters, and in those criminal matters for which the government is not obliged to provide funds for legal representation, to persons who are financially unable to compensate counsel;

(2) activities related to improving the administration of justice by simplifying the legal process

for, or increasing the availability and quality of legal services to, poor persons; and

(3) professional services to charitable, religious, civic and educational organizations in matters designed predominantly to address the needs of poor persons.

(c) Appropriate organizations for financial contributions are:

(1) organizations primarily engaged in the provision of legal services to the poor; and

(2) organizations substantially engaged in the provision of legal services to the poor, provided that the donated funds are to be used for the provision of such legal services.

(d) This Rule is not intended to be enforced through the disciplinary process, and the failure to fulfill the aspirational goals contained herein should be without legal consequence.

6.2 Reserved

6.3 Membership in a Legal Services Organization

A lawyer may serve as a director, officer or member of a not-for-profit legal services organization, apart from the law firm in which the lawyer practices, notwithstanding that the organization serves persons having interests that differ from those of a client of the lawyer or the lawyer's firm. The lawyer shall not knowingly participate in a decision or action of the organization:

(a) if participating in the decision or action would be incompatible with the lawyer's obligations to a client under Rules 1.7 through 1.13; or

(b) where the decision or action could have a material adverse effect on the representation of a client of the organization whose interests differ from those of a client of the lawyer or the lawyer's firm.

6.4 Law Reform Activities Affecting Client Interests

A lawyer may serve as a director, officer or member of an organization involved in reform of the law or its administration, notwithstanding that the reform may affect the interests of a client of the lawyer. When the lawyer knows that the interests of a client may be materially benefitted by a decision in which the lawyer actively participates, the lawyer shall disclose that fact to the organization, but need not identify the client. When the lawyer knows that the interests of a client may be adversely affected by a decision in which the lawyer actively participates, the lawyer shall disclose that fact to the client.

6.5 Participation in Limited Pro Bono Legal Service Programs

(a) A lawyer who, under the auspices of a program sponsored by a court, government agency, bar association or not-for-profit legal services organization, provides short-term limited legal services to a client without expectation by either the lawyer or the client that the lawyer will provide continuing representation in the matter:

(1) shall comply with Rules 1.7, 1.8 and 1.9, concerning restrictions on representations where there are or may be conflicts of interest as that term is defined in these Rules, only if the lawyer has actual knowledge at the time of commencement of representation that the representation of the client involves a conflict of interest; and

(2) shall comply with Rule 1.10 only if the lawyer has actual knowledge at the time of commencement of representation that another lawyer associated with the lawyer in a law firm is affected by Rules 1.7, 1.8 and 1.9.

(b) Except as provided in paragraph (a)(2), Rule 1.7 and Rule 1.9 are inapplicable to a representation governed by this Rule.

(c) Short-term limited legal services are services providing legal advice or representation free of charge as part of a program described in paragraph (a) with no expectation that the assistance will continue beyond what is necessary to complete an initial consultation, representation or court appearance.

(d) The lawyer providing short-term limited legal services must secure the client's informed consent to the limited scope of the representation, and such representation shall be subject to the provisions of Rule 1.6.

(e) This Rule shall not apply where the court before which the matter is pending determines that a conflict of interest exists or, if during the course of the representation, the lawyer providing the services becomes aware of the existence of a conflict of interest precluding continued representation.

7.1 Advertising

(a) A lawyer or law firm shall not use or disseminate or participate in the use or dissemination of any advertisement that:

(1) contains statements or claims that are false, deceptive or misleading; or

(2) violates a Rule.

(b) Subject to the provisions of paragraph (a), an advertisement may include information as to:

> **Information That Lawyers May Advertise about Themselves**

(1) legal and nonlegal education, degrees and other scholastic distinctions, dates of admission to any bar; areas of the law in which the lawyer or law firm practices, as authorized by these Rules; public offices and teaching positions held; publications of law-related matters authored by the lawyer; memberships in bar

associations or other professional societies or organizations, including offices and committee assignments therein; foreign language fluency; and bona fide professional ratings;

(2) names of clients regularly represented, provided that the client has given prior written consent;

(3) bank references; credit arrangements accepted; prepaid or group legal services programs in which the lawyer or law firm participates; nonlegal services provided by the lawyer or law firm or by an entity owned and controlled by the lawyer or law firm; the existence of contractual relationships between the lawyer or law firm and a nonlegal professional or nonlegal professional service firm, to the extent permitted by Rule 5.8, and the nature and extent of services available through those contractual relationships; and

(4) legal fees for initial consultation; contingent fee rates in civil matters when accompanied by a statement disclosing the information required by paragraph (p); range of fees for legal and nonlegal services, provided that there be available to the public free of charge a written statement clearly describing the scope of each advertised service; hourly rates; and fixed fees for specified legal and nonlegal services.

(c) An advertisement shall not:

> **Prohibitions in Advertisements**

(1) include an endorsement of, or testimonial about, a lawyer or law firm from a client with respect to a matter still pending;

(2) include a paid endorsement of, or testimonial about, a lawyer or law firm without disclosing that the person is being compensated therefor;

(3) include the portrayal of a judge, the portrayal of a fictitious law firm, the use of a fictitious name to refer to lawyers not associated together in a law firm, or otherwise imply that lawyers are associated in a law firm if that is not the case;

(4) use actors to portray the lawyer, members of the law firm, or clients, or utilize depictions of fictionalized events or scenes, without disclosure of same;

(5) rely on techniques to obtain attention that demonstrate a clear and intentional lack of relevance to the selection of counsel, including the portrayal of lawyers exhibiting characteristics clearly unrelated to legal competence;

(6) be made to resemble legal documents; or

(7) utilize a nickname, moniker, motto or trade name that implies an ability to obtain results in a matter.

(d) An advertisement that complies with paragraph (e) may contain the following:

> **Acceptable Categories of Advertisements**

(1) statements that are reasonably likely to create an expectation about results the lawyer can achieve;

(2) statements that compare the lawyer's services with the services of other lawyers;

(3) testimonials or endorsements of clients, where not prohibited by paragraph (c)(1), and of former clients; or

(4) statements describing or characterizing the quality of the lawyer's or law firm's services.

(e) It is permissible to provide the information set forth in paragraph (d) provided:

(1) its dissemination does not violate paragraph (a);

(2) it can be factually supported by the lawyer or law firm as of the date on which the advertisement is published or disseminated; and

(3) it is accompanied by the following disclaimer: "Prior results do not guarantee a similar outcome."

> **"Prior results do not guarantee a similar outcome."**

(f) Every advertisement other than those appearing in a radio, television or billboard advertisement, in a directory, newspaper, magazine or other periodical (and any web sites related thereto), or made in person pursuant to Rule 7.3(a)(1), shall be labeled "Attorney Advertising" on the first page, or on the home page in the case of a web site. If the communication is in the form of a self-mailing brochure or postcard, the words "Attorney Advertising" shall appear therein. In the case of electronic mail, the subject line shall contain the notation "ATTORNEY ADVERTISING."

(g) A lawyer or law firm shall not utilize:

> **Internet Advertising**

(1) a pop-up or pop-under advertisement in connection with computer-accessed communications, other than on the lawyer or law firm's own web site or other internet presence; or

(2) meta tags or other hidden computer codes that, if displayed, would violate these Rules.

(h) All advertisements shall include the name, principal law office address and telephone number of the lawyer or law firm whose services are being offered.

(i) Any words or statements required by this Rule to appear in an advertisement must be clearly legible and capable of being read by the average person, if written, and intelligible if spoken aloud. In the case of a web site, the required words or statements shall appear on the home page.

(j) A lawyer or law firm advertising any fixed fee for specified legal services shall, at the time of fee publication, have available to the public a written statement clearly describing the scope of each advertised service, which statement shall be available to the client at the time of retainer for any such service. Such legal services shall include all those services that are recognized as reasonable and necessary under local custom in the area of practice in the community where the services are performed.

(k) All advertisements shall be pre-approved by the lawyer or law firm, and a copy shall be retained for a period of not less than three years following its initial dissemination. Any advertisement contained in a computer-accessed communication shall be retained for a period of not less than one year. A copy of the contents of any web site covered by this Rule shall be preserved upon the initial publication of the web site, any major web site redesign, or a meaningful and extensive content change, but in no event less frequently than once every 90 days.

(l) If a lawyer or law firm advertises a range of fees or an hourly rate for services, the lawyer or law firm shall not charge more than the fee advertised for such services. If a lawyer or law firm advertises a fixed fee for specified legal services, or performs services described in a fee schedule, the lawyer or law firm shall not charge more than the fixed fee for such stated legal service as set forth in the advertisement or fee schedule, unless the client agrees in writing that the services performed or to be performed were not legal services referred to or implied in the advertisement or in the fee schedule and, further, that a different fee arrangement shall apply to the transaction.

(m) Unless otherwise specified in the advertisement, if a lawyer publishes any fee information authorized under this Rule in a publication that is published more frequently than once per month, the lawyer shall be bound by any representation made therein for a period of not less than 30 days after such publication. If a lawyer publishes any fee information authorized under this Rule in a publication that is published once per month or less frequently, the lawyer shall be bound by any representation made therein until the publication of the succeeding issue. If a lawyer publishes any fee information authorized under this Rule in a publication that has no fixed date for publication of a succeeding issue, the lawyer shall be bound by any representation made therein for a reasonable period of time after publication, but in no event less than 90 days.

(n) Unless otherwise specified, if a lawyer broadcasts any fee information authorized under this Rule, the lawyer shall be bound by any representation made therein for a period of not less than 30 days after such broadcast.

(o) A lawyer shall not compensate or give any thing of value to representatives of the press, radio, television or other communication medium in anticipation of or in return for professional publicity in a news item.

(p) All advertisements that contain information about the fees charged by the lawyer or law firm, including those indicating that in the absence of a recovery no fee will be charged, shall comply with the provisions of Judiciary Law § 488(3).

(q) A lawyer may accept employment that results from participation in activities designed to educate the public to recognize legal problems, to make intelligent selection of counsel or to utilize available legal services.

(r) Without affecting the right to accept employment, a lawyer may speak publicly or write for publication on legal topics so long as the lawyer does not undertake to give individual advice.

7.2 Payment for Referrals

(a) A lawyer shall not compensate or give anything of value to a person or organization to recommend or obtain employment by a client, or as a reward for having made a recommendation resulting in employment by a client, except that:

> **Prohibited Compensation for Recommendations**

(1) a lawyer or law firm may refer clients to a nonlegal professional or nonlegal professional service firm pursuant to a contractual relationship with such nonlegal professional or nonlegal professional service firm to provide legal and other professional services on a systematic and continuing basis as permitted by Rule 5.8, provided however that such referral shall not otherwise include any monetary or other tangible consideration or reward for such, or the sharing of legal fees; and

(2) a lawyer may pay the usual and reasonable fees or dues charged by a qualified legal assistance organization or referral fees to another lawyer as permitted by Rule 1.5(g).

(b) A lawyer or the lawyer's partner or associate or any other affiliated lawyer may be recommended, employed or paid by, or may cooperate with one of the following offices or organizations that promote the use of the lawyer's services or those of a partner or associate or any other affiliated lawyer, or request one of the following offices or organizations to recommend or promote the use of the lawyer's services or those of the lawyer's partner or associate, or any other affiliated lawyer as a private practitioner, if there is no interference with the exercise of independent professional judgment on behalf of the client:

(1) a legal aid office or public defender office:

    (i) operated or sponsored by a duly accredited law school;

    (ii) operated or sponsored by a bona fide, non-profit community organization;

(iii) operated or sponsored by a governmental agency; or

(iv) operated, sponsored, or approved by a bar association;

(2) a military legal assistance office;

(3) a lawyer referral service operated, sponsored

> **Lawyer Referral Service**

or approved by a bar association or authorized by law or court rule;

(4) any bona fide organization that recommends, furnishes or pays for legal services to its members or beneficiaries provided the following conditions are satisfied:

(i) Neither the lawyer, nor the lawyer's partner, nor associate, nor any other affiliated lawyer nor any nonlawyer, shall have initiated or promoted such organization for the primary purpose of providing financial or other benefit to such lawyer, partner, associate or affiliated lawyer;

(ii) Such organization is not operated for the purpose of procuring legal work or financial benefit for any lawyer as a private practitioner outside of the legal services program of the organization;

(iii) The member or beneficiary to whom the legal services are furnished, and not such organization, is recognized as the client of the lawyer in the matter;

(iv) The legal service plan of such organization provides appropriate relief for any member or beneficiary who asserts a claim that representation by counsel furnished, selected or approved by the organization for the particular matter involved would be unethical, improper or inadequate under the circumstances of the matter involved; and the plan provides an appropriate procedure for seeking such relief;

(v) The lawyer does not know or have cause to know that such organization is in violation of applicable laws, rules of court or other legal requirements that govern its legal service operations; and

(vi) Such organization has filed with the appropriate disciplinary authority, to the extent required by such authority, at least annually a report with respect to its legal service plan, if any, showing its terms, its schedule of benefits, its subscription charges, agreements with counsel and financial results of its legal service activities or, if it has failed to do so, the lawyer does not know or have cause to know of such failure.

7.3 Solicitation and Recommendation of Professional Employment

(a) A lawyer shall not engage in solicitation:

> **In-person, Telephone, Real-time, Computer Communication**

(1) by in-person or telephone contact, or by real-time or interactive computer-accessed communication unless the recipient is a close friend, relative, former client or existing client; or

(2) by any form of communication if:

(i) the communication or contact violates Rule 4.5, Rule 7.1(a), or paragraph (e) of this Rule;

(ii) the recipient has made known to the lawyer a desire not to be solicited by the lawyer;

(iii) the solicitation involves coercion, duress or harassment;

(iv) the lawyer knows or reasonably should know that the age or the physical, emotional or mental state of the recipient makes it unlikely that the recipient will be able to exercise reasonable judgment in retaining a lawyer; or

(v) the lawyer intends or expects, but does not disclose, that the legal services necessary to handle the matter competently will be performed primarily by another lawyer who is not affiliated with the soliciting lawyer as a partner, associate or of counsel.

(b) For purposes of this Rule, "solicitation" means any advertisement initiated by or on behalf of a lawyer or law firm that is directed to, or targeted at, a specific recipient or group of recipients, or their family members or legal representatives, the primary purpose of which is the retention of the lawyer or law firm, and a significant motive for which is pecuniary gain. It does not include a proposal or other writing prepared and delivered in response to a specific request of a prospective client.

(c) A solicitation directed to a recipient in this State, shall be subject to the following provisions:

> **Solicitations Directed to New Yorkers**

(1) A copy of the solicitation shall at the time of its dissemination be filed with the attorney disciplinary committee of the judicial district or judicial department wherein the lawyer or law firm maintains its principal office. Where no such office is maintained, the filing shall be made in the judicial department where the solicitation is targeted. A filing shall consist of:

(i) a copy of the solicitation;

(ii) a transcript of the audio portion of any radio or television solicitation; and

(iii) if the solicitation is in a language other than English, an accurate English-language translation.

(2) Such solicitation shall contain no reference to the fact of filing.

(3) If a solicitation is directed to a predetermined recipient, a list containing the names and addresses of all recipients shall be retained by the lawyer or law firm for a period of not less than three years following the last date of its dissemination.

(4) Solicitations filed pursuant to this subdivision shall be open to public inspection.

(5) The provisions of this paragraph shall not apply to:

(i) a solicitation directed or disseminated to a close friend, relative, or former or existing client;

| Web Sites |

(ii) a web site maintained by the lawyer or law firm, unless the web site is designed for and directed to or targeted at a prospective client affected by an identifiable actual event or occurrence or by an identifiable prospective defendant; or

| Business Cards |

(iii) professional cards or other announcements the distribution of which is authorized by Rule 7.5(a).

(d) A written solicitation shall not be sent by a method that requires the recipient to travel to a location other than that at which the recipient ordinarily receives business or personal mail or that requires a signature on the part of the recipient.

(e) No solicitation relating to a specific incident involving potential claims for personal injury or wrongful

| Solicitation: 30-Day Rule |

death shall be disseminated before the 30th day after the date of the incident, unless a filing must be made within 30 days of the incident as a legal prerequisite to the particular claim, in which case no unsolicited communication shall be made before the 15th day after the date of the incident.

(f) Any solicitation made in writing or by computer-accessed communication and directed to a predetermined recipient, if prompted by a specific occurrence involving or affecting a recipient, shall disclose how the lawyer obtained the identity of the recipient and learned of the recipient's potential legal need.

(g) If a retainer agreement is provided with any solicita-

| Retainer Agreement |

tion, the top of each page shall be marked "SAMPLE" in red ink in a type size equal to the largest type size used in the agreement and the words "DO NOT SIGN" shall appear on the client signature line.

(h) Any solicitation covered by this section shall include the name, principal law office address and telephone number of the lawyer or law firm whose services are being offered.

(i) The provisions of this Rule shall apply to a lawyer or members of a law firm not admitted to practice in this State who solicit retention by residents of this State.

7.4 Identification of Practice and Specialty

(a) A lawyer or law firm may publicly identify one or more areas of law in

| Specialization |

which the lawyer or the law firm practices, or may state that the practice of the lawyer or law firm is limited to one or more areas of law, provided that the lawyer or law firm shall not state that the lawyer or law firm is a specialist or specializes in a particular field of law, except as provided in Rule 7.4(c).

(b) A lawyer admitted to engage in patent practice before the United States Patent and Trademark Office may use the designation "Patent Attorney" or a substantially similar designation.

(c) A lawyer may state that the lawyer has been recognized or certified as

| Certification |

a specialist only as follows:

(1) A lawyer who is certified as a specialist in a particular area of law or law practice by a private organization approved for that purpose by the American Bar Association may state the fact of certification if, in conjunction therewith, the certifying organization is identified and the following statement is prominently made: "The [name of the private certifying organization] is not affiliated with any governmental authority. Certification is not a requirement for the practice of law in the State of New York and does not necessarily indicate greater competence than other attorneys experienced in this field of law;"

(2) A lawyer who is certified as a specialist in a particular area of law or law practice by the authority having jurisdiction over specialization under the laws of another state or territory may state the fact of certification if, in conjunction therewith, the certifying state or territory is identified and the following statement is prominently made: "Certification granted by the [identify state or territory] is not recognized by any governmental authority within the State of New York. Certification is not a requirement for the practice of law in the State of New York and does not necessarily indicate greater competence than other attorneys experienced in this field of law."

7.5 Professional Notices, Letterheads, and Signs

(a) A lawyer or law firm may use internet web sites, professional

| Business Cards, Letterheads, Web Sites, Signs, and Other Notices |

cards, professional announcement cards, office signs, letterheads or similar professional notices or devices, provided the same do not violate any statute or court rule and are in accordance with Rule 7.1, including the following:

(1) a professional card of a lawyer identifying the lawyer by name and as a lawyer, and giving

addresses, telephone numbers, the name of the law firm, and any information permitted under Rule 7.1(b) or Rule 7.4. A professional card of a law firm may also give the names of members and associates;

(2) a professional announcement card stating new or changed associations or addresses, change of firm name, or similar matters pertaining to the professional offices of a lawyer or law firm or any nonlegal business conducted by the lawyer or law firm pursuant to Rule 5.7. It may state biographical data, the names of members of the firm and associates, and the names and dates of predecessor firms in a continuing line of succession. It may state the nature of the legal practice if permitted under Rule 7.4;

(3) a sign in or near the office and in the building directory identifying the law office and any nonlegal business conducted by the lawyer or law firm pursuant to Rule 5.7. The sign may state the nature of the legal practice if permitted under Rule 7.4; or

(4) a letterhead identifying the lawyer by name and as a lawyer, and giving addresses, telephone numbers, the name of the law firm, associates and any information permitted under Rule 7.1(b) or Rule 7.4. A letterhead of a law firm may also give the names of members and associates, and names and dates relating to deceased and retired members. A lawyer or law firm may be designated "Of Counsel" on a letterhead if there is a continuing relationship with a lawyer or law firm, other than as a partner or associate. A lawyer or law firm may be designated as "General Counsel" or by similar professional reference on stationery of a client if the lawyer or the firm devotes a substantial amount of professional time in the representation of that client. The letterhead of a law firm may give the names and dates of predecessor firms in a continuing line of succession.

(b) A lawyer in private practice shall not practice under a trade name, a name that is misleading as to the identity of the lawyer or lawyers practicing under

| Nonlawyer Name as Part of Law Office Name |

such name, or a firm name containing names other than those of one or more of the lawyers in the firm, except that the name of a professional corporation shall contain "PC" or such symbols permitted by law, the name of a limited liability company or partnership shall contain "LLC," "LLP" or such symbols permitted by law and, if otherwise lawful, a firm may use as, or continue to include in its name the name or names of one or more deceased or retired members of the firm or of a

predecessor firm in a continuing line of succession. Such terms as "legal clinic," "legal aid," "legal service office," "legal assistance office," "defender office" and the like may be used only by qualified legal assistance organizations, except that the term "legal clinic" may be used by any lawyer or law firm provided the name of a participating lawyer or firm is incorporated therein. A lawyer or law firm may not include the name of a nonlawyer in its firm name, nor may a lawyer or law firm that has a contractual relationship with a nonlegal professional or nonlegal professional service firm pursuant to Rule 5.8 to provide legal and other professional services on a systematic and continuing basis include in its firm name the name of the nonlegal professional service firm or any individual nonlegal professional affiliated therewith. A lawyer who assumes a judicial, legislative or public executive or administrative post or office shall not permit the lawyer's name to remain in the name of a law firm or to be used in professional notices of the firm during any significant period in which the lawyer is not actively and regularly practicing law as a member of the firm and, during such period, other members of the firm shall not use the lawyer's name in the firm name or in professional notices of the firm.

(c) Lawyers shall not hold themselves out as having a partnership with one or more other lawyers unless they are in fact partners.

(d) A partnership shall not be formed or continued between or among lawyers licensed in different jurisdictions unless all enumerations of the members and associates of the firm on its letterhead and in other permissible listings make clear the jurisdictional limitations on those members and associates of the firm not licensed to practice in all listed jurisdictions; however, the same firm name may be used in each jurisdiction.

(e) A lawyer or law firm may utilize a domain name for an internet web site that does not include the name of the lawyer or law firm provided:

| Law Firm Web Sites |

(1) all pages of the web site clearly and conspicuously include the actual name of the lawyer or law firm;

(2) the lawyer or law firm in no way attempts to engage in the practice of law using the domain name;

(3) the domain name does not imply an ability to obtain results in a matter; and

(4) the domain name does not otherwise violate these Rules.

(f) A lawyer or law firm may utilize a telephone number which contains a domain name, nickname, moniker or motto that does not otherwise violate these Rules.

8.1 Candor in the Bar Admission Process

(a) A lawyer shall be subject to discipline if, in connection with the lawyer's own application for admission to the bar previously filed in this state or in any other jurisdiction, or in connection with the application of another person for admission to the bar, the lawyer knowingly:

| Admission to Practice |

(1) has made or failed to correct a false statement of material fact; or

(2) has failed to disclose a material fact requested in connection with a lawful demand for information from an admissions authority.

8.2 Judicial Officers and Candidates

(a) A lawyer shall not knowingly make a false statement of fact concerning the qualifications, conduct or integrity of a judge or other adjudicatory officer or of a candidate for election or appointment to judicial office.

(b) A lawyer who is a candidate for judicial office shall comply with the applicable provisions of Part 100 of the Rules of the Chief Administrator of the Courts.

8.3 Reporting Professional Misconduct

(a) A lawyer who knows that another lawyer has committed a violation of the Rules of Professional Conduct that raises a substantial question as to that lawyer's honesty, trustworthiness or fitness as a lawyer shall report such knowledge to a tribunal or other authority empowered to investigate or act upon such violation.

| Duty to Report Attorney Honesty, Trustworthiness, or Unfitness |

(b) A lawyer who possesses knowledge or evidence concerning another lawyer or a judge shall not fail to respond to a lawful demand for information from a tribunal or other authority empowered to investigate or act upon such conduct.

(c) This Rule does not require disclosure of:

(1) information otherwise protected by Rule 1.6; or

(2) information gained by a lawyer or judge while participating in a bona fide lawyer assistance program.

8.4 Misconduct

A lawyer or law firm shall not:

(a) violate or attempt to violate the Rules of Professional Conduct, knowingly assist or induce another to do so, or do so through the acts of another;

| Kinds of Attorney Misconduct |

(b) engage in illegal conduct that adversely reflects on the lawyer's honesty, trustworthiness or fitness as a lawyer;

(c) engage in conduct involving dishonesty, fraud, deceit or misrepresentation;

(d) engage in conduct that is prejudicial to the administration of justice;

(e) state or imply an ability:

(1) to influence improperly or upon irrelevant grounds any tribunal, legislative body or public official; or

(2) to achieve results using means that violate these Rules or other law;

(f) knowingly assist a judge or judicial officer in conduct that is a violation of applicable rules of judicial conduct or other law;

(g) unlawfully discriminate in the practice of law, including in hiring, promoting or otherwise determining conditions of employment on the basis of age, race, creed, color, national origin, sex, disability, marital status or sexual

| Discrimination Charge against a Lawyer |

orientation. Where there is a tribunal with jurisdiction to hear a complaint, if timely brought, other than a Departmental Disciplinary Committee, a complaint based on unlawful discrimination shall be brought before such tribunal in the first instance. A certified copy of a determination by such a tribunal, which has become final and enforceable and as to which the right to judicial or appellate review has been exhausted, finding that the lawyer has engaged in an unlawful discriminatory practice shall constitute prima facie evidence of professional misconduct in a disciplinary proceeding; or

(h) engage in any other conduct that adversely reflects on the lawyer's fitness as a lawyer.

8.5 Disciplinary Authority and Choice of Law

(a) A lawyer admitted to practice in this state is subject to the disciplinary authority of this state, regardless of where the lawyer's conduct occurs. A lawyer may be subject to the disciplinary authority of both this state and another jurisdiction where the lawyer is admitted for the same conduct.

(b) In any exercise of the disciplinary authority of this state, the rules of professional conduct to be applied shall be as follows:

(1) For conduct in connection with a proceeding in a court before which a lawyer has been admitted to practice (either generally or for purposes of that proceeding), the rules to be applied shall be the rules of the jurisdiction in which the court sits, unless the rules of the court provide otherwise; and

(2) For any other conduct:

(i) If the lawyer is licensed to practice only in this state, the rules to be applied shall be the rules of this state, and

(ii) If the lawyer is licensed to practice in this state and another jurisdiction, the rules to be applied shall be the rules of the admitting jurisdiction in which the lawyer principally practices; provided, however, that if particular conduct clearly has its predominant effect in another jurisdiction in which the lawyer is licensed to practice, the rules of that jurisdiction shall be applied to that conduct.

F. Selected Statutes from Judiciary Law (Article 15, Attorneys and Counsellors)

§ 474. Compensation of Attorney or Counsellor

The compensation of an attorney or counsellor for his services is governed by agreement, express or implied, which is not restrained by law, except that no agreement made hereafter between an attorney and a guardian of an infant for the compensation of such attorney, dependent upon the success of the prosecution by said attorney of a claim belonging to said infant, or by which such attorney is to receive a percentage of any recovery or award in behalf of such infant or a sum equal to a percentage of any such recovery or award, shall be valid or enforceable unless made as hereinafter provided.

| Fees in Cases Involving Infants |

An attorney may contract with the guardian of an infant to prosecute, by suit or otherwise, any claim for the benefit of an infant for a compensation to said attorney dependent upon the success in the prosecution of such claim, subject to the power of the court, as hereinafter provided, to fix the amount of such compensation. Whenever such a contract shall have been entered into between an attorney and a guardian of an infant, upon the recovery of a judgment, or the obtaining of an award in behalf of the said infant, or upon any compromise or settlement of such claim, the attorney may apply, upon notice to the guardian, to the judge, justice or surrogate before whom the said action or proceeding was tried, or to whom an application for compromise or settlement was made, in case the said action or proceeding was tried, or the said application was made at a court held within this state; to a special term of said court, in case the said action or proceeding was tried before some person other than a justice thereof, or said claim was compromised or settled after said suit was begun, or in case of the death or disability of the judge or justice before whom the action was tried; or to special term of the supreme court in case the recovery, award, compromise or settlement was not had in any court of this state.

Such application shall set forth briefly the contract, the services performed by the attorney and pray that there be awarded to him a suitable amount out of the recovery, award, compromise or settlement obtained through his efforts as attorney on behalf of the infant. The court, judge or surrogate to which such application is made, upon being satisfied that due notice of the said application [has] been given to the said guardian, shall proceed summarily to determine the value of the services of said attorney, taking such proof from either the attorney or the guardian by affidavit, reference or the examination of witnesses before the said court, judge or surrogate, as may seem to be necessary and proper, and shall thereupon make an order determining the suitable compensation for the attorney for his services therein, which sum shall thereafter be received by the said attorney for his services in behalf of the said infant; and no other compensation shall be paid or allowed by the guardian for such services out of the estate of said infant.

If a copy of such order awarding the compensation with notice of entry be thereafter served by the said attorney upon the adverse party to the said litigation or the person making such compromise or settlement and upon the custodian of the funds recovered, in case there be such custodian, such award shall become and constitute a lien to the amount thereof on behalf of the said attorney upon such recovery, award, settlement or fund.

§ 474-a. Contingent Fees for Attorneys in Claims or Actions for Medical, Dental or Podiatric Malpractice

1. For the purpose of this section, the term "contingent fee" shall mean any attorney's fee in any claim or action for medical, dental or podiatric malpractice, whether determined by judgment or settlement, which is dependent in whole or in part upon the success of the prosecution by the attorney of such claim or action, or which is to consist of a percentage of any recovery, or a sum equal to a percentage of any recovery, in such claim or action.

| Fees in Malpractice Cases |

2. Notwithstanding any inconsistent judicial rule, a contingent fee in a medical, dental or podiatric malpractice action shall not exceed the amount of compensation provided for in the following schedule:

   30 percent of the first $250,000 of the sum recovered;
   25 percent of the next $250,000 of the sum recovered;
   20 percent of the next $500,000 of the sum recovered;
   15 percent of the next $250,000 of the sum recovered;
   10 percent of any amount over $1,250,000 of the sum recovered.

3. Such percentages shall be computed on the net sum recovered after deducting from the amount recovered expenses and disbursements for expert testimony and investigative or other services properly chargeable to the enforcement of the claim or prosecution of the action. In computing the fee, the costs as taxed, including interest upon a judgment, shall be deemed part of the amount recovered. For the following or similar items there shall be no deduction in computing such percentages: liens, assignments or claims in favor of hospitals, for medical care, dental care, podiatric care and treatment by doctors and nurses, or of self-insurers or insurance carriers.

4. In the event that claimant's or plaintiff's attorney believes in good faith that the fee schedule set forth in subdivision two of this section, because of extraordinary circumstances, will not give him adequate compensation, application for greater compensation may be made upon affidavit with written notice and an opportunity to be heard to the claimant or plaintiff and other persons holding liens or assignments on the recovery. Such application shall be made to the justice of the trial part to which the action had been sent for trial; or, if it had not been sent to a part for trial, then to the justice presiding at the trial term calendar part of the court in which the action had been instituted; or, if no action had been instituted, then to the justice presiding at the trial term calendar part of the Supreme Court for the county in the judicial department in which the attorney has an office. Upon such application, the justice, in his discretion, if extraordinary circumstances are found to be present, and without regard to the claimant's or plaintiff's consent, may fix as reasonable compensation for legal services rendered an amount greater than that specified in the schedule set forth in subdivision two of this section, provided, however, that such greater amount shall not exceed the fee fixed pursuant to the contractual arrangement, if any, between the claimant or plaintiff and the attorney. If the application is granted, the justice shall make a written order accordingly, briefly stating the reasons for granting the greater compensation; and a copy of such order shall be served on all persons entitled to receive notice of the application.

Request for Fees That Are Higher Than the Maximum Allowed

5. Any contingent fee in a claim or action for medical, dental or podiatric malpractice brought on behalf of an infant shall continue to be subject to the provisions of section four hundred seventy-four of this chapter.

§ 475. Attorney's Lien in Action, Special or Other Proceeding

From the commencement of an action, special or other proceeding in any court or before any state, municipal or federal department, except a department of labor, or the service of an answer containing a counterclaim, the attorney who appears for a party has a lien upon his client's cause of action, claim or counterclaim, which attaches to a verdict, report, determination, decision, judgment or final order in his client's favor, and the proceeds thereof in whatever hands they may come; and the lien cannot be affected by any settlement between the parties before or after judgment, final order or determination. The court upon the petition of the client or attorney may determine and enforce the lien.

Enforcement Liens

§ 477. Settlement of Actions for Personal Injury

If, in an action commenced to recover damages for a personal injury or for death as the result of a personal injury, an attorney having or claiming to have a lien for services performed or to be performed who shall have appeared for the person or persons having or claiming to have a right of action for such injury or death, no settlement or adjustment of such action shall be valid, unless consented to in writing by such attorney and by the person or persons for whom he shall have appeared, or approved by an order of the court in which such action is brought.

Attorney Consent in Settlement

§ 479. Soliciting Business on Behalf of an Attorney

It shall be unlawful for any person or his agent, employee or any person acting on his behalf, to solicit or procure through solicitation either directly or indirectly legal business, or to solicit or procure through solicitation a retainer, written or oral, or any agreement authorizing an attorney to perform or render legal services, or to make it a business so to solicit or procure such business, retainers or agreements.

Solicitation for an Attorney

§ 480. Entering Hospital to Negotiate Settlement or Obtain Release or Statement

It shall be unlawful for any person to enter a hospital for the purpose of negotiating a settlement or obtaining a general release or statement, written or oral, from any person confined in said hospital or sanitarium as a patient, with reference to any personal injuries for which said person is confined in said hospital or sanitarium within fifteen days after the injuries were sustained, unless at least five days prior to the obtaining or procuring of such general release or statement such

Prohibited Conduct in Hospitals

injured party has signified in writing his willingness that such general release or statement be given. This section shall not apply to a person entering a hospital for the purpose of visiting a person therein confined, as his attorney or on behalf of his attorney.

§ 481. Aiding, Assisting or Abetting the Solicitation of Persons or the Procurement of a Retainer for or on Behalf of an Attorney

It shall be unlawful for any person in the employ of or in any capacity attached to any hospital, sanitarium, police department, prison or court, or for a person authorized to furnish bail bonds, to communicate directly or indirectly with any attorney or person acting on his behalf for the purpose of aiding, assisting or abetting such attorney in the solicitation of legal business or the procurement through solicitation of a retainer, written or oral, or any agreement authorizing the attorney to perform or render legal services.

§ 482. Employment by Attorney of Person to Aid, Assist or Abet in the Solicitation of Business or the Procurement Through Solicitation of a Retainer to Perform Legal Services

It shall be unlawful for an attorney to employ any person for the purpose of soliciting or aiding, assisting or

| Solicitation for an Attorney |

abetting in the solicitation of legal business or the procurement through solicitation either directly or indirectly of a retainer, written or oral, or of any agreement authorizing the attorney to perform or render legal services.

§ 483. Signs Advertising Services as Attorney-at-Law

It shall be unlawful for any person to maintain on real property or to permit or allow any other person to maintain, on such property a sign, in any language, to the effect that an attorney-at-law or legal services are available therein unless the full name of the attorney-at-law or the firm rendering such services is set forth thereon. In any prosecution for violation of the provisions of this section the existence of such a sign on real property shall be presumptive evidence that it was placed or permitted to exist thereon with the knowledge and consent of the person or persons in possession of said premises.

§ 487. Misconduct by Attorneys

An attorney or counselor who:

1. Is guilty of any deceit or collusion, or consents to

| Deceit of Collusion by Attorney |

any deceit or collusion, with intent to deceive the court or any party; or,
2. Wilfully delays his client's suit with a view to his own gain; or, wilfully receives any money or allowance

for or on account of any money which he has not laid out, or becomes answerable for,

Is guilty of a misdemeanor, and in addition to the punishment prescribed therefor by the penal law, he forfeits to the party injured treble damages, to be recovered in a civil action.

§ 491. Sharing of Compensation by Attorneys Prohibited

1. It shall be unlawful for any person, partnership, corporation, or association to divide with or receive from, or to agree to divide with or receive from, any attorney-at-law or group of attorneys-at-law, whether practicing

| Dividing Fees |

in this state or elsewhere, either before or after action brought, any portion of any fee or compensation, charged or received by such attorney-at-law or any valuable consideration or reward, as an inducement for placing, or in consideration of having placed, in the hands of such attorney-at-law, or in the hands of another person, a claim or demand of any kind for the purpose of collecting such claim, or bringing an action thereon, or of representing claimant in the pursuit of any civil remedy for the recovery thereof. But this section does not apply to an agreement between attorneys and counsellors-at-law to divide between themselves the compensation to be received.
2. Any person violating any of the provisions of this section is guilty of a misdemeanor.

§ 497. Attorneys Fiduciary Funds; Interest-Bearing Accounts

1. An "interest on lawyer account" or "IOLA" is an unsegregated interest-bearing deposit account with a banking institution for the deposit by an attorney of qualified funds.

| IOLA: Interest on Lawyer Account |

2. "Qualified funds" are moneys received by an attorney in a fiduciary capacity from a client or beneficial owner and which, in the judgment of the attorney, are too small in amount or are reasonably expected to be held for too short a time to generate sufficient interest income to justify the expense of administering a segregated account for the benefit of the client or beneficial owner. In determining whether funds are qualified for deposit in an IOLA account, an attorney may use as a guide the regulation adopted by the board of trustees of the IOLA fund pursuant to subdivision four of section ninety-seven-v of the state finance law.
2-a. "Funds received in a fiduciary capacity" are funds received by an attorney from a client or beneficial owner in the course of the practice of law, including but not limited to funds received in an escrow capacity, but not including

funds received as trustee, guardian or receiver in bankruptcy. . . .

6. a. An attorney or law firm which receives qualified funds in the course of its practice of law and establishes and maintains an IOLA account shall do so by (1) designating the account as "(name of attorney/law firm IOLA account)" with the approval of the banking institution; and (2) notifying the IOLA fund within thirty days of establishing the IOLA account of the account number and name and address of the banking institution where the account is deposited. . . .

   c. With respect to IOLA accounts, the banking institution shall:

     (i) Remit at least quarterly any interest earned on the account directly to the IOLA fund, after deduction of service charges or fees, if any, are applied. . . .

§ 498. Professional Referrals

1. There shall be no cause of action for damages arising against any association or society of attorneys

Lawyer Referrals

and counsellors at law authorized to practice in the state of New York for referring any person or persons to a member of the profession for the purpose of obtaining legal services, provided that such referral was made without charge and as a public service by said association or society, and without malice, and in the reasonable belief that such referral was warranted, based upon the facts disclosed.

2. For the purposes of this section, "association or society of attorneys or counsellors at law" shall mean any such organization, whether incorporated or unincorporated, which offers professional referrals as an incidental service in the normal course of business, but which business does not include the providing of legal services.

G. More Information

Rules of Professional Conduct
www.nycourts.gov/rules/jointappellate/NY%20Rules%20of%20Prof%20Conduct_09.pdf
www.nycourts.gov/rules/jointappellate/NY%20Rules%20of%20Prof%20Conduct.pdf
22 NYCRR 1200.0 to 22 NYCRR 1200.59.

Lawyer's Code of Professional Responsibility
www.law.cornell.edu/ethics/ny/code
www.nysba.org
(click "For Attorneys" then "Professional Standards for Attorneys")

American Bar Association Model Rules of Professional Conduct
www.abanet.org/cpr/mrpc/mrpc_toc.html

New York Ethics Materials
www.law.cornell.edu/ethics/ny.html

Ethics Opinions in New York
New York State Bar Association
www.nysba.org
(click "For Attorneys" then "Ethics Opinions")

New York County Lawyers' Association
www.nycla.org
(click "News & Publications" then "Ethics Opinions")

Nassau County Bar Association
www.nassaubar.org
(under "For the Legal Profession" click "Ethics Opinions")

Association of the Bar of the City of New York
www.abcny.org
(click "Reports/Publications/Forms" then "Ethical Responsibilities and Opinions")

Defender Ethics Resources
www.nysda.org/html/ethics_resources.html

New York Ethics on Lexis
www.lexis.com
New York Library, NYETOP file

New York Ethics on Westlaw
www.westlaw.com
NYETH-EO database
NYETH-CS database
NY-RULES database

Legal Ethics in General
www.abanet.org/cpr/links.html
www.legalethics.com
ww3.lawschool.cornell.edu/faculty-pages/wendel/ethlinks.htm

American Legal Ethics Library
www.law.cornell.edu/ethics
(click "Listing by Jurisdiction" then "New York")

H. Something to Check

1. Use the online sites for New York court opinions (see section 5.1) to find and summarize (brief) one opinion from any New York state court on attorney solicitation.

2. Run the following search ("New York" "rules of professional conduct") in any three general search engines (e.g., *www.google.com*, *www.yahoo.com*, *www.bing.com*, *www.ask.com*). Prepare a report on the categories of sites to which each search engine leads you. Cluster the same kinds of sites you find into categories (sites giving you the text of the rules, opinions interpreting the rules, law firms that represent attorneys charged with violating the rules, etc.). Give a brief description of each category with a minimum of five examples of sites under each category. After you finish the report for the three general search engines, comment on which engine was the most productive and why.

3.3 Ethical Opinions and Guidelines on Paralegals and Other Employees

A. Introduction

B. Table of Contents

C. Index of Issues Covered in Ethics Opinions

D. Chronological Table of Ethics Opinions

E. Ethical Opinions: Questions and Answers

F. Rule 5.3 of the Rules of Professional Conduct

G. New York State Bar Association Guidelines on Paralegals

H. More Information

I. Something to Check

A. Introduction

According to a major bar association ethics committee in New York, the "burgeoning use and expanding role of legal assistants, employed widely by law firms and bank and corporate law departments, necessary to enable the lawyer to provide quality service at reasonable cost, has indicated the need to remind the Bar of the essential guidelines to be followed in the employment of such assistants." New York County Lawyers' Association Committee on Professional Ethics, Opinion 666 (1985). Our goal in this section is to examine the "essential guidelines" on paralegals that have been pronounced by the following ethics committees:

- New York State Bar Association Committee on Professional Ethics
- Bar of the City of New York Committee on Professional and Judicial Ethics
- New York County Lawyers' Association Committee on Professional Ethics

The Nassau County Bar Association also issues ethics opinions. Some of them are covered here; others are covered in section 3.1 on the unauthorized practice of law. Finally, we have included ethics opinions of the New York Advisory Commission on Judicial Ethics because they raise important issues involving paralegals.

The ethical rules for attorneys are contained in the Lawyer's Code of Professional Responsibility (22 NYCRR 1200 et. seq.). The requirements in the code are called Disciplinary Rules (DR) and the explanatory guidelines are called Ethical Considerations (EC). See section 3.2 for the text of this Code. The ethics opinions of these committees are advisory in the sense that the courts are the ultimate authority on whether an attorney has violated ethical standards and should be punished.

Ethical opinions and guidelines that involve the practice of law and the unauthorized practice of law are treated separately in section 3.1.

B. Table of Contents

The following issues are covered in the ethical opinions presented in this section:

1. Paralegal Titles
2. Paralegal Tasks
3. Paralegal Compensation; Payments for Referrals
4. Letterhead and Business Cards
5. Attorney Supervision
6. Conflict of Interest
7. Real Estate Closings
8. Signatures
9. Execution of Wills
10. Conducting Depositions
11. Confidentiality
12. Unauthorized Practice of Law
13. Disbarred or Suspended Lawyer as Paralegal
14. Outsourcing

C. Index of Issues Covered in Ethics Opinions

Abbreviations

Nassau Nassau County Bar Association Committee on Professional Ethics

NY State New York State Bar Association Committee on Professional Ethics

NY City Bar of the City of New York Committee on Professional and Judicial Ethics

NY County New York County Lawyers' Association Committee on Professional Ethics

Op Ethical opinion

PEC Professional Ethics Committee

WL Westlaw

- **Advertising**, NY State 640
- **Advocate**, NY State 640
- **Bonus**, NY City 1995-11; NY State 733
- **Business card**, NY City 1996-2; NY County 673; NY State 640, 695
- **Certified Legal Assistant**, NY State 695
- **Closings**, NY State 677
- **Compensation**, NY City 1995-11; NY State 731, 733
- **Confidentiality**, NY City 1995-11; NY State 386, 422, 503, 700
- **Conflict of interest**, NY State 774
- **Deposition**, NY State 304
- **Escrow**, NY State 693
- **Investigator**, NY State 255
- **Letterhead**, NY City 1996-2; NY County 673; NY State 255, 500, 640, 695
- **Paralegal titles**, NY State 640
- **Real estate closings**, NY State 677

D. Chronological Table of Ethics Opinions

E. Ethical Opinions: Questions and Answers

1. Paralegal Titles

Opinion 640 (December 7, 1992)
New York State Bar Association Committee on Professional Ethics
(*www.nysba.org/AM/Template.cfm?Section=Ethics_Opinions&
TEMPLATE=/CM/ContentDisplay.cfm&CONTENTID=
18728*) (1992 WL 450730)

Question: **What titles can be used for paralegals on business cards, letterheads, publicity, or advertising?**

Answer: **Titles such as paralegal and senior paralegal are acceptable because they make the holder's nonlawyer status clear. Unacceptable titles that do not make this status clear include paralegal coordinator, legal associate, public benefits specialist, legal advocate, family law advocate, housing law advocate, disability benefits advocate, and public benefits advocate.**

The manner in which nonlawyer employees including paralegals hold themselves out to the public is the responsibility of the employer lawyer. The contents of professional notices, letterheads, publicity, advertising and the like are governed by DR 2-101(A) and (D) and DR 2-102, as well as *Bates v. State Bar of Arizona*, 433 U.S. 350 (1977) and its progeny. We join with Indiana, Kansas and Texas in holding that the employing lawyer is responsible to insure that the content of the business cards of the lawyer's paralegals meet the same standards as those applied to lawyer advertising.

The listing of paralegals and their services on business cards and letterheads provides the public with information of the type specified in DR 2-101(D). Thus, the primary concern is to insure that the listing is not false, deceptive or misleading as proscribed by DR 2-101(A). In N.Y. State 500 (1978), this Committee opined that if it was made clear that the employee was not a lawyer, the practice of listing nonlawyers, including paralegals, on the firm's letterhead was permissible. The term "paralegal" is sufficient without further qualification to make clear the employee's nonlawyer status. N.Y. State 500 (1978). A paralegal may use a business card that lists the name of the law firm, the name of the paralegal and a designation of the paralegal's nonlawyer status. N.Y. County 673 (1989). As that Committee noted, paralegals hold an important position in the efficient delivery of legal services by all types of organizations including legal services offices. See also ABA Inf. 89-1527 (1989) [where the terms "Staff Investigator," "Office Manager," and "Secretary" were authorized for use by a nonlawyer for inclusion on a firm's letterhead, but the term "Executive Director" was found to be ambiguous and therefore prohibited unless the letterhead, business card or other listing makes it clear that either the person is a nonlawyer or is responsible only for the administration of the law office and is not responsible for the professional practice].

Based upon the foregoing, the inquiry is largely whether the various titles clearly demonstrate that the paralegal is not an attorney. One of the titles is clearly permissible in that it uses the word "paralegal." The term "Senior Paralegal" unambiguously conveys that the employee is a paralegal. The term "Paralegal Coordinator," however, is ambiguous as it is not clear whether the coordinator is a paralegal. The person may be an attorney coordinating the firm's paralegals. Accordingly, the term "Paralegal Coordinator" may not be used unless the letterhead, business card or other listing makes it clear that either the person is a nonlawyer or is responsible only for the administration of the paralegals and is not responsible for the professional practice. See ABA Inf. 89-1527 (1989).

The title "Legal Associate" is clearly impermissible. The term "associate" is applied regularly with respect to lawyers and generally connotes a nonpartner attorney in a law firm. See ABA 90-357 (1990) and ABA 84-351 (1984).

The public would in all likelihood be confused by use of the term "Legal Associate" if listed as a paralegal's only title. The term "Public Benefits Specialist" also presents the likelihood of confusion. DR 2-105(B) allows an attorney to hold himself out as a specialist in a particular area of the law, if he or she has been so certified by an authority with jurisdiction under New York law under the subject of specialization. New York to date has not implemented the specialization provision. The use of the term by an attorney, a fortiori by a paralegal, would be misleading. N.Y. State 487 (1978).

The terms "Legal Advocate," "Family Law Advocate" and "Housing Law Advocate" present the same issue. Although few lawyers in the United States refer to their professional title as "advocate," the Spanish word for a lawyer is "abogado," and a significant segment of the U.S. population is Spanish speaking. The risk of confusion is present and the policy behind the proscription not to mislead the public requires at the very least that ambiguous language be clarified. The terms "Disability Benefits Advocate" and "Public Rights Advocate" are only slightly less ambiguous, as they do not contain the term "legal" or "law" within term. Nevertheless, they retain the potential for confusion found in the other "advocate" titles and, therefore, are misleading. A layperson could believe that a person who is a "Disability Advocate" or "Public Benefits Advocate" is in fact a lawyer.

Opinion 695 (August 25, 1997)

New York State Bar Association Committee on Professional Ethics

(*www.nysba.org/AM/Template.cfm?Section=Ethics_Opinions& TEMPLATE=/CM/ContentDisplay.cfm&CONTENTID= 18817*) (1997 WL 1068499)

> *Question:* Can an attorney identify a legal assistant as a "Certified Legal Assistant" on business cards, letterheads, and promotional material?
>
> *Answer:* Yes, but to avoid misleading the public, the designation must be accompanied by a reference to NALA and the lawyer must be satisfied of the bona fides of NALA.

Lawyers are ethically responsible for how their legal assistants are held out or designated to the public. Designations that are false, deceptive, or misleading must be avoided. In *Peel v. Attorney Registration and Disciplinary Commission*, 496 U.S. 91 (1990), the Supreme Court held that an attorney has a constitutional right under the commercial free speech doctrine to advertise certification as a specialist, subject to any disclaimer required by the state to make the claim of specialization not misleading. In light of this decision, a lawyer may include on letterhead and other materials the identification of a nonlegal employee as a Certified Legal Assistant "provided that term is accompanied by the statement that the certification is afforded by the National Association of Legal Assistants ("NALA"), and

provided further that the attorney has satisfied himself or herself that NALA is a bona fide organization that provides such certification to all who meet objective and consistently applied standards relevant to the work of legal assistants.

Formal Opinion 1996-2 (February 26, 1996)

Association of the Bar of the City of New York Committee on Professional and Judicial Ethics

(*www.nycbar.org/Publications/reports/show_html.php?rid=1 56&searchterm=1996-2*) (1996 WL 93063)

> *Question:* May a law firm issue an announcement of the employment of a nonlawyer?
>
> *Answer:* Yes, if the announcement makes clear that the person is not a lawyer.

We have found no opinions on this issue from any ethics committees within New York State. Those ethics committees from other states that have addressed the issue of announcements pertaining to nonlawyers are divided:

- Hawaii ruled that a paralegal may be listed on professional notices distributed or mailed by a law firm, provided that the paralegal is clearly identified as such and no misleading statements are made as to his or her status in the firm. Hawaii 78-8-19 (1984).

- A 1980 Wisconsin opinion held that a lawyer could not formally announce that he had hired a paralegal. The Committee reasoned that a paralegal was not authorized to practice law and could only assist a lawyer under a lawyer's supervision. Because a lawyer's advertising was limited to the lawyer's ability to perform legal services, he could not announce the employment of a nonlawyer. Wisconsin E-80-15. See also Wisconsin E-83-3.

- South Carolina held that a law firm could not send an announcement to lawyers and accountants stating that it had hired a nonlawyer to handle administrative tax matters involving IRS. It deemed such an announcement misleading in that it might have created an unjustified expectation that the employee would handle legal matters as a lawyer and by virtue of prior employment, be able to influence IRS rulings. South Carolina 83-16.

There are many opinions that address related issues, such as whether nonlawyers may be listed on a law firm's letterhead or issued business cards. Most opinions permit such listings and issuance of business cards as long as they are not false or misleading. Some opinions approve the issuance of business cards but not letterhead listings. Many of the favorable opinions arose from questions involving paralegals and legal assistants. See, e.g., Chicago 92-3("[a] law firm may supply its paralegals business cards containing the paralegal's name and nonlawyer position and the firm's name, address and telephone number, all listed in a manner compatible with the lawyer ethics rules"). See generally ABA/BNA Lawyers Manual on Professional Conduct 81:3007-10 (1995).

We believe that it would be unduly restrictive to prohibit the announcement of the hiring of a non-lawyer employee solely on the grounds of his or her status as a nonlawyer, particularly in light of the broad use of nonlawyer professionals and paraprofessionals today. Law firms now employ a variety of nonlawyers whose employment is intended both to support the practice and to attract business, such as paralegals, marketers, specialists in information technology and scientists of different disciplines. . . . Prohibitions and restrictions on announcements of the hiring of nonlawyers have been aimed at assuring that the nonlawyer status of the employee is made clear or preventing lawyers from suggesting that the hiring of the employee is calculated to achieve some improper advantage for the firm and its clients. See DR 2-101(A). Thus, the Committee concludes that as long as a law firm makes clear in an announcement that the person employed is working in a nonlawyer capacity, an announcement that otherwise conforms with the ethical considerations and sections of the Code would be permissible.

2. Paralegal Tasks

Opinion 666 (October 29, 1985)
New York County Lawyers' Association Committee on Professional Ethics
(*www.nycla.org/siteFiles/Publications/Publications440_0.pdf*)
(1985 WL 287691)

Question: What tasks may a paralegal perform?

Answer: A paralegal can perform any supervised task that does not require independent professional judgment or participation.

The burgeoning use and expanding role of legal assistants, employed widely by law firms and bank and corporate law departments, [is] necessary to enable the lawyer to provide quality service at reasonable cost. . . . He or she may conduct legal research, prepare memoranda of law, prepare all legal papers, interview prospective witnesses and, in general, perform all services that do not require the exercise of independent professional judgment or participation, all subject to the continuing supervision of the lawyer by whom the legal assistant is employed. N.Y. County 641 N.Y. City 884 N.Y. State 44 (1967); N.Y. City 78 (1927-28); EC 3-6.

The legal assistant may also deal directly with the public either by oral or written communication, provided that he or she properly identifies him or herself from the outset as a nonlawyer (N.Y. City 884; N.Y. State 500 [1978]) and, again, provided that such dealings do not call for the independent exercise of professional

judgment. He or she may also deal directly with and appear before courts and other tribunals on routine matters, such as responding to calendar calls, provided no oral argument or exercise of judgment of any kind is required (N.Y. City 884; N.Y. State 44) and, of course, provided that such appearance would not contravene a standing rule of the court of tribunal. See DR7-106(A); see also Canons 1 and 9.

The determination of what matters, moreover, require the exercise of professional judgment is not one which should be left to the legal assistant. Rather, before delegating any task, the lawyer should determine whether any such matters may arise. If it appears that any questions may rise calling for the exercise of such judgment during the performance of the task, the lawyer should not delegate it to the legal assistant or so circumscribe the assignment as to avoid the need for the legal assistant to exercise judgment. Should any questions calling for the exercise of professional judgment arise unexpectedly, it is the duty of the legal assistant to immediately refer such matters to the lawyer under whose supervision he or she is performing the work.

3. Paralegal Compensation; Payments for Referrals

Opinion 733 (October 5, 2000)
New York State Bar Association Committee on Professional Ethics
(*www.nysba.org/AM/Template.cfm?Section=Ethics_Opinions& TEMPLATE=/CM/ContentDisplay.cfm&CONTENTID= 18964*) (2000 WL 33347719)

Questions:
(1) Can a paralegal's salary or participation in a retirement plan be based on a profit-sharing arrangement?
(2) Can a paralegal be compensated by receiving a percentage of profits or fees attributable to particular clients referred to the firm by the paralegal?

Answers:
(1) Yes, so long as the paralegal is not paid a percentage of profits or fees attributable to a particular client.
(2) No. A nonlawyer cannot receive part of a particular fee and a lawyer cannot compensate a nonlawyer for referrals.

DR 3-102(A)(3) of the New York Lawyer's Code of Professional Responsibility permits nonlawyer employees to be compensated based on a profit-sharing arrangement. The rule allows them "to participate in a profit-sharing plan with respect to their salaries and bonuses and otherwise to be compensated, in whole or in part, based on the profitability of the lawyer or law firm." The rule is not limited to retirement plans of the firm in which the nonlawyer is allowed to participate. Profit sharing is ethical in salaries, bonuses, and retirement plans so long as the nonlawyer is not sharing in the fees of particular clients—even if the nonlawyer referred those clients to the firm. No such compensation can be given to a nonlawyer for referrals. DR 2-103(B) provides that "a lawyer shall not compensate or give anything of value to a person or organization to recommend or obtain employment by a client or as a reward for having made a recommendation resulting in employment by a client." Cf. N.Y. State 731 (2000) (lawyer may not compensate employees for making a referral to a title company owned by the lawyer).

Formal Opinion 1995-11 (July 6, 1995)
Association of the Bar of the City of New York Committee on Professional and Judicial Ethics
(*www.nycbar.org/Publications/reports/show_html.php?rid=169&searchterm=1995–11*) (1995 WL 607778)

> *Question:* **What categories of compensation to a paralegal are unethical?**
>
> *Answer:* **Compensation cannot be tied to a particular client, the volume of business development, or the referral of clients.**

Nonlawyer compensation does not interfere with the lawyer's professional independence. DR 3-102(A)(3) prohibits lawyers or law firms from sharing fees with nonlawyers, except that "[a] lawyer or law firm may include nonlawyer employees in a retirement plan, even though the plan is based in whole or in part on a profit-sharing arrangement." See also DR 3-103(A). The compensation of a nonlawyer employee may not be a commission or bonus that is directly linked to a percentage of profits or fees received from any client or the volume of business development, or be a reward for clients brought or referred by the nonlawyer to the firm. See, e.g., ABA 316 (1967); N.Y. State 633 (1992); Maryland 84-103. Nonlawyer compensation may, however, be tied to the net profits and business performance of a firm. See ABA Inf. 1440 (1979) (noting that the source of a law firm's funds to pay any nonlawyer employee is fees for legal services, and approving compensation of a nonlawyer administrator based in part on a percentage of net profits of the firm). Similarly, discretionary bonuses, which are almost always tied to the profitability of the firm, may properly be paid to nonlawyer employees without violating the rule against sharing legal fees. See Virginia 767 (1986) & 806 (1986).

Opinion 687 (November 11, 1991)
New York County Lawyers' Association Committee on Professional Ethics
(*www.nycla.org/siteFiles/Publications/Publications460_0.pdf*) (1991 WL 755943)

> *Question:* **Can a nonlawyer be paid a percentage of the net profits of a firm as a bonus or a percentage of the nonlawyer's salary?**
>
> *Answer:* **Yes, so long as the payments are not tied to particular fees and are not for referrals.**

A nonlawyer employee may not be paid, in addition to his or her salary, a percentage of the business brought into the firm, since such an arrangement would constitute sharing legal fees with a nonlawyer in contravention of DR 3-102 and EC 3-8. See N.Y. State 302 (1973) (unadmitted law school graduate). Such a practice would also directly implicate the rationale of discouraging nonlawyers from acting as "runners" or otherwise soliciting legal business. For the same reason, a nonlawyer may not be paid extra compensation for bringing in business that is fixed at an arbitrary amount to avoid the prohibition against fee-splitting. See N.Y. State 302, supra. See also N.Y. County 80 (1915), N.Y. County 666 (1985), N.Y. State 302 (1973).

Nevertheless, a law firm's compensation arrangement may include payment of a percentage of the net profits of the law firm, since such compensation is related to the business performance of the entire firm, and not to the receipt of particular fees. See ABA Inf. Opin. 1440 (1979) (payment to nonlawyer office administrator). It therefore does not implicate any of the dangers set forth above. Similarly, we believe the nonlawyer employee could be paid a bonus calculated as a percentage of his or her salary without implicating DR 3-102. Cf. ABA 88-356 (1988), in which the ABA approved an arrangement under which law firm paid a placement agency a fee based upon a percentage of the compensation of temporary lawyers placed by the agency.

In 1980, the ABA amended DR 3-102(A)(3) of the Model Code to clarify that lawyers may include nonlawyer employees in compensation plans, as well as retirement plans, based wholly or partially on a profit-sharing arrangement. This extension to compensation plans is also reflected in Rule 5.4(a)(3) of the ABA Model Rules of Professional Conduct. Although the Code in New York does not include this change, it includes the same language that ABA Informal Opinion 1440 interpreted to permit a compensation arrangement based on the net profits of the firm.

We agree with the rationale of ABA Informal Opinion 1440. Where the nonlawyer employee is paid a bonus based on the profitability of the firm or calculated as a fixed amount or a percentage of the employee's salary, rather than being based on billings attributed directly to the nonlawyer employee, fees to the client are likely to be reasonable, there is no incentive to the employee to influence the lawyer's professional judgment on behalf of the client, and the possibility that the nonlawyer employee will engage in prohibited solicitation in order to increase his or her total billings is minimized.

Opinion 731 (July 27, 2000)
New York State Bar Association Committee on Professional Ethics
(*www.nysba.org/AM/Template.cfm?Section=Home&CONTENTID=18959&TEMPLATE=/CM/ContentDisplay.cfm*) (2000 WL 1692833)

> **Question:** Can a lawyer compensate his or her nonlawyer employees for making a referral to a title company owned by the lawyer?
>
> **Answer:** No.

When a lawyer is representing a lender in a real estate transaction, the lawyer may not compensate the lawyer's employees for referring the borrower or lender to a title insurance company in which the lawyer holds an interest, regardless of whether the lawyer's client (or any other party to the transaction) consents to the lawyer's dual role.

4. Letterhead and Business Cards

Opinion 500 (December 6, 1978)

New York State Bar Association Committee on Professional Ethics

(*www.nysba.org/AM/Template.cfm?Section=Ethics_Opinions& TEMPLATE=/CM/ContentDisplay.cfm&CONTENTID= 18339*) (1978 WL 14163)

> **Question:** Can a paralegal be listed on law firm letterhead?
>
> **Answer:** Yes, if the inclusion was not deceptive (the employee's nonlawyer status must be clear) and might provide information that is reasonably relevant to the selection of counsel.

At one time the rule in New York was that the listing of all nonlawyers on law firm letterhead was prohibited. The Supreme Court's decision in *Bates v. State Bar of Arizona*, 433 U.S. 350 (1977), led to rules liberalizing the free flow of reliable and useful information about lawyers and their services. See, N.Y. State 487 (1978). Lawyers were now allowed to include on their letterheads the names of their nonlawyer employees whenever the inclusion of such names would not be deceptive and might reasonably be expected to supply information relevant to the selection of counsel. The term "paralegal," albeit somewhat imprecise, is sufficient without further qualification to make clear the employee's nonlawyer status. (N.Y. State 261 is overruled on this issue.)

Formal Opinion 1995-11 (July 6, 1995)

Association of the Bar of the City of New York Committee on Professional and Judicial Ethics

(*www.nycbar.org/Publications/reports/show_html.php?rid= 169&searchterm=1995-11*) (1995 WL 607778)

> **Question:** Can a paralegal be listed on law firm letterhead and business cards? Can a paralegal be credited in a brief?
>
> **Answer:** Yes, if the paralegal's nonlawyer status is clear.

DR 2-101(A) counsels that a lawyer cannot be involved in the dissemination of communications containing false, deceptive, or misleading statements.

To this end, any communication generated out of the law firm that does not properly designate the nonlawyer status of any nonlawyer named therein is prohibited. See, e.g., Nassau County 87-14. To allow otherwise is to allow the public to be misled given the imprimatur of lawyer status and all it entails that a firm document automatically conveys. Therefore, a lawyer may not list paralegals on letterhead or business cards without clearly identifying their nonlawyer status. Cf. *New York Criminal & Civil Courts Bar Ass'n v. Jacoby*, 61 N.Y.2d 130, 136, 460 N.E.2d 1325, 1328, 472 N.Y.S.2d 890, 894 (1984). Cf. N.Y. City 1987-1 (lawyer sharing an office with a nonlawyer must avoid misleading public into believing that the nonlawyer office-mate is a lawyer). Similarly, a legal assistant, designated as such, may be credited in a brief.

Further, in corresponding either orally or in writing with a client, another lawyer or member of the public, the legal assistant must make known his or her lay status. Ambiguous titles which do not make clear that the individual is a nonlawyer are prohibited. See N.Y. State 640 (1992); see also N.Y. County 673 (1989).

Opinion 673 (October 23, 1989)

New York County Lawyers' Association Committee on Professional Ethics

(*www.nycla.org/siteFiles/Publications/Publications446_0.pdf*) (1989 WL 572098)

> **Question:**
> (1) May a paralegal employee have a business card with the name of the firm or corporate legal office and the name of the paralegal, without the name of a supervising lawyer?
> (2) May the letterhead of a law firm or law department list paralegals?
>
> **Answer:**
> (1) & (2) Yes, so long as there is an appropriate designation of nonlawyer status.

One of the by-products of lawyers' attempts to provide efficient and reasonably priced legal services to their clients is the increasing use of legal assistants (also known as paralegals) to perform certain functions previously performed by lawyers. Such use is recognized in the Code of Professional Responsibility, EC 3-6 (Delegation of tasks to clerks is proper if the lawyer maintains a direct relationship with the client, supervises the delegated work and remains professionally responsible for the work product). See generally N.Y. County 666 (1985). Use of paralegal employees is common not only in law firms but also in corporate law departments, government offices, public defender offices, legal services offices and in unincorporated associations, such as trade groups and unions (hereinafter referred to collectively as "law departments").

Since paralegals may have to deal with clients and members of the court system and the public while performing their duties, it will often be convenient for them to identify themselves and their affiliation by means of a business card. DR 2-102(A) specifically deals with the professional cards of a lawyer or law firm, and permits the professional card of a law firm to give the names of members and associates. It does not specifically address legal assistants. However, DR 2-101(A), the general rule with respect to advertising by lawyers, implicitly allows a lawyer to use or disseminate any public communications as long as they are not false, deceptive or misleading. Accordingly, we believe that an agent of the lawyer, including a paralegal, may also use a business card as long as it names the agent, identifies him or her as a nonlawyer, and sets forth his or her affiliation. See N.Y. County 666 (1985), N.Y. City 884 (1974). . . . In the case of a law firm, the name of the law firm should appear on the card, and in the case of law department, we believe the name of the entity (with or without the designation "Legal Department") should appear on the card.

DR 2-102(A)(4) authorizes a lawyer to use letterhead that is in accordance with DR 2-101 (i.e., not false, deceptive or misleading), including letterhead identifying the lawyer by name and as a lawyer, and giving other information, including "the names of members and associates, and names and dates relating to deceased and retired members." The section does not specifically authorize the listing of legal assistants. Before the Bates amendments to the Code, the listing of nonlawyer employees on a lawyer's letterhead was prohibited. See, e.g., N.Y. State 261 (1972)(paralegals), N.Y. City 884 (1984)(paralegals), N.Y. County 589 (patent agents), ABA Inf. 1367 (paralegals). However, as noted in N.Y. State 500 (1978), the effect of the Bates amendments was that nonlawyer status will no longer preclude the use of a person's name on a firm's letterhead, as long as the name is accompanied by language that makes clear his or her nonlawyer status.

DR 2-101(D) provides: Advertising and publicity shall be designed to educate the public to an awareness of legal needs and to provide information relevant to the selection of the most appropriate counsel. Information other than that specifically authorized in subdivision (C) that is consistent with these purposes may be disseminated providing that it does not violate any other provisions of this rule.

We believe that the fact that the law firm or law department uses paralegals is relevant to its work and to the persons who may deal with the paralegals. Moreover, identifying paralegals as such on the letterhead of the law firm or law department may be useful to confirm their nonlawyer status. Accordingly, we believe a law firm or law department may list legal assistants on their letterhead as long as such listing clearly and in a non-misleading fashion indicates their nonlawyer status.

5. Attorney Supervision

Attorney Supervision under the Rules of Professional Conduct

See Rule 5.3 on attorney supervision in the Rules of Professional Conduct printed in full in section 3.2 of this book.
(*www.nycourts.gov/rules/jointappellate/NY%20Rules%20of%20Prof%20Conduct_09.pdf*)

Formal Opinion 1995-11 (July 6, 1995)

Association of the Bar of the City of New York Committee on Professional and Judicial Ethics
(*www.nycbar.org/Publications/reports/show_html.php?rid=169&searchterm=1995-11*) (1995 WL 607778)

Question: **What supervisory responsibility does an attorney have over a paralegal?**

Answer: **"Fairly strict" supervision is required, including instruction on ethics and taking steps to ensure that office procedures comport with ethical standards.**

DR 1-104(A) provides: A lawyer shall be responsible for a violation of the Disciplinary Rules by another lawyer or for conduct of a nonlawyer employed or retained by or associated with the lawyer that would be a violation of the Disciplinary Rules if engaged in by a lawyer if (1) [t]he lawyer orders the conduct; or (2) [t]he lawyer has supervisory authority over the other lawyer or the nonlawyer, and knows or should have known of the conduct at a time when its consequences can be avoided or mitigated but fails to take reasonable remedial action.

The Code clearly contemplates that lawyers will delegate tasks to lay personnel. See EC 3-6. In delegating tasks, the lawyer should provide instruction regarding the ethical constraints under which those in the law office must work. While the nonlawyer may receive some guidance in this regard elsewhere [e.g., the ethics codes of NALA and NFPA], the lawyer should not rely on others to perform this important task.

Employers generally require formal paralegal training. . . . Others prefer on-the-job training, often hiring persons with college education but no legal training or promoting experienced legal secretaries. Given the fact that paralegals do not have legal training and are not subject to discipline, the lawyer has a heightened standard of supervision from that generally owed toward a subordinate attorney pursuant to DR 1-104(A). The standard of supervision is fairly strict. See *In re Bonanno*, 208 A.D.2d 1117, 617 N.Y.S.2d 584 (3d Dept., 1994) (attorney censured for lack of supervision of legal assistant who unbeknownst to attorney held himself out as attorney, represented clients and embezzled client funds). The lawyer must ensure that office procedures comport with the Code as well. See *In re Kiley*, 22 A.D.2d 527, 256 N.Y.S.2d 848 (1st Dept., 1965) (submission of false reports);

In re Neimark, 13 A.D.2d 676, 214 N.Y.S.2d 12 (2d Dept., 1961) (failure to supervise office operations).

> Note: For the unauthorized-practice-of-law implications of attorney supervision, see section 3.1.

6. Conflict of Interest

Opinion 774 (March 23, 2004)
New York State Bar Association Committee on Professional Ethics
(*www.nysba.org/AM/Template.cfm?Section=Ethics_Opinions&*
CONTENTID=13619&TEMPLATE=/CM/ContentDisplay
.cfm) (2004 WL 5200056)

> *Question:* What are the duties of a law firm that hires a paralegal who has worked at another law firm?
>
> *Answer:* Take steps to avoid letting the paralegal breach the confidentiality of the client of the other firm. Screening of the paralegal and obtaining the consent of the client of the other firm may be required.

When a New York law firm hires a nonlawyer who has previously worked at another law firm, the hiring firm must, as part of its supervisory responsibilities under DR 1-104(C) and DR 4-101(D), exercise adequate supervision to ensure that the nonlawyer does not reveal any confidences or secrets that the nonlawyer acquired while working at the other law firm. A law firm should (i) instruct all newly hired nonlawyers not to divulge any such information and (ii) instruct lawyers not to exploit such information if proffered. The hiring law firm need not always check for conflicts, but should do so in circumstances where the nonlawyer may be expected to have acquired confidences or secrets of an opposing party. If a law firm learns that a nonlawyer did acquire information protected by DR 4-101(B) that is material to a matter in which the adversary is represented by the nonlawyer's former employer, the law firm should adopt appropriate measures to guard against improper disclosure of protected information.

A lawyer should ensure that nonlawyers under the lawyer's supervision are trained to protect the confidences and secrets learned at another law firm where the nonlawyer previously worked. Training might include instructing the nonlawyer not to accept any work assignment involving a matter on which the nonlawyer worked at the former firm. As an additional element of its general supervisory duties under DR 1-104(A), it is advisable that a law firm instruct its lawyers not to solicit or listen to confidential information if the nonlawyer fails to comply with this instruction, and to alert the other firm lawyers involved with the matter. As we concluded in N.Y. State 700 (1998): "A lawyer who receives an unsolicited and unauthorized communication from a former employee of an adversary's law firm may not seek information from that person if the communication would exploit the adversary's confidences or secrets."

"DR 5-105(E) does not require law firms to search for conflicts that may be created when nonlawyers join the firm laterally." Yet in some circumstances, the duty to supervise nonlawyers may make it "advisable for a law firm to check for conflicts when hiring a nonlawyer. For example, where a litigation paralegal is being hired by a small firm and worked for a sole practitioner who is now opposing counsel in litigation that was pending while the paralegal worked at the former firm, the risk that the paralegal acquired the opposing party's confidences and secrets is high and the law firm should check for conflicts. In such a case, the law firm should ask the paralegal about his or her role in the matter in question and whether he or she did in fact acquire confidences and secrets. On the other hand, when a personal injury firm hires a paralegal to perform work that is entirely unrelated to the real estate matters the paralegal worked on at the former employer's firm, we do not think a formal conflict check is necessary."

If the paralegal did acquire confidential information at a prior firm, the current employer of the paralegal must not exploit that information by encouraging the paralegal to reveal it. The greater the responsibilities of the prospective nonlawyer employee in a matter while at an opposing law firm, the more likely it is that ethics problems will arise in the matter at the new firm, and the greater the degree of supervision that will be merited. If, for example, at a former employer a secretary occasionally typed letters or took phone messages relating to a current matter of the new firm but does not recall any confidential information about it, a simple warning to the nonlawyer not to disclose any confidences and secrets acquired at the former firm would constitute adequate supervision. If, however, the secretary had played more than a ministerial role in the matter at the former firm and recalls confidential information, screening of the nonlawyer may be required to prevent the misuse of confidential information.

"Occasionally, however, a law firm will conclude that screening the nonlawyer will not adequately protect an opposing party's confidences and secrets. For example, if the nonlawyer had substantial exposure to relevant confidential information at the old firm and will now be working closely with the lawyers who are handling the opposite side of the same matter, or where the structure and practices of the firm make it difficult to isolate a nonlawyer from confidential conversations or documents pertaining to a given matter, a law firm may be obliged to adopt measures more radical than screening." Those measures may include the following:

(a) Obtaining consent from the opposing law firm's client;

(b) Terminating the nonlawyer, see *Riddell Sports, Inc. v. Brooks,* 1994 WL 67836 (S.D.N.Y., 1994) (denying a motion to disqualify where a large firm had terminated a paralegal upon learning that the paralegal had worked on a case still pending between the firms, even though the paralegal had no role in that case at the firm); or

(c) Withdrawing from the matter in question. Cf. *Glover Bottled Gas Corp. v. Circle M. Beverage Barn, Inc.*, 129 A.D.2d 678, 514 N.Y.S.2d 440 (2d Dept., 1987) (disqualifying law firm that hired paralegal who had previously worked for opposing counsel and "had worked on the litigation pending between the parties and had interviewed the plaintiff's manager concerning the facts of this case").

Note: See Part 1, section A of this book for more on the *Riddell* and *Glover* cases as well as another case cited by the ethics committee in Opinion 774: *Mulhern v. Calder.*

94-108 (November 15, 1994)
New York Advisory Commission on Judicial Ethics
(*www.scjc.state.ny.us*) (1994 WL 907359)

> *Question:* **Is recusal of a town judge required in cases handled by a law firm that employs the judge as a paralegal?**
> *Answer:* **Yes, another town judge must hear such cases.**

88-152 (March 16, 1989)
New York Advisory Commission on Judicial Ethics
(*www.scjc.state.ny.us*) (1989 WL 572212)

> *Question:* **Can a judge's daughter work as a paralegal at a law firm that handles matters before the judge?**
> *Answer:* **Yes, so long as the judge discloses to all parties the fact of the paralegal's employment.**

99-87 (June 18, 1999)
New York Advisory Commission on Judicial Ethics
(*www.scjc.state.ny.us*) (1999 WL 33721217)

> *Question:* **Is recusal of a town judge required in cases handled by a law firm that employs the judge's spouse as a paralegal?**
> *Answer:* **Yes, unless both sides agree that the judge should preside.**

The Rules Governing Judicial Conduct require a judge to "disqualify himself or herself in a proceeding in which the judge's impartiality might reasonably be questioned." 22 NYCRR 100.3(E). In our opinion, the relationship of judge and spouse and spouse and employer create a reasonable basis for a questioning of impartiality in cases in which the law firm appears. Under such circumstances, the judge should disclose the nature and extent of the relationship to the parties and disqualify him or herself. The parties, however, may execute a remittal of disqualification by agreeing, without participation by the judge, that the judge may

preside. If the parties reach such an agreement, it should be incorporated in the record of the proceeding in open court, and the judge may preside, provided that "the judge believes that he or she will be impartial and is willing to participate . . ." 22 NYCRR 100.3(F).

7. Real Estate Closings

Opinion 677 (December 12, 1995)
New York State Bar Association Committee on Professional Ethics
(*www.nysba.org/AM/Template.cfm?Section=Ethics_Opinions& TEMPLATE=/CM/ContentDisplay.cfm&CONTENTID= 18764*) (1995 WL 870964)

> *Question:* **Can an attorney delegate attendance at a real estate closing to a paralegal if the attorney is available by telephone?**
> *Answer:* **Yes, if the tasks of the paralegal are ministerial and do not require professional judgment or discretion. The attorney must determine whether adequate supervision can exist by telephone availability in light of the complexity of the closing and the capabilities of the paralegal.**

A lawyer cannot delegate the practice of law to a paralegal where the exercise of professional judgment is required. A lawyer can delegate tasks that are incident to but do not constitute legal practice in themselves. A nonlawyer cannot argue motions or conduct deposition examinations. "A clerk may, without his employer being present, attend mortgage closings and other out-of-court matters, but only so long as his responsibilities are clearly limited to those functions not involving independent discretion or judgment." (N.Y. State 44 (1977).) "We assume that real estate and mortgage closings, or some of them, are as unlikely now as ever they were to require either 'independent discretion or judgment' from a paralegal assigned to monitor the ceremony. So long as the closing is properly described as 'ministerial,' a lawyer may ethically delegate attendance at such a closing to a paralegal, provided the lawyer discharges his or her duty to the client properly in the delegation of this task."

This conclusion applies whether the paralegal's attorney represents the buyer, seller, or lender. "As distinct from the representation of the institutional lender, the buyer or seller may be expected to be present at the closing and ask questions that a paralegal ought not answer. In light of this we believe that if a lawyer for buyer or seller concludes that a paralegal can properly appear at the closing, it would likely be the wiser practice to inform the client in advance that the lawyer plans to have a paralegal attend the closing."

The attorney must judge whether he or she can properly supervise the paralegal if the attorney is available only by telephone. "If the lawyer has rightly assessed the nature and complexity (or lack of it) of the task, and the suitability and background of the paralegal, and if an adequate plan has been made to cope with the unforeseen, the telephone may be all the tool that could be desired. If this proves not to be the case, however, the lawyer's ethical obligations may be found wanting."

The "delegating attorney is completely responsible for the work-product of the delegation. . . . [F]rom an ethical standpoint the lawyer who assigns a nonlawyer to work on a client's matter had better be right about the suitability of that task for delegation, and the suitability of that employee for the task at hand. The delegating lawyer is 'completely responsible.'"

8. Signatures

Opinion 693 (August 22, 1997)
New York State Bar Association Committee on Professional Ethics
(*www.nysba.org/AM/Template.cfm?Section=Ethics_Opinions& CONTENTID=18811&TEMPLATE=/CM/ContentDisplay. cfm*) (1997 WL 1068496)

> *Question:* **Can a lawyer allow a paralegal to use a stamp bearing the lawyer's signature to execute checks on a client's escrow account?**
>
> *Answer:* **Yes, if the paralegal is properly supervised on how the checks will be used and the lawyer later reviews the accuracy of what the paralegal has done.**

An attorney is personally and professionally liable for funds and property entrusted to him or her by a client and must exercise the highest degree of care in preserving and protecting such funds and property. DR 9-102(E) provides that "[o]nly an attorney admitted to practice law in New York State shall be an authorized signatory of a special account." A nonlawyer may not be a signatory on a special account and a lawyer may not give such a person signatory power on such account. *In re Gambino*, 205 A.D.2d 212, 619 N.Y.S. 2d 305, (2d Dept., 1994) (lawyer violated DR 9-102(E) by permitting nonlawyer daughter to be signatory on special account); *In re Stenstrom*, 194 A.D.2d 277, 605 N.Y.S. 2d 603 (4th Dept., 1993) (lawyer violated DR 9-102(E) by permitting nonlawyer ex-wife to be signatory on special account).

"Although it is clear that only a lawyer may control the lawyer's client escrow account and be a signatory of it, the Rule does not address whether a lawyer may delegate the task of signing his or her name to escrow account checks to others, and if so whether a signature stamp can be used for that purpose. Based on the analysis of proper delegation in our previous opinions, we believe that it is ethically permissible for a lawyer to authorize a paralegal to make use of the lawyer's signature stamp on checks drawn from a special account at closings under certain conditions and with proper controls. As with the rest of a paralegal's duties at a real estate closing, N.Y. State 677, the lawyer must consider in advance how the paralegal will use the signature stamp—including approving the purpose of the anticipated payments to be made by such checks, the nature of the payee and the authorized dollar amount range for each check to be issued—and review afterwards what actually happened to assure that the delegation of authority has been utilized properly. As a practical matter, compliance with these restrictions will limit the use of the signature stamp by a paralegal to those circumstances in which the lawyer can reliably forecast events at the closing. Attorneys must be aware that responsibility for client funds may not be delegated, and attorneys authorizing paralegals to use signature stamps on checks drawn from escrow accounts are 'completely responsible' to the client for any errors or misuse of the stamp. N.Y. State 677; DR 1-104. Attorneys must take steps to safeguard the use of the signature stamp to avoid any misappropriation of client funds."

Opinion 255 (June 26, 1972)
New York State Bar Association Committee on Professional Ethics
(*www.nysba.org/AM/Template.cfm?Section=Ethics_Opinions& TEMPLATE=/CM/ContentDisplay.cfm&CONTENTID= 17811*)

> *Question:* **Can a paralegal sign letters on lawyer's letterhead?**
> *Answer:* **Yes, if clearly identified as a nonlawyer.**

"It is not improper for a paralegal employee to sign appropriate letters on his employer's letterhead. The signature should be followed by an appropriate designation so there is no connotation that the person so signing is a lawyer." Acceptable designations for nonlawyer employees include legal assistant and investigator.

9. Execution of Wills

Opinion 343 (May 5, 1974)
New York State Bar Association Committee on Professional Ethics
(*www.nysba.org/AM/Template.cfm?Section=Ethics_Opinions& CONTENTID=18923&TEMPLATE=/CM/ContentDisplay .cfm*)

> *Question:* **Can a paralegal supervise a will execution?**
> *Answer:* **No. The supervision of a will requires professional judgment that cannot be delegated.**

A delegation of a will execution is "tantamount to counseling a client about law matters and [thereby] permitting a paralegal to engage in the practice of law. . . . The presence of the attorney provides added assurance that the Will was properly executed by a competent testator." "The subsequent examination of a will executed under the supervision of a person other than an attorney does not provide [the attorney] with sufficient knowledge to allow him to vouch for its due execution."

10. Conducting Depositions

Opinion 304 (October 17, 1973)
New York State Bar Association Committee on Professional Ethics
(*www.nysba.org/AM/Template.cfm?Section=Ethics_Opinions&TEMPLATE=/CM/ContentDisplay.cfm&CONTENTID=17612*)

Question: **Can a nonlawyer take a deposition if a lawyer is present during the deposition?**

Answer: **No. Taking a deposition requires professional judgment that cannot be delegated.**

A lawyer cannot delegate to a nonlawyer "any function which calls for the professional judgment of a lawyer." The taking of a deposition necessarily involves an exercise of professional legal judgment, which cannot be delegated even in the presence of a lawyer. Allowing a nonlawyer to perform such a task would be aiding a nonlawyer in the unauthorized practice of law.

11. Confidentiality

Opinion 700 (May 7, 1998)
New York State Bar Association Committee on Professional Ethics
(*www.nysba.org/AM/Template.cfm?Section=Ethics_Opinions&TEMPLATE=/CM/ContentDisplay.cfm&CONTENTID=18828*) (1998 WL 957912)

Question: **May an attorney ask questions of a former nonlawyer employee of an opposing law firm who has called the attorney in order to provide confidential information about the opponent?**

Answer: **No. The attorney must not seek further information from the nonlawyer that might compromise the adversary's right to confidentiality.**

An attorney for a government agency responsible for prosecuting an administrative proceeding received an unsolicited telephone call from a person who identified himself as a former nonlawyer employee of a law firm that represents the respondent in the proceeding. In substance, the former employee told the attorney that certain key records submitted to the government agency in connection with its investigation of respondent had been materially altered prior to submission. We assume that the communication from the former employee of respondent's law firm regarding the alteration of documents was unauthorized and may have violated the attorney-client privilege. A lawyer has an ethical obligation to "exercise

reasonable care to prevent his or her employees, associates, and others whose services are utilized by the lawyer from disclosing or using confidences or secrets of a client. . . ." DR 4-101(D). See also EC 4-5 ("lawyer should be diligent in his or her efforts to prevent the misuse of such information by employees and associates"). Although the attorney did not solicit the unauthorized communication or the breach of the former employee's duty of confidentiality, the attorney may not exploit the willingness of the former employee to undermine the confidentiality rule. Just as a lawyer should never initiate contact with a former employee of an adversary's law firm for the purpose of obtaining confidential information of the adversary, neither may a lawyer take advantage of a former employee's willingness to violate the duty of confidentiality to the former employer's client.

Formal Opinion 1995-11 (July 6, 1995)
Association of the Bar of the City of New York Committee on Professional and Judicial Ethics
(*www.nycbar.org/Publications/reports/show_html.php?rid=169&searchterm=1995-11*) (1995 WL 607778)

Question: **How should attorneys supervise paralegals to avoid breaches of confidentiality?**

Answer: **Attorneys should develop mechanisms for prompt detection of breach of confidentiality problems.**

The lawyer is responsible for maintaining the confidentiality of client information. DR 4-101(A), EC 4-4. DR 4-101(D) provides:

> A lawyer shall exercise reasonable care to prevent his or her employees, associates, and others whose services are utilized by the lawyer from disclosing or using confidences or secrets of a client, except that a lawyer may reveal the information allowed by DR 4-101(C) through an employee.

A "secret" under DR 4-101(A) must be kept inviolate even if it does not reach the level of attorney-client privilege. See N.Y. State 503 (1979). It is especially important to supervise nonlawyers in this area since client conversations with lay personnel may not always be treated the same as communications with an attorney. Compare *People v. Mitchell*, 86 A.D.2d 976, 976, 448 N.Y.S.2d 332, 333 (4th Dept., 1982) (statements made in law office waiting room to paralegal and two secretaries in attorney's absence found not privileged), aff'd, 58 N.Y.2d 368, 448 N.E.2d 121, 461 N.Y.S.2d 267 (1983) with CPLR 4503(a) (confidential communication made between the attorney or his employee and the client in the course of professional employment protected).

Further, the transient nature of lay personnel is cause for heightened attention to the maintenance of confidentiality. See generally Kelly A. Randall, Note, *Do Your Clients' Confidences Go Out the Window When Your Employees Go Out the Door?*, 42 Hastings L.J. 1667 (1991) (proposing conflict of interest rule for nonlawyers). Similar to instances where a law firm has been disqualified due to the confidentiality imputed from a lawyer in the firm, so too may it be due to a nonlawyer employee. See *Glover Bottled Gas Corp. v. Circle M. Beverage Barn, Inc.*, 129 A.D.2d 678, 678, 514 N.Y.S.2d 440, 441 (2d Dept., 1987) (attorneys disqualified after hiring paralegal who had worked on subject litigation while previously employed by opponent). Lawyers should be attentive to these issues and should sensitize their nonlawyer staff to the pitfalls, developing mechanisms for prompt detection of potential conflict of interest or breach of confidentiality problems.

Opinion 503 (February 1, 1979)

New York State Bar Association Committee on Professional Ethics

(*www.nysba.org/AM/Template.cfm?Section=Ethics_ Opinions&TEMPLATE=/CM/ContentDisplay.cfm& CONTENTID=18475*) (1979 WL 15758)

Question: **Can a lawyer reveal confidential information that the lawyer acquired while was working as a paralegal?**
Answer: **No.**

In recent years, the use of legal assistants, or "paralegals," has become commonplace. Accompanying the widespread use of paralegals has been a noticeable increase in the degree of sophistication in the tasks to which they are assigned. Another understandably related phenomenon has been the dramatic rise in the number of paralegals who are entering the ranks of our profession. It is against this background that we turn to consider the question posed.

A lawyer, while employed as a paralegal in a law firm, prior to his admission to the Bar, became privy to certain confidential information relating to one of the firm's clients. The lawyer, now associated in the practice of law with another firm, has been asked to participate in a matter involving his former employer's client wherein the information he obtained as a paralegal may be of some relevance.

DR 4-101(D) provides in relevant part, "A lawyer shall exercise reasonable care to prevent his employees, associates, and others whose services are utilized by him from disclosing or using confidences or secrets of a client. . . ." See also, EC 4-3 and N.Y. State 473 (1977). While the Code's mandate to preserve the confidences and secrets of a client is addressed only to lawyers, it will be noted that to some extent the ethical rule is by statute brought to bear on all persons acquiring knowledge of client confidences. Cf., CPLR 4503 with EC 4-4 (explaining that "[t]he attorney client privilege is more limited than the ethical obligation of a lawyer to guard the confidences and secrets of his client"). Hence, regardless of the paralegal's subsequently acquired status upon admission to the Bar, the law would still require him to hold inviolate the confidences of his erstwhile

employer's client. To the extent that his conduct in revealing those confidences would violate the provisions of CPLR 4503, *ipso facto*, such conduct when undertaken by him as a lawyer would violate the Code. See, EC 1-5, DR 1-101(A)(4) and DR 7-102(A)(8).

Even if the information obtained by the former paralegal was not by its nature subject to the attorney client privilege, but merely constituted a "secret" within the meaning of DR 4-101(A), we nevertheless believe that the same may not be revealed. The ethical restraints imposed upon the former paralegal's erstwhile employer are identical to the ethical restraints imposed upon the former paralegal himself, *qua* lawyer. Just as the lawyer could not undertake to cause another's employee to divulge information protected by Canon 4, so too he himself could not reveal information acquired by him when employed by another lawyer. See, e.g., N.Y. State 422 (1975) and N.Y. State 386 (1975).

386 (April 24, 1975)

New York State Bar Association Committee on Professional Ethics

(*www.nysba.org/AM/Template.cfm?Section=Ethics_ Opinions&TEMPLATE=/CM/ContentDisplay.cfm& CONTENTID=17940*)

Question: **Can lawyer #1 hire clerical staff on a part-time basis if she continues her prior employment at the law office of lawyer #2 with whom lawyer #1 has periodic adversarial contact?**
Answer: **No.**

To avoid the possible appearance of impropriety in contravention of Canon 9, it is impermissible to allow a situation to exist where the leaking of confidential information may be foreseeable.

Opinion 422 (November 6, 1975)

New York State Bar Association Committee on Professional Ethics

(*www.nysba.org/AM/Template.cfm?Section=Ethics_ Opinions&TEMPLATE=/CM/ContentDisplay.cfm& CONTENTID=18057*)

Question: **May lawyer #1 employ a secretary who has just left the employ of lawyer #2 against whom lawyer #1 has adversarial matters pending?**
Answer: **Yes, if appropriate steps are taken to prevent a breach of confidentiality.**

No problem exists if the secretary does not possess any confidential information regarding the pending adversarial matters. If the secretary has confidential information, the lawyer may employ her "provided he cautions the secretary not to divulge any confidential information and will not permit the secretary to do so."

11. Unauthorized Practice of Law

See section 3.1 for ethics opinions on the unauthorized practice of law.

12. Disbarred or Suspended Lawyer as Paralegal

See section 3.1 for ethics opinions on allowing a disbarred or suspended attorney act as a paralegal.

13. Outsourcing

See section 3.1 for ethics opinions on outsourcing and the unauthorized practice of law.

F. Rule 5.3 of the Rules of Professional Conduct

The major rule in the Rules of Professional Conduct (RPC) that governs the attorney-paralegal relationship is Rule 5.3. We examined that and related RPC rules in section 3.2 of the book.

G. New York State Bar Association Guidelines on Paralegals

The state bar has issued guidelines on paralegals. The purpose of the guidelines is to assist attorneys in understanding the role of the paralegal in the delivery of "high quality, cost-effective legal services to the public" in accordance with ethical rules. The guidelines were created before the New York Court of Appeals promulgated the Rules of Professional Conduct (RPC). Hence the guidelines refer to the code that the RPC replaced, the Code of Professional Responsibility. Nevertheless, the guidelines are valuable in understanding how the New York legal community views the paralegal profession. Most of the provisions in the guidelines are equally applicable under the RPC.

New York State Bar Association, *Guidelines for Utilization by Lawyers of the Services of Legal Assistants* (1997) (*www.cdpa.info/files/NY_Paralegal_guidelines.pdf*). Reprinted with the permission of the New York State Bar Association.

Table of Contents of the Guidelines

Abbreviations Used in the Guidelines

ABA # Opinion of the American Bar Association Committee on Ethics and Professional Responsibility.

Code Code of Professional Responsibility of the NYSBA.

Canon Canon of the Code.

DR Disciplinary Rule of the Code.

EC Ethical Consideration of the Code.

N.Y. State # Opinion of the New York State Bar Association Committee on Professional Ethics.

N.Y. City # Opinion of the Bar of the City of New York Committee on Professional and Judicial Ethics.

N.Y. County # Opinion of the New York County Lawyers' Association Committee on Professional Ethics.

Nassau County # Opinion of the Nassau County Bar Association Committee on Professional Ethics.

Definition

A legal assistant/paralegal is a person who is qualified through education, training or work experience to be employed or retained by a lawyer, law office, governmental agency, or other entity in a capacity or function that involves the performance, under the ultimate direction and supervision of, and/or accountability to, an attorney, of substantive legal work, that requires a sufficient knowledge of legal concepts such that, absent such legal assistant/paralegal, the attorney would perform the task. The terms "legal assistant" and "paralegal" are synonymous and are not to be confused with numerous other legal titles which have proliferated with the public and within the legal community. Throughout the text of the following Guidelines, the term "legal assistant" will be used; however it is not intended to exclude nor infer a preferred status over the term "paralegal."

Value of Legal Assistants

The New York State Bar Association Code of Professional Responsibility (hereinafter "Code of Professional Responsibility") commits members of the bar to the provision of legal services to the public at a reasonable fee. This goal is embodied in Canon 2: "A lawyer should assist the legal profession in fulfilling its duty to make legal counsel available"; and also in Canon 8: "A lawyer should assist in improving the legal system." The employment of educated and trained legal assistants presents an opportunity to expand the public's access to legal services at a reduced cost while preserving attorneys' time for attention to legal services which require the independent exercise of an attorney's judgment. This should enhance the quality of legal services and, at the same time, reduce the total cost of those services. The legal profession recognizes legal assistants as dedicated professionals with skills and abilities which contribute to the delivery of cost-effective, high quality legal services. The New York State Bar Association Ad Hoc Committee on NonLawyer Practice studied the role of the legal assistant and in its report, approved by the House of Delegates in 1995, made the recommendation to support the expanded use and role of traditional legal assistants. The committee indicated its belief that the expanded use of the traditional legal assistant will benefit both the client and the bar. It recommended that court rules and ethics rules be developed to encourage the expanded use of traditional legal assistants. . . .

Purpose of These Guidelines

The New York State Bar Association, in 1976, recognized the importance of legal assistants in the delivery of legal services by adopting the *Guidelines for the Utilization by Lawyers of the Services of Legal Assistants.* It has become necessary to restructure and update these guidelines for clarity and to reflect recent ethics opinions and court decisions. The following guidelines revise those adopted by the House of Delegates in 1976 and supplement the Code of Professional Responsibility as applied to practicing with legal assistants. These guidelines are intended to assist attorneys in understanding the role of legal assistants in the delivery of high quality, cost-effective legal services to the public in accordance with the Code of Professional Responsibility, statutes, court rules and decisions, rules and regulations of administrative agencies, and opinions rendered by the attorney general and committees on professional ethics. It is recognized that these Guidelines are not static but are subject to modification due to revisions in statutes, rules or regulations, or by reason of new opinions of courts or relevant bar association committees. Attorneys who desire further advice on questions of utilization may contact the New York State Bar Association.

Guideline I: LAWYERS' PROFESSIONAL RESPONSIBILITY

A lawyer may permit a legal assistant to perform services in the representation of a client provided the lawyer:

(a) retains a direct relationship with the client;

(b) supervises the legal assistant's performance of duties; and

(c) remains fully responsible for such representation, including all actions taken or not taken in connection therewith by the legal assistant, except as otherwise provided by statute, court rule or decision, administrative rule or regulation, or by the Code of Professional Responsibility.

Commentary on Guideline I

EC 3-6 recognizes the value of utilizing the services of legal assistants, but provides certain conditions for such employment, *viz:* A lawyer often delegates tasks to clerks, secretaries, and other lay persons. Such delegation is proper if the lawyer maintains a direct relationship with his client, supervises the delegated work, and has complete professional responsibility for the work product. This delegation enables a lawyer to render legal service more economically and efficiently.

As stated in N.Y. County 641 (1975), quoting N.Y. County 420 (1953):

> What an employee, who is not a lawyer, does in the course of his employment by the law office is deemed a professional service by the law firm for which it is charged with full responsibility. Consequently, his work must be done under the supervision and direction of one or more lawyers in the firm. . . . In order to retain a "direct relationship" with the client, a lawyer need not be in contact with the client with any specified degree of regularity or frequency, nor is the language of EC 3-6 to be construed as contradicting any statutes, rules or administrative regulations which permit representation by persons who are not attorneys. The lawyer should, however, at all reasonable times be available for consultation by the client, and whenever in the course of supervising the legal assistant's work it appears that communication with the client is desirable he should act accordingly in the client's interest. Of course, the obligations imposed upon a lawyer with respect to the services of his legal assistant do not in any way relieve the latter from his personal obligation to obey the law and his employer's instructions.

In order to maintain a direct relationship with the client, a lawyer need not be in contact with the client with any specified degree of regularity or frequency. However, the lawyer should at all reasonable times be available for consultation by the client. See N.Y. State 677 (1995) (lawyer may delegate attendance at real estate closing to a legal assistant under attorney supervision). See also Nassau County 90-13 (1990).

An attorney has the further responsibility to instruct the legal assistant regarding ethics. In delegating tasks, the lawyer should provide instruction regarding the ethical constraints under which those in the law office must work. While the nonlawyer may receive some guidance in this regard elsewhere, as for instance through the Code of Ethics and Professional Responsibility and Model Standards and Guidelines adopted by the National Association of Legal Assistants ("NALA") and the National Federation of Paralegal Associations ("NFPA"). . . . The lawyer should not rely on others to perform this important task. N.Y. City 1995-11.

Legal assistants, though not members of the bar and not technically bound by the Code of Professional Responsibility, have recognized the need for adherence to ethical guidelines. The foremost national organizations of legal assistants, NALA and NFPA, have adopted a Code of Ethics and Professional Conduct which incorporate the Professional Code of Responsibility for the applicable jurisdiction and go beyond. . . .

> ### Guideline II: UNAUTHORIZED PRACTICE OF LAW
> A lawyer shall not assist a legal assistant in the performance of an activity that constitutes the unauthorized practice of the law.

Commentary on Guideline II

The unauthorized practice of law is prohibited by statute, the Code of Professional Responsibility and court decisions. Sections 478 and 484 of the Judiciary Law prohibit individuals who are not licensed members of the Bar of the State of New York (with certain exceptions hereinafter noted) from engaging in the practice of the law. Any person, including a legal assistant, who violates the statute may be punished for criminal contempt and that conduct may be enjoined. *See* Judiciary Law, § 750(B), § 476-a, 476-b.

The Code of Professional Responsibility provides in Canon 3 that "[a] lawyer should assist in preventing the unauthorized practice of law." Furthermore, DR 3-101(A) mandates that "[a] lawyer shall not aid a non-lawyer in the unauthorized practice of law."

There is no all-inclusive definition of the phrase "practice of law." It has been referred to as an act requiring the exercise of "independent professional legal judgment." N.Y. State 304 (1973).

A legal assistant may not represent a client in court, give legal advice or set legal fees. However, depending on court rule, a legal assistant may answer calendar calls provided no oral argument is necessary, and the role is confined to purely ministerial activity. N.Y. County 682 (1990); N.Y. County 666 (1985) (a lawyer may not assign a legal assistant to perform any services which involve the independent exercise of professional legal judgment). See also N.Y. City 1995-11 (comprehensive analysis of a lawyer's responsibility toward nonlawyer personnel under his or her supervision); N.Y. State 44 (1967) (law clerk's role is that of student, and attorney must provide supervision and not permit clerk to be involved in matters involving independent discretion or judgment).

As defined by the *Ad Hoc* Committee on NonLawyer Practice, a freelance paralegal, "an independent contractor with supervision by and/or accountability to a lawyer," satisfies existing ethical rules which require the direct supervision of an attorney.

> ### Guideline III: AUTHORIZED PRACTICE
> A legal assistant may perform certain functions otherwise prohibited when and only to the extent authorized by statute, court rule or decision, or administrative rule or regulation.

Commentary on Guideline III

A legal assistant is not engaged in the unauthorized practice of law when acting in compliance with statutes, court rules or decisions, or administrative rules and regulations which establish authority in specific areas for a lay person to appear on behalf of parties to proceedings before certain administrative agencies.

The Federal Administrative Procedure Act, Title 5, U.S.C. § 555(b), authorizes Federal administrative agencies to permit representation by nonlawyers. *Sperry v. Florida ex rel. Florida Bar*, 373 U.S. 379 (1963). *Sperry* held that no state may prohibit, through its UPL provisions, a nonlawyer from practice before a Federal administrative agency if the agency itself and Federal statute authorizes such practice.

Examples of Federal Agencies That Authorize Nonlawyer Practice

- Bureau of Indian Affairs: 25 CFR § 20
- Consumer Product Safety Commission: 16 CFR § 1025.61
- Department of Agriculture (food stamps): 7 CFR § 273
- Department of Health and Human Services: 45 CFR § 205
- Department of Homeland Security (Immigration and Naturalization): 8 CFR §§ 292.1–3
- Department of Veterans Affairs: 38 CFR § 14
- Internal Revenue Service: 13 CFR Part 10; 31 U.S.C. § 330
- Patent & Trademark Office: 35 CFR §§ 31–33
- Social Security Administration: 42 U.S.C. § 406(a)

Many New York State agencies permit nonlawyer advocacy pursuant to statute and regulation. According to a survey of the New York County Lawyers' Association, fourteen New York State agencies permit nonlawyer advocacy and twelve New York City agencies permit it.

Examples of New York City Agencies That Authorize Nonlawyer Practice

- Office of Administrative Trials and Hearings
- Department of Agriculture and Markets
- Department of Consumer Affairs
- Department of Transportation
- Housing Authority
- Tax Commission
- Taxi and Limousine Commission

Several bar associations have considered what actions may be delegated to a legal assistant. These services typically include, but are not limited to: researching legal matters; developing an action, procedure, technique, service or application; preparing and interpreting legal documents; selecting, compiling and using technical information; assisting the lawyer in court; handling administrative matters with tribunals; handling real estate closings; and analyzing and following procedural problems that involve independent decisions. Nassau County 90-13 (1990) (an attorney may assign a legal assistant to attend a closing of title but only if the attorney strictly supervises); see also N.Y. State 667 (1995); N.Y. City 884 (1974); N.Y. State 44 (1967).

Guideline IV: CONFIDENTIALITY AND CONFLICT OF INTEREST

It is the responsibility of a lawyer to take reasonable measures to ensure that all client confidences are preserved by the legal assistant and take appropriate measures to avoid potential conflicts of interest arising from employment of legal assistants.

Commentary on Guideline IV

DR 1-104 (Responsibilities of a Supervisory Lawyer) imposes responsibility for nonlawyer conduct on the supervising lawyer when the lawyer ordered, knew or should have known of the conduct at the time when its consequences could be avoided or mitigated, and the lawyer fails to take reasonable remedial action. Thus, the supervising lawyer must ensure that the conduct of the nonlawyer in no way compromises a client's confidentiality or secrets and that no conflict of interest will arise therefrom.

Confidentiality

DR 4-101(D) provides, in part, that "[a] lawyer shall exercise reasonable care to prevent his/her employees, associates, and others whose services are utilized by the lawyer from disclosing or using confidences or secrets of a client." This obligation is emphasized in EC 4-2, which provides: "It is a matter of common knowledge that the normal operation of a law office exposes confidential professional information to nonlawyer employees of the office, particularly secretaries and those having access to the files; and this obligates a lawyer to exercise care in selecting and training employees so that the sanctity of all confidences and secrets of clients may be preserved. See also N.Y. City 1995-11 (lawyer responsible for maintaining confidentiality should sensitize nonlawyers to pitfalls) and N.Y. State 503 (1979) (lawyer bound not to reveal confidences and secrets acquired while employed as legal assistant prior to admission to bar).

Conflict of Interest

The avoidance of, or even the appearance of, conflict of interest is embodied throughout the Code of Professional Responsibility. Lawyers should be attentive to these issues and should sensitize their nonlawyer staff to the pitfalls and develop mechanisms for prompt detection of potential conflict of interest. *Glover Bottled Gas Corp. v. Circle M. Beverage Barn, Inc.*, 129 A.D. 2d 678, 514 N.Y.S. 2d 440, 441 (2d Dept., 1987) (counsel disqualified from further representation after employing legal assistant from adversary firm). The ABA's "Model Guidelines for the Utilization of Legal Assistant Services" (1991) addresses a lawyer's responsibility as follows:

> A lawyer must make reasonable efforts to ensure that a legal assistant's conduct is compatible with the professional obligations of the lawyer. Model Rule 5.3. These professional obligations include the duty to exercise independent professional judgment on behalf of a client, "free of compromising influences and loyalties." ABA Model Rules 1.7 through 1.13. The guideline intentionally speaks to other employment rather than only past employment, since there are instances where legal assistants are employed by more than one law firm at the same time. The guideline's reference to "other interests" is intended to include personal relationships, as well as instances where a legal assistant may have a financial interest (*i.e.*, as a stockholder, trust beneficiary or trustee . . .) that would conflict with the client's in the matter in which the lawyer(and/or legal assistant) has been employed.

Legal assistants are bound to inform the supervising attorney of any interest that could result in a conflict of interest or even give the appearance of a conflict.

If a conflict arises, it may be possible to isolate the legal assistant. To the extent that such a mechanism is appropriate for a lawyer, it should be appropriate for a legal assistant. The American Bar Association takes the position that "an ethical wall will allow legal assistants who are in the possession of confidential client information to accept employment with a law firm opposing the former client so long as an ethical wall is observed and effectively screens the nonlawyer from confidential information." ABA Informal Opinion 1526 and NFPA publication, "The Ethical Wall—Its Application to Paralegals" (1990). See also DR 9-101 and Canon 5.

Guideline V: PROFESSIONAL INDEPENDENCE OF LAWYERS

A lawyer shall not form a partnership with a legal assistant if any part of the firm's activities consists of the practice of law, nor shall a lawyer share legal fees with the lawyer's legal assistant.

Commentary on Guideline V

Nonlawyer compensation may be tied to the net profits and business performance of a firm; thus, discretionary bonuses may properly be paid to nonlawyer employees without violating the rule against sharing legal fees. N.Y. City 1995-11. See also N.Y. City 884 (1974); N.Y. State 282 (1973); ABA 325 (1970). This guideline implements the express provisions of DR 3-102 and DR 3-103, which provide:

DR 3-102. A lawyer or law firm shall not share legal fees with a nonlawyer, except that:

1. An agreement by a lawyer with his or her firm, partner, or associate may provide for the payment of money, over a reasonable period of time after the lawyer's death, to the lawyer's estate or to one or more specified persons.

2. A lawyer who undertakes to complete unfinished legal business of a deceased lawyer may pay to the estate of the deceased lawyer that proportion of the total compensation which fairly represents the services rendered by the deceased lawyer.

3. A lawyer or law firm may include nonlawyer employees in a retirement plan, even though the plan is based in whole or in part on a profit-sharing arrangement.

DR 3-103. A lawyer shall not form a partnership with a nonlawyer if any of the activities of the partnership consist of the practice of law.

Guideline VI: DISCLOSURE OF NONLAWYER STATUS

A lawyer shall require that a legal assistant, when dealing with the client, disclose at the outset that the legal assistant is not a lawyer. The lawyer shall also require such disclosure at the outset when the legal assistant is dealing with a court, an administrative agency, attorneys or the public if there is any reason for their believing that the legal assistant is a lawyer or associated with a lawyer.

Commentary on Guideline VI

Disclosure of legal assistant status when dealing with persons in connection with legal matters is necessary to assure that there will be no misunderstanding as to the responsibilities and role of the legal assistant. Disclosure must be made in a way that avoids confusion. Common sense suggests a routine disclosure at the outset of communication. N.Y. City 884 (1974). When a legal assistant is designated as the individual for contact, disclosure of status should be made at the time of such designation.

Guideline VII: PROFESSIONAL DEVELOPMENT

A lawyer should promote the professional development of the legal assistant.

Commentary on Guideline VII

Professional development is important to all members of the legal team. EC 6-2 provides:

A lawyer is aided in attaining and maintaining competence by keeping abreast of current legal literature and developments, participating in continuing legal education programs, concentrating in a particular area of law, and by utilizing other available means. The lawyer has the additional ethical obligation to assist in improving the legal profession, and may do so by participating in bar activities intended to advance the quality and standards of members of the profession. Of particular importance is the careful training of younger associates and the giving of sound guidance to all lawyers who consult the lawyer. In short, a lawyer should strive at all levels to aid the legal profession in advancing the highest possible standards of integrity and competence and personally meet those standards.

Legal assistants should be provided with opportunities for continuing legal education, participation in pro bono projects and participation in professional organizations.

H. More Information

Rules of Professional Conduct
www.nycourts.gov/rules/jointappellate/NY%20Rules%20 of%20Prof%20Conduct_09.pdf
www.nycourts.gov/rules/jointappellate/NY%20Rules%20 of%20Prof%20Conduct.pdf
22 NYCRR 1200.0 to 22 NYCRR 1200.59.

Lawyer's Code of Professional Responsibility
www.law.cornell.edu/ethics/ny/code
www.nysba.org
(click "For Attorneys" then "Professional Standards for Lawyers")

New York Ethics Materials
www.law.cornell.edu/ethics/ny.html

Ethics Opinions in New York
New York State Bar Association
www.nysba.org
(click "For Attorneys" then "Ethics Opinions")

New York County Lawyers' Association
www.nycla.org
(click "News & Publications" then "Ethics Opinions")

Nassau County Bar Association
www.nassaubar.org
(under "For the Legal Profession" click "Ethics Opinions")

Association of the Bar of the City of New York
www.abcny.org
(click "Reports/Publications/Forms" then "Ethical Responsibilities and Opinions")

Defender Ethics Resources
www.nysda.org/html/ethics_resources.html

New York Ethics on Lexis
www.lexis.com
New York Library, NYETOP file

New York Ethics on Westlaw
www.westlaw.com
NYETH-EO database
NYETH-CS database
NY-RULES database

Legal Ethics in General
www.abanet.org/cpr/links.html
www.legalethics.com
ww3.lawschool.cornell.edu/faculty-pages/wendel/ethlinks.htm

I. Something to Check

Go to the ethics opinions sites of one of the four New York bar association committees listed in "More Information." Find and summarize (brief) one opinion (not mentioned in this section) on each of the following topics:

(a) "attorney advertising"
(b) "in-person solicitation"

3.4 New York Bar Associations, Related Attorney Organizations, and Paralegal Membership Opportunities

A. Introduction
B. Attorneys in New York: A Snapshot
C. Bar Membership Categories for Paralegals
D. New York State Bar Association (NYSBA)
E. Other Statewide or Regional Bar Associations
F. County, Local, and Other Bar Associations
G. More Information

A. Introduction

This section identifies every major bar association in the state. Many of the web sites for these groups have search boxes. To find out what the group may have said about paralegals, type "paralegal" or "legal assistant" in

the search box. You could be led to news, committee or section activities, or ethical material pertaining to paralegals and related nonattorneys.

For related material on New York attorneys, see:

- Part 1, Appendix A (Becoming an Attorney in New York)
- Part 3, Appendix A (Disciplinary Proceedings against an Attorney)

B. Attorneys in New York: A Snapshot

Before examining attorney associations, see Exhibit 3.4A for an overview—a snapshot—of New York attorneys.

EXHIBIT 3.4A	New York Attorneys

Membership of New York State Bar Association	74,000
Top Areas of Concentration of State Bar Members	
Real property	15%
Corporate law	11%
Trusts and estates	10%
Business law	10%
General practice	8%
Family law	6%
Gender of Members of State Bar	
Male	69%
Female	31%
Bar Exam	
Total taking exam	14,765
Number taking exam for first time	10,570
Number of repeat takers	3,916
Total passing	10,128
Percentage passing (total)	69%
Percentage passing (first-time takers)	81%
Percentage passing (repeat takers)	35%
Number taking exam with law office study rather than law school	18
Number passing	3

Sources: *www.abanet.org/marketresearch/2008_NATL_LAWYER_by_State.pdf*; *www.ncbex.org/fileadmin/mediafiles/downloads/Bar_Admissions/2008_Stats. pdf*; New York State Bar Association, *Report on Gender Equity in the Legal Profession: A Survey, Observations and Recommendations* (2002); *www.nysba.org/Content/NavigationMenu/NewsCenter/VitalStatistics/Vital_ Statistics.htm*

C. Bar Membership Categories for Paralegals

As you will see in the links in this section, the following bar associations have membership categories for paralegals and other nonlawyers:

- Albany County Bar Association
- Asian American Bar Association of New York
- Bar Association of Erie County
- Capital District Women's Bar Association
- Greater Rochester Association for Women Attorneys

- Lesbian, Gay, Bisexual and Transgender Law Association
- Metropolitan Black Lawyers Association
- Monroe County Bar Association
- Nassau Lawyers' Association of Long Island
- New York Association of Collaborative Professionals
- New York City Chapter, National Lawyers Guild
- New York State Academy of Trial Lawyers
- New York State Association of Criminal Defense Lawyers
- New York State Defenders Association
- New York State Trial Lawyers Association
- Onondaga County Bar Association
- Oswego County Bar Association
- Saratoga County Bar Association
- Westchester County Bar Association

D. New York State Bar Association (NYSBA)

New York State Bar Association
One Elk St.
Albany, NY 12207
518-463-3200
www.nysba.org

The NYSBA is the most important bar association in the state, particularly for topics such as professional responsibility (ethics). It does not license attorneys. The licensing bodies are the four Appellate Divisions of the New York Supreme Court, which, through the New York State Office of Court Administration (OCA) administer attorney licenses to practice law. (See Part 1, Appendix A.)

NYSBA operates a voluntary specialization program that allows attorneys to become certified as specialists in seven areas of practice: estates and probate, family law, federal tax law, labor and employment law, real property-business law, real property-residential law, and workers' compensation.

Paralegals and the NYSBA

New York State Bar Association, *Guidelines for Utilization by Lawyers of the Services of Legal Assistants* (1997) (see section 3.3 for the text of the guidelines)
(*www.cdpa.info/files/NY_Paralegal_guidelines.pdf*)

New York State Bar Association Ad Hoc Committee on NonLawyer Practice, *Final Report* (May 1995) (see section 3.1 for the text of this report)
(*www.cdpa.info/files/NY_Paralegal_guidelines.pdf*)

Committees of the NYSBA of Particular Concern to Paralegals
- Law Practice Management Committee (800-699-5636)
www.nysba.org
(click "Sections/Committees" then "View Committees")
- Committee on Standards of Attorney Conduct
www.nysba.org
(click "Sections/Committees" then "View Committees")

Activity of the Special Committee on the Unlawful Practice of Law: "Develop recommendations and goals to increase the role of law students and paralegals working under the supervision of attorneys."
www.nysba.org
(click "Sections/Committees" then "View Committees")

Job Leads for Paralegals
www.nysba.org
(click "For Attorneys" then "Jobs and Careers")
(select "Paralegal" and "New York" within NYSBA Instant Job Search)

More Information: Type "Paralegal" or "Legal Assistant" in the search box of the home page
www.nysba.org

E. Other Statewide or Regional Bar Associations

Association of Corporate Counsel, New York Chapters
www.acc.com
www.acc.com/chapters/index.cfm

Capital Region Bankruptcy Bar Association
www.crbba.org

Central New York Women's Bar Association
315-475-3425
www.cnywba.org
www.wbasny.bluestep.net
(click "Chapters")

Converging Technologies Bar Association
212-591-CTBA
www.convergingtechnologies.org/default2.asp

Counselors of Real Estate, New York Chapter
www.cre.org/chapters/chapter_info.cfm?cid=NYM

Dominican Bar Association
www.dominicanbarassociation.org

Bar Association of Erie County (BAEC)
716-852-8687
www.eriebar.org
Membership for Affiliate Members: $65
www.eriebar.org/displaycommon.cfm?an=1& subarticlenbr=79

Federal Bar Association, New York Chapters
www.fedbar.org/chapters.html

Injured Workers Bar Association
516-654-7791
www.injuredworkersbar.org

Korean American Lawyers Association of Greater New York
www.kalagny.org

New York Association of Collaborative Professionals (Family Law)
212-712-0121
www.collaborativelawny.com
Membership for nonlawyers (e.g., CPA): $1,000
www.collaborativelawny.com/join.php

Lesbian, Gay, Bisexual and Transgender Law Association of Greater New York
212-353-9118
www.le-gal.org/site
Legal Assistant Membership: $75
www.le-gal.org/site/form.pdf
www.le-gal.org/join/legalform.html

Metropolitan Black Lawyers Association
212-964-1645
www.mbbanyc.org
Membership for Nonlawyers: $25

New York Criminal & Civil Courts Bar Association
212-766-4030
www.nycccba.org

New York State Academy of Trial Lawyers
518-364-4044
www.trialacademy.org
Paralegal Membership: $75
*www.trialacademy.org/NYSA/index.cfm?event=showPage&
    pg=MemberApp*

New York State Association of Criminal Defense Lawyers
212-532-4434
www.nysacdl.org
Associate Membership for Nonlawyers: $175
www.nysacdl.org/index.php?doc_id=6

New York State Defenders Association
518-465-3524
www.nysda.org
Associate Membership for Nonlawyers: $40
www.nysda.org/html/about_nysda.html#Membership

New York State Intellectual Property Law Association
201-634-1870
www.nyipla.org

New York State Trial Lawyers Association
212-349-5890
www.nystla.org
Paralegal Membership: $75
*www.nystla.org/index.cfm?fuseaction=archives&category
    ID=136*

Nigerian Lawyers Association
212-566-9926
www.nigerianlawyers.org

Puerto Rican Bar Association
www.prba.net

Women's Bar Association of the State of New York
212-362-4445
www.wbasny.bluestep.net

F. County, Local, and Other Bar Associations

There are local bar associations in almost every New York county. This section identifies most of them. Some of the bar associations do not have permanent addresses. They may operate out of the personal law office of an individual member of the association. For information on contacting such associations:

- Check the web site of the courts in the area (see section 4.2); they may link to local bar associations.
- Phone your neighborhood public library; its research desk may be able to give you contact information.
- Do a "bar association" search in Google (or in any other major search engine) by typing the name of the county (or large city) plus the phrase "bar association" followed by "New York." You may be given links that will lead you to current addresses. For example:

"Erie County" "bar association" "New York"
Rochester "bar association" "New York"

Table of Contents

Suffern	Ulster County	Warwick
Suffolk County	Upper Nyack	Westchester
Sullivan County	Utica	White Plains
Syracuse	Valley Cottage	Yorktown
Tioga County	Wampsville	
Tompkins County	Warren County	

Adirondack Women's Bar Association
www.wbasny.bluestep.net
(click "Chapters")

Albany
(see also Capital District)

Albany County Bar Association
518-445-7691
www.albanycountybar.com
Affiliate Membership for Paralegals: $25
www.albanycountybar.com/membership

Allegany County Bar Association
585-268-5800 (Belmont)
www.amtands.com/BarAssociations.htm
(click "A")

Amistad Long Island Black Bar Association
alibba.org

Amistad Suffolk County Black Bar Association
631-423-9131
www.nationalbar.org/about/affiliates2.shtml

Asian American Bar Association of New York
212-571-5662
www.aabany.org
Paralegal Membership: $30
www.aabany.org/registernewmembers.cfm
(A "Paralegal Member shall be entitled to all privileges
and rights of Active Members, excluding the right to
vote at any/all meetings and/or hold office.")

Association of Black Women Attorneys
(see Black Women Attorneys)

Association of the Bar of the City of New York
(see New York City)

Bar Association of Erie County
(see Erie County)

Bar Association of the City of Niagara Falls
(see Niagara Falls)

Belmont
(see Allegany County)

Binghamton
(see Broome County)

Black Women Attorneys, Association of
212-300-2193
www.abwanewyork.org
www.nationalbar.org/about/affiliates2.shtml

Bronx County Bar Association
718-293-2227
www.bronxbar.com

Bronx County, Black Bar Association of
www.nationalbar.org/about/affiliates2.shtml

Bronx Women's Bar Association
www.wbasny.bluestep.net
(click "Chapters")

Brooklyn
(see also Kings County)

Brooklyn Bar Association
718-624-0675
www.brooklynbar.org

Brooklyn Women's Bar Association
www.brooklynwomensbar.org
www.wbasny.bluestep.net
(click "Chapters")

Broome County Bar Association
607-723-6331
www.bcbar.org

Buffalo
(see Erie County)

Burnt Hills
(see Adirondack)

Capital District Black Bar Association
www.nationalbar.org/about/affiliates2.shtml

Capital District Women's Bar Association
cdwba.org
www.wbasny.bluestep.net
(click "Chapters")
Membership for Non-Attorneys: $50

Carmel
(see Putnam County)

Carthage
(see Jefferson County)

Central Islip
(see Suffolk County)

Central New York Women's Bar Association
315-475-3425
www.cnywba.org
www.wbasny.bluestep.net
(click "Chapters")

Chemung County Bar Association
607-734-9687
www.nycourthelp.gov/lawyers2.html

Chestnut Ridge
(see Rockland County)

Clinton County Bar Association
518-562-2600
www.amtands.com/BarAssociations.htm

Converging Technologies Bar Association
212-591-CTBA
www.convergingtechnologies.org/default2.asp

Cortland County Bar Association
www.cortlandbar.com

Delaware County Bar Association
www.hancock.net/%7Edcba/dcba.html

Dominican Bar Association
www.dominicanbarassociation.org

Dutchess County Bar Association
845-473-2488
www.dutchesscountybar.org

Elmsford
(see Rockland County, Westchester)

Erie County, Bar Association of
716-852-8687
www.eriebar.org

Forest Hills
(see Queens)

Garden City
(see Nassau County)

Glen Falls
(see Adirondack, Warren County)

Goshen
(see Orange County)

Greater Rochester Association for Women Attorneys
(see Rochester)

Great River
(see Suffolk County)

Hauppauge
(see Suffolk County)

Haverstraw
(see Rockland County)

Huntington
(see Suffolk County)

Ithaca
(see Tompkins County)

Jamaica
(see Queens)

Jefferson County Bar Association
315-493-6619
www.amtands.com/BarAssociations.htm

Kings County Criminal Bar Association
718-237-1900
www.kccba.org

Kingston
(see Ulster County)

Korean American Lawyers Association of Greater New York
www.kalagny.org

Latino Lawyers Association of Queens County
718-989-2161
www.latinolawyers.org

[Laurelton] Macon B. Allen Black Bar Association
www.nationalbar.org/about/affiliates2.shtml

Lesbian & Gay Bar Association of Greater New York
212-353-9118
www.le-gal.org/site
Legal Assistant Membership: $75
www.le-gal.org/site/form.pdf
www.le-gal.org/join/legalform.html

Lewis County Bar Association
www.nycourts.gov/courts/5jd/lewis/bar.shtml

Long Island
(see Amistad, Nassau County, Suffolk County)

Madison County
(see Mid-New York)

Metropolitan Black Lawyers Association
(see New York City)

Mid-Hudson Women's Bar Association
www.wbasny.bluestep.net
(click "Chapters")

Mid-York Women's Bar Association
www.wbasny.bluestep.net
(click "Chapters")

Mineola
(see Nassau County)

Monroe County Bar Association
585-546-1817
www.mcba.org
Affiliate Membership for Paralegals: $95
*www.mcba.org/Data/Documents/Membership%
    20Application%2009-10.pdf*

Mt. Kisco
(see Westchester)

Nanuet
(see Rockland County)

Nassau County Bar Association
516-747-4070
www.nassaubar.org

Nassau County Women's Bar Association
516-942-2006
www.wbasny.bluestep.net
(click "Chapters")

Nassau Lawyers' Association of Long Island
www.nassaulawyersassociation.com
Associate Membership for Nonlawyer Businesses: $50

New City
(see Rockland County)

New York City
(see also Asian American, Bronx, Brooklyn, Metropolitan, Queens, Staten Island)

[New York City] Association of the Bar of the City of New York
212-382-6600
www.nycbar.org

New York City Chapter, National Lawyers Guild
212-679-6018
www.nlgnyc.org
Membership for Nonlawyer Legal Workers: $45+

[New York] Metropolitan Black Lawyers Association
212-964-1645
www.mbbanyc.org
Membership for Nonlawyers: $25

New York County Lawyers' Association
212-267-6646
www.nycla.org

New York Women's Bar Association
212-490-8202
www.nywba.org
www.wbasny.bluestep.net
(click "Chapters")

Newburgh
(see Orange-Sullivan)

New Windsor
(see Orange-Sullivan)

Niagara Falls, Bar Association of
716-284-4101
www.amtands.com/BarAssociations.htm
www.nycourthelp.gov/lawyers2.html

Nyack
(see Rockland County)

Oneida County
(see also Central New York, Mid-New York)

Oneida County Bar Association
315-724-4901
www.oneidacountybar.com

Onondaga County Bar Association
315-471-2667
www.onbar.org
Affiliate Membership for Paralegals: $60
www.onbar.org/about/join.htm

Orange County Bar Association
845-294-8222
www.orangelaw.org

Orange-Sullivan Women's Bar Association
www.wbaosc.org
www.wbasny.bluestep.net
(click "Chapters")

Oswego County Bar Association
315-343-4016
www.oswego-bar.org
Affiliate Membership for Paralegals: $25
www.oswego-bar.org/members.htm

Pearl River
(see Rockland County)

Plattsburgh
(see Clinton County)

Port Chester-Rye Bar Association
914-761-1300
www.amtands.com/BarAssociations.htm

Poughkeepsie
(see Dutchess County, Mid-Hudson)

Puerto Rican Bar Association
www.prba.net

Putnam County Bar Association
845-225-4904
www.amtands.com/BarAssociations.htm

Queens County Bar Association
718-291-4500
www.qcba.com

Queens County, Latino Lawyers Association of
718-989-2161
www.latinolawyers.org

Queens County Women's Bar Association
www.qcwba.com
www.wbasny.bluestep.net
(click "Chapters")

Rensselaer County Bar Association
www.nycourthelp.gov/lawyers2.html

Richmond County Bar Association
718-442-4500
www.richmondcountybar.org

Riverhead
(see Suffolk County)

Rochester Association for Women Attorneys, Greater
585-234-2394
grawa.org
Affiliate Membership for Non-attorneys: $60
grawa.org/grawa_join.htm

Rockland County Bar Association
845-634-2149
www.rocklandbar.org

Rockland County Women's Bar Association
www.rcwba.org

Rochester
(see also Greater Rochester, Monroe County)

Rochester Black Bar Association
www.nationalbar.org/about/affiliates2.shtml

Rye
(see Port Chester-Rye, Westchester)

Saratoga County Bar Association
518-587-5829
www.saratogacountybar.org
Associate Membership for Paralegals: $25
www.saratogacountybar.org/membership.html

Schenectady Bar Association
518-393-4115
www.amtands.com/BarAssociations.htm

Seneca County Bar Association
www.amtands.com/BarAssociations.htm

South Salem
(see Westchester)

Spring Valley
(see Rockland County)

Staten Island
(see also New York City, Richmond County)

Staten Island Women's Bar Association
www.wbasny.bluestep.net
(click "Chapters")

Suffern
(see Rockland County)

Suffolk County Bar Association
631-234-5511
www.scba.org

Suffolk County Women's Bar Association
www.scwba.net
www.wbasny.bluestep.net
(click "Chapters")

Sullivan County
(see also Orange-Sullivan)

Sullivan County Bar Association
www.amtands.com/BarAssociations.htm

Syracuse
(see Central New York, Onondaga County)

Tioga County Bar Association
www.amtands.com/BarAssociations.htm

Tompkins County Bar Association
607-533-8222
www.tcbaweb.com

Ulster County Bar Association
845-331-0969
www.amtands.com/BarAssociations.htm

Upper Nyack
(see Rockland County)

Utica
(see Mid-New York, Oneida County)

Valley Cottage
(see Rockland County)

Wampsville
(see Mid-New York)

Warren County Bar Association
518-792-9239
www.wcba-ny.com

Warwick
(see Orange-Sullivan)

Westchester County, Association of Black Lawyers of
www.nationalbar.org/about/affiliates2.shtml

Westchester County Bar Association
914-761-3707
www.wcbany.org
Affiliate Membership for NonLawyers: $80
m360.wcbany.org/frontend/portal/SignupOptions.aspx

Westchester Women's Bar Association
914-347-3662
www.wwbany.org
www.wbasny.bluestep.net
(click "Chapters")

White Plains
(see Port Chester-Rye, Rockland County, Westchester)

Yorktown Bar Association
914-245-7500
www.amtands.com/BarAssociations.htm

G. More Information

Lists of New York Bar Associations
www.amtands.com/BarAssociations.htm
abanet.org/barserv/map/ny.html
www.findlaw.com/11stategov/ny/associations.html
www.hg.org/bar-associations-new-york.asp
www.nationalbar.org/about/affiliates2.shtml
www.nyls.edu/pages/2761.asp
www.courts.state.ny.us/attorneys/nybarassociations.shtml
*www.brooklynbar.org/index.php?option=com_weblinks&catid
=95&Itemid=49*
www.nycourthelp.gov/lawyers2.html

Lists of New York Attorneys
www.legaldockets.com/attorneys/index.html
www.nysba.org
(click "For the Community" then "Find a NY Attorney")

Statistics on New York Attorneys

www.abanet.org/marketresearch/2009_NATL_LAWYER_by_State.pdf

Gender Equality in the Legal Profession

Report on Equity

www.nysba.org/AM/Template.cfm?Section=Home&TEMPLATE=/CM/ContentDisplay.cfm&CONTENTID=2846

New York Attorney Earnings

www.infirmation.com/shared/insider/payscale.tcl

www.payscale.com/research/US/Job=Attorney_%2F_Lawyer/Salary

www.indeed.com/salary?q1=attorney&l1=New+York%2C+NY

swz.salary.com

APPENDIX A

Timeline: Disciplinary Proceedings against an Attorney

A. Introduction

B. Timeline

C. Lawyers' Fund for Client Protection

D. Fee Disputes

E. Grading the New York Disciplinary System

F. More Information

G. Something to Check

A. Introduction

In this section we will outline the steps involved in bringing a complaint against a New York attorney for violating one or more of the rules of the Code of Professional Responsibility presented earlier in section 3.2. The power to discipline attorneys for professional misconduct resides in the Appellate Division of the Supreme Court in each of the state's four departments.

There are three major categories of discipline that can be imposed on New York attorneys:

- **Disbarment.** A revocation of the right to practice law. After seven years, the attorney can usually apply for reinstatement.
- **Suspension.** A removal of the right to practice law for a specified minimum time, e.g., a year. After this period, the suspended attorney can apply for reinstatement.
- **Letter of Caution, Admonition, or Reprimand.** A letter is sent to the attorney and placed in his or her file stating that his or her conduct was not proper. (The letter is not made public.)

Before examining the procedural steps that can result in such sanctions, Exhibit A.1 presents an overview of disciplinary data on attorneys in the state.

EXHIBIT A.1	Attorney Discipline in New York
Number of complaints received by disciplinary agency	13,004
Number of complaints pending from prior years	5,672
Number of complaints summarily dismissed for lack of jurisdiction	6,101
Number of complaints investigated	8,710
Number of complaints dismissed after investigation	4,853
Number of lawyers charged after probable cause determination	508
Number of private sanctions	403
Number of public sanctions	238
Number of disbarments (involuntarily)	79
Number of disbarments (on consent)	41
Number of suspensions (other than interim suspensions)	53
Number of interim suspensions	33
Number of public reprimands/censures	32
Staff of disciplinary agency:	
Number of attorneys	56
Number of paralegals	7
Number of investigators	17
Average caseload per attorney (1st Jud. Dept.)	36
Average caseload per attorney (3rd Jud. Dept.)	388
Average time from receipt of complaint to the filing of formal charges (1st Jud. Dept.)	24 months

Source: ABA Center for Professional Responsibility, *Survey on Lawyer Discipline Systems* (2007) (*www.abanet.org/cpr/discipline/sold/home.html*)

B. Timeline

The main body in the disciplinary process is the grievance committee appointed by the each of the Appellate Divisions. These committees have both attorney and nonattorney members. (In addition, each county's bar association may be asked to help resolve a case.) The four departments do not all follow the same disciplinary procedure, although there is considerable similarity among the departments.

1. Filing a Complaint

Complaints against attorneys are made in writing to the grievance committee where the attorney has an office (there is no official complaint form):

First Judicial Department
Departmental Disciplinary
Committee
61 Broadway, 2nd Fl.

New York, NY 10006
212-401-0800
www.courts.state.ny.us/courts/
ad1/Committees&Programs/
DDC/index.shtml

Second Judicial Department
Grievance Committee, 2nd &
11th Districts
Renaissance Plaza
335 Adams St., Ste 2400
Brooklyn, NY 11201
718-923-6300
www.courts.state.ny.us/courts/
ad2/attorneymatters_Complaint
AboutaLawyer.shtml

Grievance Committee, 10th
District
150 Motor Parkway, Ste 102
Hauppauge, NY 11788
631-231-3775

Grievance Committee,
9th District
399 Knollwood Rd., Ste 200
White Plains, NY 10603
914-949-4540

Third Judicial Department
Committee on Professional
Standards

40 Steuben St., #502
Albany, NY 12207
518-474-8816
www.courts.state.ny.us/ad3/
cops/index.html

Fourth Judicial Department
Attorney Grievance
Committee, 5th District
465 South Salina St.
Syracuse, NY 13202
315-471-1835
www.courts.state.ny.us/ad4/
AG/AG_welcome.htm

Attorney Grievance
Committee, 7th District
42 East Ave., Ste 404
Rochester, NY 14604
585-546-8340

Attorney Grievance
Committee, 8th District
438 Main St., Rm 800
Buffalo, NY 14202-3212
716-858-1190

2. Grievance Committee

Once a written complaint is filed, the following
steps can occur:

- The grievance committee and its staff determine
  whether the complaint states a claim of misconduct
  that can be investigated.
- An investigation can take different forms: obtaining
  a written response from the attorney in question,
  interviewing the relevant witnesses, examining documents and records, etc.
- If the respondent is asked to attend a hearing, it
  might be conducted by a staff attorney or by a
  panel of grievance committee members.
- At the conclusion of the investigation, the grievance
  committee can (a) dismiss the matter if it finds no
  misconduct, (b) recommend that the Appellate
  Division institute a formal disciplinary proceeding
  against the attorney because serious misconduct is
  apparent, or (c) issue letters of caution, admonition,
  or reprimand if less serious misconduct is found.

(In the second, third, and fourth departments, the
grievance committee can delegate minor matters to the
local bar association for resolution.)

3. Formal Disciplinary Proceeding

The Appellate Division will conduct a formal disciplinary proceeding if the grievance committee finds serious
misconduct such as theft of client funds. Although the
four departments do not follow the same procedures, an
example of the process can include the following steps:

- A Petition of Charges is served on the attorney.
- The attorney can file a response.

- A referee can be assigned to conduct a hearing to
  resolve factual issues and report his or her findings
  to the court.
- The Appellate Division will then hear arguments on
  whether the findings of fact should be confirmed.
- If the court sustains the findings, it will impose a
  sanction such as censure, suspension, or disbarment.

4. New York Court of Appeals

The accused attorney has the right to appeal the
actions of the Appellate Division. The appeal is to the
New York Court of Appeals.

C. Lawyers' Fund for Client Protection

The Lawyers' Fund for Client Protection is an
organization that reimburses losses (up to $300,000 per
client loss) caused by the dishonest conduct of New York
attorneys in the course of their practice. It is funded by
a portion of the registration fee paid by all practicing
attorneys in the state. Examples of losses covered by
the fund include theft of estate and trust assets, money
embezzled in investment transactions with law clients,
and unearned fees paid in advance to lawyers who falsely
promise their legal services. In 2007, the Fund made 185
awards totaling $7 million. Since 1982, over 6,300 awards
have been made totaling over $130 million.

Lawyers' Fund For Client Protection
119 Washington Ave.
Albany, NY 11210
800-442-FUND
www.nylawfund.org

D. Fee Disputes

The New York State Court System has established
a Statewide Fee Dispute Resolution Program (FDRP)
(877-FEES-137) to resolve attorney-client disputes
over legal fees through arbitration (and in some
cases mediation). In general, a lawyer may not sue a
client in court over a fee dispute unless he or she
first provides the client with notice of the client's
right to use the FDRP. If the client decides not to use
FDRP, the lawyer can pursue the fee dispute in court.
www.nycourts.gov/admin/feedispute/index.shtml

E. Grading the New York Disciplinary System

HALT—An Organization of Americans for Legal
Reform (*www.halt.org*) grades the disciplinary system of
every state by issuing its Lawyer Discipline Report Card.
The 2006 grade it gave New York was D+. See Exhibit A.2.
Its 2002 grade was also D+. New York's system was ranked
36th in the nation.

EXHIBIT A.2	Grading the New York Disciplinary System

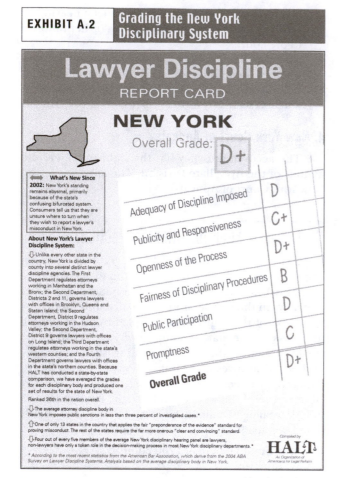

Lawyer Discipline
REPORT CARD

NEW YORK

Overall Grade: **D+**

What's New Since
2002: New York's standing remains abysmal, primarily because of the state's confusing bifurcated system. Consumers tell us that they are unsure where to turn when they wish to report a lawyer's misconduct in New York.

About New York's Lawyer Discipline System:

☞ Unlike every other state in the country, New York is divided by county into several distinct lawyer discipline agencies. The First Department regulates attorneys working in Manhattan and the Bronx; the Second Department, Districts 2 and 11, governs lawyers with offices in Brooklyn, Queens and Staten Island; the Second Department, District 9 regulates attorneys working in the Hudson Valley; the Second Department, District 9 governs lawyers with offices on Long Island; the Third Department regulates attorneys working in the state's western counties; and the Fourth Department governs lawyers with offices in the state's northern counties. Because HALT has conducted a state-by-state comparison, we have averaged the grades for each disciplinary body and produced one set of results for the state of New York.

Ranked 36th in the nation overall.

☞ The average attorney discipline body in New York imposes public sanctions in less than three percent of investigated cases.*

☞ One of only 13 states in the country that applies the fair "preponderance of the evidence" standard for proving misconduct. The rest of the states require the far more onerous "clear and convincing" standard.

☞ Four out of every five members of the average New York disciplinary hearing panel are lawyers; non-lawyers have only a token role in the decision-making process in most New York disciplinary departments.*

According to the most recent statistics from the American Bar Association, which derive from the 2004 ABA Survey on Lawyer Discipline Systems. Analysis based on the average disciplinary body in New York.

Adequacy of Discipline Imposed	D
Publicity and Responsiveness	C+
Openness of the Process	D+
Fairness of Disciplinary Procedures	B
Public Participation	D
Promptness	C
Overall Grade	D+

Compiled by
HALT
An Organization of Americans for Legal Reform

Source: HALT (*www.halt.org/reform_projects/lawyer_accountability/report_card_2006/pdf/NY_LDRC_06.pdf*). Reprinted with permission, *Lawyer Discipline Report Card*, HALT, Inc., Washington, DC (*www.HALT.org*).

F.	More Information

Overview of Discipline
www.nysba.org
(click "For the Community" then "Resolving Conflict with a New York Attorney?")

How to File an Attorney Complaint (Ninth Judicial District)
www.nylawfund.org/gc9/instruct.htm

NYS Attorney Directory, Status of Attorneys
portal.courts.state.ny.us/pls/portal30/INTERNETDB_DEV.MENU_INTERNETDB.show

Report Card on Effectiveness of New York's System of Disciplining Attorneys (2006)
www.halt.org/reform_projects/lawyer_accountability/report_card_2006

Report Card on Effectiveness of New York's System of Disciplining Attorneys (2002)
www.halt.org/reform_projects/lawyer_accountability/report_card

Report Card on Effectiveness of New York's Lawyer-Client Fee Arbitration System (2007)
www.halt.org/reform_projects/lawyer_accountability/lawyer-client_fee_arbitration

ABA Survey on Lawyer Disciplinary Systems
www.abanet.org/cpr/discipline/sold/home.html

New York State Commission on Judicial Conduct
www.scjc.state.ny.us
www.scjc.state.ny.us/Related%20Groups/lawyer.htm

Professional Discipline in New York
www.op.nysed.gov/opd.htm

Legal Ethics Resources on the Web
ww3.lawschool.cornell.edu/faculty-pages/wendel/ethlinks.htm

G.	Something to Check

Find and summarize (brief) three Appellate Division opinions: one involving paralegals, one involving the marketing of legal forms by a business, and one involving the sale of client files and lists. All attorney discipline cases are captioned "In the Matter of (attorney name)." On finding state court opinions, see section 5.1.

Legal System

4.1 Introduction to the State Government of New York

A. Introduction

B. Overview

C. More Information

D. Something to Check

A. Introduction

In this section we present an overview of New York state government. More detailed information about the major components of our government can be found in:

- Section 4.2 on our state courts
- Section 4.4 on the state legislature
- Section 4.5 on administrative agencies in the executive branch
- Section 4.6 on county and city government

B. Overview

The New York Constitution divides the powers of government into three branches: executive, legislative, and judicial. Exhibit 4.1A presents an overview of the major units of our state government.

Executive Branch

Governor

Under Article IV of the New York Constitution, the "executive power shall be vested in the governor," who is the chief executive officer of the state. The governor carries out the laws of the state by appointing department directors and members of boards and commissions and by supervising a large state bureaucracy under these officials. For a list of these government bodies and how to contact them, see section 4.5.

Through the power to sign or veto bills passed by the legislature, the governor also has a major role in the enactment of legislation. For a description of this role, see section 4.4.

Governor
State Capitol
Albany, NY 12224
518-474-8390
www.ny.gov/governor

Lieutenant Governor

The major function of the lieutenant governor is to run the state if the governor is unable to do so (Article IV of the New York Constitution). In addition, the lieutenant governor carries out other duties assigned by the governor.

Lieutenant Governor
State Capitol
Albany, NY 12224
www.state.ny.us/governor/ltgov

Attorney General

As the state's chief law officer, the attorney general serves as legal counsel to all statewide elected officials, the New York Legislature, and all state departments, agencies, boards, and commissions. In addition, the attorney general's office "is charged with the statutory and common law powers to protect consumers and investors, charitable donors, the public health and environment, civil rights, and the rights of wage-earners and businesses across the State." (*www.oag.state.ny.us/our_office.html*)

The attorney general provides (1) *formal* opinions to executive branch departments and agencies, public authorities, the office of court administration, and the state's public university system and (2) *informal* advisory opinions to municipal attorneys to assist local governments. See section 5.1 on locating these opinions.

Attorney General
The Capitol
Albany, NY 12224-0341
800-771-7755; 518-474-7330
www.oag.state.ny.us

EXHIBIT 4.1A	Overview of New York State Government

New York State Government		
EXECUTIVE BRANCH	**LEGISLATIVE BRANCH**	**JUDICIAL BRANCH**
• Governor • Lieutenant Governor • Attorney General • Secretary of State • Comptroller	• State Senate • State Assembly	• Court of Appeals • Appellate Divisions of the Supreme Court • Supreme Courts • Other trial courts

State Comptroller

The New York State Comptroller is the chief financial officer of the state. The primary functions of the comptroller include oversight of the state's finances, operating the state's retirement system, and auditing government operations.

Office of the State Comptroller
110 State St.
Albany, NY 12236
518-474-4044
osc.state.ny.us

Department of State (Secretary of State)

The office of the secretary of state is the state's record keeper. The office is responsible for the licensing and regulation of many businesses and professions. The division of corporations handles many filings of corporations, partnerships, and related entities.

Department of State
99 Washington Ave.
Albany, NY 12231
518-474-4752
dos.state.ny.us

State Departments, Agencies, Offices, Boards, and Commissions

In addition to the Department of State, there are 19 other departments, as well as a large number of state offices, boards, and commissions. For a list of the major state departments, agencies, offices, boards, and commissions, see section 4.5.

State Government Listings
nysegov.com
megalaw.com/ny/nygov.php

Legislative Branch

For an overview of how a bill becomes a law in New York, see section 4.4.

Under Article III of the New York Constitution, the "legislative power of this state shall be vested in the senate and assembly." Similar to the federal government, state senators (62) represent by area and state assembly members (150) represent by population.

New York State Assembly
assembly.state.ny.us

Individual Assembly Members
assembly.state.ny.us/mem

Assembly Committees, Commissions, and Task Forces
assembly.state.ny.us/comm

Senate
senate.state.ny.us

Individual Senators
senate.state.ny.us
(click "Senators")

Senate Committees
senate.state.ny.us
(click "Senators" then "Senate Committees")

State Statues
public.leginfo.state.ny.us/menugetf.cgi
public.leginfo.state.ny.us/menuf.cgi
caselaw.lp.findlaw.com/nycodes
megalaw.com/ny/nycode.php

Bill Search
assembly.state.ny.us/leg

Legislature Session Information
public.leginfo.state.ny.us/menuf.cgi

Judicial Branch

The major state courts created by the New York Constitution are the New York Court of Appeals, Appellate Divisions of the Supreme Court, countywide Supreme Courts, and many other trial courts (Article VI of the New York Constitution). For an overview of the jurisdiction of these courts, see section 4.2. Federal courts in New York are covered in section 4.3.

New York State Unified Court System
courts.state.ny.us/home.htm

State Courts
nycourts.gov/courts

Court of Appeals
nycourts.gov/ctapps

Supreme Court, Appellate Divisions
First Department: *nycourts.gov/courts/ad1/index.shtml*
Second Department: *nycourts.gov/courts/ad2/index.shtml*
Third Department: *nycourts.gov/ad3*
Fourth Department: *nycourts.gov/ad4*

Court of Claims
nyscourtofclaims.state.ny.us

Justice Courts, Town and Village Courts
nycourts.gov/courts/townandvillage

Court Decisions
nycourts.gov/decisions
See also sections 4.2 and 5.1.

C. More Information

Overview of State Government
ny.gov

Structure/Branches of Government
www.senate.state.ny.us/sws/aboutsenate/branches_gov.html#leg
www.budget.state.ny.us/citizen/structure/structure.html

State Government Listing
nysegov.com

Lobbying State Government
www.nyintegrity.org/local

Archives of State Government Records
nysl.nysed.gov

State Government Information Locator
www.nysl.nysed.gov/ils

Local Government
www.nysl.nysed.gov/ils/topics/local.htm

New York State Unified Court System
courts.state.ny.us/home.htm

NYS Senate
senate.state.ny.us

NYS Assembly
assembly.state.ny.us

NYS Constitution
senate.state.ny.us/lbdcinfo/senconstitution.html
www.dos.state.ny.us/info/constitution.htm

D. Something to Check

1. Use the online resources in this section to determine the current state government deficit (or surplus) in New York's budget.
2. Identify any problem that you think exists in your community. Use the online sites in this section to identify government entities or persons in the executive and legislative branches that would probably have authority to solve or address this problem.

4.2 State Courts in New York

A. Introduction and Summary

Our court system is arguably the most complicated state court system in the United States. There are 1,210 judges and approximately 15,000 nonjudicial personnel throughout the court system. There are also over 2,200 town and village justices who are elected and paid by their localities.

In this section, we present an overview of the courts in the system and their interrelationship, with an emphasis on subject-matter jurisdiction and lines of appeals.

First, a word about terminology:

- Trial courts are sometimes categorized as *superior* courts (supreme court, county court) and as *local* courts (justice courts, city courts, district courts, and NYC courts). Strictly speaking, however, the terms *superior* and *local* apply only to criminal cases (see Criminal Procedure Law §10.10). Yet the terms are often applied generally so that they include civil cases. For example, a person might refer to his or her breach-of-contract case in a local court or in a superior court even though breach-of-contract cases are civil cases.
- Civil trial courts are referred to as either *general jurisdiction* courts (the supreme court has jurisdiction for virtually every type of case, with no monetary limits) or as *limited jurisdiction* courts (all other trial courts, which have limits on the types of cases they can hear, many with monetary limits).

General Information about New York State Courts
800-COURT-NY
www.courts.state.ny.us
www.courts.state.ny.us/contactus/index.shtml

Elsewhere in this book, see the following related sections:

- Section 4.3 (federal courts in New York)
- Section 6.1 (timeline of a civil case in state court)
- Section 6.4 (timeline of a criminal case in state court)

The major categories of New York State courts are outlined in Exhibit 4.2A.

The courts of the state are divided into four judicial departments and twelve judicial districts. See Exhibit 4.2B.

The jurisdiction of each court is established either by Article VI of the New York State Constitution or by statute. The courts of original jurisdiction, or trial courts, hear cases in the first instance, and the appellate courts hear and determine appeals from the decision of the trial courts.

Exhibit 4.2C summarizes the subject-matter jurisdiction of state courts.

EXHIBIT 4.2A Categories of New York State Courts

APPELLATE COURTS
Court of Appeals
Appellate Divisions of the Supreme Court
Appellate Terms of the Supreme Court
County Court*

TRIAL COURTS
Statewide:
Supreme Court*
Court of Claims
Family Court
Surrogate's Court

New York City:
Criminal Court
Civil Court

Outside New York City:
County Court*
City Courts
Town & Village Courts
District Court (Long Island)

*Primarily a trial court, but in some jurisdictions can hear appeals.

Source: www.courts.state.ny.us/courts/10jd/suffolk/structure.shtml

B. Court of Appeals

The highest court in New York is the New York Court of Appeals, which sits in Albany. The court consists of a chief judge and six associate judges, appointed by the governor for 14-year terms. It is the "court of last resort," taking appeals of both civil and criminal matters. With few exceptions, the court chooses which appeals to accept. It must take appeals regarding the imposition of the death penalty, although currently the death penalty cannot be imposed. Also, a losing litigant in an Appellate Division case may appeal as a matter of right if two justices of the Appellate Division dissent or if a state or federal constitutional question is presented. The vast majority of appeals, however, are heard at the discretion of the court. They are called appeals by permission, or certiorari. The court is responsible for establishing rules governing the admission of attorneys to the bar.

EXHIBIT 4.2B Judicial Departments and Districts

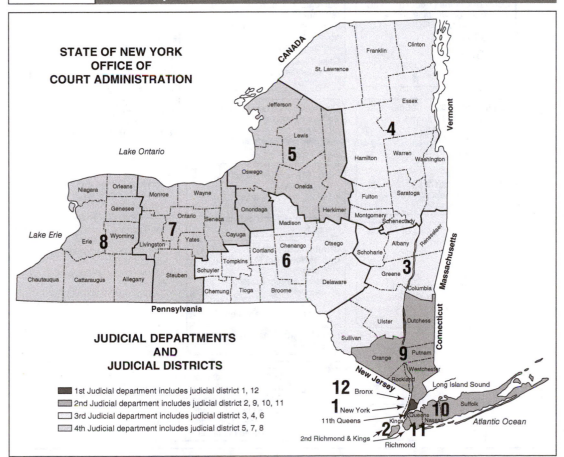

Source: *Report of the Chief Administrator of the Courts (2005)*
(*www.nycourts.gov/reports/annual/pdfs/2005annualreport.pdf*)

EXHIBIT 4.2C | **Subject–Matter Jurisdiction of New York State Courts**

Court of Appeals COLR
7 judges

Case Types:
- Mandatory jurisdiction in civil, capital criminal, administrative agency, juvenile, original proceedings cases.
- Discretionary jurisdiction in civil, criminal, administrative agency, juvenile, disciplinary, original proceedings cases.

Appellate Divisions of Supreme Court IAC
60 justices sit in panels in 4 departments A

Case Types:
- Mandatory jurisdiction in civil, criminal, administrative agency, juvenile, lawyer disciplinary, original proceedings, interlocutory decision cases.
- Discretionary jurisdiction in civil, criminal, juvenile, original proceedings, interlocutory decision cases.

Appellate Terms of Supreme Court IAC
14 justices sit in panels in 3 terms

Case Types:
- Mandatory jurisdiction in civil, criminal, juvenile, interlocutory decision cases.
- Discretionary jurisdiction in criminal, juvenile, interlocutory decision cases.

Supreme Court (12 districts) GJC
326 justices plus 50 judges from the A
Court of Claims
Jury trials

Case Types:
- Tort, contract, real property, miscellaneous civil.
- Exclusive marriage dissolution.
- Felony, misdemeanor.

County Court (57 counties outside NYC) LJC
129 judges (of which 57 serve the Surrogates' IAC
Court and/or the Family Court)
Jury trials

Case Types:
- Tort, contract, real property ($0–$25,000), civil appeals, miscellaneous civil.
- Criminal.

Court of Claims (1 court) LJC
86 judges (of which 59 act
as Supreme Court justices)
No jury trials

Case Types:
- Tort, contract, real property involving the state.

Surrogates' Court LJC
(62 counties)
31 surrogates plus 51 judges
from the County Court
Jury trials in probate/estate

Case Types:
- Probate/estate.
- Adoption.

City Court (61 courts) LJC
158 judges
Jury trials for highest level
misdemeanor

Case Types:
- Tort, contract, real property ($0–$15,000), small claims (up to $5,000)
- Felony, misdemeanor, preliminary hearings.
- Traffic infractions, ordinance violations.

Family Court (62 counties) LJC
127 judges plus 6 judges from
the County Court and 81
quasi-judicial staff
No jury trials

Case Types:
- Guardianship.
- Domestic relations.
- Domestic violence.
- Exclusive juvenile.

District Court (Nassau and LJC
Suffolk counties)
50 judges
Jury trials except in traffic

Case Types:
- Tort, contract, real property ($0–$15,000), small claims (up to $5,000)
- Felony, misdemeanor, preliminary hearings.
- Traffic infractions, ordinance violations.

Town and Village Justice LJC
Court (1,487 courts)
2,300 justices Locally funded
Jury trials in most cases

Case Types:
- Tort, contract, real property ($0–$3,000), small claims (up to $3,000)
- Misdemeanor, preliminary hearings.
- Traffic/other violations.

Civil Court of the City of LJC
New York (1 court)
120 judges
Jury trials

Case Types:
- Tort, contract, real property ($0–$25,000), small claims, (up to $5,000), miscellaneous civil.

Criminal Court of the LJC
City of New York (1 court)
107 judges
Jury trials for highest level
misdemeanor

Case Types:
- Misdemeanor, preliminary hearings.
- Traffic infractions, ordinance violations.

Legend

( ) = Appellate level

( ) = Trial level

COLR = Court of Last Resort
IAC = Intermediate Appellate Court
GJC = General Jurisdiction Court
LJC = Limited Jurisdiction Court
A = Appeal from Admin. Agency
↑ = Route of appeal

Source: *National Center for State Courts (2007)*
(*www.ncsconline.org/D_Research/Ct_Struct/state_inc.asp?STATE=NY*)

Court of Appeals: Address
New York State Court of Appeals
20 Eagle St.
Albany, NY 12207
518-455-7700
www.nycourts.gov/ctapps
www.nycourts.gov/ctapps/phone.htm

Court of Appeals: Jurisdiction
www.nycourts.gov/ctapps/forms/Practice.htm
(click entries on jurisdiction)
www.nycourts.gov/ctapps/forms/coacase.htm

Court of Appeals: Decisions
www.nycourts.gov/ctapps/latdec.htm
www.nycourts.gov/reporter/Decisions.htm
www.nycourts.gov/decisions
www.law.cornell.edu/nyctap
www.courts.state.ny.us/decisions
www.findlaw.com/11stategov/ny/courts.html
(See section 5.1 for other places to find opinions.)

Court of Appeals: Calendar and New Case Filings
www.nycourts.gov/ctapps
(Click "Court Calendar" and "New Case Filings")

Court of Appeals: Rules of Practice
www.courts.state.ny.us/ctapps/500rules.htm
www.nycourts.gov/ctapps/forms/crtrules05.htm

Court of Appeals: Practice Questions
www.nycourts.gov/ctapps/forms/coafaq.htm
www.nycourts.gov/ctapps/forms/Practice.htm

Court of Appeals: Forms
www.nycourts.gov/ctapps/forms/forms.htm

Court of Appeals: Filings by CD-ROM
www.nycourts.gov/ctapps/techcdrul.htm

Court of Appeals: Guide for Counsel
www.nycourts.gov/ctapps/counsguide.htm

Court of Appeals: Pro Se Appeals
www.nycourts.gov/ctapps/forms/ProSeApp.pdf

Court of Appeals: Background and History
www.law.cornell.edu/nyctap/court/background.htm

C. Appellate Divisions

The middle appeals or intermediate appellate court in New York is the Appellate Division of the Supreme Court, usually referred to as the Appellate Division. As indicated, the state is geographically divided into four appellate districts, referred to as judicial departments. An Appellate Division of the Supreme Court exists in each of the state's four judicial departments. The primary responsibilities of Appellate Divisions are:

- Resolving appeals from judgments or orders of lower courts of original jurisdiction in civil and criminal cases

- Reviewing civil appeals taken from the Appellate Terms and the County Courts acting as appellate tribunals
- Conducting proceedings to admit, suspend, or disbar attorneys

Each Appellate Division has jurisdiction over appeals from final orders and judgments, as well as from some intermediate orders rendered in county-level courts, and original jurisdiction over selected proceedings.

The governor designates the presiding and associate justices of each Appellate Division from among the justices of the Supreme Court. Presiding justices serve for the remainder of their term; associate justices are designated for five-year terms, or for the remainder of their unexpired term, if less than five years.

Appellate Terms

Appellate Terms have been established in the First and Second Departments. They exercise jurisdiction over civil and criminal appeals taken from local courts and, in the Second Department, over nonfelony appeals from county courts. The chief administrator designates the Appellate Term justices from among the justices of the Supreme Court, with the approval of the presiding justice of the appropriate Appellate Division. (*www.courts.state.ny.us/reports/annual/pdfs/2006annualreport.pdf*)

Appellate Divisions (Listed by County)
www.nycourts.gov/courts/appellatedivisions.shtml

Appellate Division, First Department (NY, NY)
212-340-0400
www.nycourts.gov/courts/ad1

Appellate Division, First Department (Decisions)
www.nycourts.gov/reporter/slipidx/aidxtable_1.htm
www.nycourts.gov/reporter/Decisions.htm

Appellate Division, First Department (Rules)
www.courts.state.ny.us/courts/ad1/Practice&Procedures/rules.shtml

Appellate Division, First Department (Fees)
www.courts.state.ny.us/courts/ad1/Practice&Procedures/fees.shtml

Appellate Division, First Department (Practice Guide)
www.courts.state.ny.us/courts/ad1/Practice&Procedures/index.shtml

Appellate Division, Second Department (Brooklyn)
718-875-1300
www.courts.state.ny.us/courts/ad2

Appellate Division, Second Department (Decisions)
www.courts.state.ny.us/reporter/slipidx/aidxtable_2.htm
www.nycourts.gov/reporter/Decisions.htm

Appellate Division, Second Department (Rules)
www.courts.state.ny.us/courts/ad2/pdf/rulesofprocedure.pdf
www.courts.state.ny.us/courts/ad2/howacaseisdecided.shtml

Appellate Division, Second Department (Fees: § 670.22)
www.courts.state.ny.us/courts/ad2/pdf/rulesofprocedure.pdf

Appellate Division, Second Department (Forms)
www.courts.state.ny.us/courts/ad2/formsandpracticeaids.shtml

**Appellate Division, Second Department
(Guide to Civil Practice)**
*www.courts.state.ny.us/courts/ad2/pdf/Guide%20to%20
Practice%20-%2020081106.pdf*

Appellate Division, Third Department (Albany)
518-471-4777
www.nycourts.gov/ad3

Appellate Division, Third Department (Decisions)
decisions.courts.state.ny.us/ad3/Search/AppDiv3Intro.htm
www.nycourts.gov/reporter/Decisions.htm

Appellate Division, Third Department (Rules)
www.nycourts.gov/ad3/Rulesofthecourt.html

Appellate Division, Third Department (Fees: § 800.23)
www.nycourts.gov/ad3/Rulesofthecourt.html

Appellate Division, Third Department (Forms)
www.nycourts.gov/ad3/Forms.html

Appellate Division, Fourth Department (Rochester)
585-530-3100
www.nycourts.gov/ad4

Appellate Division, Fourth Department (Decisions)
www.nycourts.gov/reporter/Decisions.htm
www.courts.state.ny.us/ad4
(Click "Decisions")

Appellate Division, Fourth Department (Rules)
www.courts.state.ny.us/ad4
(Click "Rules")

Appellate Division, Fourth Department (Fees)
nycourts.gov/ad4/perfecting_appeals.htm

Appellate Division, Fourth Department (Forms)
nycourts.gov/ad4/Court/Forms/Forms.htm
nycourts.gov/ad4/lg/lg_forms_default.htm

**Appellate Term of Supreme Court:
First Judicial Department (NY, NY)**
646-386-3040
www.courts.state.ny.us/courts/appterm_1st.shtml
www.courts.state.ny.us/supctmanh/appellate_term.htm
www.courts.state.ny.us/courts/lowerappeals.shtml

**Appellate Term of Supreme Court:
Second Judicial Department (Brooklyn)**
347-401-9580
www.courts.state.ny.us/courts/appterm_2nd.shtml
www.courts.state.ny.us/courts/lowerappeals.shtml

D. Supreme Court

The Supreme Court is the trial court of general jurisdiction in the state. It has no limits on money awards in civil cases, and is a superior criminal court. In general,

it hears cases outside the jurisdiction of other courts, such as:

- Civil matters in which parties seek damages (over $25,000) that are beyond the monetary limits available in lower trial courts
- Divorce, separation, and annulment
- Felony prosecutions (in some parts of the state outside New York City, however, felonies are heard in county court)

The Commercial Division is a part of the Supreme Court of the State of New York. Branches of the Division are located in the Seventh and Eighth Judicial Districts, and in other designated counties. The Commercial Division handles complicated commercial cases. (*www.courts .state.ny.us/courts/comdiv*)

Supreme Court justices are elected by judicial district to 14-year terms.

Supreme Court: Addresses
*www.courts.state.ny.us/ea/XML/ASP_Transform/
Court_transform.asp*
*www.ncsconline.org/D_KIS/CourtWebSites/
CtWeb_NYsupreme.htm*
www.courts.state.ny.us/courts/comdiv

Supreme Court: Court Guides by County
www.nycourts.gov/litigants/courtguides

Supreme Court: Uniform Rules for Trial Courts
www.courts.state.ny.us/rules/trialcourts

Supreme Court: Filing Fees and Forms
www.courts.state.ny.us/litigants/forms.shtml

Supreme Court: WebCivil
(WebCivil provides online access to information about cases in Civil Supreme Court in all 62 counties.)
iapps.courts.state.ny.us/webcivil/FCASMain

Supreme Court: Decisions
www.nycourts.gov/decisions/index.shtml
www.nycourts.gov/reporter/slipidx/miscolo.htm

**Supreme Court: New York County
(First Judicial District)**
646-386-3600 (civil term); 212-374-0667 (criminal term)
www.nycourts.gov/supctmanh
www.courts.state.ny.us/courts/1jd/criminal
www.courts.state.ny.us/courts/1jd
www.courts.state.ny.us/courts/nyc/supreme

**Supreme Court: Kings County
(Second Judicial District)**
347-296-1183 (civil term); 646-386-4500 (criminal term)
www.courts.state.ny.us/courts/2jd/kings.shtml

Supreme Court: Upstate (Third Judicial District)
518-285-8300 (administrative office for the district)
www.courts.state.ny.us/courts/3jd/supreme

Supreme Court: Upstate (Fourth Judicial District)
518-587-3019 (administrative office for the district)
www.courts.state.ny.us/courts/4jd/courtdescriptions.shtml

Supreme Court: Upstate (Fifth Judicial District)
315-671-2111 (administrative office for the district)
www.nycourts.gov/courts/5jd

Supreme Court: Upstate (Sixth Judicial District)
607-721-8541 (administrative office for the district)
www.nycourts.gov/courts/6jd

Supreme Court: Upstate (Seventh Judicial District)
www.courts.state.ny.us/courts/7jd

Supreme Court: Upstate (Eighth Judicial District)
716-845-2505 (administrative office for the district)
www.courts.state.ny.us/courts/8jd

Supreme Court: Upstate (Ninth Judicial District)
914-824-5100 (administrative office for the district)
www.courts.state.ny.us/courts/9jd

Supreme Court: Nassau County (Tenth Judicial District)
516-571-2400; 516-571-3542
www.courts.state.ny.us/courts/10jd/nassau
www.courts.state.ny.us/courts/10jd/nassau/supreme.shtml

Supreme Court: Suffolk County (Tenth Judicial District)
631-852-2334
www.courts.state.ny.us/courts/10jd/suffolk/supreme.shtml
www.courts.state.ny.us/courts/10jd/suffolk

Supreme Court: Queens County (Eleventh Judicial District)
718-298-1000
www.courts.state.ny.us/courts/11jd

Supreme Court: Bronx County (Twelfth Judicial District)
718-618-1200 (civil); 718-618-3100 (criminal)
www.courts.state.ny.us/courts/12jd
www.courts.state.ny.us/courts/12jd/civil.shtml
www.courts.state.ny.us/courts/12jd/criminal.shtml

Supreme Court: Richmond County (Thirteenth Judicial District)
718-390-5201
www.nycourts.gov/courts/13jd
www.courts.state.ny.us/courts/13jd/richmond.shtml

Supreme Court: Commercial Divisions
www.nycourts.gov/courts/comdiv

E. Court of Claims

The New York State Court of Claims is a state-wide court with exclusive jurisdiction over civil litigation that seeks damages against the State of New York or certain other state-related entities such as the N.Y. State Thruway Authority, the City University of New York, and the N.Y. State Power Authority (claims for the appropriation of real property only). The Court of Claims has no jurisdiction over any city, county, or town government, or over any individual defendant.

New York State Court of Claims
518-432-3411 (Albany)
nyscourtofclaims.courts.state.ny.us

Court of Claims: Decisions
nyscourtofclaims.courts.state.ny.us/decisions.shtml

Court of Claims: Uniform Rules for Trial Courts
www.courts.state.ny.us/rules/trialcourts/206.shtml

Court of Claims: Forms
nyscourtofclaims.courts.state.ny.us/forms.shtml

F. Family Court

There is a family court in every county. This court has jurisdiction over non-matrimonial family matters such as:

- Adoption, guardianship, and foster care
- Delinquency and PINS (persons in need of supervision)
- Domestic violence
- Child protective proceedings (abuse and neglect)
- Termination of parental rights
- Paternity
- Support

In addition, parts of a matrimonial action, like support or custody, may be referred to a family court from a supreme court. Because of the large volume of cases, all counties have administrative judges called Support Magistrates who handle initial proceedings for child support and paternity.

Family Court: Addresses
www.courts.state.ny.us/ea/XML/ASP_Transform/Court_transform.asp

Family Court: Court Guides by County
www.nycourts.gov/litigants/courtguides

Family Court: Uniform Rules for Trial Courts
www.courts.state.ny.us/rules/trialcourts

Family Court: Filing Fees
www.courts.state.ny.us/litigants/forms.shtml

Family Court: Forms
www.courts.state.ny.us/litigants/forms.shtml
www.courts.state.ny.us/forms/familycourt/general.shtml

Family Court: Decisions
www.nycourts.gov/reporter/slipidx/miscolo.htm

Family Court: New York County (First Judicial District)
646-386-5206
www.courts.state.ny.us/courts/1jd
www.courts.state.ny.us/courts/1jd/index.shtml#family

Family Court: Kings County (Second Judicial District)
347-401-9600
www.courts.state.ny.us/courts/2jd/kings.shtml

Family Court: Upstate (Third Judicial District)
518-285-8300 (administrative office for the district)
www.courts.state.ny.us/courts/3jd/family

Family Court: Upstate (Fourth Judicial District)
518-587-3019 (administrative office for the district)
www.courts.state.ny.us/courts/4jd/courtdescriptions.shtml

Family Court: Upstate (Fifth Judicial District)
315-671-2111 (administrative office for the district)
www.nycourts.gov/courts/5jd

Family Court: Upstate (Sixth Judicial District)
607-721-8541 (administrative office for the district)
www.nycourts.gov/courts/6jd

Family Court: Upstate (Seventh Judicial District)
www.courts.state.ny.us/courts/7jd

Family Court: Upstate (Eighth Judicial District)
716-845-2505 (administrative office for the district)
www.courts.state.ny.us/courts/8jd

Family Court: Upstate (Ninth Judicial District)
914-824-5100 (administrative office for the district)
www.courts.state.ny.us/courts/9jd

Family Court: Nassau County (Tenth Judicial District)
516-571-9033; 516-571-3542
www.courts.state.ny.us/courts/10jd/nassau
www.courts.state.ny.us/courts/10jd/nassau/family.shtml

Family Court: Suffolk County (Tenth Judicial District)
631-853-4289; 631-852-3905
www.courts.state.ny.us/courts/10jd/suffolk/family.shtml
www.courts.state.ny.us/courts/10jd/suffolk/index.shtml

Family Court: Queens County (Eleventh Judicial District)
718-298-0197
www.courts.state.ny.us/courts/11jd

Family Court: Bronx County (Twelfth Judicial District)
718-618-2098
www.courts.state.ny.us/courts/12jd

Family Court: Richmond County (Thirteenth Judicial District)
718-390-5460; 718-390-5461
www.nycourts.gov/courts/nyc/family/infobycounty.shtml#s5
www.courts.state.ny.us/courts/13jd/richmond.shtml

G. Surrogate's Court

There is a surrogate's court in every county. Its primarily function is to handle:

- Probate of wills
- Administration of decedent's estates
- Adoption

Surrogate's Court: Addresses
www.courts.state.ny.us/ea/XML/ASP_Transform/
   Court_transform.asp

Surrogate's Court: Court Guides by County
www.nycourts.gov/litigants/courtguides

Surrogate's Court: Filing Fees
www.courts.state.ny.us/litigants/forms.shtml

Surrogate's Court: Forms
www.nycourts.gov/forms/surrogates
www.courts.state.ny.us/litigants/forms.shtml

Surrogate's Court: Decisions
www.nycourts.gov/reporter/slipidx/miscolo.htm

**Surrogate's Court: New York County
(First Judicial District)**
646-386-5000
www.courts.state.ny.us/courts/1jd/surrogates
www.courts.state.ny.us/courts/1jd/index.shtml#surrogate
www.courts.state.ny.us/courts/1jd

**Surrogate's Court: Kings County
(Second Judicial District)**
347-404-9700
www.courts.state.ny.us/courts/2jd/kings.shtml

Surrogate's Court: Upstate (Third Judicial District)
518-285-8300 (administrative office for the district)
www.courts.state.ny.us/courts/3jd/surrogates

Surrogate's Court: Upstate (Fourth Judicial District)
518-587-3019 (administrative office for the district)
www.courts.state.ny.us/courts/4jd/courtdescriptions.shtml

Surrogate's Court: Upstate (Fifth Judicial District)
315-671-2111 (administrative office for the district)
www.nycourts.gov/courts/5jd

Surrogate's Court: Upstate (Sixth Judicial District)
607-721-8541 (administrative office for the district)
www.nycourts.gov/courts/6jd

Surrogate's Court: Upstate (Seventh Judicial District)
www.courts.state.ny.us/courts/7jd

Surrogate's Court: Upstate (Eighth Judicial District)
716-845-2505 (administrative office for the district)
www.courts.state.ny.us/courts/8jd

Surrogate's Court: Upstate (Ninth Judicial District)
914-824-5100 (administrative office for the district)
www.courts.state.ny.us/courts/9jd

Surrogate's Court: Nassau County
(Tenth Judicial District)
516-571-2847
www.courts.state.ny.us/courts/10jd/nassau
www.courts.state.ny.us/courts/10jd/nassau/surrogates.shtml

Surrogate's Court: Suffolk County
(Tenth Judicial District)
631-852-1746
www.courts.state.ny.us/courts/10jd/suffolk/surrogates.shtml

Surrogate's Court: Queens County
(Eleventh Judicial District)
718-298-0400
www.courts.state.ny.us/courts/11jd/surrogates/index.shtml

Surrogate's Court: Bronx County
(Twelfth Judicial District)
718-618-2300
www.courts.state.ny.us/courts/12jd/index.shtml

Surrogate's Court: Richmond County
(Thirteenth Judicial District)
718-390-5400
www.courts.state.ny.us/courts/13jd/richmond.shtml
www.nycourts.gov/courts/nyc/surrogates/index.shtml

H. County Court

Every county outside of New York City has a county court. It is a limited jurisdiction court in civil matters and a superior court for criminal cases. These courts handle:

- Criminal prosecutions of both felonies and lesser offenses committed within the county, although in practice most minor offenses are handled by lower courts
- Civil cases generally involving amounts up to $25,000

Although primarily a trial court, the county court in some counties can hear appeals from lower courts.

County Court: Addresses
www.ncsconline.org/D_KIS/CourtWebSites/
CtWeb_NYcounty.htm
www.courts.state.ny.us/ea/XML/ASP_Transform/
Court_transform.asp

County Court: Court Guides by County
www.nycourts.gov/litigants/courtguides

County Court: Uniform Rules for Trial Courts
www.courts.state.ny.us/rules/trialcourts

County Court: Filing Fees
www.courts.state.ny.us/litigants/forms.shtml

County Court: Upstate (Third Judicial District)
518-285-8300 (administrative office for the district)
www.courts.state.ny.us/courts/3jd/county

County Court: Upstate (Fourth Judicial District)
518-587-3019 (administrative office for the district)
www.courts.state.ny.us/courts/4jd/courtdescriptions.shtml

County Court: Upstate (Fifth Judicial District)
315-671-2111 (administrative office for the district)
www.nycourts.gov/courts/5jd

County Court: Upstate (Sixth Judicial District)
607-721-8541 (administrative office for the district)
www.nycourts.gov/courts/6jd

County Court: Upstate (Seventh Judicial District)
www.courts.state.ny.us/courts/7jd

County Court: Upstate (Eighth Judicial District)
716-845-2505 (administrative office for the district)
www.courts.state.ny.us/courts/8jd

County Court: Upstate (Ninth Judicial District)
914-824-5100 (administrative office for the district)
www.courts.state.ny.us/courts/9jd

County Court: Nassau County (Tenth Judicial District)
516-571-2800; 516-571-3542
www.courts.state.ny.us/courts/10jd/nassau
www.courts.state.ny.us/courts/10jd/nassau/county.shtml

County Court: Suffolk County (Tenth Judicial District)
631-852-2120
www.courts.state.ny.us/courts/10jd/suffolk/county.shtml
www.courts.state.ny.us/courts/10jd/suffolk

I. Courts in New York City

Courts in New York City: Addresses
www.courts.state.ny.us/ea/XML/ASP_Transform/
Court_transform.asp

Courts in New York City: Court Guides
www.courts.state.ny.us/litigants/courtguides/
CtUsersinNYC02.pdf
www.nycourts.gov/litigants/courtguides

Courts in New York City: Uniform Rules
for Trial Courts
www.courts.state.ny.us/rules/trialcourts/208.shtml
www.courts.state.ny.us/rules/trialcourts

Courts in New York City: Filing Fees
www.courts.state.ny.us/litigants/forms.shtml

Courts in New York City: Supreme Court
(see Supreme Court above)

Courts in New York City: Family Court
(see Family Court above)

Courts in New York City: Surrogate's Court
(see Surrogate's Court above)

Courts in New York City: Civil Court of the City
of New York
www.courts.state.ny.us/courts/nyc/civil

The Civil Court of the City of New York is a limited jurisdiction civil court. It has three divisions: the Civil Division (known as the Civil Court), which hears and determines civil matters involving monetary damages up to $25,000; the Housing Part (known as the Housing Court), which handles residential landlord/tenant disputes; and the Small Claims Court, which hears matters involving monetary damages not exceeding $5,000.

Courts in New York City: Criminal Court of the City of New York

www.courts.state.ny.us/courts/nyc/criminal/index.shtml

The Criminal Court of the City of New York has authority over all misdemeanors and minor offenses committed within New York City. It is a local criminal court. It also handles preliminary proceedings in felony matters, after which the case is transferred to the criminal term of the supreme court.

J. District Courts

There are two District Courts, both on Long Island, one for Nassau County and one for western Suffolk County. Each is a court of limited jurisdiction in civil matters and is a local criminal court. The courts handle:

- Civil lawsuits involving claims up to $15,000
- Felony arraignments
- Misdemeanors

District Court: Addresses

www.courts.state.ny.us/ea/XML/ASP_Transform/ Court_transform.asp

District Court: Court Guides

www.nycourts.gov/litigants/courtguides

District Court: Uniform Rules for Trial Courts

www.courts.state.ny.us/rules/trialcourts/212.shtml
www.courts.state.ny.us/rules/trialcourts

District Court: Filing Fees and Forms

www.courts.state.ny.us/litigants/forms.shtml

District Court: Nassau County (Tenth Judicial District)

516-572-2355; 516-571-2400
www.courts.state.ny.us/courts/10jd/nassau
www.courts.state.ny.us/courts/10jd/nassau/district.shtml
www.courts.state.ny.us/litigants/courtguides/CtUsers NasSuff02.pdf

District Court: Suffolk County (Tenth Judicial District)

631-853-7500
www.courts.state.ny.us/courts/10jd/suffolk/dist/index.shtml
www.courts.state.ny.us/courts/10jd/suffolk/index.shtml
www.courts.state.ny.us/litigants/courtguides/ CtUsersNasSuff02.pdf

K. City Courts outside New York City

A city court exists in every city except New York City. It is also a local criminal court, and a limited jurisdiction civil court. City courts hear:

- Civil lawsuits involving claims up to $15,000
- Felony arraignments
- Misdemeanors

Some city courts have small claims parts for the informal disposition of matters involving claims of up to $5,000 and/or housing parts to handle landlord-tenant matters and housing violations.

City Courts: Addresses

www.courts.state.ny.us/ea/XML/ASP_Transform/ Court_transform.asp

City Courts: Court Guides

www.nycourts.gov/litigants/courtguides

City Courts: Uniform Rules for Trial Courts

www.courts.state.ny.us/rules/trialcourts

City Courts: Filing Fees

www.courts.state.ny.us/litigants/forms.shtml

L. Town and Village Courts

Every county outside of New York City is divided into towns, villages, and cities. Every town has a town court, and some villages have a village court. Town and village courts are referred to as justice courts and are governed by the same rules. They are local criminal courts and limited jurisdiction civil courts. There are about 900 town courts and 500 village courts for a total of over 1,400 justice courts. Town justices are also referred to as justices of the peace. They do not have to be attorneys, and most are not. These courts hear:

- Civil lawsuits involving claims up to $3,000 (including small claims up to this amount)
- Felony arraignments
- Misdemeanors
- Non-felony vehicle and traffic infractions

Town and Village Courts: Addresses

www.courts.state.ny.us/ea/XML/ASP_Transform/ Court_transform.asp

Town and Village Courts: Overview

www.nycourts.gov/ea/XML/ASP_Transform/ homepage_transform.asp
www.nysmagassoc.homestead.com

Town and Village Courts: Court Guides

www.nycourts.gov/litigants/courtguides

Town and Village Courts: Filing Fees

www.courts.state.ny.us/litigants/forms.shtml

New York Association of Magistrates Court Clerks

www.nysamcc.com

M. Problem-Solving Courts

Within some of the courts described above, special attention is given to certain categories of cases. The special attention can include extra judicial monitoring and community resources. Although the providers of this attention are not separate courts, they are referred to in general as problem-solving courts and in particular by the category of problem involved, e.g., domestic violence courts and drug treatment courts.

Problem-Solving Courts: Overview
www.courts.state.ny.us/courts/problem_solving
www.courts.state.ny.us/courts/problem_solving/
  PSC-FLYER4Fold.pdf

Drug Treatment Courts
www.courts.state.ny.us/courts/problem_solving/drugcourts

Integrated Domestic Violence Courts
www.courts.state.ny.us/courts/problem_solving/idv/home.shtml

Domestic Violence Courts
www.courts.state.ny.us/courts/problem_solving/dv/home.shtml

Youthful Offender Domestic Violence Courts
www.courts.state.ny.us/courts/problem_solving/yo/home.shtml

Mental Health Courts
www.courts.state.ny.us/courts/problem_solving/mh/home.shtml

Sex Offense Courts
www.courts.state.ny.us/courts/problem_solving/so/home.shtml

Community Courts
www.courts.state.ny.us/courts/problem_solving/cc/home.shtml

N. More Information

New York State Unified Court System
www.courts.state.ny.us/home.htm

Overview of New York State Courts
www.courts.state.ny.us/admin/NYCourts-IntroGuide.pdf
www.nycourts.gov/admin/NYCourts-IntroGuide.pdf
www.courts.state.ny.us/courthelp/cfacts3.html
www.courts.state.ny.us/courts/10jd/suffolk/structure.shtml
www.nycourts.gov/reports/annual/pdfs/2006annualreport.pdf
www.nysba.org
(click "For the Community" then "Guide to the Courts of New York")

Court Dockets
www.legaldockets.com

Justice Works: Guide to New York Courts
www.courts.state.ny.us/litigants/JusticeWorks07.pdf

State Court Guides
www.courts.state.ny.us/litigants/courtguides/index.shtml

Addresses of Courts
www.courts.state.ny.us/ea/XML/ASP_Transform/
  Court_transform.asp

New York Court Decisions
www.courts.state.ny.us/decisions
www.nycourts.gov/decisions/index.shtml
www.nycourts.gov/reporter/slipidx/miscolo.htm
www.findlaw.com/11stategov/ny/courts.html

NY CourtHelp
nycourthelp.gov
nycourthelp.gov/cfacts2.html

Information about State Judges
www.courts.state.ny.us/judges/directory.shtml

Selection of Judges and Justices
www.judicialselection.us/judicial_selection/
  index.cfm?state=NY

Historical Society of the Courts of the State of New York
www.nycourts.gov/history/Courts.htm

Memorable New York State Trials
www.courts.state.ny.us/history/Cases.htm

Careers in the Court System
www.courts.state.ny.us/careers

O. Something to Check

1. Go to sites that give you online access to court opinions of the New York Court of Appeals. (See sites above and section 5.1.) Use the search features of the sites to find an opinion on any broad legal topic, e.g., capital punishment, adoption. Summarize what the opinion says about your topic.

2. Go to the web sites of any three courts mentioned in this section. For the same general kind of litigant filing (e.g., a complaint, an amendment to a prior filing) state the filing fee in each of the three courts.

3. Find a biography of one of the justices sitting on the Court of Appeals. Identify a prior job of this justice that might indicate a possible conservative or liberal philosophy of deciding cases. Explain your answer.

4.3 Federal Courts in New York

A. Introduction

B. Specific Federal Court Details

C. PACER

D. More Information

E. Something to Check

A. Introduction

There are four types of federal courts that either sit in New York or have jurisdiction over the state (not including the United States Supreme Court):

- United States Court of Appeals for the Second Circuit
- United States District Courts (Southern District, Western District, Eastern District, and Northern District)

- United States Bankruptcy Courts (Southern District, Western District, Eastern District, and Northern District)
- United States Immigration Courts

In this section we will present an overview of these courts, how they operate, and some of the major resources that are available when working with them.

The Federal Judiciary
www.uscourts.gov
www2.maxwell.syr.edu/plegal/scales/court.html

B. Specific Federal Court Details

United States Court of Appeals for the Second Circuit

The United States is divided geographically into 11 numbered federal judicial circuits (also called regional circuits). Each circuit has a U.S. court of appeals (U.S. Court of Appeals for the First Circuit, U.S. Court of Appeals for the Second Circuit, etc.). These federal courts of appeals are intermediate appellate courts just below the U.S. Supreme Court. In addition to the 11 numbered circuits, there are 2 other circuits: the District of Columbia Circuit and the Federal Circuit, both located in Washington, D.C. (The Federal Circuit is a separate and unique court of appeals that has nationwide jurisdiction in specialized cases.)

Each of the 50 states (plus the territories of Guam, Puerto Rico, and the U.S. Virgin Islands) is assigned to one of the 11 numbered circuits. New York, Vermont, and Connecticut are in the second circuit. The court of appeals for our circuit is the United States Court of Appeals for the Second Circuit, sometimes abbreviated as CA2 or 2d Cir.

The United States Court of Appeals for the Second Circuit hears appeals (1) from the United States district courts in New York, Vermont, and Connecticut and (2) from the United States Tax Court and from certain federal administrative agencies where the non-governmental parties are from one of the three states that make up the Second Circuit. The other regional circuits do the same for their circuits. Decisions of the United States courts of appeals are final except as they are subject to review on writ of certiorari by the United States Supreme Court. Judges on the court of appeals have lifetime tenure; they are nominated by the president and confirmed by the U.S. Senate.

2d Circuit: Address
United States Court of Appeals, Second Circuit
500 Pearl St.
New York, NY 10007
212-857-8500
www.ca2.uscourts.gov

2d Circuit: Clerk's Office in New York
United States Court of Appeals, Second Circuit
40 Foley Sq.
New York, NY 10007
212-857-8585
www.ca2.uscourts.gov/clerk/index.htm

2d Circuit: Biographies of Judges
www.ca2.uscourts.gov (click "Circuit Judges")

2d Circuit: Opinions
www.ca2.uscourts.gov (click "Decisions")
www.findlaw.com/casecode/courts/2nd.html
www.law.cornell.edu/federal/opinions.html

2d Circuit: PACER login
www.ca2.uscourts.gov/Docket.htm

2d Circuit: Docket
www.ca2.uscourts.gov/Docket.htm

2d Circuit: Forms
www.ca2.uscourts.gov/clerk/Forms_and_instructions/ forms_home.htm

2d Circuit: Rules
- Federal Rules of Appellate Procedure (FRAP)
www.ca2.uscourts.gov/clerk/Rules/Rules_home.htm
www.uscourts.gov/rules/newrules4.html
www.uscourts.gov/rules/appel2007.pdf
- Local Rules of the Second Circuit
www.ca2.uscourts.gov/clerk/Rules/LR/Local_Rules.htm

2d Circuit: Second Circuit Case-filing
www.ca2.uscourts.gov/clerk

2d Circuit: Fees (§ 0.17)
www.ca2.uscourts.gov/clerk/Overview/Costs_and_ billing.htm

2d Circuit: Appellate Briefs (Rule 28)
www.ca2.uscourts.gov/clerk/Rules/FRAP/Rule_28.htm

2d Circuit: Employment
www.ca2.uscourts.gov/jobs.htm
www.uscourts.gov/employment.html

United States District Courts

United States district courts exist within the judicial districts that are part of the regional circuits. In the 50 states, there are 89 district courts. Each state has at least 1 district court; New York has 4: Southern District, Western District, Eastern District, and Northern District. In addition to a district court for the District of Columbia, the Commonwealth of Puerto Rico has a district court with jurisdiction corresponding to that of district courts in the various states. Finally, district courts also exist in the territories of the Virgin Islands, Guam, and the Northern Mariana Islands for a total of 94 district courts in the federal judicial system.

United States district courts are trial courts of general federal jurisdiction. Within limits set by Congress and the U.S. Constitution, they can hear nearly all categories of federal cases, including both civil and criminal matters. Typically, federal courts hear civil cases in which the United States is a party or those involving the U.S. Constitution, laws enacted by Congress, treaties, and laws relating to navigable waters. Examples include bankruptcy and violations of federal environmental laws. Other large sources of civil cases in district courts are those involving disputes between citizens of different states (diversity of citizenship) if the amount in dispute exceeds $75,000. Federal criminal cases in district courts are filed by the United States attorney who represents the United States. Examples of federal crimes prosecuted in district court include illegal importation of drugs and certain categories of bank fraud.

At present, each district court has from 2 to 28 federal district judgeships, depending upon the amount of judicial work within its boundaries. Only one judge is usually required to hear and decide a case in a district court, but in limited cases, 3 judges are called together to comprise the court. Judges of district courts have lifetime tenure; they are nominated by the president and confirmed by the U.S. Senate.

Each district court has one or more of the following: magistrate judge and bankruptcy judge, a clerk, a United States attorney, a United States marshal, probation officers, and court reporters. A United States magistrate judge is a federal trial judge appointed for a term of eight years by the life-tenured judges of a district court. Magistrates do not have all the powers of a district judge. The latter can assign some trials to magistrates upon consent of the parties.

Cases from a district court are reviewable on appeal by the United States court of appeals in the circuit where the district court sits.

As indicated, there are four United States district courts sitting in New York:

- United States District Court, Southern District of New York
- United States District Court, Western District of New York
- United States District Court, Eastern District of New York
- United States District Court, Northern District of New York

United States District Court, Southern District of New York

Southern District: Addresses
United States District Court
Southern District of New York
500 Pearl St.
New York, NY 10007
212-895-0136
www.nysd.uscourts.gov
www1.nysd.uscourts.gov

United States District Court
Southern District of New York
300 Quarrapas St.
White Plains, NY 10601
914-390-4100

Southern District: Biographies of Judges
www1.nysd.uscourts.gov/judges.php

Southern District: Opinions
www1.nysd.uscourts.gov/cases.php
www.nysd.uscourts.gov/courtweb
www.law.cornell.edu/federal/districts.html#circuit

Southern District: CM/ECF
ecf.nysd.uscourts.gov
www1.nysd.uscourts.gov/pacer.php

Southern District: Forms
www1.nysd.uscourts.gov/forms.php

Southern District: Local Rules
www1.nysd.uscourts.gov/courtrules.php
www.nyed.uscourts.gov/localrules.pdf

Southern District: Federal Rules of Civil Procedure
www.law.cornell.edu/rules/frcp
www.uscourts.gov/rules/newrules4.html
www.federalrulesofcivilprocedure.info/frcp

Southern District: Federal Rules of Criminal Procedure
www.law.cornell.edu/rules/frcrmp
www.uscourts.gov/rules/newrules4.html

Southern District: Fees
www1.nysd.uscourts.gov/fees.php

Southern District: General Filing Procedures
www1.nysd.uscourts.gov/forms.php

Southern District: Self-Representation (Pro Se)
www1.nysd.uscourts.gov/courtrules_prose.php

Southern District: Employment
www1.nysd.uscourts.gov/human_resources.php
www.uscourts.gov/employment.html

United States District Court, Western District of New York

Western District: Addresses
United States District Court
Western District of New York
304 United States Courthouse
68 Court St.
Buffalo, NY 14202
716-332-1700
www.nywd.uscourts.gov

United States District Court
Western District of New York
2120 United States Courthouse
100 State St.
Rochester, NY 14614
585-613-4000

Western District: Opinions
www.law.cornell.edu/federal/districts.html#circuit
www.nywd.uscourts.gov
(click "Attorney Information" then "Judge's
Decisions")

Western District: PACER Login
ecf.nywd.uscourts.gov
ecf.nywd.uscourts.gov/cgi-bin/ShowIndex.pl

Western District: Forms
www.nywd.uscourts.gov
(click "Clerk's Office Information" then "Forms"
entries)

Western District: Local Rules
www.nywd.uscourts.gov
(click "Clerk's Office Information" then "Local Rules")

Western District: Federal Rules of Civil Procedure
www.law.cornell.edu/rules/frcp
www.uscourts.gov/rules/newrules4.html
www.federalrulesofcivilprocedure.info/frcp

Western District: Federal Rules of Criminal Procedure
www.law.cornell.edu/rules/frcrmp
www.uscourts.gov/rules/newrules4.html

Western District: Fees
www.nywd.uscourts.gov
(click "Financial Information")

Western District: Self-Representation (Pro Se)
www.nywd.uscourts.gov
(click "Representing Yourself in Federal Court")

Western District: Employment
www.uscourts.gov/employment.html

United States District Court, Eastern District of New York

Addresses
United States District Court
Eastern District of New York
225 Cadman Plaza East
Brooklyn, NY 11201
718-613-2600
www.nyed.uscourts.gov

United States District Court
Eastern District of New York
100 Federal Plaza
Central Islip, NY 11722
631-712-6000

Eastern District: PACER Login
*www.nyed.uscourts.gov/General_Information/
Pacer_Access/pacer_access.html*

Eastern District: CM/ECF (Case Management/
Electronic Case Files)
ecf.nyed.uscourts.gov

Eastern District: Opinions
www.law.cornell.edu/federal/districts.html#circuit
*www.nyed.uscourts.gov/Decisions_of_Interest/
decisions_of_interest.html*

Eastern District: Calendar
www.nyed.uscourts.gov/calendar/calendar.cfm

Eastern District: Forms
*www.nyed.uscourts.gov/Local_Documents/local_documents.
html*
(click "Court Forms")
*www.nyed.uscourts.gov/General_Information/Court_Forms/
court_forms.html*

Eastern District: Local Rules
www.nyed.uscourts.gov/localrules.pdf

Eastern District: Federal Rules of Civil Procedure
www.law.cornell.edu/rules/frcp
www.uscourts.gov/rules/newrules4.html
www.federalrulesofcivilprocedure.info/frcp

Eastern District: Federal Rules of Criminal Procedure
www.law.cornell.edu/rules/frcrmp
www.uscourts.gov/rules/newrules4.html

Eastern District: Fees
www.nyed.uscourts.gov
(click "General Information" then "Schedule of Fees")

Eastern District: Self-Representation (Pro Se)
www.nyed.uscourts.gov/probono

Eastern District: Employment
*www.nyed.uscourts.gov/General_Information/Job_Openings/
job_openings.html*
www.uscourts.gov/employment.html

United States District Court, Northern District of New York

Northern District: Addresses
United States District Court
Northern District of New York
445 Broadway, Rm 509
Albany, NY 12207
518-257-1800
www.nynd.uscourts.gov

157 Genesee St., 2nd Floor
Auburn, NY 13021
315-252-6555

15 Henry St.
Binghamton, NY 13902
607-773-2893

Lewis Ave.
Fort Drum, NY 13602
315-234-8500

100 S. Clinton St.
P.O. Box 7367
Syracuse, NY 13261
315-234-8500

10 Broad St.
Utica, NY 13501
315-793-8151

317 Washington St., 10th Floor
Watertown, NY 13601
315-779-8935

Web Site
www.nynd.uscourts.gov

Northern District: Biographies of Judges
www.nynd.uscourts.gov/judgebio.htm

Northern District: PACER
ecf.nynd.uscourts.gov/cgi-bin/login.pl

Northern District: CM/ECF
www.nynd.uscourts.gov/cmecf

Northern District: Opinions
www.nynd.uscourts.gov/CourtWeb.htm
www.law.cornell.edu/federal/districts.html#circuit

Northern District: Forms
www.nynd.uscourts.gov/forms.htm

Northern District: Local Rules
www.nynd.uscourts.gov/localrul.htm

Northern District: Federal Rules of Civil Procedure
www.law.cornell.edu/rules/frcp
www.uscourts.gov/rules/newrules4.html
www.federalrulesofcivilprocedure.info/frcp

Northern District: Federal Rules of Criminal Procedure
www.law.cornell.edu/rules/frcrmp
www.uscourts.gov/rules/newrules4.html

Northern District: Fees
www.nynd.uscourts.gov/documents/FeeSched7_1_2006.pdf

Northern District: Self-Representation (Pro Se)
www.nynd.uscourts.gov/prose.cfm
www.nynd.uscourts.gov/documents/ProSeHandbook2008.pdf

Northern District: Employment
www.nynd.uscourts.gov/employ.htm
www.uscourts.gov/employment.html

United States Bankruptcy Courts

Federal courts have exclusive jurisdiction over bankruptcy cases. Such cases cannot be filed in state court. Although United States district courts have jurisdiction over all bankruptcy matters (28 U.S.C. § 1334), they have authority to delegate or refer bankruptcy cases to the United States bankruptcy courts. There is a bankruptcy court in each of the 94 federal judicial districts. Bankruptcy courts are usually in the same physical location as the United States district courts. However, in some areas, based on local space availability, the bankruptcy court may be located in space other than the United States courthouse where the district court is situated. A United States bankruptcy judge is a judicial officer of the United States district court and is appointed for a 14-year term by the majority of judges of the United States court of appeals in the circuit.

The primary purposes of bankruptcy law are: (1) to give an honest debtor a "fresh start" in life by relieving the debtor of most debts and (2) to repay creditors in an orderly manner to the extent that the debtor has property available for payment.

Kinds of Bankruptcy
www.uscourts.gov/bankruptcycourts/bankruptcybasics.html

Bankruptcy Overview
www.uscourts.gov/bankruptcycourts/bankruptcybasics/
   process.html
www.uscourts.gov/bankruptcycourts/
   BB101705final2column.pdf

United States Code: Title 11 (Bankruptcy)
uscode.house.gov/download/title_11.shtml
www.law.cornell.edu/uscode/html/uscode11/
   usc_sup_01_11.html

Federal Rules of Bankruptcy Procedure
www.law.cornell.edu/rules/frbp

Filing for Bankruptcy without an Attorney
www.uscourts.gov/bankruptcycourts/prose.html

United States Bankruptcy Court, Southern District of New York
212-668-2870 (NY); 845-452-4200 (Poughkeepsie); 914-390-4060 (White Plains)
www.nysb.uscourts.gov

United States Bankruptcy Court, Western District of New York
716-362-3200 (Buffalo); 585-613-4200 (Rochester)
www.nywb.uscourts.gov

United States Bankruptcy Court, Eastern District New York
347-394-1700 (Brooklyn); 631-712-6200 (Central Islip)
www.nyeb.uscourts.gov

United States Bankruptcy Court, Northern District of New York
518-257-1661 (Albany); 315-793-8101 (Utica); 315-295-1600 (Syracuse)
www.nynb.uscourts.gov

United States Immigration Courts

The Executive Office for Immigration Review (EOIR) (*www.usdoj.gov/eoir*) adjudicates matters brought under various immigration statutes to its three administrative tribunals: the Board of Immigration Appeals, the Office of the Chief Immigration Judge, and the Office of the Chief Administrative Hearing Officer.

The Board of Immigration Appeals has nationwide jurisdiction to hear appeals from certain decisions made by immigration judges and by district directors of the Department of Homeland Security (DHS). The Office of the Chief Immigration Judge provides overall direction for more than 200 immigration judges located in 53 immigration courts throughout the nation. Immigration judges are responsible for conducting formal administrative proceedings and act independently in their decision-making capacity. Their decisions are administratively final, unless appealed or certified to the Board. New York has six court locations.

Immigration Court Locations in New York
(Batavia; Buffalo; Fishkill; New York City, Federal Plaza and Varick St.; Ulster)
www.usdoj.gov/eoir/sibpages/ICadr.htm
www.usdoj.gov/eoir/sibpages/ICadr.htm#NY

Immigration Court Practice Manual
www.usdoj.gov/eoir/vll/OCIJPracManual/ocij_page1.htm

C. PACER

Public Access to Court Electronic Records (PACER) is an electronic public access service that allows users to obtain case and docket information from Federal Appellate, District, and Bankruptcy courts, and from the U.S. Party/Case Index. PACER is a service of the United States Judiciary. The PACER Service Center is operated by the Administrative Office of the United States Courts (*pacer.psc.uscourts.gov*).

Currently most courts are accessible on the Internet. Links to these courts are provided at the PACER site (*pacer.psc.uscourts.gov/cgi-bin/links.pl*). However, a few systems are not available on the Internet and must be dialed directly using communication software (such as Procomm Plus, pcAnywhere, or HyperTerminal) and a modem. Electronic access is available for most courts by registering with the PACER Service Center, the judiciary's centralized registration, billing, and technical support center. You can register online or by phone (at 800-676-6856 or 210-301-6440).

Each court maintains its own databases with case information. Because PACER database systems are maintained within each court, each jurisdiction will have a different URL or modem number. Accessing and querying information from each service is comparable. The format and content of information provided, however, may differ slightly. See the PACER court directory (*pacer.psc.uscourts.gov/psco/cgi-bin/links.pl*).

D. | **More Information**

Federal Judiciary Overview
www.uscourts.gov
www.uscourts.gov/links.html
www.usa.gov/Agencies/Federal/Judicial.shtml

Guide to the Federal Courts
www.fjc.gov/federal/courts.nsf
www.uscourts.gov/journalistguide/welcome.html
www.uscourts.gov/understand03

Bankruptcy Courts in New York
www.llrx.com/courtrules-gen/state-New-York.html
www.bankruptcyinformation.com/NY_courts.htm
www.bankruptcyaction.com/bankruptcycourts.htm
www.lawdog.com/bkrcy/bkk34.htm

Employment Opportunities in the Federal Courts
www.uscourts.gov/employment/vacancies.html#

Federal Judicial Center
www.fjc.gov

E. | **Something to Check**

1. Go to the sites that give you online access to court opinions of the 2nd Circuit. Use the search features of the sites to find an opinion on any broad legal topic, e.g., capital punishment, adoption. Summarize (brief) what the opinion says about your topic.
2. For one of the four United States district courts in New York, find the calendar of any judge on the court you select. Name one case on the calendar of that judge.

A. Introduction

In this section we provide an overview of the legislative process in New York, specifically, how a bill becomes a law. For related information, see:

- Section 4.1 (introduction to the state government of New York, including the major units and offices of the state legislature)
- Section 5.1 (doing legal research in New York law, including finding state statutes online and on the shelves)

Under the State Constitution (Art. III, § 1), the New York State Legislature is bicameral, meaning that it is made up of two houses or legislative bodies:

Senate
(*www.senate.state.ny.us*)

Assembly
(*www.assembly.state.ny.us*)

There are 62 senators and 150 assembly members, each of whom serves a two-year term. The legislature meets every year, typically for several days a week from January through mid-June and at the call of the legislative leaders at other times during the year. The governor may call the legislature into extraordinary session for a limited agenda identified by the governor.

The Senate alone has the power to confirm the governor's appointment on non-elected state officials and court judges. The Constitution provides that such appointments are subject to the advice and consent of the Senate, which approves or disapproves them, after hearings on the candidate's qualifications. (*www.senate. state.ny.us/sws/aboutsenate/branches_gov.html#leg*)

B. How a Bill Becomes a New York Statute
Idea for a Bill

Ideas for bills can come from many sources: individual legislators, the governor, administrative agencies, lobbyists, businesses, community groups, and citizens. The first step is to have a legislator (a senator or assembly member) introduce (sponsor) the bill.

Bill Drafting and Introduction

The idea for the law must first be put into a bill in order to be considered. A legislator usually sends the idea for the bill to the Legislative Bill Drafting Commission (LBDC), where the Commission's staff drafts the bill in its proper form. The draft of the bill is returned to the legislator-sponsor for introduction.

The sponsor of the bill includes a sponsor's memorandum (also called an introducer's memorandum) with the bill. The memorandum states the desired impact (intent) of the bill and provides related information such as references to similar bills.

Normally a bill is introduced in one house and, if voted upon favorably, is then submitted to the other house for consideration. A bill that is considered by one house before the other house considers it is called a one-house bill. It is also possible for a bill to be simultaneously introduced in both houses using a special "uni-bill" process. Once introduced, the bill can be read online on the legislature's web site.

Text of Introduced Bills
public.leginfo.state.ny.us/menuf.cgi

Three Readings

Bills go through three readings in the legislative process. At one time this meant that the bill was read aloud in full in public session three times before final action could be taken on it. Today the three readings take other forms. In the Senate, for example, the first and second readings are deemed to have occurred once the bill is introduced in the Senate, examined and corrected by the Introduction and Revision Office, given a number, sent to the appropriate standing committee, and entered into the Senate computer.

Committee Structure

There are two major kinds of committees in the state legislature:

- Joint Legislative Committees that operate year-round and have members from both houses
- Standing Committees that are organized in each house to operate during the session (although some operate year-round as well)

Committees in the Assembly
assembly.state.ny.us/comm

Committees in the Senate
public.leginfo.state.ny.us/statdoc/scomlist.html

Committee Action

After introduction, a bill goes to an appropriate policy committee (and usually to one of its subcommittees) for consideration. Bills are assigned to policy committees according to subject area. For example, a Senate bill on environmental standards will be assigned to the Senate Environmental Conservation Committee for policy review. A committee will usually hold public hearings in order to give individuals and organizations an opportunity to present opposing points of view on a bill. Committee members debate the bill, often offering amendments for consideration.

Once a bill is amended, it may be sent back to the Legislative Bill Drafting Commission (LBDC) to redraft it in its proper form. Amendments are designated by a letter (A, B, C, etc.) after the bill number. (See Floor

Action below.) It takes a majority vote of the committee membership for a bill to be passed (reported out of committee) and sent to the next committee or to the floor. Bills that require an expenditure of state funds must go to the Assembly Ways and Means Committee or the Senate Finance Committee before they can reach the floor.

(Note: We will assume in the remainder of this overview that the bill originated in the Senate.)

The Calendar

The Daily Calendar is the agenda for Senate sessions and contains those measures that have come through the committee process. Bills go on the calendar (in order) as they are reported from committee, and at this point are referred to by their Calendar Number. Each bill must be on senators' desks for three days before it can be voted on, unless the governor authorizes and the Senate accepts a Message of Necessity for a certain bill. When bills reach the Order of Third Reading, they become ready for a final vote. If the sponsor of a bill realizes at this point that the bill may not have enough support for passage, or that the bill has a defect that may require an amendment, he or she may ask that it be laid aside, returned to committee for further study, or "starred" (placed in an inactive file). The majority leader also may ask that a bill be starred. Once starred, it cannot be acted on until one day after removal of the star. When the bill comes up for consideration on the Order of Third Reading, it is subject to debate, discussion, or explanation.

Floor Action; Amendments

A bill can still be amended after it has been introduced, reported out by a committee, and placed on the calendar for consideration by the full Senate. The sponsor of the bill (or any other senator) can submit the changes to the LBDC. Such a bill, now in its amended form, retains its original number, but amended versions are denoted by a letter suffix A, B, C, D, etc. for each time the bill is altered. For example 33B is the second amendment to the bill, 33E is the fifth. Since the amendments are offered in open session, all members can ask questions and discuss the merits of the proposed amendments.

Passing a Bill and Sending It to the Other House

After explanation, discussion, or debate, a vote is taken. If a majority of the senators approves, the bill is sent to the Assembly. The bill then moves through a process basically the same as that in the Senate. (Sometimes an identical bill, referred to as a "same as," is already making its way through the process in the other house.) In the Assembly, the bill is referred to a committee for discussion, and if approved there, goes to the full membership of the Assembly for a vote. If the bill is approved in the Assembly without amendment, it goes

to the governor. However, if it is changed, it is returned to the Senate for concurrence in the amendments.

Conference Committee

Sometimes the Senate and Assembly pass similar bills but cannot easily reconcile the differences between them in a reasonable time frame. In such cases, a conference committee can be used to iron out the differences. The Senate Majority Leader and Assembly Speaker each appoint five members from their respective houses to serve on this committee to try to agree on a single bill. If they reach such an agreement, the bill then goes to the full membership of both houses for a final vote.

Governor

While the Legislature is in session, the governor has 10 days (not counting Sundays) to sign or veto bills passed by both houses. The governor's failure to sign or veto a bill within the 10-day period means that it becomes law automatically. Vetoed bills are returned to the house that first passed them, together with a statement of the reason for the disapproval. A vetoed bill can become law if two-thirds of the members of each house vote to override the governor's veto.

If a bill is sent to the governor when the legislature is out of session, the governor has 30 days in which to make a decision. The governor's failure to act has the same effect as a veto. The result is known as a pocket veto. As a practical matter, this rarely occurs because the current practice is that the legislature never formally adjourns its session.

Session Chapters; Chapters in Consolidated Laws; Unconsolidated Laws

When a bill becomes a law, it is assigned a chapter number for the session in which it was passed. (Example: Chapter 23 of the Laws of 1998.) It is known as a session chapter. This definition of chapter is different from the meaning of chapter in consolidated laws. Most laws passed by the legislature are organized or consolidated into approximately 90 subject-matter areas called chapters, e.g., Labor and Insurance. An unconsolidated law is one that does not fit within any of the chapters of the consolidated laws. An example of an unconsolidated law is the Local Emergency Housing Rent Control Act of 1962.

Exhibit 4.4A presents an overview of the legislative process we have been outlining.

C. **More Information**

Overview of the Legislative Process
www.senate.state.ny.us/sws/aboutsenate/how_idea_becomes_law.html
63.118.56.3/sws/aboutsenate/how_idea_becomes_law.html
www.ll.georgetown.edu/states/newyork-in-depth.cfm

| EXHIBIT 4.4A | How a Bill Becomes a Law in New York State |

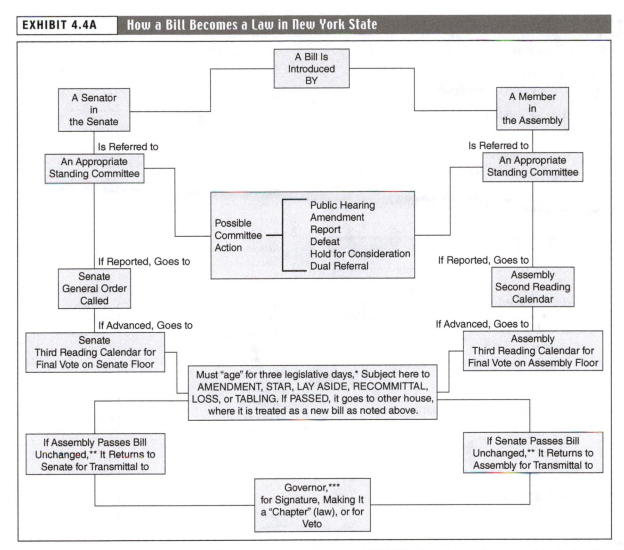

*The State Constitution requires the printed bill to be on members' desks for three calendar legislative days. The procedures may only be shortened by "Message of Necessity" for immediate vote from the governor.

**If changed, the house of origin must concur before it goes to the governor.

***The governor has 10 days, excluding Sundays, to act on bills sent by 10 days before adjournment. If the governor does not act in that time, the bills automatically become law. The governor has 30 calendar days after the legislature adjourns to act on other bills; these bills may not become law without the governor's approval ("pocket veto").

Source: *Citizen's Guide to Laptop Lobbying of State Government in New York*; New York Temporary State Commission on Lobbying; www.pcny.org/legislation/legis_how2.asp

www.pssny.org/web/2006/03/legislative_process_in_new_york.aspx
www.bcnys.org/inside/sb/billlaw.htm

Assembly
www.assembly.state.ny.us
assembly.state.ny.us/mem

Assembly Legislative Reports
assembly.state.ny.us/Reports

Senate
www.senate.state.ny.us

Senate: District Map
www.senate.state.ny.us/Senatorbio.nsf/Public_NYSMap?openform

Bill Information and Search
public.leginfo.state.ny.us
www.albanylaw.edu/sub.php?navigation_id=1267

Committee Agenda
public.leginfo.state.ny.us
(click "Senate" or "Assembly" for Committee Agenda)

Assembly Legislative Calendar
assembly.state.ny.us/leg
(click "Calendar" entries)

Floor Calendar
public.leginfo.state.ny.us
(click "Senate/Assembly" for Floor Calendars)

Legislative Intent
library.buffalo.edu/libraries/asl/guides/busdoc/legislation.html
(click "New York State")

State Legislative History
www.albanylaw.edu/sub.php?navigation_id=842

New York State Legislative Service
www.nyls.org

New York State Documents
www.columbia.edu/cu/lweb/indiv/usgd/nys.html#Official

New York State Law Revision Commission
www.lawrevision.state.ny.us

D. Something to Check

1. Find a bill currently before the legislature on any:
   a. family law topic
   b. criminal law topic
2. Cite one bill or statute that was introduced, authored, or sponsored:
   a. by your state senator
   b. by your assembly member

4.5 State Agencies, Offices, and Boards
A. Introduction
B. Contacts
C. More Information
D. Something to Check

A. Introduction

This section covers the major state agencies and commissions in New York. See also:

- Section 4.1 (overview of state government)
- Section 4.2 (state courts)
- Section 4.4 (state legislature)
- Section 4.6 (county and city governments)
- Section 5.9 (hotline resources and complaint directories)

For legal research leads to issues that pertain to many of these agencies and commissions, see the starter cites in section 5.5.

Main Information on New York Government
New York State Government
www.ny.gov

NYS Government Toll-Free Numbers
www6.oft.state.ny.us/telecom/phones/tollfreelist.jsp
www.tollfreenumber.org/forum/about45.html

B. Contacts

Accountants	Energy
Acupuncture	Engineering
Administration	Environment
Administrative Law	Equalization
Adoption	Estate Tax
Aerospace Support	Ethics
Aging	Families
Agriculture	Finance
AIDS	Fire Prevention and
Air	Control
Alcohol and Drugs	Fish
Antitrust	Food and Beverage
Architecture	Forensic Sciences
Archives	Forestry
Arts and Humanities	Funeral Services
Assembly	Gambling
Athletics	Game
Attorney General	Genealogy Records
Audiology	Governor
Audits	Health
Automotive Repair	Horse Racing
Banks	Housing
Bar Associations	Identity Theft
Birth Records	Information on
Boating	New York Government
Building	Insurance
Business	Interior Design
Cemetery	Investigation
Child Support Services	Jobs
Chiropractic	Justice
Civil Rights	Labor
Claims against State	Landscape Architecture
Commerce	Land Surveying
Complaints Directory	Law Enforcement
Comptroller	Law Library
Computers and	Legislature
Technology	Library
Conservation	Licensing
Construction	Lieutenant Governor
Consumer Services	Lobbying
Corporations	Local Government
Corrections	Lottery
Courts	Marriage Records
Credit Unions	Massage Therapy
Crime	Mediation
Death Records	Medicaid
Dentistry	Medicine
Dietetics-Nutrition	Mental Health
Disabilities	Midwifery
Dissolution/	Military
Divorce Records	Missing Persons
DMV	Mortgages
Domestic Partnership	Motor Vehicles
Domestic Violence	National Guard
Drugs	Natural Resources
Economic Development	Nursing
Education	Nutrition
Elections	Occupational Safety
Emergency	Occupational Therapy
Employment	Ophthalmic Dispensing

Opticians
Optometry
Parks
Parole
Permits
Personnel
Pharmacy
Physical Therapy
Podiatry
Police
Prison
Privacy
Probate
Probation
Psychology
Public Accountancy
Public Assistance
Public Defender
Public Utilities
Racing
Real Estate
Recreation
Recycling
Respiratory Therapy
Retirement
Secretary of State
Senate
Seniors
Sex Offenders

Shorthand Reporting
Social Services
Social Work
Speech Language
   Pathology and
   Audiology
Sports
State Agencies
State Police
Tax
Teachers
Therapy
Tourism
Traffic Safety
Transportation
Treasurer
Troopers
Unclaimed Property
Unemployment
   Insurance
Universities, Public
Utilities
Veterinary Medicine
Victim Services
Vital Records
Voting
Water
Welfare
Workers' Compensation

Accountants

(see public accountancy)

Acupuncture

State Board for Acupuncture
518-474-3817 x279
www.op.nysed.gov/acupun.htm

Administration

(see also audits, employment, governor)

New York State Government
www.ny.gov

Agencies of State Government
www.nysl.nysed.gov/ils/nyserver.html
www.ny.gov
(click "Listing of State Agencies")

Office of General Services
518-474-5987 (public affairs)
www.ogs.state.ny.us

Government Information Locator Service
www.nysl.nysed.gov/ils

Government Toll-Free Numbers
www6.oft.state.ny.us/telecom/phones/tollfreelist.jsp
www.tollfreenumber.org/forum/about45.html

Administrative Law

Office of Administrative Hearings, Department of State
212-417-5776
www.dos.state.ny.us/ooah/index.htm

Division of Administrative Rules
518-474-6957
www.dos.state.ny.us/info/register.htm

Adoption

Adoption and Foster Care
NYS Office of Children & Family Services
800-345-KIDS
www.ocfs.state.ny.us/main/fostercare

NYS Adoption Service
800-345-5437
www.ocfs.state.ny.us/adopt

Adoption Information Registry
www.health.state.ny.us/vital_records/
   adoption.htm

Adoption Records
www.health.state.ny.us/contact

Aerospace Support

(see military)

Aging

Office for the Aging
800-342-9871
www.aging.ny.gov

Office of Long Term Care Ombudsman
800-342-9871; 518-474-7329
www.ltcombudsman.ny.gov

Protective Services for Adults
518-473-7793
www.ocfs.state.ny.us/main/psa

Medicaid Fraud, Department of Health
877-87FRAUD
www.health.state.ny.us/health_care/medicaid/
   fraud

Senior Citizens Hotline
www.aging.ny.gov
800-342-9871

Agriculture

Department of Agriculture & Markets
800-554-4501 (information)
www.agmkt.state.ny.us

AIDS

Department of Health AIDS Institute
800-541-AIDS
www.health.state.ny.us/diseases/aids

Air

(see also environment)

**Department of Environmental Conservation
Division of Air Resources**
518-402-8452
www.dec.ny.gov/about/644.html

Alcohol and Drugs

(see also drugs, food and beverage, health, law enforcement, pharmacy)

Office of Alcoholism and Substance Abuse Services
800-522-5353; 800-553-5790; 518-473-3460
www.oasas.state.ny.us

Liquor Authority (Alcohol Beverage Control)
518-486-4767
www.abc.state.ny.us

Professional Assistance Program (Substance Abuse)
518-474-3817 x480
www.op.nysed.gov/prof/pap.htm

Antitrust

(see also business)

Attorney General Antitrust Bureau
212-416-8262; 800-771-7755
www.oag.state.ny.us/bureaus/antitrust/about.html

Architecture

(see construction, landscape architecture)

Archives

(see also genealogy records, library; and section 5.7)

State Archives
518-474-8955; 518-474-6926
www.archives.nysed.gov/a/directories/dir_programs.shtml

Arts and Humanities

(see also tourism)

Council on the Arts
800-510-0021; 212-627-4455
www.nysca.org

New York State Museum
518-474-5877
www.nysm.nysed.gov

New York Council for the Humanities
212-233-1131
www.nyhumanities.org

Assembly

State Assembly
(see also section 4.4)
518-455-4218
assembly.state.ny.us

Athletics

NYS Athletic Commission
212-417-5700; 866-BOXERNY
www.dos.state.ny.us/athletic

Empire State Games
www.empirestategames.org

Office of Parks, Recreation and Historic Preservation
518-474-0445
www.nysparks.state.ny.us/boating/services.asp

State Board for Athletic Training
518-474-3817 x270
www.op.nysed.gov/athlet.htm

Attorney General

(see also law enforcement)

Office of the Attorney General
800-771-7755
www.oag.state.ny.us

Audiology

(see speech language pathology and audiology)

Audits

Office of the State Comptroller
518-474-4044
www.osc.state.ny.us

Automotive Repair

Department of Motor Vehicles
Division of Vehicle Safety Services
518-474-4653
www.nydmv.state.ny.us/repairshop.htm

Banks

(see also finance)

Banking Department
877-BANKS-NYS
www.banking.state.ny.us

Federal Deposit Insurance Corporation
877-275-3342
www.fdic.gov

Federal Reserve Bank of New York
212-720-5000
www.ny.frb.org

Federal Reserve Board
www.federalreserve.gov

Bar Associations

(see also section 3.4)

New York State Bar Association
518-463-3200
www.nysba.org

4.5 STATE AGENCIES, OFFICES, AND BOARDS

Birth Records

(see also section 5.7 on public records)

Department of Health
(birth, death, marriage, and divorce records)
877-854-4481 (VitalChek)
www.health.state.ny.us/vital_records
www.health.state.ny.us/vital_records/birth.htm

Boating

(see also water)

Office of Parks, Recreation and Historic Preservation
518-474-0445
nysparks.state.ny.us

Building

(see construction)

Business

Empire State Development
800-STATE-NY
www.empire.state.ny.us

Division for Small Business
518-292-5220; 800-782-8369
www.nylovessmallbiz.com
www.nylovesmwbe.ny.gov/TechAssistance/SBDC.htm

Department of Labor (Business Services)
518-457-6821; 800-HIRE-992
www.labor.state.ny.us/businessservices/
BusinessServicesIndex.shtm

Division of Corporations
518-473-2492
www.dos.state.ny.us/corp/corpwww.html

Division of Licensing Services
212-417-5790
www.dos.state.ny.us/LCNS/licensing.html

New York Business Promotion
800-STATE-NY
www.empire.state.ny.us

Cemetery

(see also funeral services)

Division of Cemeteries
518-474-6226; 212-417-5713
www.dos.state.ny.us/cmty

Child Support Services

(see also social services)

Office of Children and Family Services
518-473-7793
www.ocfs.state.ny.us/main

Council on Children and Families
518-473-3652
www.ccf.state.ny.us

Division of Child Support Enforcement
888-208-4485
newyorkchildsupport.com

Permanent Judicial Commission on Justice for Children
518-285-8780
www.nycourts.gov/ip/justiceforchildren/index.shtml

Chiropractic

(see also health)

State Board for Chiropractic
518-474-3817 x250
www.op.nysed.gov/chiro.htm

Civil Rights

(see also consumer services, law enforcement, privacy)

Attorney General's Civil Rights Bureau
800-771-7755; 212-416-8250
www.oag.state.ny.us/bureaus/civil_rights/about.html

Division of Housing & Community Renewal
866-ASK-DHCR; 866-275-3427
www.dhcr.state.ny.us

Division of Human Rights
718-741-8400
www.dhr.state.ny.us

Equal Employment Opportunity Commission
800-669-4000
www.eeoc.gov

New York City Commission on Human Rights
212-306-5070
www.nyc.gov/html/cchr

U.S. Department of Justice
Civil Rights Division
202-514-4609
www.usdoj.gov/crt

Claims against State

Court of Claims
518-432-3411
www.nyscourtofclaims.state.ny.us

Commerce

(see also business)

Empire State Development
800-STATE-NY
www.empire.state.ny.us

Complaints Directory

Government Complaint Departments
www.nysl.nysed.gov/ils/topics/complaint.htm

Consumer Protection Board
800-697-1220
www.consumer.state.ny.us

Comptroller

(see also estate tax, finance, unclaimed property)

Office of the State Comptroller
888-OSC-4555; 518-474-4044
www.osc.state.ny.us

Computers and Technology

(see also business, identity theft)

Office of Cyber Security & Critical Infrastructure Coordination
518-474-0865
www.cscic.state.ny.us

Office for Technology
866-789-4OFT; 518-402-2537
www.oft.state.ny.us

Foundation for Science, Technology and Innovation
518-292-5700
www.nystar.state.ny.us

Conservation

(see also emergency, environment, natural resources)

Department of Environmental Conservation
518-402-8013
www.dec.state.ny.us

Bureau of Solid Waste, Reduction & Recycling
518-402-8704
www.dec.ny.gov/chemical/294.html

Construction

(see also business, consumer services, interior design, landscape architecture)

Division of Code Enforcement
518-474-4073
www.dos.state.ny.us/CODE/ls-codes.html

State Board for Architecture
518-474-3817 x250
www.op.nysed.gov/arch.htm

State Board for Engineering
518-474-3817 x250
www.op.nysed.gov/pe.htm

Consumer Services

(see also law enforcement)

Consumer Frauds Bureau
800-771-7755
www.oag.state.ny.us/bureaus/consumer_frauds/about.html

Consumer Protection Board
800-697-1220; 518-474-3514
www.consumer.state.ny.us

Consumer Law Help Manual
www.consumer.state.ny.us/clhm.htm

County Consumer Affairs Offices
www.consumer.state.ny.us/consumer_affairs_offices.htm

Federal Trade Commission
800-FTC-HELP
www.ftc.gov

Corporations

(see also business)

Division of Corporations
518-473-2492
www.dos.state.ny.us/corp/corpwww.html

Corrections

(see also law enforcement)

Commission of Correction
518-485-2346
www.scoc.state.ny.us

Department of Correctional Services
518-457-8126
www.docs.state.ny.us

Division of Parole
518-473-9400
parole.state.ny.us

Probation and Correctional Alternatives
518-485-2395
dpca.state.ny.us

Courts

(see also sections 4.2 and 4.3)

Unified Court System
www.nycourts.gov/home.htm
www.courts.state.ny.us
www.courts.state.ny.us/courts

Office of Court Administration
518-474-3828; 212-428-2700
www.nycourts.gov/admin/oca.shtml

Commission on Judicial Conduct
518-474-5617; 212-809-0566
www.scjc.state.ny.us

Court of Appeals
518-455-7711
www.nycourts.gov/ctapps

Federal Courts in New York
www.uscourts.gov/courtlinks
(click "NY" on the map)

Credit Unions

(see finance)

Crime

(see attorney general, identity theft, law enforcement)

Death Records

(see vital records; see also section 5.7)

Department of Health
(birth, death, marriage, and divorce records)
877-854-4481 (VitalChek)
www.health.state.ny.us/vital_records
www.health.state.ny.us/vital_records/death.htm

Dentistry

(see also health)

State Board for Dentistry
518-474-3817 x270
www.op.nysed.gov/dent.htm

Dietetics-Nutrition

(see also health)

State Board for Dietetics-Nutrition
518-474-3817 x270
www.op.nysed.gov/diet.htm

Disabilities

(see also health, workers' compensation)

Advocacy Programs for Persons with Disabilities
www.cqc.state.ny.us/advocacy/advocacy.htm

Commission for the Blind and Visually Handicapped
866-871-3000
www.ocfs.state.ny.us/main/cbvh

Commission on Quality of Care and Advocacy for Persons with Disabilities
800-624-4143; 518-388-1281
www.cqcapd.state.ny.us

Developmental Disabilities Planning Council
800-395-3372; 518-486-7505
www.ddpc.state.ny.us

Office of Temporary and Disability Assistance
518-474-9516
www.otda.state.ny.us/main

Social Security Disability
800-522-5511
www.otda.state.ny.us/main/ddd

State Rehabilitation Council
800-222-JOBS; 518-474-1711
www.vesid.nysed.gov/src

Dissolution/Divorce Records

(see vital records; see also section 5.7)

Department of Health
(birth, death, marriage, and divorce records)
www.health.state.ny.us/vital_records
www.health.state.ny.us/vital_records/divorce.htm

DMV

(see motor vehicles)

Domestic Partnership

Office of the City Clerk of the City of New York
www.cityclerk.nyc.gov
*www.cityclerk.nyc.gov/html/marriage/
    domestic_partnership_reg.shtml*

Domestic Violence

(see also law enforcement)

Office for the Prevention of Domestic Violence
518-457-5800; 800-942-6906
opdv.state.ny.us

Drugs

(see also health, law enforcement, pharmacy)

Bureau of Narcotic Enforcement
866-811-7957
www.health.state.ny.us/professionals/narcotic

Office of Alcoholism and Substance Abuse Services
518-473-3460; 518-485-1768
www.oasas.state.ny.us

Professional Assistance Program (Substance Abuse)
518-474-3817 x480
www.op.nysed.gov/prof/pap.htm

Economic Development

(see also business)

Empire State Development
800-STATE-NY
www.empire.state.ny.us

Education

(see also teachers)

Board of Regents
518-474-5889
www.regents.nysed.gov

City University of New York
212-794-5555
www.cuny.edu

Education (school directory)
www.nysed.gov/admin/admindex.html

New York Higher Education Services Corporation
866-944-HESC
www.hesc.com

Office of College and University Evaluation
518-474-2593
www.highered.nysed.gov/ocue

Office of Teaching Initiatives
www.highered.nysed.gov/tcert

State Education Department
518-474-3852
www.nysed.gov

State University of New York
518-443-5555
www.suny.edu

SUNY Campus Listing
www.suny.edu/Student/campuses_complete_list.cfm

Teacher Certification Examinations
518-474-3901
www.nystce.nesinc.com

Teachers' Retirement System
800-348-7298
www.nystrs.org

Elections

Board of Elections in the City of New York
866-VOTE-NYC
www.vote.nyc.ny.us

Board of Elections, State
518-474-6220; 800-458-3453
www.elections.state.ny.us

Commission on Public Integrity
518-408-3976
www.nyintegrity.org

County Boards of Elections
www.elections.state.ny.us/CountyBoards.html

Emergency

(see also environment, health)

State Emergency Management Office
518-292-2310
www.semo.state.ny.us

Emergency Preparedness and Response (Department of Health)
www.health.state.ny.us/environmental/emergency/index.htm

Employment

(see also labor, unemployment insurance, workers' compensation)

Department of Civil Service
877-NYS-JOBS; 518-457-2487
www.cs.state.ny.us

Department of Labor
888-4-NYSDOL; 800-HIRE-992; 518-457-9000
www.labor.state.ny.us

Division of Safety and Health
518-457-3518
www.labor.state.ny.us/workerprotection/safetyhealth/dosh_programs.shtm

Governor's Office of Employee Relations
518-473-8766
www.goer.state.ny.us

Personnel Council
518-474-2685
www.cs.state.ny.us/personnelcouncil/index.htm

Public Employment Relations Board
518-457-2578
www.perb.state.ny.us

State and Local Retirement System
866-805-0990; 518-474-7736
www.osc.state.ny.us/retire

State Rehabilitation Council
800-222-JOBS; 518-474-1711
www.vesid.nysed.gov/src

State Teachers' Retirement System
800-348-7298; 518-447-2900
www.nystrs.org

Energy

(see also environment, natural resources)

Energy Research and Development Authority
866-NY-SERDA; 518-862-1090
www.nyserda.org

Engineering

(see construction)

Environment

(see also emergency, natural resources, water)

Bureau of Pesticide Management
518-402-8748
www.dec.ny.gov/chemical/298.html

Department of Environmental Conservation
518-402-8013
www.dec.ny.gov

Division of Air Resources
518-402-8402
www.dec.ny.gov/chemical/8568.html

Division of Coastal Resources
www.nyswaterfronts.com/index.asp

Division of Solid and Hazardous Materials
518-402-8579
www.dec.ny.gov/chemical/296.html

Emergency Preparedness and Response
www.health.state.ny.us/environmental/emergency

Geographic Information Systems Association
www.nysgislis.org

Hudson River Valley Greenway
518-473-3835
www.hudsongreenway.state.ny.us

Equalization

(see tax)

Estate Tax

(see also tax)

Estate Tax Publications
800-641-0004
www.tax.state.ny.us
(click "Other Taxes" then "Estate Tax")

Ethics

(on attorney ethics, see sections 3.2 and 3.3)

Commission on Public Integrity
518-408-3976
www.nyintegrity.org

Families

(see child support services, domestic partnership, health, social services)

Finance

(see also banks, housing)

NYS Banking Department
800-BANK-NYS
www.banking.state.ny.us

Department of Taxation and Finance
800-443-3200; 888-698-2908
www.tax.state.ny.us

Fire Prevention and Control

(see also emergency)

Fire Departments
www.dos.state.ny.us/fire/firelinks.htm#firedepts
www.nysfirechiefs.com

Office of Fire Prevention and Control
518-474-6746
www.dos.state.ny.us/fire/firewww.html

Fish

(see also environment, natural resources)

Bureau of Fisheries
518-402-8924
www.dec.ny.gov/outdoor/fishing.html

Division of Fish, Wildlife and Marine Resources
518-402-8924
www.dec.ny.gov/about/634.html

Food and Beverage

(see also alcohol and drugs)

Department of Agriculture and Markets
800-554-4501
www.agmkt.state.ny.us

Division of Food Safety and Inspection
518-457-4492
www.agmkt.state.ny.us/FS/FSHome.html

Liquor Authority (Alcohol Beverage Control)
518-486-4767
www.abc.state.ny.us

Forensic Sciences

(see also law enforcement)

Office of Forensic Services
800-262-3257
criminaljustice.state.ny.us/forensic/aboutofs.htm

Forensic Science Laboratory (State Police)
www.troopers.state.ny.us/Forensic_Science

Forestry

(see also environment, natural resources)

Division of Lands and Forests
518-402-9405
www.dec.ny.gov/lands/4966.html

Funeral Services

Department of Health
Bureau of Funeral Directing
518-402-0785
www.health.state.ny.us/healthaz
(under letter "F" click "Funerals")

Division of Cemeteries
www.dos.state.ny.us/cmty/cemetery.html

Gambling

(see also athletics, law enforcement)

Racing and Wagering Board
518-395-5400
www.racing.state.ny.us

Game

(see also environment, natural resources, parks)

Bureau of Wildlife
518-402-8883
www.dec.ny.gov/outdoor/hunting.html

Bureau of Fisheries
518-402-8924
www.dec.ny.gov/outdoor/fishing.html

Division of Fish, Wildlife and Marine Resources
518-402-8924
www.dec.ny.gov/about/634.html

Genealogy Records

(see also archives)

Department of Health
www.health.state.ny.us/vital_records/genealogy.htm

Governor

Office of the Governor
518-474-8390
www.state.ny.us/governor

Governor's Office of Regulatory Reform
518-486-3292
www.gorr.state.ny.us

Health

(see also chiropractic, dietetics-nutrition, emergency, insurance, massage therapy, mental health, midwifery, occupational therapy, ophthalmic dispensing, optometry, pharmacy, physical therapy, podiatry, psychology, respiratory therapy, speech language pathology and audiology, veterinary medicine)

AIDS/HIV (Department of Health)
800-541-AIDS
www.health.state.ny.us/diseases/aids

Committee for Occupational Health and Safety
212-227-6440
www.nycosh.org

Department of Health
518-474-2011
www.health.state.ny.us

Emergency Preparedness and Response
www.health.state.ny.us/environmental/emergency/index.htm

Medicaid
800-505-5678; 518-486-9057
www.health.state.ny.us/health_care/medicaid/index.htm

Office of Alcoholism and Substance Abuse Services
800-522-5353; 518-473-3460
www.oasas.state.ny.us
www.oasas.state.ny.us/pio/caudes.cfm

Office of Mental Health
800-597-8481
www.omh.state.ny.us

Office of Mental Retardation and Developmental Disabilities
866-946-9733
www.omr.state.ny.us

Office of the Medicaid Inspector General
518-473-3782
www.omig.state.ny.us

State Board for Clinical Laboratory Technology
518-474-3817 x150
www.op.nysed.gov/clp.htm

State Board for Dentistry
518-474-3817 x550
www.op.nysed.gov/dent.htm

State Board for Medical Physics
518-474-3817 x560
www.op.nysed.gov/medphys.htm

State Board for Medicine
518-474-3817 x260
www.op.nysed.gov/med.htm

State Board for Nursing
518-474-3817 x280
www.op.nysed.gov/nurse.htm

State Board for Respiratory Therapy
518-474-3817 x270
www.op.nysed.gov/rt.htm

State Board for Psychology
518-474-3817 x270
www.op.nysed.gov/psych.htm

State Board of Pharmacy
518-474-3817 x250
www.op.nysed.gov/prof/pharm

State Rehabilitation Council
800-222-JOBS; 518-474-1711
www.vesid.nysed.gov/src

Vital Records Office (Department of Health)
www.health.state.ny.us/vital_records

Horse Racing

Racing and Wagering Board
518-395-5400
www.racing.state.ny.us

Housing

(see also real estate)

Office of Real Property Services
518-486-5446
www.orps.state.ny.us

Division of Housing and Community Renewal
866-ASK-DHCR
www.dhcr.state.ny.us

Dormitory Authority
518-257-3000
www.dasny.org

Identity Theft

(see also law enforcement, privacy)

Identity Theft Information
800-697-1220; 518-474-8583
www.consumer.state.ny.us/internet_security.htm

Information on New York Government

NYS Government Information Locator Service
www.nysl.nysed.gov/ils

New York State Government Public Phone Directory
www6.oft.state.ny.us/telecom/phones/

Insurance

(see also unemployment insurance, workers' compensation)

NYS Insurance Department
800-342-3736
www.ins.state.ny.us

Health Insurance Information, Counseling and Assistance
800-701-0501
www.nyconnects.org/services/medical/insurance/hiicap.shtml

New York State Insurance Fund
877-435-7743; 888-875-5790
ww3.nysif.com

Interior Design

(see also construction)

State Board for Interior Design
518-474-3817 x250
www.op.nysed.gov/interior.htm

Investigation

(see also attorney general, law enforcement)

Bureau of Criminal Investigation
www.troopers.state.ny.us/Criminal_Investigation

Commission of Investigation
212-344-6660
criminaldivision.com/articles/34/1/New-York-State-Commission-Of-Investigation/CommissionContinued.html

Department of Investigation (NYC)
212-825-5900
www.worldcat.org/arcviewer/1/AO%23/2009/04/02/H1238693215513/viewer/file33.htm

Office of Forensic Services
800-262-3257
criminaljustice.state.ny.us/forensic/aboutofs.htm

Office of the Inspector General
800-DO-RIGHT
www.ig.state.ny.us

Jobs

(see employment, labor)

Justice

(see attorney general, law enforcement)

Labor

NYS Department of Labor
800-4-NYSDOL; 518-457-9000
www.labor.state.ny.us

Industrial Board of Appeals
518-474-4785
www.labor.state.ny.us/iba/index.htm

Public Employment Relations Board
518-457-2578
www.labor.state.ny.us/erb/index.asp

State Employment Relations Board
518-474-7724
www.labor.state.ny.us/erb/index.asp

New York Job Services Employer Committee
www.nyjsec.org

Landscape Architecture

(see also architecture, construction)

State Board for Landscape Architecture
518-474-3817 x110
www.op.nysed.gov/larch.htm

Land Surveying

(see also construction)

Professional Engineering & Land Surveying
518-474-3817 x140
www.op.nysed.gov/prof/pels

Law Enforcement

(see also corrections, missing persons, public defender)

Bureau of Narcotic Enforcement
866-811-7957
www.health.state.ny.us/professionals/narcotic

Crime Victims Board
800-247-8035
www.cvb.state.ny.us

Criminal Justice (Attorney General)
800-771-7755
www.oag.state.ny.us/our_office.html

Division of Criminal Justice Services
800-262-3257
criminaljustice.state.ny.us

Marine Law Enforcement
518-474-0456
nysparks.state.ny.us/recreation/boating/marine-law-enforcement.aspx

New York State Police
www.troopers.state.ny.us

Bureau of Criminal Investigation
www.troopers.state.ny.us/Criminal_Investigation

Commission of Investigation
877-SIC-4NYS; 212-344-6660
*www.worldcat.org/arcviewer/1/AO%23/2009/04/02/
H1238693215513/viewer/file33.h*

Forensic Science Laboratory
www.troopers.state.ny.us/Forensic_Science

Office for the Prevention of Domestic Violence
800-942-6906, 518-457-5800
opdv.state.ny.us

Office of Forensic Services
800-262-3257
criminaljustice.state.ny.us/forensic/aboutofs.htm

Office of Homeland Security
866-SAFE-NYS; 518-402-2227
www.security.state.ny.us

Office of Public Safety
800-262-3257; 518-457-2667
criminaljustice.state.ny.us/ops/index.htm

Sex Offender Registry
800-262-3257
criminaljustice.state.ny.us/nsor

Law Library

(see also library; and section 5.8)

Public Access Law Libraries
www.nycourts.gov/lawlibraries/publicaccess.shtml

Legislature

(see also section 4.4)

NY State Assembly
518-455-4218
assembly.state.ny.us

NY State Senate
www.senate.state.ny.us

Library

(see archives, law library; see also section 5.8)

New York State Library
518-474-5355
www.nysl.nysed.gov

Licensing

(see also business, consumer services)

Division of Licensing Services
518-474-4429
www.dos.state.ny.us/LCNS/licensing.html

Lieutenant Governor

Office of the Lieutenant Governor
518-474-8390
www.ny.gov/governor/ltgov

Lobbying

(see also elections)

Commission on Public Integrity
518-408-3976
www.nyintegrity.org

Local Government

(see also section 4.6)

Local Government Index
www.nysl.nysed.gov/ils/topics/local.htm

State Association of Counties
518-465-1473
www.nysac.org

New York Conference of Mayors and Municipal Officials
518-463-1185
www.nycom.org

Lottery

New York Lottery
518-388-3300
www.nylottery.org/index.php

Marriage Records

(see vital records; see also section 5.7)

Department of Health
(birth, death, marriage, and divorce records)
877-854-4481 (VitalChek)
www.health.state.ny.us/vital_records
www.health.state.ny.us/vital_records/marriage.htm

Massage Therapy

(see also health)

State Board for Massage Therapy
518-474-3817 x270
www.op.nysed.gov/massage.htm

Mediation

(see also labor)

Dispute Resolution Association
518-687-2240
www.nysdra.org

Medicaid

Medicaid
518-486-9057
www.health.state.ny.us/health_care/medicaid/index.htm

Medicine

(see chiropractic, dentistry, dietetics-nutrition, emergency, health, insurance, massage therapy, mental health)

Mental Health

(see also health)

Office of Mental Health
800-597-8481
www.omh.state.ny.us

State Board for Mental Health Practitioners
518-474-3817 x592
www.op.nysed.gov/mhp.htm

Midwifery

(see also health)

State Board for Midwifery
518-474-3817 x250
www.op.nysed.gov/midwife.htm

Military

Division of Military & Naval Affairs
518-786-4581
dmna.state.ny.us/index.php

Division of Veterans' Affairs
888-838-7697; 518-474-6114
veterans.ny.gov

New York Army National Guard
518-786-4581
dmna.state.ny.us/arng/nyarng.php

New York Air National Guard
518-786-4581
dmna.state.ny.us/ang/nyang.php

New York Guard

dmna.state.ny.us/nyg/nyg.php

New York Naval Militia
518-786-4583
dmna.state.ny.us/nynm/naval.php

Missing Persons

(see also law enforcement)

NYS Missing and Exploited Children Clearinghouse
800-FIND-KID
www.criminaljustice.state.ny.us/missing

Mortages

(see housing, real estate)

Motor Vehicles

(see also automotive repair, transportation)

Department of Motor Vehicles
800-CALL-DMV
www.nydmv.state.ny.us

Governor's Traffic Safety Committee
518-474-5111
www.nysgtsc.state.ny.us

National Guard

(see military)

Natural Resources

(see also environment)

Bureau of Fisheries
518-402-8924
www.dec.ny.gov/outdoor/fishing.html

Bureau of Lands and Forests
518-402-9405
www.dec.ny.gov/lands/309.html

Bureau of Wildlife
518-402-8883
www.dec.ny.gov/outdoor/hunting.html

Department of Environmental Conservation
800-TIPP-DEC; 518-402-8013
www.dec.ny.gov

Division of Coastal Resources
nyswaterfronts.com/index.asp

Division of Water
518-402-8086
www.dec.ny.gov/lands/26561.html

Energy Research and Development Authority
866-NYS-ERDA; 518-862-1090
www.nyserda.org

Marine Law Enforcement
518-474-0456
nysparks.state.ny.us/recreation/boating/marine-law-enforcement.aspx

Office of Parks, Recreation and Historic Preservation
518-474-0456; 800-354-CAMP
www.nysparks.state.ny.us

State Council of Parks
518-474-0456
nysparks.state.ny.us/state-council/default.aspx

Nursing

(see also health, licensing)

State Board for Nursing
518-474-3817 x280
www.op.nysed.gov/nurse.htm

Nurse Practitioner Unit
518-474-3817 x270
www.op.nysed.gov/nurse.htm

Nutrition

(see dietetics-nutrition, health)

Occupational Safety

(see also health, employment, workers' compensation)

Division of Safety and Health
518-485-9263
www.labor.state.ny.us/workerprotection/safetyhealth/dosh_programs.shtm

Occupational Therapy

(see also health)

State Board for Occupational Therapy
518-474-3817 x270
www.op.nysed.gov/ot.htm

Ophthalmic Dispensing

(see also health, optometry)

State Board for Ophthalmic Dispensing
518-474-3817 x250
www.op.nysed.gov/prof/od

Opticians

(see ophthalmic dispensing)

Optometry

(see ophthalmic dispensing)

State Board for Optometry
518-474-3817 x250
www.op.nysed.gov/prof/optom

Parks

(see also environment, natural resources)

Adirondack Park Agency
518-891-4050
www.apa.state.ny.us

Lake George Park Commission
518-668-9347
www.lgpc.state.ny.us

Office of Parks, Recreation and Historic Preservation
518-474-0456; 800-456-CAMP
www.nysparks.state.ny.us

State Council of Parks, Recreation and Historic Preservation
518-474-0456
nysparks.state.ny.us

Parole

(see corrections, law enforcement)

Permits

(see business)

Personnel

(see employment, labor)

Pharmacy

(see also health)

State Board of Pharmacy
518-474-3817 x250
www.op.nysed.gov/pharm.htm

Physical Therapy

(see also health)

State Board of Physical Therapy
518-474-3817 x270
www.op.nysed.gov/pt.htm

Podiatry

(see also health)

State Board of Podiatry
518-474-3817 x250
www.op.nysed.gov/prof/pod

Police

(see corrections, law enforcement, military)

Prison

(see corrections, law enforcement)

Privacy

(see civil rights, identity theft, law enforcement)

Probate

(see courts; see also section 4.2)

Probation

(see corrections, law enforcement)

Psychology

(see also health)

State Board for Psychology
518-474-3817 x270
www.op.nysed.gov/prof/psych

Public Accountancy

State Board of Public Accountancy
518-474-3817 x270
www.op.nysed.gov/prof/cpa

Public Assistance

(see child support services, social services)

Public Defender

Capital Defender Office
212-608-3352
www.nycdo.org

Public Defender Offices
www.nysda.org/html/chief_defenders.html
www.nysda.org/08_Chief_Defender_List2008-08-05.pdf

Public Utilities

(see also natural resources)

New York Power Authority
914-681-6200
www.nypa.gov

Public Service Commission
518-474-7080
800-342-3377 (complaint hotline)
www.dps.state.ny.us

Racing

(see also athletics, law enforcement)

Racing and Wagering Board

518-395-5400
www.racing.state.ny.us

Real Estate

(see also housing)

Office of Real Property Services
518-474-2982
www.orps.state.ny.us

State of New York Mortgage Agency
800-382-HOME; 212-688-4000
www.nyhomes.org/home

Recreation

(see also environment, natural resources)

Office of Parks, Recreation and Historic Preservation
518-474-0456
www.nysparks.state.ny.us

Recycling

(see also conservation, environment)

Bureau of Solid Waste, Reduction and Recycling
518-402-8704
www.dec.ny.gov/chemical/294.html

Respiratory Therapy

(see also health)

State Board for Respiratory Therapy
518-474-3817 x270
www.op.nysed.gov/prof/rt

Retirement

(see also employment, labor)

New York State and Local Retirement System
866-805-0990; 518-474-7736
www.osc.state.ny.us/retire/

New York State Teachers' Retirement System
518-447-2900; 800-348-7298
www.nystrs.org

Secretary Of State

(see also business, corporations)

Office of the Secretary of State
518-474-4752
www.dos.state.ny.us

Senate

(see legislature; see also section 4.4)

Seniors

(see aging)

Sex Offenders

(see also law enforcement)

Sex Offender Registry
800-262-3257
www.criminaljustice.state.ny.us/nsor

Shorthand Reporting

State Board for Certified Shorthand Reporting
518-474-3817 x270
www.op.nysed.gov/csr.htm

Social Services

(see adoption, child support services, domestic partnership, health)

Office of Children and Family Services
518-473-7793
www.ocfs.state.ny.us/main

Office of Temporary and Disability Assistance
888-342-3009; 518-474-9516
www.otda.state.ny.us/main

Social Work

(see also health)

State Board for Social Work
518-474-3817 x592
www.op.nysed.gov/prof/sw

Speech Language Pathology and Audiology

(see also health)

State Board for Speech Language Pathology and Audiology
518-474-3817 x270
www.op.nysed.gov/speech.htm
www.op.nysed.gov/prof/slpa

Sports

(see athletics, racing)

State Agencies

(see administration)

Agency Web Sites and Publications
www.nysl.nysed.gov/ils/nyserver.html

Government Toll-Free Numbers
www6.oft.state.ny.us/telecom/phones/tollfreelist.jsp
www.tollfreenumber.org/forum/about45.html

State Police

(see also law enforcement, motor vehicles)

Division of State Police
www.troopers.state.ny.us
www.troopers.state.ny.us/Contact_Us/Troop_Information

Tax

(see also estate tax)

Department of Taxation and Finance
800-225-5829 (personal); 888-698-2908 (corporate)
www.tax.state.ny.us
www.nysegov.com/citGuide.cfm?superCat=212

Taxpayer Rights (Office of Real Property Services)
518-474-2982; 518-486-5446
www.orps.state.ny.us/home/tri_index.cfm

Teachers

(see education, employment)

Therapy

(see health, occupational therapy, physical therapy, psychology, respiratory therapy)

Tourism

(see also arts and humanities, athletics)

Empire State Development
800-CALL-NYS
www.iloveny.com

Traffic Safety

(see law enforcement, motor vehicles, transportation)

Transportation

(see also motor vehicles)

Department of Transportation
518-457-6195
www.nysdot.gov

New York State Thruway Authority
800-THRUWAY; 518-436-2983
www.nysthruway.gov

New York State Canal System
800-4CANAL4
www.nyscanals.gov

Treasurer

Division of the Treasury (Department of Taxation)
518-474-4250
www.nystreasury.com

Troopers

(see state police)

Unclaimed Property

(see also comptroller)

Unclaimed Funds–Office of the State Comptroller
800-221-9311
www.osc.state.ny.us/ouf

Unemployment Insurance

(see also section 2.8; employment, insurance, labor, workers' compensation)

Unemployment Insurance Division (Department of Labor)
888-209-8124
www.labor.state.ny.us/ui/ui_index.shtm

Universities, Public

(see education)

Utilities

(see also consumer services, energy)

Public Service Commission
www.dps.state.ny.us

New York Power Authority
914-681-6200
www.nypa.gov

Veterinary Medicine

State Board for Veterinary Medicine
518-474-3817 x250
www.op.nysed.gov/vet.htm
www.op.nysed.gov/prof/vetmed

Victim Services

(see also law enforcement)

Crime Victims Board
800-247-8035
www.cvb.state.ny.us

Office for the Prevention of Domestic Violence
518-457-5800; 800-942-6906
opdv.state.ny.us

Vital Records

(see also birth records, death records, dissolution/divorce records, marriage records)

Vital Records Office (Department of Health)
www.health.state.ny.us/vital_records

Voting

(see elections)

Water

(see also environment, natural resources, parks)

Division of Coastal Resources
nyswaterfronts.com/index.asp

Division of Water (Department of Environmental Conservation)
518-402-8086
www.dec.ny.gov/lands/26561.html

Office of Parks, Recreation and Historic Preservation
518-474-0445
nysparks.state.ny.us

Public Service Commission
www.dps.state.ny.us

Welfare

(see child support services, social services)

Workers' Compensation

(see also employment, labor, unemployment insurance)

Division of Safety and Health
518-457-3518
www.labor.state.ny.us/workerprotection/safetyhealth/dosh_programs.shtm

Committee for Occupational Health and Safety
212-227-6440
www.nycosh.org

Compensation Insurance Rating Board
212-697-3535
www.nycirb.org

State Insurance Fund
877-435-7743
ww3.nysif.com

Workers' Compensation Board
877-632-4996
www.wcb.state.ny.us

C. More Information

State Governments: Other States

www.statelocalgov.net

www.govspot.com/state

www.loc.gov/rr/news/stategov/stategov.html

www.usa.gov/Agencies/State_and_Territories.shtml

dir.yahoo.com/Government/U_S__Government/
   State_Government

en.wikipedia.org/wiki/State_governments_of_the_United_States

Council of State Governments

www.csg.org

State Government Data

www.census.gov/govs

D. Something to Check

1. Find the web sites of three New York agencies, offices, or boards that refer to paralegals employed within them.

2. What New York agencies, offices, or boards would have relevant information on (a) required credentials for high school teachers, (b) the plight of an insolvent business, and (c) police misconduct?

4.6 Counties and Cities: Some Useful Law-Related Sites

A. Introduction

B. Table of Contents

C. Sites

D. More Information

E. Something to Check

A. Introduction

This section presents law-related contact information for major counties and cities in New York. For New York counties, the following information is provided where Internet sites are available:

- Main government site
- Administrative agencies
- Local courts
- District attorney
- Public defender
- Consumer protection
- Child support enforcement
- County attorney (corporation counsel)
- Sheriff

For New York cities, the following information is provided where Internet sites are available:

- Main government site
- Administrative agencies
- Local courts
- City prosecutor
- City attorney (corporation counsel)
- Police department
- City code

For similar information:

- About state government, see section 4.1
- About state courts, see section 4.2
- About public records, see section 5.7
- About law libraries, see section 5.8
- About federal courts in New York, see section 4.3
- About bar associations, see section 3.4
- About paralegal associations, see section 1.2

B. Table of Contents

C. Sites

Albany, City of

Albany: City Government
518-438-4000
www.albanyny.org/Government.aspx

Albany: Administrative Agencies
www.albanyny.org/Government.aspx

Albany: Courts
518-462-6714
www.courts.state.ny.us/courthelp/cfacts2Albany.html
www.nycourts.gov/courts/3jd/city/albany/albanycriminal.shtml
www.courtreference.com/Albany-County-New-York-Courts.htm

Albany: Corporation Counsel
518-434-5050
www.albanyny.org/Government/Departments/Law.aspx

Albany: Police Department
518-462-8013
www.albanyny.gov/Government/Departments/Police.aspx

Albany: City Code
ecode360.com/?custId=AL0934

Albany County

Albany County: Government
www.albanycounty.com

Albany County: Administrative Agencies
www.albanycounty.com/depts-list.asp

Albany County: Courts
518-285-8777; 518-285-8300
www.courts.state.ny.us/courthelp/cfacts2Albany.html
www.nycourts.gov/courts/3jd
www.courtreference.com/Albany-County-New-York-Courts.htm

Albany County: District Attorney
518-487-5460
www.albanycountyda.com

Albany County: Public Defender
518-447-7150
www.albanycounty.com/publicdefender

Albany County: Consumer Protection
518-447-7581
www.albanycounty.com/consumeraffairs

Albany County: Child Support and Enforcement
888-208-4485; 518-447-7300
www.albanycounty.com/departments/dss/
  programs_services.asp?id=407

Albany County: County Attorney
518-447-7110
www.albanycounty.com/law

Albany County: Sheriff
518-487-5440
www.albanycountysheriff.com

Allegany County

Allegany: County Government
585-268-9217
www.alleganyco.com

Allegany: Administrative Agencies
www.alleganyco.com/default.asp?show=btn_departments
www.alleganyco.com/default.asp?show=btn_leadership

Allegany: Courts
585-268-5800
www.courts.state.ny.us/courthelp/cfacts2Allegany.html
www.nycourts.gov/courts/8jd/Allegany
www.courtreference.com/Allegany-County-New-York-
  Courts.htm

Allegany: District Attorney
585-268-9225
www.alleganyco.com/default.asp?show=btn_DA

Allegany: Public Defender
585-593-7111
www.nclas.org/NYPubDef.htm

Allegany: Child Support Enforcement
888-208-4485; 585-268-9312
www.alleganyco.com/default.asp?show=btn_dss
www.alleganyco.com/default.asp?show=btn_dss/admin_serv/
  child_support

Allegany: County Attorney
585-268-9410
www.alleganyco.com/default.asp?show=btn_leadership

Allegany: Sheriff
585-268-9204
www.alleganyco.com/default.asp?show=btn_sheriff

Bronx County

Bronx: County Government
www.nyc.gov

Bronx: Administrative Agencies
www.nyc.gov

Bronx: Courts
www.courts.state.ny.us/courthelp/cfacts2Bronx.html
www.courts.state.ny.us/courts/12jd/index.shtml
www.courtreference.com/Bronx-County-New-York-Courts.htm

Bronx: District Attorney
718-590-2000
bronxda.nyc.gov

Bronx: Public Defender
800-597-7980; 718-838-7878
www.bronxdefenders.org

Bronx: Consumer Protection
212-NEW-YORK
www.nyc.gov/html/dca/html/home/home.shtml

Bronx: Child Support Enforcement
888-208-4485; 718-590-3428
www.nyc.gov/html/hra/downloads/pdf/field_offices.pdf

Bronx: Corporation Counsel
212-788-0303
www.nyc.gov/html/law/html/home/home.shtml

Bronx: Sheriff
718-579-2820; 718-993-3880
www.nysheriffs.org/bronxsheriff

Brooklyn

(see Kings County)

Broome County

Broome: County Government
607-778-2109
www.gobroomecounty.com

Broome: Administrative Agencies
www.gobroomecounty.com/departments/index.php

Broome: Courts
www.courts.state.ny.us/courthelp/cfacts2Broome.html
www.gobroomecounty.com/courts
www.courtreference.com/Broome-County-New-York-Courts.htm

Broome: District Attorney
607-778-2423
www.gobroomecounty.com/da

Broome: Public Defender
607-778-2403
www.gobroomecounty.com/pubdef

Broome: Child Support Enforcement
888-208-4485; 607-778-8850
www.gobroomecounty.com/dss/support

Broome: County Attorney
607-778-2117
www.gobroomecounty.com/law

Broome: Sheriff
607-778-1911
www.gobroomecounty.com/sheriff

Buffalo, City of

Buffalo: City Government
716-851-4841
www.ci.buffalo.ny.us

Buffalo: Administrative Agencies
www.ci.buffalo.ny.us/Home/City_Departments

Buffalo: Courts
716-845-2600
www.nycourts.gov/courts/8jd/Erie/buffalo.shtml

Buffalo: Public Defender
716-853-9555
www.legalaidbuffalo.org

Buffalo: City Attorney
716-851-4343
*www.ci.buffalo.ny.us/Home/City_Departments/
LawDepartment*

Buffalo: Police Department
716-851-4444
www.bpdny.org

Buffalo: Municipal Code
www.ci.buffalo.ny.us
(click "City Charter")

Cattaraugus County

Cattaraugus: County Government
www.co.cattaraugus.ny.us/government

Cattaraugus: Administrative Agencies
www.cattco.org/departments

Cattaraugus: Courts
716-373-8035
www.courts.state.ny.us/courthelp/cfacts2Cattaraugus.html
www.nycourts.gov/courts/8jd/Cattaraugus/directions.shtml
*www.courtreference.com/Cattaraugus-County-New-York-
Courts.htm*

Cattaraugus: District Attorney
716-938-9111 x2220
ww2.cattco.org/district-attorney/district-attorneys-office

Cattaraugus: Public Defender
716-373-0004
www.cattco.org/public_defender

Cattaraugus: Child Support Enforcement
888-208-4485; 716-701-3441
www.cattco.org/dss/dss_info.asp?Parent=18002

Cattaraugus: County Attorney
716-938-9111 x2391
www.cattco.org/attorney

Cattaraugus: Sheriff
716-938-9191
www.sheriff.cattco.org

Cayuga County

Cayuga: County Government
www.co.cayuga.ny.us

Cayuga: Administrative Agencies
www.co.cayuga.ny.us/depart.htm

Cayuga: Courts
315-255-4320
www.courts.state.ny.us/courthelp/cfacts2Cayuga.html
www.nycourts.gov/courts/7jd/Cayuga
www.courtreference.com/Cayuga-County-New-York-Courts.htm

Cayuga: District Attorney
315-253-1391
www.co.cayuga.ny.us/da

Cayuga: Public Defender
315-253-1402 (assigned counsel)
www.co.cayuga.ny.us/counsel

Cayuga: Child Support Enforcement
315-253-1380
www.cayugacounty.us/hhs/humanservices/childsupport.html

Cayuga: County Attorney
315-253-1274
www.co.cayuga.ny.us/coatty

Cayuga: Sheriff
315-253-1222
www.co.cayuga.ny.us/sheriff

Chautauqua County

Chautauqua: County Government
www.co.chautauqua.ny.us

Chautauqua: Administrative Agencies
www.co.chautauqua.ny.us

Chautauqua: Courts
716-753-4000
www.courts.state.ny.us/courthelp/cfacts2Chautauqua.html
www.nycourts.gov/courts/8jd/Chautauqua
www.courtreference.com/Chautauqua-County-New-York-Courts.htm

Chautauqua: District Attorney
716-753-4241
www.co.chautauqua.ny.us/departments/da/Pages/default.aspx

Chautauqua: Public Defender
716-753-4376
dpca.state.ny.us/chautauqua.htm

Chautauqua: Child Support Enforcement
888-208-4485
newyorkchildsupport.com/DCSE/LocalChildOffices.do?selectDistrictCode=06

Chautauqua: Sheriff
716-753-4900
www.sheriff.us

Chemung County

Chemung: County Government
www.chemungcounty.com

Chemung: Administrative Agencies
www.chemungcounty.com/index.asp?pageId=80

Chemung: Courts
www.courts.state.ny.us/courthelp/cfacts2Chemung.html
www.nycourts.gov/courts/6jd/Chemung
www.courtreference.com/Chemung-County-New-York-Courts.htm

Chemung: District Attorney
607-737-2944
www.chemungcounty.com/index.asp?pageId=137

Chemung: Public Defender
607-737-2969
www.chemungcounty.com/index.asp?pageId=253

Chemung: Child Support Enforcement
888-208-4485; 607-737-5309
www.chemungcounty.com/index.asp?pageId=266

Chemung: County Attorney
607-737-2982
www.chemungcounty.com/index.asp?pageId=258

Chemung: Sheriff
607-737-2987
www.chemungcounty.com/index.asp?pageId=319

Chenango County

Chenango: County Government
607-337-1700
www.co.chenango.ny.us

Chenango: Administrative Agencies
www.co.chenango.ny.us/Directory.htm

Chenango: Courts
www.courts.state.ny.us/courthelp/cfacts2Chenango.html
www.nycourts.gov/courts/6jd/chenango
www.courtreference.com/Chenango-County-New-York-Courts.htm

Chenango: District Attorney
607-337-1745
pview.findlaw.com/view/1736702_1

Chenango: Public Defender
607-337-1870
www.co.chenango.ny.us/PublicDefender/pubdef.htm

Chenango: Child Support Enforcement
888-208-4485; 607-337-1500
ccdss.peppytech.com

Chenango: County Attorney
607-337-1405
www.co.chenango.ny.us/countyclerk/co.pdf

Chenango: Sheriff
607-334-2000
www.chenangosheriff.us

Clinton County

Clinton: County Government
www.clintoncountygov.com

Clinton: Administrative Agencies
www.clintoncountygov.com/DepartmentLists.html

Clinton: Courts
518-565-4715
www.courts.state.ny.us/courthelp/cfacts2Clinton.html
www.nycourts.gov/courts/4jd/Clinton
www.courtreference.com/Clinton-County-New-York-Courts.htm

Clinton: District Attorney
518-565-4770
www.clintoncountygov.com/Departments/DA/DAHome.html

Clinton: Public Defender
518-561-9251
www.nclas.org/NYPubDef.htm

Clinton: Child Support Enforcement
888-208-4485; 518-565-3394
www.clintoncountygov.com/Departments/DSS/child_support_enforcement.htm

Clinton: County Attorney
518-561-4400
www.clintoncountygov.com/DepartmentLists.html

Clinton: Sheriff
518-565-4300
www.clintoncountygov.com/Departments/Sheriff/SheriffHome.html

Columbia County

Columbia: County Government
www.columbiacountyny.com

Columbia: Administrative Agencies
www.columbiacountyny.com/dept_contacts.html

Columbia: Courts
518-828-7858
www.courts.state.ny.us/courthelp/cfacts2Columbia.html
www.nycourts.gov/courts/3jd/county/Columbia
www.courtreference.com/Columbia-County-New-York-Courts.htm

Columbia: District Attorney
518-828-3414
www.columbiacountyny.com/dept_contacts.html

Columbia: Public Defender
518-828-3410
www.columbiacountyny.com/dept_contacts.html

Columbia: Child Support Enforcement
888-208-4485; 518-828-9411
https://newyorkchildsupport.com/DCSE/LocalChildOffices.do?selectDistrictCode=10

Columbia: County Attorney
518-828-3303
www.columbiacountyny.com/dept_contacts.html

Columbia: Sheriff
518-828-0601
www.columbiacountysheriff.us

Cortland County

Cortland: County Government
www.cortland-co.org

Cortland: Administrative Agencies
www.cortland-co.org/cortlanddepts.html

Cortland: Courts
607-753-5013
www.courts.state.ny.us/courthelp/cfacts2Cortland.html
www.nycourts.gov/courts/6jd/cortland/index.shtml
www.courtreference.com/Cortland-County-New-York-Courts.htm

Cortland: District Attorney
607-753-5008
www.cortland-co.org/da/ccda2.html

Cortland: Public Defender
607-753-5046
www.cortland-co.org/pubdef

Cortland: Child Support Enforcement
888-208-4485; 607-753-5248
www.cortland-co.org/dss

Cortland: County Attorney
607-753-5095
www.cortland-co.org/cortlanddepts.html

Cortland: Sheriff
607-753-5006
www.cortland-co.org/sheriff

Delaware County

Delaware: County Government
www.co.delaware.ny.us/government.htm

Delaware: Administrative Agencies
www.co.delaware.ny.us/departments.htm

Delaware: Courts
607-746-2131
www.courts.state.ny.us/courthelp/cfacts2Delaware.html
www.nycourts.gov/courts/6jd/delaware/supreme-county.shtml
www.courtreference.com/Delaware-County-New-York-Courts.htm

Delaware: District Attorney
607-746-3557
www.co.delaware.ny.us/departments/da/da.htm

Delaware: Public Defender
607-652-9790
www.nclas.org/NYPubDef.htm

Delaware: Child Support Enforcement
607-746-2325 (Department of Social Services)
www.co.delaware.ny.us/departments/dss/dss.htm
https://newyorkchildsupport.com/DCSE/LocalChildOffices.do?
selectDistrictCode=12

Delaware: County Attorney
607-652-3443
www.co.delaware.ny.us/departments/cob/admin.htm

Delaware: Sheriff
607-746-2336
www.co.delaware.ny.us/departments/shrf/shrf.htm

Dutchess County

Dutchess: County Government
www.co.dutchess.ny.us/CountyGov/CountyGovInfo.htm

Dutchess: Administrative Agencies
www.co.dutchess.ny.us/CountyGov/AllServices.htm

Dutchess: Courts
845-486-2260
www.courts.state.ny.us/courthelp/cfacts2Dutchess.html
www.nycourts.gov/courts/9jd/Dutchess
www.courtreference.com/Dutchess-County-New-York-
Courts.htm

Dutchess: District Attorney
845-486-2300
www.co.dutchess.ny.us/CountyGov/AllServices_8902.htm
(click "District Attorney")

Dutchess: Public Defender
845-486-2280
www.co.dutchess.ny.us/CountyGov/AllServices_8902.htm
(click "Public Defender")

Dutchess: Consumer Protection
845-486-2949
www.co.dutchess.ny.us/CountyGov/AllServices.htm
(click "Consumer Affairs")

Dutchess: Child Support Enforcement
888-208-4485; 845-486-3100
www.co.dutchess.ny.us/CountyGov/AllServices_8902.htm
(click "Child Support Enforcement Unit")

Dutchess: County Attorney
845-486-2110
www.co.dutchess.ny.us/CountyGov/DeptDepartments.htm
(click "County Attorney")

Dutchess: Sheriff
845-486-3800
www.co.dutchess.ny.us/CountyGov/Departments/Sheriff/
SHIndex.htm

Erie County

Erie: County Government
www.erie.gov

Erie: Administrative Agencies
www.erie.gov/sitemap.asp

Erie: Courts
716-845-9301
www.courts.state.ny.us/courthelp/cfacts2Erie.html
www.nycourts.gov/courts/8jd/Erie
www.courtreference.com/Erie-County-New-York-Courts.htm

Erie: District Attorney
716-858-2424
www.erie.gov/depts/government/da.phtml

Erie: Public Defender
716-855-1553 x43
www.eriebar.com/lpsa_public_defender.htm
www.nclas.org/NYPubDef.htm

Erie: Child Support Enforcement
888-208-4485
www.erie.gov/depts/socialservices/ocse.asp

Erie: County Attorney
716-858-2200
www.erie.gov/depts/county_attorney.asp

Erie: Sheriff
716-858-7608
www.erie.gov/sheriff

Essex County

Essex: County Government
www.co.essex.ny.us

Essex: Administrative Agencies
www.co.essex.ny.us/departments.asp

Essex: Courts
518-873-3375
www.courts.state.ny.us/courthelp/cfacts2Essex.html
www.courts.state.ny.us/courts/4jd
www.courts.state.ny.us/courts/4jd/ESSEX2.htm
www.courtreference.com/Essex-County-New-York-Courts.htm

Essex: District Attorney
518-873-3335
www.co.essex.ny.us/departments.asp

Essex: Public Defender
518-873-3880
www.co.essex.ny.us/departments.asp

Essex: Child Support Enforcement
888-208-4485; 518-873-3760
newyorkchildsupport.com/counties/essex_county.html
https://newyorkchildsupport.com/DCSE/LocalChildOffices.do?
selectDistrictCode=15

Essex: County Attorney
518-873-3380
www.co.essex.ny.us/downloads/2008%20Directory.pdf

Essex: Sheriff
518-873-6321
www.co.essex.ny.us/Sheriff.asp

Franklin County

Franklin: County Government
www.franklincony.org

Franklin: Administrative Agencies
www.franklincony.org/content/Departments

Franklin: Courts
www.courts.state.ny.us/courthelp/cfacts2Franklin.html
www.nycourts.gov/courts/4jd/franklin
www.courtreference.com/Franklin-County-New-York-Courts.htm

Franklin: District Attorney
518-481-1544
www.franklincony.org/content/Departments/View/15

Franklin: Public Defender
518-481-1624; 518-891-7003
www.nclas.org/NYPubDef.htm

Franklin: Child Support Enforcement
888-208-4485; 518-483-6770
newyorkchildsupport.com/counties/franklin_county.html
*https://newyorkchildsupport.com/DCSE/LocalChildOffices.do?
    selectDistrictCode=16*

Franklin: County Attorney
518-483-8400
www.maloneny.us/malone_government.htm

Franklin: Sheriff
518-483-3304
www.franklincony.org/content/Departments/View/10

Fulton County

Fulton: County Government
518-736-5540; 518-736-5555
www.nysegov.com/map-NY.cfm?countyName=fulton
www.schenectadyhistory.org/local/fulton.html
www.fultoncountyny.org

Fulton: Courts
518-736-5539
www.courts.state.ny.us/courthelp/cfacts2Fulton.html
www.courts.state.ny.us/courthelp/FultonCountyCt1.htm
www.courtreference.com/Fulton-County-New-York-Courts.htm

Fulton: District Attorney
518-736-5511
*www.fultoncountyny.gov/index.php?word=departments/
    da.htm*

Fulton: Public Defender
518-661-5002
www.nclas.org/NYPubDef.htm

Fulton: Child Support Enforcement
888-208-4485
*https://newyorkchildsupport.com/DCSE/LocalChildOffices.do?
    selectDistrictCode=17*
newyorkchildsupport.com/counties/fulton_county.html

Fulton: Sheriff
518-736-2100
*www.fultoncountyny.gov/index.php?word=departments/
    sheriff.htm*

Genesee County

Genesee: County Government
www.co.genesee.ny.us

Genesee: Administrative Agencies
www.co.genesee.ny.us

Genesee: Courts
585-344-2550
www.courts.state.ny.us/courthelp/cfacts2Genesee.html
www.nycourts.gov/courts/8jd/Genesee
www.co.genesee.ny.us/dpt/courts/index.html

Genesee: District Attorney
585-344-2550 x2250
www.co.genesee.ny.us/dpt/districtattorney

Genesee: Public Defender
585-344-2550 x2280
www.co.genesee.ny.us/dpt/publicdefender

Genesee: Child Support Enforcement
888-208-4485
newyorkchildsupport.com/counties/genesee_county.html
*https://newyorkchildsupport.com/DCSE/LocalChildOffices.do?
    selectDistrictCode=18*

Genesee: Sheriff
585-345-3000
www.co.genesee.ny.us/dpt/sheriff

Greene County

Greene: County Government
518-719-3270
www.greenegovernment.com

Greene: Administrative Agencies
www.greenegovernment.com/countyinfo.htm

Greene: Courts
518-943-2230
www.courts.state.ny.us/courthelp/cfacts2Greene.html
www.courts.state.ny.us/courts/3jd
www.courtreference.com/Greene-County-New-York-Courts.htm

Greene: District Attorney
518-719-3590
www.greenegovernment.com/department/da

Greene: Public Defender
518-719-3220
www.greenegovernment.com/department/publicdefend

Greene: Child Support Enforcement
888-208-4485; 518-719-3700
*www.greenegovernment.com/department/socialserv/
   childsupport.htm*

Greene: County Attorney
518-719-3540
www.greenegovernment.com/department/attorney

Greene: Sheriff
518-943-3300
www.greenegovernment.com/department/sheriff

Hamilton County

Hamilton: County Government
518-548-6651
www.nysegov.com/map-NY.cfm?countyName=Hamilton
www.schenectadyhistory.org/local/hamilton.html

Hamilton: Courts
518-648-5411
www.courts.state.ny.us/courthelp/cfacts2Hamilton.html
*www.courtreference.com/Hamilton-County-New-York-
   Courts.htm*

Hamilton: District Attorney
518-648-5113
*web2.userinstinct.com/31488288-hamilton-county-officials-
   depts-district-attorney.htm*

Hamilton: Public Defender
518-548-6651
www.nclas.org/NYPubDef.htm

Hamilton: Child Support Enforcement
888-208-4485; 518-648-6131
*https://newyorkchildsupport.com/DCSE/LocalChildOffices.do?
   selectDistrictCode=20*

Hamilton: County Attorney
315-336-3900

Hamilton: Sheriff
518-548-3113
www.scoc.state.ny.us/sheriffsaddre.htm

Herkimer County

Herkimer: County Government
www.herkimercounty.org/content

Herkimer: Administrative Agencies
www.herkimercounty.org/content/Departments

Herkimer: Courts
www.courts.state.ny.us/courthelp/cfacts2Herkimer.html
www.courts.state.ny.us/courts/5jd/herkimer/index.shtml
www.courtreference.com/Herkimer-County-New-York-Courts.htm

Herkimer: District Attorney
315-867-1155
www.herkimercounty.org/content/Departments/View/24

Herkimer: Public Defender
315-866-0006
www.nclas.org/NYPubDef.htm

Herkimer: Child Support Enforcement
888-208-4485; 315-867-1291 (Department of Social
Services)
*https://newyorkchildsupport.com/DCSE/LocalChildOffices.do?
   selectDistrictCode=21*

Herkimer: County Attorney
315-867-1123
www.herkimercounty.org/content/Departments

Herkimer: Sheriff
315-867-1167; 315-867-1252
www.herkimercounty.org/content/Departments/View/27

Jefferson County

Jefferson: County Government
315-785-3000
www.co.jefferson.ny.us/Jefflive.nsf/index12
www.nysegov.com/map-NY.cfm?countyName=jefferson

Jefferson: Courts
315-785-7906
www.courts.state.ny.us/courthelp/cfacts2Jefferson.html
www.courts.state.ny.us/courts/5jd/jefferson/index.shtml
*www.courtreference.com/Jefferson-County-New-York-
   Courts.htm*

Jefferson: District Attorney
315-785-3053
www.co.jefferson.ny.us/Jefflive.nsf/dist_att

Jefferson: Public Defender
315-785-3152
www.co.jefferson.ny.us/Jefflive.nsf/pubdef

Jefferson: Child Support Enforcement
315-782-9030
www.co.jefferson.ny.us/jefflive.nsf/socialse

Jefferson: County Attorney
315-785-3088
www.co.jefferson.ny.us/jefflive.nsf/attorney

Jefferson: Sheriff
315-786-2700
www.co.jefferson.ny.us/jefflive.nsf/sheriff

Kings County

Kings: County Government
www.nyc.gov

Kings: Courts
347-296-1183
www.courts.state.ny.us/courthelp/cfacts2Kings.html
www.courts.state.ny.us/courts/2jd/kings.shtml
www.courtreference.com/Kings-County-New-York-Courts.htm

Kings: District Attorney
718-250-2000
www.brooklynda.org

Kings: Public Defender
718-237-2000 (Legal Aid Society)
www.legal-aid.org/en/findus/locations/brooklyn.aspx
www.nclas.org/NYPubDef.htm

Kings: Brooklyn Defender Services
718-254-0700
www.bds.org/home.aspx

Kings: Consumer Protection
212-NEW-YORK
www.nyc.gov/html/dca/html/home/home.shtml

Kings: Child Support Enforcement
888-208-4485; 718-643-8890
www.nyc.gov/html/hra/downloads/pdf/field_offices.pdf
newyorkchildsupport.com/counties/kings_county.html

Kings: Corporation Counsel
212-788-0303
www.nyc.gov/html/law/html/home/home.shtml

Kings: Sheriff
718-802-3543
www.scoc.state.ny.us/sheriffsaddre.htm
www.usacops.com/ny/s11201/index.html

Lewis County

Lewis: County Government
www.lewiscountyny.org/content

Lewis: Administrative Agencies
www.lewiscountyny.org/content/Departments/List?

Lewis: Courts
315-376-5347
www.courts.state.ny.us/courthelp/cfacts2Lewis.html
www.courts.state.ny.us/courts/5jd/lewis
www.courtreference.com/Lewis-County-New-York-Courts.htm

Lewis: District Attorney
315-376-5390
www.lewiscountyny.org/content/Departments/View/49

Lewis: Public Defender
315-376-6565
www.lewiscountyny.org/content/Departments/View/21

Lewis: Child Support Enforcement
888-208-4485; 315-376-5400
www.lewiscountyny.org/content/Departments/View/30
https://newyorkchildsupport.com/DCSE/LocalChildOffices.do?
selectDistrictCode=23

Lewis: County Attorney
315-376-5282
www.lewiscountyny.org/content/Departments/View/3

Lewis: Sheriff
315-376-3511
www.lewiscountyny.org/content/Departments/View/31

Livingston County

Livingston: County Government
www.co.livingston.state.ny.us

Livingston: Administrative Agencies
www.co.livingston.state.ny.us
(click "Departments")

Livingston: Courts
585-243-7060
www.courts.state.ny.us/courthelp/cfacts2Livingston.html
www.courts.state.ny.us/courts/7jd/Livingston
www.courtreference.com/Livingston-County-New-York-Courts.htm

Livingston: District Attorney
585-243-7020
www.co.livingston.state.ny.us/da.htm

Livingston: Public Defender
585-243-7028; 585-335-1738
www.co.livingston.state.ny.us/public_def.htm

Livingston: Child Support Enforcement
888-208-4485; 585-243-7300
www.co.livingston.state.ny.us/dss.htm

Livingston: County Attorney
585-243-7033
www.co.livingston.state.ny.us/attorney.htm

Livingston: Sheriff
585-243-7100; 585-335-1742
www.co.livingston.state.ny.us/Sheriff/home.htm

Madison County

Madison: County Government
www.madisoncounty.org

Madison: Administrative Agencies
www.madisoncounty.org/departments.html

Madison: Courts
www.courts.state.ny.us/courthelp/cfacts2Madison.html
www.courts.state.ny.us/courts/6jd/madison
www.courtreference.com/Madison-County-New-York-Courts.htm

Madison: District Attorney
315-366-2236
www.madisoncounty.org/departments.html
(click "District Attorney")

Madison: Public Defender
315-366-2585
www.nclas.org/NYPubDef.htm
www.madisoncounty.org/departments.html
(click "Public Defenders Office")

Madison: Child Support Enforcement
888-208-4485; 315-366-2211
www.madisoncounty.org/dss/dsshome.htm

Madison: County Attorney
315-366-2203
www.madisoncounty.org/departments.html
(click "County Attorney")

Madison: Sheriff
315-366-2318
www.madisoncountysheriff.us

Monroe

Monroe: County Government
www.monroecounty.gov/government-index.php

Monroe: Administrative Agencies
www.monroecounty.gov/department-index.php

Monroe: Courts
585-428-2020; 585-428-2331
www.courts.state.ny.us/courthelp/cfacts2Monroe.html
www.courts.state.ny.us/courts/7jd/Monroe
www.courtreference.com/
    Monroe-County-New-York-Courts.htm

Monroe: District Attorney
585-753-4500
www.monroecounty.gov/da-index.php

Monroe: Public Defender
585-753-4210
www.monroecounty.gov/defender-index.php

Monroe: Child Support Enforcement
888-208-4485
www.monroecounty.gov/law-cseu.php

Monroe: County Attorney
585-753-1380
www.monroecounty.gov/law-index.php

Monroe: Sheriff
585-753-4178
www.monroecountysheriff.info

Montgomery County

Montgomery: County Government
www.co.montgomery.ny.us

Montgomery: Administrative Agencies
www.co.montgomery.ny.us
(click "Departments")

Montgomery: Courts
518-853-3834
www.courts.state.ny.us/courthelp/cfacts2Montgomery.html
www.courtreference.com/
    Montgomery-County-New-York-Courts.htm

Montgomery: District Attorney
518-853-8250
www.co.montgomery.ny.us
(click "Departments")

Montgomery: Public Defender
518-853-8305
www.nclas.org/NYPubDef.htm
www.co.montgomery.ny.us
(click "Departments" then "Public Defender")

Montgomery: Child Support Enforcement
888-208-4485; 518-853-4646
https://newyorkchildsupport.com/DCSE/LocalChildOffices.do?
    selectDistrictCode=27

Montgomery: County Attorney
518-843-3717
www.co.montgomery.ny.us
(click "Departments")

Montgomery: Sheriff
518-853-5500
www.co.montgomery.ny.us/sheriff
www.nysheriffs.org/montgomerysheriff

Mount Vernon, City of

Mount Vernon: City Government
914-665-2300
cmvny.com

Mount Vernon: Administrative Agencies
cmvny.com
(click entries under "Government")

Mount Vernon: Courts
914-665-2400
www.nycourts.gov/courts/9jd/Westchester/MountVernon.shtml

Mount Vernon: Consumer Protection
914-665-2433
cmvny.com/export/sites/cmvny3/departments/cup/e-gov.html

Mount Vernon: Corporation Counsel
914-665-2366
cmvny.com/export/sites/cmvny3/departments/law

Mount Vernon: Police Department
914-665-2500
cmvny.com/export/sites/cmvny3/departments/pol

Mount Vernon: Municipal Code
cmvny.com/export/sites/cmvny3/departments/cic/
    municode.html

Nassau County

Nassau: County Government
www.nassaucountyny.gov

Nassau: Administrative Agencies
*www.nassaucountyny.gov/website/AG/Nassau/
    departments.html*

Nassau: Courts
516-571-2400
www.courts.state.ny.us/courthelp/cfacts2Nassau.html
www.courts.state.ny.us/courts/10jd/nassau
www.courtreference.com/Nassau-County-New-York-Courts.htm

Nassau: District Attorney
516-571-3800
www.nassaucountyny.gov/agencies/DA/index.html

Nassau: Public Defender
516-560-6400
www.nclas.org

Nassau: Consumer Protection
516-571-3343
www.nassaucountyny.gov/agencies/DA/consumer_info.html

Nassau: Child Support Enforcement
888-208-4485
www.nassaucountyny.gov/agencies/dss/cse/index.html
*newyorkchildsupport.com/DCSE/
    LocalChildOffices.do?selectDistrictCode=28*

Nassau: County Attorney
516-571-3056
www.nassaucountyny.gov/agencies/CountyAttorney/index.html

Nassau: Sheriff
516-571-2113
www.nassaucountyny.gov/agencies/Sheriff/index.html

New Rochelle, City of

New Rochelle: City Government
www.newrochelleny.com

New Rochelle: Administrative Agencies
www.newrochelleny.com
(click "City Government")

New Rochelle: Courts
914-654-2207
www.nycourts.gov/courts/9jd/Westchester/NewRochelle.shtml

New Rochelle: Police Department
914-654-2300
www.nrpd.com

New Rochelle: City Code
www.newrochelleny.com
(click "Municipal Code")

New York, City of

(see Bronx County, Kings County, New York County,
Queens County, Richmond County)

New York County

New York: County Government
www.nyc.gov

New York: Administrative Agencies
www.nyc.gov

New York: Courts
www.courts.state.ny.us/courthelp/cfacts2NewYork.html
www.courts.state.ny.us/courts/1jd/index.shtml
*www.courtreference.com/New-York-County-New-York-
    Courts.htm*

New York: District Attorney
212-335-9000
www.manhattanda.org

New York: Public Defender
212-298-5174 (New York County Legal Aid Society)
www.nclas.org/NYPubDef.htm
www.legal-aid.org/en/findus/locations/manhattan.aspx

New York: Consumer Protection
212-NEW-YORK
www.nyc.gov/html/dca/html/home/home.shtml

New York: Child Support Enforcement
888-208-4485; 212-385-8218
www.nyc.gov/html/hra/downloads/pdf/field_offices.pdf
newyorkchildsupport.com/counties/NYC.html

New York: Corporation Counsel
212-788-0303
www.nyc.gov/html/law/html/home/home.shtml

New York: Sheriff
212-788-8731
www.scoc.state.ny.us/sheriffsaddre.htm#New
www.usacops.com/ny/s10017/index.html

Niagara County

Niagara: County Government
www.niagaracounty.com

Niagara: Administrative Agencies
www.niagaracounty.com/departments.asp

Niagara: Courts
716-278-1800
www.courts.state.ny.us/courthelp/cfacts2Niagara.html
www.courts.state.ny.us/courts/8jd/Niagara
*www.courtreference.com/Niagara-County-New-York-
    Courts.htm*

Niagara: District Attorney
716-439-7085
*www.niagaracounty.com/departments.asp?City=
    District+Attorney*

Niagara: Public Defender
716-439-7071
*www.niagaracounty.com/departments.asp?City=
    Public+Defender*

Niagara: Child Support Enforcement
888-208-4485; 716-439-7600
www.niagaracounty.com/departments.asp?City=
Social+Services
https://newyorkchildsupport.com/DCSE/LocalChildOffices.do?
selectDistrictCode=29

Niagara: County Attorney
716-439-7105
www.niagaracounty.com/departments.asp?City=
County+Attorney

Niagara: Sheriff
716-438-3393
www.niagarasheriff.com

Oneida County

Oneida: County Government
ocgov.net

Oneida: Administrative Agencies
ocgov.net/government

Oneida: Courts
www.courts.state.ny.us/courthelp/cfacts2Oneida.html
www.courts.state.ny.us/courts/5jd/oneida
www.courtreference.com/Oneida-County-New-York-Courts.htm

Oneida: District Attorney
315-798-5766
ocgov.net/oneida/distatty

Oneida: Public Defender
315-798-5870; 315-266-6100
ocgov.net/oneida/pdcriminal
ocgov.net/oneida/pdcivil

Oneida: Child Support Enforcement
888-208-4485; 315-798-5048
ocgov.net/oneida/socialservices/childsupport

Oneida: County Attorney
315-798-5910
ocgov.net/oneida/countyattorney

Oneida: Sheriff
315-768-7804
www.oneidacountysheriff.us

Onondaga County

Onondaga: County Government
www.ongov.net

Onondaga: Administrative Agencies
www.ongov.net/departments
www.ongov.net/phoneDirectory.html

Onondaga: Courts
315-671-2111
www.courts.state.ny.us/courthelp/cfacts2Onondaga.html
www.courts.state.ny.us/courts/5jd/onondaga
www.courtreference.com/Onondaga-County-New-York-Courts.htm

Onondaga: District Attorney
315-435-2470; 315-671-1020
www.ongovda.net/section/home
www.ongov.net/departments
(click "District Attorney")

Onondaga: Public Defender
315-476-2921 (assigned counsel)
www.nclas.org/NYPubDef.htm
www.hiscocklegalaid.org

Onondaga: Child Support Enforcement
888-208-4485; 315-435-2560
www.ongov.net/dss/childSupport.html

Onondaga: County Attorney
315-435-2170
www.ongov.net/law/contact.html

Onondaga: Sheriff
315-435-3044
www.ongov.net/Sheriff

Ontario County

Ontario: County Government
www.co.ontario.ny.us

Ontario: Administrative Agencies
www.co.ontario.ny.us
(click entries under "Departments")

Ontario: Courts
585-396-4239
www.courts.state.ny.us/courthelp/cfacts2Ontario.html
www.courts.state.ny.us/courts/7jd/Ontario/index.shtml
www.courtreference.com/Ontario-County-New-York-Courts.htm

Ontario: District Attorney
585-396-4010
www.co.ontario.ny.us/da

Ontario: Public Defender
716-396-2040 (assigned counsel)
www.nclas.org/NYPubDef.htm
www.ontariocountybar.org/FreeAttorney.asp

Ontario: Child Support Enforcement
888-208-4485
www.co.ontario.ny.us/social_services/ChildSupport.html

Ontario: County Attorney
585-396-4411
www.co.ontario.ny.us/co_atty

Ontario: Sheriff
585-394-4560
www.co.ontario.ny.us/sheriff

Orange County

Orange: County Government
845-291-3000
www.co.orange.ny.us

Orange: Administrative Agencies
www.co.orange.ny.us/orgMain.asp?orgid=38&
storyTypeID=&sid=&

Orange: Courts
845-291-3111
www.courts.state.ny.us/courthelp/cfacts2Orange.html
www.courts.state.ny.us/courts/9jd/Orange/index.shtml
www.courtreference.com/Orange-County-New-York-Courts.htm

Orange: District Attorney
845-291-2050
www.co.orange.ny.us/orgMain.asp?orgid=43&
storyTypeID=&sid=&

Orange: Public Defender
845-291-2454 (Legal Aid Society of Orange County)
www.nclas.org/NYPubDef.htm

Orange: Consumer Protection
845-291-2400
www.co.orange.ny.us/orgMain.asp?orgid=83&
storyTypeID=&sid=&

Orange: Child Support Enforcement
888-208-4485; 845-291-4000
www.co.orange.ny.us/orgMain.asp?orgid=55&
storyTypeID=&sid=&
https://newyorkchildsupport.com/DCSE/LocalChildOffices.do?
selectDistrictCode=33

Orange: County Attorney
845-291-3150
www.co.orange.ny.us/orgMain.asp?orgid=91&
storyTypeID=&sid=&

Orange: Sheriff
845-291-4033
www.co.orange.ny.us/orgMain.asp?orgid=86&
storyTypeID=&sid=&

Orleans County

Orleans: County Government
www.orleansny.com

Orleans: Administrative Agencies
www.orleansny.com

Orleans: Courts
585-589-4457
www.courts.state.ny.us/courthelp/cfacts2Orleans.html
www.courts.state.ny.us/courts/8jd/Orleans
www.courtreference.com/
Orleans-County-New-York-Courts.htm

Orleans: District Attorney
585-590-4127
www.orleansny.com/PublicSafety/DistrictAttorney/tabid/68/
Default.aspx

Orleans: Public Defender
585-589-7335
www.orleansny.com/PublicSafety/PublicDefender/tabid/82/
Default.aspx

Orleans: Child Support Enforcement
888-208-4485; 585-589-7000
https://newyorkchildsupport.com/DCSE/LocalChildOffices.do?
selectDistrictCode=34

Orleans: County Attorney
585-798-2250
www.orleansny.com/Legislature/CountyAttorney/tabid/95/
Default.aspx

Orleans: Sheriff
585-589-5527
www.orleansny.com/PublicSafety/Sheriff/tabid/67/
Default.aspx

Oswego County

Oswego: County Government
www.co.oswego.ny.us/govt-home.shtml

Oswego: Administrative Agencies
www.co.oswego.ny.us/govt-home.shtml
(click "County Departments")

Oswego: Courts
315-349-3280
www.courts.state.ny.us/courthelp/cfacts2Oswego.html
www.courts.state.ny.us/courts/5jd/oswego
www.courtreference.com/Oswego-County-New-York-Courts.htm

Oswego: District Attorney
315-349-3200
www.co.oswego.ny.us/da.shtml

Oswego: Public Defender
315-598-2263 (assigned counsel)
www.nclas.org/NYPubDef.htm
www.co.oswego.ny.us/offices.shtml#ca

Oswego: Child Support Enforcement
888-208-4485
www.co.oswego.ny.us/dss/support.html

Oswego: County Attorney
315-349-8290
www.co.oswego.ny.us/offices.shtml#ca

Oswego: Sheriff
315-349-3302
www.co.oswego.ny.us/sheriff.shtml

Otsego County

Otsego: County Government
www.otsegocounty.com

Otsego: Administrative Agencies
www.otsegocounty.com
(click entries under "Dept. Directory")

Otsego: Courts
www.courts.state.ny.us/courthelp/cfacts2Otsego.html
www.courts.state.ny.us/courts/6jd/otsego/index.shtml
www.courtreference.com/Otsego-County-New-York-Courts.htm

Otsego: District Attorney
607-547-4249
www.otsegocounty.com/depts/da

Otsego: Public Defender
607-432-7410
www.otsegocounty.com/depts/pd

Otsego: Child Support Enforcement
888-208-4485; 607-547-4355
www.otsegocounty.com/depts/dss

Otsego: County Attorney
607-547-4208
www.otsegocounty.com/depts/coatty

Otsego: Sheriff
607-547-4271
www.otsegocounty.com/depts/shf

Putnam County

Putnam: County Government
845-225-3641 x200
www.putnamcountyny.com

Putnam: Administrative Agencies
www.putnamcountyny.com
(click "Department Directory")

Putnam: Courts
845-208-7830
www.courts.state.ny.us/courthelp/cfacts2Putnam.html
www.courts.state.ny.us/courts/9jd/Putnam
www.courtreference.com/
   Putnam-County-New-York-Courts.htm

Putnam: District Attorney
845-225-3641 x277
www.naco.org/Template.cfm?Section=Find_a_County&
   Template=/cffiles/counties/county.cfm&id=36079

Putnam: Public Defender
845-225-8466 (Legal Aid Society)
www.nclas.org/NYPubDef.htm

Putnam: Consumer Protection
845-225-2039
www.putnamcountyny.com/consumers

Putnam: Child Support Enforcement
845-225-7040
www.putnamcountyny.com/socialservices/index.htm
https://newyorkchildsupport.com/DCSE/LocalChildOffices.do?
   selectDistrictCode=37

Putnam: County Attorney
845-228-0480
www.putnamcountyny.com/law/index.htm

Putnam: Sheriff
845-225-4300
www.putnamsheriff.com

Queens County

Queens: County Government
www.nyc.gov

Queens: Courts
718-298-1000
www.courts.state.ny.us/courthelp/cfacts2Queens.html
www.courts.state.ny.us/courts/11jd/index.shtml
www.courtreference.com/Queens-County-New-York-Courts.htm

Queens: District Attorney
718-286-6000
www.queensda.org

Queens: Public Defender
718-286-2000 (Queens County Legal Aid Society)
www.nclas.org/NYPubDef.htm
www.legal-aid.org/en/findus/locations/queens.aspx

Queens: Consumer Protection
212-NEW-YORK
www.nyc.gov/html/dca/html/home/home.shtml

Queens: Child Support Enforcement
888-208-4485; 718-739-6231
www.nyc.gov/html/hra/downloads/pdf/field_offices.pdf

Queens: Corporation Counsel
212-788-0303
www.nyc.gov/html/law/html/home/home.shtml

Queens: Sheriff
718-298-7550
www.scoc.state.ny.us/sheriffsaddre.htm
www.usacops.com/ny/s11435/index.html

Rensselaer County

Rensselaer: County Government
www.rensco.com

Rensselaer: Administrative Agencies
www.rensco.com/departments.asp

Rensselaer: Courts
518-270-3710
www.courts.state.ny.us/courthelp/cfacts2Rensselaer.html
www.nycourts.gov/courts/3jd
www.courtreference.com/Rensselaer-County-New-York-
   Courts.htm

Rensselaer: District Attorney
518-270-4040
www.rensco.com/da.asp

Rensselaer: Public Defender
518-270-4030
www.nclas.org/NYPubDef.htm

Rensselaer: Child Support Enforcement
888-208-4485
www.rensco.com/departments_socialservices.asp

Rensselaer: County Attorney
518-270-2950
www.rensco.com/departments_countyattorney.asp

Rensselaer: Sheriff
518-270-5448
www.rensco.com/sheriff.asp

Richmond County

Richmond: County Government
www.nyc.gov

Richmond: Courts
718-876-6411
www.courts.state.ny.us/courthelp/cfacts2Richmond.html
www.courts.state.ny.us/courts/13jd
www.courtreference.com/Richmond-County-New-York-
  Courts.htm

Richmond: District Attorney
718-876-6300
rcda.nyc.gov

Richmond: Public Defender
212-577-3300 (Legal Aid Society)
www.nclas.org/NYPubDef.htm
www.legal-aid.org/en/findus/locations/statenisland.aspx

Richmond: Consumer Protection
212-NEW-YORK
www.nyc.gov/html/dca/html/home/home.shtml

Richmond: Child Support Enforcement
888-208-4485; 718-720-2793
www.nyc.gov/html/hra/downloads/pdf/field_offices.pdf

Richmond: Corporation Counsel
212-788-0303
www.nyc.gov/html/law/html/home/home.shtml

Richmond: Sheriff
718-815-8407
www.usacops.com/ny/s10301/index.html
www.scoc.state.ny.us/sheriffsaddre.htm

Rochester, City of

Rochester: City Government
585-428-5990
www.cityofrochester.gov

Rochester: Administrative Agencies
www.cityofrochester.gov/category.aspx?id=8589935105

Rochester: Courts
www.nycourts.gov/courts/7jd/monroe
www.town-court.com/getTownCourt.php?courtID=1411

Rochester: Corporation Counsel
585-428-6986; 585-428-6990
www.cityofrochester.gov/article.aspx?id=8589934900

Rochester: Police Department
585-428-7033
www.cityofrochester.gov/police

Rochester: Municipal Code
www.nycourts.gov/library/buffalo/municipalcodes.shtml

Rockland County

Rockland: County Government
www.co.rockland.ny.us

Rockland: Administrative Agencies
www.co.rockland.ny.us/departments.htm

Rockland: Courts
845-638-5393
www.courts.state.ny.us/courthelp/cfacts2Rockland.html
www.courts.state.ny.us/courts/9jd/Rockland
www.courtreference.com/
  Rockland-County-New-York-Courts.htm

Rockland: District Attorney
845-638-5001
rocklandcountyda.com

Rockland: Public Defender
845-638-5660
www.co.rockland.ny.us/Defender

Rockland: Consumer Protection
845-708-7600
www.co.rockland.ny.us/cpl

Rockland: Child Support Enforcement
888-208-4485; 845-638-5550
https://newyorkchildsupport.com/DCSE/LocalChildOffices.do?
  selectDistrictCode=39

Rockland: County Attorney
845-638-5180
www.co.rockland.ny.us/Law

Rockland: Sheriff
845-638-5400
www.co.rockland.ny.us/Sheriff

Saratoga County

Saratoga: County Government
518-885-5381
www.saratogacountyny.gov

Saratoga: Administrative Agencies
www.saratogacountyny.gov/departments.asp

Saratoga: Courts
518-885-2224
www.courts.state.ny.us/courthelp/cfacts2Saratoga.html
www.courtreference.com/Saratoga-County-New-York-Courts.htm

Saratoga: District Attorney
518-885-2263
www.jimmurphyda.com

Saratoga: Public Defender
518-884-4795
www.saratogacountyny.gov/departments.asp?did=215

Saratoga: Child Support Enforcement
888-208-4485; 518-884-4142
www.saratogacountyny.gov/subpage.asp?pageid=7

Saratoga: County Attorney
518-884-4770
www.saratogacountyny.gov/departments.asp?did=363

Saratoga: Sheriff
518-885-2450
www.saratogacountyny.gov/departments.asp?did=214

Schenectady, City of

Schenectady: City Government
518-382-5000
www.cityofschenectady.com

Schenectady: Administrative Agencies
www.cityofschenectady.com/departments.html

Schenectady: Courts
518-382-5077
www.nycourts.gov/courts/4jd/schdycty.HTM

Schenectady: Corporation Counsel
518-382-5073
www.cityofschenectady.com/law_department.htm

Schenectady: Police Department
518-382-5200
www.schenectadypd.com

Schenectady: City Code
www.cityofschenectady.com/building_inspector_code.htm
www.generalcode.com/Webcode2.html#newy

Schenectady County

Schenectady: County Government
www.schenectadycounty.com

Schenectady: Administrative Agencies
www.schenectadycounty.com/MenuItemList.aspx?m=3

Schenectady: Courts
518-388-4220
www.courts.state.ny.us/courthelp/cfacts2Schenectady.html
www.courtreference.com/Schenectady-County-New-York-Courts.htm

Schenectady: District Attorney
518-388-4364
www.schenectadycounty.com/MenuItemList.aspx?m=138

Schenectady: Public Defender
518-386-2266
www.nclas.org/NYPubDef.htm

Schenectady: Consumer Protection
518-356-7473
www.schenectadycounty.com/FullStory.aspx?m=99&amid=427

Schenectady: Child Support Enforcement
888-208-4485; 518-388-4470
www.schenectadycounty.com/MenuItemList.aspx?m=110

Schenectady: County Attorney
518-388-4700

Schenectady: Sheriff
518-388-4300
www.schenectadycounty.com/MenuItemList.aspx?m=38

Schoharie County

Schoharie: County Government
518-295-8300
www.schohariecounty-ny.gov/CountyWebSite/index.jsp

Schoharie: Administrative Agencies
www.schohariecounty-ny.gov/CountyWebSite/depts.jsp

Schoharie: Courts
518-295-8383
www.courts.state.ny.us/courthelp/cfacts2Schoharie.html
www.schohariecounty-ny.gov/CountyWebSite/CountyJudge/countyjoffice.jsp
www.courtreference.com/Schoharie-County-New-York-Courts.htm

Schoharie: District Attorney
518-295-2272
www.schohariecounty-ny.gov/CountyWebSite/DistrictAttorney/dahome.jsp

Schoharie: Public Defender
518-295-7515 (assigned counsel)
www.nclas.org/NYPubDef.htm

Schoharie: Child Support Enforcement
518-295-8405
https://newyorkchildsupport.com/DCSE/LocalChildOffices.do?selectDistrictCode=43

Schoharie: County Attorney
518-296-8844
ny.gov/CountyWebSite/CountyAttorney/countyattorneyoffice.html

Schoharie: Sheriff
518-295-8114
www.schohariecounty-ny.gov/CountyWebSite/Sheriff/sheriffservices.jsp

Schuyler County

Schuyler: County Government
www.schuylercounty.us

Schuyler: Administrative Agencies
www.schuylercounty.us

Schuyler: Courts
607-535-7015
www.courts.state.ny.us/courthelp/cfacts2Schuyler.html
www.schuylercounty.us/ccourts.htm
www.courtreference.com/Schuyler-County-New-York-Courts.htm

Schuyler: District Attorney
607-535-8383
www.schuylercounty.us/distattorney.htm

Schuyler: Public Defender
607-535-6400
www.schuylercounty.us/pubdef.htm

Schuyler: Child Support Enforcement
888-208-4485
www.schuylercounty.us/page22.htm

Schuyler: County Attorney
www.schuylercounty.us/ctyatty.htm

Schuyler: Sheriff
607-535-8222
www.schuylercounty.us/sheriff.htm

Seneca County

Seneca: County Government
www.co.seneca.ny.us/gov-index.php

Seneca: Administrative Agencies
www.co.seneca.ny.us/dpt-index.php

Seneca: Courts
315-539-7021
www.courts.state.ny.us/courthelp/cfacts2Seneca.html
www.courts.state.ny.us/courts/7jd/Seneca
www.courtreference.com/Seneca-County-New-York-Courts.htm

Seneca: District Attorney
315-539-1300
www.co.seneca.ny.us/dpt-district-attorney.php

Seneca: Public Defender
315-568-4975
www.co.seneca.ny.us/dpt-public-defender.php

Seneca: Child Support Enforcement
888-208-4485; 315-539-1774
www.co.seneca.ny.us/dpt-divhumserv-support-collection-unit.php

Seneca: County Attorney
315-539-1989
www.co.seneca.ny.us/dpt-cty-attorney.php

Seneca: Sheriff
315-220-3200
www.co.seneca.ny.us/res-sheriffs.php

Steuben County

Steuben: County Government
607-776-9631
www.steubencony.org

Steuben: Administrative Agencies
www.steubencony.org

Steuben: Courts
607-776-7879
www.courts.state.ny.us/courthelp/cfacts2Steuben.html
www.courts.state.ny.us/courts/7jd/steuben
www.courtreference.com/Steuben-County-New-York-Courts.htm

Steuben: District Attorney
607-776-9631
www.steubencony.org/da/distattorney.html

Steuben: Public Defender
607-664-2413; 607-664-2410
www.steubencony.org/pubdef.html

Steuben: Child Support Enforcement
888-208-4485; 607-664-2178
www.steubencony.org/dss.html

Steuben: County Attorney
607-664-2355
www.steubencony.org/lawdept.html

Steuben: Sheriff
800-724-7777; 607-776-7009
www.steubencony.org/Sheriff/sheriffindex1.html

St. Lawrence County

St. Lawrence: County Government
315-379-2276
www.co.st-lawrence.ny.us

St. Lawrence: Administrative Agencies
www.co.st-lawrence.ny.us/Departments

St. Lawrence: Courts
315-379-2219
www.courts.state.ny.us/courthelp/cfacts2St.Lawrence.html
www.courts.state.ny.us/courts/4jd/stlawrence
www.courtreference.com/St-Lawrence-County-New-York-Courts.htm

St. Lawrence: District Attorney
315-379-2225
www.co.st-lawrence.ny.us/District_Attorney/SLCDA.htm

St. Lawrence: Public Defender
315-379-2393
www.co.st-lawrence.ny.us/Public_Defender/SLCPD.htm

St. Lawrence: Child Support Enforcement
315-379-2147
www.co.st-lawrence.ny.us/Departments/SocialServices/
ChildSupport
https://newyorkchildsupport.com/DCSE/LocalChildOffices.do?
selectDistrictCode=40

St. Lawrence: County Attorney
315-379-2269
www.co.st-lawrence.ny.us/County_Attorney/SLCCA.htm

St. Lawrence: Sheriff
315-379-2222
www.co.st-lawrence.ny.us/Sheriff/SLCSHER.htm

Suffolk County

Suffolk: County Government
www.co.suffolk.ny.us

Suffolk: Administrative Agencies
www.co.suffolk.ny.us/departments.aspx

Suffolk: Courts
631-852-1613
www.courts.state.ny.us/courthelp/cfacts2Suffolk.html
www.courts.state.ny.us/courts/10jd/Suffolk
www.courtreference.com/Suffolk-County-New-York-Courts.htm

Suffolk: District Attorney
631-853-4161
www.co.suffolk.ny.us/da

Suffolk: Public Defender
631-854-0401 (Legal Aid Society of Suffolk County)
dpca.state.ny.us/suffolk.htm

Suffolk: Consumer Protection
631-853-4232
www.co.suffolk.ny.us/da/about.htm
www.co.suffolk.ny.us/Home/departments/CountyExec/
consumeraffairs.aspx

Suffolk: Child Support Enforcement
888-208-4485
www.co.suffolk.ny.us/departments.aspx
(click "Social Services" then "Child Support
Enforcement")

Suffolk: County Attorney
631-853-4049
www.co.suffolk.ny.us/departments/countyattorney.aspx

Suffolk: Sheriff
631-852-2200
www.co.suffolk.ny.us/departments/sheriff.aspx

Sullivan County

Sullivan: County Government
845-794-3000
www.co.sullivan.ny.us/orgMain.asp?orgId=43&sid=

Sullivan: Administrative Agencies
www.co.sullivan.ny.us/orgMain.asp?sid=&orgId=297

Sullivan: Courts
845-794-1248
www.courts.state.ny.us/courthelp/cfacts2Sullivan.html
www.nycourts.gov/courts/3jd
www.courtreference.com/Sullivan-County-New-York-
Courts.htm

Sullivan: District Attorney
845-794-3344
co.sullivan.ny.us/orgMain.asp?orgId=543&sId=
www.co.sullivan.ny.us/index.asp?orgid=544&sID=&
storyID=847

Sullivan: Public Defender
845-794-4094 (Sullivan Legal Aid Bureau)
www.nclas.org/NYPubDef.htm

Sullivan: Child Support Enforcement
888-208-4485
https://newyorkchildsupport.com/DCSE/LocalChildOffices.do?
selectDistrictCode=48

Sullivan: County Attorney
845-794-3000 x3565
www.co.sullivan.ny.us/documentView.asp?docid=544

Sullivan: Sheriff
845-794-7100
www.usacops.com/ny/s12701/index.html

Syracuse, City of

Syracuse: City Government
www.syracuse.ny.us

Syracuse: Administrative Agencies
www.syracuse.ny.us
(click entries under "Departments")

Syracuse: Courts
315-671-2700
www.nycourts.gov/courts/5jd/onondaga/syracuse

Syracuse: Department of Law
315-448-8400
www.syracuse.ny.us/Law_Department.aspx?ekmensel=
9050e624_51_0_457_15

Syracuse: Police Department
315-442-5200
www.syracusepolice.org

Syracuse: Municipal Code
www.syracuseut.com/page.php/citygovernment-
ordinances/City-Ordinances.html

Tioga County

Tioga: County Government
www.tiogacountyny.com/government

Tioga: Administrative Agencies
www.tiogacountyny.com/government
(click "Departments")

Tioga: Courts
607-687-0544
www.courts.state.ny.us/courthelp/cfacts2Tioga.html
www.courts.state.ny.us/courts/6jd/tioga
www.courtreference.com/Tioga-County-New-York-Courts.htm

Tioga: District Attorney
607-687-8650
tiogacountyny.com/departments/safety/district_attorney.php

Tioga: Public Defender
607-565-2455
tiogacountyny.com/departments/safety/public_defender.php

Tioga: Child Support Enforcement
888-208-4485; 607-687-8300 (Department of Social Services)
www.tiogacountyny.com/departments/health/social_services

Tioga: County Attorney
607-687-8253
tiogacountyny.com/departments/administration/county_attorney.php

Tioga: Sheriff
607-687-1010
www.tiogacountyny.com/departments/safety/sheriff_dept.php

Tompkins County

Tompkins: County Government
607-274-5551
www.tompkins-co.org

Tompkins: Administrative Agencies
www.tompkins-co.org/departments

Tompkins: Courts
www.courts.state.ny.us/courthelp/cfacts2Tompkins.html
www.courts.state.ny.us/courts/6jd/Tompkins
www.courtreference.com/Tompkins-County-New-York-Courts.htm

Tompkins: District Attorney
607-274-5461
www.tompkins-co.org/distatto

Tompkins: Public Defender
607-272-7487 (assigned counsel)
www.tompkins-co.org/departments/detail.aspx?DeptID=52

Tompkins: Child Support Enforcement
888-208-4485
www.tompkins-co.org/departments/detail.aspx?DeptID=41

Tompkins: County Attorney
607-274-5546
www.tompkins-co.org/ctyattorney

Tompkins: Sheriff
607-257-1345
www.tompkins-co.org/sheriff/division.aspx?sectionID=20

Ulster County

Ulster: County Government
www.co.ulster.ny.us

Ulster: Administrative Agencies
www.co.ulster.ny.us/resources.html

Ulster: Courts
845-340-3377
www.courts.state.ny.us/courthelp/cfacts2Ulster.html
www.co.ulster.ny.us/resources/courts.html
www.courtreference.com/Ulster-County-New-York-Courts.htm

Ulster: District Attorney
845-340-3280
www.co.ulster.ny.us/resources/da.html

Ulster: Public Defender
845-340-3232
www.co.ulster.ny.us/resources/publicdefender.html

Ulster: Consumer Protection
845-340-3260
www.co.ulster.ny.us/resources/da.html#Consumer

Ulster: Child Support Enforcement
888-208-4485
www.co.ulster.ny.us/resources/socservices.html#Child

Ulster: County Attorney
845-340-3685
www.co.ulster.ny.us/resources/attorney.html

Ulster: Sheriff
845-338-3640
www.co.ulster.ny.us/sheriff

Utica, City of

Utica: City Government
www.cityofutica.com/Home

Utica: Administrative Agencies
www.cityofutica.com/Home

Utica: Courts
www.courts.state.ny.us/courts/5jd/Oneida

Utica: Corporation Counsel
315-792-0171
www.cityofutica.com/CorporationCounsel

Utica: Police Department
315-223-3555
www.uticapd.com

Utica: City Code
www.cityofutica.com/Codes

Warren County

Warren: County Government
www.co.warren.ny.us/gov.php

Warren: Administrative Agencies
www.co.warren.ny.us/depts.php

Warren: Courts
518-761-6355
www.courts.state.ny.us/courthelp/cfacts2Warren.html
www.courts.state.ny.us/courts/4jd/warren
www.courtreference.com/Warren-County-New-York-Courts.htm

Warren: District Attorney
518-761-6405
www.co.warren.ny.us/depts.php

Warren: Public Defender
518-761-6460
www.co.warren.ny.us/counsel

Warren: Child Support Enforcement
518-761-6310
www.co.warren.ny.us/depts.php#SOCIALSERVICES

Warren: County Attorney
518-761-6463
www.co.warren.ny.us/depts.php#COUNTYATTORNEY

Warren: Sheriff
518-743-2500
sheriff.co.warren.ny.us/index.html

Washington County

Washington: County Government
www.co.washington.ny.us

Washington: Administrative Agencies
www.co.washington.ny.us/s_phone.htm

Washington: Courts
www.courts.state.ny.us/courthelp/cfacts2Washington.html
www.courts.state.ny.us/courts/4jd/Washing2.htm
www.courtreference.com/Washington-County-New-York-Courts.htm

Washington: District Attorney
518-746-2525
www.co.washington.ny.us/Departments/dao/dao1.htm

Washington: Public Defender
518-747-2823
www.nclas.org/NYPubDef.htm

Washington: Child Support Enforcement
888-208-4485; 518-746-2300
www.co.washington.ny.us/Departments/Dss/cseu.htm

Washington: County Attorney
518-746-2216
www.co.washington.ny.us/s_phone.htm

Washington: Sheriff
518-746-2475
www.co.washington.ny.us/Departments/Lec/shr1.htm

Wayne County

Wayne: County Government
www.co.wayne.ny.us

Wayne: Administrative Agencies
www.co.wayne.ny.us/Departments/depts.htm

Wayne: Courts
315-946-5459
www.courts.state.ny.us/courthelp/cfacts2Wayne.html
www.courts.state.ny.us/courts/7jd/Wayne
www.courtreference.com/Wayne-County-New-York-Courts.htm

Wayne: District Attorney
315-946-5905
www.co.wayne.ny.us/Departments/distattorney/distattorney.htm

Wayne: Public Defender
315-946-7472
www.co.wayne.ny.us/Departments/publicdef/publicdef.htm

Wayne: Child Support Enforcement
888-208-4485; 315-946-4881
www.co.wayne.ny.us/Departments/dss/dss.htm
https://newyorkchildsupport.com/DCSE/LocalChildOffices.do?
selectDistrictCode=54

Wayne: County Attorney
315-946-7442
www.co.wayne.ny.us/Departments/ctyattorney/ctyattorney.htm

Wayne: Sheriff
315-946-9711
www.waynecosheriff.org

Westchester County

Westchester: County Government
www.westchestergov.com

Westchester: Administrative Agencies
www.westchestergov.com/departments.htm

Westchester: Courts
914-824-5300
www.courts.state.ny.us/courthelp/cfacts2Westchester.html
www.courts.state.ny.us/courts/9jd/Westchester
www.courtreference.com/
Westchester-County-New-York-Courts.htm

Westchester: District Attorney
914-995-3414
www.westchesterda.net

Westchester: Public Defender
914-286-3472 (Legal Aid Society of Westchester County)
www.nclas.org/NYPubDef.htm

Westchester: Consumer Protection
914-995-2155
www.westchestergov.com/consumer.htm

Westchester: Child Support Enforcement
888-208-4485; 914-995-5000
www.westchestergov.com/social/default.htm

Westchester: County Attorney
914-995-2660
www.westchesterda.net

Westchester: Public Safety
www.westchestergov.com/departments.htm
(click "Public Safety")

Wyoming County

Wyoming: County Government
www.wyomingco.net

Wyoming: Administrative Agencies
www.wyomingco.net
(click "Departments")

Wyoming: Courts
585-786-3148
www.courts.state.ny.us/courthelp/cfacts2Wyoming.html
www.courts.state.ny.us/courts/8jd/Wyoming
www.courtreference.com/
    Wyoming-County-New-York-Courts.htm

Wyoming: District Attorney
585-786-8822
www.wyomingco.net/DA/main.html

Wyoming: Public Defender
716-591-1600
www.nysda.org/08_Chief_Defender_List2008-08-05.pdf

Wyoming: Child Support Enforcement
585-786-8900
https://newyorkchildsupport.com/DCSE/LocalChildOffices.do?
    selectDistrictCode=56

Wyoming: County Attorney
585-786-8814

Wyoming: Sheriff
585-786-2255
www.wyomingco.net/sherrif_dept/main.html

Yates County

Yates: County Government
www.yatescounty.org

Yates: Administrative Agencies
www.yatescounty.org/display_page.asp?pID=64

Yates: Courts
315-536-5126
www.courts.state.ny.us/courthelp/cfacts2Yates.html
www.courts.state.ny.us/courts/7jd/Yates
www.yatescounty.org/display_page.asp?pID=172
www.courtreference.com/Yates-County-New-York-Courts.htm

Yates: District Attorney
315-536-5550
www.yatescounty.org/display_page.asp?pID=79

Yates: Public Defender
315-536-0352
www.yatescounty.org/display_page.asp?pID=192

Yates: Child Support Enforcement
888-208-4485
www.yatescounty.org/upload/12/dss/frameset.html

Yates: County Attorney
www.yatescounty.org/display_page.asp?pID=77

Yates: Sheriff
315-536-4438
www.yatescounty.org/display_page.asp?pID=86

Yonkers, City of

Yonkers: City Government
914-377-6000
www.cityofyonkers.com

Yonkers: Administrative Agencies
www.cityofyonkers.com
(click "Government")

Yonkers: Courts
www.town-court.com/getTownCourt.php?courtID=418
www.courts.state.ny.us/courts/9jd/Westchester/Yonkers.shtml

Yonkers: Consumer Protection
914-377-3000
www.cityofyonkers.com/Index.aspx?page=239

Yonkers: Corporation Counsel
914-377-6250
www.yonkersny.gov/index.aspx?page=76

Yonkers: Police Department
914-377-7900
www.yonkersny.gov/Index.aspx?page=204

Yonkers: City Code
www.generalcode.com/Webcode2.html#newy

D. More Information

Assessors (Office of Real Property Services)
www.orps.state.ny.us/MuniPro

Child Support
888-208-4485
newyorkchildsupport.com
newyorkchildsupport.com/DCSE/LocalChildOffices.do

Consumer Protection
www.consumer.state.ny.us

County/City Governments
www.nysegov.com/map-NY.cfm
libguides.library.albany.edu/newyorkcounties
www.nysegov.com/citguide.cfm?context=citguide&content=
    munibyalpha

www.wowworks.com/wowcity/ny.htm
www.statelocalgov.net/state-ny.cfm
www.nycom.org
www.nysac.org

County Clerks
www.nytitle.com/faq.ivnu

County History
www.hopefarm.com/nycounty.htm

County Departments of Social Services
www.ocfs.state.ny.us/main/localdss.asp
www.health.state.ny.us/health_care/medicaid/ldss.htm

County Sheriffs
www.nysheriffs.org
oneidacountysheriff.us/main/links.aspx
www.scoc.state.ny.us/sheriffsaddre.htm

County Statistics/Profiles
quickfacts.census.gov/qfd/states/36000.html
www.columbia.edu/cu/lweb/indiv/lehman/guides/stats/ny.html
www.fedstats.gov/qf/states/36000.html

Courts
www.nycourts.gov/litigants/courtguides

District Attorneys
www.daasny.org/Members.html

Domestic Violence Resources
www.opdv.state.ny.us

Health Departments, by County
www.health.state.ny.us/nysdoh/lhu/map

New York Legislative Service
www.nyls.org

Public Defenders
www.nysda.org/08_Chief_Defender_List2008-08-05.pdf
www.nclas.org/NYPubDef.htm
www.nysda.org
www.nycdo.org

Vital Records
www.health.state.ny.us/vital_records

E. **Something to Check**

1. Pick one kind of information pertaining to law and government (e.g., enforcement of the dog leash law). Find the address of where this information would be found in any ten New York counties or cities.
2. For any county you select, identify the kind of information available online about any aspect of real property in that county.

Legal Research and Records Research

A. Introduction

In this section we answer the following question: Where can you find New York primary authority (e.g., cases, statutes) and secondary authority (e.g., legal encyclopedias and treatises) if you need to research an issue of New York law? We will cover both traditional book sources as well as what is available online. For related material, see:

- State courts in New York, including links to their opinions (section 4.2)
- Federal courts in New York, including links to their opinions (section 4.3)
- Citing New York legal materials (section 5.2)
- Research starters for 77 major state law topics (section 5.5)
- Finding New York public records (section 5.7)
- Finding law libraries in your area that often have materials on New York law (section 5.8)
- Finding continuing legal education (CLE) resources in New York (section 1.3)

B. Finding New York State Law

Exhibit 5.1A presents an overview of New York law found in traditional and online sources.

C. Publishers of Materials on New York Law

CaseClerk
www.caseclerk.com

Fastcase
www.fastcase.com

Gould Publications
www.lexisnexis.com/gould

LexisNexis
www.lexisone.com/legalresearch/states/ny.html
www.lexis.com

Loislaw
www.loislaw.com

Looseleaf Law Publications
www.looseleaflaw.com/home

NY Law Journal
law.com/ny

NY Lawyer
nylj.com/nylawyer

New York State Bar Association
www.nysba.org
(click "Publications")

Nolo Press
www.nolo.com

State Net
www.statenet.com

TheLaw.net
thelaw.net

VersusLaw
www.versuslaw.com

West/Thomson
west.thomson.com/store
(type "New York" in the search box)

D. More Information

Online Portals to New York Legal Research
www.ll.georgetown.edu/states/newyork-in-depth.cfm
www.loc.gov/law/help/guide/states/us-ny.html
www.law.cornell.edu/states/ny.html
law-library.rutgers.edu/resources/nyresearch.php
www.law.syr.edu/Pdfs/0NYS%20Research.pdf
www.findlaw.com/11stategov/ny/laws.html
www.lawsource.com/also/usa.cgi?ny
www.aallnet.org/chapter/llagny/ny.html
www.chesslaw.com/newyorklaw.htm
www.hg.org/usstates.html

E. Something to Check

1. Select any three of the sources in section C (Publishers of Materials on New York Law). Find three that sell the same New York materials. Compare what they offer, e.g., description, ease of use, cost.
2. Pick any legal issue (e.g., capital punishment, abortion, equitable distribution). Using the free online materials referred to here, find and briefly summarize one case and one statute on your topic.
3. Use any of the sites to locate a New York legal form that can be used in a family law case.

EXHIBIT 5.1A New York Law on the Shelf and Online

CATEGORY	WHERE TO FIND IT ON THE SHELF	WHERE TO FIND IT ONLINE FOR A FEE	WHERE TO FIND IT ONLINE FOR FREE (complete, partial, or links)

New York Constitution	• *McKinney's Consolidated Laws of New York Annotated* (Book 2)
	• *New York Consolidated Laws Service* (vols. 41C, 42, 42A)
		• Lexis: www.lexis.com
		  NY library, NYCONST file
		• Westlaw: www.westlaw.com
		  NY-ST-ANN database
		• Others: see addresses on p. 214 for Fast-case, Loislaw, TheLaw.net, VersusLaw, StateNet
			• www.dos.state.ny.us/info/constitution.htm
			• www.law.cornell.edu/states/ny.html
			• public.leginfo.state.ny.us/menugetf.cgi?
			  COMMONQUERY=LAWS (click "CNS")
			• www.senate.state.ny.us (click "Senate Rules" and "State Constitution")

New York Statutes or Codes	• *McKinney's Consolidated Laws of New York Annotated* (West Group)
	• *New York Consolidated Laws Service* (LexisNexis)
	• *Gould's Consolidated Laws of New York*
		• Lexis: www.lexis.com
		  NY library, CODE file
		• Westlaw: www.westlaw.com
		  NY-ST-ANN database
		• nyslrs.state.ny.us
		• Others: see addresses on p. 214 for Fastcase, Loislaw, TheLaw.net, VersusLaw, StateNet
			• public.leginfo.state.ny.us/menugetf.cgi
			• public.leginfo.state.ny.us/menugetf.cgi?
			  COMMONQUERY=LAWS
			• www.law.cornell.edu/states/ny.html
			• caselaw.lp.findlaw.com/nycodes

New York Statutes (chapter laws, session laws)	• *Laws of New York* (New York Legislative Bill Drafting Commission)
	• *McKinney's Session Laws of New York* (West Group)
	• *New York Consolidated Laws Service Session Laws* (LexisNexis)
	• *Advanced Legislative Service for the New York Consolidated Laws Service* (LexisNexis)
	• *McKinney's Session Law News of New York* (West Group)
		• Lexis: www.lexis.com
		  NY library, NYALS file
		• Westlaw: www.westlaw.com
		  NY-LEGIS database
		• nyslrs.state.ny.us
			• public.leginfo.state.ny.us/menuf.cgi
			• www.senate.state.ny.us/bills.html

Pending Bills/ Bill Tracking	• *New York State Legislative Annual*
	• *New York Legislative Digest*
	• *New York State Legislative Calendar*
		• Lexis: www.lexis.com
		  NY library NYBILL, TYTRCK files
		• Westlaw: www.westlaw.com
		  NY-BILLS, NY-BILLTRK databases
			• assembly.state.ny.us/leg
			• public.leginfo.state.ny.us/menuf.cgi
			• www.nyls.org
			• www.senate.state.ny.us/bills.html
			• assembly.state.ny.us/leg/?sh=cal

Legislative History	• *State of New York Legislative Digest*
	• *New York Legislative Annual*
		• Lexis: www.lexis.com
		  NY library NYLH file
		• Westlaw: www.westlaw.com
		  NY-LH-BILLJACKET database
			• www.nysl.nysed.gov/leghist
			• www.nyls.org
			• www.law.syr.edu/Pdfs/0NYS%20Leghis.pdf
			• iarchives.nysed.gov/PublmageWeb/listCollections.jsp?id=68007
			• www.pace.edu/page.cfm?doc_id=30027
			• purl.org/net/nysl/nysdocs/49650712
			• www.archives.nysed.gov/aindex.shtml

CATEGORY	WHERE TO FIND IT ON THE SHELF	WHERE TO FIND IT ONLINE FOR A FEE	WHERE TO FIND IT ONLINE FOR FREE (complete, partial, or links)

State Administrative Regulations	• *New York State Register* (New York State Department of State)
	• *Official Compilation of Codes, Rules and Regulations of the State of New York (NYCRR)* (New York State Department of State)
	• Some state administrative agencies publish their administrative decisions online. Examples:
	  - Unemployment insurance (www.labor.state.ny.us/ui/dande/regintro.shtm)
	  - Environmental conservation (www.dec.ny.gov/65.html)
		• *Lexis:* www.lexis.com NY library NYADMN, NYRGST files
		• *Westlaw:* www.westlaw.com NY-ADC database
		• *Others:* see addresses on p. 214 for Fastcase, Loislaw, TheLaw.net, VersusLaw, StateNet
			• www.dos.state.ny.us/info/nycrr.htm (NYCRR)
			• www.dos.state.ny.us/info/register.htm (State Register)
			• www.nyls.org
			• www.state.ny.us/governor (budget, state of the state address)
			• www.labor.state.ny.us/ui/dande/regintro.shtm (example of regulations of an individual agency: unemployment insurance)
			• www.dec.ny.gov/65.html (example of regulations of an individual agency: environmental conservation)
			• www.dos.state.ny.us/info/rulemakingmanual.html

State Administrative Decisions	Examples of published administrative decisions (see Web address in fourth column): • Legal opinions of the Office of the State Comptroller • Decisions of the Commissioner of Education • Decisions of the Department of Environmental Conservation • See also Attorney General Opinions below	• In Lexis, do a library/file search to find out if the administrative decisions of a particular agency are available Example: NY library, NYENV file (decisions of the Department of Environmental Conservation) or NY library, AGEN file • In Westlaw, do a database search to find out if the administrative decisions of a particular agency are available Example: NYENV-ADMIN database (decisions of the Department of Environmental Conservation)	Some state administrative agencies publish their administrative decisions online. Examples: • Legal opinions of the Office of the State Comptroller (www.osc.state.ny.us/legal) • Decisions of the Commissioner of Education (www.counsel.nysed.gov/Decisions) • Decisions of the Department of Environmental Conservation (www.dec.ny.gov/hearings/395.html) • See also Attorney General Opinions below
Executive Orders	• Executive Orders of the Governor of New York	• *Lexis:* www.lexis.com NY library NYADMN, NYRGST files • *Westlaw:* www.westlaw.com NY-ADC database	• www.ny.gov/governor/executive_orders • www.dos.state.ny.us/info/register.htm (State Register) • www.nysl.nysed.gov/statedoc.htm
State Court Opinions of: • **New York Court of Appeals** • **New York Appellate Division** • **Miscellaneous trial courts**	Current opinions: • *New York Reports 3d* (N.Y.3d) (Court of Appeals) • *New York Appellate Division Reports 3d* (A.D.3d) (Appellate Division) • *New York Miscellaneous Reports 3d* (Misc. 3d) (selected trial courts) • *North Eastern Reporter 2nd ed.* (N.E.2d) (Court of Appeals) • *New York Supplement 2nd ed.* (N.Y.S.2d) (all courts)	• *Lexis:* www.lexis.com NY library • *Westlaw:* www.westlaw.com NY-CS database • *Others:* see addresses on p. 214 for Fastcase, Loislaw, TheLaw.net, VersusLaw, StateNet	• www.nycourts.gov/decisions/index.shtml • www.law.cornell.edu/states/ny.html (selected cases) • www.findlaw.com/11stategov/ny/laws.html (selected cases)

CATEGORY	WHERE TO FIND IT ON THE SHELF	WHERE TO FIND IT ONLINE FOR A FEE	WHERE TO FIND IT ONLINE FOR FREE (complete, partial, or links)
Ethics Code	• *New York Lawyer's Code of Professional Responsibility* • *New York Rules of Professional Conduct* (proposed) • *Simon's New York Code of Professional Responsibility Annotated* (West Group)	• Lexis: www.lexis.com NY library, NYCPR, ETHICS files • Westlaw: www.westlaw.com NY-ADC database	• www.nysba.org (click "For Attorneys" then "Professional Standards for Attorneys") • www.abanet.org/cpr/links.html (scroll down to "New York") • www.law.cornell.edu/ethics/ny/code • www.dos.state.ny.us/info/nycrr.htm
Ethics/Disciplinary Opinions	• Ethics opinions, New York State Bar Association Committee on Professional Ethics • Ethics opinions, Bar of the City of New York Committee on Professional and Judicial Ethics • Ethics opinions, New York County Lawyers' Association Committee on Professional Ethics • The Nassau County Bar Association also issues ethics opinions	• Lexis: www.lexis.com ETHICS library, NYBAR, NYCBAR files • Westlaw: www.westlaw.com NYETH-EO, NYETH-CS databases	• www.nysba.org (click "For Attorneys" then "Ethics Opinions") • www.abcny.org (click "Reports/Publications/Forms" then "Ethical Responsibilities and Opinions") • www.nycla.org (click "News & Publications" then "Ethics Opinions") • www.nassaubar.org (under "For the Legal Profession" click "Ethics Opinions")
State Court Rules (Rules of Court)	• McKinney's New York Rules of Court—State and Federal (West Group) • New York Court Rules (in Consolidated Laws Service) (LexisNexis) • Judges' Part Rules (New York Law Journal) • Uniform Rules for N.Y. State Trial Courts • 22 NYCRR (see State Administrative Regulations above)	• Lexis: www.lexis.com NY library NYRULE file • Westlaw: www.westlaw.com NY-RULES database • Others: see addresses on p. 214 for Fastcase, Loislaw, TheLaw.net, VersusLaw, StateNet	• www.courts.state.ny.us/rules/trialcourts/index.shtml (Uniform Rules for N.Y. State Trial Courts) • courts.state.ny.us/rules/index.shtml (Uniform Rules: Standards and Administrative Policies) • www.dos.state.ny.us/info/nycrr.htm (22 NYCRR) • nycourts.law.com/cpnylj/CourtRules.asp (Judges' Part Rules)
Citators	• *Shepard's New York Court of Appeals Citations* • *Shepard's New York Appellate Division Citations* • *Shepard's New York Supreme Court Citations* • *Shepard's New York Miscellaneous Citations* • *Shepard's New York Supplement Citations* • *Shepard's New York Northeastern Citations* • *Shepard's New York Reporter Citations* • *Shepard's New York Statutes Citations*	• Shepard's: www.lexis.com NY Library • KeyCite: www.westlaw.com • Globalcite: Loislaw (see address on p. 214)	

CATEGORY	WHERE TO FIND IT ON THE SHELF	WHERE TO FIND IT ONLINE FOR A FEE	WHERE TO FIND IT ONLINE FOR FREE (complete, partial, or links)
Digests of New York State Court Opinions	• *West's New York Digest 4th* (West Group)	• Westlaw: www.westlaw.com	
New York State Attorney General Opinions	• *Opinions of the New York State Attorney General* (Lenz & Riecker)	• Lexis: www.lexis.com NY library NYAG file • Westlaw: www.westlaw.com NY-AG database	• www.oag.state.ny.us/our_office.html (click "Division of Appeals and Opinions")
Jury Instructions	• *New York Pattern Jury Instructions-Civil* (West) • *New York Criminal Jury Instructions* (Office of Court Administration)	• Westlaw: www.westlaw.com NY-PJI (civil)	• www.nycourts.gov/cji (Criminal Jury Instructions 2nd ed.)
Jury Verdicts	• *National Jury Law Reporter* • *National Jury Review & Analysis*	• Lexis: www.lexis.com VERDICT library NYJURY file • Westlaw: www.westlaw.com LRPNY-JV database	• www.juryverdicts.com/newyork.html • www.verdictsearch.com • www.morelaw.com/newyork
Forms	• Administrative Promulgated Forms found at 22 NYCRR Subchapter D (see State Administrative Rules above) • *West's McKinney's Forms* • *Bender's Forms for the Consolidated Laws of New York* • *Carmody-Wait 2nd ed.: Cyclopedia of New York Practice with Forms* (West)	• Lexis: www.lexis.com NY library • Westlaw: www.westlaw.com McKinney's Forms (MCF-ALL) • Others: see addresses on p. 214 for Fast-case, Loislaw, TheLaw.net, VersusLaw, StateNet	• megalaw.com/forms/ny/nyforms.php • www.courts.state.ny.us/forms • forms.findlaw.com (type "New York" in the search box) • www.llrx.com/courtrules (click "New York")
Local Government Laws (charters, codes, ordinances)	• See section 4.6 for local governments sites, many of which have links to municipal codes, charters, and other local laws	• Lexis: www.lexis.com NY library, NYCMUN, NYCCDE, NYCCHT files CODES library NYMCDE file • Westlaw: www.westlaw.com NYC-MUN, NYC-C, NYC-CODE databases	• www.state.ny.us (click "Government," then "Local Government Information") • www.e-codes.generalcode.com/globalsearch.asp (scroll down to New York entries) • www.generalcode.com (click "State-Specific Resources") • www.nysegov.com/citguide.cfm?context=citguide&content=munibycounty1 **All NY Municipalities:** • www.nysegov.com/citguide.cfm?context=citguide&content=munibyalpha **E-Codes for NYS (selected):** • www.generalcode.com/webcode2.html#newy
State Legal Encyclopedia	• *New York Jurisprudence 2nd ed.* (West) (N.Y. Jur. 2d)	• Lexis: www.lexis.com NY JUR2d database	

CATEGORY	WHERE TO FIND IT ON THE SHELF	WHERE TO FIND IT ONLINE FOR A FEE	WHERE TO FIND IT ONLINE FOR FREE (complete, partial, or links)
Legal Treatises on State Law	Examples: • *New York Practice 4th ed.* by Siegel (West Group) • *New York Civil Practice: CPLR* Weinstein, Korn & Miller 2nd ed. (LexisNexis) • *White on New York Corporations* (LexisNexis) • *Carmody-Wait 2nd ed.: Cyclopedia of New York Practice with Forms* (West Group) • *Harris 5th New York Estates: Probate, Administration, and Litigation* (West Group) • *Criminal Law in New York, 4th ed.* Morris (West Group) • *Warren's Weed New York Real Property, 5th ed.* (LexisNexis) • *New York Civil Appellate Practice, 2nd ed.* by Davies (West Group)	• Lexis: www.lexis.com NY library (search for files on treatises) • Westlaw: www.westlaw.com (search for New York databases on treatises)	
Citation Rules/ Guidelines	• *New York Law Reports Style Manual, Official Edition* (Law Reporting Bureau of the State of New York) • *New York Rules of Citation, 5th ed.* (St. John's Law Review)		• www.courts.state.ny.us/reporter/ New_Styman.htm
Legal Research Manuals/Guides on New York Law	Examples: • *New York Legal Research Guide, 3rd ed.* by Gibson & Manz (2004) • *New York Legal Research* by Adelman & Rowe (Carolina Academic Press)		• See Online Portals to New York Legal Research in More Information on p. 214
Appellate Briefs		• Lexis: www.lexis.com CRTFLS library NYMTBR file • Westlaw www.westlaw.com NY-BRIEF-ALL database	• www.llrx.com/features/briefsonline.htm (scroll down to New York) • www.courts.state.ny.us/courts/ad2/index .shtml (click "Briefs") • decisions.courts.state.ny.us/ad2/search/ queryad2briefs3.asp
Legal Newspapers/ Periodicals	• *New York Law Journal*	• law.com/ny • nylj.com/nylawyer	• law.com/ny (some free content) • nylj.com/nylawyer (some free content)

CATEGORY	WHERE TO FIND IT ON THE SHELF	WHERE TO FIND IT ONLINE FOR A FEE	WHERE TO FIND IT ONLINE FOR FREE (complete, partial, or links)
Blogs on New York law			• New York Paralegal Blog (www.newyork paralegalblog.com) • New York Civil Law (nylaw.typepad.com/new_york_civil_law) • New York Legal Update (www.nylegalupdate.com) • New York Attorney Malpractice Blog (blog.bluestonelawfirm.com) • New York State Bar General Practice Section Blog (nysbar.com/blogs/generalpractice) • New York Federal Criminal Practice Blog (www.nyfederalcriminalpractice.com) • It's No-Fault of NY Blog (nynofaultlaw.blogspot.com) • A Buffalo Lawyer Blog (abuffalolawyer.blogspot.com) More New York Law Blogs: • nylawblog.typepad.com • www.blawg.com
Locating New York attorneys	• *Martindale-Hubbell Law Directory* • *New York Lawyer's Diary & Manual-Bar Directory of State of New York* (Skinder-Strauss Associates)	• Lexis: www.lexis.com MARHUB library NYDIR file • Westlaw: www.westlaw.com WLD-NY database	• iapps.courts.state.ny.us/attorney/ AttorneySearch • www.martindale.com • lawyers.findlaw.com
New York Law Library Catalogs Online			• Unified Court System Library and Information Network Catalogs (LION) (www.courts. state.ny.us/lawlibraries/lion/index.shtml) • Library Catalogs (www.digital-librarian.com/ nystatelaw.html#catalogs) • Columbia Law School (www.law.columbia.edu/library) • New York Law School (lawlib.nyls.edu) • New York University Law School (julius.law.nyu.edu)
Ask a New York Librarian (submit a legal research question on New York law)			• www.nycourts.gov/lawlibraries/ document-service.shtml • iapps.courts.state.ny.us/ad4lib/ ask_librarian.jsp • www.loc.gov/rr/askalib • www.loc.gov/rr/askalib/ask-law.html • www.nypl.org/questions • library.nyu.edu/ask

---

> **5.2 Citation Examples: Some Comparisons**
> A. Introduction
> B. Comparison of Citation Formats
> C. More Information
> D. Something to Check

A. Introduction

There are three major citation systems, the first two of which are the most prominently used in New York:

Citation System Explained	Abbreviation Used Here
New York Law Reports Style Manual (New York State Law Reporting Bureau, 2007 ed.) (*www.courts.state.ny.us/reporter/ New_Styman.htm*)	Style Manual
The Bluebook: A Uniform System of Citation (Columbia Law Review Ass'n et al., eds., 18th ed. 2005)	Bluebook
ALWD Citation Manual: A Professional System of Citation (3d ed., Aspen Publishers, 2006) (Ass'n of Legal Writing Directors & Darby Dickerson)	ALWD

The Style Manual is prepared by the New York State Law Reporting Bureau and approved by the state's highest court, the New York Court of Appeals. The Style Manual contains the required format for state court opinions and the preferred format for submissions to state courts. For matters not covered in the Style Manual, writers should consult other sources such as the Bluebook and the ALWD Manual. In New York practice, the most widely consulted source after the Style Manual is the Bluebook.

There is considerable similarity in how these systems cite laws and other categories of materials. Yet there are some important differences you should know about. In this section, we will give examples of citations using all three systems. As you compare the examples, make careful note of large differences (e.g., how words are abbreviated and in what order they are used) as well as seemingly small ones (e.g., the use of spaces and commas).

Assumptions about the examples used in this section:

- The examples based on the Style Manual assume that the citations are contained in a brief or other writing that will be submitted to a state court in New York. Hence the name of the state (New York) does not always have to be repeated. For example, in a brief filed in the New York Court of Appeals, the citation Penal Law § 156.20 will be understood to refer to New York Penal Law § 156.20.

- When New York (N.Y.) is specifically mentioned in a Bluebook or ALWD example, it will be because the cite is contained in a brief or other writing that will be submitted to a court outside New York.

- The examples based on the Style Manual consist of citations found after a complete sentence or in a list. Hence they are completely within parentheses. A different citation format is often used for citations found within a sentence (referred to as "citations in running text").

- Abbreviations used in all the citation examples are covered in section 5.3.

B. Comparison of Citation Formats

New York Constitution

Style Manual:	(NY Const, art VI, § 35)
Bluebook:	N.Y. Const. art. VI, § 35
ALWD:	N.Y. Const. art. VI, § 35

New York Statutes

Style Manual:	(Domestic Relations Law § 236[B][6])
Bluebook:	N.Y. Dom. Rel. Law § 236(B)(6) (McKinney 2009)
ALWD:	N.Y. Dom. Rel. Law § 236(B)(6) (McKinney 2009)

New York Administrative Code

(Official Compilation of Codes, Rules and Regulations of the State of New York—often referred to as the New York Code of Rules and Regulations)

Style Manual:	(12 NYCRR 23-1.7[b][1])
Bluebook:	N.Y. Comp. Codes R. & Regs. tit. 12, § 23-1.7(b)(1) (2009)
ALWD:	12 N.Y. Comp. Codes, R. & Reg. 23-1.7(b)(1) (2009)

New York Court Opinions

New York Court of Appeals

Style Manual:	(Tropea v Tropea, 87 NY2d 727 [1996])
Bluebook:	Tropea v. Tropea, 665 N.E.2d 145 (N.Y. 1996)
ALWD:	Tropea v. Tropea, 665 N.E.2d 145 (N.Y. 1996)

New York Appellate Division

Style Manual:	(People v Mead, 27 AD3d 767 [2006])

Bluebook: People v. Mead, 815 N.Y.S.2d 616 (App. Div. 2006)

ALWD: People v. Mead, 815 N.Y.S.2d 616 (App. Div. 2d Dept. 2006)

New York Trial Courts

Style Manual: (Gidina Partners LLC v Marco, 11 Misc 3d 21 [2005])

Bluebook: Gidina Partners LLC v. Marco, 811 N.Y.S.2d 859 (Sup. Ct. 2005)

ALWD: Gidina Partners LLC v. Marco, 811 N.Y.S.2d 859 (Sup. Ct. 2005)

United States Supreme Court

Style Manual: (Sansone v United States, 380 U.S. 343 [1965])

Bluebook: Sansone v. United States, 380 U.S. 343 (1965)

ALWD: Sansone v. U.S., 380 U.S. 343 (1965)

United States Court of Appeals for the Second Circuit

Style Manual: (Fowlkes v Adamec, 227 F.3d 36 [2d Cir 2000])

Bluebook: Fowlkes v. Adamec, 227 F.3d 36 (2d Cir. 2000)

ALWD: Fowlkes v. Adamec, 227 F.3d 36 (2d Cir. 2000)

United States District Court in New York

Style Manual: (United States v Gotti, 219 F. Supp. 2d 296 [E.D. N.Y. 2002])

Bluebook: United States v. Gotti, 219 F. Supp. 2d 296 (E.D. N.Y. 2002)

ALWD: U.S. v. Gotti, 219 F. Supp. 2d 296 (E.D. N.Y. 2002)

New York Attorney General Opinions

Style Manual: (1999 Ops Atty Gen No. F 99-3)

Bluebook: N.Y. Att'y Gen. Op. No. F 99-3 (1999)

ALWD: N.Y. Atty. Gen. Op. F 99-3 (1999)

New York Rules of Court

Style Manual: (Rules of Prac of the Ct of Appeals [22 NYCRR] § 500.21)

Bluebook: N.Y. Comp. Codes R. & Regs. tit. 22, § 500.21 (2003)

ALWD: 22 N.Y. Comp. Codes, R. & Regs. 500.21 (2003)

Law Reviews

Style Manual: (Applegate, The Perils of Unreasonable Risk: Information, Regulatory Policy, and Toxic Substances Control, 91 Colum. L. Rev. 261 [1991])

Bluebook: John S. Applegate, The Perils of Unreasonable Risk: Information, Regulatory Policy, and Toxic Substances Control, 91 Colum. L. Rev. 261 (1991)

ALWD: John S. Applegate, The Perils of Unreasonable Risk: Information, Regulatory Policy, and Toxic Substances Control, 91 Colum. L. Rev. 261 (1991)

Encyclopedias

Style Manual: (12 NY Jur 2d, Buildings, Zoning, and Land Controls § 377)

Bluebook: 12 N.Y. Jur. 2d Buildings, Zoning, and Land Controls § 377 (2006)

ALWD: 12 N.Y. Jur. 2d Buildings, Zoning, and Land Controls § 377 (2006)

Treatises

Style Manual: (Siegel, NY Prac § 194, [3d ed])

Bluebook: David D. Siegel, New York Practice § 194 (3d ed. 2006)

ALWD: David D. Siegel, New York Practice § 194 (3d ed., West Group, 2006)

Dictionaries

Style Manual: (Black's Law Dictionary 101 [8th ed 2004])

Bluebook: Black's Law Dictionary 101 (8th ed. 2004)

ALWD: Black's Law Dictionary 101 (Bryan A. Garner ed., 8th ed., West 2004)

C. More Information

New York Law Reports Style Manual
www.courts.state.ny.us/reporter/New_Styman.htm

ALWD Citation
www.alwd.org
www.alwd.org/publications/second_edition_resources.html
(click "Appendix 2" and scroll down to "New York")

Bluebook Citation
www.law.cornell.edu/citation

Comparison Between Bluebook and ALWD
www.legalcitation.net
www.cooley.edu/library/research_guides/
   Bluebook_ALWD0809.pdf
www.alwdmanual.com/books/dickerson_alwd/updates/
   ALWD-Bluebook%20Comparison%20Charts.pdf

Citation in General
www.csulb.edu/library/eref/vref/style.html
freedomlaw.com/LegCitations.html

Cite-Checking
lib.law.washington.edu/ref/citecheck.html

Universal Citation Guide
www.aallnet.org/committee/citation/ucg/appe-index.html
(click "New York")

Citation and Style Manuals
www.law.cornell.edu/citation
www.abanet.org/tax/pubs/ttl/ttlstyle.pdf
www.bgsu.edu/colleges/library/assistance/page39954.html
www.bgsu.edu/colleges/library/assistance/page39964.html

Other Citation Systems
www.bedfordstmartins.com/online/citex.html

New York Law Reporting Bureau
www.courts.state.ny.us/reporter

Official Name and Citation Locator
iapps.courts.state.ny.us/lawReporting/SearchCitation

Wikipedia on Citation
en.wikipedia.org/wiki/Case_citation

D. Something to Check

According to the *New York Law Reports Style Manual*, what errors in format do you see in the following citations:

1. (N.Y. Const. Art III, sec. 17.)
2. (N.Y. Domestic Rel. L. § 24.)
3. (N.Y. Code of Regs. Tit. 9, § 218.)
4. (Davis v. Davis (1997) 31 N.Y.2d 344 657.)
5. (Hepter v. Jason (2001) 70 AD2d 819.(2nd Dept.)
6. (59 Ops. N.Y. Atty. Gen. 181 (1989).)

7. (New York Rules of Court, Rule 200.1.)
8. (David Ray, Court Injunctions, 67 Columbia L. Rev. 598 (1999).)
9. (34 N.Y. Jur. 2d (2000) § 7 Adverse Possession.)
10. (William Stern, Restraint of Trade, § 33, p. 122 (2d ed. 1988.)

5.3 Abbreviations in Citations
A. Introduction
B. Abbreviation Differences
C. More Information
D. Something to Check

A. Introduction

As we saw in section 5.2, there are three major citation systems: *New York Law Reports Style Manual* (Style Manual), *The Bluebook: A Uniform System of Citation* (Bluebook), and *ALWD Citation Manual: A Professional System of Citation* (ALWD). The first two are most common in New York.

One important citation concern is the abbreviation of words and phrases in legal writing. The three citation systems do not always agree on how something should be abbreviated or whether something should be abbreviated at all. In this section, we will compare how the three systems abbreviate important words and phrases. Our focus will be on those abbreviations that *differ* among any one of the three systems, although for major entries we will show the abbreviations even if all three systems agree. Note that often the only difference is a letter, a space, an apostrophe, or a period.

B. Abbreviation Differences

	New York Style Manual	Bluebook	ALWD
Administrator	Adm'r	Adm'r	Administr.
Advertising	Adv.	Adver.	Advert.
Affidavit	Aff	Aff.	Aff.
affirmed	affd	aff'd	aff'd
affirming	affg	aff'g	
American Jurisprudence	Am Jur	Am. Jur.	Am. Jur.
American Jurisprudence Second	Am Jur 2d	Am. Jur. 2d	Am. Jur. 2d
American Law Reports 6th	ALR6th	A.L.R.6th	A.L.R.6th
American Law Reports Federal	ALR Fed	A.L.R. Fed.	A.L.R. Fed.
Appellate Division Reports 1st Series	App Div	App. Div.	App. Div.

Appellate Division Reports 2d Series	AD2d	A.D. 2d	A.D. 2d
Appellate Division Reports 3d Series	AD3d	A.D. 3d	A.D. 3d
article	art	art.	art.
Association	Assn.	Ass'n	Assn.
Atlantic	A	A.	A.
Atlantic 2d	A2d	A.2d	A.2d
Attorney	Atty	Att'y	Atty.
Buffalo Law Review	Buff L Rev	Buff. L. Rev.	Buff. L. Rev.
Central	Cent.	Cent.	C.
certiorari	cert	cert.	cert.
certiorari denied	cert denied	cert. denied	cert. denied
certiorari granted	cert granted	cert. granted	cert. granted
chapter	ch.	ch.	ch.
Circuit	Cir	Cir.	Cir.
Civil Practice Law and Rules	CPL	C.P.L.R.	Civ. Prac. L. R.
clause	cl	cl.	cl.
Commission	Commn.	Comm'n	Commn.
Committee	Comm.	Comm.	Comm.
Columbia Law Review	Colum L Rev	Colum. L. Rev.	Colum. L. Rev.
Cornell Law Review	Cornell L Rev	Cornell L. Rev.	Cornell L. Rev.
County	County	County	Co.
Court of Claims Reports	NY Ct Cl	N.Y. Ct. Cl.	N.Y. Ct. Cl.
Court of Appeals	Ct App	Ct. App.	App.
Criminal Procedure Law	CPLR	Crim. Proc. Law	Crim. P.L.
Department	Dept.	Dep't	Dept.
Distributing	Distrib.	Distrib.	Distribg.
Division	Div	Div.	Div.
doing business as	doing business as	d/b/a	d/b/a
edition	ed	ed.	ed.
Eminent Domain Procedure Law	EDPL	Em. Dom. Proc. Law	Em. Dom. P.L.
Environmental Conservation Law	ECL	Envtl. Conserv. Law	Envtl. Conserv. L.
Estates, Powers and Trusts Law	EPTL	Est. Powers & Trusts Law	Est. Powers & Trusts L.
Executor	Ex'r	Ex'r	
Executrix	Ex'x	Ex'x	Execx.
Family Court Act	Family Ct Act	Fam. Ct. Act	Fam. Ct. Act
Federal Reporter First Series	F	F.	F.
Federal Reporter Second Series	F2d	F.2d	F.2d
Federal Reporter Third Series	F3d	F.3d	F.3d
Federal Supplement	F Supp	F. Supp.	F. Supp.
Federal Supplement Second	F Supp 2d	F. Supp. 2d	F. Supp. 2d
footnote	n	n.	n.
footnotes	nn	nn.	nn.
Fordham Law Review	Fordham L Rev	Fordham L. Rev.	Fordham L. Rev.
Hun's Supreme Court Reports	Hun	Hun	
Institution	Inst.	Inst.	Instn.
International	Intl.	Int'l	Intl.
judgment		judm't	judm.
Legal	Legal	Legal	Leg.
Lawyers' Edition	L Ed	L. Ed.	L. Ed.
Lawyers' Edition Second	L Ed 2d	L. Ed. 2d	L. Ed. 2d
Library	Lib.	Libr.	Lib.

Management	Mgt.	Mgmt.	Mgt.
Memorial	Mem.	Mem'l	Meml.
Miscellaneous Reports	Misc	Misc.	Misc.
Miscellaneous Reports 2d Series	Misc 2d	Misc. 2d	Misc. 2d
Miscellaneous Reports 3d Series	Misc 3d	Misc. 3d	Misc. 3d
modified	mod	modified	modified
Monthly	Monthly	Monthly	Mthy.
Municipal Court	Mun Ct.	Mun. Ct.	Mun. Ct.
National	Natl.	Nat'l	Natl.
New York City Civil Court Act	NY City Civ Ct Act	N.Y. City Civ. Ct. Act	N.Y. City Civ. Ct. Act
New York City Criminal Court Act	NY City Crim Ct Act	N.Y. City Crim. Ct. Act	N.Y. City Crim. Ct. Act
New York Jurisprudence	NY Jur	N.Y. Jur.	N.Y. Jur.
New York Jurisprudence Second	NY Jur 2d	N.Y. Jur. 2d	N.Y. Jur. 2d
New York Law Journal	NYLJ	N.Y.L.J.	N.Y.L.J.
New York Reports	NY	N.Y.	N.Y.
New York Reports 2d Series	NY2d	N.Y.2d	N.Y.2d
New York Reports 3d Series	NY3d	N.Y.3d	N.Y.3d
New York State Court of Claims Reports	NY Ct Cl	N.Y. Ct. Cl.	N.Y. Ct. Cl.
New York Supplement	NYS	N.Y.S.	N.Y.S.
New York Supplement 2d Series	NYS2d	N.Y.S.2d	N.Y.S.2d
New York University Law Review	NYU L Rev	N.Y.U. L. Rev.	N.Y.U. L. Rev.
Opinion	Op	Op.	Op.
Opinion of the Attorney General	Ops Atty Gen No.	N.Y. Att'y Gen. Op. No.	N.Y. Atty. Gen. Op.
paragraph	para	para.	para.
paragraphs	para	paras.	paras.
petition	petition	pet.	pet.
Real Property Actions and Proceedings Law	RPAPL	R.P.A.P.L.	R.P.A.P.L.
Real Property Tax Law	RPTL	R.P.T.L.	R.P.T.L.
rehearing denied	reh denied	reh'g denied	
reversed	revd	rev'd	rev'd
Supreme Court Reporter	S Ct	S. Ct.	S. Ct.
Supreme Court Reporter, Lawyers Edition	L Ed	L. Ed.	L. Ed.
Supreme Court Reporter, Lawyers Ed. 2d	L Ed 2d	L. Ed. 2d	L. Ed. 2d
title	tit.	tit.	tit.
Uniform Commercial Code	UCC	U.C.C.	U.C.C.
University	Univ.	Univ.	U.
U.S. Court of Appeals, Federal Circuit	Fed Cir	Fed. Cir.	Fed. Cir.
U.S. Court of Appeals, Second Circuit	2d Cir	2d Cir.	2d Cir.
U.S. Court of Federal Claims	Fed Cl	Fed. Cl.	Fed. Cl.
U.S. District Court Eastern District	ED NY	E.D.N.Y.	E.D.N.Y.
U.S. District Court Northern District	ND NY	N.D.N.Y.	N.D.N.Y.
U.S. District Court Southern District	SD NY	S.D.N.Y.	S.D.N.Y.
U.S. District Court Western District	WD NY	W.D.N.Y.	W.D.N.Y.
U.S. Tax Court	TC	T.C.	Tax

C. More Information

(See also the sources listed for More Information at the end of section 5.1 on citation rules.)

New York Law Reports Style Manual
www.courts.state.ny.us/reporter/New_Styman.htm

Citation and Abbreviation Sites
www.law.cornell.edu/citation
www.llrx.com/columns/reference37.htm
www.aallnet.org/sis/lisp/cite.htm
lib.law.washington.edu/pubs/acron.html
www.ulib.iupui.edu/subjectareas/gov/docs_abbrev.html

Legal Citation Guides and Abbreviation Lists
www.law.harvard.edu/library/research/guides/citation_guides.html

Abbreviations and Acronyms
www.acronymfinder.com
www.all-acronyms.com

New York Police Department Abbreviations
www.n2nov.net/nypdabbr.html

Comparison Between Bluebook and ALWD
www.tjeffersonlrev.org/Resources/comparisonchart.pdf
www.alwdmanual.com/books/dickerson_alwd/updates/ALWD-Bluebook%20Comparison%20Charts.pdf

D. Something to Check

1. Open any law book, e.g., a school textbook, a court reporter, a statutory code. Find any three abbreviations used in this book that do *not* conform with the New York Style Manual or Bluebook. Explain the discrepancies.

2. Use the examples and other material in sections 5.2 and 5.3 to determine if there are any improper abbreviations in the following citations according to the New York Style manual:
   (a) People v. Davis (1998) 253 A.D.2d 634, 677 NYS2d 541 (NY)
   (b) Civil Proc Sec 244
   (c) 35 Columb. Law Re. 226.
   (d) Jones v. Commish. Of Social Services, 133 New York 2d 344 (Court of Appeals)

5.4 Abbreviations for Notetaking

A. Introduction
B. Notetaking Abbreviations
C. More Information

A. Introduction

There are many settings in which paralegals must be able to write quickly. Examples include notetaking while:

- In class
- Studying school textbooks
- Conducting legal research
- Receiving instructions from a supervisor
- Interviewing a client or witness
- Listening to a deposition witness give testimony
- Listening to a trial witness give testimony

Using abbreviations in such settings can be helpful. This section presents some commonly used abbreviations in the law. Some entries have more than one abbreviation, e.g., c/a and coa for cause of action. When a choice is available, pick an abbreviation with which you are comfortable.

These abbreviations are for use in notetaking, *not for use in citations or formal writing*. (For abbreviations in citations, see section 5.3.) The primary purpose of the following abbreviations is to help you take notes that only you will read. Hence feel free to try out, adapt, and add to the following list.

B. Notetaking Abbreviations

a action
A Atlantic Reporter (or answer)
A2d Atlantic Reporter Second
aa administrative agency
a/b appellate brief
ABA American Bar Association
a/c appellate court
ACD adjournment in contemplation of dismissal
acct account
acctg accounting
ad administrative decision
AD Appellate Division
admr administrator
ADR alternate dispute resolution
aff affirmed
a/g attorney general
agt agent
aka also known as
alj administrative law judge
amt amount
ans answer
aple appellee

aplt appellant
app appeal
appee appellee
appnt appellant
apt apartment
ar administrative regulation
a/r assumption of the risk
ASAP as soon as possible
assn association
atty attorney
b business
b. born
b/4 before
ba bar association
bankr bankruptcy
b/c because
bd board
betw/ between
bfp bona fide purchaser
b/k breach of contract
bldg building
b/p burden of proof
bus business
b/w breach of warranty
© consideration
¢ complaint
c. about (circa)
ca court of appeals

CA2 Second Circuit
c/a cause of action
→ causes, results in
cc child custody
CC Circuit Court
c/c counterclaim
CCA Court of Claims Act
c-dr creditor
c/e cross examination
cert certiorari
cf compare
ch chapter
CiCt Circuit Court
c/l common law
cle continuing legal
    education
co company (or county)
coa cause of action
coi court ordered
    investigation
comm committee
commn commission
commr commissioner
compl complaint
    (or compliance)
conf conference
con law constitutional law
consv conservative
cont continued
corp corporation
cp community property
CPL Criminal Procedure
    Law
CPLR Civil Practice
    Laws & Rules
CPU child protective unit
cr criminal (or creditor)
cr-c criminal court
cs child support (or
    closing statement)
CSSA Child Support
    Standards Act
ct court
cty county
cv civil
cy calendar year
CyCt county court
cz cause
Δ defendant
d danger (or dangerous)
d. died (or death)
DA district attorney
DAT desk appearance
    ticket
dba doing business as
DC district court
d/e direct examination

decrg decreasing
depo deposition
dept department
df defendant
dist district
div division
dkt docket
dmg damages
DMV Department of
    Motor Vehicles
dob date of birth
dod date of death
dom date of marriage
d-r debtor
DSS Department of
    Social Services
DT deed of trust
dv domestic violence
= equals
e evidence
ebt examination before
    trial (deposition)
e/d eminent domain
ee employee
eg example
egs examples
18-b court appointed
    attorney
EIS environmental
    impact statement
emp employment
encon NYS Department
    of Environmental
    Conservation
eng engineer
    (or engineering)
ent enterprise
eq equity
eqbl equitable
er employer
est estimate (or estab-
    lished or estate)
ev evidence
exr executor
f fact
F Federal Reporter
F2 Federal Reporter
    Second
F3 Federal Reporter Third
faq frequently asked
    questions
FC Family Court
FCA Family Court Act
1st Dept. Appellate Divi-
    sion, First Department
4cb foreseeable
fed federal

fn footnote
FOIL freedom of
    information law
4th Dept. Appellate
    Division, Fourth
    Department
FRAP Federal Rules of
    Appellate Procedure
FRCP Federal Rules of
    Civil Procedure
FRCrP Federal Rules of
    Criminal Procedure
FRE Federal Rules of
    Evidence
fs facts
f-st federal statute
fy fiscal year
g govern
g/r general rule
gt government
gvt government
h husband
hb House Bill
hdc holder in due course
HR House of
    Representatives
hrg hearing
HUD-1 settlement
    statement of HUD
i interest
IAS individual assignment
    system
ij injury
immig immigration
in interest
inc incorporated
incrg increasing
indl individual
indp independent
info information
inj injunction (or injury)
ins insurance
intl international
i-p in personam
i-r in rem
IRC Internal Revenue
    Code
IRS Internal Revenue
    Service
J judge (justice or
    judgment)
JC Juvenile Court
jd juvenile delinquent
j/d judgment for
    defendant
jj judges (or justices)
jp justice of the peace

j/p judgment for plaintiff
jt judgment (or joint)
jud judicial (or judge)
jur jurisdiction
juv juvenile
jxn jurisdiction
K contract
l liable (or liability)
< less than (or smaller
    than)
l/h legislative history
liab liability (or liable)
lit litigation
ll limited liability
l/l landlord
llc limited liability
    company
llp limited liability
    partnership
LN Lexis-Nexis
lr legal research
ltd limited
Lx Lexis
max maximum
MC Municipal Court
mem memorial
mfr manufacturer
mfg manufacturing
mgf maternal grandfather
mgm maternal
    grandmother
mgmt management
min minimum
misc miscellaneous
mj major
mkt market
mo majority opinion
> more than (or greater
    than)
mtg mortgage (or
    meeting)
mtge mortgagee
mtgr mortgagor
mtn motion
mun municipal
MV-104 DMV accident
    report form
mva motor vehicle
    accident
n/a irrelevant, not
    applicable
natl national
negl negligence
≠ not equal
NOH notice of hearing
nt nothing (or note
    or not)

ntry notary
number
NYCCCA NYC Criminal Court Act (or NYC Civil Court Act)
NYCRR NY Code of Rules and Regulations
NYSBA New York State Bar Association
° degree
O owner
oa opposing attorney
obj object (or objective)
o/b/o on behalf of
oc opposing counsel
OC Orphan's Court
OCA Office of Court Administration
occ occupation
oee offeree
oer offeror
ol online
oop order of protection
op opinion
π plaintiff
p plaintiff
p. page
p/c proximate cause
pee promise
pet petition
petr petitioner
p/f prima facie
pg page
pgf paternal grandfather
pgm paternal grandmother
pgs pages
PINS person in need of supervision
pj personal judgment
pl plaintiff
PL public law
pol practice of law
por promisor
pp pages (or public policy)
p/r personal representative
prft People are ready for trial
priv private
PSI presentence investigation
pub public
pub-op public opinion

pvg privilege
pvt private
Q equity (or equitable)
QC quitclaim
? question
?d questioned
r regulation
® reasonable
re real estate (or regarding)
rec record
rec'd received
reg regulation
rel related to
rep representative (or representation)
← results from, is produced by
rev reverse
revd reversed
rf respondent father
RJI request for judicial intervention
rm respondent mother
r/o restraining order
roc rules of court
rogs interrogatories
ros right of survivorship
RP-5217 Real Property Transfer Report
RPAPL Real Property Actions and Procedure Law
RPC Rules of Professional Conduct
rr railroad
rsb reasonable
s sum
S statute
$ suppose
SB Senate Bill
s/b should be
sc supreme court
SCPA Surrogate's Court Procedure Act
SCR State Central Register of Child Abuse
SCU Support Collections Unit (DDS)
2C Second Circuit
2nd Dept. Appellate Division, Second Department

secy secretary
s/f statute of frauds
s-h self-help
Sh Shepard's Citations (or shepardize)
Sh-z shepardize
s/j summary judgment
s/l statute of limitations (or strict liability)
smj subject-matter jurisdiction
sn/b should not be
soc society
SOL statute of limitations
SOP service of process
SOS secretary of state
ss sections
s-st state statute
st something (or sometimes)
Stat United States Statutes at Large
stats statistics
std standard
st-st state statute
sub substantial
subj subject (or subjective)
t testimony
/ therefore (or per)
∴ therefore
T tort
t/c trial court
tee trustee
t/m testimony
3rd Dept. Appellate Division, Third Department
30.30 speedy trial (CPL § 30.30)
toop temporary order of protection
tp third party
tpr termination of parental rights
tro temporary restraining order
trp trespass (or trespasser)
u understanding
U university
uc unemployment compensation
ucc Uniform Commercial Code

UCCA Uniform Justice Court Act
UDCA Uniform District Court Act
UGMA Uniform Gifts to Minors Act
ui unemployment insurance
UJCA Uniform Justice Court Act
usc United States Code
ussc United States Supreme Court
UTMA Uniform Transfer to Minors Act
utt uniform traffic ticket
v versus (or against)
vs against (or versus)
VTL Vehicle & Traffic Law
V&T Vehicle & Traffic Law
w wife
w/ with
wc workers' compensation
WD warranty deed
w/i within
w/in within (or with interest)
WL Westlaw
w/o without
x cross (or times)
xe cross examination
→ causes, results in
← results from, is produced by
© consideration
¢ complaint
Δ defendant
= equals
≠ not equal
< less than (or smaller than)
> more than (or greater than)
number
π plaintiff
+ plus
? question
?d questioned
® reasonable
$ suppose
**** therefore (or per)
∴ therefore
x cross (or times)
18-b court appointed attorney

C. More Information

Taking Notes
www.nyls.edu/pages/3083.asp

Abbreviations
lib.law.washington.edu/pubs/acron.html
www.llrx.com/columns/reference37.htm
www.aboutlawschools.org/law/resources/legalabbreviations
www.abbreviations.com
www.acronymfinder.com
www.all-acronyms.com

5.5 Research Starters for 78 Major New York Topics
A. Introduction
B. Abbreviations
C. Topics Covered
D. Research Starter Cites
E. More Information
F. Something to Check

A. Introduction

Often in legal research, the first hurdle is finding your first lead. You need a *starting point* that will guide you into the various categories of case law, statutory law, administrative law, etc. You may also need a lead to a secondary authority such as a legal treatise or legal encyclopedia that will provide an overview of an area of the law that may be new to you. In this section, we provide you with such leads to 78 major topics of New York law. They are *starter cites* in the sense that they may lead you—directly or indirectly—to what you need.

See also the following related areas of the book:

- Section 4.5 (state agencies, offices, and boards)
- Section 5.1 (legal research in New York law)
- Section 5.6 (self-help resources on New York law)
- Section 5.7 (public records research)

B. Abbreviations

The starter cites use the following abbreviations for the legal materials covered:

CW2d: Carmody-Wait Second Series, New York Practice with Forms

NYD: New York Official Digest (the NYD will lead you to key numbers within the WestGroup digest system, both in print and on WESTLAW)

NYCRR New York Codes, Rules and Regulations

NY JUR2d: New York Jurisprudence 2d (the legal encyclopedia of New York law)

Statutory Abbreviations

AGM Agriculture & Markets Law
BNK Banking Law
BSC Business Corporation Law
CCA New York City Civil Court Act
CNT County Law
CPL Criminal Procedure Law
CRC New York City Criminal Court Act
CTC Court of Claims Act
CVP Civil Practice Law & Rules Law
CVR Civil Rights Law
CVS Civil Service Law
DOM Domestic Relations Law
ENV Environmental Conservation Law
EPT Estates, Powers & Trusts Law
EXE Executive Law
FCA Family Court Act
GBS General Business Law
GCT General City Law
GMU General Municipal Law
GOB General Obligations Law
ISC Insurance Law
JUD Judiciary Law
LAB Labor Law
LEG Legislative Law

LLC Limited Liability Company Law
PAR Parks, Recreation and Historic Preservation Law
PBH Public Health Law
PBL Public Lands Law
PBS Public Service Law
PEN Penal Law
PEP Personal Property Law
PTR Partnership Law
RPA Real Property Actions & Proceedings Law
RPP Real Property Law
RPT Real Property Law
SAP State Administrative Procedure Act
SCP Surrogate Court Procedure Act
SOS Social Services Law
STF State Finance Law
TAX Tax Law
TWN Town Law
UCC Uniform Commercial Code
UCT Uniform City Court Act
UDC Uniform District Court Act
UJC Uniform Justice Court Act
VAT Vehicle & Traffic Law
TWN Village Law
WKC Workers' Compensation Law

C. Topics Covered

Abortion
Administrative Law
Adoption
Affidavits
Alimony
Annulment
Appeal and Error
Arbitration
Attorney-Client Privilege
Attorneys
Banking
Child Custody
Child Support
Civil Procedure
Commercial Code
Constitutional Law
Consumer Protection
Contracts
Corporations
Courts in New York
Criminal Law

Damages
Deeds
Discovery
Divorce
Domestic Violence
Employment
Employment Discrimination
Enforcement of Judgment
Environment
Equitable Distribution
Equity
Estates
Evidence
Family Law
Fraud
Garnishment
Government
Guardianship
Illegitimacy
Injunctions
Insurance

Intellectual Property
Labor Relations
Landlord and Tenant
Legal Separation
Limited Liability Companies
Marriage
Mediation
Medical Malpractice
Mineral, Water, and Fishing
   Rights
Minors
Mortgages
Motor Vehicles
Negligence
Notary Public
Paralegals
Partnerships
Pleading
Power of Attorney

Privacy
Privileged Communications
Products Liability
Real Property
Service of Process
Statute of Frauds
Statute of Limitations
Summary Judgment
Summons
Taxation
Torts
Traffic Laws
Trusts
Unemployment Insurance
Venue
Water Rights
Wills
Workers' Compensation

D. Research Starter Cites

Abortion

Statutes: EXC § 291; PBH §§ 17, 4161, 4164; PEN §§ 125.05, 125.40–125.60; CPL § 700.5; CVR §79-i; JUD § 4
Regulations: 10 NYCRR §§ 86-4.13, 753.1, 756; 14 NYCCR § 27.6; 18 NYCCR §§ 361.4, 505.2, 505.13
Cases: NYD: check Abortion and Birth Control, key numbers (☞) 100 et seq.
Encyclopedia: NY JUR2d: Constitutional Law § 369; Criminal Law § 566; Domestic Relations § 309
Carmody-Wait Link: CW2d § 147:146
Internet:
law.findlaw.com/state-laws/abortion/new-york
www.prochoiceny.org
megalaw.com/ny/top/nyfamily.php

Administrative Law

Statutes: SAP §§ 100, 201, 301
Regulations: 19 NYCRR 400 (Administrative Procedure Act)
Cases: NYD: check Administrative Law and Procedure, key numbers (☞) 1 et seq.
Encyclopedia: NY JUR2d: check Administrative Law; Article 78
Carmody-Wait: CW2d §§ 2:326, 145:58, 145:181
Internet:
www.dos.state.ny.us/info/nycrr.htm (New York Code of Regulations)
www.gorr.state.ny.us/RegulatoryReform/rulemakingprocess.htm (The Rule Making Process)

Adoption

Statutes: DOM § 109
Regulations: 18 NYCRR § 421.3
Cases: NYD: check Adoption, key numbers (☞) 1 et seq.

Encyclopedia: NY JUR2d: check Domestic Relations §§ 584 et seq.
Carmody-Wait: CW2d §§ 1:4, 1:7, 111:3 et seq.
Internet:
www.ocfs.state.ny.us/adopt

Affidavits

Statutes: CVP §§ 4520, 4531
Regulations: 6 NYCRR § 647.1 (affidavit defined)
Cases: NYD: check Affidavits, key numbers (☞) 1 et seq.
Encyclopedia: NY JUR2d: check Acknowledgement §§ 36, 42 et seq.
Carmody-Wait: CW2d § 4:16
Internet:
www.ilrg.com/forms/affidavit-gen/us/tx (form purchase)
www.megalaw.com/ny/top/nycivpro.php

Alimony (Spousal Support)

Statutes: DOM §§ 236 Part A, 241, 246, 247; FCA Article 4
Regulations: 18 NYCRR § 347.10; 20 NYCRR § 202.16
Cases: NYD: check Divorce, key numbers (☞) 208 et seq. (Temporary Alimony), 230 (Permanent Alimony)
Encyclopedia: NY JUR2d: check Domestic Relations §§ 965, 999, 1000
Carmody-Wait: CW2d §§ 2:208, 13:206, 25:58, 64:49
Internet:
www.nycourts.gov/ip/matrimonial-matters
www.megalaw.com/ny/top/nyfamily.php

Annulment

Statutes: DOM §§ 7, 140–146, 244
Regulations: 22 NYCRR §§ 144.3, 202.6
Cases: NYD: check Marriage, key numbers (☞) 56 et seq.
Encyclopedia: NY JUR2d: check Domestic Relations §§ 178, 996, 1980, 2371
Carmody-Wait: CW2d §§ 13:200, 39:173, 91:47
Internet:
www.nycourts.gov/ip/matrimonial-matters
www.megalaw.com/ny/top/nyfamily.php

Appeal and Error

Statutes: JUD §§ 70, 140; CVP §§ 5501, 5601, 5701; CPL §§ 450.10, 460.10, 470.05
Regulations: 22 NYCRR §§ 600, 670, 800
Cases: NYD: check Appeal and Error, key numbers (☞) 1 et seq.
Encyclopedia: NY JUR2d: check Appellate Review
Carmody-Wait: CW2d Chapter 2 (Courts and Their Jurisdiction)
Internet:
www.nycourts.gov/ctapps
www.courts.state.ny.us/courts/appellatedivisions.shtml
www.megalaw.com/ny/top/nycivpro.php

Arbitration (Alternative Dispute Resolution)

Statutes: CVP §§ 7501 et seq.
Regulations: 22 NYCRR § 28.1
Cases: NYD: check Alternative Dispute Resolution, key numbers (☞) 110 et seq.; Labor Relations, key numbers (☞) 1517 et seq.
Encyclopedia: NY JUR2d: check Arbitration and Award
Carmody-Wait: CW2d §§ 2:43, 2:195, 63:531, 141.1 et seq.
Internet:
www.adr.org
www.megalaw.com/ny/top/nycivpro.php

Attorney-Client Privilege

Statutes: CVP §§ 4503, 4548
Cases: NYD: check Witnesses, key numbers (☞) 197 et seq.
Encyclopedia: NY JUR2d: check Evidence and Witnesses §§ 864 et seq.
Carmody-Wait: CW2d §§ 3:383, 64:320, 149:546
Internet:
public.leginfo.state.ny.us/menugetf.cgi?COMMONQUERY =LAWS
(type "attorney client privilege" in the search box)

Attorneys

Statutes: JUD § 90, CVP § 9401
Regulations: 22 NYCRR §§ 1200.0–1200.59
Cases: NYD: check Attorney and Client, key numbers (☞) 197 et seq.
Encyclopedia: NYJUR2d: check Attorneys at Law
Carmody-Wait: CW2d §§ 3:88, 3:249
Internet:
www.nysba.org
www.courts.state.ny.us/attorneys
iapps.courts.state.ny.us/attorney/AttorneySearch

Banking

Statutes: BNK §§ 2 et seq.
Regulations: 3 NYCRR §§ 1.1 et seq.
Cases: NYD: check Banks and Banking, key numbers (☞) 1 et seq.
Encyclopedia: NY JUR2d: check Banks and Financial Institutions
Carmody-Wait: CW2d §§ 29:33, 165:752
Internet:
www.banking.state.ny.us
www.hg.org/law-firms/Banking-Law/USA-New-York.html
topics.law.cornell.edu/wex/banking

Child Custody

Statutes: DOM §§ 75 et seq., FCA Articles 5, 6
Regulations: 18 NYCRR §§ 347.1 et seq.
Cases: NYD: check Child Custody, key numbers (☞) 1 et seq.

Encyclopedia: NY JUR2d: check Domestic Relations §§ 332 et seq.
Carmody-Wait: CW2d §§ 2:148, 111:276
Internet:
courts.state.ny.us/courthelp/faqs/childcustody.html
www.ocfs.state.ny.us/main
www.megalaw.com/ny/top/nyfamily.php

Child Support

Statutes: DOM §§ 240, FCA Article 4
Regulations: 18 NYCRR §§ 347.1 et seq.
Cases: NYD: check Child Support, key numbers (☞) 1 et seq.
Encyclopedia: NY JUR2d: check Domestic Relations §§ 521, 897
Carmody-Wait: CW2d §§ 2:142, 2:147, 67:10, 118:88 et seq.
Internet:
newyorkchildsupport.com
appsext8.dos.state.ny.us/csewarrants_public/cse_search
www.child-support-laws-state-by-state.com
www.megalaw.com/ny/top/nyfamily.php

Civil Procedure

Statutes: CVP §§ 101 et seq.
Regulations: 19 NYCRR 400 (Administrative Procedure Act)
Cases: NYD: check the vols. for Appeal and Error, key numbers (☞) 1 et seq.; Equity, key numbers (☞) 1 et seq.; Limitations of Actions, key numbers (☞) 1 et seq.; Pretrial Procedure, key numbers (☞) 1 et seq.; Trial, key numbers (☞) 1 et seq.; Witnesses, key numbers (☞) 1 et seq.
Encyclopedia: NY JUR2d: check Actions, Appellate Review, Article 78 and Related Proceedings, Courts and Judges, Evidence and Witnesses, Pleading, Process and Papers, Trial
Carmody-Wait: CW2d Chapter 2 (Courts and Their Jurisdiction), Chapter 8 (Motions and Orders), Chapter 9 (Actions and Proceedings), Chapter 27 (General Rules of Pleadings)
Internet:
www.megalaw.com/ny/top/nycivpro.php
law.lib.buffalo.edu/PDFs/nys/NYCivPro.pdf

Commercial Code

Statutes: UCC §§ 1-101 et seq.
Regulations: 3 NYCRR §§ 34.4, 41.1; 11 NYCRR 187.1; 19 NYCRR §§ 143-1.1 et seq.
Cases: NYD: check the vols. for Bills and Notes, key numbers (☞) 1 et seq.; Sales, key numbers (☞) 1 et seq., Secured Transactions, key numbers (☞) 1 et seq.
Encyclopedia: NY JUR2d: check Uniform Commercial Code
Carmody-Wait: CW2d §§ 19:201, 29:147, 84:64, 84:68

Internet:
www.dos.state.ny.us/corp/ucc.html
www.law.cornell.edu/uniform/nyucc.html
www.nysegov.com/citGuide.cfm?superCat=28

Constitutional Law, State

Cases: NYD: check Constitutional Law, key numbers
(☞) 500 et seq.
Encyclopedia: NY JUR2d: check Constitutional Law
Carmody-Wait: CW2d §§ 2:3, 2:126, 2:203, 24:3
Internet:
www.senate.state.ny.us/lbdcinfo/senconstitution.html

Consumer Protection

Statutes: EXE § 550; GBS § 349-a; PBS § 224-a;
VAT § 468
Regulations: 9 NYCRR § 5.45; 13 NYCRR § 300.1
(Lemon Law Arbitration Program); 21 NYCRR
§ 4600.1 (State Consumer Protection Board)
Cases: NYD: check Antitrust and Trade Regulation,
key numbers (☞) 1 et seq.; Consumer Credit, key
numbers (☞) 1 et seq.
Encyclopedia: NY JUR2d: check Automobiles;
Bailments; Consumer and Borrower Protection;
Uniform Commercial Code
Carmody-Wait: CW2d §§ 13:39, 126:100 et seq.
Internet:
www.consumer.state.ny.us (Consumer Protection Board)
www.oag.state.ny.us/our_office.html

Contracts

Statutes: GOB §§ 5-101; UCC §§ 2-201
Cases: NYD: check the vols. for Contracts, key numbers
(☞) 1 et seq.; Sales, key numbers (☞) 1 et seq.
Encyclopedia: NY JUR2d: check Contracts; Uniform
Commercial Code
Carmody-Wait: CW2d §§ 10:17, 3:537

Corporations

Statutes: BSC §§ 101 et seq.
Regulations: 20 NYCRR § 1-2.5
Cases: NYD: check the vols. for Corporations, key
numbers (☞) 1 et seq.; Securities Regulation,
key numbers (☞) 1 et seq.
Encyclopedia: NY JUR2d: check Business Relationships
(Corporations)
Carmody-Wait: CW2d § 121:453
Internet:
www.dos.state.ny.us/corp/corpwww.html
www.nysegov.com/citGuide.cfm?superCat=28

Courts in New York

Statutes: NY Const, Art. VI, §§ 1, 4, 6; JUD §§ 51, 70,
140; CTC; FCA; CCA; CRC; SCP; UCT; UDC; UJC

Regulations: 22 NYCRR §§ 500.1, 600.1 (1st Dept.),
670.1 (2d Dept.), 800.1 (3d Dept.), 1000.1 (4th Dept.)
Cases: NYD: check Courts, key numbers (☞) 1 et seq.
Encyclopedia: NY JUR2d: check Courts and Judges
Carmody-Wait: CW2d § 2:1
Internet:
www.courts.state.ny.us (Unified Court System)
www.nycourts.gov/ctapps (Court of Appeals)
www.courts.state.ny.us/courts/trialcourts.shtml (Trial Courts)

Criminal Law

Statutes: CPL §§ 1.00 et seq.; PEN §§ 1.00 et seq.
Regulations: 9 NYCRR §§ 525.1 (Crime Victims
Board), 6170.5 (victim compensation)
Cases: NYD: check the vols. for Criminal Law, key
numbers (☞) 1 et seq.; Sentencing and Punishment,
key numbers (☞) 1 et seq.
Encyclopedia: NY JUR2d: check Criminal Law: Procedure,
Criminal Law: Substantive Principles
Carmody-Wait: CW2d § 1:3
Internet:
www.oag.state.ny.us (state attorney general)
www.nysda.org (NYS Defenders Association)
www.docs.state.ny.us (Department of Corrections)
www.cvb.state.ny.us (Crime Victims Board)
www.megalaw.com/ny/top/nycriminal.php

Damages

Statutes: GOB § 11-100; CVP § 1411
Cases: NYD: check Damages, key numbers (☞)
1 et seq.
Encyclopedia: NY JUR2d: check Damages
Carmody-Wait: CW2d §§ 2:232, 13:82

Deeds (see also Real Property)

Statutes: RPP § 258 (Short Form Deed)
Cases: NYD: check the vols. for Deeds, key numbers
(☞) 1 et seq.
Encyclopedia: NY JUR2d: check Deeds
Carmody-Wait: CW2d §§ 13:99, 29:379, 64:178
Internet:
www.tenant.net/Other_Laws/RPL/rpltoc.html
www.orps.state.ny.us/home/varp_index.cfm (Office of
Real Property)

Discovery

Statutes: CVP § 3101
Regulations: 12 NYCRR § 68.18
Cases: NYD: check Pretrial Procedure, key numbers
(☞) 11 et seq.
Encyclopedia: NY JUR2D: check Administrative Law
§ 246, Article 78 § 323, Courts and Judges § 256,
Criminal Law: Procedure § 883

Carmody-Wait: CW2d §§ 13:215 et seq., 39:78
Internet:
www.megalaw.com/ny/top/nycivpro.php

Divorce

Statutes: DOM §§ 170, 210
Cases: NYD: check the vols. for Divorce, key numbers
(☞) 1 et seq.; Husband and Wife, key numbers (☞)
1 et seq.
Encyclopedia: NY JUR2d: check Domestic Relations
Law, §§ 2154 et seq.
Carmody-Wait: CW2d §§ 63:251, 91:47
Internet:
www.courts.state.ny.us/courthelp/faqs/divorce.html
www.divorcelawinfo.com/states/ny/newyork.htm
www.courts.state.ny.us/ip/matrimonial-matters/forms.shtml
www.health.state.ny.us/vital_records (Office of Vital
Records)
www.megalaw.com/ny/top/nyfamily.php

Domestic Violence (see also Criminal Law, Family Law)

Statutes: CPL § 530.11; EXC § 575; FCA Article 8,
Article 10; PEN § 60.12; SOS § 459-a
Regulations: 9 NYCRR §§ 525.30, 525.31 (victim
compensation); 18 NYCRR §§ 408.1
Cases: NYD: check Breach of the Peace, key number
(☞) 15; Criminal Law, key numbers (☞) 474.4(3)
et seq.
Encyclopedia: NY JUR2D: check Criminal Law § 114;
Domestic Relations §§ 364, 387; Public Welfare § 173
Carmody-Wait: CW2d §§ 2:213, 188A:65
Internet:
www.opdv.state.ny.us (NYS Office for Prevention of
Domestic Violence)
www.nyscadv.org (NYS Coalition Against Domestic
Violence)
www.megalaw.com/ny/top/nyfamily.php

Employment

(see Employment Discrimination, Labor Relations,
Workers' Compensation)

Employment Discrimination

Statutes: NY Constitution, Art. 1 § 11; EXC §§ 290 et seq.
Regulations: 9 NYCRR § 4.154
Cases: NYD: check Civil Rights, key numbers (☞)
1101 et seq.
Encyclopedia: NY JUR2D: check Civil Rights
§§ 28 et seq.
Carmody-Wait: CW2d § 38:24
Internet:
www.dhr.state.ny.us (NYS Division of Human Rights)
www.labor.state.ny.us/workerprotection/wp_index.shtm

Enforcement (Execution) of Judgment

Statutes: CVP § 5201; GOB § 12-109
Regulations: 22 NYCRR § 212.39 (Uniform Rules
for the District Courts)
Cases: NYD: check Judgment, key numbers (☞)
1 et seq.; Execution, key numbers (☞) 1 et seq.
Encyclopedia: NY JUR2D: check Enforcement and
Execution of Judgments; Judgments
Carmody-Wait: CW2d §§ 64:1 et seq.
Internet:
www.courts.state.ny.us/Ithaca/city/webpageJudgement.html
www.megalaw.com/ny/top/nycivpro.php

Environment (see also Mineral, Water, and Fishing Rights)

Statutes: ENV §§ 1-0101 et seq.
Regulations: CCR: see title 6 (Dept. of Environmental
Conservation)
Cases: NYD: check Environmental Law, key numbers
(☞) 1 et seq.
Encyclopedia: NY JUR2D: check Environmental Rights
and Remedies; Fish and Wildlife § 24
Internet:
www.dec.ny.gov (NYS Dept. of Environmental
Conservation)
www.oag.state.ny.us/bureaus/environmental/about.html
www.megalaw.com/ny/top/nyenvironmental.php

Equitable Distribution (see also Divorce)

Statutes: DOM § 236
Cases: NYD: check Divorce (Alimony, Allowances, and
Disposition of Property), key numbers (☞) 248 et seq.
Encyclopedia: NY JUR2D: Domestic Relations
§§ 2606 et seq.
Carmody-Wait: CW2d §§ 42:273, 113.181, 114:321,
147:127
Internet:
www.divorcelawinfo.com/states/ny/newyork.htm
www.divorceinfo.com/nyfaqspropertydivision.htm
www.megalaw.com/ny/top/nyfamily.php

Equity

Statutes: CVP § 103; RPP § 270; SCP § 1810;
UCC § 1-103
Cases: NYD: check Equity, key numbers (☞) 1 et seq.
Encyclopedia: NY JUR2D: check Equity
Carmody-Wait: CW2d §§ 2:16, 9:2
Internet:
www.megalaw.com/ny/top/nycivpro.php

Estates (see also Real Property; Wills)

Statutes: EPT §§ 1-2.6 (definition), 13-1.1;
SCP §§ 2101 et seq.
Regulations: 20 NYCRR § 119.1 (estate tax)

Cases: NYD: check the vols. for Estates in Property, key numbers (☞) 1 et seq.; Wills, key numbers (☞) 1 et seq.
Encyclopedia: NY JUR2D: check Decedents' Estates; Estates, Powers, and Restraints on Alienation; Trusts
Carmody-Wait: CW2d § 2:130
Internet:
www.megalaw.com/ny/top/nyprobate.php
www.tax.state.ny.us/pdf/2008/et/et85_708.pdf
(NYS Estate Tax form)
www.courts.state.ny.us/courthelp/forms.html
(Surrogate Court forms)

Evidence (see also Civil Procedure)

Statutes: CVP §§ 4501 et seq.; CPL §§ 50.10, 60.10 et seq.
Regulations: 10 NYCRR § 51.11; 12 NYCRR § 65.29
Cases: NYD: check the vols. for Evidence, key numbers (☞) 1 et seq.; Trial (☞) 32 et seq.; Witnesses, key numbers (☞) 1 et seq.
Encyclopedia: NY JUR2D: check Evidence and Witnesses
Carmody-Wait: CW2d §§ 8:146, 56:11 et seq.
Internet:
www.megalaw.com/ny/top/nycivpro.php

Family Law (see also Child Custody, Child Support)

Statutes: DOM § 1; FCA §§ 211 et seq.
Regulations: 4 NYCRR § 21.3 (Sick Leave); 18 NYCRR § 453.1 (Domestic Violence)
Cases: NYD: check the vols. for Child Custody, key numbers (☞) 1 et seq.; Child Support, key numbers (☞) 1 et seq.; Divorce, key numbers (☞) 1 et seq.; Husband and Wife, key numbers (☞) 1 et seq.; Marriage, key numbers (☞) 1 et seq.
Encyclopedia: NY JUR2D: check Domestic Relations
Carmody-Wait: CW2d §§ 2:142 et seq.
Internet:
www.megalaw.com/ny/top/nyfamily.php
www.courts.state.ny.us/courthelp/forms.html (Forms Library)
www.law.syr.edu/Pdfs/2NYFamilyLaw.pdf

Fraud (see also Criminal Law, Torts)

Statutes: WKC § 114 (Penalties for fraudulent workers' comp claims); UCC § 5-109; DOM § 7 (Voidable marriages); SOS § 134-b; GBS § 349-c (Additional civil penalty for consumer fraud against the elderly)
Regulations: 3 NYCRR § 38.8 (banking license); 10 NYCRR § 98-1.21 (HMOs); 11 NYCRR § 86.1 (insurance); 18 NYCRR §§ 348.1 (Social Services), 399.1 (Food Stamp Fraud); 20 NYCRR § 416.4 (Tax fraud)
Cases: NYD: check Fraud, key numbers (☞) 1 et seq.
Encyclopedia: NY JUR2D: check Fraud and Deceit

Carmody-Wait: CW2d § 13:202
Internet:
www.oag.state.ny.us/bureaus/consumer_frauds/about.html
www.megalaw.com/ny/top/nycriminal.php

Garnishment (see also Enforcement of Judgment)

Statutes: ISC § 7414; PEP § 46(8)
Regulations: 18 NYCRR § 346.11 (Child support enforcement)
Cases: NYD: check Garnishment, key numbers (☞) 1 et seq.
Encyclopedia: NY JUR2D: check Creditors' Rights and Remedies §§ 18 et seq.; Domestic Relations § 1114
Carmody-Wait: CW2d §§ 64:19, 64:23, 64:276

Government (see also Administrative Law, Courts)

Statutes: EXC § 1 et seq.; LEG §§ 1 et seq.; GMU §§ 1 et seq.; GCT §§ 1 et seq.; JUD §§ 1 et seq.; CNT §§ 1 et seq.; MHR §§ 1; STL §§ 1 et seq.; TWN §§ 1 et seq.; VIL §§ 1-100 et seq.
Regulations: title 9 (Executive Dept.); title 13 (Dept. of Law); title 19 (Dept. of State); title 22 (Judiciary)
Cases: NYD: check the vols. for Municipal Corporations, key numbers (☞) 1 et seq.; Officers and Public Employees, key numbers (☞) 1 et seq.; States, key numbers (☞) 1 et seq.
Encyclopedia: NY JUR2D: check Administrative Law; Counties, Towns, and Municipal Corporations; Government Tort Liability; State of New York
Internet:
www.nysl.nysed.gov/ils
www.govspot.com/state/ny.htm

Guardianship

Statutes: DOM § 80; SOS §§ 383-c, 384, 384-b; SCP §§ 1701, 1750
Regulations: 18 NYCRR § 421.1 (definition)
Cases: NYD: check Guardian and Ward, key numbers (☞) 1 et seq.
Encyclopedia: NY JUR2D: check Courts and Judges, §§ 763, 772; Domestic Relations §§ 622 (Court-appointed guardian), 1254 (Law Guardians)
Carmody-Wait: CW2d § 13:369
Internet:
www.cqc.state.ny.us/advocacy/pagrdfaq.htm
www.cqc.state.ny.us/advocacy/guardianshipforms/guardfrm.htm (forms)
www.courts.state.ny.us/courthelp/forms.html
www.nysarc.org/family/nysarc-family-guardianships.asp
www.megalaw.com/ny/top/nyfamily.php

Illegitimacy

Statutes: DOM § 24; SOS § 384-c
Regulations: 18 NYCRR § 301.2(b)

Cases: NYD: check Children Out-of-Wedlock, key numbers (☞) 1 et seq.
Encyclopedia: NY JUR2D: check Domestic Relations § 708
Carmody-Wait: CW2d § 111:28
Internet:
www.megalaw.com/ny/top/nyfamily.php

Injunctions

Statutes: CVP § 6301; CVS § 211; LAB §§ 358-a, 807 et seq.
Regulations: 9 NYCRR §§ 465.9, 2526.3
Cases: NYD: check Injunction, key numbers (☞) 1 et seq.
Encyclopedia: NY JUR2D: check Injunctions
Internet:
www.megalaw.com/ny/top/nycivpro.php

Insurance

Statutes: ISC §§ 101 et seq.
Regulations: Title 11 (Insurance Dept.)
Cases: NYD: check Insurance, key numbers (☞) 1 et seq.
Encyclopedia: NY JUR2D: check Insurance
Carmody-Wait: CW2d § 13:137
Internet:
www.ins.state.ny.us (Department of Insurance)
www.ins.state.ny.us/regclinx.htm

Intellectual Property

Statutes: GBS §§ 360-a, 550; PBA §§ 3102-b, 3152
Regulations: 11 NYCRR § 16.12
Cases: NYD: check Copyrights and Intellectual Property, key numbers (☞) 1 et seq.; Patents, key numbers (☞) 1 et seq.; Trademarks, key numbers (☞) 1 et seq.
Encyclopedia: NY JUR2D: check Declaratory Judgment § 142; Domestic Relations § 128; Patents
Carmody-Wait: CW2d: § 78:67
Internet:
www.nyipla.org

Labor Relations (see also Employment Discrimination, Workers' Compensation)

Statutes: LAB §§ 700 et seq. (Labor Relations Act)
Regulations: 12 NYCRR §§ 250.1 et seq. (Labor Relations Board)
Cases: NYD: check Labor and Employment, key numbers (☞) 1 et seq.
Encyclopedia: NY JUR2D: check Employment Relations
Carmody-Wait: CW2d: §§ 80:9, 80:19
Internet:
www.labor.state.ny.us (Dept. of Labor)
www.goer.state.ny.us (Office of Employee Relations)
www.perb.state.ny.us (Public Employee Relations Board)

Landlord and Tenant

Statutes: RPA § 711; RPP §§ 220 et seq.
Regulations: 9 NYCRR §§ 5.53, 1630-4.3, 2107.1, 2206.7
Cases: NYD: check Landlord and Tenant, key numbers (☞) 1 et seq.
Encyclopedia: NY JUR2D: check Landlord and Tenant
Carmody-Wait: CW2d: §§ 2:167, 13:142, 147:114
Internet:
www.oag.state.ny.us/bureaus/consumer_frauds/housing_ issues.html
www.megalaw.com/ny/top/nylandlord.php

Legal Separation

Statutes: DOM §§ 200, 210
Cases: NYD: check Husband and Wife, key numbers (☞) 26 et seq.; Divorce, key number (☞) 314
Encyclopedia: NY JUR2D: check Domestic Relations § 1914
Carmody-Wait: CW2d: §13:204
Internet:
www.courts.state.ny.us/courthelp/faqs/divorce.html
www.megalaw.com/ny/top/nyfamily.php

Limited Liability Companies (see also Corporations)

Statutes: LLC §§ 101 et seq.
Regulations: 3 NYCRR § 6.9(c); 20 NYCRR § 3-13.2 (Tax)
Cases: NYD: check Limited Liability Companies, key numbers (☞) 1 et seq.
Encyclopedia: NY JUR2D: check Business Relations § 1994
Carmody-Wait: CW2d: §§ 24:147, 92:177, 112:30, 126:44
Internet:
www.dos.state.ny.us/corp/llpfile.html
www.dos.state.ny.us/corp/newlegislation2006.html
www.nysegov.com/citGuide.cfm?superCat=28

Marriage (see also Family Law)

Statutes: DOM §§ 5 et seq.
Regulations: 10 NYCRR § 35.1 (Vital Records)
Cases: NYD: check Marriage, key numbers (☞) 1 et seq.
Encyclopedia: NY JUR2D: check Domestic Relations §§ 1 et seq.
Carmody-Wait: CW2d: §§ 9:22, 13:200
Internet:
www.health.state.ny.us/vital_records/married.htm
www.health.state.ny.us/vital_records
marriage.about.com/cs/marriagelicenses/p/newyork.htm
www.megalaw.com/ny/top/nyfamily.php

Mediation

Statutes: JUD § 39-a; FCA § 1018; LAB § 702-a
Regulations: 12 NYCRR § 275.1
Cases: NYD: check Alternative Dispute Resolution, key numbers (☞) 440 et seq.

Encyclopedia: NY JUR2D: check Arbitration and Award; Employment Relations § 631
Carmody-Wait: CW2d: § 2:43
Internet:
www.courts.state.ny.us/ip/adr/index.shtml
www.mediate.com/NewYork
www.megalaw.com/ny/top/nycivpro.php

Medical Malpractice

Statutes: CPLR Rule 3406; CVP § 214-a; ISC §§ 2343, 3436, 5502
Regulations: 10 NYCRR §§ 86-1.70 (insurance), 91.3 (excessive liability pool), 1000.3 (malpractice awards), 1000.4 (disclosure)
Regulations: 11 NYCRR §§ 70.0, 73.4, 73.5, 73.6
Cases: NYD: check Health, key numbers (☞) 600 et seq.
Encyclopedia: NY JUR2D: check Limitations and Laches § 250; Malpractice
Carmody-Wait: CW2d: § 13:57
Internet:
www.mcandl.com/newyork.html
www.health.state.ny.us/nysdoh/opmc/faq.htm

Mineral, Water, and Fishing Rights

Statutes: EPT § 11-A-4.11; GOB §§ 5-333, 15-304; PBL §§ 81, 92-a; ENV §§ 11-0313, 15-0503
Regulations: See title 6 (Dept. of Environmental Conservation), ch. 1 (Fish and Wildlife), §§ 550 (Mineral Resources), 601 (water supply)
Cases: NYD: check Environmental Law, key number (☞) 111 et seq.; Fish, key numbers (☞) 1 et seq.; Mines and Minerals, key numbers (☞) 1 et seq.; Waters and Water Courses, key numbers (☞) k2
Encyclopedia: NY JUR2D: check Environmental Rights and Remedies, Fish and Wildlife, Mines and Minerals, Water
Carmody-Wait: CW2d: §§ 91.20, 108:72, 157:171
Internet:
www.dec.ny.gov/outdoor/7746.html
www.citizenscampaign.org/campaigns/allegany.asp
www.encyclopedia.com/doc/1G1-53282223.html
www.megalaw.com/ny/top/nyenvironmental.php

Minors (see also Child Custody, Child Support, Family Law)

Statutes: BSC § 625 (infant shareholders); CVP § 1201 (representation); DOM §§ 15-a (marriage of), 70 (habeas); EPT § 2-1.3 (as heirs); GOB § 3-101 (contracts with); LAB § 130 (employments of)
Regulations: 12 NYCRR § 185.1
Cases: NYD: check Infants, key numbers (☞) 1 et seq.
Encyclopedia: NY JUR2D: check Decedents' Estates § 1133; Employment Relations § 17; Evidence and Eyewitnesses § 832; Infants and Other Persons Under Legal Disability

Carmody-Wait: CW2d: §§ 2:28, 13:367, 27:56
Internet:
www.labor.state.ny.us/workerprotection/laborstandards/workprot/minors.shtm
www.megalaw.com/ny/top/nyfamily.php

Mortgages (see also Real Property)

Statutes: RPP §§ 240 et seq.
Regulations: 3 NYCRR §§ 4.3, 82.1, 84.4, 410.3
Cases: NYD: check Mortgages, key numbers (☞) 1 et seq.; Chattel Mortgages, key numbers (☞) 1 et seq.
Encyclopedia: NY JUR2D: check Mortgages and Deeds of Trust
Carmody-Wait: CW2d: §§ 13:126, 13:468, 13:487, 92:16, 92:71
Internet:
www.banking.state.ny.us/rmlfees.htm

Motor Vehicles (see also Traffic Laws)

Statutes: VAT §§ 200 (Dept. of), 300 (Inspection & Safety), 400 (Registration)
Regulations: title 15 (Motor Vehicles)
Cases: NYD: check Automobiles, key numbers (☞) 1 et seq.
Encyclopedia: NY JUR2D: check Automobiles and Other Vehicles
Carmody-Wait: CW2d: §§ 14:25, 24:285, 39:181, 144:38
Internet:
www.nydmv.state.ny.us
www.nysgtsc.state.ny.us/vt-ndx.htm (Vehicle & Traffic Law)

Negligence (see also Torts)

Statutes: PEN § 15.05 (Criminal Culpability); CVP § 1411 (Contrib. Negl.); GMU § 50-j (of public officers); GOB § 3-111 (of parents not imputed to infant); PAR § 25.23 (in public parks); UCC § 3-406; VAT § 2411
Regulations: 20 NYCRR §§ 9-1.6; 21 NYCRR § 1023.1
Cases: NYD: check Negligence, key numbers (☞) 200 et seq.; Torts, key numbers (☞) 101 et seq.
Encyclopedia: NY JUR2D: check Negligence
Carmody-Wait: CW2d: §§ 13:59, 13:274, 25:48
Internet:
www.hg.org/torts.html
www.nytortreformnow.org

Notary Public

Statutes: EXC § 130
Regulations: 7 NYCRR §§ 304.8, 9 NYCRR § 7031.5
Cases: NYD: check Notaries, key numbers (☞) 1 et seq.
Encyclopedia: NY JUR2D: check Acknowledgments

Carmody-Wait: CW2d: § 4:5
Internet:
www.dos.state.ny.us/lcns/professions/notary/notary1.htm
www.notarypublicnewyork.com

Paralegals

Statutes: AGM § 308-a; CVP § 8602(b); STF § 8(17)(f)
Regulations: 2 NYCRR §§ 20.3, 20.4; 8 NYCRR
§§ 126.6(f), 200.22(f); 9 NYCRR §§ 6654.12, 7031.1(c)
Cases: NYD: Costs, key number (☞) 194.18; Prisons,
key number (☞) 4(11)
Encyclopedia: NY JUR2D: check Agency § 71; Attorneys
at Law §§ 32 (Unauthorized Practice of Law), 82, 168;
Decedents' Estates § 2059; Trial § 170
Carmody-Wait: CW2d §§ 3:190 (appearance by
nonattorney), 3:295 (sharing fees), 63:377 (affidavit
of paralegal), 159:145 (services performed by
nonattorney under supervision of attorney), 159:206
(services of nonattorney), 172:1882 (representation
by nonattorney impostor)
Internet:
empirestateparalegals.org
www.newyorkparalegalblog.com

Partnerships (see also Corporations)

Statutes: PTR §§ 1 et seq.
Regulations: 19 NYCRR §§ 156.6, 20 NYCRR §§ 1-2.6,
115.4
Cases: NYD: check Partnership, key numbers (☞)
1 et seq.; Joint Adventures, key numbers (☞) 1 et seq.
Encyclopedia: NY JUR2D: check Business
Relationships §§ 1379 et seq.
Carmody-Wait: CW2d §§ 13:404, 17:92, 24:139, 42:45,
42:64
Internet:
www.dos.state.ny.us/corp/newlegislation2006.html

Pleading (see also Civil Procedure)

Statutes: CVP §§ 402, 3011
Regulations: 9 NYCRR § 4.131; 12 NYCRR § 65.11
(Dept. of Labor); 20 NYCRR § 3000.4 (Tax);
22 NYCRR § 206.7 (Ct. of Claims)
Cases: NYD: check Pleading, key numbers (☞) 1 et seq.
Encyclopedia: NY JUR2D: check Pleading
Carmody-Wait: CW2d §§ 3:434, 19:276, 27:2 et seq.
Internet:
www.nyscourtofclaims.state.ny.us/rules/206_7.shtml
www.megalaw.com/ny/top/nycivpro.php

Power of Attorney

Statutes: EPT § 10-2.1; GOB § 5-1501
Regulations: 22 NYCRR § 207.48 (Surrogate's Court)
Cases: NYD: check Principal and Agent, key number
(☞) 10 et seq.

Encyclopedia: NY JUR2D: check Acknowledgements § 83,
Business Relationships § 1517; Decedents' Estates § 1004
Carmody-Wait: CW2d §§ 19:26, 19:205, 159:180
Internet:
www.oag.state.ny.us/bureaus/health_care/seniors/
pwrat.html
www.nylawfund.org/pubs/durpoa.pdf (Statutory Short
Form)

Privacy

Statutes: CVR §§ 50, 50-b; CVS § 80.8; GBS § 399-dd;
FCA § 166; PBH § 2997; PBS § 230
Regulations: 1 NYCRR § 360.10; 4 NYCRR § 80.8;
7 NYCRR § 6.2; 8 NYCRR § 315.2; 18 NYCRR §§ 339.2,
441.18
Cases: NYD: check Constitutional Law, key numbers
(☞) 1210 et seq.; Torts, key numbers (☞) 325 et seq.
Encyclopedia: NY JUR2D: check Defamation and
Privacy
Carmody-Wait: CW2d §§ 13:183 (civil rights), 16:27
(invasion), 19:80, 19:295, 55:11, 78:59, 172:108
Internet:
www.nysegov.com/citGuide.cfm?superCat=129&cat=289&
content=main
privacylaw.proskauer.com/tags/new-york

Privileged Communications (see also Evidence, Privacy)

Statutes: CVP §§ 4502 et seq.
Regulations: 10 NYCRR § 38.1; 22 NYCRR § 128.12
Cases: NYD: check Witnesses, key numbers (☞)
184 et seq.
Encyclopedia: NY JUR2D: check Decedents' Estates
§ 1217; Domestic Relations § 476; Evidence and
Witnesses § 490
Carmody-Wait: CW2d §§ 3:386 (attorney-client),
53:11 (attorney-client), 117:314 (spouses)
Internet:
www.megalaw.com/ny/top/nycivpro.php

Products Liability

Statutes: CVP § 1602(10); ISC § 5902(1); UCC § 2-A-216
Cases: NYD: check the vols. for Products Liability,
key numbers (☞) 1 et seq.
Encyclopedia: NY JUR2D: check Products Liability;
Courts and Judges § 655
Carmody-Wait: CW2d §§ 13:85, 29:357
Internet:
topics.law.cornell.edu/wex/products_liability

Real Property (see also Landlord and Tenant)

Statutes: RPP §§ 1 et seq.; RPA § 101; RPT §§ 101 et seq.
Regulations: see 20 NYCRR §§ 575.13, 2393.7
(transfer tax)

Cases: NYD: check the vols. for Estates in Property, key numbers (☞) 1 et seq.; Property, key numbers (☞) 1 et seq.
Encyclopedia: NY JUR2D: check Real Property-Possessory and Related Actions; Real Property Sales and Exchanges
Carmody-Wait: CW2d §§ 9:10, 38:39
Internet:
www.tenant.net/Other_Laws/RPL/rpltoc.html
www.orps.state.ny.us/home/varp_index.cfm (Office of Real Property)

Service of Process

Statutes: CVP §§ 305, 6213, 6512; FCA § 426; BSC § 306
Regulations: 11 NYCRR § 27.16; 22 NYCR § 520.13
Cases: NYD: check Process, key numbers (☞) 1 et seq.
Encyclopedia: NY JUR2D: check Process and Papers
Carmody-Wait: CW2d §§ 4:20, 24:25, 24:90
Internet:
www.nysppsa.org
www.dos.state.ny.us/corp/pdfs/0277.pdf
www.ins.state.ny.us/faqs/faqs_ind_serv_pro.htm
www.megalaw.com/ny/top/nycivpro.php

Statute of Frauds

Statutes: GOB § 5-701; UCC §§ 1-206, 2-201, 2-A-201, 8-113
Cases: NYD: check Frauds, Statute of, key numbers (☞) 1 et seq.
Encyclopedia: NY JUR2D: check Frauds, Statute of
Carmody-Wait: CW2d §§ 29:5, 30:72, 38:38
Internet:
www.law.cornell.edu/uniform/nyucc.html
(click "Sec 1-206")

Statute of Limitations

Statutes: CVP § 201; DOM § 250; GOB § 12-110; UCC § 2-725
Cases: NYD: check Limitation of Actions, key numbers (☞) 1 et seq.
Encyclopedia: NY JUR2D: check Limitations and Laches
Carmody-Wait: CW2d §§ 3:481, 13:178 et seq.
Internet:
www.expertlaw.com/library/limitations_by_state/ New_York.html
law.findlaw.com/state-laws/statute-of-limitations/new-york

Summary Judgment (see also Civil Procedure)

Statutes: CVP § 3212
Cases: NYD: check Judgment, key numbers (☞) 178 et seq.
Encyclopedia: NY JUR2D: check Summary Judgment and Pretrial Motions to Dismiss

Carmody-Wait: CW2d §§ 39:33 et seq., 39:105
Internet:
www.megalaw.com/ny/top/nycivpro.php

Summons (see also Civil Procedure)

Statutes: CVP § Rule 305
Regulations: 22 NYCRR §§ 212.6 (District Cts), 214.3 (Justice Cts)
Cases: NYD: check Process, key numbers (☞) 1 et seq.
Encyclopedia: NY JUR2D: check Process and Papers §§ 44 et seq.
Carmody-Wait: CW2d §§ 2:234, 24:10 et seq.
Internet:
www.megalaw.com/ny/top/nycivpro.php

Taxation

Statutes: TAX § 1; RPT § 499-b
Regulations: see title 20 (Dept. of Taxation and Finance)
Cases: NYD: check Taxation, key numbers (☞) 2000 et seq.
Encyclopedia: NY JUR2D: check Taxation and Assessments; Taxpayers' Actions; Decedents' Estates § 40; Estates, Powers, Etc. § 226
Carmody-Wait: CW2d Chapters 128, 143, 146, 165
Internet:
www.tax.state.ny.us
www.tax.state.ny.us/forms
www.nylovesbiz.com/Tax_and_Financial_Incentives/ Default.asp

Torts (see also Medical Malpractice, Negligence)

Statutes: CVP Rule 4533-b, CNT § 52; GMU § 50-I; GOB § 3-313; TWN § 67
Regulations: see 20 NYCRR § 9-1.6; 21 NYCRR § 56.7; 22 NYCRR § 691.20
Cases: NYD: check the vols. for Negligence, key numbers (☞) 200 et seq.; Products Liability, key numbers (☞) 1 et seq.; Torts, key numbers (☞) 101 et seq.
Encyclopedia: NY JUR2D: check Negligence, Products Liability, Torts
Carmody-Wait: CW2d §§ 2:90 et seq., 13:274, 25:48, 29:149, 38:101
Internet:
www.hg.org/torts.html
www.nytortreformnow.org

Traffic Laws

Statutes: VAT §§ 1100 et seq.
Regulations: see title 17 (Department of Transportation)
Cases: NYD: check Automobiles, key numbers (☞) 1 et seq.
Encyclopedia: NY JUR2D: check Automobiles and Other Vehicles §§ 632 et seq.

Carmody-Wait: CW2d §§ 24:285, 145:1498, 172:396 et seq.
Internet:
www.nysdot.gov/portal/page/portal/index
www.nysgtsc.state.ny.us/vt-ndx.htm

Trusts

Statutes: EPT §§ 7-1.1 et seq.; SCP §§ 1501 et seq.
Regulations: 3 NYCRR §§ 6.3, 31.2 (Trust Company)
Cases: NYD: check Trusts, key numbers (☞) 1 et seq.
Encyclopedia: NY JUR2D: check Trusts
Carmody-Wait: CW2d §§ 13:270, 15:537
Internet:
www.nycourts.gov/courts/nyc/surrogates/index.shtml
www.megalaw.com/ny/top/nyprobate.php

Unemployment Insurance

Statutes: LAB §§ 500 et seq.; WKC § 206(1)(b)
Regulations: see 12 NYCRR §§ 460.1 et seq.
Cases: NYD: check Unemployment Compensation, key numbers (☞) 1 et seq.
Encyclopedia: NY JUR2D: check Unemployment Insurance
Carmody-Wait: CW2d §§ 64:96, 72:82, 142:46, 147.42
Internet:
ui.labor.state.ny.us/UBC/home.do
www.nysegov.com/citGuide.cfm?superCat=36&cat=222&content=main

Venue (see also Civil Procedure)

Statutes: CVP §§ 501 et seq.
Regulations: 22 NYCRR § 212.9 (District Cts)
Cases: NYD: check Venue, key numbers (☞) 1 et seq.
Encyclopedia: NY JUR2D: check Actions § 67; Courts and Judges §§ 247, 931; Domestic Relations §§ 639, 2284; Trial § 200
Carmody-Wait: CW2d §§ 8:27, 17:66 et seq., 48:1 et seq.
Internet:
www.megalaw.com/ny/top/nycivpro.php
en.wikipedia.org/wiki/New_York_State_Judiciary

Water Rights

Statutes: ENV §§ 11-2101, 15-1703 et seq.
Regulations: see 6 NYCRR §§ 601.1 et seq.
Cases: NYD: check Waters and Water Courses, key numbers (☞) 2 et seq.
Encyclopedia: NY JUR2D: check Water
Carmody-Wait: CW2d §§ 108:17, 108:36, 108:189
Internet:
www.waterwebster.com/state_framebottom.htm
www.dec.ny.gov/lands/313.html
www.health.state.ny.us/environmental/water/drinking
www.megalaw.com/ny/top/nyenvironmental.php

Wills (see also Estates)

Statutes: EPT §§ 3-1.1 et seq.
Cases: NYD: check Wills, key numbers (☞) 1 et seq.
Encyclopedia: NY JUR2D: check Decedents' Estates §§ 256 et seq.
Carmody-Wait: CW2d §§ 36:184, 152:18 et seq.
Internet:
www.megalaw.com/ny/top/nyprobate.php

Workers' Compensation

Statutes: WKC §§ 1 et seq.
Regulations: see 12 NYCRR §§ 300 et seq.
Cases: NYD: check Workers' Compensation, key numbers (☞) 1 et seq.
Encyclopedia: NY JUR2D: check Workers' Compensation
Carmody-Wait: CW2d §§ 72:83 et seq.
Internet:
www.wcb.state.ny.us
www.wcb.state.ny.us/content/main/Forms.jsp
ww3.nysif.com
www.nyworkerscompensationalliance.org

E. More Information

(See also section 5.1 on New York legal research.)

New York Statutes
public.leginfo.state.ny.us/menugetf.cgi?COMMONQUERY=LAWS
caselaw.lp.findlaw.com/nycodes/index.html
law.justia.com/newyork/codes

Megalaw.com
megalaw.com/ny/ny.php

Online Portals to New York Legal Research
www.ll.georgetown.edu/states/newyork-in-depth.cfm
www.loc.gov/law/help/guide/states/us-ny.html
www.law.cornell.edu/states/ny.html
law-library.rutgers.edu/resources/nyresearch.php
www.law.syr.edu/Pdfs/0NYS%20Research.pdf
www.findlaw.com/11stategov/ny/laws.html
www.lawsource.com/also/usa.cgi?ny
www.aallnet.org/chapter/llagny/ny.html
www.chesslaw.com/newyorklaw.htm
www.hg.org/usstates.html

New York Legal Forms
megalaw.com/forms/ny/nyforms.php

F. Something to Check

One of the ways that law firms try to attract clients is to provide law summaries and overviews on their web sites. Pick any two topics covered in this section (e.g., adoption, limited liability companies). For each topic, find three New York law firm web sites that provide summaries or overviews of New York law on the topic. Compare the quality and quantity of what you learn about the law at each site. To locate the law firms, go to any search engine (e.g., *www.google.com*) and type in New York, law, or lawyer, and your topic (e.g., New York law adoption, New York lawyer adoption).

5.6 Self-Help Resources in New York

A. Introduction

B. Caution on Using Self-Help Resources

C. General Resources

D. Specific Areas of Law

E. Forms

F. Resource Centers/Self-Help Offices

G. Your Neighborhood Public Library

H. Ask a Librarian: Self-Help by E-Mail

I. More Information

J. Something to Check

A. Introduction

Where do New York citizens go when they are representing themselves but would still like some assistance? Such individuals are sometimes said to be engaged in self-help. They are proceeding pro se, acting on their own behalf. (Another meaning of self-help is taking steps to obtain redress outside the legal system.) "Among the many changes to courts in the State of New York in the past two decades has been a sharp increase in the number of self-represented litigants. There are nearly 1.8 million self-represented litigants in the New York State Unified Court System, according to a recent estimate." Association of the Bar of the City of New York, *Formal Opinion 2009-2*. (*www.nycbar.org/ Ethics/eth2009-2.htm#_ftn1*)

An American Bar Association study of self-represented litigants showed:

- Persons with incomes less than $50,000 are more likely to represent themselves.
- About 20% of self-represented litigants report that they can afford an attorney but do not want one.
- Self-represented persons are more likely to be satisfied with the judicial process than those who are represented by attorneys.
- Almost 75% of those who represent themselves in court say they would do it again. (*www.pro-selaw.org/ pro-selaw/index.asp*)

Self-help resources can play a number of roles in a law office:

- An office may provide partial (i.e., unbundled) legal services to clients who are representing themselves.
- An office will sometimes refer citizens to self-help materials when the office cannot provide representation.
- Self-help resources can provide excellent overviews of the law that everyone should know about. The overviews provide links to additional research sources that can be checked.
- Even if persons have attorney representation, they may sometimes consult self-help materials in order to be able to communicate with their attorneys more intelligently. Some law offices encourage their clients to do so.

Many of the self-help resources in this section involve family law and small claims matters. The links in the sites, however, often lead to resources for other kinds of cases as well.

For related sections, see:

B. Caution on Using Self-Help Resources

A great deal of information about law is available from many sources, particularly on the Internet. See Exhibit 5.6A for a disclaimer found on a bar association web site with self-help materials. The caution in the disclaimer applies to most of the legal materials found on the Internet.

EXHIBIT 5.6A	Caution on Using Online Self-Help Materials

Information Not Legal Advice. This Web site has been prepared for general information purposes only. The information on this Web site is not legal advice. Legal advice involves the application of legal knowledge and skills by a licensed attorney to your specific circumstances. Also, laws vary from state to state, so some information on this Web site may not be correct for where you live. Laws also change frequently so the information contained in this Web site is not guaranteed to be up to date. Therefore, the information contained in this Web site cannot replace the advice of a competent attorney licensed in your state. (*www.texaslawhelp.org*) (click "Disclaimer")

Similarly, the very useful forms web site provided by the Uniform Court System (see section C below) includes the warning that "we strongly suggest that you give serious thought to using a lawyer" for your divorce, even if you believe that the divorce will be uncontested. (*nycourts.gov/courthelp/forms.html*)

This not to suggest, however, that valuable self-help resources are not available in New York. Quite the contrary, as the following overview will demonstrate.

C. General Resources

NYCourtHelp

nycourthelp.gov

The major source of online legal self-help is *NYCourt Help.gov*, a site sponsored by the Unified State Court System. The site provides the following assistance:

- Free court forms for cases on family law issues such as divorce, custody, support, paternity; tort law issues such as medical malpractice, contract disputes, and automobile accidents; and small estate cases, including probate.
- Overview of the subject-matter jurisdiction of New York state courts (e.g., in what court to file a civil action for damages up to $25,000).
- Brief summaries on the law of a variety of topics such as divorce, support, landlord-tenant, pleadings in negligence cases, wills and estates, small claims, traffic offenses, and criminal procedure.
- Contact listings when seeking information from or about specific courts in the state.
- Lists of courts that have self-help resources such as an Office for the Self-Represented.
- Locations of law libraries throughout the state.
- A legal dictionary of frequently used legal terms.

LawHelp

www.lawhelp.org/ny

The site provides summaries and links on numerous areas of the law, including:

- Adoption
- Bankruptcy
- Child custody
- Child support
- Consumer law
- Debtors and creditors
- Disability law
- Discrimination
- Divorce
- Domestic violence
- Elder law
- Employment law
- Estate planning
- Health law
- Immigration law
- Labor law
- Landlord and tenant law
- Public assistance law
- Social security law
- Student rights
- Wills

New York State Bar Association

www.nysba.org
(click "For the Community")

Some useful self-help materials can be found on the "For the Community" links of the New York State Bar Association. For example:

- Summaries of laws governing individuals who have just turned 18 years of age
- Guides to the courts of the state
- Living wills and health care proxy forms
- Online video overviews by Peoples Law School on topics such as civil lawsuits, wills and estates, divorce, child custody, labor law, contracts, and elder law

Understanding the Law: A Practical Guide for New York Residents

204.8.127.102/peopleslaw/program3.htm

This guide provides overviews of the following legal topics:

- Kinds of law
- Citizen rights
- Negligence and other torts
- Criminal law and procedure
- Contract law
- Debtor and creditor law
- Real estate law
- Divorce and other family law issues
- Wills and estates

Attorney General Legal Guides

www.oag.state.ny.us/bureaus/intergov_affairs/publications. html

Legal materials are available at the attorney general's site on the following topics:

- Car buying
- Charitable giving
- Condominium/ Coops
- Consumer fraud
- Contractor/ Construction
- Debt collection
- Domestic violence
- Elder law
- Employment
- Health care
- Immigration
- Landlord-tenant
- Sexual harassment

New York City Bar Self-Help Legal Clinics

www.abcny.org/Public/SelfHelpLegalClinics.htm
www.abcny.org/Publications/Brochures.htm

Legal materials are available at these clinics on the following topics:

- Alternative dispute resolution
- Animal rights
- Attorney grievances
- Bankruptcy
- Child support
- Consumer protection
- Criminal justice
- Employment law
- Estates
- Family law
- Labor law
- Probate
- Trademark law
- Wills
- Workers' compensation

Small Claims Court Guide

*www.courts.state.ny.us/ithaca/city/webpageGuideto
SmallClaims.html*

tenant.net/Court/Howcourt/sclaim.html

*www.courts.state.ny.us/courthelp/Booklets/SmallClaims
Handbook.pdf,* (outside NYC)

*www.nyc.gov/html/dca/html/publications/publications_small_
claims.shtml* (NYC)

www.nycourts.gov/courts/nyc/smallclaims/index.shtml (NYC)

Representing Yourself in State Court

www.nycourts.gov/supctmanh/Representing_Yourself.htm

www.courts.state.ny.us/litigants/JusticeWorks07.pdf

www.courts.state.ny.us/publications/GuideforProSes.pdf

Representing Yourself in Federal Court

www.nynd.uscourts.gov/prose.cfm

www.nynd.uscourts.gov/documents/ProSeHandbook2008.pdf

www1.nysd.uscourts.gov/courtrules_prose.php

www.nywd.uscourts.gov

(click "Representing Yourself in Federal Court")

D. Specific Areas of Law

Adoption

*www.nycourts.gov/courts/7jd/courts/family/case_types/
adoption.shtml*

www.nycourts.gov/courts/3jd/surrogates/adoption.shtml

www.nycourts.gov/courts/nyc/family/faqs_adoption.shtml

nycourts.gov/forms/familycourt/adoption.shtml

Animal Law

www.abcny.org/Publications/Brochures.htm

Attorneys, Grievances Against

www.nylawfund.org

www.nylawfund.org/pubs/avoidinggrief.pdf

www.abcny.org/Publications/Brochures.htm

Bankruptcy

www.nyeb.uscourts.gov/filing_wo_atty.html

www.abcny.org/Publications/Brochures.htm

Child Custody

*www.nycourts.gov/courts/nyc/family/faqs_custodyandvisitation
.shtml*

nycourts.gov/forms/familycourt/custodyvisitation.shtml

nycourts.gov/forms/familycourt/childprotective.shtml

Child Neglect and Abuse

nycourts.gov/forms/familycourt/childprotective.shtml

*www.nycourts.gov/courts/nyc/family/faqs_abusedchildren
.shtml*

www.nycourts.gov/courts/3jd/Family/childabuse.shtml

preventchildabuseny.org/cpsandcourts.shtml

Child Support

newyorkchildsupport.com/custodial_parent_info.html

newyorkchildsupport.com/support_enforcement.html

www.abcny.org/Publications/pdf/childsupport.pdf

www.nycourts.gov/courts/nyc/family/faqs_support.shtml

*www.nycourts.gov/courts/7jd/courts/family/case_types/
support.shtml*

Commercial Claims

www.courts.state.ny.us/courts/comdiv

Consumer Law

*www.oag.state.ny.us/bureaus/intergov_affairs/
publications.html*

www.abcny.org/Publications/Brochures.htm

Cooperative and Condominium Conversion

*www.oag.state.ny.us/publications/COOP%20CONDO%
20Conversion%20Handbook%202-13-08.pdf*

Criminal Law

www.nycourts.gov/litigants/crimjusticesyshandbk.shtml

www.abcny.org/Publications/StateCriminalJusticeH_e.htm

Custody and Visitation

*www.nycourts.gov/courts/nyc/family/
faqs_custodyandvisitation.shtml*

Disability Law

www.lawhelp.org/ny

Divorce

www.nycourts.gov/ip/matrimonial-matters/forms.shtml

www.nycourts.gov/divorce

www.nycourts.gov/courthelp/faqs/divorce.html

www.nycourts.gov/courts/2jd/kings/Civil/matrimonial.shtml

Domestic Violence

nycourts.gov/forms/familycourt/familyoffence.shtml

*www.oag.state.ny.us/bureaus/criminal_prosecutions/pdfs/
domestic_violence.pdf*

www.nycourts.gov/courthelp/faqs/domesticviolence.html

*www.nycourts.gov/courts/nyc/family/faqs_domesticviolence
.shtml*

Education Law

www.lawhelp.org/ny

Elder Law

www.nycourts.gov/courts/2jd/kings/Civil/guardianship.shtml

*www.oag.state.ny.us/bureaus/intergov_affairs/pdfs/smart_
seniors.pdf*

*www.oag.state.ny.us/bureaus/consumer_frauds/pdfs/Senior_
Housing_Guide.pdf*

Employment Law

*www.oag.state.ny.us/publications/labor_rights_tip_card_
english.pdf*

www.lawhelp.org/ny

www.nycbar.org/pdf/report/pro_se_handbook.pdf

Estates and Probate

www.abcny.org/Publications/executor.htm

nycourts.gov/forms/surrogates/index.shtml

Family Law

www.nycourts.gov/courthelp/qa_familylaw.html

www.nycourts.gov/forms/familycourt/index.shtml

www.nycbar.org/pdf/famguide_ms.pdf

Foster Care
nycourts.gov/forms/familycourt/fostercareplacement.shtml

Guardianship
www.nycourts.gov/supctmanh/Guardianship_Cases.htm
nycourts.gov/forms/familycourt/guardianship.shtml
www.nycourts.gov/courts/2jd/kings/Civil/guardianship.shtml
www.nycourts.gov/courts/3jd/surrogates/guardianship.shtml
*www.nycourts.gov/courts/7jd/courts/family/case_types/
   guardianship.shtml*

Housing
www.nycourts.gov/courts/nyc/housing/resourcecenter.shtml

Immigration Law
www.immigrantdefenseproject.org
www.fd.org/odstb_ConstructIMMIGRATIONCON.htm
www.oag.state.ny.us/publications/immigration_brochure.pdf

Juvenile Delinquency
www.nycourts.gov/courts/nyc/family/faqs_juvenile.shtml
*www.nycourts.gov/courts/7jd/courts/family/case_types/
   juvenile_delinquency.shtml*
nycourts.gov/forms/familycourt/juveniledelinquency.shtml

Labor Law
*www.oag.state.ny.us/publications/labor_rights_tip_card_
   english.pdf*
www.nycbar.org/pdf/report/pro_se_handbook.pdf

Landlord-Tenant Law
www.courts.state.ny.us/publications/L&TPamphlet.pdf
*www.courts.state.ny.us/courts/nyc/housing/pdfs/
   tenantsguide.pdf*
www.nycbar.org/pdf/report/tenantsguide.pdf
*www.oag.state.ny.us/bureaus/real_estate_finance/pdfs/
   tenants_rights_guide.pdf*

Legal Separation
*www.nycourts.gov/courts/6jd/forms/SRForms/legal_
   separationproced.pdf*

Lemon Law
*www.oag.state.ny.us/bureaus/intergov_affairs/
   publications.html*

Name Change
www.nycourts.gov/courts/6jd/forms/SRForms/index.shtml
nycourts.gov/forms/namechange.shtml
www.nycourts.gov/courts/nyc/civil/namechanges.shtml

Paternity
nycourts.gov/forms/familycourt/paternity.shtml
www.nycourts.gov/courts/nyc/family/faqs_paternity.shtml
*www.nycourts.gov/courts/7jd/courts/family/case_types/
   paternity.shtml*

Real Estate Law
www.nytitle.com/faq.ivnu
www.orps.state.ny.us/ref/forms/index.cfm
*portal.hud.gov/portal/page/portal/HUD/program_offices/
   administration/hudclips/forms*

Tax Law
www.lawhelp.org/ny

Trademarks
www.abcny.org/Publications/Trademark.htm

Workers' Compensation
(see also section 2.9)
www.abcny.org/Publications/WorksCompensation.htm

E. Forms

Many of the sites listed above (as well as those in sections 4.2 and 4.3) contain forms that can be adapted for particular fact situations and client needs. Here are some additional sources of forms:

NYS Unified Court System Forms
nycourts.gov/forms/index.shtml

Family Court Forms
nycourts.gov/forms/familycourt/index.shtml

Divorce Forms
nycourts.gov/ip/matrimonial-matters/forms.shtml

**Forms, Permits, Registrations, Licenses,
and Certifications**
www.nysl.nysed.gov/ils/topics/forms.htm

Surrogate's Court Forms
nycourts.gov/forms/surrogates/index.shtml

Name Change Forms
nycourts.gov/forms/namechange.shtml

FindForms
www.findforms.com (type "New York" in the search box)

F. Resource Centers/Self-Help Offices

Statewide
www.nycourts.gov/courthelp

6th Judicial District Self-Represented Forms
www.nycourts.gov/courts/6jd/forms/SRForms/index.shtml

7th Judicial District Overview Assistance
www.courts.state.ny.us/courts/7jd/index.shtml

8th Judicial District Court Resource Center
*www.nycourts.gov/courts/8jd/pdfs/Resource/
   CHC_BROCHURE.pdf*

New York City Bar Self-Help Legal Clinics
www.abcny.org/Public/SelfHelpLegalClinics.htm

G. Your Neighborhood Public Library

Valuable self-help materials on New York law are often available at your neighborhood public library. For example, you might find *New York Jurisprudence 2d* and *McKinney's Consolidated Laws of New York Annotated.* For a list of other possibilities, see section 5.8. Of course, you need to find out how up-to-date any of these law books are.

H. Ask a Librarian: Self-Help by E-Mail

A potentially valuable self-help resource is the free "Ask a Librarian" program in New York and around the country. Most "Ask" programs are available by e-mail to help answer specific questions, particularly about research materials and factual information. They cannot give legal advice, but they can provide useful leads.

Ask programs are sometimes limited to designated populations such as the students of a particular university. The web site of the program will list any restrictions that exist. Don't be reluctant to contact Ask programs located outside New York. Many are eager to help no matter where the inquirer is located.

Finding Ask a Librarian Programs
Run the following search in Google or any search engine:

"ask a librarian"
"ask a librarian" law
"ask a librarian" "New York"
"ask a librarian" law "New York"

Examples of Ask Sites
www.nypl.org/questions
www.nysl.nysed.gov/ask.htm
www.nycourts.gov/lawlibraries/document-service.shtml
www.loc.gov/rr/askalib
www.ipl.org/div/askus
govtinfo.org

I. More Information

ABA Legal Information Resources
www.abalawinfo.org
www.abanet.org/legalservices/findlegalhelp/main.cfm?id=NY

ABA Practical Law
www.abanet.org/publiced/practical/home.html

American Pro Se Association
www.legalhelp.org

City Legal Guide
www.citylegalguide.com
(click "New York" on the map)

Consumers' Guide to Legal Help: Helping Yourself
www.abanet.org/legalservices/findlegalhelp/faq_selfhelp.cfm

Findlaw for the Public
public.findlaw.com

Going It Alone in Court
www.halt.org/lic/art.php?aid=33

Legal Information Institute
www.law.cornell.edu/index.html

Nolo Press Self-Help Law Center
www.nolo.com

Pro-Se Law Center
www.pro-selaw.org/pro-selaw/index.asp

Resources of Forms, Permits, Registrations, Licenses, and Certifications
www.nysl.nysed.gov/ils/topics/forms.htm

Self-Help Support
www.selfhelpsupport.org

Self-Help Law ExPress
blogs.law.harvard.edu/shlep

Unbundled Legal Services in Litigated Matters in NYS
www.courts.state.ny.us/ip/partnersinjustice/Unbundled.pdf

Yahoo Self-Help Resources
dir.yahoo.com/Government/Law/Self_Help

J. Something to Check

1. Find online self-help information on suing a police officer in your city for using excessive force in an arrest. Cite a sentence from each site (up to three) that you find.
2. Find online self-help information on suing your neighbor for damage done to a common fence. Cite a sentence from each site (up to three) that you find.

5.7 Public Records Research

A. Introduction
B. New York State Freedom of Information Law (FOIL)
C. Search Resources
D. More Information
E. Something to Check

A. Introduction

There are a large variety of public records that a law firm may seek to obtain. For example:

Business Records

Corporations	Sales Tax Registrations
Fictitious Names	Tax Liens
Limited Liability Companies	Trademarks and Service Marks
Partnerships	UCC Filings
Real Estate	

Individual Records

Accident Reports	Divorce
Bankruptcies	Marriage
Birth	Occupational Licenses
Court Judgments	Vehicle Ownership
Criminal Records	Workers' Compensation Claims
Death	

Access to these records varies. Some are available to the general public; access to others is subject to substantial restrictions.

This section will provide starting points in finding out what is available. Some of the Internet sites and phone numbers in this section will lead you to complete access to the records involved. Others will simply be locations where you can begin making inquiries about what might be available.

Local Records (County and City)

Many public records are available at the local government level. See section 4.6 for contact information on the relevant county and city agencies.

County Governments

www.nysegov.com/citguide.cfm?context=citguide&content= munibycounty1

libguides.library.albany.edu/newyorkcounties

www.statelocalgov.net/state-ny.htm

City Governments

www.nysegov.com/citguide.cfm?context=citguide&content= munibyalpha

www.statelocalgov.net/state-ny.htm

B. New York State Freedom of Information Law (FOIL)

The New York State Freedom of Information Law (FOIL) is similar to the federal Freedom of Information Act. The text of FOIL is found in sections 84–90 of Public Officers Law. Its purpose is to give private citizens greater access to government information. FOIL considers records maintained by most state agencies to be public records unless they are covered by exceptions listed in FOIL. An "agency" includes any state or municipal department, board, bureau, division, commission, committee, public authority, public corporation, council, office, or other government entity performing a governmental or propriety function.

In general, to make a FOIL request one must "reasonably describe" in writing what is requested and direct the request to the Records Access Officer of the agency. The agency must respond to your request within five days (unless additional time is reasonably needed) by granting the request or denying it for stated reasons. If disclosure of records would be damaging to an individual or preclude a government agency from carrying out its duties, access will probably be denied.

Freedom of Information Law (FOIL)

www.dos.state.ny.us/coog/Right_to_know.html

Your Right to Know: New York State Open Government Laws

www.dos.state.ny.us/coog/Right_to_know.html

How to Use FOIL

www.nycosh.org/health_safety_rights/foil.html

New Provisions of FOIL

www.dos.state.ny.us/coog/foilnews2.html

C. Search Resources

Accident Reports
Accountants
Acupuncturists
Adoption
Alarm Installer
Albany County Records
Alcohol
Allegany County Records
Apartments
Appearance Enhancement
Appraiser
Architects
Armored Car Carriers and Guards
Assessor Records
Athlete Agents
Athletic Training
Attorneys
Audiology
Automobile Inspections/ Repairs
Background Checks
Bail Enhancement Agent
Banks
Barbers
Bedding
Birth Records
Brokers
Bronx County Records
Broome County Records
Business Filings
Business Permits
Campaigns
Cattaraugus County Records
Cayuga County Records
Certified Shorthand Reporting
Charitable Organization Records
Chautauqua Public Records
Chemung County Records
Chenango County Records
Chiropractic
Clinical Laboratory Technology
Clinton County Records
Columbia County Records
Corporation Records
Cortland County Records
Cosmetology
County Boards of Election
County Clerks
County Government Records
Court Dockets
Court Opinions
Court Reporters
Credit Reports

Credit Unions
Criminal Records
Death Records
Delaware County Records
Dental Hygienists/Assistants
Dentists
Department of Motor Vehicles
Dietetics-Nutrition
Dispatch Facility, Central
Divorce/Dissolution of Marriage Records
DMV
Doctors
Dog Licensing
Driving Records
Dutchess County Records
Elections
Engineers
Erie County Records
Essex County Records
Expungement
Family Records in New York State Archives
Fictitious Names
Financial Institutions
Franklin County
Fulton County Records
Funeral Directors
Genealogy Records
Genesee County Records
Greene County Records
Hair Styling
Hamilton County Records
Health Statistics
Hearing Aid Dispenser
Herkimer County Records
Home Inspector
Inmate Locator
Insurance Brokers/ Companies
Interior Design
Investigator
Jefferson County Records
Kings County Records
Laboratory Technology
Landscape Architect
Land Surveying
Lawyers
Lewis County Records
Licenses
Lien Search
Limited Liability Company
Limited Liability Partnership
Limited Partnership
Livingston County Records
Lobbying Records
Madison County Records

Marriage Records
Massage Therapy
Medical Records, Right
 to See/Privacy
Mental Health Practitioners
Midwifery
Monroe County Records
Montgomery County
 Records
Motor Vehicles
Nassau County Records
New York County Records
Niagara County Records
Notary Public
Not-for-Profit Corporation
 Filings
Nurses
Occupational/Professional
 Licenses
Occupational Therapy
Oneida County Records
Onondaga County
 Records
Ontario County Records
Optometrists
Orange County Records
Orleans County Records
Oswego County Records
Otsego County Records
Partnership Records
Pharmacists
Physical Therapists
Physician Assistants
Physicians
Podiatry
Private Investigator
Professional/Occupational
 Licenses
Psychologists
Public Accountancy
Putative Father Registry
Putnam County Records
Queens County Records
Real Estate Appraiser
Real Estate Brokers/
 Salespersons
Records Repository
 Directory
Rensselaer County Records
Repairs
Respiratory Therapy
Richmond County Records

Rockland County Records
Sales Tax Registrations
Saratoga County Records
Savings and Loan
 Associations
Schenectady County
 Records
Schoharie County Records
School
Schuyler County Records
Security Guard
Seneca County Records
Sex Offender Registration
 Records
Shorthand Reporting
Social Workers
Speech-Language Pathology
 & Audiology
Steuben County Records
St. Lawrence County
 Records
Suffolk County Records
Sullivan County Records
Taxation
Teacher, Public School
Telemarketer Business
Therapists
Tioga County Records
Title/Lien Status Check
Tompkins County Records
Trademark Registration
Trust Companies
UCC Statements
Ulster County Records
Unclaimed Property
 Records
Uniform Commercial Code
 Filings
Vehicle History Report
Veterinarians
Vital Records
Warren County Records
Washington County Records
Watch, Guard & Patrol
 Agency
Wayne County Records
Westchester County
 Records
Workers' Compensation
Wyoming County
 Records
Yates County Records

Accident Reports
Department of Motor Vehicles
Accident Reports
www.nysdmv.com/dmvfaqs.htm#accident
www.nysdmv.com (click "if you have a traffic accident")
Accident Report Request Form (MV-198-c)
www.nysdmv.com/forms/mv198c.pdf

Accountants (license and disciplinary records)
Office of the Professions (Public Accountancy)
518-474-3817
www.op.nysed.gov/cpa.htm
www.op.nysed.gov/opsearches.htm
www.op.nysed.gov/rasearch.htm

Acupuncturists (license and disciplinary records)
Office of the Professions (Acupuncture Unit)
518-474-3817 x270
www.op.nysed.gov/acupun.htm
www.op.nysed.gov/opsearches.htm
www.op.nysed.gov/rasearch.htm

Adoption
Adoption Information Registry
www.health.state.ny.us/vital_records/adoption.htm
Putative Father Registry
800-345-KIDS
www.ocfs.state.ny.us/main/publications/Pub5040text.asp

Alarm Installer (license records)
Division of Licensing Services
518-474-4429
appsext8.dos.state.ny.us/lcns_public/chk_load

Albany County Records
publicrecords.onlinesearches.com/NY_Albany.htm
www.publicrecordcenter.com/newyorkpublicrecord.htm
www.albanycounty.com

Alcohol (license records)
Alcohol Beverage Control, State Liquor Authority
abc.state.ny.us
abc.state.ny.us/public-license-query

Allegany County Records
publicrecords.onlinesearches.com/NY_Allegany.htm
www.publicrecordcenter.com/newyorkpublicrecord.htm
www.alleganyco.com

Apartments
Apartment Information Vendor (license records)
Apartment Sharing Agent (license records)
Division of Licensing Services
518-474-4429
appsext8.dos.state.ny.us/lcns_public/chk_load

Appearance Enhancement (hair styling; cosmetology) (license records)
Division of Licensing Services
518-474-4429
appsext8.dos.state.ny.us/lcns_public/chk_load

Appraiser
(see real estate appraiser)

Architects (including landscape architects) (license and disciplinary records)
Office of the Professions
518-474-3817 x250

www.op.nysed.gov/arch.htm
www.op.nysed.gov/larch.htm
www.op.nysed.gov/opsearches.htm
www.op.nysed.gov/rasearch.htm

Armored Car Carriers and Guards (license records)
Division of Licensing Services
518-474-4429
appsext8.dos.state.ny.us/lcns_public/chk_load

Assessor Records (property ownership and valuation)
Office of Real Property Services
518-474-2982
www.orps.state.ny.us/home/varp_index.cfm
www.uspdr.com

Athlete Agents (license records)
Division of Licensing Services
518-474-4429
appsext8.dos.state.ny.us/lcns_public/chk_load

Athletic Training (license records)
Office of the Professions
518-474-3817 x270
www.op.nysed.gov/athlet.htm
www.op.nysed.gov/opsearches.htm

Attorneys (license records)
Unified Court System
212-428-2800
iapps.courts.state.ny.us/attorney/AttorneySearch

Audiology (license and disciplinary records)
Office of the Professions
518-474-3817 x270
www.op.nysed.gov/speech.htm
www.op.nysed.gov/opsearches.htm
www.op.nysed.gov/rasearch.htm

Automobile Inspections/Repairs (complaints)
www.nysdmv.com/vehsafe.htm#complaint
www.nydmv.state.ny.us/vehsafe.htm#complaint

Background Checks
www.dmv.org/background-checks.php
new_york.iaf.staging.intelius.com/states/new_york.html

Bail Enforcement Agent (license records)
Division of Licensing Services
518-474-4429
appsext8.dos.state.ny.us/lcns_public/chk_load

Banks
(see Financial Institutions)

Barbers (license records)
Division of Licensing Services
518-474-4429
appsext8.dos.state.ny.us/lcns_public/chk_load

Bedding (license records)
Division of Licensing Services
518-474-4429
appsext8.dos.state.ny.us/lcns_public/chk_load

Birth Records
Department of Health
877-854-4481; 877-854-4481 (VitalChek)
www.health.state.ny.us/vital_records/birth.htm
www.health.state.ny.us/vital_records/genealogy.htm
www.publicrecordcenter.com/newyorkpublicrecord.htm
National Center for Health Statistics: New York
www.cdc.gov/nchs/w2w/new_york.htm
www.statearchives.us/public/new-york.htm
New York City
www.nyc.gov/html/doh

Brokers
(see Insurance Brokers, Real Estate Brokers)

Bronx County Records
publicrecords.onlinesearches.com/NY_Bronx.htm
publicrecords.onlinesearches.com/NY_NewYork.htm
www.publicrecordcenter.com/newyorkpublicrecord.htm
www.nyc.gov/portal/site/nycgov/?front_door=true

Broome County Records
publicrecords.onlinesearches.com/NY_Broome.htm
www.gobcclerk.com
www.publicrecordcenter.com/newyorkpublicrecord.htm
www.gobroomecounty.com/home

Business Filings (business entity database: business corporations, not-for-profit corporations, limited partnerships, limited liability companies, and limited liability partnerships)
(see also Corporations Records, UCC Statements)
Department of State
518-473-2492
*appsext8.dos.state.ny.us/corp_public/corpsearch.entity_
    search_entry*
www.dos.state.ny.us

Business Permits
www.nys-permits.org
www.business.gov/states/new-york

Campaigns
(see Elections)

Cattaraugus County Records
publicrecords.onlinesearches.com/NY_Cattaraugus.htm
www.cattco.org/real_property/index.asp
www.publicrecordcenter.com/newyorkpublicrecord.htm
www.co.cattaraugus.ny.us

Cayuga County Records
publicrecords.onlinesearches.com/NY_Cayuga.htm
www.publicrecordcenter.com/newyorkpublicrecord.htm
www.co.cayuga.ny.us

Certified Shorthand Reporting
(see Shorthand Reporting)

Charitable Organization Records
www.oag.state.ny.us/bureaus/charities/about.html

Chautauqua County Records
publicrecords.onlinesearches.com/NY_Chautauqua.htm
www.publicrecordcenter.com/newyorkpublicrecord.htm
www.co.chautauqua.ny.us

Chemung County Records
publicrecords.onlinesearches.com/NY_Chemung.htm
www.publicrecordcenter.com/newyorkpublicrecord.htm
www.chemungcounty.com

Chenango County Records
publicrecords.onlinesearches.com/NY_Chenango.htm
www.publicrecordcenter.com/newyorkpublicrecord.htm
www.co.chenango.ny.us

Chiropractic (license and disciplinary records)
Office of the Professions
518-474-3817 x250
www.op.nysed.gov/chiro.htm
www.op.nysed.gov/opsearches.htm
www.op.nysed.gov/rasearch.htm

Clinical Laboratory Technology (license and disciplinary records)
Office of the Professions
518-474-3817 x150
www.op.nysed.gov/clp.htm
www.op.nysed.gov/opsearches.htm
www.op.nysed.gov/rasearch.htm

Clinton County Records
publicrecords.onlinesearches.com/NY_Clinton.htm
www.publicrecordcenter.com/newyorkpublicrecord.htm
www.clintoncountygov.com/Departments/CC/
*   CountyClerkHome.html*

Columbia County Records
publicrecords.onlinesearches.com/NY_Columbia.htm
www.publicrecordcenter.com/newyorkpublicrecord.htm
www.columbiacountyny.com

Corporations Records
(see also Business Filings)
Department of State, Division of Corporations,
State Records
518-473-2492
www.dos.state.ny.us
*appsext8.dos.state.ny.us/corp_public/corpsearch.entity_*
*   search_entry*

Cortland County Records
publicrecords.onlinesearches.com/NY_Cortland.htm
www.publicrecordcenter.com/newyorkpublicrecord.htm
www.cortland-co.org

Cosmetology (license records)
(see Appearance Enhancement)

County Boards of Election
www.elections.state.ny.us
(click "County Boards")

County Clerks (statewide list)
www.nysl.nysed.gov/scandoclinks/ocm36998634.htm
www.nytitle.com/faq.ivnu

County Government Records
(see also section 4.6 for sites to all county
governments)
www.nysegov.com/map-NY.cfm
www.nysegov.com/citguide.cfm?context=citguide&content=
*   munibycounty1*

Court Dockets
www.legaldockets.com

Court Opinions
(see also 5.1 on finding New York court opinions)
www.courts.state.ny.us/decisions
www.courts.state.ny.us/courts/appellate.shtml

Court Reporters
(see Shorthand Reporting)

Credit Reports
www.publicrecordcenter.com/newyorkpublicrecord.htm
www.ftc.gov/bcp/menus/consumer/credit/rights.shtm
www.ftc.gov/freereports

Credit Unions
(see Financial Institutions)

Criminal Records
(see also County Clerks, Inmate Locator, Sex Offenders)
Division of Criminal Justice Personal Criminal
History Lookup
criminaljustice.state.ny.us/ojis/recordreview.htm
criminaljustice.state.ny.us/nsor/index.htm
Office of Court Administration
Criminal History Record Search
www.nycourts.gov/apps/chrs
Expungement of Records
criminaljustice.state.ny.us/legalservices/section6193.htm
*www.publicrecordcenter.com/newyork_public_records_*
*   expungements.htm*

Death Records
Department of Health
877-854-4481 (VitalChek)
www.health.state.ny.us/vital_records/death.htm
www.health.state.ny.us/vital_records/genealogy.htm
National Center for Health Statistics: New York
www.cdc.gov/nchs/w2w/new_york.htm
www.statearchives.us/public/new-york.htm
New York City
www.nyc.gov/html/doh

Delaware County Records
publicrecords.onlinesearches.com/NY_Delaware.htm
www.publicrecordcenter.com/newyorkpublicrecord.htm
www.co.delaware.ny.us

Dental Hygienists/Assistants (license and disciplinary records)
Office of the Professions
518-474-3817
www.op.nysed.gov/prof/dent/dentcdalic.htm
www.op.nysed.gov/prof/dent/dentdhlic.htm
www.op.nysed.gov/opsearches.htm
www.op.nysed.gov/rasearch.htm

Dentists (license and disciplinary records)
Office of the Professions
518-474-3817 x270
www.op.nysed.gov/dent.htm
www.op.nysed.gov/opsearches.htm
www.op.nysed.gov/rasearch.htm

Department of Motor Vehicles
(see DMV)

Dietetics-Nutrition (license and disciplinary records)
Office of the Professions
518-474-3817 x270
www.op.nysed.gov/diet.htm
www.op.nysed.gov/opsearches.htm
www.op.nysed.gov/rasearch.htm

Dispatch Facility, Central (license records)
Division of Licensing Services
518-474-4429
appsext8.dos.state.ny.us/lcns_public/chk_load

Divorce/Dissolution of Marriage Records
Department of Health
877-854-4481 (VitalChek)
www.health.state.ny.us/vital_records/divorce.htm
National Center for Health Statistics: New York
www.cdc.gov/nchs/w2w/new_york.htm
www.statearchives.us/public/new-york.htm

DMV (Department of Motor Vehicles)
212-645-5550, 800-DIAL DMV, 800-CALL-DMV
www.nydmv.state.ny.us
Driving Records
www.nydmv.state.ny.us/driverabstract/default.html
www.dmv.org/ny-new-york/driving-records.php
Title/Lien Status Check
www.nydmv.state.ny.us/titlestat/default.html
Vehicle Registration Information
www.nydmv.state.ny.us/register.htm
Vehicle History Report
www.dmv.org/reports-records.php

Doctors
(see Dentists, Physicians)

Dog Licensing
Department of Agriculture and Markets
www.agmkt.state.ny.us/AI/Doglic.html

Driving Records
(see also DMV)
www.nydmv.state.ny.us/driverabstract/default.html
www.dmv.org/ny-new-york/driving-records.php
www.publicrecordcenter.com/newyork_dmv.htm

Dutchess County Records
publicrecords.onlinesearches.com/NY_Dutchess.htm
www.publicrecordcenter.com/newyorkpublicrecord.htm
www.dutchessny.gov

Elections (results, contribution records)
Board of Elections
916-657-2166
www.elections.state.ny.us

Engineers (license and disciplinary records)
Office of the Professions
518-474-3817 x250
www.op.nysed.gov/prof/pels/pelic.htm
www.op.nysed.gov/opsearches.htm
www.op.nysed.gov/rasearch.htm

Erie County Records
publicrecords.onlinesearches.com/NY_Erie.htm
www.publicrecordcenter.com/newyorkpublicrecord.htm
www.erie.gov

Essex County Records
publicrecords.onlinesearches.com/NY_Essex.htm
www.publicrecordcenter.com/newyorkpublicrecord.htm
ecclerk.erie.gov

Expungement
(see Criminal Records)

Family Records in New York State Archives
(see also Birth, Death, Divorce, Marriage)
www.archives.nysed.gov/a/research/res_topics_genealogy.shtml
www.statearchives.us/new-york.htm

Fictitious Names
Corporate and Business Entity Database
appsext8.dos.state.ny.us/corp_public/corpsearch.entity_search_entry

Financial Institutions (banks, credit unions, savings & loan associations, trust companies)
Banking Department
877-BANK-NYS
www.banking.state.ny.us/supinst.htm

Franklin County Records
publicrecords.onlinesearches.com/NY_Franklin.htm
www.publicrecordcenter.com/newyorkpublicrecord.htm
franklincony.org/content

Fulton County Records

publicrecordcenter.com/newyorkpublicrecord.htm

Funeral Directors (license records)
Bureau of Funeral Directing
518-402-0785
www.labor.state.ny.us/stats/olcny/funerald.shtm

Genealogy Records and Resources
(see also Birth, Death, Divorce, Marriage)
www.health.state.ny.us/vital_records/genealogy.htm

Genesee County Records

publicrecords.onlinesearches.com/NY_Genesee.htm
www.publicrecordcenter.com/newyorkpublicrecord.htm
www.co.genesee.ny.us

Greene County Records

publicrecords.onlinesearches.com/NY_Greene.htm
www.publicrecordcenter.com/newyorkpublicrecord.htm
www.greenegovernment.com

Hair Styling (license records)
(see Appearance Enhancement)

Hamilton County Records

publicrecords.onlinesearches.com/NY_Hamilton.htm
www.publicrecordcenter.com/newyorkpublicrecord.htm

Health Statistics
Department of Health
www.nyhealth.gov/nysdoh/vital_statistics/index.htm
www.health.state.ny.us/healthaz

Hearing Aid Dispenser (license records)
Division of Licensing Services
518-474-4429
appsext8.dos.state.ny.us/lcns_public/chk_load

Herkimer County Records

publicrecords.onlinesearches.com/NY_Herkimer.htm
www.publicrecordcenter.com/newyorkpublicrecord.htm
herkimercounty.org/content

Home Inspector (license records)
Division of Licensing Services
518-474-4429
appsext8.dos.state.ny.us/lcns_public/chk_load

Inmate Locator
Department of Corrections
nysdocslookup.docs.state.ny.us

Insurance Brokers/Companies (license records; disciplinary actions)
Insurance Department
www.ins.state.ny.us/licinfo.htm
www.ins.state.ny.us/das.htm

awebproxyprd.ins.state.ny.us/onepage/StartForm.jsp?
   link=/CompanyDirectory/dir_srch_optiono.jsp?c=m

Interior Design (license records)
Office of the Professions
518-474-3817 x250
www.op.nysed.gov/interior.htm
www.op.nysed.gov/opsearches.htm

Investigator
(see Private Investigator)

Jefferson County Records

publicrecords.onlinesearches.com/NY_Jefferson.htm
www.co.jefferson.ny.us/Jefflive.nsf/index12
www.publicrecordcenter.com/newyorkpublicrecord.htm

Kings County Records

publicrecords.onlinesearches.com/NY_Kings.htm
publicrecords.onlinesearches.com/NY_NewYork.htm
www.nyc.gov/portal/site/nycgov/?front_door=true
www.publicrecordcenter.com/newyorkpublicrecord.htm

Laboratory Technology
(see Clinical Laboratory Technology)

Landscape Architect (license records)
(see Architects)

Land Surveying (license and disciplinary records)
Office of the Professions
518-474-3817 x250
www.op.nysed.gov/prof/pels/lsurvlic.htm
www.op.nysed.gov/opsearches.htm
www.op.nysed.gov/rasearch.htm

Lawyers
(see Attorneys)

Lewis County Records

publicrecords.onlinesearches.com/NY_Lewis.htm
www.publicrecordcenter.com/newyorkpublicrecord.htm
lewiscountyny.org/content

Licenses

www.op.nysed.gov/proflist.htm
appsext8.dos.state.ny.us/lcns_public/chk_load

Lien Search
(see County Government; UCC Statements)

Limited Liability Company; Limited Liability Partnership; Limited Partnership
(see Business Filings, Corporation Records)

Livingston County Records

publicrecords.onlinesearches.com/NY_Livingston.htm
www.publicrecordcenter.com/newyorkpublicrecord.htm
www.co.livingston.state.ny.us

Lobbying Records
(see Elections)

Madison County Records
publicrecords.onlinesearches.com/NY_Madison.htm
www.publicrecordcenter.com/newyorkpublicrecord.htm
www.madisoncounty.org

Marriage Records
Department of Health
877-854-4481 (VitalChek)
www.health.state.ny.us/vital_records/marriage.htm
www.health.state.ny.us/vital_records/genealogy.htm
National Center for Health Statistics: New York
www.cdc.gov/nchs/w2w/new_york.htm
www.statearchives.us/public/new-york.htm

Massage Therapy (license and disciplinary records)
Office of the Professions
518-474-3817 x270
www.op.nysed.gov/massage.htm
www.op.nysed.gov/opsearches.htm
www.op.nysed.gov/rasearch.htm

Medical Records, Right to See/Privacy
www.health.state.ny.us/nysdoh/opmc/medright.htm
www.wcb.state.ny.us/content/main/forms/HIPAA-1.pdf

Mental Health Practitioners (license and disciplinary records)
Office of the Professions
518-474-3817 x592
www.op.nysed.gov/mhp.htm
www.op.nysed.gov/opsearches.htm
www.op.nysed.gov/rasearch.htm

Midwifery (license and disciplinary records)
Office of the Professions
518-474-3817 x250
www.op.nysed.gov/midwife.htm
www.op.nysed.gov/opsearches.htm
www.op.nysed.gov/rasearch.htm

Monroe County Records
publicrecords.onlinesearches.com/NY_Monroe.htm
www.publicrecordcenter.com/newyorkpublicrecord.htm
www.monroecounty.gov

Montgomery County Records
publicrecords.onlinesearches.com/NY_Montgomery.htm
www.publicrecordcenter.com/newyorkpublicrecord.htm
www.co.montgomery.ny.us/website

Motor Vehicles
(see DMV)

Nassau County Records
publicrecords.onlinesearches.com/NY_Nassau.htm
www.nassaucountyny.gov/mynassauproperty/main.jsp
www.publicrecordcenter.com/newyorkpublicrecord.htm
www.nassaucountyny.gov

New York County Records
publicrecords.onlinesearches.com/NY_NewYork.htm

www.nyc.gov/portal/site/nycgov/?front_door=true
www.publicrecordcenter.com/newyorkpublicrecord.htm

Niagra County Records
publicrecords.onlinesearches.com/NY_Niagara.htm
www.publicrecordcenter.com/newyorkpublicrecord.htm
www.niagaracounty.com

Notary Public (license records)
(see also section 2.5)
Division of Licensing Services
518-474-4429
appsext8.dos.state.ny.us/lcns_public/chk_load

Not-for-Profit Corporation Filings
(see Business Filings)

Nurses (license and disciplinary records)
Office of the Professions
518-474-3817 x280
www.op.nysed.gov/nurse.htm
www.op.nysed.gov/opsearches.htm
www.op.nysed.gov/rasearch.htm

Occupational/Professional Licenses
www.op.nysed.gov/proflist.htm
appsext8.dos.state.ny.us/lcns_public/chk_load
www.op.nysed.gov/prof
(See also Professional/Occupational Licenses)

Occupational Therapy (license and disciplinary records)
Office of the Professions
518-474-3817 x270
www.op.nysed.gov/ot.htm
www.op.nysed.gov/opsearches.htm
www.op.nysed.gov/rasearch.htm

Oneida County Records
publicrecords.onlinesearches.com/NY_Oneida.htm
www.publicrecordcenter.com/newyorkpublicrecord.htm
www.co.oneida.ny.us

Onondaga County Records
publicrecords.onlinesearches.com/NY_Onondaga.htm
www.publicrecordcenter.com/newyorkpublicrecord.htm
www.ongov.net

Ontario County Records
publicrecords.onlinesearches.com/NY_Ontario.htm
raims.com/towns.html
www.publicrecordcenter.com/newyorkpublicrecord.htm
www.co.ontario.ny.us

Optometrists (license and disciplinary records)
Office of the Professions
518-474-3817 x250
www.op.nysed.gov/optom.htm
www.op.nysed.gov/opsearches.htm
www.op.nysed.gov/rasearch.htm

Orange County Records
publicrecords.onlinesearches.com/NY_Orange.htm
www.publicrecordcenter.com/newyorkpublicrecord.htm
www.co.orange.ny.us

Orleans County Records
publicrecords.onlinesearches.com/NY_Orleans.htm
www.publicrecordcenter.com/newyorkpublicrecord.htm
www.orleansny.com/default.aspx

Oswego County Records
publicrecords.onlinesearches.com/NY_Oswego.htm
www.publicrecordcenter.com/newyorkpublicrecord.htm
www.co.oswego.ny.us

Otsego County Records
publicrecords.onlinesearches.com/NY_Otsego.htm
www.publicrecordcenter.com/newyorkpublicrecord.htm
www.otsegocounty.com

Partnership Records
(see County Clerks, Business Filings)

Pharmacists (license and disciplinary records)
Office of the Professions
518-474-3817 x250
www.op.nysed.gov/pharm.htm
www.op.nysed.gov/opsearches.htm
www.op.nysed.gov/rasearch.htm

Physical Therapists (license and disciplinary records)
Office of the Professions
518-474-3817 x270
www.op.nysed.gov/pt.htm
www.op.nysed.gov/opsearches.htm
www.op.nysed.gov/rasearch.htm

Physician Assistants (license and disciplinary records)
Office of the Professions
518-474-3817 x260
www.op.nysed.gov/med.htm
www.op.nysed.gov/opsearches.htm
www.health.state.ny.us/nysdoh/opmc/main.htm

Physicians (license and disciplinary records)
Office of the Professions
518-474-3817 x260
www.op.nysed.gov/med.htm
www.op.nysed.gov/opsearches.htm
www.health.state.ny.us/nysdoh/opmc/main.htm

Podiatry (license and disciplinary records)
Office of the Professions
518-474-3817 x250
www.op.nysed.gov/pod.htm
www.op.nysed.gov/opsearches.htm
www.op.nysed.gov/rasearch.htm

Private Investigator (license records)
Division of Licensing Services
518-474-4429
appsext8.dos.state.ny.us/lcns_public/chk_load

Professional/Occupational Licenses
www.op.nysed.gov/proflist.htm
www.op.nysed.gov/opsearches.htm
appsext8.dos.state.ny.us/lcns_public/chk_load

Psychologists (license and disciplinary records)
Office of the Professions
518-474-3817 x270
www.op.nysed.gov/psych.htm
www.op.nysed.gov/opsearches.htm
www.op.nysed.gov/rasearch.htm

Public Accountancy
(see Accountants)

Putative Father Registry
800-345-KIDS
www.ocfs.state.ny.us/main/publications/Pub5040text.asp

Putnam County Records
publicrecords.onlinesearches.com/NY_Putnam.htm
www.publicrecordcenter.com/newyorkpublicrecord.htm
www.putnamcountyny.com

Queens County Records
publicrecords.onlinesearches.com/NY_Queens.htm
publicrecords.onlinesearches.com/NY_NewYork.htm
www.nyc.gov/portal/site/nycgov/?front_door=true
www.publicrecordcenter.com/newyorkpublicrecord.htm

Real Estate Appraiser (license records)
Division of Licensing Services
518-474-4429
appsext8.dos.state.ny.us/lcns_public/chk_load

Real Estate Brokers/Salespersons (license records)
Division of Licensing Services
518-474-4429
appsext8.dos.state.ny.us/lcns_public/chk_load

Records Repository Directory
iarchives.nysed.gov/Directories/directories.jsp?who=HRR

Rensselaer County Records
publicrecords.onlinesearches.com/NY_Rensselaer.htm
www.publicrecordcenter.com/newyorkpublicrecord.htm
www.rensco.com

Repairs
(see Automobile Inspections/Repairs)

Respiratory Therapy (license and disciplinary records)
Office of the Professions
518-474-3817 x270
www.op.nysed.gov/rt.htm
www.op.nysed.gov/opsearches.htm
www.op.nysed.gov/rasearch.htm

Richmond County Records
publicrecords.onlinesearches.com/NY_Richmond.htm
publicrecords.onlinesearches.com/NY_NewYork.htm
www.nyc.gov/portal/site/nycgov/?front_door=true
www.publicrecordcenter.com/newyorkpublicrecord.htm

Rockland County Records
publicrecords.onlinesearches.com/NY_Rockland.htm
www.publicrecordcenter.com/newyorkpublicrecord.htm
www.co.rockland.ny.us

Sales Tax Registrations
Department of Taxation and Finance
800-698-2909
www.tax.state.ny.us/sbc
www7.nystax.gov/STLR/stlrHome

Saratoga County Records
publicrecords.onlinesearches.com/NY_Saratoga.htm
www.publicrecordcenter.com/newyorkpublicrecord.htm
www.saratogacountyny.gov

Savings and Loan Associations
(see Financial Institutions)

Schenectady County Records
publicrecords.onlinesearches.com/NY_Schenectady.htm
www.publicrecordcenter.com/newyorkpublicrecord.htm
www.schenectadycounty.com/default.aspx?m=2

Schoharie County Records
publicrecords.onlinesearches.com/NY_Schoharie.htm
www.publicrecordcenter.com/newyorkpublicrecord.htm
www.schohariecounty-ny.gov/CountyWebSite/index.jsp

School
(see Teacher)

Schuyler County Records
publicrecords.onlinesearches.com/NY_Schuyler.htm
www.publicrecordcenter.com/newyorkpublicrecord.htm
www.schuylercounty.us

Security Guard (license records)
Division of Licensing Services
518-474-4429
appsext8.dos.state.ny.us/lcns_public/chk_load

Seneca County Records
publicrecords.onlinesearches.com/NY_Seneca.htm
www.publicrecordcenter.com/newyorkpublicrecord.htm
www.co.seneca.ny.us

Sex Offender Registration Records
(see also Criminal Records)
800-262-3257
criminaljustice.state.ny.us/nsor/index.htm

Shorthand Reporting (license and disciplinary records)
Office of the Professions
518-474-3817 x270
www.op.nysed.gov/csr.htm
www.op.nysed.gov/rasearch.htm

Social Workers (license and disciplinary records)
Office of the Professions
518-474-3817 x592
www.op.nysed.gov/sw.htm

www.op.nysed.gov/opsearches.htm
www.op.nysed.gov/rasearch.htm

Speech-Language Pathology & Audiology (license and disciplinary records)
Office of the Professions
518-474-3817 x270
www.op.nysed.gov/speech.htm
www.op.nysed.gov/opsearches.htm
www.op.nysed.gov/rasearch.htm

Steuben County Records
publicrecords.onlinesearches.com/NY_Steuben.htm
www.publicrecordcenter.com/newyorkpublicrecord.htm
www.steubencony.org

St. Lawrence County Records
publicrecords.onlinesearches.com/NY_St.Lawrence.htm
www.publicrecordcenter.com/newyorkpublicrecord.htm
www.co.st-lawrence.ny.us

Suffolk County Records
publicrecords.onlinesearches.com/NY_Suffolk.htm
www.publicrecordcenter.com/newyorkpublicrecord.htm
www.co.suffolk.ny.us

Sullivan County Records
publicrecords.onlinesearches.com/NY_Sullivan.htm
www.publicrecordcenter.com/newyorkpublicrecord.htm
www.co.sullivan.ny.us

Taxation
State
800-225-5829 (personal); 800-972-1233 (business)
www.tax.state.ny.us

Federal
800-829-1040 (personal); 800-829-4933 (business)
www.irs.gov

Teacher, Public School (credential records)
Department of Education
518-474-3901
eservices.nysed.gov/teach/certhelp/CpPersonSearchExternal.jsp?trgAction=INQUIRY

Telemarketer Business (license records)
Division of Licensing Services
518-474-4429
appsext8.dos.state.ny.us/lcns_public/chk_load

Therapists (license and disciplinary records)
Office of the Professions
518-474-3817
www.op.nysed.gov/opsearches.htm
www.op.nysed.gov/rasearch.htm

Tioga County Records
publicrecords.onlinesearches.com/NY_Tioga.htm
www.publicrecordcenter.com/newyorkpublicrecord.htm
www.tiogacountyny.com

Title/Lien Status Check (Vehicles)
(see also DMV)
www.nydmv.state.ny.us/titlestat/default.html

Tompkins County Records
publicrecords.onlinesearches.com/NY_Tompkins.htm
www.tompkins-co.org/assessment/online.html
www.publicrecordcenter.com/newyorkpublicrecord.htm
www.tompkins-co.org/cclerk

Trademark Registration
Department of State
www.nysl.nysed.gov/tradmark.htm
www.dos.state.ny.us/corp/miscfae.html

Trust Companies
(see Financial Institutions)

UCC Statements
NYS Dept. of State
www.dos.state.ny.us/corp/ucc.html
www.dos.state.ny.us/corp/uccfaq.html
appsext8.dos.state.ny.us/pls/ucc_public/web_search.
  main_frame

Ulster County Records
publicrecords.onlinesearches.com/NY_Ulster.htm
www.publicrecordcenter.com/newyorkpublicrecord.htm
www.co.ulster.ny.us

Unclaimed Property Records
Office of the State Comptroller
800-221-9311
www.osc.state.ny.us/ouf/index.htm

Uniform Commercial Code Filings
(see UCC Statements)

Vehicle History Report
(see also DMV)
www.dmv.org/reports-records.php

Veterinarians (license and disciplinary records)
Office of the Professions
518-474-3817 x250
www.op.nysed.gov/vet.htm
www.op.nysed.gov/opsearches.htm
www.op.nysed.gov/rasearch.htm

Vital Records
(see also Birth, Death, Divorce, Marriage)
*www.archives.nysed.gov/a/research/res_topics_gen_*
  vitalstats.shtml

Warren County Records
publicrecords.onlinesearches.com/NY_Warren.htm
www.publicrecordcenter.com/newyorkpublicrecord.htm
www.co.warren.ny.us

Washington County Records
publicrecords.onlinesearches.com/NY_Washington.htm
www.publicrecordcenter.com/newyorkpublicrecord.htm
www.co.washington.ny.us

Watch, Guard & Patrol Agency (license records)
Division of Licensing Services
518-474-4429
appsext8.dos.state.ny.us/lcns_public/chk_load

Wayne County Records
publicrecords.onlinesearches.com/NY_Wayne.htm
www.co.wayne.ny.us/warnicktreasurer/propertylocation.htm
www.publicrecordcenter.com/newyorkpublicrecord.htm
www.co.wayne.ny.us

Westchester County Records
publicrecords.onlinesearches.com/NY_Westchester.htm
www.publicrecordcenter.com/newyorkpublicrecord.htm
www.westchestergov.com
(type "records" in the search box)

Workers' Compensation
(see also section 2.9)
877-632-4996
www.wcb.state.ny.us

Wyoming County Records
publicrecords.onlinesearches.com/NY_Wyoming.htm
www.publicrecordcenter.com/newyorkpublicrecord.htm
www.wyomingco.net

Yates County Records
publicrecords.onlinesearches.com/NY_Yates.htm
www.publicrecordcenter.com/newyorkpublicrecord.htm
www.yatescounty.org

D. More Information

County Clerks
www.nytitle.com/faq.ivnu

County History
www.hopefarm.com/nycounty.htm

Courts
www.nycourts.gov/litigants/courtguides

Vital Records
www.health.state.ny.us/vital_records

New York State Archives
518-474-6926
www.archives.nysed.gov/aindex.shtml

Links for New York Occupations
www.op.nysed.gov/opsearches.htm
www.op.nysed.gov/contact.htm
www.labor.ny.gov/stats/index.shtm

Public Records Search Sites
www.searchsystems.net/list.php?nid=41
www.searchsystems.net
proagency.tripod.com/skp-ny.html
www.50states.com/publicrecords/newyork.htm
www.50states.com/newyork.htm
www.casebreakers.com
www.pretrieve.com

www.publicrecordfinder.com
www.brbpub.com
*www.virtualchase.com/topics/introduction_public_
records.shtml*

Open Government Guide
www.rcfp.org/ogg/index.php
(click "New York")

County Statistics/Profiles
quickfacts.census.gov/qfd/states/36000.html
*www.columbia.edu/cu/lweb/indiv/lehman/guides/
stats/ny.html*
www.fedstats.gov/qf/states/36000.html

LexisNexis
www.lexis.com
Examples of public records in NY libraries: NYPROP file (county property records); NYJGT file (judgments and liens). Additional public records databases on LexisNexis: Bankruptcy Filings, Business Locators, Corporate Filings (Business and Corporate Information, Limited Partnership Information, Fictitious Business Name Information, Franchise Index), Civil and Criminal Court Filings, Judgments and Liens (Including UCC and State Tax Liens), Jury Verdicts and Settlements, Professional Licenses Information, Person Locators (Military Locator, Voter Registration Record Information from 26 states, Social Security Death Records from 1962, Inmate Records from 6 states, Criminal History Records from 37 states), Personal Property Records (including Aircraft Registrations, Boat Registrations, Motor Vehicle Registrations from 20 states), Real Property Records (Deed Transfers, Tax Assessor Records, Mortgage Records).

Westlaw
www.westlaw.com
Examples of public records databases: RPA-NY (real property assessments); ULJ-NY (judgments and liens). Additional public records databases on Westlaw: People Finder-Person Tracker, Name Tracker, Telephone Tracker, Address Alert, Skip Tracer, Social Security Number Alert, Death Records, Professional Licenses; People Finder Plus Assets Library-Combined Asset Locator, Aircraft Registration Records, Watercraft Registration Records, Stock Locater Records, Motor Vehicle Registration Records, Real Property Transactions; People Finder, Assets Plus Adverse Filings Library—Combined Adverse Filings, Bankruptcy Records, UCC, Liens/Civil Judgment Filings, Uniform Commercial Code Filings, Liens/Civil Judgment Filings; Public Records Library—U.S. Business Finder Records, Corporate and Limited Partnership Records, "Doing Business As" Records, Litigation Preparation Records, Executive Affiliation Records, Name Availability Records.

1. In the yellow pages select three persons or businesses in three different categories of services that probably require a license in New York (e.g., physical therapist, midwife). Go to the web site on New York licenses for each service.
   (a) What kind of information is available about that service?
   (b) What information can you find about the three persons or businesses you selected, e.g., were you able to verify that the person or business has a current valid New York license? Could you find any disciplinary actions against them?
2. Pick three corporate or business entities and search the Department of State web site. For each, state its entity type and its street address for providing services.
3. Pick a lawyer licensed in New York and search the name.
   (a) From what law school did the attorney graduate?
   (b) Find the year the attorney was admitted to practice.

A. Introduction

Elsewhere we cover the extensive availability of New York law that you can read online (see section 5.1). Suppose, however, that you want to go to a bricks-and-mortar law library to use its resources. You want to go to a facility where you can take books off the shelf. What options are available to you?

There are three major kinds of law libraries in New York to which you have full or partial access:

Court Law Libraries (CLL)
Federal Depository Libraries (FDL)
State Document Depository Libraries (SDDL)

The list below will tell you which libraries fall into these three categories. Some libraries fall into more than one category. After each entry you will find the designations

CLL, FDL, or SDDL to indicate the kind of library it is or the kind of legal materials in it to which you may be entitled to have free access.

Before you visit any of the libraries on this list, you should phone the library and check its web site to determine its location, hours, and any restrictions on using its materials.

Court Law Libraries (CLL)

Judiciary Law §§ 813 and 814 provide that each county have a "court" library, commonly referred to as the supreme court library. There are currently 63 of these public law libraries. Each typically has, at minimum, New York and federal case law, statutes, regulations, and some secondary materials. Many libraries have materials both in print and online. There is an online catalog of all the collections on LION, the court system's Library and Information Network. Section 812 of the Judiciary Law also provides for libraries for each of the appellate divisions.

Court Law Libraries
www.nycourts.gov/lawlibraries/courtlawlibraries.shtml
www.nycourts.gov/lawlibraries/publicaccess.shtml

Federal Depository Libraries (FDL)

A federal depository library is a public or private library that receives free federal government publications to which it must allow access by the general public. The publications include federal statutes, federal regulations, and federal court opinions. If the library is private, e.g., a private university library, the public right of free access may be limited to those publications the library receives from the federal government under the federal depository program. The private library has the right to prevent the public from using the rest of its collection.

Federal Depository Libraries in New York
www.nysl.nysed.gov/feddep/fdlpdata.htm

State Document Depository Libraries (SDDL)

The New York State Library is a repository of official state publications of the legislative, executive, and judicial branches. Every state officer, department, commission, institution, authority, legislative committee, and board must send 30 copies of its printed reports to the New York State Library. The State Library sends paper or microfilm copies to designated state document depository libraries throughout the state.

State Document Depository Libraries
www.nysl.nysed.gov/nysdep.htm
www.nysl.nysed.gov/edocs/education/bycounty.htm

Your Neighborhood Public Library

In the card or online catalog of your neighborhood public library, find out (1) what legal materials it has on its shelves and (2) how current (up-to-date) any particular legal material is. In the catalog, check entries under New York law. Here are examples of what you might find:

- *New York Jurisprudence 2d*, West, 2009
- *McKinney's Consolidated Laws of New York Statutes Annotated*
- *New York Consolidated Laws Service: Annotated Statutes with Forms*
- *Official Compilation of Codes, Rules and Regulations.* Title 8: Education (an example of NYCRR sections that maybe found)
- *West's New York Digest, 4th*
- *Black's Law Dictionary*, West Group
- Carmody-Wait, 2d, *Cyclopedia of NY Practice with Forms*, West Group
- *New York Practice, 4th*, David Siegel, Thompson-West
- *Martindale-Hubbell Law Directory*
- *New York Landlord and Tenant*, Joseph Rasch, West Group
- *Criminal Law Handbook of New York*, Gould Publications
- *Law and the Family New York, 2d*, Joel Brandes, West Group
- *New York City Charter and Administrative Code*
- *United States Code Service*, Michie
- *United States Code Annotated*, West

Of course, not every local public library will have all of these sets of legal materials. Furthermore, those libraries that have them may not keep them current with the latest supplementary material. Nevertheless, it is worth checking what is available.

Ask a Librarian

See section 5.6 for a discussion of another valuable library service: Ask a Librarian. There are excellent web sites available (e.g., *www.nysl.nysed.gov/ask.htm*) that you can contact by phone or e-mail to obtain leads to legal and nonlegal materials that are relevant to your research.

B. Abbreviations

CLL Court Law Library
FDL Federal Depository Library
Lib Library
NY New York
SDDL State Document Depository Library
SUNY State University of New York
Univ University

C. Law Libraries

Albany County
Albion
Allegany County
Auburn
Batavia
Bath
Belmont
Binghamton
Brockport
Bronx County
Bronxville
Brooklyn
Brookville
Broome County
Buffalo
Canandaigua
Canton
Carmel
Catskill
Cattaraugus County
Cayuga County
Central Islip
Chautauqua County
Chemung County
Chenango County
Clinton County
Columbia County
Cooperstown
Corning
Cortland County
Delaware County
Delhi
Dryden
Dutchess County
East Islip
Elizabethtown
Elmira
Erie County
Essex County
Farmingdale
Flushing
Fonda
Fort Edward
Franklin County
Fulton County
Garden City
Genesee County
Geneseo
Goshen
Greene County
Hamilton
Hamilton County
Hempstead
Herkimer County
Hudson
Ithaca
Jamaica
Jefferson County
Johnstown

Kings County
Kings Point
Kingston
Lake George
Lake Pleasant
Lewis County
Little Valley
Livingston County
Lockport
Long Island City
Lowville
Lyons
Madison County
Malone
Mayville
Middletown
Mineola
Monroe County
Montgomery County
Monticello
Mount Vernon
Nassau County
Newburgh
New City
New Paltz
New York County
Niagara County
Norwich
Oakdale
Oneida
Oneida County
Oneonta
Onondaga County
Ontario County
Orange County
Orleans County
Oswego County
Otsego County
Penn Yan
Plattsburgh
Potsdam
Poughkeepsie
Purchase
Putnam County
Queens County
Rensselaer County
Richmond County
Riverhead
Rochester
Rockland County
Saint Bonaventure
Saint Lawrence County
Saratoga County
Schenectady County
Schoharie County
Schuyler County
Seneca County
Staten Island
Steuben County

Stony Brook
Suffolk County
Sullivan County
Syracuse
Tioga County
Tompkins County
Troy
Ulster County
Utica
Warren County
Warsaw
Washington County

Watertown
Watkins Glen
Waverly
Wayne County
Westchester County
West Point
White Plains
Wyoming County
Yates County
Yonkers
Yorktown Heights

Albany County
Frances Bergan Law Lib (CLL)
518-270-3717 (Albany)
www.nycourts.gov/lawlibraries/publicaccess.shtml

Albany Law School Schaffer Law Lib (FDL) (SDDL)
518-445-2390 (Albany)
www.albanylaw.edu/sub.php?navigation_id=8
www.albanylaw.edu/sub.php?navigation_id=788

New York State Lib (FDL)
518-474-5355 (Albany)
www.nysl.nysed.gov
www.nysl.nysed.gov/feddep

State University of NY, Albany Univ Lib (FDL) (SDDL)
518-442-3558 (Albany)
library.albany.edu

Albion
(see Orleans County)

Allegany County
Allegany County Law Lib (CLL)
716-268-5813 (Belmont)
www.nycourts.gov/courts/8jd/Allegany/index.shtml
www.nycourts.gov/lawlibraries/publicaccess.shtml

Auburn
(see Cayuga County)

Batavia
(see Genesee County)

Bath
(see Steuben County)

Belmont
(see Allegany County)

Binghamton
(scc Broome County)

Brockport
(see Monroe County)

Bronx County
Bronx Supreme Court Law Lib (CLL)
718-590-3678, 718-590-3679 (Bronx)
www.courts.state.ny.us/library/bronx/board.shtml
www.nycourts.gov/lawlibraries/publicaccess.shtml

Fordham University Welsh Lib (FDL)
718-817-3586 (Bronx)
www.library.fordham.edu
www.library.fordham.edu/information/about.html

Herbert Lehman College/CUNY Lief Lib
(FDL)(SDDL)
718-960-8580 (Bronx)
www.lehman.edu/provost/library
www.lehman.edu/provost/library//govdoc/index.htm

New York City Civil Court, Bronx County (CLL)
718-466-3123 (Bronx)
www.nycourts.gov/lawlibraries/courtlawlibraries.shtml
www.courts.state.ny.us/courts/nyc/civil/bronxciviladmin.shtml

New York City Criminal Court, Bronx County
(CLL)(SDDL)
718-590-7297 (Bronx)
www.nycourts.gov/courts/nyc/criminal/generalinfo.shtml

SUNY, Maritime College Luce Lib (FDL)(SDDL)
718-409-7231 (Bronx)
www.sunymaritime.edu/Library/index.aspx
www.sunymaritime.edu/stephenblucelibrary/generalcoll.htm

Bronxville
(see Westchester County)

Brooklyn
(see Kings County)

Brookville
(see Nassau County)

Broome County
Binghamton Supreme Court Law Lib (CLL)(SDDL)
607-778-2119 (Binghamton)
www.nycourts.gov/lawlibraries/publicaccess.shtml
www.nycourts.gov/lawlibraries/courtlawlibraries.shtml

Binghamton University Bartle Lib (FDL)(SDDL)
607-777-2345 (Binghamton)
library.lib.binghamton.edu
libraryguides.binghamton.edu

Buffalo
(see Erie County)

Canandaigua
(see Ontario County)

Canton
(see Saint Lawrence County)

Carmel
(see Putnam County)

Catskill
(see Greene County)

Cattaraugus County
Cattaraugus County Law Lib (CLL)
716-938-9111 Ext. 326 (Little Valley)

www.nycourts.gov/lawlibraries/courtlawlibraries.shtml#8
www.nycourts.gov/lawlibraries/publicaccess.shtml

Saint Bonaventure University Friedsam Lib
(FDL)(SDDL)
716-375-2164 (Saint Bonaventure)
www.sbu.edu/library.aspx?id=1754
www.nysl.nysed.gov/feddep/fdlpdata.htm

Cayuga County
New York State Supreme Court Law Lib (CLL)
315-255-4310 (Auburn)
www.nycourts.gov/lawlibraries/courtlawlibraries.shtml
www.nycourts.gov/lawlibraries/publicaccess.shtml

Central Islip
(see Suffolk County)

Chautauqua County
Chautauqua County Law Lib (CLL)
716-753-7111 (Mayville)
www.courts.state.ny.us/courts/8jd/Chautauqua/index.shtml
nycourthelp.gov/LawLib.html#c

Chemung County
Charles B. Swartwood Supreme Court Lib (CLL)
607-737-2983 (Elmira)
www.nycourts.gov/lawlibraries/publicaccess.shtml
www.chemungcounty.com/index.asp?pageId=80

Elmira College Gannett-Tripp Lib (FDL)(SDDL)
607-735-1864 (Elmira)
www.elmira.edu/academics/library
research.elmira.edu/subjects/govinfo.shtml

Chenango County
David L. Follett Supreme Court Lib (CLL)
607-334-9463 (Norwich)
www.nycourts.gov/lawlibraries/publicaccess.shtml
www.nycourts.gov/courts/6jd

Clinton County
Clinton County Supreme Court Law Lib (CLL)
518-565-4808 (Plattsburgh)
www.nycourts.gov/lawlibraries/publicaccess.shtml
www.courts.state.ny.us/courthelp/ClintonSupCt1.htm

SUNY Plattsburgh Feinberg Lib (FDL)(SDDL)
518-564-5190 (Plattsburgh)
www.plattsburgh.edu/library
www.plattsburgh.edu/library/governmentinformation.php

Columbia County
Supreme Court Law Lib (CLL)
518-828-3206 (Hudson)
www.courts.state.ny.us/courthelp/ColumbiaSupCt1.htm
www.nycourts.gov/lawlibraries/publicaccess.shtml

Cooperstown
(see Otsego County)

Corning
(see Steuben County)

Cortland County
Louis H. Folmer Supreme Court Lib (CLL)
Cortland County Courthouse
607-753-5011 (Cortland)
www.nycourts.gov/library/Cortland
www.nycourts.gov/lawlibraries/publicaccess.shtml

Delaware County
Delaware County Courthouse (CLL)
607-746-3959 (Delhi)
www.courts.state.ny.us/library/delaware/index.shtml
www.nycourts.gov/lawlibraries/publicaccess.shtml

SUNY, Delhi Resnick Lib (FDL)(SDDL)
607-746-4635 (Delhi)
www.delhi.edu/library
www.nysl.nysed.gov/feddep/fdlpdata.htm

Delhi
(see Delaware County)

Dryden
(see Tompkins County)

Dutchess County
Supreme Court Law Lib (CLL)
845-486-2215 (Poughkeepsie)
www.courts.state.ny.us/courts/9jd/dutchess/index.shtml
www.nycourts.gov/lawlibraries/publicaccess.shtml

Vassar College Lib (FDL)(SDDL)
845-437-5766 (Poughkeepsie)
library.vassar.edu
library.vassar.edu/research/guides/howtofind/govdocs.html

East Islip
(see Suffolk County)

Elizabethtown
(see Essex County)

Elmira
(see Chemung County)

Erie County
Buffalo and Erie County Public Lib (FDL)(SDDL)
716-858-8900 (Buffalo)
www.buffalolib.org
www.nysl.nysed.gov/feddep/fdlpdata.htm

State University of New York, University at Buffalo Lib
(FDL)(SDDL)
716-645-2820 (Buffalo)
ublib.buffalo.edu/libraries/asl/guides/busdoc/index.html

State University of New York, University at Buffalo
Law Lib (FDL)
716-645-2047; 716-645-6765 (Buffalo)
law.lib.buffalo.edu

Supreme Court Lib at Buffalo (CLL)(SDDL)
716-845-9400 (Buffalo)
www.nycourts.gov/library/buffalo/index.shtml

www.nycourts.gov/library/buffalo/index.shtml
www.nycourts.gov/lawlibraries/publicaccess.shtml

Essex County
Essex County Court Law Lib (CLL)
518-873-3377 (Elizabethtown)
www.courts.state.ny.us/courthelp/EssexCountyCt1.htm
www.nycourts.gov/lawlibraries/publicaccess.shtml

Farmingdale
(see Nassau County)

Flushing
(see Queens County)

Fonda
(see Montgomery County)

Fort Edward
(see Washington County)

Franklin County
Franklin County Court Law Lib (CLL)
518-481-1732 (Malone)
www.nycourts.gov/lawlibraries/publicaccess.shtml
www.courts.state.ny.us/courthelp/FranklinCountyCt1.htm

Fulton County
Fulton County Court Law Lib (CLL)
518-762-0685 (Johnstown)
www.nycourts.gov/lawlibraries/publicaccess.shtml
www.courts.state.ny.us/courthelp/FultonCountyCt1.htm

Garden City
(see Nassau County)

Genesee County
Genesee County Law Lib (CLL)
585-344-2550 x2224 (Batavia)
www.nycourts.gov/lawlibraries/publicaccess.shtml
www.courts.state.ny.us/courthelp/GeneseeCountyCt1.htm

Geneseo
(see Livingston County)

Goshen
(see Orange County)

Greene County
Emory A. Chase Memorial Lib (CLL)
518-943-3130 (Catskill)
www.nycourts.gov/lawlibraries/publicaccess.shtml
www.courts.state.ny.us/courthelp/GreeneCountyCt1.htm

Hamilton
(see Madison County)

Hamilton County
Hamilton County Court Law Lib (CLL)
518-648-5411 (Lake Pleasant)
www.nycourts.gov/lawlibraries/publicaccess.shtml
www.courts.state.ny.us/courthelp/HamiltonCountyCt1.htm

Hempstead
(see Nassau County)

Herkimer County
Herkimer County Law Lib (CLL) (SDDL)
315-867-1172 (Herkimer)
www.nycourts.gov/lawlibraries/publicaccess.shtml
www.courts.state.ny.us/courthelp/HerkimerCountyCt1.htm

Hudson
(see Columbia County)

Ithaca
(see Tompkins County)

Jamaica
(see Queens County)

Jefferson County
Supreme Court Law Lib (CLL) (SDDL)
315-785-3064 (Watertown)
nycourthelp.gov/JeffersonSupCt1.htm
www.nycourts.gov/lawlibraries/publicaccess.shtml

Johnstown
(see Fulton County)

Kings County
Brooklyn College Lib (FDL) (SDDL)
718-951-5332 (Brooklyn)
library.brooklyn.cuny.edu
library.brooklyn.cuny.edu/research/govdocs/databases.html

Brooklyn Law School Lib (FDL) (SDDL)
718-780-7973 (Brooklyn)
www.brooklaw.edu/library

Brooklyn Public Lib (FDL) (SDDL)
718-230-2100; 718-623-7000 (Brooklyn)
www.brooklynpubliclibrary.org/index.jsp

Kings County Supreme Court Law Lib (CLL)
360 Adams Street, Room 349
Brooklyn, NY 11201
347-296-1144 (Brooklyn)
www.nycourts.gov/library/brooklyn/index.shtml
www.nycourts.gov/lawlibraries/publicaccess.shtml

New York City Civil Court, Kings County (CLL)
718-643-2843 (Brooklyn)
nycourthelp.gov/KingsCitywideCivCt1.htm
www.nycourts.gov/lawlibraries/courtlawlibraries.shtml

Kings Point
(see Nassau County)

Kingston
(see Ulster County)

Lake George
(see Warren County)

Lake Pleasant
(see Hamilton County)

Lewis County
Lewis County Law Lib (CLL)
315-376-538 (Lowville)

www.courts.state.ny.us/library/lewis/index.shtml
www.nycourts.gov/lawlibraries/publicaccess.shtml

Little Valley
(see Cattaraugus County)

Livingston County
SUNY, College at Geneseo Milne Lib (FDL) (SDDL)
585-245-5595 (Geneseo)
library.geneseo.edu

Wadsworth Public Lib (CLL)
24 Center Street
Geneseo, NY 14454
585-243-0440 (Geneseo)
www.wadsworthnylibrary.blogspot.com
www.nycourts.gov/lawlibraries/publicaccess.shtml

Lockport
(see Niagara County)

Long Island City
(see Queens County)

Lowville
(see Lewis County)

Lyons
(see Wayne County)

Madison County
Colgate University Case Lib (FDL)
315-228-6194 (Hamilton)
exlibris.colgate.edu

Oneida Public Lib (CLL)
315-363-3050 (Oneida)
www.midyork.org/oneida
www.nycourts.gov/lawlibraries/publicaccess.shtml

Malone
(see Franklin County)

Mayville
(see Chautauqua County)

Middletown
(see Orange County)

Mineola
(see Nassau County)

Monroe County
Monroe County Lib System (FDL) (SDDL)
585-428-7300 (Rochester)
www3.libraryweb.org/home2.aspx

Seventh Judicial District Law Lib (CLL)
585-428-1854 (Rochester)
www.nycourts.gov/lawlibraries/publicaccess.shtml
nycourthelp.gov/MonroeSupCt1.htm

SUNY, College at Brockport Drake Lib (FDL) (SDDL)
585-395-2760; 585-395-2143 (Rochester)
www.brockport.edu/~govdoc/doc1.html

University of Rochester Rhees Lib (FDL)(SDDL)
585-273-5322; 585-275-4482 (Rochester)
www.library.rochester.edu/index.cfm?PAGE=235

Montgomery County
Montgomery County Court Law Lib (CLL)
518-853-4516 (Fonda)
www.nycourts.gov/lawlibraries/publicaccess.shtml
nycourthelp.gov/MontgomeryCountyCt1.htm

Monticello
(see Sullivan County)

Mount Vernon
(see Westchester County)

Nassau County
Adelphi University Swirbul Lib (FDL)(SDDL)
516-877-3574 (Garden City)
libraries.adelphi.edu

Farmingdale State SUNY Greenley Lib (FDL)
631-420-2184 (Farmingdale)
www.farmingdale.edu/library/gov.html
www.farmingdale.edu/library/index.html

Hofstra University Axinn Lib (FDL)(SDDL)
516-463-5972 (Hempstead)
*www.hofstra.edu/libraries/axinn/axinn_libdepts_docs_*
  index.cfm

Hofstra University Deane Law Lib (FDL)(SDDL)
516-463-5898 (Hempstead)
law.hofstra.edu/Library/index.html

Long Island University Schwartz Lib (FDL)(SDDL)
516-299-2142 (Brookville)
www.liunet.edu/cwis/cwp/library/gov/docs.htm

Supreme Court Law Lib (CLL)(SDDL)
516-571-3883 (Mineola)
www.dos.state.ny.us/code/libs.htm#Mineola
www.nycourts.gov/lawlibraries/publicaccess.shtml
nycourthelp.gov/NassauSupCt1.htm

U.S. Merchant Marine Academy Bland Lib (FDL)
516-773-5503 (Kings Point)
www.usmma.edu/academics/Library

Newburgh
(see Orange County)

New City
(see Rockland County)

New Paltz
(see Ulster County)

New York County
City College/CUNY Cohen Lib (FDL)(SDDL)
212-650-7612 (New York)
www.ccny.cuny.edu/library/Divisions/Government/
  GOVPUBS.html

Columbia Law School Diamond Lib (FDL)
212-854-3922 (New York)
www.law.columbia.edu/library

Columbia University Lehman Lib (FDL)(SDDL)
212-854-3794; 212-854-5087 (New York)
www.columbia.edu/cu/lweb/indiv/usgd

Cooper Union for the Advancement of Science &
Art/Lib (FDL)
212-353-4187; 212-353-4186 (New York)
www.cooper.edu/facilities/library/gov_docs_frameset.html

Fordham University School of Law Kissam Lib
(FDL)(SDDL)
212-636-6908 (New York)
lawlib1.lawnet.fordham.edu

New York City Surrogate's Court (CLL)
212-374-8257 (New York)
www.nycourts.gov/lawlibraries/publicaccess.shtml
nycourthelp.gov/NYSurrCt1.htm

New York City Civil Court, NY County (CLL)
212-374-8043 (New York)
www.nycourts.gov/library/nyc_criminal/index.shtml
www.nycourts.gov/lawlibraries/publicaccess.shtml

New York City Criminal Court, NY County (CLL)
212-748-5085 (New York)
www.nycourts.gov/lawlibraries/publicaccess.shtml
nycourthelp.gov/NYCitywideCrimCt1.htm

New York County Supreme Court, Criminal
Term (CLL)
646-386-3890 (New York)
nycourts.gov/library/nyc_criminal/index.shtml
www.nycourts.gov/lawlibraries/publicaccess.shtml
nycourthelp.gov/NYSupCrimCt1.htm

New York County Supreme Court, Civil Term
(CLL)(SDDL)
646-386-3670 (New York)
www.nycourts.gov/lawlibraries/publicaccess.shtml
nycourthelp.gov/NYSupCivCt1.htm

New York County Public Access Law Lib (CLL)
646-386-3715 (New York)
www.nycourts.gov/lawlibraries/publicaccess.shtml
www.aallnet.org/chapter/llagny/publawlib.html

New York Law Institute (FDL)
212-732-8720 (New York)
nyli.org

New York Law School Mendik Lib (FDL)(SDDL)
212-431-2332 (New York)
www.nyls.edu/pages/220.asp

New York Public Lib (FDL)(SDDL)
Astor Branch/Lenox Branch Science, Industry
and Business
212-592-7000 (New York)
www.nypl.org/research/sibl/govt/index.html

New York Public Lib Mid-Manhattan Lib
(FDL)(SDDL)
212-340-0888 (New York)
www.nypl.org/research/sibl/govt/locate.htm

New York University Bobst Lib (FDL)(SDDL)
212-998-2601 (New York)
library.nyu.edu/research/govdocs

New York University School of Law Lib (FDL) (LSL)
212-998-6300 (New York)
www.law.nyu.edu/library/index.htm

St. John's University Davis Lib (FDL)
212-277-5135 (New York)
new.stjohns.edu/academics/libraries/campus/davis

Cardozo School of Law Chutick Lib (Yeshiva) (FDL)
New York, NY 10003-4301
212-790-0220 (New York)
www.cardozo.yu.edu
www.cardozo.yu.edu/directory.aspx?page=4
(click "Library")

Yeshiva University Pollack Lib (FDL)
212-960-5378 (New York)
www.yu.edu/libraries/index.aspx?id=33

Niagara County
Supreme Court Lib (CLL)
716-439-7145 (Lockport)
www.nycourts.gov/lawlibraries/publicaccess.shtml
nycourts.gov/courts/8jd/Niagara/index.shtml

Norwich
(see Chenango County)

Oakdale
(see Suffolk County)

Oneida
(see Madison County)

Oneida County
Oneida County Supreme Court Law Lib (CLL)(SDDL)
315-798-5703 (Utica)
www.nycourts.gov/lawlibraries/publicaccess.shtml
nycourthelp.gov/OneidaSupCt1.htm

SUNY, Institute of Technology Cayan Lib (FDL)
315-792-7245 (Utica)
web1.sunyit.edu/library

Oneonta
(see Otsego County)

Onondaga County
Onondaga County Public Lib Kinchen Lib
(FDL)(SDDL)
315-435-1900 (Syracuse)
www.onlib.org

Supreme Court Law Lib (CLL)
315-671-1150 (Syracuse)

www.nycourts.gov/lawlibraries/publicaccess.shtml
nycourthelp.gov/OnondagaSupCt1.htm

Syracuse University Bird Lib (FDL)(SDDL)
315-443-4176 (Syracuse)
libwww.syr.edu/research/internet/government/index.html

Syracuse University Barclay Law Lib (FDL)(SDDL)
315-443-9560 (Syracuse)
www.law.syr.edu/lawlibrary

Ontario County
Finger Lakes Community College Lib (CLL)(SDDL)
585-394-3500, x7371 (Canandaigua)
library.flcc.edu
www.nycourts.gov/lawlibraries/publicaccess.shtml

Orange County
Middletown Thrall Lib (FDL)(SDDL)
Middletown, NY 10940-5706
845-341-5454 (Middletown)
thrall.org/gov

Newburgh Free Lib (FDL)(SDDL)
845-563-3625 (Newburgh)
www.newburghlibrary.org/websites/federal.asp

Supreme Court Law Lib (CLL)
845-291-3138 (Goshen)
www.nycourts.gov/lawlibraries/publicaccess.shtml
nycourthelp.gov/OrangeSupCt1.htm

U.S. Military Academy Lib (FDL)(SDDL)
845-938-2230 (West Point)
usmalibrary.usma.edu

Orleans County
Orleans County Law Lib (CLL)
Orleans County Court
County Building
Albion, NY 14411
716-589-4457 (Albion)
nycourthelp.gov/OrleansCountyCt1.htm
www.nycourts.gov/lawlibraries/publicaccess.shtml

Oswego County
State University of New York, Penfield Lib
(FDL)(SDDL)
315-312-4267 (Oswego)
*www.oswego.edu/academics/library/resources/gov_*
    info.html

Supreme Court Law Lib (CLL)
315-349-3297 (Oswego)
www.nycourts.gov/lawlibraries/publicaccess.shtml
nycourthelp.gov/OswegoSupCt1.htm

Otsego County
Joseph P. Molinari Supreme Court Law Lib (CLL)
607-547-5425 (Cooperstown)
www.nycourts.gov/lawlibraries/publicaccess.shtml
nycourthelp.gov/OtsegoSupCt1.htm

SUNY, College at Oneonta Milne Lib (FDL)(SDDL)
607-436-2722 (Oneonta)
www.oneonta.edu/library

Penn Yan
(see Yates County)

Plattsburgh
(see Clinton County)

Potsdam
(see Saint Lawrence County)

Poughkeepsie
(see Dutchess County)

Purchase
(see Westchester County)

Putnam County
Supreme Court Law Lib (CLL)
845-225-3641 x297 (Carmel)
www.nycourts.gov/lawlibraries/publicaccess.shtml
nycourthelp.gov/PutnamSupCt1.htm

Queens County
CUNY School of Law (Queens) Law Lib (FDL)(SDDL)
718-340-4240 (Flushing)
www.law.cuny.edu/library.html

LaGuardia Community College/CUNY Lib (FDL)
718-482-5425 (Long Island City)
library.laguardia.edu

New York City Civil Court, Queens County
718-262-7348 (Jamaica)
www.nycourts.gov/library/queens

Queens Borough Public Lib (FDL)(SDDL)
718-990-0714 (Jamaica)
www.queenslibrary.org

Queens College/CUNY Rosenthal Lib (FDL)
718-997-3700 (Flushing)
qcpages.qc.cuny.edu/Library/information/mission.php

Queens Supreme Court Law Lib (CLL)(SDDL)
718-298-1206 (Jamaica)
www.nycourts.gov/library/queens/index.shtml
www.nycourts.gov/lawlibraries/publicaccess.shtml

Saint John's University Mail Lib (FDL)(SDDL)
718-990-6454 (Jamaica)
www.stjohns.edu/academics/libraries

Saint John's University Rittenberg Law Lib (FDL)(SDDL)
718-990-6651 (Jamaica)
lawlibrary.stjohns.edu/screens/idx_libr_catalogs.html

Rensselaer County
Supreme Court Lib (CLL)
518-285-6183; 518-270-3717 (Troy)
www.nycourts.gov/lawlibraries/publicaccess.shtml
nycourthelp.gov/RensselaerSupCt1.htm

Troy Public Lib (FDL)(SDDL)
518-274-7073 (Troy)
www.stjohns.edu/academics/libraries

Richmond County
New York City Civil Court, Richmond County (CLL)
718-390-5422 (Staten Island)
www.nycourts.gov/lawlibraries/publicaccess.shtml
nycourthelp.gov/RichmondNYCCivCt1.htm

Richmond County Supreme Court (CLL)
718-390-5291 (Staten Island)
www.nycourts.gov/lawlibraries/publicaccess.shtml
nycourthelp.gov/RichmondSupCt1.htm

Riverhead
(see Suffolk County)

Rochester
(see Monroe County)

Rockland County
Supreme Court Law Lib (CLL)
845-638-5396 (New City)
www.nycourts.gov/lawlibraries/publicaccess.shtml
nycourthelp.gov/RocklandSupCt1.htm

Saint Bonaventure
(see Cattaraugus County)

Saint Lawrence County
Clarkson University Burnap Lib (FDL)(SDDL)
315-268-2297 (Potsdam)
www.clarkson.edu/library/books_more/govdocs.html

State University of New York Crumb Lib (FDL)(SDDL)
315-267-2485 (Potsdam)
wwwx.potsdam.edu/library

St. Lawrence County Supreme Court Lib (CLL)
315-379-2279 (Canton)
www.nycourts.gov/lawlibraries/publicaccess.shtml
nycourthelp.gov/StLawrenceSupCt1.htm

St. Lawrence University Young Lib (FDL)(SDDL)
315-229-5451 (Canton)
www.stlawu.edu/library

Saratoga County
Saratoga Supreme Court Law Lib (CLL)
518-584-4862 (Saratoga Springs)
www.nycourts.gov/lawlibraries/publicaccess.shtml
www.nycourts.gov/lawlibraries/courtlawlibraries.shtml#4

Skidmore College Scribner Lib (FDL)
Saratoga Springs, NY 12866-1632
518-580-5502; 518-580-5503 (Saratoga Springs)
www.skidmore.edu/library

Schenectady County
Schenectady County Supreme Court (Egan) Lib (CLL)
518-285-8518 (Schenectady)
www.nycourts.gov/lawlibraries/publicaccess.shtml
nycourthelp.gov/SchenectadySupCt1.htm

Union College Schaffer Lib (FDL)
518-388-6635 (Schenectady)
www.union.edu/PUBLIC/LIBRARY/refroom/govinfo
  .htm

Schoharie County
F. Walter Bliss Memorial (Court House) Lib (CLL)
518-295-7900 (Schoharie)
www.nycourts.gov/lawlibraries/publicaccess.shtml

Schuyler County
Watkins Glen Public Lib (CLL) (SDDL)
607-535-2346 (Watkins Glen)
www.nycourts.gov/lawlibraries/publicaccess.shtml
www.stls.org/Watkins

Seneca County
Seneca Falls Lib (CLL)
315-568-8265 (Seneca Falls)
www.senecafallslibrary.org
www.nycourts.gov/lawlibraries/publicaccess.shtml

Staten Island
(see Richmond County)

Steuben County
Corning Community College Houghton Lib
(FDL) (SDDL)
607-962-9251 (Corning)
www.corning-cc.edu/visitors/library
www.corning-cc.edu/visitors/library/resources

Steuben County Supreme Court Lib (CLL)
607-664-2099 (Bath)
www.nycourts.gov/lawlibraries/publicaccess.shtml
nycourthelp.gov/SteubenSupCt1.htm

Stony Brook
(see Suffolk County)

Suffolk County
Dowling College Lib (FDL)
631-244-3282 (Oakdale)
www.dowling.edu/library/about/govdocs.html

Stony Brook University Melville Lib (FDL) (SDDL)
631-632-7110 (Stony Brook)
www.sunysb.edu/library/collections/collections/govdocs
  .html

Suffolk Cooperative Lib System (FDL) (SDDL)
631-286-1600 x1335 (East Islip)
www.suffolk.lib.ny.us/govdocs/webgov.shtml

Suffolk County Supreme Court Law Lib (CLL)
631-853-7530 (Central Islip)
www.nycourts.gov/lawlibraries/publicaccess.shtml
nycourthelp.gov/SuffolkSupCt1.htm

Supreme Court Law Lib (Criminal Courts) (CLL)
Riverhead, NY 11901-3312
631-852-2419 (Riverhead)
www.nycourts.gov/lawlibraries/publicaccess.shtml

Touro College Gould Law Lib (FDL) (SDDL)
631-761-7360 (Central Islip)
www.tourolaw.edu/Library

Sullivan County
New York State Supreme Court Lib
845-794-1547 (Monticello)
www.nycourts.gov/lawlibraries/publicaccess.shtml
nycourthelp.gov/SullivanSupCt1.htm

Syracuse
(see Onondaga County)

Tioga County
Waverly Free Public Lib (CLL) (SDDL)
607-565-9341 (Waverly)
www.courts.state.ny.us/library/tioga/index.shtml
www.nycourts.gov/lawlibraries/publicaccess.shtml

Tompkins County
Cornell University Mann Lib (FDL)
607-255-5406 (Ithaca)
www.mannlib.cornell.edu

Cornell University Olin Lib (FDL) (SDDL)
607-255-4144 (Ithaca)
www.library.cornell.edu/olinuris

Cornell Law School Lib (FDL) (SDDL)
Myron Taylor Hall
Ithaca, NY 14853-4901
607-255-9577 (Ithaca)
www.lawschool.cornell.edu
(click "Library")

Ernest Warren Supreme Court Lib (CLL)
607-272-0045 (Ithaca)
www.nycourts.gov/library/tompkins/index.shtml
www.nycourts.gov/lawlibraries/publicaccess.shtml

Tompkins Cortland Community College Lib (SDDL)
888-567-8211; 607-844-8222 x4363 (Dryden)
www.sunytccc.edu/library

Troy
(see Rensselaer County)

Ulster County
New York State Supreme Court Lib (CLL)
www.nycourts.gov/lawlibraries/publicaccess.shtml
nycourthelp.gov/UlsterSupCt1.htm

State University of New York Sojourner Lib
(FDL) (SDDL)
845-257-3710 (New Paltz)
lib.newpaltz.edu

Utica
(see Oneida County)

Warren County
Warren County Supreme Court Lib (CLL)
518-761-6442 (Lake George)
www.nycourts.gov/lawlibraries/publicaccess.shtml
nycourthelp.gov/WarrenSupCt1.htm

Warsaw
(see Wyoming County)

Washington County
Washington County Law Lib (CLL)
518-746-2521 (Fort Edward)
www.nycourts.gov/lawlibraries/publicaccess.shtml
nycourthelp.gov/WashingtonSupCt1.htm

Watertown
(see Jefferson County)

Watkins Glen
(see Schuyler County)

Waverly
(see Tioga County)

Wayne County
Lyons Public Lib (CLL)
315-946-9262 (Lyons)
www.lyonslibrary.blogspot.com
www.nycourts.gov/lawlibraries/publicaccess.shtml

Westchester County
Mount Vernon Public Lib (FDL)(SDDL)
914-668-1840 (Mount Vernon)
www.mountvernonpubliclibrary.org

Mercy College Lib (FDL)
Yorktown Heights, NY 10598-2997
914-245-6100 x2218 (Yorktown Heights)
www.mercy.edu/libraries

Pace University Glass Law Lib (FDL)(SDDL)
White Plains, NY 10603-3710
914-422-4273 (White Plains)
www.pace.edu/page.cfm?doc_id=29797

Sarah Lawrence College Raushenbush Lib
(FDL)(SDDL)
914-395-2474 (Bronxville)
www.slc.edu/library
www.slc.edu/library/research_tools/govdocs.htm

State University of New York College Lib (FDL)
914-251-6410 (Purchase)
*www.purchase.edu/Departments/Library/collections/
    government.aspx*

Westchester County Supreme Court Law Lib (CLL)
914-995-3900/3902 (White Plains)
www.nycourts.gov/lawlibraries/publicaccess.shtml
nycourthelp.gov/WestchesterSupCt1.htm

Yonkers Public Lib (FDL)(SDDL)
914-337-1500 (Yonkers)
www.ypl.org

West Point
(see Orange County)

White Plains
(see Westchester County)

Wyoming County
Wyoming County Law Lib (CLL)
585-786-3148 (Warsaw)
www.nycourts.gov/lawlibraries/publicaccess.shtml
nycourthelp.gov/WyomingCountyCt1.htm

Yates County
Penn Yan Public Lib (CLL)(SDDL)
315-536-6114 (Penn Yan)
www.pypl.org
www.nycourts.gov/lawlibraries/publicaccess.shtml

Yonkers
(see Westchester County)

Yorktown Heights
(see Westchester County)

D. | **More Information**

Law Library Locator
nycourthelp.gov/thelaw3.html

Public Access Law Libraries
www.nycourts.gov/lawlibraries/publicaccess.shtml

Court Law Libraries
www.nycourts.gov/lawlibraries/courtlawlibraries.shtml

Federal Depository Libraries
www.gpoaccess.gov/libraries.html

Law Library Association of Greater New York
www.aallnet.org/chapter/llagny
www.aallnet.org/chapter/llagny/llagnymembers.html

New York State Document Depository Libraries
www.nysl.nysed.gov/edocs/education/bycounty.htm

Supreme Court Libraries
www.dos.state.ny.us/code/libs.htm

E. | **Something to Check**

1. Contact the closest court law library (CLL) to you. Does it have the current paper edition of the *Martindale-Hubbell Law Directory*? Does it have Siegel's *New York Practice*?

2. Call the federal depository library (FDL) near you that is a private institution, e.g., a private university. Assume that you wanted to go to this library to use the Code of Federal Regulations (CFR) volumes on the shelves of this library. (You want to look at a "hard copy" of the CFR rather than examine it online.) Ask the library how you would do this. Do you need a special pass? In short, how do you gain admission to use the materials (like the CFR) that this private library receives under the federal depositary program?

5.9 Hotline Resources and Complaint Directories

A. Introduction
B. Help and Complaint Hotline Resources
C. More Information
D. Something to Check

A. Introduction

On the job you sometimes need quick access to phone numbers or web sites of commonly used resources. This section provides many of them. See also section 4.5 for similar leads.

B. Help and Complaint Hotline Resources

Topics Covered

Accountants
Acupuncturists
Adoption and Foster Care
Adult Abuse
Agencies of State
   Government
Aging
Agriculture
AIDS/HIV
Air Pollution
Air Travel
Alcoholism and Drug
   Abuse
Alzheimer's
Amber Alert
Architects
Arts
Asbestos
Assembly
Attorney
Attorney General
Auditor
Automobile Complaints
Banks
Bar Associations
Bar Examiners
Battered Women
Birth Records
Blind
Business
Cable TV
Cancer
Census
Charities
Child Abuse
Children

Child Support
Chiropractors
City Governments
Civil Rights
Civil Service
CLE
Cocaine
Complaints against
   Occupations
Comptroller
Congress
Consumer Information
   Center
Consumer Protection
Continuing Legal Education
Corporate Complaint
   Hotlines
Corporations
Corrections
County/City Governments
Courts
Credit Reports
Crime
Crisis Hotlines
Customs
Day Care Complaints
Death Records
Dentists
Department of Motor
   Vehicles
Diabetes
Disability
Discrimination
Disease
Divorce Records
DMV

Doctors
Domestic Violence
Do Not Call Registry
Drugs
Economic Development
Education
Elder Abuse
Elections
Electricity
Emergency
Employment
Energy
Engineers
Environment
Ethics
Fair Housing
Families
Federal Government
Fish and Game
Food Safety
Food Stamps
Foster Care
Fraud
Gambling
Gas and Electricity
Governments
Governor
Handicapped
Harassment
Hate Crimes
Health
HIPAA
HIV
HMO Complaints
Housing
Human Rights
Identity Theft
Immigration
Insurance
IOLA
IRS
Labor
Landlord and Tenant
Law Enforcement
Lawyer Referral Service
Lawyers' Fund for Client
   Protection
Lead
Legislature
Lemon Law
LexisNexis
Lottery
Marriage Records
Medicare and Medicaid
Mental Health
Military
Missing Children
Mortgages
Motor Vehicles
Natural Resources

New York State Government
Nurses
Nursing Home Complaints
Occupational Safety
Ombudsman
Ozone
Parks and Recreation
Parole
Passport
Pensions
Pesticides
Pharmacy
Physicians
Poison
Police and Sheriffs
Pollution
Port Authority
Prison
Privacy
Product Safety
Public Defender
Public Utilities
Rape
Real Estate
Recycling
Runaway
Secretary of State
Securities
Senate
Seniors
Sex Offenders
Sexual Harassment
Sexually Transmitted
   Diseases
Sheriffs
Social Security
Social Services
Social Worker
Students
Substance Abuse
Suicide
Tax
Telephone
Tourism
Transportation
Unclaimed Property
Unemployment
   Insurance
Utilities
Veterans
Veterinarian
Victim Services
Vital Records
Voting
Water
Welfare
West Group/Westlaw
Whistleblowing
White House
Workers' Compensation

Accountants

Accountants Complaint Hotline
800-442-8106
www.op.nysed.gov/opd.htm
www.op.nysed.gov/opsearches.htm

Acupuncturists

Acupuncturists Complaint Hotline
800-442-8106
www.op.nysed.gov/opd.htm
www.op.nysed.gov/opsearches.htm

Adoption and Foster Care

NYS Office of Children & Family Services
800-345-KIDS
www.ocfs.state.ny.us/main/fostercare

Adult Abuse

(see Elder Abuse, Seniors)

Agencies of State Government

(see also section 4.5)
Agency Web Sites
www.state.ny.us
www.nysl.nysed.gov/ils/nyserver.html

Government Toll-Free Numbers
www.tollfreenumber.org/forum/about45.html

State Government Information Locator Service
www.nysl.nysed.gov/ils

Aging

(see Elder Abuse, Seniors)

Agriculture

Department of Agriculture and Markets
800-554-4501
www.agmkt.state.ny.us/index.html

U.S. Department of Agriculture
202-720-HELP; 800-424-9121
www.usda.gov

Food Stamps
800-221-5689
www.fns.usda.gov/snap

Food and Drug Administration
888-INFO-FDA
www.fda.gov

Center for Food Safety
888-SAFEFOOD; 888-723-3366
402-344-5000
www.fsis.usda.gov

AIDS/HIV

www.nyaidsline.org
www.projinf.org/org/Regionrsrc/NYs.html
800-541-2437; 800-822-7422; 800-872-2777;
800-HIV-0400

Albany 800-962-5065	Jamaica 800-462-6787
Bronx 800-526-4823	Mineola 800-462-6785
Brooklyn 800-462-6788	New Rochelle 800-828-0064
Buffalo 800-962-5064	Rochester 800-962-5063
Hauppauge 800-462-6786	Syracuse 800-562-9423

Air Pollution

(see also Environment)
Air Quality
800-438-4318
www.epa.gov/iaq/iaqinfo.html

Department of Environmental Conservation
518-402-8452
800-367-4448 (Inspector General Hotline)
www.dec.ny.gov
www.dec.ny.gov/chemical/281.html

Ozone Information Hotline
800-535-1345

Air Travel

FAA Consumer Hotline
800-322-7873
www.faa.gov

Alcoholism and Drug Abuse

(see also Health, Mental Health)
Al-Anon
888-4AL-ANON
www.al-anon.alateen.org

Alcoholics Anonymous
212-870-3400; 845-331-6360
www.aa.org

Cocaine Anonymous
800-347-8998
www.ca.org

County Services
www.oasas.state.ny.us/pio/regdir.cfm

DARE (Drug Abuse Resistance Education)
800-SAY-DARE
criminaljustice.state.ny.us

Drug-Free Workplace Hotline
800-WORKPLACE
www.dol.gov/dol/siteindex.htm
(click "W" then "Workplace Substance Abuse")

Drug Relapse Hotline
800-735-2773

National Clearinghouse on Alcohol and Drug Information
800-729-6686
ncadi.samhsa.gov

Office of Alcoholism and Substance Abuse Services
800-522-5353; 800-553-5790
www.oasas.state.ny.us/index.cfm
www.oasas.state.ny.us/pio/regdir.cfm

Patient Advocacy
800-553-5790
www.oasas.state.ny.us/pio/caudes.cfm

Phoenix House New York
800-DRUG-HELP
www.phoenixhouse.org/locations/new-york

Alzheimer's

Alzheimer's Helpline
800-272-3900
www.alz.org/apps/findus.asp
www.alznyc.org
www.alz.org/rochesterny

Amber Alert

(see also Law Enforcement, Missing Children)
518-464-7134
www.amberalert.gov
nysamber.troopers.state.ny.us
www.amberalert.gov/state_contacts.htm

Architects

Architects Complaint Hotline
800-442-8106
www.op.nysed.gov/opd.htm
www.op.nysed.gov/opsearches.htm

Arts

New York State Council on the Arts
800-510-0021; 212-627-4455
www.nysca.org

Asbestos

Information Clearinghouse
800-368-5888
www.epa.gov/sbo/hotline.htm#hotline

New York Department of Health
www.health.state.ny.us/environmental/indoors/asbestos

Assembly

(see also Legislature)
assembly.state.ny.us

Attorney

Attorney Complaints
(see also section 3.4)
518-463-3200
www.nysba.org
(click "For the Community" then "Resolving Conflict with a New York Attorney?")

Attorney Fee Disputes
877-FEES-137
www.courts.state.ny.us/admin/feedispute/index.shtml

Attorney Search
iapps.courts.state.ny.us/attorney/AttorneySearch

New York State Bar Association
(see also section 3.4 for all bar associations)
518-463-3200
www.nysba.org

Board of Bar Examiners
800-342-3335; 518-452-8700
www.nybarexam.org

IOLA
Interest on Lawyer Accounts
800-222-IOLA; 646-865-1541
www.iola.org
www.nylawfund.org/pubs/guide.shtml

Lawyers' Fund for Client Protection
800-422-Fund
www.nylawfund.org

Lawyer Referral Service
800-342-3661
www.nycourthelp.gov/lawyers2.html

Attorney General

Office of the Attorney General
www.oag.state.ny.us

Consumer Helpline
800-771-7755

Consumer Frauds Bureau
800-771-7755
www.oag.state.ny.us/bureaus/consumer_frauds/about.html

Lemon Law
800-771-7755
www.oag.state.ny.us/bureaus/consumer_frauds/lemon_law.html

Auditor

(see Comptroller)

Automobile Complaints

(see also Consumer Protection)

Department of Motor Vehicles
Complaints Vehicle Repairs, Inspections and Dealers
800-DIAL-DMV; 518-474-8943
www.nydmv.state.ny.us/vehsafe.htm
www.nysdmv.com/vscontact.htm

Auto Safety Hotline
888-327-4236
www-odi.nhtsa.dot.gov/ivoq

Banks (and related financial institutions)

State Banking Department
877-BANK-NYS
800-518-8866 (credit card complaints)
www.banking.state.ny.us
www.banking.state.ny.us/ccs.htm

Controller of the Currency
800-613-6743
www.occ.treas.gov

Federal Deposit Insurance Corporation
877-ASK-FDIC
www.fdic.gov

Federal Deposit Insurance Corporation
New York Regional Office
917-320-2749; 877-275-3342
www.fdic.gov/about/contact/directory/index.html
(click "New York" regional)

Federal Reserve Bank of New York
212-720-5000
www.newyorkfed.org

Federal Reserve Consumer Hotline
888-851-1920
www.federalreserve.gov/consumerinfo/agency.htm

National Credit Union Administration
800-755-1031
www.ncua.gov

Office of Thrift Supervision
800-842-6929
www.ots.treas.gov

Savings and Loan Associations
800-842-6929
www.ots.treas.gov

Bar Associations

(see Attorney above and section 3.4)

Bar Examiners

Board of Bar Examiners
(see also Attorney)
800-342-3335; 518-452-8700
www.nybarexam.org

Battered Women

(see Domestic Violence)

Birth Records

(see also section 5.7)

Department of Health
877-854-4481 (VitalChek)
www.health.state.ny.us/vital_records/birth.htm
www.health.state.ny.us/vital_records/genealogy.htm
www.publicrecordcenter.com/newyorkpublicrecord.htm

Blind

(see Disability, Health)

Business

(see also Corporations)

Business Permit Assistance
800-342-3464
www.nys-permits.org
www.gorr.state.ny.us

Division for Small Business
518-292-5220; 800-782-8369
www.nylovessmallbiz.com
www.nylovesmwbe.ny.gov/TechAssistance/SBDC.htm

Division of Corporations
518-473-2492
www.dos.state.ny.us/corp/corpwww.html

Division of Licensing Services
212-417-5790
www.dos.state.ny.us/LCNS/licensing.html

Empire State Development
800-STATE-NY
www.empire.state.ny.us

New York Business Promotion
800-STATE-NY
www.empire.state.ny.us

Small Business Ombudsman Hotline
800-368-5888 (environmental laws)
www.epa.gov/sbo

State Resources for Business
www.sba.gov

Small Business Administration
800-U-ASK-SBA
www.sba.gov

Cable TV

Federal Communications Commission
888-CALL-FCC
www.fcc.gov

New York Public Service Commission
800-342-3377 (complaints)
www.dps.state.ny.us

Cancer

(see also Health)

Cancer Hotline
National Cancer Institute
800-4-CANCER
www.cancer.gov

Roswell Park Cancer Institute
800-ROSWELL
www.roswellpark.org

Census

U.S. Census Bureau
800-923-8282
www.census.gov

Region Covering New York
800-562-5721
www.countonchange2010.org/contactuscensusbureau

Census Statistics for New York
quickfacts.census.gov/qfd/states/36000.html

Charities (complaints against)

Office of Attorney General
800-771-7755
www.oag.state.ny.us/bureaus/charities/about.html

Child Abuse

(see also Health, Missing Children)

Childhelp USA
800-422-4452
www.cwla.org

Departments of Social Services by County
www.ocfs.state.ny.us/main/localdss.asp

National Child Abuse Hotline
800-4-A-CHILD
www.childhelpusa.org

Office of Children and Family Service
800-342-3720
www.ocfs.state.ny.us/main/cps

RAINN (Rape, Abuse, Incest) Hotline
800-656-HOPE
www.rainn.org
centers.rainn.org
(click "New York")

Stop It Now
888-PREVENT
www.stopitnow.org

Children

(see also Child Abuse, Child Support, Health, Missing Children)

Departments of Social Services by County
www.ocfs.state.ny.us/main/localdss.asp

Office of Children and Family Services
518-473-7793
www.ocfs.state.ny.us/main

Office of Juvenile Justice and Delinquency
800-851-3420
ojjdp.ncjrs.org
ojjdp.ncjrs.org/statecontacts/ResourceListDetails.asp

Office of Temporary and Disability Assistance
877-472-8411
www.otda.state.ny.us

Children with Disability Sites
www.cqc.state.ny.us/misc_pages/siteindex.htm
nichcy.org/Pages/StateSpecificInfo.aspx?State=NY

Child Support

Division of Child Support Enforcement
888-208-4485; 800-846-0773
newyorkchildsupport.com/child_support_services.html

Chiropractors

Chiropractors Complaint Hotline
800-442-8106
www.op.nysed.gov/opd.htm
www.op.nysed.gov/opsearches.htm

City Governments

All Cities, Towns, Villages, and Counties
www.citytown.info/New-York.htm
www.nysegov.com/citguide.cfm?context=citguide&content=
munibyalpha

Municipal Civil Service
518-473-5022
www.cs.state.ny.us/home/msd.cfm

Civil Rights

(see also Disability)

Attorney General's Civil Rights Bureau
800-771-7755; 212-416-8250
www.oag.state.ny.us/bureaus/civil_rights/about.html

Division of Housing & Community Renewal
866-ASK-DHCR; 866-275-3427
www.dhcr.state.ny.us

Division of Human Rights
888-392-3644; 718-741-8400
www.dhr.state.ny.us

Equal Employment Opportunity Commission
800-669-4000 (national)
www.eeoc.gov

Equal Employment Opportunity Commission
800-669-4000 (New York district)
www.eeoc.gov/newyork/index.html
www.eeoc.gov/newyork/area.html

Health Records (Privacy)
HHS Office for Civil Rights
800-369-1019 (HIPAA)
www.hhs.gov/ocr/privacy

Office of Fair Housing and Equal Opportunity
800-CALL-FHA
www.hud.gov/offices/fheo

New York City Commission on Human Rights
212-306-5070
www.nyc.gov/html/cchr

New York Civil Rights Coalition
212-563-5636
nycivilrights.org

U.S. Department of Education
Office for Civil Rights
800-421-3481
www.ed.gov/about/offices/list/ocr/index.html

U.S. Department of Justice
Civil Rights Division
202-514-4609
www.usdoj.gov/crt

Civil Service

Department of Civil Service
877-NYS-JOBS; 518-457-9375
www.cs.state.ny.us

Municipal Civil Service
518-473-5022
www.cs.state.ny.us/home/msd.cfm

State Government Employees
800-553-1322 (Career Mobility Office)
www.cs.state.ny.us/employees/state

CLE

(see Continuing Legal Education)

Cocaine

(see Alcoholism and Drug Abuse)

Complaints against Occupations

(see also Consumer Protection)

Division of Licensing Services
Complaint Review Office
212-417-5790
www.dos.state.ny.us/LCNS
www.dos.state.ny.us/forms/licensing/1507-a.pdf

Professional Misconduct Hotline
800-442-8106
www.op.nysed.gov/opd.htm
www.op.nysed.gov/opsearches.htm

Comptroller

Office of the State Comptroller
888-OSC-4555
800-221-9311 (unclaimed property)
www.osc.state.ny.us/investigations

Congress

U.S. Capitol
202-224-3121; 202-225-3121
www.house.gov
www.senate.gov
www.congress.org

Federal Information Center
800-FED-INFO
www.firstgov.gov

Consumer Information Center (Federal)

888-8-PUEBLO; 800-688-9889
www.pueblo.gsa.gov

Federal Information Center
800-FED-INFO; 800-688-9889
www.firstgov.gov

Consumer Protection

Consumer Protection Board
800-697-1220
www.consumer.state.ny.us

Better Business Bureau
800-955-5100
www.newyork.bbb.org
www.rochester.bbb.org
www.syracuse.bbb.org

Consumer Frauds Bureau
800-771-7755
www.oag.state.ny.us/bureaus/consumer_frauds/about.html

Complaints, Miscellaneous
www.ag.ny.gov/bureaus/consumer_frauds/
filing_a_consumer_complaint.html

Consumer Product Safety Commission
800-638-2772
www.cpsc.gov

County Consumer Affairs Offices
www.consumer.state.ny.us/consumer_affairs_offices.htm

Division of Licensing Services
Complaint Review Office
212-417-5790
www.dos.state.ny.us/LCNS
www.dos.state.ny.us/forms/licensing/1507-a.pdf

Government Complaint Departments
www.nysl.nysed.gov/ils/topics/complaint.htm

Lawyers' Fund for Client Protection
800-422-Fund
www.nylawfund.org

Lemon Law
800-771-7755
www.ag.ny.gov/bureaus/consumer_frauds/
   lemon_law.html

Continuing Legal Education

(see also section 1.3)
518-487-5600
www.nysba.org (select "CLE")

Corporate Complaint Hotlines

Adobe Systems (800-833-6687)
Allstate (800-255-7828)
Amazon (800-201-7575)
America Online (800-827-6364)
Apple Computer (800-676-2775)
AT&T (800-331-0500)
Bank of America (800-432-1000)
Campbell Soup Company (800-257-8443)
Chase Bank (866-879-3207)
Chevron (800-962-1223)
CompUSA (800-266-7872)
CVS/pharmacy (800-746-7287)
Dell Customer Service (800-624-9897)
Dell Technical Support (800-624-9896)
DuPont (800-441-7515)
eBay (800-322-9266)
Expedia (800-397-3342)
Exxon Mobile (800-243-9966)
Gateway Computers (800-846-2000)
General Electric (800-626-2000)
General Mills (800-249-0562)
Gillette (800-445-5388)
Hewlett-Packard Technical Support (800-752-0900)
Home Depot (800-553-3199)
IBM (800-426-4969)
Microsoft (800-642-7676)
MSN Internet Service (800-386-5550)
Orbitz (888-656-4546)
Panasonic (800-211-7262)
Radio Shack (800-843-7422)

Safeway (877-723-3929)
SBC Communications (800-464-7928)
Shell Oil (888-467-4355)
Sony (800-222-7669)
Verizon (800-621-9900)
Wal-Mart (800-925-6278)
Xerox Technical Support (800-821-2797)
Yahoo! (866-562-7219)

Corporations

(see also Business)

Department of State
518-473-2492; 518-474-4752
www.dos.state.ny.us

Corporation and Business Entity Database
*appsext8.dos.state.ny.us/corp_public/corpsearch.entity_*
   search_entry

Division of Corporations
518-473-2492
www.dos.state.ny.us/corp/corpwww.html

Corrections

(see also Law Enforcement)
Commission of Correction
518-485-2346
www.scoc.state.ny.us

Department of Correctional Services
518-457-8126
www.docs.state.ny.us

Division of Parole
518-473-9400
parole.state.ny.us

Probation and Correctional Alternatives
518-485-2395
dpca.state.ny.us

County/City Governments

(see also section 4.6)
www.nysegov.com/map-NY.cfm
libguides.library.albany.edu/newyorkcounties
www.nysegov.com/citguide.cfm?context=citguide&content=
   munibyalpha
www.nysegov.com/citguide.cfm?context=citguide&content=
   munibycounty1
www.wowworks.com/wowcity/ny.htm
www.statelocalgov.net/state-ny.cfm
www.nycom.org
www.nysac.org

Courts

(see also sections 4.2 and 4.3)

Unified Court System
800-COURT-NY (court administration)
800-NY-JUROR (juror hotline)
www.nycourts.gov/home.htm
www.courts.state.ny.us
www.courts.state.ny.us/courts

Office of Court Administration
518-474-3828; 212-428-2700
www.nycourts.gov/admin/oca.shtml

Commission on Judicial Conduct
518-474-5617; 212-809-0566
www.scjc.state.ny.us

Federal Courts in New York
www.uscourts.gov/courtlinks
(click "NY" on the map)

Credit Reports

Annualcreditreports.com
877-322-8228
www.ftc.gov/bcp/edu/pubs/consumer/credit/cre34.shtm

Credit Counseling
800-388-2227 (national)

Equifax
800-685-1111
www.equifax.com

Experian
888-397-3742
www.experian.com

TransUnion
800-916-8800
www.transunion.com

Crime

(see Alcoholism and Drug Abuse, Law Enforcement)

Crisis Hotlines

(see Alcoholism and Drug Abuse, Domestic Violence, Mental Health, Suicide)

Customs

U.S. Customs and Border Protection
800-BE-ALERT
www.cbp.gov

Day Care Complaints

Office of Children & Family Services
800-732-5207
www.ocfs.state.ny.us

Death Records

(see also section 5.7)

Department of Health
877-854-4481 (VitalChek)
www.health.state.ny.us/vital_records/death.htm
www.health.state.ny.us/vital_records/genealogy.htm

National Center for Health Statistics: New York
www.cdc.gov/nchs/w2w/new_york.htm

New York City
www.nyc.gov/html/doh

Dentists

Dentists Complaint Hotline
800-442-8106
www.op.nysed.gov/opd.htm
www.op.nysed.gov/opsearches.htm

Department of Motor Vehicles

(see DMV)

Diabetes

(see also Health)

American Diabetes Association
800-DIABETES
www.diabetes.org

Disability

(see also Alcoholism and Drug Abuse, Health, Mental Health)

ADA (Americans with Disabilities) Library
800-ADA-WORK; 800-526-7234
www.jan.wvu.edu/links/adalinks.htm

ADA Portal
800-949-4232
www.adata.org/adaportal

Americans with Disabilities Act
800-541-0301
www.ada.gov

Commission for the Blind and Visually Handicapped
866-871-3000; 518-473-7793
www.ocfs.state.ny.us/main/cbvh

Commission on Quality of Care and Advocacy for Persons with Disabilities
800-624-4143
www.cqc.state.ny.us

Disability Information and Resources
www.disabilityinfo.gov
www.makoa.org/index.htm

Disability Sites
www.cqc.state.ny.us/misc_pages/siteindex.htm

Law Help
www.lawhelp.org/NY
(click "Disability")

National Association for Rights Protection and Advocacy
205-464-0101
www.narpa.org

National Disability Rights Network
202-408-9514
www.ndrn.org

New York Disability Links
nichcy.org/Pages/StateSpecificInfo.aspx?State=NY

Office of Special Education and Rehabilitative Services
800-USA-LEARN
www2.ed.gov/about/offices/list/osers/index.html

Self-Help Advocacy Association of New York State
www.sanys.org

Speaking for Ourselves
800-867-3330
www.speaking.org

Vocational and Educational Services for Individuals with Disabilities
800-222-JOBS
www.vesid.nysed.gov

Workers' Compensation and Disability Insurance
ww3.nysif.com

Discrimination

(see Civil Rights)

Disease

(see also Cancer, Health)

Disease Control Hotline
800-CDC-INFO
www.bt.cdc.gov

Divorce Records

(see also section 5.7)

Department of Health
877-854-4481 (VitalChek)
www.health.state.ny.us/vital_records/divorce.htm

National Center for Health Statistics: New York
www.cdc.gov/nchs/w2w/new_york.htm

DMV

(see also Transportation)

Department of Motor Vehicles
212-645-5550, 800-DIAL-DMV, 800-CALL-DMV
www.nydmv.state.ny.us

Doctors

(see Dentists, Health, Mental Health, Physicians)

Domestic Violence

(see also Child Abuse, Elder Abuse, Law Enforcement)

County Services on Domestic Violence
www.nyscadv.org/directory.htm

Mayor's Office to Combat Domestic Violence
www.nyc.gov/html/ocdv/html/home/home.shtml

National Center for Victims of Crime
800-FYI-CALL
www.ncvc.org/ncvc/Main.aspx

National Domestic Violence Hotline
800-799-SAFE
www.ndvh.org

New York City Gay and Lesbian Anti-Violence Project
212-714-1141
www.avp.org

New York Coalition Against Domestic Violence
800-942-6906
www.nyscadv.org

Office for the Prevention of Domestic Violence
800-942-6906
800-621-HOPE (New York City)
www.opdv.state.ny.us

Protective Services for Adults
800-342-3009
www.ocfs.state.ny.us/main/psa

RAINN (Rape, Abuse, Incest) Hotline
800-656-HOPE
www.rainn.org
centers.rainn.org
(click "New York")

Do Not Call Registry

888-382-1222
www.donotcall.gov
www.consumer.state.ny.us/dnc_index.htm
www.ftc.gov/bcp/edu/microsites/donotcall/index.html

Drugs

(see Alcoholism and Drug Abuse)

Economic Development

(see Business)

Education

Board of Regents
518-474-5889
www.regents.nysed.gov

Education (school directory)
www.nysed.gov/admin/admindex.html

Federal Student Aid
800-4-FED-AID
www.fafsa.ed.gov
www.ifap.ed.gov/ifap/index.jsp

New York Higher Education Services Corporation
866-944-HESC
www.hesc.com

U.S. Department of Education
800-USA-LEARN
www.ed.gov

U.S. Department of Education
Office for Civil Rights
800-421-3481
www.ed.gov/about/offices/list/ocr/index.html

Elder Abuse

(see also Seniors)

Elder Crime Victim Resources
www.nyc.gov/html/dfta/html/caregiver/victims.shtml

National Center on Elder Abuse
800-677-1116
www.ncea.aoa.gov

National Committee for the Prevention of Elder Abuse
202-682-4140
www.preventelderabuse.org

New York Protective Services for Adults
800-342-3009
www.ocfs.state.ny.us/main/psa

Nursing Home Complaints
888-201-4563

Elections

Board of Elections of the City of New York
866-VOTE-NYC
www.vote.nyc.ny.us

Board of Elections, State
518-474-6220
800-367-8683 (voter registration hotline)

800-458-3453 (campaign finance)
www.elections.state.ny.us

County Boards of Election
www.elections.state.ny.us/CountyBoards.html

Vote NY
800-FOR-VOTE
www.vote-ny.com/english/faqs.php

Electricity

(see Gas and Electricity, Public Utilities)

Emergency

(see also Health, Law Enforcement)

State Emergency Management Office
866-SAFE-NYS (terrorism hotline)
518-292-2312
www.semo.state.ny.us

Federal Emergency Management Agency
800-621-FEMA
www.fema.gov

National Response Center Hotline
800-424-8802
www.nrc.uscg.mil/nrchp.html

Employment

(see also Civil Service, Discrimination, Unemployment Insurance, Workers' Compensation)

Department of Civil Service
877-NYS-JOBS; 518-457-2487
www.cs.state.ny.us

Department of Labor
888-4-NYSDOL; 800-HIRE-992; 518-457-9000
www.labor.state.ny.us

Employment in Government (Civil Service)
877-NYS-JOBS
www.cs.state.ny.us/jobseeker/public/index.cfm

State and Local Retirement System
866-805-0990; 518-474-7736
www.osc.state.ny.us/retire

State Rehabilitation Council
800-222-JOBS; 518-474-1711
www.vesid.nysed.gov/src

WorkforceNY
(matching employers and seekers)
800-HIRE-992
www.labor.state.ny.us

Energy

(see also Environment)

Energy Research and Development Authority
866-NY-SERDA; 518-862-1090
www.nyserda.org

Environmental Justice Hotline
800-962-6215
www.epa.gov/compliance/about/offices/oej.html

HEAP (Home Energy Assistance)
800-342-3009
www.otda.state.ny.us/main/heap

Public Service Commission
800-342-3377 (complaint hotline)
888-NYS-PSC4 (energy choices)
www.dps.state.ny.us/help.html

Renewable Energy
877-EERE-INF
www1.eere.energy.gov/informationcenter

U.S. Department of Energy
800-DIAL-DOE
www.energy.gov

Engineers

Engineers Complaint Hotline
800-442-8106
www.op.nysed.gov/opd.htm
www.op.nysed.gov/opsearches.htm
www.op.nysed.gov/pe.htm

Environment

Department of Environmental Conservation
800-TIPP-DEC (reporting violations)
www.dec.ny.gov

Environmental Justice
866-229-0497
www.dec.ny.gov/public/923.html

Environmental Protection Agency (EPA) (federal)
800-621-8431; 800-424-8802 (emergencies)
888-777-1000 (complaint hotline)
www.epa.gov

**Environmental Protection Agency (EPA)
(New York region)**
212-637-3660
www.epa.gov/region2
www.epa.gov/region02/state/nylink.htm

Other Hotlines
866-411-4EPA (airborne pollution)
800-438-4318 (air quality)
800-368-5888 (asbestos)
800-426-4791 (drinking water)
800-447-3813 (endangered species)
800-462-6553 (hazardous waste)

800-424-LEAD (lead)
800-296-1996 (ozone)
888-ECONSPT (penalties)
800-858-7378 (pesticides)
800-222-1222 (poison)
800-490-9198 (publications)
800-55-RADON (radon)
800-225-2566 (regulatory fee program)
800-431-9209 (Superfund)
800-424-9346 (toxic waste)
800-926-7337 (water conservation)
800-832-7828 (wetlands)
www.epa.gov/epahome/hotline.htm
www.dec.ny.gov/about/259.html

Ethics

(see also sections 3.1, 3.2, and 3.3)

Attorney Ethics
www.law.cornell.edu/ethics/ny.html
www.nysba.org
(click "For Attorneys" then "Ethics Opinions")

Commission on Public Integrity (public officials)
800-873-8442
www.nyintegrity.org

Fair Housing

(see Civil Rights, Housing)

Families

(see also Children, Child Support, Seniors)

Departments of Social Services by County
www.ocfs.state.ny.us/main/localdss.asp

HEAP (Home Energy Assistance)
800-342-3009
www.otda.state.ny.us/main/heap

Office of Children and Family Services
518-473-7793
www.ocfs.state.ny.us/main

Office of Temporary and Disability Assistance
877-472-8411
www.otda.state.ny.us

Departments of Social Services by County
www.ocfs.state.ny.us/main/localdss.asp

Federal Government

Congress
202-224-3121; 202-225-3121
www.house.gov
www.senate.gov
www.congress.org

Federal Information Center
800-FED-INFO
www.firstgov.gov

U.S. Government Manual
www.gpoaccess.gov/gmanual

Fish and Game

(see also Environment)

Division of Fish, Wildlife and Marine Resources
518-402-8924; 518-402-8920
www.dec.ny.gov/about/634.html
www.dec.ny.gov/about/32834.html

U.S. Fish and Wildlife Service
800-344-WILD
www.fws.gov

Food Safety

(see Agriculture)

Food Stamps

Supplemental Nutrition Assistance Program (SNAP)
800-221-5689
www.fns.usda.gov/snap

Foster Care

NYS Office of Children & Family Services
800-345-KIDS
www.ocfs.state.ny.us/main/fostercare

Fraud

(see also Consumer Protection, Law Enforcement)

Consumer Frauds Bureau
800-771-7755
www.oag.state.ny.us/bureaus/consumer_frauds/about.html

Consumer League's Fraud Center
800-876-7060
www.fraud.org

Medicare Fraud
800-HHS-TIPS
www.medicare.gov/fraudabuse/HowToReport.asp
www.oig.hhs.gov/fraud/hotline

Postal Fraud
877-876-2455
postalinspectors.uspis.gov

Social Security Fraud
800-269-0271
www.ssa.gov/oig/guidelin.htm

Gambling

Gamblers Anonymous
www.gamblersanonymous.org
www.gamblersanonymous.org/mtgdirNY.html

New York Council on Problem Gambling
800-437-1611
www.nyproblemgambling.org

Gas And Electricity

(see also Public Utilities)

Public Service Commission
800-342-3377 (complaint hotline)
www.dps.state.ny.us

Governments

(see Agencies of State Government, City Governments, County/City Governments, Federal Government, Legislature)

Governor

Office of the Governor
518-474-8390
www.state.ny.us/governor

Governor's Office of Regulatory Reform
518-486-3292
www.gorr.state.ny.us

Handicapped

(see Disability, Health)

Harassment

(see Sexual Harassment)

Hate Crimes

(see also Civil Rights, Domestic Violence, Law Enforcement)

Hate Crime National Hotline
206-350-HATE
www.lambda.org/hatecr2.htm

Southern Poverty Center
334-956-8200
www.splcenter.org

Health

(see also AIDS/HIV, Alcoholism and Drug Abuse, Disability, Environment, Insurance, Mental Health, Physicians)

Disease Control Hotline
800-CDC-INFO
www.bt.cdc.gov

State Department of Health
866-881-2809
www.health.state.ny.us

Health Complaint Hotlines
866-983-6722 (adult care)
866-983-6722 (assisted living)
800-7-ASTHMA (asthma)
800-3AUTISM (autism)
800-DIABETES (diabetes)
800-EFA-1000(epilepsy)
800-369-1019 (HIPAA)
800-206-8125 (HMO)
800-628-5972 (home care)
800-628-5972 (hospice)
800-804-5447 (hospitals)
800-682-6056 (laboratories)
800-206-8125 (managed care)
877-87-FRAUD (Medicaid)
800-MEDICARE (Medicare)
888-201-4563 (nursing home)
800-663-6144 (physicians)
800-227-8922 (STD)
www.health.state.ny.us/nysdoh/healthinfo/complaint.htm

Specific Ailments
800-541-2437 (AIDS)
800-522-5353 (alcoholism)
800-272-3900 (Alzheimer's)
800-368-5888 (asbestos related)
800-4-CANCER (cancer)
800-347-8998 (cocaine)

U.S. Department of Health and Human Services
877-696-6775
www.hhs.gov

HIPAA

(see also Health)

Privacy of Medical Records
800-369-1019 (HIPAA)
www.hhs.gov/ocr/hipaa

HIV

(see AIDS)

HMO Complaints

(see Health)

Housing

(see also Civil Rights)

Division of Housing and Community Renewal
866-ASK-DHCR
www.dhcr.state.ny.us

Manufactured Homes Hotline
800-432-4210
www.dhcr.state.ny.us/AboutUs/contact.htm

New York City Housing Authority
718-707-7771
www.nyc.gov/html/nycha/html/home/home.shtml

Public Housing Contacts
www.hud.gov/offices/pih/pha/contacts/states/ny.cfm

Public Housing Information Hotline
800-955-2232
www.hud.gov/offices/pih/about/css.cfm

State Housing Finance Agency
800-382-4663
www.nyhomes.org/index.aspx?page=47

State of New York Mortgage Agency
800-382-HOME (home buyers hotline)
www.nyhomes.org/index.aspx?page=48

**U.S. Department of Housing and
Urban Development**
202-708-1112 (national office)
212-264-8000 (New York regional office)
www.hud.gov
www.hud.gov/local/index.cfm?state=ny
www.hud.gov/local/index.cfm?state=ny&topic=offices

Human Rights

(see Civil Rights)

Identity Theft

(see also Credit Reports, Fraud, Law Enforcement)

Consumer Protection Board (Identity Theft)
800-697-1220; 518-474-8583
www.consumer.state.ny.us/internet_security.htm

Federal Trade Commission Identity Theft Site
(see also Privacy)
877-ID-THEFT
www.ftc.gov/bcp/edu/microsites/idtheft

Identity Theft Resource Center
858-693-7935
www.idtheftcenter.org

Identity Theft Laws in New York
*www.idtheftcenter.org/artman2/publish/states/New_York
.shtml*

Office of the Attorney General
800-771-7755
*www.ag.ny.gov/bureaus/consumer_frauds/
identity_theft.html*

Immigration

New York Citizenship/Immigration Hotline
800-566-7636
www.westchesterlibraries.org/node/20?l=sp&id=211

U.S. Citizenship and Immigration Services
800-375-5283
www.uscis.gov

Insurance

Health Insurance Information Counseling and Assistance
800-701-0501
www.aging.ny.gov/HealthBenefits/HIICAPIndex.cfm

Insurance Department
800-342-3736; 866-NYINS-HELP
www.ins.state.ny.us

Insurance Fraud Hotline
888-FRAUD-NY
www.ins.state.ny.us

National Insurance Consumer Hotline
800-942-4242; 800-331-9146
www.iii.org

State Insurance Fund
877-435-7743; 888-875-5790
ww3.nysif.com

IOLA

Interest on Lawyer Accounts
(see also Attorney)
800-222-IOLA; 646-865-1541
www.iola.org
www.nylawfund.org/pubs/guide.shtml

IRS

(see Tax)

Labor

(see also Employment)

State Department of Labor
800-4-NYSDOL; 518-457-9000
www.labor.state.ny.us

U.S. Department of Labor
866-4USA-DOL
www.dol.gov

Wage and Hour Hotline
866-4US-WAGE
www.dol.gov/whd/index.htm

Landlord and Tenant

(see Civil Rights, Housing)

Law Enforcement

(see also Domestic Violence)

Bureau of Justice Assistance Clearinghouse
866-859-2687
www.ojp.usdoj.gov/BJA/contact.html

Bureau of Narcotic Enforcement
866-811-7957
www.health.state.ny.us/professionals/narcotic

Commission of Investigation
877-SIC-4NYS; 212-344-6660
*www.worldcat.org/arcviewer/1/AO%23/2009/04/02/
H1238693215513/viewer/file33.htm*

Crime Victims Board
800-247-8035
www.cvb.state.ny.us

Criminal Justice (Attorney General)
800-771-7755
www.oag.state.ny.us/our_office.html

Division of Criminal Justice Services
800-262-3257
criminaljustice.state.ny.us

Office for the Prevention of Domestic Violence
800-942-6906, 518-457-5800
opdv.state.ny.us

Office of Forensic Services
800-262-3257
*criminaljustice.state.ny.us/forensic/
aboutofs.htm*

Office of Homeland Security
866-SAFE-NYS; 518-402-2227
www.security.state.ny.us

Office of Juvenile Justice and Delinquency
800-851-3420
ojjdp.ncjrs.org
ojjdp.ncjrs.org/statecontacts/ResourceListDatails.asp

Office of Public Safety
800-262-3257
criminaljustice.state.ny.us/ops/index.htm

Sex Offender Registry
800-262-3257
criminaljustice.state.ny.us/nsor

Lawyer Referral Service

(see Attorney)

Lawyers' Fund For Client Protection

(see Attorney)

Lead

(see also Environment)

National Lead Information Center
800-424-LEAD
www.epa.gov/lead/pubs/nlic.htm

Legislature

(see also section 4.4)

Congress
202-224-3121; 202-225-3121
www.house.gov
www.senate.gov
www.congress.org

New York State Assembly
518-455-4218
assembly.state.ny.us

New York State Senate
www.senate.state.ny.us

State Legislature
Bill Drafting Commission Hotline
800-342-9860
public.leginfo.state.ny.us/menuf.cgi

Legislative Retrieval System
800-356-6566
nyslrs.state.ny.us/news/whatslrs.html

Lemon Law

800-771-7755
www.oag.state.ny.us/bureaus/consumer_frauds/
lemon_law.html

LexisNexis

800-223-1940; 800-356-6548
www.lexisone.com

Lottery

New York Lottery
518-388-3300
www.nylottery.org/index.php

Marriage Records

(see also section 5.7)

Department of Health
877-854-4481 (VitalChek)
www.health.state.ny.us/vital_records
www.health.state.ny.us/vital_records/marriage.htm

Medicare and Medicaid

(see also Health)

Centers for Medicare and Medicaid Services
800-MEDICARE; 877-267-2323
www.cms.hhs.gov
www.cms.hhs.gov/RegionalOffices

County Contacts for Medicaid in New York
www.health.state.ny.us/health_care/Medicaid
www.health.state.ny.us/health_care/medicaid/ldss.htm

Mental Health

(see also Alcoholism and Drug Abuse, Health)

Mental Health Information Hotline
Office of Mental Health
800-597-8481
www.omh.state.ny.us

National Alliance Information Hotline
800-950-NAMI
www.nami.org

Quality of Care Complaints
800-624-4143
www.cqcapd.state.ny.us/misc_pages/howtosubmitcomplaint.htm

Other Mental Health Hotlines
800-735-2773 (drug relapse)
800-931-2237 (eating disorders)
800-DONTCUT (self-abuse)
800-848-9596 (shoplifters)
800-SUICIDE (suicide)
800-293-TALK (suicide)
smhp.psych.ucla.edu/hotline.htm

Military

(see Veterans)

Missing Children

(see also Amber Alert, Child Abuse, Law Enforcement)

Division of Criminal Justice Services
800-FIND-KID
criminaljustice.state.ny.us/missing/graphics/if_child_mis.pdf

National Center for Missing and Exploited Children
800-THE-LOST; 800-I-AM-LOST
www.missingkids.com
www.childwelfare.gov/pubs/reslist/tollfree.cfm

Mortgages

(see also Housing)

State of New York Mortgage Agency
Consumer Mortgages
800-382-HOME
www.nyhomes.org

Motor Vehicles

(see also DMV, Transportation)

Natural Resources

(see also Energy, Environment)

Bureau of Fisheries
518-402-8924
www.dec.ny.gov/outdoor/fishing.html

Bureau of Lands and Forests
518-402-9405
www.dec.ny.gov/lands/309.html

Bureau of Wildlife
518-402-8883
www.dec.ny.gov/outdoor/hunting.html

Department of Environmental Conservation
800-TIPP-DEC; 518-402-8013
www.dec.ny.gov

Division of Coastal Resources
nyswaterfronts.com/index.asp

Energy Research and Development Authority
866-NYS-ERDA; 518-862-1090
www.nyserda.org

Office of Parks, Recreation and Historic Preservation
518-474-0456; 800-456-CAMP
www.nysparks.state.ny.us

New York State Government

Agency Web Sites
www.state.ny.us
www.nysl.nysed.gov/ils/nyserver.html

Government Toll-Free Numbers
www.tollfreenumber.org/forum/about45.html

State Government Information Locator Service
www.nysl.nysed.gov/ils

Nurses

Nurses Complaint Hotline
800-442-8106
www.op.nysed.gov/opd.htm
www.op.nysed.gov/opsearches.htm

Nursing Home Complaints

888-201-4563
nursinghomes.nyhealth.gov

Ombudsman, Office of Long Term Care
800-342-9871
www.ombudsman.state.ny.us

Occupational Safety

Department of Labor, State
518-485-9263
*www.labor.state.ny.us/workerprotection/safetyhealth/
    dosh_programs.shtm*

Occupational Safety and Health Administration (OSHA)
800-321-OSHA
www.osha.gov/oshdir/ny.html

Ombudsman

(see Nursing Home Complaints)

Ozone

(see Environment)

Parks and Recreation

Office of Parks, Recreation and Historic Preservation
518-474-0456; 800-456-CAMP
www.nysparks.state.ny.us

Parole

(see Corrections, Law Enforcement)

Passport

National Passport Information Center
877-4USA-PPT
travel.state.gov/passport/passport_1738.html

Pensions

Pensions Benefits Guaranty Corporation
800-400-7242
www.pbgc.gov

Pesticides

(see also Environment)

National Pesticide Information Center
800-858-7378
npic.orst.edu/index.html

Pharmacy

Pharmacy Complaint Hotline
800-442-8106
www.op.nysed.gov/opd.htm
www.op.nysed.gov/opsearches.htm

Physicians

(see also Health)

Medical Society of the State of New York
800-523-4405
www.mssny.org

Office of Professional Medical Conduct
800-663-6114
www.health.state.ny.us (click "Physician Discipline")

Physicians Complaint Hotline
800-442-8106
www.op.nysed.gov/opd.htm
www.op.nysed.gov/opsearches.htm

Poison

(see also Environment)

Poison Control Centers
800-222-1222
www.poison.org (national)
*www.health.state.ny.us/nysdoh/poisoncontrol/
    centers.htm* (NY)

Police and Sheriffs

(see also section 4.6)
www.troopers.state.ny.us
www.usacops.com/ny
www.usacops.com/ny/shrflist.html
www.nysheriffs.org

Pollution

(see Environment)

Port Authority

Port Authority of NY and NJ
800-221-9903
www.panynj.gov

Prison

(see Corrections)

Privacy

(see Civil Rights, HIPAA, Identity Theft)

Product Safety

(see also Consumer Protection)

Consumer Product Safety Commission
800-638-2772
www.cpsc.gov

Public Defender

Capital Defender Office
212-608-3352
www.nycdo.org

Public Defender Offices
www.nysda.org/html/chief_defenders.html
www.nysda.org/08_Chief_Defender_List2008-08-05.pdf

Public Utilities

(see also Energy, Environment, Natural Resources)

New York Power Authority
914-681-6200
www.nypa.gov

Public Service Commission
518-474-7080
800-342-3377 (complaint hotline)
www.dps.state.ny.us

Rape

(see also Child Abuse, Domestic Violence, Law
Enforcement)

RAINN (Rape, Abuse, Incest) Hotline
800-656-HOPE
www.rainn.org
centers.rainn.org
(click "New York")

Real Estate

(see also Housing, Mortgages)

Office of Real Property Services
518-474-2982
www.orps.state.ny.us

Real Estate, Department of (enforcement/complaints)
www.dos.state.ny.us/LCNS/licensing.html

Recycling

Reduction, Reuse and Recycling
888-925-7329
www.nysar3.org

Runaway

(see Child Abuse, Domestic Violence, Missing Children)

Missing and Exploited Children Hotline
800-FIND-KID
criminaljustice.state.ny.us/missing/aware/runaway.htm

National Runaway Switchboard
800-RUNAWAY
www.1800runaway.org

Secretary of State

Office of the Secretary of State (New York)
212-417-5800 (Albany)
212-417-5800 (New York City)
www.dos.state.ny.us

U.S. Department of State
202-647-4000
877-487-2778 (passports)
www.state.gov

Securities

(see also Business)

Investor Protection Bureau (Attorney General)
800-771-7755; 212-416-8222
*www.oag.state.ny.us/bureaus/investor_protection/
    about.html*

New York Society of Security Analysts
800-248-0108
www.nyssa.org

U.S. Securities and Exchange Commission
888-SEC-6585
www.sec.gov

Senate

(see Legislature)

Seniors

(see Disability, Elder Abuse, Families, Health, Social Security)

Aging, Office for the
800-342-9871 (senior's hotline)
www.aging.ny.gov

AARP
888-OUR-AARP
www.aarp.org

Elderly Pharmaceutical Insurance Coverage
800-332-3742
www.health.state.ny.us
(click "EPIC for Seniors")

Office of Long Term Care Ombudsman
800-342-9871; 518-474-7329
www.ombudsman.state.ny.us

Protective Services for Adults
518-473-7793
www.ocfs.state.ny.us/main/psa

Sex Offenders

(see also Law Enforcement, Rape)

Sex Offender Registry
800-262-3257
criminaljustice.state.ny.us/nsor/index.htm

Sexual Harassment

(see also Law Enforcement)

Office of Sexual Harassment
800-HARASS-3
www.dhr.state.ny.us

U.S. Equal Employment Opportunity Commission
800-669-4000
EEOC: *www.eeoc.gov/facts/fs-sex.html*

Sexually Transmitted Diseases

(see also Health)

American Social Health Association
800-227-8922
www.ashastd.org

Sheriffs

(see Police and Sheriffs; see also section 4.6)

Social Security

Social Security Administration
800-772-1213 (information)
800-269-0271 (fraud hotline)
www.ssa.gov

Social Services

(see Children, Families, Seniors)

Social Worker

Social Worker Complaint Hotline
800-442-8106
www.op.nysed.gov/opd.htm
www.op.nysed.gov/opsearches.htm

Students

(see Education)

Substance Abuse

(see Alcoholism and Drug Abuse)

Suicide

(see also Mental Health)

National Suicide Prevention Hotline
800-273-TALK; 800-SUICIDE
www.suicidepreventionlifeline.org

Tax

Federal Taxes
Internal Revenue Service
800-829-1040 (individuals)
800-829-4933 (businesses)
www.irs.gov
www.irs.gov/localcontacts
(click "New York")

State Taxes
New York State Department of Taxation and Finance
800-225-5829 (personal); 888-698-2908 (corporate)
888-675-9437 (tax evasion)
www.tax.state.ny.us
www.nysegov.com/citGuide.cfm?superCat=212

Taxpayer Rights (Office of Real Property Services)
518-474-2982; 518-486-5446
www.orps.state.ny.us/home/tri_index.cfm

Telephone

(see also Public Utilities)

Public Service Commission
800-342-3377 (complaint hotline)
www.dps.state.ny.us

Tourism

I Love NY
800-CALL-NYS
www.iloveny.com

Transportation

Department of Motor Vehicles
212-645-5550, 800-DIAL-DMV, 800-CALL-DMV
www.nydmv.state.ny.us

Department of Transportation, State
518-457-6195
800-847-8929 (road conditions)
www.nysdot.gov

Department of Transportation, Federal
866-377-8642
www.dot.gov

National Highway Traffic Safety Administration
888-327-4236
www.nhtsa.dot.gov

New York State Thruway Authority
800-THRUWAY; 518-436-2983
www.nysthruway.gov

Unclaimed Property

Office of the State Comptroller
800-221-9311
www.osc.state.ny.us/ouf/index.htm

Unemployment Insurance

(see also section 2.8; Employment, Labor, Workers' Compensation)

Unemployment Insurance Division (Department of Labor)
888-209-8124
www.labor.state.ny.us/ui/ui_index.shtm

Utilities

(see Public Utilities)

Veterans

Division of Veterans' Affairs
888-838-7697; 518-474-6114
veterans.ny.gov

U.S. Veterans Administration
800-827-1000
www.va.gov

Veterinarian

Veterinarian Complaint Hotline
800-442-8106
www.op.nysed.gov/opd.htm
www.op.nysed.gov/opsearches.htm

Victim Services

(see also Domestic Violence, Law Enforcement)

National Organization for Victim Assistance
800-TRY-NOVA
www.trynova.org

Victim Compensation
800-247-8035
www.cvb.state.ny.us

Victim Resources
800-771-7755
www.oag.state.ny.us/bureaus/intergov_affairs/victim_rights.
  html

Vital Records

(see Birth Records, Death Records, Divorce Records, Marriage Records; see also section 5.7)

Voting

(see Elections)

Water

(see also Fish and Game, Natural Resources, Public Utilities)

Public Service Commission
800-342-3377 (complaint hotline)
www.dps.state.ny.us

Welfare

(see also Child Support, Families, Seniors)

Office of Temporary and Disability Assistance
877-472-8411
www.otda.state.ny.us

West Group/Westlaw

800-328-4880; 800-WESTLAW
west.thomson.com

Whistleblowing

(see Fraud)

White House

202-456-1414
www.whitehouse.gov

Workers' Compensation

(see also section 2.9; Employment, Labor, Unemployment Insurance)

Advocate for Injured Workers

800-580-6665

www.wcb.state.ny.us/content/main/Contact.jsp

Division of Safety and Health

518-457-3518

www.labor.state.ny.us/workerprotection/safetyhealth/dosh_programs.shtm

State Insurance Fund

877-435-7743

ww3.nysif.com

Workers' Compensation Board

877-632-4996

www.wcb.state.ny.us

C. More Information

State Government

www.ny.gov

www.nysl.nysed.gov/ils

www.state.ny.us/governor

www.nysl.nysed.gov/citizens.htm

www.nysl.nysed.gov/ils/nyserver.html

www.nysegov.com/citGuide.cfm?superCat=102&cat=449&content=main

D. Something to Check

What hotline resources might help a client concerned about the following circumstances:

1. Stalking
2. Insolvency
3. Credit discrimination

Procedure: Some Basics

Abbreviations Used in the Section

CPLR: New York Civil Practice Laws and Rules

EBT: Examination before Trial (Deposition)

GCN: General Construction Law

GMU: General Municipal Law

NYCRR: New York Code of Rules and Regulations

RJI: Request for Judicial Intervention

A. Introduction

To illustrate how the court system works, this section will present a timeline of a civil case involving more than $25,000, which must be filed in the supreme court of one of the counties. Cases involving lesser amounts are filed in one of the many local courts such as a county court, city court, town court, village court, district court, or (in New York City) civil court, all of which have their own local rules. In addition, a supreme court civil case uses essentially the same procedure in divorce cases for which the supreme court has exclusive jurisdiction. Because each type of court has its own rules, be sure to check the appropriate statutory source, such as the Civil Practice Laws and Rules (for supreme court and county court civil actions), the Family Court Act (for custody petitions), or the Surrogate's Court Act (for will probates), as well as the local court rules. In addition, the Uniform Rules for New York State Trial Courts (22 NYCRR 200.01, et seq.) apply to the trial courts.

The timeline describes many of the major events in a disputed (i.e., contested) civil case commonly filed in supreme court. Keep in mind, however, that civil cases can vary a great deal in complexity, depending on the nature of the case, the magnitude of the issues involved, the amount of potential damages, the extent of contention between the parties, and the caliber of the attorneys. Also adding diversity and complexity are the local rules that apply only to the court in which a case is being litigated. Each county has a supreme court clerk from whom you can obtain the local rules. (See sections 4.2 and 5.1 on locating such rules.) Our timeline primarily covers rules of statewide applicability.

See also the following related sections:

- Overview of New York state courts (section 4.2)
- Venue, process, pleadings, and discovery (section 6.2)
- Example of a civil complaint (section 7.1)
- Rules for (and example of) an appellate brief (section 7.4)
- Self-help resources (section 5.6)
- Overview of federal courts sitting in New York (section 4.3)
- Some comparisons between state and federal civil procedure (section 6.3)
- Timeline of a criminal case in state court (section 6.4)

B. Overview

Exhibit 6.1A presents an overview of many of the major events involved in the litigation of supreme court cases in New York.

Preliminary Considerations

Statute of limitations. The statute of limitations places time limits on filing a lawsuit. For example, a breach of contract claim must usually be filed within six years of the alleged breach. If you do not bring suit within six years, the suit is barred, meaning that you can no longer sue. (CPLR 213.)

Notice of claim. When suing a public corporation (city, county, fire district, school district, etc.) for a tort, the plaintiff must file a special notice (called a notice of claim). This notice acts like a statute of limitations. Filing the notice is a condition precedent or prior requirement for bringing the suit. Plaintiffs have only 90 days to give notice to the public corporation of the possible tort action. Although the notice itself does not have to contain much detail, failure to file it in a timely fashion precludes most actions. (GMU 50-e.)

Subject-matter jurisdiction. The trial court of general jurisdiction is the supreme court. There is one in each county. It conducts trials of all civil cases with no monetary limits, all divorce cases, and in large cities, all felonies, in addition to many other types of actions. Although the supreme court has jurisdiction for money claims of any amount, claims for less than $25,000 are typically handled in courts with jurisdiction over limited amounts of money. Small claims cases are brought in "local" courts and involve claims up to $3,000 (in town and village courts) and $5,000 (in district court, NYC civil court, and city courts). Local courts are also where most criminal matters are commenced and all non-felony trials are conducted. Claims of less than $25,000 but more than the small claims amount may be brought in a county court (the 57 non-NYC counties have county courts) or in a local court, where the maximum amount ranges from as little as $3,000 in justice court (town court or village court) to $15,000 (city courts, district courts) to $25,000 (NYC civil court). This is discussed more completely in section 4.2.

EXHIBIT 6.1A Bringing and Defending a Civil Case in New York Supreme Court

(The following overview covers many of the major events in a typical case seeking money damages of more than $25,000 in New York Supreme Court; variations will depend on the complexity of the case and the applicability of local rules.)

PRELIMINARY CONSIDERATIONS	COMMENCEMENT OF CASE; PLEADINGS AND MOTIONS	DISCLOSURE	MOTION PRACTICE	PROVISIONAL REMEDIES	PRETRIAL EVENTS	TRIAL	APPEAL

• Statute of limitations
• Notice of claim
• Subject-matter jurisdiction
• Venue
	• Summons and complaint; summons with notice
	• Summons
	• Filing, index number, and RJI
	• Complaint
	• Service on defendant
	• Proof of service
	• Answer
	• Counterclaims
	• Cross-claims
	• Reply
	• Amending the complaint
	• Demand for bill of particulars
	• Default judgment
	• Motion to vacate default judgment
		• Deposition upon oral questions
		• Interrogatories
		• Notice to admit
		• Inspection and production
		• Physical or mental examination
		• Commission or letters rogatory
		• Motion to compel disclosure
		• Motion for a protective order
			• General motion procedures
			• Responding papers
			• Cross-motion
			• Motion to dismiss
			• Motion for summary judgment
			• Motion hearing
				• Order to show cause
				• Preliminary injunction
				• Examples of provisional remedies
				  - Attachment
				  - Replevin
				  - Receivership
				  - Notice of pendency
					• Note of issue
					• Certificate of readiness
					• Preliminary conference
					• Pretrial conferences
					• Alternative dispute resolution
						• Conference prior to trial
						• Motion in limine
						• Voir dire
						• Opening statements
						• Case in chief of plaintiff
						• Examination of witnesses
						• Objections
						• Case in chief of defendant
						• Exhibits
						• Trial motions
						• Rebuttal witnesses
						• Closing arguments
						• Charging conference
						• Instructions to the jury
						• Verdict
						• Additur and remittitur
						• Costs and disbursements
						• Motion for judgment and new trial
						  - Entry of judgment and notice of entry of judgment
							• Appellate courts
							• Stay and undertaking
							• Notice of appeal
							• Perfecting the appeal
							• Appellate briefs
							• Oral argument
							• Appellate Division decision
							• Appeal to Court of Appeals
							• Court of Appeals decision

Venue. Most civil claims (transitory actions) must be filed in the county where one of the parties resides. (CPLR 503(a).) Corporate litigants are deemed to be residents of the county in which their principal office is located. (CPLR 503(c).) Claims involving real estate local actions are generally brought in the county where the property is located. (CPLR 507.)

Commencement of Case; Pleadings and Motions

Summons and complaint; summons with notice. A lawsuit is commenced by filing either a summons and complaint (CPLR 304) or a summons with notice (CPLR 305(b)) with the supreme court clerk of the appropriate county. If a summons with notice is used, the complaint is usually filed later.

Summons. Every action in supreme court must be commenced with a summons, which is produced and signed by the attorney. The summons notifies the defendants of the action ("YOU ARE HEREBY SUMMONED . . . and in case of your failure to appear, judgment will be taken against you by default for the relief demanded in the notice set forth below . . .") A complete sample of a summons may be found in the Official Forms of the Office of Court Administration. (See, for example, *www.nycourts.gov/litigants/divorce/forms_instructions/ud-1.pdf.*) The summons lists the parties and the time within which the defendants must file a response (generally 20 to 30 days depending on the type of service used). There are usually three copies stamped with filing information from the court: the original for the court files, one to be served on the defendant, and one for the plaintiff's files.

Filing, index number, and RJI. The filing of the summons marks the actual commencement of the legal action. When the initial pleading is ready, the plaintiff must first purchase an index number from the county clerk, which is written or stamped on all pleadings. Next, the summons and complaint or summons with notice is presented to the supreme court clerk. Either at filing or later, an RJI number (request for judicial intervention) must also be purchased. Pursuant to this request, the clerk randomly selects a judge to be assigned to the case. Because this step is not needed until the first court appearance, which could occur months after filing, some lawyers wait until the last minute to obtain the RJI, often hoping that the other lawyer will need judicial action first and then have to pay for the RJI.

Complaint. The complaint is usually served with the summons. (In some kinds of actions called special proceedings the complaint is called the *petition.* An example is an Article 78 Action against a governmental agency, CPLR 7801 et seq.) The complaint contains a statement of the facts constituting the cause of action (CPLR 3013) and a demand for judgment for the relief to which the pleader claims to be entitled. (CPLR 3017.) In some circumstances, no complaint is served with the summons. In such cases, a summons with notice is used to commence the action. This is most frequently done when there is not sufficient time to complete a complaint, especially when the statute of limitations problem is looming. If a complaint fails to state a cause of action, it will be dismissed after a CPLR 3211 motion to dismiss.

Service on defendant. When a party is sued, the plaintiff must provide formal notice to the defendant that the legal process has begun. This is called service. When serving the other side, copies of the papers filed in court to commence the action must be provided. For a civil case, the summons and complaint (or summons with notice) must be served on each defendant named in the summons. Proof of this service must then be filed with the court. (CPLR § 306.) For personal service, the server personally delivers the summons and complaint to the defendant or someone qualified to accept service for the defendant. (CPLR § 308.) The server must be over 18 and not be a party to the case. Servers can be friends, relatives, the sheriff, or a licensed process server. (CPLR 2103(a).)

If, after reasonable diligence, a copy of the summons and complaint cannot be served using one of the above methods, a summons may be served by (a) affixing a copy of the summons and complaint at the person's dwelling house, usual place of abode, usual place of business, or usual mailing address (other than a post office box); (b) in the presence of a competent member of the household or a person apparently in charge of his or her office, place of business, or usual mailing address (other than a post office box), at least 18 years of age; (c) who shall be informed of the contents thereof, and by thereafter (d) mailing a copy of the summons and complaint by first-class mail, postage prepaid to the person to be served at the place where a copy of the summons and complaint were left.

This is referred to as nail and mail (CPLR 308(4)). Other methods of service are also possible, such as first class mail (CPLR 312-a), designated agent (CPLR 303), and publication (CPLR 315). See CPLR Article 3 on the requirements for these alternatives.

Proof of service. The person serving the summons and complaint must complete, sign, and notarize a proof-of-service form called an affidavit of service. After the defendants are served, the proof of service together with the original summons is filed with the court. The proof of service states that a copy of the summons and complaint was served on each defendant in a designated way. The signed original proof of service and a copy of it are filed with the court clerk. Service must take place within 120 days from the commencement of the action, with an additional extension possible for good cause shown or in the interest of justice. Effecting proper service can be critical if the statute of limitations expires after commencement of an action but prior to service (CPLR 306-b).

Answer. After being served a summons and complaint or summons with notice, the defendant must file a responsive pleading or paper. The possible responsive pleadings or papers are an answer, a notice of appearance, a motion to dismiss (CPLR 320(a)), or (when served with a summons with notice) a demand for complaint (CPLR 3012(b)).

The answer to a complaint contains (1) responses to every allegation in the complaint, usually admitting the allegation, denying it, or stating a lack of knowledge or information sufficient to admit or deny; (2) a statement of any new matter constituting a defense (affirmative defense); and/or (3) a counter-claim. (CPLR 3018, 3019.)

The defendant has 20 days from the date the defendant was personally served to file an answer or other response (e.g., demand for complaint, motion to dismiss) with the clerk of the court, or 30 days if service was accomplished through an alternate means. (CPLR 320(a).)

When counting days for any time period, the first day counted is the day after the event unless that day falls on a Saturday, Sunday, or holiday, in which case the time is extended until the next business day (GCL 20). For example, if the defendant was personally served with a summons and complaint on the 2nd of the month, the first day of the 20-day period would begin on the 3rd; the 20th day would fall on the 22nd. If the 22nd was a Saturday, the answer would be due the 24th, unless the 24th was a holiday, in which case it would be due the 25th.

In addition, CPLR 2004 gives the court broad discretion in extending almost every deadline "upon good cause shown," even if the extension is requested after the deadline has passed. When one attorney asks another for extra time, common practice is to grant the request unless missing the date will extinguish a cause of action because of the statute of limitations.

Failure to file an answer within the required time period is one basis for a plaintiff to seek a default judgment (CPLR 3215(a)). Unlike missing a statute of limitations, which is a fatal error for a cause of action, a default judgment may be overturned for a myriad of reasons (CPLR 5015). See discussion of default judgments below.

The second type of responsive pleading to a summons and complaint is a motion to dismiss (CPLR 3211), which is served instead of an answer under certain circumstances and is discussed below. The third type of response is a notice of appearance, which is usually a one-page pleading with the caption of the action, indicating that a particular attorney represents the defendant. This gives the defendant additional time to respond with either an answer or a motion. (CPLR 320(a).)

When a summons with notice is served, the defendant can file a demand for a complaint. (CPLR 3012(b).)

After the complaint is served, the defendant responds with either an answer or a motion. (CPLR 320(a).)

Counterclaims. A defendant may include a counterclaim in the answer. A counterclaim is a claim against the plaintiff asserted by the defendant, even if it does not relate to the plaintiff's original claim. By bringing the initial claim, the plaintiff has consented to the court's jurisdiction, so commencement of a new action is not required. (CPLR 3019.)

Cross-claims. A defendant can also file a cross-claim against another defendant. A cross-claim asserts an independent action and is treated like a complaint, i.e., it must be properly served and the side against whom it is filed must respond at the risk of receiving a default judgment. Any cross-claim is permitted in an answer, even if it is not related to the plaintiff's claim. Cross-claims are commonly used when both the insured and the insurance company are being sued. For example, a defendant driver in a car accident could cross-claim against an insurance company (CPLR 3019(b)). Cross-claims can also be used when one plaintiff wishes to bring an action against another plaintiff in the same litigation.

Reply. A reply is an answer-like response to a counterclaim imposed by the defendant. The sole difference between a reply and an answer is that a reply is used as a responsive pleading to a counterclaim instead of to a complaint. (CPLR 3011.)

Amending the complaint. There are times when it is prudent to amend the original complaint. For instance, a complaint may have deficiencies because it was drafted under time pressures to meet a looming statute of limitations deadline. Having met the deadline, the plaintiff may now want to go back and redraft the complaint more artfully. Another reason to amend is that an opponent's motion may point out errors or omissions in the complaint. "A party may amend his pleading, or supplement it by setting forth additional or subsequent transactions or occurrences, at any time by leave of court or by stipulation of all parties. Leave shall be freely given upon such terms as may be just including the granting of costs and continuances." (CPLR 3025(b).)

Demand for bill of particulars. A bill of particulars is a more detailed statement of a claim brought against another. A defendant can demand that the plaintiff amplify the complaint through a bill of particulars.

The plaintiff must comply with such a demand. A demand for bill of particulars is similar to the disclosure devices (discovery) we will examine shortly. The focus of the demand is more limited than disclosure devices. The demand is aimed at items for which the plaintiff has the burden of proof. If, for example, a plaintiff sues for breach of contract, the date and time of the alleged agreement could be demanded in a bill of particulars, but a copy of the contract could not. To obtain the latter, a party would have to use a Demand to Produce, discussed below. (CPLR 3042.)

Default judgment. A default judgment is a judgment against a party for failure to file a required pleading or otherwise respond to the opponent's claim. If, for example, a defendant fails to appear, plead, or proceed to trial within the time period provided by law, the plaintiff can request that a default judgment be entered against the defendant for this reason. (CPLR 3215.)

Motion to vacate default judgment. Once a default judgment is entered against a defendant, the latter cannot file a response to the complaint or appear in the action unless the court vacates the default. The court will do so if the defendant can demonstrate that the default was "excusable" (CPLR 5015(a)(1)). Courts prefer to resolve a legal dispute through the litigation process by the presentation of evidence and arguments (i.e., on the merits), but the dispute will be resolved by default if there is no legitimate reason for the failure of a party to respond.

Disclosure

Chapter 31 of the CPLR (3101–3140) contains the rules of discovery, which is referred to in the CPLR as *disclosure.*

Deposition upon oral questions. A deposition is a method of discovery by which parties or their prospective witnesses are questioned outside the courtroom before trial. A deposition upon oral questions is also referred to as an oral deposition or EBT (examination before trial). A party or other witness is questioned under oath in the presence of a court reporter who takes down or records the testimony. A deposition upon oral questions is considered the single most important disclosure device in pretrial practice. (Less frequently used is a deposition upon written questions.)

Any party may take an EBT of any person, including any party to the action. (CPLR 3107.) To conduct an EBT, the party first sends a 20-day notice to the other party (with a subpoena if the target of the EBT is not a party to the action). Although the notice includes the scheduled time for the EBT, the actual time of the deposition is often set by informal agreement among the parties. The deposition is usually held in the conference room of one of the attorneys.

The costs of the EBT are borne by the demanding party. (CPLR 3107.)

Interrogatories. Interrogatories are written questions posed to a party, requiring a sworn written response (CPLR 3130). Unlike federal practice where interrogatories are freely used (often prior to depositions to help flesh out issues), New York restricts the use of interrogatories and hence they are much less common. For instance, in a matrimonial action one may not use both interrogatories and a demand for particulars; a party must choose one or the other. Further, in most personal injury actions, one may not serve interrogatories and conduct an EBT on the same party unless special leave of the court is obtained. Since the EBT is usually the most important part of discovery, interrogatories are much less important in New York practice than in other jurisdictions.

Notice to admit. A notice to admit (also called request for admission) is a written demand from a party that the other party to the action admit uncontested and uncontroverted matters prior to the beginning of a trial. This usually involves the genuineness of specified documents or the truth of easily established matters of fact. This disclosure device may be used only when the moving party "reasonably believes there can be no substantial dispute at the trial" concerning the matter. (CPLR 3123(a).) Once the notice is served, the matter is deemed admitted unless the recipient objects within 20 days. There is a penalty for a party who files an unreasonable denial (CPLR 3123(c)).

Inspection and production. Any party may obtain discovery of "documents and things" in the possession, custody, or control of any other party to the action. A party can demand that the other party produce and permit inspection, copying, testing, or photographing a document or other tangible thing; and allow entry on any land or other property for purposes of "inspecting, measuring, surveying, sampling, testing, photographing or recording by motion pictures or otherwise." (CPLR 3120.) This device may be used by either party anytime after the commencement of an action.

Physical or mental examination. Any party may serve notice on another party to submit to a physical, mental, or blood examination by a designated physician after commencement of an action in which the mental or physical condition or the blood relationship of a party is in controversy. (CPLR 3121.) The examination can also be taken of an agent, employee, or other person in the custody or legal control of a party. Such examinations are routinely used in personal injury actions.

Commission or letters rogatory. Commissions or letters rogatory are used when a witness is out of state or out of the county and unavailable for an EBT in New York.

(CPLR 3108.) The commission or letters rogatory permits a foreign judge or attorney to conduct an EBT out of state or out of the country, usually using a combination of New York and local rules.

Motion to compel disclosure. If the parties disagree on what constitutes proper discovery, or if a party fails to respond to a proper discovery request, a motion may be brought to compel a response. (CPLR 3124.) After receipt of such a motion, the judge will determine if the motion has merit, and if it does, will issue a conditional order, giving the non-complying party a set date for compliance and a designated penalty for failure to comply. (CPLR 3104.)

Motion for a protective order. A protective order is a court order that requires a party to cease improper disclosure conduct or face judicial penalties. "Such order shall be designed to prevent unreasonable annoyance, expense, embarrassment, disadvantage, or other prejudice to any person or the courts." An example of abuse is demanding information that is privileged or otherwise protected from disclosure by law. A court may impose a protective order on its own initiative or the responding party may bring a motion for the protective order. (CPLR 3103.)

Motion Practice

General motion procedures. A motion is a party's request for a court order. Most motions are brought during existing actions and are made in writing with notice to the other party. (CPLR 2212 (a).) (An alternative method to bring a motion is called an order to show cause. This method, made ex parte, is less common.) During a trial, the notice and writing requirements are generally relaxed; motions are usually made orally on the record. Written motions are brought with a single "Notice of Motion" page, which includes:

- The caption of the case,
- The nature of the motion, and
- The date, place, and time of the court appearance to present the motion. (See Office of Court Administration Form 26.)

The substance of the motion is drafted in the form of an affidavit and is attached to the Notice of Motion, along with affidavits (sworn statements), pleadings, letters, photos, and other relevant documents that support the request made in the motion. If there are issues of law, a memo is also included. At least three copies are made: the original for the court; a copy for the other parties, which is usually mailed; and one for the attorney's file. When the motion is filed with the court clerk, a court appearance for addressing the motion is scheduled, referred to as the return date, which is then written on each copy. The general rule is that there

must be at least 8 days notice before the motion hearing if the motion if personally served, 13 if served by mail. (CPLR 2214(b).)

Responding papers. The recipient of motion papers must submit responding papers at least 2 days before the return date for a motion served with 8 days notice or within 7 days if served with 16 days notice. The moving party may then respond with a reply affidavit, addressing the responding papers, with at least 1 day notice. (CPLR 2214(b).)

Cross-motion. At least three days prior to the return date of any motion, or seven days prior if the demand is made pursuant to CPLR 2124(b), the responding party may file a notice of cross-motion demanding relief, with or without supporting documents. (CPLR 2215.) This will be heard at the same time as the underlying motion.

Motion to dismiss. Often a defendant's first strategy in a civil case is to file a motion to dismiss one or more causes of action asserted by the plaintiff. If the motion is granted, the case on any affected cause of action terminates. Grounds for the motion to dismiss include:

- The complaint fails to state a cause of action
- A defense is founded upon documentary evidence; or
- The court lacks subject-matter jurisdiction or personal jurisdiction of the defendant
- The plaintiff lacks legal capacity to sue
- Statute of limitations
- Res judicata (CPLR 3211)

There is no specified time to bring a motion to dismiss; it can be brought as the first responsive pleading after being served or as the last pleading, such as when a defendant brings the motion when plaintiff neglects to move the case forward for an extended time. (CPLR 3216.)

Motion for summary judgment. A summary judgment is a judgment on a claim or defense rendered without a full trial because of the absence of genuine conflict on any of the material facts involved. Any party may move for summary judgment any time prior to trial by alleging that the action has no merit or that there is no defense to the action or proceeding. The motion will be granted if the submissions show that there is no triable issue as to any material fact and that the moving party is entitled to a judgment as a matter of law. The motion includes supporting proof such as affidavits, pleadings, deposition testimony, written admissions, and other discovery material. (CPLR 3212.)

Motion hearing. Hearings may occur for motions such as a motion to dismiss and motions for summary judgment. As mentioned above, the notice of motion includes the return date, which is the court date for the motion.

The court date is the date for oral argument before the judge regarding the merits of the motion. This appearance before the judge may be waived, either by consent of the parties or when the judge decides that an oral argument is unnecessary, which is referred to as deciding the motion "on the papers." On rare occasion, there may a question of fact that requires a hearing, for which the court may schedule a hearing prior to determining the motion. (CPLR 2218.)

Provisional Remedies

A provisional remedy is a temporary remedy, pending final court action. The remedy is designed to give a party protection against an adverse act taken by the other party prior to the resolution of the legal action such as emptying out a bank account or destroying an historic building. (CPLR 6001.) The request for a provisional remedy is brought by motion. If, however, the need for the provisional remedy is urgent, it is brought by an expedited motion called an order to show cause (see below). Provisional remedies are ordered only if the moving party is determined by the court to be likely to prevail in the lawsuit. If the provisional remedy is ordered, it remains in effect until the action is finished. The notice of pendency is the only provisional remedy that is not obtained by motion.

The chronology of injunctive relief (discussed below) is:

- Temporary restraining order, which protects the moving party from the initiation of the action until the first hearing; then
- Preliminary injunction, which protects the moving party from the first hearing until the end of the lawsuit; then
- Permanent injunction (not a provisional remedy), which provides a permanent resolution at the conclusion of the legal action.

Order to show cause. An order to show cause (OTSC) is a substitute for a notice of motion, the latter being the short document that accompanies every written motion. The OTSC can be used to bring any motion quickly in an emergency situation. (CPLR 2214(d).) The OTSC is presented to the judge ex parte with a proposed notice time, method of service, and hearing date at the earliest possible time. Because it is brought ex parte, this is one exception to the general rule that every motion must have a notice of motion attached. Often the judge will discuss the necessity for the short time period and service method. If the court grants the OTSC, the resulting provisional relief is called a temporary restraining order (TRO). The TRO can contain any type of stay the court has the power to grant. The stay maintains the status quo until the hearing such as by stopping the demolition of a building in order to establish whether it is an historic

landmark. A TRO will not be granted unless there is a showing of immediate and irreparable injury and a likelihood that the plaintiff will eventually prevail. (CPLR 6313.) Other examples include an order not to publish salacious material, not to sell real property, not to picket a building, or for a person not to leave the jurisdiction. If the judge signs the order, it must be served on the opposing party as specified in the order.

Preliminary injunction. A TRO protects the moving party from the time the OTSC is signed until the preliminary hearing is held. At the preliminary hearing, the moving party seeks a preliminary injunction, which continues the protection given in the TRO from the end of the preliminary hearing through the final disposition of the legal action. (CPLR 6311.)

Examples of Provisional Remedies

- *Attachment.* The act of seizing a party's property by the sheriff (CPLR 6201), usually to conserve it for eventual execution following litigation seeking a money judgment or to secure a debt if the plaintiff prevails in the action.
- *Receivership.* Taking control of property (e.g., a business) during litigation to preserve it for the party who eventually prevails in the litigation. (CPLR 6401.)
- *Replevin.* An action to recover possession of personal property (chattel) that has been wrongfully held. (CPLR 7101.) Replevin also refers to an order to have the sheriff seize the chattel (which is the subject of the litigation) in order to secure it during the litigation. This is similar to attachment except that the goal of replevin is recovery of the chattel itself, not just money.
- *Notice of pendency.* A notice of pendency (also called a lis pendens) is a recorded notice that a court action has been filed affecting the title to or right to possession of the real property described in the notice.

Pretrial Events

A pending case cannot be placed on the trial calendar until all pretrial events have been concluded, the most important of which is disclosure. Once on the trial calendar, certain scheduling preferences are applied, pursuant to court rules. Next a pretrial conference is scheduled, and then, if the case is not settled, a trial date is set.

Note of issue. For a case to be placed on the trial calendar, a note of issue must be filed with the court. A note of issue is a court form that includes the caption of the case, the type of action involved, some basic statistics about the case (which are collected and published annually by the Office of Court Administration), and calendar preferences, if any (CPLR 3402). Although most cases are tried chronologically based on the filing date of the note of issue, preferences can impact the calendar. There is the "general preference" designed to keep cases with money amounts less than $25,000 out of supreme court and back in limited jurisdiction courts where possible. There is also a "special" or "statutory" preference that can speed a case to trial. (CPLR 3403.) The note of issue is also where a demand for a jury can be made on all or some issues. Either party may demand a jury, but failure to do so is waiver of a jury. There are usually separate calendars for jury trials and nonjury trials.

Certificate of readiness. The certificate (or statement) of readiness is another court form that is filed with the note of issue. (22 NYCRR 202.21.) It is checklist for important steps of the case such as the service of pleadings, the completion of discovery, and the readiness of the case for trial.

Preliminary conference. While there is an optional "preliminary conference" that can be requested anytime after service of process (22 NYCRR 202.12), it is not common. The goals of the conference are to simplify the issues to be tried, confirm stipulations and admissions, discuss settlement possibilities, and handle other trial-related administrative matters.

Pretrial conference. A pretrial conference, on the other hand, is required unless the judge dispenses with it (22 NYCRR 202.26). The pretrial conference (also called a settlement conference) is generally held between 15 and 45 days prior to the trial. The goals of the conference are to simplify the issues to be tried, confirm stipulations and admissions, discuss settlement possibilities, and handle other trial-related administrative matters. In practice, it is often the equivalent of a judge-supervised settlement conference because of the pressure exerted by some judges on the parties to settle. To the extent practicable, pretrial conferences shall be held not less than 15 nor more than 45 days before trial is anticipated.

Alternative dispute resolution. While there is no statutory arbitration or mediation required prior to trial, some courts have mandatory arbitration for matters under a specified dollar amount. One example is known as the Alternative Method of Dispute Resolution by Arbitration, which requires arbitration for cases of $10,000 or less in NYC Civil Court, and $6,000 or less in other courts. (22 NYCRR 28 et. seq.) Courts, however, may not use this provision to deprive litigants of the opportunity to use small claims court (*Lortz v. Lortz*, 162 Misc. 2d 539 [Mon. Co. Ct., 1994]). Further, the loser of an arbitration has the right to have a trial do novo

(new trial). In addition, a reluctant party to an agreement to arbitrate may be ordered to arbitrate by court action (CPLR 7503).

Trial

Conference prior to trial. The judge will meet with the attorneys prior to the commencement of trial to go over administrative and other trial matters, sometimes immediately prior to the trial. The agenda can include the number of witnesses, scheduling matters, pretrial motions, proposed jury instructions, etc.

Motion in limine. A motion in limine is a request for a ruling (often on the admissibility of evidence) prior to the trial or at a preliminary time during the trial. The motion is a way for parties to prevent the jury from hearing their objections to evidence the other side is likely to try to introduce during the trial. A favorable ruling results in the evidence being excluded before the jury sees or hears it.

Voir dire. In jury trials, prospective jurors are examined in a process called voir dire in order to select a jury that can be fair and impartial. For example, attorneys question the prospective jurors to determine whether any of them might have a bias (prejudice) for or against any of the parties. (CPLR 4110.) In addition, the parties can exercise a limited number of peremptory challenges, usually three for each side. (CPLR 4109.) A peremptory challenge is a right to challenge and remove a prospective juror without giving any reasons. (Such challenges, however, cannot be used to discriminate against a protected minority.) The judge is not present during voir dire but is usually nearby to resolve any disputes. After voir dire is concluded, the jury of six (CPLR 4104) with one or two alternates (CPLR 4106) will be sworn in by the judge and empanelled to hear the evidence in the case.

Opening statements. The court will give each side an opportunity to make an opening statement to the jury in a jury trial or to the judge alone in nonjury trial. (CPLR 4016.) The party with the burden of proof (the plaintiff) goes first. An opening statement tells the jury what the side expects the evidence to show.

Case in chief of plaintiff. Although CPLR 4011 gives the court the power to determine the sequence of the trial, in practice the traditional common law trial sequence has been adopted. The plaintiff presents its case first, since plaintiff has the burden of proof. The plaintiff must establish each element of each cause of action it asserts, such as the existence of consideration if the cause of action is breach of contract. Although there are many types of evidence, such as physical evidence, photographs, public records, and business records, the most common type of evidence is witness or testimonial evidence. The defense typically presents evidence, but is not required to.

Examination of witnesses. A party that calls or subpoenas a witness conducts the direct examination of that witness. After the direct examination is concluded the sequence can be as follows:

- The other side may cross-examine the witness on the subject matter of the direct examination.
- The party that called the witness may conduct a redirect examination, limited to matters brought up on cross-examination.
- The other side may conduct a recross-examination, limited to matters brought up on redirect examination.

After all the plaintiff's witnesses have testified, the plaintiff "rests." Then it is the defendant's turn to present its case in chief.

Objections. If a party believes that a question or answer of a witness violates a rule of evidence, the party will state "Objection" and indicate the nature of the alleged violation. This halts the testimony. The judge then makes a ruling that the evidence is:

- Improper (sustaining the objection),
- Proper (overruling the objection), or
- Proper and improper, necessitating an appropriate adjustment in going forward

Each such ruling is a potential ground for appeal. (CPLR 4017.)

Case in chief of defendant. The defendant presents its case by conducting a direct examination of the witnesses it calls and by offering physical evidence. The plaintiff can cross-examine the plaintiff's witnesses. The defendant then rests.

Exhibits. Exhibits, such as photos, maps, and other physical items to be introduced into evidence, are usually pre-marked before the start of the trial. The court clerk labels each exhibit with a number (for the plaintiff's exhibits) or a letter (for the defendant's exhibits). When introducing an exhibit, it is necessary to establish a legal basis for considering the exhibit. This is usually done through witness questions that are related to the exhibit. Establishing a legal basis for evidence is called "laying an evidentiary foundation." Before accepting the exhibit into evidence, the judge will ask the opposing side if it has any objection to admitting the exhibit into evidence. If an objection is raised, the judge will rule on it.

Trial motions. At the beginning of a trial, motions to dismiss may be made such as a defense motion to dismiss for lack of subject-matter jurisdiction or for failure to state a cause of action. (CPLR 3211.) Either party can make a *motion for judgment during trial*, often called a *directed verdict*, which is made at the end of the other party's evidence. (CPLR 4401.) If granted, the court essentially instructs the jury that there is no issue of fact for them to resolve, and as a matter of law, the result of the case must be decided a certain way. If the motion is granted, the jury does not deliberate. For example, if the plaintiff is suing for a breach of contract, but cannot prove during the case in chief that there was a contract, after the plaintiff rests, the defendant will move for a directed verdict, on the grounds that the plaintiff did not prove an essential part of the case.

Other trial motions include a motion to conform the pleadings to the proof (CPLR 3025(c)) and a motion for a new trial (mistrial) (CPLR 4402).

Rebuttal witnesses. At the end of the defendant's case, the plaintiff's attorney will be asked for rebuttal witnesses, limited to matters brought up by the defense. For example, if in a breach of contract case the defendant asserts that her signature is a forgery, the plaintiff may want to call a handwriting expert to rebut that testimony. Because it was brought up for the first time by the defense, the plaintiff could not have called the expert in the plaintiff's case in chief.

Closing arguments. Closing arguments are made after the defendant rests or after the plaintiff has put on rebuttal witnesses. A closing argument (also called a summation) is the final statement of counsel to the jury (or to the trial judge alone in nonjury cases) that summarizes the evidence presented during the trial and argues for a favorable decision. The defendant makes the first closing argument, followed by the plaintiff. (CPLR 4016.)

Charging conference. The judge must give instructions to the jury on how to go about finding the facts in order to reach a verdict. This process is called charging the jury. Anytime prior to charging, attorneys can propose specific jury instructions. More formally, the judge will meet the attorneys during the trial for a "charging conference" at which the parties will propose their instructions and the judge will decide what the instructions will be. In proposing instructions, the parties usually consult the standard jury instructions (called Pattern Jury Instructions (PJI)). Parties are free, however, to propose changes in them. Each side tries to obtain instructions that are favorable, so this can be a contentious conference.

Instructions to the jury. After deciding what the instructions will be, the judge delivers them to the jury—he or she charges the jury. The jury is then sent to a private room to deliberate on the verdict. The first juror sworn becomes the foreperson (22 NYCRR 220.1), whose duty is to moderate the discussion so that every juror is given an opportunity to participate.

Verdict. Several kinds of jury verdicts are possible:

- A *general verdict*, which finds in favor of one of the parties; the verdict states which side wins (CPLR 4111(a))
- A *special verdict*, which consists of the jury's answers to specific questions put to it by the court (CPLR 4111(b)); the jury does not find in favor of one of the parties
- A *general verdict accompanied by answers to interrogatories*, which consists of a finding in favor of one of the parties and answers to questions (interrogatories) put to it by the court (CPLR 4111(c))

To reach a verdict, five of the six jurors must agree (CPLR 4113(a)). If a jury cannot arrive at a verdict within a reasonable time (sometimes referred to as being a hung jury), the judge may declare a mistrial, dismiss the jury, and direct a new trial before another jury (CPLR 4113(b)).

Additur and remittitur. After the jury returns a verdict, the losing side routinely asks for a new trial, often because the jury award is too large. The winning party may ask for a new trial if the amount is too small. There is no authority for a judge to change the amount of the jury award. Instead, the judge picks an amount of increase (additur) or decrease (remittitur) to which the parties must agree or risk the granting of an order for a new trial by the judge. *O'Connor v. Papertsian*, 309 NY 465 [1956]. (CPLR 5501(c).)

Costs and disbursements. The winning party is entitled to a payment from the other party for "costs." (CPLR 8101.) These costs, however, are not related to actual litigation expenditures, but are an arbitrary amount based on how far the case proceeded:

- $200 if the case is terminated prior to the note of issue being filed
- An additional $200 if the case is terminated after that but prior to trial
- An additional $300 if the case goes to trial, for a maximum amount of $700

In addition, costs of up to $100 may be awarded for a motion. The winning party is also entitled to "disbursements" from the other party, which *are* related to actual litigation expenditures subject to designated limitations such as $250 for deposition (EBT) expenses. (CPLR 8301.) Other common disbursements include witness fees, payments for title searches, and fees for certified copies of documents.

Motion for judgment and new trial. After a jury returns a verdict, either party may bring a motion for judgment and a new trial. This motion asks the court to disregard the jury's verdict if it is not supported by the evidence (or is otherwise contrary to law) and to replace it with a different verdict. (CPLR 4404.) The court may set aside the verdict or any judgment and redirect the verdict, or it may order a new trial, either in response to the motion or upon the court's own initiative. When this motion is granted because a party is entitled to judgment as a matter of law, it is like a directed verdict or a judgment notwithstanding verdict (n.o.v.).

Entry of judgment and notice of entry of judgment. As soon as possible after the verdict, the prevailing party drafts the actual judgment and delivers it to the court clerk for signing and entry. The step is called entry of judgment, which is the act of noting the existence of the judgment in the judgment book. This book exists in each county clerk's office. (CPLR 9702.) A copy of the judgment with notice of entry is then served upon the losing party. It is important to have an affidavit of service for this event because service of the notice of entry marks the starting time for the 30 days that the losing party has to file a notice of appeal (CPLR 5513) as well as the commencement of the time for the enforcement (collection) of the judgment. (CPLR Article 52.)

Appeal

Appellate courts. Any litigant may appeal a supreme court trial verdict once as a matter of right (CPLR 5701). Appeals of supreme court verdicts and most county-wide courts are made to one of the four Appellate Divisions of the supreme court, depending on the county where the trial took place. Appeals from lower courts are made to an appellate term of the supreme court, or to the county court. (See exhibit 4.2C in section 4.2.) After an adverse result from an appeal as a matter of right, the next step is to appeal to the Court of Appeals. Most commonly, the litigant must obtain permission from the Court of Appeals. However, under certain circumstances, the appeal to the Court of Appeals may be taken as a matter of right. (CPLR 5601.) Examples:

- When there were two dissents in the Appellate Division
- Where the appeal may be taken as a matter of right for certain constitutional issues
- "Certification" from another court, whereby the other court requests the Court of Appeals to review an issue (NY Const., Art. VI, Sec. 3(b))

The party appealing is the appellant. The party against whom the appeal is filed is the respondent. The following sequence of events applies primarily to the appeal of civil cases, but is basically the same for all appeals. Many of the rules for appeal are found in the New York Rules of Court, also called the Uniform Rules, found in 22 NYCRR. For more on the appellate courts in New York, see section 4.2.

Stay and undertaking. At any time during a legal proceeding, any party may make a motion to the court to stay (pause) the proceeding (CPLR 2201). The judgment debtor may automatically obtain a stay of enforcement of the judgment upon service of the notice of appeal on the other party so long as the judgment debtor provides assurance that the judgment will be paid if the appeal is lost. This is usually done by posting an "undertaking" with the court in the amount of the judgment.

Notice of appeal. A notice of appeal of a judgment (a) is filed by the appellant with the clerk in the supreme court that rendered the judgment and (b) is served upon the other party. The notice is a one-page document that must be filed within 30 days of the appellant's service of the notice of entry of the judgment. Failure to do so waives the right to appeal. (CPLR 5513.)

Perfecting the appeal. After the notice of appeal, the record of what happened at trial must be assembled. It is up to the appellant to perfect the appeal by:

- Ordering a stenographic transcript of all court proceedings
- Assembling all pleadings

If the parties disagree about what should be part of the record, they try to resolve their differences in a process called settling the record. (CPLR 5525.)

Appellate briefs. After perfecting the record, the next step is preparing appellate briefs. An appellate brief is a document submitted by a party to an appellate court in which arguments are presented on why the appellate court should affirm (approve), reverse, or otherwise modify what a lower court has done. The appellant files its brief with the court and serves a copy on the respondent. The brief states reasons the judgment appealed from was in error. In response, the respondent files and serves an opposing brief. Finally, in response to this opposing brief, the appellant can file a reply brief.

Oral argument. The case is not retried on appeal. Rather, the parties make oral arguments before four or five Appellate Division judges randomly selected from the panel of about 10 to 22 to hear a case. Oral argument is usually limited to between 5 and 15 minutes per side. During an attorney's presentation, judges frequently interrupt with questions about the case.

Appellate Division decision. The decision of the Appellate Division (or other appellate court) will be to affirm (approve), reverse, or otherwise modify the judgment. Alternatively, the court can send the case back to the lower court (remand it) for further proceedings. Decisions are determined by majority vote. Judges in the minority can file dissenting or concurring opinions, although this does not occur often.

Appeal to the Court of Appeals. The highest court in New York is the Court of Appeals in Albany. Appeals to it may be taken as a matter of right if there are two dissenting Appellate Division justices or if certain constitutional and statutory issues are raised in the appeal (CPLR 5601). Other appeals are by permission of the court (referred to as discretionary appeals). To seek permission, a party first asks the Appellate Division for permission to appeal to the Court of Appeals. If it is not granted, the party can ask the Court of Appeals directly for leave (permission) to file the appeal. (CPLR 5602.) Two of the seven Court of Appeals judges must agree to hear a case for leave to be granted. A denial of leave to appeal means that judgment below stands. If leave is granted the request, the initial appeals process is repeated. Appellate briefs are filed and oral argument is scheduled.

Court of Appeals decision. The Court of Appeals can affirm (approve), reverse, or otherwise modify the judgment. Alternatively, the court can send the case back to the lower court (remand it) for further proceedings.

C. More Information

Civil Appeals Structure
(Figure 1b)
www.courts.state.ny.us/reports/annual/pdfs/2006annualreport.pdf

Civil Practice Law and Rules (CPLR)
public.leginfo.state.ny.us/menugetf.cgi?COMMONQUERY=LAWS
caselaw.lp.findlaw.com/nycodes
(click "CVP")

Criminal Appeals Structure
(Figure 1a)
www.courts.state.ny.us/reports/annual/pdfs/2006annualreport.pdf

Forms and Filing Fees for New York Courts
www.courts.state.ny.us/forms/index.shtml

How to Try or Defend a Case When You Don't Have a Lawyer
www.courts.state.ny.us/publications/GuideforProSes.pdf

Law Clerk's Guide to Serving Papers in New York's Courts
www.nysba.org/AM/Template.cfm?Section=Home&TEMPLATE=/CM/HTMLDisplay.cfm&CONTENTID=14531

Overview of a Civil Action
(commencement, service, motions)
www.nycourts.gov/courts/6jd/forms/SRForms/civilact_howtocommence.pdf
www.nycourts.gov/COURTS/5JD/onondaga/syracuse/civil.shtml

Memorable New York State Trials
www.courts.state.ny.us/history/Cases.htm

New York Consolidated Laws
caselaw.lp.findlaw.com/nycodes
public.leginfo.state.ny.us/menugetf.cgi?COMMONQUERY=
LAWS

New York State Court System
www.courts.state.ny.us/courts/

Procedures for Collecting a Judgment
nycourts.gov/courts/6jd/chemung/elmira/civil_collect.shtml
www.nycourts.gov/courts/nyc/smallclaims/collectingjudgment
.shtml
www.courts.state.ny.us/Ithaca/city/webpageJudgement.html

Summary of Courthouse Procedures
(commencement, motions, ADR, jury)
www.nycourts.gov/supctmanh/CourtHouse_Procedures.htm

Uniform Rules for New York Courts
www.courts.state.ny.us/rules/index.shtml

Uniform Rules for New York Trial Courts
www.nycourts.gov/rules/trialcourts/202.shtml

What Happens in a Trial? (Petit Juror's Handbook)
www.nyjuror.gov/general-information/hbPetitJuror42007.pdf

D. | Something to Check

Go to the web site of the supreme court in your county and to the Appellate Division to which decisions of that court are appealed (see the web sites in section 4.2).

1. What assistance is available on these sites for trials and appeals of civil cases in those courts?
2. Go to the online local rules of the supreme court. Find any three court rules that are different from the procedural rules in the CPLR.

6.2 Venue, Process, Pleadings, and Disclosure: 43 Rules Even Non-Litigation Paralegals Should Know

A. Introduction
B. The Rules
C. More Information
D. Something to Check

A. Introduction

Even if you do not work in litigation now, at some time in your career there is a good chance that you will. Close to a majority of the paralegals you will meet at paralegal association gatherings work in some phase of litigation, either on the front lines or in indirect capacities. Even attorneys and paralegals who work in transaction practices often have litigation on their

mind—from the perspective of how to avoid it! In short, litigation dominates a large portion of the legal world. Knowing some of the essential rules of civil litigation in the New York courts will help you communicate intelligently with (and perhaps be better prepared one day to join) attorneys and paralegals in the world of litigation.

In this section, we introduce excerpts from 43 of the most important litigation rules in New York, primarily in areas where paralegals have their most prominent roles: pleadings, disclosure, and discovery. Because the rules are excerpted rather than presented in full, you, of course, will need to go to the codes or rules themselves to obtain the full text whenever working on a client's case.

Consider this recommendation: Read through these 43 excerpts at least once or twice a year. Each time you do, you will increase your "litigation literacy" and gain a richer context for many of the non-litigation tasks you perform.

For related material in this book, see:

- Section 4.2 (state courts in New York)
- Section 4.3 (federal courts in New York)
- Section 6.1 (timeline: a civil case in the New York state courts)
- Section 6.3 (state vs. federal civil litigation in New York)
- Section 7.1 (example of a civil complaint)
- Section 7.4 (example of an appellate brief)

B. The Rules

Table of Contents

- Subject-Matter Jurisdiction
- Venue
- Institution of Suit
- Pleadings
- Service of Process
- Disclosure: Overview
- Disclosure: Depositions
- Disclosure: Demand for Address
- Disclosure: Discovery and Production of Documents and Things
- Disclosure: Physical or Mental Examination
- Disclosure: Requests for Admissions
- Disclosure: Interrogatories

Subject-Matter Jurisdiction

See section 4.2 for the subject-matter jurisdiction of the following state courts:

- Court of Appeals
- Appellate Division of the Supreme Court
- County Court
- Supreme Court
- Court of Claims
- Family Court

- Surrogate's Court
- District Court
- City Court
- Civil Court of the City of New York
- Criminal Court of the City of New York
- Town and Village Justice Court

Venue

Venue. Based on residence (§ 503, CPLR)

§ 503(a). Generally. Except where otherwise prescribed by law, the place of trial shall be in the county in which one of the parties resided when it was commenced; or, if none of the parties then resided in the state, in any county designated by the plaintiff. A party resident in more than one county shall be deemed a resident of each such county.

| Residence as Basis of Venue: Where Lawsuits Shall Be Brought |

§ 503(b). An executor, administrator, trustee, committee, conservator, general or testamentary guardian, or receiver shall be deemed a resident of the county of his appointment as well as the county in which he actually resides.

§ 503(c). Corporation. A domestic corporation, or a foreign corporation authorized to transact business in the state, shall be deemed a resident of the county in which its principal office is located; except that such a corporation, if a railroad or other common carrier, shall also be deemed a resident of the county where the cause of action arose.

Venue. Real property actions (§ 507, CPLR)

§ 507. The place of trial of an action in which the judgment demanded would affect the title to, or the possession, use or enjoyment of, real property shall be in the county in which any part of the subject of the action is situated.

| Venue in Land Cases |

Institution of Suit

Institution of Suit. Actions and special proceedings (§ 304, CPLR)

§ 304. An action is commenced by filing a summons and complaint or summons with notice. A special proceeding is commenced by filing a petition. Where a court finds that circumstances prevent immediate filing, the signing of an order requiring the subsequent filing at a specific time and date not later than five days thereafter shall commence the action. For purposes of this section, . . . filing shall mean the delivery of the summons with notice, summons and complaint or petition to the clerk of the court in the county in which the

| Filings to Commence an Action or Special Proceeding |

action or special proceeding is brought or any other person designated by the clerk of the court for that purpose together with any fee required as specified in rule twenty-one hundred two of this chapter for filing. At such time of filing, the original and a copy of such papers shall be date stamped by a court clerk who shall file the original and maintain a record of the date of the filing and who shall immediately return the copy to the party who brought the filing.

Institution of Suit. Summons (§ 305, CPLR)

§ 305. A summons shall specify the basis of the venue designated and if based upon the residence of the plaintiff it shall specify the plaintiff's address, and also shall bear the index number assigned and the date of filing with the clerk of the court.

| Basis of Venue Stated in the Summons |

Pleadings

Pleadings: Kinds allowed (§ 3011, CPLR)

§ 3011. There shall be a complaint and an answer. An answer may include a counterclaim against a plaintiff and a cross-claim against a defendant. A defendant's pleading against another claimant is an interpleader complaint, or against any other person not already a party is a third-party complaint. There shall be a reply to a counterclaim denominated as such, an answer to an interpleader complaint or third-party complaint, and an answer to a cross-claim that contains a demand for an answer. If no demand is made, the cross-claim shall be deemed denied or avoided. There shall be no other pleading unless the court orders otherwise.

| Complaints, Answers, and Other Kinds of Pleadings |

Pleadings: Certificate of merit with complaint (§ 3012-a, CPLR)

§ 3012-a(a). In any action for medical, dental or podiatric malpractice, the complaint shall be accompanied by a certificate, executed by the attorney for the plaintiff, declaring that:

| Medical Malpractice Cases |

(1) the attorney has reviewed the facts of the case and has consulted with at least one physician in medical malpractice actions, at least one dentist in dental malpractice actions or at least one podiatrist in podiatric malpractice actions who is licensed to practice in this state or any other state and who the attorney reasonably believes is knowledgeable in the relevant issues involved in the particular action, and that the attorney has concluded on the basis of such review and consultation that there is a reasonable basis for the commencement of such action; or [indicate why the consultation did not occur].

Pleadings: Particularity (§ 3013, CPLR)

§ 3013. Statements in a pleading shall be sufficiently particular to give the court and parties notice of the transactions, occurrences, or series of transactions or occurrences, intended to be proved and the material elements of each cause of action or defense.

Pleadings: Statements in pleadings (§ 3014, CPLR)

§ 3014. Every pleading shall consist of plain and concise statements in consecutively numbered paragraphs. Each paragraph shall contain, as far as practicable, a single allegation. Reference to and incorporation of allegations may subsequently be by number. Prior statements in a pleading shall be deemed repeated or adopted subsequently in the same pleading whenever express repetition or adoption is unnecessary for a clear presentation of the subsequent matters. Separate causes of action or defenses shall be separately stated and numbered and may be stated regardless of consistency. Causes of action or defenses may be stated alternatively or hypothetically. A copy of any writing which is attached to a pleading is a part thereof for all purposes.

> **Guidelines for Drafting Pleadings**

Pleadings: Fraud, mistake, and personal injury cases (§ 3016, CPLR)

§ 3016(b). Fraud or mistake. Where a cause of action or defense is based upon misrepresentation, fraud, mistake, wilful default, breach of trust or undue influence, the circumstances constituting the wrong shall be stated in detail.

> **Pleading Fraud and Personal Injury**

§ 3016(g). Personal injury. In an action designated in § 5104(a) of the insurance law, for personal injuries arising out of negligence in the use or operation of a motor vehicle in this state, the complaint shall state that the plaintiff has sustained a serious injury, as defined in § 5102(d) of the insurance law, or economic loss greater than basic economic loss, as defined in § 5102(a) of the insurance law.

Pleadings: Demand for relief (§ 3017, CPLR)

§ 3017(a). Generally. Except as otherwise provided in subdivision (c) of this section, every complaint, counterclaim, cross-claim, interpleader complaint, and third-party complaint shall contain a demand for the relief to which the pleader deems himself entitled. Relief in the alternative or of several different types may be demanded. . . .

> **Demand for Relief in Personal Injury or Wrongful Death Cases**

§ 3017(c). Personal injury or wrongful death actions. In an action to recover damages for personal injuries or wrongful death, the complaint, counterclaim, cross-claim, interpleader complaint, and third-party complaint shall contain a prayer for general relief but shall not state the amount of damages to which the pleader deems himself entitled. If the action is brought in the supreme court, the pleading shall also state whether or not the amount of damages sought exceeds the jurisdictional limits of all lower courts which would otherwise have jurisdiction. Provided, however, that a party against whom an action to recover damages for personal injuries or wrongful death is brought, may at any time request a supplemental demand setting forth the total damages to which the pleader deems himself entitled. . . .

Pleadings: Responsive pleadings (§ 3018, CPLR)

§ 3018(a). Denials. A party shall deny those statements known or believed by him to be untrue. He shall specify those statements as to the truth of which he lacks knowledge or information sufficient to form a belief and this shall have the effect of a denial. All other statements of a pleading are deemed admitted, except that where no responsive pleading is permitted they are deemed denied or avoided.

> **Drafting Answers**

§ 3018(b). Affirmative defenses. A party shall plead all matters which if not pleaded would be likely to take the adverse party by surprise or would raise issues of fact not appearing on the face of a prior pleading such as arbitration and award, collateral estoppel, culpable conduct claimed in diminution of damages as set forth in article fourteen-A, discharge in bankruptcy, facts showing illegality either by statute or common law, fraud, infancy or other disability of the party defending, payment, release, res judicata, statute of frauds, or statute of limitation. The application of this subdivision shall not be confined to the instances enumerated.

Pleadings: Counterclaims (§ 3019(a), CPLR)

§ 3019(a). A counterclaim may be any cause of action in favor of one or more defendants or a person whom a defendant represents against one or more plaintiffs, a person whom a plaintiff represents or a plaintiff and other persons alleged to be liable.

Service of Process

Service of Process: Service of Pleadings (§ 3012(a), CPLR)

§ 3012(a). The complaint may be served with the summons. A subsequent pleading asserting new or additional claims for relief shall be served upon a party who has not appeared in the manner provided for service of a summons. In any other case, a pleading shall be served in the manner provided for

> **Service of Complaint with Summons**

service of papers generally. Service of an answer or reply shall be made within twenty days after service of the pleading to which it responds.

Service of Process: Personal service (§§ 308, 311, 311-a CPLR)

| Serving a Natural Person, a Corporation, or a Limited Liability Company |

§ 308. Personal service upon a natural person shall be made by any of the following methods:

1. by delivering the summons within the state to the person to be served; or
2. by delivering the summons within the state to a person of suitable age and discretion at the actual place of business, dwelling place or usual place of abode of the person to be served and by either mailing the summons to the person to be served at his or her last known residence or by mailing the summons by first class mail to the person to be served at his or her actual place of business in an envelope bearing the legend "personal and confidential" and not indicating on the outside thereof, by return address or otherwise, that the communication is from an attorney or concerns an action against the person to be served, . . .
4. where service under paragraphs one and two cannot be made with due diligence, by affixing the summons to the door of either the actual place of business, dwelling place or usual place of abode within the state of the person to be served and by either mailing the summons to such person at his or her last known residence or by mailing the summons by first class mail to the person to be served at his or her actual place of business. . . .

§ 311(a). Personal service upon a corporation . . . shall be made by delivering the summons . . . upon any domestic or foreign corporation, to an officer, director, managing or general agent, or cashier or assistant cashier or to any other agent authorized by appointment or by law to receive service.

§ 311-a(a). Service of process on any domestic or foreign limited liability company shall be made by delivering a copy personally to (i) any member of the limited liability company in this state, if the management of the limited liability company is vested in its members, (ii) any manager of the limited liability company in this state, if the management of the limited liability company is vested in one or more managers, (iii) to any other agent authorized by appointment to receive process, or (iv) to any other person designated by the limited liability company to receive process, in the manner provided by law for service of a summons as if such person was a defendant. . . .

Service of Process: Proof of service (§ 306, CPLR)

§ 306(a). Generally. Proof of service shall specify the papers served, the person who was served and the date, time, address, or, in the event there is no address, place and manner of service, and set forth facts showing that the service was made by an authorized person and in an authorized manner.

| Proof of Service |

§ 306(b). Personal service. Whenever service is made pursuant to this article by delivery of the summons to an individual, proof of service shall also include, in addition to any other requirement, a description of the person to whom it was so delivered, including, but not limited to, sex, color of skin, hair color, approximate age, approximate weight and height, and other identifying features. . . .

Disclosure: Overview

Disclosure: Methods of obtaining disclosure (§ 3102(a), CPLR)

§ 3102(a). Disclosure devices. Information is obtainable by one or more of the following disclosure devices: depositions upon oral questions or without the state upon written questions, interrogatories, demands for addresses, discovery and inspection of documents or property, physical and mental examinations of persons, and requests for admission.

| Forms of Disclosure |

Disclosure: Scope (§ 3101(a), CPLR)

§ 3101(a). Generally. There shall be full disclosure of all matter material and necessary in the prosecution or defense of an action, regardless of the burden of proof, by:

| What Is Discoverable? (Matters That Are "Material and Necessary") |

(1) a party, or the officer, director, member, agent or employee of a party;
(2) a person who possessed a cause of action or defense asserted in the action;
(3) a person about to depart from the state, or without the state, or residing at a greater distance from the place of trial than one hundred miles, or so sick or infirm as to afford reasonable grounds of belief that he or she will not be able to attend the trial, or a person authorized to practice medicine, dentistry or podiatry who has provided medical, dental or podiatric care or diagnosis to the party demanding disclosure, or who has been retained by such party as an expert witness; and
(4) any other person, upon notice stating the circumstances or reasons such disclosure is sought or required.

Disclosure: Scope (§§ 3101(b)(c)(d), CPLR)

Privileged Matter and Attorney Work Product

§ 3101(b). Privileged matter. The work product of an attorney shall not be obtainable.

§ 3101(c). Attorney's work product. The work product of an attorney shall not be obtainable.

§ 3101(d)(1). Trial preparation, materials. Subject to the provisions of paragraph one of this subdivision, materials otherwise discoverable under subdivision (a) of this section and prepared in anticipation of litigation or for trial by or for another party, or by or for that other party's representative (including an attorney, consultant, surety, indemnitor, insurer or agent), may be obtained only upon a showing that the party seeking discovery has substantial need of the materials in the preparation of the case and is unable without undue hardship to obtain the substantial equivalent of the materials by other means. In ordering discovery of the materials when the required showing has been made, the court shall protect against disclosure of the mental impressions, conclusions, opinions or legal theories of an attorney or other representative of a party concerning the litigation.

Disclosure: Protective orders (§ 3103(a), CPLR)

§ 3103(a). Prevention of abuse. The court may at any time on its own initiative, or on motion of any party or of any person from whom discovery is sought, make a protective order denying, limiting, conditioning or regulating the use of any disclosure device. Such order shall be designed to prevent unreasonable annoyance, expense, embarrassment, disadvantage, or other prejudice to any person or the courts.

Disclosure: Depositions

Disclosure: Priority of depositions (§ 3106, CPLR)

§ 3106(a). Normal priority. After an action is commenced, any party may take the testimony of any person by deposition upon oral or written questions. . . .

Deposition upon Oral or Written Questions

§ 3106(b). Witnesses. Where the person to be examined is not a party or a person who at the time of taking the deposition is an officer, director, member or employee of a party, he shall be served with a subpoena. Unless the court orders otherwise, on motion with or without notice, such subpoena shall be served at least twenty days before the examination. . . .

§ 3106(d). Designation of deponent. A party desiring to take the deposition of a particular officer, director, member or employee of a person shall include in the notice or subpoena served upon such person the identity, description or title of such individual.

Disclosure: Notice of taking oral depositions (§ 3107, CPLR)

§ 3107. A party desiring to take the deposition of any person upon oral examination shall give to each party twenty days' notice, unless the court orders otherwise. The notice shall be in writing, stating the time and place for taking the deposition, the name and address of each person to be examined, if known, and, if any name is not known, a general description sufficient to identify him or the particular class or group to which he belongs. The notice need not enumerate the matters upon which the person is to be examined. . . .

Disclosure: Production of things at the examination (§ 3111, CPLR)

§ 3111. The notice or subpoena may require the production of books, papers and other things in the possession, custody or control of the person to be examined to be marked as exhibits, and used on the examination. The reasonable production expenses of a non-party witness shall be defrayed by the party seeking discovery.

Exhibits at the Deposition

Disclosure: Demand for Address

Disclosure: Demand for address (§ 3118, CPLR)

§ 3118. A party may serve on any party a written notice demanding a verified statement setting forth the post office address and residence of the party, of any specified officer or member of the party and of any person who possessed a cause of action or defense asserted in the action which has been assigned. The demand shall be complied with within ten days of its service.

Obtaining a Verified Address

Disclosure: Discovery and Production of Documents and Things

Discovery and production of documents and things for inspection, testing, copying, or photographing (§ 3120, CPLR)

§ 3120. 1. After commencement of an action, any party may serve on any other party a notice or on any other person a subpoena duces tecum:

Subpoena Duces Tecum

(i) to produce and permit the party seeking discovery, or someone acting on his or her behalf, to inspect, copy, test or photograph any designated documents or any things which are in the possession, custody or control of the party or person served; or

(ii) to permit entry upon designated land or other property in the possession, custody or control of the party or person served for the purpose of inspecting, measuring, surveying, sampling, testing, photographing or recording by motion pictures or otherwise the property or any specifically designated object or operation thereon.

2. The notice or subpoena duces tecum shall specify the time, which shall be not less than twenty days after service of the notice or subpoena, and the place and manner of making the inspection, copy, test or photograph, or of the entry upon the land or other property and, in the case of an inspection, copying, testing or photographing, shall set forth the items to be inspected, copied, tested or photographed by individual item or by category, and shall describe each item and category with reasonable particularity.

3. The party issuing a subpoena duces tecum as provided hereinabove shall at the same time serve a copy of the subpoena upon all other parties and, within five days of compliance therewith, in whole or in part, give to each party notice that the items produced in response thereto are available for inspection and copying, specifying the time and place thereof. . . .

Disclosure: Physical or Mental Examination

Disclosure: Physical or mental examination (§ 3121(a), CPLR)

§ 3121(a). Notice of examination. After commencement of an action in which the mental or physical condition or the blood relationship of a party, or of an agent, employee or person in the custody or under the legal control of a party, is in controversy, any party may

Physical or Mental Examination by a Physician

serve notice on another party to submit to a physical, mental or blood examination by a designated physician, or to produce for such examination his agent, employee or the person in his custody or under his legal control. The notice may require duly executed and acknowledged written authorizations permitting all parties to obtain, and make copies of, the records of specified hospitals relating to such mental or physical condition or blood relationship; where a party obtains a copy of a hospital record as a result of the authorization of another party, he shall deliver a duplicate of the copy to such party. A copy of the notice shall be served on the person to be examined. It shall specify the time, which shall be not less than twenty days after service of the notice, and the conditions and scope of the examination.

Disclosure: Requests for Admissions

Admissions as to matters of fact, papers, documents, and photographs (§ 3123(a), CPLR)

§ 3123(a). Notice to admit; admission unless denied or denial excused. At any time after service of the answer or after the expiration of twenty days from service

of the summons, whichever is sooner, and not later than twenty days before the trial, a party may serve upon any other party a written request for admission by the

Request to Admit Genuineness, Correctness, Fairness, or Truthfulness

latter of the genuineness of any papers or documents, or the correctness or fairness of representation of any photographs, described in and served with the request, or of the truth of any matters of fact set forth in the request, as to which the party requesting the admission reasonably believes there can be no substantial dispute at the trial and which are within the knowledge of such other party or can be ascertained by him upon reasonable inquiry. Copies of the papers, documents or photographs shall be served with the request unless copies have already been furnished. Each of the matters of which an admission is requested shall be deemed admitted unless within twenty days after service thereof or within such further time as the court may allow, the party to whom the request is directed serves upon the party requesting the admission a sworn statement either denying specifically the matters of which an admission is requested or setting forth in detail the reasons why he cannot truthfully either admit or deny those matters. If the matters of which an admission is requested cannot be fairly admitted without some material qualification or explanation, or if the matters constitute a trade secret or such party would be privileged or disqualified from testifying as a witness concerning them, such party may, in lieu of a denial or statement, serve a sworn statement setting forth in detail his claim and, if the claim is that the matters cannot be fairly admitted without some material qualification or explanation, admitting the matters with such qualification or explanation. . . .

Disclosure: Interrogatories

Use of interrogatories (§ 3130, CPLR)

§ 3130. 1. Except as otherwise provided herein, after commencement of an action, any party may serve upon any other party written interrogatories. Except in a matrimonial action, a party may not serve written interrogatories on another party and also demand a bill of

Disclosure by Interrogatories

particulars of the same party pursuant to § 3041. In the case of an action to recover damages for personal injury, injury to property or wrongful death predicated solely on a cause or causes of action for negligence, a party shall not be permitted to serve interrogatories on and conduct a deposition of the same party pursuant to Rule 3107 without leave of court.

2. After the commencement of a matrimonial action or proceeding, upon motion brought by either party, upon such notice to the other party and to the

non-party from whom financial disclosure is sought, and given in such manner as the court shall direct, the court may order a non-party to respond under oath to written interrogatories limited to furnishing financial information concerning a party, and further provided such information is both reasonable and necessary in the prosecution or the defense of such matrimonial action or proceeding.

Scope of interrogatories (§ 3131, CPLR)

§ 3131. Interrogatories may relate to any matters embraced in the disclosure requirement of § 3101 and the answers may be used to the same extent as the depositions of a party. Interrogatories may require copies of such papers, documents or photographs as are relevant to the answers required, unless opportunity for this examination and copying be afforded.

Service of interrogatories (§ 3132, CPLR)

After commencement of an action, any party may serve written interrogatories upon any other party. Interrogatories may not be served upon a defendant before that defendant's time for serving a responsive pleading has expired, except by leave of court granted with or without notice. A copy of the interrogatories and of any order made under this rule shall be served on each party.

Service of answers or objections to interrogatories (§ 3133, CPLR)

§ 3133(a). Service of an answer or objection. Within twenty days after service of interrogatories, the party upon whom they are served shall serve upon

| Answering Interrogatories |

each of the parties a copy of the answer to each interrogatory, except one to which the party objects, in which event the reasons for the objection shall be stated with reasonable particularity.

§ 3133(b). Form of answers and objections to interrogatories. Interrogatories shall be answered in writing under oath by the party served, if an individual, or, if the party served is a corporation, a partnership or a sole proprietorship, by an officer, director, member, agent or employee having the information. Each question shall be answered separately and fully, and each answer shall be preceded by the question to which it responds. . . .

C. More Information

New York Code of Civil Procedure
public.leginfo.state.ny.us/menugetf.cgi?COMMONQUERY=LAWS
(click "CVP")
www.law.cornell.edu/states/ny.html
(click "Consolidated Laws" then "CVP")

New York Court Rules
www.nycourts.gov/rules/trialcourts/index.shtml
www.llrx.com/courtrules-gen/state-New-York.html

Megalaw: New York Civil Procedure
www.megalaw.com/tx/top/txcivpro.php

D. Something to Check

Go to a site that contains the New York Code of Civil Procedure (see More Information above). Do a search for any three topics covered in the rules excerpted here in section 6.2. Look for additional rules on these topics. Summarize what you find.

6.3 State and Federal Civil Litigation in New York: Some Comparisons

A. Introduction

B. Comparisons

C. More Information

D. Something to Check

A. Introduction

In this section, we will briefly outline some comparisons between litigating civil cases in New York state courts and in the federal courts. See also the following related sections:

- Section 4.2, state court subject-matter jurisdiction
- Section 4.3, federal court subject-matter jurisdiction
- Section 6.1, timeline: a civil case in New York state courts
- Section 6.2, selected litigation rules in New York state courts
- Section 6.4, timeline: a criminal case in state court
- Section 7.1, example of a civil complaint filed in state court
- Section 7.2, example of a civil complaint filed in federal court
- Section 7.4, example of an appellate brief filed in state court

Abbreviations

FRCP: Federal Rules of Civil Procedure

CPLR: New York Civil Practice Law and Rules

NYCRR: New York Code of Rules and Regulations

USC: United States Code

B. Comparisons

Comparisons between state and federal civil litigation are presented in Exhibit 6.3A.

EXHIBIT 6.3A	State and Federal Civil Litigation: Some Points of Comparison
State Litigation	**Federal Litigation**
Major Courts • Court of Appeals • Appellate Division of the Supreme Court • County Court • Supreme Court • Court of Claims • Family Court • Surrogate's Court • District Court • City Court • Civil Court of the City of New York • Criminal Court of the City of New York • Town and Village Justice Court	**Major Courts** • Supreme Court of the United States • United States Court of Appeals • United States District Court • United States Immigration Court • United States Court of International Trade • United States Court of Federal Claims • United States Court of Appeals for the Armed Services • United States Tax Court • United States Court of Appeals for Veterans Claims • Judicial Panel on Multidistrict Litigation

Subject-Matter Jurisdiction of Main Trial Courts
• Supreme Court
  - Civil matters over $25,000
  - Divorce
  - Felonies (concurrent with county court) (see section 4.2)
• Court of Claims
  - Damages sought against the state
• Family Court
  - Adoption
  - Paternity
  - Support (see section 4.2)
• Surrogate's Court
  - Probate
  - Adoption (see section 4.2)
• County Court
  - Civil matters up to $25,000
  - Felonies (concurrent with supreme court) (see section 4.2)
• New York City Courts, District Courts, Town and Village Justice Courts
  - Small claims
  - Traffic tickets
(see section 4.2)
	Subject-Matter Jurisdiction of Main Trial Court
	• United States District Court
	  - Federal questions
	  - Diversity cases (over $75,000) (28 USC §§ 1331; 1332; 1345; 1346)

Venue • Transitory actions. Except where otherwise prescribed by law, the place of trial shall be in the county in which one of the parties resided when it was commenced (CPLR 503) • Local actions (e.g., actions involving real property). The place of trial shall be in the county in which any part of the subject of the action is situated (CPLR 507)	**Venue** Examples: • district where a substantial part of the events or omissions giving rise to the claim occurred or where the property in dispute is located • any district if the defendant is an alien (28 USC § 1391)
Forum Non Conveniens When the court finds that in the interest of substantial justice the action should be heard in another forum, the court, on motion of any party, may stay or dismiss the action in whole or in part on any conditions that may be just (CPLR 327(a))	**Forum Non Conveniens** For the convenience of parties and witnesses, in the interest of justice, a district court may transfer any civil action to any other district or division where it might have been brought (28 USC § 1404(a))
Joinder of Parties • Necessary (e.g., CPLR 1001(a)) • Permissive (e.g., CPLR 1002(a))	**Joinder of Parties** • Compulsory (FRCP 19) • Permissive (FRCP 20)
Pleadings Allowed The major pleadings are: (1) A complaint (2) An answer to a complaint	**Pleadings Allowed** Only these pleadings are allowed: (1) A complaint (2) An answer to a complaint
(3) A reply to a counterclaim (4) An answer to a cross-claim (5) An interpleader complaint (6) An answer to an interpleader complaint (7) A third-party complaint (8) An answer to a third-party complaint (CPLR 3011)	(3) An answer to a counterclaim designated as a counterclaim (4) An answer to a crossclaim (5) A third-party complaint (6) An answer to a third-party complaint (7) If the court orders one, a reply to an answer (FRCP (7)(a))
Complaint Statements in a pleading shall be sufficiently particular to give the court and parties notice of the transactions, occurrences, or series of transactions or occurrences, intended to be proved and the material elements of each cause of action or defense (CPLR 3013) Complaints are subject to a motion to dismiss if they fail to state a cause of action (CPLR 3211(a)(7))	**Complaint** A pleading that states a claim for relief must contain: (1) A short and plain statement of the grounds for the court's jurisdiction, unless the court already has jurisdiction and the claim needs no new jurisdictional support (2) A short and plain statement of the claim showing that the pleader is entitled to relief (3) A demand for the relief sought, which may include relief in the alternative or different types of relief (FRCP (8)(a)) By motion, a party can raise the defense that the complaint fails to state a claim upon which relief can be granted (FRCP (12)(b)(6))
Demand for Relief; Relief in the Alternative Every complaint shall contain a demand for the relief "to which the pleader deems himself entitled." Relief in the alternative or of several different types may be demanded (CPLR 3017)	**Demand for Relief; Relief in the Alternative** A pleading that states a claim for relief must contain: a demand for the relief sought, which may include relief in the alternative or different types of relief (FRCP (8)(a))
Caption Each paper served or filed shall begin with a caption setting forth the name of the court, the venue, the title of the action, the nature of the paper and the index number of the action if one has been assigned. In a summons, a complaint, or a judgment the title shall include the names of all parties, but in all other papers it shall be sufficient to state the name of the first named party on each side with an appropriate indication of any omissions (CPLR 2101(c))	**Caption** Every pleading must have a caption with the court's name, a title, a file number, and a Rule 7(a) designation. The title of the complaint must name all the parties; the title of other pleadings, after naming the first party on each side, may refer generally to other parties (FRCP 10(a))
Signature Every pleading, written motion, and other paper served on another party or filed or submitted to the court shall be signed by an attorney, or by a party if the party is not represented by an attorney, with the name of the attorney or party clearly printed or typed directly below the signature. (22 NYCRR 130.1.1a(a).) By signing a paper, an attorney or party certifies that, to the best of that person's knowledge, information and belief, formed after an inquiry reasonable under the circumstances . . . the presentation of the paper or the contentions therein are not frivolous . . . (and) was not obtained through illegal conduct (22 NYCRR 130.1.1a (b)) **Verification** A verification is a statement under oath that the pleading is true to the knowledge of the deponent, except as to matters alleged on information and belief, and that as to those matters he believes it to be true. (CPLR 3020(a).) Verification is generally optional except for certain pleadings that must be verified (e.g., many non-adultery matrimonial pleadings and most pleadings that respond to verified pleadings)	**Signature** Every pleading, written motion, and other paper must be signed by at least one attorney of record in the attorney's name—or by a party personally if the party is unrepresented (FRCP 11(c)) **Certification** By presenting to the court a pleading, written motion, or other paper . . . an attorney or unrepresented party certifies that to the best of the person's knowledge, information, and belief, formed after an inquiry reasonable under the circumstances: . . . the factual contentions have evidentiary support (FRCP 11(b)(3))

State Litigation	Federal Litigation

Time Limit for Service
Service of the summons and complaint . . . shall be made within one hundred twenty days after the filing of the summons and complaint . . . If service is not made upon a defendant within the time provided in this section, the court, upon motion, shall dismiss the action without prejudice as to that defendant, or upon good cause shown or in the interest of justice, extend the time for service. (CPLR 306-b)

Time Limit for Service
If a defendant is not served within 120 days after the complaint is filed, the court—on motion or on its own after notice to the plaintiff—must dismiss the action without prejudice against that defendant or order that service be made within a specified time. But if the plaintiff shows good cause for the failure, the court must extend the time for service for an appropriate period. (FRCP 4(m))

Answer
- Particularity. Statements in a pleading shall be sufficiently particular to give the court and parties notice of the transactions, occurrences, or series of transactions or occurrences, intended to be proved and the material elements of each cause of action or defense (CPLR 3013)
- Denials. A party shall deny those statements known or believed by him to be untrue. He shall specify those statements as to the truth of which he lacks knowledge or information sufficient to form a belief and this shall have the effect of a denial. All other statements of a pleading are deemed admitted, except that where no responsive pleading is permitted they are deemed denied or avoided. (CPLR 3018(a))

Answer
- In General. In responding to a pleading, a party must:
  (A) State in short and plain terms its defenses to each claim asserted against it; and
  (B) Admit or deny the allegations asserted against it by an opposing party. (FRCP (8)(b)(1))
- Denials—Responding to the Substance. A denial must fairly respond to the substance of the allegation.
- General and Specific Denials. A party that intends in good faith to deny all the allegations of a pleading—including the jurisdictional grounds—may do so by a general denial. A party that does not intend to deny all the allegations must either specifically deny designated allegations or generally deny all except those specifically admitted. (FRCP (8)(b)(2))

Motion for More Definite Statement
If a pleading is so vague or ambiguous that a party cannot reasonably be required to frame a response he may move for a more definite statement. (CPLR 3024 (a))

Motion for More Definite Statement
A party may move for a more definite statement of a pleading to which a responsive pleading is allowed but which is so vague or ambiguous that the party cannot reasonably prepare a response. (FRCP 12(e))

Time Limit for Answer
Except as otherwise required by statute, a response to a summons and complaint shall be made in 20 days if personally served, otherwise 30 days. (CPLR 320)

Time Limit for Answer
Unless a different time is prescribed in a statute of the United States, a defendant shall serve an answer within 20 days after being served with the summons and complaint. (FRCP 12(a)(1))

Amendments to Pleadings
- Amendments without leave. A party may amend his pleading once without leave of court within twenty days after its service, or at any time before the period for responding to it expires, or within twenty days after service of a pleading responding to it. (CPLR 3025(a))
- Amendments and supplemental pleadings by leave. A party may amend his pleading, or supplement it by setting forth additional or subsequent transactions or occurrences, at any time by leave of court or by stipulation of all parties. Leave shall be freely given upon such terms as may be just including the granting of costs and continuances. (CPLR 3025(b))

Amendments to Pleadings
(1) Amending as a Matter of Course. A party may amend its pleading once as a matter of course: (A) Before being served with a responsive pleading; or (B) Within 20 days after serving the pleading if a responsive pleading is not allowed and the action is not yet on the trial calendar.
(2) Other Amendments. In all other cases, a party may amend its pleading only with the opposing party's written consent or the court's leave. The court should freely give leave when justice so requires. (FRCP 15(a))

What is Discoverable: Scope of Disclosure and Discovery
- There shall be full disclosure of all matter material and necessary in the prosecution or defense of an action, regardless of the burden of proof. (CPLR 3101(a))
- "Our courts possess broad discretion to decide whether information sought is 'material and necessary,' but that discretion is not unlimited. . . . [The] test is one of 'usefulness and

What is Discoverable: Scope of Discovery
Parties may obtain discovery regarding any nonprivileged matter that is relevant to any party's claim or defense—including the existence, description, nature, custody, condition, and location of any documents or other tangible things and the identity and location of persons who know of any discoverable matter. For good cause, the court may order

reason' . . . if the material is sought in good faith for possible use as evidence-in-chief or in rebuttal or for cross-examination, it should be considered material." *State v. DeGroot*, 35 A.D.2d 240, 241–242 (3rd Dept. 1970)
- Upon objection by a person entitled to assert the privilege, privileged matter shall not be obtainable. (CPLR 3101(b))

discovery of any matter relevant to the subject matter involved in the action. Relevant information need not be admissible at the trial if the discovery appears reasonably calculated to lead to the discovery of admissible evidence. (FRCP Rule 26(b)(1))

Work-Product Rule
- The work product of an attorney shall not be obtainable. (CPLR 3101(c))
- As a general matter, the work-product rule applies only to documents prepared principally or exclusively to assist in anticipated or ongoing litigation. *Stenovich v. Wachtell, Lipton, Rosen & Katz*, 195 Misc.2d 99, 116 (Sup. Ct., NY Co., 2003)
- [Materials otherwise discoverable under § 3101(a)] and prepared in anticipation of litigation or for trial by or for another party, or by or for that other party's representative . . ., may be obtained only upon a showing that the party seeking discovery has substantial need of the materials in the preparation of the case and is unable without undue hardship to obtain the substantial equivalent of the materials by other means. In ordering discovery of the materials when the required showing has been made, the court shall protect against disclosure of the mental impressions, conclusions, opinions or legal theories of an attorney or other representative of a party concerning the litigation. (CPLR 3101(d)(2))

Work-Product Rule
- Documents and Tangible Things. Ordinarily, a party may not discover documents and tangible things that are prepared in anticipation of litigation or for trial by or for another party or its representative (including the other party's attorney, consultant, surety, indemnitor, insurer, or agent). But, subject to Rule 26(b)(4), those materials may be discovered if: (i) they are otherwise discoverable under Rule 26(b)(1); and (ii) the party shows that it has substantial need for the materials to prepare its case and cannot, without undue hardship, obtain their substantial equivalent by other means. (FRCP 26(b)(3)(A))
- Protection Against Disclosure. If the court orders discovery of those materials, it must protect against disclosure of the mental impressions, conclusions, opinions, or legal theories of a party's attorney or other representative concerning the litigation. (FRCP 26(b)(3)(B))

Attorney-Client Privilege
- Upon objection by a person entitled to assert the privilege, privileged matter shall not be obtainable in the disclosure process. (CPLR 3101(b))
- The attorney-client privilege requires a confidential communication between client and attorney, in the course of a professional relationship, for the purpose of seeking or providing legal advice or assistance; and the communication itself must have been primarily or predominantly of a legal character. *Aetna Cas. and Sur. Co. v. Certain Underwriters*, 176 Misc.2d 605, 608 (Sup. Ct., NY Co., 1998)

Attorney-Client Privilege
- The privilege attaches when the following is established: relationship of attorney and client, a communication by the client relating to the subject matter upon which professional advice is sought, and the confidentiality of the expression for which the protection is claimed. The privilege also covers communications made to certain agents of an attorney assisting in the rendition of legal services. *U.S. v. Schwimmer*, 892 F.2d 237, 243 (2d Cir. 1989)

Methods of Disclosure and Discovery
- Interrogatories
- Depositions upon oral questions (EBT) (examination before trial)
- Depositions upon written questions
- Notice to admit (requests for admission)
- Demands for addresses, discovery, and inspection of documents or property
- Physical or mental examination of persons (CPLR 3102(a))

Methods of Disclosure and Discovery
- Interrogatories (FRCP 33)
- Deposition by oral examination (FRCP 30)
- Deposition by written questions (FRCP 31)
- Requests for admissions (FRCP 36)
- Production of documents, electronically stored information, and tangible things, or entry on land for inspection and other purposes (FRCP 34)
- Physical or mental examination of a party (FRCP 35)

Default Judgment
Default and entry.
- When a defendant has failed to appear, plead or proceed to trial of an action reached and called for trial, or when the court orders a dismissal for any other neglect to proceed, the plaintiff may seek a default judgment against him.

Default Judgment
- (a) Entering a Default. When a party against whom a judgment for affirmative relief is sought has failed to plead or otherwise defend, and that failure is shown by affidavit or otherwise, the clerk must enter the party's default. (FRCP 55(a))

State Litigation	Federal Litigation
• If the plaintiff's claim is for a sum certain or for a sum which can by computation be made certain, application may be made to the clerk within one year after the default. The clerk, upon submission of the requisite proof, shall enter judgment for the amount demanded in the complaint or stated in the notice . . . plus costs and interest. • Where the case is not one in which the clerk can enter judgment, the plaintiff shall apply to the court for judgment. (CPLR 3215(a))	• Entering a Default Judgment. (1) By the Clerk. If the plaintiff's claim is for a sum certain or a sum that can be made certain by computation, the clerk—on the plaintiff's request, with an affidavit showing the amount due—must enter judgment for that amount and costs against a defendant who has been defaulted for not appearing and who is neither a minor nor an incompetent person. (2) By the Court. In all other cases, the party must apply to the court for a default judgment . . . . The court may conduct hearings or make referrals—preserving any federal statutory right to a jury trial—when, to enter or effectuate judgment, it needs to: (A) conduct an accounting; (B) determine the amount of damages; (C) establish the truth of any allegation by evidence; or (D) investigate any other matter. (FRCP 55(b))
Summary Judgment • Any party may move for summary judgment in any action, after issue has been joined; provided however, that the court may set a date after which no such motion may be made, such date being no earlier than thirty days after the filing of the note of issue. If no such date is set by the court, such motion shall be made no later than one hundred twenty days after the filing of the note of issue, except with leave of court on good cause shown. (CPLR 3212(a)) • A motion for summary judgment shall be supported by affidavit, by a copy of the pleadings and by other available proof, such as depositions and written admissions. The affidavit shall be by a person having knowledge of the facts; it shall recite all the material facts; and it shall show that there is no defense to the cause of action or that the cause of action or defense has no merit. The motion shall be granted if, upon all the papers and proof submitted, the cause of action or defense shall be established sufficiently to warrant the court as a matter of law in directing judgment in favor of any party. (CPLR 3212(b))	***Summary Judgment*** • A party claiming relief may move, with or without supporting affidavits, for summary judgment on all or part of the claim. The motion may be filed at any time after: (1) 20 days have passed from commencement of the action; or (2) the opposing party serves a motion for summary judgment. (FRCP 56(a)) • A party against whom relief is sought may move at any time, with or without supporting affidavits, for summary judgment on all or part of the claim. (FRCP 56(b)) • The motion must be served at least 10 days before the day set for the hearing. An opposing party may serve opposing affidavits before the hearing day. The judgment sought should be rendered if the pleadings, the discovery and disclosure materials on file, and any affidavits show that there is no genuine issue as to any material fact and that the movant is entitled to judgment as a matter of law. (FRCP 56(c))
Formal Planning Procedures • Preliminary conference (Uniform Rules for the New York State Trial Courts 202.12) • Pretrial conference (Uniform Rule for the New York State Trial Courts 202.26)	***Pretrial Planning Procedures*** • Pretrial conferences (FRCP 16(a–c)) • Final pretrial conferences (FRCP 16(d))
Alternate Dispute Resolution Arbitration of certain claims. The chief judge of the court of appeals may promulgate rules for the arbitration of claims for the recovery of a sum of money not exceeding six thousand dollars, exclusive of interest, pending in any court or courts except the civil court of the city of New York, and not exceeding ten thousand dollars, exclusive of interest, pending in the civil court of the city of New York. Such rules must permit a jury trial de novo upon demand by any party following the determination of the arbitrators and may require the demander to pay the cost of arbitration. (CPLR 3405)	***Alternate Dispute Resolution*** An alternative dispute resolution process includes any process or procedure, other than an adjudication by a presiding judge, in which a neutral third party participates to assist in the resolution of issues in controversy, through processes such as: • Early neutral evaluation, • Mediation, • Minitrial, and • Arbitration Each United States district court shall authorize, by local rule, the use of alternative dispute resolution processes in all civil actions. Each United States district court shall devise and implement its own alternative dispute resolution program to encourage and promote the use of alternative dispute resolution in its district. (28 USC § 651)

C. More Information

Federal Rules of Civil Procedure
www.law.cornell.edu/rules/frcp/?
www.lectlaw.com/tcrf.htm

New York Code of Civil Procedure
public.leginfo.state.ny.us/menugetf.cgi?
   COMMONQUERY=LAWS
(click "CVP")
www.law.cornell.edu/states/ny.html
(click "Consolidated Laws" then "CVP")

New York Court Rules
www.nycourts.gov/rules/trialcourts/index.shtml

Federal Courts Overview
www.uscourts.gov/journalistguide/welcome.html

D. Something to Check

Using the online sites that give the text of statutes and rules (see the sites under More Information), compare the state and federal provisions on:

1. Interrogatories
2. Sanctions for failure to comply with disclosure and discovery requests

6.4 Timeline: Criminal Case in the New York State Courts

  A. Introduction

  B. Overview of a Criminal Case

  C. More Information

  D. Something to Check

A. Introduction

In this section, we will focus on the major procedural steps involved in prosecuting serious criminal cases in the New York state courts. Such cases can vary a great deal in complexity depending on the nature of the charge, the extent of contention between the state and the accused, and the caliber of attorneys representing both sides. With this qualification in mind, the overview presented here will apply to many serious criminal cases brought in the New York state courts. See also the following related sections:

- Overview of New York state courts (section 4.2)
- Example of a criminal complaint (section 7.5)
- Rules for (and an example of) an appellate brief (section 7.4)
- Legal research in state law (section 5.1)
- Overview of federal courts sitting in New York (section 4.3)

Abbreviations Used in the Section

CPL: New York Criminal Procedure Law

CPLR: New York Civil Practice Law & Rules

PEN: New York Penal Law

B. Overview of a Criminal Case

A criminal case begins when a prosecutor files formal charges, a suspect is arrested, or a grand jury issues an indictment. The first court appearance for all crimes and offenses is in local court (city court, town court, village court, district court, or NYC Criminal Court). Subsequently, felonies transfer to superior court for further proceedings (supreme court or county court), whereas misdemeanors and offenses remain in local court. Exhibit 6.4A presents an overview of a typical criminal case in New York state courts.

Acts Alleged

There are three major categories of actions that are prosecuted in New York: felonies, misdemeanors, and offenses.

Felony. A crime for which a sentence to a term of imprisonment in excess of one year may be imposed. (PEN § 10.00(5).)

Misdemeanor. A crime punishable by up to a year in county jail. (PEN § 10.00(4).)

Offense. A minor prohibited act such a traffic violation, a disorderly conduct penal law violation, or municipal code infraction for which the maximum sentence is a fine and/or 30 days or less in jail. An offense is neither a felony nor a misdemeanor, and it is not a crime. (PEN §§ 10.00(1)(2)(3).)

Commencement of Case

Arrest with a warrant. A judge or other designated court official can issue a warrant that directs a police officer to arrest a person if satisfied that the latter probably violated the criminal law. (CPL § 120.10.)

Arrest without a warrant. A police office can arrest someone without a warrant if the officer has probable cause to believe that the person has committed a crime or if the person has committed an infraction in the presence of the officer. (CPL § 140.10.)

Appearance ticket in lieu of arrest. Instead of arresting someone, the officer can issue an appearance ticket (sometimes referred to as a desk appearance ticket [D.A.T.]) when an arrest is not needed to assure the accused's attendance in court. (CPL § 150.) An appearance ticket serves the function of a complaint and summons by informing the accused of the alleged violation and when he or she must appear in court.

Citizen's arrest. A private citizen can arrest someone (a) for a felony that has in fact been committed and (b) for any offense that has in fact been committed in the citizen's presence. (CPL § 140.30.)

Filing an accusatory instrument. A criminal case against a person formally begins in court when an accusatory instrument against that person is filed in court. Accusatory instruments include a felony complaint, a misdemeanor complaint, an information, and a simplified information. To prosecute a crime, the accusatory instrument must at some point include sworn allegations of every element of the crime charged, whether in the accusatory instrument or in a supplemental pleading. (CPL §100.05.)

Grand jury indictment prior to arrest; sealed indictment. Another way to begin a criminal case is for the grand jury to issue a formal accusation (called an indictment) against a person for whom an accusatory instrument has not yet been filed. In most cases, the grand jury becomes involved *after* arrest, but it is possible for the grand jury to indict someone who has not yet been arrested or involved in court proceedings. This is called a sealed indictment. (CPL § 210.10.)

Arraignment

Procedure. The arraignment is the first court appearance for anyone charged with a crime or offense. At the arraignment, the defendant is told what crime or infraction he or she is charged with, and is advised of the constitutional rights:

- To a jury trial (or a nonjury trial for offenses)
- To an appointed attorney
- To the presumption of innocence, etc.

There is a single arraignment in local court for a misdemeanor, but for felonies, after the initial arraignment in local court, there is a superior court arraignment that takes place after indictment or waiver of indictment (see SCI below). All initial arraignments are based on an accusatory instrument and take place in local court (except for sealed indictments, which have only a single arraignment in superior court). For an example of an indictment, see section 7.5. (CPL §§ 170, 180.)

Bail. Bail is money or other property deposited with the court as security to ensure that the defendant will reappear at designated times. Failure to appear forfeits the security. The court sets the amount and the conditions of bail. In some cases, bail cannot be set and the judge must order "remand" (which means jail with no right to post bail). It is also possible for a judge to order release without bail, called ROR (releases on recognizance), or

EXHIBIT 6.4A	The Prosecution of a Criminal Case in New York State Courts					
ACTS ALLEGED	COMMENCEMENT OF CASE	ARRAIGNMENT	PRELIMINARY MATTERS (FELONIES)	DISCOVERY	PRETRIAL PROCEEDINGS	TRIAL	APPEAL
● Felony ● Misdemeanor ● Offense	● Arrest with warrant ● Arrest without warrant ● Appearance ticket in lieu of arrest ● Citizen's arrest ● Filing an accusatory instrument ● Grand jury indictment prior to arrest; sealed indictment	● Procedure ● Bail ● Counsel ● Plea ● Plea bargaining ● Guilty plea ● Not guilty plea in misdemeanor cases ● Not guilty plea in felony cases	● Preliminary hearing ● Grand jury indictment ● Superior court arraignment	● Informal discovery ● Mandatory disclosures	● Motions and hearings ● Pretrial conferences	● Jury selection ● Opening statements ● Presentation of evidence ● Examination of witnesses ● Exhibits ● Rebuttal witnesses ● Trial motions ● Closing arguments ● Jury instructions ● Verdict ● Probation report ● Sentencing	● Right of appeal ● Notice of appeal ● Record on appeal ● Appellate briefs ● Oral arguments ● Further appeals ● Corum nobis

under supervision of the local probation department, called RUS (release under supervision). (CPL § 520.)

Counsel. If a defendant is charged with a crime or a jailable offense and cannot afford to hire an attorney, the court will assign counsel or direct the public defender's office to represent the defendant. (CPL § 170.10.) Even if a defendant invokes the right of self-representation, the judge will assign "back-up" counsel to help the defendant with administrative matters such as marking evidence and courtroom decorum.

Plea. The court will ask the defendant to plead to the charges against him or her: guilty or not guilty. (CPL § 220.10.) If the defendant "stands mute" or remains silent when asked to plead, the court will treat the response as a plea of not guilty.

Plea bargaining. At arraignment or anytime after arraignment but prior to a trial verdict, the defendant may reach an agreement with the prosecutor to plead guilty to a lesser charge, or plead guilty with an agreed-to sentence. This is called a plea bargain.

Guilty plea. At the arraignment for a non-felony, if the defendant pleads guilty, the judge can impose sentence immediately or adjourn the case for sentencing on a future date. For felonies (and under some circumstances for misdemeanors), the judge must order a presentence investigation from the probation department prior to imposing sentence. (See "Sentencing" below.) For felonies, the local court does not have jurisdiction to accept a guilty plea, so a guilty plea can be entered only in a superior court. In many courts, a defendant can enter a contract with the prosecutor to plead guilty and enter a drug court program. Successful completion results in a substantial reduction or dismissal of the charge; failure to complete the program results in expulsion from the program and sentencing on the original charge.

Not guilty plea in misdemeanor cases. If at the arraignment the defendant pleads not guilty to a misdemeanor, the judge will announce the motion date—the date by which the defendant's pretrial motions are due. Certain documents are routinely served on the defendant by the prosecutor at arraignment, such as a statement of readiness for trial (CPL § 30.30) and a Notice of Intent to Use Evidence (CPL § 710.30). Discovery demands (CPL § 240) and pretrial motions (CPL § 255) will be made and any necessary pretrial hearings will take place. If the case is not pleaded out, a jury trial will be scheduled with a six-person jury.

Not guilty plea in felony cases. At the arraignment, if a defendant pleads not guilty to a felony, a preliminary hearing may be demanded under most circumstances. (See "Preliminary hearing" below.) Note that even if a defendant wishes to plead guilty to a felony, the local court does not have the authority to accept it. A guilty plea may be made only to a superior court.

Preliminary Matters (Felonies)

Preliminary hearing. If an incarcerated felony defendant made the demand at initial arraignment, the local court must hold a preliminary hearing (a probable cause hearing) within 120 hours of arraignment (or 144 hours if a weekend intervenes). If the prosecution shows probable cause, the defendant remains incarcerated and the local court's involvement terminates. However, the case does not automatically transfer to superior court. Indictment or SCI is still required (see below). If the prosecution fails to show probable cause, the defendant is released from custody but the case is not dismissed. The case may still proceed to the grand jury, where the defendant may be indicted, and the case continued. Since the prosecution's failure to show probable cause results in nothing beyond release of an incarcerated defendant, when the defendant is not incarcerated, a preliminary hearing is not held. (CPL § 180.)

Grand jury indictment. Superior court is the only court with subject-matter jurisdiction over a felony. The only way for a felony case to be transferred to superior court is by grand jury indictment, or if the defendant "consents" to indictment by a Superior Court Information (SCI), which is discussed below. Failure to obtain a grand jury indictment or an SCI within 180 days of the commencement of the felony action results in the dismissal of the case for failure to comply with the "speedy trial" statute. (CPL § 30.30.)

A grand jury is made up of 16 to 25 citizens who hear evidence presented by the prosecution on whether there is probable cause to believe that the defendant committed a felony. Neither the defendant or defense counsel is present (although in rare circumstances, a defendant does testify). After hearing the evidence, the grand jury votes. At least 12 grand jurors are needed to find probable cause for a "true bill of indictment." If there are not 12 votes, there is no indictment, referred to as "no true bill."

Grand jury proceedings are closed to the public and are secret. The proceedings must not be discussed outside the grand jury room by anyone involved. Once a true bill is voted, the case is scheduled for arraignment in superior court, where the arraignment process is repeated. In cases where the defendant wishes to waive indictment, usually when there is a plea agreement, an SCI is used in lieu of an indictment. (CPL § 190.)

Superior court arraignment. After the superior court obtains jurisdiction over the defendant by indictment or SCI, there must be a superior court arraignment. Just like the local court arraignment, matters considered include bail, counsel, and entry of a plea. (CPL § 210.15.)

This is when the prosecution serves documents on the defendant, such as a statement of readiness for trial (CPL § 30.30) and a notice of intent to use evidence (CPL § 710.30).

Discovery

The defendant has 30 days from arraignment to make discovery demands, which are routinely made. Although the prosecutor also makes discovery demands, most of the defense materials are protected against discovery by the defendant's fifth amendment right against self-incrimination. The only items that are demanded by and provided to the prosecutor are copies of reports of the defendant's mental or physical condition if the defendant intends to introduce them at trial, and copies of exhibits the defense intends to introduce at trial, such as photos or charts. (CPL § 240.30.)

Informal discovery. Prosecutors know what must be provided by discovery and generally (under a system referred to as informal or voluntary discovery) provide it prior to formal demands of the defendant. Otherwise, they provide it after the formal demands are made. Even if there are no demands made, discovery is usually provided, since the defendant's failure to make demands would likely be a ground for reversal on appeal (inadequate assistance of counsel).

Mandatory discovery. When routine discovery demands are made by the defendant, the prosecutor must provide:

* All written statements of the defendant
* Photos of evidence of the crime
* Audio tapes relevant to the case, etc. (CPL § 240.10)

For written materials, tapes, or other materials than can be duplicated, copies are provided. Other items, such as a gun or drugs, are made available for physical examination by the defendant. If there is any dispute involving the prosecutor's failure to provide something, or over a particular request by the defendant, a motion is made to the judge to resolve the dispute. (CPL § 240.90.) The prosecutor must also provide all *Brady* material, which includes whatever is exculpatory. Exculpatory material is anything the prosecutor has that could help the defendant prove innocence, such as the result of a DNA test indicating that blood on the defendant did not match the victim's blood.

Pretrial Proceedings

Motions and hearings. After arraignment for any crime or offense (superior court arraignment for felonies), the parties may file motions requesting rulings on evidentiary matters. The most common motion is the "omnibus" motion, which includes within it all motions and requests for relief. An omnibus motion means all possible motions are combined into one motion, to save time and increase court efficiency. This motion must be filed within 45 days of arraignment. Here are examples of three different motions that might be included in a defendant's omnibus motion:

* Motion to suppress drugs found in the trunk of the defendant's car because the police officer did not have authority for a warrantless search
* Motion to suppress the defendant's statement in the police station ("Yeah, I guess the drugs are mine") made to a police officer
* Motion to suppress the identification made in a lineup because the other "fillers" in the lineup were all much taller than the defendant, resulting in the lineup being unfairly suggestive

If the motion issues are only questions of law, both sides make written submissions and the judge rules on each motion. Usually, however, motions include allegations of fact, which require a pretrial motion hearing (often referred to as a suppression hearing) in which all issues in the motion are addressed at one time. In the example above, the same officer might testify about the search of the trunk, the defendant's comments, and even what took place at the lineup. (CPL § 255.)

Pretrial conferences. For cases going to trial, the judge will schedule one or more pretrial conferences. Various administrative matters are addressed in these conferences, such as scheduling, timing, pretrial evidentiary matters, and last-minute motions, which are often presented orally. Judges usually use the conference as a final attempt to encourage the parties to reach a plea bargain.

Trial

Criminal trials are relatively rare. Over 90 percent of the cases are disposed of by defendants' pleas of guilty. When a trial is held, the steps are often as follows:

Jury selection. In jury trials, prospective jurors are examined in a process called *voir dire* in order to select a jury that can be fair and impartial. For example, attorneys question the prospective jurors to determine whether any of them might have a bias (prejudice) for or against any of the parties. (CPL § 270.20.) In addition, the parties can exercise a limited number of *peremptory challenges*, between 10 and 20 depending on the charge. (CPL § 270.25.) A peremptory challenge is a right to challenge and remove a prospective juror without giving any reasons. (Such challenges, however, cannot be used to discriminate against a protected minority.)

Although entitled to a jury trial in any criminal case, the defendant may choose to waive a jury and let the judge decide guilt or innocence in what is called a nonjury trial or bench trial. Otherwise, 12 citizens are selected for a felony jury plus between 1 and 6 alternates who hear the case and substitute for any juror who cannot be present for deliberations due to illness, conflict, etc. A *petit jury* is a six-person jury, which is used for misdemeanor trials. The jury (or the judge in a bench trial) is the "trier of fact." (CPL §§ 260, 270, 350.)

Opening statements. The prosecutor gives an opening statement to the jury. (The party with the burden of proof makes the first opening statement and the last closing argument to the jury.) The opening statement outlines what the prosecution expects to prove. Defense counsel can then give its opening statement or can postpone it until it starts presenting defense witnesses. (CPL § 260.30.)

Presentation of evidence. The prosecutor presents first, since the prosecutor has the burden of proof. The prosecutor must establish each element of each cause of action it asserts, such as the intent to cause serious physical injury if the charge is Assault 2nd Degree. Although there are many types of evidence (e.g., photographs, public records, business records, and other physical evidence), the most common type of evidence is witness or testimonial evidence. After the prosecution has finished presenting evidence, the prosecutor announces that "the prosecution rests," meaning that the prosecution has finished presenting evidence. The defense then typically presents its evidence, but is not required to. (CPL § 260.30.)

Examination of witnesses. A party who calls or subpoenas a witness conducts the direct examination of that witness. After the direct examination is concluded the sequence can be as follows:

- The other side cross-examines the witness on the subject matter of the direct examination
- The party who called the witness conducts a redirect examination, limited to matters brought up on cross-examination
- The other side conducts a recross-examination, limited to matters brought up on redirect examination

If a party believes that a question or answer of a witness violates a rule of evidence, the party will state "Objection" and indicate the nature of the alleged violation. This halts the testimony. The judge then makes a ruling that the evidence is:

- Improper (sustaining the objection),
- Proper (overruling the objection), or
- Proper and improper, necessitating an appropriate adjustment in going forward

Each such ruling is a potential ground for appeal.

Exhibits. Exhibits (e.g., photos, maps, and other physical items) to be introduced into evidence are usually pre-marked before the start of the trial. The court clerk labels each exhibit with a number (for the plaintiff's exhibits) or a letter (for the defendant's exhibits). When introducing an exhibit, a party must establish a legal basis for considering the exhibit. This is usually done through witness questions that are related to the exhibit. Establishing a legal basis for evidence is called laying an evidentiary foundation. Before accepting the exhibit into evidence, the judge will ask the opposing side if it has any objection to admitting the exhibit into evidence. If an objection is raised, the judge rules on it.

Rebuttal witnesses. At the end of the defendant's case, the prosecutor can offer rebuttal witnesses, limited to matters brought up by the defense. (CPL § 260.30.)

Trial motions. At any point during the trial, motions may be made by either side for different kinds of relief. For instance, in a famous case during wartime, the defendant made a motion to have the prosecutor remove his American flag lapel pin because it could influence the jury. At the close of the prosecution's case, the defendant routinely moves to dismiss the case because the prosecutor failed to make a prima facie case (i.e., did not offer proof for every element of the crime charged), called a trial order of dismissal (CPL § 290.10). The judge usually denies that motion.

Then the defense begins presenting its case, repeating the process above on offering evidence.

Closing arguments. Closing arguments are made after the defendant rests or after the prosecution has put on rebuttal witnesses. A closing argument (also called a summation) is the final statement made by counsel to the jury (or to the trial judge alone in nonjury trial) that summarizes the evidence presented during the trial. The defendant makes the first closing argument, followed by the prosecution. The closing argument is a party's final summary of the case and argument for a favorable decision. (CPL § 260.30.)

Jury instructions. The judge gives the jury detailed instructions about the crimes and explains the deliberation process that the jurors should follow in reaching a verdict. Jury instructions are worked out ahead of time in a meeting between the judge and the attorneys. (CPL § 300.)

Verdict. The jury then goes to the jury room to deliberate and reach a verdict. All 12 jurors must agree on a guilty verdict. (CPL § 310.) If the defendant is acquitted, he or she must immediately be released. Bail, if any, must be returned (CPL § 330.10). Sometimes the defendant makes post-verdict motions to set aside a guilty verdict (CPL § 330), but judges rarely overturn a jury verdict.

Probation report. If the jury reaches a guilty verdict in a felony case, the judge will order a pre-sentence investigation (PSI) and schedule a sentencing hearing. In the PSI, the probation department prepares a report for the judge that summarizes the crime and gives detailed information on the defendant's life, including prior criminal activity. Generally, the victim is contacted for a recommendation of sentence. The probation officer concludes the report with a recommended sentence. The attorneys can review the PSI and submit memoranda to the judge in which they advocate for a particular sentence. (CPL § 390.)

Sentencing. After a defendant is convicted or pleads guilty, the court will schedule a date for sentencing. (CPL § 380.30; PEN §§ 60, 65, 70, 80, 85.) Possible sentences include incarceration, fines, probation (for crimes), and combinations of all three. The court can also order restitution to the victim. (CPL § 420.10.) Crime victims may be able to apply to the Crime Victims Board for compensation from the state for out-of-pocket losses associated with certain categories of crime (*www.cvb.state.ny.us*).

Appeal

Right of appeal. The party filing an appeal is called the appellant. The party against whom an appeal is filed is the respondent.

The defendant may appeal any conviction to an intermediate appellate court as a matter of right, which means that for almost every criminal conviction, the defendant is entitled to at least one appeal. (CPL § 450.10.) In some circumstances, the prosecution may file an appeal but the prohibition against double jeopardy precludes most prosecution appeals. An example of a prosecution appeal might be an adverse pretrial ruling that led to the case being dismissed prior to trial. Since the trial never occurred, jeopardy never "attached."

Notice of appeal. The first step in an appeal is filing the written notice of appeal. This notice tells the other parties in the case and the court that a party is appealing a decision of the trial court. This must be done within 30 days of sentencing. (CPL § 460.10.) All felony appeals go to one of the four Departments of the Appellate Division. Local court appeals are made to the County Court in the 3rd and 4th Departments, and the Appellate Terms of the Supreme Court in the 1st and 2nd Departments.

Record on appeal. To appeal a case, the appellant needs to assemble the "record" from the trial court. The record includes everything that was written, filed, and transcribed during the trial. This includes documentary evidence, copies of every motion, court papers, and most importantly, the stenographic transcript of the trial. After it is assembled, the respondent must agree that the record is proper. Any disputes are resolved by the trial court (CPL § 460.70). If there is only a part of the record relating to the appeal, the parties

may stipulate to a much smaller record, such as an appeal based on a pretrial hearing where the parties may stipulate to a record that includes only the pretrial hearing transcript and related documents.

Appellate briefs. An appellate brief is a document submitted by a party to an appellate court in which arguments are presented on why the appellate court should affirm (approve), reverse, or otherwise modify what a lower court has done. After filing the notice of appeal, the appellant (usually the defendant) files an appellate brief with the appellate court. The brief states reasons the judgment appealed from was in error. In response, the respondent (usually the prosecutor) files an opposing brief. Finally, in response to this opposing brief, the appellant can file a reply brief. The specifics of what can and cannot be contained in the briefs, citing requirements, and other crucial administrative rules are found in the Uniform Rules. Each Appellate Department has its own rules for appeals (e.g., 22 NYCRR 670.12), as does the Court of Appeals. Additional rules are found in the CPLR (e.g., CPLR 5531).

Oral arguments. The case is not retried on appeal. Rather, the parties present oral arguments before one or more appellate court judges on why the trial court's judgment should be affirmed, reversed, or otherwise modified. The parties, however, can waive their right to present oral arguments and rely entirely on the arguments made in their appellate briefs.

Further appeals. The intermediate appellate court can affirm the judgment, reverse it, remand the case for further proceedings, or dismiss the appeal. A further appeal is made to the Court of Appeals and is discretionary by the court, which means that the court chooses which cases it accepts for review. There are only a few exceptions to that rule, such as death penalty cases, which must be heard. (CPL § 450.70.) Like the U.S. Supreme Court, the Court of Appeals rejects the vast majority of appeal requests. When requests to appeal are granted, appellate briefs are filed and oral argument is scheduled. The court can affirm, reverse, or remand the case for further proceedings. (CPL § 470.)

Corum nobis. There is a procedure to ask the trial court for post-conviction relief. The procedure is not, strictly speaking, an appeal. Its common law name is writ of error corum nobis. It has been codified (CPL § 440) and is often referred to as a "440 motion." It differs from an appeal because it is presented to the trial court rather than to an appellate court. There is no specific time limit within which it must be brought. The basis of a 440 motion is a matter "outside the trial record." Examples include newly discovery evidence, evidence used at trial that the prosecutor knew was false, and other improper conduct that was not on the record.

EXHIBIT 6.4B   A Criminal Case in New York

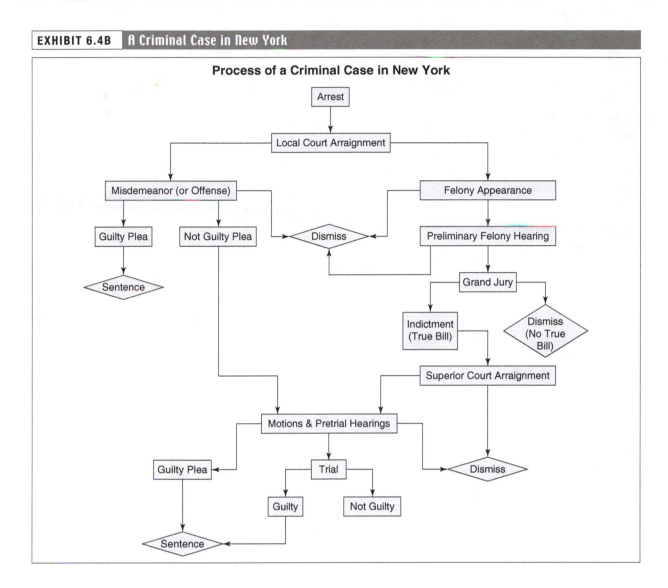

Process of a Criminal Case in New York

See Exhibit 6.4B for an outline of the major steps we have been examining.

C.   More Information

Arraignment Process
www.new-york-arraignments.com/process.htm

Arrest to Sentence
www.manhattanda.org/officeoverview/arresttosentence

Assigned Counsel in Criminal Appeals
nycourts.gov/ad4/Court/Forms/Criminal/15.%20
*   Guidelines%20for%20Criminal%20Appeals.pdf*

Criminal Appeals Structure
Twenty-Ninth Annual Report of the Chief Administrator
of the Courts (2007)
www.courts.state.ny.us/reports/annual/pdfs/2006
*   annualreport.pdf*

Criminal Court
nycourts.gov/litigants/crimjusticesyshandbk.shtml
nycourts.gov/courts/6jd/chemung/elmira/criminal.shtml

Criminal Investigation and Prosecution Procedure
in New York
www.chemungcounty.com/index.asp?pageId=143

Criminal Jury Instructions
www.nycourts.gov/cji

Criminal Justice Procedures
www.co.suffolk.ny.us/da/cjprocedures.htm

Criminal Justice Process
*www.nassaucountyny.gov/agencies/DA/criminal_justice_*
*   process.html*
albanycountyda.com/criminal%20justice%20process/
*   criminaljusticeprocess*

Criminal Law Statutes

public.leginfo.state.ny.us/menugetf.cgi?
  COMMONQUERY=LAWS
(click "CPL" for Criminal Procedure Law and "PEN"
for Penal Law)

Defense Practice Tips

www.nysda.org/html/publications.html#PracticeTips

Learn about Your Case (Bronx Defenders)

www.bronxdefenders.org/index.php?page=content&
  param=learn_about

New York Penal Law Overview

wings.buffalo.edu/law/bclc/web/cover.htm

New York Search Warrant Manual

www.courts.state.ny.us/judges/SearchWarrant_Manual.pdf

New York State Attorney General

www.oag.state.ny.us

New York State Criminal Justice Handbook

www.nycourts.gov/litigants/crimjusticesyshandbk.shtml
www.abcny.org/Publications/StateCriminalJusticeH_e.htm

Overview of Criminal Proceedings

nycourts.gov/litigants/crimjusticesyshandbk.shtml
nycourts.gov/courts/6jd/chemung/elmira/criminal.shtml

Police Abbreviations

www.n2nov.net/nypdabbr.html

Public Defenders in New York

www.nysda.org/html/chief_defenders.html

Sentencing Guide

crimetime.nypti.org

Stages of a Criminal Case

co.cayuga.ny.us/da/geninfo.htm

D. **Something to Check**

1. Go to the web site for the state courts in your county (see sections 4.2 and 4.6). What information or assistance does it provide for defendants, witnesses, or jurors in criminal cases?

2. Select any three general search engines (e.g., *www.google.com*) and any three legal search engines or portals (e.g., *www.findlaw.com*). At these sites run this search: "New York criminal cases." What are the different categories of results you find? Compare the six sites you used for this search.

PART

7

Sample Documents

7.1 Sample Civil Complaint Filed in a New York State Court

A. Introduction

B. A State Civil Complaint

C. More Information

D. Something to Check

A. Introduction

This section presents an example of a civil complaint filed in county supreme court. This complaint is from a New York woman who legally married another woman in Ontario, Canada, who entered into a civil union with the same woman in Vermont, and whose spouse was denied health benefits by her employer.

Compare this complaint to the sample *federal* civil complaint printed in section 7.2. See also:

- Section 4.2 for an overview of New York state courts
- Section 6.2 containing some of the major rules covering pretrial procedures, including the drafting of complaints and other pleadings
- Section 6.3 on some of the distinctions between state and federal civil procedure
- Section 7.6 containing a state criminal complaint

B. A State Civil Complaint

Exhibit 7.1A contains a sample civil complaint filed in a New York state court.

C. | More Information

Unified Court System: Forms and Filing Fees for State Courts
www.nycourts.gov/forms

Court Rules
www.llrx.com/courtrules-gen/state-New-York.html

Forms Library
www.nycourts.gov/courthelp/forms.html
forms.lp.findlaw.com/states/ny.html
www.uslegalforms.com/New+York.htm
www.findforms.com
(type "New York" in the search box)

Drafting and Self-Help Resources
www.selfhelpsupport.org/index.cfm
dir.yahoo.com/Government/Law/Self_Help

New York Statutes
*public.leginfo.state.ny.us/menugetf.cgi?COMMONQUERY=
LAWS*

D. | Something to Check

1. Online, find each of the statutory sections referred to in the Martinez complaint. Quote the first clause of each section.

2. What categories of information can you find online about New York lawsuits concerning benefits for same-sex partners?

3. The Martinez complaint tells who represented Martinez. Go to the web site of that attorney's office. Describe the kind of practice engaged in by this office. Is the attorney still at that office? If so, what information can you find out about him, e.g., what associations he belongs to and other kinds of cases he has brought?

4. Use Google or other search engines to find out the outcome of the litigation that began with the Martinez complaint.

EXHIBIT 7.1A | **Sample Complaint Filed in a New York State Court**

STATE OF NEW YORK
SUPREME COURT MONROE COUNTY

PATRICIA MARTINEZ,
 Plaintiff,

        COMPLAINT

vs.

        Index No.

THE COUNTY OF MONROE, MONROE
COMMUNITY COLLEGE AND MONROE
COMMUNITY COLLEGE DIRECTOR OF
HUMAN RESOURCES SHERRY RALSTON,
in her Individual and Official capacity,
 Defendants.

Plaintiff, Patricia Martinez, by her attorney, Jeffrey Wicks, PLLC, for her Complaint against the defendants, alleges as follows:

INTRODUCTION

1. Plaintiff, Patricia Martinez is an individual who is presently employed by Monroe Community College (hereinafter "MCC"). Plaintiff has been employed at MCC since April 1994. She is also in a loving, long term, committed same sex relationship that has been solemnized in both a marriage in Ontario, Canada and a civil union in the State of Vermont. However, despite the legal status of her relationship with her partner and the language in her employment contract with MCC, MCC has refused to extend health care benefits to Plaintiff's partner.

2. Plaintiff demands equal protection under the law, pursuant to both the New York Constitution and the New York Human Rights Law, whereby she and her partner should lawfully receive the myriad of benefits, including spousal health benefits, conferred by a contract of marriage or its equivalent.

THE PARTIES

3. At all times herein alleged, Plaintiff was and is a resident of the County of Monroe, State of New York, currently residing at 23 Stone Barn Road, in the Town of Gates.

-1-

EXHIBIT 7.1A

4. Upon information and belief, at all times herein alleged, defendant County of Monroe (hereinafter the "County"), was and is a municipal corporation duly organized and existing under the laws of the State of New York, and located in the County of Monroe, State of New York.

5. Upon information and belief, at all times herein alleged, defendant MCC is a unit of the State University of New York, an agency of the State of New York.

6. Upon information and belief, at all times herein alleged, Monroe Community College Director of Human Resources Sherry Ralston was and is a resident of the County of Monroe, State of New York, employed by defendant MCC.

FACTS

7. Plaintiff, a mother of three adult children, has been in a loving, long term, monogamous, committed same sex relationship with her partner, Lisa Ann Golden, since 2000. They own a home together and share financial responsibility for their expenses and for each other's needs. Moreover, they share household duties such as cleaning, cooking, laundry and outdoor chores.

8. To celebrate their relationship on July 5, 2001 the couple entered into a civil union within the State of Vermont. Said civil union was valid under the laws of the State of Vermont.

9. To celebrate their relationship further, on July 5, 2004, the couple traveled to Ontario, Canada and entered into a marriage. Said marriage was valid under the laws of the Province of Ontario, Canada.

10. Under the laws of the State of Vermont, persons, of the same sex, who enter into a civil union have the same rights and responsibilities as persons, of the opposite sex, who marry within the State of Vermont.

11. Under the laws of the Province of Ontario, Canada, persons of the same sex who marry have the same rights and responsibilities as persons of the opposite sex who marry within Ontario, Canada.

-2-

EXHIBIT 7.1A   Sample Complaint Filed in a New York State Court

12. Plaintiff and her partner hold themselves out to the public as a married couple and refer to one another as "spouse." Further, they have sought to protect each other, in the event of an emergency or calamity, by drawing up mutual wills, health care proxies and the like, just as many other married couples do.

13. Plaintiff has been employed at MCC since April 1994. Her current position at MCC is a word processing supervisor.

14. MCC is aware of the fact that Plaintiff's relationship with her same sex partner has been solemnized, as set forth above, and Plaintiff has provided MCC with legal documentation thereof.

15. The terms of Plaintiff's employment at MCC are governed by a contract between The Civil Service Employees Association Monroe County Employee Unit, Local 828 and the County (hereinafter the "CSEA Contract"). Importantly, the CSEA Contract is silent as to whether spousal health benefits or domestic partner health benefits will be provided to employees.

16. Specifically, the CSEA Contract merely states in Article 32 entitled "Health Insurance" that: "Full time employees may, by application, become members of Blue Cross/Blue Shield plan . . ."

17. Pursuant to the CSEA Contract Plaintiff has applied for, received and continues to receive health care benefits through her employment at MCC.

18. Upon information and belief, despite the CSEA Contract's silence as to spousal benefits, MCC and the County have interpreted the CSEA contract to implicitly provide for spousal health care benefits for married couples of the opposite sex. Moreover, upon information and belief, MCC and the County have provided and continue to provide health care benefits to spouses of married couples of the opposite sex for their full time employees.

19. Plaintiff, a full time MCC employee, has repeatedly sought similar health care benefits for her partner through MCC. MCC has repeatedly denied her requests for coverage despite the fact, upon information and belief, that MCC provides these same heath care benefits to spouses of its full time employees who are married to an individual of the opposite sex, and that Plaintiff and her same sex partner had their relationship legally solemnized in both the State of Vermont and in Ontario, Canada.

-3-

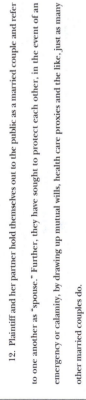

EXHIBIT 7.1A

20. In an informal opinion, dated March 3, 2004 (2004 WL 551537 [N.Y.A.G.]), the Attorney General of the State of New York, concluded that: "New York law presumptively requires that parties to such [civil] unions [solemnized by the State of Vermont] must be treated as spouses for the purposes for New York law." Moreover, the State of New York has recognized solemnized marriages which could not have been solemnized in New York.

21. New York Courts have consistently recognized, under New York common law and the Full Faith and Credit Clause, marriages between individuals of the opposite sex, solemnized in other states that could not be solemnized within the State of New York.

22. New York courts have consistently recognized, under principles of comity, marriages, between individuals of the opposite sex, solemnized in foreign countries that could not be solemnized with the State of New York.

23. Recognition of plaintiff's Vermont civil union would not violate any public policy of the State of New York.

24. Recognition of plaintiff's Ontario marriage would not violate any public policy of the State of New York.

25. Article I, Section 11 of the State of New York Constitution provides: "No person shall be denied the equal protection of the laws of this state or any subdivision thereof."

26. Defendants' failure to recognize Plaintiff's civil union is in violation of Plaintiff's civil rights.

27. The State of New York's choice of law rules require the enforcement of foreign laws governing marriage.

28. Defendants' failure to recognize Plaintiff's Canadian marriage is in violation of Plaintiff's civil rights.

29. Plaintiff has been harmed by her partner's exclusion from health care benefits routinely provided to the spouses of other married full time MCC employees simply because of the nature of her legally recognized relationship to an individual of the same sex. Plaintiff seeks nothing more than an order requiring governmental employers, like MCC, to adopt fair and equitable health

-4-

EXHIBIT 7.1A Sample Complaint Filed in a New York State Court

care policies that will allow individuals in similar same sex relationships to take on the rights and responsibilities that all other New Yorkers in solemnized relationships already have or may seek without constraint.

AS AND FOR A FIRST CAUSE OF ACTION

30. Plaintiff repeats and realleges paragraphs 1–29 as if set forth in full.

31. New York has a long and rich history of giving recognition to marriages, or its legal equivalent, performed outside of this State regardless of whether the union at issue would be permitted under the New York's Domestic Relations Law. Moreover, New York is unique in its history of recognition of such marriages on the grounds of Equal Protection pursuant to Article I, Section 11 of the State of New York Constitution, which provides that: "[n]o person shall be denied the equal protection of the laws of this state or any subdivision thereof."

32. The only exceptions to said recognition by the State of New York occur where recognition has been expressly prohibited by statute, or the union is abhorrent to New York's public policy. Neither exception is applicable here.

33. By not according plaintiff health benefits, which defendants otherwise make available to employees and their partners in opposite sex marriages, defendants have willfully violated plaintiff's civil rights, as guaranteed by the State of New York pursuant to its Constitution, and the case law of New York.

34. Plaintiff's civil rights, as guaranteed under the Constitution, statutes, common law, and case law of the State of New York were willfully violated by the acts set forth above.

AS AND FOR A SECOND CAUSE OF ACTION

35. Plaintiff repeats and realleges paragraphs 1–34 as if set forth in full.

36. Article 15 of the State of New York's Human Rights Law, as forth in Section 296 of the Executive Law, provides that it is illegal for an employer to discriminate against any individual, in terms of compensation, terms, conditions or privileges, because of sexual orientation.

-5-

EXHIBIT 7.1A

37. By their refusal to accord plaintiff health benefits, which defendants otherwise make available to employees and their partners in opposite sex marriages, defendants have willfully violated Article 15 of the State of New York's Human Rights Law, as forth in Section 296 of the Executive Law.

WHEREFORE, Plaintiff respectfully requests that this Court grant the following relief:

A. An Order declaring that Defendant's failure to recognize Plaintiff's marriage solemnized in the Province of Ontario, Canada is in violation of Plaintiff's constitutional right pursuant to the State of New York Constitution and Article 15 of the Human Right's Law;

B. An Order declaring that Defendants' failure to recognize Plaintiff's civil union solemnized in the State of Vermont is in violation of Plaintiff's constitutional right pursuant to the State of New York Constitution and Article 15 of the Human Right's Law;

C. Awarding Plaintiff money damages in an amount to be determined at trial for Defendans violations of Article I, Section 11 of the State of New York Constitution because Defendants willfully denied Plaintiff equal protection under the law;

D. Awarding Plaintiff money damages in an amount to be determined at trial for Defendants violations of Article 15 of the State of New York's Human Rights Law, as forth in Section 296 of the Executive Law;

E. Awarding Plaintiff the costs and disbursements of this action; and

F. For such other and further relief as to this Court may seem just and proper.

DATED: January 6, 2005

JEFFREY WICKS, PLLC
Attorney for Plaintiff
Cooperating Attorney to the
NYCLU Foundation
36 West Main Street
Suite 318, Executive Building
Rochester, New York 14614
Telephone: (585) 325-6070

-6-

A. Introduction

In this section, we look at a civil complaint filed in a United States district court sitting in New York. The complaint alleges copyright infringement by defendants who downloaded the plaintiffs' copyrighted recordings. Compare this complaint to the sample state court civil complaint found in section 7.1. See also section 6.3 covering some of the distinctions between state and federal civil procedure.

For more on federal courts in New York, see section 4.3.

B. A Federal Civil Complaint

Exhibit 7.2A contains a sample complaint filed in a federal court sitting in New York.

C. More Information

How to Draft a Complaint in Federal Court
forms.lp.findlaw.com/form/courtforms/fed/cir/c2/d/nyed/ nyed000023.pdf

Federal Rules of Civil Procedure
www.law.cornell.edu/rules/frcp/?
www.lectlaw.com/tcrf.htm

Federal Courts Overview
www.uscourts.gov/journalistguide/welcome.html

United States District Court Southern District of New York
www.nysd.uscourts.gov

United States District Court Eastern District of New York
www.nyed.uscourts.gov

United States District Court Western District of New York
www.nywd.uscourts.gov

United States District Court Northern District of New York
www.nynd.uscourts.gov

Components of a Complaint
www1.nysd.uscourts.gov/courtrules_prose.php?prose= no_attorney

Civil Cover Sheet
www.uscourts.gov/forms/JS044.pdf
www1.nysd.uscourts.gov/cases/show.php?db=forms&id=90

Court Forms
www1.nysd.uscourts.gov/forms.php
www.nyed.uscourts.gov/Local_Documents/local_documents .html
www.nywd.uscourts.gov/mambo/index.php?option= com_content&task=view&id=96&Itemid=1

Federal Court Rules and Forms
www.llrx.com/courtrules-gen/state-New-York.html

D. Something to Check

1. What different kinds of federal complaint forms are available on the web sites of federal courts in New York?

2. The beginning of the Capital Records complaint in this section tells you what attorneys represented the plaintiffs. Use Google (*www.google.com*) or other general search engines to find basic biographical information about each attorney.

3. Use any search engine to find information about the litigation begun by the complaint in this section. In the search engine you select, insert various combinations of party names and the case number ("04 CV 00472"). What happened in the case?

EXHIBIT 7.2A | Sample Federal Complaint Filed in a Federal Court in New York

JUDGE KAPLAN

UNITED STATES DISTRICT COURT
SOUTHERN DISTRICT OF NEW YORK

CAPITOL RECORDS, INC., a Delaware corporation; ARISTA RECORDS, INC., a Delaware corporation; INTERSCOPE RECORDS, a California general partnership; LOUD RECORDS, LLC, a Delaware corporation; UMG RECORDINGS, INC., a Delaware corporation; WARNER BROS. RECORDS INC., a Delaware corporation; ATLANTIC RECORDING CORPORATION, a Delaware corporation; FONOVISA, INC., a California corporation; SONY MUSIC ENTERTAINMENT INC., a Delaware corporation; BMG MUSIC, a New York general partnership; LONDON-SIRE RECORDS INC., a Delaware corporation; MOTOWN RECORD COMPANY, L.P., a California limited partnership; PRIORITY RECORDS LLC, a California limited liability company; MAVERICK RECORDING COMPANY, a California joint venture; ELEKTRA ENTERTAINMENT GROUP INC., a Delaware corporation; and VIRGIN RECORDS AMERICA, INC., a California corporation,

Plaintiffs,

-against-

DOES 1-250,

Defendants.

Civil Action No.: 04 CV 00472

JAN 2 1 2004

COMPLAINT FOR COPYRIGHT INFRINGEMENT

Plaintiffs, by their attorneys, for their complaint against Defendants, allege:

-1-

EXHIBIT 7.2A

JURISDICTION AND VENUE

1.   This is a civil action seeking damages and injunctive relief for copyright infringement under the copyright laws of the United States (17 U.S.C. § 101 et seq.).

2.   This Court has jurisdiction under 17 U.S.C. § 101 et seq; 28 U.S.C. § 1331 (federal question); and 28 U.S.C. § 1338(a) (copyright).

3.   Venue in this District is proper under 28 U.S.C. § 1391(b) and/or 28 U.S.C. § 1400(a). Although the true identity of each Defendant is unknown to Plaintiffs at this time, on information and belief, each Defendant may be found in this District and/or a substantial part of the acts of infringement complained of herein occurred in this District. On information and belief, personal jurisdiction in this District is proper because each Defendant, without consent or permission of the copyright owner, disseminated over the Internet copyrighted works owned and/or controlled by the Plaintiffs. Such illegal dissemination occurred in every jurisdiction in the United States, including this one. In addition, each Defendant contracted with an Internet Service Provider found in this District to provide each Defendant with the access to the Internet which facilitated Defendants' infringing activities.

PARTIES

4.   Plaintiff Capitol Records, Inc. is a corporation duly organized and existing under the laws of the State of Delaware, with its principal place of business in the State of New York.

5.   Plaintiff Arista Records, Inc. is a corporation duly organized and existing under the laws of the State of Delaware with its principal place of business in the State of New York.

6.   Plaintiff Interscope Records is a California general partnership, with its principal place of business in the State of California.

7.   Plaintiff Loud Records, LLC is a corporation duly organized and existing under the laws of the State of Delaware, with its principal place of business in the State of New York.

-2-

EXHIBIT 7.2A	Sample Federal Complaint Filed in a Federal Court in New York

8. Plaintiff UMG Recordings, Inc. is a corporation duly organized and existing under the laws of the State of Delaware, with its principal place of business in the State of California.

9. Plaintiff Warner Bros. Records Inc. is a corporation duly organized and existing under the laws of the State of Delaware, with its principal place of business in the State of California.

10. Plaintiff Atlantic Recording Corporation is a corporation duly organized and existing under the laws of the State of Delaware, with its principal place of business in the State of New York.

11. Plaintiff Fonovisa, Inc. is a corporation duly organized and existing under the laws of the State of California, with its principal place of business in the State of California.

12. Plaintiff Sony Music Entertainment Inc. is a corporation duly organized and existing under the laws of the State of Delaware, with its principal place of business in the State of New York.

13. Plaintiff BMG Music is a general partnership duly organized and existing under the laws of the State of New York, with principal place of business in the State of New York.

14. Plaintiff London-Sire Records Inc. is a corporation duly organized and existing under the laws of the State of Delaware, with its principal place of business in the State of New York.

15. Plaintiff Motown Record Company, L.P. is a limited partnership duly organized, and existing under the laws of the State of California, with its principal place of business in the State of New York.

16. Plaintiff Priority Records LLC is a limited liability company with its principal place of business in the State of California.

17. Plaintiff Maverick Recording Company is a joint venture between Maverick Records and Warner Bros. Records Inc., organized and existing under the laws of the State of California, with its principal place of business in the State of California.

18. Plaintiff Elektra Entertainment Group Inc. is a corporation duly organized and existing under the laws of the State of Delaware, with its principal place of business in the State of New York.

EXHIBIT 7.2A

19. Plaintiff Virgin Records America, Inc. is a corporation duly organized and existing under the laws of the State of California, with its principal place of business in the State of New York.

20. The true names and capacities of the Defendants are unknown to Plaintiffs at this time. Each Defendant is known to Plaintiffs only by the Internet Protocol ("IP") address assigned to that Defendant by his or her ISP on the date and time at which the infringing activity of each Defendant was observed. Exhibit A. Plaintiffs believe that information obtained in discovery will lead to the identification of each Defendant's true name.

COUNT I
INFRINGEMENT OF COPYRIGHTS

21. Plaintiffs incorporate herein by this reference each and every allegation contained in each paragraph above.

22. Plaintiffs are, and at all relevant times have been, the copyright owners or licensees of exclusive rights under United States copyright law with respect to certain copyrighted sound recordings, including, but not limited to, all of the copyrighted sound recordings on Exhibit A to this Complaint (collectively, these copyrighted sound recordings shall be identified as the "Copyrighted Recordings"). Each of the Copyrighted Recordings is the subject of a valid Certificate of Copyright Registration issued by the Register of Copyrights to each Plaintiff as specified on each page of Exhibit A.

23. Among the exclusive rights granted to each Plaintiff under the Copyright Act are the exclusive rights to reproduce the Copyrighted Recordings and to distribute the Copyrighted Recordings to the public.

24. Plaintiffs are informed and believe that each Defendant, without the permission or consent of Plaintiffs, has used, and continues to use, an online media distribution system to download, distribute to the public, and/or make available for distribution to others, certain of the Copyrighted Recordings. Exhibit A identifies on a Defendant-by-Defendant basis (one Defendant per page) a list of copyrighted recordings that each Defendant has, without the permission or consent of Plaintiffs, downloaded, distributed to the public, and/or made available for distribution to others. In doing so, each Defendant has violated Plaintiffs' exclusive rights of reproduction and distribution.

EXHIBIT 7.2A — Sample Federal Complaint Filed in a Federal Court in New York

Each Defendant's actions constitute infringement of Plaintiffs' copyrights and/or exclusive rights under copyright. (In addition to the sound recordings listed for each Defendant on Exhibit A, Plaintiffs are informed and believe that each Defendant has, without the permission or consent of Plaintiffs, downloaded, distributed to the public, and/or made available for distribution to others additional sound recordings owned by or exclusively licensed to the Plaintiffs or Plaintiffs' affiliate record labels.

25. Plaintiffs are informed and believe that the foregoing acts of infringement have been willful, intentional, and in disregard of and with indifference to the rights of Plaintiffs.

26. As a result of each Defendant's infringement of Plaintiffs' copyrights and exclusive rights under copyright, Plaintiffs are entitled to statutory damages pursuant to 17 U.S.C. § 504(c) against each Defendant for each infringement by the Defendant of each copyrighted recording. Plaintiffs further are entitled to their attorneys' fees and costs pursuant to 17 U.S.C. § 505.

27. The conduct of each Defendant is causing and, unless enjoined and restrained by this Court, will continue to cause Plaintiffs great and irreparable injury that cannot fully be compensated or measured in money. Plaintiffs have no adequate remedy at law. Pursuant to 17 U.S.C. §§ 502 and 503, Plaintiffs are entitled to injunctive relief prohibiting each Defendant from further infringing Plaintiffs' copyrights, and ordering that each Defendant destroy all copies of copyrighted sound recordings made in violation of Plaintiffs' exclusive rights.

WHEREFORE, Plaintiffs pray for judgment against each Defendant as follows:

1. For an injunction providing:

"Defendant shall be and hereby is enjoined from directly or indirectly infringing Plaintiffs' rights under federal or state law in the Copyrighted Recordings and any sound recording, whether now in existence or later created, that is owned or controlled by Plaintiffs (or any parent, subsidiary, or affiliate record label of Plaintiffs) ("Plaintiffs' Recordings"), including without limitation by using the Internet or any online media distribution system to reproduce (i.e., download) any of Plaintiffs'

-5-

EXHIBIT 7.2A

Recordings, to distribute (i.e., upload) any of Plaintiffs' Recordings, or to make any of Plaintiffs' Recordings available for distribution to the public, except pursuant to a lawful license or with the express authority of Plaintiffs. Defendant also shall destroy all copies of Plaintiffs' Recordings that Defendant has downloaded onto any computer hard drive or server without Plaintiffs' authorization and shall destroy all copies of those downloaded recordings transferred onto any physical medium or device in Defendant's possession, custody, or control."

2. For statutory damages for each infringement of each Copyrighted Recording pursuant to 17 U.S.C. § 504.

3. For Plaintiffs' costs in this action.

4. For Plaintiffs' reasonable attorneys' fees incurred herein.

5. For such other and further relief as the Court may deem just and proper.

Dated: New York, New York

[signature] day

Attorneys for Plaintiffs

By: _[signature]_

J. Christopher Jensen (JJ-1864)
Jason D. Sanders (JS-2219)
COWAN, LIEBOWITZ & LATMAN, P.C.
1133 Avenue of the Americas
New York, New York 10036-6799
Phone: (212) 790-9200
Fax: (212) 575-0671

Donald B. Verrilli, Jr. (DV-5260)
Steven B. Fabrizio (SF-8639)
JENNER & BLOCK LLP
601 Thirteenth Street, NW
Suite 1200 South
Washington, D.C. 20005-3823
Phone: (202) 639-6000
Fax: (202) 639-6006

-6-

A. Introduction

This section presents a sample memorandum of law that analyzes New York law. It is an internal memo (often called an office memo) in the sense that it will not be filed with the court nor shown to anyone outside the office. It is designed for discussion and analysis solely for members of the firm working on the case of a client. Hence the memo is *not* an advocacy document; it is not designed to convince a court or an opponent to take a particular position. Consequently, the memo does not hide or downplay the weaknesses in the client's position. It presents the strengths and weaknesses of the client's case.

All law firms do not use the same format for a memorandum of law. Most firms, however, have the same basic five components: facts, issues or questions, brief answer, analysis or discussion, and conclusion. Firms may package these components in different ways (and may add others), but all of the five basic components are often present.

The format selected for the sample memorandum in Exhibit 7.3A contains these five components and adds a sixth, an overview presented at the beginning of the memo:

  I. Overview
 II. Statement of Facts
III. Questions Presented
 IV. Brief Answer
  V. Discussion
 VI. Conclusion

C. More Information

Sample Memoranda of Law
users.ipfw.edu/vetterw/a339-research-sample-memo.htm
www.alwd.org/publications/second_edition_resources.html
(click "Legal Memorandum Example")
www.alwd.org/publications/pdf/CM2_Appendix6.pdf
www.alwd.org/publications/pdf/CM1_Appendix6.pdf

Legal Memorandum Format Guidelines
www.ualr.edu/cmbarger
(click "Format Guidelines")
sparkcharts.sparknotes.com/legal/legalwriting/section2.php

D. Something to Check

Find a memorandum of law online on any legal issue in any state. Run the search "memorandum of law" in Google or another search engine. Try to find an internal memo rather than one that was filed in court. Compare its format or structure to the sample memorandum presented here in Exhibit 7.3A.

B. Sample Memorandum of Law

EXHIBIT 7.3A Sample Memorandum of Law Applying New York Law

MEMORANDUM

TO: F. Dewey

FROM: R. Howe

RE: Wexler v. Deily; #07-0223
           Enforcement of set date in a real estate contract

DATE: April 11, 2008

I. OVERVIEW

Our client, Andrew Deily, is bringing an action against the seller of a house to recover the $50,000 deposit he paid prior to sale's collapse. The question addressed in this memo is whether the term "but in no event later than" a particular date created a "time-is-of-the-essence clause." If it did, our client's payment of $150,000 eleven days after the particular date constituted a breach of the purchase contract, which results in the forfeiture of the deposit. If, however, the term is not deemed as time-is-of-the-essence, the eleven-day delay would constitute substantial performance, and the contract would not be deemed breached, and the deposit would be returned to our client. This memo concludes that New York will likely support our client's position that no "time-is-of-the-essence" clause was created by the "but in no event later than" clause.

II. STATEMENT OF FACTS

After a three-year search, our client, Andrew Deily, made a purchase offer on July 1, 2006 for a house to Sam Wexler that Deily intended to renovate and turn into a bed and breakfast. Although the house was ideal for this purpose, it was in an area that is zoned R-1 under the zoning rules of the Town of Woodstock, and it required a zoning variance to run a business in an R-1 zone. The sales price was $500,000; Deily paid $50,000 at the time of the contract signing. The seller's attorney held this amount in escrow.

The contract did not have an explicit time-is-of-the-essence clause. Rather it stated that Deily was required to make an additional payment of $150,000 "upon the date of receipt of the variance, or by December 31, 2006, whichever comes first, but in no event later than December 31, 2006." The remaining $300,000 was to be paid at closing. A clause in the contract entitled Deily to the return of the $50,000 down payment if, despite performance of the terms of the contract, due diligence, and good faith, he failed to obtain the variance.

-1-

EXHIBIT 7.3A

The Town of Woodstock Board of Zoning Appeals (BZA) was scheduled to meet once a month in 2006. Deily filed his variance application with the BZA in July but no action was taken at that time. The BZA did not meet in August and, although Deily attended every subsequent meeting, did not take any action on the application for the remainder of the year. At the November meeting, however, the BZA indicated that they would probably grant the request in early 2007.

In November Deily called the Wexler's attorney and explained the situation, emphasizing that although he was certain that his due diligence entitled him to a return of the $50,000 deposit, he felt that he was close to obtaining the variance and would much prefer to wait for the forthcoming approval. He had no desire to renegotiate a new contract, as property values had increased. There were further negotiations, but no agreement, on increasing the price in exchange for an extension of time to pay the $150,000.

On December 28, 2006, the seller's attorney sent a fax to Deily stating that failure to pay the $150,000 by the agreed-to date would "constitute a default of the time-is-of-the-essence clause in the contract" and that the seller's attorney would avail himself of all remedies on behalf of the seller, including keeping the down payment. Deily was not certain how to proceed, but did remit the $150,000 on January 11, 2007. The seller's attorney promptly notified Deily by letter that the late payment was a breach of the purchase contract because the December 31st date was a "time-is-of-the-essence" clause. However, rather than terminate the contract, the attorney tried to renegotiate a more favorable contract for his client. On February 12, 2007 the attorney, after acrimonious negotiations, sent our client another letter declaring him in default and returning the $150,000 but keeping the $50,000 because Deily "failed to perform the contract based upon late payment."

III. QUESTIONS PRESENTED

For purposes of enforcing a real estate contract, can setting a date certain for payment, such as payment to be made "in no event later than" a designated date, or other actions by the seller, create an enforceable time-is-of-the-essence clause?

IV. BRIEF ANSWER

The basic contract rule supports our client because the term "on or before" a particular date does not create a time-is-of-the-essence clause. However, a court could deem the December 28 fax as having created a post-contract time-is-of-the-essence clause, but even then, the seller may be estopped from asserting it based on the post-breach negotiations.

-2-

EXHIBIT 7.3A   Sample Memorandum of Law Applying New York Law

V. DISCUSSION

It is well established that when a contract for the sale of real property does not specify that time is of the essence, either party is entitled to a reasonable adjournment of the closing date. (3M Holding Corp. v. Wagner, 166 AD2d 580 [3rd Dept., 1990]; Sohayegh v. Oberlander, 155 AD2d 436 [2nd Dept., 1989].) In contracts for the transfer of real estate, time is not ordinarily of the essence unless the agreement so provides (Grace v. Happa, 46 NY2d 560 [1979]). The act of designating a date for performance, without further language, is not sufficient to make the date the essence of the contract (Ballen v. Potter, 241 NY 224 [1929]). To be effective, a clause in a contract stating that time is of the essence must be clear, distinct, and unequivocal. (Miller v. Almquist, 241 AD2d 181 [1st Dept., 1988].)

Courts have held that performance "on or before" a specified date alone does not make time of the essence. In O'Conell v. Clear Holding Co. (126 AD2d 530 [2nd Dept. 1987]), the court held that "[t]ime was not made of the essence by the designation that closing would take place 'on or before' a stated date." (Id. at 530.) Other consistent cases include Kevan v. Modesta (292 AD2d 348 [2nd Dept., 2002], letter stating the closing would take place "on or prior to" a stated date did not make time of the essence); Steinberg v. Linzer (2002 WL 221104 [Sup. Ct. Suf. Co. 2002], closing to take place on or before a date in the purchase offer contract did not make time of the essence); and In re Southold Development Corp. (134 BR 705 [ED NY, 1991], where bankruptcy court held that the "in no event later than" language was not clear and unequivocal).

Even though a contract for the sale of real property does not contain an explicit time-is-of-the-essence clause, one party may unilaterally notify the other that time is of the essence if the notice is clear, distinct, unequivocal, fixes a reasonable time in which to perform, and informs the other party that a failure to perform will result in default (Mohen v. Mooney, 162 AD2d 664 [2nd Dept., 1990]; James v. James, 205 AD2d 735 [2nd Dept., 1994]; Sahayegh, supra). What constitutes a "reasonable time" must be determined by the facts and circumstances of each case (76 North Associates v. Theil Management Corp., 114 AD3d 948, 949 [2nd Dept., 1985]).

The seller will likely assert that time was made of the essence by the December 28 fax of the seller's attorney even if there was no breach of any clause in the contract. The argument is that the fax constituted a binding, unilateral modification. The terms of the fax appear to be unequivocal and clearly state the consequences of a breach, as required.

In asserting that the fax was not effective, we would rely on Levine v. Sarbello (112 AD2d 197 [2nd Dept., 1985]), which held that a post-contract attempt to make time of the essence made on the same day as the alleged breach was not effective because that was not a reasonable time. However,

EXHIBIT 7.3A

we would need to distinguish our client's contract from EC, LLC v. Eaglecrest Manufactured Home Park (275 AD2d 898 [4th Dept., 2000]), where a real estate contract formed in May 1997 called for an August 1997 closing, with no time-is-of-the-essence clause. In EC, LLC, a September 1997 addendum to the May 1997 contract provided an "on or before" January 31, 1998 date, again without a time-is-of-the-essence clause. In response to a January 13, 1998 request for an extension, a post-contract time-is-of-the-essence letter was sent. The court held that the time-is-of-the-essence clause provided a reasonable time "particularly in view of the fact that the parties initially anticipated a closing date in August 1997." (Id. at 391.) We would need to assert the fact that the "on or before" date in the original contract was not originally of the essence and that a post-contract fax only three days prior to the performance date was an inadequate notice.

Another facet regarding the validity of the post-contract fax is that the seller's attorney continued with negotiations after first asserting the breach. In Levine, the court stated that in addition to the failure of the notice, the seller's continued negotiations with the buyer after asserting the default, estopped it from reasserting the default after the negations failed. Therefore we should argue that, even if the post-contract fax did create a binding time-is-of-the-essence clause, the subsequent negotiations after the assertion of a breach estopped the seller from asserting it.

VI. CONCLUSION

Deily has many good arguments to show that no time-is-of-the-essence clause was created. Case law squarely supports the notion that "on or before" a date certain in and of itself does not make time of the essence. Hence the law would then permit a reasonable time for performance, which the January 11 payment of the $150,000, eleven days after, very likely is.

The seller will undoubtedly rely on the December 28, 2006 fax as having created a post-contract time-is-of-the-essence clause. Yet the fact that it was received three days before the performance date makes it less likely to be considered adequate. Finally, even if the court finds that the fax did make time of the essence, the seller may be estopped from asserting it based on the continued negotiation after the assertion of the breach.

7.4 Sample Appellate Brief Filed in the New York Court of Appeals

A. Introduction

This section presents an example of an appellate brief. An appellate brief is a document submitted by a party to an appellate court and served on the opposing party in which arguments are presented on why the appellate court should affirm (approve), reverse, or otherwise modify what a lower court has done. There are a number of roles that paralegals perform in this area of appellate practice. They might be asked to go through the transcript of the trial record to find references that the attorney wants to use in the brief. They might be asked to cite check the brief by making sure that:

- All quotations are accurate
- All citations are in the format required by court rules
- The brief itself is in the format required by court rules
- All laws cited are still valid

The last role is performed by using citators such as Shepard's Citations, KeyCite, or GlobalCite. A citator allows you to check each case, statute, or other law to make sure that it has not been overruled or changed since the time the appellate brief was drafted. Occasionally, an experienced paralegal will be asked to draft a portion of an appellate brief.

See also the following related sections in the book:

- New York state legal research (section 5.1)
- Citation of legal materials (section 5.2)
- Timeline of civil litigation (section 6.1)
- Selected rules of procedure (section 6.2)
- Timeline of criminal litigation (section 6.4)
- Civil complaints (section 7.1 for state and 7.2 for federal)

B. Rules on the Content and Form of Appellate Briefs

Before examining a sample brief in Exhibit 7.4A, review the following rules from the Civil Practice Laws and Rules and from the Rules of the New York Court of Appeals on the content and form of appellate briefs in the New York Court of Appeals.

Civil Practice Law and Rules

public.leginfo.state.ny.us/menugetf.cgi?COMMONQUERY=
LAWS

(click "CVP" then "Article 55" then "R5529")

Rule 5528. Content of briefs and appendices

(a) *Appellant's brief and appendix.* The brief of the appellant shall contain in the following order:

1. a table of contents, which shall include the contents of the appendix, if it is not bound separately, with references to the initial page of each paper printed and of the direct, cross, and redirect examination of each witness;

2. a concise statement, not exceeding two pages, of the questions involved without names, dates, amounts or particulars, with each question numbered, set forth separately and followed immediately by the answer, if any, of the court from which the appeal is taken;

3. a concise statement of the nature of the case and of the facts which should be known to determine the questions involved, with supporting references to pages in the appendix;

4. the argument for the appellant, which shall be divided into points by appropriate headings distinctively printed; and

5. an appendix, which may be bound separately, containing only such parts of the record on appeal as are necessary to consider the questions involved, including those parts the appellant reasonably assumes will be relied upon by the respondent; provided, however, that the appellate division in each department may by rule applicable in the department authorize an appellant at his election to proceed upon a record on appeal printed or reproduced in like manner as an appendix, and in the event of such election an appendix shall not be required.

(b) *Respondent's brief and appendix.* The brief of the respondent shall conform to the requirements of subdivision (a), except that a counterstatement of the questions involved or a counterstatement of the nature and facts of the case shall be included only if the respondent disagrees with the statement of the appellant and the appendix shall contain only such additional parts of the record as are necessary to consider the questions involved.

(c) *Appellant's reply brief and appendix.* Any reply brief of the appellant shall conform to the requirements of subdivision (a) without repetition.

(d) *Joint appendix.* A joint appendix bound separately may be used. It shall be filed with the appellant's brief.

(e) *Sanction.* For any failure to comply with subdivision (a), (b) or (c) the court to which the appeal is taken may withhold or impose costs.

Rule 5529. Form of briefs and appendices

(a) *Form of reproduction; size; paper; binding.*
1. Briefs and appendices shall be reproduced by any method that produces a permanent, legible, black image on white paper. Paper shall be of a quality approved by the chief administrator of the courts.
2. Briefs and appendices shall be on white paper eleven inches along the bound edge by eight and one-half inches.
3. An appellate court may by rule applicable to practice therein prescribe the size of margins and type of briefs and appendices and the line spacing and the length of briefs.

(b) *Numbering.* Pages of briefs shall be numbered consecutively. Pages of appendices shall be separately numbered consecutively, each number preceded by the letter A.

(c) *Page headings.* The subject matter of each page of the appendix shall be stated at the top thereof, except that in the case of papers other than testimony, the subject matter of the paper may be stated at the top of the first page of each paper, together with the page numbers of the first and last pages thereof. In the case of testimony, the name of the witness, by whom he was called and whether the testimony is direct, cross, redirect or recross examination shall be stated at the top of each page.

(d) *Quotations.* Asterisks or other appropriate means shall be used to indicate omissions in quoted excerpts. Reference shall be made to the source of the excerpts quoted. Where an excerpt in the appendix is testimony of a witness quoted from the record the beginning of each page of the transcript shall be indicated by parenthetical insertion of the transcript page number.

(e) *Citations of decisions.* New York decisions shall be cited from the official reports, if any. All other decisions shall be cited from the official reports, if any, and also from the National Reporter System if they are there reported. Decisions not reported officially or in the National Reporter System shall be cited from the most available source.

(f) *Questions and answers.* The answer to a question in the appendix shall not begin a new paragraph.

Court of Appeals Rules

www.nycourts.gov/ctapps/500rules08.htm
www.nycourts.gov/ctapps/500rules08.htm#500_13

§ 500.12. Filing of Record Material and Briefs in Normal Course Appeals

(a) *Scheduling letter.* Generally, in an appeal tracked for normal course treatment, the clerk of the Court issues a scheduling letter after the filing of the preliminary appeal statement. A scheduling letter also issues upon the termination of an inquiry pursuant to section 500.10 or 500.11 of this Part. The scheduling letter sets the filing dates for record material and briefs.

(b) *Appellant's initial filing.* On or before the date specified in the scheduling letter, appellant shall serve and file record material in compliance with section 500.14 of this Part, and shall remit the fee, if any, required by section 500.3(a) of this Part. Appellant also shall file an original and 24 copies of a brief, with proof of service of three copies on each other party. If no scheduling letter is issued, appellant's papers shall be served and filed within 60 days after appellant took the appeal by (1) filing a notice of appeal in the place and manner required by CPLR 5515, (2) entry of an order granting a motion for leave to appeal in a civil case, or (3) issuance of a certificate granting leave to appeal in a criminal case.

(c) *Respondent's filing.* On or before the date specified in the scheduling letter, respondent shall serve and file an original and 24 copies of a brief and a supplementary appendix, if any, with proof of service of three copies on each other party. If no scheduling letter is issued, respondent's papers shall be filed within 45 days after service of appellant's brief.

(d) *Reply briefs.* A reply brief is not required but may be served and filed by appellant on or before the date specified in the scheduling letter. If no scheduling letter is issued, a reply brief may be served and filed within 15 days after service of respondent's brief. Where cross appeals are filed, the cross appellant may serve and file a reply brief to the main appellant's responsive brief. An original and 24 copies of a reply brief shall be served and filed, with proof of service of three copies on each other party.

§ 500.13. Content and Form of Briefs in Normal Course Appeals

(a) *Content.* All briefs shall conform to the requirements of section 500.1 of this Part and contain a table of contents, a table of cases and authorities and, if necessary, a disclosure statement pursuant to section 500.1(f) of this Part. Such disclosure statement shall be included before the table of contents in the party's principal brief. Appellant's brief shall include a statement showing that the Court has jurisdiction to entertain the appeal and to review the questions raised, with citations to the pages of the record or appendix where such questions have been preserved for the Court's review. Respondent's brief may have a supplementary appendix attached to it. The original of each brief shall be signed and dated, shall have the affidavit of service affixed to the inside of the back cover and shall be identified on the front cover as the original. Each brief shall indicate the status of any related litigation as of the date the brief is completed. Such statement shall be included before the table of contents in each party's brief.

(b) *Brief covers.* Brief covers shall be white and shall contain the caption of the case and name, address, telephone number, and facsimile number of counsel or self-represented litigant and the party on whose behalf the brief is submitted, and the date on which the brief was completed. In the upper right corner, the brief cover shall indicate whether the party proposes to submit the brief without oral argument or, if argument time is requested, the amount of time requested and the name of the person who will present oral argument (see section 500.18 of this Part). If a time request does not appear on the brief, generally no more than 10 minutes will be assigned. The Court will determine the argument time, if any, to be assigned to each party. Plastic covers shall not be used.

C. Sample Appellate Brief Filed in the New York Court of Appeals

Exhibit 7.4A contains an example of an appellate brief filed in the New York Court of Appeals.

D. | More Information

Analyzing Effective Appellate Briefs
www.lwionline.org/grading_rubrics.html#appellate

Appellate Briefs Online: Free and Fee-Based
www.llrx.com/features/briefsonline.htm

Civil Practice Laws and Rules
*public.leginfo.state.ny.us/menugetf.cgi?COMMONQUERY=
LAWS*
(click "CVP")
www.law.cornell.edu/states/ny.html
(click "Consolidated Laws" then "CVP")

Formatting Computer-Generated Briefs
*www.courts.state.ny.us/courts/ad2/pdf/GlossaryFormatting
Terms.pdf*

Forms and Practice Aids
www.courts.state.ny.us/courts/ad2/formsandpracticeaids.shtml

Guide to Appellate Briefs Online
www.law.duke.edu/curriculum/appellateAdvocacy/guide.html
*www.llrx.com/features/briefsonline.htm#free%20by%
20jurisdiction*
www.llrx.com/columns/reference43.htm
www.legaline.com/freebriefslinks.html
www.lawsource.com/also/usa.cgi?usb
*west.thomson.com/documentation/westlaw/wlawdoc/wlres/
litbrf07.pdf*

Megalaw: New York Civil Procedure
www.megalaw.com/tx/top/txcivpro.php

New York Court Rules
www.nycourts.gov/rules/trialcourts/index.shtml
www.llrx.com/courtrules-gen/state-New-York.html

Records and Briefs
iapps.courts.state.ny.us/docprocessing/Main

E. | Something to Check

Assume that you have been asked to cite check the appellate brief in exhibit 7.4A. Pick any three cases cited in the brief. Try to find them in a large law library or online. On finding cases online, see section 5.1.

1. Check the accuracy of the location information in the citations by determining whether the three cases are found in the volumes and pages indicated in their citations.
2. Check the accuracy of what the brief says about the three cases. For example, the brief cites *Berkowitz v. Fischbein* for the position that contract claims are routinely dismissed as duplicative of the malpractice claim. Go to the *Berkowitz* opinion to determine if it does support this conclusion.

EXHIBIT 7.4A

TABLE OF CONTENTS

EXHIBIT 7.4A   Sample Appellate Brief

2007-0091

To Be Argued By:
JEFFREY A. BARR, ESQ.
Thirty minutes requested.

Surrogate's Court, New York County Clerk's File No. 4323/1993

COURT OF APPEALS
OF THE STATE OF NEW YORK

HOWARD LEDER, as Preliminary Executor
of the Estate of ABRAHAM WARSASKI,

Proponent,

- against -

MARSHALL SPIEGEL and MICHAEL SPIEGEL,

Objectants-Appellants.

BRIEF OF APPELLANT

JEFFREY A. BARR, Esq.
Attorney for Objectant-Appellant
Marshall Spiegel
225 Broadway, Suite 3504
New York, NY 10007
(212) 227-1834
(212) 964-4360 fax

February 19, 2007

EXHIBIT 7.4A

QUESTIONS PRESENTED

I. WHETHER A PLAINTIFF ASSERTING A CLAIM OF LEGAL MALPRACTICE MUST PROVE, IN OPPOSING A MOTION TO DISMISS, THAT HE WOULD HAVE PREVAILED AT TRIAL OR SUFFERED NO PECUNIARY HARM, BUT FOR THE ATTORNEY'S NEGLIGENCE.

The Court below ruled in the affirmative.

II. WHETHER A PLAINTIFF ASSERTING A LEGAL MALPRACTICE CLAIM MUST PROVE ULTIMATE SUCCESS IN THE MATTER, REGARDLESS OF THE MALPRACTICE, WHERE OTHER FORMS OF DAMAGE HAVE BEEN SUFFERED, SUCH AS REJECTED SETTLEMENT OFFERS BASED ON FAULTY ADVICE.

The Court below implicitly ruled in the affirmative.

III. WHETHER A BREACH OF CONTRACT CLAIM, PREMISED ON A RETAINER LETTER AND SEEKING RECOVERY OF A SUM OTHER THAN THE RECOVERY SOUGHT IN THE UNDERLYING MATTER, STATES A CLAIM THAT IS DISTINCT FROM A NEGLIGENCE CLAIM.

The Court below ruled in the negative.

IV. WHETHER REQUIRING A PLAINTIFF TO PROVE ULTIMATE SUCCESS AT TRIAL OR THAT HE WOULD NOT HAVE SUFFERED ANY PECUNIARY HARM AS AN ESSENTIAL ELEMENT OF PROXIMATE CAUSE IS A VIOLATION OF THE EQUAL PROTECTION CLAUSE OF THE NEW YORK STATE CONSTITUTION (ART. 1, SECTION 11).

The Court below ruled in the negative.

V. WHETHER A PLAINTIFF MUST PROVE PROXIMATE CAUSE WITH FACTUAL ALLEGATIONS IN OPPOSING A MOTION TO DISMISS ARISING UNDER N.Y. C.P.L.R. 3211(A)(7).

The Court below answered in the affirmative.

-ii-

EXHIBIT 7.4A   Sample Appellate Brief

TABLE OF AUTHORITIES

-i-

EXHIBIT 7.4A   Sample Appellate Brief

PRELIMINARY STATEMENT

Objectant-Appellant Marshall Spiegel appeals from the July 6, 2006 Order of the Appellate Division, First Department which affirmed an Order dated May 24, 2002 from the Surrogate's Court, New York County (per Roth, Surrogate) which fixed and determined the legal fees he owed to Respondent Joanne Rowland, Esq., at $16,608.00 and disbursements in the sum of $245.42 and dismissed his counterclaims for legal malpractice and breach of contract against Ms. Rowland. The Appellate Division ruled that the Surrogate's Court properly dismissed the Appellant's counterclaim on a N.Y. C.P.L.R. 3211 motion to dismiss, because after a review of the record, there was no set of facts under which the Appellant could have succeeded in his malpractice claim. The dissenting justices argued that the majority was making a finding of fact. They argued that the majority had reviewed the underlying evidence and reached a factual conclusion contradictory to the appellant's allegation of his reliance on allegedly incorrect legal advice in his rejection of a proposed settlement offer. The dissent stated emphatically that such a factual finding was improper on a motion to dismiss made under C.P.L.R. 3211.

On appeal to this Court, Appellant challenges the majority's holding, not merely because it was a factual finding, but because, at its heart, the Court determined that it was permissible to make a finding of fact on a C.P.L.R. 3211 motion, because the standard of proof in a legal malpractice case requires the plaintiff to prove a "case within a case," demonstrating even before considering the issue of the attorney's negligence, with certainty, that the plaintiff would have ultimately prevailed in the underlying action or would not have sustained any "ascertainable damages."

The Court of Appeals has never directly ruled on the issue of the appropriateness or constitutionality of the "case within a case" requirement in legal malpractice cases. Appellant submits that this Court should adopt for the state a standard in line with the standards for such cases in many other states, and consistent with the standards of proof required in other types of malpractice cases, which would require only a finding of a breach of a duty of care which

-1-

EXHIBIT 7.4A

resulted in some actual harm. Proof of the certainty of ultimate success in the underlying action should not be an intrinsic element of proximate cause when other measures of damage and harm from the attorney's malpractice can be demonstrated, such as in the case at bar. Alternatively, this Court should rule that a breach of contract claim against a lawyer for rendering faulty advice is not necessarily duplicative of a malpractice case, where it can be shown that while the plaintiff may not have prevailed at trial, he did suffer actual damage by virtue of the defective services rendered.

While the New York courts pay lip service to such a standard, it is clear from their rulings that, in practice, liability is determined solely on the issue of whether the plaintiff would have prevailed at trial.

STATEMENT OF THE CASE

In June, 1997, Respondent Joanne Rowland agreed to serve as local counsel to the Appellant and his brother, the sole distributees-at-law in a contested probate proceeding entitled Will of Abraham Warsaski. In the period June through August, 1997, as shown in Ms. Rowland's time records and records of correspondence (A-39-42, 65, 101-103), respondent Rowland substituted in as local counsel and represented that she was an expert in New York law and Surrogate's Court procedure. It is without dispute that Ms. Rowland reviewed the papers in the case, consisting inter alia of discovery proceedings conducted over the preceding four years, and was aware of the evidence available to objectants. Ms. Rowland even went to Chicago and met with and advised Appellant, his brother and their Illinois counsel regarding the case and helped them prepare for trial. (A-14-17, 34-36). In August, 1997, approximately one month prior to the scheduled trial in the Surrogate's Court, Ms. Rowland agreed to serve as sole trial counsel. (A-35).

Appellant's objection was based on the belief that, in light of numerous suicide attempts, imagined illnesses and utterly irrational writings made by his uncle Abraham Warsaski contemporaneous to the execution of a 1992 will, he lacked testamentary capacity with respect to the 1992 and certain

-2-

EXHIBIT 7.4A

decision and order dated February 23, 1999, held that the failure to have such documentation admitted into evidence was fatal to the objection. (A-118).

The counterclaims assert claims for the $108,000.00 settlement, which the estate had offered until the eve of trial, and all sums previously paid to Rowland.

By Amended Notice of Motion dated June 10, 1999, Rowland moved in the Surrogate's Court to dismiss the counterclaims. (A-42-43). Appellant opposed. (A-24-31).

By decision dated January 14, 2002, the Surrogate's Court (per Roth) granted the fee petition awarding Rowland $16,608.00 plus disbursements of $245.42, denied the request to decline jurisdiction of the malpractice claim in favor of the Illinois action (thereby ruling on an application made by Appellant *pro se* in an Affirmation dated December 3, 1997) (A-44-49), denied recusal and dismissed the counterclaims on the grounds that objectants had failed to prove as a threshold requirement that the alleged negligence was a proximate cause of any damages. (A-*iii-xv*).

By Notice of Appeal dated October 26, 2004 (A-9), an appeal was taken to the Appellate Division, First Department, challenging the Surrogate's Court's exercise of jurisdiction over the malpractice claim, its denial of a recusal motion, and its dismissal of the malpractice and breach of contract counterclaim asserted against Ms. Rowland.

By Order and Decision dated July 6, 2006, the Appellate Division unanimously held that there was jurisdiction in the Surrogate's Court to determine the counterclaim asserting attorney malpractice, and that the denial of recusal was proper. The Appellate Division was divided on the issue of whether the malpractice counterclaim should have been dismissed at the pleading stage. (A6-8).

An appeal was taken to this Court from that portion of the Appellate Division's order which affirmed the dismissal of the malpractice counterclaims asserted in the determination of the legal fee application of Ms. Rowland, based on the dissent of two members of the panel hearing the appeal on that issue.

-4-

EXHIBIT 7.4A **Sample Appellate Brief**

other prior wills. (A-71-74). The alleged malpractice concerns Ms. Rowland's alleged advice that the Dead Man's Statute, N.Y. C.P.L.R. 4519, did not apply, her failure to advise that it would bar the Objectant from testifying; and her failure to procure in time for trial, even after having been given a one-day continuance by the court to do so, a handwriting expert to authenticate the handwriting of the decedent. (A-72, A 111-114).

The will contest was tried before Surrogate Roth and a jury, and after the first day, the court directed the verdict dismissing the will challenge. (*Id*.). On the eve of trial, however, a settlement offer of $108,000 had been presented by the proponent and, based on Ms. Rowland's optimism, the offer was rejected. Surrogate Roth confirmed the existence of this settlement offer, which was made in the Court's presence on the morning of the trial. (A-*xiii*).

After the unsuccessful trial, Respondent filed an order to show cause dated October 9, 1997, in the Surrogate's Court, seeking to be relieved as counsel and seeking an order pursuant to N.Y. S.C.P.A. 2110 to have her legal fees determined. (A-32-43). Appellant Spiegel made an application to have counterclaims to the legal fee claim adjudicated in an Illinois court where appellant had already commenced a malpractice proceeding. (A-44-49). After the Surrogate appeared to have declined the application, Appellant interposed, in the Surrogate's Court, a counterclaim and answer asserting a counterclaim for malpractice seeking damages of $108,000 and a breach of contract claim seeking $115,000.00. (A-107-117).

The Counterclaims

Appellant contends that due to faulty advice, inadequate legal research and lack of preparation, Ms. Rowland misadvised him and his Chicago counsel about their prospects of prevailing at trial and, indeed, as a direct result of her lack of skill, Appellant was unable to obtain necessary authentication to admit into evidence certain manuscripts and other writings made by the decedent in the period contemporaneous to the execution of the wills and was thereby unable to present to the jury expert opinion testimony by a psychiatrist retained by Appellant to prove his uncle's lack of testamentary capacity. (A-1 12-115). The Appellate Division, First Department, in an earlier

-3-

EXHIBIT 7.4A Sample Appellate Brief

<u>ARGUMENT</u>

I. THE STANDARD OF PROOF REQUIRED IN A LEGAL MALPRACTICE ACTION, PROOF THAT ONE WOULD HAVE ACTUALLY PREVAILED AT TRIAL, IGNORES ACTUAL PECUNIARY DAMAGES WHICH LITIGANTS MAY AND DO SUFFER BY VIRTUE OF MALPRACTICE, REGARDLESS OF ULTIMATE OUTCOME IN THE UNDERLYING ACTION

The Appellate Division in rendering its opinion relied on cases which hold that in order to prevail the "plaintiff must demonstrate that 'but for' the attorney's negligence, plaintiff would either have prevailed in the matter, or would not have sustained any 'ascertainable damages.'" (A-2-8) (citing *Reibman v. Senie*, 302 A.D.2d 290, 756 N.Y.S.2d 164 (1st Dep't 2003) and *Brooks v. Lewis*, 21 A.D.3d 731, 734 (1st Dep't 2005) *leave denied*, 6 N.Y.3d 713 (2006)). The Court further termed this required showing which, apparently, is preliminary even to the analysis of whether there was malpractice, as "proximate cause," citing *Schwartz v. Olshan Grundman Frome & Rosenzweig*, 302 A.D.2d 193, 198 (1st Dep't 2003) ("The failure to demonstrate proximate cause mandates the dismissal of a legal malpractice action regardless of whether the attorney was negligent.") (A-4).

Several other states do not appear to set such rigid limits on the measure of damages available nor apply such a strict definition of proximate cause in legal malpractice cases (*see, e.g., Banker v. Nighswander, Martin & Mitchell*, 37 F.3d 866, 870-1 (2d Cir. 1994); *Royal Ins. Co. of America v. Miles and Stockbridge, P.C.*, 133 F. Supp.2d 747, 755 (D. Md. 2001)).

In no other type of malpractice action is the measure of the plaintiff's damages so limited and construed so narrowly. Holding plaintiffs who sue attorneys to a different standard than that applied with respect to other professionals and other members of society is a deprivation of due process and equal protection under the state constitution.

The Court of Appeals has never directly addressed the appropriateness of requiring proof of ultimate success at trial as an essential element of proximate cause which has been imposed by Appellate Division rulings and New York practice. *See McCoy v. Feinman*, 99 N.Y.2d 295 (2002)

-5-

EXHIBIT 7.4A

(addressing the issue of statute of limitations); and *Darby & Darby, P.C v. VSI International, Inc.*, 95 N.Y.2d 308 (2000) (finding no specific duty as alleged).

II. A MALPRACTICE CLAIM CANNOT BE DUPLICATIVE OF A CONTRACT CLAIM WHERE THE MEASURE OF DAMAGES IS DIFFERENT

The Appellate Division affirmed the Surrogate's dismissal of the appellant's breach of contract counterclaim on the ground that it was factually duplicative of the malpractice claim which it dismissed because the appellant could not meet the proximate cause standard of proving a "case within a case."

Where the measure of damages in a legal malpractice case is limited to the recovery the plaintiff would have recovered had the plaintiff prevailed in the underlying action, but where the breach of contract claim seeks damages suffered (including legal fees paid) for the reliance on faulty advice, the claims are not the same. The Surrogate's Court misapplied the standard of proof.

The breach of contract claim seeks a different sum, and the nature of the reliance on counsel's advice and performance is different. Because neither the underlying facts nor the relief sought is the same, it was error for the Court to have considered that the breach of contract claim was duplicative of the malpractice claim and therefore dismissible.

While the Appellate Division, First Department, holds out the possibility of a contract claim, such claims are routinely dismissed as duplicative of the malpractice case. *See, e.g., Berkowitz v. Fischbein, Badillo, Wagner & Harding*, 34 A.D.3d 297 (1st Dep't 2006). The requirement of proving the certainty of actually prevailing in the underlying matter ignores both the purpose for which litigants hire lawyers and the actual pecuniary damages which can legitimately be incurred by virtue of faulty legal advice. For example, there are significant costs incurred in preparing for trial, the most obvious of which is legal fees, which are now generally required to be the subject of a retainer agreement (which is a contract). *See* 22 N.Y.C.R.R., Subtitle B, Ch. IV, Subchapter E, Part 1215. In this case, in addition to the legal fees paid (which were minimal), there was the proper evaluation of a settlement offer which would have been accepted had proper advice been given by Ms. Rowland.

-6-

EXHIBIT 7.4A

IV. APPELLANT'S CONSTITUTIONAL RIGHT (N.Y. STATE CONSTITUTION, ART. I, SECTIONS 6 AND 11, U.S. CONSTITUTION, 14TH AMENDMENT) TO EQUAL PROTECTION AND DUE PROCESS IS DENIED BY THE PROXIMATE CAUSE STANDARD SET BY THE APPELLATE DIVISION, FIRST DEPARTMENT

New York State Constitution, Art. I, Section 11, provides that, "No person shall be denied the equal protection of the laws of this state or any subdivision thereof." New York State Constitution, Art. I, Section 6, provides a right to due process. These same rights are assured by the United States Constitution, 14th Amendment. *Central Sav. Bank v. City of New York*, 279 N.Y. 266 (1939).

By requiring that plaintiffs seeking to sue an attorney be held to a higher standard of proof than what is generally required were one to sue an ordinary person, or even another type of professional, the courts are depriving such litigants of due process and equal protection of the law in violation of N.Y. Constitution Art. I, Sections 6 and 11. There is an appearance that the courts are protecting attorneys from malpractice claims by requiring their former clients prove that they would have prevailed at trial but for the malpractice.

The alternate requirement that plaintiffs must prove "no ascertainable damages," seems nothing more than the corollary requirement of an aggrieved defendant in the unsuccessful action—that he would not have lost. Other than protection of the legal profession, or limiting access to the courts, there is no rationale for limiting a plaintiff in a legal malpractice action to proof of total victory at trial.

One does not need to prove that one would have recovered to full health but for medical malpractice when suing a medical professional. Indeed, the standard in a medical malpractice case is that the negligence be a substantial factor in producing the injury, not the only cause. *See, Mortenson v. Memorial Hospital*, 105 A.D.2d 151, 158 (1st Dep't 1984); *Koster v. Greenberg*, 120 A.D.2d 644, 645 (2d Dep't 1986). ("The plaintiff is not obligated to eliminate all possibility that the injuries resulted from causes other than the defendant's negligence."). (*Id.*). To require a plaintiff in a legal malpractice case to prove that they would have prevailed but for the attorney's

-8-

EXHIBIT 7.4A **Sample Appellate Brief**

To ignore these facts, as argued below, ignores a real distinction between a breach of contract claim and a negligence claim, and ignores the fact that a reasonable settlement is often the goal of a litigant and that a careful and accurate analysis of the law and evidence is needed for such purpose.

Here, Surrogate Roth appeared to acknowledge Appellant's grievance by stating that Appellant's counterclaim for legal malpractice had a direct bearing on the attorney's right to compensation (citing *Martin, Van de Walle, Guarino and Donahue v. Yohay*, 149 A.D. 2d 477, 480 (2d Dep't 1991), *app. denied*, 79 N.Y.2d 753 (1992)), noting that it would be a "defense to a fee application" and that the issue was "intertwined" with the issue of the appropriate fee. (A-x). But rather than permit discovery and permit the parties to develop the record, the Court refused to permit any inquiry into the alleged malpractice and dismissed the counterclaims. The Court applied the legal malpractice "proximate cause standard" to the breach of contract claim and ruled that unless the Objectant could prove at the pleading stage that he would have prevailed at trial regardless of the malpractice of counsel (which the Surrogate, as a potential witness, discounted), there was no basis to evaluate the malpractice even as a set-off against the legal fees claimed by Respondent.

The Appellant here was not claiming as damages the value of his intestate share of the estate which his objection sought, which would have been over $250,000. He sued for two items, the value of the rejected settlement offer from the estate, $108,000 (A-114), plus a sum equal to the fees he had already paid to Ms. Rowland. (A-116). Thus an inquiry into whether Appellant would have prevailed at trial seems surplusage and irrelevant at best.

III. THIS COURT HAS JURISDICTION UNDER ARTICLE VI, SECTION 3(b)(1) OF THE CONSTITUTION OF THE STATE OF NEW YORK TO HEAR THIS APPEAL, WHICH IS A FINAL DETERMINATION AND IS BASED ON THE DISSENT OF TWO JUSTICES OF THE APPELLATE DIVISION

New York State Constitution, Art. VI, Section 3(b)(1) provides an appeal as of right where the appeal is from an order which finally determines the issue and there were two Justices who dissented from the decision below. Here both criteria are met.

-7-

EXHIBIT 7.4A | **Sample Appellate Brief**

negligence requires them to prove that the attorney's malpractice was the sole cause of their lack of success in the matter or simply leaves them with no right of action at all.

There may be legitimate policy considerations in determining proximate causation standards. "[T]he concept stems from policy considerations that serve to place manageable limits upon the liability that flows from negligent conduct." *Mortensen*, 105 A.D.2d at 157. *See also, Ventricelli v. Kinney System Rent A Car*, 45 N.Y.2d 950, 952 (1978), *Palsgraf v. Long Island R.R. Co.*, 248 N.Y. 339, 352 (1928).

It is respectfully submitted that society is not benefited by giving a free pass to attorneys who vary from the standard of care required in a particular case by burdening the former client with a definition of proximate cause that cannot, except in extraordinary cases, be overcome. The standard applied by the Appellate Division, practically, implies that attorneys can only be found negligent in the simplest and most straightforward cases where a lesser level of skill would be required of the attorney. Indeed, the profession, and the persons it serves, would be better served were the inquiry focused on the attorney's standard of care, not whether, regardless of the standard of care applied, the plaintiff would have prevailed. Had that inquiry actually been permitted here, and the Court or the finder of fact actually been permitted to review the facts of the case, Respondent might not have been awarded her fees, and she might have been found liable for the results of her allegedly faulty advice—the improvidently rejected settlement offer.

-9-

EXHIBIT 7.4A

CONCLUSION

FOR THE FOREGOING REASONS IT IS RESPECTFULLY SUBMITTED THAT THE ORDER OF THE APPELLATE DIVISION BE REVERSED, THE JUDGMENT OF THE SURROGATE'S COURT BE VACATED AND THAT THE MATTER BE REMANDED TO THE SURROGATE'S COURT FOR FURTHER PROCEEDINGS WITH RESPECT TO THE MALPRACTICE AND BREACH OF CONTRACT COUNTERCLAIMS AND THAT THE COURT ORDER SUCH OTHER AND FURTHER RELIEF AS TO THE COURT SEEMS JUST AND PROPER.

Dated: New York, New York
February 19, 2007

Respectfully Submitted,

By: _[signature]_
JEFFREY A. BARR
Attorney for Objectant-Appellant
Marshall Spiegel
225 Broadway, Suite 3504
New York, NY 10007
(212) 227-1834

-10-

7.5 Sample Indictment Filed in a New York State Court

A. Introduction

B. An Indictment

C. Additional Materials

D. More Information

E. Something to Check

A. Introduction

This section presents an example of an indictment filed in a New York State superior court. The complaint involves a murder trial after which the defendant was convicted.

For related sections, see also:

- Section 4.2 (state court system)
- Section 6.4 (timeline of a criminal court case)

B. An Indictment

All felony cases require an indictment and are prosecuted in a superior court (i.e., supreme court or county court). With the rare exception of a sealed indictment, however, the legal process for all crimes begins in local court with a felony complaint, which serves the limited purpose of commencing the criminal process. (Local courts include district courts, city courts, and town courts.) After arraignment and a preliminary hearing (see section 6.4), the local court has no jurisdiction to proceed. At that point, a grand jury indictment is required for the case to proceed to superior court.

Once the grand jury votes an indictment, the superior court obtains jurisdiction to arraign and prosecute the defendant. Below is a sample of an indictment, which includes a summary of facts, with some of the names changed.

C. Additional Materials

Certain actions take place at a felony arraignment. For all criminal prosecutions, the prosecution must state "ready for trial" (orally or in writing) within six months of the commencement of the criminal action (Criminal Procedure Law § 30.30). Further, for some types of evidence (e.g., a confession or lineup identification)

the defendant must receive a notice within 15 days (Criminal Procedure Law § 710.30). The prosecutor can make a demand to be told about any alibi defense, but the demand must be served upon the defendant within 20 days (see Criminal Procedure Law § 250.20). Also served at arraignment are less common items that require notices within a specified time period after arraignment (e.g., notice of intent to use psychiatric evidence, notice of defenses in computer offenses, and notice of intent to seek the death penalty). In addition, for both the prosecution and the defense there are time limits for discovery and motions for which the clock starts at arraignment. Often many pretrial notices are served at arraignment. Prosecutors sometimes will serve a copy of their file on the defense (voluntary discovery), which makes the defendant's discovery demands unnecessary. Exhibit 7.5B is an example of a prosecutor's arraignment notices.

D. More Information

Criminal Justice Process

www.nycourts.gov/litigants/crimjusticesyshandbk.shtml
*www.nassaucountyny.gov/agencies/DA/criminal_justice_*
 process.html
albanycountyda.com/criminal%20justice%20process/
 criminaljusticeprocess

New York Criminal Law Statutes

public.leginfo.state.ny.us/menugetf.cgi?COMMONQUERY=
 LAWS
(click "CPL" for Criminal Procedure Law and "PEN" for Penal Law)

New York Criminal Jury Instructions 2d

www.nycourts.gov/cji

New York Penal Law Overview

wings.buffalo.edu/law/bclc/web/cover.htm

New York Search Warrant Manual

www.courts.state.ny.us/judges/SearchWarrant_Manual.pdf

Crime Time (Sentencing Guide)

www.new-york-arraignments.com/sentencing.htm
crimetime.nypti.org

New York State Attorney General

www.oag.state.ny.us

E. Something to Check

1. In the New York Penal Code (see part D above) quote from any sentence in one of the statutes mentioned in the Fenton indictment.

2. Find online information about paralegals who work in criminal law offices in New York.

EXHIBIT 7.5A | Indictment in a New York State Criminal Case

State of New York
County Court: County of Tompkins

The People of the State of New York

vs.   Indictment

Alexander Fenton   Ind. No. 00-0139
    Defendant

Count 1

The Grand Jury accuses the defendant of **Murder in the Second Degree** in violation of Penal Law 125.24(1), committed as follows:

On or about November 19, 2000, in Tompkins County, the defendant, with intent to cause the death of another person, caused the death of another person.

Count 2

The Grand Jury accuses the defendant of **Murder in the Second Degree** in violation of Penal Law 125.25(2), committed as follows:

On or about November 19, 2000, in Tompkins County, the defendant, under circumstances evincing a depraved indifference to human life, recklessly engaged in conduct creating a grave risk of death to another person, and thereby caused the death of another person.

-1-

EXHIBIT 7.5A

Count 3

The Grand Jury accuses the defendant of **Gang Assault in the First Degree** in violation of Penal Law 120.07, committed as follows:

On or about November 19, 2000, in Tompkins County, the defendant, with intent to cause serious physical injury to another person and while aided by two or more other persons actually present, caused serious physical injury to such person or to a third person.

Count 4

The Grand Jury accuses the defendant of **Assault in the First Degree** in violation of Penal Law 120.10(1), committed as follows:

On or about November 19, 2000, in Tompkins County, the defendant, with intent to cause serious physical injury to another person, caused such injury to another person by means of a deadly weapon or dangerous instrument, to wit, a knife.

Dated: December 15, 2000

James Valmount
Grand Jury Foreperson

George M. Dentes
District Attorney

-2-

EXHIBIT 7.5B

Voluntary Disclosure, CPL 710.30 Notice, Statement of Readiness in a New York State Criminal Case

State of New York

County Court: County of Tompkins

The People of the State of New York §
§
§
vs. §   **People's Voluntary Disclosure, CPL 710.30 Notices, Produce, and Statement of Readiness**
§
§
Alexander Fenton §
Defendant §   Ind. No. 00-0139

STATEMENT OF READINESS

The People are ready for trial in the above captioned matter.

CPL 710.30 NOTICES

Statement Notice: Take notice pursuant to CPL 710.30(1)(a) that the People intend to offer at trial evidence of statements made by defendant to a public servant. A description of the time, place, and substance of the statements is contained in the discovery documents served herewith bearing the following serial numbers: 124–131.

On November 19, 2000, at about 4:46 pm, defendant was interviewed by Investigators Richard Tubbs and Jeffrey Hall at the Tompkins County Sheriff's Department. Defendant admitted to stabbing Mr. Shelton three times with a kitchen knife during the attack in Michelle Cobb's bedroom, and leaving the knife in the sink. See summary of facts below and documents 126–29 for details. The interview was video taped; a copy of the video will be made for the defense if a blank video is provided.

Identification Notice: Take notice pursuant to CPL 710.30(1)(b) that the People intend to offer at trial testimony regarding an observation of defendant upon an occasion relevant to the case, to be given by a witness who has previously identified defendant. A description of the time, place, served herewith bearing the following serial numbers: 132–145.

EXHIBIT 7.5B

SUMMARY OF FACTS

On November 19, 2000, during the early morning hours, defendant was at a party at 15 Patterson Road, Newfield, the residence of Michelle Cobb and Heather Hoffman. Defendant went to the party with several friends from Elmira, including Jamie Myers, Michael Vance (aka Redeye), Robert Ortiz (aka Rex), Jason Hudson (aka JR). Also at the party was Mr. Randy Shelton. Shortly after 5:00am a fight broke out between Mr. Shelton, defendant and his friends. Defendant, together with Myers, Vance, Ortiz and Hudson, cornered Mr. Shelton in a bedroom of the residence and beat him. All five participated together in the attack on Mr. Shelton— physically trapping Shelton in a corner of the bedroom and striking him with their fists. Mr. Shelton was unarmed at the time. During the attack, defendant stabbed Mr. Shelton three times in the left side with a kitchen knife. The blade penetrated Mr. Shelton's heart. Defendant and his accomplices fled the scene.

Michelle Cobb summoned help, and fire and ambulance personnel transported Mr. Shelton to the Cayuga Medical Center. Shelton was flown by helicopter from Cayuga Medical Center to University Hospital, Syracuse, New York, where he died as a result of the stab wounds. In addition to the stab wounds, Mr. Shelton suffered contusions to his face and head as a result of the beating.

Defendant was interviewed by Investigators Richard Tubbs and Jeffrey Hall concerning this incident. Defendant admitted to stabbing Mr. Shelton three times with a kitchen knife. Defendant also stated that after the stabbing he placed the knife in the sink at the residence. Police recovered a black handled kitchen knife from the sink of the residence at 15 Patterson Road, having what appeared to be blood on the blade.

Comprehensive Legal Dictionary

A

AAA American Arbitration Association (*www.adr.org*).

AAfPE See American Association for Paralegal Education (*www.aafpe.org*).

AALS Association of American Law Schools (*www.aals.org*).

a aver et tener To have and to hold. See habendem clause.

ABA American Bar Association (*www.abanet.org*).

abaction Stealing animals, often by driving them off.

abandonee The person to whom something is abandoned or relinquished.

abandonment A total surrender of property, persons, or rights.

> Abandonment, within meaning of statute prohibiting a parent from taking any distributive share of estate of deceased child on ground that parent abandoned the child, is a voluntary breach or neglect of the duty to care for and train a child, and the duty to supervise and guide the child's growth and development. McKinney's EPTL 4-1.4. *In re Estate of Pessoni*, 11 Misc. 3d 245 (Cort. Co. Surr. Ct., 2005)

abatable nuisance A nuisance that can be diminished or eliminated.

abatement 1. Termination or nullification. 2. A suspension of proceedings. 3. A reduction of testamentary legacies because estate assets are insufficient to pay debts and other legacies.

abatement of action A complete ending or quashing of a suit.

abator Someone who abates a nuisance.

abdication A voluntary renunciation of a privilege or office.

abduction The unlawful taking away of someone (e. g., child, wife, ward, servant) by force or trickery.

> Abduct means to restrain a person with intent to prevent his liberation by either (a) secreting or holding him in a place where he is not likely to be found, or (b) using or threatening to use deadly physical force. McKinney's Penal Law § 135.00(2)

abet To encourage or assist another, often in criminal activity.

abettor A person who encourages another to commit a crime.

abeyance Suspension; not finally settled or vested.

ability The power or capacity to perform.

ab initio From the beginning.

abjuration Renunciation under oath, formally giving up rights.

abnormally dangerous Extrahazardous (ultrahazardous) even if reasonable care is used.

abode Dwelling place; residence.

abogado An advocate or lawyer (Spanish).

abolish To eliminate or cancel.

aboriginal Pertaining to inhabitants from earliest times.

abortifacient Causing abortion.

abortion 1. An induced termination of a pregnancy. 2. A miscarriage.

above 1. With a superior status. 2. Earlier or before.

abridge 1. To diminish. 2. To condense or shorten.

abrogate To annul, cancel, or destroy.

abscond To flee in order to avoid arrest or legal process.

absentee landlord A lessor who does not live on the leased premises.

absolute Unconditional; final.

absolute deed A deed that transfers land without encumbrances.

absolute law An immutable law of nature.

absolute liability See strict liability.

absolute nuisance A nuisance for which one is liable without regard to whether it occurred through negligence or other fault.

> Defendant cannot be held strictly liable for the negligence of its tenant on a theory of absolute nuisance because the runoff condition alleged by the plaintiffs does not constitute an unlawful obstruction of the sidewalk. *Placide*, 24 A.D.3d 529 (2nd Dept, 2005)

absolution Release from an obligation or penalty.

absolutism A political system in which one person has total power.

absorption The assimilation of one entity or right into another.

abstain To refrain from; to refuse to use the jurisdiction that a court has.

abstention doctrine If a matter can be tried in federal or state court, a federal court can decline its jurisdiction to avoid unnecessary interference with the state.

abstract A summary or abridgment.

abstraction Taking something, often wrongfully with intent to defraud.

abstract of record Abbreviated history of court proceedings to date.

abstract of title A condensed history or summary of conveyances, interests, and encumbrances that affect title to land.

abuse 1. Improper use. 2. Physical or mental mistreatment.

abuse of discretion A decision that is manifestly unreasonable, depriving someone of a substantive right.

abuse of process A tort consisting of (a) the use of a civil or criminal process, (b) for a purpose for which the process is not designed, (c) resulting in actual damage.

> Abuse of process is simply causing legal process to issue lawfully to accomplish some unjustified purpose, whereas malicious prosecution is maliciously causing process to issue unlawfully. *Pawlicki*, 993 F. Supp. 140 (N.D.N.Y., 1998)

abut To be next to or touch; to share a common border.

abutters Owners of property joined at a common border.

accede 1. To agree. 2. To attain an office.

accelerated depreciation Taking more depreciation deductions during the early years of the life of an asset.

acceleration Causing something to occur sooner, e.g., to pay an obligation, to enjoy a benefit.

acceleration clause A clause in a contract or instrument stating what will trigger an earlier payment schedule.

acceptance 1. Agreement (express or implied) with the terms of an offer. 2. The act of receiving a thing with the intention of retaining it. 3. The commitment to honor a draft or bill of exchange.

> Acceptance is the drawee's signed engagement to honor the draft as presented. It must be written on the draft, and

may consist of his signature alone. It becomes operative when completed by delivery or notification. McKinney's Uniform Commercial Code § 3-410(1).

access Opportunity to enter, visit with, or be intimate with.

access easement See easement of access.

accession 1. An increase through addition. 2. A country's acceptance of a treaty. 3. The right to own what is added to land by improvements or natural growth.

accessory 1. One who, without being present, helps another commit or conceal a crime. 2. A subordinate part.

accessory after the fact One who knows a crime has been committed (although not present at the time) and who helps the offender escape.

accessory before the fact One who assists or encourages another to commit a crime, although not present at the time it is committed.

accident An unexpected misfortune whether or not caused by negligence or other fault.

"Accident," for purposes of receiving accidental disability retirement benefits under the Retirement and Social Security Law, is characterized as a sudden fortuitous mischance, unexpected, out of the ordinary, and injurious in impact; to be considered an accident, it must be deemed that the event precipitating the injury was not a risk of the work performed. *Hamilton,* 28 A.D.3d 965 (3rd Dept., 2006)

accommodated party See accommodation party.

accommodation 1. A favor, e.g., making a loan, acting as a cosigner. 2. An adjustment or settlement. 3. Lodging.

accommodation indorser See accommodation party.

accommodation paper A promissory note or bill of exchange that is cosigned by a person (who does not receive payment or other consideration) in order to help someone else secure credit or a loan. The person signing is the accommodation party.

accommodation party Someone who signs a promissory note or other negotiable instrument in any capacity, e.g., as indorser, without receiving payment or other consideration, in order to act as surety for another party (called the accommodated party).

accomplice A person who participates with another in an offense before, during, or after its commission.

In order for witness to be deemed an "accomplice" as a matter of law for purposes of rule requiring corroboration of accomplice testimony, evidence presented must demonstrate that witness participated in the offense charged or an offense based on the same or some of the same facts or conduct which constitutes the offense charged. McKinney's CPL §§ 60.22, 60.22, subds. 1, 2. *People v. Gjonaj,* 179 A.D.2d 773 (2nd Dept., 2005)

accord 1. An agreement or contract to settle a dispute. 2. An agreement for the future discharge of an existing debt by a substituted performance. Also called executory accord. Once the debt is discharged, the arrangement is called an accord and satisfaction.

accord and satisfaction See accord (2).

account 1. A financial record of debts, credits, transactions, etc. 2. An action or suit to force the defendant to explain his or her handling of a fund in which the plaintiff has an interest. Also called accounting.

"Account," except as used in "account for," means a right to payment of a monetary obligation, whether or not earned by

performance, . . . McKinney's Uniform Commercial Code § 9-102(a)(2)

accountable Responsible; liable.

accountant A person skilled in keeping financial records and accounts.

account debtor The person who has obligations on an account.

accounting 1. A bookkeeping system for recording financial transactions. 2. A settling of an account with a determination of what is owed. 3. See account (2).

accounting period The period of time, e.g., a year, used by a taxpayer for the determination of tax liability.

account payable A regular business debt not yet paid.

account receivable A regular business debt not yet collected.

account stated An agreement on the accuracy of an account, stating the balance due.

accredit 1. To acknowledge or recognize officially. 2. To accept the credentials of a foreign envoy.

accredited investor An investor who is financially sophisticated.

accretion Growth in size by gradual accumulation. An increase of land by natural forces, e.g., soil added to a shore.

"Accretion" is increase of upland by a change so gradual as not to be perceived in any one moment of time. *Trustees of Freeholders,* 84 Misc. 2d 318 (Sup. Ct. Suf. Co., 1975)

accrual basis A method of accounting in which revenues are recorded when earned or due, even though not collected, and expenditures are recorded when liabilities are incurred, whether paid or not.

accrue To come into existence as a right; to vest.

accrued dividend A declared dividend yet to be paid.

accumulated earnings tax A penalty tax on a corporation that retains its earnings beyond the reasonable needs of the business.

accumulation trust A trust in which the trustee must invest trust income rather than pay it out to beneficiaries.

accumulative sentence See consecutive sentences.

accusation A charge that one has committed a crime or other wrong.

accusatory instrument A document charging someone with a crime, e.g., an indictment.

accused The person accused or formally charged with a crime.

ACD See adjournment in contemplation of dismissal.

acknowledgment 1. An affirmation that something is genuine. 2. A formal statement of a person executing an instrument that he or she is doing so as a free act. 3. An acceptance of responsibility.

"Acknowledgment" is verification of fact of execution of an instrument but not of its contents. *Pittis,* 129 N.Y.S.2d 216 (App. Term., 1st Dept., 1954)

acknowledgment of paternity A formal admission by a father that a child is his.

ACLU American Civil Liberties Union (*www.aclu.com*).

acquaintance rape Rape by someone the victim knows.

acquest Property acquired by a means other than inheritance.

acquiesce To consent passively; to comply without protest.

acquire To obtain; to gain ownership of.

acquit 1. To release someone from an obligation. 2. To declare that the accused is innocent of the crime.

acquittal 1. A discharge or release from an obligation. 2. A formal declaration of innocence of a crime.

acquittance A written discharge from an obligation.

ACRS Accelerated cost-recovery system.

act 1. Something done voluntarily; an external manifestation of the will. 2. A law passed by the legislature.

acting Temporarily functioning as or substituting for.

actio A right or claim.

action 1. A civil or criminal court proceeding. 2. Conduct.

actionable Pertaining to that which can become the basis of a lawsuit.

actionable per se Pertaining to words that on their face and without the aid of extrinsic proof are defamatory. They are called actionable words.

actionable words See actionable per se.

action at law An action in a court of law, not in a court of equity.

action on the case An action to recover for damages caused indirectly rather than directly or immediately. Also called trespass on the case.

active trust See special trust.

act of bankruptcy Debtor's conduct that could trigger involuntary bankruptcy.

act of God An unpredictable and unpreventable force of nature.

> By asserting the "act of God defense," the burden falls upon negligence defendants to show that those losses and injuries were occasioned exclusively by natural causes, such as could not be prevented by human care, skill and foresight; if there be any co-operation of man, or any admixture of human means, the injury is not, in a legal sense, the act of God. *Tel Oil Co.*, 303 A.D.2d 868 (3rd Dept., 2003)

act of state doctrine Courts of one country should not judge the validity of an act of another country that occurs within the latter.

actual Real; existing in fact.

actual authority The authority a principal intentionally confers on an agent or permits the agent to believe has been conferred.

actual cash value 1. Fair market value. 2. Replacement cost less depreciation.

actual damages Damages that compensate for an actual or proven loss.

actual fraud See positive fraud.

actual loss Amounts paid or payable as a result of a substantial loss.

actual malice 1. Conscious wrongdoing; intent to injure. Also called malice in fact. 2. Knowledge of the falsity of a defamatory statement or a reckless disregard as to truth or falsity.

actual notice Notice given to a person directly and personally. Also called express notice.

actual value Fair market value.

actuary One skilled in statistics for risk and premium calculations.

actus reus The physical deed or act that is wrongful.

ADA Americans with Disabilities Act (*www.eeoc.gov/ada*).

ad damnum clause A clause stating the damages claimed.

addict A habitual user of something, e.g., a drug.

additur A practice by which a judge offers a defendant the choice between a new trial and accepting a damage award higher than what the jury awarded.

adduce To present or introduce; to offer as evidence or authority.

ADEA Age Discrimination in Employment Act (*www.eeoc.gov/policy/adea.html*).

adeem To take away; to revoke a bequest.

ademption The extinction of a specific bequest or devise because of the disappearance of or disposition of the subject matter from the estate of the testator in his or her lifetime.

> Ademption is the extinction or withholding of a legacy in consequence of some act of the testator, which, though not directly a revocation of bequest, is considered in law as equivalent thereof. *In re Dittrich's Estate*, 853 Misc. 2d 782 (Sur. Ct. Qu. Co., 1967)

adequate compensation See just compensation.

adequate consideration Fair and reasonable consideration under the circumstances of the agreement. See also consideration.

adequate remedy at law A legal remedy, e.g., damages, that is complete, practical, and efficient.

adhesion contract A standard contract offered on a take-it-or-leave-it basis to a consumer who has no meaningful choice as to its terms.

> Adhesion is found where the party seeking to enforce the contract used high pressure tactics or deceptive language in the contract, there is inequality of bargaining power between the parties, and the contract inflicts substantive unfairness on the weaker party. *Matter of Ball*, 236 A.D.2d 158 (3rd Dept., 1997)

ad hoc For this special purpose only.

ad hominem Appealing to emotions or personal matters, not to reason.

ad idem On the same matter.

ad interim Temporarily.

adjacent Lying near or close by; next to.

adjective law Procedural law; rules of practice.

adjoining Touching; contiguous.

adjourn To postpone or suspend until another time.

adjournment Postponing of a session until another time.

adjournment in contemplation of dismissal (ACD) A possible outcome in a criminal case whereby a dismissal is granted to the defendant upon the passage of a set period of time, usually six months, and upon the defendant's compliance with designated conditions.

adjudge To decide judicially.

adjudicate To judge; to resolve a dispute judicially.

adjudication A determination or judgment by a court of law.

adjudicative facts Facts concerning the who, what, when, where, and how pertaining to a particular case.

adjunction Adding or attaching one thing to another.

adjure To request solemnly.

adjust 1. To assess and determine what will be paid under an insurance policy. 2. To set a new payment plan for debts.

adjustable-rate mortgage (ARM) A mortgage with a fluctuating interest rate tied to a market index. Also called variable-rate mortgage (VRM).

adjusted basis The cost or other original basis of an asset reduced by deductions for depreciation and increased by capital improvements.

adjusted gross income (AGI) Gross income less allowable deductions.

adjuster One who determines (or settles) the amount of a claim.

ad litem For the suit; for purposes of this litigation.

administration 1. The persons or entities managing an estate, a government agency, or other organization. 2. The management and settlement of the estate of a decedent. 3. The management and settlement of a bankruptcy estate.

administrative agency See agency (2).

administrative discretion An administrative agency's power to use judgment in choosing among available alternatives.
The Legislature in the enactment of delegative statutes must define the limits of administrative discretion conferred and fix rules or standards to govern its exercise. McKinney's Statutes § 3(d)

administrative law The laws governing and created by administrative agencies.

Administrative law judge (ALJ) A hearing officer within an administrative agency. Also called hearing examiner.

Administrative Procedure Act (APA) A federal or state statute on rulemaking and hearing procedures before administrative agencies.

administrative remedy Relief granted by an administrative agency.

administrator 1. A manager. 2. A person appointed by the court to manage the estate of someone who dies without a will (i.e., intestate) or who dies with a will that does not name a functioning executor.

administrator ad litem An administrator appointed by the court to represent an estate of a decedent in a court proceeding.

administrator cum testamento annexo (cta) See cum testamento annexo.

administrator de bonis non (dbn) See de bonis non.

administratrix A woman who administers the estate of the deceased.

admiralty The law that applies to maritime disputes or offenses involving ships and navigation. Also called maritime law.

admissible Allowed into court to determine its truth or believability.

admission 1. An assertion of the truth of a fact. 2. An official acknowledgement of someone's right to practice law.

admission against interest A statement by a party that is harmful to a position he or she is taking in the litigation.
An admission is a statement of a party made prior to trial which is inconsistent with the position the party is attempting

to establish in the case. Admissions are exceptions to the rule against hearsay and may be introduced against the declarant at trial. *People v. Ballinger*, 176 Misc. 2d 803 (Sup. Ct. Kings Co., 1998)

admit To accept as true or valid.

admonition 1. A reprimand. 2. A warning from a judge to a jury.

adopt To go through a formal process of establishing a relationship of parent and child between persons.

adoptee The person adopted.

ADR See alternative dispute resolution.

ad testificandum To or for testifying.

adult A person who has reached the age of majority (e.g., 21, 18).

adulterate To contaminate by adding something inferior.

adultery Sexual relations between a married person and someone other than his or her spouse.
An act of sodomy alleged to have been committed by husband did not constitute an act of "adultery" entitling wife to divorce. *Cohen*, 200 Misc. 2d 19 (Sup. Ct. N.Y. Co., 1951)

ad valorem tax A tax based on a percentage of the value of property.

advance 1. To lend. 2. To pay or supply something before it is due.

advance directive A statement of one's wishes regarding medical treatment upon becoming incompetent. Also called living will or healthcare proxy.

advancement A gift in advance, usually by a parent to a child. The amount or value of the gift is deducted from what the recipient eventually receives when the giver dies intestate (i.e., without a valid will).

advance sheet A pamphlet that comes out before a later volume of the same set. Most advance sheets contain court opinions, although some contain proposed legislation and enacted laws. (Online advance sheets are sometimes called electronic advance sheets or e-advance sheets.)

adventure A risky business venture, e.g., a shipment of goods at sea.

adversary An opponent.

adversary proceeding 1. A hearing involving opposing parties. 2. Litigation brought within a bankruptcy proceeding based on conflicting claims between a debtor, a creditor, or other interested party.

adversary system A method of resolving a legal dispute whereby the parties argue their conflicting claims before a neutral decision-maker.

adverse Having opposite interests; against.

adverse interest A goal or claim of one person that is different from or opposed to the goal or claim of another.
Under New York law, the adverse interest exception rebuts the usual presumption that the acts and knowledge of an agent acting within the scope of employment are imputed to the principal. Under the exception, management misconduct will not be imputed to the corporation if the officer acted entirely in his own interests and adversely to the interests of the corporation. *Wight*, 219 F. 3d 79 (C.A.2 (N.Y.), 2000)

adverse parties Parties in a suit with conflicting interests.

adverse possession A method of obtaining title to the land of another by using the land under a claim of right in a way that is open, exclusive, hostile to the current owner, and continuous.

adverse witness See hostile witness.

advice 1. An opinion offered as guidance. 2. Notice that a draft has been drawn.

advice and consent The U.S. Senate's approval power on treaties and major presidential appointments. U.S. Const. art. II, § 2.

advisement Careful consideration.

advisory jury A jury whose verdict is not binding on the court.

advisory opinion An opinion of a court that is not binding.

advocacy Arguing for or against something; pleading.

advocate One who argues or pleads for another.

AFDC See Aid to Families with Dependent Children.

aff'd Affirmed.

affect To act on (upon); to influence.

affected class 1. Persons who suffered job discrimination. 2. Persons who constitute a class for bringing a class action.

affecting commerce Involving commerce or trade.

aff'g Affirming.

affiant Someone who makes an affidavit.

affidavit A written or printed statement of facts made under oath before a person with authority to administer the oath.

affidavit of service A sworn statement that a document (e.g., summons) has been delivered (served) to a designated person.

affiliate A subsidiary; one corporation controlled by another.

affiliation order An order determining paternity.

affinity Relationship by marriage, not by blood.

> Relationship by affinity is based upon marriage, and has to do with the relationship one spouse has to the blood or adopted relatives of the other spouse. McKinney's Family Court Act § 812(1)(a). *Anstey*, 23 A.D.3d 780 (3rd Dept., 2005)

affirm 1. To declare that a judgment is valid. 2. To assert formally, but not under oath. The noun is *affirmance*.

affirmance See affirm.

affirmation A solemn declaration, often a substitute for an oath.

affirmative action Steps designed to eliminate existing and continuing discrimination, to remedy the effects of past discrimination, and to create systems to prevent future discrimination.

affirmative charge An instruction that removes an issue from the jury.

affirmative defense A defense raising new facts that will defeat the plaintiff's claim even if the plaintiff's fact allegations are proven.

affirmative easement An easement that forces the landowner to allow the easement holder to do specific acts on the land.

> In case of affirmative easement under New York law, the owner of the dominant tenement—easement holder—acquires or is granted a right to use another person's land in a particular, though limited, way; the grant carries with it those rights

necessary to effectuate the easement's exercise and enjoyment. *Sutera*, 86 F. 3d 298 (C.A.2 (N.Y.), 1996)

affirmative relief Relief (e.g., damages) a defendant could have sought in his or her own suit, but instead is sought in a counterclaim or cross-claim.

affirmative warranty An insurance warranty that asserts the existence of a fact at the time the policy is entered into.

affix To attach; to add to permanently.

affray Fighting in a public place so as to cause terror to the public.

affreightment A contract to transport goods by ship.

aforementioned See aforesaid.

aforesaid Mentioned earlier in the document.

aforethought Thought of beforehand; premeditated.

a fortiori With greater force; all the more so.

after-acquired property Property acquired after a particular event, e.g., after making a will, after giving a security interest.

after-acquired title rule When a seller does not obtain title to an asset until after attempting to sell it, title automatically vests in the buyer the moment the seller obtained it.

after-born child A child born after the execution of a will.

age discrimination Discrimination on the basis of one's age.

agency 1. A relationship in which one person acts for and can bind another. 2. A governmental body, other than a court or legislature, that carries out the law.

> Public Officers Law § 86(3) defines "agency" as "any state or municipal department, board, bureau, division, commission, committee, public authority, public corporation, council, office or other governmental entity performing a governmental or proprietary function for the state or any one or more municipalities thereof, except the judiciary or the state legislature." *Ervin*, 26 A.D.3d 633 (3rd Dept., 2006)

agency shop A business or other entity that collects union dues from all employees, even those who decided not to join the union.

agent 1. A person authorized to act for another. 2. A power or force that produces an effect.

age of consent The age at which one can marry without parental consent or have sexual intercourse without the partner committing statutory rape.

age of majority The age at which a person has the right to vote, enter a contract that cannot be disaffirmed, make a will, etc. Also called full age.

age of reason The age at which a child is deemed capable of making reasoned judgments and, therefore, can commit a crime or tort.

aggravated assault The crime of assault committed with the intent to cause serious bodily harm or other circumstances that make the crime more serious than simple assault.

aggravation Circumstances that increase the enormity of a crime or tort, e.g., using a weapon.

> Family Court Act § 827(a)(vii) defines "aggravating circumstances" as physical injury or serious physical injury to the petitioner caused by the respondent, the use of a dangerous instrument against the petitioner by the respondent, a history or repeated violations of prior orders of petitioner by the respondent, . . . *Swersky*, 93 Misc. 2d 730 (Sup. Ct. Nas. Co., 2001)

aggregate Combined into a whole.

aggregation The unpatentability of an invention because its parts lack a composite integrated mechanism.

aggregation doctrine To reach the jurisdictional amount in a federal diversity case, the total of all the claims cannot be added.

aggrieved party One whose legal rights have been invaded.

AGI See adjusted gross income.

agio Money paid to convert one kind of money into another.

agreed case Facts agreed upon by the parties, allowing a court to limit itself to deciding the questions of law on those facts. Also called case agreed, case stated.

agreement Mutual assent by the parties; a meeting of the minds.

aid and abet Assist or encourage someone to commit a crime.

aider by verdict A jury verdict cures technical pleading defects.

Aid to Families with Dependent Children (AFDC) Federal public assistance replaced by TANF (Temporary Assistance for Needy Families).

airbill A bill of lading used in a shipment of goods by air.

air rights The right of a landowner to use all or part of the airspace above his or her land.

> "Air rights" conveyed with condominium units were "real property" but were taxable by county's taxing authority as "buildings" rather than at higher rate for "land" . . . 53 P.S. §§ 25891, 25894; 68 P.S. §§ 801–803; 68 Pa.C.S.A. §§ 3101–3414. *Appeal of Bigman*, 533 A. 2d 778 (Pa.Cmwlth., 1987)

air piracy Using force or threats to seize or hijack an aircraft.

aka Also known as.

alderman A member of the local legislative body.

aleatory Depending on uncertain circumstances or contingencies.

aleatory contract A contract in which performance depends on uncertain events, e.g., an insurance contract.

ALI See American Law Institute (*www.ali.org*).

Alford **plea** A defendant's plea-bargained guilty plea that does not actually admit guilt. *North Carolina v. Alford*, 91 S. Ct. 160 (1970).

alias Otherwise known as; an assumed name.

alias summons; alias writ A new summons or writ given when the original one was issued without effect.

alibi A defense alleging absence from the scene of the crime.

alien One who is not a citizen of the country where he or she resides.

alienable Legally transferable to the ownership of another.

alienage The condition or status of an alien.

alienate To transfer; to transfer title.

alienation clause A clause in an insurance policy that voids the policy if the property being insured is sold or transferred.

alienation of affections The tort of causing a diminishment of the marital relationship between the plaintiff and his or her spouse.

The rights of action to recover sums of money as damages for alienation of affections, criminal conversation, seduction, or breach of contract to marry are abolished. *Gubbins*, 148 Misc. 2d 47 (Sup. Ct. Nas. Co., 1990)

alienee A person to whom property is conveyed or transferred.

alieni juris Under another's power.

alienor A person who transfers or conveys property.

alimony A court-ordered payment of money or other property by one spouse to another for support after divorce or separation. In New York and other states, alimony has been replaced by spousal support.

alimony in gross Alimony in the form of a single definite sum that cannot be modified. Also called lump-sum alimony.

alimony pendente lite See temporary alimony.

aliquot An exact division or fractional part.

aliunde rule Jury deliberations may not be scrutinized, unless there is evidence from a source other than a juror to impeach the jury verdict.

ALJ See administrative law judge.

allegation A statement of fact that one expects to prove.

alleged Asserted as true, but not yet proven.

allegiance Loyalty owed to a government, a cause, or a person.

Allen charge A supplementary instruction given to a deadlocked jury to encourage it to reach a verdict. Also called dynamite charge. *Allen v. U.S.*, 17 S. Ct. 154 (1896).

all faults A sale of goods "as is," in their present condition.

> [U]nless the circumstances indicate otherwise, all implied warranties are excluded by expressions like "as is," "with all faults" or other language. Unif. Commercial Code § 2-316(3)(a)

all fours See on all fours.

allocation A setting aside or designation for a purpose.

allocatur It is allowed. In Pennsylvania, the permission to appeal.

allocution 1. The inquiry made prior to sentencing by a judge who asks a defendant if he or she has anything to say before sentence is imposed. In New York, the in-court colloquy between the judge and defendant when the defendant enters a guilty plea to a crime. 2. The defendant's right to make such a statement.

allodial Owned absolutely, free and clear.

allograph A writing or signature made by one person for another.

allonge A slip of paper attached to a negotiable instrument to provide space for more indorsements.

allotment A share, e.g., the land awarded to an individual American Indian; a portion of one's pay deducted to meet an obligation such as child support.

allotment certificate A document stating the number of shares of a security to be purchased, payment terms, etc.

allowance 1. Portion assigned or bestowed. 2. Deduction or discount.

alluvion The washing up of sand or soil so as to form firm ground.

alteration Making something different, e.g., modifying real property, changing the language or meaning of a document.

alter ego rule Personal liability can be imposed on shareholders who use the corporation for personal business.

The alter ego theory permits an individual, who is not a party to a corporation's contract, to be held personally liable for its breach, if that individual, by disregarding the corporate form, exercised such dominion and control over the corporation's operations that the corporation became his alter ego, and a vehicle for his personal rather than corporate ends. *Lupien*, 5 Misc. 3d 1025(A) (Sup. Ct. West. Co., 2004)

alternate valuation The value of assets six months after death.

alternative contract A contract that gives options for performance.

alternative dispute resolution (ADR) Arbitration, mediation, and similar methods of resolving a dispute without litigation.

alternative minimum tax (AMT) A tax imposed to ensure that enough income tax is paid by persons with large deductions, credits, or exclusions.

alternative pleading Alleging facts or claims in a complaint or other pleading that are not necessarily consistent.

alternative relief Inconsistent relief sought on the same claim.

alternative writ A writ requiring a person to do a specified thing or to show cause why he or she should not be compelled to do it.

amalgamation Consolidation, e.g., two corporations into a new one.

ambassador An officer of high diplomatic rank representing a country.

ambit Boundary; the limits of a power.

ambulance chasing Soliciting injury victims by or for an attorney.

This is a classic case of ambulance chasing which originated with blatant in-person solicitation by the attorney. *Matter of Koffler*, 70 A.D.2d 252 (2nd Dept., 1979)

ambulatory 1. Revocable. 2. Able to walk.

ameliorating waste Waste by a tenant that in fact improves the land.

amenable 1. Legally accountable or answerable; subject to answer to the law. 2. Submissive.

amendment A formal change (e.g., addition, subtraction, correction) made in the text of a document (e.g., statute, legislative bill, pleading, contract).

amercement A fine or punishment imposed (e.g., on a public official) at the court's discretion.

American Law Institute (ALI) An organization of scholars that writes model acts and restatements of the law (*www.ali.org*).

American Association for Paralegal Education (AAfPE) A national association of paralegal schools (*www.aafpe.org*).

American Bar Association (ABA) A national voluntary association of attorneys (*www.abanet.org*).

American rule Each side in litigation pays its own attorney fees and court costs unless a statute provides otherwise. Under the English rule, also called loser-pays, the losing party may be required to pay the attorney fees and court costs incurred by the winning side.

The American Rule provides that attorney fees are incidents of litigation and a prevailing party may not collect them from the loser unless an award is authorized by agreement between the parties, statute or court rule. *Green Harbour*, 307 A.D.2d 465 (3rd Dept., 2003)

Americans with Disabilities Act (ADA) A federal statute that prohibits discrimination against persons with disabilities in employment and other public services. 42 USC § 12101

amicable action An action brought by mutual consent of the parties to seek a ruling on facts they do not dispute.

amicus curiae Friend of the court. A nonparty who obtains court permission to file a brief with its views on the case.

amnesty A pardon for crimes, often granted to a group.

amortization 1. The gradual elimination of a debt, often by making regular payments toward principal along with interest payments. 2. Writing off the cost of an intangible asset over its useful life.

amotion Removing or turning someone out.

amount in controversy The amount sued for. The amount needed (over $75,000) to establish diversity jurisdiction in federal court. Also called jurisdictional amount (28 U.S.C. 1332(a)).

analogous 1. Sufficiently similar to lend support. 2. Involving facts and rules that are similar to those now under consideration.

anarchist One who believes government should not exist.

anarchy The absence of political authority or order.

ancestor A person from whom one is descended; a forebear.

ancient documents Deeds and other writings 20 or more years old (states may impose different age spans) that are presumed to be genuine if kept in proper custody.

To be admissible as a so called ancient document it must be a recorded survey for more than 10 years, under CPLR 4522. *Greenberg*, 43 A.D.2d 968 (2nd Dept., 1974)

ancient lights rule Windows with outside light for a period of time (e.g., 20 years) cannot be blocked off by an adjoining landowner.

ancillary Supplementary; subsidiary.

ancillary administration An administrator appointed by the court for property or the decedent located in a different jurisdiction.

ancillary jurisdiction Authority of a court to hear claims that otherwise would not be within its jurisdiction if these claims are sufficiently related to the case properly before the court.

and his heirs Words that give a transferee a fee simple absolute.

animo With the intention.

animus 1. Intention, e.g., animus furandi (intent to steal), animus testandi (intent to make a will). 2. Animosity; ill will.

annexation 1. Merging or attaching one thing to another. 2. The formal takeover or appropriation of something (e.g., territory).

annotated statutes A collection of statutes that include research references such as case summaries interpreting the statutes.

annotation A remark or note on a law, e.g., a summary of a case.

annual exclusion The amount one can give away each year gift-tax free.

annual percentage rate (APR) The true cost of borrowing money expressed as an annual interest rate.

annual report A corporation's annual financial report to stockholders.

annuitant A beneficiary of an annuity.

annuity A fixed sum payable periodically to a person for life or a specific period of time.

> An annuity differs from an ordinary trust, whether the payments are to be made out of income and/or corpus, since the annuitant is deemed to have a vested right to payment of the stipulated amounts out of income as well as the corpus. *In re Clark's Will*, 54 Misc. 2d 1015 (Sur. Ct. Kings Co., 1967)

annuity certain An annuity that continues paying for a set period even if the annuitant dies within the period.

annuity due An annuity payable at the start of each pay period.

annul To obliterate or nullify.

annulment 1. A nullification or voiding. 2. A declaration that a valid marriage never existed or that an attempted marriage is invalid.

answer 1. The first pleading of the defendant that responds to the plaintiff's claims. 2. To assume someone else's liability.

ante Before; prior to.

ante litem motam Before the suit began or arose.

antecedent Preexisting.

antecedent debt A debt that preexists an event, e.g., filing for bankruptcy. A prior debt may be consideration for a new promise to pay.

antedate 1. To backdate; to place a date on a document that is earlier than the date the document was written. 2. To precede.

antenuptial Occurring before marriage. See premarital agreement.

antichresis An agreement giving the creditor the income from and possession of the property pledged, instead of interest.

anticipation 1. Doing something before its scheduled time. 2. Prior disclosure or use of an invention, jeopardizing its patentability.

anticipatory breach A repudiation of a contract duty before the time fixed in the contract for the performance of that duty.

> The concept of anticipatory breach entitles a plaintiff to sue for breach of contract when the other party makes a definite and final communication of the intention to forego performance. *Salvato*, 307 A.D.2d 812 (1st Dept., 2003)

anticipatory search warrant A search warrant usable only on a future date, not upon issuance.

antidumping law A law against selling imported goods at less than their fair price if the imports hurt comparable domestic products.

antilapse A gift in a will goes to the heirs of the beneficiary to prevent the gift from failing because the beneficiary predeceases the testator.

antinomy A contradiction between two laws or propositions.

anti-racketeering See RICO.

antitrust law Laws against price fixing, monopolies, and other anticompetitive practices and restraints of trade.

APA See Administrative Procedure Act.

apostille A certificate authenticating foreign documents.

apparent 1. Capable of being seen; visible. 2. Seeming.

apparent authority An agent's authority that the principal reasonably leads another to believe the agent has. Also called ostensible authority.

> Essential to the creation of apparent authority are words or conduct of the principal, communicated to a third party, that give rise to the appearance and belief that the agent possesses authority to enter into a transaction. *Clark*, 306 A.D.2d 82 (1st Dept., 2003)

apparent defects Defects observable upon reasonable inspection. Also called patent defects.

apparent heir An heir who will inherit unless he or she predeceases the ancestor or is disinherited by will. Also called heir apparent.

app. Appellate; appeal.

appeal Asking a higher tribunal to review or reconsider the decision of an inferior tribunal.

appealable Sufficiently final so that it can be appealed.

appeal bond A bond of a party filing an appeal to cover the opponent's costs if the appeal is later deemed to have been not genuine.

appearance Formally coming before a tribunal as a party or as a representative of a party.

> Making a change of venue motion by the defendant in a defamation action did not constitute an appearance so as to waive defense of lack of personal jurisdiction. McKinney's CPLR 302(a), par. 1, 320(a), 511. *Montgomery*, 263 A.D.2d 636 (3rd Dept., 1999)

appellant The person or party who brings the appeal.

appellate Concerning appeals or an appellate court.

appellate brief See brief (1).

appellate jurisdiction The power of an appellate court to review and correct the decisions of a lower tribunal.

appellee The person against whom an appeal is brought. Respondent.

append To attach.

appoint To give someone a power or authority.

appointee The person selected.

apportionment 1. A proportional division. 2. The process of allocating legislators among several political subdivisions.

> Contribution or apportionment involves a determination of relative responsibility in which respective fault of two or more defendants is determined by reviewing the contribution of each to the damage sustained and, once the tort-feasors' relative responsibilities are determined, each pays his ratable portion of the total damages. *Smith*, 83 A.D.2d 199 (4th Dept., 1981)

appraisal Estimation of value or worth.

appraisal remedy A shareholder's right to have its shares bought back by the corporation due to dissent with an extraordinary corporate decision.

appraiser Someone who impartially evaluates (appraises) property.

appreciation Increase in property value, often due to inflation.

apprehension 1. Knowledge. 2. Fear. 3. Seizure or arrest.

appropriation 1. Taking control or possession. 2. An invasion-of-privacy tort committed by the use of a person's name, likeness, or personality for commercial gain without authorization. 3. The legislature's setting aside of money for a specific purpose.

approval sale See sale on approval.

appurtenance A thing or right belonging or attached to something else.

appurtenant Belonging to; incident to the principal property.

appurtenant easement See easement appurtenant.

APR See annual percentage rate.

a priori Deductively; derived from logic or self-evident propositions, without reference to observed experience.

arbiter A referee or judge, someone who can resolve a dispute.

arbitrage Simultaneous matched purchase and sale of identical or equivalent securities in order to profit from price discrepancies.

arbitrament 1. The decision of an arbitrator. 2. The act of deciding.

arbitrary Capricious, subjective. Biased on individual preferences.

> Arbitrary action is without sound basis in reason and is generally taken without regard to facts. *O'Brien*, 24 A.D.3d 9 (2nd Dept., 2005)

arbitration A method of alternative dispute resolution (ADR) in which the parties submit their dispute to an impartial third person (the arbitrator) who renders a decision that can resolve the dispute without litigation. The decision is either nonbinding or, usually upon prior agreement of the parties, binding.

arbitration clause A contract clause providing for compulsory arbitration of disputes under the contract.

arbitrator The person rendering the decision in arbitration.

arguendo In arguing; for the sake of argument.

argument A presentation of reasons for a legal position.

argumentative Containing conclusions as well as facts; contentious.

arise 1. To stem from or originate. 2. To come into notice.

aristocracy A government ruled by a superior or privileged class.

ARM See adjustable-rate mortgage.

armed robbery Robbery committed while armed with a dangerous weapon.

arm's length As between two strangers who are looking out for their own self-interests.

> [An] arm's length transaction means a sale . . . in good faith and for valuable consideration, that reflects the fair market value of such real property or lease, or business, in the open market, between two informed and willing parties, where neither is under any compulsion to participate in the transaction . . . . McKinney's Tax Law § 480-a(1)(e)

arraignment A court proceeding in which the accused is formally charged with a crime and enters a plea of guilty, not guilty, etc. The verb is *arraign*.

arrangement with creditors A plan whereby the debtor settles with his or her creditors or obtains more time to repay debts.

array A group of persons summoned to be considered for jury duty.

arrearages, arrears Unpaid debts; overdue debts.

arrest Taking someone into custody to answer a criminal charge.

arrest of judgment A court's staying of a judgment because of errors.

arrest record 1. A form filled out when the police arrest someone. 2. A list of a person's prior arrests.

arrest warrant A written order of a judge or magistrate that a person be arrested and brought before the court.

arrogation Claiming or seizing something without authority or right.

arson The willful and malicious burning of property.

> A person is guilty of arson in the first degree when he intentionally damages a building or motor vehicle by causing an explosion or a fire and when . . . . McKinney's Penal Law § 150.20(1)

art 1. Applying knowledge and skill to produce a desired result. 2. A process or method to produce a useful result. 3. See terms of art.

art. Article.

artful pleading An attempt to phrase a federal claim as a state claim.

article A part or subdivision of a law or document.

Article I court A federal court created by legislation. Also called legislative courts.

Article III court A federal court created by the United States Constitution in article III. Also called constitutional court.

articled clerk In England, one apprenticed to a solicitor.

Articles of Confederation The governing document for the 13 original states.

articles of dissolution A document filed with the secretary of state or other state official that pertains to the dissolving of a corporation or other business entity. It must state that the debts of the entity have been settled.

articles of impeachment Formal accusations against a public official asserted as grounds for removing him or her from office.

articles of incorporation The document that establishes (incorporates) a corporation and identifies its basic functions and rules.

artifice Contrivance, trick, or fraud.

artificial person A legal person. An entity, such as a corporation, created under the laws of the state and treated in some respects as a human being. Also called fictitious person, juristic person.

artisan's lien See mechanic's lien.

ascendant An ancestor, e.g., grandparent.

as is In its present condition; no warranty given.

asportation Carrying away for purposes of larceny.

assailant One who attacks or assaults another.

assault 1. As a tort, assault is an act intended to cause harmful or offensive contact with another or an imminent apprehension of such contact and the other is thereby placed in such imminent apprehension. 2. As a crime, assault may require an intent to cause physical harm and actual contact with the victim.

A person is guilty of assault in the third degree when: 1. With intent to cause physical injury to another person, he causes such injury to such person or to a third person; or 2. He recklessly causes physical injury to another person; or 3. With criminal negligence, he causes physical injury to another person by means of a deadly weapon or a dangerous instrument. McKinney's Penal Law § 120.00

assault and battery The crime of battery. See battery.

assay An examination to test the quality and quantity of metals.

assembly 1. A gathering of people for a common goal. 2. One of the houses of the legislature in many states.

assent Agreement, approval.

assert To declare; to state as true.

assessable stock Stock that subjects the holder to an additional assessment or contribution.

assessment 1. A determination of the value of something, often for purposes of taxation. 2. A determination of the share that is due from someone; an amount assessed. 3. The requirement of an additional payment to a business.

assessed ratio The ratio of assessed value to fair market value.

assessment work Labor on a mining claim each year to maintain the claim.

assessor A technical expert or adviser, e.g., on making assessments.

asset Anything of value; tangible or intangible property.

asset depreciation range IRS's range of depreciable lives of assets.

asseveration A solemn declaration.

assign 1. To transfer or convey property or rights. 2. To point out or specify, e.g., errors. 3. See assigns.

assigned counsel A court-appointed attorney for a poor person.

Counsel is often indispensable to a practical realization of due process of law. . . . The purpose of this part is to provide a means for implementing the right to assigned counsel for indigent persons in proceedings under this act. McKinney's Family Court Act § 261

assigned risk A person an insurance company is required to insure.

assignee The person to whom property or rights are transferred.

assignment The transfer of ownership or rights.

assignment for benefit of creditors A transfer of the debtor's property to a trustee, with authority to liquidate the debtor's affairs and distribute the proceeds equitably to creditors.

assignment of errors A party's list of errors claimed to have been made by a trial court submitted to an appellate court on appeal.

assignor The person who transfers property or rights.

assigns Assignees; persons to whom property or rights are transferred.

assise; assize An old English court, law, or writ.

assistance of counsel See effective assistance of counsel.

associate An attorney employee who hopes one day to be promoted to partner.

associate justice An appellate court judge who is not the chief justice.

association 1. An organization of people joined for a common purpose. 2. An unincorporated company or other organization.

assume 1. To take upon oneself. 2. To suppose without proof.

assumpsit 1. A promise. 2. An action for breach of contract.

assumption 1. The act of taking something upon oneself. 2. Something taken for granted without proof.

assumption of mortgage A property buyer's agreement to be personally liable for payment of an already existing mortgage.

assumption of the risk The knowing and voluntary acceptance of the risk of being harmed by someone's negligence or other conduct.

Under the assumption of the risk doctrine, by engaging in a sport or recreational activity, the participant consents to those commonly appreciated risks which are inherent in and arise out of the nature of the sport generally and flow from such participation. *Sauray*, 690 N.Y.S.2d 716 (N.Y.A.D. 2 Dept., 1999)

assurance 1. A statement tending to inspire confidence. 2. Insurance. 3. A pledge or guarantee. 4. The act (and the document) that conveys real property.

assured A person who has been insured.

asylum 1. A sanctuary or hiding place. 2. A government's protection given to a political refugee from another country. Also called political asylum.

at bar Currently before the court.

at issue In dispute.

at large 1. Free. 2. An entire area rather than one of its districts.

at law Pertaining to a court of law as opposed to a court of equity.

at risk Pertaining to an investment that could lead to actual loss.

attaché A person in a diplomatic office with a specific specialty.

attachment The act or process of taking, apprehending, or seizing persons or property, by virtue of writ, summons, or other judicial order, and bringing same into custody of the law.

Attachment is a provisional remedy designed to secure a debt by a preliminary levy upon property of the debtor to conserve it for eventual execution. McKinney's CPLR 6201, subd. 3. *Michaels Elec.*, 231 A.D.2d 695 (2nd Dept., 1996)

attachment bond A bond given by one whose property has been attached in order to reclaim it and provide protection to the party who attached it.

attainder The loss of civil rights upon receiving a death sentence or being designated as an outlaw.

attaint 1. To disgrace or condemn to attainder. 2. To accuse a jury of giving a false verdict.

attempt An overt act or conduct (beyond mere preparation) performed with the intent to commit a crime that was not completed.

attendant circumstances Relevant facts surrounding an event.

attenuation Illegally obtained evidence might be admissible if the link between the illegal conduct and the evidence is so attenuated as to dissipate the taint.

attest To affirm to be true or genuine; to bear witness.

attestation clause A clause stating that you saw (witnessed) someone sign a document or perform other tasks related to the validity of the document.

attorn 1. To transfer something to another. 2. To acknowledge being the tenant of a new landlord.

attorney 1. One licensed to practice law. A lawyer. Also called attorney at law. 2. One authorized to act in place of or for another. Also called attorney-in-fact.

attorney at law See attorney (1).

attorney-client privilege A client and an attorney can refuse to disclose communications between them if their purpose was to facilitate the provision of legal services to the client.

The attorney-client privilege requires a confidential communication between client and attorney, in the course of a professional relationship, for the purpose of seeking or providing legal advice or assistance; and the communication itself must have been primarily or predominantly of a legal character. *Aetna Cas. and Sur. Co.*, 176 Misc. 2d 605 (Sup. Ct. N.Y. Co., 1998)

attorney general The chief attorney for the government.

attorney-in-fact See attorney (2).

attorney of record The attorney noted in the court files as the attorney representing a particular party.

attorney's lien The right of an attorney to retain possession of money or property of a client until his or her proper fees have been paid.

attorney work product See work product rule.

attornment See attorn.

attractive nuisance doctrine A duty of reasonable care is owed to prevent injury to a trespassing child unable to appreciate the danger from an artificial condition or activity on land to which the child can be expected to be attracted. Also called turntable doctrine.

attribution Assigning one taxpayer's ownership interest to another.

at-will employee An employee with no contract protection. An employee who can quit or be terminated at any time and for any reason.

Employment at will doctrine is a judicially created rule that where employment is for indefinite term it is presumed to be a hiring at will which may be freely terminated by either party at any time for any reason or even for no reason. *Starishevsky*, 161 Misc. 2d 137 (Sup. Ct. Suf. Co., 1994)

auction A public sale of assets to the highest bidder.

audit An examination of records to verify financial or other data.

auditor Someone who performs audits, often an accountant.

augmented estate A decedent's estate with adjustments keyed to the length of marriage and gifts decedent made shortly before death.

authentication Evidence that a writing or other physical item is genuine and is what it purports to be.

An official publication, or a copy attested as correct by an officer or a deputy of an officer having legal custody of an official record of the United States or of any state, territory or jurisdiction of the United States, or of any of its courts, legislature, offices, public bodies or boards is prima facie evidence of such record. McKinney's CPLR Rule 4540(a)

author An originator of a work in various media (e.g., print, film) plus other participants with copyright protection, e.g., translators.

authority 1. The power or right to act. 2. A source relied upon.

authorize To give power or permission; to approve.

authorized stock See capital stock (1).

automobile guest statute See guest statute.

autopsy An examination of a cadaver to identify the cause of death. Also called postmortem.

autoptic evidence See demonstrative evidence.

autrefois acquit A plea that one has already been acquitted of the offense.

autre vie Another's life.

aver To assert or allege.

average 1. Usual, ordinary, norm. 2. Mean, median. 3. Partial loss or damage.

averment A positive allegation or assertion of fact.

avoid 1. To annul or cancel. 2. To escape.

avoidable consequences See mitigation-of-damages rule.

avoidance Escaping; invalidating. See also confession and avoidance.

avowal 1. An offer to prove. 2. An acknowledgment.

avulsion The sudden loss or addition to land caused by flood or by a shift in the bed or course of a stream.

Land lost by avulsion, which is the sudden or violent action of the elements perceptible while in progress, does not cause a change of boundaries. *In re City of Buffalo*, 206 NY 319 (1912)

award What a court or other tribunal gives or grants via its decision.

axiom An established or self-evident principle.

AWOL Absent without leave or permission. See also desertion.

B

baby act A minor's defense of infancy in a breach of contract action.

BAC See blood alcohol concentration.

bachelor of laws See LL.B.

back To assume financial responsibility for; to indorse.

bad 1. Defective. 2. Void or invalid.

bad check A check dishonored for insufficient funds.

bad debt An uncollectible debt.

bad faith 1. Dishonest purpose. Also called mala fides. 2. The absence of a reasonable basis to delay or deny an insurance claim.

Principles relevant to assessment of bad-faith claim were adequately conveyed by instruction informing jury that in order to find "bad faith" by automobile insurer in failing to settle personal injury claim within policy limits, jury had to conclude that insurer acted intentionally and in gross disregard of insureds' interest and that there was deliberate or reckless decision to disregard insureds' interest in pursuing insurer's litigation strategy. *Pavia*, 589 N.Y.S.2d 510 (N.Y.A.D. 2 Dept., 1992)

badge of fraud Factors from which an inference of fraud can be drawn.

bad law 1. A court opinion that fails to follow precedent or statutes. 2. A court opinion whose broader implications are unfortunate even though probably accurate for the narrow facts before the court.

bad title Title that is so defective as to be unmarketable.

bail 1. Money or other property deposited with the court as security to ensure that the defendant will reappear at designated times. Failure to appear forfeits the security. 2. Release of the defendant upon posting this security. 3. The one providing this security.

bailable offense An offense for which an accused is eligible for bail.

bail bond A surety contract under which the surety will pay the state the amount of the bond if the accused fails to appear in court.

bailee One to whom property is entrusted under a contract of bailment.

bailiff A court officer with duties in court, e.g., keep order.

bail jumping See jump bail.

bailment A delivery of personal property by one person to another under an express or implied contract whereby the property will be redelivered when the purpose of the contract is completed.

A bailment is the delivery of personal property for a particular purpose on express or implied contract with the understanding that it shall be re-delivered to the person leaving it or kept until he reclaims it after fulfillment of the purpose for which it was delivered. *Lash*, 143 N.Y.S.2d 516 (Sup. Ct., 1955)

bailment for hire A bailment under which the bailee is paid.

bailor One who delivers property to another under a contract of bailment.

bailout 1. Financial help to one in need of rescue. 2. Seeking alternative tax treatment of income.

bait and switch Using a low-priced item to lure a customer to a merchant who then pressures the customer to buy another item at a higher price.

Both the Penal Law provision pertaining to false advertising and the General Business Law provision giving the Attorney General the right to seek a civil injunction against false advertising proscribe the sale promotional practice known as "bait and switch advertising," "bait advertising" or "fictitious bargain claims." Penal Law § 190.20; General Business Law § 396. *People v. Block & Kleaver*, 427 N.Y.S.2d 133 (Co. Ct., 1980)

balance 1. To calculate the difference between what has been paid and what is due. 2. To check to ensure that debits and credits are equal. 3. The equality of debits and credits. 4. See balancing test.

balance sheet A dated statement showing assets, liabilities, and owners' investment.

balancing test Weighing competing interests or values in order to resolve a legal issue.

balloon note A note on a loan calling for a large final payment and smaller intervening periodic payments.

balloon payment The final payment on a balloon note that is much larger than prior periodic payments that are smaller.

ballot A paper or other media on which to vote; a list of candidates.

ban 1. To prohibit. 2. An announcement.

banc Bench. See also en banc.

banish See exile.

bank A financial institution that receives money on deposit, exchanges money, makes loans, and performs similar functions.

bank bill See bank note.

bank credit Money a bank allows a customer to borrow.

bank draft A check that one bank writes on its account with another bank.

banker's lien The right of a bank to seize property of a depositor in the bank's possession to satisfy a customer's debt to the bank.

Banker's lien: a right of offset against the bank account. *Goldsmith*, 97 N.Y.S.2d 597 (1 Dept. 1950)

bank note A promissory note issued by a bank payable to bearer on demand and usable as cash. Also called bank bill.

bankrupt 1. Unable to pay debts as they are due. 2. A debtor undergoing a bankruptcy proceeding.

bankruptcy 1. The federal process by which a bankruptcy court gives a debtor relief by liquidating some or all of the unsecured debts or by otherwise rearranging debts and payment schedules. 2. Insolvency.

bankruptcy estate Assets of a debtor when bankruptcy is filed.

bankruptcy trustee See trustee in bankruptcy.

bar 1. The court or court system. 2. The courtroom partition behind which spectators sit. 3. All the attorneys licensed to practice in a jurisdiction. 4. The examination taken by attorneys to become licensed to practice law. 5. An impediment or barrier to bringing or doing something.

bar association An association of members of the legal profession.

bar examination See bar (4).

bare licensee One who enters the land for his or her own purposes, but with the express or implied consent of the occupier. Also called naked licensee.

A 15½ year old boy playing in railroad freight yard was not "invitee" but was at most a "bare licensee" to whom railroad company owed only duty to maintain no hidden engine of destruction and to abstain from inflicting intentional, wanton or willful injuries. *Rand*, 95 N.Y.S.2d 688 (Sup. Ct., 1950)

bareboat charter A document under which one who charters or leases a boat becomes for the period of the charter the owner for all practical purposes. Also called demise charter.

bargain 1. To negotiate the terms of a contract. 2. An agreement establishing the obligations of the parties.

bargain and sale deed A deed of conveyance without covenants.

bargaining agent A union bargaining on behalf of its members.

bargaining unit A group of employees allowed to conduct collective bargaining for other employees.

barratry 1. Persistently instigating or stirring up lawsuits. 2. Fraud or other misconduct by a captain or crew that harms the ship owner.

barrister An attorney in England and other Commonwealth countries who is allowed to try cases in specific courts.

barter To exchange goods or services without the use of money.

basis 1. The foundation; the underlying principle. 2. The cost or other amount assigned to an asset for accounting purposes or income tax reporting.

bastard A child born before its parents were married or born from those who never married. An illegitimate child.

bastardy proceeding See paternity suit.

battered child syndrome A diagnosis that a child's injury or injuries are not accidental and are presumed to have been caused by someone of mature strength, such as an adult caregiver.

battered woman syndrome Psychological helplessness because of a woman's financial dependence, loneliness, guilt, shame, and fear of reprisal from her husband or boyfriend who has repeatedly battered her in the past.

Government was precluded from introducing expert testimony on its direct case against defendant on charge of assault in the third degree on subject of battered woman syndrome (BWS) to explain woman's delay in reporting alleged assault for approximately nine weeks, repeated reconciliations with defendant after beatings, and why she believed defendant's threats to kill her if she reported alleged assault. *McKinney's Penal Law § 120.00, subd. 1. People v. White,* 780 N.Y.S.2d 727 (Dist. Ct., 2004)

battery An intentional touching of the person of another that is harmful or offensive. In some states, battery can be a tort and a crime.

bear 1. To produce or yield. 2. To carry.

bearer One who holds or possesses a negotiable instrument that is payable to bearer or to cash.

bearer paper Commercial paper payable to one who holds or possesses it.

belief The mind's acceptance that something is probably true or certain.

belief-action distinction Under the First Amendment, beliefs cannot be regulated by the state, but actions or practices based on those beliefs can sometimes be subject to state regulation.

belligerent A country at war or in armed conflict.

below 1. Pertaining to a lower court in the judicial system. 2. Later in the document.

bench The court, the judge's seat, or the judiciary.

bench conference A meeting at the judge's bench between the judge and the attorneys out of the hearing of the jury. Also called a sidebar conference.

bench memo A memorandum of law by a party's attorney for a trial judge or by a law clerk for a judge.

bench trial A trial without a jury. Also called nonjury trial.

bench warrant A judge's direct order for the arrest of a person.

Bench warrant, as defined in CPL 1.20(30)—i.e., process issuing after a defendant's initial arraignment "upon the accusatory instrument by which the action was commenced." *People v. Marrin,* 589 N.Y.S.2d 874 (1 Dept., 1992)

beneficial Tending to the benefit of a person.

beneficial interest A right to a benefit from property or an estate as opposed to the legal ownership of that property or estate.

A beneficial interest is a profit, benefit, or advantage resulting from a contract or the ownership of an estate as distinct from the legal ownership or control. *Sasso,* 447 N.Y.S.2d 618 (Sup. Ct., 1982)

beneficial owner See equitable owner.

beneficial use A right to the benefits of property when legal title to the property may be held by others.

beneficiary 1. A person whom a trust was created to benefit. 2. A person entitled to insurance benefits. 3. One who receives a benefit.

benefit Assistance, advantage, profit, or privilege; payment or gift.

benefit of clergy 1. A former right of clerics not to be tried in secular courts. 2. The approval or blessing given by a religious rite.

benefit of the bargain rule 1. In a fraud action, the damages should be the value as represented less the value actually received. 2. In a contract action, the damages should be what would place the victim in the position he or she would have been in if the contract had not been breached. Also called loss of bargain rule.

They are liable, pursuant to the benefit of the bargain rule, inter alia, for those costs necessary to put the property in the condition it would have been in if delivered as warranted. *Davis,* 479 N.Y.S.2d 553 (2 Dept., 1984)

bequeath To give property (sometimes only personal property) by will.

bequest Property (sometimes only personal property) given in a will.

best efforts Diligence more exacting than the duty of good faith.

best evidence rule To prove the content of a writing, recording, or phonograph (where there is an issue regarding its authenticity), the original or an acceptable duplicate should be produced unless it is unavailable. Also called original document rule.

bestiality Sexual relations between a human and an animal.

bestow To give or convey.

best use See highest and best use.

betterment A property improvement beyond mere repairs.

beyond a reasonable doubt See reasonable doubt.

BFOQ See bona fide occupational qualification.

BFP See bona fide purchaser.

BIA Bureau of Indian Affairs (*www.doi.gov/bureau-indian-affairs.html*).

biannual 1. Twice a year. 2. Every two years.

bias A tendency or inclination to think and to act in a certain way. A danger of prejudgment. Prejudice.

Bias is a condition of mind, which sways judgment and renders a judge unable to exercise his functions impartially in particular case. *People v. Bonnerwith*, 330 N.Y.S.2d 248 (Just. Ct. 1972)

bicameral Having two chambers or houses in the legislature.

bid 1. An offer to perform a contract for a designated price. 2. An offer to pay a designated price for property, e.g., auction bid.

bid and asked Price ranges quoted for securities in an over-the-counter market.

bid bond A bond to protect the government if a bidder fails to enter the contract according to its bid.

bid in A bid on property by its owner to set a floor auction price.

bid shopping A general contractor's use of a low subcontractor's bid as a tool to negotiate lower bids from other subcontractors.

biennial 1. Occurring every two years. 2. Lasting two years.

biennium A two-year period.

bifurcated trial A case in which certain issues are tried separately (e.g., guilt and punishment; liability and damages).

bigamy Marrying while still in a valid marriage with someone else.

bilateral contract A contract of mutual promises between the parties.

A bilateral contract is created when the offeror extends a promise and asks for a promise in return and where the offeree accepts offer by making requested promise. *Antonucci*, 340 N.Y.S.2d 979 (N.Y. City Civ. Ct., 1973)

bilateral mistake See mutual mistake.

bill 1. A proposed statute. Legislation under consideration for enactment by a legislature. 2. The statute that has been enacted. 3. A statement of money owed. 4. Paper money. 5. A pleading that states a claim in equity. Also called bill in equity. 6. A list of specifics or particulars. 7. A draft. See bill of exchange.

billable Pertaining to tasks for which an attorney, paralegal, or other timekeeper can charge a client fees.

bill in equity See bill (5).

bill of attainder An act of the legislature that imposes punishment (e.g., death) on a specific person or group without a trial.

bill of exchange See draft (1).

bill of health A certificate on the health of a ship's cargo and crew.

bill of indictment A document asking the grand jury to determine whether enough evidence exists to bring a formal criminal charge against the accused.

bill of lading A document from a carrier that lists (and acknowledges receipt of) the goods to be transported and the terms of their delivery.

Bill of lading is a receipt for goods, a contract for their carriage, and is documentary evidence of title to the goods. *Schwalb*, 293 N.Y.S. 842 (N.Y. Mun. Ct., 1937)

bill of pains and penalties An act of the legislature that imposes punishment (other than death) on a specific person or group without a trial. It is a similar to bill of attainder except the punishment is not death.

bill of particulars A more detailed statement of the civil claims or criminal charges brought against another.

bill of review A request that a court of equity revise a decree.

bill of rights 1. The first ten amendments to the U.S. Constitution. 2. A list of fundamental rights.

bill of sale A document that conveys title to personal property from seller to buyer.

bind To place under a legal duty.

binder 1. A contract giving temporary protection to the insured until a formal policy is issued. 2. A statement (and often a deposit) to secure the right to purchase property.

A binder is a temporary contract of insurance that binds the insurer according to its terms. *Crouse West Holding Corp.*, 670 N.Y.S.2d 640 (4 Dept., 1998)

binding instruction See mandatory instruction.

bind over 1. To hold or transfer for further court proceedings. 2. To place under an obligation.

blackacre A fictitious name for a parcel of land, commonly used in classes on real property law. Also, whiteacre.

black code Laws of southern states regulating slavery.

black letter law A statement of a fundamental or basic principle of law. Also called hornbook law.

blackmail Unlawful demand of money or property under threat of bodily harm, property damage, accusation of crime, or exposure. Extortion.

black market Illegal avenues for buying and selling.

blanket bond 1. A bond protecting against loss from employee dishonesty. 2. A bond covering a group rather than named persons.

blank indorsement An indorsement without naming a person to whom the instrument is to be paid.

Payee's signature on back of his paycheck, which did not specify any particular endorsee and merely set forth payee's mortgage number, was a "blank endorsement," which had effect of converting paycheck into a bearer instrument, so that paycheck was properly negotiated by delivery to third party and properly cashed by third party at collecting bank. McKinney's Uniform Commercial Code § 3-204(2). *Walcott*, 507 N.Y.S. 2d 961 (N.Y. City Civ. Ct., 1986)

blasphemy Language or acts showing contempt for God or sacred matters.

blind trust A trust with a trustee who acts without control or influence by the owner or settlor to avoid a conflict of interest.

blockage rule A tax rule allowing a lower value for a large block of shares than the sum of their individual values.

blockbusting Persuading homeowners to sell by asserting that minority newcomers will lower property values.

blood alcohol concentration, blood alcohol content (BAC) The percentage of alcohol in a person's blood.

blotter A book recording daily events, e.g., arrests.

bluebook 1. Popular name of *A Uniform System of Citation*, a citation guidebook. 2. A directory of government offices and employees.

blue chip Pertaining to a high-quality investment stock.

blue flu Police officers call in sick as a labor protest.

blue laws Laws regulating Sunday commerce.

blue ribbon jury A jury with members having special skills.

blue sky laws State securities laws to prevent fraud.

board 1. A group of persons with authority to manage or advise. 2. Regular meals.

boarder One to whom meals are supplied, often with a room.

board of aldermen A local legislative body, e.g., city council.

board of directors Individuals elected by shareholders to hire officers and set policy.

> The affairs of every corporation shall be managed by a board of directors, each of whom shall be at least eighteen years of age. McKinney's Banking Law § 7001(1)

board of education A government body that manages local public schools.

board of equalization A government agency with responsibility for ensuring that the tax burden is distributed fairly in a particular state or district.

board of pardons A government agency with the power to issue pardons.

board of parole See parole board.

board of supervisors The body that governs a county.

board of trade 1. An organization of businesses that promote common business interests. 2. The governing body of a commodities exchange.

bodily harm Physical damage to the body, including injury, illness, and pain.

bodily heir See heir of the body.

bodily injury Physical harm or damage to the body. Also called physical injury.

body 1. A collection or laws. 2. The main section(s) of a document. 3. A person, group, or entity.

> Body is the whole material part of human being. *Hezekiah,* 420 N.Y.S.2d 161 (N.Y. City Civ. Ct., 1979)

body corporate Another term for corporation.

body execution Taking a person into custody by order of the court.

body of the crime See corpus delicti.

body politic The people of a nation or state as a political group.

bogus Counterfeit, sham.

boilerplate Standard language commonly used in some documents.

boiler room sale A high-pressure phone sale of goods and services, e.g., securities.

bona fide In good faith; sincere.

bona fide occupational qualification (BFOQ) An employment qualification based on gender, religion, or other characteristic that is reasonably necessary for the operation of a particular business and hence can be legally required.

bona fide purchaser One who has purchased property for value without notice of defects in the title of seller or of any claims in the property by others. Also called good faith purchaser, innocent purchaser.

> This article does not affect or impair the title of a purchaser or incumbrancer for a valuable consideration, unless it appear that such purchaser or incumbrancer had previous notice of the fraudulent intent of his immediate vendor, or of the fraud rendering void the title of such vendor. McKinney's Personal Property Law § 40

bona immobilia Immovable property such as land.

bond 1. A certificate that is evidence of a debt in which the entity that issues the bond (a company or a governmental body) promises (a) to pay the bondholders a specified amount of interest for a specified amount of time and (b) to repay the loan on the expiration date. 2. An obligation to perform an act (e.g., payment of a sum of money) upon the occurrence or nonoccurrence of a designated condition. 3. A promise or binding agreement.

bond discount The difference between the selling price of a bond and its par value when the bond is sold for less than par.

bonded Placed under or secured by a bond.

bonded debt A debt that has the added backing or security of a bond.

bonded warehouse A private warehouse that stores imported goods subject to special taxes or custom duties.

bondholder One who holds a government, corporate, or commercial bond.

bond issue Bonds offered for sale at the same time.

bond premium The difference between the selling price of a bond and its par value when the bond is sold for more than par.

bondsman A surety; a person or business that guarantees a bond.

bonification A forgiveness of taxes, usually on exports.

bonus Extra; a consideration paid in addition to what is strictly due.

book 1. To enter charges against someone on a police register. The process is called booking. 2. To engage the services of someone. 3. Books: original financial or accounting records. Also called books of account. See also shop-book rule.

book entry 1. A note in a financial ledger or book. 2. A statement acknowledging ownership of securities.

booking See book (1).

bookkeeper One who records financial accounts and transactions.

bookmaking Taking or placing or offering to take or place a bet for another.

bookie One engaged in bookmaking.

books; books of account See book (3).

book value 1. The value at which an asset is carried on a balance sheet. 2. Net worth.

> The term "book value of all tangible assets," as used in termination provision of shareholders' agreement for corporation which used cash method of accounting, included only those items traditionally taken into consideration in a cash method system of accounting, and thus did not include items such as accounts receivable. *Ehrlich,* 721 N.Y.S.2d 23 (1 Dept., 2001)

Boolean search A computer search that allows words to be included or excluded by using operatives such as AND, OR, and NOT in the query.

boot 1. The taxable component in a transaction that is otherwise not taxable. 2. An additional payment or consideration.

bootlegger One who deals in (e.g., copies, sells) products illegally.

bootstrap sale Using the future earnings of a business to acquire that business.

border search A search upon entering the country, usually at the border.

borough 1. A political subdivision of a state with self-governing powers. 2. The five political subdivisions of New York City, each of which is also a county: Bronx, Brooklyn (Kings County), Manhattan (N.Y. County), Queens, and Staten Island (Richmond County).

borrowed servant rule See loaned servant doctrine.

bottomry A contract by which the owner of a ship borrows money for a voyage, giving the ship as security for the loan.

bought and sold notes Written confirmations of a sale from a broker to the buyer and seller.

bound 1. To identify the boundary. 2. Obligated. See also bind.

bound over See bind over.

bounty 1. A reward. 2. Generosity.

boycott A concerted refusal to work or do business with a particular person or business in order to obtain concessions or to express displeasure with certain practices of the person or business.

A combination of many to cause a loss to one by coercing others to withdraw from him their beneficial business intercourse through threats that unless others do so, the many will cause similar loss to them. *Alexander's Department Stores*, 40 N.Y.S. 2d 631 (Sup. Ct., 1943)

Brady **material** Evidence known by the prosecution to be favorable to the defense that must be disclosed to the defendant. *Brady v. Maryland*, 83 S. Ct. 1194 (1963).

brain death Irreversible cessation of circulatory and respiratory functions, or irreversible cessation of all functions of the entire brain, including the brain stem. Also called legal death.

Determination of death. (a) An individual who has sustained either: (1) irreversible cessation of circulatory and respiratory functions; or (2) irreversible cessation of all functions of the entire brain, including the brain stem, is dead. 10 NYCRR 400.16

branch A subdivision, member, or department.

Brandeis brief An appellate brief in which economic and social studies are included along with legal principles.

breach The breaking or violation of a legal duty or law.

breach of contract The failure to perform a contract obligation.

breach of promise to marry Breaking an engagement (promise) to marry.

breach of the peace A violation or disturbance of the public tranquility and order. Disorderly conduct.

A disturbance of public order by an act of violence, or by an act likely to produce violence, or which, by causing consternation and alarm, disturbs peace and quiet of community. *Cherno*, 282 N.Y.S.2d 114 (Sup. Ct., 1967)

breach of trust Violation of a fiduciary obligation by a trustee.

breach of warranty Breaking an express or implied warranty.

breaking a close Trespassing on land.

breaking and entering See burglary.

breaking bulk Unlawful opening by a bailee of a container entrusted to his or her care and stealing of the contents.

breathalyzer A device to measure blood alcohol concentration.

breve A writ.

bribe An offer, acceptance, or solicitation of an unlawful payment with the understanding that it will corruptly affect the official action of the recipient.

Any person, who while holding any public office, or in nomination for, or while seeking a nomination or appointment for any public office, shall corruptly use or promise to use, whether directly or indirectly, any official authority or influence, whether then possessed or merely anticipated, in the way of conferring upon any person, or in order to secure or aid any person in securing any office or public employment, or any nomination, confirmation, promotion or increase of salary, upon the consideration that the vote or political influence or action of the last-named person, or any other, shall be given or used in behalf of any candidate, officer or party, or upon any other corrupt condition or consideration, shall be deemed guilty of bribery or an attempt at bribery. McKinney's Civil Service Law § 107(4)

bridge loan A short-term loan given until other funding is arranged.

brief 1. Shorthand for appellate brief, which is a document submitted by a party to an appellate court in which arguments are presented on why the appellate court should affirm (approve), reverse, or otherwise modify what a lower court has done. 2. A document submitted to a trial court in support of a particular position. 3. A summary of the main or essential parts of a court opinion. 4. Shorthand for a trial brief, which is an attorney's personal notes on how to conduct a trial.

bright-line rule A clear-cut (but sometimes overly simple) legal principle that resolves a dispute.

bring an action To sue someone.

broad interpretation See liberal construction.

broker An agent who arranges or negotiates contracts for others.

A broker shall mean and include any person, firm, association or corporation, other than a dealer, engaged in the business of effecting transactions in securities for the account of others within or from this state, but does not include a bank unless such bank is considered a broker under the federal securities exchange act of 1934. McKinney's General Business Law § 359-e(1)(b)

brokerage 1. The business or occupation of a broker. 2. The wages or commissions of a broker.

broker-dealer A firm that buys and sells securities as an agent for others and as a principal, buying or selling in its own name.

brutum fulmen 1. An empty threat. 2. An invalid judgment.

bubble An extravagant commercial project based on deception.

bucket shop A fraudulent business that pretends to be engaged in securities transactions.

buggery Sodomy or bestiality.

building code Laws that provide standards for constructing buildings.

building line Distances from the ends and sides of the lot beyond which construction may not extend.

bulk goods Goods not divided into parts or packaged in separate units.

bulk sale or transfer The sale of all or a large part of a seller's inventory, not in the ordinary course of the seller's business.

bulletin An ongoing or periodic publication.

bull market A stock market climate of persistent rising prices.

bumping 1. Depriving someone of a reserved seat due to over-booking. 2. Replacing a worker with someone more senior.

burden 1. A duty or responsibility. 2. A limitation or hindrance.

burden of going forward The obligation to produce some evidence tending to prove (not necessarily conclusive evidence) its case. Also called burden of producing evidence, burden of production.

burden of persuasion The obligation to convince the trier of fact (judge or jury) that the party has introduced enough evidence on the truth of its version of the facts to meet the standard of proof, e.g., preponderance of the evidence. Also called risk of nonpersuasion.

burden of producing evidence See burden of going forward.

burden of production See burden of going forward.

burden of proof The obligation of proving the facts of one's claim. This obligation is met by meeting the burden of going forward and the burden of persuasion.

> Burden of proof denotes the duty of establishing truth of given proposition or issue by such quantum of evidence as the law demands in the case; thus, it is the quantum of evidence that must be produced to establish prima facie any particular fact. *Spaid*, 642 N.Y.S.2d 783 (Sup. Ct., 1996)

Burford **abstention** To avoid unnecessary federal-state friction, a federal court can refuse to review a state court's decision involving complex state regulations or sensitive state policies. *Burford v. Sun Oil Co.*, 63 S. Ct. 1098 (1943).

burglary 1. At common law, breaking and entering the dwelling house of another in the nighttime with the intent to commit a felony therein. 2. Most states have changed the common law. Example: Burglary is breaking and entering any building with the intent to commit any crime therein.

burgle To commit burglary; to burglarize.

bursar Someone in charge of funds, especially at a college.

business agent 1. One selected by union members to represent them. 2. A manager of another's business affairs.

business compulsion Exerting improper economic coercion on a business in a weak or vulnerable position. Also called economic duress.

business entry rule An exception to the hearsay rule allowing the introduction into evidence of entries (records) made in the ordinary course of business. Also called the business records exception.

business expense An amount paid for goods or services used in operating a taxpayer's business or trade.

business invitee Someone who has been expressly or impliedly invited to be present or to remain on the premises, primarily for a purpose directly or indirectly connected with business dealings between them. Also called business guest, business visitor.

business judgment rule Courts will defer to good-faith decisions made by boards of directors in business dealings and presume the decisions were made in the best interests of the company.

> Business-judgment rule is a common-law doctrine by which the courts exercise restraint and defer to good-faith decisions made by boards of directors in business settings, and rule applies to determinations of residential cooperative board. *13315 Owners Corp.*, 782 N.Y.S.2d 554 (N.Y. City Civ. Ct., 2004)

business records exception See business entry rule.

business trust An unincorporated business in which a trustee manages its property for the benefit and use of the trust beneficiaries. Also called common law trust, Massachusetts trust.

business visitor See business invitee.

but-for test A test for causation: an event (e.g., injury) would not have happened without the act or omission of the defendant.

> The leading test utilized in determining legal causation is the "sine qua non" or "but for" test. Under this approach one asks if the event would not have happened "but for" the action which is being considered as a possible legal "cause" of the alleged damage. *Bebber*, 729 N.Y.S.2d 844 (Sup. Ct., 2001)

buy and sell agreement An arrangement under which there is a right or duty of one or more owners of an entity to buy another owner's interest upon the occurrence of certain events, e.g., an owner dies or withdraws.

buyer in the ordinary course of business One who buys goods in good faith, without knowledge that the sale violates the rights of another person in the goods, and in the ordinary course from a person (other than a pawnbroker) in the business of selling goods of that kind. McKinney's Uniform Commercial Code § 1-201(b)(9)

by-bidding Planting someone to make fictitious auction bids. Also called puffing.

bylaws Rules governing internal affairs of an organization.

by operation of law See operation of law.

bypass trust A trust designed to take full advantage of the unified credit against estate taxes by reducing the surviving spouse's estate.

by the entirety See tenancy by the entirety.

C

c Copyright, often printed as ©.

CA Court of Appeals.

cabinet An advisory board or council of a chief executive.

caduary Subject to forfeiture.

c.a.f. See cost and freight.

calendar A list of cases awaiting court action or bills awaiting legislative action.

calendar call 1. A hearing to determine the status of, and establish court dates for, cases on the court calendar. 2. In a court-room where there are a large number of cases scheduled at the same session, such as an arraignment day or a motion term, the process of a court clerk or judge calling every case on the court calendar to which each attorney responds, such as stating present, or giving the status of the case.

call 1. A demand for payment. 2. A demand to present bonds or other securities for redemption before maturity. 3. A property boundary landmark. 4. See call option.

callable Subject to be called and paid for before maturity.

callable bonds See redeemable bond.

call option The right to buy something at a fixed price.

call premium The added charge paid to redeem a bond prior to maturity.

calumny A false and malicious accusation.

camera See in camera.

cancellation 1. Striking or crossing out. 2. Invalidation, termination.

To cancel an instrument means to blot it out, to set at naught provisions of instrument cancelled and to declare them void; to do away with an existing agreement. *551 Fifth Ave.*, 103 N.Y.S.2d 265 (Sup. Ct., 1950)

c&f See cost and freight.

cannabis The plant from which marijuana is prepared.

canon A rule, law, or principle.

canonical disability An impediment justifying a church annulment.

canon law Ecclesiastical law; Roman Church jurisprudence.

canons of construction Rules for interpreting statutes and contracts.

canvass 1. To examine carefully, e.g., the votes cast. 2. To solicit votes, contributions, opinions, etc.

capacity 1. Legal qualification or competency to do something. 2. The ability to understand the nature of one's acts. 3. Occupation, function, or role.

Capacity concerns a litigant's power to bring its grievance before a court. Standing involves inquiry into whether that litigant has a sufficiently cognizable stake in the outcome so as to cast the dispute in a form traditionally capable of judicial resolution. *Saratoga Lake Protection*, 809 N.Y.S.2d 874 (Sup. Ct., 2006)

capias A writ requiring that someone be taken into custody.

capias ad respondendum A writ commanding the sheriff to bring the defendant to court to answer the claims of the plaintiff.

capias ad satisfaciendum A writ commanding the sheriff to hold a judgment debtor until the latter satisfies its judgment debt.

capias pro fine A writ commanding the sheriff to arrest someone who has not paid a fine.

capita Head, person. See also per capita.

capital 1. Assets available for generating more wealth. 2. Assets less liabilities; net worth. 3. Relating to the death penalty.

capital asset See fixed asset.

capital budget Projected spending to buy long-term or fixed assets.

capital gains tax A tax on the sale or exchange of a capital asset.

capital goods Assets (e.g., tools) used to produce goods and services.

capitalization 1. The total value of stocks and other securities used for long-term financing. 2. See capitalize.

capitalize 1. To treat an asset as capital; to classify an expenditure as a long-term investment. 2. To provide with investment funds. 3. To determine current value of cash flow. 4. To allocate the cost of an asset over future periods; to depreciate or amortize.

capital loss Loss realized on the sale or exchange of a capital asset.

capital market The market for long-term securities.

capital punishment A death sentence.

capital stock 1. All of the stock a corporation is authorized to issue. Also called authorized stock. 2. The total par value of stock a corporation is authorized to issue.

Shares of stock are the intangible property itself, and "capital stock" is the substance or the thing of real value, while "certificate of stock" is but the evidence of ownership of part or share of capital stock. *Medex*, 98 N.Y.S.2d 269 (Sup. Ct., 1950)

capital surplus The amount received in excess of par when a company sells its stock. This amount is seen in the Owner's Equity section of a balance sheet.

capitation tax See poll tax.

capitulary A collection or code of laws.

capricious Impulsive; not based on evidence, law, or reason.

A verdict is capricious within the meaning of rule that court must set aside an arbitrary or capricious verdict and order a new trial when such verdict is against overwhelming weight of evidence, and verdict is "arbitrary" within such rule when it is without any supporting evidence. *Gruhn*, 40 N.Y.S.2d 765 (Sup. Ct., 1943)

caption 1. The heading or introductory part of a pleading, court opinion, memo, or other document that identifies what it is, the names of the parties, the court involved, etc. 2. The arrest of someone.

care 1. Caution in avoiding harm. 2. Heed. 3. Supervision or comfort.

career criminal See habitual criminal.

careless Absence of reasonable care; negligent.

carjacking Using violence or threats to take a vehicle from the driver.

carnal knowledge Sexual intercourse.

carrier 1. A person or company engaged in transporting passengers or goods for hire. See also common carrier. 2. An insurance company.

Carrier means a stock or mutual corporation or a reciprocal insurer or a nonprofit property/casualty insurance company, if such corporation or insurer is authorized to transact the business of workers' compensation insurance in this state, but not including any such corporation or insurer which is insolvent. McKinney's Workers' Compensation Law § 106

carrier's lien The legal right of a carrier to hold cargo until its owner pays the agreed shipping costs.

carry 1. To transport. 2. To bear the burden of. 3. To have in stock. 4. To list on one's accounts as a debt.

carryback Applying a loss or deduction from one year to a prior year.

carrying charge 1. Charges of a creditor, in addition to interest, for providing credit. 2. Costs involved in owning land, e.g., taxes.

carryover Applying a loss or deduction from one year to a later year.

carryover basis When property is transferred in a certain way (e.g., by gift) the basis of the property in the transferee is the same as (is carried over from) the transferor's basis.

cartel 1. An association of producers or sellers of any product joined together to control the production, sale, or price of the product. 2. An agreement between enemies while at war.

carve out To separate income from the property that generates it.

CASA Court appointed special advocate (*www.nationalcasa.org*).

case 1. A court's written explanation of how it applied the law to the facts to resolve a legal dispute. See also opinion. 2. A pending matter on a court calendar. 3. A client matter handled by a law office. 4. A statement of arguments and evidence. See also action on the case.

> The term "case" in statute providing that "the court shall not . . . impose a sentence of probation in any case where it sentences a defendant for more than one crime and imposes a sentence of imprisonment for any one of the crimes" referred to criminal action which is commenced by filing of accusatory instrument. *People v. Cerilli*, 575 N.Y.S.2d 557 (2 Dept., 1991)

case agreed See agreed case.

casebook A law school textbook containing many edited court opinions.

caselaw (case law) The law found within court opinions. See also common law.

case method Learning law by studying court opinions.

case of first impression See first impression.

case-in-chief The presentation of evidence by one side, not including the evidence it introduces to counter the other side.

case or controversy For a federal court to hear a case, the plaintiff must have suffered a definite and concrete injury.

case reports See reporter (3).

case stated See agreed case.

cash basis Reporting or recognizing revenue only when actually received and expenses only when actually paid out.

cash dividend A dividend paid by a corporation in money.

cash flow 1. Cash from income-producing property. 2. The periodic or recurring receipt of cash.

cashier's check A check drawn by a bank on its own funds, signed by a bank officer, and payable to a third party named by a customer.

cash out To receive cash for one's total ownership interest.

cash price A lower price if paid in cash rather than with credit.

cash sale A sale in which the buyer and seller exchange goods and full payment in cash at the same time.

cash surrender value Cash available upon surrender of an insurance policy before it becomes payable in the normal course (e.g., at death). Also called surrender value.

> The term cash surrender, as used in a life policy, means cash on surrender. *Evans*, 33 N.Y.S.2d 19 (N.Y. Sup., 1941)

cash value See fair market value.

castle doctrine See retreat rule.

casual 1. Unexpected. 2. Occasional. 3. Without formality.

casual ejector A fictitious defendant who casually enters the land to eject the person lawfully in possession of it.

casualty 1. A serious accident. 2. A person injured or killed.

> Casualty is an accident, an unfortunate occurrence. Disaster is a sudden and extraordinary misfortune, an event regarded as a terrible misfortune. *I Q Originals*, 447 N.Y.S.2d 174 (1 Dept., 1981)

casualty insurance Insurance against loss from accident. (Covers many different kinds of insurance.)

casualty loss Damage to property due to an event that is sudden, unexpected, and unusual in nature.

catching bargain An unconscionable purchase from one who has an estate in reversion or expectancy.

caucus 1. A meeting of the members of a particular group, e.g., a political party. 2. The political party itself.

causa A cause; what produces an effect.

causa causans The predominating effective cause.

causa mortis In contemplation of approaching death. Also phrased mortis causa.

causa proxima The immediate cause.

causa sine qua non "But-for" cause. Without (but-for) the act or omission, the event in question would not have occurred.

causation Bringing something about. Producing an effect.

cause 1. Bringing something about. Producing an effect. 2. A reason, justification, or ground. 3. A lawsuit.

cause of action The facts that give a person a right to judicial relief. A legally acceptable reason for suing.

> A cause of action is a set of operative facts which give rise to a separate and distinct legal right and to a right to seek separate and distinct redress for a violation of that legal right. *Benson*, 413 N.Y.S.2d 600 (Co. Ct., 1979)

cautionary instruction A judge's caution or warning to the jury to avoid outside contact about the case, to ignore certain evidence, or to consider the evidence for a limited purpose.

caveat 1. A warning or admonition. 2. A party's notice filed in court asking that the case be stopped.

caveat actor Let the doer (the actor) beware.

caveatee The person being challenged by someone who files a caveat. The latter is the caveator.

caveat emptor Let the buyer beware. A buyer should examine and judge the product on his or her own.

> Doctrine of caveat emptor imposes no duty upon a vendor to disclose any information concerning the property in an arms' length real estate transaction; however, if some conduct by the vendor exceeding mere silence rises to the level of active concealment, the vendor may have a duty to disclose. *Bethka*, 672 N.Y.S.2d 494 (N.Y.A.D. 3 Dept., 1998)

CC Circuit Court; County Court; City Court; Civil Code; courtesy copy.

C corporation A corporation whose income is taxed at the corporate level; it has not chosen S corporation status. Also called subchapter C corporation.

CD Certificate of deposit.

cease and desist order A court or agency order prohibiting the continuation of a course of conduct.

cede 1. To surrender or yield. 2. To assign or transfer.

cedent A person who transfers something. One who cedes.

censor A person who examines material in order to identify and remove what is objectionable.

censure 1. An official reprimand. 2. To express formal disapproval.

census An official counting of a population.

center of gravity doctrine In conflict-of-law cases, courts apply the law of the place that has the most significant contacts or relationship with the matter in dispute.

The parties are in agreement that the choice of law applicable to the insurance policy is governed by the center of gravity or "grouping of contacts" theory, which looks to such factors as the place of contracting, negotiation and performance; the location of the subject matter of the contract; and the domicile of the contracting parties. *Allstate Ins. Co.*, 670 N.Y.S. 2d 469 (1 Dept., 1998)

ceremonial marriage A marriage entered in compliance with statutory requirements, e.g., obtaining a marriage license.

cert. See certiorari.

certificate A document that asserts the truth of something or that something has been done, e.g., that requirements have been met.

certificated Having met the qualifications for certification from a school or training program.

certificate of acknowledgement Confirmation that the signature on a document was made by a person who is who he or she claimed to be.

certificate of convenience and necessity An authorization from a regulatory agency that a company can operate a public utility.

certificate of deposit (CD) A document from a bank confirming that a named person has a designated amount of money in the bank, usually for a fixed term earning a fixed rate of interest. A time deposit.

certificate of incorporation A document issued by the state to a company that grants its status as a corporation.

certificate of occupancy A document confirming that the premises comply with building codes and regulations.

certificate of title A document confirming who owns personal designated property, including who holds encumbrances such as liens.

"Certificate of title" means a certificate of title with respect to which a statute provides for the security interest in question to be indicated on the certificate as a condition or result of the security interest's obtaining priority over the rights of a lien creditor with respect to the collateral. McKinney's Uniform Commercial Code § 9-102(a)(10)

certification 1. The act of affirming the truth or authenticity of something. 2. A request by a federal court that a state court resolve a state issue relevant to a case in the federal court. 3. The process by which a nongovernmental organization grants recognition to a person who has met the qualifications established by that organization.

certification mark Any word, name, symbol, or device used to certify some aspect of goods or services, e.g., their origin.

certified Having complied with the qualifications for certification.

certified check A check drawn on funds in a depositor's account whose payment is guaranteed by the bank on which it is drawn.

certified copy A duplicate of an original document, certified as an exact reproduction. Also called exemplified copy.

Certified copies of papers filed to be evidence. Copies of all official documents and orders filed or deposited according to law in the office of the commission, certified by a commissioner or by the secretary or assistant secretary of the commission to be true copies of the originals, under the official seal of the division, shall be evidence in like manner as the originals. McKinney's Public Service Law § 17

Certified Legal Assistant (CLA) The credential bestowed by the National Association of Legal Assistants (NALA) (*www.nala.org*) for meeting its criteria such as passing a national, entry-level certification exam. Individuals can select the alternative designation, Certified Paralegal (CP).

Certified Paralegal (CP) See Certified Legal Assistant.

Certified Public Accountant (CPA) An accountant who has met the requirements to be licensed as a public accountant (*www.aicpa.org*).

certiorari (cert.) An order (or writ) by a higher court that a lower court send up the record of a case because the higher court has decided to use its discretion to review that case.

cession A surrender or yielding up.

cestui ("he who") One who benefits, a beneficiary.

cestui que trust Beneficiary of a trust. See also trust.

cf. Compare.

CFI Cost, freight, and insurance.

CFR See Code of Federal Regulations (*www.gpoaccess.gov/cfr*).

Ch. Chancellor; chancery; chapter.

chain of causation The sequence of actions and omissions that led to or resulted in the harm or other event in question.

chain of custody A list of places an item of physical evidence has been in and the name of anyone who has possessed it over a period of time.

chain of title The history of ownership of land from the original title holder to the present holder.

The "chain of title" to real property is the succession of deeds or other instruments by which title is traced back to its original source and when the records of all transactions impinging upon given piece of land are available through pertinent indices, the law assumes that a prudent person will inspect them and treat them on basis of his having knowledge of contents whether he has seen them or not. *Eltman*, 403 N.Y.S.2d 428 (Sup. Ct., 1978)

challenge 1. A formal objection to the selection of a particular prospective juror. 2. A protest or calling into question.

challenge for cause An objection to selecting a prospective juror because of specified causes or reasons, e.g., bias.

challenge to the array A formal protest to the manner in which the entire pool or panel of prospective jurors has been selected.

chamber 1. A room, e.g., a judge's office. 2. A legislative body.

champerty Conduct by an individual (called the champertor) who promotes or supports someone else's litigation, often by helping to finance the litigation in exchange for a share in the recovery.

"Champerty" is species of common law generic offense of maintenance and involves unlawful maintenance of suit in consideration of bargain for some part of thing involved, with gist of offense consisting in mode of compensation. Judiciary Law § 489. *Coopers and Lybrand*, 384 N.Y.S.2d 804 (1 Dept., 1976)

chancellor 1. Judge in a court of equity. 2. An officer of high rank.

chancery 1. Equity jurisprudence. 2. A court of equity.

change of venue The transfer of a suit begun in one court to another court in the same judicial system.

chapter 1. A subdivision of a code. 2. A division of an organization.

Chapter 11 A category of bankruptcy (found in chapter 11 of the bankruptcy code) in which the debtor is allowed to postpone payment of debts in order to reorganize the capital structure of his or her business.

character evidence Evidence of a person's habits, personality traits, and moral qualities.

charge 1. To instruct a jury, particularly on the law pertaining to the verdict it must reach. 2. A jury instruction. 3. To accuse someone of a crime. 4. To impose a burden or obligation; to assign a duty. 5. To defer payment. 6. A person (e.g., a child) entrusted to the care of another. 7. Price.

chargé d'affaires A diplomatic officer of a lower rank.

charge off To treat or report as a loss.

charitable Having the character or purpose of the public good; philanthropic, eleemosynary.

charitable contribution A gift of money or other property to a charitable organization.

charitable deduction An income tax deduction taken for gifts to a qualified tax-exempt charitable organization.

charitable remainder annuity trust A trust that pays designated amounts to beneficiaries for a period of time after which the trust property goes to a charity.

A "charitable remainder annuity trust" is a trust which must pay the noncharitable income beneficiary or beneficiaries a sum certain annually, or more frequently, if desired, which is not less than 5% of the initial net fair market value of all property placed in the trust as finally determined for federal tax purposes. *In re Danforth's Will*, 366 N.Y.S.2d 329 (Sur., 1975)

charitable trust A trust established to serve a purpose that is beneficial to a community. Also called public trust.

charter 1. The fundamental law governing a municipality or other local unit of government, authorizing it to perform designated functions. 2. A document creating an organization that states its fundamental purposes and powers. 3. The legal authorization to conduct business 4. To rent for temporary use.

chattel Personal property.

chattel mortgage A mortgage or lien on personal property as security for a debt.

chattel paper A document that is evidence of both a monetary obligation and a security interest in specific goods.

"Chattel paper" means a record or records that evidence both a monetary obligation and a security interest in specific goods, a security interest in specific goods and software used in the goods, a security interest in specific goods and license of software used in the goods, a lease of specific goods, or a lease of specific goods and license of software used in the goods. McKinney's Uniform Commercial Code § 9-102(11)

check 1. A written order instructing a bank to pay on demand a certain amount of money from the check writer's account to the person named on the check (the payee). See also negotiable instrument. 2. To control; to hold within bounds. 3. To examine for accuracy; to investigate. 4. To deposit for safekeeping.

check kiting A form of bank fraud in which the kiter opens accounts at two or more banks, writes checks on insufficient funds on one account, and then, taking advantage of bank processing delays, covers the overdraft by depositing a check on insufficient funds from the other account. Also called kiting.

checkoff An employer's deduction of union dues from employee wages and turning the dues over to the union.

A "check off" is accomplished by employer deducting, with employee's consent, a certain sum from employee's wages for union dues and initiation fees, and employer's obligation thereunder to make deduction and transmittal to union rests purely on contract. *Greenwald*, 57 N.Y.S.2d 765 (Sup. Ct., 1945)

checks and balances An allocation of powers among the three branches of government (legislative, executive, and judicial) whereby one branch can block, check, or review what another branch wants to do (or has done) in order to maintain a balance of power among the branches.

chief justice The presiding judge (called a justice) in a higher court. In a lower court, he or she is often called the chief judge.

child 1. A son or daughter. 2. A person under the age of majority.

child abuse Physically or emotionally harming a child, intentionally or by neglect.

"Abused child" means a child less than eighteen years of age whose parent or other person legally responsible for his care (i) inflicts or allows to be inflicted upon such child physical injury by other than accidental means which causes or creates a substantial risk of death, or serious or protracted disfigurement, or protracted impairment of physical or emotional health or protracted loss or impairment of the function of any bodily organ, . . . McKinney's Family Court Act § 1012(e)

child abuse report law A law that requires designated individuals (e.g., teachers) to report suspected child abuse to the state.

child molestation Subjecting a child to sexual advances, contact, or activity.

"Child abuse" shall mean any of the following acts committed in an educational setting by an employee or volunteer against a child: (a) intentionally or recklessly inflicting physical injury, serious physical injury or death, or (b) intentionally or recklessly engaging in conduct which creates a substantial risk of such physical injury, serious physical injury or death, or (c) any child sexual abuse as defined in this section, or (d) the commission or attempted commission against a child of the crime of disseminating indecent materials to minors pursuant to article two hundred thirty-five of the penal law. McKinney's Education Law § 1125(1)

child neglect The failure to provide a child with support, medical care, education, moral example, discipline, and other necessaries. See McKinney's Family Court Act § 1012(f).

child pornography Visual portrayal of a person under the age of 18 engaged in sexual activity, actual or simulated.

child support The obligation of a parent to pay a child's basic living expenses. The statute in New York that governs the determination of child support payments is the Child Support Standards Act (CSSA). FCA 413(1)(A).

chilling effect Being hindered or inhibited from exercising a constitutional right, e.g., free speech.

Chinese wall Steps taken in an office to prevent a tainted employee from having any contact with a particular case in order to avoid a disqualification of the office from the case. The employee is tainted because he or she has a conflict of interest in that case.

chit 1. A voucher for food and drinks. 2. A short letter or note.

choate Complete; perfected or ripened.

choate lien A perfected lien, enforceable without further steps.

> A "choate lien" is a lien which is definite in respect to identity of lienor, property subject to lien, and amount of lien. *In re Rosenberg's Will*, 308 N.Y.S.2d 51 (Sur., 1970)

choice of evils Acts otherwise criminal may be justifiable if performed under extraordinary circumstances out of some immediate necessity to prevent a greater harm from occurring. Also called necessity.

choice of law Deciding which jurisdiction's law should govern when an event involves the law of more than one jurisdiction.

chose Chattel; a thing.

chose in action 1. A right to recover something in a lawsuit, e.g., money. 2. The thing itself that embodies the right to sue. Also called thing in action.

> A right to receive or recover a debt, demand, or damages on a cause of action ex-contractu or for a tort or omission of a duty. *Sheahan*, 753 N.Y.S.2d 664 (Sur., 2002)

churning A broker's excess trading in a customer's account to benefit the broker (via commissions), not the client.

CI See confidential informant.

CIF See cost, insurance, and freight.

circuit 1. One of the 13 appellate subdivisions in the federal judicial system. 2. Pertaining to a court that has jurisdiction in several counties or areas. 3. A district traveled by a judge.

circular note See letter of credit.

circumstantial evidence Evidence of a fact that is not based on personal knowledge or observation from which another fact might be inferred. Also called indirect evidence.

citation; cite 1. A reference to any legal authority printed on paper or stored in a computer database. 2. An order to appear in court to answer a charge. 3. An official notice of a violation.

citator A book, CD-ROM, or online service with lists of citations that can help assess the current validity of an opinion, statute, or other authority and give leads to additional relevant material.

cite checking Examining citations in a document to assess whether the format of the citation is correct, whether quoted material is accurate, and whether the law cited is still valid.

citizen A person born or naturalized in a country to which he or she owes allegiance and who is entitled to full civil rights.

citizen's arrest A private person making an arrest for a crime that is a breach of the peace committed in his or her presence or for reasonably believing the person arrested has committed a felony.

> Subject to the provisions of subdivision two, any person may arrest another person (a) for a felony when the latter has in fact committed such felony, and (b) for any offense when the latter has in fact committed such offense in his presence. Such an arrest, if for a felony, may be made anywhere in the state. If the arrest is for an offense other than a felony, it may be made only in the county in which such offense was committed. McKinney's Criminal Procedure Law § 140.25(1)&(2)

civil Pertaining to (a) private rights, (b) noncriminal cases, (c) the state or citizenship, (d) public order and peace, and (e) legal systems of Western Europe other than England.

civil action A lawsuit to enforce private rights.

civil arrest The arrest of the defendant until he or she satisfies the judgment.

civil assault The tort of assault.

civil code 1. A collection of statutes governing noncriminal matters. 2. The code containing the civil law of France, from which the civil code of Louisiana is derived.

civil commitment Noncriminal confinement of those who because of incompetence or addiction cannot care for themselves or who pose a danger to themselves or to society. Also called involuntary commitment.

civil conspiracy A combination of two or more persons acting in concert to commit an unlawful act and an overt act that results in damages.

civil contempt The refusal of a party to comply with a court order, resulting in punishment that can be avoided by compliance.

> To find that "civil contempt" has occurred in a given case it must be determined that a lawful order of the court, clearly expressing an unequivocal mandate was in effect, and it must also appear with reasonable certainty that the order has been disobeyed and the party to be held in contempt had knowledge of the court's order. McKinney's Judiciary Law §§ 753, 773. *People v. Simplice*, 733 N.Y.S.2d 855 (N.Y. City Crim. Ct., 2001)

civil court A court that hears noncriminal cases.

civil damage law See Dram Shop Act.

civil death The status of a person who has lost civil rights (e.g., to vote) because of a conviction of certain crimes. Also called legal death.

civil disabilities Civil rights (e.g., the right to vote) that are lost when a person is convicted of a serious crime.

civil disobedience Breaking the law (without using violence) to show the injustice or unfairness of the law.

civilian One who is not a police officer or in the military.

civil law 1. The law governing civil disputes. Any law other than criminal law. 2. The statutory or code law applicable in Louisiana and many Western European countries other than England.

civil liability Damages or other noncriminal responsibility.

civil liberties Basic individual rights that should not be unduly restricted by the state (e.g., freedom of speech).

civil penalty A fine or assessment for violating a statute or administrative regulation.

civil procedure Laws governing the mechanics of resolving a civil (noncriminal) dispute in a court or administrative agency.

civil rights Basic individual rights (e.g., to vote) guaranteed by the U.S. Constitution and by special statutes.

Civil rights, as distinguished from naturally inherent rights, being those defined and given by positive law enacted for maintenance of government. *Green*, 295 N.Y.S. 672 (N.Y.A.D. 4 Dept., 1937)

civil service Nonmilitary government employment, often obtained through merit and competitive exams.

civil union A same-sex relationship with the same *state* benefits and responsibilities the state grants spouses in a marriage.

CLA or **CP** The certification credential bestowed by the National Association of Legal Assistants. CLA (Certified Legal Assistant); CP (Certified Paralegal) (*www.nala.org*). See also Certified Legal Assistant.

Claflin trust A trust that cannot be terminated by a beneficiary. Also called indestructible trust.

claim 1. A right to sue. 2. To demand as one's own or as one's right. 3. To assert something.

A claim accrues when it matures and damages become ascertainable. *Scherman*, 355 N.Y.S.2d 162 (2 Dept., 1974)

claim and delivery A suit to recover personal property that was wrongfully taken or kept.

claimant One who makes a demand or asserts a right or claim.

claim jumping Asserting a mining claim that infringes on the claim of another.

claim of right 1. A good-faith assertion that one was entitled to do something. 2. If a taxpayer receives income (without restrictions) that he or she claimed the right to have, it must be reported in the year received even if it may have to be returned in a later year.

claim preclusion See res judicata.

claims court A court in which a party seeks to resolve claims against the government, e.g., U.S. Court of Federal Claims, New York State Court of Claims.

claims-made policy Insurance that covers only claims actually filed (i.e., made) during the period in which the policy is in effect.

Basic "claims made" or "discovery" insurance policy provides for indemnity, regardless of when the act complained of occurred, if the act is discovered and brought to the attention of the insurer during the policy period. *Oot*, 676 N.Y.S.2d 715 (N.Y.A.D. 4 Dept., 1998)

class A group with common characteristics, e.g., persons injured by the same product.

class action A lawsuit in which one or more members of a class sue (or are sued) as representative parties on behalf of everyone in the class, all of whom do not have to be joined in the lawsuit. Also called representative action.

class gift A gift to a group containing an unknown number of persons at the time the gift is made.

clause A subdivision of a sentence in a law or other document.

Clayton Act A federal antitrust statute prohibiting price discrimination and other monopolistic practices. 15 USC § 12.

CLE See continuing legal education.

clean bill A proposed statute (bill) that has been substantially revised and introduced to the legislature as a new bill.

clean bill of lading A bill of lading without qualifications.

clean hands doctrine A party may not be allowed to assert an equitable claim or defense if his or her conduct has been unfair or in bad faith. Also called unclean hands doctrine.

Those who come into a court of equity must come with clean hands. Seeking relief against the illegal acts of others, they must themselves be free from the imputation of illegality in respect of the transaction of which they complain. *Vandershoot*, 72 N.Y.S.2d 121 (Sup. Ct., 1947)

clear 1. Free from encumbrance. 2. To vindicate or acquit. 3. To pay a check according to the instructions of the maker. 4. To pass through a clearinghouse. 5. Obvious, unambiguous.

clearance card A letter from an employer given to a departing employee stating facts such as the duration of the latter's employment.

clear and convincing evidence Evidence demonstrating that the existence of a disputed fact is much more probable than its nonexistence. This standard is stronger than preponderance of the evidence but not as strong as beyond a reasonable doubt.

clear and present danger Imminent risk of severe harm, the test used to help determine whether the state can restrict First Amendment freedoms.

clearing 1. The process by which checks are exchanged and pass through the banking system. 2. A ship leaving port in compliance with laws.

clearinghouse A place where banks exchange checks and drafts drawn on each other and reconcile accounts.

clearly erroneous The definite and firm conviction of an appellate court that a mistake has been made by a lower court.

clear title 1. Title that is free of reasonable doubt as to its validity. Marketable title. 2. Title that is free of encumbrances.

clemency Leniency from the president or a governor to a criminal, e.g., a pardon or reduction in sentence. Also called executive clemency.

clergy-penitent privilege A privilege preventing spiritual advisors from disclosing confessions or religious confidences made to them. Also called priest-penitent privilege.

Unless the person confessing or confiding waives the privilege, a clergyman, or other minister of any religion or duly accredited Christian Science practitioner, shall not be allowed [to] disclose a confession or confidence made to him in his professional character as spiritual advisor. McKinney's CPLR § 4505

clerical error A minor mistake such as a copying error, typographical error, or inadvertent omission.

clerk 1. An official who manages records and files and performs other administrative duties, e.g., a court clerk.

2. A law student or recent law school graduate who works for a law office or judge, usually for a short period of time. 3. One who performs general office duties.

clerkship Employment as a clerk in a legal office. See clerk (2).

client One who hires or receives services from a professional, e.g., an attorney.

client security fund A fund (often run by the bar association) used to compensate victims of attorney misconduct.

client trust account An attorney's bank account that contains client funds that may not be used for office operating expenses. Also called trust account.

Clifford trust A fixed-term trust in which the principal is returned to the grantor after a period of time.

A Clifford Trust is a short-term trust which is measured by a term of years and which at the end of the term reverts to the settler. *In re Durland's Will*, 315 N.Y.S.2d 1011 (Sur., 1970)

close 1. Land that is enclosed. 2. In real property, the principle that every metes-and-bounds description must end where it began, thus enclosing the described property. 3. To bring to completion.

close corporation; closed corporation; closely held corporation A corporation whose shares are held by a small group, e.g., a family.

closed-end mortgage A mortgage loan whose principal cannot be increased during the life of the loan and cannot be prepaid.

closed shop A business whose employees must be members of a union as a condition of employment.

closing 1. The meeting in which a transaction is finalized. Also called settlement. 2. A meeting in the transfer of real estate in which the buyer receives the deed and the seller receives the money.

closing statement 1. The final statements by opposing trial attorneys to the jury (or to the trial judge alone in non-jury cases) summarizing the evidence presented during the trial and requesting a favorable decision. Unrepresented parties make the statement themselves. Also called closing statement, final argument, summation, summing up. 2. A list of all costs and adjustments for parties involved in a real estate transaction; sometimes called a statement of sale.

closing costs Expenses incurred in the purchase, sale, or mortgage financing of real estate in addition to the purchase price.

cloture A legislative procedure to end debate and allow a vote.

cloud on title A claim or encumbrance on land, which, if valid, would affect or impair the title rights of the owner.

cluster zoning Modifications in zoning restrictions in exchange for other land being set aside for public needs, e.g., a park.

"Cluster development" is an optional planning technique permitting planning boards to exercise greater flexibility in subdivision approval for purpose of achieving more efficient use of land containing unusual features, for facilitating economical provision for streets and utilities, as well as for preserving natural and scenic qualities of open lands .... McKinney's Town Law §§ 281, 281(b). *Bayswater Realty*, 560 N.Y.S.2d 623 (Ct. of App., 1990)

coaching Telling a witness how to give testimony on the stand.

COBRA See Consolidated Omnibus Budget Reconciliation Act.

coconspirator One who engages in a conspiracy with another. Under the conspirator exception to the hearsay rule, statements of one coconspirator can be admitted against another coconspirator if made in furtherance of the conspiracy.

COD Collect on delivery; cash on delivery.

code A systematic collection of laws, rules, or guidelines, usually organized by subject matter.

code civil The code containing the civil law of France. Also called the Code Napoléon.

codefendant One of two or more defendants sued in the same civil case or prosecuted in the same criminal case.

Code Napoléon See code civil.

code pleading See fact pleading.

codicil A supplement that adds to or changes a will.

A "codicil" is a written supplement or addition to already executed will, and its purpose is to change, add to, enlarge or restrict, or annul provisions of will to which it refers, or it may revoke the will altogether. *In re Smith's Estate*, 300 N.Y.S. 1057 (N.Y. Sur., 1937)

codification Collecting and systematically arranging laws or rules by subject matter.

coercion Compelling something by force or threats. Overpowering another's free will by force or undue influence.

cognizable 1. Pertaining to what can be heard and resolved by a court. 2. Capable of being known.

cognizance 1. The power of a court to hear and resolve a particular dispute. 2. Judicial notice. 3. Awareness or recognition.

cognovit A written statement that acknowledges liability or the validity of a debt. The statement confesses judgment. A cognovit note (also called judgment note) is a promissory note containing a cognovit.

cohabitation Living together as a couple or in a sexual relationship.

"Cohabitation" in an action for annulment of marriage means something more than merely living in the same house or even occupying the same bed, but is the living together of the parties as husband and wife and includes sexual relations. *Zoske*, 64 N.Y.S.2d 819 (Sup. Ct., 1946)

coheir One of several persons to whom an inheritance passes or descends. A joint heir.

coif A ceremonial cap or other headpiece. See also Order of the Coif.

coinsurance A sharing of the risks between two or more insurers or between the insurer and the insured.

COLA Cost of living adjustment.

cold blood Premeditated killing.

collapsible corporation A corporation set up to be sold or liquidated before it earns substantial income.

collateral 1. Property pledged as security for the satisfaction of a debt. 2. Not in the direct line of descent. 3. Not directly relevant. 4. Accompanying but of secondary importance.

collateral attack A challenge or attack against the validity of a judgment that is not raised in a direct appeal from the court that rendered the judgment.

collateral estoppel When parties have litigated and resolved an issue in one case, they cannot relitigate the issue in another case against each other even if the two cases raise different claims or causes of action. Also called direct estoppel, estoppel by judgment, estoppel by record, issue preclusion.

"Collateral estoppel," or "issue preclusion," operates to preclude a party to a prior action or proceeding, or a person or entity in privity with such a party, from relitigating in a subsequent action or proceeding an issue that previously was decided against it in the prior action or proceeding. *Pouncy*, 814 N.Y.S.2d 641 (N.Y.A.D. 2 Dept., 2006)

collateral fraud Deception by one party that does not pertain to the actual issues that were resolved in a trial but which prevented the other party from presenting its case fairly. Also called extrinsic fraud.

collateral heir One who is not of the direct line of the deceased, but comes from a collateral line, as a brother, aunt, or a cousin of the deceased. Also called heir collateral.

collateral order doctrine An appeal of a nonfinal order will be allowed if the order conclusively determines the disputed question, resolves an important issue that is completely separate from the merits of the dispute, and is effectively unreviewable on appeal from a final judgment.

collateral source rule The amount of damages caused by the tortfeasor shall not be reduced by any injury-related funds received by the plaintiff from sources independent of the tortfeasor such as a health insurance policy of the plaintiff.

Common-law "collateral source rule," which provided that a personal injury award may not be reduced or offset by amount of any compensation that injured person may receive from a source other than tortfeasor. *Inchaustegui*, 725 N.Y.S.2d 627 (Ct. of App., 2001)

collateral warranty A warranty of title given by someone other than the seller.

collation 1. A comparison of a copy with the original to determine the correctness of the copy. 2. Taking into account property already given to some heirs as an advancement.

collecting bank A bank handling a check for collection other than the payor bank.

collective bargaining Negotiations between an employer and representatives of its employees on working conditions.

collective mark A mark used by members of an organization (e.g., a union) to indicate membership or to identify what it offers.

colloquium Extrinsic facts showing that a defamatory statement was of and concerning the plaintiff. A complaint alleging such facts.

colloquy A formal discussion, e.g., between the judge and the defendant to determine if the defendant's plea is informed.

collusion 1. An agreement to commit fraud. 2. An agreement between a husband and wife that one or both will lie to the court to facilitate the obtaining of their divorce.

"Collusion," in the matrimonial law, is an agreement between husband and wife for one of them to commit, or appear to commit, or be represented in court as having committed, a breach of matrimonial duty so that the other may obtain a divorce. *Fuchs*, 64 N.Y.S.2d 487 (Sup. Ct., 1946)

colorable 1. Plausible. Having at least some factual or legal support. 2. Deceptively appearing to be valid.

color of law 1. Acting or pretending to act in an official, governmental capacity. 2. The pretense of law.

color of office Asserted official or governmental authority.

color of title A false appearance of having title to property.

comaker See cosigner.

combination The union or association of two or more persons or entities to achieve a common end. See also conspiracy, restraint of trade.

combination in restraint of trade An agreement among businesses to create a monopoly or otherwise stifle competition.

combination patent A combination of known elements which, when combined, accomplish a patentable function or result.

coming and going rule See going and coming rule.

comity Giving effect to the laws of another state, not as a requirement, but rather out of deference or respect.

Common-law doctrine of "judicial comity" is principle in accordance with which courts of one state or jurisdiction will give effect to laws and judicial decisions of another, not as matter of obligation, but out of deference and mutual respect. *Will of Brown*, 466 N.Y.S.2d 988 (N.Y. Sur., 1983)

Comity Clause A provision in the U.S. Constitution which provides that "The Citizens of each State shall be entitled to all Privileges and Immunities of Citizens in the several States." U.S. Const. art. IV, § 2, cl. 1.

commerce Buying, selling, or exchanging goods or services.

Commerce Clause The clause in the U.S. Constitution (art. I, § 8, cl. 3) giving Congress the power to regulate commerce among the states, with foreign nations, and with Indian tribes.

commercial bank A bank with a variety of services such as providing loans, checking accounts, and safety deposit boxes.

commercial bribery The advantage secured over a competitor by corrupt dealings with agents of prospective purchasers.

commercial frustration An excuse not to perform a contract due to an unforeseen event not under the control of either party.

commercial impracticability See impracticability.

commercial law The law governing commercial transactions such as the sale and financing of goods and services.

commercial paper 1. A negotiable instrument (e.g., a draft, a promissory note) used in commerce. 2. A short-term, unsecured negotiable note, often sold to meet immediate cash needs.

commercial speech Expression related solely to the economic interests of the speaker and its audience.

"Commercial speech," limitations on which are permitted under First Amendment, is speech which does no more than propose a commercial transaction, and is removed from any exposition of ideas. *Lacoff*, 705 N.Y.S.2d 183 (N.Y. Sup., 2000)

commercial unit Goods considered a single whole for purposes of sale, the value of which would be materially impaired if divided into parts.

commingling Mixing what should be kept separate, e.g., depositing client funds in a single account with general law firm funds or an attorney's personal funds.

"Commingling" takes place when client's money is intermingled with that of attorney and its separate identity is lost. *Matter of Friscia*, 526 N.Y.S.2d 13 (2 Dept., 1988)

commission 1. The granting of powers to carry out a task. 2. A government body granted power to carry out a task. 3. Compensation, often a percentage of the value of the transaction. 4. The act of committing something, usually a crime.

commitment 1. An agreement or pledge to do something. 2. The act of institutionalizing someone as to a prison or mental hospital.

commitment fee A fee paid by a loan applicant for a lender's promise to lend money at a defined rate on a specified date.

committee 1. A group appointed to perform a function on behalf of a larger group. 2. A special guardian appointed to protect the interests of an incompetent person.

committee of the whole A special committee consisting of the entire membership of a deliberative body.

commodity Something useful; an article of commerce.

common 1. The legal right to use another's land or waters. 2. Land set apart for use by the general public. 3. Shared. See also tenancy in common.

common carrier A company that holds itself out to the general public as engaged in transporting people or goods for a fee.

common disaster An event causing the death of two or more persons with shared interests, without clear evidence of who died first.

common enemy doctrine Landowners can fend off surface waters (e.g., rain) as needed, without liability to other landowners.

common law 1. Judge-made law in the absence of controlling statutory law or other higher law. Law derived from court opinions. 2. Law based on the legal system of England.

common law action An action based on the common law. See also action at law.

common law copyright The author's proprietary interest in his or her creation before it has been made available to the public.

common law marriage A marriage entered without license or ceremony by persons who have agreed to marry, have lived together as husband and wife, and have held themselves out as such.

common law trust See business trust.

common nuisance See public nuisance.

Common Pleas The name of a trial court in some states (e.g., Ohio) and an intermediate appellate court in others.

common situs picketing Picketing an entire construction project even though the labor grievance is with only one subcontractor.

common stock Stock in a corporation with voting rights and the right to dividends after preferred stockholders have been paid.

commonwealth 1. A nation or state as a political entity. (In the United States, four states are officially designated commonwealths: Kentucky, Massachusetts, Pennsylvania, and Virginia.) 2. A political unit that is voluntarily united with the United States but is self-governing, e.g., Northern Mariana Islands.

community 1. A section or neighborhood in a city or town. 2. A group of people with common interests. 3. The marital entity that shares or owns community property.

community notification law See Megan's law.

community property Property in which each spouse has a one-half interest because it was acquired during the marriage (by a method other than gift or inheritance to one spouse only) regardless of who earned it.

community trust An entity (e.g., a foundation) that operates a trust to dispense funds for educational, health, or other charitable goals.

commutation 1. A change of punishment to one that is less severe. 2. An exchange or substitution.

A "commutation of sentence" reduces and terminates a sentence, except as otherwise provided. Correction Law, § 241. *Lehrman*, 29 N.Y.S.2d 635 (N.Y. Ct. Cl. 1941)

commutative contract A contract in which what each party promises or exchanges is considered equal in value.

commutative justice A system of justice in which the goal is fundamental fairness in transactions among the parties.

commuted value The present value of a future interest or payment.

compact An agreement, often between states or nations.

company An association of persons who are engaged in a business.

company union An employer-controlled union of employees in a single company.

comparable worth Jobs requiring the same levels of skill should receive equal pay whether performed by men or women.

comparative negligence In a negligence action, the plaintiff's damages will be reduced in proportion to the plaintiff's negligence in causing his or her own injury.

Damages recoverable when contributory negligence or assumption of risk is established. In any action to recover damages for personal injury, injury to property, or wrongful death, the culpable conduct attributable to the claimant or to the decedent, including contributory negligence or assumption of risk, shall not bar recovery, but the amount of damages otherwise recoverable shall be diminished in the proportion which the culpable conduct attributable to the claimant or decedent bears to the culpable conduct which caused the damages. McKinney's CPLR § 1411

comparative rectitude When both spouses have grounds for a divorce, it will be granted to the spouse least at fault.

compelling state interest A substantial need for the state to act that justifies the resulting restriction on the constitutional right claimed by the person challenging the state's action.

compensating balance The minimum balance a bank requires one of its borrowers to have on deposit.

compensation 1. Payment of wages or benefits for services rendered. 2. Payment for a loss incurred. Indemnification.

compensatory damages Money to restore an injured party to his or her position prior to the injury or wrong. Actual damages.

competency proceeding A hearing to determine if someone has the mental capacity to do something, e.g., to stand trial.

competent 1. Having the knowledge and skill reasonably necessary to represent a particular client. 2. Having sufficient understanding to be allowed to give testimony as a witness. 3. Having the ability to understand the criminal proceedings, to consult with one's attorney, and to assist in one's own defense. 4. Having the capacity to manage one's own affairs.

For purposes of grand jury proceedings, "competent evidence" is evidence admissible pursuant to statute governing rules of evidence before grand jury. McKinney's CPL §§ 70.10, 190.30, 190.65, subd. 1. *People v. Young*, 620 N.Y.S.2d 223 (Sup. Ct., 1994)

competent evidence Evidence that is relevant and admissible.

compilation 1. A collection of laws, usually statutes. 2. An original work formed by the collection and assembling of preexisting works.

complainant One who files a complaint to initiate a civil lawsuit or who alleges that someone has committed a crime.

complaint 1. A plaintiff's first pleading, stating a claim against the defendant. Also called petition in some states. 2. A formal criminal charge.

completion bond A bond given as insurance to guarantee that a contract will be completed within the agreed-upon time. Also called performance bond, surety bond.

A "performance bond" or as it is sometimes referred to, "completion bond," is given to insure public authority that contract once awarded will be completed as awarded within fixed period of time. *Extruded Louver Corp.*, 226 N.Y.S.2d 220 (Sup. 1962)

complex trust See discretionary trust.

composition An agreement between a debtor and two or more creditors on what will be accepted as full payment.

compos mentis Of sound mind; competent.

compound 1. To adjust or settle a debt or other claim by paying a lesser amount. 2. To accept an illegal payment in exchange for not prosecuting a crime. 3. To calculate interest on both the principal and on interest already accrued. 4. A mixture of parts.

compound interest See compound (3).

compounding a crime Receiving something of value in exchange for an agreement to interfere with a prosecution or not to prosecute.

compromise To settle a dispute through mutual concessions.

compromise verdict A verdict that results when jurors resolve their inability to reach unanimity by conceding some issues to entice agreement on others.

comptroller A fiscal officer of an organization appointed to examine accounts, issue financial reports, and perform other accounting duties. Also spelled controller.

compulsion 1. Forcing someone to do or refrain from doing something. 2. An irresistible impulse.

compulsory arbitration Arbitration that parties are required to undergo to resolve their dispute.

"Compulsory arbitration," also known as "interest arbitration," deals with terms and conditions of employment not previously agreed upon, and mandates arbitration pursuant to applicable statute if impasse occurs with respect to such issues in collective negotiations involving public employees. McKinney's Civil Service Law § 209. *In re Board of Educ. of Watertown City School Dist.*, 688 N.Y.S.2d 463 (Ct. of App., 1999)

compulsory counterclaim A claim that arises out of the same subject matter as the opposing party's claim.

compulsory joinder Someone who must be joined as a party if his or her absence means that complete relief is not possible for the parties already in the lawsuit or that one or more of the parties may be subject to inconsistent or multiple liability.

compulsory process A summons or writ that compels a witness to appear in court, usually by subpoena or arrest.

compurgator Someone called to give testimony for the defendant.

computer crime The use of a computer to commit an illegal act, e.g., accessing or damaging computer data without authorization.

concealed weapon A weapon carried on a person in such a manner as to conceal it from the ordinary sight of another.

concerted Planned or accomplished together. Concerted activity is the conduct of employees who have joined together to achieve common goals on conditions of employment.

concert of action 1. A person cannot be prosecuted for both a substantive offense and a conspiracy to commit that offense where an agreement between two or more persons is a necessary element of the substantive offense. Also called Wharton's rule. 2. Concerted action (conduct planned by persons) results in liability for each other's acts.

Concert of action liability creates joint and several liability. *Matter of New York State Silicone Breast Implant Litigation*, 631 N.Y.S.2d 491 (Sup. Ct., 1995)

conciliation 1. Conduct taken to restore trust in an effort to resolve a dispute. 2. Settlement of a conflict without undue pressure or coercion.

conclusion of fact An inference of fact drawn from evidence of another fact. See also finding of fact.

conclusion of law The result of applying the law to the facts. See also holding.

conclusive 1. Decisive. 2. Supported by substantial evidence.

conclusive presumption An inference of fact that the fact finder must find despite any evidence to the contrary. Also called irrebuttable presumption.

A "conclusive presumption" is an inference which as a matter of law cannot be rebutted; it is, in reality, a rule of substantive law expressed in terms of rules of evidence. *Hanley*, 428 N.Y.S. 2d 865 (Fam. Ct., 1980)

conclusory Pertaining to an argument that states a conclusion without providing the underlying facts to support the conclusion.

concur 1. To agree. 2. To accept a conclusion but for different reasons. See also concurring opinion.

concurrent 1. At the same time. 2. With the same authority.

concurrent cause A cause that acts together (simultaneously) with another cause to produce an injury or other result.

concurrent condition A condition that one party must fulfill at the same time that another party must fulfill a mutual condition.

concurrent covenants Two covenants that must be performed or be ready to be performed simultaneously.

concurrent jurisdiction The power of two or more courts to resolve the same dispute. Also called coordinate jurisdiction.

"Concurrent jurisdiction" means that different courts have jurisdiction over same subject matter at same time. *Van Gorder*, 623 N.Y.S.2d 935 (3 Dept., 1995)

concurrent negligence Negligence by two or more persons who, though not working in concert, combine to produce a single injury.

concurrent power A legislative power that can be exercised by the federal or state government, or by both.

concurrent resolution A measure that is adopted by both houses of the legislature but that does not have the force of law.

concurrent sentence A sentence served simultaneously, in whole or in part, with another sentence.

concurring opinion A court opinion in which a judge agrees with the result of the majority opinion but for different reasons.

condemn 1. To set apart or expropriate (take) property for public use in exercise of the power of eminent domain. 2. To judge someone to be guilty. 3. To declare to be unfit.

condemnee A person whose property is taken for public use.

The EDPL broadly defines a "condemnee" as a "holder of any right, title, interest, lien, charge or encumbrance" in or on real property acquired by eminent domain (EDPL 103[C]). *Village of Port Chester*, 788 N.Y.S.2d 422 (2 Dept., 2005)

condition 1. An uncertain future event upon which a legal result (e.g., a duty to pay) is dependent. 2. A prerequisite.

conditional Depending on or containing a condition.

conditional bequest A gift in a will that will be effective only if a specific event (condition) occurs or fails to occur.

conditional contract An executory (i.e., unperformed) contract whose existence and performance depends on a contingency.

conditional fee 1. See contingent fee. 2. See fee simple conditional.

conditional privilege A right to do or say something that can be lost if done or said with malice. Also called a qualified privilege.

conditional sale A sale in which the buyer does not receive title until making full payment.

Essentially, a "conditional sale" is a credit device, whereby buyer is the substantial owner, in joint possession, use, control, and equity of redemption, whereas seller reserves title to goods solely as security for payment by buyer. *Snyder*, 185 N.Y.S.2d 110 (Sup. Ct., 1959)

conditional use Permitted land use upon compliance with specified conditions. Also called special exception, special use.

condition of employment A job requirement.

condition precedent An act or event (other than a lapse of time) that must occur before performance becomes due.

condition subsequent An act or event that will, if it occurs, render an obligation invalid.

condominium A real estate interest that combines two forms of ownership: exclusive ownership of an individual unit of a multiunit project and common ownership of the common project areas.

"Condominium" form of ownership of real property is division of parcel of real property into individual units and common elements into which owner holds title in fee to his individual unit as well as retaining undivided interest in common elements of parcel. *Schoninger*, 523 N.Y.S.2d 523 (2 Dept., 1987)

condonation Overlooking or forgiving, e.g., one spouse's express or implied forgiveness of the marital fault of the other.

conference committee A committee consisting of members of both houses of the legislature that seeks to reach a compromise on two versions of the same bill the houses passed.

confession A statement acknowledging guilt.

"Confession" is voluntary express acknowledgment by accused that he engaged in conduct which constitutes crime charged, or essential part of it. *People v. Alexander*, 544 N.Y.S.2d 595 (1 Dept., 1989)

confession and avoidance A plea that admits some facts but avoids their legal effect by alleging new facts.

confession of judgment See cognovit.

confidence game Obtaining money or other property by gaining a victim's trust through deception.

confidential communication An exchange of information that is privileged—the exchange cannot be disclosed against the will of the parties involved.

confidential informant (CI) A person with pending charges who agrees to provide information or testify in exchange for a lesser plea or lesser sentence. Because of the risk of exposing the informant to harm, or the risk of impairing an ongoing investigation, the identity of the informant is not disclosed in court papers or in court, unless good cause is shown by the defendant. See also informer.

confidential relationship 1. See fiduciary relationship. 2. A relationship that requires non-disclosure of certain facts.

confirmation 1. Giving formal approval. 2. Corroboration. 3. Rendering enforceable something that is voidable.

confiscation Seizing private property under a claim of authority.

conflict of interest Divided loyalty that actually or potentially harms someone who is owed undivided loyalty.

conflict of laws Differences in the laws of two coequal legal systems (e.g., two states) involved in a legal dispute. The choice of which law to apply in such disputes.

conformed copy An exact copy of a document with notations of what could not be copied.

conforming In compliance with the contract or the law.

conforming use A use of land that complies with zoning laws.

confrontation Being present when others give evidence against you and having the opportunity to question them.

The right of confrontation is essentially the right to have witness produced and physically present for questioning. *People v. Sorrell*, 241 N.Y.S.2d 586 (Co. Ct. 1963)

confusion of goods The mixing of like things belonging to different owners so that sorting out what each originally owned is no longer possible. Also called intermixture of goods.

conglomerate A corporation that has diversified its operations, usually by acquiring enterprises in widely different industries.

Congress 1. The national legislature of the United States. 2. A formal meeting of representatives of different groups (congress).

Congressional Record (Cong. Rec.) The official record of the day-to-day proceedings of Congress.

conjoint Joined together; having a joint interest.

conjugal Pertaining to marriage or spouses, e.g., the rights that one spouse has in the other's companionship, services, support, and sexual relations.

connecting-up Evidence demonstrating the relevance of prior evidence.

connivance A willingness or a consent by one spouse that a marital wrong be committed by the other spouse.

"Connivance," as a defense in action for divorce on grounds of adultery, is the corrupt consenting of a married party to that offense of the spouse for which that party afterwards seeks a divorce. *Santoro*, 55 N.Y.S.2d 294 (Sup. Ct., 1945)

consanguinity Relationship by blood or a common ancestor.

conscience of the court The court's power to apply equitable principles.

conscientious objector A person who for religious or moral reasons is sincerely opposed to war in any form.

conscious parallelism A process, not in itself unlawful, by which firms in a concentrated market might share monopoly power.

consecutive sentences Sentences that are served one after the other—in sequence. Also called accumulative sentences, cumulative sentences.

consensus ad idem A meeting of the minds; agreement.

consent Voluntary agreement or permission, express or implied.

consent decree A court decree agreed upon by the parties.

consent judgment An agreement by the parties (embodied in a court order) settling their dispute.

A consent judgment is merely an agreement of the parties entered upon the record with the sanction and approval of the Court. It is the act of the parties rather than the Court. It is a judicially recorded supposed agreement and, as such, is admissible in evidence. *Town of Oyster Bay*, 219 N.Y.S.2d 456 (Sup. Ct., 1961)

consent search A search consented to by the person affected who has the authority to give the consent.

consequential damages Losses or injuries that do not flow directly from a party's action, but only from some of the consequences or results of such action.

conservator A person appointed by the court to manage the affairs of someone, usually an incompetent. A guardian.

consideration A bargained-for promise, act, or forbearance. Something of value exchanged between the parties.

"Consideration" consists of either a benefit to the promisor or a detriment to the promisee; it is enough that something is promised, done, forborne or suffered by the party to whom the promise is made as consideration for the promise made to him. *Weiner*, 457 N.Y.S.2d 193 (Ct. of App., 1982)

consignment Transferring goods to someone, usually for sale by the latter. The one transferring the goods is the consignor; the person receiving them is the consignee.

consignee, consignor See consignment.

consolidated appeal An appeal from two or more parties who file a joint notice of appeal and proceed as a single appellant.

Consolidated Omnibus Budget Reconciliation Act (COBRA) A federal statute that gives workers limited rights to keep their health insurance policy when they leave a job.

consolidation 1. A joining together or merger. 2. Combining two or more corporations that dissolve into a new corporate entity. 3. Uniting the trial of several actions into one court action.

consolidation loan A new loan that pays the balances owed on previous loans that are then extinguished.

consortium 1. The benefits that one spouse is entitled to receive from the other, e.g., companionship, cooperation, services, affection, and sexual relations. 2. The companionship and affection a parent is entitled to receive from a child and that a child is entitled to receive from a parent. 3. An association or coalition of businesses or other organizations.

Concept of "consortium" includes not only loss of support or services, but also such elements as love, companionship, affection, society, sexual relations, solace and more. *Millington*, 293 N.Y.S.2d 305 (Ct. of App., 1968)

conspiracy An agreement between two or more persons to commit a criminal or other unlawful act or to perform a lawful act by unlawful means. Also called criminal conspiracy.

constable A peace officer whose duties (e.g., serving writs) are similar to (but not as extensive as) those of a sheriff.

constitution The fundamental law that creates the branches of government, allocates power among them, and defines some basic rights of individuals.

constitutional Pertaining to or consistent with the constitution.

constitutional court See Article III court.

constitutional fact A fact whose determination is decisive of constitutional rights.

constitutional law The body of law found in and interpreting the constitution.

constitutional right A right guaranteed by a constitution.

construction An interpretation of a law or other document. The verb is *construe*.

constructive True legally even if not factually.

constructive bailment An obligation imposed by law on a person holding chattels to deliver them to another.

A "constructive bailment" arises when person having possession of personal property holds it under such circumstances that law imposes on him an obligation to deliver property to another. *Mays*, 97 N.Y.S.2d 909 (Sup. Ct., 1950)

constructive contempt See indirect contempt.

constructive contract See implied in law contract.

constructive delivery Acts that are the equivalent of the actual delivery of something.

constructive desertion The misconduct of the spouse who stayed home that justified the other spouse's departure from the home.

constructive discharge Acts by an employer that make working conditions so intolerable that an employee quits.

constructive eviction A landlord's causing or allowing premises to become so uninhabitable that a tenant leaves.

constructive fraud A breach of a duty that violates a fiduciary relationship. Also called legal fraud.

"Constructive fraud" refers to an act done or omitted not with actual design to perpetrate positive fraud or injury upon other persons, but which, nevertheless, amounts to positive fraud, or is construed as fraud by the court because of its detrimental effect upon public interests and public or private confidence. *Ajettix Inc.*, 804 N.Y.S.2d 580 (N.Y. Sup., 2005)

constructive knowledge What one does not actually know, but should know or has reason to know and, therefore, is treated as knowing.

constructive notice Information the law assumes one has because he or she could have discovered it by proper diligence and had a duty to inquire into it.

constructive possession Control or dominion one rightfully has over property that he or she does not actually possess.

constructive receipt of income Having control over income without substantial restriction even though not actually received.

constructive service See substituted service.

constructive trust A trust implied as an equitable remedy to prevent unjust enrichment by one who has obtained the legal right to property by wrongdoing. Also called implied trust, involuntary trust, trust de son tort, trust ex delicto, trust ex maleficio.

To state a legally sufficient cause of action for the imposition of a "constructive trust," a plaintiff must plead and prove four essential elements: (1) a confidential or fiduciary relationship; (2) a promise; (3) a transfer in reliance thereon; and (4) unjust enrichment caused by breach of the promise. *Satler*, 675 N.Y.S.2d 644 (2 Dept., 1998)

construe See construction.

consul An official in a foreign country who promotes the commercial and other interests of his or her own country.

consumer A buyer of goods and services for personal use rather than for resale or manufacturing.

consumer credit Credit to buy goods or services for personal use.

consumer goods Products used or bought for personal, family, or household use.

"Consumer goods" means goods that are used or bought for use primarily for personal, family, or household purposes. McKinney's Uniform Commercial Code § 9-102(a)(23)

consumer lease A lease of personal property for personal, family, or household use.

consumer price index (CPI) A measurement by the Bureau of Labor Statistics of average monthly changes in prices of basic goods and services bought by consumers (*www.bls.gov/cpi*).

consummate 1. To complete or bring to fruition. 2. To engage in the first act of sexual intercourse after marriage.

contemner (contemnor) One who commits contempt.

contemplation of death The thought of death as a primary motive for making a transfer of property.

contemporaneous Existing or occurring in the same period of time.

contempt Disobedience of or disrespect for the authority of a court or legislature.

"Civil contempt" is one in which rights of person have been harmed by contemnor's failure to obey court order; conversely, "criminal contempt" involves offense against judicial authority and is used to protect the integrity of the judicial process and to compel respect for court's mandates. *People v. Wright*, 619 N.Y.S.2d 525 (N.Y. City Ct., 1994)

contest To challenge; to raise a defense against a claim.

contested Challenged; litigated.

contingency 1. A possible event. 2. Uncertainty. 3. A contingent fee.

contingent 1. Uncertain; pertaining to what may or may not happen. 2. Dependent; conditional.

contingent annuity An annuity whose commencement or exact terms of payment depend on an uncertain future event.

contingent beneficiary A person who receives a gift or insurance proceeds if a condition occurs.

contingent estate An estate that will become a present or vested estate if an event occurs or condition is met.

contingent fee A fee that is paid only if the case is successfully resolved by litigation or settlement. Also called conditional fee.

contingent interest An interest whose enjoyment is dependent on an uncertain event.

contingent liability Liability that depends on an uncertain event.

contingent remainder A remainder that is limited to take effect either to an uncertain person or upon an uncertain event. Also called executory remainder.

Contingent remainders: where there is no person having immediate right of possession on cessation of intermediate or precedent estate. *In re Barnes' Estate*, 279 N.Y.S. 117 (Sur., 1935)

continuance An adjournment or postponement of a session.

continuing jurisdiction A court's power (by retaining jurisdiction) to modify its orders after entering judgment.

continuing legal education (CLE) Training in the law (often short term) received after completing one's formal legal training.

continuing offense An offense involving a prolonged course of conduct.

Coercion is crime that can be committed by series of acts over period of time and can be characterized as "continuing offense." McKinney's Penal Law § 135.65. *People v. Belden*, 627 N.Y.S.2d 110 (3 Dept., 1995)

continuing trespass Allowing a structure or other permanent invasion on another's land.

contra Against; in opposition to.

contraband Property that is unlawful to possess, import, export, or trade.

For purpose of law prohibiting inmates from promoting prison contraband, "dangerous contraband" includes knife-like weapons known as "shanks." McKinney's Penal Law § 205.25, subd. 2. *People v. Mendoza*, 666 N.Y.S.2d 260 (3 Dept., 1997)

contract A legally enforceable agreement. A promise that, if breached, will entitle the aggrieved to a remedy.

contract carrier A private company that transports passengers or property under individual contracts, not for the general public.

Contract Clause A clause in the U.S. Constitution (art. I, § 10, cl. 1) providing that no state shall pass a law impairing the obligation of contracts.

contract for deed An agreement to sell property in which the seller retains title or possession until full payment has been made. Also called land sale contract.

contract implied in fact See implied in fact contract.

contract implied in law See implied in law contract.

contract of adhesion See adhesion contract.

contract under seal A signed contract that has the waxed seal of the signer attached. Consideration was not needed. Also called special contract, specialty.

contractor A person or company that enters contracts to supply materials or labor to perform a job.

contributing to the delinquency of a minor Engaging in conduct by an adult that is likely to lead to illegal or immoral behavior by a minor.

contribution 1. The right of one tortfeasor who has paid a judgment to be proportionately reimbursed by other tortfeasors who have not paid their share of the damages caused by all the tortfeasors. 2. The right of one debtor who has paid a common debt to be proportionately reimbursed by the other debtors.

Contribution or apportionment involves a determination of relative responsibility in which respective fault of two or more defendants is determined by reviewing the contribution of each to the damage sustained and, once the tort-feasors' relative responsibilities are determined, each pays his ratable portion of the total damages. *Smith*, 443 N.Y.S.2d 922 (4 Dept., 1981)

contributory 1. Helping to bring something about. 2. Pertaining to one who pays into a common fund or benefit plan.

contributory negligence Unreasonableness (negligence) by the plaintiff that helps cause his or her own injury or loss. Where recognized, it bars any recovery due to the defendant's negligence.

controlled substance A drug whose possession or use is prohibited or otherwise strictly regulated.

controller See comptroller.

controlling interest Ownership of enough of the stock of a company to be able to control it.

controversy A dispute that a court can resolve; a justiciable dispute. An actual rather than a hypothetical dispute.

Any difference which can be the subject of a suit at law or equity. *Osborne & Thurlow*, 172 N.Y.S.2d 522 (N.Y. Sup., 1958)

contumacy Refusal to obey a court order. Contempt.

convenience and necessity See certificate of convenience and necessity.

convention 1. An agreement or treaty. 2. A special assembly.

conventional 1. Customary. 2. Based on agreement rather than law.

conventional mortgage A mortgage that is not government insured.

conversation See criminal conversation.

conversion 1. An intentional interference with personal property that is serious enough to force the wrongdoer to pay its full value. An action for conversion is called trover. 2. Changing the nature of property.

In order to assert a cause of action for "conversion," which is the unauthorized assumption and exercise of the right of ownership of goods belonging to another, to the exclusion of the owner's rights, plaintiff must have exercised ownership, possession or control of the property in the first place. *Soviero*, 813 N.Y.S.2d 49 (1 Dept., 2006)

convertible security One kind of security (e.g., bond) that can be exchanged for another kind (e.g., stock).

convey See conveyance.

conveyance A transfer of an interest in land. A transfer of title. The verb is *convey*.

conveyancer One skilled in transferring interests in land.

convict 1. To find a person guilty of a crime. 2. A prisoner.

conviction 1. A finding that a person is guilty of a crime. 2. A firm belief.

cooling off period 1. A period of time during which neither side can take any further action. 2. The time given to a buyer to cancel the purchase.

cooperative 1. A business owned by customers that use its goods and services. 2. A multiunit building owned by a corporation that leases units to individual shareholders of the corporation.

coordinate jurisdiction See concurrent jurisdiction.

coparcenary An estate that arises when several persons inherit property from the same ancestor to share equally as if they were one person or one heir. Also called estate in coparcenary, parcenary.

coparcener A concurrent or joint heir through coparcenary. Also called parcener.

copyhold Tenure as laid out in a copy of the court roll (an old form of land tenure).

copyright (©) The exclusive right for a fixed number of years to print, copy, sell, or perform original works. 17 U.S.C. § 101.

coram nobis ("before us") An old remedy allowing a trial court (via a writ of error) to vacate its own judgment because of factual errors. If the request to vacate is made to an appellate court, the remedy is called coram vobis ("before you").

"Writ of error coram nobis" is application to vacate judgment of conviction on grounds that defendant has been deprived of substantial justice, predicated upon error which does not appear on the record. *People v. Marino*, 273 N.Y.S.2d 5 (N.Y. Dist. Ct., 1966); McKinney's Criminal Proc. Law § 440

coram vobis See coram nobis.

core proceeding A proceeding that invokes a substantive bankruptcy right. 28 U.S.C.A. § 157(b).

corespondent 1. The person who allegedly had sexual intercourse with a defendant charged with adultery. 2. A joint respondent.

corner Dominance over the supply of a particular commodity.

coroner A public official who inquires into suspicious deaths.

corporal punishment Punishment inflicted on the physical body.

corporate-opportunity doctrine Corporate directors and officers must not take personal advantage of business opportunities they learn about in their corporate role if the corporation itself could pursue those opportunities.

> Officer or director of corporation may not appropriate corporate assets or opportunities to himself or to new corporation formed for that purpose and "corporate opportunity" is defined as any property, information or prospective business dealing in which corporation has interest or tangible expectancy or which is essential to its existence or logically and naturally adaptable to its business. *Matter of Greenberg*, 614 N.Y.S.2d 825 (4 Dept., 1994)

corporate veil Legitimate corporate actions are not treated as shareholder actions. See piercing the corporate veil.

corporation An organization that is an artificial person or legal entity that has limited liability and can have an indefinite existence separate from its shareholders.

corporation counsel An attorney who works for an incorporated municipality.

corporeal Tangible; pertaining to the body.

corporeal hereditament Anything tangible that can be inherited, e.g., land.

corpus 1. Assets in a trust. Also called res, trust estate, trust fund. 2. Principal as opposed to interest or income. 3. A collection of writings. 4. The main part of a body (anatomy).

corpus delicti ("body of the crime") The fact that a loss or injury has occurred as a result of the criminal conduct of someone.

> The fact that the crime has been actually perpetrated. *People v. Palmer*, 16 N.E. 529 (Ct. of App., 1888)

corpus juris A collection or body of laws.

correction 1. The system of imposing punishment and treatment on offenders. 2. Removing an error. 3. A market adjustment.

correspondent An intermediary for an organization that needs access to a particular market.

corroborating evidence Supplemental or supporting evidence.

corruption of blood Punishment by taking away the right to inherit or transfer property to blood relatives.

corrupt practices act A statute regulating campaign contributions, spending, and disclosure.

cosigner One who signs a document along with another, often to help the latter secure a loan. The cosigner can have repayment obligations upon default of the other. Also called comaker.

cost and freight (c&f) (c.a.f.) The price includes the cost of the goods and of transporting them.

cost basis The acquisition costs of purchasing property.

cost, insurance, and freight (CIF) The price includes the cost of purchasing, insuring, and transporting the goods.

cost-of-living clause A clause providing an automatic wage or benefit increase tied to cost-of-living rises as measured by indicators such as the Consumer Price Index.

costs Court-imposed charges or fees directly related to litigation in that court, e.g., filing fees. (Usually does not include attorney fees.) Also called court costs.

> "Costs" are sums awarded to prevailing party as compensation for expense of litigation, but bear no relation to actual cost. *Selby Marketing Associates*, 647 N.Y.S.2d 927 (City Ct., 1996)

costs to abide event Court costs that will be awarded to the prevailing party at the conclusion of the case.

cotenancy An interest in property whereby two or more owners have an undivided right to possession.

cotrustees Two or more persons who administer a trust together.

council An assembly or body that meets to advise or to legislate.

counsel 1. An attorney. A client's lawyer. Also called counselor, counselor at law. 2. Advice. 3. To give advice, to advise.

counselor See counsel (1).

count In pleading, a separate claim (cause of action) or charge.

counterclaim An independent claim by one side in a case (usually the defendant) filed in response to a claim asserted by an opponent (usually the plaintiff).

> In a "counterclaim," a cause of action is generally asserted by one or more defendants against one or more plaintiffs and other persons alleged to be liable; in contrast, a "cross-claim" is asserted against one or more codefendants and others also alleged to be liable. CPLR 203, 203(c), 3019(a, b). *Seligson*, 376 N.Y.S.2d 899 (1 Dept., 1975)

counterfeit To copy without authority in order to deceive by passing off the copy as genuine; fraudulent imitation, forgery.

countermand To change or revoke instructions previously given.

counteroffer A response by someone to whom an offer is made that constitutes a new offer, thereby rejecting the other's offer.

counterpart A corresponding part or a duplicate of a document.

countersign To sign in addition to the signature of another in order to verify the identity of the other signer.

county The largest territorial and governmental division within most states.

county commissioners Officers who manage county government.

coupon An interest or dividend certificate attached to a bond or other instrument that can be detached and presented for payment.

course of business What is usually and normally done in a business. Also called ordinary or regular course of business.

course of dealing A pattern of prior conduct between the parties.

course of employment Conduct of an employee that fulfills his or her employment duties.

Whether activity is "within course of employment" or purely personal, under workers' compensation scheme, depends upon whether activity is both reasonable and sufficiently work related under the circumstances. *Knaub*, 674 N.Y.S.2d 799 (3 Dept., 1998)

course of performance Repeated occasions for performing a contract in the past by either party with knowledge of the nature of the performance and opportunities for objection to it.

court 1. A unit of the judicial branch of government that applies the law to disputes and administers justice. 2. A judge or group of judges on the same tribunal.

court costs See costs.

court en banc See en banc.

court-martial A military court for trying members of the armed services for offenses violating military law.

court of appeals The middle appeals court in most judicial systems and the highest appellate court in a few.

court of chancery See chancery (2), equity (1).

court of claims A court that hears claims against the government for which sovereign immunity has been waived. The New York State Court of Claims hears claims against the state (*nyscourtofclaims.courts.state.ny.us*).

court of common pleas (C.P.) 1. A trial court in several states, e.g., Ohio, Pennsylvania. 2. An appellate court in some states.

court of equity See court of law, equity (1).

court of law 1. A court that applied the common law as opposed to a court of equity that applied equitable principles. 2. Any court or judicial tribunal.

court reporter See reporter.

covenant A promise or contract, e.g., a promise made in a deed or other legal instrument.

A "covenant" is simply contract of special nature and is a promise usually enforced by action at law for money damages for breach or, in case of covenants running with land, by specific performance. Real Property Law, § 500 et seq. *Birnbaum*, 232 N.Y.S.2d 188 (Sup. Ct., 1962)

covenantee One to whom a promise by covenant is made.

covenant for quiet enjoyment A grantor's promise that the grantee's possession of real property will not be disturbed by any other claimant with a superior lawful title.

covenant marriage A form of marriage that requires proof of premarital counseling, a promise to seek marital counseling when needed during the marriage, and proof of marital fault to dissolve.

covenant not to compete A promise in an employment contract or contract for the sale of a business not to engage in competitive activities, usually within a specified geographic area and for a limited time. Also called restrictive covenant.

covenant of seisin An assurance that the grantor has the very estate in quantity and quality that he or she purports to convey to the grantee. Also called right-to-convey covenant.

covenant of warranty An assurance that the grantee of real property has been given good title and a promise to provide compensation if a claim is made against the title or if the title is otherwise challenged.

covenantor One who makes a promise by covenant to another.

covenant running with the land A covenant whose benefits or duties bind all later purchasers of the land.

cover The right of a buyer, after breach by the seller, to purchase goods in substitution for those due from the seller.

coverage The amount and extent of risk included in insurance.

coverture The legal status of a married woman whereby her civil existence for many purposes merged with that of her husband.

craft union A labor union whose members do the same kind of work (e.g., plumbing) across different industries. Also called horizontal union.

credibility Believability; the extent to which something is worthy of belief.

credit 1. The ability to acquire goods or services before payment. 2. Funds loaned. 3. An accounting entry for a sum received. 4. A deduction from the amount owed.

credit bureau A business that collects financial information on the creditworthiness of potential customers of businesses.

credit insurance Insurance against the risk of a debtor's nonpayment due to insolvency or other cause.

credit line See line of credit.

creditor One to whom a debt is owed.

creditor beneficiary A third person who is to receive the benefit of the performance of a contract (of which he or she is not a direct party) in satisfaction of a legal duty owed to him or her by one of the parties of that contract.

A "donee beneficiary" is payee receiving gift; a "creditor beneficiary" is a payee to whom insured owes a legal duty; and an "incidental beneficiary" is neither donee nor creditor. *Wargo*, 265 N.Y.S.2d 37 (Sup. Ct., 1965)

creditor's bill An equitable proceeding brought by a judgment creditor to enforce the judgment out of the judgment debtor's property that cannot be reached by ordinary legal process.

credit rating An assessment of one's ability to repay debts.

crime Conduct defined as criminal by the government. Typically all felonies and misdemeanors are crimes.

crime against humanity Conduct prohibited by international law that is knowingly committed as part of a widespread or systematic attack against any civilian population.

crime against nature See sodomy.

crimen falsi A crime involving false statements, e.g., perjury.

crime of passion A crime committed in the heat of an emotionally charged moment.

criminal 1. One who has committed or been convicted of a crime. 2. Pertaining to crimes.

criminal action A prosecution for a crime.

criminal assault See assault.

criminal attempt See attempt.

criminal conspiracy See conspiracy.

criminal contempt An act directed against the authority of the court that obstructs the administration of justice and tends to bring the court into disrepute.

> "Criminal contempt" involves vindication of an offense against judicial authority and is utilized to protect integrity and dignity of judicial process and to compel respect for its mandates. McKinney's Judiciary Law §§ 750, 753. *Department of Housing Preservation and Development of City of New York*, 620 N.Y.S. 2d 837 (2 Dept., 1995)

criminal conversation (crim. con.) A tort that is committed when the defendant has sexual relations with the plaintiff's spouse.

criminal forfeiture An action against a defendant convicted of a crime to seize his or her property as part of the punishment.

criminalize To declare that specific conduct will constitute a crime.

criminal law Laws defining crimes, punishments, and procedures for investigation and prosecution. Also called penal law.

criminal mischief See malicious mischief.

criminal negligence Conduct that is such a gross deviation from the standard of reasonable care that it is punishable as a crime.

> "Criminal negligence" is synonymous with "culpable negligence," which encompasses a reckless and wanton disregard for the safety of life or limb. *People v. Brucato*, 32 N.Y.S.2d 689 (Co. Ct., 1942)

criminal procedure The law governing the investigation and prosecution of crimes, including sentencing and appeal.

criminal syndicalism Advocacy of crime or other unlawful methods of achieving industrial or political change.

criminal trespass Knowingly entering or remaining on land with notice that this is forbidden.

criminology The study of the causes, punishment, and prevention of crime.

critical legal studies (CLS) The theory that law is not neutral but exists to perpetuate the interests of those who are rich and powerful. *Critical race theory* emphasizes the disadvantages imposed on racial minorities under this theory.

critical stage A step in a criminal investigation or proceeding that holds significant consequences for the accused, at which time the right to counsel applies.

cross action 1. A claim brought by the defendant against the plaintiff in the same action. Sometimes called a counterclaim. 2. A claim brought by one defendant against another defendant or by one plaintiff against another plaintiff in the same action. Also called a cross-claim.

cross appeal An appeal by the appellee in the case that the appellant has appealed.

cross bill An equitable claim brought by the defendant against the plaintiff or another defendant in the same suit.

cross-claim See cross action (2).

cross collateral 1. Pooling collateral among participants. 2. Collateral used to secure additional loans or accounts.

cross-complaint 1. A claim by the defendant against another party in the same case. 2. A claim by the defendant against someone not now a party in the case that is related to the claim already filed against the defendant.

cross-examination Questioning a witness by an opponent after the other side called and questioned that witness.

crown cases A criminal case brought in England.

cruel and unusual punishment Degrading or disproportionate punishment, shocking the conscience and offending human dignity.

cruelty The intentional or malicious infliction of serious mental or physical suffering on another.

> "Cruelty" for purposes of divorce action on ground of cruel and inhuman treatment implies wantonness or intent to inflict suffering by actions of such character as to show pattern of actual physical violence or other conduct which seriously affects or impairs health of complaining spouse and renders cohabitation unsafe or improper. McKinney's DRL § 170(1). *Wilson*, 663 N.Y.S.2d 710 (3 Dept., 1997)

CSSA (Child Support Standards Act) See child support.

cta See cum testamento annexo.

culpable At fault; blameworthy.

cum Together with, along with.

cum testamento annexo (cta) Concerning administration of an estate where no executor is named in the will, or where one is named but is unable to serve. Administration with the will annexed.

cumulative That which repeats earlier material and consolidates it with new material. Added and combined into one unit.

> The definition is cumulative, so that an obscene publication or performance must contain all of them. *People v. Thousand*, 469 N.Y.S.2d 991 (City Ct., 1983)

cumulative dividend A dividend that, if not paid in one period, is added to dividends to be paid in the next period.

cumulative evidence Additional evidence tending to prove the same point as other evidence already given.

cumulative legacy An additional gift of personal property in the same will (or its codicil) to the same person.

cumulative sentences See consecutive sentences.

cumulative voting A type of voting in which a voter is given as many votes as there are positions to fill and can use the votes for one candidate or spread them among several candidates.

curative Tending to correct or cure a mistake or error.

curator 1. A guardian or custodian of another's affairs. 2. One appointed by the court to be in charge of a decedent's estate until letters are issued.

cure 1. To remove a legal defect or error. 2. The seller's right, after delivering defective goods, to redeliver conforming goods.

current asset 1. Property that can readily be converted into cash. 2. An asset that will be converted into cash within one year.

current liabilities A debt that is likely to be paid within the current business cycle, usually a year.

curtesy A husband's right to lifetime use of land his deceased wife owned during the marriage if a child was born alive to them.

> Curtesy is a life estate which the common law gives to a husband upon his wife's death in the real property of which she dies seized of an estate of inheritance, provided live issue was born of the marriage. *Terwilliger*, 426 N.Y.S.2d 684 (Sup. Ct., 1980)

curtilage The land (often enclosed) immediately surrounding and associated with a dwelling house.

custodial interrogation Questioning by law enforcement officers after a person is taken into custody or otherwise deprived of his or her freedom in any significant way.

custodian One with responsibility for the care and custody of property, a person, papers, etc.

custody The protective care and control of a thing or person.

custom 1. An established practice that has acquired the force of law. 2. A tax (duty) on the importation and exportation of goods.

cy-pres As near as possible. The intention of the author of an instrument (e.g., will, trust) will be carried out as closely as possible if carrying it out literally is impossible. To prevent the failure of the instrument, the court reforms the instrument using this guideline.

D

DA 1. District Attorney. 2. Deposit account.

dactylography The study of identification through fingerprints.

damage An injury or loss to person, property, or rights.

damages Monetary compensation a court can award for wrongful injury or loss to person or property.

damnum absque injuria A loss that cannot be the basis of a lawsuit because it was not caused by a wrongful act.

dangerous instrumentality An object or condition that in its normal operation is an implement of destruction or involves grave danger.

> "Dangerous instrument" means any instrument, article or substance, including a "vehicle" as that term is defined in this section, which, under the circumstances in which it is used, attempted to be used or threatened to be used, is readily capable of causing death or other serious physical injury. McKinney's Penal Law § 10.00(13)

date of issue The date fixed or agreed upon as the beginning or effective date of a security or document in a series (e.g., bonds).

date rape Rape committed by the victim's social escort.

day in court The right to assert your claim or defense in court.

daybook A book on which daily business transactions are recorded.

dba (d/b/a) Doing business as. A trade name; an assumed name.

dbn See de bonis non.

DC District Court; District of Columbia.

dead freight The amount paid for the portion of a ship's cargo space that is contracted for but not used.

deadlock 1. A standstill due to a refusal of the parties to compromise. 2. The threatened destruction of a business that results when contending shareholders owning an equal number of shares cannot agree.

deadly force Force that is likely or intended to cause death or great bodily harm.

deadly weapon A weapon or other instrument intended to be used or likely to be used to cause death or great bodily harm. Also called lethal weapon.

> Cannister of mace, like a handgun, was capable of inflicting serious injury when operable, and, thus, the mace was a "deadly or dangerous instrument," for purposes of statute criminalizing possession of a weapon. McKinney's Penal Law § 265.01. *People v. McCullum*, 706 N.Y.S.2d 616 (N.Y. City Crim. Ct., 2000)

dead man's statute A rule making some statements of a dead person inadmissible for designated purposes such as to support a claim against the estate of the dead person.

> The Dead Man's Statue "precludes a party or person interested in the underlying event from offering testimony concerning a personal transaction or communication with the decedent." *Miller* 876 N.Y.S.2d 211 (3 Dept., 2009). McKinney's CPLR 4519.

dealer 1. One who buys goods for resale to others. 2. One who buys and sells securities on his or her own account rather than as an agent.

death Permanent cessation of all vital functions and signs.

> For purposes of homicide conviction, "death" occurs upon cardiorespiratory failure or upon irreversible cessation of brain function. *People v. Lai*, 516 N.Y.S.2d 300 (2 Dept., 1987)

deathbed declaration See dying declaration.

death certificate An official record of someone's death, often including vital information such as the date and cause of death.

death knell exception A nonfinal order is appealable if delaying the appeal will cause a party to lose substantial rights.

death penalty Capital punishment; a death sentence.

death qualified rule In a death penalty case, prospective jurors who oppose the death penalty should not be selected.

death tax See estate tax, inheritance tax.

death warrant A court order to carry out a death sentence.

debar To prohibit someone from possessing or doing something.

de bene esse Conditionally allowed for now.

debenture A bond or other debt backed by the general credit of a corporation and not secured by a lien on any specific property.

de bonis non (dbn) Of the goods not administered. An administrator de bonis non is an administrator appointed (in place of a former administrator or executor) to administer the remainder of an estate.

> When the office of administrator becomes vacant for any reason the court may grant letters of administration de bonis non to one or more eligible persons and the proceedings to procure such letters shall be the same as upon an application for original letters of administration. McKinney's SCPA § 1007(1)

debit 1. A sum owed. 2. An entry made on the left side of an account.

debt An amount of money that is due; an enforceable obligation.

debt capital Money raised by issuing bonds rather than stock.

debtor One who owes a debt, usually money.

debtor in possession A debtor in bankruptcy while still running its business.

debt service Payments to be made to a lender, including interest, principal, and fees.

deceased A dead person; dead.

decedent A dead person.

decedent's estate Property (real and personal) in which a person has an interest at the time of his or her death.

deceit Willfully or recklessly misrepresenting or suppressing material facts with the intent to mislead someone.

decertify 1. To withdraw or revoke certification. 2. To declare that a union can no longer represent a group of employees.

decision A determination of a court or administrative agency applying the law to the facts to resolve a conflict.

decisional law Case law; the law found in court opinions.

declarant A person who makes a declaration or statement.

declaration 1. A formal or explicit statement. 2. An unsworn statement. 3. The first pleading of the plaintiff in an action at law.

declaration against interest A statement made by a nonparty that is against his or her own interest. The statement can be admitted as an exception to the hearsay rule if it was made by someone with personal knowledge who is now not available as a witness.

A declaration against interest may be received if four conditions are satisfied: (1) the declarant is unavailable; (2) the declaration when made was against the pecuniary, proprietary or penal interest of the declarant; (3) the declarant had competent knowledge of the facts; and (4) there was no probable motive to misrepresent the facts. *McDonald*, 684 N.Y.S.2d 414 (Sup. Ct., 1998)

declaration of trust The establishment of a trust by one who declares that he or she holds the legal title to property in trust for another.

declaratory judgment A binding judgment that declares rights, status, or other legal relationships without ordering anything to be done.

The objective of a declaratory judgment is to enable a party whose rights, privileges, and powers are endangered, threatened, or placed in uncertainty to invoke the aid of the court to obtain a declaration of his rights or legal relations. *Kopit*, 35 N.Y.S.2d 558 (Sup. Ct., 1942)

declaratory statute A statute passed to remove doubt about the meaning of an earlier statute. Also called expository statute.

decree 1. A court order. 2. The decision of a court of equity.

decree nisi A decree that will become absolute unless a party convinces the court that it should not be. Also called order nisi, rule nisi.

decretal Pertaining to a decree.

decriminalization A law making legal what was once criminal.

dedication A gift of private land (or an easement) for public use.

deductible 1. What can be taken away or subtracted. 2. The amount of a loss the insured must bear before insurance payments begin.

deduction The part taken away, e.g., an amount that can be subtracted from gross income when calculating adjusted gross income.

deed 1. A document transferring (conveying) an interest in land. 2. An act; something that is done or carried out.

deed of trust A security instrument (similar to a mortgage) in which title to real property is given to a trustee as security until the debt is paid. Also called trust deed, trust indenture.

deem To treat as if; to regard something as true or present even if this is not actually so.

deep pocket An individual, business, or other organization with resources to pay a potential judgment. The opposite of *shallow pocket*.

Deep Rock doctrine A controlling shareholder's loan to its own company that is undercapitalized may, in fairness, be subordinated in bankruptcy to other loan claims.

deface To mar or destroy the physical appearance of something.

de facto 1. In fact. 2. Functioning or existing even if not formally or officially encouraged or authorized.

de facto corporation An enterprise that attempts to exercise corporate powers even though it was not properly incorporated in a state where it could have incorporated and where it made a good faith effort to do so.

Where corporate term of existence has expired but the corporation carries on its affairs and exercises corporate powers as before, it is a de facto corporation. *Ludlum Corp.*, 548 N.Y.S. 2d 292 (2 Dept., 1989)

de facto government A government that has assumed the exercise of sovereignty over a nation, often by illegal or extralegal means.

de facto segregation Segregation caused by social, economic, or other factors rather than by state action or active government assistance.

defalcation 1. A fiduciary's failure to account for funds entrusted to it. Misappropriation; embezzlement. 2. The failure to comply with an obligation.

defamation The publication of a written (or gestured) defamatory statement (libel) or an oral one (slander) of and concerning the plaintiff that harms the plaintiff's reputation.

Defamation is a false statement that exposes a person to public contempt, ridicule, aversion or disgrace. *Town of Massena*, 749 N.Y.S.2d 456 (Ct. of App., 2002)

default 1. The failure to carry out a duty. 2. The failure to appear.

default judgment A judgment against a party for failure to file a required pleading, appear in court, or otherwise respond to the opponent's claim.

defeasance 1. The act of rendering something null and void. 2. An instrument that defeats the force or operation of an estate or deed upon the fulfillment of a condition.

defeasible Subject to being revoked or avoided.

defeasible fee See fee simple defeasible.

defeat To prevent, frustrate, or circumvent; to render void.

defect A shortcoming; the lack of something required.

defective Lacking in some particular that is essential to completeness, safety, or legal sufficiency.

defend 1. To protect or represent someone. 2. To contest or oppose.

defendant One against whom a civil action or criminal prosecution is brought.

defender 1. One who raises defenses. 2. One who represents another.

defense 1. An allegation of fact or a legal theory offered to offset or defeat a claim or demand. 2. The defendant and his or her attorney.

deferred annuity An annuity that begins payment at a future date.

deferred compensation Work income set aside for payment in the future.

deferred income Income to be received in the future, after it was earned.

deficiency 1. A shortage or insufficiency. 2. The amount still owed.

> Deficiency compensation is difference between amount actually collected from a third party and benefits to which he is entitled under the Workmen's Compensation Law. Workmen's Compensation Law, § 29. *Schreckinger*, 194 N.Y.S.2d 67 (3 Dept., 1959)

deficiency judgment A judgment for an unpaid balance after the creditor has taken the secured property of the debtor.

deficit 1. An excess of outlays over revenues. 2. An insufficiency.

defined benefit plan A pension plan where the amount of the benefit is fixed but the amount of the contribution is not.

defined contribution plan A pension plan where the amount of the contribution is generally fixed but the amount of the benefit is not.

> Defined contribution plan means any service award program that provides to a participant a benefit as the result of definite and determinable contributions made to the program on behalf of the participant without reference to any income, expense, gains or losses or forfeitures of other participants under the program. McKinney's General Municipal Law § 219-c(2)

definite failure of issue See failure of issue.

definite sentence See determinate sentence.

definitive Complete; settling the matter.

defraud To use deception to obtain something or harm someone.

degree 1. The measure or scope of the seriousness of something; a grade or level of wrongdoing. 2. One of the steps in a process. 3. A step in the line of descent.

degree of care The standard of care that is required.

degree of proof The level of believability or persuasiveness that one's evidence must meet.

dehors Beyond the scope, outside of.

de jure Sanctioned by law; in compliance with the law.

de jure segregation Segregation allowed or mandated by the law.

del credere agent A business agent or factor who guarantees the solvency and performance of the purchaser.

delectus personae The right of a partner to exercise his or her preference on the admission of new partners.

delegable duty A responsibility that one can ask another to perform.

delegate 1. To appoint a representative. 2. A representative.

delegation 1. The granting of authority to act for another. 2. The persons authorized to act as representatives.

deliberate 1. To weigh or examine carefully. 2. Intentional.

deliberative process privilege The government can maintain secrecy when needed to ensure the free exchange of ideas in the making of policy.

delict, delictum A tort or offense; a violation of the law.

delinquency 1. A violation of duty. 2. The failure to pay a debt. 3. Antisocial, unruly, or immoral behavior by a minor.

delinquent 1. Pertaining to that which is still due; in arrears. 2. Failing to abide by the law or to conform to moral standards. 3. In some states, a minor who has committed an offense or other serious misconduct. See also juvenile delinquent.

delisting Removing a security from the list of what can be traded on an exchange.

delivery 1. The act by which something is placed in the possession or control of another. 2. That which is delivered.

demand 1. To claim as one's due or right. 2. The assertion of a right.

demand deposit Any bank deposit that the depositor may withdraw (demand) at any time without notice.

> The term, "demand deposits," when used in this chapter, and except as provided otherwise by regulation of the banking board, means deposits payment of which can legally be required within fourteen days. McKinney's Banking Law § 2(13)

demand loan A loan without a set maturity date that the lender can demand payment of at any time. A call loan.

demand note A note that must be paid whenever the lender requests (demands) payment.

demeanor Outward or physical appearance or behavior; deportment.

demesne 1. Domain. 2. Land a person holds in his or her own right.

de minimis Very small; not significant enough to change the result.

demise 1. A lease. A conveyance of land to another for a term. 2. The document that creates a lease. 3. To convey or create an estate or lease. 4. To transfer property by descent or by will. 5. Death.

demise charter See bareboat charter.

democracy A system of government controlled by the people directly or through elected representatives.

demonstrative bequest; demonstrative legacy A gift by will payable out of a specific fund.

demonstrative evidence Evidence (other than testimony) addressed to the senses. Physical evidence offered for illumination and explanation, but otherwise unrelated to the case. Also called autoptic evidence.

"Demonstrative evidence" is concerned with real objects which illustrate some verbal testimony and has no probative value in itself. *People v. Diaz*, 445 N.Y.S.2d 888 (Sup. Ct., 1981)

demur 1. To state a demurrer. 2. To take exception.

demurrer A pleading that admits, for the sake of argument, the allegations of fact made by the other party in order to show that even if they are true, they are do not entitle this party to relief.

denial 1. A declaration that something the other side alleges is not true. 2. Rejection; refusing to do something.

de novo Anew; as if for the first time. See trial de novo.

depecage Under conflicts of law principles, a court can apply the laws of different jurisdictions to different disputes in the same case.

dependency 1. A geographically separate territory under the jurisdiction of another country or sovereign. 2. A relationship in which one person relies on another for society or a standard of living.

dependent 1. One who derives his or her main support from another. 2. A person who can be claimed as a personal exemption by a taxpayer.

dependent covenant A party's agreement or promise whose performance is conditioned on and subject to prior performance by the other party.

dependent relative revocation The revocation of an earlier will was intended to give effect to a later will, so if the later will is inoperative, the earlier will shall take effect.

Under doctrine of "dependent relative revocation," under which revocation of a will fails and original will remains in force if attempted disposition is inoperative, penned alterations to testator's will did not revoke the will in light of testator's intent to change, rather than revoke, the will. *Matter of Collins' Will*, 458 N.Y.S.2d 987 (Sur., 1982)

depletion An exhausting or reduction during the taxable year of oil, gas, or other mineral deposits and reserves.

deponent One who gives testimony at a deposition.

deport To banish or exile someone to a foreign country.

depose 1. To question a witness in a deposition. 2. To give testimony. 3. To remove from office or power.

deposit 1. To place for safekeeping. 2. An asset placed for safekeeping. 3. Money given as security or earnest money for the performance of a contract. Also called security deposit.

depositary A person or institution (e.g., bank) that receives an asset for safekeeping.

depositary bank The first bank to which checks or other deposits are taken for collection.

"Depositary bank" means the first bank to which an item is transferred for collection even though it is also the payor bank. McKinney's Uniform Commercial Code § 4-105(a)

deposition A method of discovery by which parties or their prospective witnesses are questioned outside the courtroom before trial.

deposition de bene esse A deposition of a witness who will not be able to testify at trial, taken in order to preserve his or her testimony.

depository The place where an asset is placed and kept for safekeeping.

depreciable life 1. The period over which an asset may reasonably be expected to be useful in a trade or business. Also called useful life. 2. The time period over which an asset is depreciated for the purpose of determining depreciation expense for either financial reporting or tax calculation.

depreciation 1. A gradual decline in the value of property caused by use, deterioration, time, or obsolescence. 2. The act of matching the cost of an asset's decrease in value over the time period over which the decrease occurs, resulting in the determination of depreciation expense for either financial accounting or tax calculation.

deputy One duly authorized to act on behalf of another.

deregulate To lessen government control over an industry or business.

derelict 1. Abandoned property. 2. Delinquent in a duty.

dereliction 1. A wrongful or shameful neglect or abandonment of one's duty. 2. The gaining of land from the water as a result of a shrinking back of the sea or river below the usual watermark.

derivative 1. Coming from another; secondary. 2. A financial instrument whose value is dependent on another asset or investment.

derivative action 1. A suit by a shareholder to enforce a corporate cause of action. Also called a derivative suit, representative action. 2. An action to recover for a loss that is dependent on an underlying tort or wrong committed against someone else.

A "stockholder's derivative action" is one to redress a wrong done to a corporation and not to a stockholder individually. *Kerekes*, 186 N.Y.S.2d 90 (Sup. Ct., 1959)

derivative evidence Evidence that is inadmissible because it is derived or spawned from other evidence that was illegally obtained. See also fruit of the poisonous tree doctrine.

derivative suit See derivative action (1).

derivative work A translation or other transformation of a preexisting work.

derogation 1. A partial repeal or abolishing of a law, as by a subsequent act that limits its scope or force. 2. Disparaging or belittling, or undermining something or someone.

descend To be transferred to persons entitled to receive a deceased's assets by intestate succession. To pass by inheritance.

descendant Offspring; persons in the bloodline of an ancestor.

descent A transfer to persons entitled to receive a deceased's assets by intestate succession. Passing by inheritance.

descent and distribution 1. See intestate succession. 2. The passing of a decedent's assets by intestacy or will.

desecrate To violate something that is sacred; to defile.

desegregation The elimination of policies and laws that led to racial segregation.

desertion 1. The voluntary, unjustified leaving of one's spouse for an uninterrupted period of time with the intent not to return to resume marital cohabitation. Also called abandonment. 2. The willful failure to fulfill a support obligation. 3. Remaining absent (without authority) from one's military place of duty with the intent to remain away permanently.

Abandonment has been defined as the desertion of a spouse with intent not to return or with an intent that the marriage should no longer exist. *In re Goethie's Will*, 161 N.Y.S.2d 785 (Sur., 1957)

design defect A flaw rendering a product unreasonably dangerous because of the way in which it was designed or conceived.

designer drug A synthetic substitute for an existing controlled substance or drug, often made to avoid anti-drug laws.

destination contract A contract in which the risk of loss passes to the buyer when the seller tenders the goods at the destination.

destructibility of contingent remainders A contingent remainder must vest before or at the end of the preceding estate, or it fails (is destroyed).

desuetude 1. Discontinuation of use. 2. The equivalent of a repeal of a law by reason of its long and continued nonuse.

detainer 1. Withholding possession of land or goods from another. Keeping someone or something in your custody. See also unlawful detainer. 2. A request or writ that an institution continue keeping someone in custody.

detention Holding in custody; confinement.

determinable 1. Capable of coming to an end (terminable) upon the occurrence of a contingency. 2. Susceptible of being determined, ascertained, or settled.

Where realty was conveyed to railroad for railroad purposes and for "so long as" the railroad should use the realty for its railroad, and deed provided that, when realty should cease to be permanently used for railroad, then realty should revert to the grantor or his heirs or assigns, the estate created was a "determinable fee" rather than a fee on "condition subsequent." *Thypin*, 28 N.Y.S.2d 262 (Sup. Ct., 1941)

determinable fee See fee simple determinable.

determinate sentence A sentence to confinement for a fixed period. Also called definite sentence.

determination 1. The final decision of a court or administrative agency. 2. The ending of an estate or property interest.

detinue An action for the recovery of personal property held (detained) wrongfully by another.

detraction Transferring property to another state upon a transfer of the title to it by will or inheritance.

detriment 1. Any loss or harm to person or property. 2. A legal right that a promisee gives up. Also called legal detriment.

Something that causes damage, harm or loss. [The plain meaning of detriment] when used in the subject statute is that the emission of certain strong odors and visible dust have harmful effects on, inter alia, human health. *New Amber Auto Service*, 619 N.Y.S.2d 496 (Sup. Ct., 1994)

detrimental reliance A loss, disadvantage, or change in one's position for the worse because of one's reliance on another's promise.

devaluation A reduction in the value of a currency in relation to other currencies.

devastavit An act of omission, negligence, or misconduct of an administrator or other legal representative of an estate.

devest See divest.

deviation Departure from established or usual conduct or ideology.

deviation doctrine A variation in the terms of a will or trust will be allowed to avoid defeating the purposes of the document.

device 1. A mechanical or electronic invention or gadget. 2. A scheme.

devise The gift of property (sometimes only real property) by a will.

Use of the word "devise" in residuary gift symbolized a conveyance of realty and supported contention that testator intended that realty should vest as such in residuary devisees. *In re Wanninger's Estate*, 34 N.Y.S.2d 326 (Sur. Ct., 1942)

devisee The person to whom property is devised or given in a will.

devisor The person who devises or gives property in a will.

devolution The transfer or transition of a right, title, estate, or office to another or to a lower level. The verb is *devolve*.

devolve See devolution.

dicta See dictum, which is the singular form of dicta.

dictum 1. An observation made by a judge in an opinion that is not essential to resolve the issues before the court; comments that go beyond the facts before the court. Also called obiter dictum. 2. An authoritative, formal statement or announcement.

dies A day; days, e.g., dies non juridicus: A day on which courts are not open for business.

diet The name of the legislature in some countries.

digest An organized summary or abridgment. A set of volumes that contain brief summaries of court opinions, arranged by subject matter and by court or jurisdiction.

dilatory plea A plea raising a procedural matter, not on the merits.

diligence 1. Persistent activity. 2. Prudence, carefulness.

dilution Diminishing the strength or value of something, e.g., voting strength by increasing the number of shares issued, uniqueness of a trademark by using it on too many different products.

diminished capacity or **responsibility** A mental disorder not amounting to insanity that impairs or negates the defendant's ability to form the culpable mental state to commit the crime. Also called partial insanity.

diminution in value As a measure of damages, the difference between the fair market value of the property with and without the damage.

diplomatic immunity A diplomat's exemption from most laws of the host country.

direct 1. To command, regulate, or manage. 2. To aim or cause to move in a certain direction. 3. Without interruption; immediate. 4. In a straight line of descent, as opposed to a collateral line.

direct attack An attempt to have a judgment changed in the same case or proceeding that rendered the judgment, e.g., an appeal.

"Direct attack" on judgment is attempt to avoid same in proceeding in same action, while "collateral attack" is attempt to impeach judgment by matters outside record in different action. *James Mills Orchards Corp.*, 244 N.Y.S. 473 (Sup. Ct., 1930)

direct cause See proximate cause.

direct contempt A contempt committed in the presence of the court or so near the court as to interrupt its proceedings.

direct damages See general damages.

directed verdict A judge's decision not to allow the jury to deliberate because only one verdict is reasonable. In federal court, the verdict has been replaced by a *judgment as a matter of law* (see this phrase).

direct estoppel See collateral estoppel.

direct evidence Evidence that, if believed, proves a fact without using inferences or presumptions; evidence based on what one personally saw, heard, or touched. Also called positive evidence.

Evidence is "direct evidence" when principal or res gestae facts of case are communicated by those who have actual knowledge of them by means of their senses. *People v. Duffy*, 508 N.Y.S. 2d 267 (3 Dept., 1986)

direct examination The first questioning of a witness by the party who has called the witness. Also called examination in chief.

direct line A line of descent traced through those persons who are related to each other directly as descendants or ascendants.

director 1. One who directs or guides a department, organization, or activity. 2. A member of the board that oversees and controls the managers or officers of an entity such as a corporation.

directory Nonmandatory. Pertaining to a clause or provision in a statute or contract that is advisory rather than involving the essence of the statute or contract.

directory trust A trust whose details will be filled out by later instructions.

direct tax A tax imposed directly on property rather than on the transfer of property or on some other right connected with property.

disability 1. Legal incapacity to perform an act. 2. A physical or mental condition that limits one's ability to participate in a major life activity such as employment. Also called incapacity.

The term "disability" is defined as physical, medical or mental impairments that do not prevent the complainant from performing in a reasonable manner the activities involved in the job. *Pimentel*, 811 N.Y.S.2d 381 (1 Dept., 2006)

disaffirm To repudiate; to cancel or revoke consent.

disallow To refuse to allow; to deny or reject.

disavow To repudiate; to disclaim knowledge of or responsibility for.

disbar To expel an attorney or revoke his or her license to practice law.

disbursement Paying out money; an out-of-pocket expenditure.

discharge 1. To relieve of an obligation. 2. To fulfill an obligation. 3. To release or let go. 4. To cancel a court order. 5. To shoot. 6. To release from employment or service.

The doctrine of "provoked discharge," for unemployment compensation purposes, is limited to those circumstances where the employer had no choice but to discharge the employee where the latter's acts were voluntary. *In re Williams*, 798 N.Y.S.2d 546 (3 Dept., 2005)

discharge in bankruptcy The release of a bankrupt from all nonexempted debts in a bankruptcy proceeding.

disciplinary rule (DR) A rule stating the minimum conduct below which no attorney should fall without being subject to discipline.

disclaimer The repudiation of one's own or another's claim, right, or obligation.

disclosure 1. The act of revealing that which is secret or not known. 2. Complying with a legal duty to provide specified information.

discontinuance 1. The plaintiff's withdrawal or termination of his or her suit. 2. In zoning, the abandonment of a use.

discount 1. An allowance or deduction from the original price or debt. 2. The amount by which interest is reduced from the face value of a note or other financial instrument at the outset of the loan. 3. The amount by which the price paid for a security is less than its face value.

discounting Converting future cash flows into a present value.

discount rate 1. A percentage of the face amount of commercial paper (e.g., note) that an issuer pays when transferring the paper to a financial institution. 2. The interest rate charged by the Federal Reserve to member banks.

discoverable Pertaining to information or other materials an opponent can obtain through a deposition or other discovery device.

discovered peril doctrine See last clear chance doctrine.

discovery Compulsory exchanges of information between parties in litigation. Pretrial devices (e.g., interrogatories) to obtain information about a suit from the other side.

discredit To cast doubt on the credibility of a person, an idea, or evidence.

discretion 1. The power or right to act by the dictates of one's own judgment and conscience. 2. The freedom to decide among options. 3. Good judgment; prudence.

"Discretion" is not simply a judge's sense of moral right or what is just, but it is a liberty or privilege to decide and act in accordance with what is fair and equitable under the peculiar circumstances of the particular case, guided by the spirit, principles, and analogies of the law. *Gielski*, 155 N.Y.S.2d 863 (Ct. Cl., 1956)

discretionary review An appeal that an appellate court agrees to hear when it has the option of refusing to hear it.

discretionary trust A trust giving the trustee discretion to decide when a beneficiary will receive income or principal and how much. Also called complex trust.

discrimination 1. Differential imposition of burdens or granting of benefits. 2. Unreasonably granting or denying privileges on the basis of sex, age, race, nationality, religion, or handicap.

Discrimination means differential treatment on in-State and out-of-State economic interests that benefits the former and burdens the latter. *City of New York*, 709 N.Y.S.2d 122 (Ct. of App., 2000)

disenfranchise To deprive someone of a right or privilege, e.g., the right to vote. Also called disfranchise.

disfranchise See disenfranchise.

disgorge To surrender unwillingly.

dishonor To refuse to accept or pay a draft or other negotiable instrument when duly presented.

disinheritance Taking steps to prevent someone from inheriting property.

disinterested Objective; without bias; having nothing to gain or lose.

disintermediation The withdrawal by depositors of funds from low-yielding bank accounts for use in higher-yielding investments.

disjunctive allegations Assertions pleaded in the alternative, e.g., he stole the car or caused it to be stolen.

dismissal 1. An order that ends an action or motion without additional court proceedings. 2. A discharge; an order to go away.

dismissal without prejudice Termination of the action that is not on the merits, meaning that the party can return later with the same claim.

dismissal with prejudice Termination of the action that is the equivalent of an adjudication on the merits, meaning that the party is barred from returning later with the same claim.

disorderly conduct Behavior that tends to disturb the peace, endanger the health of the community, or shock the public sense of morality.

A person is guilty of disorderly conduct when, with intent to cause public inconvenience, annoyance or alarm, or recklessly creating a risk thereof: 1. He engages in fighting or in violent, tumultuous or threatening behavior; or 2. He makes unreasonable noise; or 3. In a public place, he uses abusive or obscene language, or makes an obscene gesture; or 4. Without lawful authority, he disturbs any lawful assembly or meeting of persons; or 5. He obstructs vehicular or pedestrian traffic; or 6. He congregates with other persons in a public place and refuses to comply with a lawful order of the police to disperse; or 7. He creates a hazardous or physically offensive condition by any act which serves no legitimate purpose. McKinney's Penal Law § 240.20

disorderly house A dwelling where acts are performed that tend to corrupt morals, promote breaches of the peace, or create a nuisance.

disparagement The intentional and false discrediting of the plaintiff's product or business (sometimes called trade libel when written or slander of goods when spoken) or the plaintiff's title to property (sometimes called slander of title) resulting in specific monetary loss.

Now, although defamation and disparagement in the commercial context are allied in that the gravamen of both are falsehoods published to third parties, there is a distinction. Where a statement impugns the basic integrity or creditworthiness of a business, an action for defamation lies and injury is conclusively presumed. Where, however, the statement is confined to denigrating the quality of the business' goods or services, it could support an action for disparagement, but will do so only if malice and special damages are proven. *Ruder*, 439 N.Y.S.2d 858 (N.Y., 1981)

disparate impact Conduct that appears neutral on its face but that disproportionately and negatively impacts members of one race, sex, age, disability, or other protected group.

disparate treatment Intentionally treating some people less favorably than others because of sex, age, race, nationality, religion, or disability.

dispensation An exemption from a duty, burden, penalty, or law.

disposition 1. The act of distributing or transferring assets. 2. The final ruling or decision of a tribunal. 3. An arrangement or settlement. 4. Temperament or characteristics.

dispossess To evict from land; to deprive of possession.

disputable presumption See rebuttable presumption.

dispute 1. A controversy. 2. The conflict leading to litigation.

disqualification That which renders something ineligible or unfit.

disseisin Wrongful dispossession of another from property.

dissent 1. A judge's vote against the result reached by the judges in the majority on a case. 2. A dissenting opinion.

dissipation 1. Wasting, squandering, or destroying. 2. The use of marital property by a spouse for a personal purpose.

dissolution 1. Cancellation. 2. The act or process of terminating a legal relationship or organization. 3. A divorce.

"Dissolution" of corporation is termination of corporate existence in any manner, whether by expiration of charter, decree of court, act of Legislature, or other means. *New York Title & Mortg. Co.*, 276 N.Y.S. 72 (N.Y. Mun. Ct., 1934)

dissolution of marriage See divorce.

dist. ct. District court.

distinguish To point out an essential difference; to demonstrate that a particular court opinion is inapplicable to the current legal dispute.

distrain To take and hold the personal property of another until the latter performs an obligation.

distrainee A person who is distrained.

distrainer or **distrainor** One who seizes property under a distress.

distraint Property seized to enforce an obligation.

distress Seizing property to enforce an obligation, e.g., a landlord seizes a tenant's property to secure payment of delinquent rent.

The term "distress" as used in statute providing that the warrant shall authorize a town collector to levy taxes by distress and sale in case of nonpayment, means the taking and holding of another's chattel to apply it in satisfaction of the distrainer's demand, or to hold it until satisfaction is rendered. *City of Utica*, 41 N.Y.S.2d 248 (Sup. Ct., 1943)

distress sale 1. A foreclosure sale; a forced sale to pay a debt. 2. A sale at below market rates because of a pressure to sell.

distributee One who shares in the distribution of an estate. An heir.

distribution 1. The apportionment and division of something. 2. The transfer of property under the law of intestate succession after estate taxes and other debts are paid. 3. The transfer of proceeds from the sale of assets by a bankruptcy trustee to creditors of the estate.

distributive finding A jury's finding in part for the plaintiff and in part for the defendant.

distributive justice A system of justice where the goal is the fair allocation of available goods, services, and burdens.

district A geographic division for judicial, political, electoral, or administrative purposes.

district attorney 1. A prosecutor representing the government in criminal cases in an area or district. Also called prosecuting attorney or state attorney. 2. The elected county-wide prosecutor of all criminal cases in each New York county.

district court 1. A trial court in the federal and some state judicial systems. 2. A county-wide local court in Nassau and Suffolk counties.

disturbance of the peace See breach of the peace.

divers Various, several.

diversion 1. Turning aside or altering the natural course or route of a thing. 2. An alternative to criminal prosecution leading to the dismissal of the charges if the accused completes a program of rehabilitation. Also called diversion program, pretrial diversion, or pretrial intervention.

diversity of citizenship The disputing parties are citizens of different states. This fact gives jurisdiction (called diversity jurisdiction) to a U.S. District Court when the amount in controversy exceeds $75,000.

divest To dispose of or be deprived of rights, duties, or possessions. Also spelled devest.

divestiture 1. The selling, spinning off, or surrender of business assets. 2. The requirement that specific property, securities, or other assets be disposed of, often to avoid a restraint of trade.

divided custody A custody arrangement in which the parents alternate having full custody (legal and physical) of a child.

dividend A share of corporate profits given pro rata to stockholders.

divisible Capable of being divided.

divisible contract A contract with parts that can be enforced separately so that the failure to perform one part does not bar recovery for performance of another.

Where sales contract for delivery of goods in installments provided that each delivery was to stand as separate contract and each shipment was to be paid for on delivery, independently of others, contract was "divisible." *Koppel*, 47 N.Y.S.2d 443 (City Ct. 1944)

divisible divorce A divorce decree that dissolves the marriage in one proceeding but that resolves other marital issues such as property division and child custody in a separate proceeding.

divorce A declaration by a court that a validly entered marriage is dissolved. Also called dissolution of marriage.

divorce a mensa et thoro See legal separation.

divorce a vinculo matrimonii An absolute divorce that terminates the marital relationship.

DNA fingerprinting The process of identifying the genetic makeup of an individual based on the uniqueness of his or her DNA pattern. Deoxyribonucleic acid (DNA) is the carrier of genetic information in living organisms.

DNR Do not resuscitate (a notice concerning terminally ill persons).

dock 1. The space in a criminal court where prisoners stand when brought in for trial. 2. A landing place for boats.

docket 1. A list of pending court cases. 2. A record containing brief notations on the proceedings that have occurred in a court case.

docket number A consecutive number assigned to a case by the court and used on all documents filed with the court during the litigation of that case.

doctor of jurisprudence See Juris Doctor.

doctor-patient privilege A patient and doctor can refuse to disclose communications between them concerning diagnosis or treatment. Also called physician-patient privilege.

Confidential information is privileged. Unless the patient waives the privilege, a person authorized to practice medicine, registered professional nursing, licensed practical nursing, dentistry, podiatry or chiropractic shall not be allowed to disclose any information which he acquired in attending a patient in a professional capacity, and which was necessary to enable him to act in that capacity. McKinney's CPLR § 4504(a)

doctrine A rule or legal principle.

document 1. Any physical or electronic embodiment of words or ideas (e.g., letter, X-ray plate). 2. To support with documentary evidence or with authorities. 3. To create a written record.

documentary evidence Evidence in the form of something written.

document of title A document giving its holder the right to receive and dispose of goods covered by the document (e.g., a bill of lading).

doing business Carrying on or conducting a business.

doli capax Capable of having the intent to commit a crime.

dolus Fraud; deceitfulness.

domain 1. Land that is owned; an estate in land. 2. Absolute ownership and control. 3. The territory governed by a ruler.

Dombrowski doctrine To protect First Amendment rights, a federal court can enjoin state criminal proceedings based on a vague statute. *Dombrowski v. Pfister*, 85 S. Ct. 1116 (1965).

domestic Concerning one's own country, state, jurisdiction, or family.

domestic corporation A corporation established in a particular state.

domestic partners Persons in a same-sex (or unmarried opposite-sex) relationship who are emotionally and financially interdependent and who register with the government to receive marriage-like benefits.

"Domestic partner" means a person who, with respect to another person: (i) is formally a party in a domestic partnership entered into pursuant to the laws of the United States or of any state, local or foreign jurisdiction; or (ii) is formally recognized as a beneficiary or covered person under the other person's employment benefits or health insurance; or (iii) is at least eighteen years of age and dependent or mutually interdependent on the other person for support, indicating a mutual intent to be domestic partners. McKinney's Public Health Law § 4201(1)(c)

domestic relations 1. Law relating to marital and family matters. 2. Domestic Relations Law, the New York law relating to marriage and divorce.

domestic violence Actual or threatened physical injury or abuse by one member of a family or household on another member.

domicile 1. The place where someone has physically been present with the intention to make that place a permanent home; the place to which one would intend to return when away. 2. The place where a business has its headquarters or principal place of business. 3. The legal residence of a person or business. (Residence and domicile are sometimes used interchangeably.)

The primary difference between a residence and a domicile is that residence merely means "being in a particular locality," but it is the "intent to make it a fixed and permanent home" that makes "it one's domicile." *In re Estate of Orejas*, 12 Misc. 3d 1172(A) (Sur., 2006)

domiciliary Someone who has established a domicile in a place.

domiciliary administration The administration of an estate in the state where the decedent was domiciled at the time of death.

dominant estate The parcel of land that is benefited from an easement. Also called dominant tenement. The estate on which the easement is imposed or burdened is the servient estate.

dominant tenement See dominant estate.

dominion Ownership or sovereignty; control over something.

donated surplus Assets contributed by shareholders to a corporation.

donatio A gift or donation.

donative intent The donor's intent that title and control of the subject matter of the gift be irrevocably and presently transferred.

Accountholder's donative intent: that he intended, at operative time, to make present transfer of ownership to petitioner. *Leonard*, 643 N.Y.S.2d 199 (2 Dept., 1996)

donee One to whom a gift or power of appointment is given.

donee beneficiary A nonparty to a contract who receives the benefit of the contract as a gift.

donor One who makes a gift, confers a power, or creates a trust.

dormant In abeyance, suspended; temporarily inactive.

dormant judgment An unsatisfied judgment that has remained unexecuted for so long that it needs to be revived before it can be executed.

dormant partner A partner who receives financial benefits from a business, but does not run it and may be unknown to the public. Also called a silent partner, a sleeping partner.

double hearsay A hearsay statement contained within another hearsay statement.

double indemnity Twice the benefit for losses from specified causes.

double insurance Overlapping insurance whereby an insured has two or more policies on the same subject and against the same risks.

double jeopardy A second prosecution for the same offense after acquittal or conviction; multiple punishments for the same offense.

"Double jeopardy" exists where a person is tried and punished twice for the same offense. *In re Smith*, 114 N.Y.S.2d 673 (Dom. Rel. Ct., 1952)

double taxation Taxing the same thing twice for the same purpose by the same taxing authority during identical taxing periods.

double will See mutual wills (1).

doubt Uncertainty of mind. See also reasonable doubt.

doubtful title Title that raises serious doubts as to its validity.

dower A wife's right to a life estate in one-third of the land her deceased husband owned in fee at any time during the marriage.

down payment An amount of money paid by the buyer to the seller at the time of sale, which represents only a part of the total cost.

dowry Property that a woman brings to her husband upon marriage.

DR See disciplinary rule.

draft 1. An unconditional written order (e.g., a check) by the first party (called the drawer) instructing a second party (called the drawee or payor, e.g., a bank) to pay a specified sum on demand or at a specified time to a third party (called the payee) or to bearer. Also called bill of exchange. 2. A preliminary version of a plan, drawing, memo, or other writing. 3. Compulsory selection; conscription.

"Draft" is bill of exchange payable on demand purporting to be drawn on deposit, while "cashier's check" is primary obligation of bank which issues it and constitutes its written promise to pay on demand. *In re Bank of U.S.*, 277 N.Y.S. 96 (1 Dept., 1935)

Dram Shop Act A law imposing civil liability on a seller of liquor to one whose intoxication causes injury to a third person. Also called civil damage law.

draw 1. To prepare a legal document. 2. To withdraw money. 3. To make and sign (e.g., draw a check to pay the bill). 4. To pick a jury. 5. An advance against profits or amounts owed.

drawee The bank or other entity ordered to pay the amount on a draft.

drawer One who makes and signs a draft for the payment of money.

Dred Scott case The U.S. Supreme Court case holding that slaves and former slaves were not citizens even if they lived in states where slavery was not legal. *Scott v. Sanford*, 60 U.S. 393 (1857).

driving under the influence (DUI) The offense of operating a motor vehicle while impaired due to alcohol or drugs.

driving while ability impaired (DWAI) The offense of operating a motor vehicle while impaired due to alcohol, an offense less than driving while intoxicated (DWI).

Driving while ability impaired. No person shall operate a motor vehicle while the person's ability to operate such motor vehicle is impaired by the consumption of alcohol. McKinney's Vehicle and Traffic Law § 1192(1)

driving while intoxicated (DWI) 1. Generally, the offense of operating a motor vehicle while impaired due to alcohol or drugs. 2. In New York, the crime of operating a motor vehicle while impaired due to alcohol while being intoxicated or having a blood alcohol content of greater than .08%.

Driving while intoxicated. No person shall operate a motor vehicle while the person has .08 of one per centum or more by weight of alcohol [McKinney's Vehicle and Traffic Law § 1192(2)] or while the person is in an intoxicated condition. McKinney's Vehicle and Traffic Law § 1192(3)

droit A legal right; a body of law.

drug-free zone Geographic areas (e.g., near schools) where conviction of a drug offense will lead to increased punishment.

dry 1. Without duties. 2. Prohibiting the sale or use of liquor.

dry trust See passive trust.

dual capacity doctrine An employer may be liable in tort to its employee if it occupies, in addition to its capacity as employer, a second capacity that confers on it obligations independent of those imposed on an employer.

dual citizenship The status of a person who is a citizen of the United States and of another country at the same time.

dual contract Two contracts by the same parties for the same matter or transaction, something entered to mislead others.

dual-purpose doctrine An employee injured on a trip serving both business and personal purposes is covered under workers' compensation if the trip would have been made for the employer even if there were no personal purpose.

dubitante Having doubt.

duces tecum Bring with you. See also subpoena duces tecum.

due 1. Payable now or on demand; owing. 2. Proper, reasonable.

due-bill An acknowledgement of indebtedness; an IOU.

due care See reasonable care.

due course See holder in due course.

due diligence Reasonable prudence and effort in carrying out an obligation.

"Due diligence" is measure of prudence, activity, or assiduity, as is properly to be expected from and ordinarily exercised by reasonable and prudent man under particular circumstances; it is not measured by absolute standard but depends on relative facts of each case. *People v. Seto*, 616 N.Y.S.2d 890 (Sup. Ct., 1994)

due notice Notice likely to reach its target; legally prescribed notice.

due process of law Fundamental fairness in having a dispute resolved according to established procedures and rules, e.g., notice, hearing.

DUI See driving under the influence.

duly In due and proper form or manner.

dummy 1. One who buys property and holds the legal title for someone else, usually to conceal the identity of the real owner. 2. Sham.

dummy corporation A corporation formed to avoid personal liability or conceal the owner's identity, not to conduct a legitimate business.

dumping 1. Selling in quantity at a very low price. 2. Selling goods abroad at less than their fair market price at home. 3. Shifting a nonpaying patient onto another health care provider.

dun To make a demand for payment.

duplicate A copy or replacement of the original.

duplicity 1. Deception. 2. Improperly uniting two or more causes of action in one count or two or more grounds of defense in one plea. 3. Improperly charging two or more offenses in a single count of an indictment.

duress 1. Coercion; the unlawful use of force or threat of force. 2. Wrongful confinement or imprisonment.

"Duress" requiring contract to be set aside may be by physical compulsion, by threat, or by the exercise of undue influence, tantamount to self-interested cheating. *Silver*, 674 N.Y.S. 2d 915 (Sup. Ct., 1998)

duress of goods A tort of seizing or detaining another's personal property and wrongfully requiring some act before it is returned.

***Durham* test** See insanity (3).

duty 1. A legal or moral obligation that another has a right to have performed. 2. The obligation to conform to a standard of conduct prescribed by law or by contract. Also called legal duty. 3. A function or task expected to be performed in one's calling. 4. A tax on imports or exports.

duty of tonnage See tonnage (2).

dwelling house The building that is one's residence or abode.

DWAI See driving while ability impaired.

DWI See driving while intoxicated.

dying declaration A statement of fact by one conscious of imminent death about the cause or circumstances of his or her death. An exception to the hearsay rule. Also called deathbed declaration.

dynamite instruction See *Allen* charge.

E

E&O See errors and omissions insurance.

earmarking To set aside or reserve for a designated purpose.

earned income Income (e.g., wages) derived from labor and services.

earned income credit A refundable tax credit on earned income for low-income workers who have dependent children and who maintain a household.

earned premium The portion of an insurance premium that has been used thus far during the term of a policy.

earned surplus The surplus a corporation accumulates from profits after dividends are paid. Also called retained earnings.

earnest money Part of the purchase price paid by a buyer when entering a contract to show the intent and ability to carry out the contract.

earnings report A company report showing revenues, expenses, and losses over a given period and the net result. Also called an income statement, profit-and-loss statement.

easement A property interest in another's land that authorizes limited use of the land, e.g., a right-of-way across private property.

An easement is an interest in land created by grant or agreement, express or implied, which confers a right upon the holder thereof to some profit, benefit, dominion, enjoyment or lawful use out of or over the estate of another; thus, holder of easement falls within scope of generic term "owner." *Copertino*, 473 N.Y.S.2d 494 (2 Dept., 1984)

easement appurtenant An easement interest that attaches to the land and passes with it when conveyed.

easement by implication See implied easement.

easement by prescription See prescriptive easement.

easement in gross A personal right to use the land of another that usually ends with the death of the person possessing this right. An easement that does not benefit a particular piece of land.

easement of access The right to travel over the land of another to reach a road or other location.

easement of necessity A right-of-way that arises by implication or operation of law in favor of a grantee who has no reasonable access to its land or to a road except over other lands owned by the grantor or by a stranger.

eavesdrop To listen to another's private conversation without consent.

ecclesiastical Pertaining to the church. See also canon law.

ECF See electronic court filing.

economic duress See business compulsion.

economic realities test The totality of commercial circumstances that a court will examine to determine the nature of a relationship.

Plaintiff contends that she was employed by both Ms. Feinberg and her mother. In order to determine this issue, the Court must apply, as plaintiff urges, the "economic reality" test, which has four factors: whether the alleged employer (1) had the power to hire and fire the employees, (2) supervised and controlled employee work schedules or conditions of employment, (3) determined the rate and method of payment, and (4) maintained employment records. *Bauin*, 800 N.Y.S.2d 342 (City Civ. Ct., 2005)

economic strike A strike over wages, hours, working conditions, or other conditions of employment, not over an unfair labor practice.

edict A formal decree, command, law, or proclamation.

EEOC Equal Employment Opportunity Commission (*www.eeoc.gov*).

effect 1. That which is produced. 2. To bring about or cause.

effective assistance of counsel Representation provided by an attorney using the skill, knowledge, time, and resources of a reasonably competent attorney in criminal cases.

effective date The date a law, treaty, or contract goes into effect and becomes binding or enforceable.

effective tax rate The percentage of total income actually paid for taxes.

effects Personal property; goods.

efficient cause See proximate cause.

efficient market A market in which material information on a company is widely available and accurately reflected in the value of the stock or some other asset.

eggshell skull An unusually high vulnerability to injury.

egress The means or right to leave a place. The act of leaving.

Eighth Amendment The amendment to the U.S. Constitution that prohibits cruel and unusual punishment and excessive fines and bails.

ejectment An action for the recovery of the possession of land and for damages for the wrongful dispossession.

The usual form of action for determination of a right to possession of realty is an ejectment action, which is known in New York as action to recover immediate possession of realty. *Wright*, 67 N.Y.S.2d 63 (Mun. Ct., 1946)

ejusdem generis Where general words follow a list of particular words, the general words will be interpreted as applying only to things of the same class or category as the particular words in the list.

election A selection among available persons, conduct, rights, etc.

election by spouse The right of a widow or widower to choose between what a deceased spouse gives the surviving spouse by will or the share of the decedent's estate designated by statute.

election of remedies A choice by a party between two inconsistent remedies for the same wrong.

The doctrine of election of remedies is only applicable when the choice which has been exercised proceeds upon a claim that is irreconcilable with another right. Put in other words, the cause of action pursued cannot be so inconsistent with an alternative cause of action as to be irreconcilable. *Peterson*, 599 N.Y.S.2d 686 (3 Dept., 1993)

elective share The statutory share a surviving spouse chooses over what the will of his or her deceased spouse provides.

A surviving spouse can choose either the amount designated to the spouse in the will of the deceased spouse, or the greater of $50, 000 or the 1/3 of the net estate of the deceased spouse. McKinney's EPTL § 5-1.1-A

elector 1. A voter. 2. A member of the electoral college.

electoral college A body of electors chosen to elect the president and vice president based on the popular vote in each individual state.

electronic court filing (ECF) A method of filing documents in court electronically.

electronic signature Any letters, characters, or symbols, manifested by electronic or similar means, executed or adopted by a party with an intent to authenticate a writing.

eleemosynary Having to do with charity.

element 1. A constituent part of something. 2. A portion of a rule that is a precondition of the applicability of the entire rule.

elisor A person appointed by the court to perform duties of a disqualified sheriff or coroner.

eloign To remove something in order to conceal it from the court.

emancipation 1. Setting free. 2. The express or implied consent of a parent to relinquish his or her control and authority over a child.

Children of employable age are emancipated, and parents no longer have obligation to support them, if children become economically independent of their parents through employment and are self-supporting. McKinney's Family Court Act § 413. *Fortunato*, 662 N.Y.S.2d 579 (2 Dept., 1997)

embargo A government prohibition of ships into or out of its waters or of the exchange of goods and services to or from a particular country.

embezzlement Fraudulently taking personal property of another, which was initially acquired lawfully because of a position of trust.

emblements The crops produced by the labor of a tenant.

embracery The crime of corruptly trying to influence a jury by promises, entertainments, etc. Also called jury tampering.

emend To correct or revise.

emergency doctrine 1. One will not be liable for ordinary negligence when confronted with an emergency situation he or she did not aid in creating. Also called imminent peril doctrine, sudden emergency doctrine. 2. A warrantless search is allowed if the police have an objectively reasonable belief that an emergency has occurred and that someone within the residence is in need of immediate assistance. 3. In an emergency, consent to medical treatment for a child or unconscious adult will be implied if no one is available to give express consent.

eminent domain The power of government to take private property for public use upon the payment of just compensation. The exercise of eminent domain is called *condemnation.*

> The power of eminent domain is the right of the State, as sovereign, to take private property for public use upon making just compensation. *West 41st Street Realty*, 744 N.Y.S.2d 121 (1 Dept., 2002)

emolument Payment or other benefit for an occupation or office.

emotional distress Mental or emotional suffering or pain, e.g., depression, shame, worry. Also called mental anguish, mental distress, mental suffering.

empanel To enlist or enroll. To enroll or swear in (a list of jurors) for a particular case. Also spelled impanel.

employee One hired by another who has the right to control the employee in the material details of how the work is performed.

Employee Retirement Income Security Act (ERISA) A federal statute creating the Pension Benefit Guaranty Corporation to regulate private pension plans (29 USC § 1001) (*www.pbgc.gov*).

employee stock ownership plan (ESOP) An employee benefits plan that primarily invests in the shares of stock of the employer creating the plan.

employers' liability See workers' compensation.

employment at will See at-will employee.

emptor A buyer or purchaser. See also caveat emptor.

enabling statute The statute that allows (enables) an administrative agency to carry out specified delegated powers.

enact To make into a law, particularly by a legislative body.

enacting clause A clause in a statute (often in the preamble) that states the authority by which it is made (e.g., "Be it enacted . . .").

enactment 1. The method or process by which a bill in a legislature becomes a law. 2. A statute.

en banc or **in banc** By the full membership of a court as opposed to one of its smaller groupings or panels. Also called by the full bench or full court.

encroach To trespass, interfere with, or infringe on another's property or rights. Also spelled incroach.

encumbrance Every right to, interest in, or claim on land that diminishes the value of land, e.g., a mortgage or easement. Also spelled incumbrance.

> An encumbrance is every right to or interest in real property, other than an easement for a highway, to the diminution of the value of the real property, though consistent with conveyance of the fee interest therein. *Village of Spring Valley Urban Renewal Agency*, 371 N.Y.S.2d 579 (Co. Ct., 1975)

encumbrancer Someone who holds an encumbrance (e.g., a lien) against land.

endorsee See indorsee.

endorsement 1. See indorsement. 2. A modification to an insurance policy. An insurance policy rider.

endorser See indorser.

endowment 1. A special gift or fund for an institution. 2. An endowment insurance policy will pay the insured a stated sum at the end of a definite period, or, if the insured dies before such period, pay the amount to the person designated as beneficiary.

> The term endowment, as used in will, means the bestowment of money as a permanent fund, the income of which is to be used in the administration of a proposed work. *In re Hendricks' Will*, 148 N.Y.S.2d 245 (Sup. Ct., 1955)

enfeoff To invest someone with a freehold estate. See also feoffment.

enforcement Forcing someone to comply with a law or other obligation.

enfranchisement 1. Giving a right or franchise, e.g., the right to vote. 2. Freeing someone from bondage.

engage 1. To hire or employ. 2. To participate.

English rule See American rule.

engrossment 1. Copying or drafting a document (e.g., a bill) for its final execution or passage. 2. Preparing a deed for execution. 3. Buying up or securing enough of a commodity in order to obtain a monopoly.

engrossed bill The version of a bill passed by one of the chambers of the legislature after incorporating amendments or other changes.

enjoin 1. To require a person to perform or to abstain from some act. 2. To issue an injunction.

enjoyment 1. The ability to exercise a right or privilege. 2. Deriving benefit from possession.

enlarge 1. To make or become bigger. 2. To allow more time.

Enoch Arden doctrine The presumption that a spouse is dead after being missing without explanation for a designated number of years.

> The story of Enoch Arden and the current New York Law Domestic Relations Law 220 that presumes a missing person is dead after five years and the one-year waiting time for the abandonment of a spouse to be declared, provide some parameters. *Watertown Housing Authority*, 546 N.Y.S.2d 929 (City Ct., 1989)

enroll To register or record officially.

enrolled agent An attorney or nonattorney authorized to represent taxpayers at the Internal Revenue Service.

enrolled bill A bill that is ready to be sent to the chief executive after both chambers of the legislature have passed it.

entail To impose a limitation on who can inherit real property; it does not pass to all the heirs of the owner.

enter 1. To place anything before a court or on the court record. 2. To go into or onto. 3. To become part of or party to.

enterprise 1. A venture or undertaking, often involving a financial commitment. 2. Any individual, partnership, corporation, association, or other legal entity, and any union or group of individuals associated in fact although not a legal entity. 18 USC § 1961(4). See also RICO.

enterprise liability theory Liability for harm caused by a product is spread over the entire industry or enterprise that made the product.

enticement 1. The tort of wrongfully (a) encouraging a wife to leave or stay away from her husband or (b) forcing or encouraging a child to leave or stay away from his or her parent. 2. The crime of luring a child to an area for sexual contact.

entire Whole, without division; indivisible.

entirety The undivided whole; the entire amount or extent. See also tenancy by the entirety.

entitlement 1. The right to benefits, income, or other property. 2. The right to receive a government benefit that cannot be abridged without due process.

entity An organization that has a legally independent existence that is separate from its members.

entrapment Conduct by a government official that instigates or induces the commission of a crime by someone not ready and willing to commit it in order to prosecute him or her for that crime.

> Entrapment is an affirmative defense and depends for its validity on an act of inducement or encouragement by a public servant or by a person acting in cooperation with a public servant. Penal Law 1965, § 40.05. *People v. Taylor*, 300 N.Y.S.2d 20 (Co. Ct., 1969)

entry 1. The act of making a notation or record; the notation or record itself. 2. The act of presenting something before the court for or on the record. 3. The right or act of going into or onto real property. 4. Entering a building with one's whole body, a part of the body, or a physical object under one's control (for purposes of burglary).

enumerated Specifically or expressly listed or mentioned (e.g., the enumerated powers of Congress in the U.S. Constitution).

enure See inure.

en ventre sa mere In its mother's womb; an unborn child. Also spelled in ventre sa mere.

environmental impact statement (EIS) A detailed report on the potential positive and negative environmental effects of a proposed project or law.

envoy A diplomat of the rank of minister or ambassador.

EO See executive order.

eo die On that day.

eo instanti At that instant.

eo nomine By that name.

Equal Employment Opportunity Commission (EEOC) The federal regulatory agency that enforces antidiscrimination laws (*www.eeoc.gov*).

equality The status of being equal in rights, privileges, immunities, opportunities, and duties.

equalization 1. The act or process of making equal; bringing about uniformity or conformity to a common standard. 2. Adjusting tax assessments to achieve fairness.

> Equalization rate indicates the percentage of full value at which the assessor in a locality is assessing, on the average, taxable property in his locality. *City of New York*, 739 N.Y.S.2d 333 (Ct. of App., 2001)

equal protection of the law A constitutional guarantee that the government will not deny a person or class of persons the same treatment it gives other persons or other classes under like circumstances. 14th Amendment, U.S. Constitution.

Equal Rights Amendment A proposed amendment to the U.S. Constitution that did not pass. ("Equality of rights under the law shall not be denied or abridged by the United States or by any State on account of sex.")

equipment Implements needed for designated purposes or activities, including goods that do not qualify as consumer goods, farm products, or inventory.

> Equipment means goods other than inventory, farm products, or consumer goods. McKinney's Uniform Commercial Code § 9-102(33)

equitable 1. Just; conformable to the principles of what is right. 2. Available or sustainable in equity or under the principles of equity.

equitable adoption A child will be considered the adopted child of a person who agreed to adopt the child but failed to go through the formal adoption procedures.

equitable abstention doctrine Where an order of a state agency predominantly affects local matters, a federal court should refuse to exercise its equity powers to restrain enforcement of the order if adequate state judicial relief is available to the aggrieved party.

equitable action An action seeking equitable remedy relief (e.g., an injunction) rather than damages.

equitable assignment An assignment that, though invalid at law, will be enforced in equity.

equitable defense A defense (e.g., unclean hands, laches) that was once recognized only by courts of equity but is now recognized by all courts.

> "Equitable defense" over which city court has jurisdiction is one that is destructive of petitioner's rights; "equitable counterclaim" for which city court's jurisdiction is limited requires equitable decree which declares respondent's rights to be superior to those of petitioner and affords affirmative relief. McKinney's N.Y. City Civ. Ct. Act §§ 208, 905. *Rocconi*, 503 N.Y.S.2d 677 (City Ct., 1986)

equitable distribution The fair, but not necessarily equal, division of all marital property upon divorce in a common law property state.

equitable election An obligation to choose between two inconsistent or alternative rights or claims (e.g., a party cannot accept the benefits of a will and also refuse to recognize the validity of the will in other respects).

equitable estate An estate recognized by courts of equity.

equitable estoppel The voluntary conduct of a person will preclude him or her from asserting rights against another who justifiably relied on the conduct and who would suffer damage or injury if the person is now allowed to repudiate the conduct. Also called estoppel in pais.

An "equitable estoppel" may be imposed to prevent injustice suffered by a person who, in justifiable reliance upon the words or conduct of another, is induced to act or forbear. *Charles*, 745 N.Y.S.2d 572 (2 Dept., 2002)

equitable lien A restitution right enforceable in equity to have a fund or specific property, or its proceeds, applied in whole or part to the payment of a particular debt or class of debts.

equitable mortgage Any agreement to post certain property as security before the security agreement is formulized.

equitable owner The person who is recognized in equity as the owner of the property even though bare legal title to the property is in someone else. Also called beneficial owner.

equitable recoupment Using a claim barred by the statute of limitations as a defense to offset or diminish another party's related claim.

Under doctrine of equitable recoupment, transactions and occurrences which were subject of corporation's counterclaim against shareholder could be utilized to defend against and offset any liability that corporation otherwise might incur on shareholder's claims, irrespective of whether counterclaim was itself time-barred. McKinney's CPLR 203(d). *In re Watson*, 778 N.Y.S.2d 658 (4 Dept., 2004)

equitable relief An equitable remedy (e.g., injunction, specific performance) that is available when remedies at law (e.g., damages) are not adequate.

equitable restraint doctrine A federal court will not intervene to enjoin a pending state criminal prosecution without a strong showing of bad faith and irreparable injury. Also called *Younger* abstention. *Younger v. Harris*, 91 S. Ct. 746 (1971).

equitable servitude See restrictive covenant (1).

equitable title 1. The right (enforceable against the trustee) to the beneficial enjoyment of the trust property or corpus under the terms of the trust. 2. The right of the person holding equitable title to have legal title transferred to him or her upon the performance of specified conditions.

equitable tolling A litigant may sue after the statute of limitations has expired if, despite due diligence, he or she was prevented from suing due to inequitable circumstances, e.g., wrongful concealment of vital information by the other party.

equity 1. Justice administered according to fairness in a particular case, as contrasted with strictly formalized rules once followed by common-law courts. 2. Fairness, justice, and impartiality. 3. The monetary value of property in excess of what is owed on it. Net worth. 4. Shares of stock in a corporation.

Equity under the law is defined as the application of the dictates of conscience or the principles of natural justice to the settlement of controversies. It is a system of jurisprudence, a body of rules and doctrines serving to supplement and remedy the limitations and inflexibility of the common law. *Flushing Nat. Bank*, 379 N.Y.S.2d 978 (Sup. Ct., 1975)

equity capital The investment of owners in exchange for stock.

equity court A court with the power to apply equitable principles.

equity financing Raising capital by issuing stock, as opposed to bonds.

equity loan A loan to a homeowner that is secured by the amount of equity in the home at the time of the loan. A home equity loan.

equity of redemption Before foreclosure is finalized, the defaulting debtor-mortgagor can recover (redeem) the property upon payment of the debt plus interest and costs. Also called right of redemption.

equivalent 1. Equal in value or effect; essentially equal. 2. Under the doctrine of equivalents, an accused patent infringer cannot avoid liability for infringement by changing only minor or insubstantial details of the claimed invention while retaining the invention's essential identity.

ERA See Equal Rights Amendment.

erase 1. To wipe out or obliterate written words or marks. 2. To seal from public access.

ergo Therefore; consequently.

***Erie* doctrine** Federal courts in diversity cases will apply the substantive law of the state in which the federal court is situated, except as to matters governed by the U.S. Constitution and acts of Congress. *Erie v. Tompkins*, 58 S. Ct. 817 (1938).

ERISA See Employee Retirement Income Security Act.

erroneous Involving error, although not necessarily illegal.

error A mistaken judgment or incorrect belief as to the existence or the consequences of a fact; a false application of the law.

errors and omissions insurance (E&O) Insurance against liability for negligence, omissions, and errors in the practice of a particular profession or business. A form of malpractice insurance for nonintentional wrongdoing.

"Errors and omissions policy" is intended to insure a member of a designated calling against liability arising out of the mistakes inherent in the practice of that particular profession or business. *Watkins Glen Central School Dist.*, 732 N.Y.S.2d 70 (2 Dept., 2001)

escalator clause A clause in a contract or lease providing that a payment obligation will increase or decrease depending on a measurable standard such as changing income or the cost-of-living index. Also called fluctuating clause.

escape clause A provision in a contract or other document allowing a party to avoid liability or performance under defined conditions.

escheat A reversion of property to the state upon the death of the owner when no one is available to claim it by will or inheritance.

In origin, word "escheat" was a term of art applicable only to real property, descriptive of the forfeiture to the lord of the manor in certain contingencies of lands held in feudal tenure, but now word is understood as referring broadly to reversion of property, real and personal, to State on death of owner without distributees or claimants. *In re O'Brine's Estate*, 371 N.Y.S.2d 453 (Ct. of App., 1975)

Escobedo **rule** Statements of a suspect in custody who is the focus of a police investigation are inadmissible if the suspect is not told of his or her right to counsel and to remain silent. *Escobedo v. Illinois*, 84 S. Ct. 1758 (1964).

escrow Property (e.g., money, a deed) delivered to a neutral person (e.g., bank, escrow agent) to be held until a specified condition occurs, at which time it is to be delivered to a designated person.

ESOP See employee stock ownership plan.

espionage Spying to obtain secret information about the activities or plans of a foreign government or rival company.

Esq. See esquire.

esquire (Esq.) A courtesy title given to an attorney.

essence 1. The gist or substance of something. 2. That which is indispensable. See also time is of the essence.

establish 1. To make or institute. 2. To prove. 3. To make secure.

establishment 1. A business or institution. 2. The act of creating, building, or establishing. 3. Providing governmental sponsorship, aid, or preference. 4. The people or institutions that dominate a society.

Establishment Clause Government cannot establish an official religion, become excessively entangled with religion, nor endorse one form of religion over another. First Amendment, U.S. Constitution.

estate 1. An interest in real or personal property. 2. The extent and nature of one's interest in real or personal property. 3. All of the assets and liabilities of a decedent after he or she dies. 4. All of the property of whatever kind owned by a person. 5. Land.

[T]he term "estate" shall mean the assets held by an executor or an administrator, with or without the will annexed, of the goods, chattels and credits of a decedent. . . . McKinney's Banking Law § 100-c

estate at sufferance The interest that someone has in land he or she continues to possess after the permission or right to possess it has ended. Also called holdover tenancy, tenancy at sufferance.

estate at will See tenancy at will.

estate by the entirety See tenancy by the entirety.

estate for years An estate whose duration is known at the time it begins. A tenancy for a term.

estate from year to year See periodic tenancy.

estate in common See tenancy in common.

estate in expectancy See future interest.

estate of inheritance An estate that may be inherited.

estate planning Presenting proposals on how a person can have assets distributed at death in a way that will achieve his or her goals while taking maximum advantage of tax and other laws.

estate pur autre vie See life estate pur autre vie.

estate tail See fee tail.

estate tax A tax on the transfer property at death; the tax is based on the value of what passes by will or intestacy. Also called death tax.

"Inheritance tax" is tax on privilege of survivor to receive property of deceased, whereas "estate tax" is tax on interest which ceased upon deceased's death. *In re Wise's Will*, 244 N.Y.S.2d 960 (1 Dept., 1963)

estimated tax The current year's anticipated tax that is paid quarterly on income not subject to withholding.

estop To stop or prevent something by estoppel.

estoppel 1. Stopping a party from denying something he or she previously said or did, especially if the denial would harm someone who reasonably relied on it. 2. Stopping a party from relitigating an issue.

Equitable estoppel is imposed by law in the interest of fairness where enforcement of one party's rights would work a fraud or injustice upon the person against whom enforcement is sought, and where the party against whom enforcement is sought has, in justifiable reliance on the opposing party's words and conduct, been misled into acting, or refraining from acting, upon the belief that the opposing party would not seek to enforce the right. *Piacentino*, 816 N.Y.S.2d 674 (Sup. Ct., 2006)

estoppel by deed A party to a deed will be stopped from denying the truth of a fact stated in a deed (e.g., that the party owns the land being transferred) as against someone induced to rely on the deed.

estoppel by judgment See collateral estoppel.

estoppel by laches Denial of relief to a litigant who unreasonably delayed enforcing his or her claim.

estoppel by record See collateral estoppel.

estoppel by silence Estoppel against a person who had a duty to speak, but refrained from doing so and thereby misled another.

estoppel certificate A signed statement certifying that certain facts are correct (e.g., that mortgage payments are current) as of the date of the statement and can be relied upon by third parties.

estoppel in pais See equitable estoppel.

estover 1. The right to use, during a lease, any timber on the leased premises to promote good resource management. 2. Support or alimony.

et al. And others.

ethical 1. Conforming to minimum standards of professional conduct. 2. Pertaining to moral principles or obligations.

ethics 1. Rules that embody the minimum standards of behavior to which members of an organization are expected to conform. 2. Standards of professional conduct.

et seq. And following. When used after a page or section number, the reference is to several pages or sections after the one mentioned.

et ux. And wife.

et vir. And husband.

Euclidian zoning Comprehensive zoning in which every square foot of the community is within some fixed zone and is subject to the predetermined set of land use restrictions applicable to that zone. Zoning by district.

Euclidian zoning concepts mandate that such zoning requirements be equally binding on all property in a particular zoning classification. *Moriarty*, 506 N.Y.S.2d 184 (2 Dept., 1986)

eurodollar A U.S. dollar on deposit in a bank outside the United States, especially in Europe.

euthanasia The act of painlessly putting to death those persons who are suffering from incurable diseases or conditions. Also called mercy killing.

evasion 1. The act of avoiding something, usually by artifice. 2. The illegal reduction of tax liability, e.g., by underreporting income.

evasive answer An answer that neither admits nor denies a matter.

evergreen agreement A contract that automatically renews itself.

eviction 1. The use of legal process to dispossess a land occupier. 2. Depriving one of land or rental property he or she has held or leased.

evidence Anything that could be offered to prove or disprove an alleged fact. Examples: testimony, documents, fingerprints.

evidence aliunde See extrinsic evidence.

evidentiary fact 1. A subsidiary fact required to prove an ultimate fact. 2. A fact that is evidence of another fact.

"Evidentiary facts" are those obtained or perceived by senses, while "ultimate facts" are conclusions or opinions acquired by reflection and by reasoning upon evidentiary facts. *Jacobson*, 234 N.Y.S.2d 780 (Sup. Ct., 1962)

evidentiary harpoon Deliberately introducing inadmissible evidence in order to prejudice the jury against the accused.

ex; Ex. Without, from, example; Exchequer.

ex aequo et bono According to dictates of equity and what is good.

examination 1. Questioning someone under oath. 2. An inspection.

examination in chief See direct examination.

examined copy A copy of a record or other document that has been compared with the original and often sworn to be a true copy.

examiner One authorized to conduct an examination; one appointed by the court to take testimony of witnesses.

except 1. To leave out. 2. Other than.

exception 1. An objection to an order or ruling of a hearing officer or judge. 2. The act of excluding or separating something out (e.g., a judge excludes something from an order; a grantor retains an interest in property transferred). 3. That which is excluded.

excess Pertaining to an act, amount, or degree that is beyond what is usual, proper, or necessary.

excess insurance Supplemental insurance coverage available once the policy limits of the other insurance policies are exhausted.

excessive Greater than what is usual, proper, or necessary.

Fine is considered constitutionally "excessive" if (1) it constitutes payment to government for offense, and (2) amount of payment is grossly disproportionate to gravity of offense. *Street Vendor Project*, 811 N.Y.S.2d 555 (Sup. Ct., 2005)

excessive bail A sum that is disproportionate to the offense charged and beyond what is reasonably needed to deter evasion by flight.

excess of jurisdiction Action taken by a court or other tribunal that is not within its authority or powers.

excessive verdict A verdict that is clearly exorbitant and shocking.

exchange 1. A transaction (not using money) in which one piece of property is given in return for another piece of property. 2. Swapping things of value. 3. The conversion of the money of one country for that of another. The price of doing so is the rate of exchange. 4. Payment using a bill of exchange or credits. 5. An organization bringing together buyers and sellers of securities or commodities, e.g., New York Stock Exchange.

Exchequer The treasury department in England.

excise A tax that is not directly imposed on persons or property but rather on performing an act (e.g., manufacturing, selling, using), on engaging in an occupation, or on the enjoyment of a privilege.

excited utterance A statement relating to a startling event or condition, made while under the stress of excitement caused by the event or condition. An exception to the hearsay rule. See also res gestae.

Generally, an "excited utterance," for purposes of hearsay exception, is one made under the immediate and uncontrolled domination of the senses, and during the brief period when consideration of self-interest could not have been brought fully to bear by reasoned reflection; among the factors that courts will consider is whether there has been physical shock or trauma. *People v. Vega*, 771 N.Y.S.2d 30 (1 Dept., 2004)

exclusion 1. Denial of entry, admittance, or admission. 2. A person, event, condition, or loss not covered by an insurance policy. 3. Income that does not need to be included in gross income.

exclusionary rule Evidence obtained in violation of the constitution (e.g., an illegal search and seizure) will be inadmissible.

exclusive Not allowing others to participate; restricted; belonging to one person or group.

exclusive agency An agreement in which the owner grants a broker the right to sell property to the exclusion of other brokers, but allows the owner to sell the property through his or her own efforts.

Plaintiff was employed as the "sole and exclusive agent" of defendant for the sale of defendant's property. This created an exclusive agency as distinguished from an exclusive right of sale. Under an exclusive agency agreement, an owner may make a sale himself, without the broker's aid, and, if the sale is made in good faith to a purchaser not procured by the broker, the owner does not become liable for commissions to the broker. *Levy*, 140 N.Y.S.2d 519 (2 Dept., 1955)

exclusive jurisdiction The power of a court to hear a particular kind of case to the exclusion of all other courts.

exclusive listing An agreement giving only one broker the right sell the owner's property for a defined period. Also called exclusive agency listing.

ex contractu Arising from or out of a contract.

exculpate To free from guilt or blame.

exculpatory clause A clause in a lease or other contract relieving a party from liability for injury or damages he or she may wrongfully cause.

exculpatory evidence Any evidence tending to show excuse or innocence.

exculpatory-no doctrine An individual who merely supplies a negative and exculpatory response to an investigator's questions cannot be prosecuted for making a false statement to a government agency even if the response is false.

The doctrine preserves the individual's self-incrimination protection.

ex curia Out of or away from court.

excusable neglect The failure to take the proper step (e.g., to file an answer) at the proper time that will be excused (forgiven) because the failure was not due to carelessness, inattention, or recklessness but rather was due to (a) an unexpected or unavoidable hindrance or accident, (b) reliance on the care and vigilance of one's attorney, or (c) reliance on promises made by an adverse party.

To be relieved of judgment on ground of "excusable default," party must establish that there was reasonable excuse for default and meritorious claim or defense. McKinney's CPLR 5015(a), par. 1. *Pagano*, 636 N.Y.S.2d 188 (3 Dept., 1996)

excuse A reason one should be relieved of a duty or not be convicted.

ex delicto Arising from a tort, fault, crime, or malfeasance.

ex dividend (x)(xd) Without dividend. Upon purchase of shares ex dividend, the seller, not the buyer, receives the next dividend.

execute 1. To complete, perform, or carry into effect. 2. To sign and do whatever else is needed to finalize a contract or other instrument to make it legal. 3. To enforce a judgment. 4. To put to death.

executed contract 1. A contract that has been carried out according to its terms. 2. See execute (2).

executed trust A trust in which nothing remains to be done for it to be carried out.

execution 1. Carrying out or performing some act to its completion. 2. Signing and doing whatever else is needed to finalize a document and make it legal. 3. The process of carrying into effect the decisions in a judgment. A command (via a writ) to a court officer (e.g., sheriff) to seize and sell the property of the losing litigant in order to satisfy the judgment debt. Also called general execution, writ of execution. 4. Implementing a death sentence.

"Execution" is formal document issued by court that authorizes sheriff to levy upon property of judgment debtor. McKinney's CPLR 5230. *Liggett*, 534 N.Y.S.2d 973 (1 Dept., 1988)

execution sale See forced sale.

executive 1. Pertaining to that branch of government that is charged with carrying out or enforcing the laws. 2. A managing official.

executive agreement An agreement between the United States and another country that does not require the approval of the Senate.

executive clemency See clemency.

executive order (EO) An order issued by the chief executive pursuant to specific statutory authority or to the executive's inherent authority to direct the operation of government agencies and officials.

"Executive orders" are simply voluntary arrangements or directions to implement current interpretation of legislative policy, subject to revocation at sole discretion of Governor. *New York Citizens Utility Bd.*, 659 N.Y.S.2d 933 (3 Dept., 1997)

executive privilege The privilege, based on the separation of powers, that exempts the executive branch from disclosing information in order to protect national security and also to protect confidential advisory and deliberative communications among government officials.

executive session A meeting of a board or governmental unit that is closed to the general public.

executor A person appointed by someone writing a will (a testator) to carry out the provisions of the will.

executory Yet to be executed or performed; remaining to be carried into operation or effect; dependent on a future performance or event.

executory contract A contract that is wholly unperformed or in which substantial duties remain to be performed by both sides.

executory interest A future interest created in one other than the grantor, which is not a remainder and vests upon the happening of a condition or event and in derogation of a vested freehold interest.

executory trust A trust that cannot be carried out until a further conveyance is made. Also called imperfect trust.

executrix A woman appointed by a will to carry it out. A female executor.

exemplar 1. Nontestimonial identification evidence, e.g., fingerprints, blood sample. 2. A typical example; a model.

exemplary damages See punitive damages.

exemplification An official copy of a public record, ready for use as evidence.

exemplified copy See certified copy.

exempt Relieved of a duty others still owe.

Under New York law, an "exempt class" means that there is no requirement that person appointed to civil service position pass a civil service examination and that appointment of such position vests in the discretion of the appointing officer or body. *Perfetto*, 635 N.Y.S.2d 407 (Sup. Ct., 1995)

exemption 1. Release or freedom from a duty, liability, service, or tax. 2. A right of a debtor to retain a portion of his or her property free from the claims of creditors. 3. A deduction from adjusted gross income.

exercise 1. To make use of. 2. To fulfill or perform; to execute.

ex facie On its face; apparently.

ex gratia As a matter of grace; as a favor rather than as required.

exhaustion of remedies Using available dispute-solving avenues (remedies) in an administrative agency before asking a court to review what the agency did.

Generally, the doctrine of "exhaustion of administrative remedies" requires litigants to address their complaints initially to administrative tribunals, rather than to courts, and to exhaust all possibilities of obtaining relief through administrative channels before appealing to courts. *Pantel*, 735 N.Y.S.2d 228 (3 Dept., 2001)

exhibit 1. A document, chart, or other object offered or introduced into evidence. 2. An attachment to a pleading, instrument, or other document.

exigency (exigence) An urgent need, requiring an immediate response.

exigent circumstances 1. An emergency justifying the bypassing of normal procedures. 2. An emergency requiring swift action to prevent imminent threat to life or property, escape, or destruction of evidence.

exile 1. Banishment from the country. 2. A person banished.

ex officio Because of or by virtue of one's position or office.

exonerate To free or release from (a) guilt, blame or (b) responsibility, duty.

exoneration 1. Releasing or freeing from (a) guilt, blame or (b) responsibility, duty. 2. The right to be reimbursed by reason of having paid what another should be compelled to pay. 3. A surety's right, after the principal's debt has matured, to compel the principal to honor its obligation to the creditor.

ex parte With only one side present; involving one party only.

ex parte order A court order requested by one party and issued without notice to the other party.

expatriation 1. The abandonment of one's country and becoming a citizen or subject of another. 2. Sending someone into exile.

expectancy 1. The bare hope (but more than wishful thinking) of receiving a property interest of another, such as may be entertained by an heir apparent. 2. A reversion or remainder.

expectation damages The cost of restoring the non-breaching party to the position in which it would have been if the contract not been breached. Also called expectancy damages.

expectation of privacy The belief that one's activities and property would be private and free from government intrusion.

"Legitimate expectation of privacy" exists, such that a defendant has standing to challenge search, where the defendant has manifested an expectation of privacy either in the place that was searched or in the item that was searched, and the circumstances are such that the expectation is one that society is prepared to recognize as reasonable. *People v. Bell*, 780 N.Y.S. 2d 373 (2 Dept., 2004)

expenditure 1. The act of spending or paying out money. 2. An amount spent. An expense.

expense 1. What is spent for goods and services. 2. To treat (write off) as an expense for tax and accounting purposes. 3. A decrease in assets or an increase in liabilities to generate revenue.

experience rating A method of determining insurance rates by using the loss record (experience) of the insured over a period of time.

expert One who is knowledgeable, through experience or education, in a specialized field.

expert witness A person qualified by scientific, technical, or other specialized knowledge or experience to give an expert opinion relevant to a fact in dispute.

export 1. To carry or send abroad. 2. A commodity that is exported.

expository statute See declaratory statute.

ex post facto After the fact; operating retroactively.

ex post facto law A law that punishes as a crime an act that was innocent when done, that makes punishment more burdensome after its commission, or that deprives one of a defense that was available when the act was committed.

exposure The financial or legal risk one has assumed or could assume.

express Definite; unambiguous and not left to inference. Direct.

express agency The actual agency created when words of the principal specifically authorize the agent to take certain actions.

express authority Authority that the principal explicitly grants the agent to act in the principal's name.

express condition A condition agreed to by the parties themselves rather than imposed by law.

Express conditions in contract are those agreed to and imposed by parties themselves, but "implied or constructive conditions" are those imposed by law to do justice. *Oppenheimer*, 636 N.Y.S.2d 734 (Ct. of App., 1995)

express contract An oral or written agreement whose terms were stated by the parties rather than implied or imposed by law.

expressio unius est exclusio alterius A canon of interpretation that when an author (e.g., the legislature) expressly mentions one thing, we can assume it intended to exclude what it does not mention.

express malice 1. Ill will, the intent to harm. Actual malice; malice in fact. 2. Harming someone with a deliberate mind or formed design.

For purposes of overcoming qualified privilege as defense to defamation, "express malice" necessitates proof of personal spite, ill will or culpable recklessness or negligence and conclusory averments, surmise, conjecture or suspicion will not suffice. *Elite Funding Corp.*, 629 N.Y.S.2d 611 (Sup. Ct., 1995)

express notice See actual notice.

express power A power that is specifically listed or mentioned.

express repeal An overt statement in a statute that it repeals an earlier statute.

express trust A trust created or declared in explicit terms for specific purposes, usually in writing.

express waiver Oral or written statements intentionally and voluntarily relinquishing a known right or privilege.

express warranty A seller's affirmation of fact, description, or specific promise concerning a product that becomes part of the basis of the transaction or bargain.

"Express warranty" or "warranty" means the written affirmation of fact or promise made by a manufacturer or supplier to a consumer in connection with the sale of farm equipment which relates to the nature of the material or workmanship, including any terms or conditions precedent to the enforcement of obligations under that warranty. McKinney's General Business Law § 697(3)

expropriation The government's taking of private property for public purposes. See also eminent domain.

expulsion A putting or driving out; a permanent cutting off from the privileges of an institution or society.

expunge To erase or eliminate.

expungement of record The process by which the record of a criminal conviction, an arrest, or an adjudication of delinquency is destroyed or sealed after the expiration of a designated period of time.

ex rel. (ex relatione) Upon relation of information. A suit ex rel. is brought by the government in the name of the real party in interest (called the realtor).

ex rights (x)(xr) Without certain rights, e.g., to buy additional securities.

extension 1. An increase in the length of time allowed. 2. An addition or enlargement to a structure.

extenuating circumstances See mitigating circumstances.

exterritoriality See extraterritoriality.

extinguishment The destruction or cancellation of a right, power, contract, or estate.

extort To compel or coerce; to obtain by force, threats, or other wrongful methods.

extortion 1. Obtaining property from another through the wrongful use of actual or threatened force, violence, or fear. 2. The use of an actual or apparent official right (i.e., color of office) to obtain a benefit to which one is not entitled. See also blackmail.

> Essence of crime of "extortion" is the obtaining of property by a wrongful use of fear, induced by threat to do an unlawful injury and fear of economic loss or harm satisfies the ingredients of fear necessary to the crime. *People v. Dioguardi*, 203 N.Y.S.2d 870 (Ct. of App., 1960); McKinney's Penal Law § 155.05(e)

extra 1. Additional. 2. Beyond or outside of.

extradition The surrender by one state (or country) to another of an individual who has been accused or convicted of an offense in the state (or country) demanding the surrender.

extrajudicial Outside of court and litigation. Pertaining to what is done or given outside the course of regular judicial proceedings.

extralegal Not governed, regulated, or sanctioned by law.

extraneous evidence See extrinsic evidence.

extraordinary remedy A remedy (e.g., habeas corpus, writ of mandamus) allowed by a court when more traditional remedies are not adequate.

extraordinary session A session of the legislature called to address a matter that cannot wait till the next regular session. Also called special session.

extraordinary writ A special writ (e.g., habeas corpus) using a court's discretionary or unusual power. Also called prerogative writ.

extraterritoriality The exemption of diplomatic personnel from the jurisdiction of the local law of countries where they are posted. Also called exterritoriality.

extrinsic evidence External evidence; evidence that is not contained in the body of an agreement or other document; evidence outside of the writing. Also called extraneous evidence, evidence aliunde.

extrinsic fraud See collateral fraud.

ex warrants (x)(xw) Without warrants. See also warrant (3).

eyewitness A person who saw or experienced the act, fact, or transaction about which he or she is giving testimony.

F

fabricated evidence Evidence that is manufactured or made up with the intent to mislead.

face 1. That which is apparent to a spectator; outward appearance. 2. The front of a document.

> Term "face" as used in statute providing that application shall contain on its face a notice that purpose of hearing is to punish accused for contempt of court is to be given its usual dictionary meaning of a front, upper or outer surface or surface presented to view. . . . Judiciary Law § 756. *Stevens Plumbing Supply Co.*, 404 N.Y.S.2d 964 (Sup. Ct., 1978)

face amount 1. The amount of coverage on an insurance policy. 2. See par value.

face value See par value.

facial Pertaining to what is apparent in a document—the words themselves—as opposed to their interpretation.

facilitation Aiding; making it easier for another to commit a crime.

facility of payment clause A provision in an insurance policy permitting the insurer to pay the death benefits to a third person on behalf of the beneficiary.

facsimile 1. An exact copy of the original. 2. Transmitting printed text or pictures by electronic means. Fax.

fact A real occurrence. An event, thing, or state of mind that actually exists or that is alleged to exist, as opposed to its legal consequences.

fact-finder The person or body with the duty of determining the facts. If there is a jury, it is the fact-finder; if not, it is the judge or hearing officer. Also called trier of fact.

fact-finding The determination of the facts relevant to a dispute by examining evidence.

factor 1. One of the circumstances or considerations that will be weighed in making a decision, no one of which is usually conclusive. 2. A circumstance or influence that brings about or contributes to a result. 3. An agent who is given possession or control of property of the principal and who sells it for a commission. 4. A purchaser of accounts receivable at a discount.

factoring The purchase of accounts receivable at a discounted price.

factor's act A statute that protects good-faith buyers of goods from factors or agents who did not have authority to sell.

fact pleading Pleading those alleged facts that fit within the scope of a legally recognized cause of action. Also called code pleading.

fact question See issue of fact.

factual impossibility Facts unknown by or beyond the control of the actor that prevent the consummation of the crime he or she intends to commit.

> An example of factual impossibility would be the case of a defendant who stole a purse believing that it contained credit cards when in fact the purse was empty. *People v. McMurty*, 538 N.Y.S.2d 127 (Sup. Ct., 1987)

factum 1. A fact, deed, or act, e.g., the execution of a will. 2. A statement of facts.

factum probandum The fact to be proved.

factum probans The evidence on the fact to be proved; an evidentiary fact.

failure 1. The lack of success. 2. An omission or neglect of something expected or required. Deficiency.

failure of consideration Failure of performance. The neglect, refusal, or failure of one of the contracting parties to perform or furnish the agreed upon consideration.

failure of issue Dying without children or other descendants who can inherit. Also called definite failure of issue.

failure to prosecute A litigant's lack of due diligence (e.g., failure to appear) in pursuing a case in court. Want of prosecution.

faint pleader Pleading in a misleading or collusive way.

fair Free from prejudice and favoritism, evenhanded; equitable.

fair comment The honest expression of opinion on a matter of legitimate public interest.

fair hearing A hearing that is conducted according to fundamental principles of procedural justice (due process), including the rights to an impartial decision maker, to present evidence, and to have the decision based on the evidence presented.

fair market value The price agreed upon by a willing buyer and a willing seller, neither being under any compulsion to enter the transaction and both having reasonable knowledge of the relevant facts. Also called cash value, market value, true value.

Assessment of property may in no circumstances exceed property's "fair market value," or most probable price which could be obtained in fair sale in competitive market, with both parties acting prudently, knowledgeably, and with price not affected by undue stimulus. McKinney's Const. Art. 16, § 2. *Grandview Heights Ass'n*, 674 N.Y.S.2d 571 (Sup. Ct., 1998)

fairness doctrine A former rule of the Federal Communications Commission that a broadcaster must provide coverage of issues of public importance that is adequate and that fairly reflects differing viewpoints. Replaced by the equal-time doctrine.

fair preponderance of the evidence See preponderance of the evidence.

fair trade laws Statutes that permitted manufacturers or distributors of brand goods to fix minimum retail prices.

fair trial A trial in which the accused's legal rights are safeguarded, e.g., the procedures are impartial.

fair use The privilege of limited use of copyrighted material without permission of the copyright holder.

fair warning A due process requirement that a criminal statute be sufficiently definite to notify persons of reasonable intelligence that their planned conduct is criminal.

faith 1. Confidence. 2. Reliance or trust in a person, idea, or thing.

false 1. Knowingly, negligently, or innocently untrue. 2. Not genuine.

false advertising A misdescription or deceptive representation of the specific characteristics of products being advertised.

false arrest An arrest made without privilege or legal authority.

false impersonation See false personation.

false imprisonment 1. The intentional and unjustified confinement within fixed boundaries of someone who is conscious of the confinement or is harmed by it. 2. The crime of wrongfully restraining another person. McKinney's Penal Law §§ 135.05, 135.10.

Claim for false arrest or false imprisonment requires a showing by plaintiff that (1) the defendant intended to confine him, (2) the plaintiff was conscious of the confinement, (3) the plaintiff did not consent to the confinement and (4) the confinement was not otherwise privileged. *Nadeau*, 707 N.Y.S.2d 704 (3 Dept., 2000)

false light An invasion-of-privacy tort committed by unreasonably offensive publicity that places another in a false light.

false personation The crime of falsely representing yourself as someone else for purposes of fraud or deception. Also called false impersonation.

false pretenses Obtaining money or other property by using knowingly false statements of fact with the intent to defraud.

In the context of a prosecution for scheme to defraud, false pretenses means false statements about some prior or existing facts, thus contemplating a misrepresentation or an untrue statement of fact or facts. McKinney's Penal Law § 190.65, subd. 1(b). *People v. Brigham*, 702 N.Y.S.2d 119 (3 Dept., 1999)

false representation See misrepresentation.

false return 1. A false statement filed by a process server, e.g., falsely stating that he or she served process. 2. An incorrect tax return. A tax return that is knowingly incorrect.

false statement 1. A falsehood. 2. Knowingly stating what is not true. Covering up or concealing a fact.

false swearing See perjury.

false verdict A verdict that is substantially unjust or incorrect.

falsi crimen See crimen falsi.

falsify To forge or alter something in order to deceive. To counterfeit.

family 1. A group of people related by blood, adoption, marriage, or domestic partnership. 2. A group of persons who live in one house and under one head or management.

Immediate family means parent, spouse, child, brother, sister, first cousin, aunt and uncle of such person, whether such relationship arises by reason of birth, marriage or adoption. McKinney's Mental Hygiene Law § 32.39(b)(3)

family car See family purpose.

family court A special court with subject-matter jurisdiction over family law matters such as adoption, paternity, and divorce. Every New York county has a family court that has jurisdiction over custody, visitation, support, paternity, child protection actions, adoption, PINS, juvenile delinquency, and family offenses.

family farmer A farmer whose farm has income and debts that qualify it for Chapter 12 bankruptcy relief. 11 USC § 101(18).

family law The body of law that defines relationships, rights, and duties in the formation, existence, and dissolution of marriage and other family units.

family purpose (automobile/car) doctrine The owner of a car who makes it available for family use will be liable for injuries that result from negligent operation of the car by a family member.

Fannie Mae Federal National Mortgage Association (FNMA) (*www.fanniemae.com*).

FAS See free alongside ship.

fascism A system of government characterized by nationalism, totalitarianism, central control, and often, racism.

fatal Pertaining to or causing death or invalidity.

fatal error See prejudicial error.

fatal variance A variance between the indictment and the evidence at trial that deprives the defendant of the due process guarantee of notice of the charges or exposes him or her to double jeopardy.

> We consider first its claim of a fatal variance between plaintiffs' pleading and proof and as to which no motion was made to conform. *Leonard*, 60 N.Y.S.2d 78 (3 Dept., 1946)

***Fatico* hearing** A proceeding to hear arguments on a proposed sentence for the defendant. *Fatico v. U.S.*, 603 F. 2d 1053 (2d Cir. 1979).

fault An error or defect in someone's judgment or conduct to which blame and culpability attaches. The wrongful breach of a duty.

favored beneficiary A beneficiary in a will who is suspected of exerting undue influence on the decedent in view of the relative size of what this beneficiary receives under the will.

FBI Federal Bureau of Investigation (*www.fbi.gov*).

FCC Federal Communications Commission (*www.fcc.gov*).

FDA Food and Drug Administration (*www.fda.gov*).

FDIC Federal Deposit Insurance Corporation (*www.fdic.gov*).

fealty Allegiance of a feudal tenant (vassal) to a lord.

feasance The performance of an act or duty.

featherbedding Requiring a company to hire more workers than needed.

Fed 1. Federal. 2. Federal Reserve System (*www.federalreserve.gov*).

federal United States; pertaining to the national government of the United States.

Federal Circuit Court of Appeals for the Federal Circuit (*www.cafc.uscourts.gov*), one of the 13 federal courts of appeal.

federal common law Judge-made law created by federal courts when resolving federal questions.

federal courts Courts with federal jurisdiction created by the U.S. Constitution under Article III or by Congress under Article I. The main federal courts are the U.S. district courts (trial courts), the U.S. circuit courts of appeals, and the U.S. Supreme Court.

federalism The division of powers between the U.S. (federal) government and the state governments.

federal magistrate See magistrate.

federal preemption See preemption.

federal question A legal issue based on the U.S. Constitution, a statute of Congress, a treaty, or a federal administrative law.

Federal Register (Fed. Reg.) The official daily publication for rules, proposed rules, and notices of federal agencies and organizations, as well as executive orders and other presidential documents (*www.gpoaccess.gov/fr*).

federal rules Rules of procedure that apply in federal courts (*www.uscourts.gov/rules/newrules4.html*).

Federal Tort Claims Act (FTCA) The federal statute that specifies the torts for which the federal government can be sued because it waives sovereign immunity for those torts (28 USC §§ 2671 et seq., 1346).

federation An association or joining together of states, nations, or organizations into a league.

fee 1. Payment for labor or a service. 2. An estate in land that can be passed on by inheritance.

fee simple An estate over which the owner's power of disposition is without condition or limitation, until he or she dies without heirs. Also called fee simple absolute.

> Estates in property as to duration are classified as follows: (1) Fee simple absolute. (2) Fee on condition. (3) Fee on limitation. McKinney's EPTL § 6-1.1(a)

fee simple absolute See fee simple.

fee simple conditional A fee that is limited or restrained to particular heirs, exclusive of others. Also called conditional fee.

fee simple defeasible A fee that is subject to termination upon the happening of an event or condition.

fee simple determinable A fee subject to the limitation that the property automatically reverts to the grantor upon the occurrence of a specified event.

fee splitting A single bill to a client covering the fee of two or more attorneys who are not in the same law firm.

fee tail An estate that can be inherited by the lineal heirs, e.g., children (not the collateral heirs) of the first holder of the fee tail. Also called estate tail. If the estate is limited to female lineal heirs, it is a fee tail female; if it is limited to male lineal heirs, it is a fee tail male.

> Estates tail have been abolished, and every estate which would be a fee tail, according to the law of this state as it existed before the twelfth day of July, seventeen hundred eighty-two, shall be a fee simple; and if no valid future estate is limited thereon, a fee simple absolute. Where a future estate in fee is limited on any estate which would be a fee tail, according to the law of this state as it existed previous to such date, such future estate is valid and vests in possession on the death of the first taker without issue living at the time of his death. McKinney's EPTL § 6-1.2

fee tail female; fee tail male See fee tail.

fellow servant rule An employer will not be liable for injuries to an employee caused by the negligence of another employee (a fellow servant). This rule has been changed by workers' compensation law.

felon Someone convicted of a felony.

felonious 1. Malicious. Done with the intent to commit a serious crime. 2. Concerning a felony.

felonious assault A criminal assault that amounts to a felony.

felonious homicide Killing another without justification or excuse.

felony Any crime punishable by death or imprisonment for a term exceeding a year; a crime more serious than a misdemeanor.

> A felony is a crime punishable by death or imprisonment in a state prison and any other crime is a misdemeanor. *McKinney*, 26 N.E.2d 949 (Ct. of App., 1940)

felony murder rule An unintended death resulting from the commission or attempted commission of certain felonies is murder.

feme covert A married woman.

feme sole An unmarried woman.

fence 1. A receiver of stolen property. 2. To sell stolen property to a fence. 3. An enclosure or boundary about a field or other space.

feoffee One to whom a feoffment is conveyed. A feoffor conveys it.

feoffment The grant of land as a fee simple (i.e., full ownership of an estate). The grant of a freehold estate.

ferae naturae Of a wild nature; untamed, undomesticated.

Feres **doctrine** The federal government is not liable under the Federal Tort Claims Act for injuries to members of the armed services where the injuries arise incident to military service. *Feres v. U.S.*, 71 S. Ct. 153 (1950).

fertile octogenarian rule A person is conclusively presumed to be able to have children (and therefore heirs) at any age.

feudalism A social and political system in medieval Europe in which laborers (serfs) were bound to and granted the use of land in return for services provided to their lords.

FHA Federal Housing Administration (*www.hud.gov/offices/hsg/fhahistory.cfm*).

fiat 1. An authoritative order or decree. 2. An arbitrary command.

FICA Federal Insurance Contributions Act (a statute on social security payroll taxes).

fiction of law See legal fiction.

fictitious 1. Based on a legal fiction. 2. False; imaginary.

fictitious name 1. The name to be used by a business. A d/b/a (doing business as) name. 2. An alias.

fictitious payee A payee on a check named by the drawer or maker without intending this payee to have any right to its proceeds.

Fictitious payee rule creates an exception to the general principle that a drawer is not liable on a forged indorsement in situations where the drawer is the party best able to prevent the loss. A forged endorsement is treated as if it were the actual indorsement of the stated payee, and the payment by a transferee in the transactional chain is proper. McKinney's Uniform Commercial Code § 3-405(1)(b). *Kersner*, 695 N.Y.S. 2d 369 (2 Dept., 1999)

fictitious person See artificial person.

fidelity bond or **insurance** A contract whereby the insurer agrees to indemnify the insured against loss resulting from the dishonesty of an employee or other person holding a position of trust.

fides Faith, honesty, veracity.

fiduciary One whose duty is to act in the interests of another with a high standard of care. Someone in whom another has a right to place great trust and to expect great loyalty, especially regarding financial matters.

[T]he term "fiduciary" means a person acting for the benefit of another party as a bona fide trustee; executor; administrator; custodian; guardian of estates or guardian ad litem; receiver; conservator; committee of estates of incapacitated person; personal representative; trustee. McKinney's ECL § 27-1323(a)(1)

fiduciary bond A bond that a court requires of fiduciaries (e.g., trustees, executors) to guarantee the performance of their duties.

fiduciary duty A duty to act with the highest standard of care and loyalty for another's benefit, always subordinating one's own personal interests.

fiduciary relationship A relationship in which one owes a fiduciary duty (see this phrase) to another, e.g., attorney-client relationship. Also called confidential relationship.

fiduciary shield doctrine A person's business in a state solely as a corporate officer does not create personal jurisdiction over that person.

field warehousing Financing by pledging inventory under the control of the lender or a warehouser working on behalf of the lender.

fieri facias (fi. fa.) A writ or order to a sheriff to seize and sell the debtor's property to enforce (satisfy) a judgment.

fi. fa. See fieri facias.

FIFO First in, first out. An inventory flow assumption by which the first goods purchased are assumed to be the first goods used or sold. Used to value the cost of goods sold in determining income.

Fifth Amendment The amendment to the U.S. Constitution that provides rights pertaining to grand juries, double jeopardy, self-incrimination, due process of law, and just compensation for the taking of private property.

fighting words Words likely to provoke a violent reaction when heard by an ordinary citizen and consequently may not have free-speech protection.

Fighting words, which are words that are likely to provoke a violent reaction when heard by an ordinary citizen, and "true threats" may be proscribed without offending the First Amendment. *People v. Bonitto*, 777 N.Y.S.2d 900 (N.Y. City Crim. Ct., 2004)

file 1. To deliver a document to a court officer so that it can become part of the official collection of documents in a case. To deliver a document to a government agency. 2. To commence a lawsuit. 3. A law firm's collection of documents for a current or closed case.

file wrapper The entire record of the proceedings on an application in the U.S. Patent and Trademark Office. Also called prosecution history.

file wrapper estoppel One cannot recapture in an infringement action the breadth of a patent previously surrendered in the patent office.

filiation 1. The relationship between parent and child. 2. A court determination of paternity.

filiation proceeding A judicial proceeding to establish paternity.

filibuster A tactic to delay or obstruct proposed legislation, e.g., engaging in prolonged speeches on the floor of the legislature.

filing A document delivered to a court or government agency.

filius nullius ("son of nobody") An illegitimate child.

final 1. Not requiring further judicial or official action. 2. Conclusive. 3. Last.

final argument See closing statement.

final judgment; final decree A judgment or decree that resolves all issues in a case, leaving nothing for future determination other than the execution or enforcement of the judgment.

Order being appealed from was in fact an "order and a final judgment," in that it determined the rights of the parties and was dispositive of all factual and legal issues in the case and judicially settled the case between the parties, and thus brought up for review any nonfinal judgment or order which necessarily affected the judgment, including an order denying a motion to dismiss the complaint. McKinney's CPLR 411, 3001, 5011, 5501(a), par. 1. *State v. Wolowitz*, 468 N.Y.S.2d 131 (2 Dept., 1983)

final submission Completing the presentation (including arguments) of everything a litigating party has to offer on the facts and law.

finance 1. To supply with funds; to provide with capital or loan money to. 2. The management of money, credit, investments, etc.

finance charge The extra cost (e.g., interest) imposed for the privilege of deferring payment of the purchase price.

finance company A company engaged in the business of making loans.

financial institution A bank, trust company, credit union, savings and loan association, or similar institution engaged in financial transactions with the public such as receiving, holding, investing, or lending money.

"Financial institution" means any bank, trust company, savings bank, savings and loan association or cooperative bank chartered by the state or any national banking association, federal savings and loan association or federal savings bank; provided, however, that the financial institution has its principal office located in the state. McKinney Unconsol.Laws § 6266-k(1)(a)

financial responsibility law A law requiring owners of motor vehicles to prove (through personal assets or insurance) that they can satisfy judgments against them involving the operation of the vehicles.

financial statement A report summarizing the financial condition of an organization or individual on or for a certain date or period.

financing statement A document filed as a public record to notify third parties, e.g., prospective buyers or lenders, that there may be an enforceable security interest in specific property. Financial statements usually contain an income statement, a balance sheet, a statement of owners' equity, and a statement of cash flows.

Financing statement means a record or records composed of an initial financing statement and any filed record relating to the initial financing statement. McKinney's Uniform Commercial Code § 9-102(a)(39)

find To make a determination of what the facts are.

finder Someone who finds or locates something for another. An intermediary who brings parties together (e.g., someone who secures mortgage financing for a borrower).

finder of fact See fact-finder.

finder's fee A fee paid to someone for finding something or for bringing parties together for a business transaction.

finding of fact The determination of a fact. A conclusion, after considering evidence, on the existence or nonexistence of a fact.

fine 1. To order someone to pay a sum of money to the state as a criminal or civil penalty. 2. The money so paid.

fine print The part of an agreement or other document containing exceptions, disclaimers, or other details, often difficult to read.

fingerprint The unique pattern of lines on a person's fingertip that can be made into an impression, often for purposes of identification.

firefighter's rule Negligence in causing a fire or other dangerous situation furnishes no basis for liability to a firefighter, police officer, or other professional who is injured while responding to the danger.

Common law doctrine known as the "firefighters' rule" bars recovery by a firefighter against a property owner or occupant for injuries related to the risks firefighters are expected to assume as part of their job. *Galapo*, 721 N.Y.S.2d 857 (Ct. of App., 2000)

firm 1. A business or professional entity. 2. Fixed, binding.

firm offer An offer that remains open and binding (irrevocable) for a period of time until accepted or rejected.

First Amendment The amendment to the U.S. Constitution that provides rights pertaining to the establishment and free exercise of religion, freedom of speech and press, peaceful assembly, and petitioning the government.

first degree The most serious level of an offense.

first-degree murder Killing another with premeditation, with extreme cruelty or atrocity, or while committing another designated felony.

In New York, first-degree murder requires intentional killing by someone more than 18 years of age with an aggravating factor present, such as the killing of a particular category of person, (police officer or witness to a crime), or killing more than one person, or extreme cruel and wanton manner, or as an act of terrorism, or while committing another designated felony. McKinney's Penal Law § 125.27.

first impression Concerning an issue being addressed for the first time.

first in, first out See FIFO.

first lien; first mortgage A lien or mortgage with priority that must be satisfied before other liens or mortgages on the same property.

First mortgage of record, within meaning of statute giving all sums unpaid on a first mortgage of record priority over a condominium board of managers' lien for unpaid common charges, means any first mortgage of record, regardless of whether it was for the purpose of purchasing the condominium. McKinney's Real Property Law § 339-z. *Greenpoint Bank*, 711 N.Y.S.2d 275 (Sup. Ct., 2000)

first offender A person convicted of a crime for the first time and, therefore, may be entitled to more lenient sentencing or treatment.

first refusal See right of first refusal.

fiscal Pertaining to financial matters, e.g., revenue, debt, expenses.

fiscal year Any 12 consecutive months chosen by a business as its accounting period (e.g., 7/01/08 to 6/30/09).

fishing expedition Unfocused questioning or investigation. Improper discovery undertaken with the purpose of finding an issue.

fitness for a particular purpose See warranty of fitness for a particular purpose.

fix 1. To determine or establish something, e.g., price, rate. 2. To prearrange something dishonestly. 3. To fasten or repair. 4. An injection or dose of heroin or other illegal drug.

fixed asset An asset (e.g., machinery, land) held long-term and used to produce goods and services. Also called capital assets.

fixed capital Fixed assets. Money invested in fixed assets.

fixed charges Expenses or costs that must be paid regardless of the condition of the business (e.g., tax payments, overhead).

fixed income Income that does not fluctuate (e.g., interest on a bond).

fixed liability 1. A debt that is certain as to obligation and amount. 2. A debt that will not mature soon; a long-term debt.

fixed rate An interest rate that does not vary for the term of the loan.

fixture Something that is so attached to land as to be deemed a part of it. An item of personal property that is now so connected to the land that it cannot be removed without substantial injury to itself or the land.

> Under the common law, a "fixture" is personalty which is (1) actually annexed to real property or something appurtenant thereto, (2) applied to the use or purpose to which that part of the realty with which it is connected is appropriated, and (3) intended by the parties as a permanent accession to the freehold. *Mastrangelo*, 793 N.Y.S.2d 94 (2 Dept., 2005)

flagrante delicto See in flagrante delicto.

flat rate A fixed payment regardless of how much of a service is used.

flight Fleeing to avoid arrest or detention.

float 1. The time between the writing of a check and the withdrawal of the funds that will cover it. 2. The total amount representing checks in the process of collection. 3. To allow a given currency to freely establish its own value as against other currencies in response to supply and demand.

floater policy An insurance policy that is issued to cover items that have no fixed location (e.g., jewelry that is worn).

floating capital Funds available for current needs; capital in circulation.

floating debt Short-term debt for current needs.

floating interest rate A rate of interest that is not fixed; the rate may fluctuate by market conditions or be pegged to an index.

floating lien A lien on present and after-acquired assets of the debtor during the period of the loan.

> § 9-204. After-acquired Property. Official Comment. This section adopts the principle of a "continuing general lien" or "floating lien." It validates a security interest in the debtor's existing and (upon acquisition) future assets, even though the debtor has liberty to use or dispose of collateral without being required to account for proceeds or substitute new collateral. McKinney's Uniform Commercial Code § 9-204

floating zone A special detailed use district of undetermined location; it "floats" over the area where it may be established.

floor 1. The minimum or lowest limit. 2. Where legislators sit and cast their votes. 3. The right of someone to address the assembly.

floor plan financing A loan secured by the items for sale and paid off as the items are sold.

flotsam Goods that float on the sea when cast overboard or abandoned.

FLSA Fair Labor Standards Act (29 USC § 201) (*www.dol.gov/esa/whd/flsa*).

FNC See forum non conveniens.

FOB See free on board.

FOIA See Freedom of Information Act.

follow 1. To accept as authority. 2. To go or come after.

forbearance Deciding not to take action, e.g., to collect a debt.

for cause For a reason relevant to one's ability and fitness to perform a duty as a juror, employee, fiduciary, etc.

force Strength or pressure directed to an end; physical coercion.

forced heir A person who by law must receive a portion of a testator's estate even if the latter tries to disinherit that person.

forced sale 1. A court-ordered sale of property to satisfy a judgment. Also called execution sale. 2. A sale one is pressured to make.

> A "forced sale" within rent control statute forbidding the use of forced sale price as basis for computing allowable net return, refers to sale in which owner, through economic pressure or stress of other circumstances, has little, if any, real voice in transaction. McK.Unconsol.Laws, § 8584. *Quittner*, 210 N.Y.S. 2d 568 (Sup. Ct., 1961)

force majeure An unexpected event; an irresistible and superior force that could not have been foreseen or avoided.

forcible detainer 1. Unlawfully (and often by force) keeping possession of land to which one is no longer entitled. 2. See forcible entry and detainer.

forcible entry Taking possession of land with force or threats of violence. Using physical force to enter land or gain entry into a building.

forcible entry and detainer 1. A summary, speedy, and adequate remedy to obtain the return of possession of land to which one is entitled. Also called forcible detainer. 2. Using physical force or threats of violence to obtain and keep possession of land unlawfully.

foreclosure The procedure to terminate the rights of a defaulting mortgagor in property that secured the mortgagor's debt. The lender-mortgagee can then sell the property to satisfy the remaining debt.

> "Foreclosure" is a judicial act invoked by one party to compel the other party to fulfill his mortgage agreement, and when invoked, irrevocably cuts off beyond the possibility of recall, the mortgagor's rights, including his equity of redemption. *Harlem Savings Bank*, 101 N.Y.S.2d 641 (Sup. Ct., 1950). See also McKinney's ECL § 27-1323(4).

foreign Pertaining to another country or to one of the 50 states of the United States other than the state you are in.

foreign administrator A person appointed in another state or jurisdiction to manage the estate of the deceased.

foreign commerce Trade involving more than one nation.

foreign corporation A corporation chartered or incorporated in one state or country but doing business in another state or country.

foreign exchange 1. The currency of another country. 2. Buying, selling, or converting one country's currency for that of another.

foreman 1. The presiding member and spokesperson of a jury. 2. A superintendent or supervisor of other workers. Also called foreperson.

forensic 1. Belonging to or suitable in courts of law. 2. Pertaining to the use of scientific techniques to discover and examine evidence. 3. Concerning argumentation. 4. Forensics: ballistics or firearms evidence.

forensic medicine The science of applying medical knowledge and techniques in court proceedings to discover and interpret evidence.

foreperson See foreman.

foreseeability The extent to which something can be known in advance; reasonable anticipation of something.

forestalling the market Buying products on their way to market in order to resell them at a higher price.

forfeiture The loss of property, rights, or privileges because of penalty, breach of duty, or the failure to make a timely claim of them.

Forfeiture actions. A civil action may be commenced by the appropriate claiming authority against a criminal defendant to recover the property which constitutes the proceeds of a crime, the substituted proceeds of a crime, an instrumentality of a crime or the real property instrumentality of a crime or to recover a money judgment in an amount equivalent in value to the property which constitutes the proceeds of a crime, the substituted proceeds of a crime, an instrumentality of a crime, or the real property instrumentality of a crime. McKinney's CPLR § 1311(1)

forgery 1. Making a false document or altering a real one with the intent to commit a fraud. 2. The document or thing that is forged.

form 1. Technical matters of style, structure, and format not involving the merits or substance of something. 2. A document, usually preprinted as a model, to be filled in and adapted to one's needs. 3. See forms of action.

formal 1. Following accepted procedures or customs. 2. Pertaining to matters of form as opposed to content or substance. 3. Ceremonial.

formal contract 1. A contract under seal or other contract that complies with prescribed formalities. 2. A contract in writing.

forma pauperis See in forma pauperis.

former adjudication See collateral estoppel and res judicata on when a former adjudication (prior judgment) on the merits will prevent relitigating issues and claims.

former jeopardy, defense of A person cannot be tried or prosecuted for the same offense more than once. See also double jeopardy.

Former jeopardy occurs where prior trial results in judgment of acquittal or conviction or where defendant is actually placed on trial on valid charge, jury is duly impaneled, and trial is terminated arbitrarily without defendant's consent. *People, on Complaint of McKinney*, 43 N.Y.S.2d 114 (Mag. Ct., 1943)

forms of action The procedural devices or actions (e.g., trespass on the case) that are used to take advantage of common-law theories of liability.

fornication Sexual relations between unmarried persons or between married persons who are not married to each other.

forswear 1. To give up something completely. To renounce something under oath. 2. To swear falsely; to commit perjury.

forthwith Without delay; immediately.

fortiori See a fortiori.

fortuitous Happening by chance or accident rather than by design.

forum 1. The court; the court where the litigation is brought. 2. A setting or place for public discussion.

forum domicilii The court in the jurisdiction where a party is domiciled.

forum non conveniens (FNC) The discretionary power of a court to decline the exercise of the jurisdiction it has when the convenience of the parties and the ends of justice would be better served if the action were brought and tried in another forum that also has jurisdiction.

Doctrine of "forum non conveniens" permits a court to either dismiss or stay an action when it determines that, although jurisdictionally sound, the matter would more properly be adjudicated in another forum. *American Guarantee and Liability Ins.*, 703 N.Y.S.2d 661 (Sup. Ct., 1999)

forum rei The court in the jurisdiction where the defendant is domiciled or the subject matter of the case is located.

forum selection clause A contract clause stating that any future litigation between the parties will be conducted in a specified forum (jurisdiction).

forum shopping Choosing a court or jurisdiction where you are most likely to win.

forward contract An agreement to buy or sell goods at a specified time in the future at a price established when the contract is entered. The agreement is not traded on an exchange.

foster home A home that provides shelter and substitute family care temporarily or for extended periods when a child's own family cannot properly care for him or her, often due to neglect or delinquency.

Child was "foster child" in care of "foster parent" within meaning of Social Services Law; family court could place child outside child's family to protect welfare of child; a "foster child" is a person in care of "authorized agency" who is place for temporary or long-term care. McKinney's Family Court Act §§ 1013(d) 1052(a)(iii), 1055(a); McKinney's Social Services Law §§ 371, subds. 10(b), 19, 374, subd. 1. *Matter of Dale P.*, 595 N.Y.S.2d 970 (2 Dept., 1993)

foundation 1. A fund for charitable, educational, religious, or other benevolent purpose. 2. The underlying basis or support for something. Evidence that shows the relevance of other evidence.

founder One who establishes something, e.g., an institution or trust fund.

founding father A leader in establishing a country or organization.

four corners The contents of a written document; what is written on the surface or face of a document.

four-corners rule 1. The intention of the parties to a contract or other instrument is to be ascertained from the document as a whole and not from isolated parts thereof.

2. If a contract is clear on its face, no evidence outside the contract may be considered to contradict its terms.

frame 1. To formulate or draft. 2. To produce false evidence that causes an innocent person to appear guilty.

franchise 1. The right to vote. 2. A contract that allows a business (the franchisee) the sole right to use the intellectual property and brand identity, marketing experience, and operational methods of another business (the franchisor) in a certain area. 3. A government authorization to engage in a specified commercial endeavor or to incorporate.

"Franchise" is a special privilege which authorizes use of the public streets, thereby creating a right where none existed before and which commensurately requires that the one to whom the privilege is granted assume the risk of relocation during street repair projects. *City of New York*, 713 N.Y.S.2d 40 (1 Dept., 2000)

franchisee The person or entity granted a franchise.

franchise tax A tax on the privilege of engaging in a business.

franchisor The person or entity that grants a franchise.

franking privilege The privilege given to designated government officials of sending certain matter through the mail without paying postage. Also called frank.

fraternal benefit association or **society** A nonprofit association of persons of similar calling or background who aid and assist one another and promote worthy causes.

fratricide The killing of a brother or sister.

fraud A false statement of material fact made with the intent to mislead by having the victim rely on the statement. A tort is committed if the victim suffers actual damage due to justifiable reliance on the statement. Fraud can also be a crime.

To constitute "fraud," a misrepresentation must have been knowingly and intentionally made to the plaintiff, whose damages follow from reasonable reliance upon the misstatement. *Mayes*, 723 N.Y.S.2d 151 (1 Dept., 2001)

fraud in fact See positive fraud.

fraud in law Constructive or presumed fraud.

fraud in the factum A misrepresentation about the essential nature or existence of the document itself.

fraud in the inducement Misrepresentation as to the terms or other aspects of a contractual relation, venture, or other transaction that leads (induces) a person to agree to enter into the transaction with a false impression or understanding of the risks or obligations he or she has undertaken.

fraud on the market theory When false information artificially inflates the value of a stock, it is presumed that purchasers on the open market relied on that information to their detriment.

frauds, statute of See statute of frauds.

fraudulent Involving fraud.

fraudulent concealment 1. Taking affirmative steps to hide or suppress a material fact that one is legally or morally bound to disclose. 2. An equitable doctrine that estops a defendant who concealed his or her wrongful conduct from asserting the statute of limitations.

fraudulent conveyance Transferring property without fair consideration in order to place the property beyond the reach of creditors.

FRCP Federal Rules of Civil Procedure. See federal rules.

free 1. Not subject to the legal constraint of another. 2. Not subject to a burden. 3. Having political rights. 4. To liberate. 5. Without cost.

free alongside ship (FAS) The quoted price includes the cost of delivering the goods to a designated point alongside of the ship. The risk of loss is with the seller up to this point.

Unless otherwise agreed the term F.A.S. vessel (which means "free alongside") at a named port, even though used only in connection with the stated price, is a delivery term under which the seller must (a) at his own expense and risk deliver the goods alongside the vessel in the manner usual in that port or on a dock designated and provided by the buyer; and (b) obtain and tender a receipt for the goods in exchange for which the carrier is under a duty to issue a bill of lading. McKinney's Uniform Commercial Code § 2-319(2)

free and clear Not subject to liens or other encumbrances.

freedom of association The right protected in the First Amendment to join with others for lawful purposes.

freedom of contract The right of parties to enter a bargain of their choice subject to reasonable government regulation in the interest of public health, safety, and morals.

freedom of expression The rights protected in the First Amendment concerning freedom of speech, press, and religion.

Freedom of Information Act (FOIA) A federal statute making information held by federal agencies available to the public unless the information is exempt from public disclosure (5 USC § 552). Many states have equivalent statutes for state agencies.

Freedom of Information Law (FOIL) A New York statute (Public Officers Law, Article 6) making information held by state and municipal entities available to the public unless the information is exempt from public disclosure.

freedom of religion The right protected in the First Amendment to believe and practice one's form of religion or to believe in no religion. In addition, the right to be free of governmental promotion of religion or interference with one's practice of religion.

"Freedom of religion" means freedom to individually believe and to practice or exercise one's belief. Const. art. 1, § 3. *In re Elwell*, 284 N.Y.S.2d 924 (Fam. Ct., 1967)

freedom of speech The right protected in the First Amendment to express one's ideas without government restrictions subject to the right of the government to protect public safety and to provide a remedy for defamation.

freedom of the press The First Amendment prohibition against government restrictions that abridge the freedom of the press such as imposing prior restraint or censorship.

freedom of the seas The right of ships to travel without restriction in the sea beyond the territorial waters of any nation.

free exercise clause The clause in the First Amendment stating that "Congress shall make no law . . . prohibiting the free exercise" of religion.

freehold An estate in land for life, in fee simple, or in fee tail. An estate in real property of uncertain or unlimited duration, unlike a leasehold, which is for a definite period of time.

freelance paralegal See independent paralegal.

free on board (FOB) In a sales price quotation, the seller assumes all responsibilities and costs up to the point of delivery on board.

(1) Unless otherwise agreed the term F.O.B. (which means "free on board") at a named place, even though used only in connection with the stated price, is a delivery term under which (a) when the term is F.O.B. the place of shipment, the seller must at that place ship the goods in the manner provided in this Article (Section 2-504) and bear the expense and risk of putting them into the possession of the carrier; or (b) when the term is F.O.B. the place of destination, the seller must at his own expense and risk transport the goods to that place and there tender delivery of them in the manner provided in this Article (Section 2-503); . . . McKinney's Uniform Commercial Code § 2-319(1)

freeze To hold something (e.g., wages, prices) at a fixed level; to immobilize or maintain the status quo.

freeze-out Action by major shareholders or a board of directors to eliminate minority shareholders or to marginalize their power.

fresh Prompt; without material interval.

fresh complaint rule A victim's complaint of sexual assault made to another person soon after the event is admissible.

fresh pursuit 1. Promptly; without undue delay. 2. The right of a police officer, engaged in a continuous and uninterrupted pursuit, to cross geographic or jurisdictional lines to arrest a felon even if the officer does not have a warrant. 3. The right of a victim of property theft to use reasonable force to obtain it back just after it is taken. Also called hot pursuit.

friendly Pertaining to someone who is favorably disposed; not hostile.

"Friendly fire" for purposes of fire policy is fire under control and fire beyond control is "hostile," whether in or out of its proper place. *Barcalo Mfg. Co.*, 263 N.Y.S.2d 807 (4 Dept., 1965)

friendly suit A suit brought by agreement between the parties to obtain the opinion of the court on their dispute.

friend of the court See amicus curiae.

friendly takeover The acquisition of one company by another that is approved by the boards of directors of both companies.

fringe benefits Benefits provided by an employer that are in addition to the employee's regular compensation (e.g., vacation).

frisk To conduct a pat-down search of a suspect in order to find concealed weapons.

frivolous 1. Involving a legal position that cannot be supported by a good-faith argument based on existing law or on the need for a change in the law. 2. Clearly insufficient on its face.

"Frivolous lawsuit," as basis for imposing sanctions, is one for which there is no genuine basis either in law or fact, or good faith argument for a change in the law. *Costanza*, 693 N.Y.S.2d 897 (Sup. Ct., 1999)

frivolous appeal An appeal that is devoid of merit or one that has no reasonable chance of succeeding.

frolic Employee conduct outside the scope of employment because it is personal rather than primarily for the employer's business.

front A person or organization acting as a cover for illegal activities or to disguise the identity of the real owner or principal.

frontage The land between a building and the street; the front part of property.

front-end load A sales fee or commission (the load) levied at the time of making a stock or mutual fund purchase.

frozen assets 1. Nonliquid assets. Assets that cannot be easily converted into cash. 2. Assets that are prohibited from transfer or liquidation by court order in anticipation of the owner's wrongful transfer or liquidation of the assets during the pendency of a legal proceeding.

fructus The fruit or produce of land.

fruit 1. The effect, consequence, or product of something. 2. Evidence resulting from an activity.

fruit and tree doctrine One cannot avoid taxation on income simply by assigning it to someone else.

fruit of the poisonous tree doctrine Evidence derived directly or indirectly from illegal governmental activity (e.g., an illegal search and seizure), is inadmissible as trial evidence.

Evidence derived from unlawful seizure is not inadmissible under the "fruit of the poisonous tree" doctrine when it is shown that such evidence would inevitably have been gained without the unlawful action. *People v. Steg*, 380 N.Y.S.2d 270 (2 Dept., 1976)

fruits of crime Stolen goods or other products of criminal conduct.

frustration Preventing something from occurring. Rendering something ineffectual.

frustration of contract or **purpose** See commercial frustration.

FTC Federal Trade Commission (*www.ftc.gov*).

fugitive One who flees in order to avoid arrest, prosecution, prison, service of process, or subpoena to testify (18 USC § 1073).

full age See age of majority.

full bench; full court See en banc.

full coverage Insurance with no exclusions or deductibles.

full faith and credit A state must recognize and enforce (give full faith and credit to) the legislative acts, public records, and judicial decisions of sister states. U.S. Constitution, art. IV, § 1.

full settlement An adjustment of all pending matters and the mutual release of all prior obligations existing between the parties.

full warranty A warranty that covers labor and parts for all defects.

functus officio Without further official authority once the authorized task is complete.

fund 1. Money or other resources available for a specific purpose. 2. A group or organization that administers or manages money. 3. To convert into fixed-interest, long-term debt.

fundamental Serving as an essential component; basic.

fundamental error See plain error.

fundamental law Constitutional law; the law establishing basic rights and governing principles.

fundamental right A basic right that is either explicitly or implicitly guaranteed by the constitution.

funded debt 1. A debt that has resources earmarked for the payment of interest and principal as they become due. 2. Long-term debt that has replaced short-term debt.

fungible Commercially interchangeable; substitutable; able to be replaced by other assets of the same kind. Examples: grain, sugar, oil.

"Fungible" with respect to goods or securities means goods or securities of which any unit is, by nature or usage of trade, the equivalent of any other like unit. McKinney's Uniform Commercial Code § 1-201(17)

future advances Funds advanced by a lender after a mortgage or other security agreement is created, yet which are still secured by the original mortgage or other security instrument.

future damages Sums awarded for future pain and suffering, impairment of earning capacity, future medical expenses, and other future losses.

future earnings Income that a party is no longer able to earn because of injury or loss of employment.

future estate See future interest.

future interest An interest in real or personal property in which possession, use, or other enjoyment is future rather than present. Also called estate in expectancy, future estate.

futures Commodities or securities sold or bought for delivery in the future.

futures contract A contract for the sale or purchase of a commodity or security at a specified price and quantity for future delivery.

FY Fiscal year.

G

GAAP Generally Accepted Accounting Principles.

gag order 1. A court order to stop attorneys, witnesses, or media from discussing a current case. 2. An order by the court to bind and gag a disruptive defendant during his or her trial.

gain 1. Profit; excess of receipts over costs. 2. Increments of value. 3. The excess of the net selling price over the book value of an asset.

gainful employment Available work for pay.

gambling Risking money or other property for the possibility—chance—of a reward. Also called gaming.

game laws Laws regulating the hunting of wild animals and birds.

gaming See gambling.

GAO General Accountability Office (*www.gao.gov*).

gaol A place of detention for temporary or short-term confinement; jail.

garnishee; garnishor (garnisher) A garnishee is the person or entity in possession of a debtor's property that is being reached or attached (via garnishment) by a creditor of the debtor. The creditor is the garnishor (garnisher).

A garnishee is defined in CPLR 105(i) as "a person other than the judgment debtor who has property in his possession or custody in which a judgment debtor has an interest." *CanWest Global*, 804 N.Y.S.2d 549 (Sup. Ct., 2005)

garnishment A court proceeding by a creditor to force a third party in possession of the debtor's property (e.g., wages) to turn the property over to the creditor to satisfy the debt.

gavelkind A feudal system under which all sons shared land equally upon the death of their father.

GDP See gross domestic product.

gender discrimination Discrimination based on one's sex or gender.

GBMI Guilty but mentally ill. See also insanity.

general administrator A person given a grant of authority to administer the entire estate of a decedent who dies without a will.

general agent An agent authorized to conduct all of the principal's business affairs, usually involving a continuity of service.

general appearance Acts of a party from which it can reasonably be inferred that the party submits (consents) to the full jurisdiction of the court.

Generally, when a defendant becomes an actor in an action to the extent of participating in the merits, he makes a "general appearance" and submits to the court's jurisdiction. *Odiens*, 40 N.Y.S.2d 179 (1 Dept., 1943)

general assembly A legislative body in some states.

general assignment A transfer of a debtor's property for the benefit of all creditors. See also assignment for benefit of creditors.

general average contribution rule When one engaged in a maritime venture voluntarily incurs a loss (e.g., discards part of the cargo) to avert a larger loss of ship or cargo, the loss incurred is shared by all who participated in the venture.

general bequest A gift in a will payable out of the general assets of the estate. A gift in a will of a designated quantity or value of property.

general contractor One who contracts to construct an entire building or project rather than a portion of it; a prime contractor who hires subcontractors, coordinates the work, etc. Also called original contractor, prime contractor.

general counsel The chief attorney or law firm that represents a company or other organization in most of its legal matters.

General Court The name of the legislature in Massachusetts and in New Hampshire.

general creditor See unsecured creditor.

general court-martial A military trial court consisting of five members and one military judge, which can impose any punishment.

general damages Damages that naturally, directly, and frequently result from a wrong. The law implies general damages to exist; they do not have to be specifically alleged. Also called direct damages.

> Damages that are natural and probable consequence of party's breach of contract. *American List Corp.*, 550 N.Y.S.2d 590 (Ct. of App., 1989)

general demurrer A demurrer challenging whether an opponent has stated a cause of action or attacking a petition in its entirety. See also demurrer.

general denial A response by a party that controverts all of the allegations in the preceding pleading, usually the complaint.

general deposit Placing money in a bank to be repaid upon demand or to be drawn upon from time to time in the usual course of banking business.

general devise A gift in a will to be satisfied out of testator's estate generally; it is not charged upon any specific property or fund.

general election A regularly scheduled election.

general execution See execution (3).

general finding A finding in favor of one party and against the other.

general jurisdiction The power of a court to hear any kind of case, with limited exceptions.

general intent The state of mind in which a person is conscious of the act he or she is committing without necessarily understanding or desiring the consequences of that action.

> General intent has been defined as an intent to do knowingly and wilfully that which is condemned as wrong by the law and is presumed from the criminal act itself. 1 Callaghan, Criminal Law. *People v. Maxam*, 557 N.Y.S.2d 534 (3 Dept., 1990)

general law A law that applies to everyone within the class regulated by the law.

general legacy A gift of personal property in a will that may be satisfied out of the general assets of the testator's estate.

general lien A lien that attaches to all the goods of the debtor, not just the goods that caused the debt.

general partner A business co-owner who can participate in the management of the business and is personally liable for its debts.

general partnership A partnership in which all the partners are general partners, have no restrictions on running the business, and have unlimited liability for the debts of the business. An association of two or more persons to carry on as co-owners of a business for profit.

general power of appointment A power of appointment exercisable in favor of any person that the donee (i.e., the person given the power) may select, including the donee him or herself.

> General power of appointment.—The term "general power of appointment" means a power which is exercisable in favor of the decedent, his estate, his creditors, or the creditors of his estate. McKinney's Tax Law I.R.C. § 2041(b)(1)

general power of attorney A grant of broad powers by a principal to an agent.

general statute A statute that operates equally upon all persons and things within the scope of the statute. A statute that applies to persons or things as a class. A statute that affects the general public.

general strike Cessation of work by employees throughout an entire industry or country.

general verdict A verdict for one party or the other, as opposed to a verdict that answers specific questions.

general warrant A blanket warrant that does not specify the items to be searched for or the persons to be arrested.

general warranty deed See warranty deed.

General Welfare Clause The clause in the federal constitution giving Congress the power to impose taxes and spend for defense and the general welfare. U.S. Constitution, art. I, § 8, cl. 1.

generation-skipping transfer A transfer of assets to a family member who is more than one generation below the transferor, e.g., from grandparent to grandchild.

generation-skipping trust Any trust having younger generation beneficiaries of more than one generation in the same trust. A trust that makes a generation-skipping transfer.

generic 1. Relating to or characteristic of an entire group or class. 2. Not having a brand name. Identified by its nonproprietary name.

generic drug A drug not protected by trademark that is the same as a brand name drug in safety, strength, quality, intended use, etc.

genetic markers Separate genes or complexes of genes identified as a result of genetic tests. In paternity cases, such tests may exclude a man as the biological father, or may show how probable it is that he is the father.

> A non-marital child is the legitimate child of his father so that he and his issue inherit from his father and his paternal kindred if: . . . (D) a blood genetic marker test had been administered to the father which together with other evidence establishes paternity by clear and convincing evidence. McKinney's EPTL § 4-1.2(2)

Geneva Conventions International agreements on the conduct of nations at war, e.g., protection of civilians, treatment of prisoners of war.

genocide Acts committed with intent to destroy, in whole or in part, a national, ethnic, racial, or religious group, e.g., killing members of the group, causing them serious mental harm, or imposing measures designed to prevent births within the group.

gentleman's agreement An agreement, usually unwritten, based on trust and honor. It is not an enforceable contract.

genuine Authentic; being what it purports to be; having what it says it has.

germane Relevant; on point.

gerrymander Dividing a geographic area into voting districts in order to provide an unfair advantage to one political party or group by diluting the voting strength of another party or group.

gestational surrogacy The sperm and egg of a couple are fertilized in vitro in a laboratory; the resulting embryo is then implanted in a surrogate mother who gives birth to a child with whom she has no genetic relationship.

gift A transfer of property to another without payment or consideration. To be irrevocable, (a) there must be a delivery of the property; (b) the transfer must be voluntary;

(c) the donor must have legal capacity to make a gift; (d) the donor must intend to divest him or herself of title and control of what is given; (e) the donor must intend that the gift take effect immediately; (f) there must be no consideration (e.g., payment) from the donee; (g) the donee must accept the gift.

> A gift is a voluntary transfer of property without consideration or compensation and cannot be dependent upon an agreement. *Signacon Controls*, 329 N.Y.S.2d 175 (Sup. Ct., 1972)

gift causa mortis A gift made in contemplation of imminent death subject to the implied condition that if the donor recovers or the donee dies first, the gift shall be void.

gift in contemplation of death See gift causa mortis.

gift inter vivos See inter vivos gift.

gift over A gift of property that takes effect when a preceding estate in the property ends or fails.

gifts to minors act The Uniform Transfers to Minors Act covering adult management of gifts to minors, custodial accounts for minors, etc. Formerly the Uniform Gifts to Minors Act.

gift tax A tax on the transfer of property by gift, usually paid by the donor, although a few states tax the donee.

gilt-edged 1. Of the highest quality. 2. Pertaining to a very safe investment.

Ginnie Mae (GNMA) Government National Mortgage Association (*www.ginniemae.gov*).

gist The central idea or foundation of a legal action or matter.

give To make a gratuitous transfer of property. See also gift.

giveback A reduction in wages or other benefits agreed to by a union during labor bargaining.

gloss A brief explanatory note. An interpretation of a text.

GNP See gross national product.

go bare To engage in an occupation or profession without malpractice insurance.

go forward 1. To proceed with one's case. 2. To introduce evidence.

going and coming rule The scope of employment usually does not include the time when an employee is going to or coming from work. Respondeat superior during such times does not apply.

> An injury sustained by an employee is compensable under the Workers' Compensation Law if it arises out of and in the course of the employment. The general rule is that injuries sustained during travel to and from the place of employment do not come within the statute. *Neacosia*, 626 N.Y.S.2d 44 (Ct. of App., 1995)

going concern An existing solvent business operating in its ordinary and regular manner with no plans to go out of business.

going-concern value What a willing purchaser, in an arm's length transaction, would offer for a company as an operating business as opposed to one contemplating liquidation.

going private Delisting equity securities from a securities exchange. Going from publicly owned corporation to a close corporation.

going public Issuing stock for public purchase for the first time; becoming a public corporation.

golden parachute Very high payments and other economic benefits made to an employee upon his or her termination.

golden rule 1. A guideline of statutory interpretation in which we presume that the legislature did not intend an interpretation that would lead to absurd or ridiculous consequences. 2. Urging jurors to place themselves in the position of the injured party or victim.

good 1. Sufficient in law; enforceable. 2. Valid. 3. Reliable.

good behavior Law-abiding. Following the rules. A standard used to grant inmates early release.

good cause A cause that affords a legal excuse; a legally sufficient ground or reason. Also called just cause, sufficient cause.

> Good cause means and shall be limited to: (i) (A) The implementation by a brewer of a national or regional policy of consolidation which is reasonable, nondiscriminatory and essential. McKinney's Alcoholic Beverage Control Law § 55-c(e)

good consideration Consideration based on blood relationship or natural love and affection. Also called moral consideration.

good faith A state of mind indicating honesty and lawfulness of purpose; the absence of an intent to seek an undue advantage; a belief that known circumstances do not require further investigation.

good faith bargaining Going to the bargaining table with an open mind and a sincere desire to reach agreement.

good faith exception Evidence is admissible (in an exception to the exclusionary rule) if the police reasonably rely on a warrant that is later invalidated because of the lack of probable cause.

good faith purchaser See bona fide purchaser.

goods 1. Movable things other than money or intangible rights. 2. Any personal property.

Good Samaritan Someone who comes to the assistance of another without a legal obligation to do so. Under Good Samaritan laws of most states, a person aiding another in an emergency will not be liable for ordinary negligence in providing this aid.

> "Good samaritan" shall mean a person who, other than a law enforcement officer, acts in good faith (a) to apprehend a person who has committed a crime in his presence or who has in fact committed a felony, (b) to prevent a crime or an attempted crime from occurring, or (c) to aid a law enforcement officer in effecting an arrest. McKinney's Executive Law § 621(7)

goods and chattels 1. Personal property. 2. Tangible personal property.

good time Credit for an inmate's good conduct that reduces prison time.

good title A valid title; a title that a reasonably prudent purchaser would accept. Marketable title.

goodwill 1. The reputation of a business that causes it to generate additional customers. The advantages a business has over its competitors due to its name, location, and owner's reputation. 2. An asset that represents the excess value of the purchase price over the fair market value of an acquired business entity.

govern 1. To direct or control by authority; to rule. 2. To be a precedent or controlling law.

government 1. The process of governing. 2. The framework of political institutions by which the executive, legislative, and judicial functions of the state are carried on. 3. The sovereign power of a state.

governmental function 1. An activity of government authorized by law for the general public good. 2. A function that can be performed adequately only by the government. An essential function of government.

A purely governmental function is undertaken for the protection and safety of the public pursuant to the general police powers, while a purely proprietary function is a governmental activity which substitutes for or supplements a traditionally private enterprise. *Johnson City Cent. School Dist.*, 709 N.Y.S.2d 225 (3 Dept., 2000)

governmental immunity See sovereign immunity.

government contract A contract in which at least one of the parties is a government agency or branch.

government corporation A government-owned corporation that is a mixture of a corporation and a government agency created to serve a predominantly business function in the public interest.

government security A security (e.g., a treasury bill) issued by the government or a government entity.

governor A chief executive official of a state of the United States.

grace period Extra time past a due date given to avoid a penalty (e.g., cancellation) that would otherwise apply to the missed date.

graded offense A crime that can be committed in different categories or classes of severity, resulting in different punishments.

graduated lease A lease for which the rent will vary depending on factors such as the amount of gross income produced.

graduated payment mortgage (GPM) A mortgage that begins with lower payments that increase over the term of the loan.

Graduated payment mortgage: payments are lower in the first few years and increase over the term of the loan. McKinney's RPL sec. 279(1); *Danyluk*, 784 N.Y.S.2d 919 (N.Y. Civ. Ct., 2004)

graduated tax See progressive tax.

graft Money or personal gain unlawfully received because of one's position of public trust.

grandfather clause A special exemption for those already doing what will now be prohibited or otherwise restricted for others.

grand jury A jury of inquiry that receives accusations in criminal cases, hears the evidence of the prosecutor, and issues indictments when satisfied that a trial should be held.

grand larceny Unlawfully taking and carrying away another's personal property valued in excess of a statutorily set amount (e.g., $1,000).

grant 1. To give property or a right to another with or without compensation. 2. To transfer real property by deed or other instrument. 3. Something given or transferred.

grantee The person to whom a grant is made or property is conveyed.

grant-in-aid Funds given by the government to a person or institution for a specific purpose, e.g., education or research.

granting clause That portion of a deed or instrument of conveyance that contains the words of transfer of an interest.

grantor The person who makes the grant or conveys property.

grantor-grantee index A master index by grantor name to all recorded instruments (e.g., deeds, mortgages) allowing you to trace the names of sellers and buyers of land up to the present owner.

grantor trust A trust in which the grantor is taxed on its income because of his or her control over the income or corpus.

gratis Without reward or consideration. Free.

gratuitous 1. Given or granted free, without consideration. 2. Unwarranted; unjustified.

gratuitous bailment A bailment in which the care and custody of the bailor's property by the bailee is without charge or expectation of payment.

A gratuitous bailment is, by definition, a transfer of possession or use of property without compensation. *Fili*, 590 N.Y.S.2d 961 (4 Dept., 1992)

gratuitous promise A promise made by one who has received no consideration for it.

gravamen The essence of a grievance; the gist of a charge.

gray market A market where goods are legally sold at lower prices than the manufacturer would want or that are imported bearing a valid United States trademark, but without consent of the trademark holder.

great bodily injury A significant or substantial injury or damage; a serious physical impairment. Also called serious bodily harm.

great care The amount of care used by reasonable persons when involved in very important matters. Also called utmost care.

Great Charter See Magna Carta.

Great Writ See habeas corpus.

green card The government-issued registration card indicating the permanent resident status of an alien.

greenmail Inflated payments to buy back the stock of a shareholder (a raider) who has threatened a corporate takeover.

Green River ordinance An ordinance that prohibits door-to-door commercial solicitations without prior consent.

grievance 1. An injury or wrong that can be the basis for an action or complaint. 2. A charge or complaint. 3. A complaint about working conditions or about a violation of a union agreement.

grievance procedure Formal steps established to resolve disputes arising under a collective bargaining agreement.

The practice of grievance arbitration permits public sector parties to submit grievances under a collective bargaining agreement (CBA) to arbitration pursuant to statute. McKinney's Civil Service Law § 204. *In re Board of Educ. of Watertown City School Dist.*, 688 N.Y.S.2d 463 (Ct. of App., 1999)

gross 1. Glaring, obvious. 2. Reprehensible. 3. Total; before or without diminution or deduction.

gross domestic product (GDP) The total value of all goods and services produced in a country in a given period.

gross estate The total assets of a person at his or her death before deductions are taken.

gross income All income from whatever source before exemptions, deductions, credits, or other adjustments.

gross lease A lease in which the tenant pays only rent; the landlord pays everything else, e.g., taxes, utilities, insurance, etc.

gross national product (GNP) The total value of all goods and services produced by a country in a given period. Has been replaced in general usage by gross domestic product (GDP).

gross negligence 1. The intentional failure to perform a manifest duty in reckless disregard of the consequences to the life or property of another. 2. The failure to use even slight care and diligence. Also called willful negligence.

Gross negligence differs in kind as well as degree from ordinary negligence; it is conduct that evinces a reckless disregard for the rights of others or smacks of intentional wrongdoing. *Sutton Park Development Corp.*, 745 N.Y.S.2d 622 (3 Dept., 2002)

gross receipts The total amount of money (and any other consideration) received from selling goods or services.

ground 1. Foundation; points relied on. 2. A reason that is legally sufficient to obtain a remedy or other result.

ground rent 1. Rent paid to the owner for the use of undeveloped land, usually to construct a building on it. 2. A perpetual rent reserved to the grantor (and his or her heirs) from land conveyed in fee simple.

group annuity A policy that provides annuities to a group of people under a single master contract.

group boycott Agreements among competitors within the same market tier not to deal with other competitors or market participants.

group insurance A single insurance policy covering a group of individuals, e.g., employees of a particular company.

group legal services See prepaid legal services.

growth stock The stock in a company that is expected to have higher than average growth, particularly in the value of the stock.

GSA General Services Administration (*www.gsa.gov*).

guarantee 1. An assurance that a particular outcome will occur, e.g., a product will perform as stated or will be repaired at no cost. Also called guaranty. 2. A promise to fulfill the obligation of another if the latter fails to do so. 3. To give security. 4. Security given.

guaranteed stock The stock of one corporation whose dividends are guaranteed by another corporation, e.g., by a parent corporation.

guarantor One who makes a guaranty; one who becomes secondarily liable for another's debt or performance.

guaranty 1. A promise to fulfill the obligation of another if the latter fails to do so. 2. See guarantee (1).

guardian A person who lawfully has the power and duty to care for the person, property, or rights of another who is incapable of managing his or her affairs (e.g., a minor, an insane person).

guardian ad litem (GAL) A special guardian appointed by the court to represent the interests of another (e.g., a minor) in court. See also ad litem, law guardian.

A guardian ad litem is a special guardian appointed by the court to prosecute or defend, in behalf of an infant, a suit to which he is a party, and such guardian is considered an officer of the court to represent the interests of the infant in the litigation. *Kossar*, 179 N.Y.S.2d 71 (Ct. Cl. 1958)

guardianship 1. The office, duty, or authority of a guardian. 2. The fiduciary relationship that exists between guardian and ward.

guest 1. A passenger in a motor vehicle who is offered a ride by someone who receives no benefits from the passenger other than hospitality, goodwill, and the like. 2. One who pays for the services of a restaurant or place of lodging. 3. A recipient of one's hospitality, especially at home.

guest statute A statute providing that drivers of motor vehicles will not be liable for injuries caused by their ordinary negligence to nonpaying guest passengers.

guilty 1. A defendant's plea that accepts (or does not contest) the criminal charge against him or her. 2. A determination by a jury or court that the defendant has committed the crime charged. 3. Responsible for criminal or civil wrongdoing.

H

habeas corpus ("you have the body") A writ designed to bring a party before a court in order to test the legality of his or her detention or imprisonment. Also called the Great Writ.

A writ of habeas corpus is designed to safeguard rights of persons and to challenge in court the legality of their detention. *Morhous*, 293 N.Y. 131 (N.Y., 1944)

habeas corpus ad faciendum et recipiendum A writ to move a civil case (and the body of the defendant) from a lower to a higher court.

habeas corpus ad prosequendum A writ issued for the purpose of indicting, prosecuting, and sentencing a defendant already confined within another jurisdiction.

habeas corpus ad testificandum A writ used to bring in a prisoner detained in a jail or prison to give evidence before the court.

habendum clause The portion of a deed (often using the words, "to have and to hold") that describes the ownership rights being transferred (i.e., the estate or interest being granted).

habitability The condition of a building that allows it to be enjoyed because it is free from substantial defects that endanger health or safety.

habitable Suitable or fit for living.

habitation 1. Place of abode; one's dwelling or residence. 2. Occupancy.

habitual Customary, usual, regular.

habitual criminal A repeat offender. Also called career criminal, recidivist.

half blood (half brother, half sister) The relationship between persons who have the same father or the same mother, but not both.

halfway house A house in the community that helps individuals make the adjustment from prison or other institutionalization to normal life.

hand down To announce or file an opinion by a court.

handicap A physical or mental impairment or disability that substantially limits one or more of a person's major life activities.

harassment Intrusive or unwanted acts, words, or gestures (often persistent and continuing) that have a substantial adverse effect on the safety, security, or privacy of another and that serve no legitimate purpose.

A person is guilty of harassment in the second degree when, with intent to harass, annoy or alarm another person: 1. He or she strikes, shoves, kicks or otherwise subjects such other person to physical contact, or attempts or threatens to do the same; or 2. He or she follows a person in or about a public place or places; or 3. He or she engages in a course of conduct or repeatedly commits acts which alarm or seriously annoy such other person and which serve no legitimate purpose. McKinney's Penal Law § 240.26

harbor To shelter or protect, often clandestinely and illegally.

hard cases Cases in which a court sometimes overlooks fixed legal principles when they are opposed to persuasive equities.

hard labor Forced physical labor required of an inmate.

harm 1. Loss or detriment to a person. 2. To injure.

harmless Not causing any damage.

harmless error An error that did not prejudice the substantial rights of the party alleging it. Also called technical error.

Hatch Act A federal statute that prohibits federal employees from engaging in certain types of political activities (5 USC § 1501).

hate crime A crime motivated by hatred, bias, or prejudice, based on race, color, religion, national origin, ethnicity, gender, or sexual orientation of another individual or group of individuals.

A person commits a hate crime when he or she commits a specified offense and either: (a) intentionally selects the person against whom the offense is committed or intended to be committed in whole or in substantial part because of a belief or perception regarding the race, color, national origin, ancestry, gender, religion, religious practice, age, disability or sexual orientation of a person, regardless of whether the belief or perception is correct, or (b) intentionally commits the act or acts constituting the offense in whole or in substantial part because of a belief or perception regarding the race, color, national origin, ancestry, gender, religion, religious practice, age, disability or sexual orientation of a person, regardless of whether the belief or perception is correct. McKinney's Penal Law § 485.05(1)

have and hold See habendum clause.

hazard 1. A risk or danger of harm or loss. The chance of suffering a loss. 2. Danger, peril.

hazardous Exposed to or involving danger. Risky.

H.B. house bill. A proposed statute considered by the House of Representatives.

headnote A short-paragraph summary of a portion of a court opinion printed before the opinion begins. Also called syllabus.

head of household 1. The primary income earner in a household. 2. An unmarried taxpayer (or married if living and filing separately) who maintains a home that for more than one-half of the taxable year is the principal place of abode of certain dependents, such as an unmarried child.

head tax See poll tax.

healthcare proxy See advance directive.

health maintenance organization (HMO) A prepaid health insurance plan consisting of a network of doctors and healthcare institutions that provide medical services to subscribers.

hearing 1. A proceeding designed to resolve issues of fact or law. Usually, an impartial officer presides, evidence is presented, etc. The hearing is *ex parte* if only one party is present; it is *adversarial* if both parties are present. 2. A meeting of a legislative committee to consider proposed legislation or other legislative matters. 3. A meeting in which one is allowed to argue a position.

hearing officer; hearing examiner One who presides at a hearing. See also administrative law judge.

hearsay 1. What one learns from another rather than from first-hand knowledge. 2. An out-of-court statement offered to prove the truth of the matter asserted in the statement. A "statement, other than one made by the declarant while testifying at the trial or hearing, offered in evidence to prove the truth of the matter asserted." Federal Rule of Evidence 801(c).

Hearsay is an out-of-court statement offered to prove the truth of the matter asserted therein. *Gelpi*, 721 N.Y.S.2d 380 (2 Dept., 2001)

heart balm statute A law abolishing heart balm actions, which are actions based on a broken heart or loss of love (e.g., breach of promise to marry, alienation of affections, criminal conversation).

The rights of action to recover sums of money as damages for alienation of affections, criminal conversation, seduction, or breach of contract to marry are abolished. McKinney's Civil Rights Law § 80-a

heat of passion Fear, rage, or resentment in which a person loses self-control due to provocation. Also called hot blood, sudden heat of passion.

hedge To safeguard oneself from loss on a bet, bargain, or speculation by making compensatory arrangements on the other side. To reduce risk by entering a transaction that will offset an existing position.

hedge fund A special investment fund that uses aggressive (higher risk) strategies such as short selling and buying derivatives.

hedonic damages Damages that cover the victim's loss of pleasure or enjoyment of life.

heinous Shockingly odious or evil.

heir 1. One designated by state law to receive all or part of the estate of a person who dies without leaving a valid will (intestate). Also called heir at law, legal heir. 2. One who inherits (or is in line to inherit) by intestacy or by will.

The word "heirs" may be construed as meaning legatees when other provisions of will indicate testator's intent to make bequests to persons other than his blood relatives. *In re Mercereau's Will*, 177 N.Y.S.2d 393 (Sur., 1958)

heir apparent See apparent heir.

heir at law See heir (1).

heir collateral See collateral heir.

heir of the blood One who inherits because of a blood relationship with the decedent in the ascending or descending line.

heir of the body A blood relative in the direct line of descent, e.g., children, grandchildren (excluding adopted children).

heir presumptive See presumptive heir.

heirs and assigns Words used to convey a fee simple estate.

held Decided. See also hold.

henceforth From this (or that) time on.

hereafter 1. From now on. 2. At some time in the future.

hereditament 1. Property, rights, or anything that can be inherited. 2. Real property.

hereditary Capable of being inherited. Pertaining to inheritance.

hereditary succession See intestate succession.

herein In this section; in the document you are now reading.

hereto To this (document or matter).

heretofore Before now; up to now.

hereunder 1. By the terms of or in accordance with this document. 2. Later in the document.

herewith With this or in this document.

heritable Capable of being inherited.

hermeneutics The science or art of interpreting documents.

hidden asset Property of a company that is either not stated on its books or is stated at an undervalued price.

hidden defect A deficiency in property that could not be discovered by reasonable and customary observation or inspection and for which a lessor or seller is generally liable if such defect causes harm. Also called inherent defect, latent defect.

high crime A major offense that is a serious abuse of governmental power. Can be the basis of impeachment and removal from office.

highest and best use The use of property that will most likely produce the highest market value, greatest financial return, or the most profit.

Highest and best use, for purposes of determining value of condemned property, is not static concept, but one that fluctuates pursuant to changes in market value, demand, land use regulations, and available engineering techniques. *Metropolitan Transp. Authority*, 601 N.Y.S.2d 768 (Sup. Ct., 1993)

high-low agreement A compromise agreement under which the parties set a minimum (floor) and maximum (ceiling) for damages. The defendant will pay at least the floor (if the jury awards less than this amount) but no more than the ceiling (if the jury awards over that amount).

high seas That portion of the ocean or seas that is beyond the territorial jurisdiction of any country.

high-water line or mark The line on the shore to which high tide rises under normal weather conditions.

hijack To seize possession of a vehicle from another; to seize a vehicle and force it to go in another direction.

HIPAA Health Insurance Portability and Accountability Act. A federal statute providing protections such as maintaining the privacy of personal health information (*www.hhs.gov/ocr/hipaa*).

hire 1. To purchase the temporary use of a thing. 2. To engage the services of another for a fee.

hiring hall An agency or office operated by a union (or by both union and management) to place applicants for work.

hit and run The crime of leaving the scene of an accident without being identified.

Insureds' accident fell within ambit of "hit and run" provision of Insurance Law, even though other driver involved in accident did not immediately leave scene; police officers spoke to insureds and other driver, as they did not speak much English, insureds did not personally attempt to obtain any information from other driver or police officers, insureds were subsequently told that there was no police accident report, and insureds were unable to ascertain identity of other driver. *Matter of Country Wide Ins. Co*, 607 N.Y.S.2d 648 (1 Dept., 1994)

HMO See health maintenance organization.

hoard To accumulate assets beyond one's reasonable needs, often anticipating an increase in their market price.

Hobbs Act A federal anti-racketeering act that makes it illegal to obstruct, delay, or affect interstate commerce or attempt to conspire to do so by robbery, physical violence, or extortion (18 USC § 1951).

hobby losses A nondeductible loss suffered when engaged in an activity that is not pursued for profit.

hodgepodge See hotchpot.

hold 1. To possess something by virtue of lawful authority or title. 2. To reach a legal conclusion; to resolve a legal dispute. 3. To restrain or control; to keep in custody. 4. To preside at.

holder 1. One who has possession of something, e.g., a check, bond, document of title. 2. One who has legally acquired possession of a negotiable instrument (e.g., a check, a promissory note) and who is entitled to receive payment on the instrument.

holder for value Someone who has given something of value for a promissory note or other negotiable instrument.

holder in due course (HDC)(HIDC) One who gives value for a negotiable instrument in good faith, without any apparent defects, and without notice that it is overdue, has been dishonored, or is subject to any claim or defense.

A holder . . . who takes the instrument (a) for value; and (b) in good faith; and (c) without notice that it is overdue or has been dishonored or of any defense against or claim to it on the part of any person. McKinney's Uniform Commercial Code § 3-302(1)

hold harmless To assume any liability in a transaction thereby relieving another from responsibility or loss. Also called save harmless.

holding 1. A court's answer to or resolution of a legal issue before it. 2. A court ruling. 3. Property owned by someone.

holding company A company that owns stock in and supervises the management of other companies.

holding period The length of time a taxpayer owns a capital asset, which determines whether a gain or loss will be short-term or long-term.

holdover tenancy See estate at sufferance.

holdover tenant A tenant who retains possession of the premises after the expiration of a lease or after a tenancy at will has been ended.

holograph A handwritten document.

holographic will A will written entirely by the testator in his or her own handwriting, often without witnesses.

A will is holographic when it is written entirely in the handwriting of the testator, and is not executed and attested in accordance with the formalities prescribed by 3-2.1. McKinney's EPTL § 3-2.2(a)(2)

home equity conversion mortgage A first mortgage that provides for future payments to a homeowner based on accumulated equity.

homeowner's policy A multiperil insurance policy covering damage to a residence and liability claims based on home ownership.

homeowner's warranty (HOW) A warranty and insurance protection program offered by many home builders, providing protection for 10 years against major structural defects. A construction warranty.

home port doctrine A vessel engaged in interstate and foreign commerce is taxable only at its home port (e.g., where it is registered).

home rule A designated amount of self-government granted to local cities and towns.

homestead The dwelling house and adjoining land where the owner or his or her family lives.

homestead exemption laws Laws that allow a householder or head of a family to designate a residence and adjoining land as his or her homestead that, in whole or part, is exempt from execution or attachment for designated general debts.

homicide The killing of one human being by another. Whether the killing is a crime depends on factors such as intent.

homologate To approve; to confirm officially.

Hon. Honorable. Used as an honorific for judges and other officials.

honor To accept or pay a check or other negotiable instrument when presented for acceptance or payment.

"Honor" of a letter of credit means performance of the issuer's undertaking in the letter of credit to pay or deliver an item of value. McKinney's Uniform Commercial Code § 5-102(a)(8)

honorable discharge A declaration by the government that a member of the military left the service in good standing.

honorarium A fee for services when no fee was required.

honorary trust A trust that may not be enforceable because it has no beneficiary to enforce it. Example: a trust for the care of a pet.

horizontal agreement An agreement between companies that directly compete at the same level of distribution, often in restraint of trade.

horizontal merger The acquisition of one company by another company producing the same or a similar product and selling it in the same geographic market. A merger of corporate competitors.

horizontal price fixing An agreement by competitors at the same market level to fix or control prices they will charge for their goods or services.

"Horizontal price-fixing," which is prohibited under the fair trade laws, is price fixing engaged in by those in competition with each other at the same level. General Business Law, § 369-a. *Eastman Kodak Co.*, 133 N.Y.S.2d 908 (Sup. Ct., 1954)

horizontal privity The relationship between a supplier and a nonpurchasing party who is affected by the product, such as a relative of the buyer or a bystander.

horizontal property acts A statute on condominiums or cooperatives.

horizontal restraint See horizontal agreement.

horizontal union See craft union.

hornbook A book summarizing the basics or fundamentals of a topic.

hornbook law See black letter law.

hostile environment sexual harassment A work setting in which severe and pervasive conduct of a sexual nature creates a hostile or offensive working environment.

A workplace that is permeated with discriminatory intimidation, ridicule, and insult that is sufficiently severe or pervasive as to alter conditions of victim's employment and to create an abusive working environment. *Espaillat*, 642 N.Y.S.2d 875 (1 Dept., 1996)

hostile fire 1. A fire that breaks out or spreads to an unexpected area. 2. Gunfire from an enemy.

hostile possession Possession asserted to be superior to or incompatible with anyone else's claim to possession.

hostile witness A witness who manifests bias or prejudice, who appears aligned with the other side, or who refuses to answer questions. Also called adverse witness.

hot blood See heat of passion.

hot cargo 1. Goods produced or handled by an employer with whom a union has a dispute. 2. Stolen goods.

hotchpot Mixing or blending all property, however acquired, in order to divide it more equally. Also called hodgepodge.

hot pursuit See fresh pursuit.

house 1. Living quarters; a home. 2. One of the chambers of a legislature (e.g., U.S. House of Representatives, Md. House of Delegates).

house bill (H.B.)(H.) Proposed legislation considered by the House of Representatives.

housebreaking Breaking and entering a dwelling-house with the intent to commit any felony therein. Also called burglary.

house counsel An attorney who is an employee of a business or organization, usually on salary. Also called in-house counsel.

household 1. Belonging or pertaining to the house and family. 2. A group of persons living together.

House of Representatives (H.R.) See house (2).

H.R. See House of Representatives.

H. Res. House resolution. See also concurrent resolution.

H.R. 10 plan See Keogh plan.

HUD-1 A settlement statement required for real estate closings involving federally related mortgage loans. It includes the purchase price and all closing costs. The statement is required by the Real Estate Settlement Procedure Act (RESPA).

humanitarian doctrine See last clear chance doctrine.

hung jury A jury so irreconcilably divided in opinion that a verdict cannot be agreed upon.

husband-wife immunity See interspousal immunity.

husband-wife privilege See marital communications privilege.

hybrid security A security that combines the features of a debt instrument and an equity instrument.

hypothecate To pledge property as security or collateral for a debt without transferring title or possession.

hypothesis An assumption or theory to be proven or disproven.

hypothetical 1. Based on conjecture; not actual or real, but presented for purposes of discussion and analysis. 2. A set of assumed facts presented for the sake of argument and illustration.

hypothetical question A question in which the person being interviewed (e.g., an expert witness) is asked to give an opinion on a set of facts that are assumed to be true for purposes of the question.

I

IAS See Individual assignment system.

ibid. In the same place; in the work previously cited or mentioned. See also id.

ICE Immigration and Customs Enforcement (*www.ice.gov*).

ICJ See International Court of Justice (*www.icj-cij.org*).

id. The same. (Id. refers to the case or other authority cited immediately above or before in the text or footnotes.) See also ibid.

idem sonans Sounding the same. A misspelled signature can be effective if the misspelled name sounds the same as the correct spelling.

identify 1. To establish the identity of someone or something. 2. To associate or be associated with. 3. To specify the subject of a contract.

identity of interests Two persons being so closely related that suing one acts as notice to the other. Being only nominally separate.

identity of parties Two persons being so closely related that a judgment against one will bar (via res judicata) a later suit against the other.

identity theft Knowingly transferring or using a means of identification of another person with the intent to commit any unlawful activity.

A person is guilty of identity theft in the second degree when he or she knowingly and with intent to defraud assumes the identity of another person by presenting himself or herself as that other person, or by acting as that other person or by using personal identifying information of that other person, and thereby: 1. obtains goods, money, property or services or uses credit in the name of such other person in an aggregate amount that exceeds five hundred dollars; . . . McKinney's Penal Law § 190.79

i.e. That is; in other words.

IFP See in forma pauperis.

ignoramus We do not know. (A notation by a grand jury indicating a rejection of the indictment.)

ignorance The absence of knowledge.

ignorantia juris non excusat Ignorance of the law excuses no one.

illegal Against the law; prohibited by law.

illegal entry 1. Unauthorized entry with intent to commit a crime. 2. Entry into a country by an alien at the wrong time or place or by fraud; or eluding immigration officers when here.

illegality That which is contrary to law.

illegally obtained evidence Evidence collected in violation of a suspect's statutory or constitutional rights.

illegitimate 1. Born out of wedlock. 2. Contrary to law.

illicit Not permitted, illegal; improper.

illicit cohabitation Two unmarried persons living together as man and wife.

Illinois Land Trust See land trust.

illusory Deceptive, based on false appearances; not real.

illusory contract An agreement in which one party's consideration is so insignificant that a contract obligation cannot be imposed.

illusory promise An apparent promise that leaves the promisor's performance entirely within the discretion of the promisor.

Normally, if a promise is indefinite, or if promisor is free to perform it or not as he wills, it is wholly "illusory" and will not be enforced, but a promise which requires an affirmative cancellation cannot be regarded as illusory whether cancellation is for cause or otherwise. *Murphy Chemical Corp.*, 57 N.Y.S.2d 899 (Sup. Ct., 1945)

imbecility Severe mental retardation or cognitive dysfunction.

imitation Substantial duplication; resembling something enough to cause confusion with the genuine article.

immaterial Not material. Tending to prove something not in issue.

immaterial variance A discrepancy between the pleading and the proof that is so slight it misleads no one.

immediate annuity An annuity bought with a lump sum that starts making payments soon after its purchase.

immediate cause The last of a series or chain of events that produced the occurrence or result; a cause immediate in time to what occurred.

immemorial Beyond human memory. Exceptionally old.

immigrant A foreigner who comes into a country with the intention to live there permanently.

imminent Near at hand; about to occur.

imminent peril doctrine See emergency doctrine.

immoral Contrary to good morals; inimical to public welfare according to the standards of a given community.

immovables Land and those things so firmly attached to it as to be regarded as part of it; property that cannot be moved. See also fixture.

immunity 1. Exemption or freedom from a duty, penalty, or liability. 2. A complete defense to a tort claim whether or not the defendant committed the tort. 3. The right not to be subjected to civil or criminal prosecution.

immunize To grant immunity to; to render immune.

impact rule A party may recover emotional distress damages in a negligence action only if he or she suffered accompanying physical injury or contact.

Although the impact rule—which permits recovery only if the plaintiff can show that he suffered some contemporaneous physical impact in conjunction with the mental suffering—was the majority opinion for many years in various jurisdictions, New York has for some time now rejected it in favor of the "zone of danger" test. *Khan,* 487 N.Y.S.2d 700 (Sup. Ct., 1985)

impair To cause something to lose some or all of its quality or value.

impair the obligation of contracts To nullify or materially change existing contract obligations. See also Contract Clause.

impanel See empanel.

imparl 1. To delay a case in an attempt to settle. 2. To seek a continuance for more time to answer and pursue settlement options.

impartial Favoring neither side; unbiased.

impasse A deadlock in negotiations. The absence of hope of agreement.

impeach To attack; to accuse of wrongdoing; to challenge the credibility of.

To attack the credibility of a witness. *People v. Casanova,* 422 N.Y.S.2d 307 (Sup. Ct.,1979)

impeachment 1. An attack or challenge because of impropriety, bias, or lack of veracity. 2. A procedure against a public officer before a quasi-political court (e.g., a legislative body), instituted by written accusations called articles of impeachment that seek his or her removal from office.

impediment A legal obstacle that prevents the formation of a valid marriage or other contract.

imperfect Missing an essential legal requirement. Unenforceable.

imperfect trust See executory trust.

impersonation Pretending or representing oneself to be another.

impertinent Irrelevant or not responsive to the issues in the case.

implead To bring a new party into the lawsuit on the ground that the new party may be liable for all or part of the current claim. The procedure is called impleader or third-party practice.

Impleader is a means by which primary liability of the original defendant and alleged liability over of a third party may be settled in one action. *Horoch,* 143 N.Y.S.2d 327 (3 Dept., 1955); McKinney CPLR 1007

implied Expressed by implication; suggested by the circumstances.

implied acquittal A guilty verdict on a lesser included offense is an implied acquittal of the greater offense about which the jury was silent.

implied agency An actual agency established through circumstantial evidence.

implied authority Authority that is necessary, usual, and proper to perform the express authority delegated to the agent by the principal.

implied consent Consent inferred from the surrounding circumstances.

implied consent law A law providing that a person who drives a motor vehicle in the state is deemed to have given consent to a test that determines the alcoholic or drug content of that person's blood.

implied contract An implied in fact contract or an implied in law contract (see these terms).

implied in fact Inferred from the facts and circumstances.

implied in fact contract An actual contract whose existence and the parties' intentions are inferred from facts rather than by express agreement.

To create "contracts implied in fact," circumstances must warrant inference that one expected compensation and other intended to pay it. *In re Altmann's Will,* 266 N.Y.S. 773 (Sur., 1933)

implied in law Imposed by law; arising by operation of law.

implied in law contract An obligation created by the law to avoid unjust enrichment. Also called constructive contract, quasi contract.

implied easement An easement created by law when land is conveyed that does not contain an express easement, but one is implied as an intended part of the transaction. Also called easement by implication, way of necessity.

implied malice Malice that is inferred from conduct, e.g., reckless disregard for human life. Also called legal malice, malice in law.

implied notice Knowledge implied from surrounding facts so that the law will treat one as knowing what could have been discovered by ordinary care. See also constructive notice.

implied powers Powers presumed to have been granted because they are necessary to carry into effect expressly granted powers.

implied promise A fictional promise created by law to impose a contract liability, and thereby avoid fraud or unjust enrichment.

implied trust See constructive trust, resulting trust.

implied warranty A warranty imposed by operation of law regardless of the parties' intent. See also warranty of fitness for a particular purpose, warranty of habitability, warranty of merchantability.

There was "an implied warranty" that food served at restaurant was reasonably fit for consumption. *Frier,* 39 N.Y.S.2d 794 (4 Dept., 1943)

imply 1. To suggest; to state something indirectly. 2. To impose or declare something by law.

import To bring goods into a country from a foreign country.

impossibility That which no person in the course of nature or the law can do or perform; that which cannot exist.

impossibility of performance doctrine A defense to a breach of contract when performance becomes objectively impossible, not due to anyone's fault.

imposts A duty that is levied. An import tax.

impotence The inability to perform the act of sexual intercourse.

imposter One who deceives by pretending to be someone else.

impound To seize and take into custody of the law.

impoundment 1. Seizing and taking something into custody of the law. 2. Refusing to spend money appropriated by the legislature.

impracticability 1. A defense to breach of contract when performance can be undertaken only at an excessive and unreasonable cost. 2. Difficulty or inconvenience of joining all parties because of their large number.

impracticable Excessively burdensome to perform.

> Personal service . . . shall be made . . . 1. by delivering the summons within the state to the person to be served; . . . 5. in such manner as the court . . . directs, if service is impracticable under paragraphs one. . . . McKinney's CPLR § 308. Impracticability can be established by a detailed showing of reasonably thorough efforts to unearth information regarding defendant's current place of abode and place of business. *Franklin*, 592 N.Y.S.2d 726 (1st Dept., 1993)

impress 1. To force someone into public service, e.g., military service. 2. To impose a constructive trust. The noun is *impressment.*

impression See first impression.

imprimatur ("let it be printed") Official approval to publish a book.

imprison To put in prison; to place in confinement.

improper 1. Not in accord with proper procedure or taste. 2. Wrongful.

improved land Land that has been developed such as by adding roads or buildings.

improvement An addition to or betterment of land (usually permanent) that enhances its capital value. Something beyond mere repairs.

> The erection, alteration, or repair of any structure connected with any real property. Lien Law § 2. *W. L. Development Corp.*, 406 N.Y.S.2d 437 (Ct. of App., 1978)

improvident Lacking in care and foresight. Ill-considered.

impulse A sudden urge or thrusting force within a person.

impunity Exemption or protection from penalty or punishment.

impute To credit or assign to; to ascribe. To attribute to another or to make another responsible because of a relationship that exists.

imputed disqualification If one attorney or employee in a firm has a conflict of interest with a client, the entire firm is ineligible to represent that client. Also called vicarious disqualification.

imputed income A monetary value assigned to certain property, transactions, or situations for tax purposes (e.g., the value of a home provided by an employer for an employee).

imputed knowledge Information that a person does not actually know, but should know or has reason to know and, therefore, is deemed to know.

imputed negligence Negligence of one person that is attributed to another solely because of a special relationship between them.

in absentia In the absence of.

inadequate remedy at law An ineffective legal remedy, e.g., damages, justifying a request for an equitable remedy, e.g., injunction.

inadmissible Cannot be received and considered.

inadvertence An oversight; a consequence of carelessness, not planning.

inalienable Incapable of being bought, sold, transferred, or assigned. Also called unalienable.

> Inalienable means that it is incapable of being surrendered. *Byrn*, 335 N.Y.S.2d 390 (Ct. of App., 1972)

in banc See en banc.

in being In existence; existing in life.

in blank Not identifying a particular indorsee. Not filled in.

Inc. Incorporated.

in camera In private with the judge; in chambers; without spectators.

incapacity 1. The existence of a legal impediment preventing action or completion. 2. Physical or mental inability. 3. See disability (2).

incarcerate To imprison or confine in jail.

incendiary 1. A bomb or other device designed to cause fire. 2. One who maliciously and willfully sets fire to property.

incest Sexual intercourse between a man and woman who are related to each other within prohibited degrees (e.g., brother and sister).

in chief 1. Main or principal. 2. See case-in-chief.

inchoate Begun but not completed; partial.

> An "inchoate subordination" gives senior creditor priority over subordinated creditor only with respect to debtor's assets, and becomes operative only when voluntary or involuntary distribution of debtor's assets is made to creditors; the specific event which makes the subordination operative is to be mentioned in the agreement. *Standard Brands*, 260 N.Y.S.2d 913 (Sup. Ct., 1965)

inchoate crime A crime in its early stage, constituting another crime. The inchoate crimes are attempt, conspiracy, and solicitation.

inchoate dower A wife's interest in the land of her husband during his life; a possibility of acquiring dower.

inchoate lien A lien in which the amount, exact identity of the lienor, and time of attachment must await future determination.

incident 1. Connected with, inherent in, or arising out of something else. 2. A dependent or subordinate part. 3. An occurrence.

incidental Depending upon and secondary to something else.

incidental beneficiary One who will be benefited by performance of a promise but who is neither a promisee nor an intended beneficiary.

An "incidental beneficiary" of a contract is a third party who may derive a benefit from the performance of a contract though he is neither the promisee nor the one to whom performance is to be rendered. *Cole*, 708 N.Y.S.2d 789 (4 Dept., 2000)

incidental damages 1. The additional expenses reasonably incurred because of a breach of contract. 2. In class actions, those damages that flow directly from liability to the class as a whole on claims forming the basis of the injunctive or declaratory relief.

incident of ownership An ownership right retained in an insurance policy, e.g., the right to change beneficiaries.

incite To urge, persuade, stir up, or provoke another.

included offense See lesser included offense.

income 1. Money or other financial gain derived from one's business, labor, investments, and other sources. 2. The difference between revenue and expense for a given time period.

In construing a trust, ordinarily "income" is some thing produced by capital which leaves the capital unimpaired, and as a legal concept it implies a severance from capital and not merely a capital increment, and its usual signification is net after subtraction of expenses necessary to preserve the corpus. *In re James' Trust*, 159 N.Y.S.2d 989 (Sup. Ct., 1957)

income in respect of a decedent (IRD) The right to income earned by a decedent at death that was not included in his or her final income tax return.

income splitting Seeking a lower total tax by allocating income from persons in higher tax brackets to those in lower tax brackets.

income statement See earnings report.

income tax A tax on the net income of an individual or entity.

in common Shared together equally.

incompatibility Such discord between a husband and wife that it is impossible for them to live together in a normal marital relationship.

incompetent 1. Failing to meet legal requirements; unqualified. 2. Not having the skills needed. Physically or mentally impaired.

incompetent evidence Evidence that is not admissible.

inconsistent Not compatible. Mutually repugnant; the acceptance of one fact, position, or claim implies the abandonment of the other.

in contemplation of death With a view toward death. See contemplation of death.

incontestability clause An insurance policy clause providing that after a period of time (e.g., two years), the insurer cannot contest it on the basis of fraud, mistake, or statements made in the application.

The "incontestability clause" in life policy applies to the policy as a whole, and is not a stipulation absolute to waive all defenses and to condone fraud, but is in the nature of a statute of limitations by providing ample time and opportunity within which defenses may be, but beyond which they may not be established. *Berkshire Life Ins. Co.*, 47 N.E. 2d 418 (Ct. of App., 1943)

inconvenient forum See forum non conveniens.

incorporate 1. To form a corporation. 2. To combine or include within.

incorporation by reference Making one document a part of another document by stating that the former shall be considered part of the latter.

incorporation doctrine See selective incorporation.

incorporator A person who is one of, or who acts on behalf of, the original founders (formers) of a corporation.

incorporeal Not having a physical nature; intangible.

incorporeal hereditament An intangible land right that is inheritable.

The title or right which a lot owner obtains by purchase from a cemetery corporation is "property" and "real property," because it is an "incorporeal hereditament," but is not "land." Membership Corporation Law, §§ 70, 84–86; Real Property Law, §§ 2, 290, 337 et seq.; General Construction Law, § 40. *Mount Hope Cemetery Ass'n*, 45 N.Y.S.2d 249 (Sup. Ct., 1943)

incorrigible Incapable of being corrected or reformed. Unmanageable.

increment An increase or addition in amount or quality.

incriminate 1. To charge with a crime; to accuse someone. 2. To show involvement in the possibility of crime or other wrongdoing.

incriminating Tending to demonstrate criminal conduct.

Waiver of witness' Fifth Amendment privilege should be found only when witness' statements are "incriminating," meaning that they did not merely deal with matters collateral to the events surrounding commission of the crime but directly inculpated the witness on the charges at issue and thus contained information that the witness was privileged not to reveal. *People v. Bagby*, 492 N.Y.S.2d 562 (Ct. of App., 1985)

incriminating statement A statement that tends to establish a person's guilt.

incriminatory Charging or showing involvement with a crime.

incroach See encroach.

inculpatory Tending to show involvement with crime.

incumbent 1. One presently holding an office. 2. Obligatory.

incumbrance See encumbrance.

incur To become liable or subject to; to bring down upon oneself.

indebitatus assumpsit An action based on undertaking a debt.

indecent Sexually vulgar, but not necessarily obscene.

indecent assault Unconsented sexual contact with another.

indecent exposure Displaying one's self in public (especially one's genitals) in such manner as to be offensive to common decency.

A person is guilty of public lewdness when he intentionally exposes the private or intimate parts of his body in a lewd manner or commits any other lewd act (a) in a public place, or (b) in private premises under circumstances in which he may readily be observed from either a public place or from other private premises, and with intent that he be so observed. McKinney's Penal Law § 245.00

indecent speech Vulgar or offensive (but not necessarily obscene) speech concerning sexual or excretory activities and organs.

indefeasible Not capable of being defeated, revoked, or made void.

indefinite Not definite or fixed; lacking fixed boundaries.

indefinite failure of issue A failure of issue (dying without descendants who can inherit) whenever it occurs.

indefinite sentence See indeterminate sentence.

indemnify To compensate or promise to compensate someone for a specified loss or liability that has resulted or that might result.

indemnitee A person who is indemnified by another.

indemnitor A person who indemnifies another.

indemnity 1. The duty of one person to pay for another's loss, damage, or liability. 2. A right to receive compensation to make one person whole from a loss that has already been sustained but which in justice ought to be sustained by the person from whom indemnity is sought.

"Indemnity" involves an attempt to shift the entire loss from one who is compelled to pay for a loss, without regard to his own fault, to another party who should more properly bear responsibility for that loss because it was the actual wrongdoer. *Trump Village Section 3*, 764 N.Y.S.2d 17 (1 Dept., 2003)

indemnity insurance Insurance covering losses to the insured's person or to his or her own property. Also called first-party insurance.

indenture 1. A deed with the top of the parchment having an irregular (indented) edge. 2. A written agreement under which bonds and debentures are issued; the agreement sets forth terms such as the maturity date and the interest rate. 3. An apprenticeship agreement.

independent 1. Not subject to control or limitation from an outside source. 2. Not affiliated; autonomous.

independent agency A government board, commission, or other agency that is not subject to the policy supervision of the chief executive.

independent contractor One who operates his or her own business and contracts to do work for others who do not control the method or administrative details of how the work is performed.

An "independent contractor" is one who, exercising an independent employment, contracts to do a piece of work according to his own methods, and without being subject to the control of his employer except as to the result of his work. *Ostrander*, 386 N.Y.S.2d 597 (Dist. Ct., 1976)

independent counsel 1. An outside attorney hired to conduct an investigation or perform other special tasks. 2. Counsel chosen by an insured or with the approval of the insured, but paid by the insurer.

independent covenant An obligation that is not conditioned on performance by the other party.

independent paralegal An independent contractor (a) who sells his or her paralegal services to, and works under the supervision of, one or more attorneys or (b) who sells his or her paralegal services directly to the public without attorney supervision. Also called freelance paralegal or legal technician. Note, however, that in some states (e.g., California), the paralegal and legal assistant titles are limited to those who work under attorney supervision. See section 1.1 for the definition of paralegal in New York.

independent source rule Illegally obtained evidence will be admitted if the government shows that it is also obtained through sources wholly independent of the illegal search or other constitutional violation.

indestructible trust See Claflin trust.

indeterminate Not designated with particularity; not definite.

indeterminate sentence A prison sentence that is not fixed by the court but is left to the determination of penal authorities within minimum and maximum time limits set by the court. Also called indefinite sentence.

"Indeterminate term," for purposes of sentencing, is limited to felonies; minimum and maximum periods are fixed and term is completed at expiration of maximum period and parole eligibility arises after service of minimum period. *People ex rel. Johnson*, 636 N.Y.S.2d 581 (Sup. Ct., 1995); McKinney's Penal Law § 70.00(1)

index fund A mutual fund that seeks to match the results of a stock market index, e.g., the S&P 500.

indexing 1. Adjusting wages or other payments to account for inflation. 2. Tracking investments to an index, e.g., the S&P 500.

index number In supreme court and in county court, an action is commenced by filing the summons and complaint, which requires the payment of a filing fee, which in turn triggers the assignment of an index number and the creation of a court file. A judge may not act on any part of a case, such as granting a temporary order or deciding a motion, without the presence of an index number.

Indian reservation Land set apart for tribal use of Native Americans (American Indians).

indicia Signs or indications of something; identifying marks.

indict To bring or issue an indictment.

indictable Subject or liable to being indicted.

indictable offense A crime that must be prosecuted by indictment.

indictment A formal accusation of crime made by a grand jury.

indigent 1. Impoverished. 2. Without funds to hire a private attorney.

indignity Humiliating, degrading treatment of another.

indirect contempt Behavior outside the presence of the judge that defies the authority or dignity of the court. Also called constructive contempt.

indirect evidence See circumstantial evidence.

indirect tax A tax upon some right, privilege, or franchise.

indispensable evidence Evidence essential to prove a particular fact.

indispensable party A party so essential to a suit that no final decision can be rendered without his or her joinder. The case cannot be decided on its merits without prejudicing the rights of such a party.

"Indispensable party" is one whose presence is absolutely necessary in order for court to render a final judgment. *Brown*, 358 N.Y.S.2d 579 (Sup. Ct., 1973); McKinney's CPLR 3211(a)(10)

Individual Assignment System (IAS) The process by which a judge is assigned to a case in most trial courts where there are multiple judges.

There shall be established for all civil actions and proceedings heard in the Supreme Court and County Court an individual assignment system which provides for the continuous supervision of each action and proceeding by a single judge. 22 NYCRR 202.3

individual retirement account (IRA) A special account in which qualified persons can set aside a certain amount of tax-deferred income each year for savings or investment. The amount is subject to income tax upon withdrawal at the appropriate time.

indorse To place a signature on a check or other negotiable instrument to make it payable to someone other than the payee or to accept responsibility for paying it. Also spelled endorse.

indorsee The person to whom a check or other negotiable instrument is transferred by indorsement. Also spelled endorsee.

indorsement 1. Signing a check or other negotiable instrument to transfer or guarantee the instrument or to acknowledge payment. 2. The signature itself. Also spelled endorsement.

> An indorsement in blank includes an indorsement to bearer. A special indorsement specifies to whom a security is to be transferred or who has power to transfer it. A holder may convert a blank indorsement to a special indorsement. . . . An indorsement, whether special or in blank, does not constitute a transfer until delivery of the certificate on which it appears or, if the indorsement is on a separate document, until delivery of both the document and the certificate. McKinney's Uniform Commercial Code § 8-304(a)&(c)

indorser One who transfers a check or other negotiable instrument by indorsement.

inducement 1. The benefit or advantage that motivates a promisor to enter a contract. 2. An introductory statement in a pleading, e.g., alleging extrinsic facts that show a defamatory meaning in a libel or slander case. 3. Persuading or influencing someone to do something.

industrial relations The relationship between employer and employees on matters such as collective bargaining and job safety.

industrial union A labor union with members in the same industry (e.g., textiles) irrespective of their skills or craft. Also called vertical union.

industry An occupation or business that is a distinct branch of manufacture and trade, e.g., the steel industry.

inebriated Intoxicated; drunk.

ineffective assistance of counsel See effective assistance of counsel.

in equity Pertaining to (or in a court applying) equitable principles.

inescapable Being helpless to avoid a result by oneself; inevitable.

in esse In being, actually existing.

in evidence Before the court, having been declared admissible.

inevitable accident See unavoidable accident.

inevitable discovery doctrine Illegally obtained evidence is admissible if it inevitably would have been discovered by lawful means.

> According to the doctrine of "inevitable discovery," evidence illegally seized will not be suppressed where it is shown that such evidence would have been properly gained even without the unlawful action. *People v. Green*, 363 N.Y.S.2d 753 (Sup. Ct., 1975)

infamous 1. Having a notorious reputation; shameful. 2. Denied certain civil rights due to conviction of a crime.

infamous crime A crime punishable by imprisonment or the loss of some civil rights.

infancy 1. See minority (1). 2. Childhood at its earliest stage.

infanticide The murder or killing of an infant soon after its birth.

inference 1. A process of reasoning by which a fact to be established is deduced from other facts. Reaching logical conclusions from evidence. 2. A deduction or conclusion reached by this process.

> In criminal law, a "presumption" is a rule of law attaching definite probative value to a specific fact, as distinguished from an "inference," which is a permissive conclusion by trier of fact, unaided by any rule or theory of law directly applicable. *People v. Hildebrandt*, 126 N.E. 2d 377 (Ct. of App., 1955)

inferior court Any court that is subordinate to a higher court within its judicial system. Also called lower court.

infeudation Granting legal possession of land in feudal times.

infirm Lacking health; weak or feeble.

infirmative Tending to weaken a criminal charge.

infirmity Physical or mental weakness; frailty due to old age.

in flagrante delicto In the act of committing an offense.

infliction of emotional distress See intentional infliction of emotional distress.

in force In effect; legally operative.

informal Not following formal or normal procedures or forms.

informal contract 1. An oral contract. 2. A binding contract that is not under seal.

informal proceedings Proceedings that are less formal (particularly in applying the rules of evidence) than a court trial.

informant See informer.

in forma pauperis (IFP) With permission (as a poor person) to proceed without paying filing fees or other court costs.

information A formal accusation of a criminal offense from the prosecutor rather than from a grand jury indictment.

information and belief Good faith belief as to the truth of an allegation, not based on firsthand knowledge.

informed consent Agreement to let something happen based on having a reasonable understanding of the benefits and risks involved.

> The gist of the informed consent theory of liability is that a physician is under a duty in certain circumstances to warn his patient of the known risks of proposed treatment so that the patient will be in a position to make an intelligent decision as to whether he or she will submit to such treatment. *Petterson*, 299 N.Y.S.2d 244 (Sup. Ct., 1969)

informed intermediary A skilled and knowledgeable individual (e.g., a doctor) in the chain of distribution between the manufacturer of a product and the ultimate consumer. Also called learned intermediary.

informer A person who informs against another; one who brings an accusation against another on the basis of a suspicion that the latter has committed a crime. Also called informant. See also confidential informant.

informer's privilege The government's limited privilege to withhold the identity of persons who provide information of possible violations of law.

infra Below; later in the text.

infraction A violation (often minor) of a law, agreement, or duty.

infringement An invasion of a right; a violation of a law or duty.

infringement of copyright The unauthorized use of copyrighted material (17 USC § 106).

infringement of patent An unauthorized making, using, offering for sale, selling, or importing an invention protected by patent (35 USC § 271(a)).

infringement of trademark The unauthorized use or imitation of a registered trademark on goods of a similar class likely to confuse or deceive (15 USC § 1114).

> The Federal statute defines trade-mark infringement as the use of "Any . . . colorable imitation of any registered mark in connection with . . . any goods or services on or in connection with which such use is likely to cause confusion or mistake or to deceive purchasers as to the source of origin of such goods or services" (15 U.S.C.A. s 1114(1)). *Dell Pub. Co.*, 211 N.Y.S.2d 393 (Ct. of App., 1961)

in futuro At a future time.

ingress The act or right of entering.

in gross In a large sum or quantity; undivided.

in haec verba In these words; verbatim.

inherent Existing as a permanent or essential component.

inherently dangerous Being susceptible to harm or injury in the nature of the product, service, or activity itself. Requiring great caution.

inherent defect See hidden defect.

inherent power A power that must necessarily exist in the nature of the organization or person, even if not explicitly granted.

inherent right A fundamental, nontransferable right that is basic to the existence of a person or organization. An inalienable right.

inherit 1. To take by inheritance. 2. To take by will.

inheritance 1. Property received by an heir when an ancestor dies without leaving a valid will (i.e., intestate). 2. Property received through the will of a decedent.

inheritance tax A tax on the right to receive property by descent (intestate succession) or by will. Also called death tax, succession tax.

> "Inheritance tax" is tax on privilege of survivor to receive property of deceased, whereas "estate tax" is tax on interest which ceased upon deceased's death. *In re Wise's Will*, 244 N.Y.S.2d 960 (1 Dept., 1963)

in hoc In this regard.

in-house counsel See house counsel.

in invitum Against an unwilling party.

initial appearance The first criminal court appearance by the accused during which the court informs him or her of the charges, makes a decision on bail, and determines the date of the next proceeding. See also arraignment.

initiative The electorate's power to propose and directly enact a statute or change in the constitution or to force the legislature to vote on the proposal.

injunction A court order requiring a person or organization to do or to refrain from doing something.

injuria absque damno A legal wrong, from which no loss or damage results, will not sustain a lawsuit for damages.

injuria non excusat injuriam One wrong does not justify or excuse another wrong.

injurious falsehood 1. The publication of a false statement that causes special damages. 2. The publication of a false statement that is derogatory to plaintiff's business of a kind calculated to prevent others from dealing with the business or otherwise to interfere with its relations with others, to its detriment. Sometimes called disparagement.

> The tort of trade libel or injurious falsehood consists of the knowing publication of false matter derogatory to the plaintiff's business of a kind calculated to prevent others from dealing with the business or otherwise interfering with its relations with others, to its detriment. *Pusch*, 816 N.Y.S.2d 700 (Sup. Ct., 2003)

injury 1. Any harm or damage to another or oneself. 2. An invasion of a legally protected interest of another.

in kind 1. Of the same species or category. 2. In goods or services rather than money.

in lieu of In place of.

in limine At the outset. Preliminarily. See also motion in limine.

in loco parentis In the place of a parent; assuming the duties of a parent without adoption.

> "In loco parentis" refers to a person who has fully put himself in situation of lawful parent by assuming all obligations incident to parental relationship and who actually discharges those obligations. *Rutkowski*, 143 N.Y.S.2d 1 (3 Dept., 1955)

inmate A person confined in a prison, hospital, or other institution.

innocence 1. The absence of guilt. 2. The lack of cunning or deceit.

innocent Free from guilt; untainted by wrongdoing.

innocent agent One who engages in illegal conduct on behalf of the principal wrongdoer without knowing of its illegality.

innocent construction rule If words can be interpreted as harmless or defamatory, the harmless interpretation will be adopted.

innocent party 1. One who has not knowingly or negligently participated in wrongdoing. 2. One without actual or constructive knowledge of any limitations or defects.

innocent purchaser See bona fide purchaser.

innocent spouse An affirmative defense to a tax offense asserting that a spouse did not know or have reason to know that the other spouse understated the taxes due on their joint tax return.

innocent trespasser One who enters the land of another under the mistaken belief that it is permissible to do so.

inn of court An association or society of the main trial attorneys (called barristers) in England that has a large role in their legal training and admission to practice.

innominate Belonging to no specific class.

innuendo 1. The portion of a complaint that explains a statement's defamatory meaning when this is not clear on its face. 2. An indirect derogatory comment or suggestion.

> An "innuendo" in libel designates the allegation which sets forth the pleader's explanation of the alleged libelous words

and its office is to point out the libelous meaning of which the plaintiff claims the words are susceptible and it is not an averment of an extrinsic fact but a fact which when examined in the light of words apparently innocent, would convey a libelous accusation. *Murray,* 232 N.Y.S.2d 74 (Sup. Ct., 1962)

inoperative No longer in force or effective.

in pais Done informally or without legal proceedings.

in pari delicto In equal fault; equally culpable.

in pari materia Upon or involving the same matter or subject. Statutes in pari materia are to be interpreted together to try to resolve any ambiguity or inconsistency in them.

The anti-injunction act and the State Labor Relations Act are "in pari materia" and should be read together and reconciled so far as possible, although they were passed at different sessions of the legislature. *Petrucci,* 27 N.Y.S.2d 718 (Sup. Ct., 1941)

in perpetuity Forever.

in personam Against the person. See also personal judgment.

in personam jurisdiction See personal jurisdiction.

in posse Capable of being; not yet in actual being or existence.

in praesenti At the present time; now.

in propria persona (in pro per) In one's own person. See pro se.

inquest An inquiry by a coroner or medical examiner to determine the cause of death of a person who appears to have died suddenly or by violence.

inquiry 1. A careful examination or investigation. 2. A question.

inquiry notice Knowledge of facts that would lead a reasonably cautious person to inquire further.

inquisitorial system The fact-finding system in some civil law countries in which the judge has a more active role in questioning the witnesses and in conducting the trial than in an adversary system.

in re In the matter of. A way of designating a court case in which there are no adversary parties in the traditional sense.

in rem (against the res or thing) Pertaining to a proceeding or action binding the whole world in which the court resolves the status of a specific property or thing. The action is not against a person.

in rem jurisdiction The court's power over a particular res, which is a thing within the territory over which the court has authority.

In rem jurisdiction involves an action in which a plaintiff is after a particular thing, rather than seeking a general money judgment; he wants possession of the particular item of property, or to establish his ownership or other interest in it, or to exclude the defendant from an interest in it. *Majique Fashions,* 414 N.Y.S.2d 916 (1 Dept., 1979)

INS Immigration and Naturalization Service, now U.S. Citizenship and Immigration Services (*www.uscis.gov*).

insane delusion An irrational, persistent belief in nonexistent facts.

insanity 1. That degree of mental illness that negates an individual's legal responsibility or capacity to perform certain legal actions. Also called lunacy. 2. Model Penal Code test: As a result of a mental disease or defect, the accused lacks substantial capacity to appreciate the criminality of his or her conduct or to conform the conduct to the law. Also called substantial capacity test. 3. *Durham* test: The unlawful act was the product of mental disease or mental defect. 4. *M'Naghten* test: Laboring under such a defect of reason, from disease of the mind, as not to know the nature and quality of the act the accused was doing, or if the accused did know it, he or she did not know that it was wrong. Also spelled *McNaghten.* Also called right-from-wrong test. 5. Irresistible impulse test: An urge to commit an act induced by a mental disease so that the person is unable to resist the impulse to commit the act even if he or she knows that the act was wrong.

In any prosecution for an offense, it is an affirmative defense that when the defendant engaged in the proscribed conduct, he lacked criminal responsibility by reason of mental disease or defect. Such lack of criminal responsibility means that at the time of such conduct, as a result of mental disease or defect, he lacked substantial capacity to know or appreciate either: 1. The nature and consequences of such conduct; or 2. That such conduct was wrong. McKinney's Penal Law § 40.15.

inscription Entering, enrolling, or registering a fact or name on a list or record.

in se In and of itself. See malum in se.

insecurity clause A clause stating that a party may accelerate payment or performance or require collateral (or additional collateral) when he or she feels insecure because of a danger of default.

insider 1. One with knowledge of facts not available to the general public. 2. An officer or director of a corporation or anyone who owns more than 10 percent of its shares.

insider trading Conduct by corporate employees (or others who owe a fiduciary duty to the corporation) who trade in their company's stock based on material, nonpublic information, or who tip others about confidential corporate information. Trading in securities based on material, nonpublic information acquired in violation of a duty of confidence owed to the source of the information.

insolvency The condition of being unable to pay one's debts as they mature or fall due in the usual course of one's trade and business.

in specie In kind; in the same or like form.

inspection An examination of the quality or fitness of something.

installment A part of a debt payable in stages or successive periods.

installment contract A contract that requires or authorizes the delivery of goods in separate lots to be separately accepted or paid for. UCC 2-612.

installment credit A commercial arrangement in which the buyer pays for goods or services in more than one payment (often at regular intervals), for which a finance charge may be imposed.

installment loan A loan to be repaid in specified (often equal) amounts over a designated period.

installment note See serial note.

installment sale A commercial arrangement in which a buyer makes an initial down payment and agrees to pay the balance in installments over a period of time. The seller may keep title or take a security interest in the goods sold until full payment is made.

"Retail instalment sale" or "sale" means a sale, other than for a commercial or business use or for the purpose of resale, of a motor vehicle by a retail seller to a retail buyer for a time sale price payable in two or more instalments, payment of which is secured by a retail instalment contract. McKinney's Personal Property Law § 301(4)

instance 1. Bringing of a law suit. 2. Occurrence. 3. Urgent insistence.

instant 1. Now under consideration. 2. The present.

instanter At once.

in statu quo In the same condition in which it was.

instigate To stimulate or goad someone to act; to incite.

in stirpes See per stirpes.

institute 1. To inaugurate or begin. 2. An organization that studies or promotes a particular area. 3. Legal treatise or textbooks.

institution 1. The commencement of something. 2. An enduring or established organization. 3. A place for the treatment of those with special needs. 4. A basic practice or custom, e.g., marriage.

instruction See charge (1).

instrument 1. A formal written document that gives expression to or embodies a legal act or agreement, e.g., contract, will. 2. See negotiable instrument. 3. A means by which something is achieved.

instrumentality A means or agency by which something is done.

insubordination Intentional disregard of instructions. Disobedience.

insufficient evidence Evidence that cannot support a finding of fact.

insurable Capable of being insured against loss.

insurable interest Any actual, legal, and substantial economic interest in the safety or preservation of the subject of the insurance.

insurance A contract to provide compensation for loss or liability that may occur by or to a specified subject by specified risks.

In this article: (1) "Insurance contract" means any agreement or other transaction whereby one party, the "insurer," is obligated to confer benefit of pecuniary value upon another party, the "insured" or "beneficiary," dependent upon the happening of a fortuitous event in which the insured or beneficiary has, or is expected to have at the time of such happening, a material interest which will be adversely affected by the happening of such event. McKinney's Insurance Law § 1101(a)

insurance adjuster A person who investigates, values, and tries to settle insurance claims.

insurance broker An intermediary or middleman between the public and an insurer on insurance matters such as the sale of an insurance policy. A broker is not tied to a particular insurance company.

insurance policy An instrument in writing by which one party (insurer) engages for the consideration of a premium to indemnify another (insured) against a contingent loss by providing compensation if a designated event occurs, resulting in the loss.

insurance trust A trust containing insurance policies and proceeds for distribution under the terms of the trust.

insure 1. To obtain insurance. 2. To issue a policy of insurance.

insured The person covered or protected by insurance.

insurer The underwriter or insurance company that issues insurance.

insurgent One in revolt against government or political authority.

insurrection A rising of citizens or subjects in revolt against civil authority. Using violence to overthrow a government.

intangible 1. Without physical form. 2. Property or an asset that is a "right" (e.g., copyright, option) rather than a physical object even though the right may be evidenced by something physical such as a written contract.

"General intangible" means any personal property, including things in action, other than accounts, chattel paper, commercial tort claims, deposit accounts, documents, goods, instruments, investment property, letter-of-credit rights, letters of credit, money, and oil, gas, or other minerals before extraction. The term includes payment intangibles and software. McKinney's Uniform Commercial Code § 9-102(42)

intangible asset; intangible property See intangible (2).

integrated bar A bar association to which all lawyers must belong if they want to practice law. Also called unified bar.

integrated contract A contract that represents the complete and final understanding of the parties' agreement.

integration 1. Bringing together different groups, e.g., different races. 2. Making something whole or entire. Combining into one.

integration clause A contract clause stating that the writing is meant to represent the parties' entire and final agreement. Also called merger clause.

intellectual property Intangible property rights that can have commercial value (e.g., patents, copyrights, trademarks, trade names, trade secrets) derived from creative or original activity of the mind or intellect.

intend 1. To have in mind as a goal; to plan. 2. To mean or signify. See also intent.

intended use doctrine Manufacturers must design their products so that they are reasonably safe for their intended users.

intendment The true meaning or intention of something.

intent 1. Design, plan, or purpose in performing an act. 2. The desire to cause the consequences of one's acts (or failure to act) or the knowledge with substantial certainty that the consequences will follow from what one does (or fails to do).

intention 1. The purpose or design with which an act is done. Goal. See also intent. 2. Determination or willingness to do something.

intentional Deliberately done; desiring the consequences of an act or knowing with substantial certainty that they will result.

intentional infliction of emotional distress (IIED) The tort of intentionally or recklessly causing severe emotional distress by an act of extreme or outrageous conduct. Also called outrage.

A cause of action for the IIED lies when one who by extreme and outrageous conduct intentionally or recklessly causes severe emotional distress to another. *Freihofer*, 477 N.Y.S.2d 847 (3 Dept., 1984)

inter alia Among other things.

intercept 1. To seize benefits owed to a parent to cover delinquent child support obligations. 2. To covertly acquire the contents of a communication via an electronic or other device. To wiretap.

interdict 1. To forbid, prevent, restrict. 2. To intercept and seize. 3. An injunction or prohibition. 4. One incapacitated by an infirmity.

interest 1. A right, claim, title, or legal share in something; a right to have the advantage accruing from something. 2. A charge that is paid to borrow money or for a delay in its return when due.

interested Involved, nonobjective; having a stake in the outcome.

Interest on Lawyer Account Fund (IOLA) A program in which designated client funds held by an attorney are deposited in a bank account, the interest from which can be used (often through a foundation) to help finance legal services for low-income persons. Called Interest on Lawyers' Trust Accounts in some states (*www.iola.org*).

An ... unsegregated interest-bearing deposit account with a banking institution for the deposit by an attorney of qualified funds. "Qualified funds" are moneys received by an attorney in a fiduciary capacity from a client or beneficial owner and which, in the judgment of the attorney, are too small in amount or are reasonably expected to be held for too short a time to generate sufficient interest income to justify the expense of administering a segregated account for the benefit of the client or beneficial owner. McKinney's Judiciary Law § 497

Interest on Lawyers' Trust Accounts (IOLTA) See Interest on Lawyer Account Fund.

interference 1. Hindering or obstructing something. 2. Meddling. 3. A patent proceeding to determine who has priority in an invention.

interference with prospective advantage The tort of intentionally interfering with a reasonable expectation of an economic advantage, usually a commercial or business advantage.

interim 1. Intervening time; meantime. 2. Temporary.

interim order A temporary order that applies until another order is issued.

interlineation Writing between the lines of an existing document.

interlocking director A member of the board of directors of more than one corporation at the same time.

interlocutory Not final; interim.

interlocutory appeal An appeal that occurs before the trial court reaches its final judgment.

interlocutory decree An intermediate decree or judgment that resolves a preliminary matter or issue.

"Interlocutory judgment" determines some rights in action but does not finally dispose of action and is generally followed by a final judgment. *In re Adoption of Anonymous*, 337 N.Y.S.2d 428 (Sur., 1972)

interlocutory injunction See preliminary injunction.

interlocutory order An order made before final judgment on an incidental or ancillary matter. Also called intermediate order.

interloper One who meddles in the affairs of others.

intermeddler See officious intermeddler.

intermediary A go-between or mediator who tries to resolve conflicts.

intermediary bank Any bank (other than a depositary or payor bank) to which an item is transferred in the course of collection.

intermediate In the middle position.

intermediate court An appellate court below the court of last resort.

intermediate order See interlocutory order.

intermittent easement An easement that is used only occasionally.

intermixture of goods See confusion of goods.

intern 1. To restrict or confine a person or group. 2. A student obtaining practical experience and training outside the classroom.

internal law The law within a state or country; local law.

internal revenue Tax revenue from internal (not foreign) sources.

Internal Revenue Code (IRC) The federal statute in title 26 of the U.S. Code that codifies federal tax laws.

Internal Revenue Service (IRS) The federal agency responsible for enforcing most federal tax laws (*www.irs.gov*).

internal security Laws and government activity to counter threats from subversive activities.

international agreements Contracts (e.g., treaties) among countries.

International Court of Justice (ICJ) The judicial arm of the United Nations that renders advisory opinions and resolves disputes submitted to it by nations (*www.icj-cij.org*).

international law The legal principles and laws governing relations between nations. Also called law of nations, public international law.

International Paralegal Management Association (IPMA) An association of paralegal managers at law firms and corporations (*www.paralegalmanagement.org*).

internment The confinement of persons suspected of disloyalty.

interplead 1. To file an interpleader. 2. To assert your claim or position on an issue in a case already before the court.

interpleader A remedy or suit to determine a right to property held by a disinterested third party (called the stakeholder) who is in doubt about ownership and who, therefore, deposits the property with the trial court to permit interested parties to litigate ownership.

"Interpleader" is procedure by which one, who may be exposed to multiple liability, may require adverse claimants to litigate their claims in one action or proceeding. *Horoch*, 143 N.Y.S.2d 327 (3 Dept., 1955); McKinney's CPLR 1006

Interpol International Criminal Police Organization; a coordinating group for international law enforcement (*www.interpol.int*).

interpolation Inserting words in a document to change or clarify it.

interpose To submit or introduce something, especially a defense.

interpret To explain the meaning of language or conduct. To construe.

interpretive rule The rule of an administrative agency that explains or clarifies the meaning of existing statutes and regulations.

interrogation A methodical questioning of someone, e.g., a suspect.

The term "interrogation" under *Miranda* refers not only to express questioning, but also to any words or actions on the part of the police (other than those normally attendant to arrest and custody) that the police should know are reasonably likely to elicit an incriminating response. *Perro* 482 N.Y.S.2d 237 (Ct. of App., 1984)

interrogatories A discovery device consisting of written questions about a lawsuit submitted by one party to another.

in terrorem clause A clause with a threat, e.g., a clause in a will stating that a gift to a beneficiary will be forfeited if he or she contests the validity of the will. Also called a no-contest clause.

inter se; inter sese Among or between themselves.

interspousal Relating to or between husband and wife.

interspousal immunity Spouses cannot sue each other for personal torts, e.g., battery. Also called husband-wife immunity.

interstate Involving two or more states.

interstate commerce The exchange of goods or services (commerce) between two or more states of the United States (including a U.S. territory or the District of Columbia).

interstate compact An agreement between two or more states (and approved by Congress) that is designed to address common problems.

interval ownership See time-sharing.

intervening Coming or occurring between two times or events.

intervening cause A new and independent force that produces harm after the defendant's act or omission.

"Intervening act" will be deemed superseding cause in negligence action and will serve to relieve defendant of liability when act is of such extraordinary nature, or so attenuates defendant's negligence from ultimate injury, that responsibility for injury may not be reasonably attributed to defendant. *Carson*, 807 N.Y.S.2d 458 (3 Dept., 2006)

intervenor A person with an interest in real or personal property who applies to be made a party to an existing lawsuit involving that property.

intervention The procedure by which a third person, not originally a party but claiming an interest in the subject matter of the suit, is allowed to come into the case to protect his or her own interests.

inter vivos Between or pertaining to the living.

inter vivos gift A gift that takes effect when the donor is living.

To establish a "gift inter vivos" there must be an intention to make a gift, completed delivery pursuant to that intention, and acceptance of the gift by donee. *In re Harter's Estate*, 261 N.Y.S.2d 431 (Sup. Ct., 1965)

inter vivos trust A trust that takes effect when its creator (the settler) is living. Also called living trust.

intestacy Dying without a valid will.

intestate 1. Without making a valid will. 2. The person who dies without making a valid will.

intestate succession The transfer of property to the relatives of a decedent who dies without leaving a valid will. Also called descent and distribution, hereditary succession.

in testimonium In witness; in evidence whereof.

in the matter of See in re.

intimidate To coerce unlawfully.

in toto In total; completely.

intoxication A significantly lessened physical or mental ability to function normally, caused by alcohol or drugs.

intra Within.

intrastate commerce Commerce that occurs exclusively within one state.

intra vires Within the power; within the scope of lawful authority.

intrinsic Pertaining to the essential nature of a thing.

intrinsic evidence The evidence found within the writing or document itself.

intrinsic fraud Fraud that goes to the existence of a cause of action or an issue in the case, e.g., perjured testimony.

"Fraud" is "extrinsic" when it is collateral to matter decided by court and deprives opposing party of opportunity adequately to present his claim or defense, while fraud is "intrinsic" when it relates to very matter decided by court. *DiRusso*, 287 N.Y.S.2d 171 (Sup. Ct., 1968)

intrinsic value The true, inherent, and essential value of a thing, not depending on externals, but the same everywhere and to everyone.

intrusion 1. Wrongfully entering upon or taking something. 2. See invasion of privacy (1)(c).

inure 1. To take effect. 2. To habituate. Also spelled enure.

in utero In the uterus.

invalid 1. Having no legal effect. 2. A disabled person.

invasion 1. An encroachment on the rights of others. 2. Making payments from the principal of a trust rather than from its income.

invasion of privacy 1. Four separate torts. (a) Appropriation: The use of a person's name, likeness, or personality for commercial gain without authorization. (b) False light: Unreasonably offensive publicity that places another in a false light. (c) Intrusion: An unreasonably offensive encroachment or invasion into someone's private affairs or concerns. (d) Public disclosure of a private fact: Unreasonably offensive publicity concerning the private life of a person. 2. A constitutional prohibition of unreasonable governmental interferences with one's private affairs or effects.

invention The creation of a potentially patentable process or device through independent effort. The discovery of a new process or product.

inventory 1. A detailed list of property or assets. 2. Goods in stock held for sale or lease or under contracts of service, raw materials, works in process, or materials used or consumed in a business.

in ventre sa mere See en ventre sa mere.

inverse condemnation A cause of action for the taking of private property for public use without proper condemnation proceedings.

The courts of New York have traditionally recognized inverse condemnation as a procedural vehicle for granting damages where an entity clothed with the power of eminent domain has interfered with the property rights of a landowner to the extent that it amounts to a compensable taking. *Evans*, 410 N.Y.S.2d 199 (Sup. Ct., 1978). New York Jurisprudence, Eminent Domain § 490.

inverse order of alienation doctrine One seeking to collect on a lien or mortgage on land sold off in successive parcels must collect first from any land still with the original owner; if this land is insufficient to satisfy the debt, he or she must resort to the parcel last sold, and then to the next to the last, and so on until the debt is satisfied.

invest 1. To use money to acquire assets in order to produce revenue. 2. To give power or authority to. 3. To devote to a task; to commit.

investiture See livery of seisin.

investment advisor One who, for compensation, engages in the business of advising others (directly or through publications) on the value of securities or the advisability of investing in, purchasing, or selling securities, or who, as a part of a regular business, publishes reports about securities.

investment bank A financial institution engaged in underwriting, selling securities, raising capital, and giving advice on mergers and acquisitions.

investment company A company in the business of investing, reinvesting, or trading in securities (15 USC § 80a-3). A company that sells shares and invests in securities of other companies. Also called an investment trust.

investment contract A contract in which money is invested in a common enterprise with profits to come solely from the efforts of others.

A transaction is an "investment contract" when, disregarding form over substance, it involves an investment in a common enterprise with a reasonable expectation of profits to be derived solely from the entrepreneurial or managerial efforts of the promoter. McKinney's General Business Law § 352. *State v. Justin*, 779 N.Y.S.2d 717 (Sup. Ct., 2003)

investment income Income from investment capital rather than income resulting from labor. Also called unearned income.

investment securities Instruments such as stocks, bonds, and options used for investment.

investment tax credit A credit against taxes, consisting of a percentage of the purchase price of capital goods and equipment.

investment trust See investment company.

invidious discrimination An arbitrary classification that is not reasonably related to a legitimate purpose. Offensively unequal treatment.

invited error rule On appeal, a party cannot complain about an error for which he or she is responsible, such as an erroneous ruling that he or she prompted or invited the trial court to make.

invitee One who enters land upon the express or implied invitation of the occupier of the land to use the land for the purpose for which it is held open to the public or to pursue the business of the occupier.

invocation 1. Calling upon for assistance or authority. 2. The enforcement of something. The verb is *invoke*.

invoice A document giving the price and other details of a sale of goods or services.

involuntary 1. Not under the control of the will. 2. Compulsory.

involuntary bailment A bailment arising by an accidental, nonnegligent leaving of personal property in the possession of another.

involuntary bankruptcy Bankruptcy forced on a debtor by creditors.

involuntary commitment See civil commitment.

involuntary confession A confession obtained by threats, improper promises, or other unlawful pressure from someone in law enforcement

Pursuant to statute defining involuntary confessions, a confession induced by a promise can be admissible, so long as the promise is not of the type that would create a risk of false incrimination. McKinney's CPL § 60.45. *People v. Brown*, 474 N.Y.S.2d 927 (Sup. Ct., 1984)

involuntary conversion The loss or destruction of property through theft, casualty, or condemnation.

involuntary dismissal A dismissal of an action for failure to prosecute the action or to comply with a court rule or order.

involuntary dissolution The forced termination of the existence of a corporation or other legal entity.

involuntary intoxication Intoxication resulting when one does not knowingly and willingly ingest an intoxicating substance.

involuntary manslaughter The unintentional killing of another without malice while engaged in an unlawful activity that is not a felony and does not naturally tend to cause death or great bodily harm or while engaged in a lawful activity with a reckless disregard for the safety of others.

involuntary nonsuit The dismissal of an action when the plaintiff fails to appear, gives no evidence on which a jury could find a verdict, or receives an adverse ruling that precludes recovery.

involuntary servitude The condition of being compelled to labor for another (with or without compensation) by force or imprisonment.

involuntary trust See constructive trust.

IOLA See Interest on Lawyer Account Fund.

IOLTA See Interest on Lawyers' Trust Accounts.

IPMA See International Paralegal Management Association (*www.paralegalmanagement.org*).

ipse dixit An unproven or unsupported assertion made by a person.

ipso facto By that very fact; in and of itself.

ipso jure By the law itself; by the mere operation of law.

IRA See individual retirement account.

IRC See Internal Revenue Code.

irrational Illogical, not guided by a fair assessment of the facts.

irrebuttable presumption See conclusive presumption.

irreconcilable differences A no-fault ground of divorce that exists when persistent, unresolvable disagreements between the spouses lead to an irremediable breakdown of the marriage.

irrecusable Cannot be challenged or rejected.

irregular Not according to rule, proper procedure, or the norm.

irrelevant Not tending to prove or disprove any issue in the case.

irremediable breakdown See irretrievable breakdown.

irreparable Not capable of being repaired or restored.

irreparable injury Harm that cannot be adequately redressed by an award of monetary damages. An injunction, therefore, is possible.

> An irreparable injury can warrant a preliminary injunction if the injury that cannot be adequately compensated in damages or for which there is no set pecuniary standard for measurement of damages; a preliminary injunction is not available in an action for money only. McKinney's CPLR 6301. *475 Ninth Ave. Associates*, 773 N.Y.S.2d 790 (Sup. Ct., 2003)

irresistible impulse See insanity (5).

irretrievable breakdown A no-fault ground of divorce that exists when there is such discord and incompatibility between the spouses that the legitimate objects of matrimony have been destroyed and there is no reasonable possibility of resolution. Also called irremediable breakdown.

irrevocable Not capable of being revoked or recalled.

irrevocable trust A trust that cannot be terminated by its creator.

IRS See Internal Revenue Service (*www.irs.gov*).

issuable 1. Open to debate or litigation. 2. Allowed or authorized for issue or sale. 3. Possible.

issue 1. To send forth, announce, or promulgate. 2. A legal question. A point or matter in controversy or dispute. 3. Offspring; lineal descendants, e.g., child, grandchild. 4. A group or class of securities offered for sale in a block or at the same time. Also called stock issue. 5. The first delivery of a negotiable instrument.

issue of fact A dispute over the existence or nonexistence of an alleged fact. The controversy that exists when one party asserts a fact that is disputed by the other side. Also called question of fact or fact question.

issue of law A question of what the law is, what the law means, or how the law applies to a set of established, assumed, or agreed-upon facts. Also called legal question, question of law.

issue preclusion See collateral estoppel.

item 1. An instrument or a promise or order to pay money handled by a bank for collection or payment. 2. An entry on an account. 3. A part of something.

itemized deduction A payment that is allowed as a deduction from adjusted gross income on a tax return.

J

J Judge; justice.

jactitation False boasting; false claims causing harm.

JAG See Judge Advocate General.

jail A place of confinement, usually for persons awaiting trial or serving sentences for misdemeanors or minor crimes.

jailhouse lawyer An inmate who is allowed to give legal assistance and advice to other prisoners if the institution provides no alternatives.

> Petitioner was approved to serve as an inmate law clerk (a so-called "jailhouse lawyer"). *People ex rel. Hicks*, 571 N.Y.S.2d 367 (Sup. Ct., 1991)

Jane Doe; Jane Roe A fictitious name for a female party in legal proceedings if the real name is unknown or is being kept confidential.

***Jason* clause** A clause in a bill of lading requiring a general average contribution (see this phrase). *The Jason*, 32 S. Ct. 560 (1912).

jaywalking Failure to use crosswalks or to comply with other regulations for crossing the street.

jd See juvenile delinquent.

J.D. See Juris Doctor.

***Jencks* rule** After a witness called by the federal prosecutor has testified on direct examination, the court shall, on motion of the defendant, order the prosecution to produce any statement of the witness in the possession of the prosecution that relates to the subject matter of the testimony to aid the defendant in the cross-examination of this witness. 18 USC § 3500(b); *Jencks v. U.S.*, 77 S. Ct. 1007 (1957). See also *Rosario* rule.

jeopardy The risk of conviction and punishment once a criminal defendant has been placed on trial. Legal jeopardy.

jeopardy assessment If the collection of a tax appears to be in question, the IRS may assess and collect the tax immediately without going through the usual formalities.

jetsam Goods abandoned at sea that sink and remain underwater. Goods that the owner voluntarily throws overboard in an emergency in order to lighten the ship.

jettison To discard or throw overboard in order to lighten the load of a ship in danger. Goods thrown overboard for this purpose.

Jim Crow law A law that intentionally discriminates against blacks.

JJ Judges; justices.

JNOV See judgment notwithstanding the verdict.

jobber 1. One who buys goods from manufacturers and sells them to retailers. A wholesaler. 2. One who does odd jobs or piecework.

> A jobber is defined as one who sells to retailers, restaurants and like institutions which sell food to the public. *Sperling*, 28 N.Y.S.2d 788 (Sup. Ct., 1941)

John Doe; Richard Roe A fictitious name for a male party in legal proceedings if the real name is unknown or is being kept confidential.

joinder Uniting two or more parties as plaintiffs, two or more parties as defendants, or two or more claims into a single lawsuit.

joinder of issue The assertion of a fact by a party in a pleading and its denial by the opposing party. The point in litigation when opponents take opposite positions on a matter of law or fact.

joint 1. Shared by or between two or more. 2. United or coupled together in interest or liability.

joint account An account of two or more persons containing assets that each can withdraw in full, and, upon the death of one of them, is payable to the others rather than to the heirs or beneficiaries of the decedent.

joint adventure See joint venture.

joint and mutual will A single will executed by two or more persons disposing of property owned individually or together that shows that the devises or dispositions were made in consideration of one another.

joint and several Together as well as individually or separately.

joint and several liability Legally responsible together and individually. Each wrongdoer is individually responsible for the *entire* judgment; the plaintiff can choose to collect from one wrongdoer or from all of them until the judgment is satisfied.

Joint and several liability, which is primarily tort-law concept, imposes on each wrongdoer responsibility for the entire damages awarded, even though a particular wrongdoer's conduct may have caused only a portion of the loss. *Matter of Seagroatt Floral Co.*, 576 N.Y.S.2d 831 (Ct. of App., 1991)

joint and survivor annuity An annuity with two beneficiaries (e.g., husband and wife) that continues to make payments until both beneficiaries die.

joint annuity An annuity with two beneficiaries that stops making payments when either dies.

joint bank account See joint account.

joint committee A legislative committee whose membership is from both houses of the legislature.

joint custody This phrase can mean (a) joint legal custody in which both parents share the right to make the major decisions on raising their child, who may reside primarily with one parent, (b) joint physical custody in which the child resides with each parent individually for alternating, although not necessarily equal, periods of time, or (c) both joint legal custody and joint physical custody.

Joint custody involves sharing by parents of responsibility for and control over the upbringing of their children, and imposes upon the parents the obligation to behave in mature, civilized, and cooperative manner in carrying out the joint custody arrangement. *Fedun*, 641 N.Y.S.2d 759 (3 Dept., 1996)

joint enterprise See joint venture.

joint estate A form of joint ownership, e.g., joint tenancy, tenancy in common, tenancy by the entirety.

joint legal custody See joint custody.

joint liability Two or more parties together have an obligation or liability to a third party. Liability that is owed to a third party by two or more parties together.

joint lives The duration of an estate lasting until either one of two named persons dies.

joint obligation An obligation incurred by two or more debtors to a single performance to one creditor.

joint ownership Two or more persons who jointly hold title to, or have an interest in, property.

joint physical custody See joint custody.

joint resolution A resolution passed by both houses of a legislative body.

joint return A federal, state, or local tax return filed by a husband and wife together regardless of who earned the income.

joint stock company An unincorporated association of individuals who hold shares of the common capital they contribute. Also called stock association.

joint tenancy Property that is owned equally by two or more persons (called joint tenants) with the right of survivorship. Joint tenants have one and the same interest; accruing by one and the same conveyance, instrument, or act; commencing at one and the same time; with one and the same undivided possession.

Joint tenancy requires that tenants acquire their interest simultaneously and by the same instrument, and have an interest identical with each of the other cotenants, and that each be entitled to common possession. *Moore Lumber Co.*, 259 N.Y.S. 248 (Mun. Ct., 1932)

joint tortfeasors Two or more persons who together commit a tort. One or more persons jointly or severally liable in tort for the same loss to person or property.

jointure A widow's freehold estate in lands (in lieu of dower) to take effect on the death of her husband and to continue during her life.

joint venture An association of persons who jointly undertake some commercial enterprise in which they share profits. An agreement among members of a group to carry out a common purpose, in which each has an equal voice in the control and direction of the enterprise. Also called joint adventure, joint enterprise.

joint will A single testamentary instrument (will) executed by more than one person. It can dispose of property owned individually and jointly.

A joint will is a single testamentary instrument, which contains the wills of two or more persons, is executed jointly by them, and disposes of property owned jointly, in common, or in severalty by them; by contrast, mutual wills are separate instruments, usually executed at the same time and making similar provisions. *Schloss*, 800 N.Y.S.2d 715 (2 Dept., 2005)

joint work A work prepared by two or more authors with the intention that their contributions be merged into inseparable or interdependent parts of a unitary whole (17 USC § 101).

Jones Act The federal statute that provides a remedy to seamen injured in the course of employment due to negligence (46 USC § 30104).

journal 1. A book in which entries are made, often on a regular basis. 2. A periodical or magazine.

journalist's privilege 1. The privilege of a journalist not to disclose information obtained while gathering news, including the identity of sources. Also called reporter's privilege. 2. The qualified privilege of the media (asserted in defamation actions) to make fair comment about public figures on matters of public concern.

journeyman A person who has progressed through an apprenticeship in a craft or trade and is now qualified to work for another.

joyriding Driving an automobile without authorization but without the intent to steal it.

J.P. See justice of the peace.

J.S.D. Doctor of Juridical Science.

judge 1. A public officer appointed or elected to preside over and to administer the law in a court of justice or similar tribunal. 2. To resolve a dispute authoritatively.

judge advocate A legal officer or adviser in the military. A legal officer on the staff of the Judge Advocate General.

Judge Advocate General (JAG) The senior legal officer in the army, navy, or air force (see, e.g., *www.jag.navy.mil*).

judge-made law 1. Law created by judges in court opinions. Law derived from judicial precedents rather than from statutes. 2. A court decision that fails to apply the intent of the legislature. Also called judicial legislation.

judgment The final conclusion of a court that resolves a legal dispute or that specifies what further proceedings are needed to resolve it.

A judgment is the law's last word in a judicial controversy, it being the final determination by a court of the rights of the parties upon matters submitted to it in an action or proceeding. *Towley*, 386 N.Y.S.2d 80 (Ct. of App., 1976)

judgment as a matter of law A judgment on an issue in a federal jury trial (and in some state jury trials) ordered by the judge against a party because there is no legally sufficient evidentiary basis for a reasonable jury to find for that party on that issue. The judgment may be rendered before or after the verdict. In some state courts, the judgment is called a *directed verdict* if it is rendered before the jury reaches a verdict and a *judgment notwithstanding the verdict* (JNOV or judgment n.o.v.) if it is rendered after the jury reaches a verdict.

judgment book The book or docket in which the clerk enters the judgments that are rendered.

judgment by default See default judgment.

judgment creditor A person in whose favor a money judgment (damages) is entered or who becomes entitled to enforce it.

judgment debtor A person ordered to pay a money judgment (damages) rendered against him or her.

judgment in personam See personal judgment.

judgment in rem A judgment concerning the status or condition of property. The judgment is against or on the property, not a person. See also in rem.

A decree of divorce so far as it affects status of the parties is considered a judgment in rem and, if free from fraud and collusion, is binding on the whole world. *Urquhart*, 69 N.Y.S.2d 57 (1 Dept., 1947)

judgment lien A lien on property of a judgment debtor giving the judgment creditor the right to levy on it to satisfy the judgment.

judgment nisi ("a judgment unless") A judgment that will stand unless the party affected by it appears and shows cause against it.

judgment non obstante veredicto See judgment notwithstanding the verdict.

judgment note See cognovit.

judgment notwithstanding the verdict (JNOV) A court judgment that is opposite to the verdict reached by the jury. Also called judgment non obstante veredicto or judgment n.o.v. In federal court, it is called a *judgment as a matter of law* (see this phrase).

A court may grant judgment notwithstanding the verdict to the losing party only where there is simply no valid line of reasoning and permissible inferences which could possibly lead rational men to the conclusion reached by the jury. *Seong Sil Kim*, 812 N.Y.S.2d 485 (1 Dept., 2006)

judgment n.o.v. See judgment notwithstanding the verdict.

judgment on the merits A judgment, rendered after evidentiary inquiry and argument, determining which party is in the right, as opposed to a judgment based solely on a technical point or procedural error.

judgment on the pleadings A judgment based solely on the facts alleged in the complaint, answer, and other pleadings. See also summary judgment.

judgment proof A person without assets to satisfy a judgment.

judgment quasi in rem A judgment determining a particular person's interest in specific property within the court's jurisdiction. See also quasi in rem.

judicature 1. The judiciary. 2. The administration of justice. 3. The jurisdiction or authority of a judge.

judicial Pertaining to the courts, the office of a judge, or judgments.

judicial act A decision or other exercise of power by a court.

judicial activism Writing court decisions that invalidate arguably valid statutes, that fail to follow precedent, or that inject the court's political or social philosophy. Sometimes called judicial legislation.

judicial admission A deliberate, clear statement of a party on a concrete fact within the party's peculiar knowledge that is conclusive upon the party making it, thereby relieving the opposing party from presenting any evidence on it.

Formal judicial admissions take the place of evidence and are concessions, for purposes of the litigation, of truth of fact alleged by an adversary; informal judicial admissions are facts incidentally admitted during trial, and are not conclusive, being merely evidence of fact or facts admitted. *Wheeler*, 795 N.Y.S.2d 370 (3 Dept., 2005)

judicial bonds Generic term for bonds required by a court for appeals, costs, attachment, injunction, etc.

judicial discretion The ability or power of a court (when it is not bound to decide an issue one way or another) to choose between two or more courses of action. Also called legal discretion.

judicial economy Efficiency in the use of the courts' resources.

judicial immunity The exemption of judges from civil liability arising out of the discharge of judicial functions.

judicial legislation 1. Statutes creating or involving the courts. 2. See judge-made law (2), judicial activism.

judicial lien A lien that arises by judgment, sequestration, or other legal or equitable process or proceeding (11 USC § 101).

judicial notice A court's acceptance of a well-known fact without requiring proof of that fact.

Judicial notice is knowledge which a court takes of a matter without evidence having been introduced to establish it. *People v. Sowle*, 327 N.Y.S.2d 510 (Co. Ct., 1971)

judicial power The power of the court to decide and pronounce a judgment and carry it into effect between parties in the case.

judicial question A question that is proper for the courts to resolve.

judicial restraint Courts should resolve issues before them without reaching other issues that do not have to be resolved, follow precedent closely without injecting personal views and philosophies, and defer to the right of the legislature to make policy.

judicial review 1. The power of a court to interpret statutes and administrative laws to determine their constitutionality. 2. The power of a court to examine the legal and factual conclusions of a lower court or administrative agency to determine whether errors were made.

judicial sale A sale based on a court decree ordering the sale.

judicial separation See legal separation.

judiciary The branch of government vested with the judicial power; the system of courts in a country; the body of judges; the bench.

jump bail To fail to appear at the next scheduled court appearance after having been released on bail.

junior Subordinate; lower in rank or priority.

junior bond A bond that has a lower payment priority than other bonds.

junior lien A lien that has a lower priority than other liens on the same property.

junk science Unreliable, potentially misleading scientific evidence.

A trial judge has inherent power to keep unreliable evidence (junk science) away from the trier of fact regardless of the qualifications of the expert. *Styles*, 799 N.Y.S.2d 38 (1 Dept., 2005)

jura Rights; laws.

jural Pertaining to law, justice, rights, and legal obligations.

jurat A certificate of a person before whom a writing was sworn. A certification by a notary public that the person signing the writing (e.g., an affidavit) appeared before the notary and swore that the assertions in the writing were true.

jure By the law; by right.

juridical Relating to the law or the administration of justice.

juris Of law; of right.

jurisdiction 1. The power of a court to decide a matter in controversy. 2. The geographic area over which a particular court has authority. 3. The scope of power or authority that a person or entity can exercise. See also personal jurisdiction, in rem jurisdiction, quasi in rem jurisdiction, and subject-matter jurisdiction.

jurisdictional amount See amount in controversy.

jurisdictional dispute Competing claims by different unions that their members are entitled to perform certain work.

jurisdictional facts Those facts that must exist before the court can properly take jurisdiction of the particular case.

jurisdiction in personam See personal jurisdiction.

jurisdiction in rem See in rem jurisdiction.

jurisdiction of the subject matter See subject-matter jurisdiction.

jurisdiction quasi in rem See quasi in rem jurisdiction.

Juris Doctor (J.D.) Doctor of law. The standard degree received upon completion of law school. Also called doctor of jurisprudence.

jurisprudence The philosophy of law; a science that ascertains the principles on which legal rules are based. The system of laws.

jurist A legal scholar; a judge.

juristic person See artificial person.

juror A member of a jury.

jury A group of persons selected to resolve disputes of fact and to return a verdict based on the evidence presented to them.

jury box The courtroom location where the jury observes the trial.

jury charge See charge (1).

jury commissioner An official in charge of prospective jurors.

jury instructions See charge (1).

jury list A list of citizens who could be called for jury duty.

jury nullification A jury's refusal to apply a law perceived to be unjust or unpopular by acquitting a defendant in spite of proof of guilt.

Jury nullification occurs when a jury—based on its own sense of justice or fairness—refuses to follow the law and convict in a particular case even though the facts seem to allow no other conclusion but guilt. *People v. Douglas*, 680 N.Y.S.2d 145 (Sup. Ct., 1998)

jury panel A list or group of prospective jurors. Also called venire.

jury tampering See embracery.

jury trial The trial of a matter before a judge and jury as opposed to a trial solely before a judge. The jury decides the factual issues.

jury wheel A system for the storage and random selection of the names or identifying numbers of prospective jurors.

jus (**jura** plural) Law; system of law; right; power; principle.

jus accrescendi The right of survivorship or accrual.

jus cogens A rule or legal principle that the parties cannot change.

jus gentium The law of nations; international law.

jus publicum 1. Public law. 2. State ownership of land.

just Conforming to what is legal or equitable.

just cause See good cause.

just compensation Compensation that is fair to both the owner and the public when the owner's property is taken for public use through eminent domain. Also called adequate compensation.

Just compensation, to which property owner is entitled under Fifth Amendment where government appropriates property for public use, in most cases means fair market value of property on date it is appropriated. *Matter of New York State Urban Development Corp.*, 674 N.Y.S.2d 562 (Sup. Ct., 1998)

jus tertii The right of a third person or party.

justice 1. A judge, usually of a higher court. 2. The proper administration of the law; the fair resolution of legal disputes.

justice court A lower court (e.g., a town or village court) that can hear minor civil or criminal matters.

justice of the peace (J.P.) A judicial magistrate of inferior rank with limited jurisdiction over minor civil or criminal cases in a town or village court. In New York, this elected official does not have to be an attorney.

justiciable Appropriate for court resolution.

A justiciable controversy is one solvable by a court rather than some other forum and, with regard to the separation of powers doctrine, has to do with whether the matter is resolvable by the judicial branch of government by way of interpreting or enforcing a statutory mandate or by the executive or legislative branches in the exercise of their purely political function. *Schulz*, 629 N.Y.S.2d 316 (3 Dept., 1995)

justifiable Warranted or sanctioned by law. Defensible.

justifiable homicide Killing another when permitted by law (e.g., in self-defense).

justification A just or lawful reason to act or to fail to act.

juvenile One under 18 (or other age designated by law) and, therefore, not subject to be treated as an adult for purposes of the criminal law. See also juvenile delinquent.

juvenile court A special court with jurisdiction over minors alleged to be neglected or juvenile delinquents. In New York, juvenile cases are heard in family court.

juvenile delinquent (jd) A minor (e.g., someone under 18) who has committed an act that would be a crime if committed by an adult. Also called youthful offender in some states.

"Juvenile delinquent" means a person over seven and less than sixteen years of age, who, having committed an act that would constitute a crime if committed by an adult, (a) is not criminally responsible for such conduct by reason of infancy, or (b) is the defendant in an action ordered removed from a criminal court to the family court pursuant to article seven hundred twenty-five of the criminal procedure law. McKinney's Family Court Act § 301.2(1)

juvenile offender A person thirteen, fourteen, or fifteen years old who is criminally responsible for felonies specified in CPL § 1.20, describing the circumstance of a juvenile prosecuted as an adult.

K

k Contract.

kangaroo court A sham legal proceeding in which a person's rights are disregarded and the result is a foregone conclusion due to bias.

K.B. See King's Bench.

keeper A person or entity that has the custody or management of something or someone.

Keogh plan A retirement plan for self-employed taxpayers, the contributions to which are tax deductible. Also called H.R. 10 plan.

KeyCite The citator on Westlaw that allows online checking of the subsequent history of cases, statutes, and other laws.

key number A number assigned to a topic by West Group in its indexing or classification system of case law.

key man insurance Life insurance on employees who are crucial to a company. The company pays for the insurance and is the beneficiary.

kickback A payment made by a seller of a portion of the purchase price to the buyer or to a public official in order to induce the purchase or to influence future business transactions.

kiddie tax A popular term used for the tax paid by parents at their rate for the investment (unearned) income of their children.

kidnapping Taking and carrying away a human being by force, fraud, or threats against the victim's will and without lawful authority.

A person is guilty of kidnapping in the first degree when he abducts another person and when: 1. His intent is to compel a third person to pay or deliver money or property as ransom, or to engage in other particular conduct, or to refrain from engaging in particular conduct; or .... McKinney's Penal Law § 135.35

kin One's relatives; family, kindred.

kind Generic class; type. See also in kind.

kindred Family, relatives.

King's Bench (K.B.) One of the superior courts of common law in England. If the monarch is a queen, the court is called Queen's Bench.

kiting See check kiting.

knock-and-announce rule Police must (absent exigent circumstances such as danger to the police) announce their presence before forcibly entering premises to be searched. An exception (called the useless-gesture exception) exists if the occupants already know why the police are there.

knock down Final acceptance of a bid by an auctioneer.

knowingly With awareness or understanding; conscious or deliberate; intentionally.

A contractor acts "knowingly" if it knew or should have known that it was violating prevailing wage law. McKinney's Labor Law § 220. *Baywood Elec. Corp.*, 649 N.Y.S.2d 28 (N.Y.A.D. 2 Dept., 1996). A person acts knowingly with respect to conduct or to a circumstance described by a statute defining an offense when he is aware that his conduct is of such nature or that such circumstance exists. McKinney's Penal Law § 15.05

knowledge Acquaintance with fact or truth. Understanding obtained by experience or study. Awareness.

L

labor Mental or physical exertion or work, usually for a wage.

labor contract A collective bargaining agreement between a union and an employer covering wages, conditions of labor, and related matters.

laborer's lien A lien on property of someone responsible for paying for the work of a laborer on that property.

Labor-Management Relations Act The federal statute that covers procedures to settle strikes involving national emergencies, protects employees who do not want to join the union, and imposes other restrictions on unions (29 USC § 141). Also called Taft-Hartley Act.

labor organization A union.

labor union See union.

laches A party's unreasonable delay in asserting a legal or equitable right and another's detrimental good-faith change in position because of the delay.

To establish laches, a party must show conduct by the offending party giving rise to the situation complained of, delay by complainant in asserting a claim for relief despite opportunity to do so, lack of knowledge or notice on part of the offending party that complainant would assert a claim for relief, and injury or prejudice to the offending party in the event that relief is accorded the complainant. *Cohen*, 643 N.Y.S.2d 612 (2 Dept., 1996)

lading See bill of lading.

LAMA See International Paralegal Management Association (*www.paralegalmanagement.org*).

lame duck 1. An elected official still in office who has not been or cannot be reelected. 2. A member of a stock exchange who has overbought and cannot meet his or her obligations.

lame duck session A legislative session conducted after the election of new members but before they are installed.

land 1. The surface of the earth, anything growing or permanently attached to it, the airspace above the earth, and what exists beneath the surface. 2. An interest in real property.

land bank A federally created bank under the Federal Farm Loan Act organized to make loans on farm land at low interest rates.

land grant A gift or donation of public land by the government to an individual, corporation, or other government.

landlord The owner who leases land, buildings, or apartments to another. Also called lessor.

To be considered a landlord or lessor, the party seeking to recover possession of real property must prove he or she is possessed of ownership in an estate in land, be it ownership in fee or of lesser estate, and that he or she had leased it to another, the tenant; alternatively, party must show that he or she has authority from such person to do so. McKinney's RPAPL § 721, subd. 1. *Redhead*, 610 N.Y.S.2d 433 (N.Y. City Civ. Ct., 1994)

landlord's lien The right of a landlord to levy upon goods of a tenant in satisfaction of unpaid rents or property damage.

landmark 1. A monument or other marker set up on the boundary line of two adjoining estates to fix such boundary. 2. Historically important. A landmark case establishes new and significant legal principles.

land sales contract See contract for deed.

land trust A trust that gives legal and equitable title of real property to a trustee but management and control of the property to the trust beneficiary. Also called Illinois Land Trust.

land use planning The use of zoning laws, environmental impact studies, and coordination efforts to develop the interrelated aspects of a community's physical environment and its social and economic activities.

lapping Theft of cash receipts from a customer that is covered up by crediting someone else's receipts to that customer.

lapse 1. To end because of a failure to use or a failure to fulfill a condition. 2. To fail to vest because of the death of the prospective beneficiary before the death of the donor. 3. A slip, mistake, or error. 4. A period of time.

lapsed Expired; no longer effective.

larcenous Having the character of or contemplating larceny.

larceny The wrongful taking and carrying away of another's personal property with the intention to deprive the possessor of it permanently.

A person steals property and commits larceny when, with intent to deprive another of property or to appropriate the same to himself or to a third person, he wrongfully takes, obtains or withholds such property from an owner thereof. McKinney's Penal Law § 155.05(1)

larceny by trick Larceny by using fraud or false pretenses to induce the victim to give up possession (but not title) to personal property.

lascivious Tending to incite lust; obscene.

last antecedent rule Qualifying words will be applied only to the word or phrase immediately preceding unless the qualifying words were clearly intended to apply to other language in the document as well.

last clear chance doctrine A plaintiff who has been contributorily negligent in placing himself or herself in peril can still recover if the negligent defendant had the last opportunity (clear chance) to avoid the accident and failed to exercise reasonable care to do so. Also called discovered peril doctrine, humanitarian doctrine, supervening negligence.

Doctrine of last clear chance requires that defendant having ultimate power to do so forfend the plaintiff's injury even though the defendant might otherwise have been relieved of liability by virtue of the plaintiff's own negligence; the doctrine fixes upon a defendant the onus of rescuing the plaintiff from a peril in which the latter has placed himself and from which he cannot extricate himself provided the defendant has both actual notice of the plaintiff's plight and a reasonable opportunity to prevent the harm. *O'Connor*, 426 N.Y.S.2d 557 (2 Dept., 1980)

last in, first out (LIFO) An accounting assumption that the last goods purchased are the first ones sold or used. The assumption is used to value the cost of goods sold in determining income.

last resort The end of the appeal process, referring to a court from which there is no further appeal.

last will The testator's most recent will before dying.

latent Concealed; dormant or not active.

latent ambiguity A lack of clarity in otherwise clear language that arises when some extrinsic evidence creates a necessity for interpretation.

A latent ambiguity in will, which may be cleared up by extrinsic evidence, arises when words used are neither ambiguous nor obscure but ambiguity appears relative to persons or things meant. *In re Blodgett's Estate*, 7 N.Y.S.2d 364 (Sup. Ct., 1938)

latent defect See hidden defect.

lateral support right The right to have land in its natural state supported by adjoining land.

laundering Concealing or disguising the source or origin of something (e.g., money) that was obtained illegally.

law 1. A rule of action or conduct prescribed by a controlling authority and having binding force. 2. The aggregate body of rules governing society. 3. The legal profession.

law clerk 1. An attorney's employee who is in law school studying to be an attorney or is waiting to pass the bar examination. 2. A lawyer or non-lawyer who provides research and writing assistance to a judge.

law day 1. The date on which a mortgagor can avoid foreclosure by paying the debt on the mortgaged property. 2. May 1, the date each year set aside to honor our legal system.

law enforcement officer Someone empowered by law to investigate crime, make arrests for violations of the criminal law, and preserve the peace.

lawful Legal, authorized by law.

law guardian An attorney appointed to represent a child in some court proceedings. Called a guardian ad litem in many states.

Regarding custody and visitation in divorce, "In all proceedings under this section, a law guardian shall be appointed for the child." McKinney's DRL § 240.

law journal A legal periodical of a law school or bar association. See also law review.

law list A list or directory of attorneys containing brief information relevant to their practice.

law merchant The practices and customs of those engaged in commerce that developed into what is known today as commercial law.

law of nations See international law.

law of nature See natural law.

law of the case doctrine An appellate court's determination of a legal issue binds both the trial court and the court on appeal in any subsequent appeal involving the same case and substantially the same facts.

The law of the case doctrine is a rule of practice, an articulation of sound policy that, when an issue is once judicially determined, that should be the end of the matter as far as judges and courts of co-ordinate jurisdiction are concerned. *Oyster Bay Associates*, 801 N.Y.S.2d 612 (2 Dept., 2005)

law of the land 1. The law that applies in a country, state or region. 2. Due process of law and related constitutional protections.

law of the road Traffic laws.

law reports, law reporters See reporter (3), report (2).

law review (L. Rev.) A legal periodical (usually student-edited) published by a law school. Also called law journal.

Law School Admission Test (LSAT) A standardized aptitude test used by many law schools in making decisions on admission.

lawsuit A court proceeding that asserts a legal claim or dispute. Also called a suit.

lawyer See attorney (1).

lay 1. Nonprofessional; not having expertise. 2. Nonecclesiastical; not belonging to the clergy. 3. To state or allege in a pleading.

layaway A seller's agreement with a consumer to hold goods for sale at a later date at a specified price.

For purposes of this section, the term "layaway plan" shall mean a purchase over the amount of fifty dollars whereby the consumer agrees to pay in four or more installments for the purchase of specific merchandise, delivery of which is to be made upon the payment of the full purchase price at a definite future date or at a date to be selected by the consumer. McKinney's General Business Law § 396-t(a)

layoff A temporary or permanent termination of employment at the will of the employer.

lay witness A person giving only fact or lay (not expert) opinion testimony.

LBO See leveraged buyout.

lead counsel The attorney managing the case of a client with several attorneys. The primary attorney in a class action.

leading case An opinion that has had an important influence in the development of the law on a particular point.

leading question A question to someone being interviewed or examined that suggests the answer within the question.

learned intermediary See informed intermediary.

lease 1. A contract for the use or possession of real or personal property for a designated rent or other consideration. Ownership of the property is not transferred. 2. To let or rent.

The central distinguishing characteristic of a lease is the surrender of absolute possession and control of property to another party for an agreed-upon rent. *Plaza*, 759 N.Y.S.2d 748 (2 Dept., 2003)

leaseback The sale of property to a buyer who gives the seller the right to lease the property from the buyer. Also called sale and leaseback.

leasehold An estate in real property held by a tenant/lessee under a lease; property held by a lease.

leave 1. To give in a will; to bequeath. 2. To withdraw or depart. 3. Permission to do something, e.g., to be absent from work or military service.

leave of court A court's permission to perform or refrain from a procedural step during litigation.

ledger A book used to record business transactions.

legacy 1. Any gift in a will. 2. A gift of personal property in a will. 3. Something handed down from an ancestor.

Legacies are gifts of personal property, and depending upon their nature, are classified as general, specific or demonstrative. *In re Brown's Will*, 209 N.Y.S.2d 465 (Sur., 1961)

legal 1. Authorized, required, permitted, or involving the law. 2. Pertaining to law rather than to equity.

legal age See age of consent, age of majority, age of reason.

legal aid A system (often government-funded) of providing legal services to people who cannot afford counsel.

legal assistant See paralegal.

legal cap Long ruled paper in tablet form. Traditionally used for pleadings and litigation documents. Often has red or blue vertical margins, hence sometimes referred to as "red line" or "blue line" paper.

legal capital The par or stated value of outstanding stock. Also called stated capital.

legal cause See proximate cause.

legal certainty test A court will find federal diversity jurisdiction on the basis of the plaintiff's complaint unless it appears to a legal certainty that the claim is for less than the jurisdictional amount.

legal conclusion A statement of legal consequences, often without including the facts from which the consequences arise. See also conclusion of law.

legal consideration See valuable consideration.

legal custody 1. The right and duty to make decisions about raising a child. 2. The detention of someone by the government.

Phrase "having legal custody" in statute which provides that unless the court appoints a guardian ad litem, an infant shall appear by a parent "having legal custody" or, if there is no such parent, by another person or agency "having legal custody" is intended to designate a person whose custody was formally determined by judicial decree. CPLR 1201. *Villafane*, 387 N.Y.S.2d 183 (Sup. Ct., 1976)

legal death See brain death, civil death.

legal description A description of real property by various methods (e.g., by metes and bounds), including a description of portions subject to any easements or other restrictions.

legal detriment See detriment.

legal discretion See judicial discretion.

legal duty See duty (2).

legal entity An artificial person (e.g., a corporation) that functions in some ways as a natural person (e.g., it can sue and be sued).

legalese Technical language or jargon used by attorneys.

legal ethics Rules that embody the minimum standards of behavior to which members of the legal profession are expected to conform.

legal fiction An assumption of fact made by a court in order to dispose of a matter with justice even though the fact may not be true.

John Doe is the conventional legal fiction, and means anybody or nobody. *Smith*, 1862 WL 4277 (Sup. Ct., 1862)

legal fraud See constructive fraud.

legal heir See heir (1).

legal holiday A day designated as a holiday by the legislature. A day on which court proceedings and service of process cannot occur.

legal impossibility A defense asserting that the defendant's intended acts, even if completed, would not amount to a crime.

legal injury An invasion of a person's legally protected interest.

legal interest 1. A legally protected right or claim. A legal share of something. 2. A rate of interest authorized by law.

legal investments Those investments, sometimes called legal lists, in which banks and other financial institutions may invest.

legal issue A legal question. See also issue of law.

legality 1. Lawfulness; the state of being in accordance with law. 2. A technical legal requirement.

legalize To make or declare legal that which was once illegal.

legal list See legal investments.

legal malice 1. Pertaining to wrongful conduct committed or continued with a willful or reckless disregard for another's rights. 2. Malice that is inferred. Also called implied malice.

legal malpractice The failure of an attorney to use such skill, prudence, and diligence as reasonable attorneys of ordinary skill and capacity commonly possess and exercise under the same circumstances. Professional misconduct or wrongdoing by attorneys.

Legal malpractice consists of failure of an attorney to exercise that degree of skill commonly exercised by an ordinary member of legal community, resulting in damages to client. *Bassim*, 650 N.Y.S.2d 467 (3 Dept., 1996)

legal name The designation of a person or entity recognized by the law.

legal notice Notification of something in a manner prescribed by law.

legal opinion An attorney's interpretation (often in writing) of how the law applies to facts in a client's case.

legal positivism The legal theory that the validity of laws is based, not on natural law or morality, but on being duly enacted or decreed by the three branches of government and accepted by society.

legal proceedings Formal actions in court or administrative tribunals to establish legal rights or resolve legal disputes.

legal question See issue of law.

legal realism The legal theory that the development of law in court opinions is based on public policy and social science considerations rather than on a pure or rigid legal analysis of rules.

legal representative One who represents the legal interests of another, e.g., one who is incapacitated.

Resident's legal representative means a person duly authorized under applicable state law to act on behalf of a resident. Such legal representative could include, but is not necessarily limited to, a court appointed guardian, an attorney in-fact under a durable power of attorney, an agent under a health care proxy or a representative payee, depending upon the action to be taken. McKinney's Public Health Law § 4651(9)

legal reserve Assets that a business (e.g., insurance company, bank) must set aside to be available to meet the demands of its customers.

legal residence The residence required by law for legal purposes, e.g., receipt of process. See also domicile (3).

legal separation A court order allowing spouses to live separately and establishing their rights and duties while separated, but still married. Also called divorce a mensa et thoro, judicial separation, limited divorce.

legal technician See independent paralegal.

legal tender Coins and currencies that can be used to pay debts.

legal title 1. A title that is recognizable and enforceable in a court of law. 2. A title that provides the right of ownership but no beneficial interest in the property. See also beneficial interest.

legatee The person to whom personal property (and sometimes real property) is given by will.

A residuary legatee is one who takes what remains, or a portion of what remains, after satisfying all other gifts, charges, losses, and expenses. *In re Langdon's Will*, 50 N.Y.S.2d 100 (Sur., 1943)

legation A diplomatic mission; the staff and premises of such a mission.

legislate To enact laws through legislation. To make or pass a law.

legislation 1. The enactment of laws by a legislative body. 2. Law or laws passed by a legislature. 3. A statute; a body of statutes.

legislative Pertaining to the enactment of laws by a legislative body.

legislative council A body that plans legislative strategy, primarily between sessions of the legislature.

legislative counsel The person or office that assists legislators by conducting research and drafting proposed legislation.

legislative court See Article I court.

legislative history Hearings, debates, reports, and all other events that occur in the legislature before a bill is enacted into a statute.

legislative immunity An immunity from civil suit enjoyed by a member of the legislature while engaged in legislative functions.

legislative intent The design, aim, end, or plan of the legislature in passing a particular statute.

legislative rule A rule of an administrative agency based on its quasi-legislative power. An administrative rule that creates rights or assigns duties rather than merely interprets a governing statute. Also called substantive rule.

When a rule is legislative, the reviewing court has no authority to substitute judgment as to the content of the rule, for the legislative body has placed the power in the agency and not in the court. A legislative rule is valid and is as binding upon a court as a statute if it is (a) within the granted power, (b) issued pursuant to proper procedure, and (c) reasonable. *Calzadilla*, 286 N.Y.S. 2d 510 (4 Dept., 1968)

legislative veto A legislative method of rejecting administrative action. The agency's action (e.g., a rule) would be valid unless nullified by resolutions of the legislature. On the unconstitutionality of such vetoes, see *INS v. Chadha*, 103 S. Ct. 2764 (1983).

legislator A member of a legislative body.

legislature The assembly or body of persons that makes statutory laws for a state or nation.

legitimacy 1. The condition of being born within a marriage or acquiring this condition through steps provided by law. 2. The condition of being in compliance with the law or with established standards.

legitimate 1. Lawful, valid, or genuine. 2. Born to married parents or to parents who have legitimated the child.

At common law, "lawful issue" or "legitimate issue" includes only those who were children of legally recognized subsisting marriage. *In re Sheffer's Will*, 249 N.Y.S. 102 (N.Y. Sur., 1931)

legitimation 1. Making legitimate or lawful. 2. The procedure of legalizing (legitimating) the status of an illegitimate child.

legitime A portion of decedent's estate that must be reserved for a forced heir such as a child. See also forced heir.

lemon law A law giving a buyer of a new car with major defects the right to a refund or to have it replaced. See McKinney's General Business Law §198(b).

lend 1. To provide money to another for a period of time, often for an interest charge. 2. To give something of value to another for a fixed or indefinite time, with or without compensation, with the expectation that it will be returned.

lese majesty A crime against the sovereign, e.g., treason. Also spelled leze majesty.

lessee A person who rents or leases property from another. A tenant.

A lessee is defined as "He to whom a lease is made" . . . The terms tenant and lessee have a more general meaning than Occupant. An occupant is one who is in actual possession where the "tenant" or "lessee" need not be. *25 W. 13th Street Corp.*, 488 N.Y.S.2d 597 (N.Y. City Civ. Ct., 1985)

lesser included offense A crime composed solely of some but not all of the elements of a greater crime so that it would be impossible to commit the greater offense without committing the lesser. Also called included offense.

lessor A person who rents or leases property to another. A landlord.

let 1. To allow. 2. To lease or rent. 3. To award a contract to one of the bidders.

lethal weapon See deadly weapon.

letter A writing that grants a power, authority, or right.

letter of attornment A letter to a tenant stating that the premises have been sold and that rent should be paid to the new owner.

letter of credit (LOC) An engagement by a bank or other issuer (made at the request of a customer) to honor demands for payment by a third party upon compliance with conditions stated in the letter. Also called circular note.

Letter of credit means a definite undertaking that satisfies the requirements of section 5-104 by an issuer to a beneficiary at the request or for the account of an applicant or, in the case of a financial institution, to itself or for its own account, to honor a documentary presentation by payment or delivery of an item of value. McKinney's Uniform Commercial Code § 5-102(10)

letter of intent (LOI) A nonbinding writing that states preliminary understandings of one or both parties to a possible future contract.

letter rogatory A court's request to a court in a foreign jurisdiction for assistance in a pending case, e.g., to take the testimony of a witness in the other jurisdiction.

letter ruling A written statement issued to a taxpayer by the IRS that interprets and applies the tax laws to a specific set of facts.

letters of administration The court document that authorizes a person to manage the estate of someone who has died without a valid will.

letters of marque A government authorization to a private citizen to seize assets of a foreign country.

letters patent A public document issued by the government that grants a right, e.g., a right to the sole use of an invention.

letters testamentary A formal document issued by a court that empowers a person to act as an executor of a will.

letter stock See restricted security.

levari facias A writ of execution to satisfy a party's judgment debt out of his or her profits and other assets.

leverage 1. The use of credit or debt to increase profits and purchasing power. The use of a smaller investment to generate a larger rate of return through borrowing. 2. Added power or influence.

leveraged buyout (LBO) Taking over a company by using borrowed funds for a substantial part of the purchase. The sale of a corporation in which at least part of the purchase price is obtained through debt assumed by the corporation.

levy 1. To assess or impose a tax, charge, or fine. 2. To seize assets in order to satisfy a claim. 3. To conscript into the military. 4. To wage or carry on. 5. A tax, charge, or fine.

Levy when used in reference to taxation, has various meanings; depending on the context in which it is used, the term may mean legislative function and declaration of the subject and rate or amount of taxation, fixing of the rate of taxation rather than the physical act of applying the tax rate to the property, the ministerial function of assessing, listing and extending taxes, or the doing of whatever is necessary in order to authorize the collector to collect the tax. *Walker*, 480 N.Y.S. 2d 933 (2 Dept., 1984)

lewd Indecent, obscene; inciting to lustful desire.

lex Law or a collection of laws.

lex fori The law of the forum where the suit is brought.

LexisNexis A fee-based legal research computer service (*www.lexisnexis.com*).

lex loci contractus The law of the place where the contract was formed or will be performed.

lex loci delicti The law of the place where the wrong (e.g., the tort) took place.

leze majesty See lese majesty.

liability 1. The condition of being legally responsible for a loss, penalty, debt, or other obligation. 2. The obligation owed.

liability insurance Insurance in which an insurer pays covered damages the insured is obligated to pay a third person.

liability without fault See strict liability.

liable Obligated in law; legally responsible.

libel 1. A defamatory statement expressed in writing or other graphic or visual form such as by pictures or signs. See also defamation. 2. A plaintiff's pleading in an admiralty or ecclesiastical court.

Libel is false written, symbolic, or pictorial publication about living person which has tendency to injure person's reputation so as to render person exposed to public hatred, contempt, scorn, obloquy, or shame. *Glendora*, 616 N.Y.S.2d 138 (Sup. Ct., 1994)

libelant The complainant in an admiralty or ecclesiastical court.

libelee The defendant in an admiralty or ecclesiastical court.

libelous Defamatory; constituting or involving libel.

libel per quod A writing that requires extrinsic facts to understand its defamatory meaning. Libel that requires proof of special damages.

libel per se A written defamatory statement that is actionable without proof that the plaintiff suffered special damages. Libel that is defamatory on its face.

liberal construction An expansive or broad interpretation of the meaning of a statute or other law to include facts or cases that are within the spirit and reason of the law.

liberty 1. Freedom from excessive or oppressive restrictions imposed by the state or other authority. 2. A basic right or privilege.

license 1. Permission to do what would otherwise be illegal or a tort. 2. The document that evidences this permission.

License means any license, permit or other public document which conveys to the person to whom it was issued the privilege of pursuing, possessing or taking any wildlife regulated by statute, law, regulation, ordinance or administrative rule of a participating state. McKinney's ECL § 11-2503(h)

licensee 1. One who enters land for his or her own purposes or benefit, but with the express or implied consent of the owner or occupier of the land. 2. One who has a license.

licensor One who gives or grants a license.

licentious Without moral restraint. Disregarding sexual morality.

licit Permitted by law, legal.

lie 1. A deliberately or intentionally false statement. 2. To make a false statement intentionally. 3. To be sustainable in law.

lie detector See polygraph.

lien A charge, security, or encumbrance on property; a creditor's claim or charge on property for the payment of a debt.

Lien means a charge against or interest in goods to secure payment of a debt or performance of an obligation, but the term does not include a security interest. McKinney's Uniform Commercial Code § 2-A-103(r)

lien creditor One whose claim is secured by a lien on particular property of the debtor.

lienee One whose property is subject to a lien.

lienholder; lienor One who has a lien on the property of another.

life annuity An annuity that guarantees payments for the life of the annuitant.

life-care contract A contract (often with a nursing care facility) to provide designated health services and living care for the remainder of a person's life in exchange for an up-front payment.

life estate An interest in property whose duration is limited to the life of an individual. Also called estate for life, life tenancy.

Legal life tenant. Any person entitled for his life or for the life of another to the possession and use of real or personal property. McKinney's SCPA § 103(30)

life estate pur autre vie A life estate whose duration is measured by the life of someone other than the possessor of the estate. Also called estate pur autre vie.

life expectancy The number of years a person of a given age and sex is expected to live according to statistics.

life in being The remaining length of time in the life of a person who is in existence at the time that a future interest is created.

life insurance A contract for the payment of a specified amount to a designated beneficiary upon the death of the person insured.

"Life Insurance" means every insurance upon the lives of human beings, and every insurance appertaining thereto, including the granting of endowment benefits, additional benefits in the event of death by accident, additional benefits to safeguard the contract from lapse, accelerated payments of part or all of the death benefit or a special surrender value upon (A) diagnosis of terminal illness defined as a life expectancy of twelve months or less, (B) diagnosis of a medical condition requiring extraordinary medical care or treatment regardless of life expectancy, . . . McKinney's Insurance Law § 1113(1)

life interest An interest in property whose duration is limited to the life of the party holding the interest or of some other person.

life tenant One who possesses a life estate. A tenant for life.

LIFO See last in, first out.

lift To rescind or stop.

like-kind exchange The exchange of property held for productive use in a trade or business or for investment on which no gain or loss shall be recognized if such property is exchanged solely for property of like kind or character that is to be held either for productive use in a trade or business or for investment (26 USC § 1031).

limine See in limine, motion in limine.

limitation 1. Restriction. 2. The time allowed by statute for bringing an action at the risk of losing it. See also statute of limitations.

limited (Ltd.) 1. Restricted in duration or scope. 2. A designation indicating that a business is a company with limited liability.

limited admissibility Allowing evidence to be considered for isolated or restricted purposes.

limited divorce See legal separation.

limited jurisdiction The power of a court to hear only certain kinds of cases. Also called special jurisdiction.

limited liability Restricted liability; liability that can be satisfied out of business assets, not out of personal assets.

limited-liability company (L.L.C.) A hybrid business entity with features of a corporation and a partnership. The company has a legal existence separate from its members/owners who can participate in the management of the company and have limited liability.

"Limited liability company" and "domestic limited liability company" mean, unless the context otherwise requires, an unincorporated organization of one or more persons having limited liability for the contractual obligations and other liabilities of the business (except as authorized or provided in section six hundred nine or twelve hundred five of this chapter), other than a partnership or trust, formed and existing under this chapter and the laws of this state. McKinney's Limited Liability Company Law § 102(m)

limited-liability limited partnership (L.L.L.P.) A modified limited partnership. Similar to a limited partnership, the L.L.L.P. consists of one or more general partners and one or more limited partners. The general partners manage the business operations of the L.L.L.P., while the limited partners typically only maintain a financial interest. The key advantage of an L.L.L.P. is that the general partners receive limited liability on the debts and obligations of the L.L.L.P.

limited-liability partnership (L.L.P.) A type of partnership in which a partner has unlimited liability for his or her wrongdoing but not for the wrongdoing of other partners.

limited partner A partner who takes no part in running the business and who incurs no liability for partnership obligations beyond the contribution he or she invested in the partnership.

limited partnership (L.P.) A type of partnership consisting of one or more general partners who manage the business and who are personally liable for partnership debts, and one or more limited partners who take no part in running the business and who incur no liability for partnership obligations beyond the contribution they invested in the partnership.

A limited partnership is a partnership formed by two or more persons under the provisions of section ninety-one, having as members one or more general partners and one or more limited partners. The limited partners as such shall not be bound by the obligations of the partnership. McKinney's Partnership Law § 90

limited power of appointment A power of appointment that restricts who can receive property under the power or under what conditions anyone can receive it. Also called special power of appointment.

limited publication The distribution of a work to a selected group for a limited purpose, and without the right of reproduction, distribution, or sale.

limited purpose public figure See public figure.

limited warranty A warranty that does not cover all defects or does not cover the full cost of repair.

lineage Line of descent from a common ancestor.

lineal Proceeding in a direct or unbroken line; from a common ancestor.

lineal heir One who inherits in a line either ascending or descending from a common source, as distinguished from a collateral heir.

line item veto The chief executive's rejection of part of a bill passed by the legislature, allowing the rest to become law with his or her signature.

line of credit The maximum amount of money that can be borrowed or goods that can be purchased on credit. Also called credit line.

lineup A group of people, including the suspect, shown at one time to a witness, who is asked if he or she can identify the person who committed the crime. The procedure is called a showup if the witness is shown only one person.

link-in-chain principle The privilege against self-incrimination covers questions that could indirectly connect (link) someone to a crime.

liquid Consisting of cash or what can easily be converted into cash.

liquidate 1. To pay and settle a debt. 2. To convert non-cash assets into cash, often as part of the dissolution of a business.

liquidated claim A claim as to which the parties have already agreed what the damages will be or what method will be used to calculate the damages that will be paid.

Claim is "liquidated," within meaning of fraudulent transfer provisions of Debtor and Creditor Law (DCL), when it is ascertained, fixed, settled, or made clear or manifest. McKinney's Debtor and Creditor Law §§ 270–281. *Shelly*, 660 N.Y.S.2d 937 (Co. Ct., 1997)

liquidated damages An amount the parties agree will be the damages if a breach of contract occurs. Also called stipulated damages.

liquidity 1. The measure of how rapidly an asset can be converted into cash. 2. The ability to pay current obligations.

lis pendens 1. A pending lawsuit. 2. A recorded notice that an action has been filed affecting the title to or right to possession of the real property described in the notice. Also called notice of pendency. 3. Jurisdiction or control that courts acquire over property involved in a pending lawsuit.

list 1. A court's case docket. 2. A series or registry of names. 3. See listing.

listed security A security that is bought or sold on an exchange.

listing 1. A contract between an owner of real property and a real estate agent authorizing the latter to find a buyer or tenant in return for a fee or commission. 2. A contract between a firm and a stock exchange, covering the trading of that firm's securities on the stock exchange. 3. Making a schedule or inventory.

> The listing agreement defines this agency relationship as one which provides "that if you, as owner of the property find a buyer for your house, or if another broker finds a buyer, you must pay the agreed commission to the present broker." *Talk of the Millenium Realty Inc.*, 12 Misc. 3d 1153(A) (N.Y. City Civ. Ct., 2006)

list price The published or advertised retail price of goods.

literal construction See strict construction.

literary property 1. The corporal or physical embodiment (e.g., a book) of an intellectual production. 2. The exclusive right of an owner to possess, use, and dispose of his or her intellectual productions.

literary works Under copyright law, works, "expressed in words, numbers, or other verbal or numerical symbols or indicia, regardless of the nature of the material objects, such as books, periodicals, manuscripts, phonorecords, film, tapes, disks, or cards, in which they are embodied." Audiovisual works are not included. (17 USC § 101)

litigant A party in litigation.

litigate To resolve a dispute or seek relief in a court of law.

litigation 1. The formal process of resolving a legal dispute through the courts. 2. A lawsuit.

litigious Prone to engage in disputes and litigation.

littoral Concerning or belonging to the shore or coast.

livery of seisin A ceremony to transfer legal title of land (e.g., deliver a twig, as a symbol of the whole land). Also called investiture.

living apart As a ground for divorce, the spouses live separately for a designated period of consecutive time with no present intention of resuming marital relations.

living trust See inter vivos trust.

living will A formal document that expresses a person's desire not to be kept alive through artificial or extraordinary means if in the future he or she suffers from a terminal condition.

> Reduced to its simplest terms a "Living Will" is a document in which one states, while in good health, what measures he or she does not want used to extend one's life when one is dying. *Saunders*, 492 N.Y.S.2d 510 (Sup. Ct., 1985)

LL.B.; LL.M.; LL.D. Law degrees: bachelor of laws (LL.B.), master of laws (LL.M.), doctor of laws (LL.D.). See also Juris Doctor.

LKA Last known address.

L.L.C. See limited-liability company.

L.L.L.P. See limited-liability limited partnership.

L.L.P. See limited-liability partnership.

load The charge added to the cost of insurance or securities to cover commissions and administrative expenses. See also no-load.

loan 1. Anything furnished for temporary use. 2. The act of lending.

> The term "consumer loan" means a loan of money by a creditor to a consumer for which the consumer's obligation is payable in installments or for which a finance or other charge is or may be imposed. McKinney's General Business Law § 252(d)

loan commitment An enforceable promise to make a loan for a specified amount on specified terms.

loaned servant doctrine When an employer lends its employee to another employer for some special service, the employee becomes (for purposes of respondeat superior liability) the employee of the party to whom he or she has been loaned with respect to that service.

loan for consumption A contract in which a lender delivers to a borrower goods that are consumed by use, with the understanding that the borrower will return to the lender goods of the same kind, quantity, and quality.

loan for use A loan of personal property for normal use and then returned.

loan ratio The ratio, expressed as a percentage, of the amount of a loan to the value of the real property that is security for the loan.

loansharking Lending money at excessive rates with the threat or actual use of force to obtain repayment.

loan value The maximum amount one is allowed to borrow on a life insurance policy or other property.

lobbying Attempts to influence the policy decisions of a public official, particularly a legislator.

lobbyist One in the business of lobbying.

local action An action that must be brought in a particular state or county, e.g., where the land in dispute is located.

local agent 1. A person who takes care of a company's business in a particular area or district. 2. A person designated to accept service for another person or entity (e.g., a nonlocal business), often due to a legal requirement.

local assessment A tax upon property in a limited area for improvements (e.g., sidewalk repair) that will benefit property within that area.

local law 1. A law that is limited to a specific geographic region of the state. 2. A law passed by the local legislative branch of government (e.g., city council) that declares, commands, or prohibits something. 3. The law of one jurisdiction, usually referring to a jurisdiction other than the one where a case is in litigation.

local option The right of a city or other local government to accept or reject a particular policy, e.g., Sunday liquor sales.

local union A unit or branch of a larger labor union.

lockdown The confinement of inmates to their cells or dorms, usually as a security measure.

lockout Withholding work from employees or temporarily closing a business due to a labor dispute.

> The act of locking out; the refusal of an employer to furnish work to employees, used as a means of coercion. *Agostini*, 40 N.Y.S.2d 598 (Ct. Cl., 1943)

lockup A place of detention in a police station, court, or other facility while awaiting further official action. A holding cell.

loco parentis See in loco parentis.

locus A locality. The place where a thing occurs or exists.

locus contractus The place where the last act is performed that makes an agreement a binding contract.

locus delicti The place of the wrong. The place where the last event occurred that was necessary to make the party liable.

locus in quo The place or scene of the occurrence or event.

locus poenitentiae The last opportunity to reconsider and withdraw before legal consequences (civil or criminal) occur.

locus sigilli (L.S.) The place where a document's seal is placed.

lodestar A method of calculating an award of attorney fees authorized by statute. The number of reasonable hours spent on a case is multiplied by a reasonable hourly rate. Sometimes considered above the lodestar are the quality of representation and the risk that there would be no fee.

lodger One who uses a dwelling without acquiring exclusive possession or a property interest, e.g., one who lives in a spare room of a house.

A "boarder," "roomer" or "lodger" residing with a family means a person living within the household who pays a consideration for such residence and does not occupy such space within the household as an incident of employment therein. McKinney's Executive Law § 292(12)

logrolling Trading political votes or favors.

LOI See letter of intent.

loitering Remaining idle in essentially one place. Walking about aimlessly.

To "loiter" is to consume time idly, to linger, to delay, to spend time in place in an idle manner, to travel indolently. *People v. Nowak*, 363 N.Y.S.2d 142 (4 Dept., 1975)

long Holding securities or commodities in the hope that prices will rise.

long-arm statute A statutory method of obtaining personal jurisdiction by substituted service of process over a nonresident defendant who has sufficient purposeful contact with a state.

long-term capital gain The gain (profit) realized on the sale or exchange of a capital asset held for the required period of time.

lookout 1. Keeping careful watch. 2. One who keeps careful watch.

Lord Campbell's Act A statute giving certain relatives of a decedent a wrongful-death claim for a tort that caused the death of the decedent.

Lord Mansfield's rule Testimony of either spouse is inadmissible on whether the husband had access to the wife at the time of conception if such evidence would tend to declare the child to be illegitimate.

loser-pays See American rule.

loss 1. Damage, detriment, or disadvantage to person or property. 2. The amount by which expenses exceed revenues. 3. The amount by which the basis of property exceeds what is received for it.

loss leader An item sold by a merchant at a low price (e.g., below cost) in order to entice people to come into the store.

loss of bargain rule See benefit of the bargain rule.

loss of consortium Interference with the companionship, services, affection, and sexual relations one spouse receives from another.

loss payable clause An insurance clause designating someone other than the insured to receive insurance proceeds.

loss ratio The ratio between claims paid out and premiums received by an insurance company.

A loss ratio of 105% means that for every dollar of premiums collected the insurer paid $1.05 in claims. *Excellus Health Plan*, 757 N.Y.S.2d 345 (3 Dept., 2003)

lost property Property that the owner has parted with through neglect or inadvertence and the whereabouts of which is unknown to the owner.

lost-volume seller A seller who, upon a buyer's breach, resells the goods to a second buyer who would have bought the same kind of goods from the seller even if the first buyer had not breached.

lost will A decedent's executed will that cannot be located.

lot 1. One of several parcels into which real property is divided. 2. A number of associated persons or things taken collectively. 3. A number of units of something offered for sale or traded as one item. 4. The shares purchased in one transaction.

lottery A scheme for the distribution of prizes by chance for which a participant pays something of value to enter.

"Lottery" means an unlawful gambling scheme in which (a) the players pay or agree to pay something of value for chances, represented and differentiated by numbers or by combinations of numbers or by some other media, one or more of which chances are to be designated the winning ones; and (b) the winning chances are to be determined by a drawing or by some other method based upon the element of chance; and (c) the holders of the winning chances are to receive something of value provided, however, that in no event shall the provisions of this subdivision be construed to include a raffle. . . . McKinney's Penal Law § 225.00(10)

lower court See inferior court.

L. Rev. See law review.

L.P. See limited partnership.

LSAT See Law School Admission Test.

Ltd. See limited.

lucid interval A temporary restoration to sanity, during which an insane person has sufficient intelligence to enter a contract.

lucrative title Title acquired without giving consideration.

lucri causa The intent to derive profit. For the sake of gain.

lump-sum alimony See alimony in gross.

lump-sum payment A single amount paid at one time.

lunacy See insanity (1).

luxury tax An excise tax on expensive, nonessential goods.

lying in wait Waiting and watching for an opportune time to inflict bodily harm on another by surprise.

lynch law Seizing persons suspected of crimes and summarily punishing them without legal trial or authority.

M

MACRS See Modified Accelerated Cost Recovery System.

magistrate 1. A judicial officer who has some, but not all the powers of a judge. Also called referee. In federal court, the duties of a United States Magistrate were once performed by a United States Commissioner. 2. A public civic officer with executive power. See also support magistrate.

magistrate court An inferior court with limited jurisdiction over minor civil or criminal matters. Also called police court.

Magna Carta The Great Charter of 1215, considered the foundation of constitutional liberty in England.

Magnuson-Moss Warranty Act A federal statute requiring warranties for consumer products to be written in plain and easily understood language (15 U.S.C. § 2301 et seq.).

mail box rule 1. The proper and timely mailing of a document raises a rebuttable presumption that the document has been received by the addressee in the usual time. 2. A prisoner's court papers are deemed filed when given to the proper prison authorities. 3. A contract is formed upon the act of mailing where the use of the mail is authorized by both parties.

> Petitioner had urged the court to follow the federal procedure which recognizes "the mail box rule". This rule deems litigation papers mailed by a *pro se* prisoner to the clerk of the court as "filed" the moment the papers are deposited in the mail. The Court of Appeals rejected the "mail box rule," finding that the State Legislature in drafting CPLR § 304 had evinced the intent to treat litigation papers as "filed" only upon the clerk's physical receipt of the papers. *Lovett*, 800 N.Y.S.2d 349 (Sup. Ct., 2005)

mail fraud The use of the U.S. Postal Service to obtain money by false pretenses or to commit other acts of fraud (18 USC § 1341).

mail-order divorce Obtaining a divorce from a state or country with no jurisdiction to award it, because, for example, neither spouse was domiciled there.

maim The infliction of a serious (and often disabling) bodily injury.

main purpose rule Under the statute of frauds, contracts to answer for the debt of another must be in writing *unless* the main purpose of the promisor's undertaking is his or her own benefit or protection.

> "Main purpose" rule, that the statute of frauds does not apply when main purpose of oral agreement is party's own economic advantage, is not followed in New York. McKinney's General Obligations Law § 5-701, subd. a, par. 2. *Worlock*, 617 N.Y.S.2d 87 (4 Dept., 1994)

maintain 1. To make repairs or perform upkeep tasks. 2. To bear the expenses for the support of. 3. To declare or affirm. 4. To continue or carry forward. 5. To involve oneself or meddle in another's lawsuit.

maintenance 1. Support or assistance. See also separate maintenance. 2. Keeping something in working order. 3. Becoming involved or meddling in someone else's lawsuit.

major dispute A dispute under the Railway Labor Act that relates to the formation or alteration of a collective bargaining agreement (45 USC § 155).

major federal action Projects that require an environmental impact statement because of their significant environmental effects.

majority 1. The age at which a person is entitled to the management of his or her own affairs and to the enjoyment of adult civil rights. 2. Greater than half of any total.

majority opinion The opinion in which more than half of the voting judges on the court joined.

make To formalize the creation of an instrument; to execute.

make law 1. To enact a law. To legislate. 2. To establish or expand upon a prior legal principle or rule in a court opinion.

maker One who signs a promissory note or other negotiable instrument.

make-whole rule An insurer cannot enforce subrogation rights against settlement funds until the insured is fully compensated (made whole). An insured who settles with a third-party tortfeasor is liable to the insurer-subrogee only for any excess received over the total amount of the insured's loss.

mala fides See bad faith (1).

mala in se See malum in se.

mala prohibita See malum prohibitum.

malefactor One who is guilty of a crime or offense. A wrongdoer.

malfeasance Wrongdoing, usually by a public official.

malice 1. The intentional doing of a wrongful act without just cause or excuse. 2. The intent to inflict injury; ill will. 3. Reckless or wanton disregard.

> In defamation action, malice, defined as personal spite or ill will, or culpable recklessness or negligence, refers not to defendant's general feelings about plaintiff, but to defendant's motivation for making defamatory statements. *Pezhman*, 812 N.Y.S.2d 14 (1 Dept., 2006)

malice aforethought 1. A fixed purpose or design to do some physical harm to another. 2. In a murder charge, the intention to kill, actual or implied, under circumstances that do not constitute excuse (e.g., insanity) or justification (e.g., self-defense) or mitigate the degree of the offense to manslaughter.

malice in fact See actual malice (1).

malice in law See implied malice.

malicious 1. Doing a wrongful act intentionally and without just cause or excuse. 2. Pertaining to conduct that is certain or almost certain to cause harm.

malicious mischief Intentional, wanton, or reckless damage or destruction of another's property. Also called criminal mischief.

malicious prosecution A tort with the following elements: (a) to initiate or procure the initiation of civil or criminal legal proceedings, (b) without probable cause, (c) with malice or an improper purpose, (d) the proceedings terminate in favor of the person against whom the proceedings were brought.

> Tort of malicious prosecution requires a showing of (1) the commencement or continuation of a criminal proceeding by defendant against plaintiff, (2) the termination of the proceeding in favor of plaintiff, (3) the absence of probable cause for the criminal proceeding, and (4) actual malice. *Nadeau*, 707 N.Y.S.2d 704 (3 Dept., 2000)

malpractice 1. The failure of a professional to exercise the degree of skill commonly applied under the circumstances by an ordinary, prudent, and reputable member of the profession in good standing. 2. Professional misconduct.

malum in se A wrong in itself; an act that is inherently and essentially evil and immoral in its nature (plural: mala in se).

malum prohibitum An act that is wrong because laws prohibit it; the act is not wrong in itself (plural: mala prohibita).

manager One who administers an organization or project.

managing agent A person given general powers to exercise judgment and discretion in dealing with matters entrusted to him or her.

mandamus A court order or writ to a public official to compel the performance of a ministerial act or a mandatory duty.

mandate 1. A court order, especially to a lower court. 2. To require. 3. An authorization to act.

mandatory Compulsory, obligatory.

mandatory injunction An injunction that requires an affirmative act or course of conduct.

Mandatory injunction, which is used to compel performance of act, is extraordinary and drastic remedy that is rarely granted and then only under unusual circumstances where such relief is essential to maintain status quo pending trial of action. *Matos*, 801 N.Y.S.2d 610 (2 Dept., 2005)

mandatory instruction An instruction to the jury that if it finds that a certain set of facts (laid out by the judge) exists, then it must reach a verdict for one party and against the other. Also called binding instruction.

mandatory sentence A sentence of incarceration that, by statute, must be served; the judge has no discretion to order alternatives.

manifest 1. Evident to the senses, especially to sight. 2. A list of a vehicle's cargo or passengers.

manifest necessity Extraordinary circumstances requiring a mistrial; a retrial can occur without violating principles of double jeopardy.

manifesto A formal, public statement declaring policies or intentions.

manifest weight of the evidence, against the As a standard of review, an opposite finding is clearly called for; the verdict is unreasonable, arbitrary, or not based on the evidence.

manipulation Activity designed to deceive investors by controlling or artificially affecting the price of securities, e.g., creating a misleading appearance of active trading. Also called stock manipulation.

Mann Act A federal statute making it a crime to transport someone in interstate or foreign commerce for prostitution or other sexually immoral purpose (18 USC § 2421).

manslaughter The unlawful killing of another without malice.

Manslaughter in the second degree is the reckless causing of the death of another under circumstances wherein the defendant perceives the risk of his act against the victim but recklessly disregards it; it still requires an intentional harming of the victim. Penal Law § 125.15. *People v. Walker*, 396 N.Y.S. 2d 121 (4 Dept., 1977)

manual 1. Made or performed with the hands. 2. A book with basic practical information or procedures.

manumission The act of liberating a slave from bondage.

Mapp **hearing** A hearing in a criminal case to determine whether seized evidence is admissible. *Mapp v. Ohio*, 81 S. Ct. 1684 (1961).

Marbury v. Madison The U.S. Supreme Court case that ruled that the courts can determine whether an act of Congress is constitutional. 5 U.S. 137 (1803).

margin 1. The edge or border. 2. An amount available beyond what is needed. 3. The difference between the cost and the selling price of a security. 4. An amount a buyer on credit must give to a securities broker to cover the broker's risk of loss. 5. The difference between the value of collateral securing a loan and the amount of the loan.

margin account An account allowing a client to borrow money from a securities broker in order to buy more stock, using the stock as collateral.

margin call A demand by a broker that a customer deposit additional collateral to cover broker-financed purchases of securities.

marijuana or **marihuana** A drug prepared from cannabis plant leaves.

marine insurance Insurance that covers hazards encountered in maritime transportation, including risks of river and inland navigation.

marital agreement 1. A contract between spouses. See also postnuptial agreement, separation agreement. 2. See premarital agreement.

marital communications privilege A spouse has a privilege to refuse to disclose and to prevent others from disclosing private or confidential communications between the spouses during the marriage. Also called husband-wife privilege, spousal privilege.

Not all communications between husband and wife are confidential communications protected by marital communications privilege, but rather, only those induced by marital relation and prompted by affection, confidence, and loyalty engendered by such relationship. McKinney's CPLR 4503(b). *People v. Smythe*, 620 N.Y.S.2d 647 (4 Dept., 1994)

marital deduction The amount of the federal estate and gift tax deduction allowed for transfers of property from one spouse to another (26 USC § 2056).

marital portion The part of a deceased spouse's estate that must be received by a surviving spouse.

marital property Property acquired by either spouse during the marriage that does not constitute separate property, plus any appreciation of separate property that occurs during the marriage. See also separate property.

The term marital property shall mean all property acquired by either or both spouses during the marriage and before the execution of a separation agreement or the commencement of a matrimonial action, regardless of the form in which title is held, except as otherwise provided in agreement pursuant to subdivision three of this part. Marital property shall not include separate property as hereinafter defined. McKinney's DRL § 236(c)

maritime Pertaining to the sea, navigable waters, and commerce thereon.

maritime contract A contract on ships, commerce, or navigation on navigable waters, transportation by sea, or maritime employment.

maritime law See admiralty.

mark 1. Language or symbols used to identify or distinguish one's product or service. Short for servicemark and trademark. 2. A substitute for the signature.

market 1. The place or geographic area where goods and services are bought and sold. 2. An exchange where securities or commodities are traded. 3. The geographical or economic extent of commercial demand.

marketable Capable of attracting buyers; fit to offer for sale.

marketable title A title that a reasonably prudent buyer, knowing all the facts, would be willing to accept.

A marketable title is title free from reasonable doubt, but not from every doubt. *Gateway Development and Mfg.*, 744 N.Y.S. 2d 778 (4 Dept., 2002)

market-maker Any "dealer who, with respect to a security, holds himself out (by entering quotations in an inter-dealer communications system or otherwise) as being willing to buy and sell such security for his own account on a regular or continuous basis." 15 USC § 78c(a)(38).

market order An order to buy or sell securities at the best price currently obtainable.

market price The prevailing price in a given market. The last reported price.

market share The percentage of total industry sales made by a particular company.

market value See fair market value.

mark up 1. The process by which a legislative committee puts a bill in its final form. 2. An increase in price, usually to derive profit.

marriage 1. The legal union of one man and one woman (or in some states, of two persons of the same sex) as husband and wife. 2. The status of being a married couple.

For purposes of determining scope of statutes establishing and limiting right to enter into civil marriage contract, term marriage was defined by tradition, judicial precedent, dictionaries, and common usage as union between persons of opposite sexes. McKinney's DRL §§ 10, 13, 15, 15, subd. 2. *Shields*, 783 N.Y.S.2d 270 (Sup. Ct., 2004)

marriage certificate The document filed by the person performing a marriage ceremony containing evidence that the ceremony took place.

marriage license The document (issued by the government) giving a couple authorization to be married.

marriage settlement See premarital agreement, separation agreement.

marshal 1. A federal judicial officer (U.S. Marshal) who executes court orders, helps maintain security, and performs other duties for the court. 2. A local police or fire department official.

marshaling 1. Arranging, ranking by priority, or disposing in order. 2. An equitable principle compelling a senior creditor to attempt to collect its claim first from another source that is unavailable to a junior creditor.

Equitable rule of "marshaling assets" is that where one claimant has two funds to which he may resort to answer his demand, and another claimant has interest in only one of such funds, he can compel former to take satisfaction out of fund in which latter has no lien. *In re Creem's Will*, 147 N.Y.S. 2d 634 (Sur., 1955)

martial law Rule (or rules) imposed by military authorities over civilian matters.

Martindale-Hubbell Law Directory A set of books that contain a state-by-state list of attorneys and a digest of state and foreign laws. Also available online.

***Mary Carter* agreement** A contract in which one or more defendants (a) agree to remain in the case, (b) guarantee the plaintiff a certain minimum monetary recovery regardless of the outcome of the lawsuit, and (c) have their liability reduced in direct proportion to the increase in the liability of the nonagreeing defendants. *Booth v. Mary Carter Paint Co.*, 202 So. 2d 8 (Fla. Dist. Ct. App., 1967).

mass picketing Picketing in large numbers, usually obstructing the ingress and egress of the target's employees, customers, or suppliers.

Massachusetts trust See business trust.

master 1. An employer. A principal who hires others and who controls or has the right to control their physical conduct in the performance of their service. 2. An officer appointed by the court to assist it in specific judicial duties (e.g., take testimony). Also called special master. 3. One who has reached the summit of his or her trade, and who has the right to hire apprentices and journeymen. 4. Main or central.

master agreement A labor agreement at one company that becomes the pattern for agreements in an entire industry.

master and servant An employer-employee relationship in which the employer reserves the right to control the manner or means of doing the work.

Relationship of master and servant in the judicial sense exists only where alleged master has right to direct person alleged to be his servant, such right to direct involving a right not only to order the doing of an act but also to control the manner in which it is to be done. *Zimmerman*, 276 N.Y.S.2d 711 (Sup. Ct., 1966)

master deed The major condominium document that will govern individual condominium units within a condominium complex.

master in chancery An officer in a court of equity who acts as an assistant to the judge in tasks such as taking testimony.

master limited partnership A limited partnership whose ownership interest is publicly traded.

master of laws (LL.M.) An advanced law degree earned after obtaining a Juris Doctor (J.D.) degree.

master plan A comprehensive land-use plan for the development of an area.

master policy An insurance policy that covers a group of persons, e.g., health or life insurance written as group insurance.

material 1. Essential, important, or relevant; having influence or effect. 2. Pertaining to concrete, physical matter.

A misrepresentation is "material," so as to warrant rescission of an insurance policy, if the insurer would not have issued the policy had it known the facts misrepresented. McKinney's Insurance Law § 3105(b). *Zilkha*, 732 N.Y.S.2d 51 (2 Dept., 2001)

material allegation An allegation that is essential to a claim or defense.

material alteration A change in a document or instrument that alters its meaning or effect.

material breach A failure to perform a substantial part of a contract, justifying rescission or other remedy.

material evidence Relevant evidence a reasonable mind might accept.

material fact An influential fact; a fact that will affect the result.

material issue An important issue the parties need to resolve.

materialman One who furnishes materials (supplies) for construction or repair work.

Materialman. The term "materialman" when used in this chapter, means any person who furnishes material or the use of machinery, tools, or equipment, or compressed gases for welding or cutting, or fuel or lubricants for the operation of machinery or motor vehicles, either to an owner, contractor or subcontractor, for, or in the prosecution of such improvement. McKinney's Lien Law § 2(12)

material witness A witness who can give testimony on a fact affecting the merits of the case.

maternal Pertaining to, belonging to, or coming from the mother.

matricide The killing of one's mother.

matrimonial action A divorce, annulment, or other proceeding pertaining to the status of a marriage.

matter 1. A case or dispute; the subject for which representation is sought. 2. Something that a tribunal can examine or establish.

matter in controversy 1. The subject of litigation. 2. The amount of damages sought.

matter of See in re.

matter of fact A subject involving the truth or falsity of a fact.

matter of law A subject involving the interpretation or application of the law. See also judgment as a matter of law.

matter of record Pertaining to a subject that is part of or within an official record.

mature Due or ripe for payment, owing; developed, complete.

maxim A principle; a general statement of a rule or a truth.

mayhem The crime of depriving another of a limb or of disabling, disfiguring, or rendering it useless, especially for self-defense.

MBE Multistate bar examination.

McNabb-Mallory rule Confessions or incriminating statements can be excluded from evidence if obtained during a period of unnecessary delay in taking the accused before a magistrate. *McNabb*, 63 S. Ct. 608 (1943); *Mallory*, 77 S. Ct. 1356 (1957).

McNaghten rule See insanity (4).

M.D. 1. Middle District. 2. Doctor of medicine.

MDL See multidistrict litigation.

MDP See multidisciplinary practice.

mean high tide The average height of all the high waters (tides) over a complete or regular tidal cycle of 18.6 years.

means 1. That which is used to attain an end. A cause. 2. Assets or available resources.

means test The determination of eligibility for a public benefit based on one's financial resources.

mechanic's lien A right or interest in real or personal property (in the nature of an encumbrance) that secures payment for the performance of labor or the supply of

materials to maintain or improve the property. Also called artisan's lien.

"Mechanics' lien" is statutory creature, fashioned by Legislature to protect those who, by their labor and materials, enhance value of real property. McKinney's Lien Law §§ 3, 4. *Niagara Venture*, 565 N.Y.S.2d 449 (Ct. of App., 1990)

mediation A method of alternate dispute resolution (ADR) in which the parties submit a dispute to a neutral third person (the mediator) who helps the parties resolve their dispute without litigation; he or she does not render a decision resolving it for them.

mediator See mediation.

Medicaid A federal-state public assistance program that furnishes health care to people who cannot afford it.

medical examiner A public officer who conducts autopsies and otherwise helps in the investigation and prosecution of death cases.

Medicare A federal program of medical insurance for the elderly.

meeting of creditors A bankruptcy hearing or meeting in which creditors can examine the debtor.

meeting of the minds Mutual agreement and assent of the parties to the substance and terms of their contract.

Megan's law A state law (named in honor of a victim) requiring the registration of sex offenders and a method of notifying the community when they move into an area. Also called community notification law.

This article shall be known and may be cited as the "Sex Offender Registration Act." McKinney's Correction Law § 168. The division shall establish and maintain a file of individuals required to register pursuant to the provisions of this article which shall include the following information of each registrant: (a) The sex offender's name, all aliases used, date of birth, sex, race, height, weight, eye color, driver's license number, home address and/or expected place of domicile, any internet accounts belonging to such offender and any internet screen names used by such offender. McKinney's Correction Law § 168-b(1)

memorandum (memo) 1. A written statement or note that is often brief and informal. 2. A brief record of a transaction or occurrence. 3. A written analysis of how the law applies to a given set of facts.

memorandum decision (mem.) The decision of a court with few or no supporting reasons, often because it follows established principles. Also called memorandum opinion.

memorandum of points and authorities A document submitted to a trial court that makes arguments with supporting authorities for something a party wishes to do, e.g., have a motion granted.

memorial 1. A statement of facts in a petition or demand to the legislature or to the executive. 2. A summary or abstract of a record.

memorialize To put in writing, e.g., to memorialize a phone conversation by writing a confirming letter based on the call.

mensa et thoro Bed and board. See also legal separation.

mens rea A guilty mind that produces the act. The unlawful intent or recklessness that must be proved for crimes that are not strict liability offenses.

Intent is a purpose or objective fixed in the mind. Knowledge is the perception of the mind as to facts. Intent and knowledge constitute the mens rea (evil intent or guilty mind) of a crime while the physical act or conduct constitutes the actus reus (act of the person). *People v. Tracey A.*, 413 N.Y.S.2d 92 (Co. Ct., 1979)

mental anguish See emotional distress.

mental cruelty Conduct causing distress that endangers the mental and physical health of a spouse (a fault ground for divorce).

Grounds for divorce include "the cruel and inhuman treatment of the plaintiff by the defendant such that the conduct of the defendant so endangers the physical or mental well-being of the plaintiff as renders it unsafe or improper for the plaintiff to cohabit with the defendant." McKinney's DRL §170(1)

mental defect or **disease** See insanity (2) and (3).

mental distress; mental suffering See emotional distress.

mercantile Commercial; involving the business of merchants.

merchant A person in the business of purchasing and selling goods.

merchantable Fit for the ordinary purposes for which the goods are used. The noun is *merchantability*.

mercy killing See euthanasia.

meretricious Involving vulgarity, unlawful sexual relations, or insincerity.

merger 1. The fusion or absorption of one duty, right, claim, offense, estate, or property into another. 2. The absorption of one company by another. The absorbed company ceases to exist as a separate entity.

merger clause See integration clause.

meritorious Legally plausible. Having merit; not frivolous.

merits See on the merits.

mesne Intermediate; occurring between two periods or ranks.

mesne process Any writ or process issued between commencement of the action and execution of the judgment.

mesne profits Profits accruing between two periods while held by one in wrongful possession.

The "mesne profits" from land consist of net rents after deducting all necessary repairs and taxes, net rental value, or value of use and occupation of land. *Mercy*, 142 N.Y.S.2d 549 (Sup. Ct., 1955)

messuage A dwelling house, its outbuildings, and surrounding land.

metes and bounds A system of describing the boundary lines of land beginning at a fixed point and then describing each boundary by exact distance and direction in relation to landmarks and adjoining land.

metropolitan Pertaining to a city and its suburbs.

Mexican divorce A divorce granted by a court in Mexico by mail order or when neither spouse was domiciled there.

migratory divorce A divorce obtained in a state to which one or both spouses briefly traveled before returning to their original state.

military commission A military court for violations of martial law.

military government A government in which civil or political power is under the control of the military.

military jurisdiction Jurisdiction of the military in the areas of military law, military government, and martial law.

military law A system of laws governing the armed forces.

military will; military testament A will that may be valid even if it does not comply with required formalities when made by someone in military service. Also called sailor's will, seaman's will, soldier's will.

Certain oral statements made by decedent while in active military service were entitled to probate as a nuncupative military testament. *In re Mallery's Will*, 161 N.E. 190 (Ct. of App., 1928)

militia A citizen military force not part of the regular military.

mill One-tenth of one cent.

mineral A lifeless substance formed or deposited through natural processes and found either in or upon the soil or in the rocks beneath the soil.

mineral lease A contract or other form of authorization to explore, develop, or remove deposits of oil, gas, or other minerals. A mining lease allows such activity in a mine or mining claim.

mineral right The right to explore for and remove minerals, with or without ownership of the surface of the land.

miner's inch A unit for measuring water flow through a hole one-inch square in a miner's box (about nine gallons a minute).

minimal diversity A plaintiff is a citizen of one state and at least one of the defendants is a citizen of another state.

minimum contacts Purposely availing oneself of the privilege of conducting activities within a state, thus invoking the benefits and protections of its laws. (Basis of personal jurisdiction over a nonresident.)

minimum-fee schedule A bar association list of the lowest fees an attorney can charge for designated legal services. Such lists violate antitrust law.

minimum wage The lowest allowable wage certain employers may pay.

mining lease See mineral lease.

minister 1. An agent; one acting on behalf of another. 2. An administrator in charge of a government department. 3. A diplomatic representative or officer.

ministerial Involving a duty that is to be performed in a prescribed manner without the exercise of judgment or discretion.

"Discretionary act" that cannot be compelled in mandamus proceeding involves the exercise of reasoned judgment which could typically produce different acceptable results, whereas a "ministerial act" envisions direct adherence to a governing rule or standard with a compulsory result. McKinney's CPLR 7803, subd. 1. *New York Civil Liberties Union*, 791 N.Y.S.2d 507 (Ct. of App., 2005)

ministry The duties or functions of a religious minister.

minitrial An abbreviated presentation of each side's case that the parties agree to make to each other and to a private, neutral third party, followed by discussions that seek a negotiated settlement. An example of alternative dispute resolution.

minor A person under the legal age, often 18. One who has not reached the age of majority.

> For the purposes of this section, the word "minor" shall mean a person under eighteen years of age, but does not include a person who is the parent of a child or has married or who is emancipated. McKinney's Mental Hygiene Law § 22.11(a)

minority 1. The status of being below the minimum age to enter a desired relationship (e.g., marriage) or perform a particular task. Also called infancy, nonage. 2. The smaller number. 3. A group of persons of the same race, gender, or other trait that differs from the dominant or majority group in society and that is often the victim of discrimination.

minority opinion An opinion of one or more justices that disagrees with the majority opinion. It is often a dissenting opinion.

minority shareholder Any shareholder who owns or controls less than 50 percent of the voting shares of a corporation.

minute book The book maintained by the court clerk containing a record (the minutes) of court proceedings.

minutes A record of what occurred at a meeting.

Miranda warnings Prior to any custodial interrogation, a person must be warned that: (a) he or she has a right to remain silent, (b) any statement made can be used as evidence against him or her, and (c) he or she has the right to his or her own attorney or one provided at government expense. *Miranda v. Arizona*, 86 S. Ct. 1602 (1966).

Mirandize To give a suspect the *Miranda* warnings.

misadventure An accident or misfortune (e.g., killing), often occurring while performing a lawful act.

misapplication The wrongful use of legally possessed assets.

misappropriate To take wrongfully; to use someone else's property to one's own advantage without permission. See also appropriation (2).

misbranding The use of a label that is false or misleading.

miscarriage of justice A fundamentally unfair result.

miscegenation Marriage between persons of different races.

mischarge An erroneous charge to a jury.

mischief 1. Conduct that causes discomfort, hardship, or harm. 2. The evil or danger that a statute is intended to cure or avoid.

misconduct Wrongdoing; a breach of one's duty.

> "Misconduct," for purposes of unemployment insurance benefits, is a willful and wanton disregard of the employer's interest. *In re Pfohl*, 779 N.Y.S.2d 831 (3 Dept., 2004)

misdelivery Delivery of mail or goods to someone other than the specified or authorized recipient.

misdemeanant A person convicted of a misdemeanor.

misdemeanor A crime, not as serious as a felony, punishable by fine or by detention in an institution other than a prison or penitentiary.

> Designation of offenses. Misdemeanors. (a) Each misdemeanor defined in this chapter is either a class A misdemeanor or a class B misdemeanor, as expressly designated in the section or article defining it. (b) Any offense defined outside this chapter which is declared by law to be a misdemeanor without specification of the classification thereof or of the sentence therefor shall be deemed a class A misdemeanor. (c) Except as provided in paragraph (b) of subdivision three, where an offense is defined outside this chapter and a sentence

to a term of imprisonment in excess of fifteen days but not in excess of one year is provided in the law or ordinance defining it, such offense shall be deemed an unclassified misdemeanor. McKinney's Penal Law § 55.10(2)

misdemeanor-manslaughter The unintentional killing of a human being while committing a misdemeanor.

misfeasance Improper performance of an otherwise lawful act.

misjoinder Improper joining of parties, causes of action, or offenses.

mislay To forget where you placed something you intended to retrieve.

misleading Leading one astray or into error, often intentionally.

misprision 1. Nonperformance of a duty by a public official. 2. A nonparticipant's concealment or failure to disclose a crime. Misprision of felony occurs when the crime involved is a felony.

misrepresentation 1. Any untrue statement of fact. 2. A false statement of fact made with the intent to deceive. Also called false representation. See also fraud.

> A failure to disclose in response to a particular question on application for insurance policy is as much a "misrepresentation," for purposes of entitling insurer to rescind, as is a disclosure that is a mistruth or a half truth. *Fernandez*, 372 N.Y.S.2d 357 (Sup. Ct., 1975)

mistake An unintentional act, omission, or error arising from ignorance, surprise, imposition, or misplaced confidence.

mistake of fact 1. An unconscious ignorance or forgetfulness of the existence or nonexistence of a material fact, past or present. 2. An honest and reasonable belief in the existence of circumstances, which, if true, would make the act for which the person is indicted an innocent act.

mistake of law A misunderstanding about legal requirements or consequences.

mistrial A trial terminated before its normal conclusion because of unusual circumstances, misconduct, procedural error, or jury deadlock.

mitigate To render less painful or severe.

mitigating circumstances Facts that can be considered as reducing the severity or degree of moral culpability of an act, but do not excuse or justify it. Also called extenuating circumstances.

> Criminal Procedure Law 400.27(9)(b) provides the following definition of a mitigating factor: "The defendant was mentally retarded at the time of the crime, or the defendant's mental capacity was impaired or his ability to conform his conduct to the requirements of law was impaired but not so impaired in either case as to constitute a defense to prosecution." *People v. Bell*, 695 N.Y.S.2d 242 (Sup. Ct., 1999)

mitigation-of-damages rule An injured party has a duty to use reasonable diligence to try to minimize his or her damages after the wrong has been inflicted. Also called avoidable consequences.

mittimus 1. An order commanding that a person be detained in or conveyed to a prison. 2. An order for the transfer of records between courts.

mixed nuisance A nuisance that injures the public at large and also does some special damage to an individual or class of individuals.

mixed question of law and fact An issue involving the application of the law to the facts when the facts and the legal standards are not in dispute.

M'Naghten **rule** See insanity (4).

MO See modus operandi.

model act A statute proposed to all state legislatures for adoption.

Model Penal Code A proposed criminal law code of the American Law Institute. For its test for insanity, see insanity (2).

Model Rules of Professional Conduct The current ethical rules for attorneys recommended to the states by the American Bar Association.

modification An alteration or change; a new qualification.
Partial alteration by limiting or reducing in extent or degree. *Carpenter*, 49 N.Y.S.2d 702 (Co. Ct., 1944)

Modified Accelerated Cost Recovery System (MACRS) A method to calculate the depreciation tax deduction over a shorter period.

modus Manner or method.

modus operandi (MO) A method of doing things, e.g., a criminal's MO.

moiety 1. One-half. 2. A portion or part.

molest 1. To abuse sexually. 2. To disturb or harass.

money 1. Coins and paper currency or other legal medium of exchange. 2. Assets that are readily convertible into cash.

money demand A claim for a specific dollar amount.

money had and received An action to prevent unjust enrichment when one person obtains money that in good conscience belongs to another.

money judgment The part of a judgment that requires paying money (damages).

money laundering See laundering.

money market The financial market for dealing in short-term financial obligations such as commercial paper and treasury bills.

money order A type of negotiable draft purchased from an organization such as the Postal Service and used as a substitute for a check.

money supply The total amount of money circulating and on deposit in the economy.

monition 1. A summons to appear in an admiralty case. 2. A warning.

monopoly A market where there is a concentration of a product or service in the hands of a few, thereby controlling prices or limiting competition. A power to control prices or exclude competition.
Where the sale of any merchandise or commodity is restrained to one, or to a certain number; a monopoly has three inseparable consequences: The increase of the price, the badness of the wares, and the impoverishment of others. *Larned*, 44 N.Y.S. 857 (4 Dept., 1897)

month to month tenancy A lease without a fixed duration that can be terminated on short notice, e.g., a month. See also periodic tenancy.

monument Natural or artificial boundary markers or objects on land.

moot 1. Pertaining to a nonexistent controversy where the issues have ceased to exist from a practical point of view. 2. Subject to debate.

moot case A case that seeks to resolve an abstract question that does not rest upon existing facts.

moot court A simulated court where law students argue a hypothetical case for purposes of learning and competition.

moral 1. Pertaining to conscience or to general principles of right conduct. 2. Pertaining to a duty binding in conscience but not in law. 3. Demonstrating correct character or behavior.

moral certainty A very high degree of probability although not demonstrable to an absolute certainty. Beyond a reasonable doubt.
Phrase "to a moral certainty" contained in oft-stated rule applicable in circumstantial evidence cases does not impose upon the People a greater burden of proof than traditional "beyond a reasonable doubt" foundation, but merely draws attention to rigorous function which must be undertaken by finder of fact when presented with case of purely circumstantial evidence. *People v. Burton*, 623 N.Y.S.2d 347 (3 Dept., 1995)

moral consideration See good consideration.

moral evidence Evidence based on belief or the general observations of people rather than on what is absolutely demonstrable.

moral hazard The risk or probability that an insured will destroy the insured property or permit it to be destroyed to collect on the insurance.

moral right A right of integrity enjoyed by the creator of a work even if someone else now owns the copyright. Examples include the right to be acknowledged as the creator and to insist that the work not be distorted.

moral turpitude Conduct that is dishonest or contrary to moral rules.

moratorium Temporary suspension. A period of delay.

more or less An approximation; slightly larger or smaller.

morgue A place where dead persons are kept for identification or until burial arrangements are made.

mortality tables A guide used to predict life expectancy based on factors such as a person's age and sex.

mortgage An interest in property created by a written instrument providing security for the performance of a duty or the payment of a debt. A lien or claim against property given by the buyer to the lender as security for the money borrowed.
"Mortgage" is any conveyance of land intended by the parties at the time of making it to be a security for the payment of money or the doing of some prescribed act. *CitiFinancial Co.*, 811 N.Y.S.2d 359 (1 Dept., 2006)

mortgage bond A bond for which real estate or personal property is pledged as security that the bond will be paid as stated in its terms.

mortgage certificate Document evidencing one's ownership share in a mortgage.

mortgage commitment A written notice from a lending institution that it will advance mortgage funds for the purchase of specified property.

mortgage company A company that makes mortgage loans, which it then sells to investors.

mortgagee A lender to whom property is mortgaged.

mortgage market The existing supply and demand for mortgages, including their resale. Rates and terms being offered by competing mortgagees.

mortgagor The debtor who mortgages his or her property; one who gives legal title or a lien to the mortgagee to secure the mortgage loan.

mortis causa See causa mortis.

mortmain statute A statute that restricts one's right to transfer property to institutions such as churches that would hold it forever.

> Mortmain statutes are not based on any hostility to charities but rather on intent to prohibit improvident and unjust wills which deprive relatives and dependents of the testator of proper consideration in the distribution of the estate. EPTL 5-3.3. *Matter of Eckart's Estate*, 384 N.Y.S.2d 429 (Ct. of App., 1976)

most favored nation clause (MFN) A treaty promise that each side will grant to the other the broadest rights that it gives any other nation.

motion An application for an order or ruling from a court or other decision-making body.

motion for a more definite statement A request that the court order the other side to make its pleading more definite, since it is so vague or ambiguous that one cannot frame a responsive pleading.

motion in limine A request for a ruling (often on the admissibility of evidence) prior to the trial or at a preliminary time during the trial.

motion to dismiss A request, usually made before the trial begins, that the judge dismiss the case because of lack of jurisdiction, insufficiency of the pleadings, or the reaching of a settlement.

motion to strike A request that the court remove specific statements, claims, or evidence from the pleadings or the record.

motion to suppress A request that the court exclude from a criminal trial any illegally secured evidence.

motive A cause or reason that moves the will and induces action or inaction.

> Motive means the reason why a thing is done. *People v. Feldman*, 85 N.E. 2d 913 (Ct. of App., 1949)

movables Things that can be carried from one place to another. Personal property.

movant One who makes a motion or applies for a ruling or order.

move To make an application or request for an order or ruling.

moving papers Papers or documents submitted in support of a motion.

mug 1. To criminally assault someone, often with the intent to rob. 2. A human face. A mug shot is a photograph of a suspect's face.

mulct 1. A penalty or punishment such as a fine. 2. To defraud a person of something.

mulier 1. A woman; a wife. 2. A son who is legitimate.

multidisciplinary practice (MDP) A partnership of attorneys and nonattorney professionals that offers legal and nonlegal services.

multidistrict litigation (MDL) Civil actions with common questions of fact pending in different federal district courts that are transferred to one district solely for consolidated pretrial proceedings under a single judge before returning to their original district courts.

multifarious 1. Improperly joined claims, instructions, or parties. 2. Diverse.

multilateral agreement An agreement among three or more parties.

multiple access The defense in a paternity case that more than one lover had access to the mother during the time of conception.

multiple listing An arrangement among real estate agents whereby any member agent can sell property listed by another agent. The latter shares the fee or commission with the broker who made the sale.

multiplicity 1. A large number or variety of matters or particulars. 2. The improper charging of a single offense in several counts.

multiplicity of actions Several attempts to litigate the same right or issue against the same defendant.

> CPLR § 602(a) states: "[w]hen actions involving a common question of law or fact are pending before a court, the court, upon motion, may order a joint trial of any or all the matters in issue, may order the actions consolidated, and may make such other orders concerning proceedings therein as may tend to avoid unnecessary costs or delay. . . ." This section setting forth the power of a court, upon motion, to consolidate and/or order a joint trial of actions, expresses the modern view of joinder as a means of eliminating multiplicity of actions, trial delay, and expenses of litigation. *Mars Associates*, 513 N.Y.S.2d 125 (1 Dept., 1987)

municipal 1. Pertaining to a city, town, or other local unit of government. 2. Pertaining to a state or nation.

municipal bond A bond or other debt instrument issued by a state or local unit of government to fund public projects. Also called municipal security.

municipal corporation A city, county, village, town, or other local governmental body established to run all or part of local government. Also called municipality.

> Two types of municipal subdivisions exercise kind of governmental powers warranting delegation of power to tax: municipal corporations and district corporations; "municipal corporation" is county, city, town, village, or school district, while "district corporation" is any other territorial division of state which possesses power to contract indebtedness and levy taxes or benefit assessments upon real estate or to require levy of such taxes or assessments, and fire districts and certain conservation districts may be granted powers of district corporation. McKinney's Const. Art. 8, § 3; McKinney's General Construction Law § 66, subds. 2, 3. *Greater Poughkeepsie Library Dist.*, 601 N.Y.S.2d 94 (Ct. of App., 1993)

municipal court An inferior court with jurisdiction over relatively small claims or offenses arising within the local area where it sits.

municipal ordinance See ordinance.

municipality 1. The body of officials elected or appointed to administer a local government. 2. See municipal corporation.

municipal securities See municipal bond.

muniment of title A document (e.g., a deed) presented as evidence or proof of title.

muniments Documents used to defend one's title or other claim.

murder The unlawful, premeditated killing of a human being.

A person is guilty of murder in the first degree when: 1. With intent to cause the death of another person, he causes the death of such person or of a third person; and (a) Either: (i) the intended victim was a police officer . . . or (vii) the victim was killed while the defendant was in the course of committing or attempting to commit and in furtherance of robbery, burglary in the first degree or second degree, kidnapping in the first degree, . . . McKinney's Penal Law § 125.27

mutatis mutandis With the necessary changes in any of the details.

mutilate 1. To maim, to dismember, to disfigure someone. 2. To alter or deface a document by cutting, tearing, burning, or erasing, without totally destroying it.

mutiny An insurrection or uprising of seamen or soldiers against the authority of their commanders.

mutual Reciprocal, common to both parties. In the same relationship to each other.

mutual company A company owned by its clients or customers.

mutual fund An investment company with a pool of assets, consisting primarily of portfolio securities, and belonging to the individual investors holding shares in the fund.

mutual insurance company An insurance company that has no capital stock and in which the policyholders are the owners.

mutuality An action by each of two parties; reciprocation; both sides being bound.

mutuality of contract; mutuality of obligation 1. Liability or obligation imposed on both parties under the terms of the agreement. 2. Unless both sides are bound, neither is bound.

mutual mistake A mistake common to both parties wherein each labors under a misconception respecting the terms of the agreement. Both contracting parties misunderstand the fundamental subject matter or term of the contract. Mistake of both parties on the same fact. Also called bilateral mistake.

"Mutual mistake," warranting reformation, occurs when a signed writing does not accurately express the agreement of the parties. *K.I.D.E. Associates*, 720 N.Y.S.2d 114 (1 Dept., 2001)

mutual wills 1. Separate wills made by two persons, which are reciprocal in their provisions and by which each testator makes testamentary disposition in favor of the other. Also called double will, reciprocal will. 2. Wills executed pursuant to an agreement between testators to dispose of their property in a particular manner, each in consideration of the other.

N

naked licensee See bare licensee.

naked power A mere authority to act, not accompanied by any interest of the holder of the power in the subject-matter of the power.

naked trust See passive trust.

NALA See National Association of Legal Assistants (*www.nala.org*).

NALS See National Association of Legal Secretaries, now called NALS, the Association for Legal Professionals (*www.nals.org*).

named insured The person specifically mentioned in an insurance policy as the one protected by the insurance.

Napoleonic Code See code civil.

narcotic Any addictive drug that dulls the senses or induces sleep.

Narcotic drug means any controlled substance listed in schedule I(b), I(c), II(b) or II(c) other than methadone. McKinney's Penal Law § 220.00(7)

National Association of Legal Assistants (NALA) A national association of paralegals (*www.nala.org*).

National Association of Legal Secretaries A national association of legal secretaries and paralegals, now called NALS, the Association for Legal Professionals (*www.nals.org*).

national bank A bank incorporated under federal law.

National Federation of Paralegal Associations (NFPA) A national association of paralegals (*www.paralegals.org*).

nationality The status that arises as a result of a person's belonging to a nation because of birth or naturalization.

nationalization The acquisition and control of privately owned businesses by the government.

Native American A member of the indigenous peoples of North, South, and Central America.

natural affection The affection that naturally exists between parent and child and among other close relatives.

natural death Death not caused by accidental or intentional injury.

natural heirs Next of kin by blood (consanguinity) as distinguished from collateral heirs or those related by adoption.

naturalization The process by which a person acquires citizenship after birth.

natural law A system of rules and principles (not created by human authority) discoverable by our rational intelligence as growing out of and conforming to human nature.

natural monument Boundary markers or objects on land that are not artificial.

natural object of bounty Descendants, surviving spouse, and other close relatives who are assumed to become recipients of the estate of a decedent.

natural person A human being. See also artificial person.

natural right A right based on natural law.

navigable water A body of water over which commerce can be carried on.

Generally, if body of water may be put to a public transportation and commercial use, it is "navigable." *City of Albany*, 335 N.Y.S.2d 975 (Ct. Cl., 1972)

navigation The art, science, or business of traveling the sea or other navigable waters in ships or vessels.

N.B. (nota bene) Note well, take notice, attention.

necessaries 1. The basic items needed by family members to maintain a standard of living. 2. Food, medicine, clothing, shelter, or personal services usually considered reasonably essential for preservation and enjoyment of life. 3. Goods or services reasonably needed in a ship's business for a vessel's continued operation.

Long-standing common law holds that legal services rendered for a wife or child are considered "necessaries" for which a husband or father may be held liable. *Merrick*, 622 N.Y.S.2d 852 (Sup. Ct., 1995)

necessary 1. Essential. 2. Logically true.

Necessary and Proper Clause The clause in the U.S. Constitution (art. I, § 8, cl. 18) giving Congress the power to enact laws that are needed to carry out its enumerated powers.

necessary party A party with a legal or beneficial interest in the subject matter of the lawsuit and who should be joined if feasible.

necessity 1. A privilege to make reasonable use of someone's property to prevent immediate harm or damage to person or property. 2. See choice of evils. 3. Something necessary or indispensable.

ne exeat A writ that forbids a person from leaving the country, state, or jurisdiction of the court.

negative act Not acting when a duty to act exists.

negative averment An allegation of a fact that must be proved by the alleging party even though the allegation is phrased in the negative.

negative covenant A promise not to do or perform some act.

negative easement An easement that precludes the owner of land subject to the easement (the servient estate) from doing an act which would otherwise be lawful.

A "negative easement" is one which restrains a landowner from making certain use of his land which he might otherwise have lawfully done but for that restriction and such easements arise principally by express grant or by implication. *Huggins*, 369 N.Y.S.2d 80 (Ct. of App., 1975)

negative evidence Testimony or other evidence about what did not happen or does not exist.

negative pregnant A negative statement that also implies an affirmative statement or admission (e.g., "I deny that I owe $500" may be an admission that at least some amount is owed).

neglect 1. The failure to perform an act one has a duty to perform. 2. Carelessness. See also child neglect.

negligence Harm or damage caused by not doing what a reasonably prudent person would have done under like circumstances. A tort with the following elements: (a) a duty of reasonable care, (b) a breach of this duty, (c) proximate cause, (d) actual damages.

Negligence is conduct that falls below the standard established by law for protection of others against unreasonable risk and necessarily involves a foreseeable risk, a threatened danger of injury, and conduct unreasonable in proportion to the danger. *Morris*, 302 N.Y.S.2d 51 (3 Dept., 1969)

negligence per se Negligence as a matter of law when violating a statute that defines the standard of care.

negligent Unreasonably careless. See also neglect, negligence.

negligent entrustment Creating an unreasonable risk of harm by carelessly allowing someone to use a dangerous object, e.g., a car.

negligent homicide Death due to the failure to perceive a substantial and unjustifiable risk that one's conduct will cause the death of another person.

negligent infliction of emotional distress (NIED) Carelessly causing someone to suffer substantial emotional distress.

negotiability words Words that make an instrument negotiable, e.g., "to the order of."

negotiable 1. Legally capable of being transferred by indorsement or delivery. See also negotiation (1). 2. Open to compromise.

negotiable bill of lading A bill of lading that requires delivery of goods to the bearer of the bill or, if to the order of a named person, to that person.

negotiable instrument Any writing (a) signed by the maker or drawer, (b) containing an unconditional promise or order to pay a sum certain in money, (c) payable on demand or at a definite time, and (d) payable to order or to bearer. UCC § 3-104(a).

Where note required payment of certain sums in monthly installments, but provided that in case of the death of the maker, all payments not due at date of death should be cancelled, the note was not a "negotiable instrument" for lack of unconditional promise to pay a sum certain, and defenses of general denial, breach of warranty and breach of agreement lay against holder of note. *Reserve Plan*, 145 N.Y.S.2d 122 (Mun. Ct. 1955)

negotiate 1. To bargain with another concerning a sale, settlement, or matter in contention. 2. To transfer by delivery or indorsement. See also negotiation (1).

negotiated plea See plea bargaining.

negotiation 1. The transfer of an instrument through delivery (if the instrument is payable to bearer), or through indorsement and delivery (if it is payable to order) in such form that the transferee becomes a holder. 2. The process of submitting and considering offers.

nemo est supra leges No one is above the law.

nepotism Granting privileges or patronage to one's relatives.

net The amount that remains after all allowable deductions.

net assets See net worth.

net asset value (NAV) The per share value of a company or mutual fund measured by its assets less debts divided by the number of shares.

net estate The portion of a probate estate remaining after all allowable deductions and adjustments.

net income 1. Revenues and gains less expenses and losses. 2. Income subject to taxation after allowable deductions and exemptions have been subtracted from gross or total income.

Net income means the total receipts allocated to income during an accounting period minus the disbursements made from income during the period, plus or minus transfers under this article or under subparagraph 11-2.3(b)(5) to or from income during the period. McKinney's EPTL § 11-A-1.2(8)

net lease A lease in which the tenant pays not only rent, but also items such as taxes, insurance, and maintenance charges.

net listing A listing in which the amount of real estate commission is the difference between the selling price of the property and a minimum price set by the seller.

net operating loss (NOL) 1. The excess of expenses and losses over revenues and gains. 2. The excess of allowable deductions over gross income.

net premium 1. The amount of an insurance premium less expenses such as commission. 2. The amount required by an insurer to cover the expected cost of paying benefits.

net weight The weight of an article after deducting the weight of the box or other wrapping.

net worth The total assets of a person or business less the total liabilities. Also called net assets, net equity, owners' equity, or stockholders' equity.

> The net worth of a business is the remainder after deduction of liabilities from assets. *Castelli*, 83 N.Y.S.2d 554 (Sup. Ct., 1948)

net worth method To reconstruct the income of a taxpayer, the IRS compares his or her net worth at the beginning and end of the tax year and makes adjustments for personal expenses and allowable deductions.

neutral Not taking an active part with either of the contending sides; disinterested, unbiased.

neutrality laws Acts of Congress that forbid military assistance to either of two belligerent powers with which we are at peace.

ne varietur It must not be altered (a notary's inscription).

new and useful For an invention to be patented, it must be novel and provide some practical benefit.

newly discovered evidence Evidence discovered after the trial and not discoverable before the trial by the exercise of due diligence.

new matter In pleading, a fact not previously alleged by either party in the pleadings.

newsman's privilege See journalist's privilege.

new trial Another trial of all or some of the same issues that were resolved by judgment in a prior trial.

new value Newly given money or money's worth in goods, services, new credit, or release by a transferee of property previously transferred (11 USC § 547(a)(2)).

> New value means (i) money, (ii) money's worth in property, services, or new credit, or (iii) release by a transferee of an interest in property previously transferred to the transferee. The term does not include an obligation substituted for another obligation. McKinney's Uniform Commercial Code § 9-102(57)

next friend Someone specially appointed by the court to look after the interests of a person who cannot act on his or her own (e.g., a minor). Also called prochein ami.

next of kin 1. The nearest blood relatives of the decedent. 2. Those who would inherit from the decedent if he or she died intestate.

nexus A causal or other connection or link.

NFPA See National Federation of Paralegal Associations (*www.paralegals.org*).

NGO Nongovernmental organization.

NGRI Not guilty by reason of insanity.

nighttime 1. The period between sunset and sunrise when there is not enough daylight to discern a person's face. 2. Thirty minutes after sunset to thirty minutes before sunrise.

nihil dicit ("he says nothing") The name of the judgment against a defendant who fails to plead or answer the plaintiff.

nihil est ("there is nothing") A form of return made by a sheriff when he or she has been unable to serve a writ.

nil (nihil) Nothing.

nisi Unless. Refers to the rule that something will remain or be valid unless an opponent comes forward to demonstrate otherwise.

nisi prius (n.p.) ("unless before") A trial court; the court that originally heard the case as opposed to an appellate court.

NLRB National Labor Relations Board (*www.nlrb.gov*).

NMI No middle initial.

no action letter A letter from a government agency that no action will be taken against a person based on the facts before the agency.

no bill A grand jury statement that the evidence is insufficient to justify a formal charge or indictment. Also called not found. See also no true bill.

> A grand jury's return of "no bill" was equivalent to a "not guilty verdict." *Greiner*, 591 N.Y.S.2d 864 (3 Dept., 1992)

no contest 1. See nolo contendere. 2. See in terrorem clause.

no evidence A challenge to the legal sufficiency of the evidence to support a particular fact finding.

no eyewitness rule If there is no direct evidence (e.g., eyewitness testimony) of what decedent did or failed to do immediately before an injury, the trier of facts may infer that decedent was using ordinary care for his or her own safety.

no fault Pertaining to legal consequences (e.g., granting a divorce, paying insurance benefits) that will occur regardless of who was at fault or to blame.

no knock search warrant A warrant that authorizes the police to enter the premises without first announcing themselves.

nolle prosequi (nol-pros) A formal notice by the government that a criminal prosecution will not be pursued.

no-load Sold without a commission.

nolo contendere ("I will not contest it") A plea in a criminal case in which the defendant does not admit or deny the charges. The effect of the plea, however, is similar to a plea of guilty in that the defendant can be sentenced to prison, fined, etc. Also called no contest, non vult contendere. The plea is not available in New York.

nol-pros See nolle prosequi.

nominal 1. In name only; not real or substantial. 2. Trifling.

nominal consideration Consideration so small as to bear no relation to the real value of what is received.

nominal damages A trifling sum (e.g., $1) awarded to the plaintiff because there was no significant loss or injury suffered, although a technical invasion of rights did occur.

> Nominal damages are damages in name only having no substance but which nevertheless vindicate plaintiffs' rights. *Shearing*, 273 N.Y.S.2d 464 (Sup. Ct., 1966)

nominal party A party who has no interest in the result of the suit or no actual interest or control over the subject matter of the litigation but is present to satisfy a technical rule of practice.

nominal trust See passive trust.

nominee 1. One who has been nominated or proposed for an office or appointment. 2. One designated to act for another. An agent.

nominee trust 1. A trust in which the trustee lacks power to deal with the trust property except as directed by the trust beneficiaries. 2. A trust in which property is held for undisclosed beneficiaries.

nonaccess A paternity defense in which the alleged father asserts the absence of opportunities for sexual intercourse with the mother.

nonage See minority (1).

non assumpsit A plea in an assumpsit action that the undertaking was not made as alleged.

non compos mentis Not of sound mind. Mentally incompetent.

nonconforming use A use of land that is permitted because the use was lawful prior to a change in the zoning law even though the new law would make the use illegal.

> A use of property that is no longer authorized due to rezoning, but lawfully existed prior to the enactment of existing zoning ordinance, is a nonconforming use. *Toys R Us*, 654 N.Y.S.2d 100 (Ct. of App., 1996)

noncore proceeding A nonbankruptcy proceeding related to the debtor's estate that, in the absence of a petition in bankruptcy, could have been brought in a state court.

nondelegable duty An affirmative duty that cannot be escaped by entrusting it to a third party such as an independent contractor.

nonexclusive listing See open listing.

nonfeasance The failure to perform a legal duty.

> Misfeasance is the performance of act in improper manner. Nonfeasance is the failure to perform an act. *Daurizio*, 274 N.Y.S. 174 (Sup. Ct., 1934)

nonintervention will A will providing that the executor shall not be required to account to any court or person.

nonjoinder The failure to join a necessary person to a suit.

nonjury trial See bench trial.

nonjusticiable Inappropriate or improper for judicial resolution.

nonmailable Pertaining to what cannot be transported by U.S. mail because of size, obscene content, etc.

nonnegotiable 1. Not capable of transfer by indorsement or delivery. 2. Fixed; pertaining to what will not be bargained.

non obstante veredicto Notwithstanding the verdict. See judgment notwithstanding the verdict.

nonperformance The failure or refusal to perform an obligation.

nonprofit corporation A corporation whose purpose is not to make a profit. Also called not-for-profit corporation.

non prosequitur ("he does not prosecute") A judgment against a plaintiff who fails to pursue his or her action.

nonrecourse creditor A creditor who can look only to its collateral for satisfaction of its debt, not to the debtor's other assets.

nonresident alien One who is neither a citizen nor a resident of the country he or she is presently in.

non sequitur A conclusion or statement that does not logically follow from what precedes it.

nonstock corporation A corporation whose ownership is not determined by shares of stock.

nonsuit A termination or dismissal of an action by a plaintiff who is unable to prove his or her case, defaults, fails to prosecute, etc.

nonsupport The failure to provide food, clothing, and other support needed for living to someone to whom an obligation of support is owed.

nonuse The failure to exercise a right or claim.

non vult contendere A plea of no content without admitting guilt. ("He will not contest.") See also nolo contendere.

no par stock Stock issued without a value stated on the stock certificate.

noscitur a sociis ("it is known by its associates") A word with multiple meanings is often best interpreted with regard to the words surrounding it.

> Noscitur a sociis is a rule of statutory construction under which words employed in a statute are construed and their meaning is ascertained by reference to the words and phrases with which they are associated. *Sharrow*, 746 N.Y.S.2d 531 (Ct. Cl., 2002)

no-strike clause A commitment by a labor union not to strike during the period covered by the collective bargaining agreement.

nota bene See N.B.

notarial Performed or taken by a notary public.

notarize To certify or attest, e.g., the authenticity of a signature.

notary public One authorized to perform notarial acts such as administering oaths, taking proof of execution and acknowledgment of instruments, and attesting the authenticity of signatures.

note See promissory note.

not-for-profit corporation See nonprofit corporation.

not found See no bill, no true bill.

not guilty 1. A jury verdict acquitting the accused. 2. A plea entered by the accused that denies guilt for a criminal charge.

not guilty by reason of insanity (NGRI) A verdict of not guilty because of a finding of insanity. See also insanity.

notice 1. Information or knowledge about something. 2. Formal notification. 3. Knowledge of facts that would naturally lead an honest and prudent person to make inquiry.

> A person has "notice" of a fact when (a) he has actual knowledge of it; or (b) he has received a notice or notification of it; or (c) from all the facts and circumstances known to him at the time in question he has reason to know that it exists. McKinney's Uniform Commercial Code § 1-201(25)

notice by publication Notice given through a broad medium such as a general circulation newspaper.

notice of appeal Notice given to a court (through filing) and to the opposing party (through service) of an intention to appeal.

notice of appearance A formal notification to a court by an attorney that he or she is representing a party in the litigation.

notice of pendency See lis pendens (2).

notice pleading Pleading by giving a short and plain statement of a claim that shows the pleader is entitled to relief.

notice to quit A landlord's written notice to a tenant that the landlord wishes to repossess the leased premises and end the tenancy.

notorious 1. Well-known for something undesirable. 2. Conspicuous.

notorious possession Occupation or possession of property that is conspicuous or generally known. Also called open possession.

no true bill What occurs when a grand jury votes and fails to indict the defendant. A no true bill means the grand jury did not vote for a true bill of indictment. See also no bill, not found.

NOV See judgment notwithstanding the verdict.

novation The substitution by mutual agreement of one debtor for another or of one creditor for another, whereby the old debt is extinguished, or the substitution of a new debt or obligation for an existing one.

novelty That which has not been known or used before. Innovation.

NOW account An interest-bearing savings account on which checks can be written. NOW means negotiable order of withdrawal.

NSF check (not sufficient funds) A check that is dishonored because the drawer of the check does not have sufficient funds to cover it.

nude Lacking something essential.

nudum pactum ("a bare agreement") A promise or undertaking made without any consideration.

nugatory Without force; invalid.

nuisance A substantial interference with the reasonable use and enjoyment of private land (private nuisance); an unreasonable interference with a right that is common to the general public (public nuisance).

A nuisance, for which eviction is allowed under the Rent Stabilization Code, is a condition that threatens the comfort and safety of others in the building and key to the definition is a pattern of continuity or recurrence of objectionable conduct.... *CHI-AM Realty*, 794 N.Y.S.2d 778 (Sup. Ct., 2005)

nuisance per se An act, occurrence, or structure that is a nuisance at all times and under all circumstances.

null; null and void Having no legal effect; binding no one.

nulla bona "No goods" on which a writ of execution can be levied.

nullification 1. The state or condition of being void or without legal effect. 2. The process of rendering something void. See also jury nullification.

nullify To invalidate; to render void.

nullity Having absolutely no legal effect. Something that is void.

nullius filius ("the son of no one") An illegitimate child.

nul tiel record ("no such") A plea asserting that the record relied upon in the opponent's claim does not exist.

nunc pro tunc ("now for then") With retroactive effect. As if it were done as of the time that it should have been done.

nuncupative will An oral will declared or dictated in anticipation of imminent death.

NYSE New York Stock Exchange (*www.nyse.com*).

O

oath 1. A solemn declaration. 2. A formal pledge to be truthful.

In order to constitute a valid oath, there must be an unequivocal and present act in some form by which the affiant consciously takes upon himself the obligation of an oath; merely citing in piece of paper that one has accepted oath upon one's self is insufficient to constitute "swearing." McKinney's CPL §§ 1.20, subd. 38, 190.45, subd. 2. *People v. Coles*, 535 N.Y.S.2d 897 (Sup. Ct., 1988)

obiter dictum See dictum (1).

object 1. To express disapproval; to consider something improper or illegal and ask the court to take action accordingly. 2. The end aimed at; the thing sought to be accomplished.

objection 1. A formal disagreement or statement of opposition. 2. The act of objecting.

objective 1. Real in the external world; existing outside one's subjective mind. 2. Unbiased. 3. Goal.

obligation 1. Any duty imposed by law, contract, or morals. 2. A binding agreement to do something, e.g., to pay a certain sum.

obligee The person to whom an obligation is owed; a promisee or creditor.

obligor The person under an obligation; a promisor or debtor.

obliterate To destroy; to erase or wipe out.

obloquy Abusive language; disgrace due to defamatory criticism.

obscene Material that enjoys no free-speech protection if: (a) the average person, applying contemporary community standards, finds that the work, taken as a whole, appeals to the prurient interest in sex; (b) the work depicts or describes, in a patently offensive way, sexual conduct specifically defined by the applicable state law; and (c) the work, taken as a whole, lacks serious literary, artistic, political, or scientific value.

obscenity 1. See obscene. 2. Conduct tending to corrupt the public morals by its indecency or lewdness.

obsolescence Diminution in value caused by changes in taste or new technology, rendering the property less desirable on the market; the condition or process of falling into disuse.

obstruction of justice Conduct that impedes or interferes with the administration of justice (e.g., hindering a witness from appearing).

obvious Easily discovered or readily apparent.

occupancy 1. Obtaining possession of real property for dwelling or lodging purposes. 2. The period during which one is in actual possession of land.

Actual occupancy, such as extends time for redemption from tax sale, implies more than casual or temporary presence on land and requires elements of permanency. *Mosher*, 355 N.Y.S. 2d 831 (3 Dept., 1974)

occupation 1. Conduct in which one is engaged. 2. One's regular employment or source of livelihood. 3. Conquest or seizure of land.

occupational disease A disease resulting from exposure during employment to conditions or substances detrimental to health.

Occupational Safety and Health Administration (OSHA) A federal agency that develops workplace health and safety standards, and conducts investigations to enforce compliance (*www.osha.gov*).

occupation tax A tax imposed for the privilege of carrying on a business or occupation.

occupying the field A form of preemption (see this word) where a federal rule is so pervasive that no room is left for states to supplement it.

occurrence policy Insurance that covers all losses from events that occur during the period the policy is in effect, even if the claim is not actually filed until after the policy expires.

In contrast to the traditional occurrence policy, which generally provides liability coverage for injury or damage that occurs within the policy period, without regard to when the claim is made or suit is filed, the claims-made policy generally provides coverage only when a claim is made during the policy period. *Segal Co.*, 798 N.Y.S.2d 30 (1 Dept., 2005)

odd lot An irregular or nonstandard amount for a trade, e.g., less than 100.

odd lot doctrine For workers' compensation, permanent total disability may be found in the case of workers who, while not altogether incapacitated for work, are so handicapped that they will not be employed regularly in any well-known branch of the labor market.

odious Arousing strong dislike; base, vile, detestable, disgraceful, scandalous.

odium Contempt or intense dislike. Held in disgrace.

of age See adult, majority (1).

of counsel 1. An attorney who is semiretired or has some other special status in the law firm other than regular member or employee. 2. An attorney who assists the principal attorney in a case.

offender One who has committed a crime or offense.

offense A crime or violation of law for which a penalty can be imposed.

offensive 1. Disagreeable, objectionable, displeasing. 2. Offending the personal dignity of an ordinary person who is not unduly sensitive. 3. Taking the offensive; on the attack; aggressive.

An action for battery may be sustained without a showing that the actor intended to cause injury as a result of the intended contact, but it is necessary to show that the intended contact was itself offensive, i.e., wrongful under all the circumstances. Lack of consent is considered in determining whether the contact was offensive. *Messina*, 729 N.Y.S.2d 4 (1 Dept., 2001)

offer 1. A proposal presented for acceptance or rejection. 2. To request that the court admit an exhibit into evidence.

offeree The person to whom an offer is made.

offering The sale or offer for sale of an issue of securities.

offer of compromise An offer to settle a case.

offer of proof When a judge is uncertain or unwilling to admit evidence at trial, an offer of proof is made by the party proposing the evidence, explaining what the evidence would be in order to persuade the judge to admit the proposed evidence and, if the judge does not permit it, to make a record for appeal.

offeror The party who makes an offer.

office 1. A position of trust and authority. 2. A place where everyday administrative business is conducted. 3. A unit or subdivision of government.

officer A person holding a position of trust, command, or authority in organizations.

officer of the court A person who has a responsibility in carrying out or assisting in the administration of justice in the courts, such as judges, bailiffs, court clerks, and attorneys.

official 1. An elected or appointed holder of a public office. An officer. 2. Concerning that which is authorized. 3. Proceeding from, sanctioned by, or pertaining to an officer.

Official Gazette Publication of the U.S. Patent and Trademark Office.

official immunity The immunity of government employees from personal liability for torts they commit while performing discretionary acts within the scope of their employment.

The general rule in New York relating to a public official's immunity has been stated as follows: A public official may be held liable in damages for a wrongful act only where such act is ministerial in nature. Where, however, an act is discretionary or quasi-judicial in nature no liability attaches even if the act was wrongfully performed. *Sinhogar*, 427 N.Y.S.2d 216 (1 Dept., 1980)

official notice The equivalent of judicial notice when taken by an administrative law judge or examiner.

official report or **official reporter** A collection of court opinions whose printing is authorized by the government.

officious intermeddler One who interferes in the affairs of another without justification (or invitation) and is generally not entitled to restitution for any benefit he or she confers. Also called intermeddler.

offset A deduction; that which compensates for or counters something else. See also setoff.

Old Age, Survivors, and Disability Insurance A federal program providing financial benefits for retirement and disability. Also called Social Security.

oligarchy Government power in the hands of a few persons.

oligopoly A market structure in which a few sellers dominate sales of a product, resulting in high prices.

ombudsman One who investigates and helps resolve grievances that people have within or against an organization, often employed by the organization.

omission 1. The intentional or unintentional failure to act. 2. Something left out or neglected.

Village's failure to remove ice from the road or to salt and sand it, as well as the failure to warn of dangerous condition, were acts of omission, not acts of affirmative negligence. *Grant*, 579 N.Y.S.2d 746 (2 Dept., 1992)

omnibus bill 1. A legislative bill that includes different subjects in one measure. 2. A legislative bill covering many aspects of one subject.

omnibus clause 1. A clause in an instrument (e.g., a will) that covers all property not specifically mentioned or known at the time. 2. A clause extending liability insurance coverage to persons using the car with the permission of the named insured.

omnibus motion Motions grouped together (in order to expedite a case) rather than offered sequentially. In criminal cases all motions, with few exceptions, must be combined and made in an omnibus motion within 45 days of arraignment. McKinney's CPL §255.20.

on all fours Pertaining to facts that are exactly the same, or almost so; being a very close precedent.

on demand Upon request; when demanded.

onerous Unreasonably burdensome or one-sided.

on information and belief See information and belief.

on its face Whatever is readily observable, e.g., the language of a document. See also face.

on or about Approximately.

one man (person), one vote The equal protection requirement that each qualified voter be given an equal opportunity to participate in an election.

on point 1. Germane, relevant. 2. Covering or raising the same issue (in a case, law review article, etc.) as the one before you.

on the brief Helped to research or write the appellate brief.

on the merits Pertaining to a court decision that is based on the facts and on the substance of the claim, rather than on a procedural ground.

A ruling granting motion to dismiss petition on prior summary holdover proceeding on a technicality because of defective papers was not a final determination on the merits, and hence was not res judicata in subsequent similar proceeding. *Barone*, 61 N.Y.S.2d 673 (Mun. Ct., 1946)

on the pleadings Pertaining to a ruling based on the allegations in the pleadings rather than on evidence presented in a hearing.

on the record Noted or recorded in the official record of the proceeding.

open 1. Visible, apparent, exposed. 2. Still available or active. 3. Not restricted. 4. Not resolved or settled.

open account 1. A type of credit from a seller that permits a buyer to make purchases on an ongoing basis without security. 2. An unpaid account.

open and notorious Conspicuous, generally recognized, or commonly known.

open court A court in session to which the general public may or may not be invited.

open end 1. Without a defined time or monetary limit. 2. Allowing further additions or other changes.

open-end mortgage A mortgage that allows the debtor to borrow additional funds without providing additional collateral.

open field doctrine No violation of one's constitutional right to privacy occurs when the police search an open field without a warrant.

The "open fields" doctrine that a landowner has no constitutionally protectible interest in land outside the curtilage, did not protect citizens' fundamental rights under the State Constitution and would not be adopted as law of New York. *People v. Scott*, 583 N.Y.S.2d 920 (Ct. of App., 1992)

opening statement An attorney's statement to the jury (or to the judge alone in nonjury cases) made before presenting evidence. The statement summarizes or previews the case the attorney intends to try to establish during the trial. Unrepresented parties make the statement themselves.

open listing A listing available to more than one agent in which the owner agrees to pay a commission to any agent who produces a ready, willing, and able purchaser. Also called nonexclusive listing.

open market An unrestricted competitive market in which any buyer and purchaser is free to participate.

open order An order to purchase securities placed with a broker that remains viable (open) until filled or the client cancels the order.

open policy See unvalued policy.

open possession See notorious possession.

open price The amount to be paid has yet to be determined or settled.

open shop A business in which union membership is not a condition of employment.

operating lease A short-term lease that expires before the end of the useful life of the leased property.

operating loss See net operating loss.

operation of law The means by which legal consequences are imposed by law, regardless of the intent of the parties involved.

opinion 1. A court's written explanation of how it applied the law to the facts to resolve a legal dispute. 2. A belief or conclusion expressing a value judgment that is not objectively verifiable.

Unless the court orders otherwise, questions calling for the opinion of an expert witness need not be hypothetical in form, and the witness may state his opinion and reasons without first specifying the data upon which it is based. Upon cross-examination, he may be required to specify the data and other criteria supporting the opinion. McKinney's CPLR Rule 4515

opinion evidence Beliefs or inferences concerning facts in issue.

opinion of the attorney general Formal legal advice from the chief law officer of the government to another government official or agency.

opportunity cost Benefits a business foregoes by choosing one course of action (e.g., an investment) over another.

opportunity to be heard A due process requirement of being allowed to present objections to proposed government action that would deprive one of a right.

oppression 1. An act of cruelty; conduct intended to frighten or harm. 2. Excessive and unjust use of authority. 3. Substantial inequality of bargaining power of the parties to the contract and an absence of real negotiation or a meaningful choice on the part of the weaker party.

option 1. An agreement that gives the person to whom the option is granted (the optionee) the right within a limited time to accept an offer. The right to buy or sell a stated quantity of securities or other goods at a set price within a defined time. 2. An opportunity to choose.

Option means an agreement giving the buyer the right to buy or receive (a "call option"), sell or deliver (a "put option"), enter into, extend or terminate or effect a cash settlement based on the actual or expected price, spread, level, performance or value of one or more underlying interests. McKinney's Insurance Law § 1401

option contract A unilateral agreement to hold an offer open. See option(1).

optionee The person to whom an option is granted.

OR Own recognizance. See release on own recognizance.

oral Spoken, not written.

oral argument A spoken presentation to the court on a legal issue, e.g., telling an appellate court why the rulings of a lower tribunal were valid or were in error.

oral contract See parol contract.

oral trust A trust established by its creator (the settler) by spoken words rather than in writing.

oral will See nuncupative will.

ordeal An ancient form of trial in which the innocence of an accused person was determined by his or her ability to come away from an endurance test (e.g., hold a red-hot iron in the hand) unharmed.

order 1. A command or instruction from a judge or other official. 2. An instruction to buy or sell something. 3. The language on a check (or other draft) directing or ordering the payment or delivery of money or other property to a designated person.

"Order" being appealed from was in fact an "order and a final judgment," in that it determined the rights of the parties and was dispositive of all factual and legal issues in the case and judicially settled the case between the parties. *State v. Wolowitz*, 468 N.Y.S.2d 131 (2 Dept., 1983)

order bill of lading A negotiable instrument, issued by a carrier to a shipper at the time goods are loaded aboard ship, that serves as a receipt that the carrier has received the goods for shipment, as a contract of carriage for those goods, and as documentary evidence of title to those goods.

ordered liberty The constitutional balance between respect for the liberty of the individual and the demands of organized society.

order nisi See decree nisi.

Order of the Coif An honorary organization of law students whose membership is based on excellence.

order paper A negotiable instrument payable to a specific person or to his or her designee (it is payable to order, not to bearer).

order to show cause See show cause order.

ordinance 1. A law passed by the local legislative branch of government (e.g., city council) that declares, commands, or prohibits something. Also called municipal ordinance. See also local law. 2. A law or decree.

ordinary Usual; regularly occurring.

ordinary care Reasonable care under the circumstances.

One element of a cause of action sounding in negligence is the failure to exercise "ordinary care," i.e., failure to exercise degree of care which reasonably prudent person would have exercised under same circumstances. *Gray*, 611 N.Y.S.2d 637 (2 Dept., 1994)

ordinary course of business See course of business.

ordinary income Wages, dividends, commissions, interest earned on savings, and similar kinds of income; income other than capital gains.

ordinary life insurance See whole life insurance.

ordinary negligence The failure to use reasonable care (often involving inadvertence) that does not constitute gross negligence or recklessness. Sometimes called simple negligence.

ordinary prudent person See reasonable man (person).

organic Inherent, integral, or basic.

organic law The fundamental law or constitution of a state or nation; laws that establish and define the organization of government.

organization A society or group of persons joined in a common purpose.

organize To induce persons to join an organization, e.g., a union.

organized crime A continuing conspiracy among highly organized and disciplined groups to engage in supplying illegal goods and services.

The legislature finds and determines as follows: Organized crime in New York state involves highly sophisticated, complex and widespread forms of criminal activity. The diversified illegal conduct engaged in by organized crime, rooted in the illegal use of force, fraud, and corruption, constitutes a major drain upon the state's economy, costs citizens and businesses of the state billions of dollars each year, and threatens the peace, security and general welfare of the people of the state. McKinney's Penal Law § 460.00

organized labor Employees in labor unions.

original 1. The first form, from which copies are made. 2. New and unusual.

original contractor See general contractor.

original document rule See best evidence rule.

original intent The meaning understood by the framers or drafters of the U.S. Constitution, a statute, a contract, or other document.

original jurisdiction The power of a court to be the first to hear and resolve a case before it is reviewed by another court.

original-package doctrine Goods imported into a state cannot be taxed by that state if they are in their original packaging when shipped.

original promise A promise, made for the benefit of the promisor, to pay or guarantee the debt of another.

original writ The first process or initial step in bringing or prosecuting a suit.

origination fee A fee charged by the lender for preparing the loan documents and processing the loan.

orphan's court See probate court, surrogate's court.

OSHA See Occupational Safety and Health Administration (*www.osha.gov*).

ostensible Apparent; appearing to be accurate or true.

ostensible agency An agency that arises when the principal's conduct allows others to believe that the agent possesses authority, which in fact does not exist.

The Court of Appeals recognized as a predicate for malpractice liability apparent or ostensible agency (or, as it is sometimes called, agency by estoppel). Liability based on agency by estoppel requires a showing that the plaintiff reasonably believed that the treater was acting at the defendant's "behest." *Warden*, 772 N.Y.S.2d 299 (1 Dept., 2004)

ostensible authority The authority a principal intentionally or by lack of ordinary care allows a third person to believe the agent possesses. See also apparent authority.

OTC See over-the-counter.

our federalism Federal courts must refrain from hearing constitutional challenges to state action when federal action is regarded as an improper intrusion on the right of a state to enforce its own laws in its own courts.

oust To remove; to deprive of possession or of a right.

ouster Turning out (or keeping excluded) someone entitled to possession of property. Wrongful dispossession.

outlaw 1. To prohibit or make illegal. 2. A person excluded from the benefits and protection of the law. 3. A fugitive.

out-of-court Not part of a court proceeding.

out-of-court settlement The resolution or settlement of a legal dispute without the participation of the court.

out-of-pocket expenses Expenditures made out of one's own funds.

out-of-pocket rule The damages awarded will be the difference between the purchase price and the real or actual value of the property received.

Proper measure of damages for fraud is plaintiff's actual pecuniary loss as result of fraud, or what is known as "out-of-pocket" rule; damages are to be calculated to compensate plaintiffs for what they lost because of fraud, not to compensate them for what they might have gained. *Kaddo*, 673 N.Y.S. 2d 235 (3 Dept., 1998)

output contract A contract in which one party agrees to sell its entire output, which the other party agrees to buy during a designated period.

outrage See intentional infliction of emotional distress.

outrageous Shocking; beyond the bounds of human decency.

outside director A member of a board of directors who is not an officer or employee of the corporation.

outstanding 1. Uncollected, unpaid. 2. Publicly issued and sold.

over Passing or taking effect after a prior estate or interest ends or is terminated.

overbreadth doctrine A law is invalid, though designed to prohibit legitimately regulated conduct, if it is so broad that it includes within its prohibitions constitutionally protected freedoms.

overdraft 1. A check written on an account for an amount that exceeds the funds available in the account. 2. The act of overdrawing a bank account.

overhead The operating expenses of a business (e.g., rent, utilities) for which customers or clients are not charged a separate fee.

Overhead expense means the expense reasonably attributable to the work at hand. *Long Beach Gas Co.*, 36 N.Y.S.2d 194 (3 Dept., 1942)

overissue To issue shares in an excessive or unauthorized quantity.

overreaching Taking unfair advantage of another's naiveté or other vulnerability, especially by deceptive means.

Overreaching means to overdo matters, or get the better of one in a transaction by cunning, cheating, or sharp practice. *In re Baruch's Will*, 132 N.Y.S.2d 402 (Sur., 1954)

override 1. To set aside, supersede, or nullify. 2. A commission paid to managers on sales made by subordinates. 3. A commission paid to a real estate agent when a landowner makes a sale on his or her own (after the listing agreement expires) to a purchaser who was found by the agent.

overrule 1. To decide against or deny. 2. To reject or cancel an earlier opinion as precedent by rendering an opposite decision on the same question of law.

overt act 1. An act that reasonably appears to be about to inflict great bodily harm, justifying the use of self-defense. 2. An outward act from which criminality may be implied. 3. An outward objective action performed by one of the members of a conspiracy, a necessary element of the crime of conspiracy.

over-the-counter (OTC) 1. Sold or transferred independent of a securities exchange. 2. Sold without the need of a prescription.

owelty Money paid to equalize a disproportionate division of property.

ownership The right to possess, control, and use property, and to convey it to others. Having rightful title to property.

oyer Reading a document aloud in court or a petition to have such a reading.

oyer and terminer A special court with jurisdiction to hear treason and other criminal cases. A judge's commission to hear such cases.

oyez Hear ye; a call announcing the beginning of a court proceeding or a proclamation.

P

P.A. See professional association.

PAC See political action committee.

PACE See Paralegal Advanced Competency Exam (*www.paralegals.org*).

PACER See Public Access to Court Electronic Records (*pacer.psc.uscourts.gov*).

pack 1. To assemble with an improper purpose. 2. To fill or arrange.

pact 1. A bargain. 2. An agreement between two or more nations or states.

pactum An agreement. See also nudum pactum.

paid-in capital 1. Money or property paid to a corporation by its owners for its capital stock. 2. Surplus of proceeds from the sale of a corporation's stock in excess of par. Also referred to as additional paid-in capital.

paid-in surplus That portion of the surplus of a corporation not generated by profits but contributed by the stockholders. Surplus accumulated by the sale of stock at more than par value. Also referred to as additional paid-in capital, paid-in capital.

pain Physical discomfort and distress.

pain and suffering Physical discomfort or emotional distress; a disagreeable mental or emotional experience.

pains and penalties See bill of pains and penalties.

pais See in pais.

palimony Support payments ordered after the end of a non-marital relationship if the party seeking support was induced to sustain or initiate the relationship by a promise of support or if support is otherwise equitable.

palming off Misrepresenting one's own goods or services as those of another. Also called passing off.

The essence of unfair competition is found where simulated article is "palmed off" or "passed off" as goods of another with intent to deceive. *Oneida*, 25 N.Y.S.2d 271 (Sup. Ct., 1940)

***Palsgraf* rule** Negligence liability is limited to reasonably foreseeable harm. *Palsgraf v. Long Island R. Co.*, 162 N.E. 99 (Ct. of App.,1928).

pander To engage in pandering. A panderer is one who panders.

pandering The recruitment of prostitutes. Acting as a go-between to cater to the lust or base desires of another.

panel 1. A group of judges who decide a case in a court with a larger number of judges. 2. A list of persons summoned to be examined for jury duty or to serve on a particular jury. 3. A group of attorneys available in a group legal services plan.

paper A written or printed document that is evidence of a debt. Commercial paper; a negotiable instrument.

paper loss; paper profit An unrealized loss or gain on a security or other investment that is still held. Loss or profit that will not be realized until the asset is sold or written off.

papers Pleadings, motions, and other litigation documents filed in court.

paper title The title listed or described on public records after the deed is recorded. Also called record title.

par 1. An acceptable average or standard. 2. See par value.

paralegal A person with legal skills who works under the supervision of an attorney or who is otherwise authorized by law to use his or her skills; this person performs substantive tasks that do not require all the skills of an attorney and that most secretaries are not trained to perform. Also called legal assistant.

Paralegal Advanced Competency Exam (PACE) The certification exam of the National Federation of Paralegal Associations for experienced paralegals (*www.paralegals.org*).

parallel citation A citation to an additional reporter where you can read the same court opinion.

paramount title Superior title as among competing claims to title.

paraphernalia 1. Property kept by a married woman on her husband's death in addition to her dower. 2. Equipment used for an activity.

parcel 1. To divide into portions and distribute. 2. A small package or wrapped bundle. 3. A part or portion of land.

parcenary See coparcenary.

parcener See coparcener.

pardon An act of government exempting an individual from punishment for crime and from any resulting civil disabilities.

parens patriae The state's power to protect and act as guardian of persons who suffer disabilities (e.g., minors, insane persons).

Parens patriae allows the state to care for children who do not have proper care and custody from their natural parents; it is not, however, a basis to interfere in relationships between fit parents and their children. *C.M. v. C.H.*, 789 N.Y.S.2d 393 (Sup. Ct., 2004)

parent A biological or adoptive mother or father of another.

parental kidnapping A parent's taking and removing his or her child from the custody of a person with legal custody without the latter's consent with the intent of defeating the custody jurisdiction of the court that currently has such jurisdiction.

parental liability law A law that makes parents liable (up to a limited dollar amount) for torts committed by their minor children.

The parent . . . of an infant over ten and less than eighteen years of age, shall be liable . . . for damages caused by such infant, where such infant has willfully, maliciously, or unlawfully damaged, defaced or destroyed such public or private property, whether real or personal, . . . [P]rior to the entering of a judgment under this section in the sum total of five hundred dollars or more, the court shall provide such parent . . . with an opportunity to make an application to the court based upon such parent's or legal guardian's financial inability to pay any portion or all of the amount of such sum total which is in excess of five hundred dollars. . . . McKinney's General Obligations Law § 3-112(1)&(2)

parental rights The rights of a parent to raise his or her children, receive their services, and control their income and property.

parent corporation A corporation that controls another corporation (called the subsidiary corporation) through stock ownership.

pari delicto See in pari delicto.

pari materia See in pari materia.

parish 1. A territorial government division in Louisiana. 2. An ecclesiastical division of a city or town administered by a pastor.

parity Equality in amount, status, or value.

parliament A legislative body of a country, e.g., England.

parliamentarian An expert who provides advice on parliamentary law.

parliamentary Pertaining to the parliament or to its rules.

parliamentary law Rules of procedure to be followed by legislatures and other formal organizations.

parol 1. Spoken rather than in writing. 2. An oral statement.

parol contract A contract that is not in writing. Also called oral contract.

parole Allowing a prisoner to leave confinement before the end of his or her sentence.

Parole is a promise made with or confirmed by a pledge of one's honor; a conditional release of a prisoner serving an indeterminate sentence; it is a suspension of the execution of a convict's sentence, temporarily releasing him from imprisonment on conditions which he is at liberty to accept or reject; he is still under supervision of parole board, subject to be remanded to prison if he violates the conditions of his parole. *Cummings*, 350 N.Y.S.2d 119 (Sup. Ct., 1973)

parole board A government agency that decides if and under what conditions inmates can be released before completing their sentences.

parolee An ex-prisoner who has been placed on parole.

parol evidence rule Prior or contemporaneous oral statements cannot be used to vary or contradict a written contract the parties intended to be final.

The parol evidence rule precludes a party from introducing extrinsic evidence to add to or vary a complete written contract. *Sheriff's Silver Star Ass'n*, 811 N.Y.S.2d 512 (4 Dept., 2006)

parole officer A government official who supervises persons on parole.

partial average See particular average.

partial breach A nonmaterial breach of contract that entitles a party to a remedy but not the right to consider the contract terminated.

partial disability A worker's inability to perform jobs he or she could perform before a work injury, even though still able to perform other gainful jobs subject to the disability.

partial insanity See diminished capacity.

partial verdict A verdict that is not the same on all the counts charged or on all the defendants in the trial. A verdict that consists of a finding of guilt on some counts and innocence on others.

particeps criminis A participant in a crime; an accomplice or accessory.

participation loan A loan issued or owned by more than one lender.

particular average An accidental partial loss of goods at sea by one who must bear the loss alone. Also called partial average.

particular estate An estate less than a fee simple, e.g., life estate.

particular lien A right to hold property as security for labor or funds expended on that specific property. Also called special lien.

particulars The details. See also bill of particulars.

partition The dividing of land held by co-owners into distinct portions, resulting in individual ownership.

Partition is a division between several persons of property which belongs to them as co-owners; it may be compulsory (judicial) or voluntary. Real Property Actions & Proceedings Law § 901. *O'Brien*, 391 N.Y.S.2d 502 (Sup. Ct., 1976)

partner 1. One who has united with others to form a partnership. 2. Two or more persons engaged in a jointly owned business.

partnership A voluntary association of two or more persons to place their resources in a jointly owned business or enterprise, with a proportional sharing of profits and losses.

A partnership is defined as a contract of two or more persons to place their money, effects, labor or skill or some or all of them in lawful commerce or business and to divide the profits and bear the loss in certain proportions. *Boyarsky*, 479 N.Y.S. 2d 606 (Sup.Ct., 1984)

partnership association A hybrid type of business with characteristics of a close corporation and a limited partnership.

part performance rule When an oral agreement fails to meet the requirements of the statute of frauds, the agreement may sometimes still be enforced when a relying party has partly performed the agreement.

party 1. One who brings a lawsuit or against whom a lawsuit is brought. 2. One who is concerned with, has an interest in, or takes part in the performance of an act. 3. A formal political association.

party aggrieved See aggrieved party.

party in interest See real party in interest.

party to be charged One against whom another seeks to enforce a contract.

par value 1. An amount stated in a security, policy, or other instrument as its value. Also called face amount, face value, par, stated value. 2. Stock issued with a value stated on the stock certificate as required in some states.

pass 1. To utter or pronounce. 2. To transfer. 3. To enact into law by a legislative body. 4. To approve. 5. To forego.

passage Enactment into law by a legislative body.

passbook A bank document that records a customer's account activities.

passenger Any occupant of a motor vehicle other than the operator.

passim Here and there; in various places throughout.

passing off See palming off.

passion Any strong emotion that often interferes with cool reflection of the mind. See also heat of passion.

passive 1. Submitting without active involvement. 2. Inactive.

passive negligence The unreasonable failure to do something; carelessly permitting defects to exist.

As respects rights on indemnity, one cannot be guilty of passive negligence merely if he has been guilty of fault of commission. *Putvin*, 186 N.Y.S.2d 15 (Ct. of App., 1959)

passive trust A trust whose trustee has no active duties. Also called dry trust, naked trust, nominal trust, simple trust.

passport A document that identifies a citizen, constitutes permission to travel to foreign countries, and acts as a request to foreign powers that the citizen be allowed to pass freely and safely.

past consideration An earlier benefit or detriment that was not exchanged for a new promise.

past recollection recorded A written record of a matter about which a witness now has insufficient memory. The record may be read into evidence if it was made or adopted by the witness when the matter was fresh in his or her memory. Fed. R. Evid. 803(5). An exception to the hearsay rule. Also called recorded recollection.

Victim's grand jury testimony, which victim described as accurate when given, was admissible as a past recollection recorded to supplement his in-court testimony, which was subject to cross-examination, in prosecution for assault and other crimes; victim had not refused to testify, but, rather, at time of trial, no longer remembered details of shooting in question. *People v. Linton*, 800 N.Y.S.2d 627 (2 Dept., 2005)

patent 1. A grant of a privilege or authority by the government. 2. A grant made by the government to an inventor for the exclusive right to make, use, and sell an invention for a term of years.

patentable Suitable to be patented because the device or process is novel, useful, and nonobvious.

patent defect See apparent defects.

patentee A person to whom a patent is granted; the holder of a patent.

patent infringement See infringement of patent.

patent medicine Packaged medicines or drugs sold over the counter under a trademark or other trade symbol.

paternity The state or condition of being a father.

paternity suit A court action to determine whether a person is the father of a child for whom support is owed. Also called bastardy proceeding.

patient-physician privilege See doctor-patient privilege.

pat. pend. Patent (application is) pending.

patricide 1. Killing one's father. 2. One who has killed his or her father.

patrimony 1. Heritage from one's ancestors. 2. That which is inherited from a father. 3. The total value of a person's rights and obligations.

patronage 1. The power to offer political jobs or other privileges. 2. Assistance received from a patron. 3. The customers of a business.

pattern 1. A reliable sample of observable features. 2. A model.

pauper A person so poor that he or she needs public assistance.

pauper's affidavit See poverty affidavit.

pawn To deliver personal property to another as security for a loan.

pawnbroker A person in the business of lending money upon the deposit of personal property as security.

Under statute defining pawnbroker as any person lending money on pledge of personal property other than securities or printed evidences of indebtedness, "property" included only such articles of personalty as may be actually delivered over to possession and custody of person who advances the money. General Business Law, § 52. *Modell Pawnbrokers*, 184 Misc. 817, 55 N.Y.S.2d 73 (Sup. Ct., 1945)

payable 1. Able to be paid. 2. Money or a balance owed.

payable to bearer Payable to whoever possesses the instrument.

payable to order Payable to a named person, the payee.

payee One to whom or to whose order a check or other negotiable instrument is made payable. One who receives money.

payer or **payor** One who makes or should make payment, particularly on a check or other negotiable instrument.

payment 1. The partial or full performance of an obligation by tendering money or other consideration. 2. An amount paid.

payment bond A guarantee from a surety that laborers and material suppliers will be paid if the general contractor defaults.

Primary purpose of a contractor's performance bond is to indemnify the building owner against breach by the contractor while primary purpose of a payment bond is to assure payment to specified third parties; such bonds serve entirely separate and different purposes. *Novak & Co.*, 381 N.Y.S.2d 646 (Sup. Ct., 1976)

payment in due course Payment made in good faith at or after maturity to the holder without notice that his or her title is defective.

payment into court Property deposited into court for eventual distribution by court order.

payor See payer.

payroll tax 1. A tax on employees based on their wages. 2. A tax on employers as a percentage of wages paid to employees.

P.C. 1. See professional corporation. 2. Politically correct.

PCR See post-conviction relief.

P.D. 1. See public defender. 2. Police department.

peace Orderly behavior in the community. Public tranquility.

peaceable 1. Without force or violence. 2. Gentle, calm.

"Peaceable picketing," in which laboring men and women have right to participate during labor dispute, means tranquil conduct, conduct devoid of noise or tumult, the absence of a quarrelsome demeanor, and a course of conduct that does not violate or disturb the public peace. *Lilly Dache*, 28 N.Y.S.2d 303 (Sup. Ct., 1941)

peaceable possession 1. Possession that is continuous and not interrupted by adverse claims or attempts to dispossess. 2. Peaceful enjoyment.

peace bond A bond required of one who threatens to breach the peace.

peace officer A person designated by public authority to keep the peace and to arrest persons suspected of crime.

peculation Misappropriation of money or goods. Embezzlement.

pecuniary Relating to money.

pecuniary interest A financial interest, e.g., the opportunity, directly or indirectly, to share in the profit (or loss) derived from a transaction.

pederasty Sexual relations (oral or anal) between a man and boy.

penal Concerning or containing a penalty.

penal action 1. A civil action based on a statute that subjects a wrongdoer to liability in favor of the person wronged as a punishment for the wrongful act. 2. A criminal prosecution.

penal bond A bond obligating the payment of a specified penalty (called the penal sum) upon nonperformance of a condition.

penal code A compilation of statutes on criminal law.

penal institution See penitentiary.

penal law The statutes defining crimes in New York. See also criminal law.

penal statute A statute that defines a crime and its punishment.

Penal statute within the rules of private international law is one that awards a penalty to the state or to a public officer in its behalf or to a member of the public suing in the interest of the whole community to redress a public wrong for the purpose, not of reparation to one aggrieved, but vindication of the public justice. *Porter*, 64 N.Y.S.2d 655 (Sup. Ct., 1946)

penal sum See penal bond.

penalty 1. Punishment for a criminal or civil wrong. 2. An extra charge imposed if a stated condition (e.g., late payment) occurs.

penalty clause A contract clause imposing a stated penalty (rather than actual damages) for nonperformance.

pendency While waiting; while still undecided.

pendent Undecided; pending.

pendente lite During the progress of the suit; pending the litigation.

pendent jurisdiction The power of a court to hear a claim over which it has no independent subject-matter jurisdiction if the facts of the claim are closely enough related on the facts of a main claim over which it does have such jurisdiction.

pending Under consideration; begun but not yet completed.

penetration An intrusion, however slight, of any object or any part of the defendant's body into the genital or anal openings of the victim's body.

penitentiary A place of confinement for persons convicted of crime, usually serious crimes. Also called penal institution, prison.

Pennoyer **rule** A personal judgment requires personal jurisdiction. *Pennoyer v. Neff*, 95 U.S. 714 (1877).

penny stocks High-risk equity securities, often selling at less than $1 a share and usually not traded on an approved securities exchange.

penology The study of prisons and the rehabilitation of criminals.

pen register A device that records the numbers dialed on a telephone but not the conversations themselves.

pension Regularly paid funds as a retirement or other benefit.

A payment, not wages, made regularly to someone who has fulfilled certain conditions of service, reached a certain age, etc. A periodical payment of a fixed amount made to retired public and private employees by way of retirement pay. *Biddlecom*, 481 N.Y.S.2d 605 (Sup. Ct., 1984)

pension plan A plan of an employer, primarily to pay determinable retirement benefits to its employees or their beneficiaries.

penumbra doctrine Implied constitutional rights, e.g., the right of privacy, exist on the periphery of explicit constitutional rights.

peonage Illegally compelling one to perform labor to pay off a debt.

people The prosecution in a criminal case representing the citizenry.

peppercorn A small amount; nominal consideration.

per By; for each.

per annum Annually.

per autre vie See pur autre vie.

per capita 1. For each person. 2. Divided equally among each person.

If taking under will is "per capita," children and grandchildren take concurrently, but if "per stirpes," they take by representation. *In re Macy's Will*, 68 N.Y.S.2d 833 (Sup. Ct., 1947)

percentage depletion A method of taking a depletion deduction or calculating a depletion expense based on a percentage of gross income from an oil or gas well.

percentage lease A lease in which the rent is a percentage of gross or net sales, often with a minimum required payment.

per curiam opinion (an opinion "by the court" as a whole) A court opinion, usually a short one, that does not name the judge who wrote it.

per diem By the day; an allowance or amount of so much per day.

peremptory 1. Conclusive; final. 2. Without need for explanation.

peremptory challenge The right to challenge and remove a prospective juror without giving any reasons. Such challenges, however, cannot be used to discriminate on the basis of race, ethnicity, or gender.

peremptory instruction An instruction by the judge to the jury that it must obey. (The equivalent of a directed verdict.)

perfect 1. Complete, executed. 2. To follow all procedures needed to complete or put in final form so that it is legally enforceable.

perfected Completed, executed; legally enforceable.

Security interest becomes "perfected security interest" when it has attached and all steps for perfection under Uniform Commercial Code (UCC) have been taken. McKinney's Uniform Commercial Code § 9-303(1). *Heidelberg Eastern, Inc.*, 631 N.Y.S.2d 370 (2 Dept., 1995)

perfect tender rule Exact (perfect) performance by the seller of its obligations can be a condition of the enforceability of the contract.

performance The fulfillment of an obligation according to its terms.

performance bond See completion bond.

peril That which may cause damage or injury; exposure to danger.

peril of the sea A peril peculiar to the sea that cannot be guarded against by ordinary human skill and prudence.

periodic Happening at fixed intervals; recurring now and then.

periodic alimony Alimony paid indefinitely at scheduled intervals. Also called permanent alimony.

periodic tenancy A tenancy that continues indefinitely for successive periods (e.g., month to month, year to year) unless terminated by the parties.

perjury Making a false statement under oath concerning a material matter with the intent to provide false testimony. Also called false swearing.

"Perjury" is willful, knowing, absolute, and false swearing, in a matter material to issue or point in question, in judicial proceeding, by a person to whom a lawful oath or affirmation is administered by court. *Walther*, 339 N.Y.S.2d 386 (N.Y. City Civ. Ct. 1972)

perks See perquisites.

permanent Continuing indefinitely.

permanent alimony See periodic alimony.

permanent injunction An injunction issued after a court hearing on the merits of the underling issues. Also called perpetual injunction.

permissive 1. Allowable; optional. 2. Lenient.

permissive counterclaim A counterclaim that does not arise out of the same transaction or occurrence that is the basis of the plaintiff's claim.

permissive joinder The joinder of a party that is allowed (but not required) if the claims involved arise out of the same occurrence and there are questions of law or fact that will be common to all the parties.

permissive presumption A presumption that allows (but does not require) the fact finder to infer the presumed fact.

A "permissive presumption" is one that allows, but does not require, the trier of fact to accept the presumed fact, and does not shift to the defendant the burden of proof. *In re Raquel M.*, 752 N.Y.S.2d 268 (Ct. of App., 2002)

permissive use A use expressly or impliedly within the scope of permission.

permissive waste A tenant's failure to use ordinary care to preserve and protect the property, such as allowing deterioration for lack of repair.

permit 1. To expressly agree to the doing of an act. 2. A formal document granting the right to do something. A license.

perp (slang) Perpetrator of a crime.

perpetrate To commit or carry out an act, often criminal in nature.

perpetrator A person who commits a crime or other serious wrong.

perpetual injunction See permanent injunction.

perpetual lease A lease of land with no termination date.

perpetual succession The uninterrupted (perpetual) existence of a corporation even though its owners (shareholders) change.

perpetuation of testimony Procedures to ensure that the testimony of a deposition witness will be available for trial.

perpetuity 1. Continuing forever. 2. A future interest that will not vest within the period prescribed by law.

perquisites (perks) Incidental benefits in addition to salary.

per quod Needing additional facts or proof of special damages.

per se In itself; inherently. Without needing additional facts.

Defendant newspaper's article prima facie exposing plaintiff's newspaper to charge of commission of bribery and affecting plaintiff's credit and business was "libelous per se" and allegation of extrinsic facts or special damages was not required to make article actionable and allegations of extrinsic facts in complaint would be treated as "surplusage" notwithstanding that plaintiff was a corporation. *Harry Lee Pub. Co.*, 40 N.Y.S.2d 899 (Sup. Ct., 1943)

persecution The offensive infliction of suffering or harm upon those who differ in race, religion, sexual orientation, or beliefs.

person A natural person, plus legal entities such as corporations that the law endows with some of the rights and duties of natural persons.

personal Pertaining to a person or to personal property.

personal bond A bail bond with no sureties.

personal chattel Tangible or intangible personal property.

personal effects Articles intimately or closely associated with the person (e.g., clothing, jewelry, wallet).

personal exemption A deduction from adjusted gross income for an individual and qualified dependents.

personal injury (PI) Injury, damage, or invasion of one's body or personal rights. Harm to personal (as opposed to property) interests.

"Personal injury" as defined in General Construction Law covers every variety of injury to a person's body, feelings, or reputation. General Construction Law, § 37-a. *Bonilla*, 267 N.Y.S.2d 374 (Sup. Ct., 1966)

personality The legal status of being a person.

personal judgment A judgment against the person (over whom the court had personal jurisdiction) that may be satisfied out of any property of that person. Also called judgment in personam.

personal jurisdiction A court's power over a person to adjudicate his or her personal rights. Also called *in personam jurisdiction*. More limited kinds of jurisdiction include the court's power over a person's interest in specific property (*quasi in rem jurisdiction*) or over the property itself (*in rem jurisdiction*).

personal knowledge Firsthand knowledge rather than what others say.

personal liability An obligation that one can be forced to pay or satisfy out of personal (not just business) assets.

personal notice Information communicated directly to a person.

personal property Everything, other than real property, that can be owned, e.g., a car, a stock option.

personal recognizance See release on own recognizance (ROR).

personal representative A person appointed to administer the estate and legal affairs of someone who has died or who is incapacitated.

"Personal representative" includes executor, administrator, successor personal representative, preliminary executor, temporary administrator and persons who perform substantially the same function under the law governing their status. McKinney's EPTL § 13-4.1(f)

personal right A right that inheres in the status of an individual as opposed to his or her estate or property rights.

personal service Handing a copy of a notice or summons to the defendant.

personalty Personal property.

personam See in personam, personal judgment.

Person In Need of Supervision (PINS) A person under 18 who does not attend school, is incorrigible, or is beyond the control of parents. Article 7, Family Court Act.

per stirpes Taking the share a deceased ancestor would have been entitled to (had he or she lived) rather than taking as individuals in their own right. Taking by right of representation. Also called in stirpes.

persuasive authority Any source a court relies on in reaching its decision that it is not required to rely on.

pertinent Relevant to an issue.

petit Lesser, minor.

petition 1. A formal written request. 2. A complaint.

In general, "petition" is formal document, filed in court and served on all parties, which commences process by which party may obtain judicial relief, and provides opposing party with notice of requested relief. *Figueroa*, 645 N.Y.S.2d 290 (Fam.Ct., 1996)

petitioner One who presents a petition or complaint to a tribunal.

petition in bankruptcy A formal application from a debtor to a bankruptcy court to file for bankruptcy.

petit jury An ordinary jury called and sworn in (impaneled) to try a particular civil or criminal case. Also called petty jury, trial jury. See also grand jury.

petit larceny See petty larceny. McKinney's Penal Law 155.25.

pettifogger 1. One who quibbles over trivia. 2. An incompetent, ill-prepared attorney who sometimes engages in questionable practices.

petty Of less importance or merit.

petty jury See petit jury.

petty larceny The larceny or stealing of personal property with a value below a statutorily set amount (e.g., $200).

petty offense A minor violation of the law, e.g., a traffic violation.

Offenses carrying sentences of less than six months are "petty" offenses, to which no right to jury trial attaches. U.S.C.A. Const. Amend. 6; McKinney's Const. Art. 1, § 2. *People v. Foy*, 650 N.Y.S.2d 79 (Ct. of App., 1996)

p.h.v. See pro hac vice.

physical Pertaining to the body or other material (non-mental) things.

physical evidence See real evidence (1).

physical fact A thing or action that can be perceived by the senses.

physical-fact rule The testimony of a witness that is positively contradicted by physical facts can be disregarded.

physical injury See bodily injury.

physician-patient privilege See doctor-patient privilege.

PI See personal injury.

picket To patrol or demonstrate outside a business or other organization in order to protest something it is doing or proposing and thereby pressure it to change.

pickpocket One who secretly steals something from another's person.

piecework Work for which one is paid by the number of units produced.

piercing the corporate veil A process by which a court disregards the limited liability normally afforded corporations and instead imposes personal liability on officers, directors, and shareholders.

pilferage Stealing, often in small amounts or values; petty larceny.

pillage Using force or violence to rob someone, often in times of war.

"Pillage" or "plunder" is taking of private property not necessary for immediate prosecution of war effort, and is unlawful; where pillage has taken place, title of original owner is not extinguished. *Menzel*, 267 N.Y.S.2d 804 (Sup. Ct., 1966)

pimp One who solicits customers for prostitutes.

PINS See Person In Need of Supervision.

pioneer patent A patent concerning a function or advance never before performed or one of major novelty and importance.

piracy 1. Robbery or seizure of a ship at sea or airplane in motion. See also hijack. 2. Copying in violation of intellectual property laws.

P.J. Presiding judge.

P.L. See public law.

place of abode One's residence or domicile.

placer claim A mining claim to loose minerals in sand or gravel.

plagiarism Using another's original ideas or expressions as one's own.

To establish "plagiarism," plaintiff must show a copying of substantial portions of plaintiff's work, and similarity must be one that would be apparent upon ordinary observation. *Hewitt*, 41 N.Y.S.2d 498 (Sup. Ct., 1943)

plain error An obvious, prejudicial error an appellate court will hear even if it was not raised at trial. Also called fundamental error.

plain meaning The usual and ordinary meaning given to words by reasonable persons at the time and place of their use.

plaintiff The person who initiates a civil action (and in some states, a criminal action) in court.

plaintiff in error The appellant; the party bringing the appeal.

plain view doctrine An officer can seize objects without a warrant if they can plainly be seen, there is probable cause they are connected to a crime, and the officer is lawfully present.

"Plain view doctrine" establishes exception to requirement of warrant not to search for an item, but to seize it; because item is already in open where it may be seen, owner can have no expectation of privacy in its concealment, and thus, its viewing cannot be a "search" under the State or Federal Constitutions. McKinney's Const. Art. 1, § 12. *People v. Diaz*, 595 N.Y.S.2d 940 (Ct. of App., 1993)

planned unit development (PUD) Development of land areas where standard zoning rules are suspended to achieve mixed-use flexibility.

plant patent A patent granted to someone who invents or discovers and asexually reproduces any distinct and new variety of plant.

plat 1. A map showing streets, easements, etc. 2. A small land area.

plea 1. The first pleading of the defendant in a civil case. 2. The defendant's formal response to a criminal charge, e.g., not guilty.

plea bargaining Negotiations whereby an accused pleads guilty to a lesser included offense or to one of multiple charges in exchange for the prosecution's agreement to support a dismissal of some charges or a lighter sentence. Also called plea agreement, negotiated plea.

"Plea bargain" is the process whereby the accused and the prosecution in a criminal case work out a mutually satisfactory disposition of the case, subject to court approval. *People v. D'Amico*, 556 N.Y.S.2d 456 (Sup. Ct., 1990)

plead To file a pleading, enter a plea, or argue a case in court.

pleadings Formal litigation documents (e.g., a complaint, an answer) filed by parties that state or respond to claims or defenses of other parties.

plea in abatement A plea objecting to the timing or other defect in the plaintiff's claim without challenging its merits.

plea in bar A plea that seeks a total rejection of a claim or charge.

plebiscite A vote of the people on a proposed law or policy.

pledge 1. Delivering personal property as security for the payment of a debt or other obligation. A bailment for this purpose. 2. A solemn promise or agreement to do or forbear something.

A "pledge" is a possessory lien, and therefore barring of an underlying debt by the statute of limitations would not bar an action on the lien. *Lacaille*, 253 N.Y.S.2d 937 (Sup. Ct., 1964)

pledgee The person to whom something is delivered in pledge.

pledgor The person who pledges; the one who delivers goods in pledge.

plenary 1. Complete, unlimited. 2. Involving all members.

plenary jurisdiction A court's unlimited judicial power over the parties and subject matter of a legal dispute.

plenipotentiary Someone (e.g., a diplomat) with full powers to act.

PLI Practising Law Institute (*www.pli.edu*).

plottage The additional value of adjacent, undeveloped lots when combined into a single tract.

PLS See professional legal secretary (*www.nals.org*).

plurality The largest number of votes received even though this number is not more than half of all votes cast or that could have been cast.

plurality opinion The controlling opinion that is joined by the largest number of judges on the bench short of a majority.

pluries Process (e.g., a writ) that issues in the third (or later) instance, after earlier ones have been ineffectual.

PMI See private mortgage insurance.

pocket part A pamphlet inserted into a small pocket built into the inside back (and occasionally front) cover of a book. The pamphlet contains text that supplements or updates the material in the book.

pocket veto The president's "silent" or indirect rejection of a bill by not acting on it within ten weekdays of receiving it if the legislature adjourns during this period.

POD account Pay-on-death account. An account payable to the owner during his or her life, and upon death, to a designated beneficiary.

point 1. A distinct legal position or issue. 2. A fee or service charge equal to one percent of the principal amount of the loan. 3. A unit for measuring the price or value of stocks or other securities.

point of error A lower court error asserted as a ground for appeal.

point reserved An issue on which the trial judge will rule later in the trial, allowing the case to proceed. Also called reserved point.

points and authorities See memorandum of points and authorities.

poisonous tree doctrine See fruit of the poisonous tree doctrine.

poison pill Steps by a corporation to discourage a hostile takeover, e.g., issuing new shares that would increase the takeover costs.

police A unit of the government charged with maintaining public order primarily through the prevention and investigation of crime.

police court See magistrate court.

police power The power of the state to enact laws, within constitutional limits, to promote public safety, health, morals, and convenience.

To sustain legislation under the police power, the operation of the law must tend to prevent offense or evil or preserve public health, morals, safety or welfare; it should appear that the interests of the public generally are served and that the means used are reasonably necessary for the accomplishment of the purpose and not unduly oppressive upon individuals. *People v. Braun*, 330 N.Y.S.2d 937 (Dist. Ct., 1972)

policy 1. The principles by which an organization is managed. 2. An insurance contract. 3. A lottery-type numbers game.

policyholder An owner of an insurance policy, usually the insured.

political action committee (PAC) An organization (other than a political party or candidate committee) that uses fundraising or contributions to advocate the election or defeat of a clearly identified candidate for office or the victory or defeat of a public question.

political asylum See asylum (2).

political offense Crimes against a state or political order, e.g., treason.

political question A question that a court should not resolve because it concerns policy choices that are constitutionally committed for resolution to the legislative or executive branches or because of the absence of judicially discoverable and manageable standards for resolving it.

"Political question doctrine" is expression of constitutional separation of governmental powers among legislative, executive, and judicial branches; pursuant to that doctrine, courts will, generally, adjudicate disputes concerning allocation of power between Executive branch and Legislature. However, they are reluctant to intervene in intra-branch disputes. It is a fundamental principle of the organic law that each branch of State government should be free from interference, in the discharge of its peculiar duties, by either of the others. *Urban Justice Center*, 810 N.Y.S.2d 826 (Sup. Ct., 2005)

poll the jury To ask each juror how he or she voted on the verdict.

poll tax A tax imposed on each individual regardless of income. Also called capitation tax, head tax.

polyandry Having more than one husband at the same time.

polygamy Having more than one spouse at the same time.

"Polygamy," which constitutes the crime of bigamy, is the custom or practice, as in a group, of having a plurality of wives or husbands at the same time. *Application of Sood*, 142 N.Y.S. 2d 591 (Sup. Ct., 1955)

polygraph An instrument to record physiological processes, e.g., blood pressure, to detect lying. Also called lie detector.

polygyny Having more than one wife at the same time.

Ponzi scheme A fraudulent investment scheme whereby returns to investors are financed, not through the success of an underlying business venture, but from the funds of newly attracted investors.

pool 1. To combine for a common purpose. 2. A combination or agreement by persons or companies to carry out a joint purpose. 3. A sum of money made up of stakes contributed by bettors in a game of chance.

popular Pertaining to the general public.

pornography The portrayal of erotic behavior designed to cause sexual excitement. The portrayal is protected unless it is obscene.

port authority A government agency that plans and regulates traffic through a port by sea vessels, airplanes, public transportation, etc.

portfolio All the investments held by one person or institution.

port of entry The port where goods and travelers from abroad may enter the country. The port containing a station for customs officials.

positive evidence See direct evidence.

positive fraud Fraud that is actual or intentional rather than implied or constructive. Also called actual fraud, fraud in fact.

positive law Law actually and specifically enacted by a proper authority, usually a legislative body.

positivism See legal positivism.

posse See in posse.

posse comitatus ("the power or force of the county") Citizens called by the sheriff for special purposes, e.g., to help keep the peace.

possession 1. The actual custody or control of something. 2. That which one holds, occupies, or controls. 3. That which one owns.

> "Possession" of gun, for purposes of criminal possession of a weapon statute, means to have physical possession or otherwise exercise dominion and control over gun. McKinney's Penal Law § 10.00, subd. 8. *People v. Myers*, 697 N.Y.S.2d 178 (3 Dept., 1999)

possession is nine-tenths of the law A false adage that nevertheless reflects the truth that the law does not always make it easy for a rightful property owner to oust someone in wrongful possession.

possessor One who has possession or custody of property.

possessory Relating to, founded on, or claiming possession.

possessory action An action to assert the right to keep or maintain possession of property.

possessory interest The right to exert control over specific property to the exclusion of others whether or not the right is based on title.

possibility of reverter The interest remaining in a grantor who conveys a fee simple determinable or a fee simple conditional. Any reversionary interest that is subject to a condition precedent. Also called reverter.

> A possibility of reverter is the future estate left in the creator or in his successors in interest upon the simultaneous creation of an estate that will terminate automatically within a period of time defined by the occurrence of a specified event (§ 6-4.5 EPTL). *United Methodist Church*, 357 N.Y.S.2d 637 (Sup. Ct., 1974)

post To send by mail. See also posting.

post-conviction relief (PCR) A remedy sought by a prisoner to challenge the legality of his or her conviction or sentence. A prisoner's collateral attack of his or her final judgment.

postdate To insert a date that is later than the actual date.

posterity 1. All descendants of a person. 2. Future generations.

post hoc ergo propter hoc ("after this, therefore because of this") The false logic that because one event occurs after another, it must have been caused by the previous event.

posthumous Referring to events occurring after the death of a person.

posting 1. A form of substituted service of process by placing process in a prominent place (e.g., the front door of the defendant's residence). 2. The transfer of an original entry of debits or credits to a ledger. 3. The steps followed by a bank in paying a check. 4. Making something available on the Internet. 5. Making payment.

postmortem 1. Pertaining to what occurs after death. 2. See autopsy.

> "Post mortem examination" means an examination of a body after death, and does not necessarily imply an autopsy, which is the examination of a dead body by dissection to ascertain the cause of death. *Wehle*, 31 N.Y.S. 865 (NYC Superior Ct., 1895)

postnuptial agreement An agreement between spouses on the division of their property in the event of death or divorce.

postpone 1. To put off. 2. To subordinate or give a lower priority.

post-trial discovery Discovery procedures (e.g., deposition) conducted after judgment to help enforce (e.g., collect) a judgment. Post-trial discovery in New York occurs primarily through information affidavits.

pourover trust A trust that receives property from a will.

pourover will A will that transfers property to a trust.

poverty affidavit A written declaration of one's finances for purposes of qualifying for free legal services or other public benefit. Also called pauper's affidavit, affidavit of indigency.

power 1. The right, ability, or authority to do something. 2. The right of a person to produce a change in a given legal relation by doing or not doing a given act. 3. Control over another.

power coupled with an interest A right or power to do some act, together with an interest in the subject matter on which the power is to be executed.

power of acceptance The right of an offeree to create a contract by accepting the terms of the offer.

power of appointment A power created when one person (the donor) grants another (the donee) authority to designate beneficiaries of the donor's property.

> "Power of appointment" is an authority to do an act which owner granting power might himself lawfully perform. *In re Merseles' Will*, 292 N.Y.S. 276 (Sur., 1936)

power of attorney A document that authorizes another to act as one's agent or attorney-in-fact.

power of sale The right to sell property, e.g., the right of a trustee or mortgagee to sell the real property mortgaged in the event of a default.

pp. Pages.

PPO Preferred provider organization, a group of health care providers.

practice 1. A repeated or customary action; habitual performance. 2. The rules, forms, and methods used in a court or administrative tribunal. 3. The exercise of a profession or occupation.

practice of law Using legal skills to assist a specific person resolve his or her specific legal problem. The work of a lawyer in counseling and representing clients on legal matters.

"Practice of law" includes rendering of legal advice as well as appearing in court and holding oneself out to be lawyer. McKinney's Judiciary Law § 478. *El Gemayel*, 536 N.Y.S.2d 406 (N.Y., 1988)

praecipe 1. A formal request that a court take some action. 2. A writ ordering an action or a statement of why it should not be taken.

praedial See predial.

praesenti See in praesenti.

prayer for relief The portion of a complaint or other pleading that sets forth the requested relief (e.g., damages) sought from the court.

preamble A clause at the beginning of a law (e.g., statute) or instrument (e.g., contract) setting out its objectives.

precarious Uncertain; at the whim or discretion of someone.

precatory Embodying a recommendation, hope, or advice rather than a positive command or direction; pertaining to a wish.

precedent A prior decision that can be used as a standard or guide in a later similar case.

precept 1. A rule imposing a standard of conduct or action. 2. A warrant, writ, or order.

precinct A subdivision or other geographical unit of local government.

preclusion order An order preventing a party from introducing specific evidence, usually because of a violation of discovery rules.

precognition A pretrial questioning of a potential witness.

precontract A contract designed to prevent a person from entering another contract of the same nature with someone else.

predatory pricing A company's artificially low prices designed to drive out competition so that it can reap monopoly profits at a later time.

predecessor One who goes or who has gone before. A prior holder.

predial Pertaining or attached to land. Also spelled praedial.

predisposition A defendant's tendency or inclination to engage in certain conduct, e.g., illegal activity.

preemption 1. Under the Supremacy Clause, federal laws take precedence over (preempt) state laws when Congress (a) expressly mandates the preemption, (b) regulates an area so pervasively that an intent to preempt the entire field may be inferred, or (c) enacts a law that directly conflicts with state law. 2. The right of first purchase.

preemptive right The right of a stockholder to maintain a proportionate share of ownership by purchasing a proportionate share of any new stock issues. Also called subscription right.

Effect of "right of first refusal," also called "preemptive right," is to bind party who desires to sell not to sell without first giving other party opportunity to purchase property at price specified. *Malloy*, 661 N.Y.S.2d 34 (2 Dept., 1997)

pre-existing duty rule When a contracting party does or promises something that it is already legally obligated to do, there is no adequate consideration because the party has not incurred a detriment.

prefer 1. To submit for consideration; to file or prosecute. 2. To give advantage, priority, or privilege.

preference 1. Making a payment or a transfer by an insolvent debtor to one of the creditors, to the detriment of the other creditors. 2. The choice of one over another; the choice made.

preferential shop A job site in which union members are given priority or advantage over non-union members in hiring, promotion, etc.

preferred dividend A dividend payable to preferred shareholders, which has priority over dividends payable to common shareholders.

A "preferred dividend" is a dividend which is payable, by virtue of contract, to one class of stockholders in priority to that to be paid to another class. *Gallagher*, 19 N.Y.S.2d 789 (Sup. Ct., 1940)

preferred risk An insurance classification of people who statistically have fewer accidents or have better health records and who, therefore, are often eligible for a reduced rate.

preferred stock Stock in a corporation that has a claim to income (dividends) or liquidation assets ahead of holders of common stock.

prejudice 1. Bias. A leaning toward or against one side of a cause for a reason other than merit. 2. Detriment or harm to one's legal rights.

prejudicial error An error justifying a reversal because it probably affected the outcome and was harmful to the substantial rights of the party objecting to the error. Also called fatal error, reversible error.

preliminary Introductory; prior to the main body or theme.

preliminary examination See preliminary hearing.

preliminary hearing A pretrial hearing on whether probable cause exists that the defendant committed a crime. Also called preliminary examination, probable cause hearing.

"Preliminary hearing" before magistrate is, basically, a first screening of the charge; its function is not to try the defendant, nor does it require the same degree of proof or quality of evidence as is necessary for an indictment or for conviction at trial. *Mattioli*, 335 N.Y.S.2d 613 (Sup. Ct., 1972); McKinney's CPL § 180.10

preliminary injunction A temporary order to preserve the status quo and prevent irreparable loss of rights prior to a trial on the merits. Also called interlocutory injunction, temporary injunction.

premarital agreement A contract made by two persons about to be married that covers spousal support, property division, and related matters in the event of the separation of the parties, the death of one of them, or the dissolution of the marriage by divorce or annulment. Also called antenuptial agreement, marriage settlement, prenuptial agreement.

premeditated Considered, deliberated, or planned beforehand.

premise A statement that is a basis of an inference or conclusion.

premises 1. Land, its buildings, and surrounding grounds. 2. The part of a deed describing the interest transferred and related information, e.g., why the deed is being made. 3. The foregoing statements.

premium 1. An extra payment or bonus. 2. The payment to an insurance company to keep the policy. 3. The amount by which the market value of a bond or other security exceeds its par or face value.

prenuptial agreement See premarital agreement.

prepackaged bankruptcy (prepack) A plan negotiated between debtor and creditors prior to filing for bankruptcy.

prepaid legal services A plan by which a person pays premiums to cover future legal services. Also called legal plan, group legal services.

prepayment penalty An extra payment imposed when a promissory note or other loan is paid in full before it is due.

preponderance of evidence The standard of proof that is met when the evidence establishes that it is more likely than not that the facts are as alleged. Also called fair preponderance of the evidence.

The standard of proof is "preponderance of the evidence," often defined as the existence of the "fact" being more probable than its non-existence. *Universal Open MRI*, 12 Misc. 3d 1151(A) (N.Y. City Civ. Ct., 2006)

prerogative An exclusive right or privilege of a person or office.

prerogative writ See extraordinary writ.

prescription 1. A method of acquiring ownership or title to property or rights by reason of continuous usage over a designated period of time. 2. An order for drugs issued by a licensed health professional. 3. A direction; a practice, course, or action that is ordered. 4. The laying down or establishing of rules or directions.

prescriptive easement An easement created by an open, adverse, continuous use of another's land under claim of right over a designated period of time.

presence 1. Being physically present. 2. Being in physical proximity to or with something, including a sensory awareness of it.

present 1. Currently happening. 2. In attendance. 3. Under examination.

present danger See clear and present danger.

presentence investigation (PSI) See presentence report.

presentence report A probation report on the background of a convicted offender to assist the judge in imposing a sentence. Also called presentence investigation.

present estate An interest in property that can be possessed and enjoyed now, not just in the future. Also called present interest.

presenting bank Any bank presenting an item except a payor bank.

present interest See present estate.

present memory refreshed See present recollection refreshed.

presentment 1. A grand jury's accusation of crime that is not based on a prosecutor's request for an indictment. 2. Producing a check or other negotiable instrument for acceptance or payment.

"Presentment" is an accusation of crime made at instance of Grand Jury itself and "indictment" is an accusation of crime made at instance of public prosecutor. *Wood*, 212 N.Y.S.2d 33 (Ct. of App., 1961)

present recollection refreshed A use by witnesses of writings or other objects to refresh their memory so that testimony can be given about past events from present recollection. Also called present memory refreshed, present recollection revived, refreshing memory or recollection.

presents This document being considered; the present instrument.

present sense impression A statement describing or explaining an event or condition made while perceiving it or immediately thereafter.

"Present sense impression" exception to hearsay rule permits introduction of spontaneous descriptions of events made substantially contemporaneously with the observations, if the descriptions are sufficiently corroborated by other evidence. *People v. Mitchell*, 734 N.Y.S.2d 252 (3 Dept., 2001)

present value The amount of money you would have to be given now in order to produce or generate, with compound interest, a certain amount of money in a designated period of time. Also called present worth.

preside To be the person in authority; to direct the proceedings.

president The chief executive officer of an organization or country.

presidential elector See electoral college.

president judge The presiding or chief judge on some courts.

presume To take for granted as true before establishing it as such.

presumption An assumption or inference that a certain fact is true once another fact is established.

presumption of death A presumption that a person is no longer alive after being missing without explanation for a set period of time.

presumption of fact An inference; a logical inference or conclusion that the trier of the facts is at liberty to draw or refuse to draw.

A "presumption of fact" is an inference as to existence of one fact from the existence of some other fact founded upon a previous experience of their connection. *People v. Busco*, 46 N.Y.S.2d 859 (Sp. Sess., 1942)

presumption of innocence An accused cannot be convicted of a crime unless the government proves guilt beyond a reasonable doubt. The accused does not have the burden of proving his or her innocence.

presumption of law A particular conclusion the court must reach in absence of evidence to the contrary.

presumption of paternity; presumption of legitimacy A man is presumed to be the natural father of a child if he and the child's natural mother are married to each other and the child is conceived or born during the marriage. The presumption also applies if he receives the child into his home and holds the child out as his natural child.

presumption of survivorship In a common disaster involving multiple victims, a younger, healthier victim is presumed to have died after the others in the absence of evidence to the contrary.

presumptive 1. Providing a logical basis to believe; probable. 2. Created by or arising out of a presumption.

presumptive evidence Evidence sufficient to establish a given fact and which, if not rebutted or contradicted, will remain sufficient.

"Presumptive evidence" is evidence which permits but does not require trier of fact to find in accordance with presumed fact, although no contradictory evidence has been presented. *People v. Perez*, 516 N.Y.S.2d 70 (2 Dept., 1987)

presumptive heir A person who can inherit if a closer relative is not born before the ancestor dies. Also called heir presumptive.

presumptive trust See resulting trust.

pretermit To pass by, omit, or disregard.

pretermitted heir A child or spouse omitted in a will by a testator.

pretext arrest An arrest for a minor offense in order to investigate a more serious unrelated offense for which there is no lawful cause to arrest the person. Also called pretextual arrest.

pretrial conference A meeting of the attorneys and the judge (or magistrate) before the trial to attempt to narrow the issues, to secure stipulations, and to make a final effort to settle the case without a trial.

pretrial detention Keeping someone in custody before trial.

pretrial discovery Devices parties can use to uncover facts that will help them prepare for trial (e.g., depositions, interrogatories).

pretrial diversion; pretrial intervention See diversion (2).

pretrial order A judge's order before a trial stating the issues to be tried and any stipulations of the parties.

prevail 1. To be in general use or practice. 2. To succeed.

prevailing party The party winning the judgment.

preventive detention Detaining someone before trial to prevent fleeing, future antisocial behavior, or self-inflicted harm.

Factor to consider in deciding whether defendant can be released on bail, whether defendant is likely by reason of past conduct to commit future crimes, or whether defendant's release on bail poses unusual risk to specific persons or public in general, is referred to as preventive detention. *People v. Bosco*, 668 N.Y.S.2d 331 (Co. Ct., 1997)

preventive justice Restraining orders, peace bonds, and other remedies designed to keep the peace and prevent future wrongdoing.

price discrimination A difference in price a seller charges different customers for the same product or one of like quality.

price fixing An agreement on prices that otherwise would be set by market forces. Any means calculated to eliminate competition and manipulate price.

price supports Devices (e.g., government subsidies) to keep prices from falling below a set level.

priest-penitent privilege See clergy-penitent privilege.

prima facie 1. On the face of it, at first sight. 2. Sufficient.

prima facie case A case as presented that will prevail until contradicted and overcome by contrary evidence.

prima facie evidence Sufficient evidence of a fact unless rebutted.

prima facie tort The intentional infliction of harm without justification, resulting in special damages.

Elements of "prima facie tort" are: (1) intentional infliction of harm, (2) resulting in special damages, (3) without excuse or justification, and (4) by act or series of acts that would otherwise be lawful. *Jonas*, 665 N.Y.S.2d 189 (4 Dept., 1997)

primary activity A strike, picketing, or other action directed against an employer with whom a union has a labor dispute.

primary authority Any law (e.g., case, statute) that a court could rely on in reaching a decision.

primary boycott Action by a union to urge its members and the public not to patronize a firm with which the union has a labor dispute.

primary election An election by a party's voters to select (nominate) candidates to run in a general election.

primary evidence The best or highest quality evidence available.

primary jurisdiction doctrine Although a case is properly before a court, if there are issues requiring administrative expertise, the court can refrain from acting until the administrative agency acts.

primary liability Liability for which one is directly responsible, rather than secondarily after someone else fails to pay or perform.

primary market 1. The market where new issues of securities are first sold. 2. The main target of an initial offering of goods and services.

prime contractor See general contractor.

prime rate The lowest rate of interest charged by a bank to its best (most creditworthy) customers for short-term loans.

primogeniture 1. The status of being the first-born of siblings. 2. The right of the oldest son to inherit the entire estate.

principal 1. The amount of debt not including interest. 2. The initial sum invested. 3. A perpetrator of a crime. 4. One who permits an agent to act on his or her behalf. 5. One with prime responsibility for an obligation. 6. See corpus (2).

"Principal" means property held in trust for distribution to a remainder beneficiary when the trust terminates. McKinney's EPTL § 11-A-1.2(10)

prior 1. Before in time or preference. 2. An earlier conviction.

prior art Any relevant knowledge, acts, and descriptions that pertain to, but predate, the invention in question.

prior consistent statement An earlier statement made by a witness that supports what he or she is now saying at the trial.

prior inconsistent statement An earlier statement made by a witness that conflicts what he or she is now saying at the trial.

priority A legal preference or precedence, e.g., the right to be paid first.

prior lien A lien with rights superior to other liens.

prior restraint A judicial or other government restriction on a publication before it is published.

prison See penitentiary.

prisoner A person in police custody serving a prison sentence.

privacy The absence of unwanted attention into one's private concerns or affairs. Being left alone. See also invasion of privacy.

> The right of privacy was defined in as including an interest by the person in avoiding disclosure of personal matters and the independence to make certain kinds of important decisions without interference. *Matter of Lori M.*, 496 N.Y.S.2d 940 (Fam. Ct., 1985)

privacy law A law that restricts the public's access to personal information maintained by the government. See also invasion of privacy.

private 1. Pertaining to individual or personal matters as opposed to public or official ones. 2. Restricted in use to designated persons or groups. 3. Confidential. 4. Not sold or offered to the general public.

private act See private law (2).

private bill A proposal for a private law. See private law (2).

private corporation A corporation established by private individuals for a nongovernmental or nonpublic purpose.

private foundation A charitable organization whose main source of funds is not the general public.

privateer A privately owned ship authorized by the government to attack enemy ships.

private international law Conflict of laws involving different states or countries. See also international law.

private investigator Someone other than a police officer who is licensed to do detective work or to conduct investigations.

> "Private investigator" shall mean . . . the making for hire, reward or for any consideration whatsoever, of any investigation, or investigations for the purpose of obtaining information with reference to any of the following matters . . . crime or wrongs done or threatened against the government . . . ; the identity, habits, conduct, movements, whereabouts, affiliations, associations, transactions, reputation or character of any person . . . the credibility of witnesses or other persons; the whereabouts of missing persons; . . . McKinney's General Business Law § 71(1)

private law 1. The law governing private persons and their interrelationships. 2. A law that applies to specifically named persons or groups and has little or no permanence or general interest. A special law.

private mortgage insurance (PMI) Insurance to protect the lender if the debtor dies or defaults.

private necessity A privilege to make reasonable use of another's property to prevent an immediate threat of harm or damage to one's private property.

private nuisance A substantial interference with the reasonable use and enjoyment of private land.

> To prevail on cause of action for "private nuisance," plaintiffs must prove that defendant's interference with their right to use and enjoy their property was substantial in nature, intentional in origin, unreasonable in character, and caused by defendant's conduct or failure to act. *Stiglianese*, 637 N.Y.S. 2d 284 (N.Y. City Civ. Ct., 1995)

private offering A sale of an issue of securities to a limited number of persons. Also called private placement.

private person One who is not a public official, public figure, or member of the military.

private placement 1. The placement of a child for adoption by the parents or their intermediaries rather than by a state agency. 2. See private offering.

private sale A sale that was not open to the public through advertising, auction, or real estate agents.

private statute See private law (2).

privatize Convert from government control or ownership to the private sector.

privies See privy.

privilege 1. A special legal benefit, right, immunity, or protection. 2. A defense that authorizes conduct that would otherwise be wrongful.

privilege against self-incrimination 1. A criminal defendant cannot be compelled to testify. 2. The right not to answer incriminating questions by the government that could directly or indirectly connect oneself to the commission of a crime.

privileged Protected by a privilege, e.g., does not have to be disclosed.

privileged communication A communication that does not have to be disclosed. A statement protected by privilege.

Privileges and Immunities Clause The clause in the U.S. Constitution (art. IV, § 2) that "citizens of each state shall be entitled to all Privileges and Immunities of citizens" in every other state. A state cannot discriminate within its borders against citizens of other states.

privity A relationship that persons share in property, a transaction, or a right. Mutuality of interest.

> For purposes of res judicata, privity is an amorphous concept; it includes those who are successors to a property interest, those who control an action although not formal parties to it, those whose interests are represented by a party to the action, and possibly coparties to a prior action. *Doe*, 786 N.Y.S.2d 892 (Sup. Ct., 2004)

privity of contract The relationship that exists between persons who enter a contract with each other.

privity of estate A mutual or successive relationship to the same rights in property.

privy A person who is in privity with another; someone so connected with another as to be identified with him or her in interest (plural: privies).

prize 1. A reward given to a winner. 2. A vessel seized during war.

pro For.

probable cause 1. A reasonable belief that a specific crime has been committed and that the defendant committed the crime. Also called sufficient cause. 2. A reasonable belief that evidence of a crime will be found in a particular place. 3. A reasonable ground for a belief in the existence of supporting facts.

"Probable cause" to arrest consists of such facts and circumstances as would lead a reasonably prudent person in a similar situation to believe plaintiff guilty. *Brown v. Sears Roebuck and Co.*, 746 N.Y.S.2d 141 (1 Dept., 2002)

probable cause hearing See preliminary hearing.

probate 1. A court procedure to establish the validity of a will and to oversee the administration of the estate. 2. To establish the validity (of a will); to administer (an estate) under court supervision.

probate court A court for probating wills, supervising the administration of estates, and handling related family law issues. Also called orphan's court and, in New York, surrogate's court.

probate estate Assets owned by the decedent at death plus assets later acquired by the decedent's estate.

probation 1. The conditional release of a person convicted of a crime in lieu of a prison sentence. Conditions can include attending drug counseling and remedial training. 2. A trial or test period for a new employee to determine competence and suitability for the job.

probationer A convicted offender on probation.

probation officer A government employee who supervises probationers.

probative Furnishing proof; tending to prove or disprove.

probative evidence Evidence that contributes toward proof.

probative fact A fact from which an ultimate or decisive fact may be inferred or proven.

probative value The extent to which evidence tends to establish whatever it is offered to prove.

pro bono Concerning or involving legal services that are provided for the public good (pro bono publico) without fee or compensation. Sometimes also applied to services given at a reduced rate. Shortened to pro bono.

Eligible pro bono legal services are (1) legal services for which there is no compensation to the attorney performing the legal services or (2) legal services for which the compensation to the attorney performing the legal services is provided by someone other than the recipient of those services, and such compensation would be provided regardless of whether the attorney performed those services. 22 NYCRR 1500, Appendix A (CLE)

procedendo A writ ordering a lower court to proceed to judgment.

procedural due process Minimum requirements of procedure (e.g., notice and the opportunity to be heard) that are constitutionally mandated before the government deprives a person of life, liberty, or property.

"Procedural due process" means the ways of asserting and conducting disciplinary, punishment, or economic deprivation charges and proceedings fairly and openly, with full opportunity for legal rights and remedies to be used by the party under attack. *Gould*, 304 N.Y.S.2d 537 (Sup. Ct., 1969)

procedural law A law that governs the steps or mechanics of resolving a dispute in a court or administrative agency.

procedure A method or process by which something is done, e.g., to resolve a legal dispute in court or in an administrative agency.

proceeding 1. A part or step in a lawsuit, e.g., a hearing. 2. A sequence of events. 3. Going forward or conducting something.

proceeds Money derived from some possession, sale, or other transaction. The yield.

process 1. A summons, writ, or court order, e.g., to appear in court. 2. Procedures or proceedings in an action or prosecution.

process server Someone with the authority to serve or deliver process.

prochein ami See next friend.

proclamation An official and public declaration.

pro confesso As having accepted responsibility or confessed.

proctor One who manages the affairs of another. A supervisor.

procuration The appointment of an agent. A power of attorney.

procurement 1. Obtaining or acquiring something. 2. The persuasion of another to engage in improper sexual conduct.

procurement contract A government contract to acquire goods or services.

procuring cause 1. See proximate cause. 2. The chief means by which a sale of property was effected, entitling the broker to a commission.

It means the original discovery of a purchaser by the plaintiff, and the starting of a negotiation by the plaintiff, together with the final closing by or on behalf of the defendant, with the purchaser, through the efforts of the plaintiff. *Ware*, 38 N.Y.S. 673 (1 Dept. 1896)

prodition Treason.

produce 1. To bring forth or yield. 2. Products of agriculture.

producing cause See proximate cause.

product Something produced by physical labor, intellectual effort, or natural processes. A commercial item that is used or consumed.

production of documents See request for production.

products liability A general term that covers different causes of action (e.g., negligence, strict liability in tort, and breach of warranty) based on defective products that cause harm.

profert The document relied on in the pleading is produced in court.

professional association (P.A.) 1. Two or more professionals (e.g., doctors) who practice together. 2. A group of professionals organized for a common purpose, e.g., continuing education, lobbying.

professional conduct See Model Rules of Professional Conduct.

professional corporation (P.C.) A corporation of persons performing services that require a professional license, e.g., attorneys.

professional legal secretary (PLS) A certification credential of NALS, the Association for Legal Professionals (*www.nals.org*).

professional responsibility Ethical conduct of professionals.

proffer To tender or offer.

profiling Targeting, suspecting, or selecting out individuals based on group characteristics, e.g., race.

profit The proceeds of a business transaction less the costs of the transaction; excess of revenue over expenses. Gain.

"Profits from a crime" means (i) any property obtained through or income generated from the commission of a crime of which the defendant was convicted; (ii) any property obtained by or income generated from the sale, conversion or exchange of proceeds of a crime, . . . McKinney's Executive Law § 632-a(b)

profit-and-loss (P&L) statement See earnings statement, income statement.

profit à prendre The right to enter another's land and remove something of value from the soil or the products of the soil. Also called right of common.

profiteering Making excessive profits through unfair advantage.

profit sharing A company plan in which employees can share profits.

pro forma 1. Perfunctorily; as a formality. 2. Provided in advance for purposes of description or projection.

progressive tax A type of graduated tax that applies higher tax rates as one's income range increases. Also called graduated tax.

pro hac vice (p.h.v.) ("for this particular occasion") Pertaining to permission given to an out-of-state attorney to practice law in the jurisdiction for this case only, i.e., on a case-by-case basis.

prohibited degree A relationship too close to be allowed to marry.

prohibition 1. Suppression or interdiction; an order forbidding something. 2. A law preventing the manufacture, sale, or transportation of intoxicating liquors. 3. See writ of prohibition.

prohibitory injunction A court order that a person refrain from doing a specific act. An injunction that maintains the status quo.

A prohibitory injunction, which operates to restrain the commission or continuance of an act and to prevent a threatened injury, thereby ordinarily having the effect of maintaining the status quo, is not automatically stayed without court order upon filing of appeal by public entity. McKinney's CPLR 5519(a), par. 1. *Ulster Home Care Inc.*, 688 N.Y.S.2d 830 (3 Dept., 1999)

prolixity Superfluous statements of fact in a pleading or as evidence.

promise 1. A manifestation of an intention to act or to refrain from acting in a specified way so as to justify the promisee in understanding that a commitment has been made. 2. To make a commitment.

promisee The person to whom a promise has been made.

promisor The person who makes a promise.

promissory estoppel The rule that a promise (not supported by consideration) will be binding if (a) the promisor makes a promise he or she should reasonably expect will induce action or forbearance by the promisee, (b) the promise does induce such action or forbearance, and (c) injustice can be avoided only by enforcement of the promise.

To establish viable cause of action sounding in "promissory estoppel," plaintiff must allege (1) clear and unambiguous promise, (2) reasonable and foreseeable reliance by party to whom promise is made, and (3) injury sustained in reliance on promise. *Gurreri*, 669 N.Y.S.2d 629 (2 Dept., 1998)

promissory note A written promise to pay. An unconditional promise in writing made by one person to another, signed by the maker, engaging to pay on demand, or at a fixed or determinable future time, a certain sum of money, to order or to bearer. Also called note.

promissory warranty A commitment by the insured that certain facts will continue or remain true after the insurance policy takes effect.

promoter 1. One who promotes or furthers some venture. 2. One who takes preliminary steps in the organization of a corporation or business.

promulgate 1. To announce officially. 2. To put into effect.

pronounce To declare formally.

proof 1. The effect of being persuaded by evidence that a fact has been established or refuted. 2. Evidence that establishes something.

proof beyond a reasonable doubt See reasonable doubt.

proof of claim A written statement a creditor files with the bankruptcy court showing the amount and character of the debt owed to the creditor.

proof of loss Providing an insurer with the information and evidence needed to determine its liability under an insurance policy.

proof of service Evidence that a summons or other process has been served on a party in an action. Also called certificate of service, return of service, affidavit of service.

proof to a moral certainty See moral certainty.

pro per See in propria persona, pro se.

proper lookout The duty of a driver to see what is clearly visible or what in the exercise of due care would be visible.

proper party A person whose interest may be affected by the action and, therefore, may be joined, but whose presence is not essential for the court to adjudicate the rights of others.

property 1. That which one can possess, enjoy, or own. 2. The right of ownership. 3. The quality or characteristic of a thing.

"Property" shall mean both real and personal property. "Personal property" shall mean chattels and other tangible things of a moveable or removable nature. "Real property" shall mean lands, structures, franchises and interests in land, . . . McKinney's Public Authorities Law § 2675-c(16–18)

property settlement An agreement dividing marital property between spouses upon separation or divorce. A court judgment on this division.

property tax A tax on real or personal property that one owns, the amount often dependent on the value of the property.

prophylactic Acting to prevent something.

proponent An advocate; one who presents or offers an argument, proposal, or instrument.

proposal An offer or plan.

propound To offer or propose for analysis or acceptance.

proprietary 1. Owned by a private person or company. 2. Pertaining to ownership.

proprietary drug A drug that has the protection of a patent.

proprietary function A function of a municipality that (a) traditionally or principally has been performed by private enterprise, or (b) is conducted primarily to produce a profit or benefit for the government rather than for the public at large.

Proprietary functions are those in which governmental activities essentially substitute for or supplement traditionally private enterprises. *Karedes*, 760 N.Y.S.2d 84 (Ct. of App., 2003)

proprietary interest One's right or share based on property ownership.

proprietary lease A lease in a cooperative apartment between the owner-cooperative and a tenant-stockholder.

proprietor The owner of property, e.g., a business. See also sole proprietorship.

pro rata Proportionately; according to a certain rate or factor.

The term "pro rata" means according to a rate or in proportion, and a division pro rata under will therefore involves a division or distribution in accordance with some fixed standard. *In re DeWitt's Will*, 104 N.Y.S.2d 673 (Sur., 1951)

pro rata clause A clause in an insurance policy that the insurer will be liable only for the proportion of the loss represented by the ratio between its policy limits and the total limits of all available insurance.

prorate To divide, calculate, or distribute proportionally.

proscription A prohibition or restriction.

pro se (on one's own behalf) Appearing for or representing oneself. Also called in propria persona, pro per.

prosecute To initiate and pursue a civil case or a criminal case.

prosecuting attorney See district attorney, prosecutor (1).

prosecuting witness The person (often the victim) who instigates a criminal charge and gives evidence.

prosecution 1. Court proceedings to determine the guilt or innocence of a person accused of a crime. 2. The prosecuting attorney or the government in a criminal case. 3. Pursuing a lawsuit.

prosecution history See file wrapper.

prosecutor 1. The representative of the government in a criminal case. 2. One who instigates a prosecution or files a complaint.

prosecutorial discretion The right of prosecutors to decide whether to charge someone for a crime, whether to plea bargain, and whether to ask for a particular sentence.

prosecutory Involving or relating to a prosecution.

prospective Pertaining to or applicable in the future; expected.

prospective law A law applicable to cases or events arising after its enactment.

prospectus A document containing facts on a company designed to help a prospective investor decide whether to invest in the company.

prostitution Engaging in sexual activities for hire.

Engaging or agreeing to engage in "sexual conduct" with another person in return for a fee. Penal Law §§ 230.00. *People v. Costello*, 395 N.Y.S.2d 139 (Sup. Ct., 1977)

pro tanto For so much; to the extent of.

protected class A group of people (e.g., members of a minority race) given special statutory protection against discrimination.

protection Defending or shielding from harm; coverage.

protection order See restraining order.

protective custody Being held under force of law for one's own protection or that of the public.

protective order 1. A court order designed to protect a person from harassment or undue burden or expense during litigation. 2. See restraining order.

protective trust A trust designed to protect trust assets from the spendthrift tendencies of the beneficiary.

pro tem (pro tempore) For the time being; temporarily.

protest 1. A formal declaration of dissent or disapproval. 2. A written declaration (often by a notary public) that a check or other negotiable instrument was presented but not paid or accepted. 3. A disagreement that a debt is owed but paying it while disputing it.

prothonotary A chief clerk of court.

protocol 1. The etiquette of diplomacy. 2. A brief summary of a document, e.g., a treaty. 3. The first copy or draft of a treaty; an amendment of a treaty. 4. The formal record or minutes of a meeting.

prove To establish a fact or position by sufficient evidence.

province 1. A division of the state or country. 2. A sphere of expertise or authority.

provision 1. A section or part of a legal document. 2. A stipulation.

provisional remedy A temporary remedy, pending final court action.

proviso A condition, exception, or stipulation in a law or document.

provocation Inciting another to do a particular deed.

proximate Nearest or closest; close in causal connection.

proximate cause The legally sufficient cause of an event when (a) the defendant is the cause in fact of the event, (b) the event was the foreseeable consequence of the original risk created by the defendant, and (c) there is no policy reason why the defendant should not be liable for what he or she caused in fact. Also called direct cause, efficient cause, legal cause, procuring cause, producing cause.

In medical malpractice action, as in any negligence action, plaintiff has burden of proving, by preponderance of evidence, that defendant's negligence proximately caused injury claimed if such negligence is substantial factor in producing injury, it is "proximate cause" of injury. *Mortensen*, 483 N.Y.S. 2d 264 (1 Dept., 1984)

proxy 1. An agent; one authorized to act for another. 2. The authorization to act for another.

proxy marriage The performance of a valid marriage ceremony through agents because one or both of the prospective spouses are absent.

proxy statement A document mailed to shareholders giving information on matters for which the company is seeking proxy votes.

prudent Cautious; careful in adapting means to ends.

prudent investor rule A trustee must use such diligence and prudence in managing and investing a trust fund as a reasonable person would use.

prurient Pertaining to a shameful or morbid interest in sex. Tending to excite lasciviousness; lasciviousness is tending to arouse sexual desires. Penal Law § 235.00. *People v. Ciampa*, 394 N.Y.S.2d 727 (2 Dept., 1977)

P.S.; p.s. 1. Public Statute (P.S.). See public law (1). 2. Postscript (p.s.).

PSI Presentence investigation. See presentence report.

psychotherapist-patient privilege A patient can refuse to disclose, and can prevent others from disclosing, confidential communications between patient and psychotherapist involving the patient's diagnosis or treatment.

public 1. The community at large. 2. Open for use by everyone. 3. Traded on the open market.

Public Access to Court Electronic Records (PACER) An electronic public access service that allows subscribers to obtain case and docket information from federal courts via the Internet (*pacer.psc.uscourts.gov*).

public accommodation A business or place that is open to, accepts, or solicits the patronage of the general public. Private dentist's office was not "place of public accommodation," for purposes of antidiscrimination statute, and therefore dentist could not be found to have violated statute by refusing to treat person because dentist perceived him to have AIDS. McKinney's Executive Law §§ 292, subd. 9, 296, subd. 2(a). *Cahill*, 632 N.Y.S.2d 614 (2 Dept., 1995)

public act See public law (1).

public administrator Someone appointed by the court to administer an intestate estate when relatives or associates of the decedent are not available to do so.

publication 1. Making something known to people. 2. Communication of a statement to someone other than the plaintiff.

public bill A legislative proposal for a public law.

public contract A contract (often with a private person or business) in which a government buys goods or services for a public need.

public convenience and necessity Reasonably meeting the needs of the public, justifying the grant of public funds or a license for a project or service.

public corporation 1. A company whose shares are traded on the open market. Also called publicly held corporation. 2. A corporation owned by the government and managed under special laws in the public interest.

public defender (P.D.) An attorney appointed by a court and paid by the government to represent indigent defendants in criminal cases and some in family court cases.

public domain 1. Work product or other property that is not protected by copyright or patent. A status that allows access to anyone without fee. 2. Government-owned land.

public duty doctrine The government is not liable for a public official's negligent conduct unless it is shown that the official breached a duty owed to the injured person as an individual as opposed the breach of an obligation owed to the public in general.

public easement An easement for the benefit of the general public.

public figure A person who has assumed special prominence in the affairs of society. A public figure for a limited purpose is a person who has voluntarily become involved in a controversy of interest to the general public. Two classes of persons are considered to be "public figures" for purposes of defamation law: those who occupy positions of such persuasive power and influence that they are deemed public figures for all purposes, and those who have taken affirmative steps to attract public attention or who have thrust themselves into the forefront of a particular controversy in an attempt to influence the outcome of a situation. *Farrakhan*, 638 N.Y.S.2d 1002 (Sup. Ct., 1995)

public forum Settings or places traditionally available for public expression and debate, such as public streets and the radio.

public hearing A hearing open to the general public.

publici juris ("of public right") Being owned by the public and subject to use by anyone.

public interest 1. A matter of health or welfare that concerns the general public. 2. The well-being of the public.

public interest law Law involving broad societal issues.

public international law See international law.

public land Government-owned land.

public law (P.L.)(Pub. L.) 1. A statute that applies to the general public or to a segment of the public and has permanence or general interest. Also called public act, public statute. 2. Laws governing the operation of government or relationships between government and private persons. The major examples are constitutional law, administrative law, and criminal law.

publicly held corporation See public corporation (1).

public necessity The privilege to make a reasonable use of someone's property to prevent an immediate threat of harm or damage to the public.

public nuisance Unreasonably interfering with a right of the general public. An act that adversely affects the safety, health, morals, or convenience of the public. Also called common nuisance. A "public nuisance" consists of conduct or omissions which offend, interfere with, or cause damage to the public in the exercise of rights common to all, in a manner such as to offend public morals, interfere with use by the public of a public place, or endanger or injure the property, health, safety, or comfort of a considerable number of persons. *Wall Street Garage Parking Corp*, 779 N.Y.S.2d 745 (Sup. Ct., 2004)

public offering A sale of stock to the public on the open market.

public office A position created by law by which an individual is given power to perform a public function for a given period.

public official An elected or appointed holder of a public office.

public policy Principles inherent in customs and societal values that are embodied in a law.

public property Government-owned property.

public purpose Benefit to or welfare of the public as a goal of government action.

public record A record the government must keep that may or may not be open to the public.

public records exception Some written statements that would normally be excluded as hearsay may be admitted into evidence if they qualify as public records and reports (Federal Rules of Evidence Rule 803(8)).

Essentially, the hearsay exception for public records applies to three distinct categories of records and reports. The first category of public records includes records of activities of the office itself. The second group consists of matters observed pursuant to duty. The third category relates to investigative reports, such as the document at issue in the instant case. *People v. Selassie*, 532 N.Y.S.2d 326 (Sup. Ct., 1988)

public sale A sale in which members of the public are invited to become buyers.

public security Bonds, notes, certificates of indebtedness, and other instruments evidencing government debt.

public service commission A government commission that supervises or regulates public utilities.

public statute (P.S.) See public law (1).

public trial A trial that the general public can observe.

public trust See charitable trust.

public use 1. A use that confers some benefit or advantage to the public. A use affecting the public generally, or any number thereof, as distinguished from particular individuals. 2. A use of an invention by one under no restriction or obligation of secrecy to the inventor.

Private property can be taken by eminent domain only for a public use, and term is broadly defined to encompass any use which contributes to health, safety, general welfare, convenience or prosperity of the community. McKinney's Const. Art. 1, § 7. *Byrne*, 476 N.Y.S.2d 42 (4 Dept., 1984)

public utility A company or business that regularly supplies the public with some commodity or service that is of public consequence and need (e.g., electricity).

public works Construction, demolition, installation, or repair work on roads, dams, and similar structures done under contract with public funds.

public wrong An offense against the state or the general community, e.g., a crime, public nuisance, or breach of a public contract.

publish To make known, to make public; to distribute or disseminate.

puffing 1. A seller's opinion consisting of an exaggeration of quality or overstatement of value. 2. See by-bidding.

puisne Subordinate in rank.

***Pullman* abstention** Federal courts can refrain or postpone the exercise of federal jurisdiction when a federal constitutional issue might be mooted or presented in a different posture by a state court determination of pertinent state law. *Railroad Comm'n v. Pullman*, 61 S. Ct. 643 (1941).

punishment Any fine, penalty, confinement, or other sanction imposed by law for a crime, offense, or breach of a duty.

punitive damages Damages that are added to actual or compensatory damages in order to punish outrageous or egregious conduct and to deter similar conduct in the future. Also called exemplary damages, smart money, vindictive damages.

"Punitive damages" are warranted where conduct of party being held liable evidences high degree of moral culpability, where conduct is so flagrant as to transcend mere carelessness, or where conduct constitutes willful or wanton negligence or recklessness. *Thompson*, 787 N.Y.S.2d 563 (4 Dept., 2004)

pur autre vie For or during the life of another. Also spelled per autre vie.

purchase Acquisition by buying; receiving title to property by a means other than descent, inheritance, or gift.

purchase money mortgage A mortgage taken back when purchasing property to secure payment of the balance of the purchase price.

In order for there to be a "purchase-money mortgage" with the attendant priority, lender must either be the seller of the property or have taken back the mortgage to secure money borrowed for acquiring the property. McKinney's CPLR 5203(a), par. 2. *Beneficial Homeowner Service*, 605 N.Y.S.2d 435 (3 Dept., 1993)

purchase money resulting trust A trust imposed when title to property is transferred to one person, but the entire purchase price is paid by another.

purchase money security interest (PMSI) A security interest taken or retained by a seller to secure all or part of the price of the collateral, or a security interest taken by one who gives value that is used by the debtor to acquire the collateral.

purchaser One who acquires property by buying it for a consideration.

pure accident See unavoidable accident.

pure plea A plea stating matters not in the bill to defeat the claim.

pure race statute See race statute.

purge To clear or exonerate from a charge or of guilt.

purloin To steal.

purport 1. To appear to be; to claim or seem to be. 2. Meaning.

purpose Goal or objective.

purposely Intentionally; with a specific purpose.

purpresture An encroachment on public rights or the appropriation to private use of that which belongs to the public.

pursuant to In accordance with; under.

pursuit of happiness The phrase in the Declaration of Independence interpreted to mean the right to be free in the enjoyment of our faculties, subject to restraints that are necessary for the common welfare.

purview The body, scope, or extent of something, e.g., a statute or other law.

putative Generally regarded, reputed, believed; alleged.

putative father A man reputed or alleged to be the biological father of a child born out of wedlock.

The department shall establish a putative father registry which shall record the names and addresses of: (a) any person adjudicated by a court of this state to be the father of a child born out-of-wedlock; (b) any person who has filed with the registry before or after the birth of a child out-of-wedlock, a notice of intent to claim paternity of the child; (c) any person adjudicated by a court of another state or territory of the United States to be the father of an out-of-wedlock child, where a certified copy of the court order has been filed with the registry by such person or any other person; (d) any person who has filed with the registry an instrument acknowledging paternity pursuant to section 4-1.2 of the estates, powers and trusts law. McKinney's Social Services Law § 372-c(1)

putative marriage A marriage that has been solemnized in proper form and celebrated in good faith by one or both parties, but which, by reason of some legal infirmity, is either void or voidable.

put option The right to sell a specified security or commodity at a specified price. See also call option.

pyramid scheme A sales device or plan (illegal in many states) in which participants are recruited to pay the person who recruited them, hoping to receive payments from the persons they recruit. A pyramid scheme rewards participants for inducing other people to join the program, whereas a Ponzi scheme operates strictly by paying earlier investors with money tendered by later investors.

"Pyramid scheme" is one in which participant pays money to company or its representative and in return receives right to sell products and right to earn rewards for recruiting other participants into the scheme. McKinney's General Business Law § 359-fff. *Brown*, 638 N.Y.S.2d 873 (N.Y. City Ct., 1995)

pyramiding Speculating on stocks or commodities by using unrealized (paper) profits as margin for more purchases.

Q

Q.B. Queen's Bench. See King's Bench.

QDRO See qualified domestic relations order.

QTIP See qualified terminable interest property.

qua As; in the character or capacity of.

quaere Ask, question; a query.

qualification 1. A quality or circumstance that is legally or inherently necessary to perform a function. 2. A restriction or modification in a document or transaction.

qualified 1. Eligible; possessing legal power or capacity. 2. Restricted or imperfect.

qualified acceptance A counteroffer; an acceptance that modifies the offer.

qualified disclaimer An irrevocable and unqualified refusal by a person to accept an interest in property (26 USC § 2518).

qualified domestic relations order (QDRO) A court order that allows a nonemployee to reach retirement benefits of an employee or former employee in order to satisfy a support or other marital obligation to the nonemployee.

qualified immunity A government official's immunity from liability for civil damages when performing discretionary functions if his or her conduct does not violate clearly established statutory or constitutional rights of which a reasonable person would have known.

qualified indorsement An indorsement that limits the liability of the indorser of a negotiable instrument.

qualified privilege See conditional privilege.

qualified terminable interest property (QTIP) Property that is transferred from a decedent spouse to the surviving spouse in which the latter has a qualifying income interest for life. A valid QTIP election must be made as to such property.

qualify 1. To make oneself fit or prepared. 2. To limit or restrict.

quantum meruit ("as much as he deserves") 1. An equitable theory of recovery based upon an implied agreement to pay for benefits or goods received. 2. The measure of damages imposed when a party prevails on the equitable claim of unjust enrichment.

The phrase "quantum meruit" means as much as he deserved and is premised upon finding of implied promise to pay plaintiff as much as he reasonably deserved and it is concerned with amount of damages resulting from implied promise of defendant to pay. *Pellegrino*, 201 N.Y.S.2d 275 (3 Dept., 1960)

quantum valebant An action seeking payment for goods sold and delivered based on an implied promise to pay as much as the goods are reasonably worth.

quarantine Isolation of persons, animals, goods, or vehicles suspected of carrying a contagious disease.

quare clausum fregit See trespass quare clausum fregit.

quash To vacate or annul; to suppress completely.

quasi Somewhat the same, but different; resembling.

quasi contract See implied in law contract.

quasi corporation A body or entity (often part of the government) that has some of the characteristics of a corporation but is not a corporation in the full sense.

quasi estoppel A party should be precluded from asserting, to another's disadvantage, a right or claim that is inconsistent with a position previously taken by the party.

Quasi estoppel or estoppel against inconsistent positions. These estoppel principles forbid a party from receiving the benefits of a transaction or statute, and then subsequently taking an inconsistent position to avoid the corresponding effects. *Zemel*, 815 N.Y.S.2d 496 (Sup. Ct., 2006)

quasi in rem jurisdiction A court's power over a person, but restricted to his or her specific interest in property within the territory over which the court has authority.

quasi judicial Pertaining to the power of an administrative agency (or official in the executive branch) to hear and determine controversies between the public and individuals in a manner that resembles a judicial trial.

quasi legislative Pertaining to the power of an administrative agency (or official in the executive branch) to write rules and regulations in a manner that resembles the legislature.

quasi-suspect classification A classification such as one based on gender or illegitimacy that will receive intermediate scrutiny by the court to determine its constitutionality.

Queen's Bench (Q.B.) See King's Bench.

question 1. An issue to be resolved. 2. Something asked; a query.

question of fact; question of law See issue of fact; issue of law.

quia emptores A 1290 English statute that had the effect of facilitating the alienation of fee-simple tenants.

quia timet An equitable remedy to be protected from anticipated future injury where it cannot be avoided by a present action at law.

quick assets Cash and assets readily convertible into cash (other than inventory).

quid pro quo Something for something; giving one thing for another. Quid pro quo sexual harassment exists when an employer conditions an employment benefit upon sexual favors from an employee.

quiet 1. Free from interference or adverse claims. 2. To make secure.

quiet enjoyment Possession of land that is not disturbed by superior ownership rights asserted by a third person.

> The covenant of quiet enjoyment means to ensure to the lessee a legal right to enter and enjoy the premises, and if he is prevented from entering into the possession by a person already in, under a paramount title, the action may be sustained. *Nodine,* 79 N.Y.S.2d 834 (Ct. Cl., 1948)

quiet title action An action to resolve conflicting claims to land. An action asserting an interest in land and calling on others to set forth their claims.

quit 1. To surrender possession. 2. To cease.

qui tam action An action in which a private plaintiff is allowed to sue under a statute that awards part of any penalty recovered to the plaintiff and the remainder to the government.

quitclaim 1. To transfer or release the extent of one's interest. 2. To surrender a claim. Also spelled quit-claim, quit claim.

quitclaim deed A deed that transfers or releases any interest or claim the grantor may have, without warranting that the title is valid. Also spelled quit-claim deed, quit claim deed.

> A quitclaim deed is as effective as any to convey all the title the grantor has. *Johnson,* 175 N.Y.S. 234 (Ct. Cl., 1918)

quittance A release from debt.

quod vide (q.v.) A reference directing the reader elsewhere in the text for more information.

quorum The minimum number of members who must be present in a deliberative body before business may be transacted.

quota 1. An assigned goal; the minimum sought. 2. A proportional part or allotment.

quotation 1. A word-for-word reproduction of text from another source. 2. A statement of current price.

quotient verdict A verdict on damages reached when the jurors agree to average the figures each juror states as his or her individual verdict.

> A quotient verdict results where jurors agree to write down amount of damages to which each thinks party is entitled, and the total of the amounts is divided by the number of jurors, provided that jurors agree to be bound by the quotient. *Honigsberg,* 249 N.Y.S.2d 296 (N.Y. City Civ. Ct., 1964)

quo warranto A court inquiry (by writ) to determine whether someone exercising government power is legally entitled to do so.

q.v. See quod vide.

R

® The symbol indicating registration of a trademark or servicemark with the U.S. Patent and Trademark Office.

race The historical division of humanity by physical characteristics. A grouping based on ancestry or ethnic characteristics.

race notice statute A recording law giving priority to the first party to record a claim, unless this person had notice of an unrecorded prior claim.

> Lack of knowledge is only the first hurdle which must be met under a race-notice recording act; the alleged bona fide purchaser still must win the race to the recording office. McKinney's Debtor and Creditor Law § 278. *Roth,* 722 N.Y.S.2d 566 (2 Dept., 2001)

race statute A recording law giving priority to the first party to record a claim, even if this person had notice of another's unrecorded prior claim. Also called pure race statute.

racial discrimination Discrimination based on one's race.

racketeer One who commits racketeering.

Racketeer Influenced and Corrupt Organizations Act (RICO) A federal statute imposing civil and criminal penalties for racketeering offenses such as engaging in a pattern of fraud, bribery, extortion, and other acts enumerated in the statute (18 USC § 1961). Some states have enacted similar statutes.

racketeering Crime engaged in as a business or organized enterprise, often involving illegal activity such as extortion, bribery, gambling, prostitution, and drug sales.

> A person is guilty of enterprise corruption when, having knowledge of the existence of a criminal enterprise and the nature of its activities, and being employed by or associated with such enterprise, he: (a) intentionally conducts or participates in the affairs of an enterprise by participating in a pattern of criminal activity; or (b) intentionally acquires or maintains any interest in or control of an enterprise by participating in a pattern of criminal activity; or (c) participates in a pattern of criminal activity and knowingly invests any proceeds derived from that conduct, or any proceeds derived from the investment or use of those proceeds, in an enterprise. McKinney's Penal Law § 460.20(1)

raid 1. An effort to entice personnel or customers away from a competitor. 2. A hostile attempt to take over a corporation by share purchases. 3. A sudden attack or forcible entry by law enforcement.

railroad To rush someone through without due care or due process.

rainmaker An attorney who brings fee-generating cases into the office due to his or her contacts or reputation.

raise 1. To increase. 2. To invoke or put forward. 3. To gather or collect. 4. To create or establish.

raise a check To increase the face amount of a check fraudulently.

rake-off A share of profits, often taken as a payoff or bribe.

RAM See reverse annuity mortgage.

ransom Money or other payment sought for the return of illegally detained persons or property.

rape Nonconsensual sexual intercourse.

> A person is guilty of rape in the third degree when: 1. He or she engages in sexual intercourse with another person who is

incapable of consent by reason of some factor other than being less than seventeen years old; 2. Being twenty-one years old or more, he or she engages in sexual intercourse with another person less than seventeen years old; or 3. He or she engages in sexual intercourse with another person without such person's consent where such lack of consent is by reason of some factor other than incapacity to consent. McKinney's Penal Law § 130.25

rape shield law A law imposing limits on defendant's use of evidence of the prior sexual experiences of an alleged rape victim.

rap sheet The arrest and conviction record of someone.

rasure Erasing part of a document by scraping.

ratable 1. Able to be evaluated or apportioned. 2. Taxable. 3. Proportionate.

rate 1. Relative value. A measure or degree in relationship to another measure. 2. Cost or price.

rate base The fair value of the property of a utility (or other entity) upon which a reasonable return is allowed.

rate of exchange See exchange (3).

rate of return Earnings or profit as a percentage of an investment.

ratification 1. An adoption or confirmation of a prior act or transaction, making one bound by it. 2. Formal approval.

Ratification is the express or implied adoption of the acts of another by one for whom the other assumes to be acting, but without authority, and it relates back and supplies original authority to execute an agreement. *Rocky Point Properties*, 744 N.Y.S.2d 269 (4 Dept., 2002)

ratio decidendi The ground, reason, principle, or rule of law that is the basis of a court's decision.

rational basis test A law will be upheld as constitutional if it rationally furthers a legitimate government objective.

ravish 1. To rape. 2. To seize and carry away by force.

re In the matter of; concerning or regarding.

reacquired stock See treasury securities (1).

ready, willing, and able Having sufficient funds, capacity, and desire to complete the transaction.

reaffirmation 1. A confirmation or approval of something already agreed to. 2. An agreement by a debtor to pay an otherwise dischargeable debt.

real 1. Pertaining to stationary or fixed property such as land. 2. True or genuine.

real chattel A real property interest that is less than a freehold or fee interest. An example is a lease of land.

real defense A defense such as duress and fraud in the factum that is good against everyone, including a holder in due course.

real estate See real property.

real estate broker An agent or intermediary who negotiates or arranges agreements pertaining to the sale and lease of real property.

Whenever used in this article real estate broker means any person, firm, limited liability company or corporation, who, for another and for a fee, commission or other valuable consideration, lists for sale, sells, at auction or otherwise, exchanges, buys or rents, or offers or attempts to negotiate a sale, at auction or otherwise, exchange, purchase or rental of an estate or interest in real estate, ... McKinney's Real Property Law § 440(1)

real estate investment trust (REIT) A business that invests in real estate on behalf of its shareholders.

Real Estate Settlement Procedures Act (RESPA) A federal law on disclosure of settlement costs in the sale of residential property financed by a federally insured lender (12 USC § 2601). See also HUD-1.

real evidence 1. Evidence that was actually involved in the incident being considered by the court. Also called physical evidence. 2. Evidence produced for inspection at trial.

realization 1. Conversion of an asset into cash. 2. The receipt by a taxpayer of actual economic gain or loss from the disposition of property.

realized gain or loss The difference between the amount realized on the disposition of property and the adjusted basis of the property.

real party in interest The person who benefits from or is harmed by the outcome of the case and who by substantive law has the legal right to enforce the claim in question. Also called party in interest.

real property Land and anything permanently attached or affixed to the land such as buildings, fences, and trees. Also called real estate, realty.

The term real property shall mean lands, structures, franchises, and interest in lands, and any and all things usually included within such term, and includes not only fees simple absolute but also any and all lesser interests, such as easements, rights of way, uses, leases, licenses, and all other incorporeal hereditaments and every estate, interest or right, legal or equitable, including terms of years, and liens thereon by way of judgments, mortgages or otherwise, and also claims for damage to real estate, in the area of the city. McKinney's Public Authorities Law § 1475-b(6)

realtor A real estate broker or agent, often a member of the National Association of Realtors (*www.realtor.org*).

realty See real property.

reapportionment The redistribution of representation in a legislative body resulting in a change in the number of representatives per district to reflect changes in population. The boundaries of the districts and the total number of representatives in the legislative body do not change, but the number of representatives in each district does. *Redistricting* is the redrawing of geographic boundary lines within a legislative district. See also gerrymander.

reargument Another presentation of arguments before the same court.

reason 1. An inducement, motive, or ground for action. 2. The faculty of the mind to form judgments based on logic.

reasonable Sensible and proper under the circumstances. Fair.

reasonable care The degree of care a person of ordinary prudence and intelligence would use under the same or similar circumstances to avoid injury or damage. Also called due care, ordinary care.

reasonable diligence The care and persistence of an ordinarily prudent person under the same or similar circumstances.

reasonable doubt Doubt that would cause prudent people to hesitate before acting in matters of importance to themselves. The standard of proof needed to convict someone of a crime is proof beyond a reasonable doubt.

reasonable force Force that an average person of ordinary intelligence in like circumstances would deem necessary.

reasonable man (person) A person who uses ordinary prudence under the circumstances to avoid injury or damage. (A legal guide or standard.) Also called ordinary prudent person.

reasonable suspicion A particularized and objective reason based on specific and articulable facts for suspecting someone of criminal activity.

reasonable time As much time as is needed, under the particular circumstances involved, to do what a contract or duty requires to be done.

reasonable use A use of one's property that is consistent with zoning rules and does not interfere with the lawful use of surrounding property.

> Reasonable use theory is that a landowner who interferes with the flow of surface waters is liable for injury only when his interference is unreasonable, in view of all relevant circumstances. *Bohemian Brethren Presbyterian Church*, 405 N.Y.S.2d 926 (Sup. Ct., 1978)

reasonable woman test A female plaintiff states a prima facie case of hostile environment sexual harassment when she alleges conduct that a reasonable woman would consider sufficiently severe or pervasive to alter the conditions of employment and create an abusive working environment.

rebate A reduction or return of part to the price.

rebellion Organized, open, and armed resistance to a constituted government or ruler by a subject.

rebut To refute, oppose, or repel.

rebuttable presumption An inference of fact that can be overcome by sufficient contrary evidence. Also called disputable presumption.

> A presumption that continues until overcome by evidence. Rebuttable presumptions arise in all cases where there has been sufficient evidence to make out a prima facie case and to throw on the opponent the burden of proving the contrary. *People ex rel. Bygland*, 134 N.Y.S.2d 328 (Child. Ct., 1954)

rebuttal Arguments or evidence given in reply to explain or counter an opponent.

recall 1. Removing a public official from office before the end of his or her term by a vote of the people. 2. A request by the manufacturer to return a defective product. 3. Revocation of a judgment.

recant To repudiate or retract something formally.

recapitalization A change or adjustment in the capital structure (stock, bonds, or other securities) of a corporation.

recaption Retaking chattels once in your possession or custody.

recapture 1. To retake or recover. 2. The recalculation of tax liability in order to remove improperly taken deductions or credits.

receipt 1. Written acknowledgment of receiving something. 2. Taking physical possession of something. 3. Receipts: income, money received.

receivable 1. Awaiting collection. 2. The amount still owed.

receiver A person appointed by the court to manage property in litigation or in the process of bankruptcy.

A receiver is a fiduciary and an officer of the court who acts at its direction and on its behalf. *Coronet Capital Co.*, 720 N.Y.S. 2d 158 (2 Dept., 2001)

receivership The condition of a company or individual over whom a receiver has been appointed. See receiver.

receiving stolen property Receiving or controlling stolen movable property of another, knowing that it has been stolen.

recess An interval when business is suspended without adjourning. A temporary cessation of judicial proceedings.

recidivism The tendency to return to a life of crime.

recidivist Repeat offender; habitual criminal.

reciprocal 1. Given or owed to each other. 2. Done in return.

reciprocal negative easement When an owner sells a portion of land with a restrictive covenant that benefits the land retained by the owner, the restriction becomes mutual.

reciprocal wills See mutual wills (1).

reciprocity A mutual exchange of the same benefits or treatment.

recision See rescission.

recital The formal setting forth of facts or reasons.

reckless Consciously failing to exercise due care but without intending the consequences; wantonly disregarding risks.

> Reckless and culpable conduct arises when actor has knowledge of highly dangerous nature of his actions or knowledge of such facts as under circumstances would disclose to reasonable man the dangerous character of his action, and despite this knowledge he so acts. *People v. Fink*, 238 N.Y.S.2d 847 (3 Dept., 1963)

reckless disregard Conscious indifference to consequences.

reckless endangerment Creating a substantial risk of major injury or death.

recklessness Knowing but disregarding a substantial risk that an injury or wrongful act may occur.

reclamation 1. Converting unusable land into land that is usable. 2. A seller's right to recover possession of goods from an insolvent buyer.

recognition 1. A formal acknowledgment or confirmation. 2. The point at which a tax on gain or loss is accounted for.

recognizance An obligation recorded in court to do some act required by law, e.g., to appear at all court proceedings.

> "Personal recognizance" means an agreement by a person made at the time of issuance of the wildlife citation that such person will comply with the terms of the citation. McKinney's ECL § 11-2503(k)

recollection The act of recalling or remembering.

reconciliation 1. The voluntary resumption of full marital relations. 2. The bringing of financial accounts into consistency or agreement.

reconduction 1. Renewing a lease. 2. The forcible return of illegal aliens.

reconsideration A review or reevaluation of a matter.

reconstruction 1. Rebuilding. 2. Re-creating an event.

reconveyance A transfer back. The return of something, e.g., title.

record 1. To make an official note of; to enter in a document. 2. A formal account of some act or event, e.g., a trial. 3. The facts that have been inscribed or stored.

recordation The formal recording of an instrument (e.g., a deed) with a county clerk or other public registry.

record date A date by which a shareholder must officially own shares in order to be entitled to a dividend or to vote.

recorded recollection See past recollection recorded.

recorder 1. An officer appointed to maintain public records, e.g., recorder of deeds. 2. A magistrate or judge with limited jurisdiction in some states.

recorder's court A court with limited criminal jurisdiction.

recording act; recording statute A law on recording deeds and other property instruments in order to establish priority among claims.

record owner Anyone recorded in a public registry as the owner.

record title See paper title.

recoupment 1. The defendant's right to a deduction from the plaintiff's damages due to plaintiff's breach of duty arising from the same contract. 2. An equitable remedy that permits the offset of mutual debts based on the same transaction or occurrence. 3. A reimbursement or recovery.

> "Recoupment" means a deduction from a money claim through a process whereby cross demands arising out of the same transaction are allowed to compensate one another and the balance only to be recovered. *National Cash Register Co.*, 86 N.E. 2d 561 (Ct. of App., 1949)

recourse 1. Turning or appealing for help; a way to enforce a right. 2. The right of a holder of a negotiable instrument to recover against an indorser or other party who is secondarily liable. 3. The right to reach other assets of the debtor if the collateral is insufficient.

recover 1. To obtain by court judgment or legal process. 2. To have restored; to regain possession.

recovery 1. That which is awarded by court judgment or legal process. 2. Restoration.

recrimination 1. A charge by the accused against the accuser. 2. An accusation that the party seeking the divorce has committed a serious marital wrong that in itself is a ground for divorce.

recross-examination Another cross-examination of a witness after redirect examination. The scope of recross is limited to matters raised on redirect.

recusal A judge's (or other decision-maker's) removal of him or herself from a matter because of a conflict of interest. Also called recusation. The verb is *recuse*.

redaction Revising or editing a text. Removing confidential or inappropriate parts of a text.

reddendum A provision in a deed in which the grantor reserves something out of what had been granted (e.g., rent).

redeemable bond A bond that the issuer may call back for payment before its maturity date. Also called callable bond.

redemption 1. Buying back; reclaiming or regaining possession by paying a specific price. Recovering what was mortgaged. 2. The repurchase of a security by the issuing corporation. 3. Converting shares into cash.

red herring 1. A diversion from the main issue; an irrelevant issue. 2. A preliminary prospectus.

redhibition Avoiding a sale due to a major defect in the thing sold.

> By the civil law, an action of redhibition, to rescind a sale and to compel the vendor to take back the property and restore the purchase money, could be brought by the vendee, wherever there was error in the essentials of the agreement, although both parties were ignorant of the defect which rendered the property sold unavailable to the purchaser for the purposes for which it was intended. *Bates*, 1835 WL 2471 (Chancery Ct. of NY, 1835)

redirect examination Another direct examination of a witness after he or she was cross-examined. The scope of redirect is limited to matters raised on cross-examination.

rediscount rate The rate the Federal Reserve System charges a member bank on a loan secured by paper the bank has already resold.

redistricting See reapportionment.

redlining 1. The discriminatory practice of denying credit or insurance to geographic areas due to the income, race, or ethnicity of its residents. 2. Showing the portions of an earlier draft of a text that have been stricken out.

> They were victims of a form of predatory lending called "reverse redlining," which is a scheme that targets low-income minorities, offering them exorbitantly high interest rate loans in large amounts, even though they do not have the ability to repay, thereby approving a loan designed to fail, and resulting in loss of the home through foreclosure. *EquiCredit Corp.*, 752 N.Y.S.2d 684 (2 Dept., 2002)

redraft A second note or bill drafted by the original drawer after the first draft has been dishonored.

redress Damages, equitable relief, or other remedy.

reductio ad absurdum Disproving an argument by showing that it leads to an absurd consequence or conclusion.

reduction to practice The point in time at which an invention is sufficiently tested to demonstrate it will work for its intended purpose.

redundancy Needless repetition; superfluous matter in a pleading.

reentry Retaking possession of land.

reexchange The expenses incurred due to a dishonor of a bill of exchange in a foreign country.

refer To send for further consideration or action.

referee A person to whom a judge refers a case for specific tasks, e.g., to take testimony and to file a report with the court.

referee in bankruptcy A court-appointed officer who performs administrative and judicial functions in bankruptcy cases. Now called a bankruptcy judge.

reference 1. The act of referring or sending a case for further consideration or action. 2. A source of information. 3. A citation in a document.

referendum The electorate's power to give final approval to an existing provision of the constitution or statute of the legislature.

> A "referendum" is no more than a veto power vested in the electorate to review an act of the town board and it can in no way constitute a direction to the local legislative body to do more than that body has already determined by its own resolution to accomplish. *Olin*, 231 N.Y.S.2d 286 (Sup. Ct., 1962)

refinance To replace one loan for another on different terms.

reformation An equitable remedy to correct a writing so that it embodies the actual intent of the parties.

reformatory A correctional institution for youthful offenders.

refreshing memory or **recollection** See present recollection refreshed.

refugee One seeking refuge in one country after being unwilling or unable to return to another.

refund 1. The return of an overpayment. 2. The return of the price paid for the returned product. 3. To finance again; to refinance.

refunding Refinancing a debt. Replacing a bond with a new bond issue.

reg. See regulation.

regent 1. A member of the governing board of a school. 2. A governor or ruler.

regime 1. A system of rules. 2. The current government.

register 1. To record formally. 2. To enroll. 3. A book containing official facts. 4. One who keeps official records. 5. A probate judge.

registered bond See registered security.

registered check A check guaranteed by a bank for a customer who provides funds for its payment.

registered mail Mail that is numbered and tracked by the U.S. Postal Service to monitor a safe delivery.

registered representative A representative who meets the requirements of the Securities and Exchange Commission to sell securities to the public.

registered security 1. A stock, bond, or other security whose owner is recorded (registered) by the issuer. 2. A security for sale for which a registration statement has been filed.

register of ships A customs list containing data on vessels, e.g., their owner and country of registration. A *registry* is a list of ships under the jurisdiction of a particular country.

registrar The official in charge of keeping records.

registration Inserting something in an official record; formally applying or enrolling. The process by which persons or institutions list their names on an official roster.

Federal registration number means such number assigned by the Federal agency to any person authorized to manufacture, distribute, sell, dispense or administer controlled substances. McKinney's Public Health Law § 3302(16)

registration statement A statement disclosing relevant financial and management data to potential investors in the securities of a company.

registry 1. A book or list kept for recording or registering documents or facts, e.g., a deed, the nationality of a ship. 2. A probate judge.

regressive tax A tax whose rate decreases as the tax base increases.

regs. See regulation.

regular course of business See course of business.

regular session One of the meetings scheduled at fixed times.

regulate To adjust or control by rule, method, or principle.

regulation (reg.) 1. A rule governing conduct; the management of conduct by rules. 2. An administrative agency's rule or order that carries out statutes or executive orders that govern the agency.

Regulation D A regulation of the Securities and Exchange Commission governing the limited offer and sale of unregistered securities.

regulatory agency A government agency that regulates an area of public concern and that can implement statutes by issuing regulations.

regulatory offense 1. A crime created by statute. 2. A minor offense. Also called a public-welfare offense.

regulatory taking Government regulation that deprives a private owner of all or substantially all practical uses of his or her property.

"Regulatory taking" occurs when government regulates the property in a manner that unfairly imposes on the property owner a burden that should be borne by the public as a whole. *Sobel*, 590 N.Y.S.2d 883 (1 Dept., 1992)

rehabilitation 1. Restoration of credibility to an impeached witness. 2. Improving the character of an offender to prevent recidivism. 3. A reorganizing of debts in bankruptcy.

rehearing An additional hearing to correct an error or oversight.

reimburse 1. To pay back. 2. To indemnify.

reinstate To restore; to place again in a former condition or office.

reinsurance A contract by which one insurer (called the reinsurer) insures all or part of the risks of another insurer; insurance for insurers.

REIT See real estate investment trust.

rejection A refusal to accept something, e.g., an offer, performance.

rejoinder Defendant's response to a plaintiff's reply or replication.

relation back The rule that an act done at one time is considered by a fiction of the law to have been done at a prior time.

"Relation back" doctrine allows a claim asserted against a defendant in an amended filing to relate back to claims previously asserted against a codefendant for statute of limitations purposes where the two defendants are united in interest. *Pappas*, 773 N.Y.S.2d 108 (2 Dept., 2004)

relative A person related by blood or marriage.

relator 1. See ex rel. 2. An informer. 3. One who applies for a writ.

release 1. To set free from custody. 2. To discharge or relinquish a claim against another. 3. To allow something to be communicated or published. 4. The giving up of a right, claim, interest, or privilege.

release on own recognizance (ROR) Pretrial release of a defendant in a criminal case without posting a bond, based solely on a promise to appear. Also called personal recognizance, own recognizance (OR).

relevance Logically connected to the matter at hand. Being relevant.

relevant Logically tending to establish or disprove a fact. Pertinent. Relevant evidence is evidence having any tendency to make the existence of a fact more probable or less probable than it would be without the evidence.

reliance Faith or trust felt by someone; dependence on someone.

relict A widow or widower.

reliction The gradual alteration of land by withdrawing water.

relief 1. Redress sought from a court. 2. Assistance to the poor.

religion A belief system of faith and worship, often involving a supernatural being or power and moral or ethical rules.

rem See in rem.

remainder 1. A future estate or interest arising in someone other than the grantor or transferor (or the heirs of either) that will take effect upon the natural termination of the prior estate. 2. That which is left over; the remaining portions not otherwise disposed of.

"Remainder beneficiary" means a person entitled to receive principal when an income interest ends. McKinney's EPTL § 11-A-1.2(11)

remainderman One who holds or is entitled to a remainder.

remand 1. To send back for further action. 2. To return to custody. 3. The act of sending something or someone back for further action or proceedings.

remediable Capable of being remedied.

remedial 1. Intended to correct wrongs and abuses. 2. Providing an avenue of redress.

remedial action 1. Action to solve long-term environmental damage. 2. Action to redress an individual wrong.

remedial statute 1. A statute that provides a remedy or means to enforce a right. 2. A statute designed to correct an existing law.

remedy 1. The means by which a right is enforced or the violation of a right is prevented or redressed. 2. To correct.

remise To give up or release.

remission 1. Canceling or relinquishing a debt or claim. 2. Pardon or forgiveness.

remit 1. To send or forward. 2. To transmit (money). 3. To refer for further action. 4. To cancel or excuse; to pardon. 5. To mitigate.

remittance Money sent (or the sending of money) as payment.

remitter 1. A person who purchases an instrument from its issuer if the instrument is payable to an identified person other than the purchaser. 2. The relation back of a later defective title to an earlier valid one. 3. Sending a case back to a lower court. 4. One who sends payment to another.

remittitur The power of the court to order a new trial unless a party agrees to reduce the jury verdict in its favor by a stated amount.

remonstrance A statement of grievances or reasons against something.

remote 1. Removed in relation, space, or time. 2. Minor or slight.

remote cause 1. A cause too removed in time from the event. 2. A cause that some independent force took advantage of to produce what was not the probable or natural effect of the original act.

removal The transfer of a person or thing from one place to another, e.g., transfer of a case from one court to another.

render To pronounce or deliver. To report formally.

There is a clear distinction between rendering a judgment and entering one; the former is a judicial act of the court, the latter the ministerial act of the clerk. The entry of the judgment is per se not the judgment but rather the evidence of it. The clerk is a mere ministerial officer and without authority to enter a judgment the court did not render *Dowling*, 133 N.Y.S.2d 667 (Sup. Ct., 1954)

rendition 1. Returning a fugitive to a state where he or she is wanted. 2. Making or delivering a formal decision.

renewal A reestablishment of a legal duty or relationship.

renounce To repudiate or abandon.

rent Cash or other consideration (often paid at intervals) for the use of property.

Consideration, including any bonus, benefit or gratuity demanded or received for or in connection with the use of occupancy of housing accommodations or the transfer of a lease of such housing accommodations. *Garden Towers Co.*, 416 N.Y.S. 2d 828 (2 Dept., 1979)

rent-a-judging A method of alternative dispute resolution in which the parties hire a private person (e.g., a retired judge) to resolve their dispute.

rental 1. Something rented. 2. Rent to be paid.

rent strike An organized effort by tenants to withhold rent until grievances are resolved, e.g., repair of defective conditions.

renunciation The abandonment or waiver of a right or venture.

renvoi The doctrine under which the court of the forum, in resorting to a foreign law, adopts the rules of the foreign law as to conflict of laws, which rules may in turn refer the court back to the law of the forum.

The process of referring back to the foreign jurisdiction's conflict of laws rules is known as "renvoi," the doctrine of remission, whereby the forum state looks to the whole law of the foreign jurisdiction, which is generally not recognized in the United States except in land title and divorce cases. Uniform Commercial Code, § 9-103(3). *Reger*, 372 N.Y.S.2d 97 (Sup. Ct., 1975)

reopen To allow new evidence to be introduced in a trial that was completed. To review a closed case.

reorganization A financial restructuring of a corporation for purposes of achieving bankruptcy protection, tax benefits, or efficiency.

reorganization plan A corporation's proposal to a bankruptcy court for restructuring under Chapter 11.

rep. See report, reporter, representative, republic.

reparable injury An injury for which money compensation is adequate.

reparation Compensation for an injury or wrong. Expiation.

repeal The express or implied abrogation of a law by a legislative body. Rescind.

repeat offender Someone convicted of a crime more than once.

replacement cost The current cost of creating a substantially equivalent structure or other asset.

replevin An action to recover possession of personal property wrongfully held or detained and damages incidental to the detention.

One who by virtue of an illegal transaction obtained possession only of property cannot recover in "replevin action" against third person. *Hofferman*, 49 N.E. 2d 523 (Ct. of App., 1943)

replevin bond A bond posted by the plaintiff when seeking replevin.

replevy To regain possession of personal property through replevin.

replication A plaintiff's response to the defendant's plea or answer.

reply A plaintiff's response to the defendant's counterclaim, plea, or answer.

reply brief The appellate brief filed by the appellant in response to the appellee's brief. A brief responding to an opponent's brief.

repo 1. An agreement to buy back a security. 2. See repossession.

report (rep.) 1. A written account of a court decision. 2. A volume (or set of volumes) of court opinions. Also called reports. 3. A volume (or set of volumes) of administrative decisions. 4. A formal account or descriptive statement.

reporter (rep.) 1. The person in charge of reporting the decisions of a court. 2. The person who takes down and transcribes proceedings. 3. A volume (or set of volumes) of court opinions. Also called case reports.

reporter's privilege See journalist's privilege (1).

reports See report (2).

repose See statute of repose.

repossession (repo) The taking back of property, e.g., a creditor's seizure of property bought on credit by a debtor in default.

representation 1. The act of representing or acting on behalf of another. 2. A statement of fact expressed by words or conduct, often made to induce another's conduct. 3. See also per stirpes.

representative (rep.) 1. One who acts on behalf of another. 2. A legislator. 3. Serving as an example.

representative action See derivative action; class action.

reprieve A stay or postponement in carrying out a sentence.

reprimand An official declaration that an attorney's conduct was unethical. The declaration does not affect the attorney's right to practice law. A *private reprimand* is not disclosed to the public; a *public reprimand* is.

A severe or formal reproof; a censure, especially one given with authority. *Locust Club of Rochester*, 265 N.Y.S.2d 744 (Sup. Ct., 1965)

reprisal Action taken in retaliation.

reproductive rights Rights pertaining to one's reproductive and sexual life, e.g., using contraceptives, access to abortion.

republic Government in which supreme authority lies with the voters who act through elected representatives. A republican form of government.

republication 1. Repetition of a statement already published or communicated once. 2. Steps that reestablish a revoked will, e.g., adding a codicil to it.

repudiation 1. Denial or rejection. 2. Declaring a refusal to perform.

repugnant Incompatible; irreconcilably inconsistent.

reputation The views or esteem others have of a person.

request for admission A method of pretrial discovery in which one party asks another to admit the truth of any matter that pertains to a statement or opinion of fact or the application of law to fact.

[A] party may serve upon any other party a written request for admission by the latter of the genuineness of any papers or documents, or the correctness or fairness of representation of any photographs, described in and served with the request, or of the truth of any matters of fact set forth in the request, as to which the party requesting the admission reasonably believes there can be no substantial dispute at the trial and which are within the knowledge of such other party or can be ascertained by him upon reasonable inquiry. McKinney's CPLR § 3123(a)

request for instructions A party's request that the trial judge provide the jury with the instructions stated in the request.

request for judicial intervention (RJI) The form filed in supreme court and county court that triggers a judge being assigned to a case, part of the individual assignment system (IAS). 22 NYCRR 202.3

request for production A method of pretrial discovery consisting of a demand that the other side make available documents and other tangible things for inspection, copying, and testing. McKinney's CPLR 3120

requirements contract A contract in which the buyer agrees to buy all of its goods and services from a seller, which agrees to fill these needs during the period of the contract.

requisition 1. A formal request or demand. 2. The seizure of property by the state.

res 1. The subject matter of a trust or will. 2. A thing or object, a status.

res adjudicata See res judicata.

resale A sale of goods after another buyer of those goods breaches its contract to buy them.

resale price maintenance A form of vertical price-fixing by which a manufacturer sets the price at which its buyers resell to others.

rescind 1. To annul or repeal. 2. To cancel a contract.

rescission A party's cancellation of a contract because of a material breach by the other party or by mutual agreement. Also spelled recision.

"Rescission" is act of abrogating, cancelling, vacating or annulling; the undoing of a thing. *Carlson*, 314 N.Y.S.2d 77 (Sup. Ct., 1970)

rescript 1. A direction from a court to a clerk on how to dispose of a case. 2. The decision of the appellate court sent to the trial court.

rescue doctrine An injured rescuer can recover from the original tortfeasor who negligently caused the event that precipitated the rescue.

reservation 1. A right or interest created for the grantor in land granted to the grantee. 2. A tract of land to which a Native American tribe retains the original title or which is set aside for its use. 3. A condition through a limitation, qualification, or exception.

reserve 1. To keep back or retain. 2. A fund set aside to cover future expenses, losses, or claims.

reserve banks Member banks of the Federal Reserve System.

reserve clause A contract clause giving club owners a continuing and exclusive right to the services of a professional athlete.

reserved point See point reserved.

reserved powers Powers not delegated to the federal government by the U.S. Constitution nor prohibited by it to the states and hence reserved to the states or to the people. (U.S. Const. Amend. X.)

reserve price The minimum auction price a seller will accept.

res gestae declarations Spontaneous or unfiltered statements made in the surrounding circumstances of an event (e.g., excited utterances) are sometimes admissible as exceptions to the hearsay rule.

"Res gestae" means literally "the thing done," and when applied to a declaration made by a participant, during or after an injury or other startling event, is generally considered a matter of admissibility. *Murphy*, 183 N.Y.S.2d 787 (Sup. Ct., 1959)

residence 1. Living or remaining in a particular locality for more than a transitory period but without the intent to stay there indefinitely. If this intent existed, the place would be a domicile. Sometimes, however, residence and domicile are treated as synonyms. 2. A fixed abode or house.

residency The place where one has a residence.

resident One who occupies a dwelling and has an ongoing physical presence therein. This person may or may not be a domiciliary.

"Resident" shall mean an individual legally domiciled within the state. McKinney's Elder Law § 241(5)

resident agent One authorized to accept service of process for another.

resident alien A noncitizen who legally establishes a long-term residence or domicile in this country.

residual 1. Pertaining to that which is left over or what lingers. 2. Payment for reuse of a protected work.

residuary What is left over. See also residuary estate.

residuary bequest A bequest of the residuary estate.

residuary clause A clause in a will disposing of the residuary estate.

residuary devise A devise of the residuary estate.

residuary estate The remainder of an estate after all debts and claims are paid and after all specific bequests (gifts) are satisfied. Also called residuary, residue, residuum.

residuary legacy A legacy of the residuary estate.

residuary legatee The person who receives the residuary estate.

residue What is left over. See also residuary estate.

residuum What is left over. See also residuary estate.

res inter alios acta ("a thing done among others") A person cannot be affected by the words or acts of others with

whom he or she is in no way connected, and for whose words or acts he or she is not legally responsible.

res ipsa loquitur ("the thing speaks for itself") An inference of the defendant's negligence arises when the event producing the harm (a) was of a kind that ordinarily does not occur in the absence of someone's negligence, (b) was caused by an agency or instrumentality within the defendant's exclusive control, and (c) was not due to any voluntary action or contribution on the part of the plaintiff.

The doctrine of "res judicata," or "claim preclusion," bars a party from asserting claims that it raised or could have raised in any prior action against the same parties, or parties in privity, based on the same transaction. *Landmark West!*, 802 N.Y.S. 2d 340 (Sup. Ct., 2005)

resisting arrest Intentionally preventing a peace officer from effecting a lawful arrest.

res judicata ("a thing adjudicated") A final judgment on the merits will preclude the same parties from later relitigating the same claim and any other claim based on the same facts or transaction that could have been raised in the first suit but was not. Also called claim preclusion.

res nova A question the courts have not yet addressed.

resolution 1. An expression of the opinion or will of an assembly or group. 2. A decision or authorization. The verb is *resolve*.

resort A place or destination to obtain redress or assistance.

RESPA See Real Estate Settlement Procedures Act.

respite A delay, e.g., a temporary suspension of the execution of a sentence, additional time to pay a debt.

respondeat superior ("let the master answer") An employer or principal is responsible (liable) for the wrongs committed by an employee or agent within the scope of employment or agency.

Under the doctrine of "respondeat superior," an employer is answerable for the tortious acts of its employees if those acts were within the scope of employment and in furtherance of the employer's business. *Compass Group*, 795 N.Y.S.2d 395 (3 Dept., 2005)

respondent 1. The party against whom a claim, petition, or bill is filed. 2. The party against whom an appeal is brought; the appellee.

responsibility 1. Being accountable, liable, or at fault. 2. A duty.

responsible bidder An experienced, solvent, available contract bidder.

responsive Constituting an answer or response; nonevasive.

responsive pleading A pleading that replies to a prior pleading of an opponent.

rest To indicate to the court that a party has presented all of the evidence he or she intends to submit at this time.

Restatements Treatises of the American Law Institute (e.g., *Restatement (Second) of Torts*) that state the law and indicate changes in the law that the Institute would like to see implemented (*www.ali.org*).

restitution 1. Making good or giving an equivalent value for any loss, damage, or injury. 2. An equitable remedy to prevent unjust enrichment.

"Restitution" is return of all the fruits of a crime while "reparation" is partial return of as much as defendant can afford.

McKinney's Penal Law § 60.27. *People v. Young*, 618 N.Y.S.2d 983 (Sup. Ct., 1994)

restraining order A court order not to do a threatened act, e.g., to harass someone, to transfer assets. Also called protection order, protective order.

restraint Restriction, prohibition; confinement.

restraint of marriage An inducement or obligation not to marry that results from a condition attached to a gift.

restraint of trade Contracts or combinations that tend to or are designed to eliminate competition, artificially set prices, or otherwise hamper a free market in commerce.

restraint on alienation A provision in an instrument (e.g., a deed) that prohibits or restricts transfers of the property by the grantee.

restricted security Stock whose sale to the public is restricted. The stock is not registered with the Securities and Exchange Commission. Also called letter stock.

restrictive covenant 1. A restriction created by covenant or agreement (e.g., in a deed) on the use of land. Also called equitable servitude. 2. See covenant not to compete.

"Restrictive covenants," commonly categorized as negative easements, restrain servient landowners from making otherwise lawful uses of their property. *Breakers Motel*, 638 N.Y.S.2d 135 (2 Dept., 1996)

restrictive indorsement An indorsement that limits or conditions the further negotiability of the instrument.

resulting trust A remedy used when a person makes a disposition of property under circumstances that raise the inference that he or she did not intend to transfer a beneficial interest to the person taking or holding the property. Also called implied trust, presumptive trust.

resulting use An implied use remaining with the grantor in a conveyance without consideration.

retailer A business that sells goods to the ultimate consumer.

retain 1. To engage the services of or employ. 2. To hold.

retainage A portion of the contract price withheld to assure that the contractor will satisfy its obligations and complete the project.

retained earnings See earned surplus.

retainer 1. The act of hiring or engaging the services of someone, usually a professional. 2. An amount of money (or other property) a client pays a professional as a deposit or advance against future fees, costs, and expenses of providing services.

Retainer has been defined as the securing of an attorney at law to perform professional services in the business of another, in such manner that he cannot engage himself to, or perform any service in the employment in the interest of, the opposing party, or in any manner do anything in the business prejudicial to the party employing him. *MacPherson*, 149 N.Y.S.2d 525 (Sup. Ct., 1956)

retaliatory eviction An eviction because the tenant has complained about the leased premises.

retirement 1. Voluntarily withdrawing from one's occupation or career. 2. Taking out of circulation.

retirement plans Pension or other benefit plans for retirement.

retraction Withdrawing a declaration, accusation, or promise. Recanting.

retraxit Voluntary withdrawal of a lawsuit that cannot be rebrought.

retreat rule Before using deadly force in self-defense against a deadly attack, there is a duty to withdraw or retreat if this is a safe alternative, unless (under the castle doctrine) the attack occurs in one's home or business.

A person may not use deadly physical force upon another person . . . unless: (a) The actor reasonably believes that such other person is using or about to use deadly physical force. Even in such case, however, the actor may not use deadly physical force if he or she knows that with complete personal safety, to oneself and others he or she may avoid the necessity of so doing by retreating; except that the actor is under no duty to retreat if he or she is: (i) in his or her dwelling and not the initial aggressor; . . . McKinney's Penal Law § 35.15(2)

retrial A new trial of a previously tried case.

retribution Punishment that is deserved.

retroactive Applying or extending to a time prior to enactment or issuance. Also called retrospective.

retrocession Ceding back something, e.g., title, jurisdiction.

retrospective See retroactive.

return 1. A report of a court officer on what he or she did with a writ or other court instrument. 2. Profit. 3. See tax return.

return day The day on which a litigation event must occur, e.g., file an answer, appear in court.

return of service See proof of service.

rev'd See reversed.

revenue Gross income; total receipts.

revenue bond A government bond payable by public funds.

Revenue Procedure The position of the Internal Revenue Service on procedural requirements for matters before it.

Revenue Ruling (Rev. Rul.) The opinion of the Internal Revenue Service of how the tax law applies to a specific transaction.

revenue stamp A stamp used to certify that a tax has been paid.

reversal An appellate court's setting aside of a lower court decision.

reverse annuity mortgage (RAM) A mortgage on a residence in which the borrower receives periodic income and the loan is repaid when the property is sold or the borrower dies. Also called reverse mortgage.

reversed (rev'd) Overturned on appeal.

reverse discrimination Discrimination against members of a majority group, usually because of affirmative action for a minority group.

"Reverse discrimination," also called "benign" discrimination, may be defined as classifications that are designed to assist selected groups of persons presumed to be shown to be disadvantaged; in a somewhat broader and more coarse context, the term "affirmative action" is utilized. *Alevy*, 384 N.Y.S.2d 82 (Ct. of App., 1976)

reverse mortgage See reverse annuity mortgage.

reverse stock split Calling in all outstanding shares and reissuing fewer shares with greater value.

reversible error See prejudicial error.

reversion The undisposed portion of an estate remaining in a grantor when he or she conveys less than his or her whole estate and, therefore, retains a portion of the title. The residue of the estate left with the grantor.

A "reversion" is the residue of an estate left in the grantor to commence in possession after determination of some estate granted out by him. *Application of Board of Ed. of Utica City*, 184 N.Y.S.2d 735 (Sup. Ct., 1959)

reversionary interest The interest that a person has in the reversion of property. See reversion. Any future interest left in a transferor.

reversioner A person who is entitled to an estate in reversion.

revert To turn back; to return to.

reverter See possibility of reverter.

revest To vest again with a power or interest.

rev'g Reversing.

review 1. To examine or go over a matter again. 2. The power of a court to examine the correctness of what a lower tribunal has done. Short for judicial review (see this phrase).

Revised Statutes (R.S.)(Rev. Stat.) A collection of statutes that have been revised, rearranged, or reenacted as a whole.

revival Renewing the legal force or effectiveness of something.

revocable Susceptible of being withdrawn, canceled, or invalidated.

revocable trust A trust that the maker (settlor) can cancel or revoke.

revocation Canceling, voiding, recalling, or destroying something.

Where offeror takes definite action inconsistent with intention to enter into proposed contract, such action is considered a valid "revocation." *Norca Corp.*, 643 N.Y.S.2d 139 (2 Dept., 1996)

revolving credit An extension of credit to customers who may use it as desired up to a specified dollar limit.

Rev. Rul. See Revenue Ruling.

Rev. Stat. See Revised Statutes.

RFP Request for production; request for proposals.

Richard Roe See John Doe.

RICO See Racketeer Influenced and Corrupt Organizations Act.

rider An amendment or addition attached to a legislative bill, insurance policy, or other document.

right 1. Morally, ethically, or legally proper. 2. A legal power, privilege, immunity, or protected interest one can claim.

right-from-wrong test See insanity (4).

right of action The right to bring a suit. A right that can be enforced.

right of common See profit à prendre.

right of election See election by spouse.

right of first refusal A right to equal the terms of another offer.

A "right of first refusal" binds a party who wishes to sell property not to do so without first giving another the opportunity to purchase such property at a specified price. *Krieger*, 697 N.Y.S.2d 766 (3 Dept., 1999)

right of privacy See invasion of privacy.

right of redemption 1. A mortgagor's right to redeem property after it has been foreclosed. 2. See equity of redemption.

right of re-entry The estate that the grantor may acquire again upon breach of a condition under which it was granted.

right of survivorship A joint tenant's right to receive the entire estate upon the death of the other joint tenant.

Joint account with right of survivorship under common law entitles the survivor to recover deposit from joint tenant's administrator. *Herrick*, 290 N.Y.S. 65 (Sup. Ct., 1936)

right of way 1. The right to pass over the land of another. 2. The right in traffic to pass or proceed first.

right to bear arms The Second Amendment right "to keep and bear arms."

right-to-convey covenant See covenant of seisin.

right to counsel A constitutional right to an appointed attorney in some criminal and juvenile delinquency cases when the accused cannot afford private counsel.

right to die A right of a competent, terminally ill adult to refuse medical treatment.

right to travel A constitutional right to travel freely between states.

right-to-work law A state law declaring that employees are not required to join a union as a condition of receiving or retaining a job.

rigor mortis Muscular rigidity or stiffening shortly after death.

riot Three or more persons assembled together for a common purpose and disturbing the peace by acting in a violent or tumultuous manner.

riparian right The right of owners of land adjoining a waterway to make reasonable use of the water, e.g., for ingress, egress, and fishing.

ripeness doctrine A court will decline to address a claim unless the case presents definite and concrete issues, a real and substantial controversy exists, and there is a present need for adjudication. See also justiciable.

risk The danger or hazard of a loss or injury occurring.

risk capital An investment of money or property in a business, often a new venture involving high risk. See also venture capital.

risk of loss Responsibility for loss, particularly during transfer of goods. The danger of bearing this responsibility.

risk of nonpersuasion See burden of persuasion.

RJI See request for judicial intervention.

robbery Unlawfully taking property from the person of another (or in his or her presence) by the use of violence or threats.

"Robbery" is "larceny" that has been committed with use of or immediate threat of use of physical force. Penal Law § 155.05. *People v. Banks*, 389 N.Y.S.2d 664 (3rd Dept., 1976)

Robert's Rules of Order Rules for conducting meetings. A parliamentary manual.

rogatory letters See letter rogatory.

roll 1. The record of official proceedings. 2. An official list.

rollover 1. Refinancing or renewing a short-term loan. 2. Reinvesting funds in a plan that qualifies for the same tax treatment.

Roman Law The legal system and laws of ancient Rome that is the foundation of civil law in some European countries.

root of title The recorded conveyance that begins a chain-of-title search on specific real property.

ROR Release on own recognizance. See personal recognizance.

ROS Right of survivorship. See joint tenancy.

***Rosario* rule** Prior to a witness being called in a criminal case, all written and recorded statements of the witness, as well as the witness's criminal record and notice of any pending criminal actions against the witness, must be provided to the other side. McKinney's CPL § 240.45; *Rosario* 213 N.Y.S.2d 448 (Ct. of App., 1961)

Roth IRA An individual retirement account with nondeductible contributions but tax-free distributions after age 59½.

round lot The unit of trading securities, e.g., 100 shares.

royalty 1. Payment for each use of a work protected by copyright or patent. 2. Payment for the right to extract natural resources.

R.S. See Revised Statutes.

rubric 1. The title of a statute. 2. A rule. 3. A category. 4. A preface.

rule 1. An established standard, guide, or regulation. 2. A court procedure. 3. The controlling authority. 4. To decide a point of law.

rule against accumulations Limits on a trust's accumulation of income.

rule against perpetuities No interest is valid unless it must vest, if at all, within 21 years (plus a period of gestation) after the death of some life or lives in being (i.e., alive) at the time the interest was created.

> Under "rule against perpetuities" no interest subject to a condition precedent is good, unless condition must be fulfilled, if at all, within 21 years after some life in being at creation of the interest. *In re Sherman's Will*, 71 N.Y.S.2d 492 (Sup. Ct., 1947)

rule in Shelley's case When in the deed or other instrument an estate of freehold is given to a person and a remainder to his or her heirs in fee or in tail, that person takes the entire estate—a fee simple absolute.

rule in Wild's case If X devises land to Y and Y's children, the devise is a fee tail if Y has no children at the time of the devise but a joint tenancy if Y has children at that time.

rulemaking The process and power of an administrative agency to make rules and regulations.

rule nisi See decree nisi.

rule of completeness A party may introduce the whole of a statement if any part is introduced by the opposing party.

rule of four The U.S. Supreme Court will accept a case on certiorari if at least four justices vote to do so.

rule of law 1. A legal principle or ruling. 2. Supremacy of law.

rule of lenity When there is ambiguity in a criminal statute, particularly as to punishment, doubts are resolved in favor of the defendant.

> Under the "rule of lenity," if a statute is not clear in its scope and extent, so that reasonable minds might differ as to its intention, the court must adopt the less harsh meaning; expressed otherwise, under this rule, doubt will be resolved in favor of the accused person. *People v. Cutten*, 703 N.Y.S.2d 655 (Co. Ct., 1999)

rule of reason 1. In antitrust cases, the issue is whether the restraint's anticompetitive effects substantially outweigh the procompetitive effects for which the restraint is reasonably necessary. 2. A requirement to consider pertinent evidence and reasonable alternatives in decision making.

rules committee A legislative committee establishing agendas and procedures for considering proposed legislation.

rules of professional conduct See Model Rules of Professional Conduct.

ruling A judicial or administrative decision.

run 1. To apply or be effective. 2. To expire because of elapsed time. 3. To accompany or go with a conveyance.

runaway shop An employer who relocates or transfers work for antiunion reasons.

runner 1. One who solicits business, especially accident cases. 2. An employee who delivers and files papers.

running account A continuous record kept to show all the transactions (charges and payments) between a debtor and creditor.

running with the land See covenant running with the land.

S

sabotage Willful destruction of property or interference with normal operations of a government or employer.

safe harbor Protection from liability if acting in good faith.

said Before mentioned; aforementioned.

sailor's will See military will.

salable Fit to be offered for sale. Merchantable.

salary Compensation for services paid at regular intervals.

sale The transfer of title to property for a consideration or price. A contract for this transfer.

> Sale or sell means any transfer, gift, barter, sale, offer for sale, or advertisement for sale in any manner or by any means whatsoever, including any transfer of motor fuel from a person to itself or an affiliate at another level of distribution, but does not include product exchanges at the wholesale level of distribution. McKinney's General Business Law § 370-b(q)

sale and leaseback See leaseback.

sale by sample A sale of goods in quantity or bulk with the understanding that they will conform in quality with a sample.

sale in gross A sale of land in which the boundaries are identified but the quantity of land is unspecified or deemed to be immaterial.

sale on approval A conditional sale that is absolute only if the buyer is satisfied with the goods, whether or not they are defective.

sale or return A sale to a merchant buyer who can return any unsold goods (even if not defective) if they were received for resale.

sales tax A tax on the sale of goods and services, computed as a percentage of the purchase price.

salvage 1. Property saved or remaining after a casualty. 2. Rescue of assets from loss. 3. Payment for saving a ship or its cargo.

salvage value An asset's value after its useful life for the owner has ended.

same evidence test When the same acts violate two distinct statutory provisions, the double-jeopardy test of whether there are two offenses or one is whether each provision requires proof of a fact the other does not.

sanction 1. A penalty for a violation. 2. Approval or authorization.

S&L See savings and loan association.

sane Of sound mind; able to distinguish right from wrong.

sanitary Pertaining to health and hygiene.

sanity The condition of having a sound mind.

> One may not be technically insane but nevertheless incompetent to care for and manage one's property. *Application of Brown*, 46 N.Y.S.2d 575 (Sup. Ct., 1944). Sanity within statute establishing as standard of mental capacity to stand trial determination as to whether defendant is in such state of idiocy, imbecility or insanity as to be incapable of understanding charge against him, or proceedings, or of making his defense, involves more than superficial knowledge by defendant that he is charged with particular crime and ability to recall the incident at time of its commission. *People v. Swallow*, 301 N.Y.S.2d 798 (Sup. Ct., 1969)

sanity hearing A hearing to determine fitness to stand trial or whether institutionalization is needed.

satisfaction The discharge or performance of a legal obligation.

> An accord and satisfaction, as its name implies, has two components; an accord is an agreement that a stipulated performance will be accepted, in the future, in lieu of an existing claim, while execution of the agreement is a satisfaction. McKinney's General Obligations Law § 15-501, subd. 1. *Chappelow*, 758 N.Y.S.2d 782 (Sup. Ct., 2003)

satisfaction contract A contract in which the stated standard of performance is the satisfaction of one of the parties (e.g., a contract giving an employer sole discretion to decide if an employee should be terminated for unacceptable work).

satisfaction of judgment 1. Full payment or compliance with a judgment. 2. A document so stating.

satisfaction piece A statement by the parties that the obligation between them has been paid or satisfied.

save harmless See hold harmless.

saving clause 1. A clause in a statute that preserves certain rights, remedies, privileges, or claims. 2. See severability clause. 3. See saving-to-suitors clause.

savings and loan association (S&L) A financial institution that specializes in making mortgage loans for private homes.

saving-to-suitors clause A statutory clause allowing certain admiralty claims to be brought in nonadmiralty courts. (28 USC § 1333.) Also called saving clause.

savings bank trust See Totten trust.

savings bond A United States government bond that cannot be traded.

S.B. See senate bill.

scab A worker who crosses a picket line to work or otherwise acts in disregard of positions or demands of a union. Also called strikebreaker.

scalper One who resells something at an inflated price for a quick profit.

scandalous matter Irrelevant matter in a pleading that casts a derogatory light on someone's moral character or uses repulsive language.

scènes à faire General themes that cannot be copyrighted.

schedule A written list or plan. An inventory.

schedule A An informal term meaning a separate page (attached to a deed) containing a metes-and-bounds description of land.

scheduled property A list of properties with their values.

scheme A plan of action, often involving deception.

scienter 1. Intent to deceive or mislead. 2. Knowingly done.

> Liability for foreseeable harm will be imposed upon proof that the particular animal possessed a propensity that caused the plaintiff's injury, and that the defendant had actual or constructive knowledge of that propensity. This knowledge is termed scienter. *Giles*, 431 N.Y.S.2d 781 (Ct. Cl., 1980)

sci. fa. See scire facias.

scilicet That is to say. See ss.

scintilla A minute amount; a trace.

scire facias (sci. fa.) 1. A writ ordering one to appear on a matter of record and show cause why another should not be able to take advantage of that record. 2. The procedure by which a lienholder prosecutes a lien to judgment.

scope of authority An agent's express or implied authorization to act for the principal.

scope of employment That which is foreseeably done by an employee for an employer under the latter's specific or general control.

S corporation A corporation whose shareholders are taxed on the income of the corporation. Also called subchapter S corporation.

> The term New York S corporation means, with respect to any taxable year, a corporation subject to tax under this article for which an election is in effect pursuant to subsection (a) of section six hundred sixty of this chapter for such year, any such year shall be denominated a New York S year, and such election shall be denominated a New York S election. McKinney's Tax Law § 208(1-A)

scrip 1. A substitute for money. 2. A document entitling one to a benefit. 3. A document representing a fraction of a share.

scrip dividend A dividend in the form of the right to receive future issues of stock.

script 1. Handwriting. 2. The original document.

scrivener One who prepares documents. A professional copyist or drafter.

seal An impression or sign to attest the execution of an instrument or to authenticate the document.

sealed bid A bid that is not revealed until all bids are submitted.

sealed records Publicly filed documents that are kept confidential.

sealed verdict A jury verdict not yet officially given to the court.

   Sealed verdict is mere agreement reached by jurors, and does not become final until it is read into record and jurors discharged. *Spielter*, 249 N.Y.S. 358 (1 Dept., 1931)

seaman's will See military will.

search An examination by police of private areas (e.g., one's person, premises, or vehicle) in an attempt to discover evidence of a crime.

search and seizure See unreasonable search.

search warrant A court order allowing a law enforcement officer to search designated areas and to seize evidence of crime found there.

seasonable Within the agreed-upon time; timely; at a reasonable time.

seaworthy Properly constructed and equipped for a sea voyage.

SEC See Securities and Exchange Commission.

secession The act of withdrawing.

secondary Subordinate; inferior.

secondary authority Any nonlaw a court can rely on in its decision. Writings that describe or explain, but do not constitute, the law.

secondary boycott A boycott of customers or suppliers with whom the union has no labor dispute to induce them to stop dealing with a business with whom the union does have a labor dispute. The boycott can include picketing.

secondary easement An incident to an easement that allows those things necessary to the full enjoyment of the easement.

secondary evidence Evidence that is not the stronger or best evidence.

secondary liability Liability that applies only if the wronged party cannot obtain satisfaction from the person with primary liability.

secondary market A market for previously available goods or services.

secondary meaning Public awareness that a common or descriptive name or symbol identifies the source of a particular product or service.

   A secondary meaning is established when it is shown that a trade name has become so associated in the public's mind with the plaintiff that it identifies goods sold by that entity as distinguished from goods sold by others. *Adirondack Appliance Repair*, 538 N.Y.S.2d 118 (3 Dept., 1989)

secondary picketing See secondary boycott.

second-degree murder The unlawful taking of human life without premeditation or other facts that make the crime first-degree murder. In New York, the premeditated taking of a human life, but absent aggravating factors that make the killing first degree murder, such as killing a police officer, witness, or multiple victims; cruel and wanton killing; or killing in an act of terrorism.

second-look See wait and see.

second mortgage A mortgage with a ranking in priority that is immediately below a first mortgage on the same property.

secretary The corporate officer in charge of keeping official records.

secret partner A partner whose identity is not known by the public.

secta 1. Followers. 2. A lawsuit.

section 1. A subdivision of a law or document. 2. A square mile area.

secundum 1. Second. 2. According to.

secured Backed by collateral, a mortgage, or other security.

secured creditor; secured party A creditor who can reach collateral of the debtor if the latter fails to pay the debt.

   Secured party means: (A) a person in whose favor a security interest is created or provided for under a security agreement, whether or not any obligation to be secured is outstanding; . . . (D) a person to which accounts, chattel paper, payment intangibles, or promissory notes have been sold; . . . McKinney's Uniform Commercial Code § 9-102(72)

secured transaction A contract in which the seller or lender is a secured creditor.

securities See security (2).

Securities and Exchange Commission (SEC) The federal agency that regulates the issuance and trading of securities in order to protect investors and maintain fair and orderly markets (*www.sec.gov*).

securities broker One in the business of buying and selling securities for others.

securitize To convert an asset into a security offered for sale.

security 1. Collateral that guarantees a debt or other obligation. 2. A financial instrument that is evidence of a debt interest (e.g., a bond), an ownership/equity interest (e.g., a stock), or other specially defined rights (e.g., a futures contract). 3. Surety. 4. The state of being secure.

security agreement An agreement that creates or provides for a security interest.

security deposit See deposit (3).

security interest A property interest that secures a payment or the performance of an obligation.

   "Security interest" means an interest in personal property or fixtures which secures payment or performance of an obligation. The term also includes any interest of a consignor and a buyer of accounts, chattel paper, a payment intangible, or a promissory note in a transaction that is subject to Article 9. McKinney's Uniform Commercial Code § 1-201(37)

sedition Communicating, agreeing to, or advocating lawlessness, treason, commotions, or revolt against legitimate authority.

seditious libel Libelous statements designed to incite sedition.

seduction Wrongfully inducing another, without the use of force, to engage in sexual relations.

segregation The unconstitutional separation of people based on categories such as race, religion, or nationality.

seise To hold in fee simple.

seisin or **seizin** Possession of land under a claim of freehold estate.

seize To take possession forcibly.

seizure Taking possession of person or property.

select committee A committee set up for a limited or special task.

selective enforcement Enforcing the law primarily against a member of certain groups or classes of people, often arbitrarily.

selective incorporation The process of making only some of the Bill of Rights applicable to the states through the Fourteenth Amendment. Total incorporation makes all of them applicable.

Selective Service System A federal agency in charge of military registration and, if needed, a draft (*www.sss.gov*).

selectman An elected municipal officer in some towns.

self-authenticating Not needing extrinsic proof of authenticity.

> The certifications on the laboratory reports questioned by defendant rendered the reports self-authenticating and admissible before the Grand Jury since each contained a statement, made under penalty of perjury, that the report was a true and full copy of the original "made by me." *People v. Bennett*, 676 N.Y.S.2d 60 (1 Dept., 1998); McKinney's CPLR 4518(c)

self-dealing Acting to benefit oneself when one should be acting in the interest of another to whom a fiduciary duty is owed.

self-defense The use of force to repel threatened danger to one's person or property.

self-employment tax Social security tax on the self-employed.

self-executing Immediately or automatically having legal effect.

self-help Acting to redress a wrong without using the courts.

self-incrimination Acts or declarations by which one implicates oneself in a crime; exposing oneself to criminal prosecution.

self-insurance Funds set aside by a business to cover any loss.

> "Self-insurance," in general, is simply an assurance that the self-insurer has the financial means to pay any judgments against it, for a self-insurer is not an "insurer" of anything other than its own ability to pay for damages for which it is legally responsible. *People ex rel. Spitzer*, 745 N.Y.S.2d 671 (Sup. Ct., 2002)

self-proving Not requiring proof outside of the documents themselves.

self-serving declaration An out-of-court statement benefiting the person making it.

sell To transfer an asset by sale.

seller One who sells or enters a contract to sell.

semble It would appear.

senate The upper chamber of a two-house (bicameral) legislature.

senate bill (S.B.)(S.) A bill pending or before passage in the senate.

senior Higher in age, rank, preference, or priority.

senior interest An interest that is higher in precedence or priority.

seniority Greater rights than others based on length of service.

senior judge A judge with the longest tenure or who is semi-retired.

senior lien A lien on property that has priority over other liens.

senior mortgage A mortgage that has priority over other mortgages.

sentence Punishment imposed by the court on one convicted of a crime.

> In a criminal action the "sentence" is the judgment of conviction. *People v. Michels*, 292 N.Y.S.2d 323 (2 Dept., 1968)

SEP See simplified employee pension plan.

separability clause See severability clause.

separable Capable of being separated.

separable controversy A dispute that is part of the entire controversy, yet by its nature is independent and can be severed from the whole.

separate Distinct, not joined.

separate but equal Segregated with equal opportunities and facilities.

separate maintenance Support by one spouse to another while separated.

separate property Property acquired by one spouse alone (a) before marriage, (b) during marriage by gift, will, or intestate succession, or (c) during marriage but after separating from the other spouse.

> The term separate property shall mean: (1) property acquired before marriage or property acquired by bequest, devise, or descent, or gift from a party other than the spouse; (2) compensation for personal injuries; (3) property acquired in exchange for or the increase in value of separate property, except to the extent that such appreciation is due in part to the contributions or efforts of the other spouse; (4) property described as separate property by written agreement of the parties pursuant to subdivision three of this part. McKinney's DRL § 236(d)

separate trial An individual (separate) trial of one of the defendants jointly accused of a crime or of one of the issues in any case.

separation Living separately while still married.

separation agreement A contract between spouses who have separated or who are about to separate in which the terms of their separation (e.g., child custody, property division) are spelled out.

separation of powers The division of government into judicial, legislative, and executive branches with the requirement that each branch refrain from encroaching on the authority of the other two.

sequester 1. To separate or isolate a jury or witness. 2. To seize or take and hold funds or other property. Sometimes called sequestrate.

sequestrate See sequester.

sequestrator One who carries out an order or writ of sequestration.

sergeant at arms An officer who keeps order in a court or legislature.

serial bonds A number of bonds issued at the same time but with different maturity dates.

serial note A promissory note payable in regular installments. Also called installment note.

seriatim One by one in a series; one following after another.

series bonds Groups of bonds usually issued at different times and with different maturity dates but under the same indenture.

serious bodily harm See great bodily injury.

servant One employed to perform service, whose perform-ance is controlled by or subject to the control of the master or employer.

> While words "agent" and "servant" are not wholly synonymous, they both express the idea of service to another under an ex-pressed or implied agreement; an "agent" is employed by a principal and represents him as well, while "servant" simply acts for principal and usually according to his directions and without any discretion. *People v. Izzo*, 409 N.Y.S.2d 623 (N.Y. City Crim. Ct., 1978)

serve To deliver a legal notice or process.

service 1. Delivery of a legal notice or process. 2. Tasks per-formed for others. 3. To pay interest on.

service by publication Publishing a notice in a newspaper or other media as service of process upon an absent or nonresident defendant.

service charge An added cost or fee for administration or handling.

servicemark (SM) See mark (1).

service of process A formal delivery of notice to a defendant that a suit has been initiated to which he or she must respond.

servient estate The parcel of land on which an easement is imposed or burdened. Also called servient tenement. The estate that is benefited by the easement the dominant estate.

servitude 1. An easement or similar right to use another's land. 2. The condition of forced labor or slavery.

> An "easement" is a "servitude" upon and differs from an inter-est in or lien upon land, and it is not a part of it, but is so much carved out of the estate in the land, and is as much a thing apart from that estate as a parcel of the land itself con-veyed from it. *Town of Harrison*, 81 N.Y.S.2d 257 (Sup. Ct., 1948)

session 1. A continuous sitting of a court, legislature, council, etc. 2. Any time in the day during which such a body sits.

session laws (S.L.; sess.) Uncodified statutes enacted by a legislature during a session, printed chronologically.

set aside 1. To vacate a judgment, order, etc. 2. Set-aside: Something reserved for a special reason.

setback The distance that buildings are set back from prop-erty lines.

setoff 1. A defendant's claim against the plaintiff that is independent of the plaintiff's claim. 2. A debtor's right to reduce a debt by what the creditor owes the debtor.

settlement 1. An agreement resolving a dispute without full litigation. 2. Payment or satisfactory adjustment of an account. 3. Distributing the assets and paying the debts of an estate. 4. See closing.

> A "compromise" or "settlement" is agreement or arrangement by which, in consideration of mutual concessions, a contro-versy is terminated. *Village of Upper Nyack*, 540 N.Y.S.2d 125 (Sup.Ct., 1988)

settlement option Choices available to pay life insurance benefits.

settlor One who makes a settlement of property (e.g., one who creates a trust). Also called trustor, grantor, donor.

severability clause A clause in a statute or contract providing that if parts of it are declared invalid, the remaining parts shall continue to be effective. Also called saving clause, separability clause.

several 1. A few. 2. Distinct or separate, e.g., a person's several liability is distinct from (and can be enforced independently of) someone else's liability.

severally Apart from others, separately.

severalty The condition of being separate or distinct.

severance 1. Separating claims or parties. 2. Removing; cutting off.

severance tax A tax on natural resources removed from the land.

sewer service Falsely claiming to have served process.

sex discrimination Discrimination that is gender-based.

sexual abuse; sexual assault Rape or other unlawful sexual contact with another.

sexual harassment Unwelcome conduct of a sexual nature on the job.

> To establish a prima facie case of "sexual harassment" in em-ployment under the Human Rights Law, the employee must show that (1) she belongs to a protected group, (2) she was the subject of unwelcome sexual harassment, (3) the harass-ment was based on her gender, (4) the sexual harassment af-fected a term, condition, or privilege of employment, and (5) the employer knew or should have known of the harass-ment and failed to take remedial action. McKinney's Executive Law § 296, subd. 1(a). *Pace*, 692 N.Y.S.2d 220 (3 Dept., 1999)

sexual predator A person with a propensity to commit sexual assault.

shadow jurors Persons hired by one side to observe a trial as members of the general audience and, as the trial pro-gresses, to give feedback to a jury consultant hired by the attorney of one of the parties, who will use the feedback to assess strategy for the remainder of the trial.

shall 1. Is required to, must. 2. Should. 3. May.

sham Counterfeit, a hoax; frivolous, without substance.

> "Sham exception" to the Noerr-Pennington doctrine comes into play when the party petitioning the government is not at all serious about the object of the petition, but does so merely to inconvenience its competitor, or to preclude or delay its competitor's access to governmental processes. *Alfred Weissman Real Estate*, 707 N.Y.S.2d 647 (2 Dept., 2000)

sham transaction Conduct with no business purpose other than tax avoidance.

share 1. The part or portion that you contribute or own. 2. An ownership interest in a corporation. A unit of stock.

share and share alike To divide equally.

shareholder One who owns a share in a corporation. Also called stockholder.

shareholder's derivative action See derivative action (1).

shelf registration Registration with the Securities and Exchange Commission involving a delayed stock sale.

shell corporation A corporation with no assets or active business.

Shelley's case See rule in Shelley's case.

shelter An investment or other device to reduce or defer taxes.

shepardize To use *Shepard's Citations* to find data on the history and currentness of cases, statutes, and other legal materials. See also citator.

sheriff's deed A deed given a buyer at a sheriff's sale.

sheriff's sale A forced sale based on a court order.

shield law 1. A law to protect journalists from being required to divulge confidential sources. 2. See rape shield law.

shifting income Transferring income to someone in a lower tax bracket.

shifting the burden Transferring the burden of proof (or the burden to produce evidence) from one party to another during a trial.

shipment contract A sale in which the risk of loss passes to the buyer when the seller duly delivers the goods to the carrier.

shop A place of business or employment.

shop-book rule A rule allowing regularly kept original business records into evidence as an exception to the hearsay rule.

shoplifting The theft of goods displayed for sale.

shop steward A union official who helps enforce the union contract.

short sale 1. A sale of a security the seller does not own that is made by the delivery of a security borrowed by, or for the account of, the seller. 2. The sale of real property requiring approval of a mortgage lender as the value of the property is below the amount owed on the mortgage.

short summons A summons with a shorter-than-usual response time.

short-swing profit Profit earned on stock by a corporate insider within six months of purchase or sale.

short-term capital gain Gain from the sale or exchange of a capital asset held for less than a year or other designated short term.

show To establish or prove.

show cause order A court order to appear and explain why the court should not take a proposed action to provide relief. Also called order to show cause.

shower One who takes the jury to a scene involved in the case.

showup See lineup.

shut-in royalty A payment by a lessee to continue holding a functioning well that is not being currently utilized due to a weak oil or gas market.

shyster Slang for an unscrupulous attorney.

sic A signal alerting the reader that you are quoting exactly, including the error in the quote.

sidebar conference See bench conference.

sight draft A draft payable on demand when shown.

sign 1. To affix one's signature (or mark substitute). 2. To indicate agreement.

signatory The person or nation signing a document.

signature One's name written by oneself. A word, mark, or symbol indicating identity or intended to authenticate a document.

In accordance with ESRA [Electronic Signatures and Records Act], an electronic signature is an electronic sound, symbol, or process, attached to or logically associated with an electronic record and executed or adopted by a person with the intent to sign the record. Rules and Regs. Electronic Signatures and Records § 540.4(b)

signing statement An announcement by the president upon signing a bill into law that states the president's objections, interpretation, or intention in implementing the law.

silent partner See dormant partner.

silent witness theory Evidence such as photographs may be admitted without testimony of a witness if there is sufficient proof of the reliability of the process that produced the evidence.

silicet (ss) To wit.

silver platter doctrine The former rule that evidence obtained illegally by state police is admissible in federal court if no federal officer participated in the violation of the defendant's rights.

A foreign state police officer, not in close pursuit of a suspect and acting extraterritorially in New York State, illegally arrests that suspect, unlawfully seizes evidence from him, and surrenders it on a silver platter to New York State authorities. *People v. La Fontaine*, 603 N.Y.S.2d 660 (Sup. Ct., 1993)

simple 1. Not aggravated. 2. Uncomplicated. 3. Not under seal.

simple assault; simple battery An assault or battery not accompanied by aggravating circumstances.

simple interest Interest on the principal only, not on any interest earned on the principal.

simple negligence See ordinary negligence.

simple trust 1. A trust requiring the distribution of all trust income to the beneficiaries. 2. See passive trust.

simpliciter Simply; unconditionally.

simplified employee pension plan (SEP) An employee benefit plan consisting of an annuity or an individual retirement account.

simulated sale A sham sale in which no consideration was exchanged.

Simultaneous Death Act A statute providing that when two people die together but without evidence of who died first, the property of each may be disposed of as if each survived the other.

sine die ("without day") With no day being designated.

sine prole (s.p.) Without issue.

sine qua non An essential condition.

The leading test utilized in determining legal causation is the "sine qua non" or "but for" test. Under this approach one asks if the event would not have happened "but for" the action which is being considered as a possible legal "cause" of the alleged damage. *Bebber*, 729 N.Y.S.2d 844 (Sup. Ct., 2001)

single-juror charge A jury instruction stating that if a single juror is not reasonably satisfied with the plaintiff's evidence, the jury cannot find for the plaintiff.

single-publication rule Only one defamation cause of action exists for the same communication, even if it was heard or read by many.

sinking fund Regular deposits and interest accrued thereon set aside to pay long-term debts.

SIPC Securities Investor Protection Corporation (*www.sipc.org*).

sister corporations Corporations controlled by the same shareholders.

sistren Sisters. Female colleagues.

sit 1. To hold a session. 2. To occupy an office.

sit-down strike Employees' refusal to work while at the work site.

sitting In session.

situs Position. The place where a thing happened or is located.

S.J.D. Doctor of Juridical Science.

skip person A recipient of assets in a generation-skipping transfer.

skiptracing Efforts to locate persons (e.g., debtors) or assets.

S.L. See session laws.

slander Defamation that is oral or gestured.

slander of goods; slander of title See disparagement.

slander per se Slander that accuses a person of unchastity or sexual misconduct, of committing a crime of moral turpitude, of engaging in business or professional misconduct, or of having a loathsome disease.

> Plaintiff who has suffered no special damage may bring action for "slander per se" if statements in question charge plaintiff with serious crime, tend to injure in his or her trade, business, or profession, indicate that plaintiff has loathsome disease, or impute unchastity to a woman; when statements fall within one of those categories, law presumes damages will result, and thus damages need not be alleged or proven. *Liberman*, 590 N.Y.S.2d 857 (Ct. of App., 1992)

SLAPP See Strategic Lawsuit Against Public Participation.

slavery A status or system of enforced labor and bondage.

sleeping partner See dormant partner.

slight care More than the absence of care but less than ordinary care.

slight negligence The failure to exercise great care.

slip law One act of the legislature printed in a single pamphlet.

slip opinion The first printing of a single court opinion.

slowdown Causing production to decrease as a union or labor protest.

SM Servicemark. See mark (1).

small-claims court A court that uses more informal procedures to resolve smaller claims—those under a designated amount.

small loan acts Laws on interest-rate limits for small consumer loans.

smart money 1. See punitive damages. 2. Funds of a shrewd investor.

smuggle To import or export goods illegally without paying duties.

social guest One invited to enter or remain on another's property to enjoy private hospitality, not for a business purpose.

society 1. An association of persons united for a common purpose. 2. Companionship and love among family members.

> As respects distinction between a beneficial and a charitable society, in a "beneficial society" the world outside the society's door is essentially a stranger and the society is regardful only of its members who have been drawn together by a mutual desire to be as they are and once assembled they exclude all other persons from their society activities; whereas, a "charitable institution" is exactly the opposite in all of the stated particulars allowing of comparison, and to a "charity" the outside is a world, the inhabitants of which should all be united as brothers. *In re Rathbone's Estate*, 11 N.Y.S.2d 506 (Sur., 1939)

sodomy Oral sex or anal intercourse between humans, or between humans and animals. Also called unnatural offense.

soil bank A federal program paying farmers not to grow certain crops.

soldier's will See military will.

sole actor doctrine The knowledge of an agent is treated as the knowledge of his or her principal.

sole custody Only one parent makes all child-rearing decisions.

sole proprietorship A form of business that does not have a separate legal identity apart from the one person who owns all assets and assumes all debts and liabilities.

solicitation 1. A request for something. 2. Enticing or urging someone to commit a crime. 3. An appeal or request for clients or business.

> "Soliciting" means the asking, urging or importuning of men to commit a degenerate act and the offense need not be in any particular form of words. *People v. McCormack*, 169 N.Y.S. 2d 139 (Sp. Sess., 1957)

solicitor 1. One who solicits. 2. A lawyer for a city or government agency. 3. A British lawyer who prepares documents and gives clients legal advice but (unlike a barrister) does not do extensive trial work.

solicitor general A high-ranking government litigator.

solvent Able to meet one's financial obligations.

Son of Sam law A law against criminals earning income by selling the story of their crime to the media.

sound 1. Healthy; able. 2. Marketable. 3. Well-founded. 4. To be actionable.

source of law The authority for court opinions or statutes, e.g., constitutions, other court opinions and statutes, and custom.

sovereign 1. Having supreme power. 2. The ruler or head of state.

sovereign immunity The sovereign (i.e., the state) cannot be sued in its courts without its consent. Also called governmental immunity.

sovereignty Supreme political authority.

s.p. 1. Same principle. 2. See sine prole.

speaker The chairperson or presiding officer of an assembly.

speaking demurrer A demurrer that alleges facts that are not in the pleadings. See also demurrer.

speaking motion Saying more than called for by the motion or pleading.

special act See private law (2).

special administrator An estate administrator with limited duties.

special agent An agent delegated to do a specific act.

special appearance Appearing solely to challenge the court's jurisdiction.

special assessment An additional tax on land that benefits from a public improvement such as a new sewer or sidewalk.

special contract 1. An express contract with explicit terms. 2. See contract under seal.

special counsel An attorney hired by the government for a particular matter.

special court-martial An intermediate level of court-martial.

special damages Actual and provable economic losses, e.g., lost wages.

Special damages, i.e., the loss of something having economic or pecuniary value. *Cavallaro*, 814 N.Y.S.2d 462 (4 Dept., 2006)

special demurrer A challenge to the form of a pleading.

special deposit A deposit in a bank made for safekeeping or for some special application or purpose.

special exception 1. A challenge to the form of a claim. 2. See conditional use.

special-facts rule A duty of disclosure exists when special circumstances make it inequitable for a corporate director or officer to withhold information from a stockholder.

Under the "special facts doctrine," a duty to disclose arises where one party's superior knowledge of essential facts renders a transaction without disclosure inherently unfair. *P.T. Bank Central Asia*, 754 N.Y.S.2d 245 (1 Dept., 2003)

special finding A finding of essential facts to support a judgment.

special grand jury A grand jury called for a limited or special task.

special guaranty A guarantee enforceable only by designated persons.

special indorsement An indorsement that specifies the person to whom the instrument is payable or to whom the goods are to be delivered.

special interrogatory A separate question a jury is asked to answer.

specialist One possessing special expertise, often certified as such.

special jurisdiction See limited jurisdiction.

special jury A jury chosen for its special expertise or for a case of special importance. Also called struck jury.

special law See private law (2).

special lien See particular lien.

special master See master (2).

special meeting A nonregular meeting called for a special purpose.

special power of appointment See limited power of appointment.

special power of attorney A power of attorney with limited authority.

special prosecutor An attorney appointed to conduct a criminal investigation of a matter.

special session See extraordinary session.

special trust A trust whose trustee has management duties other than merely giving trust assets to beneficiaries. Also called active trust.

specialty See contract under seal.

special use See conditional use.

special use valuation Real property valued on its actual current use rather than on its best possible use.

special verdict A jury's fact findings on fact questions given to it by the judge, who then states the legal consequences of the findings.

special warranty deed A deed in which the grantor warrants title only against those claiming by or under the grantor. Called a quitclaim deed in a few states.

specie 1. See in specie. 2. Coined money.

specification 1. A list of contract requirements or details. 2. A statement of charges. 3. Invention details in a patent application.

Contractor must follow a "design specification" provided by owner without deviation, in carrying out required work, and bears no responsibility if design proves inadequate to achieve intended result. *Fruin-Colnon Corp.*, 585 N.Y.S.2d 248 (4 Dept., 1992)

specific bequest A gift of specific or unique property in a will.

specific denial A denial of particular allegations in a claim.

specific devise A devise of a specific property.

specific intent Desiring (intending) the precise criminal consequences that follow one's act.

An element of the crime of larceny is that the wrongful taking or withholding of the property must be with intent to deprive another of property and to appropriate the same to the taker or to a third person. This means a specific intent. *People v. Chessman*, 429 N.Y.S.2d 224 (2 Dept., 1980)

specific legacy A gift of specific or unique property in a will.

specific performance An equitable remedy directing the performance of a contract according to the precise terms agreed upon by the parties.

spectograph A machine used for voiceprint analysis.

speculation 1. Seeking profits through investments that can be risky. 2. Theorizing in the absence of sufficient evidence and knowledge.

speculative damages Damages that are not reasonably certain; damages that are too conjectural to be awarded.

speech Spoken communication.

Speech or Debate Clause The clause in the U.S Constitution (art. I, § 6, cl. 1) giving members of Congress immunity for what they say during their legislative work.

speedy trial A trial that begins promptly after reasonable preparation by the prosecution and is conducted with reasonable dispatch. "In all criminal prosecutions, the accused shall enjoy the right to a speedy and public trial. . . ." U.S. Const. Amend. VI. In New York, the requirements for a speedy trial (particularly when the prosecution must be ready for trial in criminal cases) are found in McKinney's CPL §§ 30.20, 30.30.

spendthrift One who spends money irresponsibly.

spendthrift trust A trust whose assets are protected against the beneficiary's improvidence and are beyond the reach of his or her creditors.

spin-off A new and independent corporation that was once part of another corporation whose shareholders will own the new corporation.

spirit of the law The underlying meaning or purpose of the law.

split See stock split.

split gift A gift from a spouse to a nonspouse that is treated as having been given one-half by each spouse.

split-off A new corporation formed by an existing corporation, giving shares of the new corporation to the existing corporation's stockholders in exchange for some of their shares in the existing corporation.

split sentence A sentence served in part in an institution and suspended in part or served on probation for the remainder.

splitting a cause of action Suing on only part of a cause of action now and on another part later.

split-up Dividing a corporation into two or more new corporations.

spoliation Intentionally destroying, altering, or concealing evidence.

sponsor 1. One who makes a promise or gives security for another. 2. A legislator who proposes a bill.

spontaneous declaration An out-of-court statement or utterance (made with little time to reflect or fabricate) about a perceived event. An exception to the hearsay rule.

A spontaneous declaration, an exception to the hearsay evidence rule, is a narrative of a past transaction, usually occurring immediately before the declaration is made. *People v. Little*, 371 N.Y.S.2d 726 (Co. Ct., 1975)

spot zoning Singling out a lot or small area for different zoning treatment than similar surrounding land.

spousal abuse Physical, sexual, or emotional abuse of one's spouse.

spousal privilege See marital communications privilege.

spousal support See alimony.

spread The difference between two amounts, e.g., the buyer's bid price and the seller's asked price for a security.

springing use A use that is dependent or contingent on a future event.

sprinkling trust A trust that spreads income among different beneficiaries at the discretion of the trustee.

spurious Counterfeit or synthetic; false.

squatter One who settles on land without legal title or authority.

In determining whether an occupant of an apartment was a tenant or a squatter, a "squatter" is one who settles on the land of another without legal authority. *Bistany*, 372 N.Y.S.2d 6 (N.Y. City Ct., 1975)

squeeze-out An attempt to eliminate or weaken the interest of an owner, e.g., a minority shareholder.

ss. 1. Sections. 2. Sometimes used to abbreviate scilicet, meaning to wit.

SSI See Supplemental Security Income.

stake 1. A deposit to be held until its ownership is resolved. 2. A land boundary marker. 3. A bet. 4. An interest in a business.

stakeholder See interpleader.

stale No longer effective due to the passage of time.

stalking Repeatedly following or harassing someone, who is thereby placed in reasonable fear of harm.

A person is guilty of menacing in the second degree when: . . . 2. He or she repeatedly follows a person. . . . McKinney's Penal Law § 120.14

stamp tax The cost of stamps affixed to legal documents such as deeds.

stand See witness stand.

standard 1. A yardstick or criterion. 2. Customary.

standard deduction A fixed deduction from adjusted gross income, used by taxpayers who do not itemize their deductions.

standard mortgage clause A mortgage clause stating that the interest of the mortgagee will not be invalidated by specified acts of the mortgagor.

standard of care The degree of care the law requires in a particular case, e.g., reasonable care in a negligence case.

standard of need A level of need qualifying one for public benefits.

standard of proof The degree to which the evidence of something must be convincing before a fact finder can accept it as true.

standing A person's right to seek relief from a court.

standing committee An ongoing committee.

standing mute A defendant refusing to answer or plead to the charge.

standing orders Rules adopted by a court governing practice before it.

Star Chamber 1. An early English court known for arbitrariness. 2. A term used to describe an arbitrary or secret tribunal or proceeding.

stare decisis ("stand by things decided") Courts should decide similar cases in the same way. Precedent should be followed.

"Stare decisis" rests on the principal that law by which men are governed should be fixed, definite, and known and when the law is declared and construed, it should not be changed, save for mistake or error, or until revisited by competent authority. *McGee*, 694 N.Y.S.2d 269 (Sup. Ct., 1999)

stat. Statute.

state 1. A sovereign government. 2. A body of people in a defined territory organized under one government.

state action 1. Conduct of a government. 2. Court proceedings made available to protect or enforce conduct of a private person or entity.

state bank A bank chartered by a state.

stated account See account stated.

stated capital See legal capital.

stated value See par value.

statement 1. An assertion of fact or opinion. 2. An organized recitation of facts.

statement of affairs A list of assets and debts.

state of mind 1. One's reasons and motives for acting or failing to act. 2. See mens rea. 3. The condition or capacity of a mind.

state-of-mind exception An out-of-court declaration of an existing motive or reason is admissible as an exception to the hearsay rule.

Under state of mind exception, out-of-court statement will be admissible where mere utterance of the statement without regard to its truth, may indicate circumstantially the state of mind of the hearer or of the declarant; such statements are not admitted for their truthfulness. *People v. Matthews*, 791 N.Y.S.2d 24 (1 Dept., 2005)

state's attorney The prosecutor or district attorney.

state secrets Government information that would threaten national security or compromise diplomacy if disclosed to the public.

state's evidence Testimony of one criminal defendant against another.

states' rights 1. The political philosophy that favors increased powers for state governments as opposed to expanding the powers of the federal government. 2. Powers not granted to the federal government and not forbidden to the states "are reserved to the states" and the people. U.S. Const. Amend. X.

status crime; status offense 1. A crime that consists of having a certain personal status, condition, or character. Example: vagrancy. 2. Conduct by a minor that, if engaged in by an adult, would not be legally prohibited.

status quo The existing state of things.

statute 1. A law passed by the state or federal legislature that declares, commands, or prohibits something. 2. A law passed by any legislative body.

statute of frauds A law requiring some contracts (e.g., one that cannot be performed within a year of its making) to be in writing and signed by the party to be charged by the contract.

statute of limitations A law stating that civil or criminal actions are barred if not brought within a specified period of time.

"Statute of limitations" is statute enacted to bar any right, regardless of source. *Dunkum*, 256 N.Y. 275, 176 N.E. 392 (Ct. of App., 1931)

statute of repose A law barring actions unless brought within a designated time after an act of the defendant. The law extinguishes the cause of action after a fixed period of time, regardless of when the cause of action accrued.

statute of uses An old English statute that converted certain equitable titles into legal ones.

Statutes at Large The United States Statutes at Large is the official chronological collection of the acts and resolutions of a session of Congress.

statutory Pertaining to or required by a statute.

statutory construction The interpretation of statutes.

statutory employer An employer of a worker covered by workers' compensation.

statutory foreclosure A nonjudicial foreclosure of a mortgage.

statutory lien A lien created by statute.

statutory rape Sexual intercourse with a person under a designated age (e.g., 16) even if the latter consents.

stay The suspension of a judgment or proceeding.

"Stay" is a direction of the court, usually embodied in an order, freezing an action or proceeding before it at whatever point it has reached and precluding it from going any further. *1544-48 Properties, L.L.C.*, 712 N.Y.S.2d 303 (Sup. Ct., 2000)

stealing Unlawfully taking and keeping the property of another.

stenographic record The transcript of a trial or deposition.

step-up basis The tax basis of inherited property, which is its value on the date the donor died or on the alternate valuation date.

step transaction doctrine For tax purposes, a series of formally separate steps are treated as a single transaction.

stet ("let it stand") 1. Leave the text unchanged (usually meaning undo the last correction). 2. A stay.

steward See shop steward.

sting An undercover operation to catch criminals.

stipulated damages See liquidated damages.

stipulation 1. An agreement between parties on a matter, often so that it need not be argued or proven at trial. 2. A requirement or condition.

Parties may by stipulation shape the facts to be determined at trial and thus circumscribe the relevant issues for the court. A stipulation is a contract between parties. *Mandia*, 583 N.Y.S.2d 5 (2 Dept., 1992)

stirpes See per stirpes.

stock 1. An ownership interest or share in a corporation. 2. The capital raised by a corporation, e.g., through the sale of shares. 3. Goods to be sold by a merchant.

stock association See joint stock company.

stockbroker One who buys or sells stock on behalf of others.

stock certificate Documentary evidence of title to shares of stock.

stock corporation A corporation whose capital is divided into shares.

stock dividend A dividend paid in additional shares of stock.

stock exchange The place at which shares of stock are bought and sold.

stockholder See shareholder.

stockholder's derivative action See derivative action (1).

stock in trade 1. Inventory for sale. 2. Equipment used in business.

stock issue See issue (4).

stock manipulation See manipulation.

stock market See market (2).

stock option A right to buy or sell stock at a set price within a specified period of time.

stock right A shareholder's right to purchase new stock issues before the public can make such purchases.

stock split Each individual share is split into a larger number of shares without changing the total number of shareholders.

A "stock split" differs from a "stock dividend" in that in the former the number of shares of capital is increased, with a corresponding decrease in value per share, and surplus is not altered nor earnings segregated; in the latter a transfer of surplus or undivided profits to capital takes place. *In re Sheldon's Will*, 249 N.Y.S.2d 953 (Sup. Ct., 1964)

stock warrant See warrant (3).

stolen property Property taken by theft or embezzlement.

stop and frisk Temporary detention, questioning, and "patting down" of a person whom the police reasonably believe has committed or is about to commit a crime and may have a weapon. Also called *Terry* stop. *Terry v. Ohio*, 88 S. Ct. 1868 (1968).

stop-loss order An order to buy or sell securities when they reach a particular price. Also called stop order.

stop order 1. An instruction of a customer who has written a check that his or her bank should not honor it. A stop-payment order. 2. See stop-loss order.

stoppage in transit (in transitu) A seller's right to repossess goods from a carrier before they reach the buyer when payment by the latter is in doubt.

stop-payment order See stop order (1).

straddle The option to purchase or sell the same asset.

straight bill of lading A bill of lading that names a specific person to whom the goods are to be delivered.

straight life insurance See whole life insurance.

straight-line depreciation Depreciation computed by dividing the purchase price of an asset (less its salvage value) by its estimated useful life.

stranger Someone not a participant or party to a transaction.

Strategic Lawsuit Against Public Participation (SLAPP) A meritless suit brought primarily to chill the free speech of the defendant.

straw man 1. A cover or front. 2. A fictitious person or argument.

street name A broker's name on a security, not that of its owner.

strict construction A narrow construction; nothing is taken as intended that is not clearly expressed in the literal language of the law or document. Also called literal construction.

strict foreclosure A transfer of title (of the mortgaged property) to the mortgagee without a foreclosure sale upon the mortgagor's default.

stricti juris According to a strict or narrow construction of the law.

strict liability Legal responsibility even if one used reasonable care and did not intend harm. Also called absolute liability, liability without fault.

Although no culpable mental state is expressly designated in a statute defining an offense, a culpable mental state may nevertheless be required for the commission of such offense, or with respect to some or all of the material elements thereof, if the proscribed conduct necessarily involves such culpable mental state. A statute defining a crime, unless clearly indicating a legislative intent to impose strict liability, should be construed as defining a crime of mental culpability. McKinney's Penal Law § 15.15(2)

strict scrutiny The standard requiring a government to show its law is the least restrictive way to further a compelling state interest.

strike 1. An organized work stoppage or slowdown by workers in order to press demands. 2. To remove something.

strikebreaker See scab.

strike suit A shareholder derivative action that is baseless.

striking a jury Selecting a jury for a particular or special case.

struck jury 1. A jury chosen by a process that allows the parties to take turns striking names from a large panel of prospective jurors until a sufficient number exists for a jury. 2. See special jury.

Under the "struck jury" system, prospective jurors are screened and challenged for cause until a sufficient pool of qualified jurors is created from which the parties may select a jury and an adequate number of alternate jurors; peremptory challenges to the entire pool of qualified jurors are then exercised, first by the prosecution and then by defendant. McKinney's CPL § 270.15. *People v. Webb*, 722 N.Y.S.2d 349 (Sup. Ct., 2001)

structuring Altering a currency transaction in such as way as to avoid a currency reporting requirement. 31 U.S.C. §§ 5316, 5324(c)(3)

style The title or name of a case.

suable Capable of being sued.

sua sponte On one's own motion; voluntarily. Example: A judge takes judicial notice of a fact without a motion from a litigant.

sub Under; secondary.

subagent Someone used by an agent to perform a duty for the principal.

subchapter C corporation See C corporation.

subchapter S corporation See S corporation.

subcontract A contract that performs all or part of another contract.

subcontractor One who performs under a subcontract.

subdivision 1. The division of something into smaller parts. 2. A portion of land within a development.

subinfeudation A feudal system of vassals creating vassals of their own.

subjacent support The support of land by land that lies beneath it.

subject 1. A citizen or resident under another; one governed by the laws of a sovereign. 2. A theme or topic acted upon.

subject-matter jurisdiction The power of the court to resolve a particular category of dispute.

sub judice Under judicial consideration; before a court.

sublease A lease of leased premises. A lease (called a sublease, subtenancy, or underlease) granted by an existing lessee (called a sublessor) to another (called a sublessee, subtenant, or undertenant) of all or part of the leased premises for a portion of the sublessor's original term.

"Sublease" is transfer by tenant of part of his estate or interest in whole, or in part, of leased property, with reservation unto himself of reversionary interest in leasehold estate. *Diamond*, 535 N.Y.S.2d 335 (N.Y. City Civ. Ct., 1988)

sublessee; sublessor See sublease.

subletting The granting of a sublease.

submission 1. Yielding to authority. 2. An argument to be considered.

sub modo Within limits; subject to qualifications.

sub nominee (sub nom.) Under the name or title.

subordinate 1. One who works under another's authority. 2. To place in a lower priority or rank.

subordination agreement An agreement to accept a lower priority than would otherwise be due.

suborn To induce another to commit an illegal act, e.g., perjury.

subornation of perjury Instigating another to commit perjury.

subpoena A command to appear in a court, agency, or other tribunal.

subpoena ad testificandum A command to appear to give testimony.

subpoena duces tecum A command to appear and bring specified things, e.g., records.

subrogation The substitution of one party (called the subrogee) in place of another party (called the subrogor), along with any claim, demand, or right the latter party had.

> "Subrogation" is the principle by which an insurer, having paid losses of its insured, is placed in the position of its insured so that it may recover from the third party legally responsible for the loss. *Blue Cross and Blue Shield of N.J.*, 785 N.Y.S.2d 399 (Ct. of App., 2004)

subrogee; subrogor See subrogation.

subscription 1. A signature; the act of writing one's name on a document. 2. An agreement to purchase new securities of a corporation.

subscription right See preemptive right.

subsequent Occurring or coming later.

subsidiary 1. Under another's control. 2. A branch or affiliate.

subsidiary corporation A corporation owned or controlled by another corporation.

> The term "subsidiary" means a corporation of which over fifty percent of the number of shares of stock entitling the holders thereof to vote for the election of directors or trustees is owned by the taxpayer. . . . McKinney's Tax Law § 208(3)

sub silentio Under silence; without specific reference or notice.

substance 1. The material or essential part of a thing. 2. A drug.

substantial 1. Not imaginary. 2. Considerable in amount or degree.

substantial capacity test See insanity (2).

substantial compliance Compliance with the essential requirements.

substantial evidence Relevant evidence a reasonable mind might accept as adequate to support a conclusion.

> "Substantial evidence" means such relevant proof as a reasonable mind may accept as adequate to support a conclusion or ultimate fact. *Bacik*, 815 N.Y.S.2d 118 (N.Y.A.D. 2 Dept., 2006)

substantial justice A fair proceeding or trial even if minor procedural errors are made.

substantial performance Performance of the essential terms of a contract or agreement.

substantiate To establish by supporting evidence. To support with proof.

substantive due process The constitutional requirement (based on the fifth and fourteenth Amendments) that legislation be rationally related to a legitimate government purpose.

substantive evidence Evidence offered to support a fact in issue.

substantive law Nonprocedural laws that define or govern rights and duties.

substantive rule See legislative rule.

substituted basis The basis of property in the hands of the transferor becomes the transferee's basis of that property.

substituted service Service by an authorized method (e.g., by mail) other than personal service. Also called constructive service.

substitution Taking the place of another.

subtenancy; subtenant See sublease.

subversive Pertaining to the overthrow or undermining of a government.

succession 1. Obtaining property or interests by inheritance rather than by deed or contract. The acquisition of rights upon the death of another. 2. Taking over or continuing the rights of another entity.

succession tax See inheritance tax.

successor A person or entity that takes the place of or follows another.

> "Successor" shall mean an entity engaged in work substantially similar to that of the predecessor, where there is substantial continuity of operation with that of the predecessor. McKinney's Labor Law § 220(k)

successor in interest One who follows another in ownership or control of property.

sudden emergency doctrine See emergency doctrine (1).

sudden heat of passion See heat of passion.

sue To commence a lawsuit.

sue out To ask a court for an order.

suffer 1. To feel physical or emotional pain. 2. To allow or admit.

sufferance The absence of rejection; passive consent.

sufficient Adequate for the legal purpose involved.

> Sufficient corroboration means any other evidence tending to support the reliability of the previous statements and includes proper validation testimony from an expert. McKinney's Family Court Act § 1046(a)(vi). *Matter of Katje YY*, 650 N.Y.S.2d 363 (3 Dept., 1996)

sufficient cause See good cause, probable cause (1).

sufficient consideration Consideration that creates a binding contract.

suffrage The right to vote.

suicide The voluntary termination of one's life.

sui generis ("of its own kind") Unique.

sui juris ("of one's own right") Possessing full civil rights.

suit See lawsuit.

suitor A plaintiff, one who sues.

sum certain An exact amount.

summary 1. Not following usual procedures. 2. Done quickly. 3. Short or concise.

summary court-martial The lowest-level court-martial.

summary judgment A judgment on a claim or defense rendered without a full trial because of the absence of genuine conflict on any of the material facts involved.

summary jury trial A nonbinding trial argued before a mock jury as a case evaluation technique and an incentive to settle.

summary proceeding A nonjury proceeding that seeks to achieve a relatively prompt resolution. An example is an eviction proceeding. McKinney's RPAPL Article 7.

summary process A special procedure that provides an expeditious remedy.

summation; summing up See closing statement.

summons 1. A notice directing the defendant to appear in court and answer the plaintiff's complaint or face a default judgment. 2. A notice directing a witness or juror to appear in court.

> "Summons" is only a written notice required to bring a defendant into court; it is designed to apprise the defendant that the plaintiff in the action seeks judgment against him and that at a stated time and place he is to appear and answer the complaint against him. *Hutchison*, 386 N.Y.S.2d 897 (Sup. Ct., 1976)

sumptuary Regulating personal expenditures; restricting immorality.

Sunday closing laws See blue laws.

sunset law A law that automatically terminates a program unless it is affirmatively renewed.

sunshine law A law requiring increased public access to government meetings and records.

suo nomine In one's own name.

Superfund A government fund for hazardous-waste cleanup.

superior Having a higher rank, authority, or interest.

superior court A trial court in most states.

supermajority Two-thirds, 60 percent, or any other voting requirement of greater than half plus one.

supersede To supplant; to annul by replacing.

supersedeas A writ or bond to stay the enforcement of a judgment.

superseding cause An intervening cause that is beyond the foreseeable risk originally created by the defendant's unreasonable acts or omissions and thereby cuts off the defendant's liability.

> Intervening act constitutes a "superseding cause," and relieves defendant of liability, when act is of such extraordinary nature or so attenuates defendant's negligence from the ultimate injury that responsibility for the injury may not be reasonably attributed to the defendant. *Humbach*, 686 N.Y.S.2d 54 (2 Dept., 1998)

supervening cause A superseding cause.

supervening negligence See last clear chance doctrine.

supplemental jurisdiction Jurisdiction over a claim that is part of the same controversy over which the court already has jurisdiction.

supplemental pleading A pleading that adds facts to or corrects an earlier pleading.

Supplemental Security Income (SSI) A government income benefit program (part of social security) for the aged, blind, or disabled.

supplementary proceeding A new proceeding that supplements another, e.g., to help collect a judgment.

support 1. Provide a standard of living. 2. Maintenance with necessities. 3. Foundation.

support magistrate An administrative law judge who presides over a part of family court that hears support and paternity matters. McKinney's FCA § 439.

suppress To stop or prevent.

suppression hearing A pretrial criminal hearing to decide if evidence was seized illegally and should be inadmissible (i.e., suppressed).

suppression of evidence 1. A court ruling that evidence is inadmissible. 2. A prosecutor's failure to disclose exculpatory evidence to the defense.

supra Above; mentioned earlier in the document.

supremacy Being in a higher or the highest position of power.

Supremacy Clause The clause in the U.S. Constitution (art. VI, cl. 2) that has been interpreted to mean that when valid federal law and state law conflict, federal law controls.

supreme court 1. The highest appellate court in the federal and in most state judicial systems. 2. In New York, it is the trial court of general jurisdiction in every county. 3. The Supreme Court of Appeals is the highest state court in West Virginia. 4. The Supreme Judicial Court is the highest state court in Maine and Massachusetts.

surcharge 1. An added charge or tax. 2. A charge imposed on a fiduciary for misconduct.

surety One who becomes liable for the payment of another's debt or the performance of another's contractual obligation. The surety generally becomes primarily and jointly liable with the other, the principal.

surety bond See completion bond.

suretyship The contractual relation whereby one person (the surety) agrees to answer for the debt, default, or miscarriage of another (the principal), with the surety generally being primarily and jointly liable with the principal.

> "Suretyship" may be defined as contractual relationship whereby one person engages to be answerable for debt or default of another. Every "suretyship" involves three parties: "principal," whose debt or default is subject of the transaction; "obligee," one to whom debt or obligation runs; and "surety," one that undertakes to perform debt or obligation if principal does not. *Estate of Camarda*, 425 N.Y.S.2d 1012 (Sup. Ct., 1980)

surplus What is left over. The amount remaining after the purpose of a fund or venture has been accomplished.

surplusage Extraneous matter or words in a statute, pleading, or instrument that do not add meaning.

surprise Something unexpected, often unfairly so.

surrebuttal A rebuttal to a rebuttal.

surrejoinder An answer of the defendant to a rejoinder.

surrender 1. To return a power, claim, or estate. 2. To release.

surrender value See cash surrender value.

surrogacy The status or act of being a substitute for another.

surrogate 1. A substitute for another. 2. A probate judge.

surrogate mother A woman who gestates an embryo and bears a child for another person. The surrogate relinquishes her parental rights.

surrogate's court The court in New York that hears all matters concerning decedents' estates; it also has concurrent jurisdiction for adoptions. See also probate court.

surtax 1. An additional tax added to something already taxed. 2. A tax levied on a tax.

surveillance Close and continual observation of a person or place.

survey 1. A map that measures boundaries, elevations, and structures on land. 2. A study or poll.

survival action An action brought on behalf of a decedent to recover damages the decedent suffered up to the time of his or her death. The action seeks what the decedent would have sought if he or she had not died.

> The personal representative, duly appointed in this state or any other jurisdiction, of a decedent who is survived by distributees may maintain an action to recover damages for a wrongful act, neglect or default which caused the decedent's death against a person who would have been liable to the decedent by reason of such wrongful conduct if death had not ensued. McKinney's EPTL § 5-4.1(1)

survivorship See right of survivorship.

survivorship annuity An annuity that continues paying benefits to the survivor of the annuitant after the latter's death.

suspect classification A classification in a statute whose constitutional validity (under the Equal Protection Clause) will be measured by the standard of strict scrutiny. An example would be a preference in a statute on the basis of race, alienage, or national origin.

suspended sentence A sentence that is imposed but postponed, allowing the defendant to avoid prison if he or she meets specified conditions.

suspension A temporary delay or interruption, e.g., the removal of the right to practice law for a specified period.

suspicion A belief that someone has or may have committed wrongdoing but without proof.

sustain 1. To uphold or agree with. 2. To support or encourage. 3. To endure, withstand, or suffer.

swear 1. To take or administer an oath. 2. To talk obscenely.

sweating Questioning an accused through harassment or threats.

sweetheart deal An arrangement providing beneficial treatment that is illegal or ethically questionable.

syllabus A brief summary or outline. See also headnote.

symbolic delivery The constructive delivery of property by delivering something that represents the property, e.g., a key to a building.

symbolic speech Nonverbal activity or conduct that expresses a message or thought, e.g., the hood worn by the KKK; expressive conduct.

sympathy strike A strike against an employer with whom the workers do not have a labor dispute in order to show support for other workers on strike.

synallagmatic Reciprocal, bilateral.

syndicalism A movement advocating control of industry by labor unions. Criminal syndicalism is an act or plan intended to accomplish change in industrial ownership or government by means of unlawful force, violence, or terrorism.

syndicate A group formed to promote a common interest.

synopsis A brief summary.

T

tacit Understood without being openly stated; implied by silence.

tacking 1. One claiming adverse possession adds its period of possession to that of a previous possessor to meet the statutory period. 2. Gaining priority for a lien by joining it to a superior lien.

tail Limitation in the right of inheritance. See fee tail.

tail female Limitation to female heirs. See fee tail.

tail male Limitation to male heirs. See fee tail.

taint 1. A defect or contamination. 2. A felony conviction.

tainted evidence Illegally obtained evidence.

take 1. To seize or obtain possession. 2. To acquire by eminent domain.

takeover Obtaining control, management, or ownership.

taking See take.

talesman A prospective juror. A bystander called to serve on a jury.

tamper To meddle or change something without authorization.

TANF See Temporary Assistance to Needy Families.

tangible Having physical form. Capable of being touched or seen.

> For purposes of criminal mischief and criminal tampering statutes, which require damage to tangible property, radio signals and equipment used to generate and transmit them are "tangible property," but frequency and right to use particular frequency are not "tangible property." McKinney's Penal Law §§ 145.00, 145.14. *People v. Choo*, 576 N.Y.S.2d 486 (N.Y. City Crim. Ct., 1991)

target corporation A corporation that someone wants to take over.

tariff 1. A tax paid on categories of imported or exported goods. 2. A list of rates or fees charged for services.

tax Compulsory monetary payments to support the government.

taxable Subject to taxation.

taxable estate A decedent's gross estate less allowable deductions.

taxable gift See gift tax.

taxable income Gross income less deductions and exemptions.

taxable year; tax year A calendar year or a taxpayer's fiscal year.

tax avoidance Using lawful tax-reducing steps and strategies.

tax benefit rule When already deducted losses and expenses are recovered in a later year, the recovery is listed as income in the later year.

> Federal tax benefit rule applies to exclude state and local income taxes when computing New York items of tax preference subject to New York minimum income tax under Tax Law §§

622 and 623 for tax years 1976 and 1977. 26 U.S.C.A. § 58(h); McKinney's Tax Law § 622. *Hunt*, 489 N.Y.S.2d 451 (Ct. of App., 1985)

tax bracket The range of income to which the same tax rate is applied.

tax certificate An instrument issued to the buyer of property at a tax sale entitling him or her to the property after the redemption period.

tax court A court that hears appeals involving tax disputes.

tax credit A subtraction from the tax owed rather than from income.

tax deduction A subtraction from income to arrive at taxable income.

tax deed A deed given to the purchaser by the government to property purchased at a tax sale.

tax deferred Not taxable until later.

tax evasion; tax fraud See evasion (2).

tax exempt; tax free Not subject to taxation.

tax home One's principal place of employment or business.

taxing power A government's power to impose taxes.

tax lien A government's lien on property for nonpayment of taxes.

tax preference items Regular deductions that must be factored back in when calculating the alternative minimum tax.

tax rate The percentage used to calculate one's tax.

tax refund An overpayment of taxes that can be returned or credited.

tax return The form used to report income and other tax information.

tax roll A government list of taxable assets and taxpayers.

tax sale The forced sale of property for nonpayment of taxes.

> Tax sale provisions. 1. Notwithstanding the issuance of a conditional tax receipt as herein provided, the procedure provided by a law for the sale of tax liens or properties for non-payment of taxes shall in all cases remain unchanged as if the conditional tax receipt had not been issued. . . . McKinney's RPTL § 968

tax shelter An investment or other device to reduce or defer taxes.

tax title The title obtained by a buyer of property at a tax sale.

technical error See harmless error.

teller 1. A bank employee who receives and pays out money. 2. A vote counter at an election.

temporary Lasting for a limited time; transitory.

temporary alimony An interim order of spousal support pending the final outcome of the action for divorce or legal separation. Also called alimony pendente lite.

Temporary Assistance to Needy Families (TANF) The welfare program that replaced Aid to Families with Dependent Children (AFDC) (42 U.S.C. § 601).

temporary injunction See preliminary injunction.

temporary restraining order (TRO) An order maintaining the status quo pending a hearing on the application for a permanent injunction.

tenancy 1. The possession or holding of real or personal property by right or title. 2. Possession or occupancy of land under a lease.

tenancy at sufferance See estate at sufferance.

tenancy at will A lease with no fixed term or duration. Also called estate at will.

tenancy by the entirety A form of joint tenancy for a married couple. Co-ownership of property by spouses with a right of survivorship. Also called estate by the entirety.

tenancy for years A tenancy for any predetermined time period, not just for years. Also called tenancy for a term.

tenancy from year to year See periodic tenancy.

tenancy in common Ownership of property by two or more persons in shares that may or may not be equal, each person having an equal right to possess the whole property but without the right of survivorship. Also called estate in common.

> A tenant in common is an owner of realty who has a legal estate therein, a title in the fee, distinct from that of his co-tenants with only a unity of possession between them, and a right of possession exclusive against all others, except as to his co-tenants, or as to any incumbrances placed on it by the tenancy in common. *Rapsons Cravats*, 69 N.Y.S.2d 502 (Mun. Ct., 1947)

tenant 1. One who pays rent to possess another's land or apartment for a temporary period. 2. One who holds a tenancy.

tenantable Habitable, fit for occupancy.

tenant for life One who holds a life estate.

tender 1. To offer payment or other performance. 2. An offer.

tender of delivery An offer of conforming goods by the seller.

tender offer An offer to purchase shares at a fixed price in an attempt to obtain a controlling interest in a company.

tender years doctrine In custody disputes, very young children should go to the mother unless she is unfit.

> The now repudiated tender years doctrine—that a presumption in favor of the mother arises from the greater nurture that a parent with less employment demands can provide. *J.C.D.*, 676 N.Y.S.2d 100 (1 Dept., 1998)

tenement 1. An apartment or other residence. 2. An estate of land.

ten-K (10-K) A publicly traded company's annual financial report that must be filed with the SEC.

tentative trust See Totten trust.

tenure 1. The right to permanent employment subject to termination for cause in compliance with procedural safeguards. 2. The right to hold land subordinate to a superior.

term 1. A fixed period. 2. A word or phrase. 3. A contract provision.

terminable interest An interest that ends upon a given time or condition.

termination 1. The end of something. 2. Discontinuation.

term life insurance Life insurance for a specified or limited time.

term loan A loan that must be paid within a specified date.

terms of art Words or phrases with a special or technical meaning. Also called words of art.

territorial Pertaining to a particular area or land.

territorial court A court in a U.S. territory, e.g., Guam.

territorial waters Inland and surrounding bodies of water controlled by a nation, including water extending three miles offshore.

territory 1. A geographical area. 2. A part of the United States with its own branches of government but not part of or within any state.

terrorem clause A condition in a will that voids gifts to any beneficiary who contests the will. Also called no-contest clause.

> In terrorem clauses are enforceable in New York, but are viewed with disfavor by courts and are strictly construed. McKinney's EPTL 3-3.5. *In re Estate of Marshall,* 811 N.Y.S.2d 552 (Sur., 2005)

terrorism Politically motivated violence against noncombatants. Using or threatening violence to intimidate for political or ideological goals.

Terry **stop** See stop and frisk.

testament A will.

testamentary Pertaining to a will.

testamentary capacity Sufficient mental ability to make a will. Knowing the nature of a will, the extent of one's property, and the natural objects of one's bounty.

testamentary class A group of beneficiaries under a will whose number is not known when the will is made.

testamentary disposition A transfer of assets to another by will.

testamentary gift A gift made in a will.

testamentary intent The intent to make a revocable disposition of property that takes effect after the testator's death.

> Testamentary intent really means a purpose to make a will 'according to its statutory effect. *McLean,* 160 N.Y.S. 949 (2 Dept., 1916)

testamentary trust A trust created in a will and effective on the death of the creator.

testate 1. Having died leaving a valid will. 2. See testator.

testate succession Acquiring assets by will.

testator One who has died leaving a valid will. Also called testate.

testatrix A female testator.

test case Litigation brought to create a new legal principle or right.

teste The clause in a document that names the witness.

testify To give evidence as a witness. To submit testimony under oath.

testimonium clause A clause in the instrument giving the date on which the instrument was executed and by whom.

testimony Evidence given by a witness under oath.

test oath An oath of allegiance and fidelity to the government.

theft Taking personal property with the intent to deprive the owner of it permanently. Larceny.

> A person is guilty of theft of services when, with intent to obtain railroad, subway, bus, air, taxi or "any other public transportation service" without payment of lawful charge therefor, he obtains or attempts to obtain such service by unjustifiable failure or refusal to pay. Penal Law 1965, § 165.15(3); Transportation

Law §§ 2, subd. 22, 200 et seq. *People v. Lee,* 336 N.Y.S.2d 18 (N.Y. City Crim. Ct., 1972)

theory of the case The application of the law to the facts to support the judgment you are seeking.

Thibodaux **abstention** A federal court can abstain from exercising its federal jurisdiction when facing difficult and unresolved state law issues involving policy. *Louisiana Power v. Thibodaux,* 79 S. Ct. 1070 (1959).

thief One who commits larceny or theft.

thing in action See chose in action.

third degree Overly aggressive or abusive interrogation techniques.

third party A nonparty or nonparticipant who is involved in a transaction in some way.

third-party beneficiary One for whose benefit a contract is made but who is not a party to the contract.

> In New York, two definitive classes of protected third party beneficiaries, namely creditor beneficiaries and donee beneficiaries, each of whom can sue. All other third parties are incidental beneficiaries who may not sue. The only third person who may enforce a contract to which they are not parties, are the donees and creditors of the promisee to whom by the terms of the promise performance is to be rendered. *Zweig,* 340 N.Y.S.2d 817 (N.Y. City Civ. Ct., 1972)

third-party complaint A defendant's complaint against someone who is not now a party on the basis that the latter may be liable for all or part of what the plaintiff might recover from the defendant.

third-party plaintiff A defendant who files a third-party complaint.

third-party practice See implead.

30.30 (referring to McKinney's CPL 30.30) See speedy trial.

threat An expression of an intent to inflict pain or damage.

three-judge court A panel of three judges hearing a case.

three-strikes law A statute imposing harsher sentences for persons convicted of their third felony.

through bill of lading A contract covering the transport of cargo from origin to destination, including the use of additional carriers.

ticket 1. A paper giving the holder a right. 2. A citation for a traffic violation or other small offense. A traffic ticket is often referred to a uniform traffic ticket (UTT). 3. A document that requires a defendant to appear in court for arraignment. The ticket is given instead of setting bail on a non-felony. Also called appearance ticket, desk appearance ticket (DAT). McKinney's CPL 150.10.

tideland Land covered and uncovered each day by the action of tides.

tie-in See tying arrangement.

time-barred Pertaining to a claim barred by a statute of limitations.

time bill See time draft.

time deposit A bank deposit that remains in the account for a specified time and is not payable on demand before that time without penalty.

> Time Deposit as defined in section 234, subdivision 1(a) of the New York State Banking Law, and included among the terms and conditions of the agreement that the deposit shall be payable at maturity as well as that FDIC regulations required

the imposition of a minimum penalty if withdrawal is permitted prior to maturity. *Ayala*, 468 N.Y.S.2d 306 (Sup. Ct., 1983)

time draft A draft payable on a specified date. Also called time bill.

time immemorial Time beyond the reach of memory or records.

time is of the essence The failure to do what is required by the time specified will be considered a breach of the contract.

timely Within the time set by contract or law.

time note A note payable only at a definite time.

time, place, or manner restriction The government can restrict the time, place, or manner of speech and assembly, but not their content.

time-sharing Joint ownership of property that is used or occupied for limited alternating time periods. Also called interval ownership.

tippee One who receives material inside information about a company. See also insider trading.

title The legal right to control, possess, and dispose of property. All ownership rights in property.

title company A company that issues title insurance.

title insurance Insurance for losses incurred due to defects in the title to real property.

title search A determination of whether defects in the title to real property exist by examining relevant public records.

title state See title theory.

title theory The theory that a mortgagee has title to land until the mortgage debt is paid. States that so provide are called title states.

TM See trademark.

to have and to hold See habendum clause.

toll 1. Payment for the use of something. 2. To stop the running of.

tombstone ad An advertisement (sometimes printed in a black-border box) for a public securities offering.

tonnage 1. The weight carrying capacity of ships. 2. A duty on ships.

Duty of tonnage is a tax or duty charged for privilege of entering, loading, or lying in port or harbor, and can only be imposed by Congress. *Marine Lighterage Corp.*, 248 N.Y.S. 71 (Sup. Ct., 1931)

tontine A financial arrangement among a group in which the last survivor receives the entire fund.

Torrens title system A system for land registration under which a court issues a binding certificate of title.

tort A civil wrong (other than a breach of contract) for which the courts will provide a remedy such as damages.

tortfeasor A person who has committed a tort.

tortious Pertaining to conduct that can lead to tort liability.

tortious interference with prospective advantage See interference with prospective advantage.

total breach A breach that so substantially impairs the value of the contract to the injured party at the time of the breach that it is just in the circumstances to allow recovery of damages based on all the injured party's remaining rights to performance.

total disability Inability to engage in any gainful occupation.

Where policy provided that total disability would ensue when insured was prevented from performing any and every duty pertaining to his occupation, "total disability" would still exist though in isolated instances insured attempted to perform some duties pertaining to his occupation, if incapable of safely and efficiently engaging in any of his usual duties. *McGrail*, 55 N.E.2d 483 (Ct. of App., 1944)

total incorporation See selective incorporation.

total loss Damage beyond physical repair; complete destruction.

Totten trust A trust created by a deposit of funds in a bank account in trust for a beneficiary. The trustee is the depositor, who retains the power to revoke the trust. Also called savings bank trust, tentative trust.

A Totten trust is essentially an account which the depositor holds "in trust for" or "as trustee for" another person, the beneficiary. The trust may be revoked during the lifetime of the depositor by withdrawal of the funds or other affirmative acts, but if the depositor predeceases the beneficiary without revoking the trust, the beneficiary takes the balance of the funds at the time of the depositor's death without the funds passing through the depositor's estate. The account, in effect, is an alternative testamentary provision. *Eredics*, 100 N.Y.2d 106 (Ct. of App., 2003)

to wit That is to say, namely.

township 1. A political subdivision, usually part of a county. 2. A square tract that is six miles on each side.

tract index A publicly kept index of parcels (tracts) of land.

trade Commerce. Buying, selling, or bartering goods or services.

trade acceptance A bill of exchange drawn by a seller on the buyer of goods for the amount of the purchase, and accepted for payment by the buyer at a set time.

trade association An organization of businesses in an industry that promotes the interests of the industry.

trade dress The total image or overall appearance of a product.

trade fixture Personal property affixed to the realty by a tenant who uses it in its business and has the right to remove it.

trade libel See disparagement.

trademark (TM) A distinctive word, mark, or emblem that serves to identify a product with a specific producer and to distinguish it from others. See also infringement.

trade name A name or symbol that identifies and distinguishes a business.

trade secret A business formula, pattern, device, or compilation of information known only by certain individuals in the business and used for competitive advantage.

New York courts have adopted the definition of trade secret set forth in the Restatement of Torts, which defines trade secret as any formula, pattern, device, or compilation of information which is used in one's business and which gives him an opportunity to obtain an advantage over competitors who do not know or use it. *Sylmark Holdings Ltd.*, 783 N.Y.S.2d 758 (Sup. Ct., 2004)

trade union A union of workers in the same trade or craft.

trade usage A practice or method of dealing having such regularity of observance in a place, vocation, or trade as to justify an expectation that it will be observed in the transaction in question.

traffic 1. Commerce or trade. 2. Transportation of people or things.

tranche A slice or portion of a bond offering or other investment.

transact To have dealings; to carry on.

transaction 1. The act of conducting something. 2. A business deal.

transactional immunity Immunity from prosecution for any matter about which a witness testifies.

transcript A word-for-word account. A written copy of oral testimony.

transfer To deliver or convey an interest. To place with another.

transfer agent An agent appointed by a corporation to keep records on registered shareholders, handle transfers of shares, etc.

transferee One to whom an interest is conveyed.

transfer payments Payments made by the government to individuals for which no services or goods are rendered in return.

transferred-intent rule The defendant may be held responsible for a wrong committed against the plaintiff even if the defendant intended a different wrong against a different person.

> Doctrine of transferred intent serves to ensure that person will be prosecuted for the crime he or she intended to commit even when, because of bad aim or some other "lucky mistake," intended target was not actual victim. *People v. Fernandez*, 650 N.Y.S.2d 625 (Ct. of App., 1996)

transfer tax A tax imposed on the transfer of property by will, inheritance, or gift.

transitory action An action that can be tried wherever the defendant can be personally served.

transmit To send or transfer something (e.g., an interest, a message) to another person or place.

transmutation The voluntary change of separate property into marital property or vice versa.

traveler's check A cashier's check that requires the purchaser's signature when purchased and countersigned when cashed.

traverse A formal denial of material facts stated in an opponent's pleading.

treason An attempt by overt acts to overthrow the government of the state to which one owes allegiance or to give aid and comfort to its foreign enemies. Under Article III, section 3 of the U.S. Constitution, "Treason against the United States, shall consist only in levying war against them, or in adhering to their enemies, giving them aid and comfort. No person shall be convicted of treason unless on the testimony of two witnesses to the same overt act, or on confession in open court."

treasurer An officer with responsibility over the receipt, custody, and disbursement of moneys or funds. The chief financial officer.

treasure trove Valuable property found hidden in a private place and whose owner is unknown.

treasury 1. The funds of an organization. 2. The place where such funds are stored.

Treasury bill (T-bill) A short-term debt security of the U.S. government that matures in a year or less.

Treasury bond (T-bond) A long-term debt security of the U.S. government that matures in more than ten years.

treasury certificate An obligation of the U.S. government with a one-year maturity and interest paid by coupon.

Treasury note (T-note) An intermediate-term debt security of the U.S. government that matures in more than one year but not more than ten years.

treasury securities 1. A corporation's stock that it reacquires. Also called treasury stock. 2. Debt instruments of the U.S. government.

> Upon reacquiring its own shares, corporation may, at its option, carry them as treasury stock, that is, treat them as being still issued and subject to resale. *Christie*, 211 N.Y.S.2d 787 (1 Dept., 1961)

treasury stock See treasury securities (1).

treatise A book that gives an overview of a topic, often in-depth and scholarly.

treaty A formal agreement between two or more nations.

Treaty Clause The provision in the U.S. Constitution giving the president the power to make treaties with the advice and consent of the U.S. Senate. U.S. Const., art. II, § 2.

treble damages Three times the amount of damages found to be owed.

trespass A wrongful interference with another's person or property.

trespass de bonis asportatis Wrongfully taking and carrying away the goods of another.

trespasser A wrongdoer who commits a trespass.

trespass on the case See action on the case.

trespass quare clausum fregit Wrongfully entering the enclosed land of another.

trespass to chattels An intentional interference with another's personal property, resulting in dispossession or intermeddling.

> To establish trespass to chattels, plaintiff must prove that defendant intentionally, and without justification or consent, physically interfered with use and enjoyment of personal property in plaintiff's possession, and that plaintiff was harmed thereby. *School of Visual Arts*, 771 N.Y.S.2d 804 (Sup. Ct., 2003)

trespass to land A wrongful entry on another's land.

trespass to try title The procedure or action by which rival claims to title or right of possession are adjudicated.

trespass vi et armis A wrongful interference with another's person or property through force.

trial A judicial proceeding that applies the law to evidence in order to resolve conflicting legal claims.

trial brief 1. An attorney's presentation to a trial court of the legal issues and positions of his or her client. 2. An attorney's strategy notes for trial. Also called trial book, trial manual.

trial by ordeal See ordeal.

trial court The first court that provides a complete forum to hear evidence and arguments on a legal claim. A court of original jurisdiction. Also called court of first instance.

trial de novo A new trial as if a prior one had not taken place.

trial jury See petit jury.

tribal land Reservation land held by a tribe for its community.

tribunal A court or other body that adjudicates disputes.

trier of fact See fact-finder.

TRO See temporary restraining order.

trover See conversion (1).

true bill A grand jury's notation on a bill of indictment that there is enough evidence for a criminal trial—a true bill of indictment. A grand jury indictment.

true value See fair market value.

trust A device or arrangement by which its creator (the settlor or trustor) transfers property (the corpus) to a person (the trustee) who holds legal title for the benefit of another (the beneficiary or cestui que trust).

> To constitute a trust, there must be a distinct fund which the trustee is required to preserve intact and for which he must eventually account, and, if there is no such fund but merely a general obligation ultimately to pay a sum of money, there is no trust but only a "debt." *Petition of Travers*, 32 N.Y.S.2d 742 (Sup. Ct., 1941)

trust account See client trust account.

trust company A company or bank that serves as a trustee for trusts. A trust officer is the employee in charge of a trust.

trust deed 1. The document setting up a trust. 2. See deed of trust.

trust de son tort See constructive trust.

trustee (1) The person or company holding legal title to property for the benefit of another. (2) See deed of trust for the role of trustees in such deeds.

trustee in bankruptcy A person appointed or elected to administer the estate of a debtor in bankruptcy.

trust estate See corpus (1).

trust ex delicto See constructive trust.

trust ex maleficio See constructive trust.

trust fund See corpus (1).

trust fund doctrine An insolvent corporation's assets are held in trust for its creditors.

> Trust fund doctrine, under which the officers and directors of an insolvent corporation are said to hold the remaining corporate assets in trust for the benefit of its general creditors, does not automatically create an actual lien or other equitable interest as such in corporate assets upon insolvency. *Credit Agricole Indosuez*, 708 N.Y.S.2d 26 (Ct. of App., 2000)

trust indenture 1. The document specifying the terms of a trust. 2. See deed of trust.

trust instrument The document setting up a trust.

trust officer See trust company.

trustor See settlor.

trust receipt A document stating that a dealer/borrower is holding goods in trust for the benefit of the lender.

trust territory A territory placed under the administration of a country by the United Nations.

trusty A trusted prisoner given special privileges and duties.

truth-in-lending Required disclosure of credit terms.

try 1. To litigate. 2. To decide a legal dispute in court.

turnkey contract A contract in which the builder agrees to complete the work of building and installation to the point of readiness for occupancy.

> Under the turnkey method of development, property is conveyed by town to private developer who will construct public housing thereon and, on approval of site, design, and cost estimate, housing authority will then execute contract of sale to the developer to purchase the completed project. *Grayson*, 545 N.Y.S.2d 633 (Sup. Ct., 1989)

turnover order A court order that the losing litigant transfer property to the winning litigant.

turntable doctrine See attractive nuisance doctrine.

turpitude Depravity.

twisting Deception to induce an insured to switch insurance policies.

two-dismissal rule A voluntary dismissal of a second action operates as a dismissal on the merits if the plaintiff has previously dismissed an action involving the same claim.

two-issue rule A jury verdict involving two or more issues will not be set aside if the verdict is supported as to at least one of the issues.

two-witness rule In a perjury or treason case, proof of falsity of the testimony cannot be established by the uncorroborated testimony of a single witness.

tying arrangement A seller conditions the sale of one product or service on the buyer's purchase of a separate product or service.

U

uberrima fides Highest degree of good faith.

ubi Where.

UCC See Uniform Commercial Code.

UCCC Uniform Consumer Credit Code.

UCMJ Uniform Code of Military Justice.

UFTA Uniform Fraudulent Transfer Act.

UGTMA See Uniform Gift to Minors Act

ukase An official decree or proclamation.

ultimate facts Facts essential to a cause of action or a defense.

> Ultimate facts are conclusions or opinions acquired by reflection and by reasoning upon evidentiary facts. *Jacobson*, 234 N.Y.S.2d 780 (Sup. Ct., 1962)

ultrahazardous See abnormally dangerous.

ultra vires Beyond the scope of corporate powers; unauthorized.

umbrella policy An insurance policy that covers risks not covered by homeowners, automobile, or other standard liability policies.

umpire A neutral person asked to resolve or help resolve a dispute.

unalienable See inalienable.

unanimous opinion An opinion in which all judges or justices are in full agreement.

unauthorized practice of law (UPL) Engaging in acts that require either a license to practice law or other special authorization by a person who does not have the license or special authorization.

unavoidable accident An accident that could not have been prevented by ordinary care. Also called inevitable accident, pure accident.

An unavoidable accident is an occurrence which is not intended and could not have been foreseen or prevented by the exercise of reasonable caution. Toss, 719 N.Y.S.2d 295 (2 Dept., 2001)

uncertificated security A security not represented by an instrument, the transfer of which is registered on the issuer's books.

unclean hands doctrine See clean hands doctrine.

unconditional Without contingencies or conditions.

unconscionable So one-sided as to be oppressive and grossly unfair. Shocks the conscience.

unconstitutional Contrary to or inconsistent with the constitution.

uncontested Unopposed; without opposition.

uncontrollable impulse An impulse or urge that cannot be resisted.

undercapitalized Insufficient capital to run a profitable business.

under color of law See color of law.

underlease See sublease.

under protest Waiving no rights; to be challenged later, but paid now.

undersigned The person signing at the end of the document or page.

understanding 1. A meeting of the minds; agreement. 2. Interpretation.

undertaking 1. A promise or guaranty. 2. A bail bond. 3. A task.

undertenant See sublease.

under the influence See driving under the influence.

underwriting 1. Assuming a risk by insuring it. The process of deciding whether to insure a risk. 2. An agreement to buy the shares of a new issue of securities not purchased by the public.

undisclosed principal A principal whose existence and identity are not revealed by the agent to a third party.

undivided interest; undivided right; undivided title The interest of each individual in the entire or whole property rather than in a particular part of it.

undivided profits Accrued profit a corporation has not distributed.

undue influence Improper persuasion, coercion, force, or deception that substitutes the will of one person for the free will of another.

Undue influence is not limited to fraud and duress, but also can include insidious, subtle and impalpable pressure that subverts testator or internalizes within testator the desire to do, not her intent, but intent of another. *In re Estate of Edel*, 700 N.Y.S.2d 664 (Sur., 1999)

unearned income: 1. Income from sources other than salary, such as interest and dividends. Also referred to as investment income or passive income. 2. Cash received but not yet earned, such as a lawyer's retainer. Also referred to as unearned revenue.

unemployment compensation Temporary income from the government to persons who have lost their jobs (for reasons other than misconduct) and are looking for work.

unethical In violation of standards of practice or an ethical code.

unfair competition Passing off one's goods or services as those of another. Trade practices that unfairly undermine competition.

Unfair competition is nothing but a convenient name for the doctrine that no one should be allowed to sell his goods as those of another, and each case depends upon his particular facts. *Cue Pub. Co.*, 198 N.Y.S.2d 993 (Sup. Ct., 1960)

unfair labor practice Acts by workers, employers, or unions that are illegal under laws on labor-management relations.

unicameral Having one house or chamber in the legislature.

unified bar See integrated bar.

unified transfer tax A single or unified federal tax on property transfers during one's life and at death.

uniform Without change or variation; the same in all cases.

Uniform Code of Military Justice (UCMJ) The rules governing discipline in the armed forces.

Uniform Commercial Code (UCC) A law adopted in all states (with some variations) on commercial transactions (e.g., sale of goods, negotiable instruments).

Uniform Gifts to Minors Act (UGMA, UGTMA) An act that permits tax-free gifts of cash or securities to minors without having to set up a trust or establishing a guardianship.

uniform laws Laws proposed by the National Conference of Commissioners on Uniform State Laws to state legislatures, which may adopt, modify, or reject them (*www.nccusl.org*).

Uniform traffic ticket (UTT) See ticket (2).

Uniform Transfers to Minors Act (UTMA, UTTMA) An extension of the Uniform Gift to Minors Act that added real estate, royalties, patents, and other items to permissible tax-free gifts that may be given to minors without having to set up a trust or establishing a guardianship.

unilateral Affecting only one side; obligating only one side.

unilateral contract A contract in which only one party makes a promise and the other party completes the contract by rendering performance.

A unilateral contract consists of a promise for an act, the acceptance consisting of the performance of the act requested, rather than the promise to perform it. Antonucci, 340 N.Y.S. 2d 979 (N.Y. City Civ. Ct., 1973)

unilateral mistake A mistake by only one of the parties to a contract.

unincorporated association A group of persons formed (but not incorporated) to promote a common enterprise or objective.

uninsured motorist coverage Insurance protection when injured by motorists without liability insurance.

union An association that negotiates with employers on labor issues.

union certification A government declaration that a particular union is the bargaining representative of a group of workers.

union shop A business where all workers must join the union.

Where a collective bargaining agreement contains a union shop clause, which defines or limits conditions under which a union member may resign, until member takes action in accordance with such procedure, he is bound to pay dues or their equivalent. *Lewis*, 313 N.E.2d 735, 357 N.Y.S.2d 419 (Ct. of App., 1974)

United States (U.S.) The federal government.

United States Attorney An attorney who represents the federal government.

United States Code (USC) An official codification of permanent and public federal statutes organized by subject matter.

United States Commissioner See magistrate (1).

United States courts The federal courts (*www.uscourts.gov*).

United States Marshal See marshal (1).

United States Magistrate See magistrate (1).

United States Reports (U.S.) The official collection of opinions of the U.S. Supreme Court.

United States Statutes at Large See Statutes at Large.

United States Trustee A federal official appointed by the U.S. Attorney General with statutory oversight responsibility over bankruptcy court cases (28 U.S.C. § 581).

unit investment trust A trust investing in a portfolio of securities.

unit rule Valuing shares by multiplying the sale price of one share on a stock exchange by the total number of shares.

unity The four elements of a joint tenancy: (1) *unity of interest* (the interests of all the joint tenants have the same nature, extent, and duration), (2) *unity of title* (all the joint tenants had their estate created by the same instrument), (3) *unity of time* (the interests of all the joint tenants vested at the same time), and (4) *unity of possession* (all the joint tenants have the right to possess the whole property).

The distinguishing feature of a tenancy in common form of ownership is the right of each cotenant to use and enjoy the entire property as would a sole owner; this undivided interest, usually called "unity of possession" is a right enjoyed by all the cotenants whether or not they are in actual possession of the premises. *Butler*, 762 N.Y.S.2d 567 (Ct. of App., 2003)

universal agent An agent with full powers to act for the principal.

unjust enrichment Receiving a benefit that in justice and in equity belongs to another.

The essence of unjust enrichment is that one party has received money or a benefit at the expense of another. *Wolf*, 694 N.Y.S.2d 424 (2 Dept., 1999)

unlawful Contrary to the law; illegal.

unlawful arrest An arrest without a warrant or probable cause.

unlawful assembly Three or more persons who meet to do an unlawful act or a lawful act in a violent, boisterous, or tumultuous manner.

unlawful detainer Remaining in possession of real property unlawfully by one whose original possession was lawful.

unlawful entry 1. A trespass on real property. 2. Entering a country illegally.

unlawful force The wrongful use of force against another.

unliquidated Not determined or specified; not ascertained in amount.

unlisted security A security not registered with a stock exchange.

unmarketable title A title an ordinary prudent buyer would not accept.

Title is unmarketable where it is of such a character as to expose the purchaser to the hazards of litigation and where there are outstanding possible interests in third persons. *Boecher*, 377 N.Y.S.2d 781 (3 Dept., 1976)

unnatural offense See sodomy.

unnecessary hardship Ground for a variance from a zoning regulation based on the unreasonableness of its application.

unprofessional conduct Conduct that violates the ethical code.

unrealized Pertaining to a gain or loss on paper. See realization (2).

unreasonable Irrational; arbitrary or capricious.

unreasonable restraint of trade A restraint of trade whose anticompetitive effects outweigh its procompetitive effects.

unreasonable search A search conducted without probable cause or consent, or that is otherwise illegal.

unrelated business income Income of a non-profit organization that is taxable because it is not substantially related to the organization's main purpose.

unrelated offenses Crimes that are separate and independent.

unresponsive Not answering the question or charge; irrelevant.

unreviewable Not ripe or suitable for review by a court or other body.

unsecured creditor A creditor unprotected by a lien or other security in any property of the debtor. Also called general creditor.

unsound 1. Unhealthy. 2. Not based on sufficient evidence or analysis.

unsworn Not given under oath.

untenantable Unfit for the purpose leased.

untimely Too soon or too late.

unvalued policy An insurance policy in which the value of the thing insured is not agreed upon and stated in the policy. Also called open policy.

unwritten law Law derived from custom. Law not formally promulgated but collected from court opinions and learned treatises.

UPA Uniform Partnership Act.

UPC Uniform Probate Code.

UPL See unauthorized practice of law.

upset price The lowest auction price a seller will accept.

U.S. See United States.

usage A custom or practice that is widely known or established.

A custom or usage must be so general that a presumption of law will arise that everyone knows of it and contracts with reference to it. *Shaw*, 314 N.Y.S.2d 372 (N.Y. City Civ. Ct. 1969)

USC See United States Code.

USCA United States Code Annotated.

U.S.D.C. United States District Court.

use 1. Taking, employing, or applying something. 2. The value of something. 3. The profit or benefit of land. 4. A purpose.

useful Having practical utility.

useful life See depreciable life.

use immunity Compelled statements cannot be used in a later criminal trial.

useless-gesture exception See knock-and-announce rule.

use tax A tax on goods bought outside the state.

usufruct A right to use another's property without damaging it.

usurious Pertaining to usury.

usury Lending money at an interest rate above what is authorized by law.

Intent to overcharge a borrower is an essential and necessary element of usury. *Hennessey*, 26 N.Y.S.2d 1012 (Sup. Ct., 1941)

utility 1. Usefulness, providing a benefit. 2. See public utility.

UTMA Uniform Transfers to Minors Act.

utmost care See great care.

utter 1. To place or send into circulation such as cashing a check. 2. To say or publish. See also excited utterance.

uttering Knowingly presenting false instruments with the intent to harm.

ux. (uxor) Wife. See also et ux.

V

v. Versus; volume.

VA Veterans Administration, now the Department of Veterans Affairs (*www.va.gov*).

vacant succession Succession when no one claims it, when all the heirs are unknown, or when all the known heirs to it have renounced it.

vacate 1. To cancel or set aside. 2. To surrender possession.

vacation 1. Cancellation or setting aside. 2. A period of time between sessions or terms.

vacatur ("it is annulled") Setting aside.

vagrancy Wandering without a home or lawful means of support.

The crime of common-law vagrancy contains three elements: (1) being without visible means of support, (2) being without employment, and (3) being able to work but refusing to do so. *Fenster*, 282 N.Y.S.2d 739 (Ct. of App., 1967)

vague Unclear or imprecise.

vagueness Not giving fair warning of what is commanded or prohibited.

The void for vagueness doctrine requires that a penal statute provide a defendant with adequate notice of the conduct prohibited, while affording law enforcement officials some objective standard to avoid the possibility that the law will be arbitrarily enforced. *People v. Owens*, 713 N.Y.S.2d 256 (Sup. Ct., 2000)

valid Having the force of law; legally sufficient. Meritorious.

valuable consideration A benefit to the promisor or detriment to the promisee. Any valid consideration. Also called legal consideration.

valuation 1. Determining the value of something. 2. The appraised price.

value 1. Monetary worth. 2. Usefulness; desirability. 3. Consideration.

value-added tax (VAT) A tax on whatever additional value is added at the various stages of production.

valued policy An insurance policy in which the value of the thing insured is agreed upon and stated in the policy as the amount to be paid in the event of a loss.

vandalism Willful or malicious destruction of property.

variable annuity An annuity in which benefit payments fluctuate with the performance of the fund's earnings.

variable-rate mortgage (VRM) See adjustable-rate mortgage.

variance 1. Permission not to follow a zoning requirement. 2. An inconsistency between two allegations, positions, or provisions.

The fundamental difference between a variance and a special use permit is that a variance permits the use of property in a manner otherwise proscribed by an ordinance, whereas a special use permit confers special authority to use the property in a manner that is expressly permitted by the ordinance. *Sunrise Plaza Associates*, 673 N.Y.S.2d 165 (2 Dept., 1998)

VAT See value-added tax.

vehicular homicide Killing while operating a motor vehicle illegally, particularly with gross negligence.

vel non Or not; or without it.

venal Corruptible; available for bribes.

vendee A buyer.

vendor A seller.

vendor's lien A seller's lien securing the unpaid purchase price.

venire See jury panel.

venire facias A writ requiring the sheriff to summon a jury.

venireman, veniremember, venireperson A prospective member of a jury.

venture A business enterprise or other undertaking that often has an element of risk and speculation.

venture capital An investment in a business, often involving potentially high risks and gains. Also called risk capital.

venue The proper county or geographical area in which a court with jurisdiction may hear a case. The place of the trial.

Venue, which is the proper situs of a proceeding, does not involve the jurisdiction of the court to hear and determine the action, and venue issues, unlike those involving personal and subject matter jurisdiction, do not result in the enlargement or impairment of substantive rights. *Weingarten*, 776 N.Y.S.2d 701 (Sup. Ct., 2004)

veracity Accuracy, truthfulness.

verbal Concerned with words; expressed orally.

verbal act An utterance to which the law attaches duties and liabilities.

verdict The jury's decision on the fact questions it was asked to resolve.

verification 1. Confirmation of correctness. 2. A declaration (often sworn) of the authenticity or truth of something. 3. A sworn signature required for certain pleadings, such as a divorce complaint or eviction petition.

versus (vs.)(v.) Against (e.g., *Smith vs. Jones*).

vertical integration The performance within one business of two or more steps in the chain of production and distribution.

vertical merger A merger between two businesses with a buyer-seller relationship with each other.

vertical price fixing An attempt by someone in the chain of distribution to set prices that someone lower on that chain will charge. An attempt by a supplier to fix the prices charged by those who resell its products.

vertical union See industrial union.

vest To give an immediate, fixed right of present or future enjoyment. To confer ownership or title.

vested Fixed; absolute, not subject to be defeated by a condition.

vested estate; vested interest An estate or interest in which there is a present fixed right either of present or of future enjoyment.

vested remainder An estate in land that presently exists unconditionally in a definite or ascertained person, but the actual enjoyment of it is deferred until the termination of a previous estate.

vested right A right that cannot be infringed upon or taken away.

A right is vested, for purposes of determining whether statute impairs vested rights and thus may not be applied retroactively, if it is one which is complete and consummated, that is, fixed or established and no longer open to controversy. *Johnson*, 656 N.Y.S.2d 715 (Sup. Ct., 1997)

veto A chief executive's rejection of a bill passed by the legislature.

vexatious Without reasonable or just cause; annoying.

viable 1. Able to live outside the womb. 2. Practicable.

viatical settlement A contract of a terminally ill person to sell his or her life insurance policy, allowing the buyer to collect the death benefits.

vicarious Experienced, endured, or substituting for another.

vicarious disqualification See imputed disqualification.

vicarious liability Liability imposed on one party for the conduct of another, based solely upon the status of the relationship between the two.

The doctrine of vicarious liability imputes liability to defendant for another person's fault on theory that defendant had opportunity for control of wrongdoer. *Forester*, 645 N.Y.S.2d 971 (Ct. Cl., 1996)

vice 1. In substitution for; in place of. 2. Immoral; illegal; defect.

vicinage Vicinity; the area or locale where the crime was committed from which prospective jurors will be drawn.

victim impact statement Comments made during sentencing by a victim on the impact of the crime on his or her life.

victimless crime A crime with a consenting victim or without a direct victim, e.g., drug use or possession.

victualer One who serves food prepared for eating on the premises.

videlicet See viz.

vi et armis With force and arms.

vinculo matrimonii Marriage bond. See divorce a vinculo matrimonii.

vindictive damages See punitive damages.

violation 1. Breaching a law or rule. 2. Rape or sexual assault.

violent Involving great or extreme physical or emotional force.

vir 1. A man. 2. A husband.

virtual representation doctrine A person may be bound by a judgment even though not a party if one of the actual parties in the suit is so closely aligned with that person's interests as to be his or her virtual representative.

vis (power) Force; disturbance.

visa An authorization on a passport giving the holder permission to enter or leave a country.

visitation Time allowed someone without custody to spend with a child.

vis major An irresistible force or natural disaster; a loss caused by nature that was not preventable by reasonable care.

vital statistics Public records on births, deaths, marriages, diseases, etc.

vitiate To impair or destroy the legal efficacy of something.

viva voce By word of mouth, orally.

viz (abbreviation for videlicet) Namely, in other words.

void 1. Having no legal force or binding effect. 2. To invalidate.

void ab initio Invalid from its inception or beginning.

voidable Valid but subject to being annulled or declared void.

A voidable separation agreement is one capable of ratification. *Nusbaum*, 113 N.Y.S.2d 440 (N.Y.A.D. 1 Dept., 1952)

voidable preference A debtor's transfer of assets to a creditor (before filing for bankruptcy) that constitutes an advantage over other bankruptcy creditors.

void for vagueness A law that is so obscure that a reasonable person could not determine what the law purports to command or prohibit.

voir dire ("to speak the truth") A preliminary examination of (a) prospective jurors for the purpose of selecting persons qualified to sit on a jury or (b) prospective witnesses to determine their competence to testify.

volenti non fit injuria ("to a willing person it is not wrong") There is no cause of action for injury or harm endured by consent.

voluntary 1. By choice; proceeding from a free and unconstrained will. 2. Intentional. 3. Without consideration; gratuitous.

voluntary bankruptcy A petition for bankruptcy filed by the debtor.

voluntary bar A bar association that attorneys are not required to join.

voluntary commitment Civil commitment or institutionalization with the consent of the person committed or institutionalized.

voluntary dismissal A dismissal of a suit at the plaintiff's request.

voluntary manslaughter The intentional, unlawful killing of someone without malice or premeditation. Murder reduced to manslaughter.

The common law enunciates the seemingly sound doctrine, known as voluntary manslaughter that murder by intentional killing is reduced to manslaughter by a mitigating factor variously termed heat of passion, sudden passion, provocation, and the like. *People v. Patterson*, 383 N.Y.S.2d 573 (N.Y., 1976)

voluntary trust 1. A trust created by express agreement. 2. A trust created as a gift.

voluntary waste Harm to real property committed by a tenant intentionally or negligently.

volunteer 1. One who voluntarily performs an act (e.g., pays someone's debt) without a duty to do so. 2. One who acts without coercion.

vote A formal expression of one's choice for a candidate or position.

voter One who votes or who has the qualifications to vote.

voting stock Stock entitling a holder to vote, e.g., for directors.

voting trust An agreement between stockholders and a trustee whereby the rights to vote the stock are transferred to the trustee.

vouch To give a personal assurance or to serve as a guarantee.

voucher 1. A receipt for payment. 2. An authorization to pay.

vouching-in A mechanism whereby a defendant in a proceeding may notify a non-party, the vouchee, that a suit is pending against the defendant and that, if liability is found, the defendant will look to the vouchee for indemnity and hold it to the findings in that suit.

Vouching-in is a common-law procedure in which a defendant, by notifying his indemnitor of a pending suit and offering him its defense, creates, by the judgment which may be rendered against the defendant, a determination of issues as binding on the indemnitor as on the defendant, whether or not the indemnitor has undertaken to participate in the suit. *Application of Perkins & Will Partnership*, 502 N.Y.S.2d 318 (N.Y. Sup., 1985)

VRM See adjustable-rate mortgage.

vs. See versus.

W

***Wade* hearing** A pretrial hearing on the admissibility of lineup or other identification evidence. *United States v. Wade*, 87 S. Ct. 1926 (1967).

wage Payments made to a hired person for his or her labor or services.

Wages means the earnings of an employee for labor or services rendered, regardless of whether the amount of earnings is determined on a time, piece, commission or other basis. The term "wages" also includes benefits or wage supplements as defined in section one hundred ninety-eight-c of this article, except for. . . . McKinney's Labor Law § 190(1)

wage and hour laws Statutes on minimum wages and maximum work hours.

wage assignment 1. A court order to withhold someone's wages in order to satisfy a debt. An attachment by a creditor of a debtor's wages. 2. A contract transferring the right to receive wages.

wage earner's plan A new payment schedule or plan for the payment of all or a portion of a debtor's debts in a Chapter 13 bankruptcy when the debtor still has regular income.

wager policy An insurance policy to one with no insurable interest in the risks covered by the policy.

wait and see Basing the rule against perpetuities on vesting that actually occurs rather than what might occur. Also called second look.

waiting period The time that must elapse before the next legal step can occur or a right can be exercised.

waiver The express or implied voluntary relinquishment of a right, claim, or benefit.

Waiver, as an intentional relinquishment of a contractual right, may be accomplished by express agreement or by such conduct or failure to act to evince intent not to claim purported advantage. *Starrett City Inc.*, 809 N.Y.S.2d 401 (N.Y. City Civ. Ct., 2005)

walkout A labor strike or departure in protest.

want of consideration A total lack of consideration for a contract.

wanton A conscious disregard of consequences. Malicious.

war Armed conflict between nations, states, or groups.

war crimes Conduct in violation of international laws governing wars.

ward 1. A person (e.g., minor) placed by the court under the care or protection of a guardian. 2. A division of a city or town.

warden A superintendent or person in charge.

warehouseman; warehouser Someone in the business of offering storage facilities.

warehouseman's lien A lien of a warehouseman in goods it is storing that provides security for unpaid storage charges.

warehouse receipt A receipt issued by a person engaged in the business of storing goods for hire. The receipt is a document of title.

warrant 1. A court order commanding or authorizing a specific act, e.g., to arrest someone, to search an area. 2. A document providing authorization, e.g., to receive goods or make payment. 3. A long-term option to purchase stock at a given price. Also called stock warrant. 4. To guarantee or provide a warranty.

Warrant means an instrument that gives the holder the right to purchase or sell the underlying interest at a given price and time or at a series of prices and times outlined in the warrant agreement. McKinney's Insurance Law § 1401.

warrantless arrest An arrest made without a warrant. The arrest is proper if a misdemeanor is committed in the officer's presence or if the officer has probable cause to believe that a felony has been committed.

warranty 1. A commitment imposed by contract or law that a product or service will meet a specified standard. 2. A guarantee in a deed that assures the conveyance of a good and clear title.

warranty deed A deed in which the grantor promises to convey a specified title to property that is free and clear of all encumbrances. Also called general warranty deed.

warranty of fitness for a particular purpose An implied warranty that goods will meet a buyer's special need when the seller knows the buyer is relying on the seller's expertise for such need.

warranty of habitability An implied promise by a landlord that the premises are free of serious defects that endanger health or safety.

Landlord's warranty of habitability to his tenant is a contractual promise that rented premises will be safe and habitable. Real Property Law § 235-b. *McGuinness*, 431 N.Y.S.2d 755 (Sup. Ct., 1980)

warranty of merchantability An implied promise that the goods are fit for the ordinary purposes for which they are used.

warranty of title A seller's warranty that he or she owns what is being sold and that there are no undisclosed encumbrances on it.

wash sale A deceptive transaction involving the sale and purchase of securities that does not change beneficial ownership.

waste 1. Serious harm done to real property that affects the rights of holders of future interests in the property. 2. Refuse.

wasting asset An asset with a limited life or subject to depletion.

wasting trust A trust, the res of which consists of property that is gradually being depleted by payments to the beneficiaries.

watered stock 1. Stock issued at less than par value. 2. Stock issued at an inflated price.

water rights Rights to use water in its natural state, e.g., a lake.

waybill The non-negotiable document containing details of a carrier's contract for the transport of goods and acknowledging their receipt.

way of necessity See implied easement.

ways and means Methods and sources for raising government revenue.

weapon An instrument used for combat or to inflict great bodily harm.

weight of the evidence The inclination of the evidence to support one side over another; the persuasiveness of the evidence presented.

Weight of the evidence review requires the reviewing court to weigh relative probative force of conflicting testimony and relative strength of conflicting inferences that may be drawn from testimony, and permits setting aside of verdict if it appears that the trier of fact has failed to give evidence the weight it should be accorded. *People v. Davis*, 687 N.Y.S.2d 803 (3 Dept., 1999)

welfare 1. The well-being and the common blessings of life. 2. Public assistance; government aid to those in need.

well-pleaded complaint rule Federal-question jurisdiction exists only when a federal issue is presented on the face of the plaintiff's complaint.

Westlaw (WL) West Group's system of computer-assisted legal research (*www.westlaw.com*).

Wharton rule See concert-of-action rule.

whereas 1. That being the case; since. 2. Although.

whereby By means of which; through which.

whiplash Injury to the cervical spine (neck) due to a sudden jerking of the head such as might be suffered from a rear-end auto collision.

whistleblower One who discloses wrongdoing. A worker who reports employer wrongdoing to a public body.

whiteacre See blackacre.

white-collar crime A nonviolent crime, often involving a business.

white knight One who helps prevent a hostile takeover of a target corporation.

white slavery Forced prostitution.

whole law All the law in a jurisdiction, including choice of law rules.

whole life insurance Insurance covering the insured's entire life, not just for a term. Also called ordinary life insurance, straight life insurance.

wholesale Selling goods to one who is in the business of reselling them.

widow's (or widower's) allowance Part of a decedent's estate set aside by law for the surviving spouse, which most creditors cannot reach.

widow's (or widower's) election See election by spouse.

wildcat strike A strike called without authorization from the union.

Wild's case See rule in Wild's case.

will 1. An instrument that a person makes to dispose of his or her property upon his or her death. 2. Desire or choice.

A will is the legal declaration of a man's intention to be performed after his death. *In re Schofield's Will*, 49 N.Y.S.2d 341 (Sur., 1944)

will contest A challenge to the validity of a will.

willful Voluntary, intentional, deliberate.

Voluntary and intentional, but nor necessarily malicious. *Leggio*, 737 N.Y.S.2d 259 (Fam. Ct., 2002)

willful negligence See gross negligence.

will substitute An alternative method or device (e.g., life insurance) that is used to achieve all or part of what a decedent's will is designed to accomplish.

wind up To settle the accounts and liquidate the assets of a business about to be dissolved.

wire fraud A scheme to defraud using interstate electronic communication.

wiretapping Connecting a listening device to a telephone line to overhear conversations. Electronic eavesdropping.

with all faults As is; no warranty given.

withdraw 1. To remove, take back, or retract. 2. To take (funds) out of.

withholding tax Income taxes taken from one's salary or other income.

without prejudice With no loss or waiver of rights or privileges.

Where a motion is denied or a suit dismissed without prejudice, it is meant as a declaration that no rights or privileges of the party concerned are to be considered as thereby waived or lost except in so far as may be expressly conceded or decided. A dismissal "without prejudice" allows a new suit to be brought on the same cause of action. *B. v. B.*, 320 N.Y.S.2d 843 (Fam. Ct., 1971)

without recourse Disclaiming liability to subsequent holders in the event of non-payment.

with prejudice Ending all further rights; ending the controversy.

witness 1. To see, hear, or experience something. 2. A person who gives testimony, often under oath.

witness protection A government program that relocates witnesses and gives them a new identity to protect them from retaliation because of their testimony.

witness stand The place in court where a witness gives testimony.

wobbler An offense that could be charged as a felony or a misdemeanor.

words actionable in themselves Words that constitute libel per se or slander per se.

words of art See terms of art.

words of limitation In a conveyance or will, words that describe the duration or quality of an estate being transferred.

words of negotiability See negotiability words.

words of purchase Words designating the recipients of a grant.

work The physical or mental exertion of oneself for a purpose. Labor.

workers' compensation A no-fault system of benefits for workers injured on the job. Also called employers' liability.

work for hire An employee-authored work whose copyright is owned by the employer.

workhouse A jail for persons convicted of lesser offenses.

working capital Current assets of a business less its current liabilities.

working papers A permit certifying one's right to work.

workout A restructuring of the payment and other terms of a debt.

work product rule Material prepared by or for an attorney is not discoverable. McKinney's CPLR 3101.

> Privileged matter and an attorney's work product are absolutely immune from discovery. *Bluebird Partners, L.P,* 258 A.D.2d 373 (1 Dept., 1999)

work release program A program allowing inmates to leave the institution for employment during part of the day.

work stoppage A cessation of work, often due to a labor dispute.

work-to-rule A slowdown due to excessive compliance with work rules.

World Court The International Court of Justice (*www.icj-cij.org*).

worth 1. The monetary or emotional value of something. 2. Wealth.

worthier title doctrine A person who receives by will what he or she would have inherited as an heir by intestacy, takes as an heir.

wraparound mortgage A second mortgage in which the lender of additional funds assumes the payments on the first mortgage.

wreck The cast-aside wreckage of a ship or its cargo.

writ A written court order to do or refrain from doing an act.

write-down; write-up A reduction (write-down) or an increase (write-up) in the value of an asset as noted in an accounting record.

write-off Removing a worthless asset from the books of account.

writ of assistance A writ to transfer possession of land after a court has determined the validity of its title.

writ of capias See capias.

writ of certiorari See certiorari.

writ of coram nobis See coram nobis.

writ of error An appellate court's writ that the record of a lower court proceeding be delivered for review.

writ of error coram nobis See coram nobis.

writ of execution See execution (3).

writ of habeas corpus See habeas corpus.

writ of mandamus See mandamus.

writ of ne exeat See ne exeat.

writ of possession A writ to repossess real property.

writ of prohibition A writ to correct or prevent judicial proceedings that lack jurisdiction.

writ of quo warranto See quo warranto.

writ of right A writ issued as a matter of course or right.

writ of supersedeas See supersedeas.

wrong A violation of the right of another. A breach of duty.

wrongdoer One who does what is illegal.

wrongful birth action An action by parents of an unwanted impaired child for negligence in failing to warn them of the risks that the child would be born with birth defects. The parents seek their own damages.

wrongful conception See wrongful pregnancy action.

wrongful death action An action by a decedent's next of kin for their damages resulting from a wrongful injury that killed the decedent.

wrongful discharge Terminating employment for a reason that violates a contract, the law, or public policy.

wrongful life An action by or on behalf of an unwanted impaired child for negligence that precluded an informed parental decision to avoid the child's conception or birth. The child seeks its own damages.

wrongful pregnancy action An action by parents of an unwanted healthy child for negligence in performing a sterilization procedure. Also called wrongful conception.

> A wrongful conception or wrongful pregnancy claim alleges negligent performance of a sterilization or abortion procedure by a physician, or negligent filling of a contraceptive prescription by a pharmacist, as result of which plaintiffs conceived and became parents of a healthy but unwanted child. *Miller,* 585 N.Y.S.2d 523 (3 Dept., 1992)

X

x 1. The mark used as the signature of someone who is illiterate. 2. See ex dividend. 3. See ex rights. 4. See ex warrants.

Y

year-and-a-day rule Death occurring more than one year and a day after the alleged criminal act cannot be a homicide, e.g., murder, manslaughter.

The common-law rule that no person can be convicted of homicide where the victim does not die within year and day after blow struck or other cause of death administered does not exist in New York. *People v. Legeri*, 266 N.Y.S. 86 (2 Dept., 1933)

yellow-dog contract A contract forbidding union membership.

yield 1. To relinquish or surrender. 2. Profit stated as an annual rate of return on an investment.

Younger **abstention** See equitable restraint doctrine.

youthful offender A person 16 to 18 years old charged with a crime who may be eligible for youthful offender status, which both reduces possible punishment and converts what otherwise would be a criminal conviction to a sealed adjudication. McKinney's CPL Article 720. See also juvenile delinquent.

Z

z-bond A bond payable upon satisfaction of all prior bond classes.

zealous witness A witness overly eager or anxious to help one side.

zero coupon bond A bond that does not pay interest.

zipper clause A contract clause that closes out bargaining during the contract term, making the written contract the exclusive statement of the parties' rights and obligations.

zone An area set aside or that has distinctive characteristics.

zone-of-danger test To recover for negligent infliction of emotional distress (1) the plaintiff must suffer emotional distress, (2) due to the negligence of the defendant, (3) that causes a frightened plaintiff to be in an area that is dangerous to him or herself. If these conditions are met, there can be recovery whether or not there was physical impact on the plaintiff and whether or not the plaintiff suffered physical harm or injury.

The "zone-of-danger rule" allows one who is himself or herself threatened with bodily harm in consequence of the defendant's negligence to recover for emotional distress resulting from viewing the death or serious physical injury of a member of his or her immediate family. *DeAguiar*, 734 N.Y.S.2d 212 (N.Y.A.D. 2 Dept., 2001)

zone of employment The place of employment and the area thereabout, including the means of ingress and egress under control of the employer.

zone of privacy Activities and areas of a person given constitutional protection against unreasonable intrusion or interference.

zoning Geographic divisions within which regulations impose land use requirements covering permissible uses for buildings, lot size limitations, etc.

Index

CPSIA information can be obtained
at www.ICGtesting.com
Printed in the USA
BVHW052150310820
587743BV00007B/89